CUBISM

A History and an Analysis

1907–1914

CUBISM

THIRD EDITION

A History and an Analysis 1907-1914

John Golding

THE BELKNAP PRESS OF
HARVARD UNIVERSITY PRESS
CAMBRIDGE, MASSACHUSETTS
1988

Printed in Great Britain

10 9 8 7 6 5 4 3 2 1

Library of Congress Cataloging-in-Publication Data

Golding, John.
Cubism: a history and an analysis, 1907–1914
Bibliography: p.
Includes index.
1. Cubism. 2. Painting, Modern — 20th century
I. Title
ND196.C8G6 1988 759.06'32 88 – 9435
ISBN 0-674-17929-3 (cloth)
ISBN 0-674-17930-7 (pbk.)

CONTENTS

	PREFACE TO THE THIRD EDITION	vii
	ACKNOWLEDGEMENTS	xi
	INTRODUCTION	xiii
1	THE HISTORY AND CHRONOLOGY OF CUBISM	1
2	PICASSO AND BRAQUE 1907–12	33
3	PICASSO, BRAQUE AND GRIS 1912–14	96
4	THE INFLUENCE OF CUBISM IN FRANCE 1910–14	145
	CONCLUSION	194
	BIBLIOGRAPHY	202
	LIST OF ILLUSTRATIONS	219
	INDEX	227
	THE PLATES	239

FOR JAMES

PREFACE TO THE THIRD EDITION

It is now almost exactly thirty years since I finished the first draft of this book, which began life as a doctoral thesis for the Courtauld Institute of Art. In 1953, soon after I had arrived in Europe to begin my post-graduate studies, I travelled to Paris and was fortunate enough to see there the large and important exhibition of Cubism at the Musée d'Art Moderne, an exhibition which was to be of great significance in the start of a reappraisal of the movement. I visited the exhibition repeatedly and came to realize that I could never really come to terms with all the more recent contemporary art which meant so much to me until I understood the Cubist achievement. After more than three decades my ideas about Cubism have changed very little. Paradoxically, I now feel I understand it much less well than I did then. I enjoy Cubist painting as much as I ever did, but the more I look at it, particularly at the crystalline work of 1910–12, the more infinitely mysterious it seems to me. And I have come to believe that although the intellectual quality of most Cubist art is so remarkably high, the artists themselves, having initiated a radical re-examination of the vocabulary of art, were often carried along by forces outside their control. Many of the most beautiful and significant Cubist paintings were, I suspect, begun as voyages of discovery the final destination of which was not known or appreciated until it had been achieved or reached. Maybe this helps to account for the fact that while the movement was in many ways so self-contained and its true initiators so self-sufficient, it yet seemed to countless other artists so open-ended, so adaptable to a wealth of re-interpretation and re-invention.

Just before I encountered the 1953 Cubist exhibition I had spent a term of intensive tutorials and seminars on early sixteenth-century Venetian art, working under Professor Johannes Wilde, a teacher of genius. My own starting point had always been a love and appreciation of works of art, but Wilde taught me a lot about how they can be questioned in such a way that one can come to a deeper appeciation of them. To him more than to anyone else I owe any sense of method that I have; and I think it might be fair to say that this study is one of the first of its kind to analyse twentieth-century works of art in the same sort of depth as those of the great artistic periods of the past. The analysis is primarily stylistic; and because of this the book may now seem out of step with what one currently hears referred to as 'the new art history'. Were I myself to approach the subject over again today, it would be in a slightly different way: I would try to place the movement in a broader historical setting, try to make distinctions between it and movements surrounding it more fluid, try to relate it more intimately to a general climate of thought that was informing the other arts. Younger art historians are, I know, in the process of doing these things. But it is perhaps worth remarking that several recent attempts – in articles, essays and unpublished theses – at trying to give Cubism a deeper sociological basis or at analysing it in terms of new disciplines that are essentially linguistic have been at best only partially successful and have in certain instances made their points by virtually ignoring, at times indeed by falsifying, the properties and appearances of the works of art themselves. And maybe this would suggest that although quite obviously Cubism reflected the concerns of the men and the society that produced it, it was nevertheless essentially formalist in its orientation.

Much of the most important recent scholarship on Cubism has centred around the *Demoiselles d'Avignon* and the work produced by Picasso and Braque in the very early, formative years of the movement. I am grateful to Leo Steinberg for helping me to look at the *Demoiselles* and related works in a somewhat different or additional light even if his perspectives are not my own. And I am particularly grateful to William Rubin for the wealth of information he has provided about Picasso's 'primitive' sources and for his clear, detailed assessments of the achievements of both artists in the early years of their involvement even if, once again, I see the overall picture slightly differently. I have not quoted from these two scholars or from the many others who have written illuminatingly in the intervening years since I wrote this text, because although my revisions have been extensive I decided to adhere to my original decision to quote only from contemporary sources and from statements made by the artists themselves. But I hope that my debts to new literature on the subject are acknowledged in footnotes and in additions to the bibliography. Douglas Cooper's *Catalogue raisonné* of the work of Juan Gris, and those of the Cubist periods of Picasso and Braque by the team of Pierre Daix and Joan Rosselet and by Nicole Worms de Romilly respectively are invaluable new instruments for study and I only wish I had had them before me when I embarked on my own researches. Christopher Green's *Cubism and its Enemies: Modern Movements and Reaction in French Art 1916–28* deals extensively with the latter phases of Cubism which have hitherto been far too summarily discussed; and it gives me particular pleasure that this gap in the literature on the movement should have been filled by someone who was once a student of mine and who subsequently became a valued colleague.

Finally I would like to acknowledge an awareness of certain inconsistencies of scholarship in this and previous editions of the book – for example some of the titles of paintings are given in French, some in English; I have, however, simply written what seemed most comfortable at the time. After many long years of familiarity with the works they – and even in some odd way their authors – have become my friends and I have saluted them accordingly.

ACKNOWLEDGEMENTS

In its original form this book was written as a doctoral thesis for the Courtauld Institute of Art, and I am deeply indebted to my two supervisors, Prof. Anthony Blunt and Prof. Douglas Cooper, for all their help and advice. While I was writing the thesis my researches were aided by a grant from the Research Fund of the University of London. The many private collectors in Europe and America who allowed me to see Cubist works in their possession are too numerous to mention; I am particularly grateful to those who have given me permission to reproduce paintings from their collections. Of the officials of the libraries, museums and galleries who have helped me, I should like especially to mention Mr Alfred Barr, Jr. and Mr William S. Lieberman of the Museum of Modern Art, New York. I am extremely grateful, too, to M. Daniel H. Kahnweiler, to Mme Juliette Roche Gleizes and to Mme Sonia Terk Delaunay for all the time they spared me, and for letting me see unpublished and generally inaccessible documents in their possession. I would also like to thank Mr John Richardson for calling my attention to many important points, in particular to the discovery of the very rare 'mathematical' drawings by Gris. I should like especially to thank Prof. James Joll for the advice and encouragement he has given me at every stage of the work. Finally I would like to acknowledge the unfailing help of the staff of the Witt Library and the Photographic Department of the Courtauld Institute of Art.

ABBREVIATION

Z refers to C. Zervos, *Picasso*, Vols. 1–6, Paris 1932–54.

INTRODUCTION

Cubism was perhaps the most important and certainly the most complete and radical artistic revolution since the Renaissance. New forms of society, changing patronage, varying geographic conditions, all these things have gone to produce over the past five hundred years a succession of different schools, different styles, different pictorial idioms. But none of these has so altered the principles, so shaken the foundations of Western painting as did Cubism. Indeed, from a visual point of view it is easier to bridge the three hundred and fifty years separating Impressionism from the High Renaissance than it is to bridge the fifty years that lie between Impressionism and Cubism. If social and historical factors can for a moment be forgotten, a portrait by Renoir will seem closer to a portrait by Raphael than it does to a Cubist portrait by Picasso.

Despite its revolutionary quality, and the sudden, explosive way in which it seemed, almost overnight, to come into being, Cubism owed, of course, much to the art of the preceding fifty years. While the Cubists reacted against the passion and expressionistic violence of Van Gogh and the impressionistic 'intimisme' and literary symbolism of the Nabis, they admired Seurat for his intellectual objectivity, his classical detachment and formal purity; several of the future Cubists began their artistic careers as Divisionists, that is to say as his successors. Gauguin, in an indirect fashion, was a powerful influence in the formation of Cubism, in so far as it was he, in the eyes of the young painters working in Paris in the early years of the twentieth century, who had been the true discoverer of the aesthetic worth of primitive art. Tribal art, what the Cubists called 'art nègre,' was, it will be seen, one of the main influences in the birth of Cubism in that it encouraged Picasso, both on an intellectual level and by its formal, abstract properties, to take stock afresh of traditional pictorial values. In a more general way primitive art – and here one can extend the term to include the work of that great 'primitive' painter, the Douanier Rousseau – supported the Cubists in their determination to shake themselves free of what Braque has called 'la fausse tradition', the conventions that had governed Western painting for the preceding five centuries. Only one nineteenth-century artist, however, played a positive, direct role in the formation of the style. This was Cézanne. His importance cannot be too much stressed, and in a study of the development of Cubism one finds oneself returning to him again and again. It was Cézanne, more than any other painter, who provided a link between twentieth-century painting and traditional Western art.

Many of the contemporary historians and critics of Cubism agreed in seeing a direct connection between Cubism and Fauvism, the other important style born in Paris during the first decade of the century. This existed only in the most limited sense; a move towards greater abstraction, the tendency to take greater liberties with visual appearances, was the only very concrete way in which Fauvism foreshadowed Cubism. Even so, the abstract element in Cubism was the result of an entirely different approach from that of the Fauves. For while Fauve painting at its most typical sprang from a free, spontaneous and often highly subjective response to the external world, and for this reason seemed occasionally to be far removed from conventional appearances, the Cubists, on the other hand, were led to still greater abstraction by the fact that their vision was conceptual and intellectual rather than physical and sensory. The Fauves, and particularly Matisse, admired Cézanne, and Braque may well have been led to an appreciation of him through their example; but the ends to which he put his study of Cézanne were, once again, totally different. In the same way Picasso's appreciation of tribal art went far beyond that of Matisse, Derain or Vlaminck.

Indeed, viewed in retrospect, Fauvism seems to have belonged as much to the nineteenth century as to the twentieth. For in so far as Fauvism existed as a style or movement – that is to say when, between 1904 and 1906, the works of Matisse, Derain and Vlaminck all resembled each other to a certain extent and had clearly-defined characteristics in common – it was a synthesis of elements drawn from the art of the past fifty years: Impressionism, Divisionism, the decorative rhythms of Gauguin and the expressionism of Van Gogh, all contributed equally to its appearance. And since Fauvism evolved no really consistent technique of its own and was not governed by any very clearly-defined aesthetic, it was not a style that could have anything more than a very fleeting existence. It could well be interpreted as a sort of final paroxysm of post-Impressionist painting. All this does not apply, of course, to much of Matisse, and certainly not to most of the Matisse of 1906 onwards. But the *Bonheur de Vivre*, while it is generally considered to be one of the key-works of Fauvism, and while it incontestably represents a summary of Matisse's work of the previous years, shows him in fact taking the decisive step towards the formation of his own, individual, mature style. Apart from a few isolated sketches of Derain's done under the direct influence of the painting, there are really no Fauve works quite like it. The refined, undulating outlines, the subtle blending of colour, the whole feeling of carefully calculated formal precision and intellectual control, even the arcadian symbolism, all these factors are at variance with the immediacy, the sporadic, broken or violent contours and the deliberately loose, occasionally even dislocated appearance of Fauve paintings done by Vlaminck and Derain at Chatou and in London, the Collioure landscapes of Derain and Matisse, and Matisse's portraits of his wife painted in 1905 – the sort of painting that originally earned the movement its name.

The formation of Cubism was in sharp contrast to that of Fauvism. Where the Fauves drew from a wide variety of sources, the development of Cubism, except for the joint influences of Cézanne and tribal sculpture, was remarkably self-contained. And whereas the Fauves borrowed restlessly from the art of their predecessors, the Cubists reverted to fundamental principles; they began, so to speak, from the bottom upwards. Feeling that traditional painting was exhausted, they took each of the elements that comprise the vocabulary of painting – form, space, colour, and technique – and substituted for the traditional use of every one of them a new interpretation of their own. In short Cubism was a completely new pictorial language, a completely new way of looking at the outside world, a clearly-defined aesthetic. As such it has shaped the course of almost all twentieth-century painting.

The effects of Cubism are still with us. They can be seen in much of the art of to-day. In as much as Cubism has conditioned the development of architecture and the applied arts it has become part of our daily lives. For this reason it will, perhaps, be some time before it is possible to put Cubism in its proper historical perspective, to evaluate it with complete assurance. But to-day it is possible to define the characteristics of the style, to illustrate how, from one year to the other, even from one painting to the next, the painters evolved, step by step, the means of expressing their new pictorial concepts. What these concepts were, an examination of the paintings themselves will best serve to define; but it is of value, too, to reconstruct as far as possible the attitude of the painters to their own works, to tell what they said, thought and did, to see, in other words, what were the aesthetic principles that guided them. Finally, from an historical point of view it is of interest to record what their contemporaries thought of them, how Cubism was greeted by the public and critics of its day. These are the aims of this book.

Cubism, in its first stages, was the creation of two artists, Picasso and Braque, and the first chapter of the book begins in 1907 with their meeting. This chapter is devoted to an historical survey of the rise and spread of the movement. The second chapter is dedicated to an investigation of the early Cubism of Picasso and Braque: to a study of how a new concept of pictorial form and space came into being. In 1912 Picasso and Braque were joined in their creation of Cubism by a third artist, Juan Gris (Gris was a Cubist by 1911 but his real historical importance dates from the following year). 1912 was also the year in which the new Cubist techniques, *collage* and *papier collé*, were invented. The works of Gris and the use made of the new media by all three artists between 1912 and 1914 are the subject of the third chapter. The fourth and final chapter is an account of the dissemination of the style in France and comprises a stylistic survey of the development of individual artists such as Léger and Delaunay who were temporarily attracted to Cubism and developed individual variants of the style. The book ends with the outbreak of war in 1914, when the painters were physically separated by war and the school, as such, was dissolved.

1

THE HISTORY AND CHRONOLOGY OF CUBISM

Tradition has always maintained that it was Apollinaire who introduced Braque to Picasso towards the end of 1907. In fact the two men may have met sooner; a sketchbook of Picasso's which he filled with drawings in the early spring of that year contains some short written entries which mention Braque twice.[1] Possibly it was only after they came together under the aegis of Apollinaire, one of the greatest artistic impresarios of his age, that they felt the attraction towards each other that was to result in the most unusual and intensive collaboration in the history of art.

At the time of their meeting, Picasso and Braque had very different positions in the Paris art world. Picasso had already acquired a considerable reputation for himself as an original and independent figure. The works of his so-called 'pink' and 'blue' periods were being bought by important collectors, and the fact that an established dealer like Vollard was interested in his work gave him additional prestige. With the *Demoiselles d'Avignon* (Pl. 1), finished shortly before he met Braque, he had produced a painting that was to become one of the cornerstones of twentieth-century art. Braque, on the other hand, although he was only six months younger than Picasso, was slower in his development and had not yet established himself as a particularly original or significant painter; indeed, Braque subsequently came to feel that the paintings he executed in Antwerp

[1] *Je suis le Cahier, The Sketchbooks of Picasso*, Royal Academy of Arts, London 1986, pp. 59 and 313.

during the summer of 1906 were his first creative works.[1] Braque enjoyed his first success only in 1907, when the German dealer Wilhelm Uhde bought the Fauve pictures which he exhibited at the *Salon des Indépendants*.

When he was shown the *Demoiselles d'Avignon*, Braque appears at first to have been bewildered by it,[2] though he realized that it marked an important new departure. Fauvism had by now largely spent itself, and Braque's search during the following years for a more solid foundation for his painting drew him increasingly closer to Picasso. In 1907 Picasso and Braque had been living near each other in Montmartre for some time, and after 1908 began meeting daily to talk, visit the galleries and museums, and to examine each other's work. Picasso had never exhibited at the large *Salons* or taken part in any group manifestations, and after the *Indépendants* of 1909, Braque joined him in this particular kind of artistic isolation. While both painters, and Picasso in particular, led active social lives and mixed with a wide circle of literary and artistic figures, their friendship seems to have rendered them self-sufficient. This is probably what Braque meant when he said later, 'nous étions surtout trés concentrés'.[3] In 1911, the year in which their intimacy was at its greatest and their work so close as to be often almost indistinguishable, Picasso and Braque spent the summer months together at Céret, in the Pyrenees. In the summer of 1912 they were again together at Céret and then at Sorgues, a village near Avignon where Braque rented a house, and together they visited Marseilles in search of tribal art. During the brief periods in which they were separated they corresponded. Later, in the autumn of 1912, Picasso moved to Montparnasse, and during the following years the differences in their work began to become apparent, but the same friendly relations were maintained. At the time of Picasso's removal to the Left Bank he accompanied Braque on a short trip to Le Havre, and in the early summer of the next year Braque called by on Picasso at Céret. In the summer of 1914 Braque was once more at Sorgues, while Picasso spent his time between Sorgues and Avignon, where he worked in the company of André Derain. When war was declared and

[1]Douglas Cooper, notes to the Catalogue for the Braque exhibition at the Tate Gallery, London 1956, p. 26.

[2]Fernande Olivier, *Picasso et ses Amis*, Paris 1933, p. 120. Braque's remark, quoted by Fernande Olivier, is said to have been made in connection with the *Demoiselles*.

[3]Dora Vallier, 'Braque, La Peinture et Nous' in *Cahiers d'Art*, 1954, no. 1, p. 14.

Braque and Derain returned to join their regiments in Paris, Picasso escorted them to the station in Avignon. The outbreak of war naturally marked the end of the collaboration of Picasso and Braque, but the unprecedented closeness of their artistic careers over the preceding years makes it impossible to separate completely the contribution made by each to Cubism during the most vital years of its development.

Contemporary critics and writers (except those who acknowledged no relationship between the work of Picasso and Braque and that of the other figures of the movement), however, were almost unanimous in proclaiming Picasso as founder and leader of the movement. Sometimes the name of Braque is coupled with that of Picasso, but when mentioned, Braque is almost invariably referred to as a follower of Picasso. This neglect of Braque is strange, since his were the first Cubist paintings (Pls. 37B, 38) and since, as opposed to Picasso, he actually showed Cubist works in a public *Salon*. Louis Vauxcelles already spoke of 'cubes' in his review of the exhibition which Braque gave at Kahnweiler's gallery in November 1908,[1] and the same critic referred to the paintings which Braque exhibited at the *Salon des Indépendants* of the following year as 'bizarreries cubiques',[2] from which the style derived its name (Pl. 39A). Braque had submitted some paintings to the *Salon d'Automne* in 1908 (a few of the same paintings which he later showed at Kahnweiler's), and Matisse, who was on the jury, is also said to have described these works as being composed of 'petits cubes'.[3]

The reasons for Picasso's primacy however, are obvious. In the years before 1907 Braque was almost unknown, whereas many people already saw Picasso and Matisse as leaders of *avant-garde* painting. Moreover, Picasso obviously had a more forceful and dynamic personality than Braque, and this had impressed itself strongly on influential critics such as Apollinaire, Salmon and Vauxcelles, with whom he was more friendly than was Braque. Then, although neither painter was exhibiting publicly in Paris after 1909, by 1914 Picasso had held one-man exhibitions in England, Germany, Spain and America, while Braque exhibited abroad more rarely, and then only in group shows. Then, the *Hommage*

[1] *Gil Blas*, 14 November 1908.

[2] *Gil Blas*, 25 May 1909.

[3] Matisse later denied ever having said this, but the story is probably true since it is recorded as early as 30 September 1911, in *L'Intransigeant*. The story is repeated again in the June 1912 issue of *La Revue Française*.

à Picasso (Pl. 59) with which Gris made his sensational début at the *Salon des Indépendants* of 1912, must have had the character of a tribute to the *chef d'école*. Picasso was also throughout his life astonishingly prolific and during the Cubist years produced between three and four times as many works as Braque.

The importance of Braque's contribution to Cubism and his stature as an artist began to be seen and acknowledged only after the war. Kahnweiler linked the names of Picasso and Braque together seriously in *Der Weg zum Kubismus*, written in 1915 though not published until 1920, but general recognition of their collaboration dates from the Kahnweiler and Uhde sales of the early 1920s when their pre-war Cubism could be seen together in large quantities for the first time. Uhde, a young collector and dealer who had been on friendly terms with both painters since the early pre-Cubist days, in a book entitled *Picasso et la Tradition Française* which appeared in both French and German in 1928, stressed the cardinal part played by Braque in the formation of Cubism. Uhde writes: 'The crystallization (of Cubism) as a style owed much to Braque', and summing up the differences in their characters, 'Braque's temperament was limpid, precise and bourgeois; Picasso's, sombre, excessive and revolutionary. To the spiritual marriage which they then contracted, one brought a great sensitivity, the other a great plastic gift.'[1]

Vauxcelles's attack on Braque's first Cubist paintings serves to emphasize the new and radical use to which he had put his studies of Cézanne, for in 1908 Cézanne had already been an important influence on advanced painting for some time. Indeed, Vauxcelles, in a review of the *Salon des Indépendants* of 1907, notes with satisfaction that 'The influence of Cézanne is on the wane', and adds, 'certain earlier *Salons*, in particular those of 1904 and 1905, could have borne as a banner ... "homage to Cézanne"'.[2] The main influences seen by Vauxcelles in the work of the younger painters were those of Gauguin, Derain and Matisse, to which in 1910 he adds the influence of Picasso.[3] During these years the most important of the established exhibitors at the *Indépendants* and the *Salon d'Automne* included Bonnard, Vuillard and Denis, while the strong group of Neo-Impressionist painters under the leadership of Signac were also recognized

[1]*Picasso et la Tradition Française. Notes sur la Peinture Actuelle*, p. 39.
[2]*Gil Blas*, 30 March 1907.
[3]*Gil Blas*, 18 March 1910.

and admired; by 1909 Vauxcelles was able to comment on the fact that it was no longer necessary to fight for the painters that he had christened the Fauves.[1] After the large Cézanne retrospective exhibition at the *Salon d' Automne* of 1907, his influence once again became paramount,[2] although after 1909, following the lead of Braque, certain painters began to interpret Cézanne from a more formal and intellectual, and less immediately visual point of view. Vauxcelles refers to some of the painters of the *Indépendants* of 1910 who were working under the influence of Cézanne as 'ignorant geometricians, who reduce scenery and the human body to dull cubes'.[3]

But by far the greater number of paintings to be seen at both these *Salons* in the first ten years of the century were still sub-Impressionist in character, and it was as part of the final and conclusive reaction against Impressionism that the Cubist and proto-Cubist works exhibited in 1910 were greeted. Apollinaire in a review of the *Salon des Indépendants* of that year wrote: 'If we had to describe the general trend of this exhibition, we would say without hesitation – and with great pleasure – that it means the rout of Impressionism'.[4] And to prove his point he cited beside the names of Matisse and two or three other painters who had been Fauves those of Robert Delaunay, Henri Le Fauconnier, Jean Metzinger, André Lhote and Marie Laurencin, all of whom were at some time or another involved in the Cubist movement. Reviewing the *Salon d'Automne*, Allard grouped together the work of Metzinger, Le Fauconnier and Gleizes, and, using one of the paintings shown by Metzinger an example, stated: 'there is thus being born in opposition to Impressionism an art which instead of copying natural phenomena, offers to the mind of the spectator, in their pictorial entirety, elements that as a result of synthesis are fundamental and timeless'.[5] Of Gleizes' work he said: 'Standing in front of his canvases I had the very definite impression of a sobering up after an Impressionist debauch.' Allard seems to have realized that the work of these painters was a reaction against Fauvism as well: 'away

[1]*Gil Blas*, 25 March 1909.
[2]References to the renewed influence of Cézanne and its continuance are frequent, e.g. *Gil Blas*, 25 March 1909, *Mercure de France*, March 1912, *Paris Journal*, 30 September 1912.
[3]*Gil Blas*, 18 March 1910.
[4]*L'Intransigeant*, 18 March 1910.
[5]'Au Salon d'Automne de Paris', *L'Art Libre*, Lyons, November 1910. The two following quotations are from the same article.

with posters, with visions that "compel", with "quivering slices of life", away with jottings and anecdotes. A good picture is nothing more than a perfect equilibrium, that is to say a balance of weights and a harmony of numbers. Let the painter's mind be sensitive, but not his brush.' *La Presse*, although hostile to the future Cubists, seems to have realized that something new was afoot when it referred to 'the geometric excesses of Mm. Le Fauconnier, Gleizes and Metzinger'.[1] Shortly afterwards Metzinger published an article in the literary review *Pan* on the work of Picasso, Braque, Le Fauconnier and Delaunay in which he proclaimed a new type of painting which for the first time broke with hellenic traditions.[2]

1910 is the year in which the Cubist painters, other than Picasso and Braque, came together as a conscious group, although many of them had known each other earlier. Metzinger and Delaunay had exhibited portraits of each other at the *Salon d'Automne* of 1906, when both were working in a Neo-Impressionist idiom, and by 1907 Delaunay had met Léger and Le Fauconnier as well.[3] Gleizes and Le Fauconnier became friendly in 1909 after a meeting at the home of a young socialist writer named Alexandre Mercereau,[4] where Gleizes also met Metzinger and Delaunay for the first time in the following year, although these meetings did not lead to immediate friendship, and Gleizes knew little about their work.[5] Léger appears to have joined the circle at Mercereau's later in the same year, probably introduced by Delaunay with whom he was becoming very friendly at this period. The painters also met at the Tuesday evenings held by the review *Vers et Prose* at the Closerie des Lilas. This café was the stronghold of the older generation of literary Symbolists, writers like Paul Fort, Stuart Merrill and Verhaeren, but many of the younger literary figures such as Apollinaire, Allard, Salmon and Mercereau (the last two on the staff of *Vers et Prose*) were to be seen

[1]*La Presse*, 1–2 October 1910.

[2]'Note sur la Peinture', *Pan*, Paris, October–November 1910.

[3]Unpublished biographical data on Delaunay, compiled by Sonia Terk Delaunay, definitive version 1950.

[4]Mercereau, a journalist and writer of short stories dealing with supernatural happenings, had founded, some years earlier, the *Abbaye de Creteil*, a communal artistic settlement. Gleizes had also participated in this scheme. The *Abbaye* closed down after a few years, and Mercereau busied himself in trying to bring together young Parisian painters and writers.

[5]Gleizes, *Souvenirs*, unpublished, written in the years before 1953.

there too. Allard had arrived in Paris from Lille in the spring of 1910 and his first contacts were with the future Cubists; because of this, his criticism is doubly interesting as representing their ideas unclouded by outside opinion. Older, more established painters like Signac and Sérusier also frequented these gatherings at the Closerie so that the atmosphere, though stimulating, was not particularly radical. Gustave Kahn, art-critic of the *Mercure de France*, entertained privately the same group of painters and authors.[1]

The works of Metzinger, Gleizes and Le Fauconnier had been hung together by chance at the *Salon d'Automne* of 1910, but the common characteristics which the critics saw in their styles, and the excitement expressed by the poets and authors at Mercereau's and at the Closerie des Lilas over the possibilities of a new school of painting, seem to have made the painters aware of each other; Apollinaire and Salmon in particular, although both were in many ways insensitive to painting, realized that Picasso's latest style contained the elements of a new art, and felt that the work of several other painters was evolving in a similar direction. Gleizes writes, 'it was at this moment, October 1910, that we discovered each other seriously, including Robert Delaunay . . . and that we realized what we had in common. The necessity of forming a group, of frequenting each other, of exchanging ideas, seemed imperative.'[2] Besides the meetings at Mercereau's and the Closerie, the painters began meeting regularly at Le Fauconnier's studio in the rue Visconti as well, where during the closing months of the year they watched with interest the development through successive stages of his *Abondance* (Pl. 88), a painting that all appear to have regarded as an important, revolutionary work. Early in the following year Gleizes instituted weekly *soirées* at his studio in Courbevoie. Neither Picasso nor Braque, the true creators of the movement, were present at any of these gatherings.

The first Cubist manifestation took place at the *Salon des Indépendants* of 1911. Largely at the instigation of Apollinaire, Salmon and Allard, the painters had decided to show together as a group. 'Metzinger, Le Fauconnier, Delaunay, Léger and I,' writes Gleizes, 'had decided to show at the next *Salon des Indépendants* . . . but . . . we should show as a group, everyone was agreed.' They feared

[1]Ibid.
[2]Ibid, on which the following account is based.

that if their paintings were not all shown together most of the impact would be lost; but to ensure that they were hung together, the rules of the *Salon* had to be modified. Usually the committee of the *Salon* appointed a hanging committee which was automatically and unanimously approved by the general assembly at its annual meeting held a few weeks before the opening of the exhibition. With the aid of their literary friends, the painters drew up a pamphlet to distribute to the general assembly, protesting against the chaotic hanging in previous exhibitions, and urging that the hanging committee proposed by the committee of the *Salon* be overthrown. They proposed instead a new list of candidates which included themselves 'and certain other painters whom we knew to a greater or lesser extent ... who seemed to us capable of representing if not a particular tendency at least a certain standard'. These included Lhote, Segonzac, La Fresnaye and Marchand.

The manoeuvre proved successful and Metzinger in particular received a very large number of votes. Le Fauconnier, Léger, Delaunay, Metzinger and Gleizes chose for themselves *Salle 41* and accepted a few other painters to be shown with them, among them, at the request of Apollinaire, Marie Laurencin. A neighbouring gallery contained the entries of Lhote, La Fresnaye, Segonzac, Luc Albert Moreau and André Mare. The dramatic 'coup' at the general meeting, coupled with the publicity made by the writers of the circle, sufficed to provoke an exceptional amount of interest in the contents of these rooms even before the *Vernissage*. On the opening day it was almost impossible to get into *Salle 41* owing to the crowds. Next day a violent storm of criticism and derision was let loose in the press,[1] while the long review by Apollinaire in *L'Intransigeant* served to establish him as the champion of the group.[2] The painters themselves, despite the highly organized aspect of the demonstration, appear to have been surprised at the sensation caused by their works and at the sudden notoriety which they acquired overnight. Even without the works of Picasso and Braque the public saw in this manifestation a new departure in art; yet in many ways the *succès de scandale* of the *Indepéndants* was due as much to the poets as to the painters.

Shortly after the *Salon des Indépendants*, the *Société des Artistes Indépendants*

[1]*Gil Blas*, 20–21 April 1911, and in *Comoedia*, *Excelsior*, *Action*, *L'Oeuvre* and *Cri de Paris* (quoted in Gleizes).
[2]*L'Intransigeant*, 20 April 1911.

of Brussels invited the French painters to join them in their yearly show, which was to open in June. The catalogue lists Archipenko, Delaunay, Segonzac, Gleizes, Le Fauconnier, Léger, Marchand, Moreau and Jean Plumet; Metzinger for some reason abstained. In his preface to the catalogue, Apollinaire wrote: 'The new painters who made manifest this year, at the *Salon des Artistes Indépendants* of Paris, their artistic ideals, accept the name of Cubists which has been given to them. Nevertheless Cubism is not a system, and the differences which characterize not only the talent but the styles of these artists, are an obvious proof of it.'[1]

The term 'Cubism' had become common usage in the press after the opening of the *Salon des Indépendants*, although Apollinaire himself had referred to Metzinger, who had shown a painting directly influenced by Picasso, as 'the only adept of Cubism strictly speaking'.[2] Applied to the artists showing at Brussels, the term could have no very definite meaning, and Apollinaire found it hard to identify many specific characteristics shared by the painters, or even to distinguish Cubism from Fauvism: 'One feature unites them, for if the principal merit of the painters who have been called the Fauves was the return to fundamental principles as far as colour and composition are concerned, the Cubists, in order to extend yet further the province of an art thus renewed, have sought to return to basic principles of drawing and inspiration. If I add that the majority of Cubists were formerly considered to be Fauves, I can demonstrate how far these young artists have come in a short time and the logic of their vision.

'Out of these two movements which follow upon each other and fuse so successfully, is born an art that is simple and noble, expressive and precise, passionate in its search for beauty, and ready to tackle those vast subjects which yesterday's painters feared to undertake, leaving them to antiquated, boring and pretentious daubers of the official *Salons*.'

Apollinaire concludes: 'I believe that in these few words I have conveyed the true meaning of Cubism: a new and lofty artistic movement, but not a rigid school inhibiting talent.'

The exhibits in the Brussels exhibition seem to have had in common only a

[1]*Les Indépendants, Cercle d'Art*, VIIIème Salon, 10 June–3 July 1911.
[2]*L'Intransigeant*, 21 April 1911.

concentration on clearly defined simple forms and a corresponding limitation of colour, and very few of them had anything at all in common with the work of Picasso and Braque. Certain critics like Hourcade and Allard, who did not realize the importance of what Picasso and Braque were doing, continued to take a broad view of Cubism as simply a return to a more sober, classical form of art, and thus to include within the movement a large number of artists who were not strictly speaking Cubist but had been slightly influenced by the style. In October 1912 Hourcade wrote: 'The term "Cubism" . . . means nothing if it is used to designate a school: there is no school of Cubist painting. And it is absurd to think that the painters of the *Section d'Or*[1] and others, scattered through the *Salon d'Automne*, share any concern other than that of reacting against the sloppiness of Impressionism. The true definition of Cubism seems to me: *the return to a sense of style through a more subjective vision of nature* (conveyed at times by a stronger emphasis on masses). The main interest of Cubism is the total difference of the painters from each other.'[2] However, Vauxcelles's original references to the 'cubes' in Braque's work and to his 'bizarreries cubiques' had been intended disparagingly, and the term 'Cubism' continued to be applied by hostile critics to the work of the more advanced painters whom they could not understand or appreciate, and by perceptive critics to these same artists whom they considered to be pioneers in a new movement. But as the pictorial innovations of Picasso and Braque – the construction of a painting in terms of a linear grid or framework, the fusion of objects with their surroundings, the combination of several views of an object in a single image, and of abstract and representational elements in the same picture – began to influence a widening circle of artists, the style became distinguishable by virtue of these features.

Although until late in 1912 Picasso and Braque lived in Montmartre and had relatively little contact with the other Cubists who lived mostly on the Left Bank or in the suburbs, they did not live in isolation. Picasso had never shown publicly at the big *Salons*, but Braque's Cubist works exhibited at the *Salon des Indépendants* of 1909 were widely discussed and were undoubtedly an influence on some painters, while they must have helped others to interpret Cézanne in a more

[1]For the *Section d'Or* see pp. 14–16 below.
[2]*Paris Journal*, 23 October 1912.

intellectual, objective way. The work of both painters could be seen at Kahnweiler's gallery in the rue Vignon and at the small private gallery run by Uhde.[1] Delaunay used to meet Picasso at the gatherings at the Douanier Rousseau's,[2] while Metzinger was a frequent visitor to Picasso's studio in the *Bateau Lavoir*[3] during the early years of Cubism, and was an important agent in transmitting the first discoveries of Picasso and Braque. It was Metzinger who, in his *Note sur la Peinture* of 1910, was the first to write of the fact that Picasso and Braque had dismissed traditional perspective and felt free to move around their subjects, studying them from various points of view. Discussing the painting of Picasso and Braque, he added to some general remarks about the return to a more formal and intellectual art his view that a painting by Picasso was 'the tangible equivalent of an idea, the image in its totality ... Cézanne shows us living forms revealed by light, Picasso adds a material inventory of their intellectual existence, he establishes a free, variable system of perspective ... To purely optical sensations he adds tactile sensations.' And of Braque he wrote: 'Whether he paints a face, a fruit, the entire image pulses incessantly; the painting is no longer an inert grouping of concurrent masses.' Léger was shown the works of Picasso and Braque in 1910 by Kahnweiler and met them later the same year.[4] Le Fauconnier and Gleizes did not meet Picasso until late in 1911, and Gleizes does not record having met Braque at all.

The poets and writers who had been instrumental in organizing the younger painters at the *Indépendants* also played a large part in uniting the different aspects of Cubism. Apollinaire and Raynal in particular moved freely in all artistic circles. Apollinaire, however, remained personally most intimate with Picasso, and it is certain that the literary circle which surrounded Picasso, and

[1]There was also a Picasso exhibition at Vollard's in the winter months of 1910–11. Vollard continued to buy Picasso's work until the summer of 1910, although his purchases became fewer, and this exhibition may not have included Cubist work. There appears to have been no catalogue; M. Kahnweiler could not remember the exhibition at all.

[2]*Picasso et ses Amis*, p. 77.

[3]The *Bateau Lavoir* was the studio building in the rue Ravignan (to-day known as the place Emile-Goudeau), where Picasso lived from 1904 until 1909; the name seems to have arisen from its resemblance to the washing-boats on the Seine. The building was originally a piano factory, and was known to Picasso and his friends also as *la maison du trappeur*.

[4]Douglas Cooper, *Fernand Léger et le nouvel Espace*, Geneva 1949, p. 36.

which included Max Jacob and Pierre Reverdy, was more advanced than that around Gleizes and Metzinger, whose closest friends, men like Mercereau and Nayral, belonged to the circle of Paul Fort and the older generation of Symbolists.

During 1911 and 1912 the group formed by Gleizes, Metzinger, Léger, Le Fauconnier and Delaunay was expanded to include several new figures. Archipenko and La Fresnaye, who had been unknown to Gleizes before the *Salon des Indépendants* of 1911, began to frequent the Mondays at Courbevoie.[1] Picabia was drawn into the circle, probably by Apollinaire with whom he had recently become friendly. Apollinaire himself was usually accompanied by Marie Laurencin. But most important was the contact established with the Duchamp brothers who exhibited under the names of Jacques Villon, Marcel Duchamp and Duchamp-Villon. Duchamp-Villon, although at that time not personally in touch with the group, was on the committee of the *Salon d'Automne* of 1911 and together with La Fresnaye, Desvallières and one or two others, was largely responsible for persuading the hostile jury to include the paintings submitted by the Cubists. Duchamp-Villon and La Fresnaye were also members of the hanging committee, so that the Cubist painters were able to exhibit for the second time that year as a group. Marcel Duchamp and Jacques Villon had been influenced by the demonstration at the *Indépendants*, and were included in the Cubist room at the *Salon d'Automne*. After this their studio at Puteaux became another meeting place. Franz Kupka, a Czech painter who had come to Paris in 1894 or 1895, and who lived in an adjacent studio, was also drawn into contact with the Cubists. Le Fauconnier and Mercereau continued to entertain weekly, so that the painters and writers were meeting constantly. Metzinger, Gleizes, and Le Fauconnier even planned to publish a review dedicated to the plastic arts, with the collaboration of Jacques Nayral and Mercereau.[2] The participation of many of these painters in the formation of *Les Artistes de Passy* in October 1912, an attempt to transform that district of Paris into yet another art-centre, is a further sign of the continual emphasis on communal activity.[3] Lhote, who had already established a

[1]*Souvenirs*.

[2]The plans for this review are discussed in *Paris Journal*, 17–30 October 1911.

[3]The formation of this group is discussed in an article entitled 'Passy, Nouveau Centre d'Art', in *Poème et Drame*, Paris, January 1913. The painters involved were Gleizes, Metzinger, Laurencin, Jacques Villon, Duchamp-Villon, Picabia, La Fresnaye and Tobeen. Auguste and Claude Perret were

certain independent reputation, mixed cautiously in Cubist circles, but from 1911 onwards was generally referred to as a Cubist, although his somewhat academic style often gained him exemption from the unfavourable criticism directed at the other painters.

The most significant new figure to join the group, however, was undoubtedly Juan Gris. A Spaniard like Picasso, Gris had arrived in Paris in 1906 and had moved into a studio adjacent to Picasso's in the *Bateau Lavoir*. Although he did not begin painting seriously until 1911, Gris had thus been in a position to watch at first hand the birth and development of Picasso's Cubism. Within an amazingly short time he developed into a highly accomplished and individual painter. As he was a very intellectual artist, he was the ideal figure to take over from Metzinger the task of transmitting the principles of Cubism to the other painters; and since he joined the group at a moment when the movement was striving for greater definition, his influence and importance cannot be overestimated. Marcoussis and Herbin, whose work began to be noticed during 1912 and 1913, had also approached Cubism directly through Picasso and Braque.

The influence of Cubism seems to have been immediate and extensive. One reviewer of the *Salon des Indépendants* of 1912 writes: 'Now that the Cubists have grown into a school their works occupy several rooms and are to be seen in several exhibitions',[1] and another: 'the Cubists are to be found in force'.[2] Reviewing this same exhibition, both Allard and Apollinaire noticed that for the first time in several years the influence of Matisse and Fauvism was slight.[3] Gustave Kahn wrote: 'The exhibition favours the Cubists.'[4] To add to the general impact of their work, many of the Cubists had, at the suggestion of Apollinaire, submitted very large canvases – Delaunay's *Ville de Paris* was the largest painting in the exhibition (Pl. 78B).

That same year (1912) the Cubists also exhibited in Rouen at the *Salon de Juin*, and the movement was rapidly becoming known outside France as well. As

also present at the meetings in the *Maison de Balzac*. At one of these meetings La Fresnaye read a paper on Cézanne.

[1]J. Laran, in *Bulletin de la Société de l'Histoire de l'Art Français*, 1er fascicule, 1912.

[2]Mourey, in *Journal*, 22 March 1912.

[3]*L'Intransigeant*, 19–22 March 1912; *Cote*, 19 March 1912.

[4]*Mercure de France*, 1 April 1912.

early as 1910, Mercereau had sent to Russia an exhibition of works by Gleizes, Metzinger and Le Fauconnier, and a few artists whose aims he felt to be similar.[1] Apollinaire was able to write that the *Salon d'Automne* of 1912 had been persuaded to show the Cubists because of their influence and prestige abroad;[2] the most important and sensational feature in the *Salon* was certainly the *maison cubiste*, for which André Mare and Duchamp-Villon were responsible. Indeed, a painter-critic named Lecomte had resigned from membership of the *Salon* because he felt the Cubists were too numerous and their work too well hung.[3] Finally the storm and controversy raised by the Cubists reached its climax on 3 December 1912 when they became the subject of an *interpellation* in the *Chambre des Députés*. Following the lead of a municipal councillor and amateur photographer named Lampué, who had written an open letter to Monsieur Bérard, Under-Secretary in the Ministry of Fine Arts, in the *Mercure de France*,[4] a Socialist deputy, Monsieur Jean Louis Breton, demanded that measures be taken to prevent the Cubists from exhibiting at the *Salon d'Automne*: 'It is absolutely inadmissible that our national palaces should be used for manifestations of such an obviously anti-artistic and anti-national kind.' The attack was answered by Marcel Sembat, another Socialist, and a leading member of the party, who was himself keenly interested in modern painting. 'When a painting seems bad to one,' he declared, 'one has an incontestable right, that of not looking at it and going to see others. But one doesn't call in the police.'[5] So the matter rested there; but it is a sign of the intense feeling aroused by the new school.

The most important single Cubist exhibition was that of the *Section d'Or* at the *Galerie de la Boétie* in October 1912. In the previous year the Cubists and a large number of their friends had exhibited at the *Galerie de l'Art Contemporain* in the rue Tronchet, under the auspices of the *Société Normande de Peinture Moderne*.[6] This exhibition had received little attention in the press, though *l'Autorité* and

[1]Gleizes, *Souvenirs*.
[2]*L'Intransigeant*, 30 September 1912.
[3]*Le Temps*, 12 October 1912.
[4]16 October 1912.
[5]*Journal Officiel de la Chambre des Députés*, 1ère Séance du 3 décembre 1912.
[6]This is presumably the same body as originated the exhibition at Rouen the following summer (1912), see p. 13 above, although Apollinaire calls it *Société des Artistes Normands* (*Les Peintres Cubistes*, p. 13).

Paris Journal had referred to it as an 'exhibition of Fauves and Cubists'[1] no doubt through a confusion of terms, but also partly because this seemed the only way of describing the manifold tendencies represented, which were as divergent as at Brussels.[2] The *Section d'Or*, on the other hand, was generally accepted as being Cubist in character. Over 200 works were shown, and the fact that all the artists showed painting representative of their development during the previous three years gave the exhibition an added air of being a Cubist demonstration.[3] Since Picasso and Braque had not exhibited for some time, and since they had not taken part in the manifestations at the *Salon des Indépendants* and the *Salon d'Automne*, the public were not in a position to realize that their abstention deprived the *Section d'Or* of much of its meaning. The idea of the *Section d'Or* seems to have originated in the course of conversations between Gleizes, Metzinger and Jacques Villon at Puteaux and Courbevoie. Jacques Villon, who was older than the others and seems on that account to have enjoyed a certain authority, is generally credited with having suggested the title.[4] On 2 September 1912 *Gil Blas* announced that Marcel Duchamp was planning to send to the forthcoming *Salon d'Automne* a painting which was also to be called *La Section d'Or*. All the Duchamp brothers were at this time passionately interested in mathematics; Jacques Villon was engaged in reading Leonardo's *Trattato della Pittura*,[5] while Marcel Duchamp was a close friend of an amateur mathematician named Maurice Princet, so that it is not surprising that they should have been responsible for introducing a more scientific note into Cubist discussions. The choice of *La Section d'Or* as a title for the exhibition of the group of painters who appeared at the *Galerie de la Boétie* seems to indicate some dissatisfaction with the term Cubism as applied to their work, and was probably intended to imply

[1]*Paris Journal*, 13 November; *l'Autorité*, 27 November 1911.

[2]The following painters exhibited at the *Galerie d'Art Contemporain*: Metzinger, Le Fauconnier, Gleizes, Léger, Dufy, Marcel Duchamp, La Fresnaye, Lhote, Laurencin, Picabia, Friesz, Segonzac, Jacques Villon, Mare, Le Beau, Zak, Verdilhan, Dumont, Lotiron, Marchand, Luc Albert Moreau, Vera, Tobeen, Bacque, Girieud, Ribbemont-Dessaignes, Texier, Saint-Deles; and the following sculptors: Archipenko, Duchamp-Villon, Jermant, Nadelman and Halau.

[3]*Paris Journal*,15 September 1912.

[4]This was confirmed verbally to the writer by M. Marcel Duchamp.

[5]Jacques Lassaigne, *Jacques Villon*, Paris 1950, p. 4. The *Trattato della Pittura* appeared in a French translation by Péladan in 1910.

that the paintings shown had a more profound and rational basis. Perhaps it was felt also to have a wider, more general meaning. The three organizers, however, and many of the painters most directly concerned, were at this period working in a Cubist idiom.[1]

If the Cubists had been surprised by the violent reactions which they had aroused previously, they seem to have been anxious to attract as much attention as possible with this exhibition. The *Vernissage* was held from nine until midnight, for which the only precedent was the initial opening of the *Salon d'Automne* in 1903.[2] Invitations were issued to vast numbers of people, and many of the guests had to be turned away. Lectures by Apollinaire, Hourcade and Raynal were advertised, and a review, *La Section d'Or*, was published to coincide with the opening; it was edited by Pierre Dumont and numbered Apollinaire, Reverdy, Max Jacob, Maurice Raynal, Salmon, Warnod and Hourcade among its contributors. Salmon had at one point actually hinted that the great philosopher Henri Bergson might write a preface for the exhibition.[3]

As in previous exhibitions, artists like Alcide Le Beau, Segonzac and Luc Albert Moreau, whose paintings were related to Cubism only in a most general way, were invited to show, and the title may have been chosen partly to allow for this. But as opposed to the exhibition of the *Société Normande de Peinture Moderne* of the previous year, the majority of the artists showing at the *Section d'Or* were Cubists or painters directly influenced by the movement, and the effect made must have been concentrated. Furthermore, the fact that the exhibition was organized to show the successive stages through which Cubism had passed indicates that the painters were attempting to make their work as comprehensible as possible to the public, and their purpose must have been further served by the demonstration of the affinities between Cubism and the more readily understandable paintings of other artists who shared only a few of their pictorial concerns. The exhibition was undoubtedly a great success, and it put

[1]The catalogue lists: Metzinger, Gleizes, Villon, Duchamp, Duchamp-Villon, Picabia, Gris, Lhote, La Fresnaye, Marcoussis, Archipenko, Agero, Marchand, Segonzac, Luc Albert Moreau, Vera, Léger, Pierre Dumont, Tobeen, Glanis, Le Beau, Laurencin, Hassenberg, Lewitzka, Tivnet, Ribbemont-Dessaignes, Gav, Dexter, Girieud and Valensi.

[2]*Paris Journal*, 9 October 1912.

[3]*Gil Blas*, 22 June 1912. Bergson's thought was undoubtedly a stimulus to many of the Cubists although the sage himself seems to have viewed their art with a certain amount of scepticism.

Cubism on the map more than any other exhibition that preceded it.

This same desire to render Cubism more intelligible to the general public, and to define and clarify the movement generally led Gleizes and Metzinger in the autumn of 1911 to collaborate in writing the book *Du Cubisme*, which appeared in August 1912. Salmon's *La Jeune Peinture Contemporaine*, which contained an *Histoire anécdotique du Cubisme*, was published in the following month. Earlier in 1912 Apollinaire had written a series of articles for *Les Soirées de Paris* and these were gathered together with some additional material to form the bulk of his *Les Peintres Cubistes* which was issued in March of the following year. In February and June 1912 Hourcade published articles entitled respectively 'La Tendance de la Peinture Contemporaine' and 'Le Mouvement Pictural vers une école française de peinture',[1] in which he attempted to reassess the achievements of the preceding year. Raynal's first significant essay 'Qu'est-ce que le Cubisme?' did not appear until late in 1913.[2] All these writings had certain points in common. All emphasized that Cubism was an art of realism, although natural appearances were playing an ever-diminishing part. Painting was to become intellectual, and the painters would depict the world not as they saw it, but as they knew it to be. Apollinaire and Hourcade added that this conceptual or intellectual approach led naturally to a selection of simple geometric forms. The right of the painter to move around an object and combine various views of it into a single image, first stated in writing by Metzinger in 1910[3] and elaborated a few months later by Allard,[4] was quickly adopted by most critics as a central feature of the style, and became related to the conceptual or intellectual aspect. Thus Hourcade felt that an artist could convey more clearly the real nature of an object by showing as many aspects of it as possible, and guided by intelligence rather than by his eye, would resort to geometric forms. Knowing that the opening of a cup is round, it is false to depict it simply as an ellipse; ideally the object is shown as a combination of plan, section and elevation. Emphasizing the intellectual approach, Hourcade was the first of the many writers to relate Cubist painting to Kantian aesthetics, and in one of his articles includes a quotation from Schopenhauer: 'Kant's

[1]In *La Revue de France et des Pays Français No.* 1, February 1912. *Revue Française*, June 1912.
[2]In *Comoedia Illustré*, December 1912.
[3]'Note sur la Peinture'.
[4]In 'Sur Quelques Peintres', *Les Marches du Sud-Ouest*, June 1911.

greatest service was to distinguish betwen the appearance of a thing and the thing in itself, and he showed that our intelligence stands between the thing and us.'[1] Hourcade also saw as a second feature of Cubist painting the organization of the whole surface in terms of interpenetrating or interacting planes: 'The fascination of the paintings lies not only in the presentation of the main objects represented, but in the dynamism which emerges from the composition, a strange, disturbing dynamism, but one that is perfectly controlled.' In *Du Cubisme*, this feature was discussed as deriving from Cézanne: 'He teaches us to understand a dynamism that is universal. He shows us the modifications which objects thought to be inanimate impose on each other ... He prophesies that a study of primordial volumes will open up unheard of horizons. His work, a homogeneous mass, moves in front of our eyes, contracts, expands, seems motionless or flickers, and proves that painting is not – or is no longer – the art of imitating an object by means of lines and colours, but that of giving a pictorial expression to our intuitions.'[2]

On the subject of the abstract tendencies inherent in Cubist painting, however, the writers differed sharply. Apollinaire appeared to see complete abstraction as the goal. In the second section of *Les Peintres Cubistes*[3] he stated: 'The subject no longer matters, or hardly matters.[4] ... The secret ambition of the young painters of advanced tendencies is to create a form of pure painting. This is a completely new kind of plastic expression. It is still in its infancy and not as abstract as it aspires to be.'[5] Gleizes and Metzinger, themselves painters, and fascinated by purely formal pictorial problems, also began by seeing abstraction as the logical end, although they rapidly retreated and admitted the need, for the moment at least, of a certain coefficient of realism: '... the painting imitates nothing and ... must justify its existence in itself ... Yet we must admit that reminiscences of natural forms cannot be absolutely banished, at least not yet. Art cannot be raised to a pure effusion at a single onset.'[6] Allard and Hourcade rigorously

[1] 'La Tendance de la Peinture Contemporaine'.
[2] *Du Cubisme*, pp. 8, 9.
[3] This section appeared originally in the February 1912 edition of *Les Soirées de Paris* as 'Du Sujet dans la Peinture Moderne'.
[4] *Les Peintres Cubistes*, p. 11.
[5] Ibid., pp. 13–14.
[6] *Du Cubisme*, p. 17.

opposed any suggestion of abstraction in Cubist painting. Hourcade condemned it as un-French: 'our tradition calls for a subject and the originality of Cubism lies precisely in its rejection of the anecdote in order to rediscover the subject';[1] and he repudiated the idea that all the painters of the *Section d'Or* had renounced natural appearances: '. . . it is absolutely false to say that all these painters are turning their backs on nature and want only to produce pure painting.'[2] None of the writers realized that the Cubism of this date relied on a balance between abstraction and representation to achieve its effects, and that it was this balance that gave each work a significance on more levels than one. It was only natural that the two artist-writers, Gleizes and Metzinger, should have been the ones who were forced into a position of compromise between the two poles of abstraction and representation.

But while the *Section d'Or* represented the high point of the Cubist movement as it was presented to the public, and while the influence of Cubism daily became more powerful and widespread, many painters who had been Cubist, or had moved in Cubist circles, were already abandoning the style or using certain aspects of it as points of departure for developing completely new art forms. Delaunay, who earlier in the year had held an important exhibition together with Marie Laurencin at the *Galerie Barbazanges*, did not show at the *Section d'Or*, and wrote an open letter to Vauxcelles: 'I beg to inform you that I do not subscribe to the erroneously held opinions of Monsieur Hourcade which proclaim me as a founder of Cubism together with four of my colleagues and friends. It is without my knowledge that certain young painters have made use of my latest researches. They have recently exhibited paintings which they call Cubist paintings. I am not exhibiting.'[3] And in the reviews of the *Section d'Or* and the progressive *Salons* of 1912, there are indications that the works of Kupka, Picabia and Marcel Duchamp were generally recognized as having gone in some way beyond those of the original Cubists in daring and novelty. One critic of the *Salon d'Automne* wrote: 'The prize for idiocy this year is retained by M. Picabia . . . while M. Kupka has turned to sphericism,'[4] while Hourcade felt that Picabia

[1] 'La Tendance de la Peinture Contemporaine'.
[2] *Paris Journal*, 23 October 1912.
[3] *Gil Blas*, 25 October 1912.
[4] Jean Claude, in *Petit Parisien*, 30 October 1912.

had 'pushed a bad theory as far as it can go.'[1] Allard had referred to the work of Kupka at the *Salon des Indépendants* as 'post-Cubist fantasies',[2] while at the *Section d'Or* Vauxcelles singled out as representative of the worst and most outrageous tendencies Duchamp's *Le Roi et la Reine entourés de nus vites*.[3]

Both Delaunay and Le Fauconnier, who did not exhibit at the *Galerie de la Boétie* either, were at this point on less friendly terms with the other members of the movement, and for this reason their works were not illustrated in *Du Cubisme*.[4] The differences between the painters appear to have been purely personal, but Delaunay had also moved away from the other Cubists in his works of 1912, and, using his Cubist researches as a point of departure, was developing a much more purely abstract kind of painting with colour as its principal element.

Delaunay was himself profoundly aware that he had evolved a new kind of painting and he communicated his discoveries to Apollinaire with whom he had become very friendly. Apollinaire, always ready to welcome and encourage any form of artistic novelty, christened this development 'Orphism'. Apollinaire had recently finished writing *Le Bestiaire au Cortège d'Orphée*[5] and felt the name to be applicable to Delaunay's work, partly because it was more lyrical and sensuous than the rather austere Cubism of the period, and also because he saw it as a form of 'peinture pure' which had analogies with music. In the nineteenth century music had come to be regarded as queen of the arts because of its non-imitative qualities, and throughout the Cubist period musical analogies become increasingly frequent. With the emergence of abstract painting many felt that painting had become completely 'musicalized'. In his article 'Du Sujet dans la Peinture Moderne' (which became the second section of *Les Peintres Cubistes*) Apollinaire had written: 'Thus we are progressing towards an intensely new kind of art, which will be to painting what one had hitherto imagined music was to pure literature.'[6] Arthur Eddy, an American critic who in 1914 produced the first book in English on Cubism, *Cubists and Post-Impressionism*, wrote that 'the

[1] *Paris Journal*, 30 September 1912.
[2] *Revue de France*, March 1912.
[3] *Gil Blas*, 14 October 1912.
[4] Gleizes, *Souvenirs*.
[5] Paris 1911.
[6] *Les Peintres Cubistes*, p. 12.

comparison that Picabia is fondest of making is that of absolute music'.[1] Valensi, who had shown at the *Section d'Or* in 1912, in a lecture given late in the following year asked: 'Why should we not invent pure painting? Since the musician works with notes, why should we not accept that colour by its intrinsic force is capable of expressing a painter's thought?'[2] In his lecture 'Le Cubisme écartelé' given at the *Section d'Or* on 11 October and later added to *Les Peintres Cubistes* when the book was already in proof, Apollinaire divided Cubism into four categories, Orphism being the most advanced: 'It is the art of painting new harmonies out of elements borrowed not from visual reality but created entirely by the artist and endowed by him with a powerful presence. The works of Orphist artists should offer simultaneously a sensation of pure aesthetic enjoyment, a structure of which the senses are hardly aware and a profound content, in other words a subject. This is pure art.'[3]

While waiting to move into a new apartment in the Boulevard Saint Germain, Apollinaire lived with the Delaunays for almost two months during the autumn of 1912, and at this time the Delaunays' studio became the meeting-place of a new group.[4] The poet Blaise Cendrars was drawn into the circle, and he, together with Apollinaire, Chagall, and the American painters Bruce and Frost, joined the Delaunays during the summer of 1913 at the house they had rented at Louveciennes. Early in 1913 Canudo, another friend of Apollinaire's, founded a review called *Montjoie* which was recognized to be an Orphist mouthpiece, while Apollinaire expanded and developed his ideas on the new style in *L'Intransigeant* and particularly in *Les Soirées de Paris*. Archipenko, who had been a friend of Delaunay for some time, now also denied being a Cubist; the Art column of *Gil Blas* reported on 14 December 1912: 'M. Archipenko has formally announced that he has completely detached himself from the Cubist group whose principles he rejects.'[5] The group used also to frequent the Bal Bullier, a popular Parisian dance hall. There they were sometimes joined by Arp and Arthur Cravan.

Delaunay felt that the basis of his art was 'simultaneous' contrasts of colour, a

[1]A. J. Eddy, *Cubists and Post-Impressionism*, New York 1914, p. 91.
[2]This lecture was published in *Montjoie*, November–December 1913.
[3]*Les Peintres Cubistes*, p. 25.
[4]The bulk of this paragraph is reconstructed from the Delaunay biographical data.
[5]*Gil Blas*, 14 December 1912.

concept which he adopted from Chevreul, whose colour theory had interested him for some time. He meant by this that the areas of colour in his painting were not to be blended by the eye but were to be seen as acting on each other reciprocally, thus producing pictorial form and space. Sonia Delaunay later expressed this theory in its simplest form: 'Pure colours used as planes are juxtaposed in simultaneous contrasts to create for the first time a sense of form, achieved not by *clair-obscur*, but through the relationship in depth of the colours themselves.'[1] In March 1913, writing on the *Salon des Indépendants* in *Montjoie*, Apollinaire referred to 'L'Orphisme, peinture pure, Simultanéité', and the two terms thus became largely synonymous.

The poets and critics had played a considerable part in stimulating and organizing the first manifestations of the Cubists, but the connections between Orphism and contemporary literature were stronger and more direct. Apollinaire, who at the time was fascinated by the interrelation of the arts, and was exploring the visual possibilities of poetry in his *Calligrammes* (for which one of the original titles was *Moi aussi je suis peintre*), was inspired by Delaunay's paintings *Les Fenêtres* to compose, late in 1912, his poem of the same name, in which the means are to a certain extent analogous. This poem, written in free verse, was one of the first in which Apollinaire eliminated punctuation, and was composed of seemingly disconnected, partially self-sufficient phrases and ideas, which by their placing and interaction serve to evoke both form and atmosphere. Early in 1913 Cendrars published the first 'simultaneous' book, *La Prose du Transsibérien et de la petite Jehanne de France*, a poem over six feet in length, which was printed in letters of different colours and sizes on an abstract coloured background designed by Sonia Delaunay. The avowed programme of *Montjoie* was to find the link between various arts and to investigate their common tendencies, and Canudo invented the term 'cérébrisme' to describe this attitude: 'Montjoie is the mouthpiece of Cerebrist art, for Cerebrism, according to its own definition, embraces and explains the entire artistic evolution of our age during the past forty years, and in the widest sense, being an aesthetic that is indissolubly cerebral and sensual – against all sentimentality in art and life.'[2] Writing

[1]In a preface to the programme of the *Comédie des Champs Elysées, Saison 1926–27.*
[2]Issue of April–June 1914.

about Stravinsky, Canudo gave a practical demonstration of his outlook when he claimed that: 'He partakes of our aesthetic, of Cubism, of synchronism, of the simultaneity of some and the nervous, matter of fact onyrhythm of others.' An author named Henri Martin, who wrote under the name of Barzun, published a 'Manifeste sur le simultanisme poétique',[1] and disputed with Apollinaire the invention of what he called literary Simultaneism. Apollinaire felt that he had achieved simultaneity in his *poèmes conversations*, where 'the poet at the centre of life records somehow the lyricism around him'.[2] Later in the same article 'Simultanisme-Librettisme' in which he expounded these views, Apollinaire, using Picasso's work as an example, extended the idea of Simultaneity to cover the combination of various view-points of objects in a single image.

Orphism appeared before the public at the *Salon des Indépendants* of 1913. As in the case of Cubism, Apollinaire tried to give the word as much of an all-inclusive meaning as possible: 'Orphism has already been talked about a great deal. This is the first time that this development has been made manifest. It comprises painters of very different kinds, who all, in their work, are animated by a vision of life that is more internal, more popular and more poetic. This tendency is not a sudden invention; it is a slow and logical evolution from Impressionism, from Divisionism, from the works of the Fauves and from Cubism. Only the term is new.'[3] Generally speaking, however, although Orphism was regarded as a new school its derivation from Cubism was acknowledged. This had, of course, been made clear at the *Salon des Indépendants* by Delaunay's *L'Equipe de Cardiff* (pl. 81)[4] which, compared to his more abstract works, appeared simply as a highly coloured and more *mouvementé* Cubist painting. Warnod noted in *Comoedia* that 'Cubism and Orphism belong to the same family. While Cubism aims at purity of draughtsmanship, Orphism is an attempt at "pure" painting, not that it involves pure colours, that is to say colours as they come out of the tube, but rather painting divorced from all other considerations'.[5]

[1] *Paris Journal*, 27 June 1913.
[2] *Soirées de Paris*, June 1914.
[3] *L'Intransigeant*, 25 March 1913.
[4] Two large versions of this painting exist; the slightly later, more highly finished of the two, now in the Musée National d'Art Moderne in Paris, was the one shown at the *Indépendants*.
[5] 18 March 1913.

Apollinaire, who in *Les Peintres Cubistes* had defined Orphic Cubism as being represented only by Delaunay, Léger, Picabia, Duchamp and Picasso in so far as his use of light was significant, now saw Orphic tendencies in Laurencin, Gleizes and Metzinger,[1] and later (more understandably) in La Fresnaye.[2] More often, however, the term was reserved for Delaunay and his disciples, Bruce, Frost, Sonia Delaunay and Alice Bailly, and for painters such as Picabia, Kupka and Duchamp who had all been originally classified as Cubists but whose work was becoming more abstract, although it had little or nothing to do with that of Delaunay. Léger, whose researches had always been more highly personal than those of the other Cubists with whom he showed, and whose art was now becoming more obviously divergent, is also sometimes referred to as an Orphist; this, however, is understandable since his work did have something in common with Delaunay's. At the *Salon des Indépendants* all these artists were grouped together in *Salle 45*, together with the work of Morgan Russel and MacDonald Wright, who called themselves 'Synchromists' and somewhat pretentiously purported to be representatives of a new school which was to be the culmination of all European painting; they were, in fact, rapidly absorbed into the more vital Orphist movement. The Cubists were hung in the adjacent *Salle 46*.

During 1912 many of the critics, and in particular Hourcade and Allard, had been anxious to point out that the work of the Cubists was becoming more individual and less austere and didactic. Colour had begun to reappear, particularly in the work of Léger, who had only seriously restricted his palette in 1910. Now, under the influence of Orphism, the tendency to reinstate the more sensuous aspects of painting grew stronger. At the *Salon d'Automne* of 1913 Salmon was struck by 'The range of colours used in many canvases', but added, 'however, the *Salon* of 1913 is a frankly Cubist exhibition'.[3] The Orphists were not adequately represented at this *Salon*, since Delaunay himself refused to show there, but at the *Indépendants* of 1914 the Orphist canvases were so numerous and of such large dimensions that they had to be placed in the largest and most important hall on the ground floor. The Cubists had gained new recruits also, but the impact of the Orphist section caused Salmon to write, 'Orphism and Simul-

[1] *L'Intransigeant*, 18 and 25 March 1913.

[2] *Soirées de Paris*, November 1914.

[3] *Montjoie*, November–December 1913 (nos. 11 and 12 appeared as a single issue).

tanism seem to me to represent a threat to that sense of structure so miraculously rediscovered'.[1] A few months earlier La Fresnaye, a member of the jury of the *Salon d'Automne* of 1913, had written, 'painting is clearly becoming more abstract.'[2] Even allowing for the fact that Orphism, as the most recent artistic novelty, was attracting the attention of a press and public made restless and sensation-hungry by the numerous artistic upheavals which the twentieth century had already witnessed, the fact is that by 1914 the abstract tendencies in European painting were already assuming an importance second only to that of Cubism from which they had largely sprung.

Mondrian, who had felt the impact of Cubism even before reaching Paris, had first exhibited at the *Indépendants* in 1911, submitting his painting from an address in Amsterdam. At the same *Salon* in the following year, after he had come to Paris, his entries were included in the Cubist room, and by 1913 his work was beginning to attract special attention. In one review Apollinaire referred to 'the very abstract painting of Mondrian',[3] and added in another, 'his trees and his portrait of a woman are of great interest.'[4] Apollinaire was furthermore at pains to stress that while the work of Mondrian derived from that of Picasso and Braque, it was completely different in appearance (cf. Pl. 103B). This came about through the fact that although Mondrian made use of the Cubist grid-system of composition, he had already begun to develop a new form of painting which finally culminated during the war in the purely abstract idiom of *De Stijl* and Neo-Plasticism. In Russia, too, the abstract possibilities of Cubism were being explored and developed. Cubism was known there largely through the exhibitions which involved the painter Larionov, who kept in touch with all the most recent developments in Paris and Italy. Larionov had in 1911 invented Rayonism, a movement which had a strong abstract bias, although it was closer in many ways to contemporary Futurism than to Cubism. In 1913 Malevitch, whose work at this period showed traces of both Cubist and Futurist influence, was preparing to launch the Suprematist movement which stood for a more purely abstract style than anything yet seen.

[1] *Montjoie*, March 1914.
[2] Ibid., November–December 1913.
[3] *L'Intransigeant*, 18 March 1913.
[4] *Montjoie*, Special Supplement on the *Salon des Indépendants*, March 1913.

Writing of the *Salon des Indépendants* of 1914, Apollinaire saw another influence at work: 'This year Futurism has begun to invade the *Salon*, and whereas from the reproductions they publish, the Italian Futurists appear to be ever more strongly influenced by the innovators of Paris (Picasso and Braque), it would seem that a certain number of Parisian artists are being influenced by Futurist theories.'[1] This may to a certain extent have been true. Unlike the Cubists, the Futurists had never limited the colours on their palettes and were concerned with a wide range of subject-matter, so that they may have contributed to the general 'loosening-up' process that Cubism was undergoing. Certainly pictorial Futurism owed a great deal to Cubism and was even considered by some to be, like Orphism, an off-shoot of it, although its development was exactly the converse of that of Orphism. Most of the Orphists were Cubists who had broken away and formulated new stylistic and aesthetic principles. The Futurists, on the other hand, were men who started from violent ideological principles of their own but looked to Cubism for guidance as to how they could best express themselves. Marinetti, the organizer of the movement, who launched the first Futurist manifesto in 1909, had spent much time in France and was in touch with the most advanced French thought. He had been connected with the *Théâtre de l'Oeuvre* at the height of its activity, was a friend and admirer of Jarry, and a regular visitor to the Tuesday gatherings at the Closerie des Lilas.[2] In 1910 Boccioni and his friends got to know Marinetti well,[3] and were undoubtedly excited at the prospect of creating a new form of painting to correspond to his novel ideas. But when the Futurist painting manifestos appeared early in 1910 the work of the painters themselves still lacked a sense of direction. Of the five painters who had signed the manifesto only Severini, who had been in Paris since 1905, had any claim to be considered *avant-garde*, whereas the others were mostly working in a debased divisionist technique and relied for novelty on the rather obvious imagery of their subject-matter.[4] At that same moment the Cubist painters, other than Picasso and Braque, were making contact with each other on the basis of common pictorial interests, while the Italians were banded together with an elaborate

[1]*Soirées de Paris*, March 1914.
[2]Severini, *Tutta la Vita di un Pittore*, Italy 1946, p. 97 et seq.
[3]Benedetta Marinetti, *Marinetti, Cahiers d'Art*, Paris 1950.
[4]Severini, op. cit., describes some of the pre-Parisian canvases, pp. 124–5.

programme but no adequate means of expressing it. They were, however, aware of the developments in France. In 1914 Boccioni wrote: 'We were aware of Cubism as it had been publicized in France in articles and books when we came out with the technical manifesto of Futurist painting (11 April 1910) and with our first exhibition at the Bernheim Gallery (6 February 1912).'[1] In actual fact little had been written about Cubism by April 1910, but Boccioni's work of 1911 shows some indirect Cubist influence, and he was certainly in correspondence with Severini, who, though as yet little touched by the movement, was a friend of both Picasso and Braque.[2]

Boccioni, Carrà and Russolo showed recent works at the *Esposizione d'Arte Libera* in Milan in the Spring of 1911, and owing to the polemics already aroused by Futurist propaganda their work attracted great interest.[3] The Futurists were severely criticized in *La Voce* by the painter-critic Ardengo Soffici,[4] for the triteness of their imagery and their lack of technical control. A friend of Apollinaire, Soffici was possibly the only man in Italy at the time with a clear idea of Cubism and its aims, and in contrasting it with the work of the young Futurists no doubt felt that his strictures were justified. Severini, who had signed the manifestos but was not exhibiting, had come to Milan to ask Marinetti for financial assistance, and he advised that the Italian painters should visit Paris before exhibiting there as they intended.[5] Boccioni convinced Marinetti of the necessity of the expedition, and accordingly Marinetti took Boccioni, Carrá and Russolo to Paris, arriving in the autumn of 1911. Severini, who had only recently met Carrá and Russolo, now took the Italian painters on a tour of the Paris studios and galleries. By the time that the Futurist exhibition opened at the Galerie Bernheim in February of the following year, Boccioni had reworked his *States of Mind*, a series of paintings which he felt held the key to a new range of subject-matter in painting, and Carrà and Russolo had abandoned or reworked some of their largest pre-Parisian canvases.[6]

[1]Boccioni, *Pittura Scultura Futuriste*, Milan 1914, p. 148.
[2]*Tutta la Vita di un Pittore*, p. 115.
[3]There had also been a Boccioni exhibition at the Palazzo Pésaro in Venice in 1910.
[4]*Tutta la Vita di un Pittore*, pp. 118–19.
[5]Ibid., p. 125.
[6]Ibid., p. 125 et seq.

Futurism's debt to Cubism was universally recognized. Apollinaire pointed out that Boccioni's best works were those in which he came nearest to recent works by Picasso which he had seen in Paris.[1] Hourcade wrote of the Futurist exhibition in the *Revue de France*: 'One would swear that a clever pupil of the Cubists and an even cleverer pupil of Signac had painted the works in collaboration . . . Can it be that our hot-headed guests want to burn the museums in order to destroy the evidence?'[2] Even pictorial Futurism of course contained much that was new; as opposed to Cubism it was primarily an art of movement, concerned with treating large ambitious subjects, and with an aggressively contemporary aesthetic which expressed itself in its destructive attitude towards the past and a glorification of the machine; unlike Cubism it was a highly romantic and literary kind of painting. But the means by which the Futurists were expressing themselves at this point were largely borrowed from the Cubists, and occasionally in some less well-informed criticism, the two terms became synonymous.[3] The linear Cubist grid was adapted to become the Futurist 'lines of force' by which the representational elements are traversed. The fusion of the figure and its surroundings on which the Italians insisted was something that the Cubists had already achieved, and although the Futurists went further and added that the painting must be a synthesis of things seen and things remembered, visible and invisible, this had very little effect on the means employed. The interacting transparent planes used by the Cubists to achieve this fusion and to explain and develop form, coincided with the Futurists' conception of the transparency of objects, and proved capable of adaptation to give a sense of dynamic balance or movement. Explaining one of the sections of their manifesto in the preface to the exhibition at Bernheim's, the Futurists, now aware of Cubist painting, talked for the first time of 'battles of planes'; and Boccioni summarizes most concisely the debt of Futurism to Cubism when in *Pittura Scultura Futuriste*, published in 1914, he wrote under the heading 'Compenetrazione dei Piani': 'It is the pictorial method of rendering movement in a painting, making the surrounding objects fuse with the structure of the object placed in their midst'.[4] The end is purely Futurist but the means are Cubist.

[1]*Petit Bleu*, February 1912.
[2]March–April 1912.
[3]e.g. Jean Claude, in *Petit Parisien*, 19 March 1912.
[4]*Pittura Scultura Futuriste*, p. 234.

But as the movement became more fiercely nationalistic, the Futurists began to complain that they in turn were being plagiarized in France. In articles in *Der Sturm* and *Lacerba*[1] Boccioni claimed that the Futurists had been the first to introduce the concept of Simultaneity into painting, and that Léger's article 'Les Origines de la Peinture et sa Valeur Représentative'[2] was really a Futurist statement. Léger was certainly more in sympathy with Futurism than most of the other artists associated with the Cubist movement. Delaunay, for example, violently repudiated any analogy between his own art and that of the Futurists both in an open letter to the press[3] and in a long essay written immediately after attending a lecture given by Marinetti at the time of the first Futurist exhibition in Paris.[4] Actually the quarrel was largely due to Apollinaire's careless use of terms and to a rather wilful misunderstanding on the part of Boccioni. The idea of Simultaneity first appeared in the preface to the Futurist exhibition at the Bernheim Gallery: it had its origin in Boccioni's series of *States of Mind*, and was primarily the Bergsonian concept that a picture must be a synthesis of what is remembered and what has been seen, a synthetic visual impression comprising not merely the various aspects of a single object, but any feature related to it, physically or psychologically. A painting by Carrà entitled *Simultaneità*, which shows a figure in a series of successive attitudes, indicates that Simultaneity had for the Futurists also the simpler meaning of the combination of different aspects of objects or people in motion into a single painting. For Delaunay and Léger the term had much more purely plastic connotations. For Delaunay it was the interaction of colours which produced a sense of form and space in a picture, whereas for Léger it meant the simultaneous presence in a painting of the three pictorial elements of line, form and colour, all used in a system of deliberate contrasts.

The Futurists, however, undoubtedly had an influence on the terminology of French painting and literature, and the bewildering mass of 'isms' springing up in 1913 and 1914 reflects also some of the spiritual restlessness which Futurism

[1] *Lacerba*, 1 August 1913.

[2] The article was originally delivered as a lecture at the Académie Wassilief, and was published in *Montjoie*, 29 March, 14 and 29 June 1913.

[3] *L'Intransigeant*, 10 March 1913.

[4] Unpublished. Marinetti delivered two lectures, one on 9 February at the *Maison des Etudiants* and one on 15 February at the *Galerie Bernheim*.

did so much to engender. The first Futurist manifesto was published originally in French in the *Figaro*, and the manifesto of the Futurist painters appeared in full in *Comoedia* shortly after its publication in Italy. Apollinaire, whose enthusiasm and readiness to support any new cause (often without any very deep understanding or sympathy with its aims) did much to add to the artistic confusion of the period, was himself persuaded to write a Futurist manifesto which appeared in Milan in June 1913 – *L'Anti-tradizione Futurista.* Late in 1913 he wrote on a more factual note: 'Futurism is not without importance, and its manifestos drawn up in France have had an influence on the terminology which is employed today amongst the most advanced painters.'[1]

The relations between the Cubists and the German painters with whom they came into contact were less stormy, although the internal situation in Germany was complex from an art-historical point of view owing to the fact that during the pre-war years Germany seemed to become the melting-pot for western European painting. By 1912, however, the influence of Matisse and the Fauves, which the *Brücke* had grafted on to a more purely native form of Expressionism, was definitely on the wane, and German painters were feeling the influence of both Cubism and Futurism. Picasso's work was first seen in Germany in 1909 at the Thannhauser Gallery in Munich, and paintings by many of the other painters subsequently known as Cubists were shown at the second exhibition of the *Neue Künstlervereinigung* in Munich in 1910. Throughout 1912 and 1913 the works of Picasso and Braque were to be seen at the Sturm Gallery in Berlin and in the *avant-garde* exhibitions in Cologne and Munich.

The most significant and direct connection with Germany, however, was that between Delaunay and the artists of the *Blaue Reiter.*[2] In 1911 the German painter Elizabeth Epstein, a friend of the Delaunays, drew the attention of Kandinsky to the works of Delaunay at the *Salon des Indépendants*, and later in the year Kandinsky wrote inviting Delaunay to join in the first exhibition of the reconstituted *Neue Künstlervereinigung*, now known as the *Blaue Reiter*, which was held in December at the Thannhauser Gallery in Munich. Delaunay was represented by three paintings, all of which were sold, and his reputation and

[1]*Soirées de Paris*, 15 December 1913.

[2]Most of the information in this paragraph comes from the Delaunay biographical data.

influence in Germany increased steadily. In the spring of the following year (1912) Delaunay was visited in his studio in Paris by Paul Klee, and later on by Marc and Macke. While in Paris Klee saw and admired Cubist works at Uhde's, and he may have known the rapidly growing Rupf collection in Berne, but he remained most impressed by Delaunay's scientific approach to the handling of colour, which fitted in with his own ideas; in the autumn of 1912 he translated some of Delaunay's notes on light for the review *Der Sturm*. The climax of Delaunay's success in Germany came when he was given a large one-man show at the Walden Gallery in Berlin early in 1913; both Delaunay and Apollinaire travelled to Germany for the opening. Orphism appealed particularly to the Germans, since like so much of their own painting it was brightly coloured and was simultaneously a more theoretical and a more popular type of art than Cubism.

Although the influence of Cubism on the German painters was less direct than it had been in the development of Futurism (the work of Delaunay which the Germans most admired, for instance, was no longer really Cubist at all), unlike the Italians the Germans made no attempt to disguise their interest in the movement, and several of the artists of the *Blaue Reiter* actually thought of themselves as Cubist painters. This was in a sense strange, since not only was their art far removed from true Cubism from a purely visual point of view, but their aims, though not as aggressively stated as those of the Futurists, were equally at variance with those of the French painters. The work of both Klee and Marc was tinged by a strong literary flavour, and, particularly in the case of Marc, by a strong underlying current of Germanic mysticism. In fact Marc's painting after 1911, with its intense, vibrant colour, and its sense of drama and dynamic tension, was in many ways closer to Futurism than to Cubism. In the work of Macke, even at its most controlled and classical, a jagged expressionistic feeling keeps breaking through, while his subject-matter at its most typical invites, once again, Futurist analogies. However, what all three painters learnt from Cubism, largely through Delaunay, was the means of organizing a canvas in terms of interacting and transparent facets or planes, which could be made to suggest movement and depth, while preserving the unity of the picture-plane; Chagall, another painter whose work was known and admired in Germany, and who had also flirted briefly with both Cubism and Orphism, acknowledged a similar debt to Cubist painting. But whereas Futurism had been to a large extent aimed at and against Paris and Parisian painting, the Germans were content to remain on the receiving end of things and their work, in the pre-war years at least, had little or no influence back on French art.

With the declaration of war the Cubist painters, many of whom had begun to grow apart artistically, were physically separated, and the movement rapidly broke up. Cubism, however, had already won its most important battles. Though not appreciated by the public it certainly was accepted or at least recognized by all the significant critics and by several important dealers. It had temporarily reasserted the ascendancy of painting over other art forms by overshadowing any advances in literature or music. The style was constantly attracting new figures and had influenced, directly or indirectly, almost every significant young painter in Europe; even Matisse, whose art had always seemed at the opposite pole to Cubism, was introducing a hitherto unknown severity into his painting in preparation for Cubistic experiments in 1915. Whatever directions artists were to take after the war, it was already clear that painting could never be quite the same again.

2

PICASSO AND BRAQUE 1907–12

When Picasso painted the *Demoiselles d'Avignon* (Pl. 1), those of his friends who were allowed to see it seem to have felt that in some way he had let them down. In his 'Histoire anecdotique du Cubisme' Salmon records their disappointment.[1] Gertrude Stein writes that 'Tschoukine who had so much admired the painting of Picasso was at my house and he said almost in tears, what a loss for French painting.'[2] Derain prophesied that one day Picasso would be found hanged behind it.[3] Braque was frankly bewildered by it.

The *Demoiselles* is not, strictly speaking, a Cubist painting. Most of the Cubists were united in declaring that theirs was an art of realism, and in so far as Cubism was concerned with reinterpreting the external world in a detached, objective way it was also in a sense a classical art. The first impression made by the *Demoiselles*, on the other hand, is one of violence and unrest. Indeed, the savagery of the two figures at the right-hand side of the painting (which is accentuated by the lack of expression in the faces of the other figures) would justify its classification as one of the most passionate products of twentieth-century Expres-

[1]In *La Jeune Peinture Française*, p. 43.

[2]Gertrude Stein, *Picasso*, Paris 1938. Eng. edit. New York, London 1939, p. 18. This statement of Gertrude Stein's is, however, slightly puzzling as Barr writes that it was not until 1908 that Matisse took Tschoukine to Picasso's studio (*Matisse, his Art and his Public*, Museum of Modern Art, New York 1951, p. 85). At any rate, if Tschoukine did not say this to Gertrude Stein, someone else probably did.

[3]D. H. Kahnweiler, *Mes Galeries et mes Peintres: Entretiens avec Francis Crémieux*, Paris 1961, p. 56.

sionism. But it is incontestable that the painting marks a turning point in the career of Picasso and, moreover, the beginning of a new phase in the history of art. It is, too, the logical point to begin a history of Cubism. For as an analysis of the painting will show, many of the problems that faced Picasso and Braque in their creation of the style are stated here, crudely perhaps, but clearly for the first time. 'These are stark problems, white equations on a black-board', Salmon has written of the figures in the *Demoiselles*. 'This is the first appearance of painting as algebra.'[1]

In the spring of 1907, when he began the preparatory sketches for the *Demoiselles*, Picasso was already establishing his reputation as one of the most outstanding of the younger figures in contemporary French painting. Since he did not exhibit at the big *Salons* his name may not have been as well known to the general public as those of Matisse and Derain, who in the previous years had emerged as the most important and controversial figures in the Fauve movement, but there were a large number of people who believed in his genius. There are even indications that many of Picasso's circle, the artists, writers and dealers who used to meet at his studio in the *Bateau Lavoir* and at the Steins' house in the rue Fleurus, already saw Picasso and Matisse as the two rival personalities most likely to influence the course of twentieth-century painting.[2] A year earlier Matisse had show his painting *Le Bonheur de Vivre* (Barnes Foundation, Merrion, Penn.) at the *Salon des Indépendants*, where it had received a great deal of attention, and during the winter of 1906–7 Derain was engaged in painting a canvas of bathers (Museum of Modern Art, New York) (Pl. 101B) which he intended to show at the *Indépendants* of 1907, so that it is possible that the *Demoiselles* may have been prompted by a spirit of rivalry. At any rate Picasso seems to have realized, even before he began it, that it was to be no ordinary painting. Salmon, who was an intimate friend of Picasso's at this time, described a few years later his restless state of mind: 'Picasso was unsettled. He turned his canvases to the wall and laid down his brushes . . . During long days and as many nights, he drew, giving concrete expression to abstract ideas and reducing the

[1]*La Jeune Peinture Française*, p. 43.

[2]In 1912, when he wrote *La Jeune Peinture Française*, Salmon certainly saw them in this light. And by 1906 they were the two painters who were most attracting attention of the Steins and the circle around them.

results to their fundamentals. Never was a labour more arduous, and it was without his former youthful enthusiasm that Picasso began on a great canvas that was to be the first result of his researches.'[1]

There are no fewer than eight sketchbooks concerned with the *Demoiselles* and although odd pages of these have been removed, Picasso kept them with him until the end of his life, guarding them jealously. Individual sketchbooks show him, most significantly, alternating between his ideas concerning an ambitious, multifigure composition layered in iconographical implications, and the exploration of formal problems and innovations most frequently approached in sketches of single figures or images. Many of the canvases produced in the later part of 1906 constitute what might be called a 'crisis' point in Picasso's art in that he was becoming increasingly obsessed with creating figures which were heavily volumetric, indeed often almost grotesquely bulky, but which simultaneously adhered or clung to the picture plane: the effect they produce could best be described by imagining a series of pneumatic models pushed up against heavy panes of glass and pumped up with air, so that they get larger and larger whilst simultaneously flattening up against the surface in front of them. Looking at these pictures one senses that an explosion was inevitable and in a sense the explosion was the *Demoiselles*. An important canvas of the autumn or early winter of 1906, *Two Nudes* (Pl. 2), now in the Museum of Modern Art, New York, could equally well be seen as two studies of a single figure viewed from diametrically opposed positions, an indication that Picasso was not only attempting to produce images of almost unprecedented weight and girth, but that he was also becoming impatient or dissatisfied with the idea of viewing his subjects from a single, stationary point of view. Many of the pages of the *Demoiselles* sketchbooks show single figures in upright, hieratic stances, their limbs disposed symmetrically; some are seen frontally, others from the back; sketchy ghosts and erasures unite backviews with the more definitive frontal poses and vice versa.

Although the historical importance of the *Demoiselles* cannot be overestimated, it is not hard to understand why it disappointed Picasso's friends. It must have then seemed in many ways an unresolved and unsatisfactory painting. To begin with there are the obvious inconsistencies of style. Even a cursory

[1] *La Jeune Peinture Française*, p. 42.

glance is enough to show that Picasso had several changes of mind while he was working on the canvas. Kahnweiler throughout his life was to maintain that the painting was unfinished, and on occasion was even to assert that Picasso himself saw it in this way. In fact it seems more likely that Picasso felt that the *Demoiselles* as he decided to accept or leave it represented a truly astonishing challenge with which he himself must come to terms; obviously if he had been dissatisfied with the look of the painting he would not have left it as it is,[1] and it has been argued that the stylistic discrepancies within the painting are essential to its iconography, to the message which it is intended to convey.[2] Unlike the *Joie de Vivre*, which was intended to soothe and delight the eye, the *Demoiselles* can hardly have been calculated to please. Whereas Matisse's painting is, as the title suggests, wonderfully joyful and full of rich colour and sensuous rhythms, the *Demoiselles* is angular, harsh and grating. The charm and wistfulness of so much of Picasso's earlier work has been deliberately suppressed and the mood of the *Demoiselles* is quite clearly consciously disturbing, physical and erotic yet savage, simultaneously inviting and repellent. Derain's *Baigneuses* is in many ways closer in spirit to the *Demoiselles*, and it was regarded by Vauxcelles at least,[3] as a revolutionary work, but it had the advantage that it could still be fitted into a traditional frame of reference. It looked, so to speak, like a follow on from other painting. The *Demoiselles* did not.

Nevertheless, there are many things about the *Demoiselles* that serve to relate it to other painting of the period and, more particularly, to the contemporary work of Matisse. Both the *Demoiselles* and the *Bonheur de Vivre* refer, if only indirectly, to a wealth of other art. The sources of the *Bonheur* range from the decorative '*cloisonnist*' aspect of Gauguin's painting and back through Ingres to the bacchanals of the Renaissance. Both Gauguin and Ingres are relevant to the *Demoiselles*, too, and the names of Delacroix and Manet have been invoked in connection with it.[4] During the early years of the century the influence of

[1]See William Rubin, 'From Narrative to "Iconic" in Picasso: the buried allegory in *Bread and Fruit Dish on a Table . . .*', Appendix XI, 'The supposed unfinishedness of the *Demoiselles*', *Art Bulletin*, Vol. LXV, no. 4, December 1983, pp. 647–8.

[2]Leo Steinberg, 'The Philosophical Brothel', two parts, *Art News*, September 1972, pp. 22–9, October 1972, pp. 38–47.

[3]See p. 146 below.

[4]Robert Rosenblum, 'The *Demoiselles d'Avignon* Revisited', *Arts*, 71, no. 5, September 1972.

Cézanne had become increasingly pronounced among the progressive young painters who showed at the *Salon des Indépendants*, and after its creation in 1903, the *Salon d'Automne*. Matisse, who was one of the first of the painters of his generation to appreciate the true genius of Cézanne, had been working under his influence since 1899, the year in which he bought Cézanne's *Trois Baigneuses* (Pl. 105A now in the Petit Palais: Venturi no. 381) from Vollard, choosing it in preference to an *Arlésienne* by Van Gogh,[1] and in the figure pieces that lead up to the *Bonheur*, the influence of Cézanne is immediately obvious.[2] Derain, although as early as 1904 he had executed a still life (Pl. 101A) in which he seized in a more or less superficial way on some of the aspects of Cézanne's art which were later to fascinate and influence the Cubists, did not begin to look at Cézanne really seriously until 1906. The fruits of his study can, however, already be seen in the *Baigneuses* in the firm modelling of the figures and in the angular severity of their contours which recall in particular much of Cézanne's portraiture of the 1880s.[3] Now, looking for guidance in his construction of a monumental figure composition, Picasso too turned to Cézanne, although he approached him, characteristically, not only with veneration (later in life he was to say 'Cézanne was my one and only master')[4] but also in a spirit of aggression, even of iconoclasm.

To begin with, the closest prototype for this kind of painting – a large composition of naked and partially draped women – is to be found in Cézanne's *Baigneuses*.[5] The first of the preliminary sketches for the *Demoiselles*, on the other hand, suggest that at first Picasso may have been more drawn to Cézanne's earlier, more romantic figure pieces. These sketches show that Picasso originally intended the composition to include seven figures, five women and two men, grouped in a curtained interior around still lifes of fruit and flowers. Picasso later explained, in 1939, that the man seated in the centre of the composition was a

[1]Alfred H. Barr, *Matisse, his Art and his Public*, the Museum of Modern Art, New York 1951, pp. 38–9.

[2]See e.g. *Luxe, Calme et Volupté* and almost all the succeeding figure pieces of 1905.

[3]See e.g. Venturi, nos. 516–553–555 etc.

[4]Kahnweiler, op.cit, p. 55.

[5]For similarities in composition see e.g. in particular Venturi no. 542. A photograph of Derain, taken in his studio during the winter of 1908–9, shows a reproduction of this painting hanging on the wall. This photograph is reproduced in Edward F. Fry's 'Cubism 1907–08: An Early Eye Witness Account', in *Art Bulletin*, New York, March 1966.

sailor enjoying the company of the naked women.[1] The second man (who appears at the left-hand side of the composition, drawing back a curtain) in one of the earliest sketches, carries a skull, and Picasso identified him as a medical student.[2] The entire painting was thus conceived if not exactly as a kind of *memento mori*, at least as a statement about sexual compulsion and gratification and concomitant feelings of disgust, danger and fear of disease.[3] The erotic implications of the subject, the *motif* of the figure holding back the curtain and the very prominent position of the still lifes, call to mind such works by Cézanne as *l'Eternel Féminin*, the various *Temptations of St. Anthony* and the *Après-Midi à Naples*. In the later sketches, which become cruder and less Cézannesque in style, Picasso abandoned the idea of including the two male figures in the composition. Some of the original significance of the painting was, however, preserved in its first title, *Le Bordel Philosophique*, suggested in a spirit of humour by Salmon, Max Jacob and Apollinaire.[4] The painting seems to have acquired its present name after the war, when it entered the possession of M. Jacques Doucet. Even so it is only a more oblique reference to the same theme, since the *Avignon* of the title refers to a street in the prostitutes' quarter of Barcelona.

In the last analysis, and in spite of the indoor setting, the *Demoiselles* is related more closely to Cézanne's canvases of bathing women than to his earlier, less structural figure pieces. Indeed, it would have been quite natural if, when Picasso became more interested in the purely pictorial problems involved in composing and unifying a picture the size of the *Demoiselles*, he had begun to look with greater concentration at Cézanne's later figure work. The differences between the *Demoiselles* and the late *Baigneuses* of Cézanne are, of course, much more obvious than their similarities – too obvious, indeed, to need much elaboration. Picasso's work is crude and direct both in colour and execution. Cézanne's is the reverse. There is a strong linear element about the *Demoiselles* and a lack of

[1]Alfred H. Barr, *Picasso, Fifty Years of his Art*, New York 1946, p. 57.

[2]Steinberg, op.cit., part 2, p. 38.

[3]Much of Picasso's earlier work touches on the subject of prostitution and the danger and results of venereal disease.

[4]Salmon refers to it by this name in *La Jeune Peinture Française*. In *Propos d'Atelier*, Paris 1922, he writes of the *Demoiselles*: 'On a peu à peu oublié le titre premier, suggéré, revu et adopté par les familiers de Picasso: Guillaume Apollinaire, Max Jacob et moi-même: "Le B . . . Philosophique".' Footnote to p. 16.

modelling in certain parts of it that Cézanne would never have tolerated. And any influence of Cézanne that there may be in the *Demoiselles* as it now appears is of the most general kind. Nevertheless, the liberties taken with the human body, the overall composition and the way in which the figures are closely grouped together in shallow depth and intimately related to their surroundings, all these things indicate a debt, however remote, to the Cézanne *Baigneuses*. Furthermore, when one looks at these paintings by Cézanne one is often struck by the closeness between the poses of certain figures and those of the 'demoiselles'. This is a point which it would be useless to push too far; the pose of the second figure from the left in the *Demoiselles*, for instance, was one which Picasso had already used frequently in his earlier work. But in one case at least it is likely that this similarity is not simply fortuitous. The squatting *demoiselle* with her broad back and splayed-out legs must surely be derived from the figure at the right of the *Three Bathers* owned by Matisse, a work which Picasso could well, indeed almost certainly must, have seen (Pl. 105A).[1] In a discussion of the general composition and appearance of the *Demoiselles* another possible influence should be mentioned: that of El Greco. The Spanish writer Gomez de la Serna, a friend of Picasso's at this time and an *habitué* of the *Bateau Lavoir* during his visits to Paris, recalls that Picasso's walls there were decorated with reproductions of El Grecos.[2] Moreover, some of Picasso's painting of 1906 bears testimony in a very direct way to his admiration for this Spanish master.[3] The angular, and in the case of the three women at the extreme left and right of the *Demoiselles*, rather 'faceted' appearance of the figures, and the heavy, chalky highlights found in

[1]Picasso and Matisse did not meet until 1905–6 but by 1907 they were certainly on friendly terms and must have visited each other in their studios. The radiographs of the *Demoiselles* in the Museum of Modern Art, New York, show that originally the squatting figure had a tress of hair falling down her back and that her forearm was not twisted around as it now is: this would make the similarities with Cézanne's figure even greater. The closeness of the poses of these two figures was originally pointed out to me by Mr J. Richardson.

[2]Gomez de la Serna, *Picasso*, Turin 1945, pp. 6–7. G. Coquiot also mentions this in *Cubistes, Futuristes et Passéistes*, Paris 1914, p. 148.

[3]See e.g. the *Composition* now in the Barnes Foundation, Merion, Penn. Picasso was working on this painting in August 1906, some three weeks after his return from Gosol (Stein-Picasso correspondence, Yale University Library). In an undated letter to Leo Stein written from Horta de Ebro probably in May 1909 Picasso talks of a proposed trip to Toledo: 'Je veux revoir Greco.'

certain parts of the drapery could well have come from a study of El Greco's work.

But on a more concrete level the *Demoiselles* owes most to Picasso's use of 'primitive' sources. In this respect, too, the *Demoiselles* was related to much of the most advanced painting of the period. The interest in primitive art had come about largely, of course, through the work of Gauguin. Developing certain of his ideas, the Fauves and the German painters of the *Brücke* undoubtedly saw primitive art as a liberating force, stimulating them in their attempts to achieve a more direct and spontaneous form of expression, although the Fauves, at least, were more immediately influenced in this respect by the passionate painting of Van Gogh than by primitive art.[1] By 1906 Picasso had known the work of Gauguin for some time. But while the melancholy air and the mannered, somehow archaistic appearance of much of the work of his so-called 'blue period' remind one of some of Gauguin's painting, it was not until several years later, in the work executed during the year preceding the *Demoiselles*, that Picasso's work became bolder and more direct, in some cases one might justifiably say more primitive, in appearance.

In the spring of 1939, Picasso stated to Zervos that at the time when he was painting the *Demoiselles* his attention had been centred on Iberian sculpture in the Louvre.[2] Picasso had, it is true, for some time been frequenting the different galleries of the Louvre. Indeed, one gets the impression that his painting of 1906 is in some ways a synthesis of elements derived from a whole variety of different types of ancient art: the drawings on Greek white-ground vases, archaic Greek and Etruscan marbles and bronzes, and Cycladic and Mesopotamian figurines. As a Spaniard he must have been particularly interested in seeing the important series of Iberian reliefs from Osuna when they were put on show in the Louvre in the spring of 1906. Their installation was, furthermore, widely publicized. One of these reliefs, which shows a man being attacked by a lion, is, as James Johnson Sweeney has pointed out, of obvious importance in relation to the work of Picasso (Pl. 105C).[3] It accounts in fact for the new facial type which

[1] Primitive sources are not used more directly by Matisse and Derain until late in 1906 (see e.g. some of Matisse's sculpture of this period and Derain's *Baigneuses* (Pl. 101B).

[2] Zervos, *Picasso*, Paris 1942, p. 10.

[3] J. J. Sweeney, 'Picasso and Iberian Sculpture', *Art Bulletin*, 23, no. 3, 1941.

begins to make its appearance in his work during this year,[1] and which reached its most precise definition in the work executed by Picasso on his return from Gosol (a village in the province of Lerida in Spain,[2] where he spent the early part of the summer of 1906), notably in the *Portrait of Gertrude Stein* (Metropolitan Museum, N.Y., Pl. 105B). After countless sittings during the early part of 1906 Picasso, unsatisfied with the face, wiped it out completely. Immediately on his return from Gosol, while Gertrude Stein was still in Italy, he repainted the face, using the conventions of Iberian sculpture, although, since he was anxious to achieve a likeness, they appear in a slightly modified form. The same facial type is adapted to his *Self-Portrait* (Philadelphia Museum of Art) of a few months later, and it is used again, in a more sculptural way, in the *Two Nudes* (The Museum of Modern Art, New York) also of late 1906. The *Two Nudes* represents in many ways the culmination of the 'Iberian' phase in Picasso's art.

The two central figures of the *Demoiselles* relate more closely than any other part of the picture to Picasso's work of 1906. They differ, however, in several respects from anything that had preceded them. The bodies are flatter, more distorted and more angular, and the heads more truly primitive in appearance. All this could be accounted for by the fact that Picasso was working on a very large scale and found it necessary to simplify his technique and adopt a bolder approach. But there are new elements in the treatment of the heads that cannot be so easily explained. A painting of a male head, which is almost certainly a study for the figure of the sailor that Picasso originally intended to place in the centre of the composition, while it is bolder and sketchier than a work like the *Self-Portrait*, shows all the earlier Iberian devices. On the other hand in the heads of the two central 'demoiselles' the severe, regular ovals of the typically 'Iberian' faces of 1906 give way to new, asymmetric shapes. The jaws and chins become much heavier and the bulging eyes stare out vacantly at the spectator. The ears, previously almost always small and compact, reach fantastically large proportions.

[1]During much of 1906 Picasso was, however, working simultaneously in a softer style more reminiscent of his earlier manner.

[2]It is perhaps worth noting that there is no Iberian sculpture that Picasso could have seen at Gosol; so any influence must come from the objects in the Louvre. The church and the castle at Gosol, which are in a state of almost total ruin, are mediaeval. No statuary survives.

All these new features are to be found in two Iberian stone heads of a different type, one of a man and one of a woman, which entered Picasso's possession in March 1907.[1] Both heads have the same staring expression, the same irregular contours and the same heavy jaws as the central figure in the *Demoiselles*, although the male head seems to have interested Picasso most. This head has the typically Iberian ear, with a scroll or shell-like shape at the top, but it is grotesquely exaggerated in size – a comparison of a side view of this head with a watercolour in the Museum of Modern Art in New York shows that Picasso found this feature of it particularly fascinating.[2] The Osuna reliefs were not in fact 'primitive' at all, but rather a perfectly valid reinterpretation of classical Greek sculpture. The two examples that Picasso owned on the other hand could certainly be called primitive, both in conception and execution (Pls. 105D, 106A, B).

If one is willing to discard the possibility of Picasso having focused his attention on these particular heads in the Louvre – and this is unlikely since they were

[1]The history of the two stone heads is interesting. They were among the first discoveries at Cerro de Los Santos (serious excavation was begun there in 1871) and remained for some time in the possession of Don Juan de Dios Agaudo y Alarcón, the man responsible for the first excavations there. In 1903 the archaeologist Pierre Paris bought them, as a pair, for the Louvre. They were displayed there in the *Salle des Antiquités Ibériques* together with the other minor Iberian pieces. Four years later, in March of 1907, the two heads were stolen from the Louvre on successive days. The theft was committed by a man called Géry-Piéret, a Belgian adventurer whom Apollinaire had hired a year earlier as one of his secretaries and whom he was later to use as a model for the hero of *L'Hérésiarque*, which appeared in 1910. Piéret offered the heads to Apollinaire, who suggested that Picasso might be interested in them. Picasso bought them for a small sum, without realizing where they came from. Later, in 1911, after the disappearance of the *Mona Lisa*, the minor thefts from the Louvre assumed a new importance and were reported, for the first time, apparently, in the newspapers. Picasso realized that it was dangerous to retain the objects and, afraid of being implicated, he decided to dispose of them. Fernande Olivier in *Picasso et ses Amis* (pp. 182–8) tells of Picasso and Apollinaire setting out with the intention of dropping the heads in the Seine. They felt, however, that they were being followed and returned without having accomplished their mission. The restitution of the sculptures was finally made through the newspaper *Paris Journal* in September of 1911; Salmon, still a close friend of Picasso's, was working for the paper as art critic. The affair was unfortunately not over for Apollinaire. Géry-Piéret, now operating in Belgium under the name of Baron Ignace d'Ormessan, had written a letter to the Louvre, confessing to the theft of the *Mona Lisa* which he had in fact not committed. Apollinaire was arrested on the charge of complicity but released a few days later, on 13 September, after Géry-Piéret had written the Louvre yet another letter clearing Apollinaire completely.

[2]Géry-Piéret, the man who stole the heads from the Louvre, said that he had chosen the male head because of the enormous ears, 'détail qui me séduisit', *Paris Journal*, 6 September 1911.

not shown on the ground floor like the Osuna reliefs, the *Dama de Elche* and other important Iberian pieces, but in a small room in the basement together with some twenty other heads – his acquisition of them is useful in establishing a chronological sequence for the painting of the different sections of the *Demoiselles*. For the evidence set out above suggests that the heads of the central figures, which still relate to a certain extent to the work of 1906 and which were almost certainly the first to be painted, were not executed until the Iberian stone heads came into Picasso's possession in March 1907. Throughout his life Picasso always reacted very directly to the stimulus of events in his day-to-day life, and the acquisition of two fragments of antiquity from his native land must undoubtedly have fired his imagination. Nevertheless, in the last analysis he was most influenced by the composite picture he had formed of Iberian art he had seen, although one particular head which remained in the Louvre seems especially relevant to the central figures of the great canvas (Pl. 107A). It is now generally agreed that the concept of the work as a whole dates to early 1907 and possibly to the very month in which Picasso acquired his two heads.[1]

It cannot have been long, however, before the painting began to undergo a series of striking changes. The head of the figure at the extreme left, for instance, is different in colour from those of the central figures, and even different from the body to which it is attached; in it the pale pinks that had characterized so much of the work of 1906 have been mixed with black to produce a much more sombre effect. There is a more sculptural feeling about it, too. In this it is related to the heads of the *Two Nudes* painted a few months earlier, but as opposed to them, it is more completely mask-like, and every area or section of it is clearly defined and forms a self-contained unit. Thus there is a clear division between the forehead and the lower part of the face, and a lighter line running down the edge of it suggests that if more of the forehead were seen it would be divided down its central axis. The nose is a self-subsisting pyramid that could be lifted off the rest of the face, and so on. The heads of the two women at the right are different again. They are savagely distorted, and the long thin noses, which have a flat ridge running down the centre, are pulled into the side of the face by thick black lines.

[1]See Rubin, op.cit., Appendix I, 'The Chronology of the *Demoiselles*', p. 642. Pierre Daix in *Picasso, the Cubist Years 1907–16*, London 1979, has a chapter heading 'The Concept of the *Demoiselles*, Autumn 1906–March 1907', but in the captions to the illustrations he dates the first studies to 'early 1907'.

There are touches of green on the head of the standing figure, while the face of the squatting woman is orange, relieved by strokes of blue and yellow. The bodies of both these figures are even more angular than those of the other three women, and the planes that compose them are occasionally differentiated by touches of pure colour; the body of the squatting figure is in the same darker tonalities of the head. The area behind the two central figures is a pale, chalky grey, while the curtains on the right are a bright blue with strong highlights. The still life is painted in the same direct, rather violent technique. Radiographs of the various individual heads taken for the Museum of Modern Art show that originally the faces of the figures at the right were painted in the same idiom as that of the figure at the left.[1] Since the head of the standing figure represents an intermediate stage between that of the figure at the left and the one directly below it, it follows that the squatting figure, the still life and the drapery at the right were the last parts of the picture to be painted. The first 'Iberian' state of the painting probably dates from May through into early June. Picasso then abandoned the painting briefly before beginning to make increasingly radical changes to it. Kahnweiler saw the painting in its present state 'rather early' in the summer, probably in July.[2]

These abrupt changes of style in the *Demoiselles* are due to the fact that while he was working on it Picasso came into contact with tribal art. Vlaminck always insisted that he was the first to have 'discovered' African or Negro sculpture (and he and his contemporaries used the term 'art nègre' generically to cover not only African but also Polynesian art and indeed any tribal art at all that came their way) and his claim was to pass into legend, although Gauguin himself possibly owned examples of African as well as Polynesian sculpture. Undoubtedly both Vlaminck and Derain were looking at tribal art in a somewhat unfocused way before 1906, the year in which Vlaminck purchased his first 'discoveries', as were many other young artists. But 1906 was the year in which consciousness of

[1]The standing figure was originally almost in pure profile, while the lower head was seen in a three-quarter view. The picture seems at one point to have corresponded almost exactly to the sketch in the Gallatin Collection in the Philadelphia Museum of Art, Z II, 21.

[2]Describing the evolution of the picture Salmon states that Picasso at one point abandoned the painting, painted a series of other pictures, returned from a holiday, and took the painting up again (*La Jeune Peinture Française*, p. 46). There is no record of Picasso's having left Paris in the summer of 1907.

so-called 'primitive' art began to affect and colour the aesthetic concerns and standards of young French artists, and Picasso was certainly aware of it by then.[1] Salmon, who was close to Picasso at the time and whose interest in tribal art probably antedates Picasso's, confirms this.[2] Gertrude Stein, too, wrote in her book on Picasso: 'Upon his return from Gosol he became acquainted with Matisse through whom he came to know African sculpture.'[3] In the autobiography of Alice B. Toklas she insists that this was 'just after Picasso finished painting Gertrude Stein's portrait'.[4] Matisse substantiated this story by his statement to Warnod that he had bought a negro statuette in a curiosity shop in the rue de Rennes, on his way to Gertrude Stein's, and that Picasso saw it and became enthusiastic about it.[5] Picasso himself, on the other hand, said that he became familiar with negro art only after having painted the *Demoiselles*, and that his introduction to it took place in the Trocadero.[6] In view of the appearance of certain heads in the *Demoiselles*, however, it is perhaps permissible to think that his recollections are not completely accurate. The truth of the matter is that Picasso was almost certainly aware of tribal art when Matisse showed him the piece which he admired, but that he was still not taking it very seriously and only 'discovered' it for himself during his now legendary visit to the Trocadero. And the visual evidence all goes to prove that this took place while he was working on the *Demoiselles*, probably in June. Unquestionably the visit was to alter the entire course of his development as an artist. Talking to André Malraux years later, Picasso went so far as to say that it was on this occasion that he all of a sudden received the revelation of why he was a painter at all and that 'I realized what painting was all about'.[7]

[1]For by far the most exhaustive account of the 'discovery' and availability of tribal art, see *Primitivism in Twentieth Century Art*, Museum of Modern Art, New York, 2 vols., 1984, edited by W. Rubin, and in particular Rubin's essay 'Picasso' (vol. 1, pp. 241–343).

[2]*La Jeune Peinture Française*, p. 43.

[3]*Picasso*, p. 22.

[4]In the *Autobiography of Alice B. Toklas* (New York 1933) she writes: 'In any case it was Matisse who first was influenced, not so much in his painting as in his sculpture, by the African statues and it was Matisse who drew Picasso's attention to it just after Picasso had finished painting Gertrude Stein's portrait', p. 68. Janneau, who knew Picasso at this time, states in his *L'Art Cubiste* (Paris 1929) that Picasso came to know Negro sculptures in 1906, but he says that it was through Derain, p. 12.

[5]André Warnod, 'Matisse est de retour', *Arts*, no. 26, July 1945.

[6]Zervos, *Picasso*, Vol. II (1), 1942, p. 10.

[7]Quoted in Rubin, 'Picasso', *Primitivism*, Vol. 1, pp. 242 and 334, fn. 8. The Musée d'Ethnographie,

The head of the figure at the extreme left of the *Demoiselles* is, like that of her companions in the centre of the picture, expressionless and impassive but now has about it a mask-like quality that recalls a wide variety of African tribal masks in which the component parts of the head and face have about them exactly the same quality of definition, although here the similarities may possibly be simply affinities rather than derivations; the heads of many of the paintings of late 1906 had also been severe and mask-like although they tend to resemble sculptures in stone, whereas the head of the *demoiselle* in question looks more wooden in both colour and texture. The deformations of the heads of the two right-hand figures are infinitely more radical and extreme and again evoke analogies with a wide range of tribal art which cannot be simply fortuitous. In certain respects they resemble or recall the heads of Kota and Hongue reliquary figures from the French Congo, some of the most abstract and inventive of all African tribal sculptures, and which existed in a wide and varied selection in the collections of the Trocadero at the time of Picasso's visit (Pl. 106D).[2] These heads are usually oval in shape and are mostly covered with scarifications, striations or incised lines; the ears are almost always ignored, as they are in the standing figure at the right of the *Demoiselles*. The eyes are often represented by raised lozenges, with a dot in the middle. The eyebrows meet in the centre of the forehead and their contours are continued down into the noses. The mouths are small ovals and generally appear low in the face. At a very general level these highly abstracted images were to affect Picasso's art deeply over the following year, and the visual ambiguities embedded in many of them – many of these heads are, for example, concave rather than convex – were to be relevant to subsequent Cubist aesthetic. The savagery of the heads of these *demoiselles*, the twisted, asymmetrical treatment of the head of the squatting figure and the raw colouration of both heads in terms of earthy reds and chalky, greyish white, traversed by slashes of blacks, blues and greens, relate them equally convincingly to examples of Oceanic art which were on view at the Trocadero.

which came to be popularly known as the Trocadero and which is now the Musée de l'Homme, opened in 1882. At the time of Picasso's visit it was in fact officially closed to the public, but admission could be obtained.

[1]For an account of the different kinds of art available and relevant to Picasso, see Rubin, op.cit.

Nevertheless, it is dangerous and indeed impossible to push too far the analogies between the heads of the two outer *demoiselles* and various particular kinds of tribal art. In the Trocadero large quantities of objects were displayed in a crowded, haphazard fashion, and, while Picasso was undoubtedly overwhelmed by what he saw and experienced, the impression he carried away with him must have been of a very general, metaphysical kind. It might be fair to say that the paintings Picasso executed during the following eighteen or so months tend to look like *all* tribal art, an indication that he was ultimately interested and immersed in its spirit and its formal principles rather than in any of its individual manifestations. And it is deeply revealing that recent scholarly research into what tribal art he could have encountered during the time of his first enthusiasm for it has demonstrated that he could not have seen most of the examples which art historians have previously compared and juxtaposed to his paintings.[1]

Tribal sculpture and the painting of Cézanne, both of which were used extensively by Picasso as sources for the *Demoiselles*, were to be the two major influences in the creation of Cubism; in fact the constant inspiration which Picasso and Braque drew from the art of Cézanne and the stimulation which tribal sculpture provided for Picasso were the only important outside influences in the development of a style which was to be very self-contained. It is in the *Demoiselles* that these two influences first appear together in the art of Picasso, and it is this that in part makes the picture a natural starting-point for the history of Cubism. Cézanne and tribal art are not yet, it is true, interpreted in a Cubist way. However, their influence on the *Demoiselles* is not the only feature of this painting that gives some indication of what Cubism was to achieve. In the mask-like head of the figure on the extreme left, for instance, Picasso has shown an almost sculptural interest in reducing the forms of the face to their simplest component parts. This sort of dispassionate investigation of the nature of simple, solid forms in space was one of the starting-points of the Cubism of both Picasso and Braque. On a more general level, the treatment of the figures in terms of simple, angular shapes or planes arranged in shallow depth foreshadows some of the later techniques which Picasso and Braque evolved to suggest the forms of

[1]Ibid.

solid objects and their relationship to the space around them. There are several things in the *Demoiselles* that cannot be explained completely either by the influence of Cézanne or of tribal art and which point ahead to one of the most important and revolutionary features of Cubist painting: the combination of various views of a subject in a single image. In the three figures in the left-hand half of the painting this sort of optical synthesis is accomplished in a crude, rather schematic fashion. The noses of the two figures that are seen from in front are in profile, while the figure at the left, which is in strict profile, has a full-face eye. The bodies of all three figures, however, are seen as in normal vision, from a single (or stationary) viewpoint. In the squatting figure on the right, on the other hand, all the canons of traditional linear perspective have been violated. The subject seems to be posed in what is basically a three-quarter view from the back, with the breast and the inner part of the thigh visible between the arm and leg, but the far leg and arm have been pulled around into the picture plane so that the spectator has the impression of seeing a simple back view, abnormally splayed out, as well. It is as if the painter had moved freely around his subject, gathering information from various angles and viewpoints. This dismissal of a system of perspective which had conditioned Western painting since the Renaissance marks, more than any other single feature of the *Demoiselles*, the beginning of a new era in the history of art.

Although it was a powerful but very generalized recognition of the properties of tribal art that first struck Picasso during the following years he also became familiar with a wide range of its artefacts and almost immediately began amassing a collection of his own.[1] Gomez de la Serna remembers that Picasso's studio in the *Bateau Lavoir* was filled with African and Oceanic 'idols'.[2] *Paris Journal* referred in 1911 to the enthusiasm with which Picasso would show his collection to visitors to his studio in the Boulevard de Clichy.[3] Later, after Picasso had denied any knowledge of African art in the *Enquête sur l'Art Nègre* conducted by the review *Action* in 1920,[4] Paul Guillaume, the first Parisian art-dealer to become interested

[1]Many of the first objects in Picasso's collection were acquired at the same shop in the rue de Rennes in which Matisse had found the example he claimed to have shown Picasso (Allard, in *Le Nouveau Spectateur*, 25 May 1919, reviewing an exhibition of Negro sculpture at the Galerie Devakey).

[2]*Picasso*, pp. 6–7.

[3]25 September 1911.

[4]No. 30, April 1920.

in African and other primitive sculptures as works of art, wrote: 'Picasso owns a certain number of pieces of very different origins; he makes a pretence of attaching no importance to their chronology.' In fact this ignorance was not assumed. In the early part of the twentieth century very little was known about the chronology of tribal art (most of it was considered to be much older than it is), and the stylistic differences between the work of various regions had not been examined; Guillaume himself included Oceanic work under the term tribal art, and felt that it could be extended to include Alaskan art as well. To the end of his life Picasso himself did not bother to distinguish between African and Oceanic art, although he must have been aware of distinctions between the two during his contacts with the Surrealists in the 1920s, for they tended to prefer and extol the 'marvellous' properties of the latter. By the end of 1908 Picasso owned at least five tribal objects and he went on to amass a large collection, much of it of very doubtful quality, although after the war when his own work was commanding large prices he occasionally exchanged a painting for a choice piece. But he continued to be interested in the principles behind tribal art rather than in the aesthetic appeal of individual objects; and these principles could be embodied even in the contemporary 'forgeries' which quickly began to be produced in quite large numbers to meet the demand for 'primitive' art. He knew the fine private collections that were being amassed by men like Frank Burty, who was a friend, and most of all he must have been interested in the objects bought by his painter friends. Derain in particular soon acquired a large number of excellent pieces.[1] Significantly enough Matisse tended to collect relatively conservative examples of tribal art, whereas Picasso was often most attracted to abstract, fanciful and esoteric sculptures and artefacts.[2]

Thirty years later, recalling the revelation of tribal art, Picasso spoke of the *Demoiselles* as his 'first exorcism picture': 'For me the masks were not simply sculptures, they were magical objects ... They were weapons – to keep people from being ruled by spirits, to help free themselves.'[3] And it was undoubtedly at this deeply atavistic and liberating level that he responded from the first to tribal

[1]Derain is already referred to as a 'collector' of tribal art in *Paris Journal* of 5 October 1911. His collection was sold at the Hôtel Drouot in 1955.
[2]See Rubin, op.cit.
[3]Quoted Rubin, op.cit., p.255.

art. But it must also be remembered that this statement was made after his involvement with Surrealism and that he might not have phrased his reactions in precisely this way in earlier years. To Salmon he said he admired tribal sculptures because he found them 'raisonnables'.[1] In stressing the more 'reasonable' or rational character of African art, Picasso was underlining the quality that distinguishes it most fundamentally from Western art. As opposed to Western art, tribal art is more conceptual, much less conditioned by visual appearances. The tribal sculptor tends to depict what he knows about his subject rather than what he sees. Or, to put it differently, he tends to express his *idea* of it. This leads inevitably to great simplification or stylization, and, at the same time, to a clarification and accentuation of what are felt to be the significant features or details of the object depicted. Many African pieces, for example, are characterized by their angular contours and the emphasis on the solid, simple forms of trunk and head. The navel, as the central feature of the body, is usually enlarged and emphasized and sometimes the entire stomach is thrust forward in a protruding shield-like form; the limbs are shortened and seen as simple tubular forms, or reduced to a few incisive, sharply differentiated planes. The features of the face are sometimes treated in the same simplified way, or else are so highly stylized that they become simply decorative signs. Ultimately the process of creation is one of intuitively balancing formal elements, and, in the case of the most abstract tribal sculpture, the finished product has the quality not of a representation but a symbol – a re-creation rather than reinterpretation. 'The great law that dominates the new aesthetic,' wrote Salmon in 1920, possibly still echoing his earlier conversations with Picasso on the subject, 'is the following: conception overrides perception.'

Picasso's instinctive appreciation of the aesthetic principles of tribal art was indicative of a new attitude towards primitive art. Gauguin's glorification of the art and life of the South Seas was part of a conscious revolt against what he felt was a corrupt society and the art which it inspired. Through him, more than through any other single force, the aesthetic worth of primitive art forms came to be recognized. His attitude was, however, coloured by a highly literary romanticism, and despite his efforts at identifying himself with a primitive culture,

[1] *La Jeune Peinture Française*, p. 42.

his outlook naturally remained that of a sophisticated European; he borrowed freely from primitive sources but reinterpreted them to suit his own decorative and symbolic purposes. The painters of the *Brücke*, who spiritually and intellectually were some of Gauguin's truest heirs, saw primitive art as a healthy outcry against rationalism which paralleled their own 'Nietzschean affirmation of life'. This attitude was, of course, purely subjective, and their appreciation of primitive art was almost entirely emotional. The Fauves, who owed more to Gauguin from a purely pictorial standpoint, inherited from him some of the spontaneity and decorative rhythms of Polynesian art; and by 1907 both Matisse and Derain had absorbed into their own work some of the formal properties of tribal sculpture. Primitive art may have confirmed them in their desire to achieve a greater directness of expression, but they remained interested in it from a visual point of view. Picasso, on the other hand, while he was undoubtedly fascinated by the formal and sculptured properties of tribal art, also admired it intuitively for a more fundamental reason; for its 'reasonable' or conceptual quality. This was the real link between Cubism and tribal art. For, like tribal art, the Cubism of Picasso and Braque was to be essentially conceptual. Even in the initial stages of the movement, when the painters still relied to a large extent on visual models, their paintings are not so much records of the sensory appearance of their subjects, as expressions in pictorial terms of their idea or knowledge of them. 'I paint objects as I think them, not as I see them,' Picasso said to Gomez de la Serna.[1] And it was the conceptual element of Cubism that enabled the painters at various times to detach themselves from visual appearances without losing touch with the material world around them.

In the period following the execution of the *Demoiselles* Picasso's art was informed by two main principles or types of tribal art, the one flatter, more abstract and remote from European art, in which the basic planes of the face are differentiated not by relief but by the directions of the striations or hatchings with which they are covered, the other more solid, sculptural, three-dimensional and naturalistic. Much of Picasso's work of 1907–8 falls into two complementary, though by no means exclusive categories, according to which of the general types of tribal masks inspired it. Indeed, Picasso's admiration for various complementary,

[1]*Picasso*, p. 31.

at times even formally opposed categories of tribal sculpture is indicative of the instinctive pull which he was feeling between an increased interest in solid, sculptural forms and an awareness of the need to depict them in a manner that did not violate the flat, two-dimensional plane on which he was working. When Picasso's art became truly Cubist, in 1909, he had begun to see solid forms in a new pictorial way, without the aid of linear or mathematical perspective. A new treatment of volumes required, naturally, the invention or formulation of new techniques to reconcile it with the demands of the flat picture surface. In these pre-Cubist paintings of 1907 and 1908 it is as if Picasso were preparing himself for the difficulties involved in creating a new style by taking stock afresh of some of the basic problems inherent in all painting since the invention of illusionistic perspective.

The first type of 'Negroid' painting is more purely pictorial and is represented by the sketches and series of heads which culminate in the *Nu à la Draperie*, a painting of late 1907 which is known also as the *Danseuse aux Voiles* (The Hermitage, Leningrad, Pl. 3A). In this painting the various forms of the body are distinguished from each other by heavy black outlines and, as in African bronzes, by the direction of the striations with which they are covered. The strong linear flavour emphasizes, of course, the flatness of the picture plane and this effect is further strengthened by the fact that the entire picture surface is broken down into angular forms of almost equal size, which are all dealt with in the same vigorous technique.[1] Later, when their work had become completely Cubist, Picasso and Braque devised a more elaborate and sophisticated method of dealing with solid forms but the means which they used to differentiate between the parts of planes or an object or figure and the devices they used to reconcile it to the picture plane were, it will be seen, not unlike those which Picasso used so boldly here. The colours which underly the dark linear striations of *Nu à la Draperie* and related paintings tend to be yellow or golden, coppery and metallic, tempered by passages of blues, greens and reds.

[1]The treatment of the drapery and background in terms of the heavily outlined, angular planes may also relate to tribal work, since in some Sudanese bas-reliefs (doors) in the Musée de l'Homme the areas surrounding the figures are similarly divided into striated, triangular sections of almost equal size. Many of Picasso's paintings of this period are executed in gouache, a quick-drying medium which is particularly suited to this technique, where the forms and ultimately the entire picture surface are built up by a system of cross-hatchings or by a series of individual, parallel brush strokes.

Picasso approached Cubism, however, primarily through his interest in analysing and investigating the nature of solid forms. This more sculptural approach can be seen in the second kind of Negroid painting. In fact, some of the canvases of this type have almost the appearance of being paintings of sculptures and masks.[1] This intensive investigation of simple, solid forms culminates in the paintings of the late summer and autumn of 1908, although by this time Picasso's work was becoming less specifically Negroid. *La Paysanne* (The Hermitage, Pl. 3B), executed at La Rue-des-Bois (where Picasso spent most of August),[2] or shortly after Picasso's return to Paris, is one of the largest and most powerful of the group. Whereas before, in 1906, Picasso had simplified and reinterpreted the human form in a more empirical fashion under the influence of archaic sculpture, now he explains it rationally in terms of simple self-contained planes differentiated by the use of a consistent light source. The colour harmonies of *La Paysanne* and other works of the period are mostly predominantly earthy, creating a sensation of something midway between wood and flesh. The touches or larger areas of primary colours that throw the figures into relief are now less strident, more resonant. The head of *La Paysanne* which conveys the same monolithic, blocklike quality as her body, has features, like those of so many of her immediate predecessors in Picasso's work, that are set into a concave or volumetrically negative facial plane, often set under convex foreheads. These are paintings of solid forms stripped of all their inessentials and reinterpreted with almost geometric exactitude. 'If a painter asked me what was the first step necessary for painting a table' Picasso remarked to a friend at this time, 'I should say, measure it.'[3] The subjects of Picasso's paintings have just such a measured look. One is reminded, too, that this was in actual fact the practice of the Douanier Rousseau, a painter whom Picasso much admired. Indeed, it is at exactly this stage of Picasso's evolution that one senses behind his art the presence of this great 'primitive' who in his naiveté had unconsciously succeeded in ignoring the forces which had influenced French painting for the past fifty years, the forces against which Picasso and his friends were most immediately reacting.

[1]For an early example of this type, see the male head (Z II, 56) of the winter of 1907–8 which is a reinterpretation, in more incisive terms, of the head of the left-hand figure of the *Demoiselles*.
[2]Picasso-Stein correspondence.
[3]Gomez de la Serna, *Picasso*, p. 30.

From 1909, when Cubism emerged as a fully mature idiom, through until the months immediately preceding the outbreak of war in 1914, it was to be not only very self-contained as a movement, but also in certain respects curiously unaccentuated. Pictorial discoveries and transformations succeeded each other rapidly. The quality of the works produced by Picasso and Braque was on the whole consistently high (Gris' output was more uneven in this respect despite the singlemindedness of his vision). There are landmarks and turning points in the movement's evolution but few paintings that demand to be considered or discussed at the expense of others. During the winter of 1908–9, however, Picasso produced two very large canvases (larger than any he was to produce until the summer of 1914) which seem to stand out from others that surround them and which have been the subject of much stimulating argument and discussion. These are the *Three Women* (Pl. 4), which originally belonged to Leo and Gertrude Stein and is now in Russia, and the monolithic still life *Bread and Fruit Dish on a Table* (Pl. 5), now in the Kunstmuseum in Basel.[1]

Both of these pictures throw retrospective light on some of the problems faced in the *Demoiselles*; and although, once again, neither of them is truly Cubist, they are of great significance in the emergence of the style. A photograph taken in Picasso's studio in the summer of 1908 shows an earlier, apparently more or less completed version of the *Three Women* executed in a style which makes use of rough, almost violent striations, used to emphasize the different areas to the sides of the figures, while the figures themselves appear to have the rough-hewn bulkiness of much of the most characteristic contemporary African-influenced figure pieces. The canvas was re-worked during the winter months, after the return to Paris from La Rue-des-Bois in the autumn. Each of the three women is now rendered somewhat differently. The figure at the left is the most 'African' in appearance. The body of the woman to the right is modelled in softer, riper forms. The third figure is the most abstracted and schematic. But whereas the *Demoiselles* is a stylistically disjunctive painting, here each figure seems simply to qualify

[1]See in particular, W. Rubin, 'Cézannisme and the Beginnings of Cubism', *Cézanne, The Late Work*, Museum of Modern Art, New York, 1977, pp. 151–203; Leo Steinberg, 'Resisting Cézanne: Picasso's *Three Women*', *Art in America*, Nov.–Dec. 1978, pp. 114–34, and 'The Polemical Part', *Art in America*, March–April 1979, pp. 114–28; W. Rubin, 'Pablo and Georges and Leo and Bill', *Art in America*, March–April 1979, pp. 128–47.

and reaffirm the properties and existence of her neighbours. The figures now form a tight sculptural group and the space around and behind them is limited and seems to press in upon them. In the two figures on the right in particular the earlier striations and hatchings have given way to more discreetly and subtly modelled planes delineating the component parts of the trunks and limbs of the figures; these planes are angled away from each other along clearly defined ridges in some passages, but softly opened up into each other in others. The violence of the *Demoiselles* has given way to a mood of gravity: the monumental figures appear to be in reverie or slumber.

Bread and Fruit Dish also existed in an earlier version; and it too began life as a figure piece. The composition of the painting and its original theme was developed from two ambitious watercolours of late 1908 entitled *Carnaval au bistrot*, which showed five figures, one wearing a harlequin's hat and another a beret, disposed round a drop-leaved table; the compositions of these watercolours are markedly horizontal. A presumably slightly later gouache, executed on a block-like, upright format, shows the number of figures reduced to four: three seated figures and the same female attendant advancing from the background holding a bowl of fruit. Seated from left to right are a woman, a central harlequin and a man wearing a Cronstadt hat. In the lower part of the great still life, sketchily blocked in, we see the same configuration of legs as in the studies on paper. Above, the *compotier* with fruit and drapery replaces the female figure at the left. William Rubin has suggested[1] that the Gilles-like figure in the watercolour studies is a reference to Douanier Rousseau, clad most characteristically in his beret, and that his presence is still evoked in the left-hand side of the still life through stylistic allusions to his work in terms of insistently if softly modelled forms, smoothly rendered in nuances of Douanier-like greens. The central harlequin of the studies Rubin identifies as Picasso himself (and so indeed he was wont to portray himself) and the man in the Cronstadt hat as Cézanne, who often wore one. These figures have been replaced in the still life by loaves of bread, echoing the position of their arms; their trunks and heads have been eliminated. The right-hand side of the painting, as Rubin points out, is Cézannesque in feeling. Like the *Three Women*, *Bread and Fruit Dish* is a work of

[1]Rubin, 'From Narrative to Iconic . . .'.

extraordinary *gravitas*; and it has about it a physicality and a presence seldom associated with ordinary still life. But it is deeply revealing that in neither of these paintings are the revolutionary perspectival implications of the *Demoiselles* explored or developed, or indeed more than hinted at, and that in the Basel painting figures have been transformed into still life. The formal experiments and innovations on which Picasso was about to embark, and which were to result in a fully developed Cubist language were too innovative, too complex and demanding to be developed or pursued within the context of multifigure compositions. For the next six years Picasso, like Braque, was to fix his attention on single figure compositions, still lifes, and, to a lesser extent, landscapes.[1]

Braque may have been at first bewildered by the *Demoiselles d'Avignon*, but he nevertheless responded to its stimulus, most immediately perhaps in the pen and ink drawing of three nudes published in 1910 as *La Femme* (Pl. 108A):[2] the central figure, seated on her haunches, is a clear reference to the squatting *Demoiselle*, although the composition as a whole curiously anticipates that of Picasso's *Three Women*. The left-hand figure of the drawing Braque developed into his large *Baigneuse*[3] or *Grand Nu* which occupied him over the winter months of 1907–8 (Pl. 35). It fits uncomfortably into Braque's *oeuvre* but it is nevertheless a milestone in the history of Cubism. The debt to Picasso is immediately obvious; the large canvas, the scale of the figure itself and the distortions within it, the muted pinks, buffs and greys (which if they do not closely resemble those of the *Demoiselles* are surely a response to them), the treatment of the background in terms of large angular planes – all these features are new in the work of Braque. But Braque's work contains none of the expressionistic violence of Picasso's. As opposed to the harsh angularity of the *Demoiselles*, the *Baigneuse* is dealt with in terms of free, curving rhythms which owe a lot to Fauvism and to

[1]A single exception is *Soldier and Girl* of 1911, Daix and Rosselet, C.R.394.
[2]In Gelett Burgess, 'The Wild Men of Paris', *Architectural Record*, New York, May 1910, pp. 400–14.
[3]The painting is referred to by this title in the catalogue for the third of the Kahnweiler Sales, on 4 July 1922.

the contemporary work of Matisse.[1] And, fundamentally, Braque's painting is much more thoughtful and reasoned; while the *Demoiselles* must have excited him by its immediacy and directness, it also posed for Braque various pictorial problems. For instance, in the squatting 'demoiselle' Picasso had dislocated and distended the various parts of the body in an attempt to explain it as fully as possible, without the limitations of viewing it from a single, stationary position. In the *Baigneuse* the far side of the figure is pulled round into the picture plane so that the body becomes unnaturally broad; and the *pentimenti* show that the figure was originally to have been even squatter and broader. One gets the impression that Braque wanted to show the spectator as much of the figure as he possibly could. Braque sensed, too, that by dismissing the conventional, single viewpoint perspective it was possible to synthesize into the depiction of the head a variety of information; thus in a three-quarter view the knot of hair at the back of the head is seen clearly, as if from the side. Then Braque has capitalized on the element of ambiguity in the *Demoiselles* (it is not immediately clear for instance whether the leg of the 'demoiselle' on the left is the far leg or the near leg, and the lower part of the twisted forearm of the squatting figure is left undefined) as a means of emphasizing the flatness of the canvas he was working on: the far buttock of the *Nu* is connected to the foremost leg and heightened in tone so that it appears to stand in front of the nearer part of the figure; if the outline of the neck were extended it would not join the shoulder naturalistically but pass by its outer edge, and the fact that the outline is deliberately broken allows the neck, shoulder and arm to flow into each other and fuse. Hitherto Braque had attracted attention as a significant latter-day recruit to the Fauve movement. Now his awareness of the new pictorial possibilities which Picasso had instinctively hit upon in the *Demoiselles* and his study of the work of Cézanne (whose influence, indeed, can already be sensed in the *Baigneuse*) were to make him, within the space of a few months, a major force in twentieth-century painting.

By 1907, the year that preceded the painting of the *Baigneuse*, Fauvism had already lost much of its original impetus, and Braque, like the other Fauves, had for some time been searching for some more solid basis for his art. Matisse, as has been seen, had for the past years been turning to the work of Cézanne for

[1]See e.g. the *Blue Nude* of 1907.

inspiration, and by 1906 Derain was looking at his work also, so that it was only natural that Braque, who had discovered Fauvism through them, should once again follow their example, although he was already well acquainted with Cézanne's work. The influence of Cézanne becomes very apparent in the landscapes of *La Ciotat* of the summer of 1907, which show Braque's work hanging in the balance between Fauvism and a much more structural kind of painting. The loose, undulating rhythms of trees and foliage are still of a kind seen in Fauve canvases by Matisse (and have their origin ultimately in the late work of Gauguin), while the colour is decorative and heightened to an unnatural degree. But the compositions, which are now built up of a series of flat planes mounting upwards behind each other in shallow depth, are clearly derived from Cézanne. In the *View from the Hotel Mistral* (Pl. 36A), executed on Braque's return to Paris a few months later, the influence of Cézanne is even more marked. It has been put, too, to more obviously constructive ends. The composition, in terms of vertical and horizontal elements, is stronger, even slightly rigid, and there is an obvious concern with the definition of forms that is a new element in the work of Braque. The heavy, crude outlines are now no longer broken and sporadic as they were in some of his most characteristically Fauve works, and every shape is carefully and fully outlined; only a certain emphasis on the oval forms of the foliage, and a few touches of arbitrary colour retain any flavour of Fauvism. Colour has become relatively sombre (warm earth colours, blues and greens). The radical simplification of forms which characterizes the painting can be accounted for by the fact that this was one of the first canvases in which Braque attempted to work from memory. This dismissal of a visual model marked a decisive break with Fauve procedure and an important step towards a new, more rational and intellectual kind of painting.

The influence of Cézanne on contemporary painting was renewed and strengthened by two enormously important exhibitions held in 1907. In June the Bernheim Jeune Gallery showed seventy-nine of Cézanne's watercolours and in October the *Salon d'Automne* featured a restrospective of his work,[1] the largest to date, which included some of the iridescent, highly abstracted late landscapes

[1]The catalogue lists fifty-six paintings and drawings. Cézanne had been represented, on a smaller scale, in the *Salons* of this society for the three preceding years.

and some 'unfinished' paintings – paintings in which patches of bare canvas were retained; these must have allowed painters further insights into Cézanne's thought processes and working methods. Simultaneously the *Mercure de France* published in its October issues the letters of Cézanne to Emile Bernard, including the letter which contains the passage: 'Allow me to repeat what I said to you here: deal with nature in terms of the cylinder, the sphere, the cone, all seen in perspective, so that each side of an object or plane is directed towards a central point. Lines parallel to the horizon give breadth, that is to say a section of nature . . . Lines perpendicular to this horizon give depth. However, nature for us men is more depth than surface . . .'[1] As the influence of Cézanne grew, so that of Gauguin, who had hitherto been an important influence in the work of the Fauves, waned. In one of his articles Bernard quoted Cézanne as having said of Gauguin: 'He did not understand me. I have never sought and neither will ever accept the dismissal of modelling or gradation, it makes no sense. Gauguin was not a painter, he simply made Chinese images.'[2]

Cézanne died in 1906 with the feeling of only partially having achieved the end for which he had striven so long and hard. He seems to have realized, however, that there was a younger generation of artists who were to carry on his work. 'I think that the young painters are more intelligent than the others, the old ones can see in me only a disastrous rival', he said to his son in a letter written only a few days before his death.[3] Certainly no other nineteenth-century artist was so widely studied and so differently interpreted by the painters of the succeeding age. Cézanne's intensely 'painterly' art with its brilliant use of colour and its mysterious deformations, which suggested a range of new pictorial concepts, was a source of inspiration for almost all the significant young painters working in Europe during the first quarter of the twentieth century. And no other painter was such an important influence in the formation of Cubism. Indeed, in many ways, Cubism was more justified than any other movement in claiming Cézanne as its father. Even the Cubists, however, interpreted Cézanne in a variety of ways. Léger, for example, deliberately disregarded the complexities of his art, the irregularities and 'distortions', and seized on the element of definition and struc-

[1] Letter of 15 April 1904. *Mercure de France*, 16 October 1907, pp. 617–18.
[2] *Mercure de France*, 1 October 1907, p. 400.
[3] *Paul Cézanne, Correspondance*, edited by J. Rewald, Paris 1937. Letter of 15 October 1906, p. 298.

tural precision as a starting point for his own Cubist experiments.[1] Delaunay, on the other hand, eventually concentrated on his use of colour. Roger de La Fresnaye saw him as a classicist, trying to return to a tradition of painting lost by the Impressionists,[2] while Gleizes and Metzinger emphasized his importance as a revolutionary.[3] Even Picasso and Braque, who shared their discoveries so intimately that for a while they came to share a common vision, looked, it will be seen, at Cézanne in different ways.

All the Cubists, however, studied Cézanne in a more or less constructive fashion. That is to say, all seized on an element of structural and formal strength in his work, which they saw as a corrective to the formlessness which had characterized so much French painting since the Impressionists had insisted on the validity of an instantaneous form of vision, that had so often dissolved the solidity of the material world into a haze of atmospheric colour and light. The Cubists saw, too, in Cézanne's obvious concern with purely pictorial problems an antidote to the emotionalism and decorative symbolism of so much other post-Impressionist painting. In a sense his painting was, to use an expression current in Cubist circles, 'pure' painting. But while it is impossible to overstress the importance of Cézanne in the emergence of Cubism, it is wrong to see even the earliest Cubist painting simply as a direct continuation of him. Gleizes and Metzinger, carried away by their enthusiasm for his art, went so far as to suggest at one point in *Du Cubisme* that Cubism was simply a development of his work: 'To understand Cézanne is to foresee Cubism. Nowadays we are justified in saying that there is only a difference of intensity between this school and the manifestations which preceded it.'[4] Nothing could be further from the truth. Although Cézanne's painting was profoundly original, his ambition was to use his own intensive study of nature to revivify classical or traditional painting; the means he used, although they were highly personal, were founded on the optical discoveries of the Impressionists. This art remained deeply rooted in the nineteenth century. The true Cubists, on the other hand, while they made their discoveries intuitively, were nevertheless very

[1]The influence of Cézanne on Léger and the minor Cubists is discussed in detail in Chapter IV.
[2]See R. de La Fresnaye, 'Paul Cézanne' in *Poème et Drame*, Paris, January 1913.This article was originally delivered as a lecture at a meeting of *Les Artistes de Passy*. See p. 12 above.
[3]See *Du Cubisme*, pp. 8–10.
[4]Ibid., pp. 9–10.

conscious of the fact that they were the beginning of something completely new; in a sense they were anti-traditionalists. Their way of looking at the exterior world, the means they used of recording their ideas about it, even their concept of what a painting was, all these things were different from anything that had gone before them. And they were reacting not only against the art of the past fifty years but also against the techniques and traditions of vision that had shaped Western painting since the scientific discoveries of the early Renaissance. But it was Cézanne who formed the bridge between their art and the art of the preceding five centuries.

In the *View from the Hotel Mistral* Braque had been influenced decisively by Cézanne, and a significant and till recently little known *Landscape with Houses* (Pl. 37A), executed probably a month or two later shows him putting his studies of Cézanne to daring if not totally satisfactory conclusions.[1] The painting is awkwardly and laxly structured but now the contours of many of the compositional elements have been freely and insistently opened up into each other so that the eye is led quickly not only into depth but also steeply up the picture surface, a premonition of things to come. The meeting with Picasso, which probably took place around the time this picture was being painted or soon after, must have encouraged him in turning his back completely on Fauvism. The great *Nu* bears witness not only to the impact which Picasso's work had on Braque, but also to the fact that Braque realized the extent to which the *Demoiselles d'Avignon* was a revolutionary work. But in the *Baigneuse* Braque's vision exceeded his technical means. And unlike Picasso Braque did not see in African art an answer to some of the problems of contemporary painting. Although many years later Braque recalled how strong an impression tribal art made on him,[2] it is hard to see any direct reflection of this in the paintings executed at the time when Picasso was reacting so positively to tribal sculpture; even in a painting like the *Nu* any influence from tribal art seems to have come at second hand, through Picasso's *Demoiselles*. However, Braque was sufficiently unsettled by the example of Picasso to turn his studies of Cézanne to increasingly revolutionary ends, and in the canvases executed during the summer of 1908 at l'Estaque, Braque produced a

[1]The painting is discussed at length in Rubin, 'Cézannisme and the Beginnings of Cubism'.

[2]Dora Vallier quotes Braque as saying '. . . les masques nègres aussi m'ont ouvert un horizon nouveau. Il m'ont permis de prendre contact avec des choses instinctives, des manifestations directes qui allaient contre la fausse tradition'. Op. cit., p. 14.

series of completely original works, the first group of truly Cubist paintings. These were the controversial paintings rejected by the jury of the *Salon d'Automne* and later exhibited at Kahnweiler's gallery in the rue Vignon. Reviewing the exhibition, Vauxcelles wrote: 'M. Braque is an exceedingly audacious young man . . . the misleading example of Picasso and Derain has encouraged him. Perhaps he has also been unduly obsessed by the style of Cézanne and by recollections of the static art of the Egyptians. He constructs deformed and metallic puppets which are of a terrible simplification. He despises form, reduces everything, sites and figures and houses to geometric complexes, to cubes.'[1] Apollinaire, on the other hand, although he did not entirely understand the nature of Braque's new development and failed to realize that even though Braque was beginning to paint largely from memory, his work was still often related directly to his models, instinctively realized that Braque had accomplished something important and original. In his preface to the catalogue he wrote: 'He no longer owes anything to his surroundings. His talent has chosen to evoke the twilight of reality and now he is evolving within himself a universal pictorial renaissance.'

It is instructive to compare an early work of the series, *La Route de l'Estaque*, with what was probably the last, *Maisons à l'Estaque* (Pls. 37B, 38). In both all the sensuous elements of the previous years have been banished; colour has been reduced to a severe combination of browns, dull greens and greys. In the earlier work the circular, arching and swinging elements are played off against an angular, somewhat disjointed pictorial armature. In the later work the curving rhythms have given way to a system of verticals and horizontals, broken only by the forty-five degree diagonals of roof-tops and trees. All details have been eliminated and the foliage of the trees reduced to a minimum to reveal the geometric severity of the houses. These are continued upwards almost to the top of the canvas so that the eye is allowed no escape beyond them. The picture plane is further emphasized by the complete lack of aerial perspective (the far houses are, if anything, darker and stronger in value than the foreground house), and by the fact that occasionally contours are broken and forms opened up into each other. There is no central vanishing point; indeed in many of the houses all the canons of traditional perspective are completely broken.

[1]*Gil Blas*, 14 November 1908.

The debt of this sort of painting to Cézanne is clearly visible. But it is almost immediately obvious that Braque had begun to study Cézanne in a much more intellectual and thoughtful way, and that this was resulting in the creation of an entirely new type of painting. In the first place Braque had detached himself from visual appearances to a much greater extent than Cézanne, who while he was obviously very much aware (if only instinctively) of the purely formal or abstract side of painting, relied nevertheless, in his still lifes and landscapes, on an exhaustive study of the 'motif' as his point of departure, although it is worth mentioning that in his articles Emile Bernard had suggested that Cézanne's vision 'was much more in his brain than in his eye'. At l'Estaque, Braque was working from nature but one feels that the forms in his painting have not been suggested by those of particular landscapes but rather that he has imposed on the natural scene his own austere, angular, almost geometrical form of vision. In this sense Braque's painting is, like Picasso's 'Negroid' pictures, conceptual. The forms are more crudely simplified than in Cézanne, and while there is the same sensation of recession that one gets from Cézanne's paintings, as one's eye moves from one clearly defined plane to another, Braque's paintings are composed in such a way that the feeling of depth is very restricted. Moreover, Cézanne had felt he was respecting the laws of traditional, scientific perspective. When these are violated in his painting, it is because the pictorial theory involved conflicted with his intensely visual and empirical approach, and with his desire to reconstruct the three-dimensional form of his subjects as fully as possible. The irregularities of this kind in Braque's work of 1908 are much more conscious and deliberate. In the still lifes, which have the same general characteristics as the landscapes, the Cézannian device of tipping certain objects up on to the picture plane is exaggerated to the point that one realizes at once that the artist is no longer making use of scientific perspective. Finally, there is the question of colour. Cézanne worked with a full Impressionist palette, and it is evident, not only from a visual analysis of his painting, but also from his letters and from Emile Bernard's observations on his method of work, that Cézanne relied on the exactness of tonal relationships to produce a sensation of volume and recession; indeed, the necessity he felt to verify these relationships was one of the reasons why he was compelled to turn back continually to a study of nature. With the l'Estaque paintings, Braque, on the other hand, began to limit his use of colour severely, and in this respect his work was typical of most early Cubist painting. When colour was finally re-introduced into Braque's painting, it was to appear as a completely independent pictorial element, related to solid forms and the space surrounding them, but clearly distinguishable from them as a separate artistic factor. It was to be used, in other words, in exactly the reverse way to Cézanne.

The spacial sensations evoked by Braque's L'Estaque landscapes are already of a new order although his handling of space was to become increasingly original. They are structured in such a way that while we feel our way visually into the space suggested by the subject our eyes are simultaneously being run up the picture by short thrusts in and out of a limited pictorial depth. Because the eye is allowed no escape at the top of the canvas we are also forced to 'read' the picture downwards again, through its component geometricized elements, with the result that they seem to advance towards us. Braque himself tells us that he began his L'Estaque pictures by establishing a background plane and 'advancing the picture towards myself bit by bit'.[1] Kahnweiler in *Der Weg zum Kubismus* is probably echoing conversations with Braque when he writes: 'Representation of the position of objects in space is done as follows: instead of beginning from a supposed foreground and going on from there to give an illusion of depth by means of perspective, the painter begins from a definite and clearly defined background. Starting from this background the painter now works toward the front by a sort of scheme of forms in which each object's position is clearly indicated, both in relation to the definite background and to the other objects.' In fact many of Braque's Cubist paintings have dual readings, into depth and forward again, advancing not so much from the 'background' as from the picture plane. The spatial dialogues so fundamental in Braque's art touched Picasso's but were of subsidiary concern to him.

When Picasso and Braque met, Picasso was already familiar with the work of Cézanne. He had used the figure pieces of Cézanne as a source for the *Demoiselles*, and from the middle of 1907 onwards he was executing simple still lifes of pots, bottles, glasses and fruit in which he used Cézanne's high, informative viewpoints. Indeed, some of the paintings of this type, notably the group that was most probably begun towards the middle of 1908, seem to be almost exercises

[1]Quoted in Jean Paulhan, *Braque le Patron*, Geneva–Paris 1946, p. 45.

employing the sphere, the cylinder and the cone. But it is only in the second half of 1908 that Picasso turned to a more concentrated study of Cézanne. The first group of paintings in which this new development is clearly visible are the canvases executed during the few weeks spent at La Rue-des-Bois in the autumn and in Paris during the succeeding months.

There can be little doubt that Picasso was excited by the work that Braque brought back to Paris from l'Estaque in which he was drawing such original answers from the questions he had been putting to Cézanne's art. Matisse tells us that he actually saw one of the l'Estaque pieces in Picasso's studio and that Picasso 'discussed it with his friends'.[1] The presence of Cézanne is felt strongly behind both *Three Women* and *Bread and Fruit Dish on a Table*, and the borrowed Braque may well have been in his studio when he painted them. At any rate the gravity of Picasso's great canvases probably reflects some of the thoughtfulness with which Braque had approached Cézanne's art. The period of the two painters' great intimacy and of their unique collaboration was about to begin.

It is perhaps hard to see what Picasso found to admire that was common to both tribal sculpture and the work of Cézanne, two arts which are in many ways diametrically opposed. For while the tribal sculptor is often not particularly concerned with natural appearances, Cézanne's painting is the result of the acutest kind of visual observation. It is obvious that Picasso, who had admired the formal, sculptural element in tribal art, also appreciated the abstract, structural side of Cézanne's work. But it has been seen that Picasso was also attracted to tribal sculpture because he admired its conceptual quality. Now Cézanne's art, despite its use of simple, often almost geometrical forms, could never be described as conceptual although he did of course impose a very rigorous sense of pictorial order upon his subjects. He was not so much concerned, as the tribal sculptor was, with conveying his idea about an object, but rather with recording it or interpreting it in pictorial terms. Or to put it differently, he saw in nature a storehouse of artistic forms. Nevertheless, Cézanne had intuitively evolved a means of explaining the nature of solid forms in a new, very thorough way. To start with, he generally studied the objects in his still lifes from slightly above eye-level, so that the spectator sees them in their most informative aspect; this high viewpoint

[1] E. Tériade, 'Matisse Speaks', *Art News Annual*, New York 1952, pp. 40–71.

was probably assumed largely in order to limit the pictorial depth and ensure the unity of the picture surface in so far as that looking downwards on to the subject one's eye is not allowed to wander off into limitless space. However, Cézanne very often goes further and tilts up the top of an object even more towards the picture plane, so that it appears sometimes as if seen almost from directly above, while continuing to show the rest of the object from a more normal, slightly lower point of view. It is impossible to say to what extent Cézanne was aware of the fact that he was doing this, and in the process breaking the laws of scientific linear perspective, but it seems likely that it was part of a natural desire to emphasize the two-dimensional aspect of the canvas while continuing to explain the nature of objects and also insisting on their solidity by modelling them as fully as possible. Many of these 'deformations' may also owe something to the fact that, as Cézanne moved from one section of his canvas to another, he unconsciously altered the structure of objects in an effort to relate rhythmically each passage of painting to the areas around it.[1] But apart from emphasizing the aesthetic or two-dimensional plane on which he was working, the tipping forward of certain objects or parts of objects also gives the sensation that the painter has adopted variable or movable viewpoints and that he thus has been able to synthesize into a single image of an object a lot of information gathered from looking at it from a series of successive viewpoints.[2] The way in which the contours of objects are continually broken in Cézanne's painting reinforces the impression that he looked at his subject from more than one position. Picasso, who was anxious to paint an object as he 'thought' it, or to express his ideas about it, was naturally anxious to explain as fully as possible the nature of its formal composition. He thus seized on the concept of volume implicit in Cézanne as one of the means of doing so. This was a development which of course took place in Picasso's work over a period of many months.

However, when approaching Cézanne after an intensive analysis of the pre-

[1]I am indebted for some of my ideas about Cézanne's method of work to Dr R. Ratcliffe's studies of his technique.

[2]It is perhaps worth noting, too, that since Cézanne returned again and again to his visual subject for reference, he cannot always have taken up exactly the same position in front of it, so that he must have in fact actually shifted his viewpoint from time to time, even if only very slightly. His eye was, however, clearly so highly trained that this may well have affected his vision of his subject.

dominantly simple, sculptural forms of tribal art, Picasso was naturally most immediately drawn to the precise, solid treatment of volumes that is found in so much of Cézanne's portraiture and still-life painting. The aspect of definition in Cézanne's work, its 'measurable' quality, is well illustrated by the fact that in one of his later Cubist phases Gris was able to interpret one of Cézanne's portraits of his wife in terms of a few sharply defined, superimposed planes that capture much of the structural feeling of the original. Then the landscapes at La Rue-des Bois which are influenced by Cézanne are still related in many ways to Picasso's more 'primitive' or 'Negroid' work; indeed, this series of paintings begun in La Rue-des-Bois is contemporary with other canvases which represent only a continuation of his earlier work; some of the simplest of the La Rue-des-Bois landscapes, with their almost naive interpretation of houses and trees, remind one strongly of the art of the Douanier Rousseau. However, in the more elaborate and sophisticated paintings of the series, the influence of Cézanne can be sensed in the general construction, in the technique of small, flat, rhythmically applied brush-strokes which build up the forms, and in the devices which Picasso has used to retain the picture plane. For example, besides assuming Cézanne's high viewpoint, Picasso now often continues the outlines of walls or buildings at slightly different levels or angles as they appear at intervals behind the objects in the foreground. This feature derived from Cézanne's work can be seen also in some of Braque's l'Estaque landscapes.

Indeed, the Rue-des-Bois landscapes (Pl. 6A) already have much in common with Braque's contemporary works. In both there is a reinterpretation of Cézanne in thoughtful, more conceptual, terms. Both painters take slight liberties with conventional perspective; that is to say, in their canvases the angles of vision are no longer completely consistent. Further, neither painter relies completely on the use of a single, consistent light source to model forms. Both have begun to produce a sensation of relief by arbitrarily juxtaposing lights and darks rather than by using shading in a naturalistic way. This is a feature of Cubist painting that was soon to become very apparent. Like Braque, Picasso had restricted the range of colours on his palette to browns, greys and greens, though the greens he uses are brighter and tend to predominate. And if one is forced to use the term 'geometrical' when talking about Braque's work, it is even more applicable to Picasso's. The forms are severely simplified: tubular tree-trunks, heavily stylized masses of foliage and 'cubic' houses. Picasso's approach is harder, more sculptural than Braque's. The contours of the objects are unbroken (although they are occasionally slightly dislocated as has been seen) and the modelling is more aggressively three-dimensional. Braque, on the other hand, has used Cézanne's technique of opening up the contours of objects, so that in his paintings the eye slips inwards and upwards from plane to plane without having to make a series of abrupt transitions or adjustments. This use of new spatial sensations was to become an increasingly important feature of Braque's work.

The still lifes which Picasso executed during the winter of 1908–9 and the early spring of 1909, such as for example the *Compotier* (Pl. 6B) in the Museum of Modern Art, New York (a work of late 1908), are more frankly Cézannesque than anything that preceded them. Once again the forms are more solid, more firmly drawn and roundly modelled than in Braque's contemporary work. Cézanne's method of building up form by a series of parallel hatchings or small overlapping brush-strokes is used by Picasso in a severe and logical way; indeed, in the gouaches of early 1909 this method of work becomes almost a refinement of the earlier, cruder striations. The objects in Braque's painting like the *Still Life with Fruit Dish* (Moderna Museet, Stockholm), which is roughly contemporary (Pl. 39B) with the *Compotier*, are more faceted, and the whole surface is broken up in terms of the same angular but subtly modulated planes which carry the eye back into a limited depth and then forward again on to the picture plane in a series of gentle declivities and projections. In the work of both painters one becomes increasingly aware of the fact that they are making use of a variable viewpoint. One sees more of the bowl and stem of the Picasso *Compotier*, for instance, than one would in normal vision if one assumed the same high viewpoint when looking at the top of it; and the gourd behind is painted as though in silhouette or directly at eye level. The table top is tipped up into the picture plane more sharply even than in a painting by Cézanne.

The human figure always played a much more important part in the work of Picasso than in that of Braque, and Picasso looked with particular interest at Cézanne's figure work. What seems to have fascinated Picasso about Cézanne's figure studies and portraits, besides his obvious interest in their structural formal properties, is the complete disregard of details, which is at times extended even to a disregard of the individual features of the face. This is combined in

Cézanne with an extremely elaborate build-up of form in terms of small flat planes based on empirical observations, which, following countless adjustments, fuse into the whole and become inseparable from each other. Some of Picasso's studies of single heads executed during the autumn and winter of 1908 show the earlier, more sculptural, Negroid type reinterpreted in a new idiom. The severe outlines of the facial mask are retained and the noses are the same protruding, convex forms, usually flattened into a ridge along the top. But the treatment of the rest of the face is more complex, subtler and more empirical; it is no longer divided into a few clearly defined sections, and eyes and mouth are not so precisely stylized and deliberately emphasized as they had been before.

In many of the figure paintings of the winter of 1908 and the spring of 1909 the Negroid elements are superseded (Pl. 7A), and the empirical or experimental treatment of form is extended to whole or three-quarter length figures. Under the influence of Cézanne, Picasso's work becomes once again more purely painterly, and these figures, though still simple and often clumsy and awkward in appearance, never give the impression, as did so many of the paintings of the Negroid phase, of being the pictorial counterparts of wooden sculptures. Forms become much more generalized; and they are no longer thrown into relief by the use of a single, consistent light source as in most of the Negroid work. The limbs are generally thin, but there is a marked tendency to distend or inflate the trunks of the bodies so that they become unnaturally broad. Picasso's work is, of course, by now totally different, both in spirit and appearance, from that of Cézanne. It is a great deal more abstract, and the deformations within it are much more radical. This was partly because Picasso, like Braque, was at this time working largely from memory; indeed he had been doing so for the past three years.[1] This partial detachment from natural appearances, which has already been seen in the landscapes of Picasso and Braque of 1908, is one of the factors that distinguish most clearly their approach from that of Cézanne and other nineteenth-century artists, and even from the Fauves, whose vision, with the occasional exception of Matisse, despite the liberties they took with their subjects, was still conditioned by their instantaneous reactions to their surroundings. Cézanne in particular

[1]Leo Stein, *Appreciation*, New York 1947. Stein, who knew Picasso well during these years, recalls that Picasso did not use a model during the Iberian period (he refers to it as the 'rose' period) and implies that this had been Picasso's procedure for some time (p. 174).

had as a rule relied completely on visual models, and had looked at the subjects of his paintings with a concentration and intensity as great as that shown by the artists of the early Renaissance in their rediscovery of the natural world. Only in the figure compositions did he work largely from imagination and memory. The element of distortion and the handling of the space in these paintings relates them intimately to Cubism, although most Cubist painting is close, too, in feeling to the more constructive and austere portraits, still lifes and landscapes. It was the deliberate disregard of the more sensuous and immediately appealing aspects of painting, and the temporary dismissal of all human and associational values, combined with the fact that they were working in a conceptual way, relying on memory as much as on visual models, that allowed the Cubists to distort and dislocate figures and objects to a degree hitherto unknown. This is particularly noticeable in Picasso's drastic treatment of the human body in the series of paintings under discussion; in some of them the subject's limbs are abruptly truncated. There is furthermore an atmosphere of harshness and unrest about them that makes one realize how much closer to the spirit of Cézanne Braque's contemporary work is. Some figure paintings, however, probably mostly from the spring of 1909, are, like many of the contemporary still lifes, more purely Cézannesque. Less extreme in deformation, quieter and less agitated in mood, these paintings form a prelude to the important work which was to be done by Picasso during the summer in Spain at Horta de San Juan.

Examined over a certain length of time, the course of Picasso's development, though often paradoxical and breathtaking in its rapidity, can be clearly charted. The discovery of new sources of inspiration, world events, emotional and intellectual disturbances, or the stimulus provided by new contacts in his personal life, mark starting points for various periods into which his artistic career can be divided. And in his later work the careful dating supplied by Picasso himself eliminates any chronological problem. But during the early Cubist period, when the pictures were unsigned and undated, and when the wealth of discovery and invention makes differences of months and even of weeks important, it is extremely difficult to establish an exact chronological sequence. Nearly all the signatures and dates on Cubist paintings executed by Picasso and Braque between 1907 and 1913 have been added much later. Often the paintings appear to be signed on the reverse and occasionally a date is inscribed there also. These 'signatures' were mostly added by an employee of Kahnweiler's when they reached his gallery; this was usually, though clearly not always, within a few weeks of being painted. Even in the case of Braque, whose development was more methodical than Picasso's, the dating of certain works is problematical, and Picasso's sporadic method of work makes it doubly hard. The approach of both Picasso and Braque was primarily intuitive, but Picasso's innovations and changes of style give the impression of being realized more suddenly and spontaneously. Then, after having taken the most daring steps forward he sometimes retreats a few paces, so that on comparing two paintings close in date the earlier example often seems more advanced and developed. The same themes, the same subjects and poses are reinterpreted over and over again, often in some completely original way, but sometimes also in a manner reminiscent of a previous phase; any novelty is eventually assimilated to what had preceded it; nothing is ever discarded. This overlapping of styles is seen throughout the entire pre-war period, and since every phase contains the seeds for future developments, one is forced to take as focal points works in which discoveries or innovations are fully realized, rather than those in which they are first suggested.

The problem of establishing a satisfactory chronology for Picasso's work between 1907 and 1914 is largely solved by the invaluable landmarks provided by the months, generally in the summer, spent outside Paris. Because of their subject-matter and homogeneity of style, and often also because of photographic records,[1] the paintings of these periods are usually securely datable. Furthermore, these months were usually periods of synthesis and discovery. It is in some of the drawings and sketches executed at Gosol that the facial types begin to harden towards the 'Iberian' style of the autumn. Another, contemporary series of Gosol paintings is characterized by a gentle, pastoral mood that is quite distinctive. The influence of Cézanne is seen strongly and consistently in some of the paintings Picasso brought back from La Rue-des-Bois in the autumn of 1908. Now, at Horta de San Juan,[2] in the summer of 1909, Picasso consolidated the achievements of the past years to produce the most important single group of paintings of his early Cubist period. Picasso and Fernande Olivier arrived there

[1]Some paintings furthermore have the names of the towns and villages in which they were executed inscribed on the reverse. This often allows a fairly precise dating.

[2]Horta de San Juan was known to Picasso and his friends by its colloquial name, Horta de Ebro.

in May and remained, with interruptions, until September.[1]

The Horta figure pieces in particular are of vital importance in the history of Cubism. In the more sculptural, formal, Negroid paintings the starting point for the investigation of form had been the logical or rational division of the human form and face into their component parts. Later, after he had been influenced by certain paintings by Cézanne, Picasso began to treat solid forms in a more arbitrary, empirical or experimental fashion and to explore the possibilities of representing them without the aid of traditional perspective. At Horta, Picasso fused the Negroid and the Cézannian types of painting. Looking at these canvases one gets the sensation that the time spent in Horta was a period of almost unequalled concentration in Picasso's art. (Pl. 9).

The series of Horta heads all have more or less the same basic subdivision into several clearly defined areas. That is to say, Picasso uses as a starting point the same logical or rational analysis of volume that he had evolved in his Negroid paintings. The forehead is usually divided by a central ridge or furrow as in much of the Negroid work. Two simple planes connect the sunken eye socket to the forehead, and a small disk extends below from cheekbone to the inside corner of the eye, while the jaw, the nose and the section from nose to mouth and from mouth to chin are each clearly defined. But these areas then become the starting point for further subdivision and countless small refinements conditioned by the eye alone. The same approach is applied to the whole body of a three-quarter length figure, which is the culmination of the series. The basic pyramidal or shield-like form of the stomach still recalls tribal sculpture, but the deformation of the figure is at once more geometrical and less extreme than in most of the Cézannesque paintings and less rigid than in the Negroid paintings; forms are faceted or subdivided in a more elaborate fashion than hitherto, so that one's eye passes freely from one sculptural element to another. There is, too, an increased feeling of sensitivity and subtlety. Most important, in these heads and figures the Cubist concept of form is expressed in a fully developed way. The heads are viewed from slightly above or at eye level but the undersides of nose and jaw are clearly seen. The side of the neck is swung forward in a great curving plane that is the basis of the sculptural breakdown of the neck and throat. The knot of hair

[1]Picasso–Stein correspondence.

at the back of the neck is, in some of the paintings, incorporated in an almost full-face view, and the back of the shoulder is tipped up into the picture plane. In the three-quarter length figures the sides of the body are pulled or folded outwards to broaden and expand the trunk. In other words, in each image Picasso synthesizes information obtained from viewing the subject from various angles, and, relying on his knowledge and memory of the structure of the human figure, he gives a complete and detailed analysis of the nature of the forms that compose it. The Horta still lifes show the same combination of complexity and lucidity (Pl. 8A).

The problem of combining various aspects of an object into a single image was one which, it has been seen, had concerned Picasso and Braque for some time. Indeed, it should be emphasized that Picasso had been dissatisfied with the limitations imposed on pictorial volumes by a scientific or linear system of perspective for some time before he became aware of the fact that Cézanne's painting suggested a new concept of form and space. As early as 1906, in many of Picasso's paintings influenced by Iberian sculpture, forms are distended to the point of distortion, and because of this, in the heads of figures, the features, and particularly the mouths are unnaturally elongated. This is very obvious in the *Portrait of Gertrude Stein* (Pl. 105B), where in a three-quarter view the far side of the mouth is almost duplicated, while the disparity between the eyes further accentuates the sense of breadth. In other figures where both the bust and the head are expanded in this exaggerated way, the neck clearly presented a problem: by nature a slender form, it must now be used to connect convincingly two abnormally heavy masses. (A satisfactory solution was not to be reached until the work of Horta de San Juan, where, using the tendons as an axis, the back of the neck is swung around into the front of the shoulder.) Then, in the *Demoiselles*, a further step is taken. The noses of the full-face figures are in profile, and in the squatting figure, with its distended pose and dislocated head, the canons of traditional perspective are completely violated. Braque had stated the new concept of form more consciously in the *Baigneuse* or *Nu* of early 1908, where the unnaturally squat proportions of the figure are further exaggerated by the inclusion of certain aspects of it not visible from a single point of view. In a three-quarter view of the head the knot of hair at the back of the head is seen as in a profile view, and the double outline of the foremost shoulder gives the impression that the top of it has been tipped up into the picture plane.

Picasso's *Baigneuse*, a work of early 1909, shows the painter accomplishing the desired optical synthesis in a very thorough but slightly schematic way (Pl. 7B). Here both buttocks and the far side of the back are visible in what is basically a simple three-quarter view of the figure; one leg is in strict profile, while the other is seen almost from a frontal position. The face, divided down the central axis, is a crude combination of a three-quarter and profile view, and the elongation of the mouth suggests even a purely frontal viewpoint. In Braque's *Still Life with Musical Instruments* (Pl. 36B), painted in the autumn of 1908, the neck of the mandolin is bent round to an exaggerated degree, so that the top and underneath of it are visible simultaneously. And from the middle of this year onwards, both painters had adopted and accentuated Cézanne's device of lifting the tops of objects up towards the picture plane. This aspect of Cézanne's art, and the way in which he distended forms and continually opened up their contours as though in an effort to broaden them even further, must have appeared to the Cubists as an early manifestation of the simultaneous depiction of various views of an object in a single image, and as a justification for their deliberate dismissal of linear perspective.

The new concept of form reached its fullest expression to date in the work of Picasso done at Horta de San Juan, and some sheets of drawings which date from the early days of his return to Paris (Pl. 8B), show Picasso methodically applying the Cubist concept of form to objects of different kinds and shapes: to a human head, a box, an apple and so on. But even in these drawings, which have the character of a study or demonstration, there is nothing theoretical about Picasso's approach. There are in Cubism many seemingly contradictory features, and one of the most obvious is the fact that despite the strong intellectual and rational strain that characterizes the style, the painting of Picasso and Braque remained markedly unscientific. The method of work of both artists was throughout primarily intuitive. Traditional perspective was abandoned but no new system was substituted for it. On the contrary, the painter's liberty had become absolute. He was free to move around his subject and to incorporate into his depiction of it any information gained by this process or acquired through previous contacts or experiences. Memory, therefore, played an increasingly large part in the artist's new vision of the world around him, and this led at first to a great simplification of form. But at the same time the painter now felt compelled to give in every painting a multiplicity of information about the formal properties of his subject, and this in turn rendered his task in some ways more complex than it had been hitherto. No ready-made solutions were offered for the problems posed. If the mind or memory suggested new forms, the means of expressing them were purely pictorial. Pierre Reverdy, a young friend and supporter of Picasso and Braque,[1] was quick to realize the fact that true Cubism had not been the product of pictorial doctrines and theories, and also that the search for the means of expressing a new concept of form and space had made Cubism a style of almost unequalled pictorial discipline. In the first issue of *Nord-Sud*, a periodical which appeared in 1917 with the purpose of reintegrating and stimulating artistic life in Paris, Reverdy, feeling that some kind of objective evaluation of Cubism was by this time possible, wrote: 'Today for a privileged few the discipline can be taken for granted, and as they never sought for an art that was cold, mathematical and anti-plastic, wholly intellectual, the works which they offer us appeal to the lover of painting directly through the eye and the senses.'[2]

Besides the figure work, Picasso also executed several landscapes at Horta de San Juan. Trees and natural forms are here almost completely eliminated, and the concern is with the relationships between the cubic, block-like buildings and the reconciliation of their obvious solidity with the picture plane. Colour is even more limited than before, and the palette for the succeeding years is established: some of the paintings are in earth colours, greys and blacks, with a few touches of dull green, while others are in softer grey-blues and buffs. In all the paintings the deviations from traditional perspective, which in landscape painting had hitherto been only slight, are carried to new lengths. Not only is there no central vanishing point, but the perspective, rather than being convergent is actually divergent, so that the roof tops and sides of the buildings are often broadest at their furthest ends, and have the effect of opening up, fan-wise, on to the picture plane. Picasso's use of light is by now completely arbitrary: darks and lights are opposed to each other simply to accentuate the incisive quality of the outlines and to throw form more sharply into relief. Since atmospheric perspective is disregarded

[1]Reverdy, who was born in 1889, was the youngest of the contemporary writers on Cubism, but was already friendly with the painters before the outbreak of the war and lived at the *Bateau Lavoir*.
[2]*Nord-Sud* 1, 1–15 March 1917. Reverdy and Paul Dermée were the editors of this review.

also, the furthest buildings appear to be placed above rather than behind the ones in the foreground. The picture plane is further stressed by the device of dropping the small doors or openings below the bases of the buildings, and by the way in which some of the forms are opened up into each other and fused. The sky, too, is treated as a series of planes continuing the composition up to the top of the canvas, so that there is very little suggestion of depth even behind the buildings and mountains on the horizon (Pl. 14A).

This particular feature in the landscapes at Horta de Ebro, the solid, almost tangible, treatment of the sky, had been developed first in Cubist painting by Braque as a result of his new ideas about pictorial space. It is particularly noticeable in the *Port*, a work painted from memory in the spring of 1909 (Pl. 39A). In the late landscapes of Cézanne the sky is often treated in much the same way – as a complicated system of small, thickly painted facets or planes inextricably fused, and having a quality of weight and material existence. Despite the austerity of his early Cubism, Braque's interpretation of Cézanne was more painterly than that of Picasso, and he was undoubtedly fascinated by the surface quality and the actual technique of Cézanne; there is in the handling of the sky in the *Port*, and indeed throughout the whole picture, a much greater emphasis on the richness of the pigment itself than there is in contemporary works by Picasso. The forms of lighthouses and boats, while almost toy-like in their basic simplicity, are developed internally in terms of a large number of planes or facets, and since the sky receives the same treatment, the painting resolves itself into a mass of small, shifting planes, jointed together or hanging behind each other in shallow depth. Out of this, forms emerge, solidify, and then disintegrate again as the spectator turns his attention back from the individual forms to the painting as a whole. In Braque's l'Estaque landscapes of the previous year, the two-dimensional surface of the picture is retained partly by allowing the eye no way of escape beyond the mountains, buildings and trees, and here the same effect is achieved by the concrete treatment of the sky, which is as elaborately and solidly painted as the rest of the canvas, and which is fused with the landscape below by the extension into it of all the main compositional lines. A few years later, in 1912, La Fresnaye, attempting to describe a certain aspect of Cézanne's work and to assess his influence on contemporary painting said: 'Each object, in one of the late canvases, has ceased to exist only in itself, and becomes little by little a cell within the whole organism of the painting. That is the really fruitful aspect of Cézanne's painting and the reason for which it is at the root of all the modern tendencies.'[1] The first sentence describing Cézanne's late work, could equally well be applied to this kind of painting by Braque.

Something has already been said, in connection with the landscapes and still lifes of 1908 and early 1909, about the emergence of a new spatial sensation in Braque's work. In the *Port* this had become very marked. The treatment of the sky and of the areas between the various landscape objects, the boats, lighthouses and breakwaters, in terms of the same facets or pictorial units into which the objects themselves are dissolved, has the effect of making space seem as real, as material, one might almost say as 'pictorial' as the solid objects themselves. The whole picture surface is brought to life by the interaction of the angular, shaded planes. Some of these planes seem to recede away from the eye into shallow depth, but this sensation is always counteracted by a succeeding passage which will lead the eye forward again up on to the picture plane. The optical sensation produced is comparable to that of running one's hand over an immensely elaborate, subtly carved sculpture in low relief. It has been suggested that the *Port* was shown, together with another painting by Braque since destroyed, at the *Salon des Indépendants* of 1909.[2] If the *Port* is indeed the landscape listed in the catalogue, it is the first surviving Cubist painting to have been seen in a large public exhibition (the Braque exhibition in the previous year had been at Kahnweiler's gallery which was small and at that time known to relatively few people). Braque's entries in the *Salon des Indépendants* were hung in the Fauve room. Reviewing the exhibition for *Gil Blas*, Vauxcelles wrote: 'everything, down to the cubic, and I must admit barely intelligible eccentricities of Bracke [*sic*]' (there is someone, Pascal would have said, who abuses the geometric spirit!) makes this room passionately interesting.'[3]

By 1909 then, Picasso and Braque had initiated the first phase of Cubism; the art which both painters were producing was the result of a new freedom which

[1]'Paul Cézanne' in *Poème et Drame*, January 1913.

[2]Henry R. Hope, *Braque*, Museum of Modern Art, New York, 1949, p. 37. This must have been the *Paysage*, Cat. no. 215. The exhibition opened on 25 March so that if the *Port* was shown there it must have been painted very early in the spring of 1909.

[3]*Gil Blas*, 25 March 1909.

arose from their having discarded all scientific systems and theories. But despite the spirit of communal research which had begun to characterize their work, it had already become apparent that there was still a fundamental difference of approach between them. The similarity of subject-matter between Picasso's Horta landscapes and those which Braque was executing at exactly the same time at La Roche Guyon (that is to say in mid 1909) (Pl. 40A) enables one to appreciate with clarity the fact that, although they were reaching much the same conclusions, it was for different reasons. Braque's paintings show a continuation of the fragmentation of form and the elaborate surface treatment already seen in *Le Port*. The brush-strokes have become smaller and more numerous, and perspective is distorted to such an extent that the buildings occasionally appear to be composed of completely dislocated or dissociated walls and roofs. Picasso's landscapes are more incisive and linear, and the solidity of the forms is deliberately emphasized. The paint quality is less seductive and the technique itself less conscious. The Braques are softer, shapes and objects tend to fuse and merge more, and there is almost a suggestion of the atmospheric shimmer of light. Picasso has said, 'Cubism is an art dealing primarily with forms.'[1] Braque, on the other hand, is quoted as saying, 'what especially attracted me – and what was the main preoccupation of Cubism – was the materialization of that new space which I sensed.'[2]

Picasso's dismissal of traditional perspective had been the result of his interest in investigating the nature of solid form and of a desire to express it in a new, more thorough and comprehensive, pictorial way. This accounts for the strong sculptural feeling that characterizes so much of his early Cubist painting; and, indeed, from the Negro period onwards, he was executing small experimental sculptures which relate directly to the contemporary paintings. In his bronze *Head*, for example (a more important work, which will be discussed below) he dealt in three dimensions with the problems he had faced in the figure paintings at Horta de San Juan. Because of his interest in the properties of pictorial volumes, the device of combining into a single image various views of an object,

[1]Statement by Picasso, made in 1923 to de Zayas. It was translated into English and published in *Arts* under the title 'Picasso Speaks', New York, 1923. The entire statement is reproduced by Barr in his *Picasso*, pp. 270–1.

[2]Dora Vallier, 'Braque, la Peinture et Nous', *Cahiers d'Art*, 1954, p. 15.

one of the fundamental features of Cubism, was worked out more consistently in Picasso's work than in Braque's. Furthermore, Picasso was anxious to present in each image as much essential information about the subject as he could. When he subdivides and facets form, it is in an attempt to break through to its inner structure. This is exactly the effect achieved, for example, by the treatment of the necks in the Horta figures. One gets the impression that Picasso is striving for some ultimate pictorial truth, some absolute representation of reality. Braque was dissatisfied with traditional perspective for many of the same reasons as Picasso. 'Since it is mechanical, this perspective can never lead to a complete possession of objects', he has said.[1] But while he was interested in giving as complete an idea as possible of the nature of his subjects, he was not so much interested in the formal, sculptural properties of individual objects as in their relationships to each other and to the space surrounding them. Linear, scientific perspective allows for a fairly accurate mental reconstruction of the distances separating objects. Thus, in front of a still life by Chardin or Courbet, for example, one can say that one object must be separated from another behind it by so many inches, and so on. Braque, on the other hand, wanted to *paint* these distances or spaces, to make them as real and concrete for the spectator as the objects themselves. In order to accomplish this it was necessary to convey the sensation of having walked around his subjects, of having seen or 'felt' the spaces between them. Braque has said 'there is in nature a tactile space, I might almost say a manual space . . . This is the space that fascinated me so much, because that is what early Cubist painting was, a research into space.'[2] And Braque's early Cubist work gives exactly that impression of 'manual' space which he has talked about. Every object in these paintings is separated from those surrounding it by layers of tactile, visible space which enable the spectator's eye to reach from one part of the canvas to another, from one object to another, by a series of clearly defined pictorial passages. When he fragments and decomposes the objects in his still lifes and landscapes, it is not in order to strip form bare or to disengage some essential quality, but it is rather as a means of creating a completely new kind of pictorial space. And it was probably because of his desire to 'touch' space that he

[1]Ibid., p. 14.
[2]Ibid., p. 16.

began to abandon landscape painting and to devote himself increasingly to still life, in which the depth was naturally more restricted and could be more easily controlled.[1] Braque's interest in space gives his work an 'overall' quality, which has ever since remained one of the main features of his style, whereas in Picasso's painting the attention is usually riveted on the subject while the background or surround is often treated in a simpler or more cursory fashion.

Before going on to discuss the stylistic changes in the Cubism of Picasso and Braque during 1910, it is necessary to interject a word about Picasso's bronze *Head*, the most important early Cubist sculpture (Pl. 10). It might have been expected that the tribal masks and statuettes that had such a profound effect on Picasso's painting would have excited him to a new activity in the field of sculpture as they did Derain[2] and, to a certain extent, Matisse. And during 1907 and 1908 Picasso did produce a handful of wood-carvings (many of which have the appearance of being unfinished), a couple of small bronze heads and masks, and one or two incidental pieces in plaster. But most of these can be regarded as experimental works designed to clarify the problems that Picasso was facing in his painting. Picasso, it has been seen, was anxious to introduce into his paintings what might almost be called a 'sculptural completeness'. One of the things that he objected to about a tradition of painting that was governed by a scientific, single viewpoint system of perspective was that it gave the spectator an incomplete picture or idea about the subject. In other words, he wished to give his own canvases a dimension that in a sense already existed in sculpture, or at least in free-standing sculpture. For clearly one of the principal characteristics of sculpture in the round is that the spectator is able, and is indeed often encouraged or compelled, to walk around it and study it from all angles. In other words, he is free to do what Picasso was trying to do for him in his painting. This is probably why, even when a 'school' of Cubist painting came into existence, there was at first very little Cubist sculpture. On a more general level it is possible to say that since painting is in any case an art of illusion, in so far as it conveys sensations of volume and depth on a two-dimensional surface, it was easier for the Cubists to break with traditional conventions, to push the 'illusion' one step

[1]Braque has also said: 'Quand une nature morte n'est plus à la portée de la main, elle cesse d'être une nature morte.' Requoted by Braque, ibid., p.16.
[2]See p. 180 below.

further, and to invent a new pictorial language, than it was to find a new way of dealing with the solid, tangible forms themselves.

Nevertheless, Picasso's bronze *Head* is in many ways a revolutionary work. It is clearly related to the Horta figure work although it came a few months later, and it shows the same intensive analysis of the nature of solid forms. Picasso makes full use of the play of light across the rough, irregular texture of the bronze to accentuate the dissolution of the face into sharp, angular and incisive planes. Certain sections, when they fall into deep shadow, give the effect of having been gouged out in order to show the interior as well as the exterior structure of the head. This was something that Picasso had also conveyed in the necks of the Horta figures, where the area between the projecting tendons appears to have been cut back into a deep recess. Then the head is distorted in a sweeping spiral movement so that the spectator is obliged to move completely around it and thus gathers a very complete idea about it; and, owing to the element of distortion, from several positions one sees more of the head than would be possible in ordinary vision. But this sculpture remains an isolated example, emphasizing the fact that in its earliest stage Cubism was primarily a pictorial revolution. And it was not until several years later, after Picasso and Braque evolved new methods of dealing with solid forms in their paintings, through their *papier collés* and constructions, that there emerged with the work of men like Laurens and Lipchitz a real school of Cubist sculpture.

During the latter part of 1909 and the early months of 1910 the work of Picasso and Braque became increasingly elaborate and complex. In Picasso's Horta work there had still been some reference to the earlier, simpler and more rational forms derived from tribal art, but in the paintings done on his return to Paris this aspect is completely abandoned, and in the figure work, the approach becomes once again less rational and more empirical (Pl. 11). To control the elaborate complex of facets or planes to which forms are now reduced, Picasso had to resort again to the use of a consistent light source, and there is in many of these paintings a new and strong sense of chiaroscuro. Inside the objects and figures the planes begin to be opened up into each other more fully and are less clearly differentiated than hitherto. And by the spring of 1910, in works such as the *Portrait of Uhde* (Pullitzer Collection, St. Louis) figures and objects have become partially fused with their surroundings or with the background (Pl.13). In the work of Cézanne, where the outlines of objects are stressed again and again, and then as often broken, the eye, while conscious of the limitations of normal vision, has the sensation of being carried around the object beyond its boundaries. Here, in the work of Picasso, the device of fusing or merging the subject with its surroundings allows the painter to insist on the surface unity of the picture but also has the same effect of allowing the spectator to reconstruct form beyond the boundaries stated. These works of Picasso's produce, too, some of the same spatial sensation that is conveyed by Braque's.

The move towards this more complex kind of painting reaches a climax in the still lifes that Braque painted late in 1909 and early in the following year, for example *Violon et Cruche* and *Violin and Palette* (Pls. 41, 42). These paintings give the sensation that Braque has felt his way visually around each object and examined its relationships with the other objects around it from several viewpoints. By rendering the areas between the objects in a tactile, material fashion, Braque succeeds in fusing objects and space into a spatial continuum composed of small, fluid, interpenetrating planes. It is this concrete rendering of the space around the highly fragmented objects that gives these paintings a sensation of almost unprecedented complexity. The intense visual concentration and the technical discipline underlying these paintings transmits itself to the spectator in a feeling of tension, almost of unrest. Although it has been seen that early Cubism was in no sense simply a continuation of Cézanne, the paintings of Picasso and Braque of this period represent, in many ways, the culmination of the investigation of form and pictorial space initiated by him thirty years earlier. They mark also the final phase of the first period in Cubist painting. Both painters, and Braque in particular, seem to have realized that the technique of Cubist painting must become more suggestive, more abstract.

Of the two painters Braque was the more 'painterly'. He was always more conscious than Picasso of the actual surface quality of his work, and moreover more consistently conscious of the need for respecting the demands of the picture plane. It was therefore natural that it should have been Braque who solved the present problem, largely a technical one, of finding a new, easier means of representing the new concepts of pictorial form and space in all their fullness and complexity. In a couple of landscapes executed at Carrières Saint-Denis (Pl. 40B), where he had spent a week or so working in the company of Derain, late in the autumn of 1909, Braque had already begun to transform the subtlety and observational quality of the Roche Guyon landscapes into tighter, more arbitrary compositions, reminiscent in the emphasis on the vertical and horizontal structure broken by forty-five degree diagonals (and also in colour, which is once again darker and harsher) of the *Maisons à l'Estaque*. Next, in a few small still lifes of early 1910, such as the *Glass on a Table* (Pl. 43A), the objects are blocked in a much more direct manner than hitherto. The linear quality of the original idea or sketch is retained, and these outlines become the starting point for the breakdown of the entire surface in terms of flat or tilted planes, a few of which are quite arbitrary. Another still life, *Les Poissons* (Pl. 43B), probably begun a few months later, during the summer (but finished later), shows the new compositional methods carried a step further.[1] The table top and the bottle provide the main compositional accents, while the remainder of the surface is broken down in secondary vertical and horizontal sections. Through these planes the bodies of the fish, fragmented and dislocated, can be traced in a series of subsidiary diagonals. Only their heads remain immediately legible, and these provide the spectator with a starting point for the reconstruction of the subject. A contemporary landscape, *Les Usines de Rio Tinto à l'Estaque* (Pl. 45A), though the subject is still quite recognizable, is markedly more abstract than anything Braque had painted before. By now the painting is virtually constructed in terms of a loose grid or framework of vertical and horizontal lines suggested by the outlines of the buildings. The buildings themselves are no longer self-contained or fully circumscribed forms but are opened up completely into the space around them to form a composition of interpenetrating, shifting planes, suggesting an extremely complicated transparent sculpture in low relief. Braque himself has best described his new method of work when he said, 'the fragmentation (of objects) enabled me to establish space and movement within space, and I was unable to introduce the object until I had created the space.'[2]

Picasso's *Jeune Fille à la Mandoline* (also known as the *Portrait of Fanny*

[1]This painting shows signs of extensive re-working (see the *Tate Gallery Report 1961–62*): it was probably begun in 1909 and may not have been completely finished until 1911–12. But stylistically it belongs, together with the Prague National Gallery *Violin and Glass* (Pl. 44) to the middle or latter half of 1910.

[2]D. Vallier, 'Braque, la Peinture et Nous', p. 16.

Tellier) (Pl. 12) is not only one of the most beautiful, lyrical and accessible of all Cubist paintings, but is also a valuable document of the period. For the fact that at the time Picasso saw the work as unfinished, allows us an insight into his aesthetic intentions and his technical procedure. In the first place, the legibility of this canvas demonstrates conclusively that although Cubist paintings were becoming more abstract in appearance, the artists were still deeply conditioned, at least in the early stages of their works, by the material existence and the physical appearance of their subjects. Then again the painting illustrates in a very concrete fashion the pull Picasso felt between the desire to give forms an explicit, volumetrical treatment, and the need to flatten them up onto the picture plane (compare, for example, the almost sculptural treatment of the breasts and the arms with that of the head, which is rendered in terms of two flat planes). Had the painting reached completion it would have become simultaneously more elaborate, more abstract and more consistent in style; closer, for instance, to his *Portrait of Vollard* (Z II, no. 214).

In Picasso's subsequent move towards a more abstract kind of painting, the work of Braque may once again have been a stimulus, and Picasso's remark to Braque, quoted by Michel Georges-Michel, 'I have tried your methods and I feel one can do excellent things with them'[1] was perhaps made in connection with the new kind of painting Braque had invented in his still lifes of the first half of 1910. Always more extreme than Braque, Picasso, in his work at Cadaquès in the summer of 1910, used the same grid type of composition to produce some of the most abstract and hermetic of all Cubist paintings. At Horta Picasso had been concerned with the breakdown of the human figure into its sculptural units and the relationships between them. Now, working from sketches (often of a type relating to the work of 1909 and early 1910) Picasso uses the outlines or the main directional lines of the body and its limbs as the starting point for his compositions. Around this linear framework is built up a complex system of open and interacting planes, which sometimes seem to represent the forms of the body but which are often quite arbitrary compositional elements. This system of transparent, interpenetrating shapes or planes suggests form in shallow depth, and from it the figure re-emerges as the spectator studies the canvas. This new

[1]Michel Georges-Michel, *Peintres et sculpteurs que j'ai connus*, New York 1942, p. 225.

method of composition can be seen clearly by comparing an etching of a figure done as an illustration for Max Jacob's *Saint Matorel*[1] and securely datable to Cadaquès, with a drawing done a few months earlier. The oil paintings of this period are considerably more abstract than the etchings and drawings, and many cannot be deciphered or reconstructed without the aid of preliminary sketches. Picasso had abandoned the use of a consistent light source a year earlier only to reinstate it a few months later in the paintings done in Paris during the winter. Now once again lights and darks are juxtaposed arbitrarily to create a sense of shallow relief, and are evenly scattered over the entire picture surface to maintain a compositional balance (Pls. 14B, 15A, 15B).

Kahnweiler, who was in continual contact with both Picasso and Braque at this time, realized at once that with the type of painting created by these artists in 1910 (and of which the Cadaquès paintings are the most extreme examples) Cubism was entering a new phase. In 1915 he wrote: 'Much more important, however, was the decisive advance which freed Cubism from the language previously used by painting. This occurred in Cadaquès ... where Picasso spent his summer. Dissatisfied even after weeks of painful struggle, he returned to Paris in the fall with his unfinished works. But he had taken the great step. Picasso had pierced the closed form. A new technique had been invented for new purposes.'[2] Already there existed in Braque's work a dialogue between objects and the tactile space in which they were embedded; now, in Picasso's work and subsequently in Braque's, there was initiated a dialogue between the subject matter and the highly abstract way in which it was rendered. Looking at works of this second analytical phase of Cubism we are always aware of the presence of images, but sometimes they materialize only gradually from the complex of interacting transparent planes which surround and indeed constitute them, only to be reabsorbed into the painting's overall spatial flux.

If Picasso was dissatisfied with the Cadaquès paintings, this was probably because he felt them to be too hermetic and abstract. And it was at this time, in 1910, that Cubism entered its most 'difficult' or hermetic phase, which subsequently gave rise to so much misunderstanding. The ignorant, baffled by the

[1]Published by Kahnweiler, Paris, February 1911. The engravings were printed by Delatre.
[2]*Der Weg zum Kubismus*, p. 27.

appearance of Picasso's and Braque's paintings, tended, indeed, to classify them as complete abstractions. Even the critic Arthur Jerome Eddy, who was the author of the first English book on Cubism and a cautious supporter of the movement, was able to write: 'In short Picasso and a few followers have reached a degree of abstraction in the suppression of the real and the particular that their paintings represent the same degree of emotion as the demonstration of a difficult geometrical proposition.'[1] It is therefore perhaps necessary to pause here to reaffirm some of the intentions of the movement which have hitherto been suggested only in passing.

Cubism, despite the strong intellectual bias and obvious concern with purely formal pictorial values, was never at any stage an abstract art. In fact the painters themselves and the contemporary writers who were genuinely anxious to understand their work, claimed that Cubism was an art of realism. Even Apollinaire who, excited by the complete break that Cubism had effected with traditional painting, had tended to suggest that the ideal programme would be a move towards complete abstraction, could still insist that the Cubist was a realist, since his inspiration was drawn from some transcendental truth beyond the world of appearances. As early as 1911 at least one commentator was viewing Picasso's art as a plastic search for the essential.[2] Maurice Raynal, although less extreme and volatile in his thought than Apollinaire, adopted much the same idealist view while realizing that abstraction was not the end or goal of Cubist painting. In 1913, in his first attempt to define the movement, he wrote: 'Sincere artists today feel the need to canalize and tame their inspiration in order to extract from their faculties the maximum returns, and to strike a balance between sensitivity and reason ... They therefore no longer imitate the misleading appearances of visual phenomena but the truer ones of the mind.'[3]

When writing on a less metaphysical level, and in face of the paintings themselves, even Apollinaire had to admit that the subject played an important part, and that the realism of the movement lay in its attempt to make a totally new but nevertheless very concrete statement about the visual world. Apollinaire describes Picasso's method of work in this way: 'Using planes to render volumes,

[1]*Cubists and Post-Impressionism*, New York 1914, p. 101.

[2]John Middleton Murray, quoted in *New Age*, London, 23 March 1911.

[3]Raynal, 'Qu'est ce que ... le Cubisme', in *Comoedia Illustré*, December 1913.

Picasso enumerates the different elements composing objects in such a complete and penetrating manner that they only assume the aspect of objects thanks to the spectators' efforts, who are of necessity aware of their simultaneity, precisely because of their arrangement. Is this art more profound than it is elevated? It doesn't dispense with the observation of nature and it works on us as familiarly as nature itself.'[1] Apollinaire further stresses the realistic character of the movement when he writes, simply and perhaps instinctively: 'Courbet is the father of the new painters.'[2] Gleizes and Metzinger also emphasize in the opening section of *Du Cubisme* that to evaluate Cubism it is necessary to go back to Courbet – '(He) initiated a move towards realism which has touched all modern endeavours.'[3] Two years earlier, in 1910, Metzinger had written: 'Picasso doesn't negate the object and he illuminates it with his mind and his spirit', and again, 'Picasso openly declares himself a realist.'[4] Discussing Cubism, Picasso himself has said: 'in our subjects, we keep the joy of discovery, the pleasure of the unexpected; *our subjects must be a source of interest.*'[5] And Braque: 'When the fragmentation of objects appeared in my painting around 1910, it was as a technique for getting closer to the object . . .'[6]

The iconography of Cubist painting in itself serves to confirm the realistic intentions of the painters. Picasso and Braque turned to the objects closest to hand for their subject-matter, objects forming part of their daily lives and relating to their most immediate and obvious physical necessities and pleasures. The wine glasses, tumblers, pipes and so on were articles which each painter handled regularly in the course of day-to-day life. The fans and musical instruments which become recurrent themes in the still lifes were part of the equipment or decoration of many typical advanced studios in Montmartre; Braque who had been responsible in 1908 for the introduction of musical iconography into Cubist painting was furthermore seriously interested in music. Picasso worked mostly from memory, but when he used models for his figure pieces they were

[1] *Les Peintres Cubistes*, p. 36.
[2] Ibid., p. 26.
[3] *Du Cubisme*, p. 6.
[4] 'Note sur la peinture', *Pan*, October–November 1910 (the article was written in September).
[5] From the interview with de Zayas, in Barr's *Picasso*, p. 271 (the italics are my own).
[6] 'Braque, la Peinture et Nous', p. 16.

usually people he knew well, his friends and mistresses. So even in the first exploratory or formative phase, when human values were largely suppressed, the Cubism of Picasso and Braque was in some ways an expression of the private life and experience of the painter. The early researches had required the acceptance of a severe discipline, and individualities and personal tastes had been sacrificed in a common urge. But after the new concepts of form and space had been clearly formulated Cubist painting at once became much more personal, more human. Through some of his paintings of 1912 Picasso went so far as to say candidly to the spectator, 'j'aime Eva'; at the same time he wrote to Kahnweiler of Eva, 'I love her very much and I shall write it on my paintings.'[1] In 1913 and 1914, after all the most important discoveries had been made, Cubist painting naturally became freer and more decorative, but the same simple subject-matter was retained. In a vein of intimacy the Cubists introduced into their compositions the names of popular songs,[2] the programmes of theatres they had visited, the packets of cigarettes they had smoked, or the headings of newspapers they read – elements which, as Apollinaire put it, were 'already drenched in humanity'.[3] And yet, despite the extremely personal aspect of so much Cubist painting, the movement remained free from introspection, and the painters continued to view and record their ideas of the material world of their immediate experience in a detached and objective way. This seemingly contradictory combination of an extreme objectivity of vision with a strong vein of intimacy and personal humour emerges as one of the main characteristics of the classical and immediately pre-war Cubism of Picasso and Braque.

The desire of the Cubists to keep closely in touch with visual reality explains Picasso's uneasiness about his Cadaquès paintings: clearly he could not go back to his earlier, more laborious methods of dealing with form, and yet at a single stroke he had carried the new technique suggested in the work of Braque to something very near complete abstraction. The *Portrait of Kahnweiler* (Pl. 16), painted in Paris soon after Picasso's return from Cadaquès in the early autumn of 1910, may have helped Picasso towards a solution of his problem, since in dealing

[1]Letter to Kahnweiler of 12 June 1912. 'Eva' was the name given to Marcelle Humbert, Picasso's companion of the moment.

[2]These song-titles appear in paintings of 1912 as well.

[3]*Les Peintres Cubistes*, p. 35.

with a particular individual he was forced to find a less difficult and hermetic means of expression; in any case the portrait serves to illustrate what steps Picasso took to make his work once again more legible. Picasso worked from a photograph he had taken of his friend and dealer who recorded that Picasso nevertheless demanded some twenty sittings.[1] The basic method of composition of this painting is the same as in the Cadaquès work, but the subject is made identifiable by the retention or introduction of 'keys' or 'signs' within the looser, more generalized, structure of the figure. Distinctive features of the sitter, his eyes and hands for example, are rendered with a greater degree of naturalism, and these, together with the stimuli provided by other details such as a button on M. Kahnweiler's coat, a lock of hair, or the still life to the side of him, permit a reconstruction of the subject and his surroundings; (one of the New Caledonian sculptures owned by Picasso appears in a ghost-like form to the left of the sitter); and these more realistic touches in turn forced the painter to restore or preserve the naturalistic proportions of the figure. The distortion of scale which had appeared in the Cadaquès paintings is not encountered again in the following year, and while all subsequent paintings are understandably not as easily legible as this portrait, almost all of them do contain some kind of clue or stimulus which serves to identify the subject, and which renders it immediately recognizable to anyone familiar with Cubist iconography. Kahnweiler, who himself often helped the painters to choose titles for their paintings, in *Der Weg zum Kubismus* emphasizes the importance of the descriptive titles attached to the works as further means of enabling the spectator to reconstruct fully the subjects.

Although Braque had been responsible for taking the first steps towards a more abstract type of painting, his own use of the new procedure was much more cautious than Picasso's. In a painting such as the *Female Figure* (Pl. 46), executed in the winter of 1910–11, the subject is still much more easily recognizable than it had been in Picasso's Cadaquès work, or even in the *Portrait of Kahnweiler*. When, a year later, with paintings such as *Man with Violin* (Pl. 48), Braque's Cubism reached a second climax of complexity and became also highly difficult to read or interpret, one senses that it was not owing to the excitement of working

[1]*D. H. Kahnweiler, Marchand, Editeur, Ecrivain*, Centre Georges Pompidou, Musée National d'Art Moderne, Paris 1984, p. 103.

with a new, more abstract technique as it had been with Picasso, but because his interest in elaborately breaking up the picture surface so as to analyse the relationships between the objects and the space surrounding them, slowly and inevitably led him to this kind of painting. And whereas Picasso had been forced to reintroduce clues, small fragments of legibility, into his work to render it more accessible to the spectator, Braque, even at his most abstract, instinctively retained them as a link with reality. This is very clear, for example, in the beautiful crystalline *Hommage à J. S. Bach* (Pl. 50A); not only do the stencilled letters and the graphic marks enable us to reconstruct the musical subject matter of the still life, but the painting as a whole seems to become an analogy of its musical connotations.

The method of composition used by the painters brought with it a new element of ease and fluidity. Most important, since form was now largely suggested rather than clearly defined, and since a strong linear quality was retained in the finished painting, it became much easier to combine the various views of an object or to synthesize in its depiction a greater amount of information. For example (although the painters never worked in such an obvious and theoretical way), plan, section and elevation of an object could be laid or drawn over each other, and then adjusted and fused to form a single, legible and highly informative image. Secondly, it was now obviously much easier to fuse figure and surroundings, thus emphasizing the 'materiality' of space and also ensuring the unity of the picture surface, while the greater complexity and concentration of the central areas generally serves to isolate and emphasize the subject. Thirdly, with this method of composition the lack of a fixed light source, the arbitrary juxtaposition of light and dark, becomes a consistent and, indeed, a salient feature of the style. In some ways the dismissal of a single light source can be regarded as a natural consequence of the dismissal of a single viewpoint.

In the work of Cadaquès Picasso had moved ahead of Braque with characteristic impetuosity, and then late in 1911, when Picasso's painting is once again comparatively legible, Braque had in turn produced a series of unusually elaborate and highly personal paintings (of which the *Man with Violin* (discussed above) and the still life *Soda* in the Museum of Modern Art in New York are good examples) which represent the most hermetic stage of his Cubism and which have no counterpart in the work of Picasso. But on the whole the canvases of 1911 show the painters at their closest point, and the year and a half from the autumn of 1910 until the spring of 1912 was the period during which Cubist painting of the pre-war period appeared to change least radically. Perhaps no pictorial revolution of the magnitude and depth of Cubism had been effected with such extreme rapidity, and during the years between 1907 and 1910 every few months had witnessed some radical change in the appearance of Cubist painting. Now the style reached a moment of poise and equilibrium. The series of figure compositions executed by Picasso during the summer of 1911 at Céret (Pl. 17) and in Paris on his return, represent the culmination and perfection of this particular phase in his Cubism. These paintings do not differ fundamentally from his work of the previous autumn and represent only a very gentle movement towards a softer, more lyrical kind of painting. Another *Man with Guitar* by Braque (the one now in the Museum of Modern Art, New York, Pl. 45B) is a close parallel to Picasso's Céret work of 1911 (although it is slightly richer in the actual paint quality) and was probably executed in Céret also. Two etchings of early 1912, *Fox* by Braque (Pl. 34) and *Still Life with Bottle* by Picasso (Pl. 33), would, if unsigned, present a problem of identification except to the highly trained eye. As a result of the feeling of greater ease, decorative touches and small colouristic accents begin to appear in the smaller canvases of both men. In the work of Picasso of early 1912 certain objects are discreetly tinted, while in many contemporary Braques small, rippling strokes begin to be applied in bright reds and greens. Both painters were by now introducing stylized, almost illusionistically painted strips of decorative roping or braiding. The oval format, too, is used frequently.

But if Cubist methods of composition did not change fundamentally between 1910 and 1912, in the spring of 1911 Braque introduced a new element into one of his paintings which was of vital significance. Across a painting entitled *Le Portugais* (Kunstmuseum, Basel)[1] Braque stencilled the letters BAL, and under them numerals (Pl. 47). Braque had first introduced letters into a still life, probably of early 1910 (*Le Pyrogène et 'Le Quotidien'*), but they are blended into the composition and have no function other than that of identifying as a newspaper the object over which they are painted. More important was the introduc-

[1]Braque has stated that the subject is a musician he had seen in a bar in Marseilles – Notes to the Catalogue of the Braque exhibition at the Tate Gallery, September–November 1956, p. 32.

tion of illusionistic nails into three still lifes of early 1910.[1] At a time when the Cubists were beginning to restrict severely their use of colour, when all details and incidentals had been suppressed and eliminated, when the objects in their paintings had been dislocated and fragmented to a degree where they are occasionally almost unrecognizable, there is an element of contradiction, almost of perversity in this inclusion of a *trompe l'oeil* detail. But this particular device had a deep significance. Intensely concerned with retaining contact with external reality, Braque must have realized, unconsciously perhaps, that at this particular time Cubism's means of expression could become only more abstract, and the illusionistically painted nail may be regarded as an affirmation of the realistic intentions of the movement (Pl. 42).

The stencilled letters and numbers are assertions of this also – 'as part of a desire to come as close as possible to a certain kind of reality, in 1911 I introduced letters into my paintings', Braque has said[2] – but the implications are wider. In *Le Portugais* they fulfil several obvious functions. In the first place, in a style in which one of the fundamental problems had always been the reconciliation of solid form with the picture plane, the letters written or stencilled across the surface are the most conclusive way of emphasizing its two-dimensional character; Braque has stressed this when he said of the letters: 'they were forms which could not be distorted because, being quite flat, the letters existed outside space and their presence in the painting, by contrast, enabled one to distinguish between objects situated in space and those outside it.'[3] In other words Braque is in effect saying 'My picture is an object, a flat surface, and the spatial sensations it evokes are a painter's space which is intended to inform and not to deceive.' Gertrude Stein expressed much the same idea when she wrote, 'Picasso in his early Cubist pictures used printed letters as did Juan Gris to force the painted surface to measure up to something rigid and the rigid thing was the printed letter.'[4] Secondly, the letters in Cubist painting always have some associative

[1]Kahnweiler claims that the illusionistically painted nail appears for the first time in the *Still Life with a Pitcher* (Kunstmuseum, Basel). A nail also appears in two other still lifes (one in the Guggenheim Museum, New York) supporting a palette hanging on the wall (Pl. 42).

[2]'Braque, la Peinture et Nous', p. 16.

[3]Ibid., p. 16.

[4]*The Autobiography of Alice B. Toklas*, p. 102.

value; in Picasso's *Ma Jolie* series (Pl. 21) the words, from the title of a popular song, relate through their musical connotations to the still lifes with musical instruments and paintings of figures playing them. Here the letters D and BAL (the D must be the last letter of the word GRAND) were probably suggested by a dance hall poster hanging in a bar, and help to convey a 'café' atmosphere. Then, in the *Portugais* the letters have a purely compositional value, providing a terminal note for a system of ascending horizontal elements. Fourthly, they have a certain decorative value.

But the stencilled letters and numbers have yet another effect on the paintings in that they serve to stress their quality as *objects*. When, during the first years of their friendship, at Braque's suggestion[1] he and Picasso stopped signing their works they were automatically emphasizing the autonomous existence of their creations. Now, the introduction of elements of reality, such as the stencilled letters and numerals in *Le Portugais*, affirms clearly the material existence of the painting as an object in its own right. For in the same way in which the number or title of a painting in an exhibition catalogue gives it an identity as a material object different from all others of the same type, so the letters and numbers on a Cubist painting serve to individualize it, to isolate it from all other paintings. Then, again, and in this they point ahead to the invention of *collage*, the letters and numerals stress the material existence of the painting in another way: by applying to a canvas or sheet of paper letters, other pieces of paper or fragments of glass and tin – elements generally considered to be foreign to the technique of painting or drawing – the artist makes the spectator conscious of the canvas, panel or paper as a material object capable of receiving and supporting other objects.

Kahnweiler recalls that the painters themselves talked a great deal about 'le tableau objet'. In their studios the canvases stood on the floors, on the chairs and other pieces of furniture, or hung high on the walls. When their work was framed they preferred the frames to be 'en fuite', or to project the canvas forward, rather than traditional frames which enclosed paintings and made them recede. It would obviously be dangerous to deduce too much from this, but at the same time the painters' attitude towards their work unconsciously mirrored a whole new

[1] 'Braque, la Peinture et Nous', p. 18.

concept of painting. Reacting against the momentary quality of Impressionism, which had been like a window suddenly opened out on to nature from a sheltered interior, against all forms of violent personal expression, against the decorative and symbolic element which had characterized the work of the Nabis and Gauguin and so much late nineteenth-century painting, and even against the Fauves (and the strong *fin de siècle* flavour of Fauvism has never been sufficiently acknowledged or stressed), the Cubists saw their paintings as constructed objects having their own independent existence, as small, self-contained worlds, not reflecting the outside world but recreating it in a completely new form. Gleizes and Metzinger stressed that Cubist painting had no specifically decorative function, and that it did not attain its full meaning only when hung on the wall at eye level. In *Du Cubisme* they wrote: 'A decorative work exists only by virtue of its destination, comes to life only in relationship to determinate objects . . . A painting justifies its own existence. One can just as reasonably move it from a church to a gallery, from a museum to a bedroom ... It doesn't harmonize with a particular ensemble, it harmonizes with things in their entirety, with the universe; it is an organism.'[1] Later in 1925, Gleizes wrote again: '. . . what will come out of Cubism . . . will be the painting as an emotive event in itself with nothing descriptive about it, having the quality of an object and the same relationship to nature.'[2] The Cubist painters had claimed for themselves the right to move around their subject and incorporate aspects of it not visible from a single point of view, and they bestowed, in theory if not in actual practice, the same liberty on the spectator in relationship to their own work.[3]

During the war the Cubist concept of the work of art as an autonomous, constructed object became more and more widespread and was to have a profound effect on the emergence of Purism, one of the pictorial styles to which Cubism helped give birth. In an article entitled 'Quand le Symbolisme fut mort' which appeared in *Nord-Sud* in 1917, Paul Dermée attempted to sum up the new aesthetic trends. He proclaimed a classic revival in the arts in which the work of art was to be judged as whole and not on the merits of its parts or in relation to its

[1]p. 11.

[2]'Chez les Cubistes' in *Bulletin de la Vie Artistique*, 1924–5.

[3]This is implied in the painters' attitude to their works, although in actual fact the spectator's only really satisfactory viewpoint is, of course, from in front.

creator: '... the work of art should be conceived as a pipe or a hat is conceived by the craftsman who produces it; all parts should have a strictly determined place according to their function and importance. It is the object which matters and not any one of its elements.'[1] In the same periodical, Reverdy, who admitted that much contemporary literature at this time reflected an aesthetic first developed in Cubist painting, added: 'the poet's aim is to create a work which lives independently from him, from his private life, which existes in a special realm.'[2] Max Jacob, who had been a friend of the painters and in particular of Picasso, published in 1917 in *Le Cornet à Dés* one of the most lucid definitions of contemporary aesthetic. After condemning the 'Baudelairean' atmosphere of the nineteenth century ('it is the triumph of romantic disorder'),[3] and its cult of individual genius, Jacob goes on to stress the objectivity of modern poetry (which is by contrast 'a universal poetry') and the fact that a work of art 'is of value in itself and not because of any confrontation one can make with reality'.[4] Discussing the prose poem – a form of literature which, as used by Jacob, provides one of the closest literary parallels to Cubist painting in that it embodies simultaneously actions or events normally separated by time and space, which are fused into formal, difficult but rational and understandable creations – Jacob warns the poet and artist against 'the too dazzling precious stones which attract the eye at the expense of the whole', and adds 'The poem is a constructed object and not the display window of a jeweller's shop. Rimbaud is the jeweller's shop window, and not the jewel; the prose poem is a jewel.'[5]

The stencilled letters and numerals in Braque's *Portugais* are the prelude to the introduction of *collage* into Cubist painting, and *collage* was in many ways the logical outcome of the Cubist aesthetic. In the work of Picasso and Braque it ushered in a new phase of Cubist painting.

[1]*Nord-Sud*, 15 March 1917 – Dermée had obviously been influenced by Gris and by the nascent ideals of Purism in *L'Elan*, on which Ozenfant worked during 1915 and 1916.
[2]Ibid.
[3]p. 20. This was written some years before its publication, which was delayed by the outbreak of the war. In the preface to the 1922 edition, Gabory wrote: '(*Le Cornet à Dés*) donne naissance à toute une partie de littérature dit Cubiste et plus récemment "dadaïste"' – p. 7.
[4]p. 21 (from the 1916 preface).
[5]Ibid., p. 21.

3

PICASSO, BRAQUE AND GRIS 1912–14

In 1911 Picasso and Braque were joined in their creation of Cubism by a third painter, the Spaniard Juan Gris. Gris has, in a sense, no real history before this. Younger than Picasso and Braque by some five years, Gris arrived in Paris in 1906 at the age of nineteen. Knowing no one there, he sought out Picasso, and soon he installed himself in the same studio building in the rue Ravignan. In Spain Gris had begun to work as a commercial illustrator, and he continued to do so for several years in Paris, but, finding himself in the midst of a creative and original circle of people, he soon began to take his work more seriously. Apart from the commercial work only a few examples of Gris' earliest works are known. These are drawings and gouaches executed in a tight, refined, highly decorative, *art nouveau* style. By 1910, however, he had begun to work simultaneously in a more straightforward, naturalistic way, and by 1911 he was painting in oils. On 1 January 1912, *Paris Journal* announced that some fifteen of his pictures were on show at Clovis Sagot's gallery. A few months later, in March, Gris made his début at the *Salon des Indépendants* with three canvases, one of which was an *Hommage à Picasso* (Pl. 59), and during the year he contributed to three exhibitions of Cubist painting.[1] After showing at the *Section d'Or* he signed an exclusive contract with Kahnweiler and, like Picasso and Braque, stopped showing his work publicly.

[1]At the Galeries Dalmau, Barcelona, 20 April–10 May 1912; Société de Peinture Moderne, Rouen, 15 June–15 July 1912; *La Section d'Or*, October 1912.

Gris became familiar with the art of Picasso just as it was entering its most crucial stage, that is to say in the months before he began the *Demoiselles d'Avignon*. Gris was an intelligent and intensely serious and thoughtful young man, and must have followed the development of Picasso's Cubism step by step, so that when he began to paint seriously in 1911 he might have been expected to join Picasso and Braque at the most recent stage of their development, for he was already a highly experienced draughtsman. His approach to Cubism, however, was fundamentally different from theirs. More cerebral and with a much more coldly analytical mind than either Picasso or Braque, Gris was more interested in the implications of the discoveries they had made than in the appearance of their paintings. And his methodical, more purely intellectual interpretation of Cubism formed in many ways the necessary complement to the more instinctive Cubism of Picasso and Braque. His work, therefore, was of the greatest importance in serving to define the aims of true Cubism for the public and the minor figures of the movement, for from the first his uncompromising approach served to concentrate attention on the bare mechanics of the style.

Because of their seriousness and obvious originality, the paintings shown by Gris at the *Salon des Indépendants* attracted a great deal of attention. Furthermore, they were hung in a room devoted mainly to Russian exhibitors and the *Hommage à Picasso* was placed next to an *Improvisation* of Kandinsky's, so that the freedom and spontaneity of Kandinsky's technique and the extravagance of his colour must have made Gris' canvas look particularly cold and forbidding. An anonymous reviewer in *Gil Blas* wrote: 'it isn't at M. Juan Gris' painting that visitors will warm themselves ... in front of his *Homage to Picasso*, ludicrous assemblage of tubes, someone murmurs "one would take them for fragments of a stove" – "fragment" is kind but "stove" is harsh.'[1] Allard, who had supported the Cubist manifestations of 1911, in his review of the exhibition referred to 'the post-Cubist fantasies of Kupka and Juan Gris'.[2] Allard's contact with Cubism was through Gleizes and his circle, and he had probably seen very little of the work of Picasso and Braque, so that he was baffled by Gris' paintings and felt them to be fundamentally foreign to the style. Apollinaire, although the section

[1]*Gil Blas*, 20 March 1912.

[2]'Le Salon des Indépendants, 1912', *Revue de France*, March 1912.

dedicated to Gris in *Les Peintres Cubistes* indicates that he was not entirely in sympathy with Gris' painting, once again sensed instinctively what it was that Gris was striving for and what his position in the movement was to be. He wrote: 'Juan Gris shows an *Homage to Picasso* in which one must praise above all the great effort and the great disinterestedness. The entry of Juan Gris could be called integral Cubism.'[1]

It is characteristic of Gris' painstaking and methodical approach that he should have felt he could master Cubism only after a fresh study of Cézanne. In his first still lifes of 1911, the influence of Cézanne is immediately apparent in the simple forms, the high angles of vision and in the way in which the tops of the tables on which the objects stand are distorted and thrown up sharply on to the picture plane. A less immediately obvious feature of these paintings which also derives from the work of Cézanne is the treatment of the outlines of the table-edges, which, when broken by an object, are continued beyond it at a slightly different angle. This was a feature of Cézanne's style that Picasso and Braque had also seized on in some of their work of 1908 and 1909. All this early group of paintings, however, indicates a study of Cézanne by a painter whose vision was already Cubist. In many of Cézanne's still lifes the angle of vision is not consistent, but Gris' distortion of perspective is much more obvious and deliberate. The outlines are rendered in an angular and incisive fashion, and then deliberately broken at intervals, to create areas in which forms fuse or merge with each other and with the backgrounds. Form is not laboriously built up by a system of closely-knit hatchings or small planes, as in the paintings of Cézanne, or, for that matter, in some of the works of Braque and Picasso influenced by him, but smoothly and simply modelled. But the simplicity and initial impression of directness given by these paintings is deceptive. With some of them one has the sensation that having started with a more naturalistic drawing, Gris then began slowly dislocating or distorting the objects, sharpening the outlines and arbitrarily breaking them, while introducing simultaneously a series of intellectual and pictorial refinements.[2] In *The Eggs*, for example, the upper, empty part of the

[1]*L'Intransigeant*, 20 March 1912.

[2]It is known that in connection with his later work Gris destroyed almost all the many preliminary calculations that went into the construction of each painting. See p. 136 below. It is possible that there originally existed drawings for the early paintings which would have illustrated the steps by which

bottle is rendered by setting it against the darker background, and one side of it is smoothly rounded while the other is squared off in deliberate contrast. Below, the transparent glass of the bottle vanishes against the white cloth, so that the dark wine becomes a self-subsisting cylinder of liquid. The use of the flowered wall-paper or curtain in the background emphasizes in a very direct, concrete way that this sort of painting has its origins in the work of Cézanne (Pl. 58A).

The first and most obvious difference between the early Cubism of Gris and that of Picasso and Braque is that Gris never abandoned colour to the extent that they did. Some of the earliest paintings, such as the views of Paris, are in silvery, rather muted tones, but in others Gris uses a palette composed of a single bright colour, mixed with black and white to form a full range from dark to light. Sometimes a second or third colour is subsequently introduced, but the original monochromatic effect is retained. This schematization of colour, which can be seen even in the portrait of Picasso, colouristically one of the most elaborate of the early works, is accompanied by a corresponding move to a more abstract method of composition. In a series of paintings begun probably in the winter of 1911–12, of which the *Still Life with a Cylindrical Pot*, a small rectangular canvas in the Kröller-Müller Museum (Pl. 58B), is an example, the subjects are distorted as if by forces moving diagonally across the canvases, and the emphasis is on the organization of the picture surface in terms of clearly defined, carefully balanced shapes. The fusion of subject and background is more complete than hitherto in the work of Gris, and there is very little sense of depth, even in paintings, like the one referred to above, where the objects are arranged behind each other in successive layers. The forms, however, continue to be heavily modelled and are lit from a single light source. This is another distinctive feature of Gris' Cubism, for he remained preoccupied with the problem of light, and for a long time used it rationally or naturalistically to develop form, unlike Picasso and Braque who in 1909 were already using it in a purely arbitrary fashion. In many of the small still lifes of the period the background is as incisively and elaborately treated as the subjects themselves, so that the subject appears to lose its sense of importance. Already in many of them one gets the sensation that the

Gris reached the final incisive stage in which many of the objects are quite highly abstracted or distorted.

subject is being superimposed on to a schematic or geometric pictorial substructure. While these paintings are more immediately legible than many contemporary still lifes of Picasso and Braque, Gris' dispassionate and intellectual concern with the solution of purely pictorial problems renders them in a sense more abstract. Cold and formal, even these early paintings have no direct counterpart in the work of Picasso and Braque.

Nevertheless, it is from Picasso's work of 1909 that Gris' first truly Cubist paintings most directly derived, probably because it was in the works of Picasso of this period that Gris saw the essential features of the style most clearly stated; Gris knew Braque's work much less well and did not become really friendly with him until after 1912. In the still lifes the debt to Picasso was largely intellectual, but *L'Homme à la Pipe* (a portrait of Gris's friend Legua), a work of 1911, shows a purely visual influence as well (Pl. 57). The division of the forehead down the centre and the treatment of the areas around the eyes point to a thorough knowledge of the Horta de San Juan figure work. And here Gris was preoccupied with solving exactly the same problems that had concerned Picasso two years earlier; the problem of combining various views of an object into a single image, and representing them on a two-dimensional surface. In a basically three-quarter view the far side of the face is pulled around into the picture plane, and the cleft in the forehead and the bisection of the chin imply a profile view as well. The *Portrait of Picasso* (Pl. 59), painted some months later (winter 1911–12), shows Gris dealing with the combination of different views of the head in a much more stylized, intellectual fashion. Indeed, the way in which the face is divided down the central axis, suggesting simultaneously a profile and full-face view, is reminiscent of Picasso's *Baigneuse* of 1909, one of the first paintings in which the new concept of form was most clearly and deliberately stated. The abnormally long chin is typical of Gris' figure work, but the device of repeating the jaw line recalls again Picasso's heads in the Horta paintings, although in Picasso's work this had helped to convey a sculptural quality that is not present here. This portrait has a distinctly experimental quality, and naturally enough (for Gris was still a novice by comparison), it is not as accomplished as the works of Picasso to which it most closely corresponds. In the *Portrait of Picasso* the areas around the nose and mouth are not fully explained and in the work of a painter who was so obviously striving for a logical and clear pictorial expression, passages such as these are particularly disturbing. However, in his subsequent work of 1912 Gris emerges as a more completely assured painter.

Developing in the same direction as Picasso and Braque, Gris now evolved a more linear type of composition. In the work of Picasso and Braque the invention of a kind of grid or linear framework, which was suggested by the outlines or directional lines of the subject, had led to a looser, more fluid type of painting. Gris, on the other hand, used a similar procedure to achieve a greater precision and explicitness. Some of the still lifes of the first half of 1912 show Gris taking the first steps towards this new method of composition. Many of the thick black outlines are retained (rather than being blended into the composition as they had been hitherto) and left unbroken, while the curving shapes and receding ellipses of the past months are reduced to triangles and cones. The diagonal movement across the canvas is replaced by a more static composition of verticals and horizontals (Pl. 60A). By the time that Gris painted the *Portrait of Germaine Raynal* (Private collection, Paris), in the summer of 1912, the new technique was fully developed. A linear framework, like an irregularly constructed leaded window or a metal grille, is clamped down over the figure and its setting, and then within each of the sections or compartments the subject is studied from a different point of view. One eye, for instance, looks directly out, while the other, enclosed in a separate rectangular form, is tipped sideways, carrying with it a portion of the nose. A view of the nose, seen from underneath, is enclosed in an oval form and placed in the centre of the face, while below, by joining together two profile mouths the full-face image is reconstructed. The tops of the shoulders are lifted on to the picture plane, making one think, once again, of Picasso's figure work of 1909, and one of them is made transparent so that the bricks of the paving in the street behind are seen through it. But, unlike Picasso and Braque, Gris never uses a complex of partially transparent, interpenetrating planes to suggest form, which is, on the contrary always clearly defined. The main parts of the face and torso are firmly painted and solidly modelled. In this kind of painting, the linear framework is thus fused to a solid, carefully painted image. This framework itself is of course to a large extent suggested by the contours and features of the subject, and, before the painting reaches its final state, undergoes a whole series of adjustments and modifications, so that the process is by no means as simple as it might at first appear (Pl. 60B).

This sort of painting of Gris' illustrates what is perhaps the fundamental difference between his early Cubism and that of Picasso and Braque, for whereas their painting gives the impression that they moved freely around their subjects, painting them from a variable viewpoint, Gris, on the other hand, dissects his subjects, examines each part from a different, but single viewpoint, and then reconstructs the total image from these various sections. In the painting of all three painters the result is a highly informative kind of optical synthesis. But at this point Gris is still really adapting and elaborating scientific perspective (by fusing a series of different but consistent viewpoints in a single painting) to achieve the very effects for which Picasso and Braque had abandoned it.

Gris exploited the logical possibilities of this new technique to the full in the still lifes of the second half of 1912, in which he used mostly man-made or manufactured objects with basically geometric forms which allowed for even greater precision. Never before had the possibilities of Cubist form been stated so fully or explicitly. In *Le Lavabo* (private collection, Paris) the curtain and the shelf at the top establish a frontal viewpoint, but the table-top, which forms a perfect rectangle, is seen directly from above. The plan, section and elevation of each object could be almost literally reconstructed. Having found a means of expressing very accurately all the essential information about his subjects, Gris began to widen his palette and the colour in these works becomes almost naturalistic (Pl. 62A).

Gris' intellectual approach to Cubism inevitably led him to an interest in its mathematical implications. During the war he became a serious student of the works of Poincaré and Einstein, and later, in 1921, he was able to write a letter to Ozenfant in which he claimed to be able to reduce any given composition to purely geometric terms.[1] But even if before 1914 Gris had not yet reached this point, he was always ready to discuss Cubism in intellectual language.[2] The Spanish sculptor Manolo, a friend of Picasso and Gris, is reported to have said: 'the one who explained Cubism was poor Gris.'[3] In connection with the intel-

[1] *The Letters of Juan Gris*, compiled by D. H. Kahnweiler, edited by D. Cooper, London 1956, pp. 105–6 (the letter is of March 1921).

[2] D. H. Kahnweiler, *Juan Gris*, Eng. ed. translated by D. Cooper, London 1947, p. 8.

[3] Quoted by D. H. Kahnweiler, ibid., p. 8, from Josef Pla's *Vida de Manolo contada por ell mateix*, Sabadell 1928, p. 131.

lectual and theoretical side of Cubism much has been written about the influence of Maurice Princet; indeed many contemporary critics and writers saw him as an important force in the movement.[1] The employee of an insurance company and an amateur mathematician, Princet lived for a while in the *Bateau Lavoir* and was undoubtedly on terms of fairly close friendship with many of the Cubist painters. The pictorial revolution that Picasso and Braque effected was, it has been seen, primarily an intuitive one. Pictorial theory played very little, or perhaps even no part at all in their creation of Cubism. Gris, who as his later writings show, had a considerable capacity for original thought, was obviously capable of formulating for himself a more rational and intellectual interpretation of the style. But even if Princet had no influence on these three figures, his presence as one of their friends seems to show that there was a good deal of theoretical talk in Cubist circles, and that Gris contributed to it. Both he and Princet, it will be seen, were influential in encouraging many of the minor painters to approach Cubism in a more theoretical fashion. And then even if in fact the 'legendary' question that André Lhote tells us Princet posed to Picasso and Braque was never formulated so precisely, it suggests that he recognized the obvious implications of what the Cubists were doing. 'You represent by means of a trapezoid a table, just as you see it, distorted by perspective, but what would happen if you decided to express the universal table (*la table type*)? You would have to straighten it up onto the picture plane, and from the trapezoid return to a true rectangle. If that table is covered with objects equally distorted by perspective, the same straightening up process would have to take place with each of them. Thus the oval of a glass would become a perfect circle. But this is not all: this glass and this table seen from another angle are nothing more than, the table a horizontal bar a few centimetres thick, the glass a profile whose base and rim are horizontal. Hence the need for another displacement . . .'[2] While Picasso and Braque never planned a painting in such an intellectual and calculating way, this passage illustrates, in a crude and simplified way, the sort of problem with which Gris was preoccupied.

Gris' quick mind rapidly assimilated the most advanced Cubist techniques.

[1]e.g. Warnod, *Les Berceaux de la Jeune Peinture*, Paris 1926, pp. 40, 87. Carco, *De Montmartre au Quartier Latin*, p. 30. There are also references to him in writings by Metzinger, Salmon, Janneau etc.

[2]'La Naissance du Cubisme' in R. Huyghe's *Histoire de l'Art Contemporain*, Paris 1935, p. 80.

Thus on to the canvas of *Le Lavabo* he glued a small fragment of mirror. It was only about half a year earlier that Picasso had inaugurated what was to be one of the most important stages of twentieth-century art by the invention of *collage*. Early in 1912 Picasso had painted a still life, *Still Life with Chair-caning* (Pl. 24A) into which he incorporated a piece of oil cloth, overprinted to imitate chair-caning.[1] This was the first *collage*, that is to say the first painting in which extraneous objects or materials are applied to the picture surface. Then in another still life of the period Picasso introduced a postage stamp[2] and by the early part of 1913 was working with strips of cloth, bits of paper and even, occasionally, small pieces of tin or zinc foil. In the meantime, in September of 1912, Braque had executed the first *papier collé*, a drawing entitled *Compotier et Verre* (Pl. 49B) on which three pieces of wall-paper, printed to imitate wooden panelling, are pasted. Picasso and Braque spent the early part of the summer together at Céret,[3] and then were together again at the end of the summer in Sorgues, a village near Avignon. Picasso was in Paris at the beginning of September for a fortnight, but soon returned to Sorgues, where he remained for several weeks.[4] It was during Picasso's absence in Paris that Braque bought in a shop in Avignon the piece of wall-paper, simulating wood graining, which inspired him with the idea for the first *papier collé*.[5]

The invention of *collage* struck the most violent blow yet at traditional painting, and particularly at the idealized and romantic conception of the 'work of art' as the expression not only of technical skill but also almost of some absolute beauty. Now the Cubist painters were constructing works of art from odd bits of

[1]This painting has been dated 1911–12, but on stylistic grounds it is hard to place it in 1911. A certain softness in the handling of some areas, the positive colouring of the lemon and the fact that several of the objects are left almost intact (e.g. lemon and shell) all point to a date in the first half of 1912.

[2]This painting could, on stylistic grounds, be placed in 1911. However, both Picasso and Kahnweiler insist that the *Still Life with Chair-caning* is the first *collage*, so that one is forced to assume that this other painting followed it.

[3]Picasso arrived in Céret in March. He returned there in December and again at intervals during the following year.

[4]From Picasso's correspondence with the Steins (Yale University) it is possible to reconstruct his movements during the period. He returned to Sorgues on 13 September.

[5]Braque stated specifically to Mr D. Cooper that he had seen this paper for some days in a shop window and that he waited to buy it till Picasso went away.

material – one might almost say from bits of rubbish – generally considered to have no aesthetic value, and not even to serve any good or useful purpose. And the invention of *collage* was, to a large extent, a revolt against slickness of brushwork and other forms of technical facility. Sabartès quotes Picasso as saying, 'we sought to express reality with materials we did not know how to handle, and which we prized precisely because we knew their help was not indispensable to us, that they were neither the best nor the most adequate.'[1] Raynal, as became clear in some of his later writings, did not really understand or approve of Picasso's latest innovation,[2] but in his article on *collage* in the *Section d'Or* of 1912, the first written discussion of *collage*, he implies that its appearance was largely due to the artists' distaste for photographic illusionism in painting, and that they felt it preferable to substitute for an exact copy of an object (for example the label on a bottle), a portion of the object itself.

Salmon, in *La Jeune Sculpture Française*, which was written before the war but did not appear until 1919, gives an account of a discussion between the painters that must have taken place at about this time: 'Braque was arguing one day with Picasso about the inimitable in painting. Should one, if one paints a newspaper in the hands of an individual, apply oneself to reproducing the words PETIT JOURNAL or reduce the enterprise to actually sticking the newspaper on the canvas. Out of this they came to vaunt the ability of house painters who extract so much marble and so much precious wood from imaginary quarries and forests.'[3] Thus the illusionism that Picasso and Braque condemned was not that of the artisan, producing rich and exciting effects with the minumum of means, but the elaborate and pretentious productions to be seen in the fashionable *Salons* and galleries. Braque, as the son and grandson of house painters, 'peintres-décorateurs', naturally played an important part in the introduction of new methods hitherto considered to be beneath the dignity of a class of artists who in France traditionally referred to themselves as 'artistes-peintres'. Salmon goes on to tell how Braque initiated Picasso into the professional secrets of the humbler forms of commerical painting, by teaching him the use of the house-

[1]Sabartès, *Picasso*, English edition, London 1949, p. 241.

[2]In *Anthologie de la Peinture en France de 1906 à nos Jours*, Paris 1927, Raynal condemned *collage* and the incorporation of new textures (sand, etc.) into Cubist paintings as subversive tricks.

[3]p. 13.

painters' 'comb', an instrument which drawn through wet brown pigment gives the effect of wood-graining. Picasso, characteristically, used it at once (according to Salmon) not for its obvious and traditional purpose, but to suggest some stylized locks of hair and the beard in a painting of a man's head (the particular painting referred to by Salmon may be the *Male Head*, also known as *The Poet*, now in the Kunstmuseum, Basel). Even if this is simply one of the characteristic legends which have grown up around Picasso at all periods of his career, it is certain that by the summer of 1912 he and Braque were using this means of reproducing wood-graining in their paintings.

Daring as *collage* must have seemed, many of the innovations of Picasso and Braque during the preceding years had pointed towards it. Braque, at a time when he seemed to be moving inevitably towards greater abstraction, had introduced – arbitrarily in several cases – *trompe l'oeil* nails into some of his still lifes, partly at least as an assertion that he did not intend to lose contact with external reality. Picasso's use of illusionistically painted, or at least immediately legible details, coat-buttons, moustaches and so on, which help the spectator to identify his subjects, asserts in a more obvious way the realistic character of the style. Then the stencilled letters in Braque's *Le Portugais* and the words or titles written over his and Picasso's paintings, were in a sense also clues for the reconstruction of the subject. But these keys or clues did not only serve to make the painting more legible; they were also elements of reality, which as Braque himself put it, could not undergo pictorial distortion.[1] From the desire to evoke as concretely and immediately as possible fragments of external reality in their paintings to the insertion of the fragments themselves was a short step. Indeed, the painters' distaste for photographic kinds of painting and for the too obviously accomplished and showy techniques of illusionistic painters demanded it.

Furthermore, *collage* was the logical outcome of the Cubists' conception of their works as self-contained, constructed objects. And indeed the invention of *collage* was preceded by the construction of exactly such an object. Early in 1912 Picasso produced *Guitar*, now in the Museum of Modern Art, New York, made of sheet metal and wire.[2] A cardboard maquette for the *Guitar* can be seen in a contem-

[1]See p. 91–2 above.

[2]For a discussion of *Guitar*, see William Rubin, *Picasso in the Collection of the Museum of Modern Art*, New York 1972 pp. 74, 207–8.

porary photograph of Picasso's studio in the Boulevard Raspail, placed on a wall covered with large drawings in such a way as to suggest that Picasso was investigating its formal, sculptural properties on two-dimensional surfaces. Another slightly later photograph taken by Kahnweiler shows the *Guitar* transformed into a more elaborate still life by the addition of further elements, one of them a bottle painted onto a sheet of paper. Working with the opacity of sheet metal at a time when his painting was relying on effects of fluidity and transparency faced Picasso with a new challenge: the left-hand side of the guitar is seen in outline on a plane corresponding to that of the wall on which the object was designed to be hung; the right-hand side of the instrument, however, is projected forward, thus creating a sense of spatial tension and ambiguity and also giving the impression that we are seeing both its inner and outer structure simultaneously. The hole of the sounding board is an empty cylinder which projects forward further than any of the other component elements and acts as a positive sculptural form which confounds our expectations as to how a negative element—a hole—is customarily perceived. Picasso was now responding to a new kind of tribal African sculpture or artefact—masks from the Ivory Coast or Liberia.[1] Picasso acquired two such pieces although once again he seems to have apprehended their sculptural principles before he fixed his attention on individual examples (Pl. 19B, 106E). This kind of mask consists basically of flat oblong or oval wooden boards or supports. From the top of these project smaller boards or ledges representing the forehead; continued down from them, at right angles, there is generally a thin strip representing the nose. The eyes are indicated by projecting circular pegs, while the mouths, also projecting, are rendered by crescents or simply by incised or painted rectangular blocks. The properties and even the appearances of these masks were to have a deep effect on Picasso's subsequent reliefs and paintings. By contrast with some of these *Guitar* is a somewhat conservative work, simply because the side elements have so clearly been fashioned in such a way as to represent the actual appearance of the guitar's body. Nevertheless his pioneering object stands behind the foundation of the whole Constructivist movement and its aesthetic. Like the *Guitar* Cubist

[1]Until relatively recently these were characterized as being Wobe but are in fact Grebo. For a discussion of Picasso's pieces, see Rubin, 'Picasso' in *Primitivism*, p. 305.

collages and *papiers collés* are in a very real sense constructions, objects built up of various different substances and materials, a protest against the conventional oil painting proudly displayed on an easel or elaborately framed on a wall (Picasso, for instance, framed the *Still Life with Chair-caning* simply by surrounding it with a single thickness of ordinary rope). And the strips of paper, fragments of canvas and other materials that the painters applied to their pictures emphasized in a very concrete way their weight and solidity as material objects. The care required in the handling of the *collages* and *papiers collés* to-day, and the methods of restoration which will eventually have to be devised to preserve them, emphasize the fact that they form a new category of works of art, totally distinct from traditional painting.

The aesthetic implications of *collage* as a whole were vast, and its invention was to lead to a whole series of developments in twentieth-century art. The fragments of extraneous matter almost invariably undergo some kind of alteration or transmutation in their incorporation into Cubist pictures, but the curiosity in exploring unorthodox technical procedures and the ability to see aesthetic possibilities in objects and materials hitherto not thought to have any artistic value, relate this aspect of Cubism to the 'ready mades' of Dada, and to the Surrealists' *objets trouvés* and juxtaposition of incongruous materials to evoke new sensations and images. Indeed, the 'ready made' aspect of *collage* is illustrated by the fact that Gris felt that the engraving incorporated in his *Violon et Gravure* (Museum of Modern Art, New York) could be replaced by something else, the owner's portrait for example, without upsetting the pictorial balance or the 'actual merits' of the painting.[1] It is, however, necessary to make a distinction between *collage* in general and the Cubists' use of a particular kind of *collage*, namely *papier collé*. It is characteristic that Picasso should have invented *collage*, which was subsequently to be used by Dadaists as a weapon to destroy all art, and by the Surrealists to achieve the most disconcerting and disturbing of psychological effects, while Braque should have been the author of the first *papier collé*, an equally original pictorial technique at the service of more purely formalistic ends.

Braque's first *papier collé, Fruit Dish and Glass* (Pl. 49B), executed in Septem-

[1]*The Letters of Juan Gris*, p. 3. Letter to Kahnweiler, from Céret, 17 September 1913.

ber 1912, already shows a full and sophisticated command of the medium. The three strips of wood-grained paper boldly establish the basic composition of the picture to which the object is subsequently related by overdrawing. Each strip has a clear representational function: the two uppermost suggest wood-panelled walls behind the still life, while the lower one by the addition of a circular knob becomes the drawer of the table on which it stands. The strips of paper also have a pronounced aesthetic effect on the picture in that, like all fragments of Cubist *collage*, they make one conscious of it as a constructed or 'built-up' object or entity, which differs from most traditional drawings and paintings. To recapitulate: the fragments of *papier collé* here can be said to exist on three levels. They are flat, coloured, pictorial shapes. They represent or suggest certain objects in the picture by analogies of colour and texture or by the addition of keys or clues. Thirdly, and this is the aspect of *papier collé* that most relates it to other forms of Cubist *collage*, the pieces of paper exist as themselves, that is to say one is always conscious of them as solid, tactile pieces of extraneous matter incorporated into the picture and emphasizing its material existence. In this still life the small pencil marks around the fragments of paper (which are visible even in a photograph) indicate that the composition was worked out with care before the paper was finally pasted on.

Picasso's use of *papier collé* was both visually and mentally more acrobatic than Braque's. Many of the first to be produced by him cover virtually the entire surfaces with overlapping, superimposed or interacting strips of paper so that they have the appearance of almost being surrogate paintings. *The Violin* (Pl. 25), a highly complex work of the autumn or early winter of 1912, illustrates a use of *papier collé* more like the original use of *collage*. Five illusionistic colour reproductions of fruit are incorporated into the composition without any subsequent modification. Here, as in Gris' *Violin and Engraving*, the pieces of fruit are in a sense 'ready-made' objects, used to represent only pieces of fruit in a fruit bowl, and transformed only in so far as they are assimilated into a new context. The fruits are depicted prosaically and literally, but what appears to be a chair-back in the lower left-hand corner is rendered in a somewhat casual and highly abstract form. The newspaper headlines that appear at the top left ('. . . arition', which evokes at once *apparition*), and inverted at the base of the work ('La Vie Sportive') have been carefully selected to comment on the visual games and ambiguities embedded in the work as a whole. The work is more layered, both physically and in its intellectual implications, than anything to be found in Braque's contemporary works. Salmon's story of Picasso immediately putting the house-painter's comb to new ends and producing with it something totally unexpected is symbolic of a whole aspect of Picasso's talent which was given for the first time full rein by the discovery of *collage* and *papier collé*.

Bouteille de Vieux Marc, Verre, Journal (private collection, Paris) (Pl. 24B), one of Picasso's finest *papiers collés*, conveys at once a sense of greater richness and exuberance than Braque's *Fruit Dish and Glass*. For while Braque limited himself to the use of fragments of newspaper and imitation wood-graining, and to a few other black and soberly coloured types of paper, Picasso turned as well to more brightly coloured and elaborately patterned varieties of paper. Here one is more immediately aware of the representational aspect of the pieces of *papier collé* than of their purely pictorial or compositional value. The largest piece of wall-paper is the table cloth. But whereas in *Fruit Dish and Glass* Braque used the *faux-bois* paper as imitation wood, that is to say he used it to represent wood in his picture just as the interior decorator would have used it to represent or simulate wood-panelling on the wall of a room, the wall-paper in *Bouteille de Vieux Marc, Verre, Journal* undergoes a subsidiary transmutation in that it represents or becomes a flowered table-cloth. Or in other words, Braque's *faux-bois* remains *faux-bois*, whereas Picasso's wall-paper becomes *faux-tissu*. In the same way the strip below it becomes the ornate moulding along the edge of the table. The piece of newspaper represents itself, or to be more precise, represents the whole of the newspaper of which it was originally a part. The fourth and smallest fragment represents the liquid in the glass. It is cut out to suggest the *marc* seen from above and also the curved rim of the glass. At the same time it is prolonged downwards so as to suggest the depth of the liquid, while the space around it gives an idea of the thickness of the goblet. And, as opposed to the *Still Life with Guitar*, where the drawing of the objects extends over the strips of paper, in this work the drawing is at several points actually continued on underneath the fragments of *papier collé*, although Picasso did subsequently draw the outline of the table over the 'cloth' and added the shading on the newspaper to integrate the pieces of paper into the picture. This implies that Braque saw more quickly than Picasso that *papier collé* could be used as a means of establishing the basic composition of a picture in a simple and direct way, while Picasso was more interested in the possibilities of transforming the elements applied to his pictures by giving them a new and specific meaning.

Simultaneously Picasso continued to produce very dense impacted works where he combines the pasted paper with oil paint on a canvas support. Even when the applied matter is used sparingly Picasso's work tends to have about it a strongly physical, manipulative feel. In *L'Etudiant à la Pipe* (Pl. 29B), another somewhat later work of 1913 or early the following year, a piece of paper is cut out to represent the typical student beret and its crumpled appearance even suggests the texture of heavy cloth. It is obviously impossible to distinguish completely *papier collé* from *collage*, except in cases where the strips of paper involve a particular technique, that is to say when the effects could not be achieved by the use of materials other than paper. This is true for example of the *Compotier et Verre*, and generally speaking, of all the *papiers collés* of Braque. It could, broadly speaking, be said of Picasso's *Violin* also, although the paper fruits are not used primarily for their compositional or pictorial value as are the other fragments of paper in this same picture, and as the fragments are almost always in the work of Braque. They are used rather in a purely literal way to suggest the presence of the fruit. Neither are they the fruit itself in the way that the newspaper is itself in the *Bouteille de Vieux Marc*. One gets the feeling that if the fruits had been over-printed on cloth, or for that matter on any other material, they would have served Picasso's purpose equally well. It is on this somewhat abstract, metaphysical plane that the dividing line between *papier collé* and *collage* becomes confused. In the case of the *Etudiant à la Pipe* the fundamental pictorial property of the paper, its flatness, is deliberately destroyed so that one would be justified in classifying it simply as a *collage* rather than as a *papier collé*.

The deliberate casualness of many of Picasso's *papiers collés* and *collages* served to emphasize both the daring use of new, 'unsuitable' materials and the material existence of the pictures themselves: the student's cap, for example, is not evenly glued on to the canvas, and the loose edges give a sense of actual relief, while the overlapping of the layers of paper in *The Violin* gives a sensation of density and weight. Braque, although he was working with the same humble materials, is always more consciously craftsman-like and respectful in his use of them; torn and ragged edges are rarely found in his *papiers collés*, and the strips of paper are smoothly applied so that their physical assimilation into the picture is more complete.

Although Braque's use of *papier collé* was less intellectual than Picasso's, he realized that, besides providing a new compositional technique, the pieces of paper could be made to play a part in rendering the spatial effects that continued to be one of the main preoccupations of his art. *The Clarinet* (Pl. 52A), a work of 1913, despite its appearance of simplicity, is spatially extremely sophisticated. The four pieces of paper on the right, all of different colours, are pasted over each other to give a sensation of recession and depth. The large piece of black paper at the back, however, since it is darker in tone than the others seems to come forward again onto the picture surface. Its bottom end furthermore appears to stand on the front of the table. The flatness of the picture is also emphasized by the piece of black paper at the extreme left, which does not pass behind the long, horizontal strip of imitation wood graining but simply rests upon its upper edge. On the other hand it recedes, since it is smaller in size than the other piece of black paper. A series of spatial complications are also created by the relationship between the subject and the pieces of paper. Thus the clarinet is drawn over the newspaper, and the newspaper is in turn pasted over the brown wood-grained paper, which although it suggests the material of which the clarinet is made, nevertheless breaks up the drawing of it. In the same way the bowl of the wine-glass is drawn over the newspaper but its base disappears behind it. And although Braque's approach to *papier collé* was more purely pictorial than Picasso's he was not unaware of the intellectual refinements that the medium made possible. In the *papier collés* of both Picasso and Braque the simple, solid shapes cut out of paper occasionally cast shadows that do not echo or repeat their outlines, but rather reverse or complement them. Braque was to use words, typographical insertions and captions in his *papiers collés* in thoughtful provocative ways, but the associations they evoke are generally of a poetic and informative nature, directly related to the iconography of the work containing them.

Gris' approach to *collage*, as one might expect, is perfectly straightforward and logical. In 1912 he glued a piece of mirror on to *Le Lavabo* and during the following years he incorporated an etching, playing cards and fragments of chair-caning into his still lifes. The mirror in *Le Lavabo* (Pl. 62A) is used in a purely representational way, and as it is in a sense an inimitable material, its use seems completely rational. 'You want to know why I had to stick on a piece of mirror?' Gris asked a friend. 'Well, surfaces can be re-created and volumes reinterpreted in a picture, but what is one to do about a mirror whose surface is always changing and which should reflect even the spectator? There is nothing else to do but stick on a real piece.'[1] The elements of *collage* in his other paintings are generally used in the same literal way. In Picasso's *Still Life with Chair-caning* the line representing the edge or moulding of the chair was added after the chair-caning had been incorporated into the painting, and the chair-caning appears below it so that it does not cover only the seat as it normally would in an actual chair. Although Gris frequently overpaints, too, the fragments of chair-caning in his painting always give the impression of being 'tailored' or cut to fit exactly the seats of the chairs in his paintings.

Gris' *papiers collés*, however, are very different from those of Picasso and Braque. Kahnweiler has pointed out the basic distinctions in the three painters' use of the medium;[2] Picasso used it both in drawings and paintings, Braque only in drawings (although at least one of them is on canvas and many are very large), and Gris made use of it only in paintings. Unlike Picasso and Braque, who first painted *trompe l'oeil* details into their painting and then progressed to incorporating into them the actual fragments of reality, Gris seems to have begun to use illusionistic detail and *collage* almost simultaneously, and in 1913, when he was painting sections of some of his canvases to represent wood-graining and wall-paper, he was already incorporating strips of paper into others. But it is only in 1914 that Gris began to use *papier collé* seriously as a means of expression. When this occurs, however, his use of the medium is a great deal more complex than that of either Picasso or Braque; indeed it almost constitutes a completely new technique. As with some of Picasso's first *papiers collés* the entire pictorial surface is covered with fragments of paper, although the deliberate unevenness of Picasso's surfaces is avoided in favour of more 'ironed', cleaner and flatter effects. It was now that Gris began to become fully aware of the abstract compositional possibilities of the medium. That is to say he began to realize that

[1]Quoted by Kahnweiler in *Juan Gris*, pp. 87–8.
[2]Ibid., p. 87.

by adjusting or juggling the pieces of differently coloured paper he could achieve unusual compositional effects of great subtlety and of almost knife-like balance. This discovery was to affect all his subsequent work. But at this time the fragments of paper almost always continue to have some literal or representational value as well, and very often they still have (as opposed to many of the pieces of *papier collé* in the work of Picasso and Braque) the appearance of having been trimmed or cut out to fit some preconceived plan. Sometimes the scraps of paper are cut out to correspond exactly to the shapes or contours of the objects which they represent, and each is subsequently carefully modelled or made more completely representational by the addition of over-drawn or over-painted detail. There is, too, a great deal of over-drawing and over-painting of additional objects. The *papier collé* is thus assimilated into works that have the appearance of being immensely elaborate and complex paintings, and what distinguishes Gris' original approach to *papier collé* from that of Braque and Picasso is that he used it primarily to give his work a sense of definition and certainty, a precision and exactitude that he could not achieve by any other means (Pls. 65, 66).

For some time before the invention of *papier collé* Picasso and Braque had been preoccupied by the problem of reintroducing colour into their painting. The initial limitation of colour in the work of Picasso, which began in his Negroid phase, was the natural result of his attitude towards form. The touches of primary colour in the right-hand figures of the *Demoiselles* had served to give a certain sense of weight and form, but this empirical method of painting was soon abandoned for a more conceptual and rational approach, and colour thus became naturally, if not an inessential, as least a very secondary consideration. In the landscapes of La Rue-des-Bois and La Roche Guyon, Picasso and Braque had restricted themselves to browns, greys and one other colour (green) in order to control better the formal and spatial relationships which they were seeking to convey. Soon even the bright greens were suppressed, and towards the middle of 1910 Cubism entered what could almost be called a monochrome period. In other words, the discipline involved in creating a style which was revolutionizing traditional concepts of form and space forced both painters to discard the more immediately sensuous and appealing aspects of painting. Braque has said, 'I sensed that colour could produce sensations which would interfere a bit with space, and it is because of that I abandoned it.'[1] However, in such a complete visual and pictorial revolution an important factor such as colour could not be ignored for ever. Furthermore, the austerity and asceticism of early Cubism was too intense to continue without a corresponding reaction towards a more highly coloured and decorative kind of painting.

As early as the spring of 1910, that is to say when he had been forced to adopt a nearly monochrome palette, Picasso was attempting to reintroduce areas of positive, bright colour into his paintings. However, he seems to have found that strong colour could not be satisfactorily combined with the complex rendering of volumes that characterized his work at that period, since he almost invariably painted it out again.[2] Towards the end of 1911 small colour accents began to appear in the work of both painters, but while they have a definite decorative value, they remained incidental to the formal and spatial effects and did not fundamentally alter the general sobriety of the paintings. During the first half of 1912 these small areas of colour become bolder and begin to assume more importance, and finally in *Le Modèle* (Pl. 23), a painting executed by Picasso at Sorgues in the early autumn of this year, the whole figure is painted in muted pinks. However, the use of naturalistic colour was probably felt to be at variance with a style that had developed a highly abstract means of expressing form. The head of the *Aficionado* (in the Kunstmuseum, Basel), a more complex painting from the same series as *Le Modèle*, was originally also painted in flesh pink, but was then reworked in the more usual early Cubist colour harmonies.[3] In many other paintings of the period small areas of brighter colour appear to have been over-painted (Pl. 22).

Braque's remarks on colour in Cubist painting indicate that the painters wished to use it in a direct way, dissociating it from the modifications imposed on it by variations of light and the modelling of form. They wanted to find a way of using colour in a simple, direct, constructive way. That is to say they felt that it could exist as an independent pictorial entity, contributing to spatial and formal sensations but not conditioned by effects of atmospheric light and perspective or

[1]'Braque, la Peinture et Nous', p. 16.

[2]Kahnweiler describes these paintings in *Der Weg zum Kubismus*, p. 24. He recalls also that in one case the colour was not painted out. This painting, however, appears to have been since destroyed.

[3]Where the paint has cracked it reveals under the area of the face an under-painting of bright pink.

by the modelling of forms from lights to darks. This is borne out by an experiment of Picasso's that is described by Kahnweiler in his book on Gris.[1] In a painting called *The Piano* (dated 1909 by Kahnweiler), Picasso used ridges of plaster to achieve a sense of relief in order that colour might then be applied as an independent element, without any subsequent need for chiaroscuro or shading to convey a sense of form. Waldemar Georges, who was the author of what is perhaps the first serious article on Braque's work, saw his invention of *papier collé* as an experiment designed to solve the problem of reintroducing colour into Cubist painting: 'Anxious almost to excess to render not the ephemeral effect produced by colour, but its very essence, Braque introduced into his paintings extrapictorial substances. He thus produces ingenious compositions, in which the parts, felt to be important, are rendered in paper and don't represent reality but embody it and become confounded with it. This phase of Cubism indicates already the desire felt by certain painters to objectify their sensations.'[2]

Clearly *papier collé* was more than simply a colouristic experiment, but at the same time it solved the problems that were facing Picasso and Braque. '... the problem of colour was brought into focus with the *papiers collés*', Braque has said.[3] It has already been seen how the strips of coloured paper could be used as an abstract compositional structure over which an ordinary Cubist drawing could be overlaid; form was thus preserved independently of the colour beneath it, although a subsidiary relation between colour and form is almost always established subsequently. In Picasso's *papiers collés*, and very occasionally in Braque's, the pieces of paper are cut out to represent specific objects, and in the work of both painters they often relate to objects in the pictures in a general way by analogies of shape or of texture, or are made actually to represent the objects by the addition of details or keys drawn over them. But in these cases the drawing conveys, in a kind of pictorial shorthand, all the necessary information about the form of the objects so that colour can exist, once again, free from modifications of light and modelling. The point is made with great clarity in Braque's *Still Life with Guitar* (Pl. 51). The piece of wood-graining to the right tells of the guitar's substance and colour, but the piece of paper to the left which is subsumed into the

[1] p. 47.
[2] 'Braque' in *L'Esprit Nouveau*, 6 March 1921.
[3] 'Braque, la Peinture et Nous', p. 17.

guitar by overdrawing (although it suggests a bottle) is a slaty blue.

Besides the re-awakening interest in colour, there had been in Picasso's work of early 1912 a move towards a clearer, more explicit kind of painting. This becomes clear on comparing *Bottle and Glasses* (Solomon Guggenheim Museum, New York, Pl. 18A), a work of the winter of 1911–12 and typical of the kind of painting that Picasso had been producing all that year, with the slightly later *Bouteille de Pernod* (Hermitage, Leningrad, Pl. 18B). In the former it is hard to detach any of the objects from its surroundings, or to reconstruct any one of them independently of the other objects around it. The second painting is by contrast much more immediately legible; the objects are kept more intact and stand apart from each other and from the background; they are more heavily painted and are even occasionally differentiated in colour. Whereas in the earlier work one has the impression of a complex of planes inextricably involved with each other, in the *Bouteille de Pernod* the glass and bottle are composed of a series of distinct planes, which seem to pass through and behind each other as they do in the exactly contemporary *Guitar* construction. In some of the still lifes of the summer, the subjects are extended to include dead birds, and the shells which had appeared in a few earlier paintings become a recurrent theme. In keeping with the movement towards the more sensuous kind of painting, many of these canvases have a new quality of softness. The *Modèle*, painted at Sorgues in 1912, while it is still quite hermetic or hard to read, is considerably less complex in handling than any of the Céret figures of the previous year. Braque's *Hommage à J. S. Bach* (collection Sidney Janis, New York) shows that in the spring of 1912 he was moving along parallel lines to Picasso. The objects in this painting are, however, still more fully opened up into the planes surrounding them than those in the contemporary paintings of Picasso, and the simplification tends to give a sense of increased airiness or spaciousness rather than of solidity (Pl. 50A). In a work like *Violin, 'Jolie Eva'*, (Pl. 20A) of the summer of 1912, however, one senses some of Braque's spatial clarity informing Picasso's work.

Later in 1912, after the invention of *papier collé*, there was a much more radical change in the appearance of Cubist paintings by Picasso and Braque, and it has now become usual for scholars to divide Cubism into two periods, an 'analytical' phase, which is generally acknowledged to end in 1912 or 1913, and a succeeding 'synthetic' phase. Kahnweiler, in *Der Weg zum Kubismus*, noted that the discoveries made by Picasso at Cadaquès in 1910 enabled him to combine or 'synthesize' a great deal of information about an object into a single image, and that the new method of work dispenses with the early 'analytical description' of objects.[1] Carl Einstein, a German writer and poet, uses the term 'synthesis' in the same way. In an article entitled 'Notes sur le Cubisme', which appeared in *Documents* in 1929, he distinguished three successive phases in Cubist painting: 'first a period of simplistic distortion, then a period of analysis and fragmentation, and finally a period of synthesis.' In actual fact, however, during the period of 'analysis' to which these writers refer, Picasso and Braque had already broken with traditional perspective and were combining or 'synthesizing' various views of an object into a single image. The development of a more abstract technique during 1910 only enabled them to effect this kind of synthesis in a freer, more suggestive manner. It was Ozenfant and Jeanneret in *La Peinture Moderne*, published in Paris in 1925, who were the first to see that if there was any real break in Cubism, it occurred in 1912. The early period from 1908 to 1912 they called 'hermetic' or 'collective' to differentiate it from the succeeding phase in which, according to them, the painters lost all sense of restraint and discipline, and indulged in excessive self-assertion. In his *Juan Gris* Kahnweiler refers to the fact that the years 1909–13 have been called the 'hermetic period' of Picasso and Braque;[2] that is to say that some people have seen a 'hermetic' phase coinciding with an analytical one. Other critics have used the term 'hermetic' simply to describe the extremely complex, rather abstract appearance of Picasso's and Braque's paintings of 1911 and 1912. These paintings, it has been seen, were not different in kind from those of 1910.

But it was in the writings of Gris that the difference between an analytical and synthetic approach was elaborated. Gris, in a reply to a questionnaire, 'Chez les Cubistes', sent out by the *Bulletin de la Vie Artistique* in 1924 and published in January of the following year,[3] made a distinction between an early period of analysis in Cubist painting, which he felt to be purely descriptive and therefore of no real artistic value, and a later phase in which 'the analysis of yesterday has become a synthesis'. Three years earlier in *L'Esprit Nouveau* he had written: 'I

[1] p. 34.
[2] p. 49.
[3] The text is given in full in Kahnweiler's *Juan Gris*, pp. 144–5.

work with the elements of the intellect, with the imagination. I try to make concrete that which is abstract. I proceed from the general to the particular, by which I mean that I start with an abstraction in order to arrive at a true fact. Mine is an art of synthesis and deduction, as Raynal has said.'[1] Kahnweiler records a conversation with Gris, which took place in 1920, in which Gris expressed himself even more explicitly: 'I begin by organizing my picture; then I qualify the objects. My aim is to create new objects which cannot be compared with any object in reality. The distinction between synthetic and analytical Cubism lies precisely in this. These new objects, therefore, avoid distortion. My *Violin*, being a creation, need fear no comparision.'[2]

For Gris, then, synthetic Cubism involved a clearly defined procedure. To describe it crudely: the composition of a painting was established in purely abstract, and in the case of his work, often mathematical terms. The subject then emerged from or was superimposed over this framework or substructure of flat coloured forms. As the subject-matter materialized in these paintings, as the flat, coloured shapes were converted into objects and figures, the rigidity of the underlying geometric framework was naturally softened, and by the time that the paintings reached completion, it is usually entirely disguised. Sometimes while Gris was evolving this method of work the paintings were begun with specific subjects in mind (this was obviously true, for example, of the portrait of his wife and of the paintings executed after Cézanne and Corot,[3] all works of 1916 and 1917), but even in these paintings Gris used two distinct approaches in that at a certain point the representational values were ignored while he established

[1]*L'Esprit Nouveau*, no. 5, 1921. Reprinted in *Juan Gris*, pp. 137–8. Gris refers to an article by Raynal in the same no. of this periodical. In this lecture *Quelques Intentions du Cubisme*, published in 1919, Raynal made the point that the Cubist painter first analysed the objects he wanted to depict, in order to extract their significance, and then, 'par un travail synthétique qu'il exécute à l'aide de tous ses moyens pictoraux, il constitue un ensemble nouveau de tous ces éléments.' It is not clear, however, whether the process he describes is simply an extension of the original idea of 'synthesis' as Kahnweiler first saw it, or whether Raynal is trying to suggest some more radical difference of approach. He is a critic to whose terms it is often hard to give a precise meaning, and in this passage does not appear to resolve the formal contradiction between 'synthesis' and 'deduction'.

[2]*Juan Gris*, p. 104.

[3]The exhibition of Corot's figure paintings at the *Salon d'Automne* of 1909 must certainly have interested the Cubists, and his classically composed, pyramidal compositions of women playing musical instruments may well have been an important stylistic and iconographic influence.

to his satisfaction the desired formal, abstract relationships between the flat, coloured shapes which he had come to see as the raw material of painting (Pl. 68B).

Applied to Gris' work the terms 'analytical' and 'synthetic' thus have a real and very precise meaning. On the other hand, they cannot be used in quite the same way in relation to Picasso and Braque. It will be seen that, in some of his painting executed in techniques influenced by *papier collé*, Braque really appears to have first established an abstract compositional framework on the canvas and to have only subsequently objectified the pictorial forms and given them a literal, representational value. And there is no doubt that *papier collé* made both Picasso and Braque much more aware of the possibilities of combining two distinct approaches, an abstract and a representational one, in a single painting, since they were working with pictorial elements, flat, coloured shapes which remained abstract until given a representational value by their incorporation into a picture. Previously Cubist paintings had owed their final appearance to the gradual fragmentation of forms and to the break-up of the space surrounding them; after the general composition had been established the pictures were obviously elaborated section by section until the composition was perfectly balanced. Now, in the *papiers collés*, the compositions, and the forms of objects themselves, could be built up rapidly by a few ready-made elements, while in the contemporary paintings the same effect could be achieved by a few, large, boldly painted planes or shapes. The process thus became that of adding together or combining compositional elements, which were subsequently made to play their part in the rendering of solid forms and the space around them. Painted objects and eventually the whole painting, even, one might say, pictorial reality itself, was 'built up to' rather than dissected or taken apart. To this extent it is possible to differentiate between an analytical and a synthetic approach in the Cubism of Picasso and Braque, although neither of them evolved as completely as Gris a system of working from abstraction to representation; there are very few paintings by Picasso and Braque of this more synthetic type that do not contain 'analytical' passages as well. Braque certainly often created spatial relationships between planes of colour that were only subsequently given a representational function; in the work of Picasso, on the other hand, one feels that the subject almost always comes first. In Braque there is always retained a dialogue between the subject and the space in which it is embedded. Picasso, on the other hand, is more manual, even more sculptural in his approach, often seizing on unlikely elements that were lying to hand and welding or fusing them together to form vivid, unique and even startling images.

The distinction between an analytic and a synthetic phase of Cubism is, then, a useful and a valid one, provided one acknowledges that the methods employed by the three major Cubists during the second phase differed considerably. In so far as there is a definite break in the work of Picasso and Braque it occurred in 1912 after the discovery of *papier collé*, whereas Gris himself did not feel that he had achieved a synthetic kind of painting until long afterwards.[1] Gris was justified in distinguishing a series of different phases in his art, but if one tries to use these as the starting point for generalizing about the nature of Cubism, one is apt to succeed only in accentuating the differences between the approach of Picasso and Braque and that of Gris. Thus Kahnweiler rightly points out that it is in 1914 and 1915 that Gris took the first steps towards a more 'synthetic' kind of painting by attempting to convey the maximum information with the minimum means; that is to say by creating a series of generalized, significant images into each of which is synthesized all the painter's knowledge and experience of his subject. This was something that Picasso and Braque had been doing all along, or at least ever since they had adopted a variable viewpoint. Gris, on the other hand, as has been seen, originally dissected his subject, examined each part from a different angle and then reconstructed the total image again from the various parts. Then Kahnweiler tends to equate synthetic Cubism with a conceptual approach. The Cubism of Picasso and Braque was conceptual from the start, in that even when they were still relying to a certain extent on visual models, their paintings were more the depictions of ideas about types or categories of objects than representations of individual examples. The objects in Gris' pre-1914 paintings, on the contrary, often convey the impression of having been derived from particular models, or at least of having an exact counterpart in the material world. And even though during 1914 and 1915 Gris' art became more conceptual and to this extent more like that of Picasso and Braque, his approach remained very

[1]By Gris' first definitions of synthetic painting it would seem that he had achieved it by 1918. Later, just before his death, he stated that he had only just entered a synthetic period, op. cit., p. 146.

different and he continued to evolve towards a more mathematical, precise kind of painting. It was, however, his experiments with *papier collé* during 1914 that conditioned the development of his art, just as it was *papier collé* that affected the painting of Picasso and Braque when they began to use it extensively after Braque's discovery of it in the autumn of 1912.

But it should be emphasized that while *papier collé* involved new methods of work and initiated almost at once a new phase in the art of Picasso and Braque, it did not involve any fundamental change of aesthetic. *Papier collé* was, in part at any rate, an experiment designed to solve certain problems that the painters were concerned with in their creation of the style. It was not a fortuitous discovery that altered their view of the world around them, but rather a technical invention that conditioned the appearance of their paintings. Or, to put it differently, while *papier collé* affected their pictorial vision, the nature of the movement remained unchanged. Cubism continued to be an art of realism; its subject-matter remained the same, as did the interests and intentions of the painters. But it might also be fair to say that whereas analytic Cubism had been the result of the painters looking at external reality in a new and questioning way, synthetic Cubism was just as much involved in new ways of making art. And it was to have even profounder repercussions on subsequent art than its earlier analytical manifestations. It has already been seen to what extent *collage* and *papier collé* were the natural result of the painters' aesthetic beliefs. As new techniques they speeded up the natural reaction from an austere, complex form of art towards a simpler, clearer kind of painting into which sensuous values could be re-introduced.

Braque's *Composition* or *Violon et Verre* and Picasso's *Violon au Café* (Pls. 54, 26), both of early 1913, show at once the influence that the *papiers collés* had on their painting. The subjects of both paintings are treated in terms of long upright or slightly tilted planes that recall the strips of paper used in *papier collé*: both paintings are flatter than hitherto, and there is an element of directness and immediacy, particularly in the *Violon au Café*. The objects in Picasso's paintings of 1912 had been built up of overlapping and interlocking planes, and the method used here is basically the same. However, each of the planes that goes to compose the violin in this painting is a separate entity, clearly defined and differentiated from the others around it in colour and texture. The earlier effect of transparency has completely disappeared, and a work like *Violin* (Pl. 20B), executed some months earlier, looks almost fragile and insubstantial by comparison. Braque's *Composition* is a more transitional work, although once again the forms are larger and bolder than in his earlier work. A contemporary painting by Braque, *Composition à l'As de Trèfle* (Pl. 53) relates directly to his first *papier collé*, *Compotier et Verre*. The painting is more elaborate and a few alterations have taken place, but apart from these, it is obviously developed from the *papier collé* in a perfectly straightforward manner, although, once again, the painting has become aggressively flattened. Braque had painted imitation wood-graining into his pictures before he began pasting pieces of paper on to them, but here a note of further sophistication is introduced into his work by the fact that in transposing the *papier collé* into a painting the wall-paper, printed to simulate wood-graining, is replaced by a painted imitation of it.

The technique of many of Braque's paintings of 1913 and 1914 was in fact developed directly from his experiments with *papier collé*. In a canvas such as *La Table du Musicien* (Pl. 52B), for example, a work of the summer of 1913, tack or pin marks can be seen in the corners of the planes or shapes that serve to establish the basic composition of the picture – and marks like these can be found on most of the canvases of this year. This suggests that before he actually began to paint or draw on the canvas, Braque experimented by laying strips of paper on it in various positions or combinations. Then, when he had decided upon the arrangement or composition that pleased him most, the pieces of paper were pinned to the canvas and lines were drawn around them, or their positions noted by pencil marks at the corners. After the papers were removed a drawing or blueprint was left behind, from which Braque began to work. A few of the shapes were solidly painted (a characteristic of Braque's work of the period is that much of the canvas shows through), some were made to represent specific objects, while others retained a purely pictorial function. The keys which enable the spectator to identify the objects (in the case of this particular painting the lines of music, the ace of spades and so on), are kept more intact and used more boldly than hitherto, so that the subject-matter becomes more immediately obvious.

These paintings by Braque introduced a third, and totally new method of composition into Cubist painting. Originally the analysis or break-down of form and the break-up of space itself had been the starting-point for the break-up of the picture surface. Next, the linear grid suggested by the outlines or directional lines of the objects or figures had been the point of departure. Now the basic composition, worked out in terms of strips of paper, could exist independently of the subject, which was superimposed or laid over it. Waldemar Georges, after an interview with Braque, described his method of work in his article in *L'Esprit Nouveau* in 1921.[1] After discussing the early stages of Cubism and the part that Braque played in the creation of the style, Georges goes on to say, 'It remains to us to study the creative process of Braque which differs perceptibly from that of former artists. This artist paints without a model. Instead of setting up the elements of a still life and working from this pre-established theme, he composes directly on the canvas and conjures up themes to obey only the laws of the painting ... Whereas Matisse reduces surrounding objects to patches of colour, Braque transforms the patches of colour into objects, which suggest themselves to his fancy. For example if he transforms a white patch into a sheet of music, it is because he imagines rightly or wrongly that visual memory intervening, the impression of whiteness produced by a bare patch would be less than that produced by the spectacle of a book or a newspaper which one knows through practice to be white.' The insistence on colour implies that Georges is referring to Braque's post-war paintings, but the technique described is one which he developed during 1913. The process was not, of course, simply that of laying a subject over an abstract compositional background: a series of adjustments always take place that make objects and background inseparable from each other, and very often the shapes that establish the composition seem to have been suggested by specific objects. But, using Gris' definitions, these were perhaps the first synthetic Cubist paintings in so far as Braque was virtually working from abstraction to representation. Cubism had always been concerned with the balance between abstraction and representation, and now both approaches could be fused in a single painting. It is this that makes Braque's work of the period enjoyable on so many different levels, both pictorial and intellectual; and an appreciation of these paintings provides the key to the understanding of all his subsequent work.

During 1913 Picasso's work also continued to evolve under the influence of

[1] *L'Esprit Nouveau*, no. 6, p. 644.

papier collé, although not in quite the same way as Braque's. Most of Picasso's paintings are heavier and more solid than Braque's, and in a work like *Violin and Guitar* (Arensberg Collection, Philadelphia Museum of Art, Pl. 27), probably dating from the middle of the year, the long slab-like shapes that build up the composition develop also the form of the objects depicted. The part of the violin which is a piece of paper painted in imitation wood-graining and then glued to the surface clearly belongs to an early state of the composition, and this suggests that Picasso had a definite subject in mind when he actually began the painting. The preliminary pencil lines show that the fragment of violin drawn into the central white shape was part of the original subject and was not simply added as an afterthought. In this painting and others like it the original compositional ideas may have been developed by the arrangement of a few abstract pictorial shapes, but the subject soon suggested itself, or was decided upon and conditioned the subsequent development of the painting. There is thus never quite the same duality of approach in Picasso's work as there is in Braque's and his work of this period is in a sense more straightforward and direct.

There is a fundamental difference, too, in the two painters' use of colour. This can be seen by comparing the *Violin and Guitar* with a more or less contemporary work by Braque, *Violon et Verre* (Pl. 54), similar in form. Each of the coloured planes or shapes that make up the central mass of Picasso's painting seems to belong in some way to the objects depicted; if any of these areas were removed the objects would begin to disintegrate. In Braque's painting, however, although the large, irregular brown shape in the centre of the painting is clearly related to the violin, it is not inseparable from it, and gives indeed almost the effect of a plane passing through it. The violin and the glass are in fact drawn or painted over the composition of flat, coloured shapes in the same way in which objects were drawn over the fragments of paper in *papiers collés*, and their forms exist independently, although as in so many of the *papiers collés*, colour produces a subsidiary interaction betwen the objects and the shapes underneath them. Picasso, on the other hand, makes colour more an integral part of form. With Braque it exists autonomously, creating spatial relationships which are then made even more complex when the subject is superimposed. The colours in Braque's painting are browns, blacks and dull greens (imitation marbling begins to appear in this year). In other paintings of the period these more severe tones are relieved by brighter blues and by areas painted in pale colours in imitation of patterned wall-papers. Picasso's *Violin and Guitar* is painted mostly in slaty blues and grey-browns, but in other paintings of the same type the artist uses bright, rather acid greens and reds as well. By the end of the year he was working with a full palette, and his colour schemes were becoming increasingly light and decorative.

At the same time that Picasso and Braque were reintroducing colour into their paintings they began to experiment with a whole new range of materials to enhance the tactile qualities of their canvases and to give a sense of textural variety and richness. In a letter written to Kahnweiler from Sorgues in the summer of 1912 Braque mentions mixing sand into his pigments;[1] *Fruit Dish, Bottle and Glass* is one of the pictures on which he was working at the time (Pl. 49A). Certain areas in Picasso's *Violin and Guitar* are built up of plaster mixed with coarse sand, so that the effect given is almost that of a very low sculptural relief. In many of Braque's paintings of 1913, like the *Violon et Verre*, shapes are built up of gesso mixed with white oil paint. Both painters applied strips of paper dipped in paint on to their canvases. Braque was fascinated by the physical properties of different media, and by the way in which the quality of colour changed when it was blended with them: 'later on I introduced into my paintings sand, sawdust, iron filings . . . I saw to what extent colour depended on matter (*matière*) . . . and what pleased me greatly was precisely that "materiality" which I achieved through the different materials I introduced into my paintings.'[2] In their appeal to the tactile senses, the new materials represented an extension of a certain aspect of *collage* and *papier collé*, and like the fragments of paper, the gravel, sawdust and so on served to emphasize the material existence of the pictures to which they were applied.[3] They represented, too, a reaction against traditional media and facility of technique, while contributing at the same time to the new sensuous appeal that was beginning to find its way back into the work of Picasso and Braque.

[1] *Donation Louise et Michel Leiris (Collection Kahnweiler-Leiris)*, Centre Georges Pompidou, Musée National d'Art Moderne, Paris, 1984–5, p. 27.

[2] 'Braque, la Peinture et Nous', p. 17.

[3] This point is illustrated particularly well by Picasso's *Violon au Café* discussed above. Strips of cloth and paper have been incorporated into the picture, and are overpainted with forms that recall the cut-out shapes in *papier collé* but do not correspond to the shapes of the cloth and paper underneath.

In many ways the discovery of *collage* and the invention of *papier collé* represent a climax and a turning point in the pre-war Cubism of Picasso and Braque. *Collage* was, to start with, the natural outcome of their concept of the work of art as an autonomous, constructed object. It seems to have given them a sense of certainty in that they were producing works of art which were part of external reality and not just representations of it. Considered simply as pictorial media, *collage* and *papier collé* effected a conclusive break with traditional means. Then *papier collé* enabled the painters to reintroduce colour directly into their work, as an independent pictorial element. It suggested, too, a new, more abstract and in a sense freer method of composition. Hitherto both painters had submerged their individualities in a common urge; the creation of a new pictorial language and the complete reassessment of traditional artistic values had involved a rigid discipline and an intense degree of concentration. Their work of 1913, on the other hand, has a feeling of relaxation; one gets the sensation that a tension has been broken. The differences between the personalities of Picasso and Braque begin to reassert themselves. The work of Picasso, who had suppressed his natural restlessness in his anxiety to master completely the mechanics of the new style, becomes increasingly more varied and inventive, combining a sense of wit with a new feeling of gaiety that occasionally reaches the point of exuberance. Braque's work remains more static, more calm and withdrawn, although he gives freer expression to his enjoyment of the physical properties of the different materials with which he was working. The relationship between the two painters remained as intimate as before, but they no longer found it necessary to rely on each other's resources and talents for support and stimulation. Although they continued to see each other frequently, after Picasso moved to the Left Bank in the autumn of 1912, they were no longer in almost daily contact as they had been during the previous years; letters to Kahnweiler from both artists, written in 1913, speak of their not having seen each other for some time. Picasso was in Céret in the spring and intermittently over the summer. Braque visited him there briefly but spent the summer in Sorgues.[1]

Two contemporary figure pieces of the spring of 1913, Braque's *Woman with a*

The bits of *collage* therefore have no representational or compositional value and serve primarily to convey a sense of solidity and materiality (Pl. 26).

[1]*Donation . . . Leiris*, p. 27.

Guitar (Pl. 55) and Picasso's *Harlequin* (Pl. 28) show the way in which the two painters were moving apart in their work. Both paintings are still clearly related to *papiers collés* although Braque's painting differs from many of his contemporary still lifes influenced by *papier collé* in that the exact nature and form of the subject were obviously established from the start. Both paintings are less sober and austere in mood than hitherto. But the *Woman with a Guitar*, although the planes that compose the figure are larger and fewer and in some cases quite self-contained, still relates to an earlier style in which form is built up of interlocking, transparent planes – indeed the painting is closer in many respects to Braque's *Female Figure* of 1910–11 than to his more hermetic figure pieces of the following winter. Picasso's *Harlequin*, on the other hand, is flatter and more stylized than anything that had preceded it. The shapes that build up the figure are for the most part clearly defined and some of the sense of fluidity and interpenetration has disappeared. The combination of various views of the head is now accomplished by laying next to each other a series of stylized forms or symbols that represent its component parts: to the right of the central section is added a profile ear and beyond it a circular form which represents the back of the head. There is, too, an element of fantasy about the painting that is absent from Braque's, which has a feeling of calm enjoyment. Braque's incorporation of a perfectly drawn naturalistic mouth in the woman's head has an element of humour about it, but Picasso's reduction of the features of the face to small dots and sharp, thin lines (in addition to putting in the stylized moustache) is more frankly amusing. The legs of the harlequin accentuate this effect: one is stylized in an angular fashion, while the other is composed of curving, lumpy shapes. The theme of the harlequin was one which Picasso had abandoned four years earlier, before his work had become truly Cubist.[1] After 1913 it becomes a recurrent theme in Picasso's Cubist painting.

Many of the new elements in Picasso's work at this time, in 1913, can be accounted for by the fact that he was becoming increasingly fascinated by Grebo masks; by now he probably owned the two examples that were to remain in his collection throughout his life.[2] The facial conventions in Picasso's *Harlequin*

[1]See e.g. Z II(1), 138 and 145.

[2]In his preface to *The Sculpture of Picasso* (London 1949) Kahnweiler describes this type of mask, and states that Picasso owned an example. He also discusses this kind of tribal art at great length in his

clearly derive directly from this type of African mask. The eyes are the same circular forms, but reduced almost to pin points, and there is the same line above them (here it has become a small black carnival mask), with another line running straight down from it to denote the nose. Picasso furthermore clearly appreciated and understood the principles of this type of tribal art. The harlequin's hands and feet, for example, are represented by completely unnaturalistic shapes that acquire a literal meaning only because of their placing in relation to each other and to the other parts of the figure. That is to say that if shown almost any one of the various elements of the body or the features of the face (the moustache is, of course, an exception) in isolation, one might well be unable to identify it, whereas by its placing in the painting each becomes immediately legible. And in the sense that his works are now built up of abstract shapes given a representational role only by the suggestive or symbolic way in which they are assembled to depict a particular subject, Picasso's procedure is in a different way as truly synthetic as Braque's. The device of using the mouth as a focal point from which a second view of the face is opened out was one which Picasso had been exploring since 1910; now the new formal conventions he had developed enabled him to carry out this kind of displacement more freely.

From the first, tribal art had been an aesthetic revelation to Picasso, and he had been as much impressed by its 'reasonable' or conceptual qualities as by its formal, sculptural properties. But his interpretation of Grebo sculpture was perhaps still more intellectual and sophisticated. Besides realizing that the principles involved in it corresponded to the new elements which appeared in Cubist painting towards the end of 1912, Picasso seized at once upon the psychological possibilities inherent in this anti-naturalistic kind of art, in which shapes bearing very little resemblance to the original parts of the body are used as conventional symbols for them. The reduction of the student's features in

article 'Negro Art and Cubism' which appeared in the December 1948 issue of *Horizon* (London). Kahnweiler, who minimizes any direct influence from tribal art in the creation of early Cubism, feels that it is only with Picasso's study of Grebo masks that tribal art begins to be an important influence on Cubism. He emphasizes the fact that this kind of African sculpture enabled the Cubists to break with 'imitation' and to achieve a more 'synthetic' kind of painting. It is interesting to note that in a drawing of Picasso's of 1917, which shows the interior of his house at Montrouge, a Grebo mask appears on the wall. I am indebted to Mr Douglas Cooper for calling my attention to this point. (This drawing is reproduced in *Portrait of Picasso*, London 1956, pl. 96.)

L'Etudiant à la Pipe to small circles, dots, crosses and crescents, together with the displacements of the ears, produces a highly comic effect. In the *Femme en Chemise dans un Fauteuil*, a work from the end of 1913, there is an element of satire in the way in which the features of the face are reduced in size and importance to an absolute minimum, while the breasts, each of which is duplicated, are unnaturally prominent (Pl. 30A). By comparison, Braque's *Woman with a Guitar* looks almost naturalistic, even though the colours in the *Femme en Chemise* are surprisingly descriptive for the period. In some of the heads of the period the 'shorthand' treatment of the features in terms of a few insignificant dots and crosses has an almost disquieting effect. And indeed some of the pictorial devices first evolved by Picasso during 1913 and 1914 were to influence profoundly the Surrealism of Miro and Ernst. It is not surprising that the *Femme en Chemise* should have been much venerated by the Surrealists.

The constructions in paper, wood, tin and other materials which Picasso was making at this period continued to be influenced by the Grebo masks he owned. None of the paper constructions which Kahnweiler recalls having seen in Braque's studio in the Hôtel Roma, rue Caulaincourt, still exists, although he, too, was experimenting with paper sculptures and constructions during 1912. Another letter to Kahnweiler of the summer of 1912 talks of them[1] and they were an important prelude to the discovery of *papier collé* that autumn. Certainly Braque's constructions must have helped him to achieve the kind of spatial definition that exists in his *papiers collés* and paintings of 1913. Certain later paintings by Braque, such as *Music* of 1914, seem to have been even more directly influenced by these constructions (Pl. 56A, 108B). *Music* looks almost as if it had been constructed from paper or cardboard forms, attached to the background at their lower ends and inclined forwards at the top, casting shadows behind them. A large number of Picasso's drawings of 1913 and 1914 are undoubtedly projects for sculptures in paper or cardboard.

The more solid, predominantly wooden constructions by Picasso which have survived are important because they are so intimately connected with the paintings of the period and because they serve to establish many of the principles of Cubist sculpture. The debt to Grebo art is obvious. The forms, which are often

[1]*Donation . . . Leiris*, p. 27.

unnaturalistic and unrepresentational, are, by their arrangement, endowed with the quality of symbols which enable the spectator to reconstruct the subject-matter. Thus in the *Bouteille et Guitare* (a work which no longer exists) the bottle was composed of a strip of wooden moulding which represents the neck and top; the level of the liquid was shown by a small projection of wood or cardboard (Pl. 29A). The circular opening of the guitar was replaced by a projecting cone of wax. In other examples the hole of the guitar is given by a projecting circular form. This method of representing part of an object by a shape that is the reverse of its counterpart in real life, and of replacing voids by solids and solids by voids, becomes one of the distinguishing features of Cubist sculpture. In the same way the dice that appear in some of Picasso's constructions are tubular or cylindrical forms rather than cubes, and are covered with dots that act as keys or clues, enabling the spectator to identify them; in many of the paintings and constructions of the period there are references to games and gaming, rendered, in turn, in terms of pictorial games. This method of work enabled Picasso, in both his paintings and his sculptures, to work in a direct, easily legible manner, while at the same time avoiding all traditional forms of realism or imitation. By 1913 Archipenko was also producing polychromed 'sculpture-constructions' (he called them 'sculpto-paintings') which, while they are not particularly Cubist in appearance or spirit, were created in much the same way as Picasso's constructions. Thus an assortment of cones, cylinders and cubes of wood, celluloid, tin and so on were imaginatively assembled to represent human figures. When during the war Laurens and Lipchitz began to produce Cubist sculptures[1] it was the *papiers collés* and constructions of Picasso and Braque and the work of Archipenko that they used as their starting point. It is interesting to note that while the principles of their Cubist sculpture were derived from the constructions and *papiers collés* and ultimately from the Cubist painting of Picasso and Braque, towards the end of the war the bas-reliefs of Lipchitz and Laurens were in turn influencing the appearance of paintings by Picasso, Braque and Gris.

The constructions account for the simplifications and distortions that begin to

[1]Some of Lipchitz's small bronzes of 1913 and1914 (e.g. the *Danseuse* in the Petit Palais, and the *Marin* in the Musée d'Art Moderne) make use of certain Cubist devices, such as representing convex forms by concave ones and so on, but it was not until the early war years that Lipchitz emerged as a fully mature, significant artist.

appear in Picasso's painting towards the end of 1913. In *L'Homme au Livre*, perhaps the only surviving figure construction, which is in paper and zinc, the man's arms are two long, thin strips of paper, the shoulders a projecting ledge shaped like the contours of the body of a guitar, and so on. The limbs of the *Homme Assis au Verre* (Pl. 32) a large canvas of the summer of 1914, are conceived in much the same way; although working in a different medium the forms could be more freely conceived and more wildly distorted. The flat, oblong head with the peg-like eyes still relates clearly to the type derived from the Grebo mask the previous year. The effect of the whole is produced by bending and interweaving a few large planes into the representation of a human figure. The naturalism of the pose, however, suggests that at this date Picasso was already developing his figure paintings from more representational drawings, a method he was certainly using by the following year. In a work like this the element of fantasy that had begun to appear in Picasso's work during the past year reaches a climax. The colour has become frankly decorative; the background is emerald green and there are touches of bright blues, oranges and yellows. In 1914 both Picasso and Braque made free use of the decorative possibilities of a 'pointilliste' technique, covering large areas of their paintings with small, brightly coloured dots of paint. The idea may have suggested itself to Picasso through his use of stippled or patterned wall-papers in some of his contemporary *papiers collés*. During 1914 Picasso, who had during the past year often used ordinary enamel paints, began to experiment with other, less shiny types of cheap, commercially manufactured paints. These account for the unusually bright, rather metallic colour harmonies of some of his paintings.

The mood of gaiety and release is typical of Picasso's work of 1914. The *Seated Woman* (Musée d'Art Moderne, Paris), illusionistically painted to imitate *papier collé*, is almost a parody of Cubist techniques. It has been seen that in many of Picasso's and Braque's paintings there are forms which look like fragments of pasted paper, and there are several Picasso still lifes that, like the *Seated Woman*, are completely painted in direct imitation of *papier collé*. This is one of the contradictions of the style: having dispensed with the need for illusionism by incorporating fragments of external reality into their pictures Picasso and Braque then occasionally replaced these fragments by *trompe l'oeil* effects. On the other hand, the style was highly sophisticated and open to all kinds of intellectual refinements, and having definitively broken with traditional concepts of painting the artists felt at liberty to play as many variations as possible on the themes that occupied them. Humour also played a considerable part in the later, more mature phases of the style, and many of Picasso's paintings of 1913–14 have the quality of being pictorial *jeux d'esprit*. The *Seated Woman*, which is based on a whole selection of cut out papers,[1] some of which are painted in imitation of elaborately patterned, commercially manufactured wall-papers, is in fact a technical *tour de force* requiring a complete knowledge and command of academic and illusionistic techniques (Pl. 30B).

Braque painted no figure pieces during 1914, and a still life of this year, *Nature Morte à la Pipe* (collection Girardin, Petit Palais, Paris), shows only a steady and logical evolution from his work of the previous year. The objects are now kept almost completely intact; although none of the innovations and discoveries of the past years have been discarded, there is a sense of ease in the way in which they are incorporated into the picture. Every object combines aspects not visible from a single point of view, but in the dice, for instance, this is now accomplished simply by unfolding two adjoining sides of it on to the picture plane. The painting is essentially flat but the spatial relations between the objects are made clear and there is a definite sense of recession. A typical feature of the work of both Braque and Picasso at this time is the way in which objects are sometimes accompanied by flat, opaque shapes which seem to be a part of them and yet to stand behind them, like shadows or reflections. The wine-glass in this picture is reinforced by two heavy, square shapes. This, and the fact that one side of the bowl is curving and the other straight, gives the impression that not only has Braque combined various views of the glass into a single image, but that he has also synthesized into it various different types of wine-glasses. Some of the shapes are built up of sand and some of gesso, while the whole painting is covered with pointilliste dots; the resulting effect is one of great variety and richness (Pl. 56B).

By 1914 Picasso was working in several different ways so that it is necessary to compare two of his still lifes to the single one by Braque in order to show the stages reached by the two artists when they were separated in the early autumn of that year, soon after the outbreak of the war. *Le Violon* (Pl. 31A) is flatter than

[1]See Z II (2), 792–803.

Braque's *Nature Morte à la Pipe* and at first sight more abstract. The composition has been built up of large flat, overlapping shapes, like brightly coloured strips of *papier collé*. Each of these, with the exception of the patterned strip down the centre is, however, given a specific meaning so that three musical instruments can be discerned: a violin, a clarinet (both placed horizontally across the canvas) and a guitar. In other words, the shapes become the objects; and here we have an instance of Picasso working in what Gris would have agreed was a completely 'synthetic' way. In contradistinction to Braque's painting, the spatial relationships between the objects here are not clearly defined and remain a sort of intellectual puzzle. The *Green Still Life* (Pl. 31B), on the other hand, a later work of 1914, is simpler, more naturalistic and more obviously decorative than *Nature Morte à la Pipe*. It has the same brilliant colour scheme as the *Homme assis au Verre* and the same feeling of spontaneous gaiety. In the *Homme assis au Verre* the poster behind the man and the table at which he is seated seem to become almost part of the figure. In the *Green Still Life* every object gives birth to a series of shapes or planes that are fused with the background or projected into it, producing an effect almost of movement. The fusion of subject and background had, of course, been accomplished much earlier in Picasso's and Braque's work of 1909–10. In these works of Picasso of 1914, however, there is a new feeling of dynamic interaction between the subject and its surroundings which was to become one of the distinguishing features of much of his work of the following years.

While Picasso and Braque were moving, largely under the influence of *papier collé*, towards a flatter, simpler and more decorative kind of painting, Gris' work was becoming increasingly complex and more refined. Gris, who had always been an original painter, had during 1912 asserted himself as an important influence on the minor figures of the Cubist movement. Now, in 1913, he was executing works which match the contemporary paintings of Picasso and Braque in quality and invention. Gris began to use pieces of *papier collé* in his paintings during 1913, and this naturally conditioned the appearance of his work, but there is not the same fundamental change in his style at this time as there was in the case of Picasso and Braque, who were both deeply influenced in all their work not only by the appearance of *papier collé* but also by the new pictorial techniques which it involved. Gris' work of 1913 shows rather a steady progression towards an increasingly accomplished and commanding kind of painting. It is true that in 1913 a greater element of abstraction begins to make itself felt in Gris' work, but this, it will be seen, was not altogether due to the influence of *papier collé*. And it was not until later, in the series of elaborate *papiers collés* which he did in 1914, that Gris started to become really interested in the possibilities of a new kind of painting in which formal abstraction played a much greater part.

Glass of Beer and Playing Cards is built up of the same upright, oblong forms (strips of *papier collé* and other shapes derived from them) that characterize so much of Picasso's and Braque's contemporary work (Pl. 62B). But while the heavy, linear 'grid' effect of some of the paintings of the previous year has disappeared, the system of vertical shapes that is imposed on the subject is made to serve much the same purpose. Within each shape the subject is seen from a different point of view, as it had been earlier within each compartment of the linear framework laid over it. Now, however, each part of the object is rendered also in a different way. The main part of the glass is painted solidly and naturalistically, while the fragments adjoining it are rendered flatly in different colours. Sometimes the contours are shown simply by opposing a light area to a dark one, but, in other cases, a dark line is drawn over a light background or, reversing the process, a white line is drawn over a dark background. What is new, too, in the work of Gris is the way in which the component parts of an object are often completely displaced: thus the left-hand side of the glass in this painting is slipped several inches downwards on a vertical axis. While most of the vertical compositional forms have literal meanings, some are coloured in an arbitrary way, and the displacement of others (for example an area patterned in the same way as the wall-paper appears at the bottom left-hand side) gives a feeling of greater freedom of invention. While the fundamental premises of Gris' art were calculated and intellectual he had, of course, also a strong intuitive pictorial sense. In the works of 1913, the inventive, empirical aspect of his talent becomes increasingly obvious. The difference between this sort of painting and a work like *Le Lavabo* of the previous year is that now one has the impression that the composition, in terms of vertical, oblong planes, was not suggested or conditioned to such a great extent by the subject. That is to say that the framework or background of the painting has begun to assume more importance, and can be considered independently of the subject with which it is fused and related.

It has always been known that in connection with his later work Gris made a large number of preparatory sketches and calculations of a mathematical nature. These he generally destroyed after the paintings were completed; on his death, and at his request, his wife and Kahnweiler destroyed the drawings of this type which remained in his studio. But recently a few of these preliminary studies, which somehow escaped destruction, have come to light. Some of these relate stylistically to the paintings of 1913 and 1914 – surprisingly early for this kind of 'mathematical' drawing. They provide, needless to say, a new insight into Gris' method of work at this time. The simplest and perhaps the earliest of the drawings is of a single guitar, executed in heavy pencil or charcoal (Pl. 64B). By using the thin, carefully ruled pencil lines underneath as a starting point, it is possible to reconstruct some sort of underlying geometric framework. But an analysis of the drawing shows that any 'geometry' involved amounts simply to the fact that all the main lines composing the guitar are either rigid verticals or else diagonals inclined at forty-five degrees from them. Strictly speaking, there is nothing scientific about this or any of the other drawings of the series. Gris has neither used nor tried to formulate optical laws or theories about the nature of volumes in space. Neither, at this point, are the compositions established according to consistent geometrical systems. Rather Gris has used a series of unrelated, arbitrary, angular and modular relationships and proportions to carry out his Cubist displacements and his Cubist analysis of volumes with a feeling of greater explicitness and exactitude. In the drawing discussed above, the two sides of the guitar are of exactly the same thickness, the distance from the centre of the hole of the guitar to the ends of each of the two handles or necks is the same, and so on. The other, slightly later, drawings are all more complicated but they appear also to be based on sets of angular relations combined with various arbitrary, aesthetic or mathematical modules. In all the drawings there are free-hand lines (as opposed to the majority of lines which are drawn with rulers and compasses) which have been put down in a purely intuitive way and which do not fit into any kind of mathematical scheme. The pure, precise beauty of the drawings that survive make the destruction of the majority of them a subject of deep regret.

This type of preparatory drawing explains the presence of the abstract areas which begin to appear in the work of Gris during 1913. In the *Violin and Guitar* in the collection of Mr and Mrs Ralph D. Colin in New York, a work stylistically very close to the first drawing of the guitar, most of the shapes or planes around the objects are given a literal meaning, but each of the three main sections of the violin carries next to it an abstract plane of bright colour, and in other contemporary still lifes there are often important compositional areas which seem to have no literal meaning. The drawing of the guitar discussed above suggests that Gris originally used these studies in order to find a means of explaining more fully and accurately the formal properties of his subjects. Indeed, the naturalism and solidity of the objects in his paintings of this period, and his later condemnation presumably of this phase of his Cubism[1] as analytical and descriptive, both indicate that this was still one of his main concerns. However, the drawings of this series show that as he experimented with geometrical equipment, compasses, protractors, set squares and so forth, his fascination with formal relationships and proportions led him to break down the space or areas around his subject, often in an arbitrary or abstract way. In the paintings some of these shapes are given a representational meaning, but others are retained for purely formal or pictorial reasons. This painting also serves to show the greater naturalism and the emphasis on three-dimensional form that become a characteristic of the later work of 1913 (Pl. 64A).

Gris had never abandoned colour to the extent that Picasso and Braque had, and when these two painters began to widen their palettes during 1913, Gris increased the intensity of his colour so that his works, which during 1912 had been more highly coloured, remain more brilliant than theirs. The colours in *Glass of Beer and Playing Cards*, a work of early 1913, are varied but still relatively subdued. In the slightly later paintings of the same year colour reaches an intensity that is unequalled in the contemporary work of any other Cubist painter; even Delaunay's and Kupka's experiments in pure colour look subdued by comparison. Often Gris applied the colours directly as they came out of the tube, unmixed with white, and their brilliance is accentuated by the areas of black which appear in his work at this time. Although at this point Gris' desire to convey a detailed, exhaustive and precise account of the nature of his subjects prevented him from opening up the contours of objects and allowing them to

[1]See Kahnweiler, *Juan Gris, pp. 114–5, The Letters of Juan Gris*, pp.25–6.

merge with their surroundings to create the sense of spatial continuity found in Picasso and Braque, here, as in some of their contemporary work, the shapes and planes behind the objects help to convey an impression of great compositional and spatial complexity and sophistication.

During the latter part of 1911 and the first half of 1912 Gris had done a series of landscapes, views of Paris, that relate closely to Picasso's landscapes at Horta de San Juan. These paintings of Gris, however, despite their simplicity and the grasp they show of early Cubist principles of composition, still have a slight *art nouveau* quality about them: the decorative, curving outlines of the buildings in particular recall his earlier commercial illustration. At Céret, where he spent the summer of 1913, Gris painted a second series of landscapes, which are a great deal more assured and accomplished. Since 1911 Picasso and Braque had virtually abandoned landscapes because the analysis and fragmentation to which they were subjecting objects and the space around them could not be so rigorously applied to subjects viewed at a distance or in deep space. For these landscapes Gris adopts an abnormally high viewpoint. In *Landscape at Céret* (Pl. 63), for example, the spectator seems to look down on the foreground houses almost directly from above. The sides of the houses, the far sides of the roofs and the chimney-tops are arbitrarily folded outwards on to the picture plane. The furthest houses show no diminution of scale and are piled upwards, accentuating the effect of flatness; only the small, dot-like trees on the horizon give a sense of recession. Dealing with a lot of small, distant objects, Gris was not able to exercise the same intellectual control that he shows in his contemporary still lifes, and compositional unity is achieved by two abstract diagonal shapes that are superimposed over the subject, or into which the subject is fitted. These paintings by Gris are important since they were to become the prototype for much subsequent Cubist landscape.

Whereas the last months of 1912 had marked a turning-point in the work of Picasso and Braque, 1914 was a more vital year in the evolution of Gris' art. *Papier collé* did not lead Gris to a simpler, more relaxed kind of painting as it did Picasso and Braque, and in the large series of *papiers collés* that he executed in this year Gris continued to exploit the literal, representational possibilities of the medium. Nevertheless, certain more abstract elements had begun to find their way into Gris' painting during 1913, and when he began to cover the entire surface of his canvases with pieces of paper of different sizes and shapes he undoubtedly started to become very aware of the possibilities of building up a composition in terms of large, abstract, coloured shapes onto which a subject could be overlaid. The *papiers collés* mark the move, perhaps still unconscious, towards Gris' later 'synthetic' styles.

However, this is looking ahead. More immediately the *papiers collés* of 1914 represent the climax of Gris' exploration of the intellectual possibilities of Cubism and of the new techniques it had introduced. Clearly certain pieces of paper were introduced originally as pictorial shapes, to balance the composition, to pick up a note of colour, and so on, but almost every one of them can also be ascribed some literal meaning. In *Glasses and Newspaper* (Smith College Museum of Art, Northampton, Mass.), for example, the newspaper represents itself, the paper painted in a diamond pattern becomes the table cloth, while the piece of wood-grained paper in the middle of it relates to the legs of the table and tells the spectator the nature of the material that composes the table underneath the cloth. Pieces of this same imitation wood-graining are glued on to the chair behind the table, again informing the spectator of its properties. Over the pieces of paper, standing on the table, are two identical glasses, each seen from at least two points of view; as opposed to the way in which successive images were fanned out from below in many of the paintings of 1913, here in one of the glasses they are swung outwards to either side from a central point at the top. This same, detailed, intellectual analysis can be applied to every one of these *papiers collés* of Gris. The harsh, often garish, colour schemes of the previous year give way to rich, sombre effects; blacks, browns and dark blues and greens, predominate (Pls. 65, 66). The fragments of newspapers incorporated into these works contain puns or visual metaphors and frequently comment on different ways of perceiving things.

By 1914 the principles of the Cubism of Picasso and Braque had been definitively established. At this point Braque's career was interrupted by the war. When he was able to resume his normal life in 1917, after a brief period of uncertainty he began to use his earlier discoveries to achieve a richer, more human and more completely personal style. The works of the pre-war period in a sense invite analysis; those of the post-war period reject and to a large extent defy it. Picasso painted on during the war, but the stylistic unity and continuity that had characterized the pre-war period was destroyed. By 1920 his Cubist works had been interspersed not only by a large number of naturalistic drawings and paintings but also by canvases in which he employed a variety of different forms of distortions, and even by a few experiments in a Divisionist technique. Detached from the rest of his work, however, Picasso's Cubist paintings executed during and immediately after the war represent a more or less straightforward progression from his earlier work. On the whole, he simplified his style and, as Braque was to do when he began painting again, he slowly widened his range of vision and subject-matter. In 1915 and the succeeding years Picasso made relatively little use of *papier collé* and *collage*, and there are only a few constructions which can be ascribed to this period. On the other hand, after 1914 the purely pictorial possibilities suggested by these techniques are examined in a more detached and objective way. Generally speaking, the *trompe l'oeil* effects are abandoned; the ebullience and sardonic wit of the preceding years are temporarily held in check; the paintings become simpler, grander, one might almost say more structural or architectural.

But in 1914 Gris' art was just entering one of its most crucial phases. And it is thus necessary to look ahead and give a brief summary of his work during the succeeding years in order to complete the picture of his evolution as a Cubist painter. Most immediately, in the series of large canvases finished in the early part of 1915, the complexity of his work of the previous years reached a climax. In paintings like *Livre, Pipe et Verres* (Pl. 68A) the number of objects that compose the still lifes is increased; their fragmentation is more elaborate and the spatial relationships between them more intricate. There is, too, a greater skill and sophistication in the combination of various different techniques used to establish the nature of individual forms; in *Livre, Pipe et Verres*, for example, the central part of a coffee-pot is painted illusionistically (with the lid suspended above it), the right-hand side is indicated by a white line on a green ground, while the ground itself becomes the left-hand section by the application of a black shadow, which at once gives a sense of relief and conveys the contour of the spout and bowl. In this series of still lifes the use of successive viewpoints is made particularly apparent by the bold repetition of the large forms of the table-tops, which are generally seen from slightly above, as in normal vision, and a second time as though from directly above.

The *Still Life in Front of an Open Window* (Pl. 67), a painting of the middle of this year, furthermore introduced a new factor into Cubism. Hitherto, although Braque had done paintings of scenes through open windows, the Cubists had avoided relating interior and exterior space. By placing his still life in front of a landscape background, Gris was faced with the problem of introducing a new sense of depth and recession into his paintings. Gris, however, succeeds in conveying a very precise sensation of spatial definition. The still life is intimately related to its surroundings – indeed it is inseparable from them – but each object retains its separate identity. Furthermore, the objects on the table stand well in front of the balustrade of the window, which in turn appears to be separated from the trees and houses behind by a considerable distance. There is a diminution of scale between foreground and background, lines at the sides of the picture lead the eye inwards, and the use of a paler tonality in the central section of the background is, in fact, a form of atmospheric perspective. But the sense of depth is conveyed primarily by less traditional methods. The objects and the areas to the sides and above them are encased by flat planes hung or placed in front of each other and given relief by shading around their outer edges; this was a method which Picasso and Braque in particular had been using for some time, but Gris' application of it to a more elaborate subject, treated in a wide range of colours, represents an extension and refinement of Cubist techniques. Many of the later works of this year and the first paintings of 1916 show Gris introducing into his work the pointilliste technique, favoured by Picasso and Braque during 1913 and 1914. And in works such as the *Blue Guitar on a Table* (Rijksmuseum Kröller-Müller, Otterlo) Gris produced some of the most strikingly decorative effects in all Cubist painting.

Gris' art, however, was at this time undergoing a much more fundamental change. In March 1915 he wrote to Kahnweiler: 'I think I have really made progress recently and that my pictures begin to have a unity which they have lacked till now. They are no longer those inventories of objects which used to depress me so much.'[1] It is true that the objects in Gris' paintings had always given the impression of having been derived from specific models, or at least of having an exact equivalent in the material world: in fact that was one of the

[1] *The Letters of Juan Gris*, pp. 25–6.

characteristics of his Cubism that differentiated it from that of Picasso and Braque. Now, in 1915, while the objects in his paintings remain clearly defined, they begin to be much more generalized in appearance. This can be seen clearly in the *Still Life in Front of an Open Window*. The *compotier*, water-flask and glass no longer have the quality of being particular objects. The descriptive, naturalistic details of the previous years are suppressed. Neither are the objects broken up into their component parts, dislocated and examined from different points of view. Instead Gris effects the same kind of optical synthesis in a single image that Picasso and Braque had evolved in the early years of their Cubism and that Gris had hitherto forced the spectator to accomplish for himself by piecing together the various fragments and views of the subject.

This new element in Gris' art was, as Kahnweiler has pointed out, the first step towards a more conceptual approach. The objects in Gris' paintings were now the products of his memory, or of some inner, mental vision of the world. The effect of this on his painting was an almost immediate move towards a more abstract method of composition. With the *papiers collés* of 1914, Gris must have been made increasingly aware of the possibilities of building up a composition in a purely abstract way, in terms of the 'flat, coloured forms' that he came to regard as the basic material of painting. Now that he was no longer conditioned or influenced to such a great extent by the appearance of objects in the material world surrounding him, Gris felt free to interpret or represent them in terms of fanciful, coloured shapes, provided that he could subsequently objectify them for the spectator by relating them in some way to their counterparts in real life. Technically, this enabled him to relate the subjects to the compositional planes around them in a much more intricate way, since all the component parts of a picture were now conceived primarily in terms of pictorial units. In the years following 1915, the objects in Gris' work became increasingly generalized, one might almost say increasingly abstract, in their conception. Many of the paintings of 1916 and the following years were clearly begun with specific subjects in mind but in other cases a geometrical proportion or the formal relations between a few coloured shapes were the basis for his paintings, and the subject-matter only later suggested itself to Gris and was subsequently worked into the background. It is possible, too, that the sketches or calculations that preceded these paintings were by now more scientific, or at least more geometrically and mathematically consistent than earlier examples studied above. This is not to say that as Gris progressed towards the intellectual certainty he so desired he suppressed his more spontaneous, intuitive pictorial gifts. As the subject-matter was fused into the abstract substructure in these paintings, or emerged from it, Gris' eye, his instinctive pictorial sense, took over. The *pentimenti* in almost all his paintings after 1916 testify to the countless adjustments made before a work reached its ultimate conclusion. Nevertheless, the paintings executed between 1917 and 1920 have a precision and exactitude that mark the closest approach of Cubism to a mathematical science (Pl. 68B).

Gris has described both his aesthetic and his method of work with great clarity: 'It would be true to state that, with rare exceptions, elements of concrete reality have been rendered pictorial, a given subject has been made into a picture.

'My method of work is exactly the opposite ... It is not picture 'X' which manages to correspond with my subject, but subject 'X' which manages to correspond with my picture.

'I call this method a deductive method because the pictorial relationships between the coloured forms suggest to me certain private relationships between the elements of an imaginary reality. The mathematics of picture-making lead me to the physics of representation. The quality or the dimensions of a form or a colour suggest to me the appellation or the adjective for an object. Hence, I never know in advance the appearance of the object represented. If I particularize pictorial relationships to the point of representing objects, it is in order that the spectator shall not do so for himself, and in order to prevent the combination of coloured forms suggesting to him a reality which I have not intended.

'I do not know if one can give to this aesthetic, this technique and this method the name of Cubism ...'[1]

All this amounts, of course, to a recapitulation of Gris' definition of synthetic Cubism. To his uncertainty as to whether 'this aesthetic, this technique and this method' could be given the name of Cubism, the answer is that they represented only certain aspects of Cubism pushed to their ultimate formal and intellectual conclusions. But because of his detachment, his refusal to deviate from the task

[1]'Notes on my Painting', addressed to Carl Einstein, published first in *Der Querschnitt*, nos. 1 and 2, pp. 77 and 78, Frankfurt-on-Main, summer 1923. Reprinted in Kahnweiler's *Juan Gris*, pp. 138–9.

he had set himself of analysing and defining the nature and aesthetic of Cubism, Gris remained in some ways its purest exponent. Years later, when he himself was still making use of the discoveries and principles of his Cubist years, Braque was able to say 'The only one who was conscientious in following Cubist investigations through to the end is, in my opinion, Gris'.[1]

[1]'Braque, la Peinture et Nous', p.19.

4

THE INFLUENCE OF CUBISM IN FRANCE 1910–14

In *Les Peintres Cubistes*, Apollinaire wrote of the rise of Cubism: 'this new aesthetic was first formulated in the mind of André Derain.'[1] Although Derain never became a Cubist, Apollinaire's statement is not as unreasonable as it might at first seem, for Derain has some place, albeit a very hard one to define, in the history of the movement. In 1906 he was certainly regarded as one of the three or four most significant young painters working in Paris. Prodigiously gifted and intelligent, he was both intellectually and visually restless, and because of this he reflects better than almost any other painter the various influences that were at work at this time. Like all young painters of his generation he had been aware of Cézanne's art at an early stage in his career. At the *Salons* of 1903 and 1904 the influence of Cézanne was already everywhere. But Kahnweiler, who was getting to know the artists who were to form his stable in subsequent years, was always to stress Derain's importance in getting his friends to look at Cézanne in a new light.[2] And in an isolated early example, a *Still Life* of 1904 (now in a private collection in Paris), Derain had seized on many of the aspects of Cézanne which were to influence the Cubists. In it he adopted Cézanne's high, informative viewpoint; forms are boldly simplified, and there is an interest

[1]p. 22. Ozenfant and Jeanneret in *Après le Cubisme*, Paris 1918, make almost exactly the same point as Apollinaire.
[2]Kahnweiler stressed the point in his *André Derain*, Leipzig 1920, p. 7, and in conversations with the author.

in reconciling three-dimensional form with the flat picture surface. He avoids, it is true, any intensive analysis of form, and his work lacks the concentration and structural precision of the paintings executed by Picasso and Braque when they in turn came under the influence of Cézanne (Pl. 101A).

Then, largely through his admiration for Gauguin (and this influence can be seen even in the Cézannesque still life discussed above) in 1906 Derain began to explore the aesthetic possibilities of 'primitive' art just before Picasso did. As has been seen, by 1906 an awareness of tribal art was beginning to permeate the consciousness of many progressive young artists working in Paris. However, Derain was perhaps the first of the painters to appreciate tribal work in a more serious and thoughtful or intellectual way, and to absorb some of its formal qualities into his own painting. Apollinaire stressed this point in a little-known article entitled 'Les Commencements du Cubisme', which appeared in *Le Temps* on 14 October 1912. Since this is the first purely factual account of the discovery of 'Negro' art by painters, it is perhaps worth summarizing it here. After describing the way in which Vlaminck first discovered African art,[1] when he chanced to come across some tribal masks in a curiosity shop in a village on the banks of the Seine, Apollinaire goes on to say, 'these strange African apparitions made a profound impression on André Derain who examined them sympathetically, admiring the art with which the image makers from Guinea and the Congo succeeded in reproducing the human figure without using any of the elements borrowed from direct observation. The taste acquired by Maurice Vlaminck for Negro sculptures and the aesthetic meditations of André Derain on these strange objects at a time when the Impressionists had finally freed painting from its academic fetters were to have a decisive influence on the fate of French painting.'

But what gives Derain a place as a true forerunner of Cubism is that he was the first painter to combine in a single work the influence of both Cézanne and Negro art, in his large *Baigneuses* (now in the Museum of Modern Art, New York, Pl. 101B) which was painted in the winter of 1906–7 and shown at the *Salon des Indépendants* of 1907. Vauxcelles, in his review of the exhibition, wrote: 'a movement which I believe to be dangerous stands out. A chapel has been founded

[1]Apollinaire's account of all this is more or less confirmed by Vlaminck himself in *Portraits avant Décès*, Paris 1943.

where two imperious priests officiate, Derain and Matisse ... this religion charms me hardly at all.'[1] The movement to which Vauxcelles refers is, of course, Fauvism, but his remarks are puzzling since two years before he himself had given the movement its name, even if contemptuously, and had been a cautious supporter of Matisse and Derain for some time; he seems to have felt that there was some new element in their recent work. This was to a certain extent true. The paintings shown by both painters were less colourful and more structural than their most typically Fauve works of the previous years. Matisse was represented by his large *Blue Nude* (now in the Baltimore Museum of Art). After criticizing it for its crudity, Vauxcelles passed on to Derain's *Baigneuses*: 'the barbaric simplifications of Monsieur Derain don't offend me any less: Cézannesque mottlings are dappled over the torsos of bathers plunged in horribly indigo waters.'[2] There were, however, significant differences between these two paintings. As opposed to the *Blue Nude* the colours in Derain's work are earthier in the renderings of the bodies themselves, although their surroundings are of a resonant, saturated blue; and whereas the contours of Matisse's figure are free and sensuous, Derain's bathers are seen in terms of simple, angular, almost geometric forms that remind one of certain paintings by Cézanne (Pl. 101B).

The most original feature of Derain's painting is the treatment of the heads of the two right-hand figures in which the features are represented as geometrical wedges or indentations, set into mask-like, generalized facial structures; in this respect, the head of the central figure looks forward to the facial structure of Picasso's *Paysanne* painted at Horta a year and a half later. The heads of the figures in Derain's later *Last Supper* (Pl. 102A),[3] more extreme variants of the heads in the *Baigneuses*, bear in turn a striking resemblance to certain Fang masks which could be seen in the Trocadéro, and in particular to an example in

[1]*Gil Blas*, 20 March 1907.

[2]Ibid.

[3]This work is extremely hard to date. It was not shown publicly in Paris and did not pass through Kahnweiler's hands. Critics have dated it from 1907 (Salmon) to 1913 (Leymarie) and 1914 (Einstein). It seems most likely to have been executed in the years immediately following the *Baigneuses*. It might possibly be the picture subsequently referred to in a note in *Paris Journal* on 25 October 1911: 'Derain, le collectionneur de statues nègres . . . avait presque décidé à envoyer un grand tableau d'une beauté certaine (au Salon d'Automne): *Le Déjeuner*. Or Derain barbouilla le tableau: la nature morte, disait-il, avait trop d'importance.' The following year, 1912, Derain entered his 'Gothic' period.

the collection of Derain's friend Frank Haviland[1] (Pls. 102B,C). It is not known exactly when it entered Haviland's possession, but it may possibly be significant that Maurice de Zayas chose to illustrate the piece in *African Negro Art and its Influence on Modern Art*, published in New York in 1915; Fang masks were amongst Derain's early acquisitions of tribal art. If Derain's *Baigneuses* does indeed combine the influences of Cézanne and tribal art this would help to explain the prominence given to him by Apollinaire in his discussions of the emergence of Cubism.[2] In 'Les Commencements du Cubisme' Apollinaire discusses the relationship between Derain and Matisse during 1905 and then goes on to say: 'The following year (1906) Derain became close to Picasso and the result of this closeness was the almost immediate birth of Cubism.' Apollinaire continues: 'By the end of the year Cubism had ceased to be an exaggeration of the painting of the Fauves whose violent colours were a frenzied kind of Impressionism. The new meditations of Picasso, of Derain and of another young painter, Georges Braque, resulted in true Cubism which was above all the art of painting new harmonies derived not from visual reality but from conceptual reality.'[3] While Derain had no such positive role in the creation of Cubism one can see how the concern with solid formal values and the presence of the influences of Cézanne and tribal art in his work would have led Apollinaire to associate him with the birth of the movement.

In a review of the *Salon des Indépendants* of 1914 Apollinaire looked back over the past years and once again emphasized Derain's role in the formation of Cubism: 'There are two great streams, one of which derives from the Cubism of Picasso the other from the Cubism of André Derain, both alike come from Cézanne.'[4] This time Apollinaire was obviously overstressing the importance of

[1]Frank Haviland was also known as Frank Burty. The mask was reproduced again in Carl Einstein's *Negerplastik*, Munich 1920, Pls. 14 and 15.

[2]Jack Flam in his essay 'Matisse and the Fauves' in *Primitivism and Twentieth Century Art*, Vol. 1, p. 219, discounts any influence of African art in the *Baigneuses*.

[3]A note in *Gil Blas* on 8 October 1912 about a proposed exhibition of Negro sculpture also links the name of Picasso with those of Derain and Matisse: 'On sait que Matisse, Derain et Picasso furent les premiers à remplacer les moulages grecs par les simulacres d'une beauté barbare mais souvent saisissante. Ils les étudièrent et les imitèrent même, imitation qui marqua le déclin du fauvisme et l'aurore du Cubisme.'

[4]*L'Intransigeant*, 26–8 February 1914.

Derain. In actual fact the *Demoiselles d'Avignon* seems to have thrown Derain completely off balance. He was to destroy virtually all his figure pieces of the following years; to judge from photographs, *La Toilette* which he showed at the *Indépendants* of 1908, and which was clearly an immediate response to the *Demoiselles*, must have been an unsatisfactory, lifeless painting. And yet until the outbreak of the war Derain was to remain a close colleague of both Picasso and Braque and his work of the period is of the greatest significance not only because of its intrinsic merit, but because it demonstrates how an artist of comparable natural gifts could produce work which at times showed an awareness of what they were doing and even at times rivalled it in quality, but was nevertheless unprepared to jettison the past and to step over the threshold into a totally new pictorial idiom.

During the years immediately following 1907 it became obvious that a general movement towards a more thoughtful and formal kind of painting was taking place. At the *Salon des Indépendants* of 1907 Fauvism was still a force (Vauxcelles counted some twenty-five painters whom he felt had been touched by it),[1] but the movement had lost much of its original impetus. In 1908, at the *Salon d'Automne*, Vauxcelles was able to say 'the era of the sketch seems to be nearly over'.[2] By this time many of the former Fauves, painters like Braque, Dufy, Vlaminck and Friesz had renounced the unnaturally bright or arbitrary colours which had been one of the distinguishing features of the style and were turning for inspiration to the more structural aspects of Cézanne's work; the influence of Gauguin, on the other hand, was declining. With the exhibition at Kahnweiler's in 1907 and the paintings he showed at the *Salon des Indépendants* of 1909, Braque had emerged as a controversial and original painter; the influence of Cézanne could still be seen in his work, but it was obvious that he had achieved something new and important. Derain, who continued to be influenced by Picasso, Cézanne and primitive art, was producing works that were becoming increasingly austere and archaistic. Only Matisse had followed up the decorative and sensuous aspects of Fauvism to produce a highly individual style of his own, and he, it is true, remained an important influence. Yet despite the

[1] *Gil Blas*, 20 March 1907.
[2] *Gil Blas*, 30 September 1908.

quintessentially French quality of his art his disciples tended to be foreign painters, and they grouped themselves around an acknowledged master rather than constituting a spontaneous movement. Van Dongen, who had been associated with the Fauves and had been singled out as an important and promising young painter, but who was essentially a brilliant painter of fashion, was, significantly enough, losing his sense of purpose.

Another important indication of the direction in which contemporary painting was moving was the fact that for the first time the work of the Douanier Rousseau was being taken seriously by a large number of people. Rousseau had been exhibiting regularly at the *Salon des Indépendants* since 1886, but for a long time had received encouragement only from a few individual painters such as Signac, Luce and Lautrec. Shortly before the turn of the century, his original personality attracted the attention of Alfred Jarry and the circle around him; Apollinaire later became a close friend. Nevertheless, Rousseau's literary friends seem to have regarded his painting with a certain amount of amusement, and it was only towards the end of the first decade of the twentieth century that his painting began to enjoy a success with the serious critics. Vauxcelles reviewed his work favourably for the first time in 1909,[1] and in his review of the *Salon des Indépendants* of the following year, Apollinaire dedicated a long and enthusiastic passage to Rousseau's large painting *Le Rêve*.[2] In fact, though, the new taste for Rousseau's work was one which was dictated by the painters rather than by the critics. In 1908 Picasso had bought Rousseau's *Portrait of Yadwriga* (now in the Musée Picasso, Paris), and in the same year he honoured the old painter with a banquet in his studio in the *Bateau Lavoir*, which was attended by many of the most advanced painters and poets in Montmartre and by a few distinguished visitors from the Left Bank as well; the influence of Rousseau can, perhaps, be seen in some of Picasso's landscapes executed at La Rue-des-Bois in the autumn of 1908. At the same time, other painters were being drawn to Rousseau's work independently. By 1909 both Léger and Delaunay were friendly with Rousseau and used to frequent his musical *soirées*; the *Snake Charmer*, which was shown at the *Indépendants* of 1907, had been commissioned by Delaunay's mother. It is not

[1] *Gil Blas*, 25 March 1909.
[2] *L'Intransigeant*, 18 March 1910.

strange that a generation of artists who had discovered the aesthetic worth of tribal sculpture should also have felt sympathy for the art of this old 'primitive'. For as in African and other primitive art they found in Rousseau directness of vision and formal simplicity, unperverted by the over-refinement and sophistication with which so much traditional art had become overlaid. Although he dealt with elaborate literary and allegorical themes of the most hackneyed kind, the freshness and uncompromising realism of his vision gave the impression of an artist who was seeing the world for the first time and revealing in his work only its most essential formal and human qualities. In other words, the naiveté of his approach had the effect of deflating these subjects of their pretensions. Then with his painstaking approach and his refusal, or inability, to conceal technical difficulties and problems, he seemed to be 'redoing' painting from the beginning. To this extent he, too, was a 'pure' painter. Rousseau died in 1910. The following year a large retrospective exhibition of his work was held at the *Salon des Indépendants*. The exhibition was hung in the hall between the two rooms occupied by the paintings of the Cubists and their friends.

By 1909 the work of some of the future Cubists, apart from Picasso and Braque, was beginning to attract attention. In the same review of the *Salon des Indépendants* in which he referred to Braque's 'bizarreries cubiques', Vauxcelles attacked the work of Le Fauconnier and Metzinger. Metzinger had abandoned Divisionism the previous year, after Max Jacob had introduced him into the circle that revolved around Picasso. 'Let Metzinger chase after Picasso or Derain or Braque', wrote Vauxcelles of the paintings Metzinger showed at the *Indépendants*.[1] Le Fauconnier was criticized for his extreme simplification of form; he exhibited a portrait of a child and a landscape which he had executed at Ploumanach in Brittany during the previous year when he had been working under the influence of Derain. In 1909, however, Le Fauconnier developed a more personal style, and at the *Salon d'Automne* of this year he exhibited a *Portrait of Jouve* (Pl. 89A) a work that was to have a profound effect on the work of another of the future Cubists. Albert Gleizes wrote of this painting in his *Souvenirs* 'I at once drew a lesson from it'.

To-day it seems hard to think that the *Portrait of Jouve* could have been

[1]*Gil Blas*, 25 March 1909.

regarded as a progressive and revolutionary work, but it serves as a reminder that even weak paintings which reflect new tendencies can at the time seem fresh and significant; and the picture has certain features in common with more advanced paintings of the period. It is executed in severe harmonies of browns and greys, similar to those used by Picasso and Braque at this time, and there is a simplicity about it which is equalled only in contemporary canvases by Matisse and, perhaps, in the decorative creations of Marie Laurencin (Pl. 103A) and Van Dongen. Furthermore, there is an attempt (however unsuccessful) to deal with the figure in terms of elementary geometric shapes that serves to relate the painting in a very general way to Picasso's and Derain's work of the previous years. Gleizes was particularly impressed with the way in which Le Fauconnier deliberately suppressed all inessential details and used colour merely as a support for the 'armature' of the design: 'Draughtsmanship (*le dessin*) which I had come to see as holding the key to my ambitions and which I had been unable to dominate, as it was used in the portrait of Jouve showed me the true direction'.[1]

At the *Salon d'Automne* of 1909, where Le Fauconnier showed the *Portrait of Jouve*, Léger was represented by a Corsican seascape and a landscape entitled *Le Jardin*.[2] These paintings were executed in Léger's early style, which was a fusion of elements borrowed from Impressionism, Neo-Impressionism and Fauvism. *La Couseuse* (collection Kahnweiler, Paris), however, a work of the summer of 1909, marks a break in Léger's art (Pl. 69). In it colour is reduced to a scheme of blue-greys and pale buffs, while the human body is interpreted in terms of simple, cylindrical or tubular forms, faceted in a simple, rather primitive fashion, that give the figure something of the appearance of a mechanical robot. In contrast to the basic flatness of Le Fauconnier's work, Léger's forms are so insistently modelled that their three-dimensional quality becomes almost aggressive. Léger always claimed that Cézanne was the starting point for his art. In a lecture entitled 'Les Origines de la Peinture Moderne', which he delivered at

[1]Gleizes, *Souvenirs*.

[2]The seascape is reproduced in Descargues, *Léger*, 1955, p. 11. The *Jardin* is the painting shown at the posthumous Paris exhibition of Léger in 1956 (at the Musée des Arts Décoratifs), cat. no. 3. This information from the artist was passed on to me by Mr D. Cooper. The *Jardin* is, however, dated 1905 in the Paris Catalogue so that Léger was exhibiting in 1909 a painting done four years earlier.

the Académie Wassilief in 1913,[1] Léger said, 'one painter amongst the Impressionists, Cézanne, understood all that was lacking in it (i.e. Impressionism)'. What Léger felt that Cézanne had restored to painting was, of course, a sense of form and structure and a feeling for volumes in space. Léger emphasized, too, the fact that Cézanne had seen the necessity of reintroducing the use of lines or contours as a means of expressing visual reality. This was an aspect of Cézanne that had escaped the attention of many of Léger's contemporaries, who, although they all admired the solidity and formal clarity of Cézanne's art, tended to take the opposite point of view and to stress the fact that he had broken the contours of objects and had thus given painting a greater sense of fluidity and freedom. There was a certain amount of truth in both views. As opposed to the Impressionists, Cézanne was always anxious to delineate each object in his painting as fully and clearly as possible, while at the same time the contours of the objects in his paintings are constantly broken and rebroken in an attempt to expand volumes as much as possible and to reconcile them with the two-dimensional picture plane. What is significant is that Léger should have seized on the element of definition in Cézanne's work. Nevertheless, in *La Couseuse* any debt to Cézanne is of a very intellectual or generalized kind, and the work belongs to a generalized category of simplified, strongly volumetric painting pioneered to some extent by Derain in his *Baigneuses*.

The painting of Delaunay, with whom Léger was becoming particularly friendly at this time, was moving in a similar direction. In 1908 Delaunay was still working in a Divisionist technique, but in the first of his paintings of Saint Séverin, begun early in 1909, and in the first *Eiffel Towers* painted later in the same year, the influence of Cézanne began to assert itself strongly; in the case of the *Eiffel Towers* the choice of subject-matter may have been inspired by the Douanier Rousseau whom Delaunay greatly admired. In one of the first of this series (Pl. 80A), in the Arensberg Collection in the Philadelphia Museum of Art, the treatment of the foliage in terms of a few clearly defined shapes is a feature obviously derived from Cézanne; indeed, the painting recalls some of Braque's Cézannian landscapes of the previous year, although Delaunay's work has a

[1]The lecture was delivered on 5 May 1913, and was published in the issues of 29 May and 14 and 29 June 1913 of *Montjoie*.

bluntness and crudity that still relates it to his earlier Divisionist work. Like Léger, Delaunay at this point was striving for a new definition of form, and the outlines of the Tower are carefully preserved. As opposed to Léger, however, Delaunay did not limit his use of colour, and this painting is executed with a full palette. In his notebooks, under a photograph of one of his contemporary Saint Séverin pictures, Delaunay wrote: 'period of transition from Cézanne to Cubism ... In *Saint Séverin* one can see an urge towards construction but the form is traditional ... the breaking of contours still seems timid ... colour is in terms of *clair-obscur* despite the decision not to copy nature objectively, with the result that there is still perspective. As with Cézanne the contrasts are binary and not simultaneous.[1] The interaction of colour produces line ... This canvas shows an emotional desire for a new form but doesn't achieve it. Great influence on Expressionism, on the film Caligari, on Russian theatre.'[2]

By 1910 Metzinger had known Delaunay and Léger for some time, and he saw that, like Picasso and Braque, these two painters were using the discoveries of Cézanne to new ends. Although Metzinger was not a painter of very great originality, he was one of the first people to realize that Picasso and Braque were evolving a completely new style of painting, and he was anxious to organize the efforts of his friends into a modern school of painting with a clearly defined aesthetic. When his own paintings were hung by chance next to those of Gleizes and Le Fauconnier at the *Salon d'Automne* of 1910 he was quick to notice the similarities between them. In his 'Note sur la Peinture' which was written in September of 1910, after the opening of the *Salon d'Automne*, Metzinger proclaimed the birth of a new movement in painting, which was neither romantic nor decorative, and which had as its foundation a concept of form which was the result of a peculiarly modern sensibility. 'For us the Greeks invented the human form; we must reinvent it for others ... Form, taken for too many centuries as the inanimate support for colour, is recovering at last its right to life, to instability.'

[1]For Delaunay's definition of 'simultaneous' colour contrasts see pp. 184–5 below.
[2]Soon after Mme Sonia Terk Delaunay showed me these notebooks they were edited and transcribed by M. Pierre Francastel and were published in Paris in 1957, together with a catalogue of Delaunay's work compiled by M. Guy Habasque. Despite the scholarly editing it is still uncertain when many of the entries were made; most appear to date from the latter part of Delaunay's life. The sense of Delaunay's prose is often a little hard to grasp and my translation is very free.

This new art, Metzinger felt, was represented in the work of Picasso, Braque, Delaunay and Le Fauconnier.

Metzinger was one of the leading spirits in the campaign to reform the laws about the hanging of paintings in the *Salon des Indépendants*.[1] The result of this was, as we have seen, that he and his friends were able to show together as a group at the *Indépendants* of 1911, the first of the Cubist *Salons*. Metzinger himself was represented by four works; the largest and most important of these was a painting of two nudes against a background of trees (present whereabouts unknown). The figures in this painting with their featureless faces and faceted bodies, lit from a single, strong light source, are derived directly from Picasso's figure pieces executed in Paris after his return from Spain in the autumn of 1909. Metzinger therefore took as his starting point works in which Picasso's analysis of solid forms was at its most intensive. However, if Metzinger was able to appreciate intellectually the importance of Picasso's art, in his own painting he was influenced only by its most superficial aspects. In the *Two Nudes* Metzinger has learned from Picasso how to reconcile three-dimensional form with the picture plane, by placing the subject in shallow depth and fusing it with its surroundings, but there is no great interest in analysing solid forms. In his early, analytical Cubism Picasso distended and distorted form, seeking to convey a sense of solidity and to synthesize as much information as possible into a single image. Metzinger, on the other hand, elongates his figures in a mannerist fashion, denying their sculptural solidity. His vision is still fundamentally naturalistic, and he views his subject from the single, static point of view of traditional painting. In short, the *Two Nudes* is only Cubist in the most superficial and obvious sense of the word, in that there is a deliberate 'cubification' of volumes (Pl. 86A).

Léger's major painting at this exhibition was a large canvas entitled *Nus dans un Paysage* (Pl. 70A), which he had begun as early as the autumn of 1909, while Delaunay showed three Parisian landscapes, one of which was a painting of his *Eiffel Tower* series. The work of both painters was much more interesting than what they had been producing a year earlier. The *Nus* can, however, be regarded as a perfectly logical development of the *Couseuse*. For like the *Couseuse* it shows

[1]See p. 8 above.

Léger investigating the nature of solid, geometrical forms and exploring the pictorial relationships between them. The *Nus* is, of course, a much more ambitious and complex painting. 'I wanted to push volumes as far as possible,' Léger later recalled.[1] There is a great deal more subdivision within the basically simple forms of the figures, and whereas the *Couseuse* stands out against the background in sharp relief, here Léger has retained a balance between solid forms and the two-dimensional picture plane by reducing everything, figures, trees, landscape and background, to geometrical shapes of more or less equal size, as Picasso and Braque were doing in many of their paintings of 1909. Indeed, the faceted, elaborate and analytical treatment of the bodies in the *Nus* reminds one of Picasso's work of the Horta period. But, unlike Picasso, Léger shows no interest in summarizing or synthesizing various views of his models into a single image. And this, it will be seen, remained one of the fundamental differences between Léger's Cubism and that of Picasso and Braque, even after he dispensed completely with traditional linear perspective. Here perspective is suggested by the abrupt foreshortening of the lower limbs of all three figures; these are the sort of poses that Picasso and Braque deliberately avoided. Neither is Léger's painting conceptual in the sense that theirs was. He does not express his idea of the human body but uses his subject rather as a starting point for a geometric, cubistic experiment. And Léger was faced with a different problem from Picasso and Braque, that of retaining the geometric solidity, the sculptural quality of his figures and yet conveying the sense of motion that is implied in the active poses of the figures. This he has done simply by the vigorous, muscular subdivision of the forms of the bodies and by building up the composition by a series of short, emphatic diagonal movements; even the verticality of the tree-trunks is destroyed. For the *Couseuse* Léger had used a consistent, bright and direct form of illumination. Here he has substituted a generalized, 'sous-bois' effect. The forest setting, the solid, tubular forms, and the grey-green tonalities recall once again the work of the Douanier Rousseau. Léger, discussing this painting, has said, 'it has been said that there was an influence from Douanier in this canvas. Perhaps it is true because at that time I was seeing Douanier, but it is unconscious . . . The *Nus dans la forêt* (the painting subsequently became known

[1]Quoted in the Catalogue for the Léger exhibition at the Musée des Arts Décoratifs 1956, p. 78.

by this name) was for me simply a battle of volumes. I felt I couldn't cope with colour. Volume was enough for me.'[1] The dispassionate, almost brutal way in which Léger was attacking the problem of analysing solid forms disturbed Apollinaire who, in his review of the exhibition, wrote: 'Léger strikes once more the least human note in this *salon*. His art is difficult, he creates, if one dare say it, cylindrical painting and he has not avoided giving his composition the wild appearance of a pile of pneumatic tyres. Never mind! The discipline to which he has subjected himself will put his ideas in order and one can already sense the originality of his talent and his palette.'[2]

The *Eiffel Tower* shown by Delaunay at the 1911 *Indépendants* has since been destroyed but was closely related to a slightly later version (Pl. 76). In the spring of 1910 Kahnweiler had bought the *Couseuse* and had begun to become seriously interested in Léger's work. Soon Léger was frequenting the gallery in the rue Vignon. 'There, I saw, together with the burly Delaunay, what the Cubists were doing. Delaunay, surprised at seeing their grey canvases, cried "but they paint with cobwebs, these fellows!".'[3] This remark must have been inspired by Picasso's and Braque's most recent canvases in which they were evolving the linear, grid-like kind of composition that enabled them to suggest form and space more freely than when they were still working with closed contours. At any rate, both Léger and Delaunay were immensely impressed by what they saw, and the *Eiffel Tower* by Delaunay bears witness to the fact that he looked at the work of Picasso and Braque in a very intelligent if subjective way. Unlike Picasso, Braque and Léger (and for that matter unlike almost all Cubists), Delaunay was never interested in analysing, or even in portraying, solid forms. On the other hand, he realized at once (and more fully than any of the other painters showing at the *Salon des Indépendants* of 1911 in Room 41) that by dismissing traditional perspective Picasso and Braque had revolutionized traditional ideas of pictorial form, and, more important from his point of view, pictorial space. In this painting the lower part of the Eiffel Tower is seen diagonally, while the upper part is seen as though from in front. However, in the top half, three sides of the tower are seen

[1]Ibid., p. 78.
[2]*L'Intransigeant*, 20 April 1911.
[3]Catalogue cit., p. 27. Delaunay had met Picasso several years before this, and may even have seen some of his early Cubist paintings before he went with Léger to Kahnweiler's.

simultaneously (as opposed to one side that would be seen in normal vision), and below fragments of a third side of the base are scattered through the houses clustered at its foot, so that Delaunay is in fact achieving the same kind of optical synthesis which was one of the most important features of the Cubism of Picasso and Braque. Furthermore, by pushing the middle of the tower inwards, away from the spectator (or by bending the upper part of it forwards towards the spectator), Delaunay creates a new spatial effect whereby the structure of the painting cannot be grasped at a single glance but has to be read in two sections;[1] many of Braque's later works produce the same visual sensation.[2] As in works by Picasso and Braque, forms are opened up into each other and into their surroundings. As opposed to Léger, Delaunay felt that Cézanne's importance lay in the fact that he had broken the contours of forms and had thus given painting a greater sense of mobility. Delaunay later referred to this phase in his own art as 'the destructive period'. In his notebooks, accompanying a reproduction of one of his *Eiffel Towers*, he wrote this comment: 'Cézanne is definitely broken to pieces by us the first Cubists. After having broken the *compotier* no one could put it together again.' But whereas in the contemporary work of Picasso and Braque space is made concrete and fused with material objects, the work of Delaunay gives one the sensation that forms have been forcibly shattered, and this produces a sensation of energy and movement. In his 'Note sur la Peinture' Metzinger had written that Delaunay's paintings seemed to sum up the 'paroxysm' of a disordered and restless age.

Le Fauconnier and Gleizes represented the more conservative faction in Room 41, although Le Fauconnier's *Abondance* received a great deal of critical attention. This was strange since there was nothing revolutionary about Le Fauconnier's work, which was less Cubist than that of Léger, Delaunay, and Metzinger, or even that of Gleizes. Despite the squat, broad proportions of the figures in *L'Abondance*, Le Fauconnier shows no interest in going very deeply into any kind of analysis of solid form. In fact, he has simply seized upon the most accessible aspect of Cubism, that is to say the treatment of forms in terms of simple, angular facets, as an easy way of dealing with a monumental subject. There is no

[1]This is an aspect of Delaunay's work that is discussed by de la Tourette.

[2]For a discussion of the spatial inventions in Braque's later works see J. Richardson, 'The Ateliers of Braque' in the *Burlington Magazine*, June 1955.

atmospheric recession, but the perspective is completely traditional. The houses and road have a more or less consistent vanishing point (the road undoubtedly leads the eye inwards, into depth) and there is a logical diminution of scale from one background plane to the next. Gleizes' *La Femme aux Phlox*, on the other hand, although it derives from Le Fauconnier, is a more serious attempt to come to grips with the problem of reducing figures and objects to their simplest, most elementary shapes and has something in common with Léger's *Couseuse*, although the painting is full of inconsistencies and lacks Léger's forthright unequivocal approach. At the same exhibition Gleizes also showed a *Landscape*, now in the Musée d'Art Moderne in Paris, and this, while it had superficial similarities with Braque's paintings executed at l'Estaque in 1908, showed that Gleizes was still unable to impose satisfactorily his own geometric vision on the natural scene (Pls. 88 and 83A).

In Room 43, which was separated from Room 41 by the retrospective exhibition of the Douanier Rousseau, the Cubists placed the works of painters whom they felt had aims similar to their own. The most important of these painters was Roger de La Fresnaye, who showed a large canvas called *Le Cuirassier* (Musée d'Art Moderne, Paris), based on Géricault's painting in the Louvre; La Fresnaye had turned to military subjects during 1910 when he was working on the illustrations for Claudel's *Tête d'Or*. Stylistically the *Cuirassier* relates most closely to Derain's work of the previous years; indeed it has much in common with both the *Baigneuses* and the *Last Supper*. Any reference to primitive or archaic art form is, however, less direct, and La Fresnaye uses the simple forms and expressionless faces to achieve a tasteful, consciously classical effect that is far removed from the aims of true Cubism. The work of the other painters in this room, artists like Luc Albert Moreau, André Lhote and Segonzac was, like that of La Fresnaye, related to Cubism only in so far as it showed an emphasis on simple, clearly defined volumes and a corresponding limitation of colour. The *Cuirassier*, for example, is in greys, browns and a muted russet-red; only a year earlier La Fresnaye had been painting with the Gauguinian palette of greens, purples, blues and crimsons (Pl. 98A).

Reconstructing the Cubist section of the *Salon des Indépendants* of 1911 one is struck by how little it had to do with the work of Picasso and Braque, the creators of true Cubism. Léger, it is true, had devoted himself to an intensive analysis of form, making a sincere effort to extract structural, geometric properties from the visual world. Delaunay had appreciated the fact that Picasso and Braque had revolutionized traditional concepts of form and space, but he had already turned their discoveries to purely personal ends. Of all the painters from Room 41 and Room 43 Metzinger's work resembled most the Cubism of Picasso and Braque, but he was copying the superficial appearances of their art without any real appreciation of the problems which had gone to create it and those which it was still facing. Moreover, taken as a group, the Cubists at the *Indépendants* had found no genuine iconography as Picasso and Braque had done. In their creation of a new pictorial idiom, Picasso and Braque had found it necessary to limit themselves in almost every way. Their subject-matter was severely restricted to the things which played a part in their everyday life; their vision and their art were essentially realistic. Because of the conceptual nature of their art they had been able to detach themselves from external reality without lessening a sense of realism. It was an interior, formalistic and often extremely personal vision that they were imposing on the world immediately around them. The other Cubists were, on the contrary, painting large, elaborate works, many of which were deliberately painted as *Salon* pieces; their choice of subject-matter ranged from the literary allegory of Le Fauconnier's *Abondance* to the consciously heroic classicism of La Fresnaye's *Cuirassier* or Delaunay's brilliant but disturbing visions of the Parisian scene. Whereas the total effect of the Cubist rooms at the *Indépendants* had been sombre, by 1911 Picasso and Braque had gone further and had discarded colour completely, and only Gleizes' *Femme aux Phlox* and Léger's *Nus* matched their work in sobriety and restraint, although Metzinger was in fact working in what amounted to a decoratively tinted *grisaille*. And whereas the Cubism of Picasso and Braque was born out of some inner necessity, at the *Indépendants* the general impression was one of a much more superficial and contrived form of painting.

Metzinger, in an article entitled 'Cubisme et Tradition', which appeared in *Paris Journal* in September 1911, selected the work of Delaunay and Le Fauconnier as marking the two limits of the style, which, if passed, would lead on one side to 'esoterism' and on the other to 'academicism'. Just from looking at the display at the *Indépendants* in 1911 this was a fair statement of the case. However, when Léger exhibited the *Nus dans un Paysage*, early in that year, it was not wholly representative of his artistic development at that time. Some time around the spring of 1911 Léger moved from the Avenue du Maine to a new studio in the rue de l'Ancienne Comédie, and there he began an important series of landscapes or cityscapes, which represent a very different and in some ways revolutionary aspect of his work. The small *Fumée sur les Toits* given by Léger as a wedding present to the bride of his friend the painter André Mare is one of the freshest and liveliest of the series. (Pl. 70B). In the *Couseuse* and the *Nus* the emphasis is on solid forms; here, on the other hand, the houses are sketched in in a purely linear fashion and the painting is composed of flat, clearly defined planes of different colours, which are arranged in a limited space. And Léger had clearly been influenced by the 'cobweb' type of Cubism of Picasso and Braque which he and Delaunay saw at Kahnweiler's gallery. Indeed, the organization of the picture surface in terms of a loose framework or grid suggests that Léger may have seen the paintings and drawings which Picasso brought back to Paris from Cadaquès in the autumn of 1910. Léger's painting differs, however, from the contemporary work of Picasso and Braque in that it is quite brightly coloured (in blues, reds and pinks). His use of perspective, too, while it is obviously inconsistent, is still much more conventional. These features are due to the fact that in this painting Léger was still relying much more on the visual stimulus of his subject or model, as opposed to Picasso and Braque whose art was more conceptual and thus more detached from visual appearances. Then as opposed to them Léger was always much more interested in the life outside his studio. It is this that makes his art at once more impersonal and less contemplative than theirs. It is interesting to note that he found he had little in common with Apollinaire and Max Jacob, two of Picasso's closest friends, but that he felt at once drawn to Cendrars whom he also came to know at this time. For, 'he is like me, he picks up everything that is going on around him. Together we became tangled up in modern life . . .'[1]

In these first cityscapes Léger was instinctively developing a pictorial theory which was to affect almost all of his subsequent work. Looking at the urban landscape from his studio window, Léger was fascinated by the way in which the inert masses of the buildings were brought to life by the contrast of the billowing

[1]Catalogue cit., p. 27.

smoke coming out of the chimney tops. The round evanescent forms acquired a special pictorial meaning in relationship to the square, solid cubes of the houses. And from his high viewpoint the triangular forms of the pitched red roofs made further contrasts of colour and form. When in 1914 Léger delivered his second lecture at the Académie Wassilief,[1] he stressed the fact that a painting must be built up of a series of deliberate contrasts, not only of colour but of forms as well. To illustrate his point Léger took as an example exactly such a scene as he had painted in the *Fumées sur les Toits*: 'Concentrate your curves with as much variety as possible, but without separating them; frame them by the hard and spare interaction of the surfaces of the buildings, "dead" surfaces which will take on movement by the fact that they will be coloured contrastingly to the central mass and that they are juxtaposed to "live" forms. You will get the maximum effect.' The sense of dynamism and movement which is implicit even in an early work like *Les Fumées sur les Toits*, and which Léger developed in his work of the following years, is in sharp contrast to the classical balance and stability found in the contemporary Cubism of Picasso and Braque. In this respect Léger's landscapes relate more closely to Delaunay's *Eiffel Towers*, in which solid forms are broken or interrupted by cloud-like forms in much the same way, and it is possible that Léger may have been influenced by Delaunay. Léger's work was, however, more structural and solid than that of Delaunay and had none of that explosive quality which had led Apollinaire, before he became converted to Delaunay's art, to say: '(his) canvases unfortunately seem to commemorate an earthquake.'[2]

Léger used the puffs of white smoke again in a literal way in *Les Fumeurs* (or *Le Fumeur* – the work has been given both titles) painted in the winter of 1911–12 (Pl. 71). As in the cityscapes this device served to give a sense of movement and formal variety, and this effect has been further enhanced by the fact that Léger now contrasts flat forms with three-dimensional forms as well; the strong linear quality of the *Fumées sur les Toits* has been retained, but is combined with the same emphasis on solid volumes that had characterized the *Couseuse* and the *Nus dans un Paysage*. The figures are consciously 'cubified' or reduced to cylin-

[1]This lecture was published in the June 1914 issue of the *Soirées de Paris* under the title 'Réalisations picturales actuelles'.

[2]*L'Intransigeant*, 18 March 1910.

drical and block-like shapes, while the open linear framework around them allows Léger to attain a sense of precision and fluidity at the same time. In this respect Léger's work resembles that of Picasso and Braque at this period. The line of trees in the background, which runs back into depth, still gives a sense of recession, but apart from this Léger has by now also abandoned traditional perspective. Léger, however, used a variable viewpoint not so much as a means of combining different aspects of a figure or an object into a single image but as a means of manipulating pictorial forms more freely in order to create a sense of pictorial dynamism. Occasionally individual objects are foreshortened in an orthodox, traditional way, but they are likely to be placed next to others in which the perspective is either divergent or has been disregarded completely.

La Noce (Pl. 72), a contemporary painting which was almost certainly the work shown at the 1912 *Indépendants* as *Composition avec Personnages*, represents the next stage in Léger's development. Here the round, billowing white forms in the centre of the painting have no literal meaning, and are simply abstract pictorial elements which unify the composition and enliven the picture surface. The system of contrasts is further developed since these central forms are contrasted not only in shape but also in size with the more elaborately worked forms of the figures behind them. This phase in Léger's art reaches a climax in *La Femme en Bleu* (Kunstmuseum, Basel, Pl. 73), exhibited at the *Salon d'Automne* of 1912. In this painting the whole composition is organized in terms of large flat or slightly rounded shapes, some of which are completely abstract, while others have been suggested by the forms of the figure seated in the centre of the painting; the figure itself and the setting can be reconstructed only with the help of the smaller areas which contain details such as the hands and the objects on the two tables (or the table and stool). Léger achieves a sense of movement and variety not only by contrasting the large bold shapes with the smaller rounded forms between them but by contrasting them with each other as well. Some are curving and have a suggestion of shading at the edges, others are completely flat and angular; the predominant colour is blue, but there are areas of black, white, red, green and yellow. This type of painting by Léger resembles the slightly later paintings of Braque, which had been influenced by the techniques of *papier collé*, in that two distinct approaches, one completely abstract and the other more naturalistic or representational, are fused together in a single painting. This was a method of work that Léger never abandoned, and it can be seen in its most obvious form in paintings of the 1930s and 1940s in which objects and figures are drawn over a background pattern of abstract coloured shapes, which become intimately related to them, but which at the same time continue to exist independently. However, whereas in a work like the *Table du Musicien* Braque worked in a 'synthetic' way, first juggling with strips of paper, abstract pictorial elements, in order to establish a compositional substructure, and then subsequently individualizing and objectifying certain shapes by making them represent specific objects, Léger, on the other hand, begins with a fully developed idea of the subject-matter, which is elaborated with considerable detail and care, while the large abstract and semi-abstract shapes are subsequently developed from it or superimposed over it. That is to say, in the Cubist period occasionally Braque works from abstraction to representation, but Léger invariably starts with representation and works towards abstraction.

During 1911 Delaunay, whose *Eiffel Towers* had been exciting but formally slightly precarious, was trying to find a more stable basis for his art. *La Ville* (Pl. 77), now in the Guggenheim Museum in New York, is one of a new group of views of Paris, seen from an open window, that Delaunay began in this year.[1] Here Delaunay has strictly limited his use of colour, and has concentrated on building up the picture surface in a pattern of small black and grey planes; to control the tonal distinctions between them Delaunay has resorted to a schematic technique of square or rectangular brush-strokes, each distinct from the ones around it, so that the effect is of a *grisaille* Divisionism. The areas between the

[1]Delaunay, like Picasso and Braque, did not sign and date his work of this period until long afterwards. The dates he then inscribed on his paintings are often misleading, and the situation is complicated by the fact that he developed a habit of ascribing the paintings to the date of the phase of his development to which he felt they belonged. The catalogue to an exhibition which he held at the Galerie Barbazanges from 28 February until 13 March 1912, enables one to establish a sequence for his work up to this time, as dates are given, and many of the works are illustrated, so that it is possible to place exactly paintings of a series which have the same title. For example the first, more '*grisaille*', *Ville* which is dated 1911 on the painting is dated in the same way in the catalogue, but the example from the Musée d'Art Moderne which is signed and dated 1910 is illustrated in the Catalogue and dated there 1912. It must, however, have been begun in 1911 as it undoubtedly precedes the Laon paintings which were done in the first months of 1912 and were included in the exhibition. The preface to the catalogue is by Maurice Princet; unfortunately it does not tell us much about the author's personality.

houses are, however, a dull, dark green, while the Eiffel Tower, which can be seen in the background, is orange. Superficially this painting has something in common with certain Cubist landscapes by Picasso and Braque (it recalls Braque's *View of Montmartre*, painted from his studio in 1910 and now in the collection of M. Jean Masurel in Roubaix), and it seems likely that in these paintings Delaunay had again been directly influenced by what he saw at Kahnweiler's gallery. On the other hand, there is none of the subtlety of spatial definition that is found in the work of Picasso and Braque, and despite the disregard of any conventional system of perspective one has the impression that these paintings were systematically evolved from more naturalistic sketches. Unlike Léger in his treatment of similar scenes, Delaunay makes no use of contrasts of form and he avoids any kind of linear emphasis. His vision of Paris is less immediate and direct than Léger's, and by contrast more poetic and mysterious. Delaunay himself claimed that the inspiration for these paintings of scenes through open windows came to him on reading a poem by Mallarmé.

Delaunay spent January of 1912 in Laon. The *Villes* (there are some four paintings in the series)[1] had been painted in his studio in Paris (they show a view from the Place de l'Etoile towards rooftops between Avenue Kleber and Avenue d'Iena) but now, working from nature, he produced a series of paintings in a different style. In these paintings Delaunay seems to have turned back once again to the work of Cézanne, although he now interprets Cézanne in a freer, more open way. The buildings in *Les Tours de Laon* (Musée d'Art Moderne, Paris) are rendered in terms of planes loosely hinged together and opened up into each other, while the sky is subdivided into facets of more or less equal size in order to unify the picture surface. Once again there is no rigid system of perspective, although in the avenue of trees in the lower right-hand corner the recession is perfectly conventional. In one of the last of the *Villes* (another, oblong canvas, also in the Guggenheim Museum, New York), Delaunay had begun to cover some of the small grey planes with strokes of bright colour applied in accordance with Divisionist technique. The Laon paintings are once again executed with a full palette, and the importance of this series lies in the fact that it was at this time

[1]One of these is in the Musée d'Art Moderne, two are in the Guggenheim Museum, and one unfinished example was in the collection of Madame Sonia Terk Delaunay.

that Delaunay first became excited with the possibility of dealing with large pictorial surfaces in terms of flat, interpenetrating planes of colour. The concepts of form and space latent in the work of Cézanne had been seized on, simplified and exaggerated by the Cubists. Now Delaunay was to do the same thing with Cézanne's painstaking juxtaposition of contrasting or complementary warm and dark tones (Pl. 78A).

On his return to Paris Delaunay painted *La Ville de Paris* (Musée d'Art Moderne, Paris), a vast canvas that dominated the Cubist section at the *Salon des Indépendants* of 1912 (Pl. 78B). It was intended by Delaunay to synthesize all his researches of the past years. It is in fact composed of three separate paintings, joined together in a mosaic-like frieze of small, coloured shapes; the mannerist central figures were evolved from a photograph of a Pompeian painting of Three Graces, now in Naples. The elegant, elongated proportions and the insistence on obvious geometric shapes recall Metzinger's *Two Nudes* painted a year earlier, and since Delaunay was not essentially a figure painter it is likely that in this painting he turned to another artist for guidance. Delaunay, however, once again differs from the other Cubists in his refusal to use line as a means of defining or suggesting form. The forms of the three women in this painting are broken up into small planes of colour ranging from light areas of pale pinks and yellows into shadows of light blues, mauves and greens. The subject-matter of the landscape on the left recalls Delaunay's enthusiasm for Rousseau. Indeed, this section of the painting is close to the background of Rousseau's *Self-Portrait* (Prague) and to a landscape entitled *Notre Dame* (Phillips Collection, Washington). The right-hand section is a reinterpretation of the earlier *Eiffel Towers*. Apollinaire, impressed by the size of the painting, wrote in a review of the exhibition: 'Decidedly Delaunay's painting is the most important in this *Salon*. *La Ville de Paris* is more than an artistic manifestation: this painting marks the advent of a concept of art lost perhaps since the great Italians. And if it sums up all the endeavours of the painter who composed it, it sums up also and without any scientific apparatus all the endeavours of modern painting.'[1] Later, Delaunay came to feel that this marked the end of the 'destructive' or Cubist phase in his art since after this he abandoned all idea of fragmenting solid forms in a Cubistic manner (he had

[1]*L'Intransigeant*, 20 March 1912.

never been interested in showing volumes in any case), and devoted himself to his researches into the nature of pure colour.

In 1911, to the general public, who did not know the achievements of Picasso and Braque, the work of Delaunay, Léger, Metzinger, Gleizes and Le Fauconnier, represented Cubism in its most advanced and developed form. However, even at the *Salon des Indépendants* of 1911 Delaunay's *Eiffel Tower* had stood apart from the work of the other painters as an individual and independent variant of the style. Personally, too, Delaunay began to drift away from the other painters almost immediately after Cubism had been launched as a recognized movement, and he retained a close friendship only with Léger and Le Fauconnier. Léger himself, while he continued to frequent Cubist gatherings,[1] was in 1911 also beginning to assert himself as an independent personality to whom the group activities of the remaining painters meant very little. At the *Salon d'Automne* of 1911 his independence was noticed by Apollinaire, who wrote: 'Léger is in search of his personality.'[2] And Gleizes, who reviewed the same exhibition in *Les Bandeaux d'Or*, was slightly disturbed by the most recent trends in Léger's art: 'the absolute determination to express himself in purely plastic terms gives his composition a look that is at first slightly disturbing'.[3] Only Gleizes, Metzinger and Le Fauconnier, excited by the sensation caused by Room 41 at the *Indépendants*, were still anxious to consolidate Cubism into a cohesive and militant movement. Metzinger had begun to write about painting in 1910, and by 1911 Gleizes was doing critical work also; in the summer of this year these two painters began their collaboration on *Du Cubisme*. Together with Le Fauconnier, they planned to publish a review dedicated to the plastic arts which would serve as a platform for the expression of their ideas about contemporary painting and sculpture.[4]

In accordance with his desire to codify the laws which governed Cubist painting, Metzinger exhibited at the *Salon d'Automne* of 1911 a highly schematized painting entitled *Le Goûter* (Arensberg Collection, Philadelphia Museum of Art), his most famous Cubist painting; because of the smile on the

[1]See pp. 6, 12, above.
[2]*L'Intransigeant*, 30 September 1911.
[3]*Les Bandeaux d'Or*, November 1911.
[4]See p. 12 above.

face of the woman this painting became known as 'la Joconde du Cubisme'.[1] Although as early as 1910 Metzinger had written of the way in which Picasso and Braque had dismissed traditional perspective, his *Two Nudes* shown at the *Indépendants* of 1911 had shown that he did not understand what it really was that Picasso and Braque were getting at in their painting. This is still fundamentally true of *Le Goûter*, which has the same sort of academic 'cubification' as the earlier work. In the head, however, Metzinger has schematically combined a profile and a full-face view, while half the teacup is seen from above and the other half exactly at eye level. Since this kind of optical synthesis is found only in these two areas, and since Metzinger shows little interest in analysing and expanding solid forms, the effect is a bit contrived. Indeed, one is reminded at once of Princet's theoretical discussions about Cubism; Metzinger certainly knew this 'mathematician', and it is very likely that Princet had an influence on his art. In his 'Note sur la Peinture' written the previous year he went so far as to say, 'Picasso . . . creates a free, mobile perspective, *from which the shrewd mathematician Princet has deduced a whole system of geometry*' (my own italics). One is left with the impression that Metzinger's Cubism is the result more of intellectual influences than of a genuine new vision of the world (Pl. 86B).

A contemporary work by Gleizes such as the painting that was originally entitled *Passy*[2] but which is now known as *The Bridges of Paris* (Pl. 82), shows that Gleizes' painting was developing along slightly different lines. When he was collaborating with Metzinger in writing *Du Cubisme*, Gleizes had objected to the dryness of Metzinger's theorizing,[3] and this painting is certainly freer and more imaginative than Metzinger's *Le Goûter*. The canvas is broken down into various large, transparent planes, into which the different elements of the landscape are fitted. The new breadth of handling in this work and the presence of the small circular cloud forms in the centre of the composition suggest that Gleizes was beginning to study the work of Léger. A comparison of this painting with the *Femme aux Phlox* which Gleizes had shown at the *Indépendants* a few months earlier shows that Gleizes was maturing rapidly as a painter. In turning to the

[1]The painting is first referred to in this way in a note signed 'la Palette', in *Paris Journal* on 30 October 1911.
[2]The painting is reproduced under this title in the first editions of *Du Cubisme*.
[3]*Souvenirs*.

work of Léger for inspiration, Gleizes was once again following Le Fauconnier's lead, for Le Fauconnier, after returning to Paris from Italy where he had spent the summer of 1911, had fallen completely under the influence of Léger's art. His *Chasseur* (Pl. 89B), which he showed at the *Salon des Indépendants* of 1912 is clearly derived from the type of painting Léger had created in *La Noce* and *Les Fumeurs*. However, Le Fauconnier had never at any point shown any real understanding of the problems which faced Cubism, and now he failed to appreciate the fact that the strength and vitality of Léger's work of this period derived from the very careful balance that Léger maintained between abstraction and representation. Le Fauconnier turns the hard, dynamic precision of Léger's art into a bland, amorphous, badly organized and highly abstract kind of painting which has little or nothing to do with Cubism. At this time Le Fauconnier's friendship with Gleizes and Metzinger also came to an abrupt end, and for this reason his work was not illustrated in *Du Cubisme* when it appeared in March of 1912. During 1913 and 1914 Le Fauconnier's work became more representational again, and though at the advanced *Salons* his work continued to be shown with that of the Cubists, in actual fact after the *Salon des Indépendants* of 1911 he had ceased to be of any real importance as a painter. On the other hand, Le Fauconnier was an influence in encouraging young painters to look at Cubist painting and to adopt a Cubist form of expression; he was in a position to do this, since in February of 1912 he was appointed to succeed Jacques Emile Blanche as director of one of the teaching studios at the *Académie de la Palette*. Metzinger was made a teacher there at the same time.

The *Section d'Or* exhibition, held at the *Galerie de la Boétie* in October 1912, marked the climax of Cubism as a movement. In the year-and-a-half since the first Cubist manifestation at the *Salon des Indépendants* of 1911, the style had spread with astonishing speed. More than thirty painters showed at the *Section d'Or*, and while not all of them were Cubist, each of them had to some extent been influenced by the style. Delaunay and Le Fauconnier, two of the original Cubists from Room 41 of the 1911 *Indépendants*, both abstained from showing, but the exhibition was given added weight by the fact that Gris had contributed two paintings, one the very large *l'Homme au Café*, now in the Arensberg Collection in the Philadelphia Museum of Art. Gris had exhibited publicly for the first time at the *Salon des Indépendants* of this year (1912) and his work had attracted a great deal of attention;[1] his paintings, however, had been hung separately from those of the other Cubists. Furthermore, in the intervening months between the exhibition and the *Section d'Or*, Gris had evolved a much more personal and assured style, and in the absence of paintings by Picasso and Braque, his work represented Cubism in its purest and most uncompromising form (Pl. 61).

Even before the opening of the *Section d'Or*, Gris had begun to have an influence on the minor figures of the movement. At the *Salon d'Automne* which opened a week or so before the exhibition at the *Galerie de la Boétie*, Metzinger had shown a large painting, *La Danseuse au Café* (Pl. 85) (Albright Knox Gallery, Buffalo), in which he had adopted Gris' technique of superimposing a thick linear grid over his figures, although what had been evolved by Gris as a means of synthesizing different aspects of an object or a figure into a single image became in Metzinger's hands a decorative or schematic, mannerist device. This painting is, however, interesting in that it is one of the few Cubist pictures in which the influence of Seurat, a painter much admired by the Cubists, can be seen in a direct and obvious form; the flat, stylized forms of the lamp-brackets, and for that matter the entire subject-matter, suggest that Metzinger had been looking at works like the *Chahut* or *Parade*. Metzinger may have been led to a closer study of Seurat by Severini, a painter with whom he was friendly, and who was at this time reinterpreting Seurat in Futurist terms. Each of the painters of the *Section d'Or* showed several paintings, chosen to illustrate their development over the previous years. Metzinger's most recent work was *La Plume Jaune* (there are two versions of this work) which is in the same style as the *Danseuse au Café*. Both paintings are brighter than Metzinger's work of the previous year, although until 1914 he continued to favour pale, silvery colour schemes. In all Metzinger's work of this period there is a strong emphasis on decorative detail: Apollinaire referred to the drawing which Metzinger showed at the *Salon d'Automne* of 1913 as 'a delicious piece of *chinoiserie*'[2] (Pl. 87).

At the *Section d'Or* Gleizes showed *Le Dépiquage des Moissons* (Pl. 83B), one of the largest Cubist paintings ever executed, which occupied a whole wall at the *Galerie de la Boétie*. During the months before the exhibition Gleizes had come

[1]See p. 97 above.
[2]*L'Intransigeant*, November 14.

increasingly under the artistic domination of Léger. In a work like *L'Homme au Balcon* (now in the Arensberg Collection, Philadelphia Museum of Art), Gleizes deliberately contrasts angular and curved shapes, while the tubular, block-like forms of the figure and head are derived directly from works by Léger such as *Les Fumeurs*. In *Le Dépiquage* the circular white forms in the centre of the painting recall the clouds of smoke that Léger had introduced into his slightly earlier works. However, while Léger was moving towards a more dynamic kind of painting in which abstract and representational elements are contrasted or juxtaposed, Gleizes' vision remained, for the time being, more naturalistic; the circular shapes in this painting, for example, represent specific things, trees, clouds and the sacks or baskets of the gleaners. As in the contemporary work of almost all Cubist painters, there is a strong linear quality about Gleizes' work. And in *Le Dépiquage* and *L'Homme au Balcon* Gleizes also felt the need to use brighter colours again (Pl. 84).

Another of the *Section d'Or* painters who had felt the influence of Léger was Picabia. Picabia, a Spanish painter who was a few years older than most of the Cubists (he was born in 1878), had during the early years of the century gained a considerable reputation for his landscapes executed in a highly coloured, richly impasted Impressionist style. By 1909, however, his work was becoming flatter and more decorative, and he began to become interested in the formal relationships between simple, brightly coloured masses. Shortly after the *Salon des Indépendants* of 1911 he came into personal contact with some of the Cubists, through Apolliniare, who had become a close friend. He showed with the Cubists for the first time in the summer of 1912, when he was invited to join them at the *Salon de Juin* in Rouen. At the *Salon d'Automne* of this year he became recognized as an advanced and controversial painter.[1] Picabia was represented at the *Section d'Or* by *Danseuses à la Source* (Arensberg Collection, Philadelphia Museum of Art), a work for which the closest prototype is perhaps Léger's *Nus dans un Paysage*, although there may also be some influence from Marcel Duchamp's contemporary figure work. Picabia's dancers have the same wooden, rough-hewn quality as Léger's *Nus*, and the landscape background is dealt with in a similar, though more drastic fashion. But whereas Léger's interest lay

[1]See pp. 19–20 above.

primarily in examining the relationships between solid forms, Picabia reduces the whole picture surface to intricate patterns of coloured shapes (the painting is in oranges, creams and browns) with only an occasional suggestion of volume or depth; the flatness of the canvas is stressed, for example, by the way in which the further and nearer legs of the foremost figure are joined together by planes of colour which seem to belong to them both. Picabia, like many of the painters of the *Section d'Or*, could be considered a Cubist only if the term is interpreted in a broad sense, in that he took superficial aspects of Cubism and used them for different ends (Pl. 99A).

In his lecture at the *Section d'Or* Apollinaire spoke of Francis Kupka's work as Orphist; it is, however, not absolutely sure whether Kupka's work was in fact actually included in the exhibition.[1] At the *Salon d'Automne* he had just shown his *Amorpha* and at the *Indépendants* of 1914 he was to show a *Plans Verticaux*, the first non-figurative works ever to be exhibited. Kupka, who was born in 1871, was older than any of the Cubists. He must have been stimulated by the young painters whom he used to meet in Jacques Villon's studio at Puteaux; and his contacts with a younger generation of progressive painters may have encouraged him to make the final break with representation. They in turn must have been impressed as well as baffled by these enormous, totally original works. But in many respects Kupka belonged to a totally different world from that of the Cubists: a mystic who was deeply influenced by science, spiritualism, the esoteric and the occult, he was also politically a convinced anarchist. The arrangements of upright interlocking forms in some of his early abstractions relate to certain Cubist compositional procedures, but only in the most superficial way; and the fact that his work can have been seen as relating to what was on view at the *Section d'Or* helps to underline the exhibition's eclecticism. Kupka's aims, however, were never at any point those of the Cubists (Pl. 99B).

Louis Marcoussis, on the other hand, was as close to true Cubism as any of the painters at the *Section d'Or*, except for Gris, and, in a particularized way, Léger. Marcoussis (whose real name was Markous) was a Polish painter, who in 1910 met Apollinaire, and through him Picasso and Braque; he had given up painting,

[1]For a discussion of whether or not Kupka showed work in the *Section d'Or*, see Virginia Spate, *Orphism*, Oxford 1979, Appendix A, pp. 367–9.

but took it up again after meeting them. A still life of 1912 entitled *Nature Morte au Damier* (Pl. 100) shows that Marcoussis was reinterpreting the latest developments in Picasso's art with sensitivity. The flat, rather insubstantial quality of this painting may owe something to the fact that it was originally executed as part of a scheme for the decoration of the Café Azon, a Montmartre restaurant frequented by the Cubists and their friends. Marcoussis was a gifted if not very original painter, and his work at the *Section d'Or* was of some importance since it reflected something of what Picasso and Braque were doing at this time. Apollinaire wrote in his review of the exhibition, 'Marcoussis is very modern',[1] and certainly his work must have seemed advanced beside that of painters like Lhote (Pl. 104A), Luc Albert Moreau, Marchand and Segonzac. La Fresnaye, whose work belonged to the same general category as that of these painters, had, it is true, cautiously developed a more Cubist form of expression. In his still lifes of 1912 such as the *Nature Morte aux Trois Anses* (Pl. 98B) the objects are all seen from a high, generalized viewpoint, and are opened up into a background of large, flat, interlocking planes. La Fresnaye refused, however, to break completely with traditional ideas about perspective, and his work represents an elegant, somewhat decorative variant of the style.

The work of Marcel Duchamp and of Jacques Villon, who had been largely responsible for the organization of the *Section d'Or*, represented an aspect of Cubism that was different both from that of the groups dominated by Gris and Léger, and from that of the more conservative wing which was headed by La Fresnaye and Lhote. The adherence to Cubism of these two painters and of their brother, the sculptor Duchamp-Villon, was an event of importance in the history of the movement. All three were intelligent, open-minded men, interested in the intellectual possibilities of contemporary painting and anxious to relate Cubism to some of the movements which surrounded it. Duchamp-Villon had been instrumental in persuading the selection committee of the *Salon d'Automne* of 1911 to accept the work of the Cubists, and the entries of both his brothers had been placed in the Cubist section of this exhibition. During 1911 the studio at Puteaux, which was shared by Jacques Villon and Duchamp-Villon, became an important meeting-place for Cubist painters. It was here that the plans for the

[1]*L'Intransigeant*, 10 October 1912.

large exhibition at the *Galerie de la Boétie* were formulated.[1]

While most of the Cubist painters claimed to have evolved from the art of Cézanne, Marcel Duchamp saw himself rather as an artistic descendant of Redon.[2] The influence of Redon is clearly seen in *Yvonne et Magdeleine Déchiquetees*, dated September 1911 (Arensberg Collection, Philadelphia Museum of Art), in the strong, rather mysterious use of chiaroscuro and in the way in which the heads float, bodiless, in an undefined space. The faces of Duchamp's sisters are each seen twice, rendered each time in a different way. So that here it does seem to have occurred to Duchamp that it was possible to combine various views of a subject into a single painting, though not into a single image. In the Cubist section of the *Salon d'Automne* of 1911 he exhibited a painting entitled *Portrait* (now in the Arensberg Collection, Philadelphia Museum of Art), which showed the same sitter in five different positions. In this work, Duchamp was coming more directly under the Cubist influences. This can be seen also in a contemporary work, *The Sonata* (Arensberg Collection, Philadelphia Museum of Art) in which the figures are treated in an angular way and occasionally opened up into their surroundings; in the standing figure there is a crude attempt to combine a profile and a full face view. However, the painting, which is executed in pale pastel colours, lacks any sense of precision or discipline, and the forms remain vague and indistinct (Pl. 93).

The first real turning point in Marcel Duchamp's art came towards the end of 1911, when he became interested in the problem of rendering figures in successive stages of motion. In December of 1911 Duchamp was engaged in painting a picture of two chess players, each of which is seen in two different positions as he bends forward over the chess-board,[3] and at the same time he was working on the first version of his famous *Nude Descending a Staircase* (Arensberg Collection, Philadelphia Museum of Art). In these paintings Duchamp severely restricted the range of colours on his palette and reduced his subject to a few simple, geometric shapes; in short, Duchamp's intellectual interest in solving a new pictorial problem forced him to come to grips with one of the fundamental

[1]See pp. 14–15 above.

[2]Information received from M. Duchamp, May 1956.

[3]The study for this painting is in the Musée d'Art Moderne in Paris, and is dated December 1911. The finished painting in the Arensberg Collection in the Philadelphia Museum of Art is also dated 1911.

problems of painting that he had hitherto ignored, that of representing three-dimensional forms on a two-dimensional surface. The result is that these works are much closer in spirit to Cubism than anything else he ever produced. The colour scheme of blacks and browns, the fusion of the subjects and their surroundings, and the linear framework which shows through underneath the solid forms, recall similar features in the work of Picasso and Braque; Duchamp was in fact introduced to Picasso and Braque at about this time by his friend Maurice Princet. In the final version of the *Nude Descending a Staircase* (Arensberg Collection, Philadelphia Museum of Art), which was rejected by the *Salon des Indépendants* in April of 1912, the forms have been elaborated, multiplied and fused together in a fashion that suggests more convincingly the downward motion of the figure as it moves from step to step (Pls. 95A,B).

This painting has, of course, affinities with certain aspects of Futurism. Marcel Duchamp was above all else an intellectual, and he cannot have failed to be aware of developments in Italy, even before the Futurist painters descended on Paris in the autumn of 1911. The Futurist Manifesto was published in France in *Le Figaro* of 20 February 1909. The technical manifesto on painting was issued in Milan in April 1910, but it appeared soon after in a French translation, in the periodical *Comoedia*. Later Duchamp may even have met the Futurist painters on their visit to Paris, since Severini took them on an extensive tour of the studios of advanced French painters.[1] On the other hand, when Duchamp began work on the *Chess Players* and the *Nude Descending a Staircase* he could have seen no Futurist painting to influence him. Even if the Italian painters had brought examples of their work with them to Paris, it was only in the paintings executed after their return to Italy that they evolved a definite style of their own. Severini, who at this time was a main link between the Italian painters and the Cubists, was dealing with the problem of motion in his contemporary work, but while he was dislocating and displacing the limbs of his figures to achieve this effect, he had as yet made no attempt to indicate successive stages of motion in the same logical, schematic way as Duchamp. Duchamp's painting at this time was thus an independent and original variation of Cubism, and was part of the logical development of his intellectual desire to show several aspects of a model in

[1]See pp. 26–7 above.

a single painting. Duchamp was at this time also looking at the chronophotographs of Marey and Muybridge which undoubtedly had an influence on his painting.

Nevertheless, the *Nude Descending a Staircase* provides one of the most obvious and schematic illustrations of the well-known passage in the manifesto of the Futurist painters, 'Indeed all things move, all things run, all things are rapidly changing. A profile is never motionless before our eyes, but constantly appears and disappears. On account of the persistence of an image upon the retina, moving objects constantly multiply, becoming deformed as they succeed each other, like vibrations hurled into the space they traverse. Thus a running horse had not four legs but twenty and their movements are triangular.' The first Futurist exhibition in Paris was held in February 1912 at the Galerie Bernheim, and had the *Nude Descending a Staircase* been seen a few weeks later at the *Indépendants* the analogies between it and the work of the Futurists would have been clearly apparent, although Balla, whose solution to the problem of depicting figures in movement was closest at this time to that evolved by Duchamp, was not represented at the Futurist exhibition. But the *Nude* of Duchamp is linked to Futurism only in the most superficial way, and Duchamp's vision differed fundamentally from that of the Futurists. Futurism was a dynamic, romantic movement. Duchamp's work, on the other hand, was cool and detached, and the *Nude Descending a Staircase* reflects none of the Futurists' enthusiasm for contemporary life, but was rather a prelude to his later mechanistic works. This painting violates, too, the final demand of the manifesto of the Futurist painters: 'We demand the total suppression of the nude in painting for ten years.'

The *Nude Descending a Staircase* was accepted for exhibition at the *Section d'Or*, together with a more recent painting *Le Roi et La Reine entourés de nus vites* (now also in the Arensberg Collection in the Philadelphia Museum of Art). *The Bride* (Pl. 94) is a contemporary work and belongs to the same series. In the *Nude* Duchamp had conceived the idea of reducing the human figure to semi-mechanical forms. Then, late in 1911, Duchamp-Villon had asked a group of artists including Léger, Metzinger, La Fresnaye, Gleizes and his brother Marcel Duchamp, to make pictures for the decoration of his kitchen, and Duchamp produced a picture of a *Coffee-grinder* (Tate Gallery, London) in which its mechanical aspect is burlesqued or treated in a semi-humorous fashion.

Duchamp became fascinated with the mechanics of the coffee-grinder, and assimilated them to those of the human form, so that he began to interpret the figures in his paintings in terms of more obviously mechanical forms; metal cylinders, pistons, cog-wheels, rubber tubes and so on. The colour scheme of *The Bride* is still that of the *Nude*, but the forms that compose the figure are varied and each is fully modelled and carefully distinguished from the shapes around it. Once again, in the emphasis on commercially manufactured, machine-like forms, there is a parallel with the Futurists. However, while the Italians exalted the machine as one of the most glorious features of the dynamic civilization in which they lived, Duchamp uses it as a means of passing a very different kind of comment on modern life. Duchamp's attitude to contemporary civilization was aloof, wryly humorous and deliberately equivocal. *The Bride* and the paintings and sketches surrounding it culminated in *The Bride stripped bare by her Bachelors, Even* (Arensberg Collection, Philadelphia Museum of Art), a work executed on glass, which was begun in 1915 and finished eight years later, but which had been partially conceived as early as 1913. André Breton has described this work as a 'mechanistic and cynical interpretation of love; the passage of woman from the state of virginity to that of non-virginity taken as the theme of a fundamentally a-sentimental speculation, almost that of an extra-human being training himself to consider this kind of operation'.[1] *The Bride* has practically nothing that recalls Cubism, and there is an element of destructive humour about it that already relates it to the spirit of Dada. At the *Salon des Indépendants* of 1912 *The Nude Descending a Staircase* had been rejected by the Cubists clearly because they sensed that Duchamp's aims were at variance with their own. At the *Section d'Or* Vauxcelles, who had bitterly opposed the Cubists, was now frankly shocked and disgusted by Duchamp's work.[2] Even Apollinaire, for all his thirst for novelty, found it disquieting.[3]

Jacques Villon was drawn to Cubism perhaps through the enthusiasm of his younger brother, Marcel. Except for Kupka (who in any case was never really a Cubist) Villon was the oldest of the figures associated with the movement. When he began to paint seriously in 1910 at the age of thirty-five, Villon had already

[1]'Lighthouse of the Bride', *View*, Series V, New York, January 1945.
[2]*Gil Blas*, 14 October 1912.
[3]*L'Intransigeant*, 10 October 1912.

been working for over ten years as a commercial illustrator for various Parisian periodicals such as *l'Assiette au Beurre* (to which Gris also contributed). Because of his age and experience, Villon's approach to Cubism was cautious, and his methodical temperament furthermore led him to search for a scientific basis for the style. His first Cubist paintings, like the *Portrait of his Brother, Duchamp-Villon* (Musée d'Art Moderne, Paris) which was exhibited together with four other portraits at the *Salon d'Automne* of 1911, show an analytical treatment of form that may have been inspired in a very general way by the work of Cézanne or possibly even by that of Picasso and Braque. In this portrait his desire to investigate and explain the solid mass of the head has led him to distend it abnormally, so that, as in certain early Cubist paintings by Picasso, the far side of the face can be seen in what is basically a three-quarter view. As opposed to Picasso and Braque, however, Villon never abandoned the use of colour, and in this painting there is still a very strong impression of atmospheric light. Eluard quotes Villon as having said in later years, 'I was the Impressionist Cubist, and I think I remained such.'[1] (Pl. 91A).

Jacques Villon was represented at the *Section d'Or,* by four canvases. One of them, *Jeune Femme* (Arensberg Collection, Philadelphia Museum of Art), when compared to the portraits printed a year earlier, shows how rapidly Villon had moved to a more abstract and sophisticated form of expression. At this time, Marcel Duchamp was experimenting with geometry, but not applying it directly to his painting. Jacques Villon, on the other hand, who had suggested the *Section d'Or* as a title for the exhibition, was actually introducing mathematical and geometrical calculations into his work; Marcel Duchamp has been quoted as saying that his brother was familiar with the work of geometricians from Pythagoras to Dom Verkade.[2] In the *Jeune Femme* the underlying geometrical framework is fairly simple. As the basis for his composition Villon has joined the corners of the canvas by two clearly marked diagonals, while two large circles meet at their point of intersection; one of these is transformed into the section of the woman's body from her waist to her knees, while her shoulders and head are inscribed into the second. The geometrical severity of the composition is sub-

[1]P. Eluard and René Jean, *Jacques Villon ou l'Art Glorieux*, Paris 1948, p. 61.

[2]Jerome Melquist, 'Jacques Villon, Maître de Puteaux', *Art Documents*, Geneva, no. 3, December 1950.

sequently disguised and refined by a series of more instinctive pictorial adjustments: the two major diagonals are broken and shifted very slightly so that they do not coincide exactly with the four corners, and the circular forms are lost, or at least made less insistent, in the left-hand side of the picture. The intellectual quality of Villon's painting relates it to that of Gris, but while Gris was interested in exploring the intellectual possibilities opened up by the new Cubist concepts of form and space, and only subsequently became interested in establishing a mathematical basis for his art, Villon was perhaps at first primarily interested in the scientific possibilities of painting, and was drawn to Cubism largely because he saw that it was a type of painting that could be interpreted in these terms (Pl. 90).

As in the case of Marcel Duchamp, there are analogies between Villon's work and that of the Futurists. Indeed, a work like the *Jeune Femme* is in many ways more Futurist than anything produced by his brother. By repeating the forms of the shoulder Villon creates the impression that the young woman can be seen in successive stages of motion as she bends forward, and instead of simply opening the subject up into its surroundings as the Cubists would have done, here Villon suggests that the figure is vanishing into the background in a more dynamic way. The insistence on diagonal lines gives a sensation of movement which could be interpreted as a manifestation of the Futurists' theory of universal dynamism. The colour scheme in this picture, too, is hot and smouldering as in so many Futurist paintings such as, for example, Carrá's *Funeral of the Anarchist Galli* (Musée National d'Art Moderne, Paris). A painting of 1913, *Soldats en Marche* (collection Galerie Louis Carré, Paris) is more specifically Futurist (Pl. 91B). Here the composition is established by a series of vigorous diagonal 'lines of force', which indicate the forward motion of the marching soldiers; the subject-matter also is one which would have appealed to the Futurists who constantly exalted the virility and healthiness of war. It is interesting to compare this painting with contemporary works by Balla, such as his painting of a *Speeding Automobile* (Museum of Modern Art, New York). While in the work of Balla the diagonal, wedge-shaped force lines become more jagged and pointed as they progress towards the edges of the canvas, in order to give a sense of increasing velocity, in Villon's painting the marching motion is arrested by a strong counteracting diagonal at the extreme right of the composition. Villon's art remains more controlled and withdrawn than that of the Futurists, and his insistence on the more formal, classical aspects of painting gives his art of this period a place half way between Futurism and Cubism. In his work of 1914, however, Villon reverted to a highly coloured Cubistic form of expression (Pl. 92).

At the time of the *Section d'Or* exhibition, Duchamp-Villon, the third of the brothers, was the most active of the sculptors attached to the Cubist movement; a review of the *Salon d'Automne* of 1913 stated that, 'the principal exponent of Cubist sculpture is Duchamp-Villon.'[1] In actual fact, in 1912 no truly Cubist sculpture existed except for the bronze head by Picasso and the experimental constructions which he and Braque were executing to supplement their researches into pictorial form and space. However, by 1911 several sculptors were developing styles which corresponded to the Cubists' shift towards a more sober, formal kind of painting. The names of the four sculptors, Brancusi, Agero, Archipenko and Duchamp-Villon became associated in a general way with those of the Cubist painters who were exhibiting at the advanced *Salons*. All these sculptors had been influenced to a certain extent by tribal art or by other primitive and archaic forms of sculpture, and their work had in common an insistence on large, simple and clearly defined volumes.[2] Archipenko, who by 1910 was already employing a very simple and vigorous form of stylization in his work, showed at the Brussels exhibition in 1911 where Apollinaire accepted the name 'Cubists' on behalf of the exhibitors.[3] Both Archipenko and Agero showed at the *Section d'Or*. Little is known of Agero's work of this period, but on 24 January 1912 *Paris Journal* referred to a portrait of Braque executed under the influence of tribal sculpture. Shortly after the exhibition in the *Galerie de la Boétie* had closed, Archipenko declared formally to the press that he had broken completely with the Cubists whose principles he rejected.[4] Brancusi never became involved with the Cubists, and his work of this period was related to that of Archipenko and Duchamp-Villon only in its basic simplicity.

[1]Review by Henri Revers, *Paris Journal*, 14 November 1913.

[2]As early as 1906 Derain had begun to execute sculptures in stone under the combined influences of Gauguin and ethnic art. Salmon, in *La Jeune Peinture Française*, which was written before the war, although it did not appear until 1919, wrote: 'En sculpture comme en peinture l'influence d'André Derain est chaque jour plus sensible', p. 85.

[3]See pp. 80–9 above.

[4]*Gil Blas*, 14 December 1912. See p. 21 above.

Duchamp-Villon's early sculpture was purely naturalistic, but after 1910 his work became increasingly simple and stylized. The Cubistic phase of his sculpture reached a climax in a series of bas-reliefs which he showed at the *Salon d'Automne* of 1913, and which showed the influence of Archipenko. In one of the bas-reliefs, *l'Amour* (one cast is in the Museum of Modern Art, New York and another in Paris), the puppet-like figures have been distorted and reduced to a few bold and suggestive shapes, while all the subtlety of modelling which could still be found in his earlier work was suppressed. Just as the Cubist painters had revolted against the Impressionists' concern with fleeting and momentary appearances, so sculptors like Duchamp-Villon, Archipenko and Brancusi were reacting against over-elaborate surface modelling and the ephemeral effects of light, which Rodin and Medardo Rosso had introduced into sculpture. Duchamp-Villon, asked by the review *Montjoie* to comment on the sculptures shown at the *Salon d'Automne* of 1913, said: 'Unfortunately they almost all belong to the domain of modelling, so removed from that of sculpture.'[1]

Le Cheval (Museum of Modern Art, New York), Duchamp-Villon's most important single sculpture, which was executed in 1914 from studies begun in the previous year, shows that his work, like that of his brothers, had affinities with Futurism. Even in the preliminary *maquette* which is now in the Gemeente Museum in Amsterdam, the anatomy of the horse is reduced to semi-mechanical forms which serve to give a sense of power and strength. The finished work is more abstract, and the machine-like quality of the forms has been deliberately exaggerated. The spatial effects that Duchamp-Villon uses are Futurist, too: the hind quarters of the animal, for example, are treated in terms of spiral forms which seem to bore their way into the interior structure of the horse. During June of 1913 the *Galerie de la Boétie* held an exhibition of Futurist sculptures by Boccioni, and Duchamp-Villon must have been influenced by what he saw there. As opposed to the sculpture of Boccioni, however, in Duchamp-Villon's work there is no feeling of solid forms being decomposed by motion or light. Nevertheless, a letter written by Duchamp-Villon to Walter Pach at this time is a purely Futurist statement: 'The power of the machine imposes itself, and we can scarcely conceive living beings any more without it. We are strangely moved by the rapid

[1]*Montjoie*, November–December 1913.

brushing by of men and things, and accustom ourselves without knowing it to perceive the forces of the former through the forces they dominate. From that to an opinion of life in which it appears to us simply under its form of higher dynamism, there is only a step, which is quickly made.'[1] (Pl. 96).

At the time of the *Section d'Or* exhibition, however, Duchamp-Villon's major work was the façade which he designed for the *Maison Cubiste* at the *Salon d'Automne* of 1912. In 1910 the *Salon d'Automne* had included a large exhibition of decorative art from Munich, and the superiority of the Germans in this field had led the President of the *Salon*, Franz Jourdain, to launch an appeal asking French artists to take a greater interest in the applied arts. The call was answered by André Mare, a young painter whom Léger had known at the Académie Julian (they did their military service together) and with whom he shared a studio until 1908. Mare persuaded Duchamp-Villon, who was interested in architecture, to co-operate with him in the project for a *Maison Cubiste*. Mare himself was in charge of the interior decoration. The 'house' was decorated with paintings and wall panels by Jacques Villon, La Fresnaye, Marie Laurencin and Paul Vera and other *Section d'Or* painters. Both Villon and Vera were working in a Cubist idiom, but others like Laurencin were never more than peripheral figures in the movement. Marie Laurencin had been influenced by Picasso's Negroid work, and later adapted some of the devices of Cubism to her own decorative and feminine style, but her work was included in the Cubist exhibitions and manifestations mainly because she was a friend of Apollinaire, who was devoted to her and was anxious to encourage her as much as possible. Other artists who worked on the *Maison Cubiste*, like Ribbemont-Dessaignes and the sculptor Desvalliers, had nothing at all to do with Cubism. Judging from photographs, the general effect of the interiors was decidedly un-Cubist, and must have been reminiscent of earlier *art nouveau* ensembles executed by the Nabis for the theatrical productions of Lugné-Poë and Paul Fort in the 1890s. Warnod complained of the over-elaborate colour schemes and the general feeling of unnecessary complication.[2] The façade

[1]This letter of 16 January 1913 is quoted, in an English translation, in Pach's *Queer Thing, Painting*, New York 1938, p. 145, and again in an abridged form and in a different translation in the catalogue to the exhibition of works by the Duchamp brothers, organized by the Guggenheim Museum and the Museum of Fine Arts, Houston, 1957. The second, later, version is used here.
[2]*Comoedia*, 20 October 1912.

itself was basically perfectly traditional. It consisted of a flat wall, subdivided symmetrically by the openings of the door and windows, and surmounted by a small pitched roof. The only novelty lay in the heavy, angular, rather mannerist decoration that was applied in large quantities around the door and windows. Unfortunately the project was not completed in time for the opening of the exhibition, so that it was not noticed much by the critics in their reviews;[1] and shortly after the opening of the *Salon d'Automne* all critical attention was focused on the *Section d'Or'*.

These manifestations of 1912, while they demonstrated the existence of a powerful new movement, also served to show how divergent the aims of the self-styled Cubists had become. Apollinaire attempted to clarify the situation in a lecture entitled 'Le Cubisme Ecartelé', which he delivered at the *Galerie de la Boétie* on 12 October 1912, a few days after the opening of the *Section d'Or*.[2] He distinguished four types of Cubism; two of these, 'Scientific' Cubism and 'Orphic' Cubism, he felt to be pure developments. Scientific Cubism Apollinaire defined as 'the art of painting new structures out of elements borrowed not from the reality of sight, but from the reality of insight'.[3] The artists whom Apollinaire placed in this category were Picasso, Braque, Metzinger, Gleizes, Laurencin and Gris, that is to say (if one excepts Marie Laurencin), the painters who were working in a Cubist style. About Orphic Cubism Apollinaire was slightly vaguer, but he implies that its goal is abstraction and its purpose is to convey some sort of absolute truth. The artists in whom Apollinaire saw Orphist tendencies were simply those whom he sensed were breaking away from Cubism as it had been originally created by Picasso and Braque. These artists were Delaunay, Léger, Picabia and Marcel Duchamp. Picasso was placed in this category too, but only because of his use of light, and (one suspects) because Apollinaire realized his importance and could not bear to exclude him from any significant new movement. A third category, Physical Cubism, was invented to cover the work of all the peripheral figures who were working in a more naturalistic idiom but who belonged to Cubism because of the 'discipline' they showed in the construction of

[1]Apollinaire commented only on the sense of comfort which the interior of the *Maison Cubiste* gave. *L'Intransigeant*, 30 September 1912.

[2]See p. 16 above.

[3]*Les Peintres Cubistes*, p. 24.

their work. A fourth denomination, Instinctive Cubism, is applied to artists whose inspiration was not drawn from visual reality, and whose work was related to that of the Orphists, but lacked lucidity and any definite aesthetic principles. At first one might be tempted to think that Apollinaire was referring to painters like Kandinsky, who were formulating an abstract style of their own, but he goes on to say that this movement had already spread throughout Europe, and in a note at the end of *Les Peintres Cubistes* he generously extends the term to cover all the developments in twentieth-century painting from Fauvism to Futurism.

The term Orphism was originally invented by Apollinaire to describe the most recent development in Delaunay's art. The paintings by Delaunay that so impressed Apollinaire were a series of canvases which Delaunay brought back from the Valley of the Chevreuse where he had spent the summer of 1912, and which he called *Fenêtres*. These paintings by Delaunay did in fact mark the beginning of a new phase in his art which broke fundamentally with the principles of Cubism proper. Delaunay later came to feel that the series marked the beginning of the 'constructive' phase in his art which he opposed to the 'destructive' or Cubist period which preceded them; in his notebooks he wrote: 'The *Fenêtres* belong to a whole series which really initiates my artistic career.'

Delaunay had begun his artistic career as a Divionist painter, and as a student had read Chevreul and Rood on the theory of colour. Now, with the *Fenêtres*, colour once again became the principle element of his art. In some notes on painting written in the autumn of 1912 and published in the December issue of *Soirées de Paris* under the heading 'Réalité, Peinture Pure', Delaunay tried to make his position clear.[1] He stressed the importance of El Greco and 'certain English painters' (presumably Turner and Constable) whose interest in light had anticipated the researches of the Impressionists. The work of the Impressionists, Delaunay continues, was carried to its logical conclusions by Seurat, whose importance could not be overemphasized, since, 'out of light (he) extracted the contrast of complementaries'. On the laws of complementary colours Delaunay based all his own art. His own aesthetic, he goes on to say, differed from that of Seurat and the Divisionists in that, while they used colour contrasts as a technique to record their vision of nature, for him the painting of light had become an

[1]The article was published with an introductory note by Apollinaire.

end in itself. And while the Impressionists and Divisionists had covered their canvases with small strokes or dots of colour which were intended to be blended by the eye of the spectator, Delaunay conceived of a type of painting in which the colours used to produce a sensation of light would not blend but would retain their separate identities; by their interaction these colours could furthermore be made to produce a sensation of depth and movement. Since movement implies duration, time was also an element of this new art. Using the terminology of Chevreul, Delaunay called these colour contrasts 'simultaneous' to distinguish them from the colour contrasts used by the Impressionists and their successors, which were 'binary' and tended to fuse together when seen at a distance.[1]

Delaunay's writings are, unfortunately, illogical and contradictory, so that one is forced to reinterpret them in the light of his paintings. For example, in 'Réalité, Peinture Pure' he stresses the importance of studying nature, and talks about the necessity of a subject in painting, but presumably he felt (as Apollinaire did) that his own work was 'pure' painting because it was tending towards abstraction. Light and reality were for some reason inexplicably related to each other in his mind, and for this reason he felt that his art was an art of realism. Nevertheless, Delaunay would have been the first to admit that the kind of metaphysical reality he was striving for in his work had no connection with the realism of Cubism as it was created by Picasso and Braque. Writing of this period in his notebooks, Delaunay described the new developments in his art in a much simpler way; 'at this moment, towards 1912, I had the idea of a painting which would be based technically only on colour, on contrasts of colour, but developing in time and being perceived simultaneously. I used Chevreul's scientific term "simultaneous contrasts".'

Although the *Fenêtres* do mark a new departure in painting, looked at in retrospect Delaunay's evolution seems perfectly logical. With the series of *Eiffel Tower* paintings, begun in 1910, Delaunay had broken with traditional perspective and had investigated the possibilities of a new pictorial space. By his dislocation of objects he had also produced a sensation of movement in his paintings. Next, in the *Villes* he had submitted himself to a more purely Cubist

[1]The work of Chevreul that Delaunay read was *De la Loi du Contraste Simultané des Couleurs*, a book which was first published in 1839; a revised edition appeared in 1889. The chapter from which Delaunay seems to have derived his theories is entitled 'Définition du Contraste Simultané'.

discipline by virtually abandoning colour and organizing his canvases in terms of small planes or shapes arranged in shallow depth. The last of these paintings had become increasingly abstract and difficult to read; in them touches of bright colour were introduced in a tentative way. The paintings executed at Laon, although they are some of his most nearly Cubist works, lie somewhat outside the main stream of Delaunay's development. However, at this time, colour reasserted itself strongly in his art, and he abandoned the chequered, square brush-strokes he had used in the *Villes*. The *Villes de Paris*, as has been seen, was an attempt to incorporate all the researches of the previous years into a monumental *Salon* piece. The *Fenêtres* which represent the next step in his development are simply a reinterpretation of the earlier *Villes* in terms of brilliant colours, and without the Divisionist brush-strokes. The rainbow-like effects produce a new sense of light and transparency, as Delaunay had intended that they should, and there is a greater sense of depth and movement; these canvases, however, are still composed of a series of small, flat or tilted, interlocking planes. This serves to relate them, superficially at least, to the canvases of Picasso and Braque of the period between 1910 and 1912. Indeed, at first glance, the paintings of the *Fenêtres* series look like brilliantly coloured Cubism (Pl. 79).

However, if in the last of the *Villes* the subject-matter had become of secondary importance, in many of the *Fenêtres* it counts for almost nothing at all. In almost all the paintings of the series the Eiffel Tower can be seen in the background, in the centre of the composition, and some of the larger paintings of the series show ferris-wheels and houses as well, but these forms are used by Delaunay merely as the starting-point for the break-up of the picture surface in terms of transparent, interacting coloured shapes. The real subject-matter of these paintings is, as Delaunay himself said, light itself. Nevertheless, despite Delaunay's interest in colour theory, his approach remained to a large extent intuitive and empirical, and the disposition of colours in the *Fenêtres* is not governed by any very rigid system, although there is generally a careful balancing of the parts of the spectrum. In the example in the Guggenheim Museum, Delaunay uses the three primary colours (blue, yellow and a pinky-red) and three secondary colours (purple, orange and green), but they are not placed on the canvas in a logical order; they are not arranged according to the spectrum, neither is there a systematic juxtaposition of complementaries. A long horizontal *Fenêtre* in the

Gallatin Collection in the Philadelphia Museum of Art, is divided into three sections, the first predominantly yellow, the second blue and the third red, but each of these basic areas is broken by planes of various different colours that are introduced in a spontaneous and instinctive fashion. The earth colours and blacks of the *Villes*, however, are completely discarded.

The *Fenêtres* broke the balance between abstraction and representation that Cubism had always sought to maintain. The next stage in Delaunay's development is represented by a series of paintings mostly executed at Louveciennes in the first half of 1913, and which are all composed of circular motifs inspired by celestial bodies. Despite their astronomical appearance, these paintings have no real subject-matter, and Delaunay himself regarded them as 'non-figurative'. With the circular forms Delaunay was able to achieve a greater sense of movement, and he felt, furthermore, that they enabled him to eliminate the last vestiges of any linear element from his art. Line, he felt, was detrimental to the free interaction of colour. On the other hand, these paintings still had a 'faceted' appearance that related them to his more Cubist work, and Delaunay was dissatisfied, too, with the gradations which he had to employ to achieve a transition from one area to another. Later in the year he produced his first *Simultaneous Disk* (presaged by a spectral disk on the floor of one of his *Saint Séverins*), a round terra-cotta plaque covered with concentric bands of bright, unmodelled colour, and almost immediately he began to introduce these harder, disk-like forms into his paintings as well. With these works the final break with Cubism was completed. (Pl. 80B.)

Apollinaire classified Léger as an Orphist, both in the lecture that he gave at the *Galerie de la Boétie* and in his review of the *Salon des Indépendants* of 1913,[1] in which he tried to promote and organize the new movement which he had invented. Léger and Delaunay had worked together closely during the previous years, and during 1913 it is true that in certain aspects, Léger's art, like that of Delaunay, was becoming more abstract. On the other hand, the fundamental differences between the painters were also becoming more apparent. Whereas Delaunay was evolving a lyrical and poetic kind of painting with a hazy, illogical aesthetic, Léger's aims were much more concrete and realistic. And while Delaunay

[1] *L'Intransigeant*, 18 March 1913.

indulged in metaphysical speculation, Léger was primarily concerned with creating a form of painting that reflected modern life. In one of the two lectures which he deliverd at the Académie Wassilief at this time Léger said, 'we have never been more truly realist or more tied to our times than we are today.'[1] This is a point which he stressed again and again. Modern life, he felt, differed from that of other periods in that it was swifter, more compressed, and more complicated than anything that had preceded it. These qualities could best be captured by a more dynamic, vigorous and abstract form of art: 'The modern concept is not thus a passing abstraction valid for a few initiates only; it is the total expression of a new generation whose requirements it reflects and whose every aspiration it answers.'[2]

Léger's thought was clearly influenced by the theories and propaganda of the Futurists. He constantly refers to the dynamic quality of modern life; he praises the new, swift means of locomotion and derides the ridiculous reactionaries who wish to preserve the landscape by forbidding the erection of large, commercial posters along the highways. Like the Futurists, and in opposition to the Cubists, Léger expresses his admiration for the Impressionists. 'The Impressionists', he insisted, 'are the great innovators of the modern movement.'[3] However, his attitude differed from that of the Futurists in many respects. Whereas they had approved of the Impressionists because they had concerned themselves with a representation of contemporary life in a lively and direct way, Léger, on the contrary, felt that their importance lay in the fact that they had taken the first step towards a kind of painting in which formal, pictorial values predominated, while the subject itself was only of secondary importance: 'The Impressionists were the first to reject *the absolute value of the subject* and to consider its *value as relative*.'[4] Delaunay admired the Impressionists, too, but only because their canvases produced a sensation of light. While Léger sympathized with the Futurists in their glorification of contemporary life, he was untouched by their highly romantic and literary approach. He was anxious to produce a painting that would reflect the modernity and vitality of his age, but he felt that this could best be

[1]'Les Réalisations Picturales Actuelles'.
[2]'Les Origines de la Peinture et sa Valeur Représentative'.
[3]Ibid.
[4]Ibid.

achieved by the creation of a more abstract style, and not simply by the painting of movement in a schematic way or by the adoption of mechanical or up-to-date subject-matter: 'modern mechanical achievements such as colour photography, the cinema, the profusion of more or less popular novels, the vulgarization of theatres, efficiently replace and render from now on completely useless, in pictorial art, the development of the visual, sentimental, representational and popular subject.'[1] Léger's art thus remained more visual than that of the Futurists, and the problems with which he concerned himself were, in the last analysis, purely pictorial. Finally, to the intense chauvinism of the Futurists he opposed the concept of a new, universal pictorial idiom.

Léger repeatedly stressed the fact that his was an art of realism; so did the Cubists and the Futurists, and, for that matter, so did Delaunay. The Cubists aimed at an art that was anti-naturalistic but representational. They were intent on interpreting the world around them in new pictorial terms; their vision was untouched by any literary or romantic considerations, and they ignored all forms of metaphysical speculation. The Futurists, on the other hand, felt that they were realists because their work reflected the most up-to-date aspects of life in the twentieth century; in actual fact, their outlook, like that of all anarchists, was highly emotional and over-coloured. Delaunay saw himself as a realist simply because he felt that his work embodied a higher metaphysical truth than that of other painters. While in some of his work of 1913 and 1914 Léger moved away from Cubism, his claim to realism was more justified than that of either Delaunay or the Futurists. Unlike the Futurists, his view of contemporary life was objective and unromantic, and unlike Delaunay, even at his most abstract, he was concerned with relating his art to external reality by his conscious attempt to parallel the sense of immediacy and directness of modern life in his own paintings. And while at this period in his career Léger was advocating a more abstract form of expression he never excluded all the representational possibilities of art. He was to prove, too, the underlying realism of his vision by the fact that total abstraction satisfied him only for very brief periods.

The concrete, forthright nature of Léger's aesthetic was reflected in his paintings. In the years before 1913, Léger had evolved a type of painting which was

[1]Ibid.

based on a system of pictorial contrasts. A few bright colours had been juxtaposed, representational elements had been contrasted with abstract elements, solid forms with flat forms and curving or rounded shapes with angular ones. Now, during 1913, Léger produced a series of paintings which he called simply *Contrastes de Formes* (or, occasionally, *éléments géométriques*) in which the representational element is completely absent. Contemporary with these paintings, however, and closely related to them, are others which have specific subjects, although even these paintings are less immediately legible than most of Léger's work that had preceded them. The *Contrastes de Formes* are composed of contrasting shapes, some cylindrical and solid, others flat and angular; some are large and others small. All are outlined boldly in black, and are brightly coloured, generally in primary colours. There is no consistent source of illumination, but the use of vigorous white highlights enhances the solidity of the cylindrical and tubular mechanical shapes. These contrasts produce a dynamic sense of movement which was one of the aims of Léger's art; as opposed to the Futurists, however, Léger achieves this sensation by purely pictorial means, and never resorts to the device of showing a solid form in successive stages of movement. The more figurative paintings of the period are treated in exactly the same way; indeed, the *Soirées de Paris* of August 1914 reproduced a painting of Léger's of a seated woman, which had as a subtitle, *application des contrastes au sujet*. Despite the fact that the *Contrastes* are some of the most exciting of all early non-figurative works, ultimately their importance for Léger lay in the fact that they convinced him that, like Picasso, Braque and Gris, he was interested above all in the dialogue between representation and abstraction. The *Contrastes* all seem to belong to 1913. By 1914 he had returned to his earlier subject-matter while broadening his iconography in works like *L'Escalier* (Pls. 74, 75).

While Léger's experiments in abstraction were related to his more representational work, and while his art continued to have a starting point in visual reality, Delaunay, on the other hand, during 1913 had developed a completely abstract form of painting which had no connection whatsoever with the external world. Disagreements began to arise between the two painters. Léger had always been more interested in the representation of three-dimensional forms and in linear design than Delaunay had, and in his second lecture at the Académie Wassilief[1] he specifically stated that he thought it wrong for painters to rely only on the interaction of colouristic elements to produce their effects. Léger felt that the work of Delaunay and his followers was simply an extension of the theories of Neo-Impressionism, and in his lecture he went on to say that their style was not suited to paintings of large proportions such as they had shown at the *Indépendants* of 1914: 'It is what I would call additive painting as opposed to multiplicative painting.' The term 'multiplicative' Léger applied to his own work in which he stressed the importance of line and solid form as well as that of colour. Delaunay, infatuated with colour, complained that Léger was developing along the wrong lines. In his notebooks, under the reproduction of one of his *Disks*, he noted: 'influence on Léger, who didn't understand its influence. (Here) colour *is* drawing. There is no drawing with colour applied over it, as there is in Léger, as well as in Cormon and the rest.'

In retrospect, and particularly in the light of their subsequent developments, it becomes clear that the aims of both these artists, Léger and Delaunay, were never quite those of the pure Cubists, Picasso, Braque and Gris. Like these three painters, and independently of them, in his paintings of 1909 and 1910 Léger had purged his art of all inessentials and had tackled squarely the problem of creating a more classical, structural sort of art, in which simple volumes played the leading role. But the sense of movement implicit in his *Nus*, the vigorous foreshortening of the poses, the very subject itself, indicated that Léger's talent and aesthetic were of a more dynamic, less subtle and personal nature than theirs. And despite their complexity, his most purely Cubist works, paintings like *La Femme en Bleu* (Pl. 73), remained in a sense less sophisticated and more easily accessible than the contemporary work of Picasso and Braque. What he admired in their Cubism was the dismissal of what he, too, felt to be outmoded pictorial conventions. It has been seen how through their example he was led to break with traditional perspective. This gave him the freedom to manipulate pictorial forms in a new, more abstract, highly dynamic and original way, and eventually to evoke the spatial and formal sensations that enabled him to adapt his art to what he felt were the needs of twentieth-century society. In his painting there is always a feeling for the reality and significance of objects that derives,

[1]'Les Réalisations Picturales Actuelles'.

ultimately, from Cubist aesthetic. Delaunay, on the other hand, despite his pretensions to establishing a universally significant art form, remained a much more purely subjective painter. The earliest painting of his pre-Cubist phases already showed that colour, which was only one of the many pictorial factors that concerned the Cubists, was to be the all-important factor in his art. From the Cubists he learned how to organize a painting independently of perspectival considerations, and when he began to re-introduce pure, prismatic colours into his work, he came to feel almost at once that Cubism was merely the starting point for a more lyrical, more abstract kind of painting. He slipped almost imperceptibly, but very quickly, into the formalism and abstraction that the Cubists had been aware of but had deliberately avoided. His *Villes* and his *Laon* paintings can justifiably be called Cubist, but by 1913 he had made a complete break with Cubist aesthetic. While by 1914 Léger, like Delaunay, had moved away from Cubism in his abstractions, in most of his work he remained as close to Cubism, both in technique and in spirit, as he had been for the past four years.

So, although Cubism was daily making new converts, of the original painters who had launched Cubism as a movement only Gleizes and Metzinger continued to work in a strictly Cubist style. By 1913 Metzinger had fallen completely under the artistic domination of Gris, and during the following year he followed Gris' development in so far as he was capable of doing so. Gleizes in 1913 had begun to feel the influence of Gris, and also that of Delaunay, although he continued to refer to Léger's earlier Cubist work as well. Both painters occasionally introduced lettering and stencilled numbers into their paintings, but always in a literal or representational way, and never with any true understanding of what had led Picasso and Braque to do so. What is most remarkable is that in the period before the war, of the Cubist painters only Picasso, Braque and Gris made any extensive use of *collage* and *papier collé*. In 1909, 1910 and 1911 Léger and, to a lesser extent, Delaunay, had submitted themselves to an intense pictorial discipline and in this their Cubism was related to that of Picasso and Braque, but both saw in Cubism only the starting-point or the means towards a very different art. When they had extracted what they thought was most important from Cubism, they passed on to something else. Gleizes and Metzinger, less gifted and original painters, appreciated intellectually the significance of Cubism, and produced valid and important documents for the visual history of the time. After the war both painters continued to follow developments in Cubism and its offshoots, but by 1914 when Cubism was widely known, they had ceased to have any great importance within the movement. And they and other, more academic representatives of the style could not stand out against the disruptive influences, both personal and artistic, which the war was to produce.

CONCLUSION

'One can already foresee the approaching day when the term Cubism will have no more than a nominative value to designate in the history of painting certain researches carried out by painters between 1907–14.' So Blaise Cendrars wrote in 1919 in an article entitled 'Le Cube s'effrite'.[1] To the majority of people this obituary of Cubism must have seemed rather premature. For Cubism, it was obvious, had survived the war. Léonce Rosenberg, the dealer who had temporarily taken over Kahnweiler's role as the chief patron and supporter of the movement, had by 1919 presented at his *Galerie de L'Effort Moderne* large one-man exhibitions by five well-known Cubists, and was busily encouraging newcomers to the school.[2] Exhibitions by Picasso and by Severini, who had by this time abandoned Futurism in favour of a purely Cubist idiom, were scheduled for the following year. Then, in January 1920, a second exhibition of the *Section d'Or* was held at the *Galerie de la Boétie* with the intention of demonstrating the continued vitality and coherence of the movement.[3] Almost all the Cubists, with the important exception of Picasso, showed at the *Salon des Indépendants* of this same year. After the opening Gris was able to write to Kahnweiler: 'the *Salon des Indépendants* opened with something of a success for the Cubists, who were taken

[1]In *La Rose Rouge*, no. 3, 15 May 1919.

[2]By 1919 there had been exhibitions of Braque, Léger, Metzinger, Herbin and Gris. Rosenberg had also shown Laurens and was planning a Hayden exhibition, two new recruits to Cubism.

[3]Yet a third exhibition called *La Section d'Or* was held at the Galerie Vavin Raspail in 1925.

seriously by the whole – or almost – of the press. Even Monsieur Vauxcelles admits that he has wronged us.'[1]

But if at the end of the war Cubist activity was resumed on a large scale, the character of the movement was deeply changed. The great revolutionary days were past. In art, as in politics, things which had seemed outrageous in 1914 were accepted almost without a murmur in 1919. As far as Cubism goes, this is proved by the fact that Vauxcelles, who before the war had been its bitterest opponent, was now able, as Gris noted, to look at it in a more detached and objective way. And in fact, as Kahnweiler has pointed out in his book on Gris, the united front presented by the Cubists in 1920 was not based on any very solid foundations. Gleizes, who was one of the organizers of the 1920 *Section d'Or* and had seen the exhibition as a conscious attempt to revive the spirit and principles of pre-war Cubism, was forced to admit that it served only to show how 'the idea (of Cubism) as it developed had burst the tidy envelope of the *word* Cubism'.[2]

As a movement, then, Cubism had lost the quality of unity and concentration which had made it seem so vital and revolutionary in the years before the war. During the war most of the painters were physically separated from each other, and many of them were temporarily forced to abandon their work.[3] When they were able to resume their normal lives they found that they had lost a sense of continuity in their art. Some, like Braque, hesitated for a while before recovering their sense of direction. Others, like Gleizes and Villon, were immediately drawn towards a more abstract form of expression. For a few painters, such as Léger for example, the war itself provided an intense and positive experience that had an immediate and lasting effect on their artistic development. Then those artists who, like Picasso and Gris, had been in a position to keep Cubism alive during the war, had been forced to work in comparative isolation, and this had served to accentuate the differences between them. New figures, most notably the two sculptors Laurens and Lipchitz, were giving the style a new interpretation.

Nevertheless, although after 1918 Cubism was more diffuse than it had been

[1] *The Letters of Juan Gris*, p. 75. Letters of 31 January 1920. Kahnweiler was in Switzerland.

[2] 'L'Epopée' in *Le Rouge et le Noir*, June-July 1929.

[3] Léger, Braque, Gleizes (very briefly), Marcoussis, Metzinger, Jacques Villon and Duchamp-Villon were in the army as were La Fresnaye, Lhote and the majority of the peripheral figures who had been attached to the movement.

four years earlier, it is dangerous to overestimate the part played by the war in the disintegration of the school. During 1913 and 1914 Picasso and Braque had already been moving apart stylistically. Gris was asserting himself more and more as an individual artist who was giving the style a different emphasis. In his *Contrastes de Formes*, Léger's researches into the pictorial properties and possibilities of form had reached a point of individuality that placed them outside any category. The Orphism of Delaunay was growing steadily further away from its parent movment. La Fresnaye, who had in any case never been a central figure in the movement, had fallen under the influence of Delaunay and was moving out of the Cubist orbit. Jacques Villon and more especially Duchamp-Villon had amalgamated some of the principles of Cubism with some of the aesthetic of Futurism. By 1914 both Marcel Duchamp and Picabia, whose allegiance to Cubism had in any case always been rather doubtful, were completely Dada in spirit. Lhote and a large number of painters like him, who were referred to as 'Cubist', had really only seized on the most superficial aspects of the style and were using them to create an up-to-date academicism; indeed, applied to their work, Vauxcelles' definition of Cubism as 'an offensive return to the academy' was apt enough.

It is true that as the original nucleus of the movement was breaking up, the style was constantly attracting new figures. By 1914 a host of minor painters, many of whom have long since been forgotten, had become Cubist or had been touched in a positive fashion by the movement. These were the painters who were, perhaps, most affected by the war. For like Gleizes and Metzinger and the other minor Cubist figures, it was they who felt the conscious need to be part of an organized, revolutionary movement. When the major Cubists were physically separated by the war and Paris was temporarily abandoned as the home of the artistic *avant-garde*, Cubism lost the impetus that was necessary to sustain the efforts of the lesser artists. After the painters were able to reassemble again, new forces were making themselves felt; many artists experienced a sense of disillusion and disorientation that prevented them from taking up where they had left off. Although much pre-war Cubism had a strong intellectual flavour, its origin had been notably unscientific; it offered no hard and fast rules, no signposts to artistic security and success. Many of the lesser painters began to search for some definite pictorial certainty in the realms of abstraction or in coldly didactic movements such as Purism. Others turned to forms of expression more suited to an emotional and disturbed state of mind. The fact that Picasso, who was still generally regarded as the central figure of the Cubist movement, was working in a naturalistic as well as in a Cubist idiom must have made many people doubtful about the future of the style. In short, Cubism no longer held out the possibilities of a universal pictorial idiom.

And although even before 1914 Cubism had spread with unprecedented rapidity to almost every part of the Western world, it was never to become an international style. For, just as many of the painters who had been originally attached to the school used Cubism as a point of departure for the realization of totally different ends, so artists in Holland, Russia and Germany reinterpreted, indeed occasionally even misinterpreted Cubism to found a whole succession of schools and pictorial idioms that were completely divorced from its ideals. This, it has been seen, was exactly what had been done first of all by the Futurists when they had seen in the pictorial techniques evolved by the Cubists the means of expressing their own violent ideologies. By 1914 abstraction was already a force in European art, and during the war more and more painters became attracted to it. An increasing number of artists, painters like Mondrian, Malevitch, Rodchenko, and even at one point, it appeared, Klee, had come to see in Cubism only the first step towards a completely abstract form of painting.

It is easy to understand how such an interpretation could be placed on Cubism. With Cubism, painting had become further removed from ordinary visual appearances than ever before; the Cubist painters were acutely aware of the formal or abstract side of their art. And we have already seen how from an interest in reducing objects and figures to their simplest basic forms, Léger had passed on to an interest in those forms for their own sake, endowing them with a life and independent existence of their own. Delaunay, by introducing what was really a traditional use of colour (as opposed to a Cubist use of it) into Cubist painting, had become fascinated by the spatial and formal interaction between planes of pure colour, and had soon come to feel that there was no need for a subject, since these formal problems were really the theme of his art. Mondrian, without entering deeply into the spirit and significance of Cubism, had seized at once on the methods of composition evolved by the Cubists, and fascinated by the technical innovations in the work of Picasso and Léger (whom, as he himself admitted, he most admired) he embarked on a series of exciting experiments that resulted eventually in the aesthetic of *De Stijl*.

The fact that Cubism gave birth to so much abstract art may be one of the reasons why it was so often misunderstood by the public, and even occasionally by serious critics and historians. Cubism, it must be stressed again, was an art of realism, and it was as far removed from abstraction as from, for instance, Futurism. All the true Cubists had at one time or another come near to complete abstraction, but each of them had almost immediately retracted and reasserted the representational element of their art. After the Cadaquès paintings Picasso produced the comparatively legible portrait of Kahnweiler, and devised a system of pictorial 'keys' that would render his paintings more accessible to the spectator. When in the winter of 1911–12 Braque's fascination with the tactile qualities of pictorial space had resulted in a complicated, highly hermetic group of paintings, he hastily reverted to a more comprehensible idiom. In 1915 Gris' dissatisfaction with the descriptive quality of much of his earlier work led him to produce the most abstract of all his works, a still life (now in a private collection in Paris) in which it is impossible to reconstruct with any certainty the nature of most of the objects that compose it; this painting, however, did not solve the problems he was facing and remained an isolated phenomenon in his work. It was in his *Contrastes de Formes* that Léger first detached himself from Cubist aesthetic, although he paralleled these paintings with other, more figurative work, and soon abandoned abstraction altogether. Indeed, it is perhaps not altogether fortuitous that the naturalistic portraits executed by Picasso in the second half of 1915 were more or less contemporary with some of his most hermetic Cubist canvases since those done at Cadaquès five years earlier.

But whatever the future of the movement might have been if it had not been for the war, it is certainly true that by 1914 the fundamental principles of Cubism had been established and all the most important discoveries and innovations had been made. To the system of perspective which had governed European painting since the Renaissance the Cubists had opposed the right of the painter to move freely around his subject and to incorporate into his depiction of it information gathered from previous experience or knowledge. For the first time in the history of art, space had been represented as being as real and as tangible, one might almost say as 'pictorial', as the objects which it surrounded (here one must distinguish between an Impressionistic depiction of atmosphere and the painting of empty, clear space, such as is found before Cubism only in the late work of Cézanne). While the Cubists had not denied the interrelation of colour and volume, they had formulated a means of allowing them to exist independently of each other in a single painting; that is to say they were using various pictorial elements in their simplest, purest form, allowing each to retain its separate identity while contributing at the same time to the total effect. Partly in order to solve the pictorial problems that had confronted them in their creation of a completely new pictorial idiom, and partly as a natural result of their concept of the painting as an independent organism, a constructed object with a life of its own rather than as a traditional 'work of art', the Cubists had evolved two revolutionary pictorial techniques: *papier collé* and *collage*.

Finally, in their desire to take stock afresh of the world that surrounded them, the Cubists had effectively stripped bare many of the problems that had underlain painting and sculpture since the beginning of time. Artists, except those intent only on duplicating their subject in an illusionistic way, had always been aware of the need to reconcile their representation of it with the abstract demands of the aesthetic medium in which they were working; forms must be balanced to achieve a satisfactory composition, in painting volumes in depth must be arranged to produce also a harmonious surface pattern, and so on. The outlook of the Cubists, it has been seen, was intensely realistic, and a true appreciation of their painting depends ultimately on the spectators' ability to reconstruct or identify its subject-matter. But because they were less directly conditioned by visual appearances than any other school of painting since the Renaissance, they were able to evolve more abstract pictorial and sculptural techniques to solve the problems of recreating or reinterpreting the material world through an artistic medium. Never before had the duality between representation and abstraction been so clearly stated as it was in the Cubist paintings of Picasso, Braque and Gris, in the years immediately preceding the war. In these paintings one is aware at once of the presence of an easily identifiable subject, but the eye is simultaneously stimulated by the presence of an equally obvious underlying abstract pictorial structure with which the representational elements are fused and related. Had any of the problems facing the Cubists remained unsolved before the painters were physically separated by the war, they might have found it necessary to come together again in the same spirit of co-operation that had given the movement such intensity and concentration in the pre-war years. But because the nature of the style had been so firmly established during these years preceding 1914, the history of Cubism after the war is largely the history of the artistic development of a series of individual artists who used its principles as the foundation for the creation of their own particular idioms.

In so far as Cubism was a new concept of form and space, involving new pictorial techniques, it is still alive to-day. Picasso never relinquished the right to synthesize into his subjects any amount of information or detail, gained by using a variable viewpoint, that he felt necessary to convey more forcefully his vision or ideas of them. *Guernica* is not a Cubist painting, but equally obviously it could not have come into being without Cubism behind it. In Braque's late *Ateliers* there is much the same feeling of spatial materiality and continuity as there is in the works of his classical Cubist period. At the end of his career, when Gris' work could not always be classified as strictly Cubist, he was still using a 'synthetic' Cubist procedure, working from abstraction to representation, marrying a subject to an abstract pictorial substructure. This same process was used at different times and in modified ways by Braque, Picasso and even Léger; indeed Léger, more than any other French artist of his generation, after the war was able to produce a totally independent variant of synthetic Cubism just as he adapted its earlier, analytic manifestations to such personal and original ends.

It is often easy to pinpoint the beginnings of a new artistic idiom, much harder to say when it ends. To many the death of Juan Gris in 1927 must have appeared to mark the end of the Cubist epoch. Already in 1925 Picasso had painted his great *Three Dancers* (now in the Tate Gallery), a turning point in his art almost as important as the *Demoiselles d'Avignon*; the *Three Dancers* ushered in for Picasso a phase of involvement with Surrealism, which he himself had done so much to invent. Braque's work was becoming increasingly personal and meditative. Léger, who had always been open to the aesthetic of any vital new movement, and was yet able to remain always so completely himself, had looked hard at the abstraction of *De Stijl*, had co-operated with the Purists and was now also showing an awareness of Surrealism. Yet during the succeeding decades there was not an artistic movement partaking of the modernist spirit which did not show the influence, if only indirectly, of pre-war Cubism. All the subsequent art of Picasso, Braque and Léger was informed by it, and the legacy of their late work, particularly that of the two founders of the movement, still remains to be fully assimilated and assessed. There can be no doubt that to the historian of the future Cubism will appear as one of the major turning points in the evolution of Western art, a revolution comparable in its effects to any of those which have altered the course of European art, and one which has produced a series of works capable of holding their place among the great masterpieces of the past. To-day the art itself looks as fresh and as vital as ever.

BIBLIOGRAPHY

I. UNPUBLISHED MATERIAL

Delaunay, R. *Notebooks*, written over a long period of years before his death in 1941. The most significant entries were published in 1957 under the title *Du Cubisme à l'Art Abstrait* (see general section below).

Gleizes, A. *Souvenirs*, written in the years before his death in 1953 (fragments of these memoirs relating to the Cubist period were privately published in 1957 by the Association des Amis d'Albert Gleizes, under the title *Cahiers: Albert Gleizes*).

Picasso, P. Letters to Gertrude and Leo Stein, 1906–14. In the Stein correspondence, Yale University Library.

II. NEWSPAPERS AND PERIODICALS

Important articles are listed under the author's name in the general section below

Abstraction Création, Art non-Figuratif, Paris 1932.

Action (l'), Paris, 25 February–24 March 1912; February 1920.

Art Libre (l'), Lyons, November 1910.

Autorité (l'), Paris, 27 November 1912.

Bandeaux d'Or (les), Paris, November 1911.
Blast, London 1914–15.
Bulletin de l'Effort Moderne, Paris 1924–35.
Bulletin de la Société de l'Histoire de l'Art Français, Paris 1912.
Comoedia, Paris, 27 June 1911; 30 September 1912; 13 October 1912; 18 March 1913; 1 April 1914; 15 April 1914; 2 June 1914.
Cote, Paris, 19 March 1912; 20 March 1912; 30 September 1912; 12 October1912.
Ecrits Français (les), Paris, 5 April 1914.
Elan (l'), Paris 1915–16.
Esprit Nouveau (l'), Paris 1920–5.
Excelsior, Paris, 4 March 1914.
Festin d'Esope (le), Paris, November 1903–August 1904.
Figaro (le), Paris, 20 September 1909; 24 September 1911.
Gazette des Beaux Arts, Paris, November 1910.
Gazette de la Capitale, Paris, 23 April 1911.
Gil Blas, Paris 1906–14.
Intransigeant (l'), Paris 1906–14.
Je sais tout, Paris, April 1913.
Journal, Paris, 22 March 1912.
Journal Officiel de la Chambre des Députés, Paris, 3 December 1912.
Lacerba, Florence, 1 and 15 August 1913.
Matin (le), Paris, 1 December 1913.
Mercure de France (le), Paris 1906–14.
Montjoie, Paris, February 1913–June 1914.
Nord-Sud, Paris, 1917–18.
Nouveau Spectateur (le), Paris, 25 May 1919.
Opinion (l'), Toulouse, 7 April 1912; 3 May 1913.
Paris Journal, Paris, 1906–14.
Paris Midi, Paris, 10 October 1912; 21 February 1914.
Petit Bleu, Paris, February 1912.
Petit Parisien, 19 March 1912; 30 September 1912; 30 October 1912.
Petite Gironde (la), Bordeaux, April 1912.
Poème et Drame, Paris, January 1913.
Presse (la), Paris, 1–2 October 1910.

Revue de France (la), Paris, March 1912.
Revue Française (la), Paris, June 1912.
Revue Indépendante (la), Paris, August 1911.
Rue (la), Paris, April 1911.
Section d'Or (la), Paris, 9 October 1911.
Soirées de Paris (les), Paris, February 1912–August 1914.
Sturm (der), Berlin 1910–15.
Télégramme (le), Toulouse, 5 January 1909.
Temps (le), Paris, 14 October 1912.
Vers et Prose, Paris, 1907–12.
Voce (la), Florence, 24 August 1911; 7 December 1911.

III. CATALOGUES
(of exhibitions and sales)

Only contemporary catalogues are listed below. Later catalogues containing important critical or historical material are included in the general section.

Armoury Show (International Exhibition of Modern Art), New York, 1913.
Braque, at the Galerie Kahnweiler, Paris, 9–28 November 1908.
Delaunay, at the Galerie Barbazanges, Paris, February–March 1912.
Gleizes, Metzinger, Léger at the Galerie Berthe Weill, Paris, January 1913.
Herbin, at the Galerie Moderne, Paris, March 1914.
La Fresnaye, at Galerie Levesque, Paris, April–May 1914.
Les Indépendants, Cercle d'Art, VIIIème Salon, Brussels, 10 June–3 July 1911.
Kahnweiler Sales, at the Hôtel Drouot, Paris, Part 1, June 1921; Part 2, 17 and 18 November 1921; Part 3, 4 July 1922; Part 4, 7 and 8 May 1923.
Le Salon d'Automne, Paris, 1906–14.
Le Salon des Indépendants, Paris, 1906–14.
Uhde Sale, Hôtel Drouot, Paris, 30 May 1921.

IV. GENERAL

Allard, A. 'Au Salon d'Automne de Paris', in *L'Art Libre*, Lyons, November 1910; 'Quelques Peintres', in *Les Marches du Sud-Ouest*, June 1911; 'Léger', in *Les Soirées de Paris*, Paris 1913; Preface to an exhibition of works by La Fresnaye at the Galerie Levesque, Paris, April–May 1914; 'L'Avenir de la Peinture', in *Le Nouveau Spectateur*, no. 1, Paris, May 1919; *Marie Laurencin*, Paris 1921; *R. de la Fresnaye*, Paris 1922.

Apollinaire, G. Preface to the Catalogue of the Braque Exhibition at the Galerie Kahnweiler, Paris, 9–28 November 1908; *L'Hérésiarque et Cie*, Paris 1910; 'Mes Prisons', in *Paris Journal*, Paris, 14 September 1911; Preface to the Catalogue of *Les Indépendants, Cercle d'Art*, 8me Salon, 10 June–3 July 1911, Brussels; 'Les Commencements du Cubisme', in *Le Temps*, Paris, 14 October 1912; *Les Peintres Cubistes, Méditations Esthétiques*, Paris 1913; 'Pablo Picasso', in *Montjoie*, 14 March 1913; *L'Antitradition Futuriste*, Milan and Paris 1913; 'Simultanisme, Librettisme', in *Soirées de Paris*, Paris, June 1914; 'Pablo Picasso', in *Sic*, Paris, May 1917; 'L'Esprit Nouveau et Les Poètes', *Le Mercure de France*, Paris, December 1918; *Sculptures Nègres*, Paris 1917; *Peintures de Léopold Survage*, Paris 1917 (introduction to a catalogue); *Chroniques d'Art* (1902–1918), Paris 1960; Special issue of *L'Esprit Nouveau*, Paris, 26 October 1924 (with essays by Salmon, Roche Grey, Picabia, etc.).

Aragon, L. *La Peinture au Défi*, Paris 1930.

Archipenko, A. *Sturm-Bildebücher*, Berlin 1923.

Arp, H. and Neitzel, L. H. *Neue Französische Malerei*, Leipzig 1913.

Barr, A. *Cubism and Abstract Art*, Museum of Modern Art, New York 1936; *Picasso*, Museum of Modern Art, New York 1946; *Matisse*, Museum of Modern Art, New York 1951.

Barr, A. and Soby, J. T. *Twentieth Century Italian Art*, Museum of Modern Art, New York 1949.

Barzun, H. 'Après le Symbolisme', in *Poème et Drame*, Paris, May 1913; 'Manifeste sur le Simultanisme Poétique', in *Paris Journal*, Paris, 27 June 1913.

Berger, J. *The Success and Failure of Picasso*, London 1964.

Billy, A. *Max Jacob*, Paris 1947; *Apollinaire*, Paris 1947.

Bissière, R. 'Georges Braque', in *Bulletin de l'Effort Moderne*, Paris, March 1920.

Blaue Reiter (der). Munich 1912.

Blunt, Sir A. and Pool, P. *Picasso, The Formative Years*, London, 1962.

Boccioni, U. Introduction to his exhibition of Futurist Sculpture at the *Galerie de la Boétie*, Paris, June–July 1913; 'Il Dinamismo Futurista e la Pittura Francese', in *Lacerba*, Florence, 1 August 1913; *Pittura Scultura Futuriste*, Milan 1914.

Braque, G. Special issue of *Cahiers d'Art*, nos. 1–2, Paris 1933; *Cahiers de Georges Braque*, 1917–47, Paris 1948.

Braque, Les papiers collés. Centre Georges Pompidou, Musée National d'Art Moderne, Paris 1982.

Breton, A. *Francis Picabia*, Barcelona 1922.

Breunig, L. C. 'Apollinaire et le Cubisme', in *Revue des Lettres Modernes*, no. 69–70, Paris 1962. (See also the most recent and most fully documented edition of Apollinaire's *Les Peintres Cubistes*, Paris 1965, annotated by L. C. Breunig and J. C. Chevalier).

Brielle, R. *Lhote*, Paris 1931.

Buffet-Picabia, Gabrielle. 'Some Memories of Pre-Dada, Picabia and Duchamp', in *The Dada Painters and Poets* (the Documents of Modern Art), New York 1951.

Bulletin de la Vie Artistique, Enquête sur le Cubisme, Paris 1924–5. (A questionnaire about the nature of Cubism with answers from Gleizes, Metzinger, Jacques Villon, Angel Zarraga, etc.)

Burgess, Gelett, 'The Wild Men of Paris', in *Architectural Record*, New York, May 1910.

Cabanne, P. *L'Epopée du Cubisme*, Paris 1963.

Calvesi, 'Il Futurismo di Boccioni', in *Arte Antica e Moderna*, April–June 1958.

Camòn Aznar, J. *Picasso y el Cubismo*, Madrid 1956.

Carco, F. *Du Montmartre au Quartier Latin*, Paris (?) 1929.

Carrà, C. and others. *Nous Les Peintres Futuristes*, Milan 1910 (this pamphlet is not to be confused with the more important manifestos of Futurist painting); *Guerra-Pittura*, Milan 1915; *Derain*, Rome 1924.

Carrieri, R. *Pittura, Scultura d'Avanguardia*, 1890–1950, Milan 1950; *Il Futurismo*, Milan 1961 (English edition 1963).

Cendrars, B. and Delaunay, S. T. *La Prose de Transsibérien et de la Petite de France*, Paris 1913.

Cendrars, B. 'Essai' in *La Rose Rouge*, Paris, 19 June 1919; 'Le Cube s'effrite', in *La Rose Rouge*, Paris, 15 May 1919.

Cézanne, P. 'Letters to Emile Bernard', in *Le Mercure de France*, Paris, 1 and 15 October 1907. (The letters, and Bernard's accompanying articles, later appeared as *Souvenirs sur Paul Cézanne, et Lettres*, Paris 1920.)

Chadourne, M. 'R. de la Fresnaye', in *Cahiers d'Art*, Paris 1928.

Chamot, M. 'The Early Work of Goncharova and Larionov', in *Burlington Magazine*, London, June 1955.

Chevreul, M. E. *De la Loi du Contraste Simultané des Couleurs*, Paris 1839. (A revised edition appeared in 1889).

Circi-Pellicer, A. *Picasso avant Picasso*, Geneva 1950.

Cocteau, J. 'Autour de la Fresnaye', in *L'Esprit Nouveau*, no. 3, Paris, December 1920; *André Lhote*, Paris 1920; *Picasso*, Paris 1923; *Le Rappel à l'Ordre*, Paris 1926.

Cogniat, R. 'Le Cubisme Méthodique: Léger et l'Effort Moderne', in *Amour de l'Art*, vol. 14, Paris 1933.

Cooper, D. *Braque: Paintings 1909–47*, London 1948; *Fernand Léger et le Nouvel Espace*, Geneva 1949; Preface to the Léger Exhibition at the Tate Gallery, London 1950; *Fernand Léger, Dessins de Guerre 1915–16*, Paris 1956; Catalogue to the Gris Exhibition at the Berne Kunstmuseum, October 1955–January 1956; Preface and Notes to the Braque Exhibition at the Tate Gallery, London 1956; *Fernand Léger, Contrastes de Forme, 1912–15*, Paris 1962; Catalogue to the Braque exhibition, Munich 1963; *The Cubist Epoch*, London 1971; *Juan Gris, Catalogue raisonné de l'oeuvre peint (établi avec la collaboration de Margaret Potter)*, Paris 1977.

Cooper, D. and Tinterow, Gary. *The Essential Cubism, Braque, Picasso and their Friends, 1907–1920*, Tate Gallery, London 1983.

Coquiot, G. *Cubistes Futuristes et Passéistes*, Paris 1914; *Les Indépendants 1884–1920*, Paris 1920.

Courthion, P. *André Lhote*, Paris 1926; 'Ateliers et Académies', in *Nouvelles Littéraires*, Paris, 19 November and 3 December 1932.

Les Créateurs du Cubisme. Catalogue to an exhibition at the Galerie des Beaux Arts, Paris, March 1935.

Le Cubisme 1911–18. Catalogue to an exhibition at the Galerie de France, Paris, May 1945.

Le Cubisme. Catalogue to an exhibition at the Musée d'Art Moderne, Paris, January 1953.

Daix, Pierre. *La Vie de Peintre de Pablo Picasso*, Paris 1977.

Daix, Pierre and Rosselet, Joan. *Picasso, The Cubist Years, A Catalogue Raisonné of the Paintings and Related Works*, London 1979.

Dasburg, A. 'Cubism, its Rise and Influence', in *Arts*, Vol. 4, New York 1923.

De Francia, Peter. *Fernand Léger*, London 1983.

Delaunay, R. 'Réalité Peinture Pure', in *Les Soirées de Paris*, Paris, December 1912 (Prefaced and edited by Apollinaire); Letter to H. Rouveyre (undated) published under the title of 'Elément pour l'Histoire du Cubisme', in *Art-Documents*, Geneva, January 1951 (the letter discusses Delaunay's relations with Apollinaire and the birth of Orphism); *Album*, produced in connection with an Exhibition of Delaunay's work at Der Sturm in Berlin, 1913, Berlin (?) 1913 (the album is prefaced by Apollinaire's poem *Les Fenêtres*); 'Uber das Licht', in *Der Sturm*, Berlin, January 1913 (translated by Paul Klee); 'Lettre ouverte au Sturm', in *Der Sturm*, Berlin, January 1914 (the letter written to Herwarh Walden, is dated 17 December 1913); *Le Simultanéisme* reproduced in Arp and Lissitzky, *Les Ismes*, Zurich 1925, and in Raynal's *Anthologie de la Peinture en France de 1906 à nos Jours*, Paris 1927; *Du Cubisme à l'Art Abstrait*, Paris 1957 (edited by Pierre Francastel with a catalogue of Delaunay's work by Guy Habasque).

Delaunay. Catalogue to an exhibition at the Musée d'Art Moderne (edited by Guy Habasque), Paris 1957.

Delaunay, Sonia Terk. Preface to a programme of the *Comédie des Champs Elysées*, Saison 1926–7.

Delevoy, R. *Léger*, Lausanne 1962.

Derain. Catalogue to an exhibition at the Musée d'Art Moderne, Paris 1954.

Dermée, P. 'Quand le Symbolisme fut mort', in *Nord-Sud*, 1, Paris, March 1917; 'Jean Metzinger – Une Esthétique', in *Sic*, Paris, March–April 1919; 'Lipchitz', in *L'Esprit Nouveau*, Paris, November 1920.

Duchamp, Marcel. In *View*, New York, March 1945. Special issue devoted to M. Duchamp with essays by André Breton, Gabrielle Buffet-Picabia, James Thrall Soby, etc.; catalogue to an exhibition held at the Tate Gallery 1966 (notes by R Hamilton).

Duchamp, M. Preface to a Picabia exhibition at the Galerie de Beaune, Paris, November–December 1937.

Duthuit, G. *Les Fauves*, Geneva 1949.

Eddy, A. J. *Cubists and Post-Impressionism*, Chicago 1914, London 1915.

Einstein, C. *Negerplastik*, Munich 1920; 'Notes sur le Cubisme', in *Documents*, Paris 1929; *Georges Braque*, Paris 1934.

Elgar, F. 'Une Conquête du Cubisme: Le Papier Collé', in *XXme Siècle*, Paris, January 1956.

Eluard, P. and René Jean. *Jacques Villon ou l'Art Glorieux*, Paris 1948.

'Enquête sur l'Art Nègre', In *Action*, Paris, April 1920, with answers by Gris, Paul Guillaume, etc.

Fierens, P. 'R. de la Fresnaye', in *Art Vivant*, Paris, February 1931.

Fillia. *Il Futurismo*, Milan 1932.

Flechter, P. *Der Expressionismus*, Munich 1914.

Fleuret, F., Preface to the Catalogue of the Marie Laurencin Exhibition at the Galerie Barbazanges, Paris, February–March 1912.

Forthuny, P. *Conférence sur les tendances de la Peinture Moderne*, Nantes 1910.

Fosca, F. *Bilan du Cubisme*, Paris 1956.

Fry, E. 'Cubism 1907–08: An Early Eye Witness Account', in *Art Bulletin*, New York, March 1966; *Cubism*, London 1966.

Fumet, S. *Braque*, Paris 1945 (in *Couleur des Maîtres* series); *Braque*, Paris 1945 in *Collection des Maîtres* series).

Futurism. Manifestes Futuristes 1909–23, Milan 1923 (printed in English, French and Italian); *Archivi del Futurismo* (edited by M. Drudi Gambillo and T. Fiori), 2 vols., Rome 1958–62.

Garcia y Bellido, A. *La Dama de Elche y el conjunto de piezas arqueológicas reingresadas en España 1941*, Madrid 1943.

Gaya-Nuño, Juan Antonio. *Juan Gris*, London 1975.

Gedo, Mary Mathews. *Picasso: Art as Autobiography*, London 1980.

Geelhaar, Christian. 'Pablo Picasso's Stilleben, "Pains et compotier aux fruits sur une table": Metamorphosen einer Bildidee', *Pantheon*, xxviii, 2, 127–40.

Geiser, B. *L'Oeuvre Gravé de Picasso*, Lausanne 1955.

Georges, W. 'Le Cubisme', review of the *Salon des Indépendants*, in *L'Esprit Nouveau*, no. 5, Paris, February 1921; 'Braque', in *L'Esprit Nouveau*, Paris, no.

6, March 1921; Preface to an exhibition of Constructivist sculpture by Gabo and Pevsner at the Galerie Percier, Paris, June–July 1924; *Fernand Léger*, Paris 1929.

Georges-Michel, M. *Peintres et Sculpteurs que j'ai connus*, New York 1942.

Gieure, M. *G. Braque*, Paris 1956.

Gleizes, A. 'Jean Metzinger', in *Revue Indépendante*, Paris, September 1911; 'Le Fauconnier et son Oeuvre', in *Revue Indépendante*, Paris, October (?) 1911.

Gleizes, A. and Metzinger, J. *Du Cubisme*, Paris 1912.

Gleizes, A. 'Le Cubisme et la Tradition', in *Montjoie*, Paris, February 1913; 'Opinion', in *Montjoie*, Paris, November–December 1913; *Art Européen, Art Américain*, New York 1919; 'Choses Simples, à propos du Salon d'Automne de 1920', in *La Vie des Lettres et des Arts*, Paris 1920; *Du Cubisme et les Moyens de le Comprendre*, Paris 1920; 'Originalité Collective, l'Art Moderne et la Société Nouvelle', in *Cahiers Idéalistes*, Paris (?) 1921; *La Peinture et ses Lois. Ce qui devait sortir du Cubisme*, Paris 1924; 'A Propos de la Section d'Or', in *Les Arts Plastiques*, no. 1, Paris 1925; *Tradition et Cubisme*, Paris 1927; 'L'Epopée', in *Le Rouge et le Noir*, Paris, June–July 1929; *Vers une Conscience Plastique*, Paris 1932; *Homocentrisme*, Sablons 1937.

Albert Gleizes, Hommage. Atelier de la Rose, Lyons 1954. With essays, statements and fragments of works by Gleizes, Metzinger, André Beaudin, Severini, etc.

Gilot, Françoise and Lake, Carlton. *Life with Picasso*, London 1964.

Gleizes, 50 Ans de Peinture. Catalogue to an exhibition at Lyons 1947; catalogue to the Gleizes retrospective exhibition, Musée d'Art Moderne, Paris 1964–5.

Golding, J. 'Les Demoiselles d'Avignon', in *Burlington Magazine*, London, May 1958.

Golding, John and Green, Christopher. *Léger and Purist Paris*, Tate Gallery, London 1970.

Goldwater, R. J. *Primitivism in Modern Painting*, New York 1938; *Artists on Art*, New York 1945; *Lipchitz*, Berlin 1954.

Gomez de la Serna, R. 'Completa y Veridica Historia de Picasso y el Cubismo', in *Revista del Occidente*, Madrid, July–August 1929. (These articles appeared in book form in Turin 1945 under the title *Picasso*.)

Granié, J. Preface to an exhibition of works by Gleizes, Metzinger and Léger at the Galerie B. Weill, Paris, January 1913.

Green, Christopher. *Léger and the Avant-Garde*, London 1976; 'Synthesis and the "synthetic process" in the Painting of Juan Gris 1915–19' and 'Purity, poetry and the painting of Juan Gris', *Art History*, Vol. 5, nos. 1 and 2, March and June 1982; *Cubism and its Enemies. Modern Movements and Reaction in French Art, 1916–28*, London 1987.

Grey, C. *Cubist Aesthetic Theories*, Baltimore 1953.

Gris, J. Collected Writings, reprinted in *Juan Gris* by D. H. Kahnweiler, translated by D. Cooper, London 1947; *Letters* compiled by D. H. Kahnweiler, edited by D. Cooper, London 1956.

Gris. Special issue of *Cahiers d'Art*, Paris 1933, published on the occasion of a Gris exhibition at the Zurich Kunsthaus. Texts by Apollinaire, Ozenfant, Salmon, etc.

Gris, Juan. Catalogue to the exhibition held in Madrid 1985.

Guillaume, P. *A Propos de l'Art des Noirs* (with a preface by Apollinaire), Paris 1917; *Sculptures Nègres*, Paris 1917.

Guillaume, P. and Munro. *Primitive Negro Sculpture*, New York 1926.

Gybal, A. *Le Fauconnier*, Amiens 1922.

Habasque, G. 'H. Laurens, le Taciturne', in *L'Oeil*, Paris, January 1956; *Le Cubisme*, Lausanne 1959.

Herkovits, S. *African Art*, Denver 1945.

Hildebrandt, H. *Alexander Archipenko*, Berlin 1923.

Hire, M. de la. *Francis Picabia*, Paris 1920.

History of Modern Painting. Geneva 1956. With texts and documentation by Raynal, Jacques Lassaigne, Werner Schmalenbach, Arnold Rudlinger, and Hans Bolliger.

Hogg, M. 'La Ville de Paris', in *Revue du Louvre et des Musées de France*, XV, Paris 1965.

Hope, H. R. *Braque*, Museum of Modern Art, New York 1949.

Hourcade, O. 'La Tendance de la Peinture Contemporaine', in *La Revue de France et des Pays Français*, February 1912; 'Enquête sur le Cubisme', organized by Hourcade, in *L'Action*, Paris, 25 February–24 March 1912; 'Le Mouvement Pictural, vers une Ecole Française', in *Revue Française*, June 1912.

Huntingdon-Wright, W. *Modern Painting*, New York 1915.

Huyghe, R. *Histoire de l'Art Contemporain*, Paris 1935.

Isarlov, G. *Picabia Peintre*, Paris 1929; *Georges Braque*, Paris 1932.

Jacob, M. *Le Cornet à Dés*, Paris 1917.

Jaffé, H. *De Stijl 1917–31*, Amsterdam 1956.

Jakovski, A. H. *Herbin*, Paris 1933; *A. Lhote*, Paris 1947.

Janneau, G. *L'Art Cubiste*, Paris 1929.

Johnson, Ron. 'Primitivism in the early sculpture of Picasso', *Arts Magazine*, 49, no. 10, June 1975; 'The Demoiselles d'Avignon and Dionysian Destruction', *Arts Magazine*, October 1980.

Jourdain, F. *Le Salon d'Automne*, Paris 1928.

Judkins, W. O. 'Towards a Reinterpretation of Cubism', *Art Bulletin*, New York, December 1948.

Kahnweiler, D. H. *Der Weg zum Kubismus*, Munich 1920; *Juan Gris*, translated by D. Cooper, London 1947; 'Negro Art and Cubism', in *Horizon*, London, December 1948; *The Sculptures of Picasso*, London 1949; *Mes Galeries et mes peintres. Entretiens avec Francis Crémieux*, Paris 1961; *Daniel-Henri Kahnweiler, marchand, éditeur, écrivain*, Centre Georges Pompidou, Musée National d'Art Moderne, Paris 1984.

Kirchner, L. *Chronik der Brücke*, 1913 (reprinted in *College Art Journal*, New York, Fall 1950).

Kupka, F. 'Les Peintres et la Lutte pour le Pain', in *Opinion*, Paris, 3 May 1913.

Kupka. Catalogue to an exhibition at the Galerie Louis Carré, New York, June 1951.

Kuppers, P. E. *Der Kubismus*, Leipzig 1920.

La Franchis, J. *Louis Marcoussis*, Paris 1961.

La Fresnaye, R. de. 'Paul Cézanne', in *Poème et Drame*, Paris, January 1913.

La Fresnaye. Catalogue to a retrospective exhibition at the Galerie Barbazanges, Paris, December 1926.

Laporte, P. 'Cubism and Science', in *Journal of Aesthetics*, Cleveland, March 1949.

Larrande, C. 'André Lhote', in *Revue Française*, May 1912.

Lassaigne, J. *Jacques Villon*, Paris 1950.

Laurens, M. *Henri Laurens*, Paris 1955.

Lebel, R. *Marcel Duchamp*, London 1959.

Le Fauconnier. Catalogue for an exhibition at the Neumann Gallery, New York

1948–9 (the preface contains a photograph of the galley proof of a page, subsequently altered, of *Les Peintres Cubistes*).

Léger, F. 'Les Origines de la Peinture et sa Valeur Représentative', in *Montjoie*, Paris, May–June 1913; 'Les Réalisations Picturales Actuelles', in *Les Soirées de Paris*, Paris, June 1914; 'Pensées', in *Valori Plastici*, Rome, February–March 1919 and in *Selection*, Antwerp, 15 September 1920; 'L'Esthétique de la Machine', in *Bulletin de l'Effort Moderne*, Paris, nos. 1–2, 1924; Answer to a questionnaire 'Où va la peinture moderne?' in *Bulletin de l'Effort Moderne*, Paris, no. 2, 1924; Correspondence with Léonce Rosenberg in *Bulletin de l'Effort Moderne*, no. 4, Paris 1924; 'Le Spectacle', in *Bulletin de l'Effort Moderne*, no. 7, 1924; *Avant Propos* (collected documents), Paris 1959.

Léger. Cahiers d'Art, Paris 1933, special issue published on the occasion of a Léger Exhibition at the Zurich Kunsthaus. Texts by Giedion, Cendrars, Salmon, etc.

Léger. Catalogue to a retrospective exhibition at the Musée d'Art Moderne, Paris 1949.

Léger. Catalogue to an exhibition at the Musée des Arts Décoratifs, Paris 1956.

Leiris, I. and M. *Donation Louise et Michel Leiris (Collection Kahnweiler-Leiris)*, Centre Georges Pompidou, Musée National d'Art Moderne, Paris 1984.

Lemaître, G. E. *From Cubism to Surrealism in French Literature*, Cambridge Mass. 1945.

Level, A. *Picasso*, Paris 1928.

Leymarie, J. *Derain*, Paris 1949.

Lhote, A. 'Le Cubisme est-il Mort?' in *Les Feuilles Libres*, Paris, April–May 1922; *La Peinture, le Coeur et l'Esprit*, Paris 1933; *Cézanne*, Lausanne 1949.

Longhi, R. *Scultura Futurista, Boccioni*, Florence 1914.

Lozowick, *Modern Russian Art*, New York 1925.

McCully, Marilyn. *A Picasso Anthology; Documents, Criticism, Reminiscences*, London 1981.

MacOrlan, P. *Chronique de la Vie Contemporaine*, Paris 1928; *Montmartre*, Brussels 1946.

Marcoussis. Essays by Apollinaire, Tzara, etc., Antwerp 1920.

Marinetti, Benedetta. 'Marinetti', in *Cahiers d'Art*, Paris 1950.

Marinetti, F. T. 'Fondation et Manifeste du Futurisme', in *Figaro*, 20 February

1909; Le Futurisme, Paris 1911; *A bas le Tango et Parsifal*, Milan 1914.

Marinetti, F. T. (and others). *Noi Futuristi*, Milan 1917; *Les Mots en Liberté Futuristes*, Milan 1919; *I Manifesti del Futurismo*, Milan 1920.

Marx, R. *L'Art Social*, Paris 1913; *Maîtres d'hier et d'aujourd'hui*, Paris 1914.

Mauclair, C. *Trois Crises de l'Art Actuel*, Paris 1906.

Melquist, J. 'Jacques Villon, Maître de Puteaux', in *Art-Documents*, no. 3, Geneva, December 1950.

Messens, E. and Melville, R. *The Cubist Spirit in its Time*, London 1947.

Metzinger, J. 'Note sur la Peinture', in *Pan*, Paris, October–November 1910; 'Alexandre Mercereau', in *Vers et Prose*, Paris, October–December 1911; 'Le Cubisme et la Tradition', in *Paris Journal*, 15 (?) September 1911; 'Art et Esthétique', in *Lettres Parisiennes*, Paris, suppl. 9, April 1920; 'L'Evolution du Coloris', in *Le Bulletin de l'Effort Moderne*, Paris 1925; 'Un Souper chez G. Apollinaire', in *Apollinaire*, Paris 1946.

Mondrian, P. *Plastic Art and Pure Art 1937 and Other Essays 1941–43*, New York 1945.

Montaigne, N. 'G. Braque, sa Vie Racontée par lui-meme', in *Les Amis de l'Art*, Berne, nos. 4–7, January–April 1949.

Nebelthau, E. *Roger de la Fresnaye*, Paris 1935.

Olivier, Fernande. *Picasso et ses Amis*, Paris 1933.

Ozenfant, A. *Art*, Paris 1929 (translated as the *Foundations of Modern Art*, London 1931).

Ozenfant, A. and Jeanneret. *Après le Cubisme*, Paris 1918; 'Le Purisme', in *L'Esprit Nouveau*, no. 4, January 1921; *La Peinture Moderne*, Paris 1925.

Pach, W. *Queer Thing, Painting*, New York 1938.

Palau i Fabre, Josep. *Picasso: The Early Years 1881–1907*, New York 1981.

Papini, G. *Il Mio Futurismo*, Florence 1914.

Paulhan, J. *Braque le Patron*, Paris 1945.

Penrose, R. *Portrait of Picasso*, London (I.C.A.) 1956; *Picasso, His Life and Work*, London 1958, 3rd edition, Berkeley and Los Angeles 1981.

Picabia, P. *Cubism by a Cubist*, preface to the Catalogue of a Picabia exhibition in New York 1913; 'Francis Picabia et Dada', in *L'Esprit Nouveau*, no. 9, June 1921.

Picasso. Catalogue to an exhibition at the Musée des Arts Décoratifs, Paris 1955.

Picasso, A Retrospective (ed. William Rubin). Museum of Modern Art, New York 1980.

Pierre, José. *Le Cubisme*, Lausanne 1966.

Piot, R. 'A Propos les Cubistes', in *Bulletin du Salon d'Automne*, special no., 1917.

Princet, M. Preface to the Catalogue of the Delaunay Exhibition at the Galerie Barbazanges, Paris, February–March 1912.

Ragghianti, C. 'Revisioni sul Cubismo', in *Critica d'Arte*, nos 46–8, Florence, July–December 1961.

Raynal, M. 'Qu'est ce que . . . le Cubisme?' in *Comoedia Illustré*, Paris, December 1913; *Quelques Intentions du Cubisme*, Paris 1919; *Lipchitz*, Paris 1920; 'F. Léger', in *L'Esprit Nouveau*, Paris, no. 4, January 1921. The article was subsequently expanded in the *Bulletin de l'Effort Moderne*, nos. 18–19, Paris 1925; *Juan Gris*, Paris 1920 (reprinted in the *Bulletin de l'Effort Moderne*, no. 16, Paris, June 1925); 'Juan Gris', in *L'Esprit Nouveau*, Paris, February 1921; *Picasso*, Paris 1922; *G. Braque*, Rome, Paris 1923; *Anthologie de la Peinture en France de 1906 à nos Jours*, Paris 1927.

Reverdy, P. 'Sur le Cubisme', in *Nord-Sud*, Paris, March 1917; 'Le Cubisme, Poésie Plastique', in *L'Art*, Paris 1919; 'L'Esthétique et l'Esprit', in *L'Esprit Nouveau*, Paris, no. 6, March 1921; *Picasso*, Paris 1924; *Le Gant de Crin*, Paris 1926.

Rewald, J. *Paul Cézanne, Correspondence*, Paris 1937.

Rey, E. *Picabia*, Paris 1908.

Richardson, J. 'The Ateliers of Braque', in *Burlington Magazine*, London, June 1955; *Georges Braque*, London 1959; *G. Braque*, London 1961; preface and notes to the Gris Exhibition, Dortmund, 1965.

Robbins, D. Preface and notes to the Gleizes Exhibition, Solomon R. Guggenheim Museum, New York 1964; *Albert Gleizes, 1881–1953*, Musée National d'Art Moderne, Paris 1965.

Roger-Milés, L. Preface to a Picabia Exhibition at the Galerie Haussmann, Paris, February 1905; Preface to a Picabia Exhibition at the Galerie Georges Petit, Paris, March 1909.

Romains, J. *Le Fauconnier*, Paris 1921.

Rosenberg, L. *Cubisme et Tradition*, Paris 1920; *Cubisme et Empirisme*, Paris 1921.

Rosenblum, R. *Cubism and Twentieth Century Art*, New York and London 1960; 'The Demoiselles d'Avignon Revisited', *Art News*, 71, no. 5, September 1972; 'Picasso and the Typography of Cubism' in *Picasso 1881–1973* (ed. Penrose and Golding), London 1973.

Roskill, Mark. *The Interpretation of Cubism*, Philadelphia 1986.

Rubin, William. 'Cézannisme and the Beginnings of Cubism', in *Cézanne, The Late Work* (ed. W. Rubin), Museum of Modern Art, New York 1977; 'Pablo and Georges and Leo and Bill', *Art in America*, March–April 1979; 'From Narrative to "Iconic" in Picasso: the buried allegory in *Bread and Fruitdish on a Table* and the role of the *Demoiselles d'Avignon*', *Art Bulletin*, December 1983, Vol. LXV, no. 4; Ed., *'Primitivism' in Twentieth Century Art*, 2 vols., Museum of Modern Art, New York 1984.

Russell, J. *G. Braque*, London 1959.

Sabartés, J. *Picasso*, Milan 1937. English edition, London 1949; *Picasso–Documents Iconographiques*, Geneva 1954.

Salmon, A. *La Jeune Peinture Française*, Paris 1912; *La Jeune Sculpture Française*, Paris 1919; 'Les Origines et Intentions du Cubisme', in *Demain*, Paris, April 1919; *L'Art Vivant*, Paris 1920; *Propos d' Atelier*, Paris 1922; *Derain*, Paris 1924; *Derain*, Paris 1929; *L'Air de la Butte, Souvenirs sans Fin*, part 1, Paris 1945; *Souvenirs sans Fin*, part 2, 1908–20, Paris 1956.

Schwartz, Paul Waldo. *The Cubists*, London 1971.

Seligman, G. *R. de la Fresnaye*, New York 1954.

Seuphor, M. *Mondrian*, London 1956.

Severini, G. Preface to an Exhibition of his work at the Sackville Gallery, London, March 1912; *Du Cubisme au Classicisme*, Paris 1921; 'Vers une Synthèse Esthétique', in *Bulletin de l'Effort Moderne*, October–November 1924; *Tutta la Vita di un Pittore*, Milan 1946.

Siblik, E. *Francis Kupka*, Prague 1929.

Soby, J. T. *Jaun Gris*, Museum of Modern Art, New York 1958.

Soffici, A. 'Arte Francese', in *La Voce*, Florence 1913; *Cubismo e Futurismo*, Florence 1914.

Spate, Virginia. *Orphism*, Oxford 1979.

Spies, Werner (ed.). *Pour Daniel-Henry Kahnweiler*, New York 1965.

Stein, G. *The Autobiography of Alice B. Toklas*, New York 1933; *Picasso*, Paris

1938. English edition, New York, London 1939.

Stein, L. *Appreciation*, New York 1947.

Steinberg, Leo. 'The Philosophical Brothel' (2 parts), *Art News*, September and October 1972; 'Resisting Cézanne; Picasso's *Three Women*' and 'The Polemical Part', *Art in America*, November–December 1978, March–April 1979.

Sweeney, J. J. *African Negro Art*, Museum of Modern Art, New York 1935; 'Picasso and Iberian Sculpture', in *Art Bulletin*, New York, no. 3, 1941; *Modern Art and Tradition*, New York 1948.

Taylor, J. C. *Futurism*, Museum of Modern Art, New York, 1961.

Tourette, G. de la. *Delaunay*, Paris 1950.

Trillo-Clough, R. *Looking Back on Futurism*, New York 1942.

Uhde, W. *Rousseau*, Paris 1913; *Picasso et la Tradition Française*, Paris 1928.

Ungaretti, G. 'La Doctrine de Lacerba', in *L'Esprit Nouveau*, Paris, no. 2, November 1920.

Vachtová, Ludmila. *Frank Kupka*, London 1968.

Valensi. 'La Couleur et les Formes', in *Montjoie*, Paris, November–December 1913.

Vallier, D. 'Braque, la Peinture et Nous', in *Cahiers d'Art*, no. 1, 1954; *Jacques-Villon*, Paris 1957.

Villon, J. Special issue of *Cahiers d'Art*, 1951.

Villon, J. Catalogue to an exhibition at the Musée d'Art Moderne, Paris 1951.

Villon, J. Catalogue to an exhibition at the Muśee Toulouse-Lautrec, Albi 1955.

Villon, J., Duchamp, M., and Duchamp-Villon. Catalogue to an Exhibition at the Guggenheim Museum, New York 1957.

Vitrac, R. *Jacques Lipchitz*, Paris 1929.

Vlaminck, M. *Tournant Dangereux*, Paris 1929; *Portraits avant Décès*, Paris 1943.

Vriesen, Gustav and Imdhal, Max. *Robert Delaunay: Light and Colour*, New York 1967.

Wadley, Nicholas. *Cubism*, London 1972.

Warnod, A. *Les Berceaux de la Jeune Peinture*, Paris 1925.

Werth, L. *Quelques Peintres*, Paris 1923; *La Peinture et la Mode*, Paris 1924.

Wiese, E. *Alexander Archipenko*, Leipzig 1923.

Wilenski, R. *The Modern Movement in Art*, London 1927.

Worms de Romilly, Nicole. *Braque, le cubisme, fin 1907–1914* (introductory essay by Jean Laude), Maeght, Paris 1982.

Zayas, M. de. *African Negro Art, its Influence on Modern Art*, New York 1915.

Zervos, C. *Picasso, Cahiers d'Art*, Paris, Vol. 1, 1932; Vol. 2, 1942; Vol. 3, 1949; Vol. 4, 1951; Vol. 5, 1952, Vol. 6, 1954; *Histoire de l'Art Contemporain*, Paris 1938.

LIST OF ILLUSTRATIONS

PICASSO

1 *Les Demoiselles d'Avignon*, 1907. Oil. Museum of Modern Art, New York
2 *Two Nudes*, 1906. Oil. Museum of Modern Art, New York
3A *Nu à la Draperie*, 1907. Oil. The Hermitage, Leningrad
3B *La Paysanne*, 1908. Oil. The Hermitage, Leningrad
4 *Three Women*, 1908–9. Oil. The Hermitage, Leningrad
5 *Bread and Fruit Dish on a Table*, 1909. Oil. Kunstmuseum, Basel
6A *Landscape, La Rue-des-Bois*, 1908. Oil. Pushkin Museum of Fine Art, Moscow
6B *Le Compotier*, 1908. Oil. Museum of Modern Art, New York
7A *Nude Woman*, 1908–9. Oil. Louise and Walter Arensberg Collection, Philadelphia Museum of Art
7B *Baigneuse*, 1909. Oil. Private Collection, New York
8A *Still Life, Carafe, Jug and Fruit Bowl*, 1909. Oil. Solomon R. Guggenheim Museum, New York
8B *Casket, Cup, Apple*, 1909. Ink and wash on paper. Museum of Modern Art, New York
9 *La Femme aux Poires*, 1909. Oil. Private Collection
10 *Head of a Woman*, 1909. Bronze. Museum of Modern Art, New York
11 *Seated Woman*, 1910. Oil. Tate Gallery, London
12 *Girl with a Mandolin (The Portrait of Fanny Tellier)*, 1910. Oil. Museum of Modern Art, New York
13 *Portrait of Uhde*, 1910. Oil. Collection Joseph Pullitzer, St Louis

14A *Houses on the Hill, Horta de Ebro (Horta de San Juan)*, 1909. Oil. Museum of Modern Art, New York
14B *Nude (Cadaquès)*, 1910. Oil. National Gallery of Art, Washington
15A *Nude*, 1910. Ink and wash. Private Collection
15B *Mademoiselle Léonie*, 1910. Etching. Museum of Modern Art, New York
16 *Portrait of Monsieur Kahnweiler*, 1910. Oil. The Art Institute of Chicago, bequest of Mrs Gilbert Chapman
17 *L'Homme à la Pipe*, 1911. Oil. Kimbell Art Museum, Fort Worth
18A *Bottle and Glasses*, 1911–12. Oil. Solomon R. Guggenheim Museum, New York
18B *Bouteille de Pernod*, 1912. Oil. The Hermitage, Leningrad
19A *Guitar*, 1912. Sheet metal and wire. Museum of Modern Art, New York
19B Mask. Grebo, Ivory Coast or Liberia. Painted wood and fibre. Musée Picasso, Paris. Formerly Collection Picasso
20A *Violin, 'Jolie Eva'*, 1912. Oil. Staatsgalerie, Stuttgart
20B *Violin*, 1912. Oil. Rijksmuseum Kröller-Müller, Otterlo
21 *'Ma Jolie'*, 1911–12. Oil. Museum of Modern Art, New York
22 *L'Aficionado (Le Toréro)*, 1912. Oil. Kunstmuseum, Basel
23 *Le Modèle*, 1912. Oil. Private Collection, New York
24A *Still Life with Chair-caning*, 1912. Oil and pasted oil-cloth. Musée Picasso, Paris
24B *Bouteille de Vieux Marc*, 1913. *Papier collé.* Musée National d'Art Moderne, Paris
25 *The Violin*, 1912. *Papier collé.* A. E. Gallatin Collection, Philadelphia Museum of Art
26 *Violon au Café*, 1913. Oil. Collection M. Siegfried Rosengart, Lucerne
27 *Violin and Guitar*, 1913. Oil, pasted cloth, pencil and plaster. Louise and Walter Arensberg Collection, Philadelphia Museum of Art
28 *Harlequin*, 1913. Oil. Gemeente Museum, The Hague
29A *Bouteille et Guitare*, 1913. Construction. No longer in existence
29B *L'Etudiant à la Pipe*, 1913–14. Oil, charcoal, *papier collé* and sand. Museum of Modern Art, New York
30A *Femme en Chemise assise dans un Fauteuil*, 1913. Oil. Mr and Mrs Victor W. Ganz, New York
30B *Seated Woman (Portrait de Jeune Fille)*, 1914. Oil. Musée National d'Art Moderne, Paris
31A *Le Violon*, 1914. Oil. Musée National d'Art Moderne, Paris
31B *Green Still Life*, 1914. Oil. Museum of Modern Art, New York
32 *Homme Assis au Verre*, 1914. Oil. Private Collection
33 *Still Life with Bottle*, 1911–12. Drypoint. Museum of Modern Art, New York

BRAQUE

34 *Fox*, 1911–12. Drypoint. Museum of Modern Art, New York

35 *Grand Nu*, 1908. Oil. Collection M. Alex Maguy, Paris

36A *View from the Hotel Mistral*, 1907. Private Collection, New York

36B *Still Life with Musical Instruments*, 1908. Oil. Private Collection

37A *Landscape with Houses*, 1907. Oil. Private Collection

37B *La Route de l'Estaque*, 1908. Oil. Musée National d'Art Moderne, Paris

38 *Maisons à l'Estaque*, 1908. Oil. Kunstmuseum, Berne, Rupf Foundation

39A *Le Port (Harbour in Normandy)*, 1909. Oil. The Art Institute of Chicago

39B *Still Life with Fruit Dish*, 1908–9. Oil. Moderna Museet, Stockholm

40A *Landscape, La Roche Guyon*, 1909. Oil. Stedelijk Van Abbe Museum, Eindhoven

40B *Landscape, Carrières Saint-Denis*, 1909. Oil. Private Collection

41 *Violon et Cruche*, 1910. Oil. Kunstmuseum, Basel

42 *Violin and Palette*, 1910. Oil. Solomon R. Guggenheim Museum, New York

43A *Glass on a Table*, 1910. Oil. Collection Lady Hornby, London

43B *Les Poissons*, 1910. Oil. Tate Gallery, London

44 *Violin and Glass*, 1910–11. Oil. National Gallery, Prague

45A *Les Usines de Rio Tinto*, 1910. Oil. Musée National d'Art Moderne, Paris

45B *Man with a Guitar*, 1911. Oil. Museum of Modern Art, New York

46 *Female Figure*, 1910–11. Oil. H. Carey Walker Foundation, New York

47 *Le Portugais*, 1911. Oil. Kunstmuseum, Basel

48 *Man with a Violin*, 1911. Oil. Bührle Collection, Kunsthaus, Zurich

49A *Fruit Dish, Bottle and Glass*, 1912. Oil and sand. Private Collection, Paris

49B *Compotier et Verre (Fruit Dish and Glass)*, 1912. *Papier collé*. Private Collection

50A *Hommage à J. S. Bach*, 1912. Oil. Sidney Janis Collection, New York

50B *Composition (The Violin)*, 1913. Oil. Private Collection

51 *Still Life with Guitar*, 1912–13. *Papier collé*. Louise and Walter Arensberg Collection, Philadelphia Museum of Art

52A *Clarinet*, 1913. *Papier collé*. Museum of Modern Art, New York

52B *La Table du Musicien*, 1913. Oil and pencil. Kunstmuseum, Basel

53 *Still Life with Playing Cards (Composition à l'As de Trèfle)*, 1913. Oil and charcoal. Musée National d'Art Moderne, Paris

54 *Violon et Verre*, 1913. Oil. Kunstmuseum, Basel

55 *Woman with a Guitar*, 1913. Oil. Musée National d'Art Moderne, Paris

56A *Music*, 1914. Oil with gesso and sawdust. Philips Collection, Washington D.C. (Katherine Drier Gift)

56B *Still Life (Nature Morte à la Pipe)*, 1914. Oil with sand and gesso. Girardin Collection, Petit Palais, Paris

GRIS

57 *L'Homme à la Pipe*, 1911. Oil. Collection Mr and Mrs Jacques Gelman, New York

58A *The Eggs*, 1911. Oil. Staatsgalerie, Stuttgart

58B *Still Life with Cylindrical Pot*, 1911. Oil. Rijksmuseum Kröller-Müller, Otterlo

59 *Hommage à Picasso (Portrait of Picasso)*, 1911–12. Oil. The Art Institute of Chicago

60A *Grey Still Life*, 1912. Oil. Rijksmuseum Kröller-Müller, Otterlo

60B *Portrait of Germaine Raynal*, 1912. Oil. Private Collection, Paris

61 *The Man in the Café*, 1912. Oil. Louise and Walter Arensberg Collection, Philadelphia Museum of Art

62A *Le Lavabo*, 1912. Oil with mirror and *papier collé*. Private Collection

62B *Glass of Beer and Playing Cards*, 1913. Oil and *papier collé*. Columbus Gallery of Fine Arts (Howald Collection), Columbus, Ohio

63 *Landscape at Céret*, 1913. Oil. Private Collection, Spain

64A *Violin and Guitar*, 1913. Oil. Collection Mr and Mrs Ralph D. Colin, New York

64B *The Guitar*, 1913. Charcoal on paper. Private Collection, France

65 *Glasses and Newspaper*, 1914. *Papier collé*. Smith College Museum of Art, Northampton, Mass.

66 *Guitar, Glasses and Bottle*, 1914. *Papier collé*. Private Collection, New York

67 *Still Life in Front of an Open Window*, 1915. Oil. Louise and Walter Arensberg Collection, Philadelphia Museum of Art

68A *Livre, Pipe et Verres*, 1915. Oil. Collection Mr and Mrs Ralph D. Colin, New York

68B *Bouteille et Compotier*, 1917. Oil. Institute of Art, Minneapolis

LÉGER

69 *La Couseuse*, 1909. Oil. Private Collection, Paris

70A *Nus dans un Paysage*, 1909–11. Oil. Rijksmuseum Kröller-Müller, Otterlo

70B *Fumées sur les Toits*, 1910. Oil. Collection Mr Richard Weil, New York

71 *Les Fumeurs*, 1911. Oil. Solomon R. Guggenheim Museum, New York

72 *La Noce*, 1911–12. Oil. Musée National d'Art Moderne, Paris

73 *La Femme en Bleu*, 1912. Oil. Kunstmuseum, Basel

74 *Contrastes de Formes*, 1913. Oil. Solomon R. Guggenheim Museum, New York

75 *L'Escalier*, 1914. Oil. Kunstmuseum, Basel

DELAUNAY

76 *The Eiffel Tower*, 1910. Oil. Solomon R. Guggenheim Museum, New York
77 *La Ville*, 1911. Oil. Solomon R. Guggenheim Museum, New York
78A *Les Tours de Laon*, 1912. Oil. Musée National d'Art Moderne, Paris
78B *La Ville de Paris*, 1912. Oil. Musée National d'Art Moderne, Paris
79 *La Fenêtre*, 1912. Oil. Solomon R. Guggenheim Museum, New York
80A *The Eiffel Tower*, 1909. Oil. Louise and Walter Arensberg Collection, Philadelphia Museum of Art
80B *Simultaneous Contrasts: Sun and Moon*, 1912–13. Oil. Museum of Modern Art, New York
81 *L'Equipe de Cardiff*, 1912–13. Oil. Stedelijk Van Abbe Museum, Eindhoven

GLEIZES

82 *The Bridges of Paris*, 1912. Oil. Museum des 20 Jahrhunderts, Vienna
83A *La Femme aux Phlox*, 1910–11. Oil. Museum of Fine Arts, Houston
83B *Le Dépiquage des Moissons (Harvest Threshing)*, 1912. Oil. Solomon R. Guggenheim Museum, New York
84 *L'Homme au Balcon*, 1912. Oil. Louise and Walter Arensberg Collection, Philadelphia Museum of Art

METZINGER

85 *La Danseuse au Café*, 1912. Oil. Albright Knox Gallery, Buffalo
86A *Two Nudes*, 1910–11. Oil. Present whereabouts unknown
86B *Le Goûter*, 1911. Oil. Louise and Walter Arensberg Collection, Philadelphia Museum of Art
87 *La Plume Jaune*, 1912. Oil. Collection Mr R. S. Johnson, Chicago

LE FAUCONNIER

88 *L'Abondance*, 1910–11. Oil. Gemeente Museum, The Hague
89A *Portrait of Jouve*, 1909. Oil. Musée National d'Art Moderne, Paris
89B *The Huntsman (Chasseur)*, 1912. Oil. Museum of Modern Art, New York

VILLON

90 *Young Woman*, 1912. Oil. Louise and Walter Arensberg Collection, Philadelphia Museum of Art
91A *Portrait of Duchamp-Villon.* Oil. Musée National d'Art Moderne, Paris
91B *Soldats en Marche*, 1913. Oil. Musée National D'Art Moderne, Paris
92 *La Femme Assise*, 1914. Oil. Collection Galerie Louis Carré, Paris

DUCHAMP

93 *The Sonata*, 1911. Oil. Louise and Walter Arensberg Collection, Phildelphia Museum of Art
94 *The Bride*, 1912. Oil. Louise and Walter Arensberg Collection, Philadelphia Museum of Art
95A *Nude Descending a Staircase, no. 1*, 1911. Oil. Louise and Walter Arensberg Collection, Philadelphia Museum of Art
95B *Nude Descending a Staircase*, 1912. Oil. Louise and Walter Arensberg Collection, Philadelphia Museum of Art

DUCHAMP-VILLON

96 *The Horse*, 1913–14. Bronze. Museum of Modern Art, New York

LA FRESNAYE

97 *La Conquête de l'Air*, 1913. Oil. Museum of Modern Art, New York
98A *Le Cuirassier*, 1910–11. Musée National d'Art Moderne, Paris
98B *Nature Morte aux Trois Anses*, 1912. Oil. Girardin Collection, Petit Palais, Paris

PICABIA

99A *Danseuses à la Source*, 1912. Oil. Louise and Walter Arensberg Collection, Philadelphia Museum of Art

KUPKA

99B *Le Langage des Verticales* (study), 1911–12. Oil. Collection Galerie Louis Carré, Paris

MARCOUSSIS

100 *Nature Morte au Damier*, 1912. Oil. Musée National d'Art Moderne, Paris

DERAIN

101A *Still Life*, 1904. Oil. Private Collection, Paris
101B *Baigneuses*, 1906–7. Oil. Museum of Modern Art, New York
102A *The Last Supper*, 1911(?)–13. Oil. The Art Institute of Chicago
102B,C Head of a Monkey (?). Ubangi (?), Central African Republic. Wood. Private Collection

LAURENCIN

103A *Group of Artists*, 1908 (Self portrait with Apollinaire, Picasso and Fernande Olivier). Oil. Cone Collection, Baltimore Museum of Art

MONDRIAN

103B *Composition*, 1913. Oil. Rijksmuseum Kröller-Müller, Otterlo

LHOTE

104A *Portrait of Marguerite*, 1913. Oil. Marlborough Gallery, London

LIPCHITZ

104B *Danseuse*, 1913–14. Bronze. Girardin Collection, Petit Palais, Paris

COMPARATIVE MATERIAL

CÉZANNE

105A *Trois Baigneuses*. Oil. Petit Palais, Paris

PICASSO

105B *Portrait of Gertrude Stein*, 1906 (detail of head). Metropolitan Museum of Art, New York

105C *Hunting Scene*. Iberian Sculpture (Osuna). Museo Arqueológico, Madrid
105D *Head of a Man* (full face view). Iberian Sculpture. Museo Arqueológico, Madrid
106A *Head of a Man* (threequarter view). Iberian Sculpture. Museo Arqueológico, Madrid

PICASSO

106B *Head of a Man*, 1907. Ink and watercolour. Museum of Modern Art, New York

106C Wooden Mask, Dan, Ivory Coast. Musée de l'Homme, Paris
106D Bronze ancestral figure from the French Congo. British Museum, London
106E Grebo Ceremonial Mask, Sassandra, Ivory Coast. Musée de l'Homme, Paris
107A Head of a Woman. Iberian Sculpture. Museo Arqueológico, Madrid
107B Mask, Fang, Gabon. Wood. Vérité Collection, Paris
107C Mask, Bambara, Mali. Wood. Private Collection, Italy

BRAQUE

108A *Three Women*, 1907. Ink on paper. Lost
108B Cardboard and Paper Construction, 1914. Destroyed

INDEX

abstract art, 18–19, 85–7, 197–8
Académie de la Palette, 169
Académie Julien, 182
Académie Wassilief, 153, 162, 188, 190–1
Action, 48
African art *see* Tribal art
Agero, 180
Allard, R., 5–7, 10, 13, 17, 18–20, 24, 97
Apollinaire, Guillaume, 3, 5, 6, 38, 88, 161, 171, 177, 180, 185
on Braque, 62
Calligrammes, 22
'Le Cubisme Ecartelé', 183–4
on Delaunay, 162, 166
on Derain, 145, 146, 148
and the development of Cubism, 7, 11–12, 13, 14
and the first Cubist manifestations, 8, 9
and Futurism, 26, 28, 29, 30
on Gris, 97–8
introduces Braque to Picasso, 1
on Kupka, 172
on Léger, 157, 167, 187
on Marcoussis, 173
and Marie Laurencin, 182
on Metzinger, 170
on Mondrian, 25
and Orphism, 20–4, 183, 184
Les Peintres Cubistes, 17, 18, 20, 21, 24, 98, 145, 184
on Picasso, 86–7
and Rousseau, 150
and the *Section d'Or*, 16
Archipenko, Alexander, 9, 12, 21, 131, 180, 181
Arp, Jean, 21
Les Artistes de Passy, 12
L'Assiette au Beurre, 178
L'Autorité, 14–15

Bailly, Alice, 24
Balla, Giacomo, 176
Speeding Automobile, 179
Bambara mask, Pl. 107C
Les Bandeaux d'Or, 167
Barzun (Henri Martin), 23
Bérard (under-secretary in the Ministry of Fine Arts), 14

Bergson, Henri, 16
Bernard, Émile, 59, 63
Bernheim Jeune Gallery, 58
Blanche, Jacques Emile, 169
Der Blaue Reiter, 30–1
Boccioni, Umberto, 26–9, 181
Bonnard, Pierre, 4
Brancusi, Constantin, 180, 181
Braque, Georges, 178, 183, 198
  background, 1, 3–4
  Cézanne's influence on, 47, 57–8, 60, 61, 63, 76–7, 146, 149
  chronology, 70–1
  collaboration with Picasso, 1–3, 4, 65, 127
  constructions, 81, 130, 131, 180, Pl. 108B
  and Gris, 100, 144
  'hermetic' phase, 118
  importance to Cubism, 4–5, 10–11, 25, 26, 152, 154–5, 159–60, 163, 168, 172–3, 175
  influence in Germany, 30
  influence on Léger, 161
  interest in spatial effects, 76–7, 79–80, 82, 112, 120–1, 130
  interest in tribal art, 61
  l'Estaque landscapes, 61–5, 67–8, 69, 76, 159
  methods of composition, 101, 123–4, 157
  moves towards abstraction, 85–6, 89–90
  paintings at La Roche Guyon, 78, 83, 114
  papier collé and *collages*, 81, 95, 104, 108–9, 110–14, 116, 120, 122–3, 127, 192
  Picasso's influence, 56–7, 61
  pointillism, 132, 133
  post-war work, 195, 200–1
  still lifes, 80, 82–3
  subjects, 87
  surface textures, 126
  trompe l'oeil, 92, 106, 132
  use of colour, 63–4, 114–16, 125–6
  use of stencilled letters, 91–3, 95, 106
  Ateliers, 200
  Baigneuse (La Grand Nu), 56–7, 61, 73–4, Pl. 35
  La Ciotat landscapes, 58
  The Clarinet, 112, Pl. 52A
  Composition (The Violin), Pl. 50B
  Composition à l'As de Trèfle (Still Life with Playing Cards), 123, Pl. 53
  Composition or *Violon et Verre*, 122, 123
  Compotier et Verre, 104, 111, 123, Pl. 49B
  Female Figure, 89, 128, Pl. 46
  La Femme, 56
  Fox, 91, Pl. 34
  Fruit Dish and Glass, 108–9, 110
  Fruit Dish, Bottle and Glass, 126, Pl. 49A
  Glass on a Table, 83, Pl. 43A
  Hommage à J.S. Bach, 90, 117, Pl. 50A
  Landscape, La Roche Guyon, Pl. 40A
  Landscape, Carrières Saint-Denis, Pl. 40B
  Landscape with Houses, 61, Pl. 37A
  Maisons à l'Estaque, 62, 83, Pl. 38
  Man with Guitar, 91, Pl. 45B
  Man with Violin, 89–90, Pl. 48
  Music, 130, Pl. 56A
  Nature Morte à la Pipe, 133–4, Pl. 56B
  Les Poissons, 83, Pl. 43B
  Le Port, 76, 77, 78, Pl. 39A
  Le Portugais, 91, 92, 93, 95, 106, Pl. 47
  Le Pyrogène et 'Le Quotidien', 91
  La Route de l'Estaque, 62, Pl. 37B
  Soda, 90
  Still Life with Fruit Dish, 68, Pl. 39B

Still Life with Guitar, 116–17, Pl. 51
Still Life with Musical Instruments, 74, Pl. 36B
La Table du Musicien, 123, 164, Pl. 52B
Three Women, Pl. 108A
Les Usines de Rio Tinto à l'Estaque, 83, Pl. 45A
View from the Hotel Mistral, 58, 61, Pl. 36A
View of Montmartre, 165
Violin and Glass, Pl. 44
Violin and Palette, 82, Pl. 42
Violin et Cruche, 82, Pl. 41
Violin et Verre, 125, 126, Pl. 54
Woman with a Guitar, 127–8, 130, Pl. 55
Breton, André, 177
Breton, Jean Louis, 14
Bruce, Patrick Henry, 21, 24
Die Brücke, 30, 40, 51
Bulletin de la Vie Artistique, 118
Burty (Haviland), Frank, 49

Café Azon, 173
Canudo, 21, 22–3
Carrà, Carlo, 27
Funeral of the Anarchist Galli, 179
Simultaneità, 29
Cendrars, Blaise, 21, 22, 161, 194
Cézanne, Paul, 10–11, 55, 62, 82, 149, 178, 199
exhibitions, 5, 58–9
figure work, 68–70
importance of to Cubists, 4, 5, 18
influence on Braque, 47, 57–8, 60, 61, 63, 76–7, 146, 149
influence on Delaunay, 153–4, 158, 165–6
influence on Derain, 37, 58, 145–6, 148
influence on Gris, 98–9, 119
influence on Léger, 59–60, 152–3
influence on Matisse, 37, 57–8
influence on Picasso, 37–9, 47–8, 60, 64–70, 71–2, 146
still lifes, 98
Aprés-Midi à Naples, 38
Baigneuses, 37, 38–9
L'Eternel Féminin, 38
Temptations of St. Anthony, 38
Trois Baigneuses, 37, 39, Pl. 105A
Chagall, Marc, 21, 31–2
Chardin, Jean-Baptiste-Siméon, 79
Chevreul, M.E., 22, 184, 185
Claudel, Paul, 159
cloisonnisme, 36
Closerie des Lilas, 6–7, 26
Comoedia, 30, 175
Constable, John, 184
Constructivism, 107
Cormon, 191
Corot, Jean-Baptiste Camille, 119
Courbet, Gustave, 79, 87
Cravan, Arthur, 21
Cubism: and abstraction, 18–19, 85–7, 197–8
affinities with music, 20–1
'analytical' and 'synthetic' phases, 117–22, 139, 143–4, 200
Apollinaire's divisions of, 183–4
Braque's importance to, 4–5, 10–11
Cézanne's influence, 47–8, 57–61, 63–70, 73, 76–7
collage, 199
and Fauvism, 9
first manifestations, 7–10
and German painting, 30–2
'hermetic' phase, 85–6, 118
history of, 1–32

iconography, 87–8
influence on Futurism, 26–9
influence of tribal art, 44–53
intellectual and conceptual
nature of, 17–19, 22–4, 51, 102–3
and mathematics, 102–3, 143, 178–9
new concept of form, 52–3, 72–5, 82
origin of term, 9, 10
and Orphism, 20, 21–5, 183, 184, 187, 196
post-war, 194–201
and Purism, 94
sculpture and constructions, 78, 80–1,
130–2, 180–2
and the *Section d'Or*, 15–17
use of *collage* and *papier collé*, 93, 95,
104–14, 116, 120, 122–3, 126–7, 192
use of colour, 114–17
use of light, 67
use of stencilled letters, 91–3, 95, 106,
192

Dada, 108, 177, 196
De Stijl, 25
Delacroix, Eugène, 36
Delaunay, Robert, 5–6, 11, 12, 150, 160,
161, 169, 188, 196
abstraction, 190–1
and *Der Blaue Reiter*, 30–1
Cézanne's influence, 153–4, 158, 165–6
first Cubist manifestations, 7–9
and Futurism, 29
interest in colour theory, 60, 184–6,
191–2, 197
moves away from Cubism, 19–20
Orphism, 20, 21–2, 24, 29, 183, 184, 196
realism, 189
use of colour, 137, 167
Eiffel Tower series, 153–4, 155, 157–8,
162, 164, 166, 167, 185, Pls. 76, 80A
L'Equipe de Cardiff, 23, Pl. 81
Fenêtres, 22, 184, 185, 186–7, Pl. 79
Saint Séverin series, 153, 154, 187
Simultaneous Disk, 187, 191, Pl. 80B
Les Tours de Laon, 165, 192, Pl. 78A
La Ville, 164–6, 185–6, 187, 192, Pl. 77
La Ville de Paris, 13, 166, 186, P. 78B
Delaunay, Sonia, 21, 22, 24
Denis, Maurice, 4
Derain, André, 2, 4, 33, 34, 62, 82, 151, 152
Cézanne's influence on, 58, 145–6, 148
and the formation of Cubism, 145, 148–9
interest in primitive and tribal art, 44,
49, 51, 146, 147–8
sculpture, 80
Baigneuses, 36, 37, 146–8, 153, 159,
Pl. 101B
Last Supper, 147, 159, Pl. 102A
Still Life, 145–6, Pl. 101A
La Toilette, 149
Dermée, Paul, 94–5
Desvallières, Georges, 12
Desvalliers (sculptor), 182
Divisionism, 23, 140, 151, 153, 154, 164,
165, 184–5
Documents, 118
Doucet, Jacques, 38
Duchamp, Marcel, 12, 19, 24, 171, 173–7,
178, 179, 183, 196
The Bride, 177, Pl. 94
*The Bride stripped bare by her Bachelors,
Even*, 176, 177
Chess Players, 174, 175
Coffee-grinder, 176–7
Nude Descending a Staircase, 174, 175,
176, 177, Pls. 95A, 95B
Portrait, 174

Le Roi et la Reine entourés de nus vites, 20, 176
La Section d'Or, 15
The Sonata, 174, Pl. 93
Yvonne et Magdeleine Déchiquetées, 174
Duchamp-Villon, 12, 14, 173–4, 176, 180–2, 196
L'Amour, 181
Le Cheval, 181, Pl. 96
Dufy, Raoul, 149
Dumont, Pierre, 16

Eddy, Arthur Jerome, 20–1, 86
Einstein, Albert, 102
Einstein, Carl, 118
El Greco, 39–40, 184
Eluard, Paul, 178
Epstein, Elizabeth, 30
Ernst, Max, 130
Esposizione d'Arte Libera, 27
L'Esprit Nouveau, 118–19, 124
Expressionism, 30, 33–4, 154

Fang masks, 147–8, Pl. 107B
Fauvism, 2, 5, 9, 13, 23, 30, 34, 40, 51, 57–8, 59, 69, 94, 147, 148, 149–50, 152
Le Figaro, 30, 175
First World War, 2–3, 32, 139–40, 193, 194, 195–6
Fort, Paul, 6, 12, 182
Friesz, Othon, 149
Frost, A. B., 21, 24
Futurism, 25, 26–30, 31–2, 170, 175–6, 177, 179–80, 181, 188–9, 194, 196, 197

Galerie de l'Art Contemporain, 14–15
Galerie Barbazanges, 19
Galerie Bernheim, 27, 28, 29, 176
Galerie de la Boétie, 14, 15, 20, 169, 170, 174, 180, 181, 183, 187, 194
Galerie de L'Effort Moderne, 194
Gauguin, Paul, 4, 36, 40, 44, 50–1, 58, 59, 94, 146, 149
Georges, Waldemar, 116, 124
Georges-Michel, Michel, 84
Géricault, Théodore, 159
Gil Blas, 15, 21, 77, 97
Gleizes, Albert, 5–6, 7–9, 11–12, 14, 15, 18–19, 24, 97, 151, 152, 154, 158, 167, 176, 183, 192–3, 195, 196
The Bridge of Paris, 168–9, Pl. 82
Le Dépiquage des Moissons, 170–1, Pl. 83B
Du Cubisme, 17, 18, 20, 60, 87, 94, 167, 168, 169
La Femme aux Phlox, 159, 160, 168, Pl. 83A
L'Homme au Balcon, 171, Pl. 84
Landscape, 159
Gomez de la Serna, 39, 48, 51
Grebo masks, 128–9, 130–1, 132, Pls. 19B, 106E
Gris, Juan, 54, 92, 131, 169–70, 178, 183, 194–5
abstraction, 198
colours, 99, 137
death, 200
early work, 96–8
in the First World War, 195
importance of, 13
influence of Cézanne, 67, 98–9, 119
influence on minor Cubists, 103, 134, 170, 192
intellectual approach to Cubism, 102–4, 139, 143–4, 179
landscapes, 138

methods of composition, 101–2, 136–7
preliminary studies, 136, 142–3
relationship with Picasso, 97, 100
still lifes, 99–100, 101–2, 140–2
and synthetic Cubism, 118–22, 139, 143–4, 200
use of *collage* and *papier collé*, 104, 112–14, 122, 134–5, 138–9, 142
use of light, 99
Blue Guitar on a Table, 141
Bouteille et Compotier, Pl. 68B
The Eggs, 98–9, Pl. 58A
Glass of Beer and Playing Cards, 135, 137, Pl. 62B
Glasses and Newspaper, 139, Pl. 65
Grey Still Life, Pl. 60
The Guitar, Pl. 64B
Guitar, Glasses and Bottle, Pl. 66
Hommage à Picasso, 3–4, 96, 97–8, Pl. 59
L'Homme au Café, 169, Pl. 61
L'Homme à la Pipe, 100, Pl. 57
Landscape at Céret, 138, Pl. 63
Le Lavabo, 102, 104, 112–13, 135, Pl. 62A
Livre, Pipe et Verres, 140, Pl. 68A
Portrait of Germaine Raynal, 101, Pl. 60B
Portrait of Picasso, 100–1
Still Life with a Cylindrical Pot, 99, Pl. 58B
Still Life in Front of an Open Window, 141, 142, Pl. 67
Violin and Guitar, 136–7, Pl. 64A
Violon et Gravure, 108, 109, 119
Guillaume, Paul, 48–9

Haviland (Berty), Frank, 148
Herbin, Auguste, 13
Hourcade, Olivier, 10, 16, 17–20, 24, 28

Iberian sculpture, Pls. 105C, 105D, 106A, 107A
Impressionism, 5, 23, 60, 63, 94, 146, 152, 153, 181, 184–5, 188
Ingres, Jean Auguste Dominique, 36
Instinctive Cubism, 184
L'Intransigeant, 8, 21
Ivory Coast masks, Pl. 106C

Jacob, Max, 12, 16, 38, 85, 95, 151, 161
Jarry, Alfred, 26, 150
Jeanneret, Pierre, 118
Jourdain, Franz, 182

Kahn, Gustave, 7, 13
Kahnweiler, D.H., 3, 4, 11, 36, 44, 62, 64, 71, 77, 85, 88–9, 93, 96, 107, 113, 116, 117–18, 119, 121, 126, 127, 136, 141, 142, 145, 149, 157, 161, 165, 194, 195, 198
Kandinsky, Wassily, 30, 184
Improvisation, 97
Kant, Immanuel, 17–18
Klee, Paul, 31, 197
Kupka, Franz, 12, 19–20, 24, 97, 137, 172, 177
Le Langage des Verticales, Pl. 99B
Plans Verticaux, 172
Kupka, Franz, 12

La Fresnaye, Roger de, 8, 12, 24, 25, 60, 76–7, 173, 176, 182, 196
La Conquête de l'Air, Pl. 97
Le Cuirassier, 159, 160, Pl. 98A
Nature Morte aux Trois Anses, 173, Pl. 98B
Lacerba, 29
Lampué, 14
Larionov, M., 25

Laurencin, Marie, 5, 8, 12, 19, 24, 152, 182, 183
Group of Artists, Pl. 103A
Laurens, Henri, 81, 131, 195
Le Beau, Alcide, 16
Le Fauconnier, Henri, 5–6, 7–9, 11–12, 14, 20, 151, 154–5, 167
L'Abondance, 7, 158–9, 160, Pl. 88
The Huntsman (*Chasseur*), 169, Pl. 89B
Portrait of Jouve, 151–2, Pl. 89A
Lecomte, 14
Léger, Fernand, 6, 8, 9, 11–12, 150, 154, 159–60, 167, 176, 182, 187–92
abstraction, 197
Cézanne's influence, 59–60, 152–3
cityscapes, 161–2, 165
in the First World War, 195
and Futurism, 29, 188
influence on Gleizes and Le Fauconnier, 168–9, 171
and Orphism, 24, 29, 183, 187
post-war work, 200–1
Contrastes de Formes, 190, 196, 198, Pl. 74
La Couseuse, 152, 153, 155–6, 157, 159, 161, 162, Pl. 69
L'Escalier, 190, Pl. 75
La Femme en Bleu, 163–4, 191, Pl. 73
Fumées sur les Toits, 161, 162, Pl. 70B
Les Fumeurs, 162–3, 169, 171, Pl. 71
Le Jardin, 152
La Noce, 163, 169, Pl. 72
Nus dans un Paysage, 155–7, 160–1, 162, 171–2, 191, Pl. 70A
Legua, 100
Leonardo da Vinci, 15
Lhote, André, 5, 8, 12–13, 103, 159, 173, 196
Portrait of Marguerite, Pl. 104A
Lipchitz, Jacques, 81, 131, 195
Danseuse, Pl. 104B
Louvre, 40, 42–3
Luce, Maximilien, 150
Lugné-Poë, 182

Macke, Auguste, 31
Maison Cubiste, 182–3
Malevitch, Kasimir, 25, 197
Mallarmé, Stéphane, 165
Malraux, André, 45
Manet, Edouard, 36
Manolo, 102
Marc, Franz, 31
Marchand, Jean, 8, 9, 173
Marcoussis, Louis, 13, 172–3
Nature Morte au Damier, 173, Pl. 100
Mare, André, 8, 14, 161, 182
Marey, E-J., 176
Marinetti, Filippo, 26, 27, 29
Martin, Henri (Barzun), 23
Matisse, Henri, 3, 32, 39, 65, 69, 124, 152
Cézanne's influence, 37, 57–8
declining influence, 13, 30
importance of, 4, 149
interest in tribal art, 45, 49, 51
sculpture, 80
Blue Nude, 147
Le Bonheur de Vivre, 34, 36–7
Mercereau, Alexandre, 6, 7, 12, 14
Mercure de France, 7, 14, 59
Merrill, Stuart, 6
Metzinger, Jean, 5–6, 7–8, 9, 11–12, 13, 14, 15, 18–19, 24, 151, 154–5, 158, 160, 167, 176, 183, 192–3, 196
La Danseuse au Café, 170, Pl. 85
Du Cubisme, 17, 18, 20, 60, 87, 94, 167, 168, 169

Le Goûter, 167–8, Pl. 86B
La Plume Jaune, 170, Pl. 87
Two Nudes, 155, 166, 168, Pl. 86A
Miro, Joan, 130
Mondrian, Piet, 25, 197–8
Composition, Pl. 103B
Montjoie, 21, 22, 181
Moreau, Luc Albert, 8, 9, 16, 159, 173
Muybridge, Eadweard, 176

Nabis, 94, 182
Nayral, Jacques, 12
Neo-Impressionism, 4–5, 152, 191
Neo-Plasticism, 25
Neue Künstlervereinigung, 30
Nord-Sud, 75, 94–5

Oceanic art, 46, 48–9
Olivier, Fernande, 71–2
Orphism, 20, 21–5, 26, 31, 172, 183, 184, 187, 196
Osuna sculpture, Pl. 105C
Ozenfant, Amédée, 102, 118

Pach, Walter, 181
Pan, 6
Paris Journal, 15, 48, 96, 160, 180
Physical Cubism, 183–4
Picabia, Francis, 12, 19, 21, 24, 171–2, 183, 196
Danseuses à la Source, 171–2, Pl. 99A
Picasso, Pablo, 178, 183, 194
analysis of form, 53, 80–1, 84–5
analytical Cubism, 118
at Céret, 91
background, 1, 3–4
'blue period', 40
Cadaquès paintings, 85, 89, 90, 118, 161, 198
Cézanne's influence, 37–9, 47, 60, 64–70, 71–2, 146
chronology, 70–1
collaboration with Braque, 1–3, 4, 65, 127
constructions, 81, 130–2, 140, 180
figure paintings, 69–70
in the First World War, 195
'hermetic' phase, 118
importance to Cubism, 25, 26, 28, 152, 154–5, 159–60, 168, 172–3, 175
influence on Braque, 56–7, 61
influence in Germany, 30
influence on Léger, 161
influence on Metzinger, 155
interest in primitive and tribal art, 40–3, 44–53, 63, 65, 69, 72, 107, 128–9, 130–1
and Juan Gris, 97, 100
methods of composition, 84–5, 90, 101, 157
moves towards abstraction, 85–6, 88
and the origins of Cubism, 7, 10–11, 13
Orphism, 24
paintings at Horta de San Juan, 71–6, 78–9, 81, 84, 100, 138, 156
papier collés, 81
pointillism, 132
post-war work, 197, 200–1
Rue-des-Bois landscapes, 65, 67–8, 69, 71, 114, 150
sculpture, 78, 80–1
still lifes, 68
subjects, 87–8
trompe l'oeil, 132, 140
use of *collage* and *papier collé*, 93, 95, 104–6, 108, 109–14, 116, 120, 122, 127, 140, 192
use of colour, 114–16, 125–6, 132

use of stencilled letters, 93, 106
L'Aficionado, 115, Pl. 22
Baigneuse, 74, 100, Pl. 7B
Bottle and Glasses, 117, Pl. 18A
Bouteille de Pernod, 117, Pl. 18B
Bouteille de Vieux Marc, Verre, Journal, 110, 111, Pl. 24B
Bouteille et Guitare, 131, Pl. 29A
Bread and Fruit Dish on a Table, 54, 55–6, 65, Pl. 5
Carnaval au bistrot, 55
Casket, Cup, Apple, Pl. 8B
Le Compotier, 68, Pl. 6B
Les Demoiselles d'Avignon, 1, 2, 33–49, 54, 56–7, 61, 64, 73, 114, 149, 200, Pl. 1
L'Etudiant à la Pipe, 111, 129–30, Pl. 29B
La Femme aux Poires, Pl. 9
Femme en Chemise assise dans un Fauteuil, 130, Pl. 30A
Girl with a Mandolin, Pl. 12
Green Still Life, 134, Pl. 31B
Geurnica, 200
Guitar, 106–8, 117, Pl. 19A
Harlequin, 128–9, Pl. 28
Head, 78, 80–1, 180
Head of a Man, Pl. 106B
Head of a Woman, Pl. 10
L'Homme à la Pipe, Pl. 17
Homme Assis au Verre, 132, 134, Pl. 32
L'Homme au Livre, 132
Houses on the Hill, Horta de San Juan, Pl. 14A
Jeune Fille à la Mandoline, 83–4
Landscape, La Rue-des-Bois, Pl. 6A
'Ma Jolie', 93, Pl. 21
Mademoiselle Léonie, Pl. 15B
Male Head (The Poet), 106
Le Modèle, 115, 117, Pl. 23
Nu à la Draperie (Danseuse aux Voiles), 52, Pl. 3A
Nude, Pl. 15A
Nude (Cadaquès), Pl. 14B
Nude Woman, Pl. 7A
La Paysanne, 53, 147, Pl. 3B
The Piano, 116
Portrait of Gertrude Stein, 41, 73, Pl. 105B
Portrait of Kahnweiler, 88–9, 198, Pl. 16
Portrait of Uhde, 81, Pl. 13
Portrait of Vollard, 84
The Seated Woman, 132, 133, Pl. 11
Seated Woman (Portrait de Jeune Fille), Pl. 30B
Self-Portrait, 41
Still Life, Carafe, Jug and Fruit Bowl, Pl. 8A
Still Life with Bottle, 91, Pl. 33
Still Life with Chair-caning, 104, 108, 113, Pl. 24A
Still Life with Guitar, 110
Three Dancers, 200
Three Women, 54–6, 65, Pl. 4
Two Nudes, 35, 41, 43, Pl. 2
The Violin (1912), 123, Pl. 20B
The Violin (*papier collé*), 109–10, 111, Pl. 25
Violin and Guitar, 125–6, Pl. 27
Violin, 'Jolie Eva', 117, Pl. 20A
Le Violon (1914), 133–4, Pl. 31A
Violon au Café, 122–3, Pl. 26
Plumet, Jean, 9
Poincaré, Jules Henri, 102
pointillism, 132, 133, 141
La Presse, 6
Princet, Maurice, 15, 103, 168, 175
Purism, 94, 196, 200

Raynal, Maurice, 11, 16, 17, 86, 105, 119
Rayonism, 25
Redon, Odilon, 174
Reverdy, Pierre, 12, 16, 75
Revue de France, 28
Ribbemont-Dessaignes, 182
Rimbaud, Arthur, 95
Rodchenko, Alexander, 197
Rodin, Auguste, 181
Rood, 184
Rosenberg, Léonce, 194
Rosso, Medardo, 181
Rousseau, Henri 'Le Douanier', 11, 53, 55, 67, 150–1, 153, 156, 159
  Notre Dame, 166
  Portrait of Yadwriga, 150
  Le Rêve, 150
  Self-Portrait, 166
Rubin, William, 55
Rupf collection, 31
Russel, Morgan, 24
Russolo, Luigi, 27

Sabartès, Jaime, 105
Sagot, Clovis, 96
Salmon, André, 3, 7, 16, 17, 24–5, 33, 34–5, 38, 45, 50, 105–6, 110
Salon d'Automne, 4, 15, 37, 62, 172
  1903, 16
  1906, 6
  1907, 5, 58–9
  1908, 3, 149
  1909, 151, 152
  1910, 7, 154, 182
  1911, 167, 173, 174, 178
  1912, 14, 19, 163, 171, 182
  1913, 24, 25, 170, 180, 181
Salon de Juin, 13, 171
Salon des Indépendants, 15, 30, 37, 150, 155
  1906, 34
  1907, 2, 4, 34, 146–7, 149, 150
  1908, 3, 149
  1909, 10, 77, 149
  1910, 5, 150
  1911, 7–8, 12, 25, 151, 155, 157, 159–60, 167, 169, 171
  1912, 4, 13, 19–20, 96, 97, 163, 166, 169–70, 175, 176, 177
  1913, 22, 23, 24, 187
  1914, 24, 26, 148, 172, 191
  1920, 194–5
Schopenhauer, Artur, 17–18
Scientific Cubism, 183
Section d'Or, 10, 14, 15–17, 19, 20, 21, 96, 169, 170, 171, 172, 173, 176, 177, 178, 180, 182–3, 194, 195
Section d'Or (periodical), 105
Segonzac, Dunoyer de, 8, 9, 16, 159, 173
Sembat, Marcel, 14
Sérusier, Paul, 7
Seurat, Georges, 170, 184
  Chahut, 170
  Parade, 170
Severini, Gino, 26–7, 170, 175, 194
Signac, Paul, 4–5, 7, 28, 150
Simultaneism *see* Orphism
Société des Artistes Indépendants, 8–10
Société Normande de Peinture Moderne, 14–15, 16
Soffici, Ardengo, 27
Les Soirées de Paris, 17, 21, 184, 190
Stein, Gertrude, 33, 41, 45, 54, 92
Stein, Leo, 54
De Stijl, 198, 200
Stravinsky, Igor, 23

Der Sturm, 29, 31
Suprematism, 25
Surrealism, 49, 50, 108, 130, 200
Sweeney, James Johnson, 40
Symbolists, 6, 12
Synchromists, 24
synthetic Cubism, 117–22, 139, 143–4, 200

Le Temps, 146
Thannhauser Gallery, Munich, 30
Théâtre de l'Oeuvre, 26
Toulouse Lautrec, Henri de, 150
Tribal art, 44–53, 61, 65, 69, 72, 81, 107, 128–9, 146, 147–8, 151
Tschoukine, Sergei, 33
Turner, J.M.W., 184

Uhde, Wilhelm, 2, 4, 11, 31

Valensi, 21
Van Dongen, Kees, 150, 152
Van Gogh, Vincent, 40
  Arlésienne, 37
Vauxcelles, Louis, 3, 4–5, 10, 19–20, 36, 62, 77, 146–7, 149, 150, 151, 177, 195, 196
Vera, Paul, 182
Verhaeren, Emile, 6
Vers et Prose, 6
Villon, Jacques, 12, 15, 172, 173–4, 177–80, 182, 195, 196
  La Femme Assie, Pl. 92
  Jeune Femme, 178–9
  Portrait of his Brother, Duchamp-Villon, 178, Pl. 91A
  Soldats en Marche, 179, Pl. 91B
  Young Woman, Pl. 90
Vlaminck, Maurice, 44, 146, 149
  La Voce, 27
Vollard, Ambroise, 1, 37
Vuillard, Edouard, 4

Walden Gallery, Berlin, 31
Warnod, André, 16, 23, 45, 182
Wright, MacDonald, 24

Zayas, Maurice de, 148
Zervos, Christian, 40

PLATES

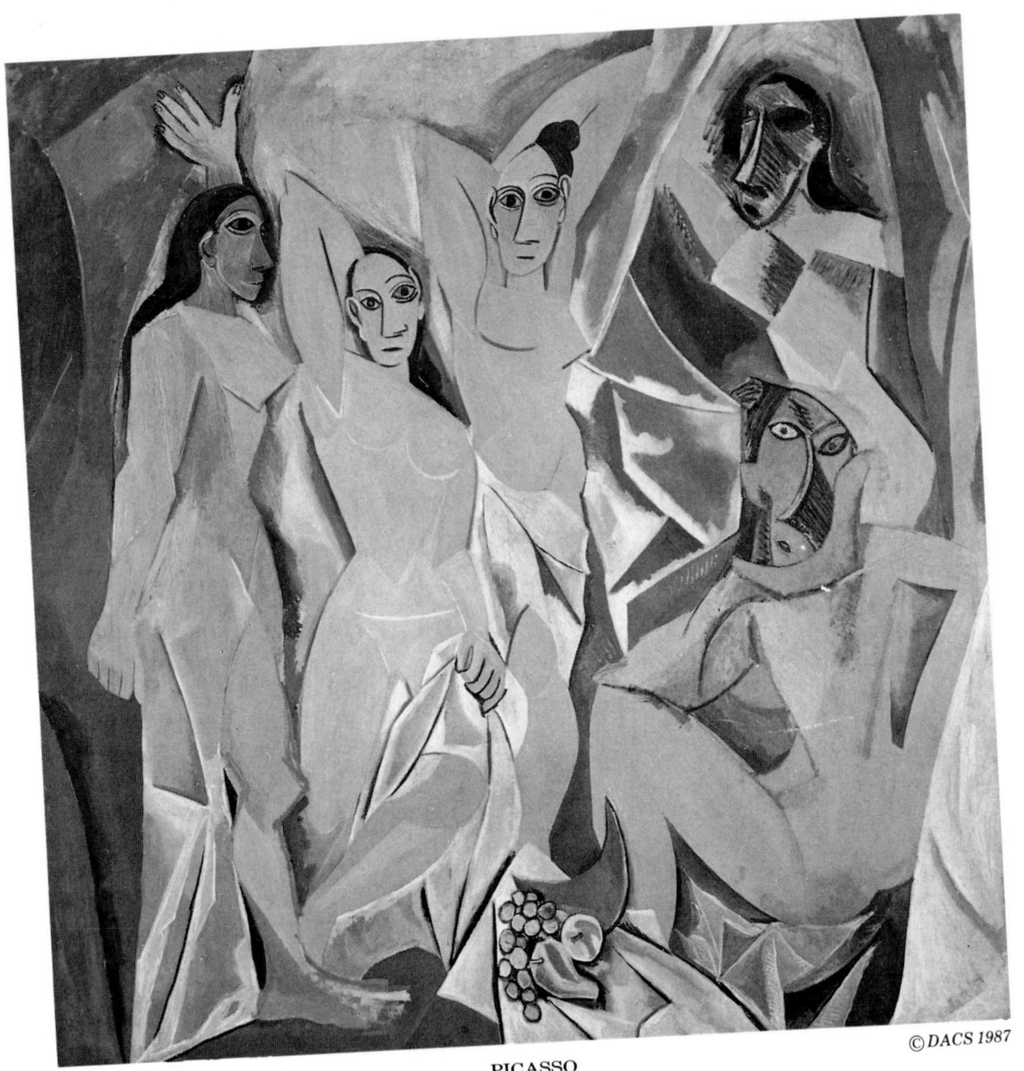

PICASSO
1 Les Demoiselles d'Avignon, 1907
Oil, 243.8 × 233.7 cm (96 × 92 in)
Collection, The Museum of Modern Art, New York
Acquired through the Lillie P. Bliss Bequest

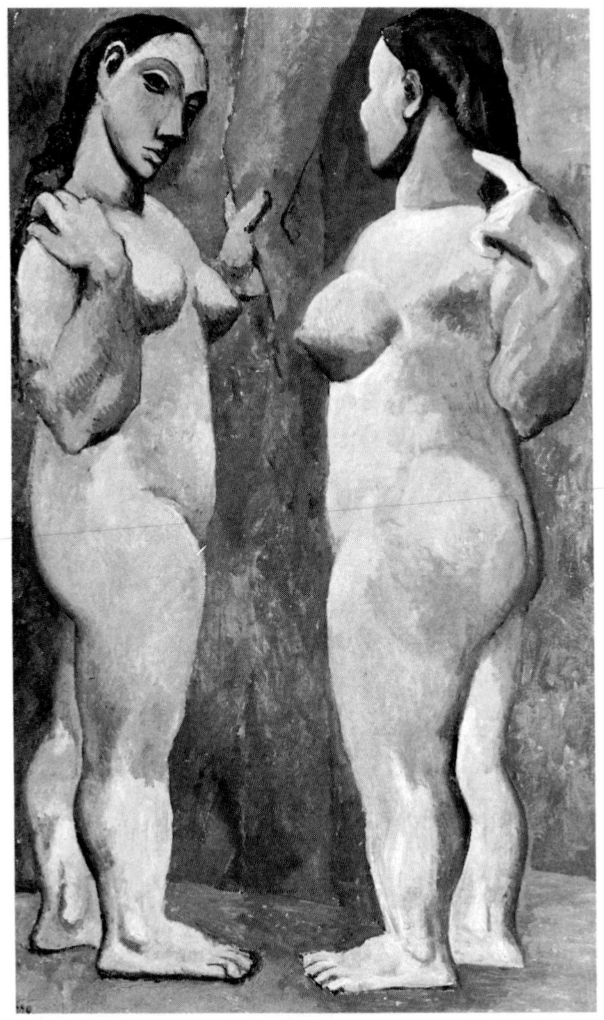

PICASSO
2 Two Nudes, 1906
Oil, 151.4 × 93 cm (59⅝ × 36⅝ in)
Collection, The Museum of Modern Art, New York
Gift of G. David Thompson in honour of Alfred H. Barr, Jr

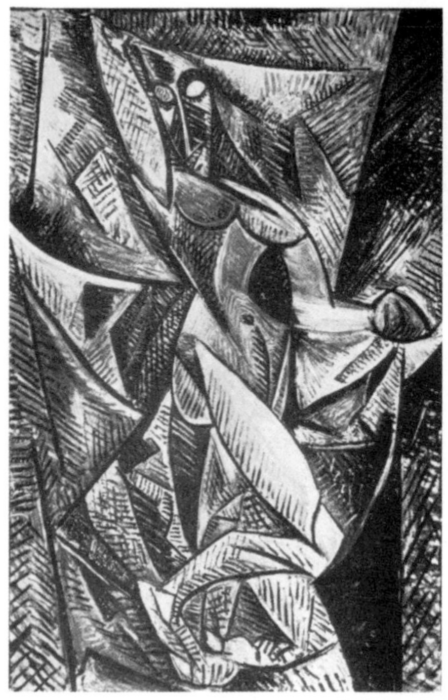

PICASSO
3A Nu à la Draperie, 1907
Oil, 154.3 × 102.8 cm (60¾ × 40½ in)
The Hermitage, Leningrad

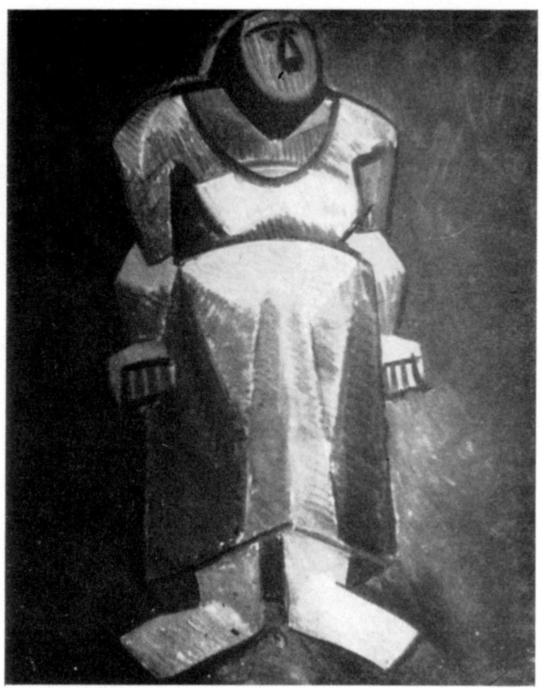

PICASSO
3B La Paysanne, 1908
Oil, 90.1 × 56.2 cm (35½ × 22⅛ in)
The Hermitage, Leningrad

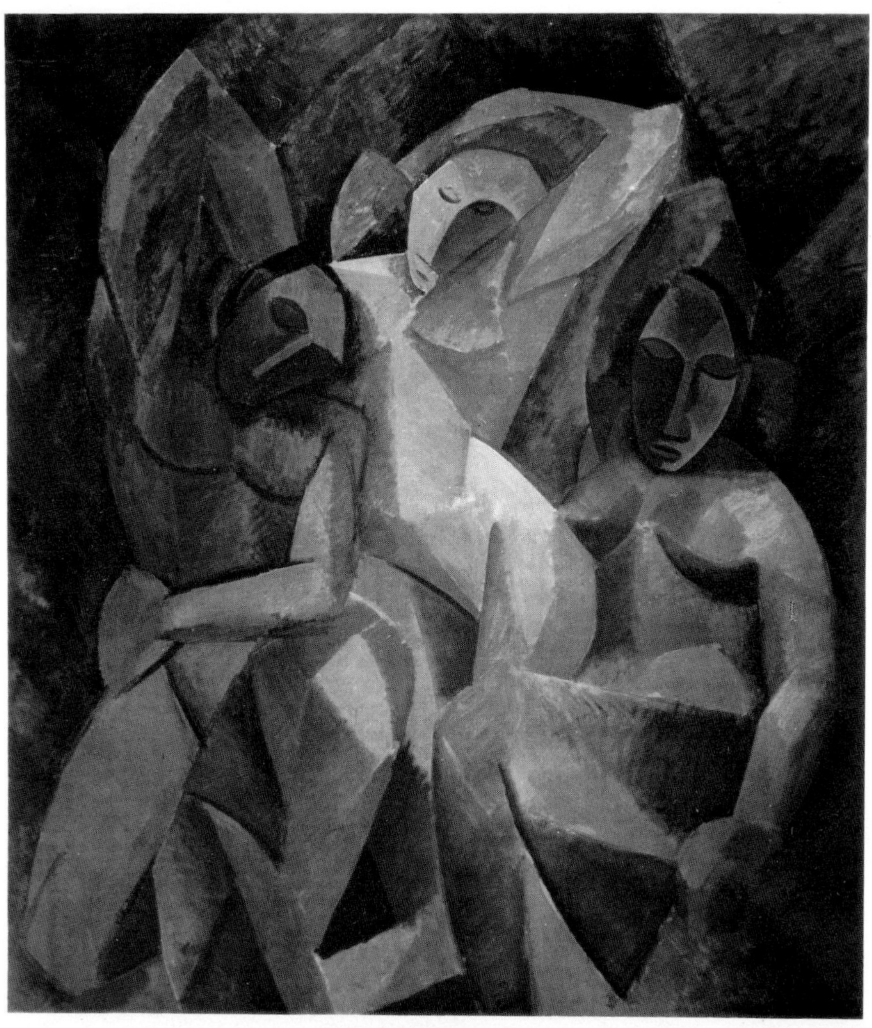

PICASSO

4 Three Women, 1908–9

Oil, 200 × 178.1 cm (78¾ × 70⅛ in)

The Hermitage, Leningrad

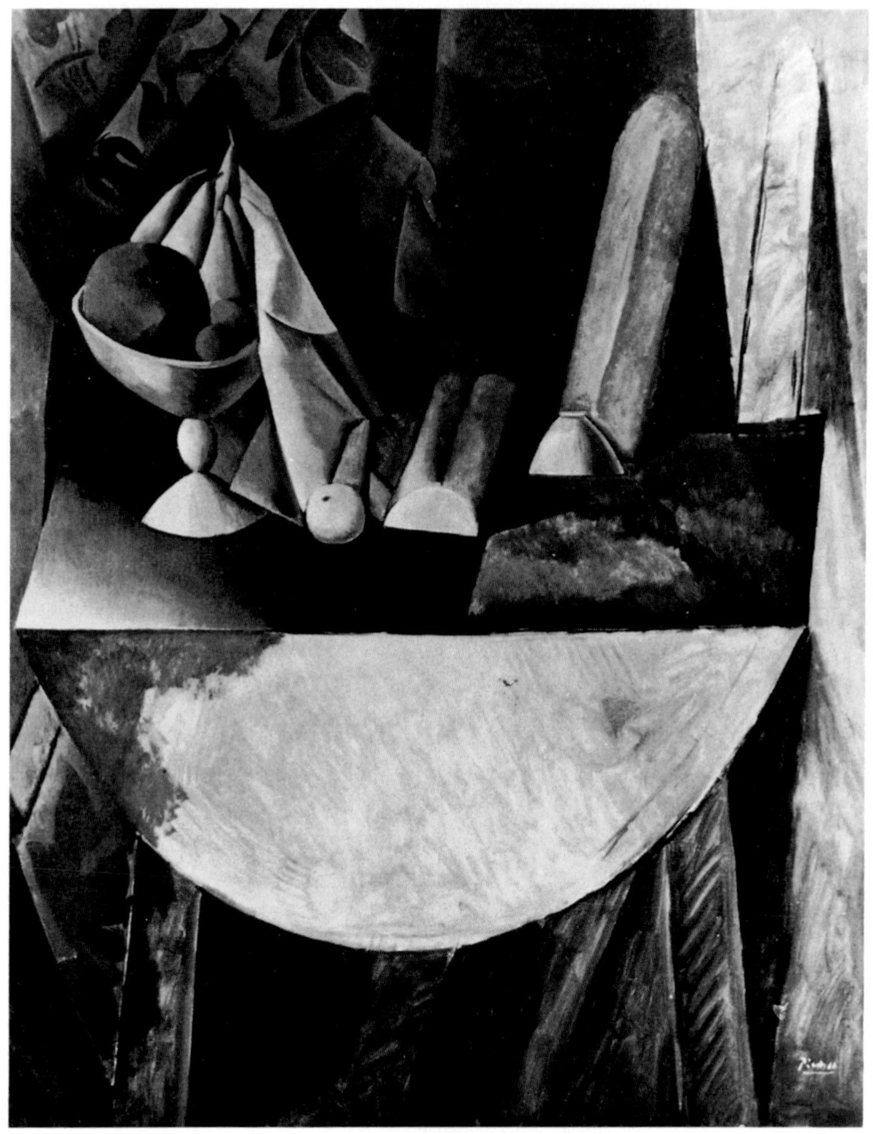

PICASSO
5 Bread and Fruit Dish on a Table, 1909
Oil, 166.7 × 132.7 cm (65⅝ × 52¼ in)
Kunstmuseum, Basel

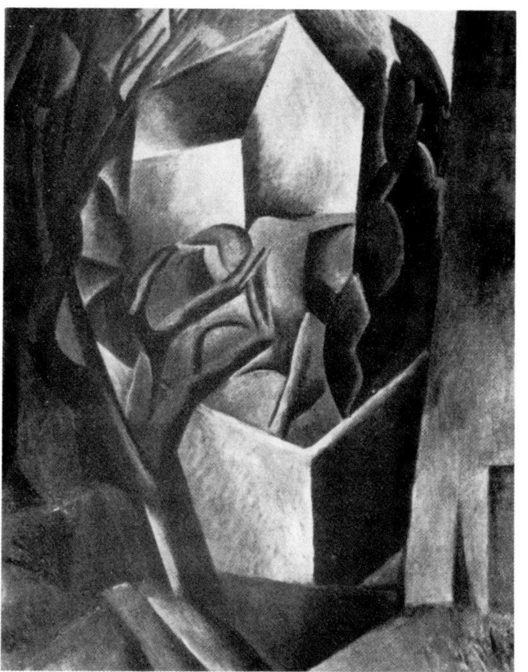

PICASSO

6A Landscape, La Rue-des-Bois, 1908
Oil, 92.7 × 74.3 cm (36½ × 29¼ in)
Pushkin Museum of Fine Art, Moscow

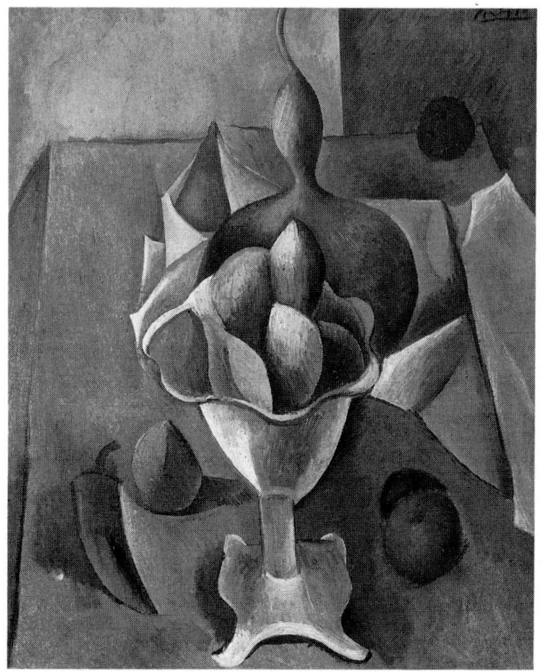

PICASSO

6B Le Compotier (Fruit Dish), 1908
Oil, 74.3 × 60.9 cm (29¼ × 24 in)
Collection, The Museum of Modern Art, New York
Acquired through the Lillie P. Bliss Bequest

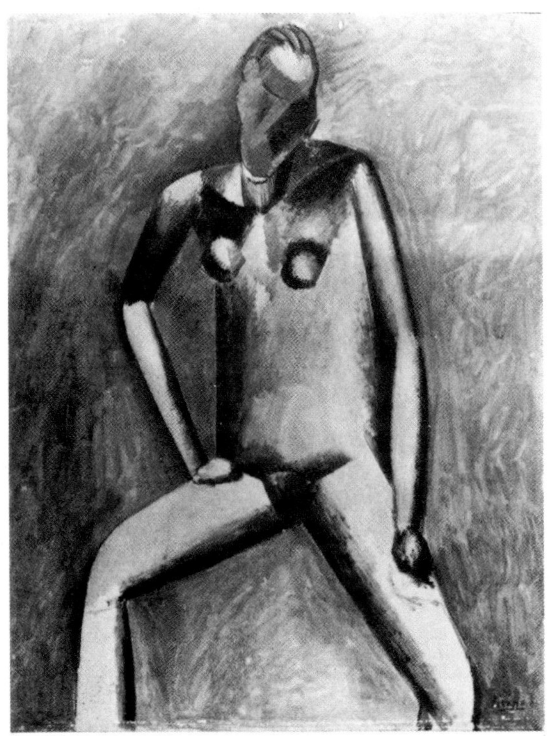

PICASSO

7A Nude Woman, 1908–9

Oil, 116.2 × 88.9 cm (45¾ × 35 in)

Louise and Walter Arensberg Collection, Philadelphia Museum of Art

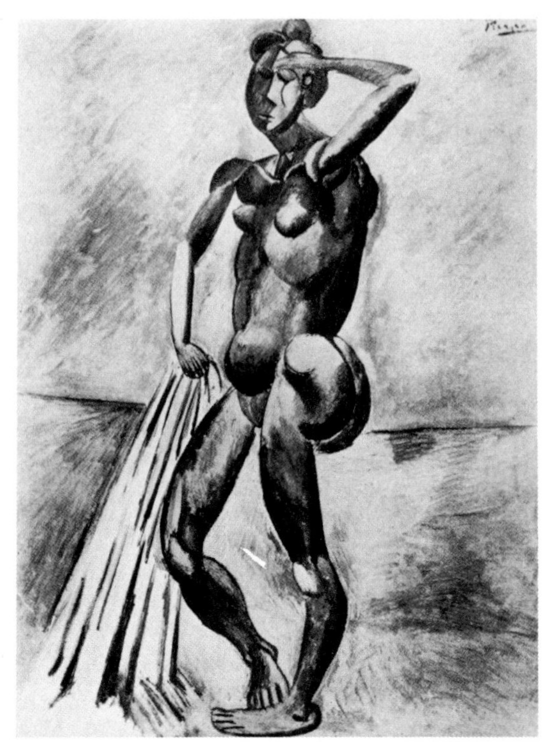

PICASSO

7B Baigneuse, 1909

Oil, 130.2 × 97.1 cm (51¼ × 38¼ in)

Private Collection, New York

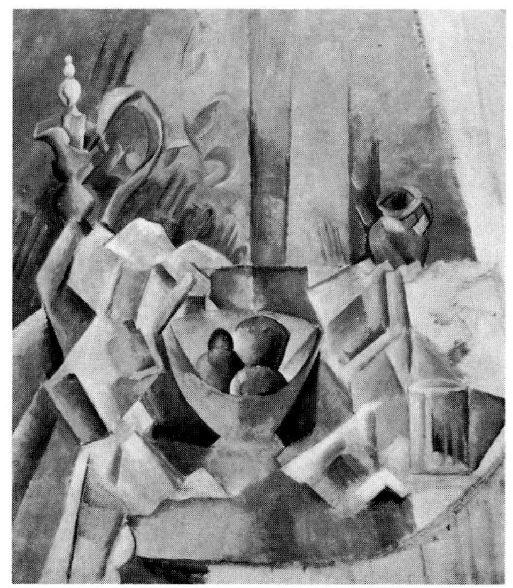

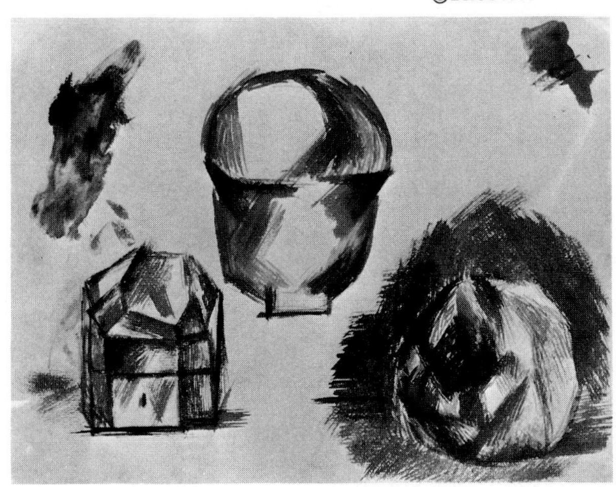

PICASSO

8A Still Life, Carafe, Jug and Fruit Bowl, 1909
Oil, 60.3 × 65.7 cm (23¾ × 25⅞ in)
Solomon R. Guggenheim Museum, New York

8B Casket, Cup, Apple, 1909
Ink and wash on paper, 24.1 × 31.4 cm (9½ × 12⅜ in)
Collection, The Museum of Modern Art, New York
Gift of Justin K. Thannhauser

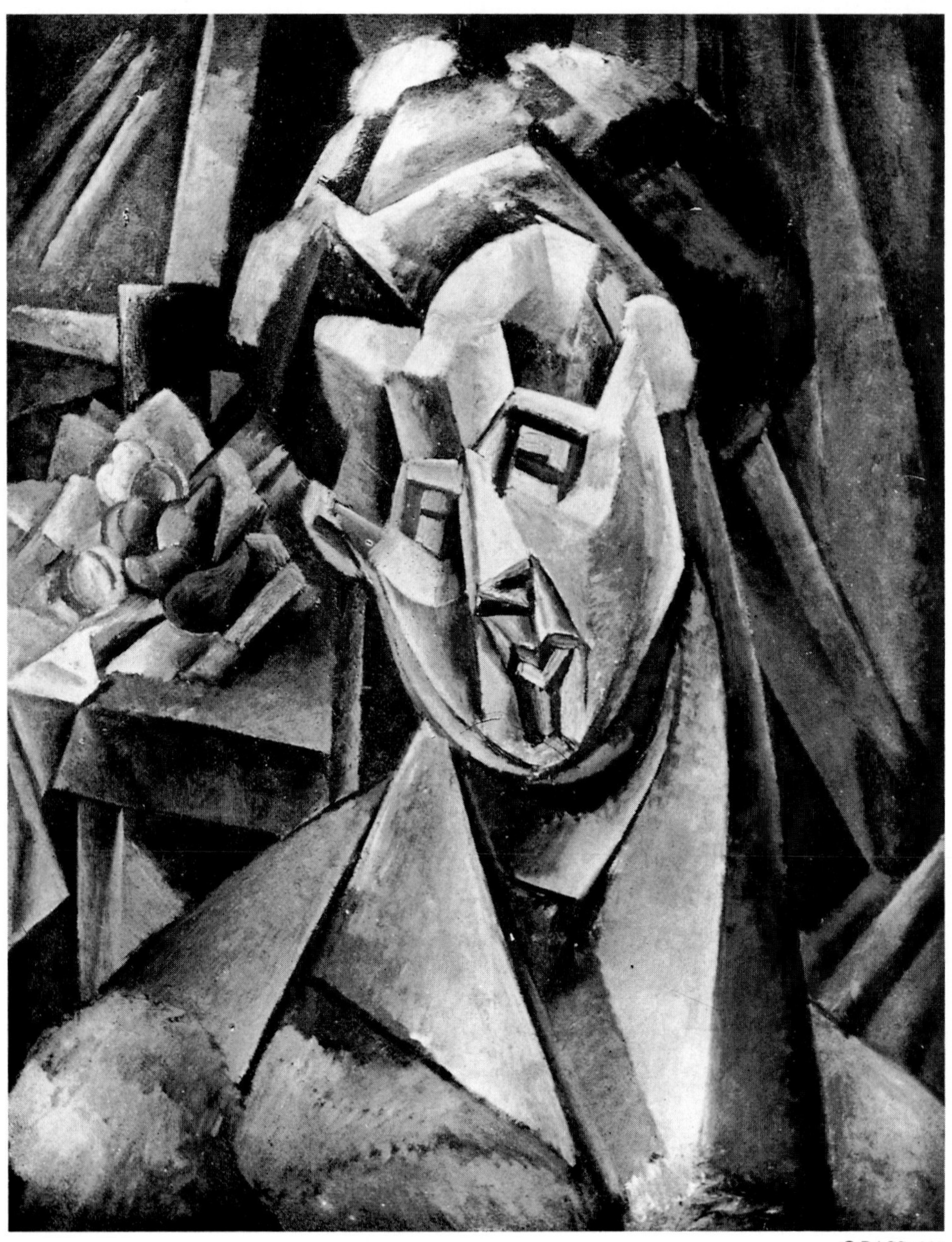

PICASSO
9 La Femme aux Poires, 1909
Oil, 92.7 × 61.6 cm (36½ × 24¼ in)
Private Collection

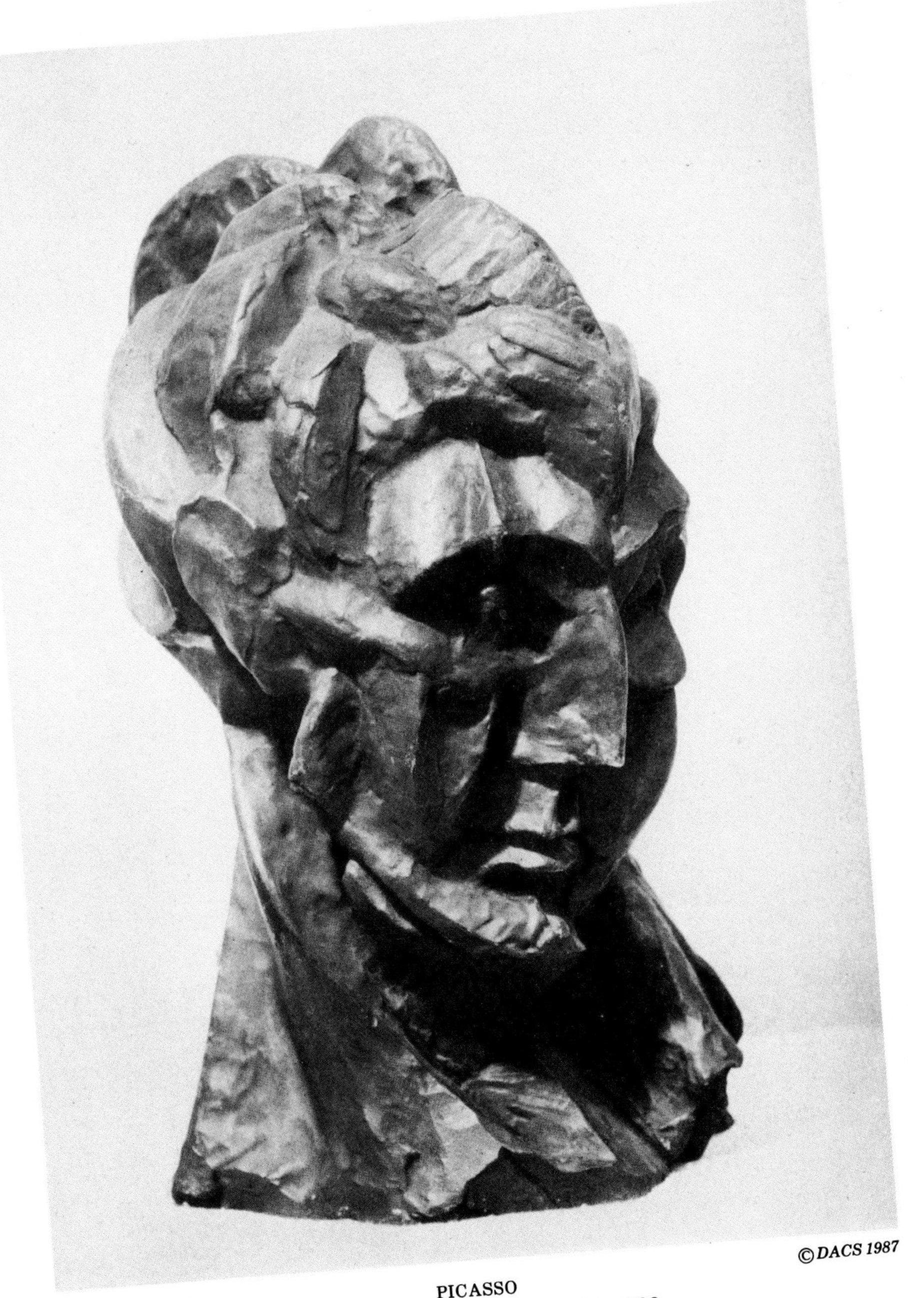

PICASSO
10 Head of a Woman (Fernande), 1909
Bronze, height 41.3 cm (16¼ in)
Collection, The Museum of Modern Art, New York. Purchase

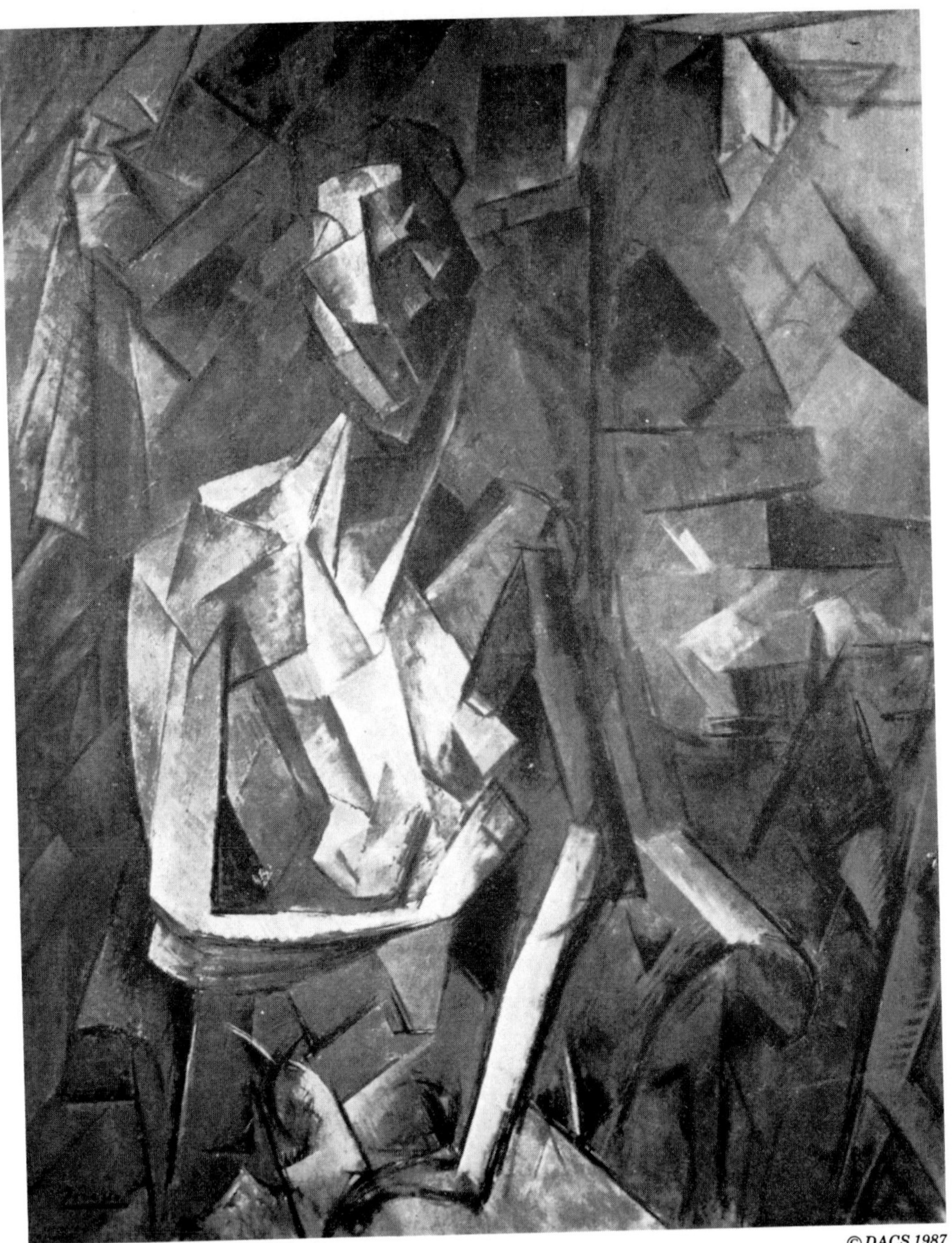

PICASSO
11 Seated Woman, 1910
Oil, 92.7 × 61.6 cm (36½ × 24¼ in)
Tate Gallery, London

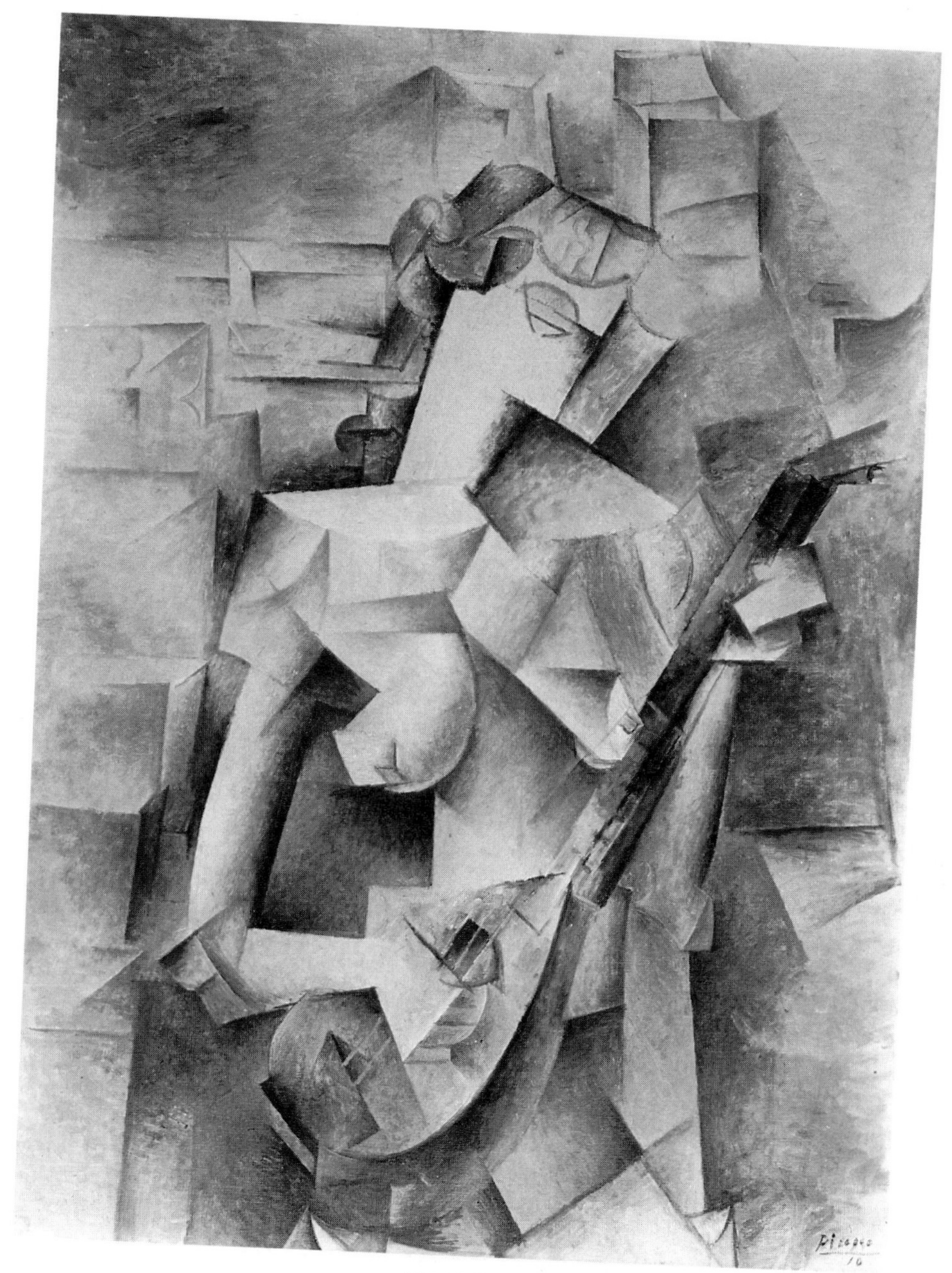

PICASSO

12 Girl with a Mandolin (The Portrait of Fanny Tellier), 1910

Oil, 100.3 × 73.6 cm (39½ × 29 in)

Collection, The Museum of Modern Art, New York

Nelson A. Rockefeller Bequest

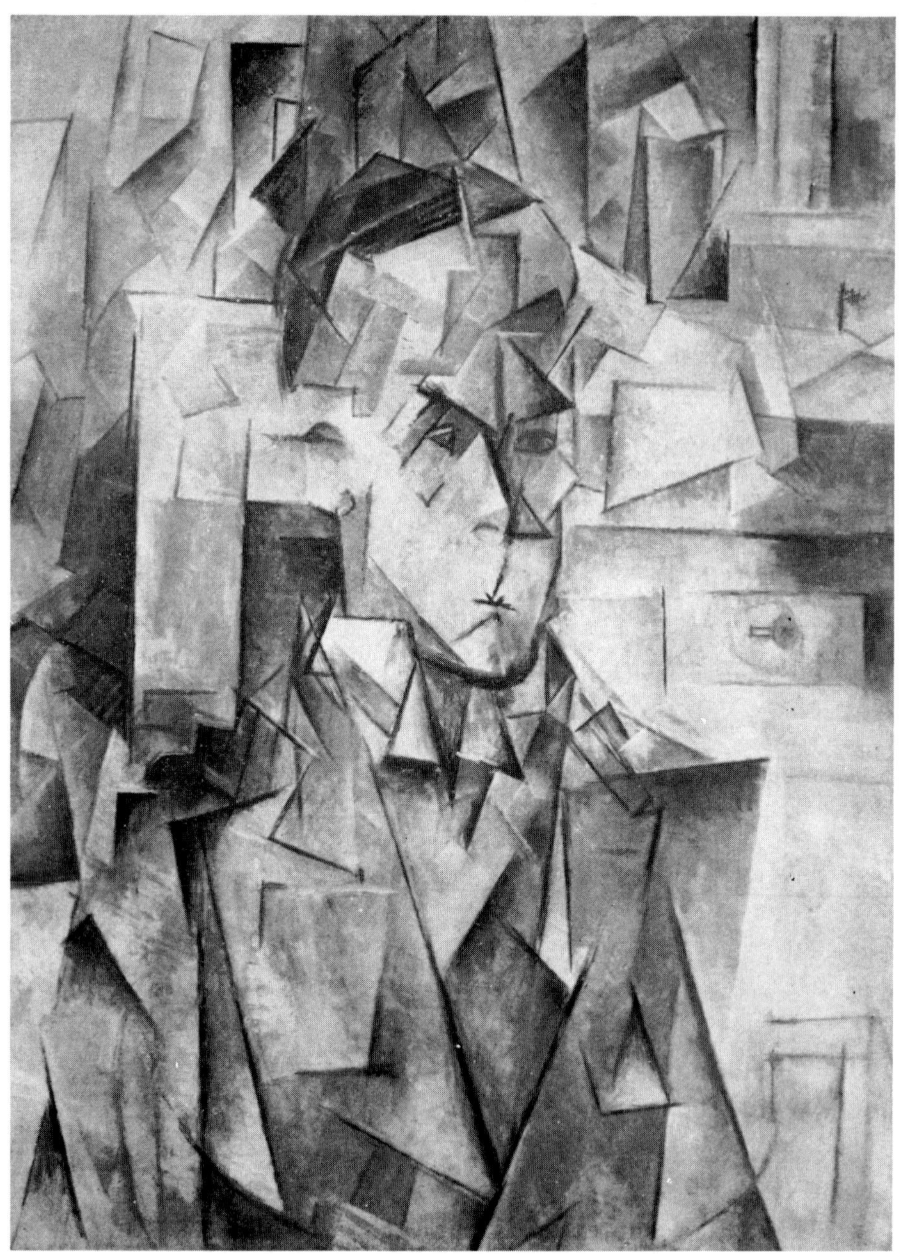

PICASSO
13 Portrait of Uhde, 1910
Oil, 78.1 × 57.8 cm (30¾ × 22¾ in)
Collection Joseph Pullitzer, St. Louis

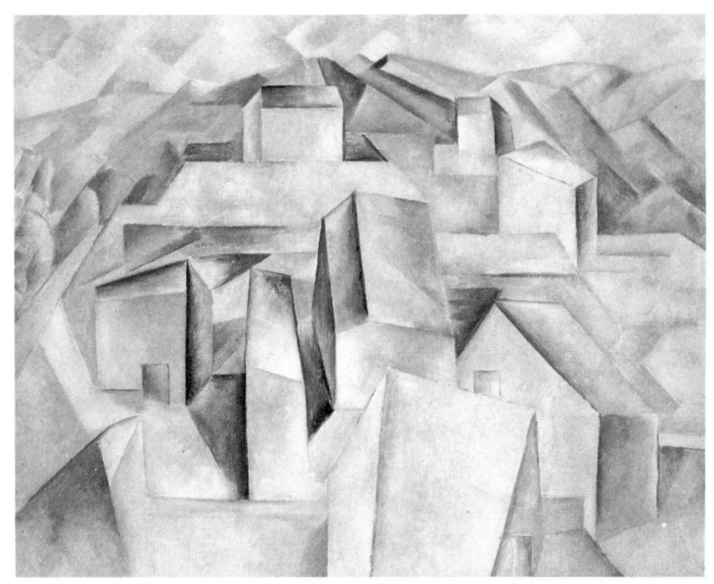

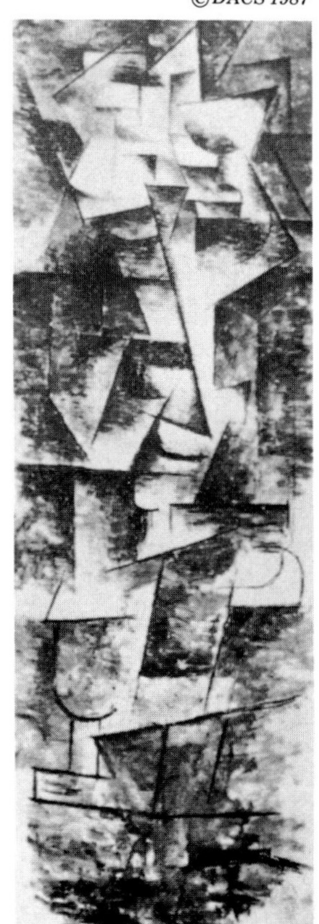

PICASSO

14A Houses on the Hill, Horta de Ebro (Horta de San Juan), 1909
Oil, 65.1 × 80.6 cm (25⅝ × 31⅞ in)
Collection, The Museum of Modern Art, New York

14B Nude (Cadaquès), 1910
Oil, 187 × 60.9 cm (73⅝ × 24 in)
National Gallery of Art, Washington

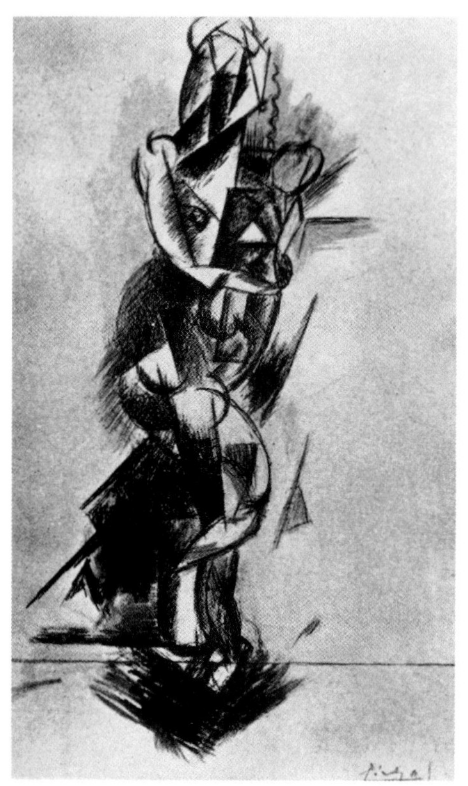

PICASSO

15A Nude, 1910.

Ink and wash, 74 × 46.7 cm (29⅛ × 18⅜ in)

Private Collection

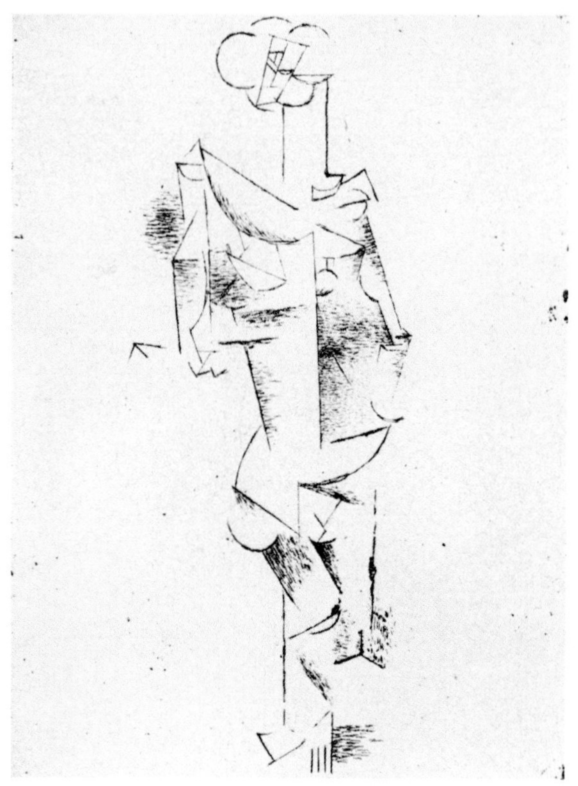

PICASSO

15B Mademoiselle Léonie, 1910

Etching, 20 × 14.1 cm (7⅞ × 5$\frac{9}{16}$ in)

Collection, The Museum of Modern Art, New York

Purchase

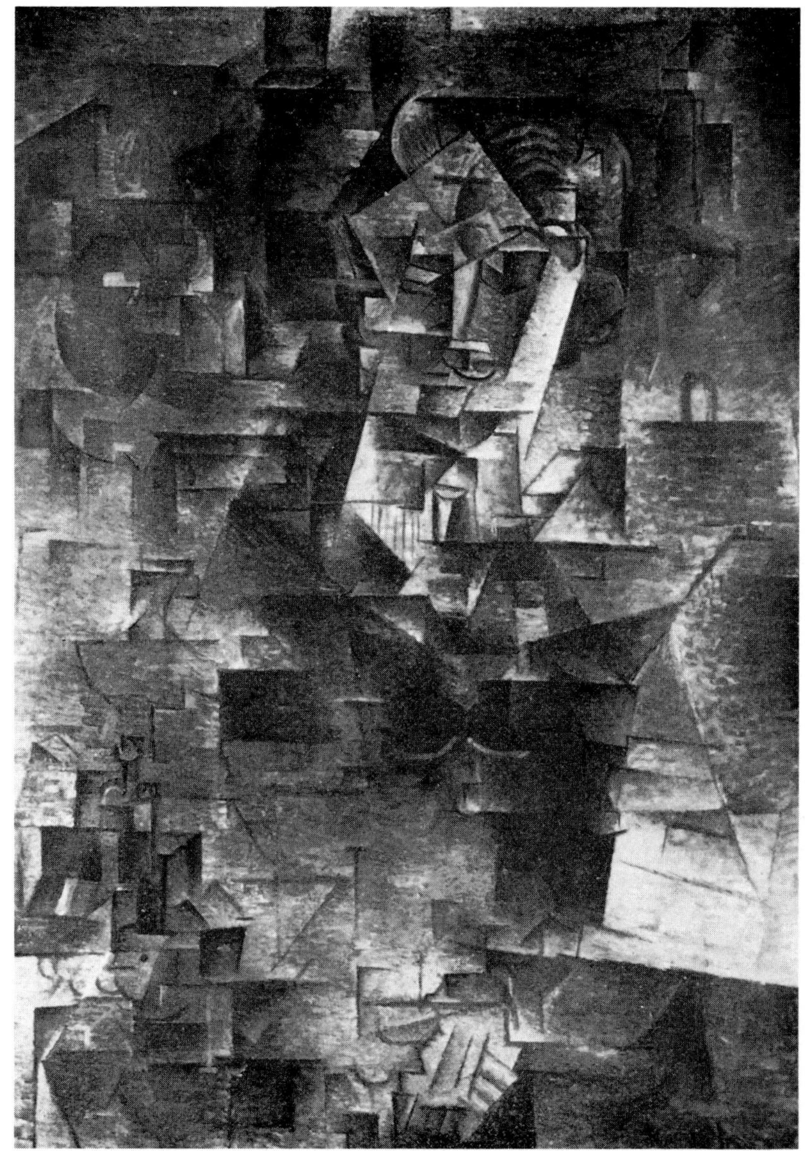

PICASSO
16 Portait of Monsieur Kahnweiler, 1910
Oil, 99.7 × 71.7 cm (39¼ × 28¼ in)
The Art Institute of Chicago, bequest of Mrs Gilbert Chapman

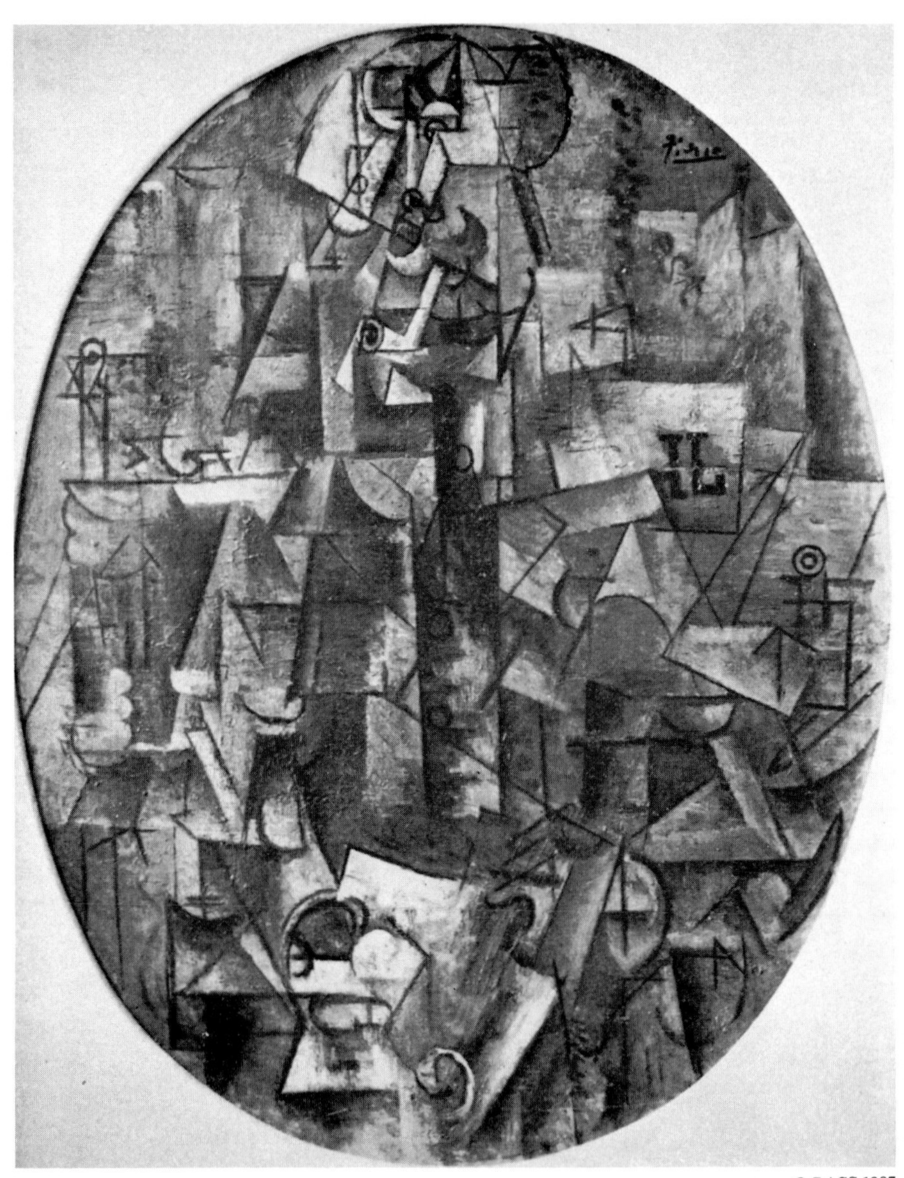

PICASSO
17 L'Homme à la Pipe, 1911
Oil, 90.1 × 71.7 cm ($35\frac{1}{2} \times 28\frac{1}{4}$ in)
Kimbell Art Museum, Fort Worth

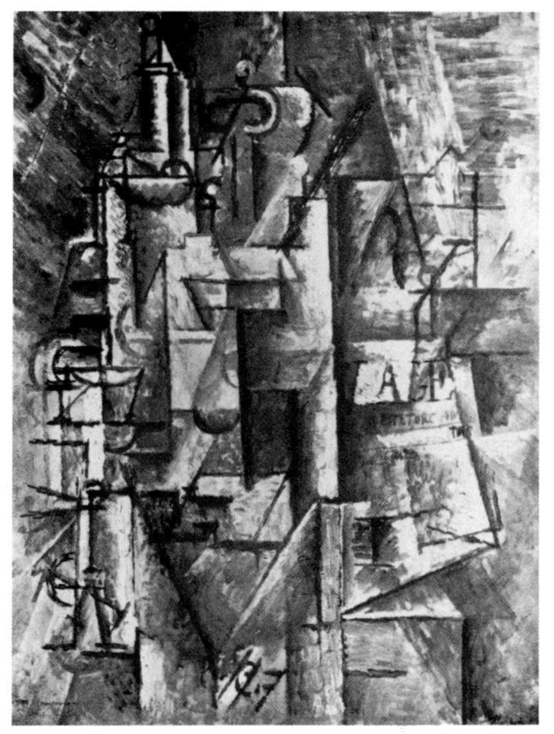

PICASSO

18A Bottle and Glasses, 1911–12

Oil, 66 × 61 cm (26 × 24 in)

Solomon R. Guggenheim Museum, New York

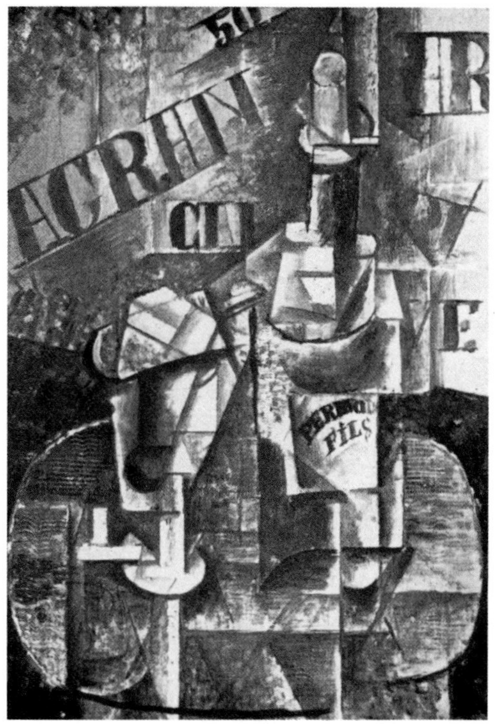

PICASSO

18B Bouteille de Pernod, 1912

Oil, 47 × 33.6 cm (18½ × 13¼ in)

The Hermitage, Leningrad

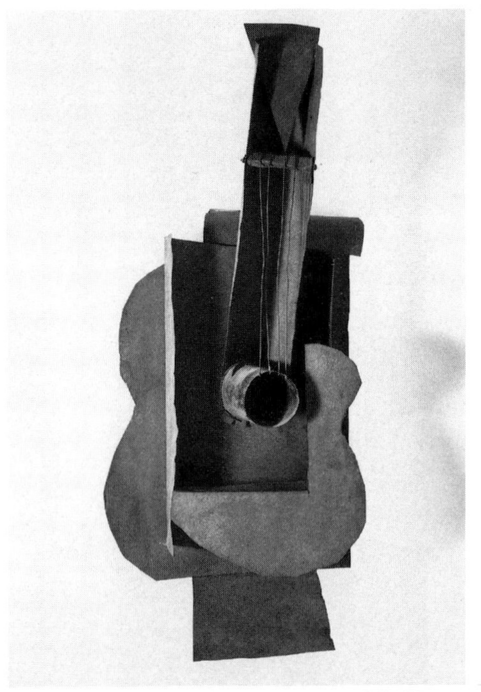

PICASSO ©*DACS 1987*

19A Guitar, 1912

Sheet metal and wire, 77.5 × 33.3 × 19.3 cm
(30½ × 13⅛ × 7⅝ in)

Collection, The Museum of Modern Art, New York
Gift of the artist

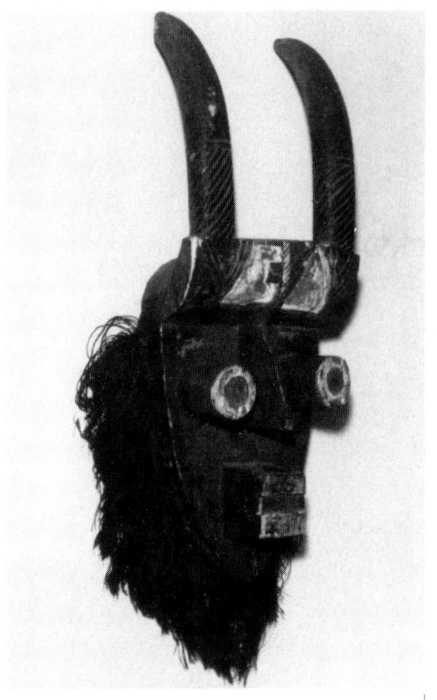

19B Mask. Grebo, Ivory Coast or Liberia
Painted wood and fibre, 63.8 cm (25⅛ in)

Musée Picasso, Paris. Formerly Collection Picasso

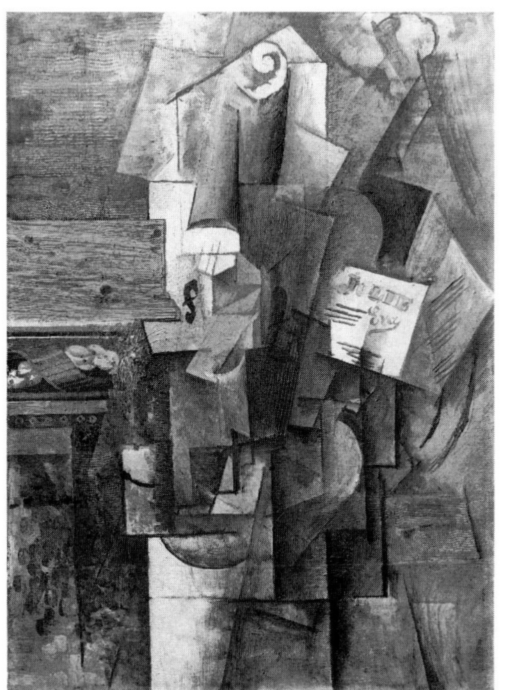

PICASSO

20A Violin, 'Jolie Eva', 1912

Oil, 60 × 80.9 cm (23⅝ × 31⅞ in)

Staatsgalerie, Stuttgart

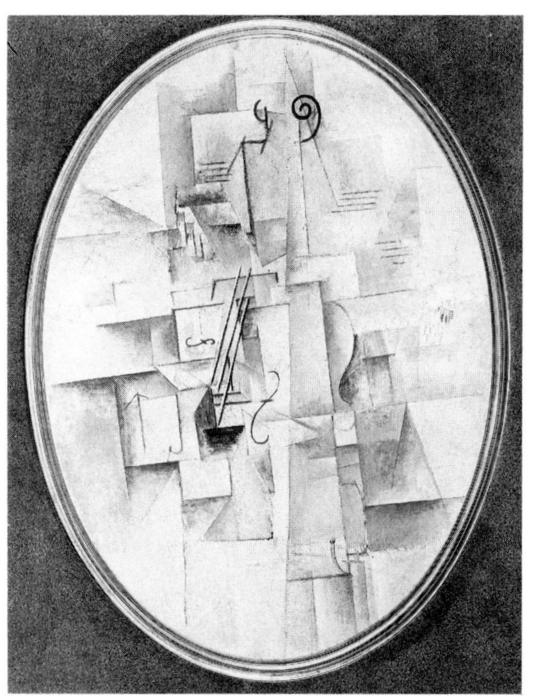

PICASSO

20B Violin, 1912

Oil, 99 × 71.1 cm (39 × 28 in)

Rijksmuseum Kröller-Müller, Otterlo

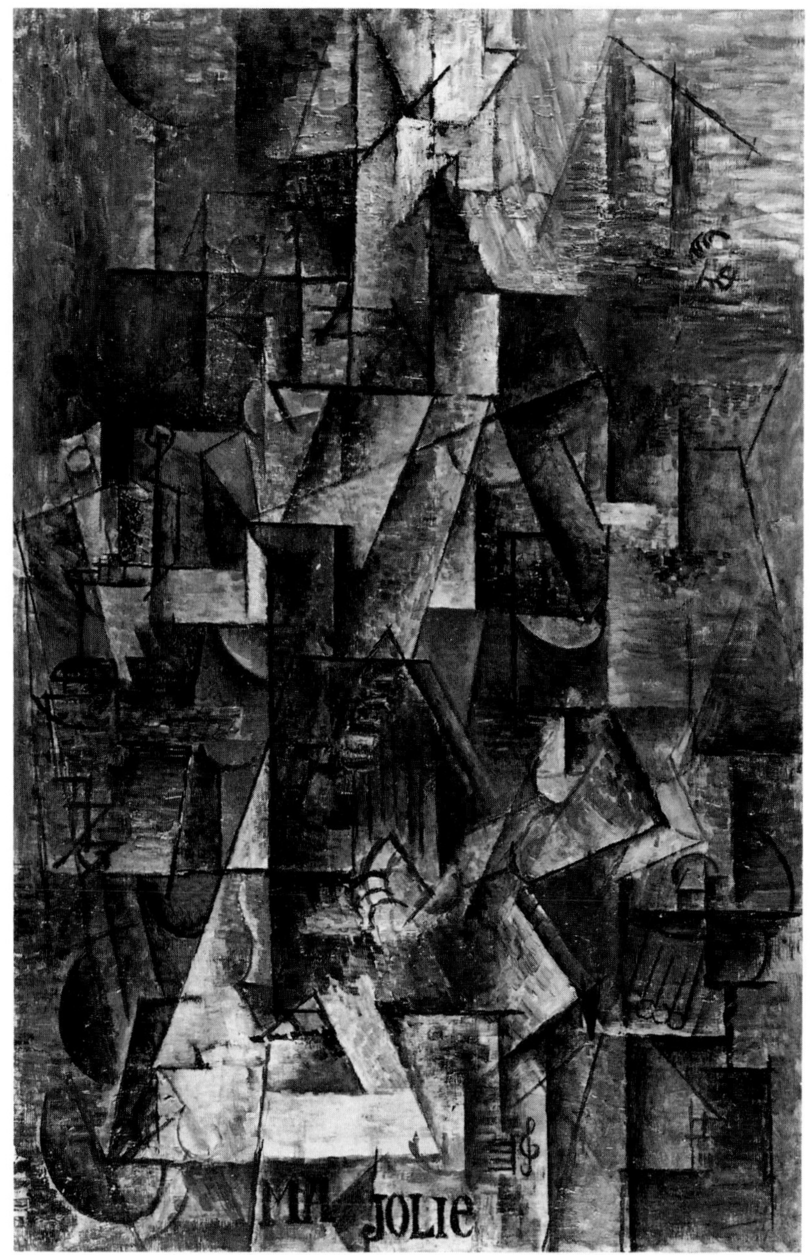

PICASSO

21 'Ma Jolie' (Woman with a Zither/Woman with a Guitar), 1911–12
Oil, 100 × 65.4 cm (39⅜ × 25¾ in)
Collection, The Museum of Modern Art, New York
Acquired through the Lillie P. Bliss Bequest

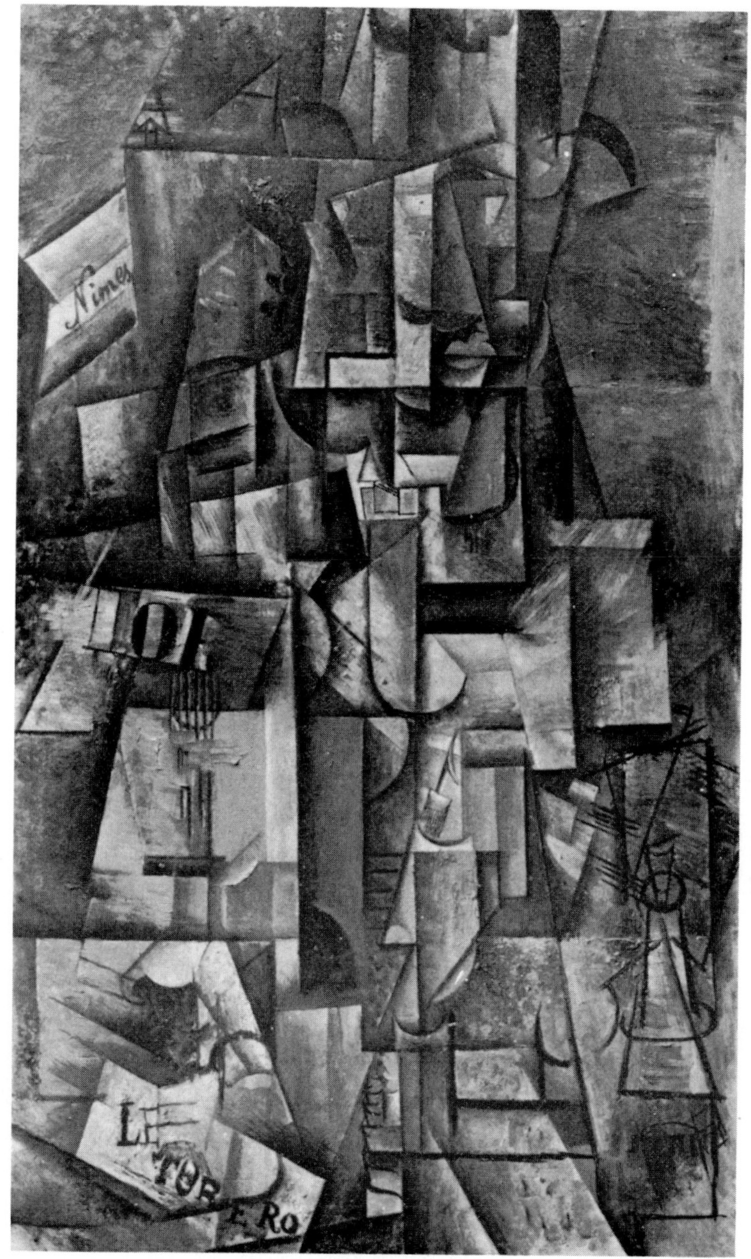

PICASSO

22 L'Aficionado (Le Toréro), 1912
Oil, 214.3 × 127.6 cm ($84\frac{3}{8} \times 50\frac{1}{4}$ in)
Kunstmuseum, Basel

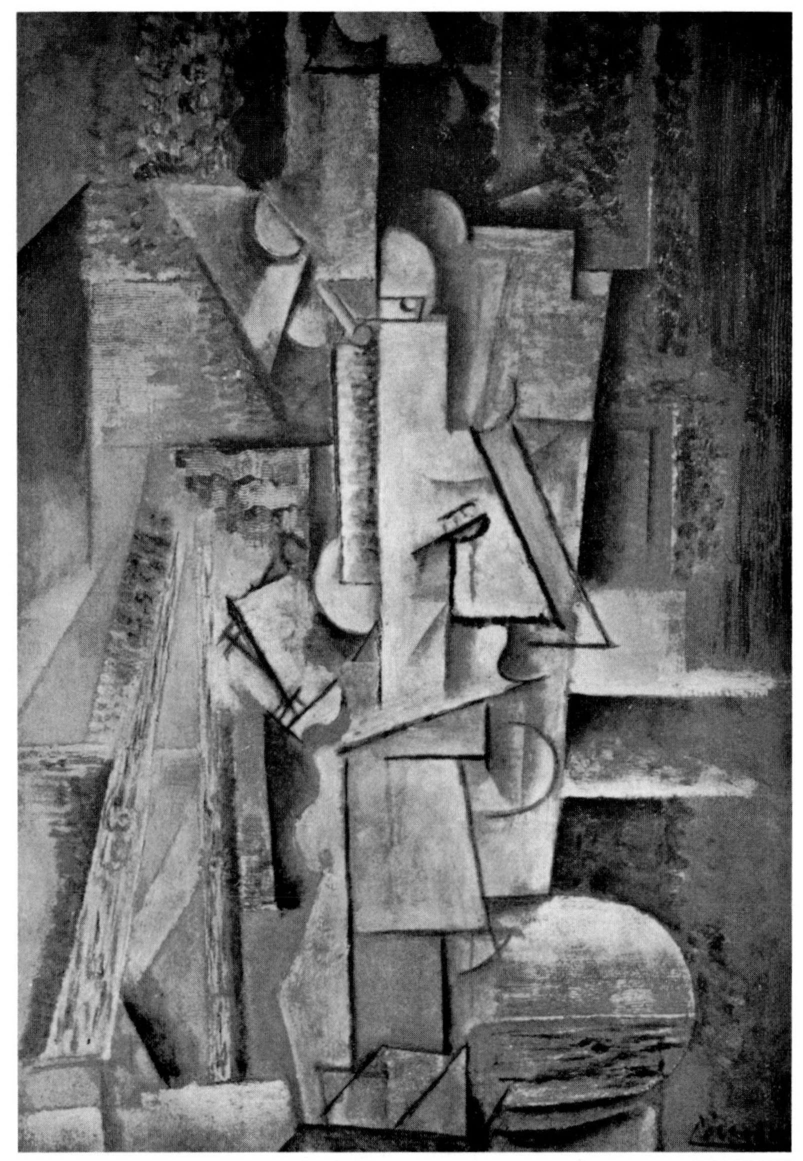

PICASSO

23 Le Modèle, 1912

Oil, 118.1 × 92.7 cm (46½ × 36½ in)

Private Collection, New York

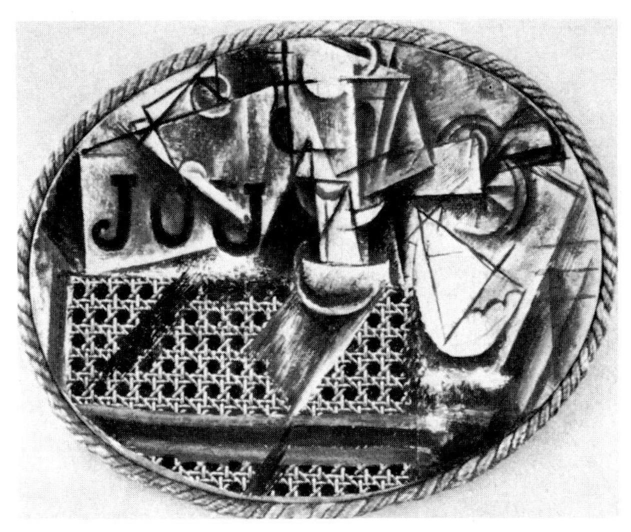

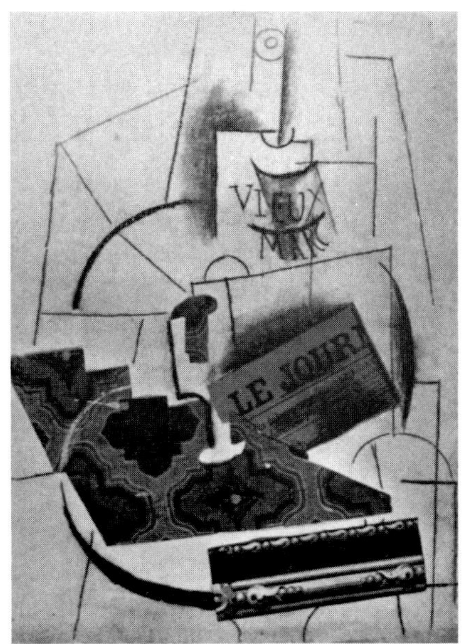

PICASSO

24A Still Life with Chair-caning, 1912

Oil and pasted oil-cloth, 27 × 34.9 cm (10⅝ × 13¾ in)

Musée Picasso, Paris

24B Bouteille de Vieux Marc, 1913

Papier collé, 77.4 × 62.2 cm (30½ × 24½ in)

Musée National d'Art Moderne, Paris

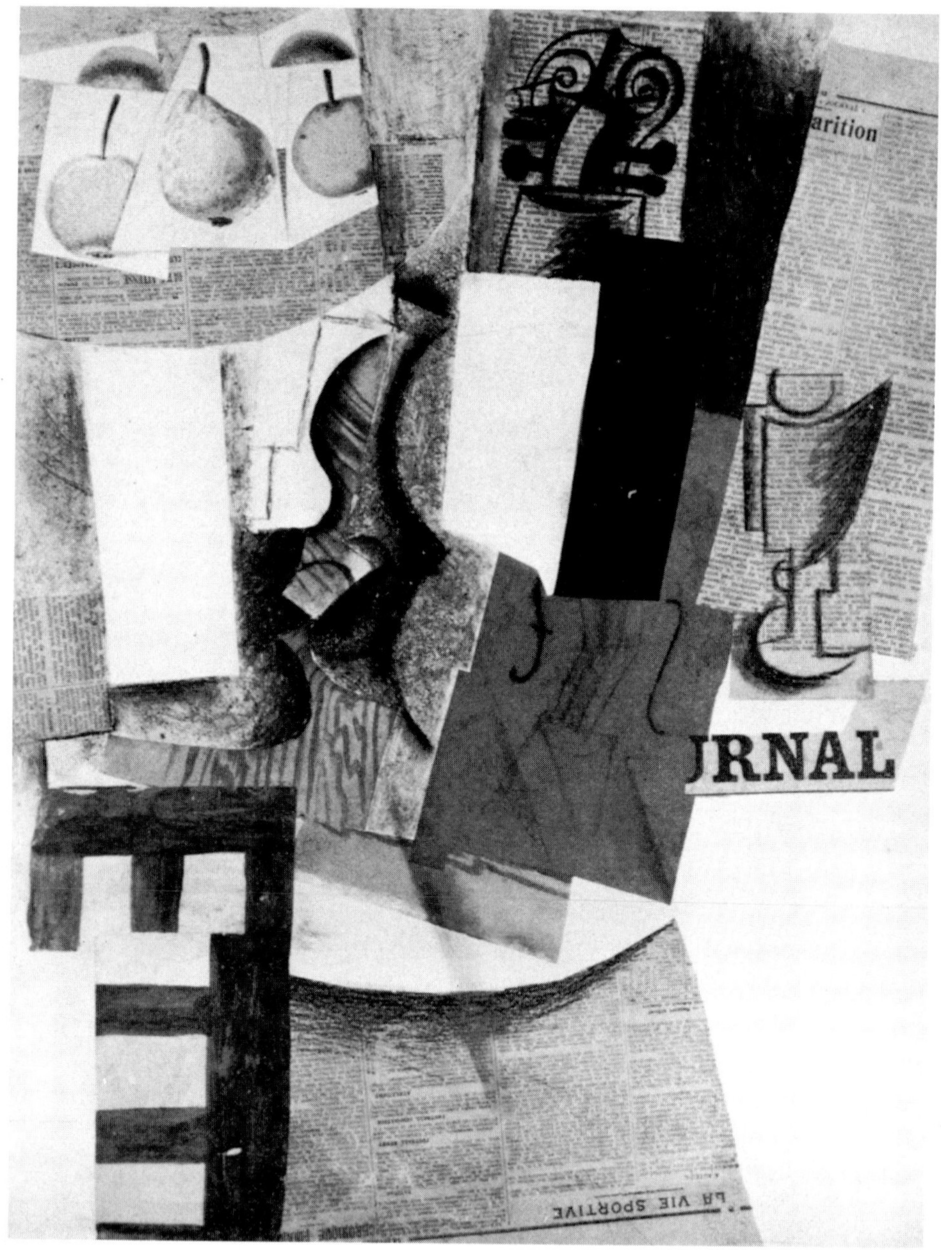

PICASSO
25 The Violin, 1912
Papier collé, 66 × 50.8 cm (26 × 20 in)
A. E. Gallatin Collection, Philadelphia Museum of Art

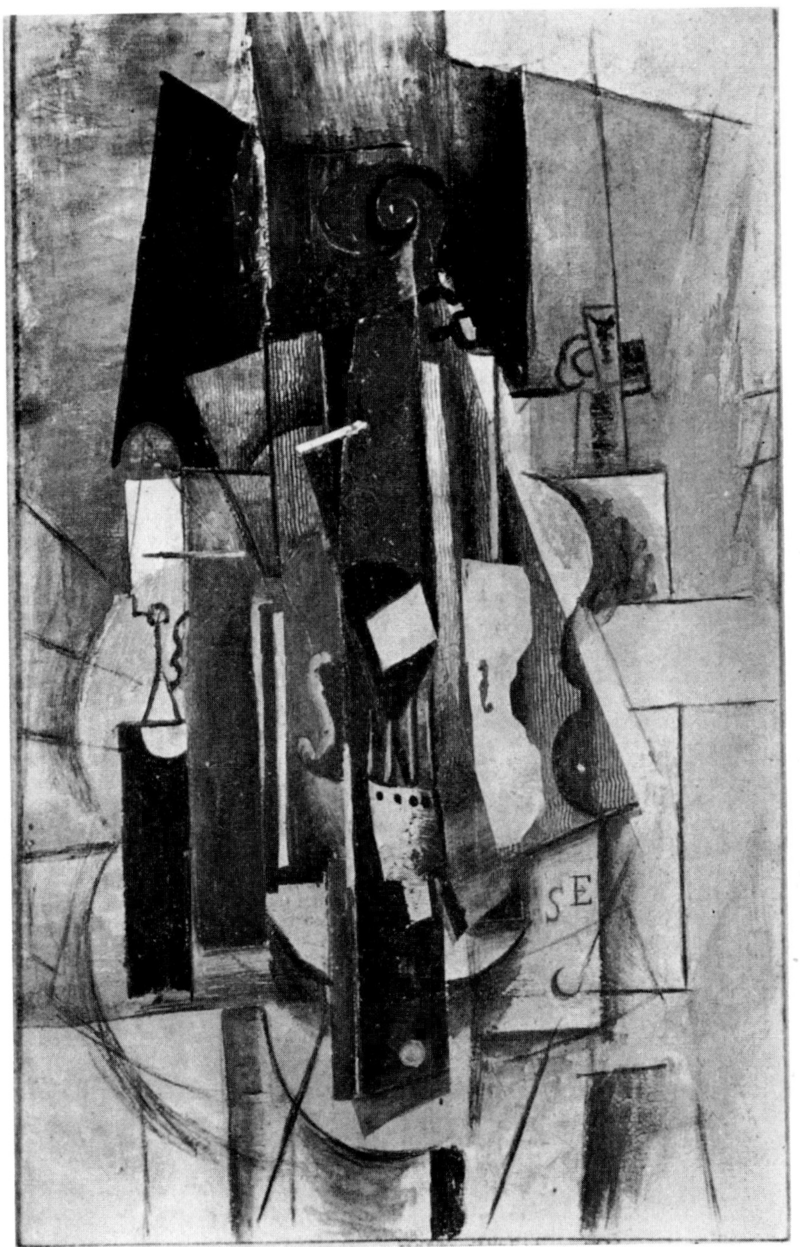

PICASSO
26 Violon au Café, 1913
Oil, 81.3 × 47 cm (32 × 18½ in)
Collection M. Siegfried Rosengart, Lucerne

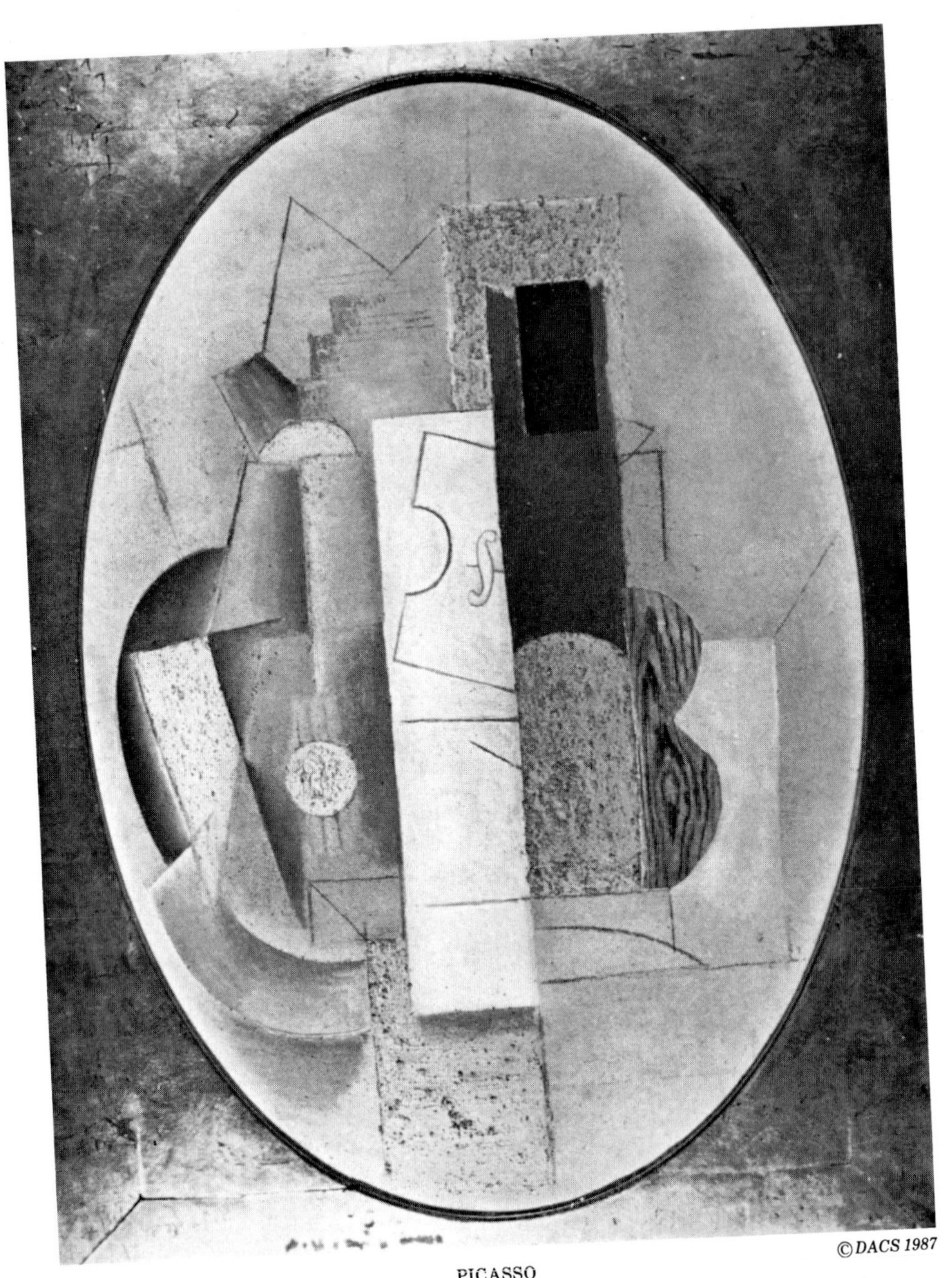

PICASSO

27 Violin and Guitar, 1913

Oil, pasted cloth, pencil and plaster, 91.4 × 63.5 cm (36 × 25 in)

Louise and Walter Arensberg Collection, Philadelphia Museum of Art

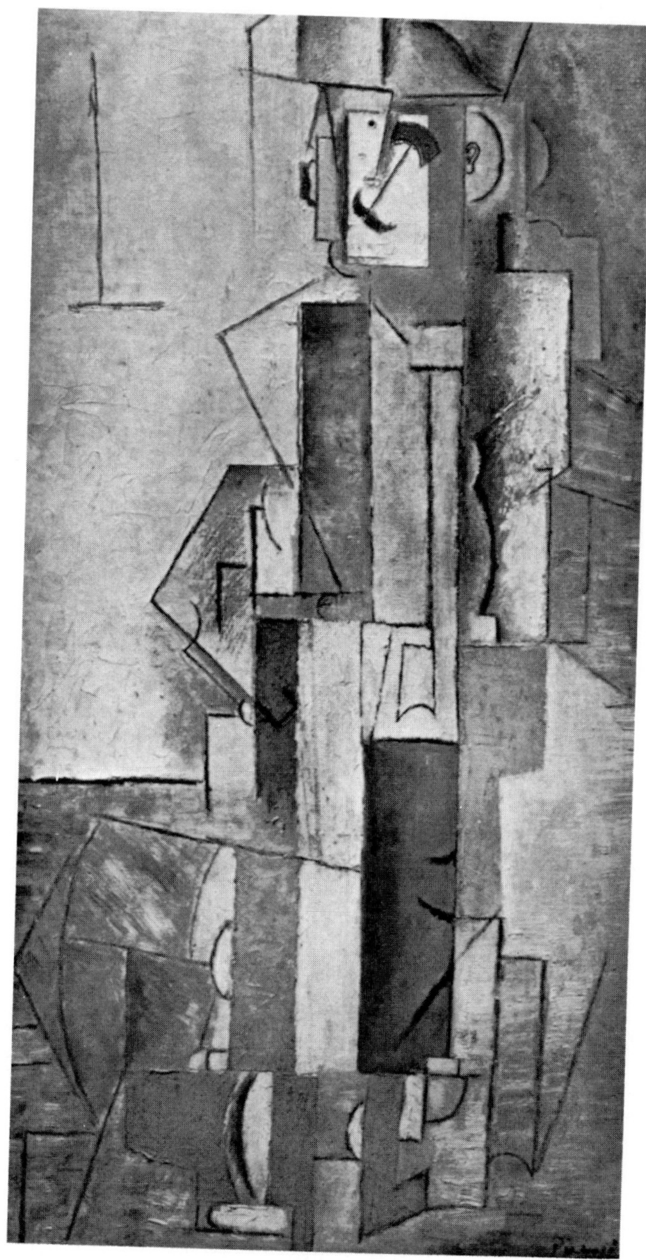

PICASSO

28 Harlequin, 1913

Oil, 85.7 × 51.4 cm (33¾ × 20¼ in)

Gemeente Museum, The Hague

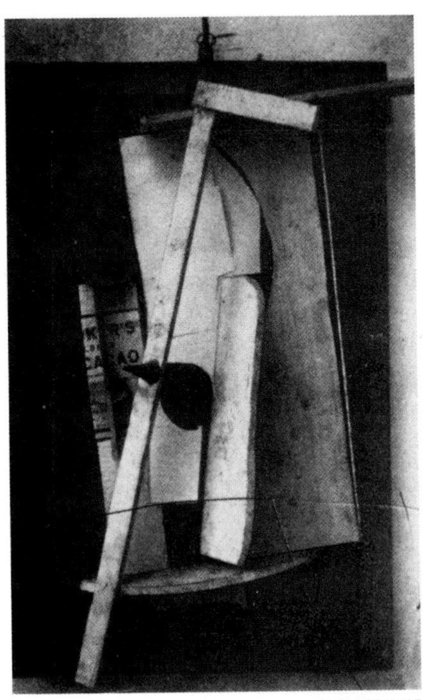

PICASSO

29A Bouteille et Guitare, 1913. Construction

No longer in existence

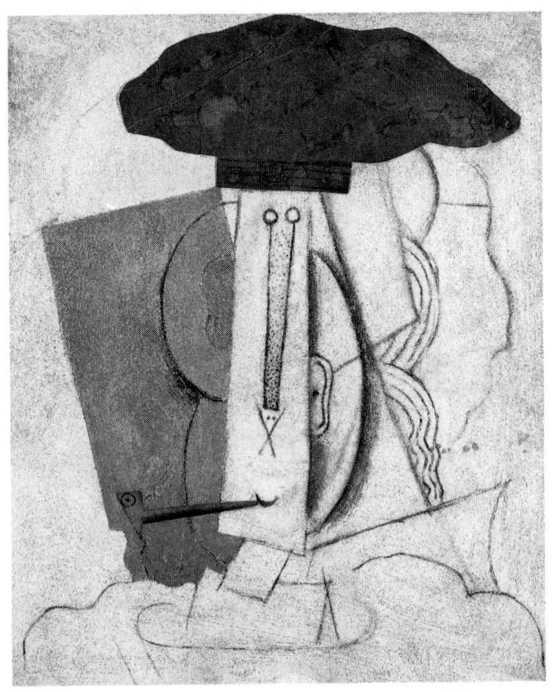

PICASSO

29B L'Etudiant à la Pipe (Student with a Pipe), 1913–14

Oil, charcoal, *papier collé* and sand, 73 × 58.7 cm

(28$\frac{3}{4}$ × 23$\frac{1}{8}$ in)

Collection, The Museum of Modern Art, New York

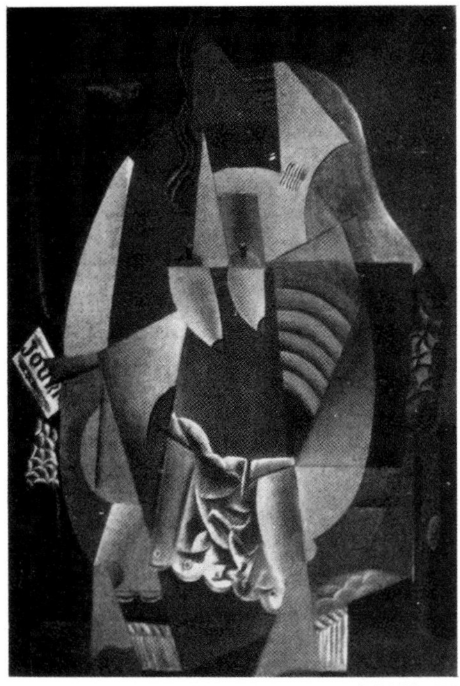

PICASSO ©*DACS 1987*

30A Femme en Chemise assise dans un Fauteuil, 1913
Oil, 129.5 × 99 cm (51 × 39 in)
Mr and Mrs Victor W. Ganz, New York

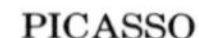

PICASSO ©*DACS 1987*

30B Seated Woman (Portrait de Jeune Fille), 1914
Oil, 129.5 × 92 cm (51 × 36¼ in)
Musée National d'Art Moderne, Paris

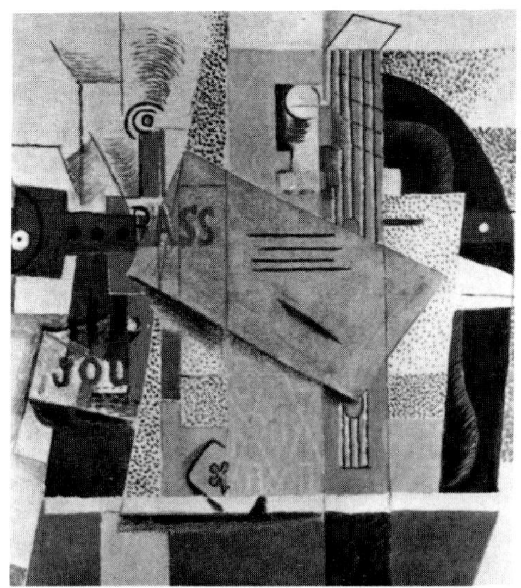

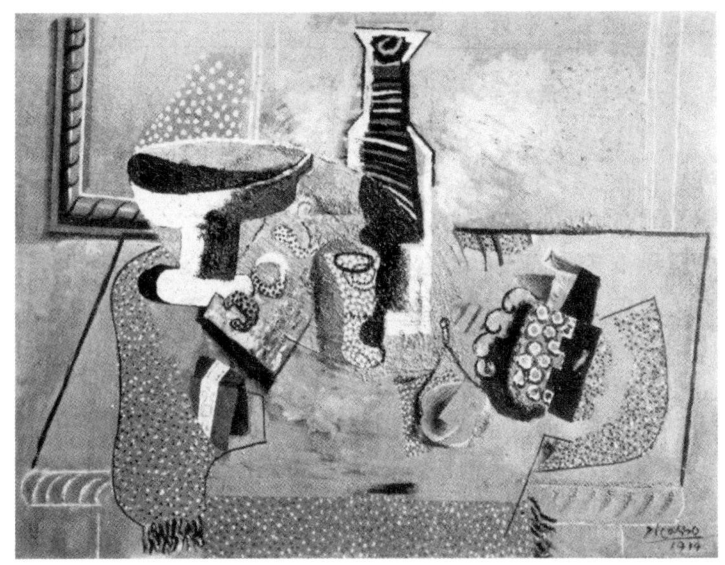

PICASSO

31A Le Violon, 1914
Oil, 83.2 × 71.1 cm (32¾ × 28 in)
Musée National d'Art Moderne, Paris

31B Green Still Life, 1914
Oil, 59.7 × 79.4 cm (23½ × 31¼ in)
Collection, The Museum of Modern Art, New York
Lillie P. Bliss Collection

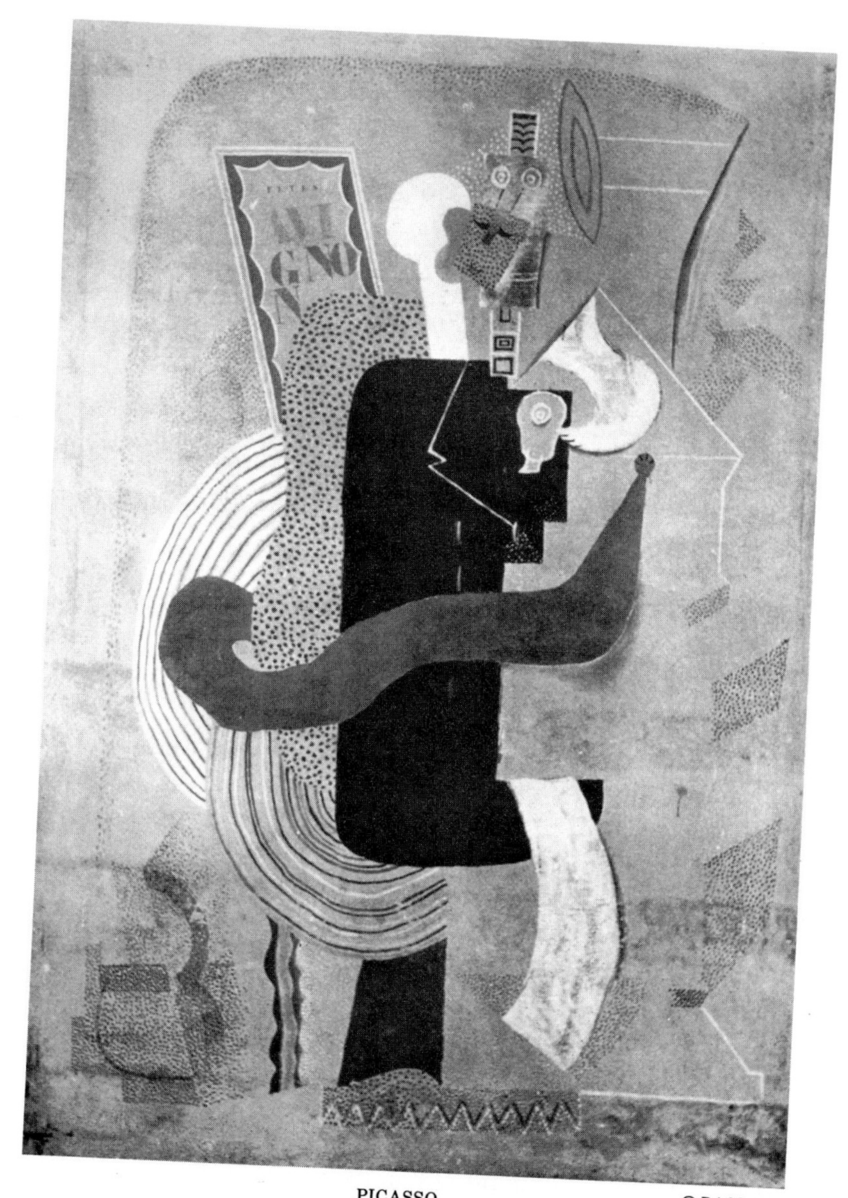

PICASSO

32 Homme Assis au Verre, 1914

Oil, 239.4 × 166.3 cm (94¼ × 65½ in)

Private Collection

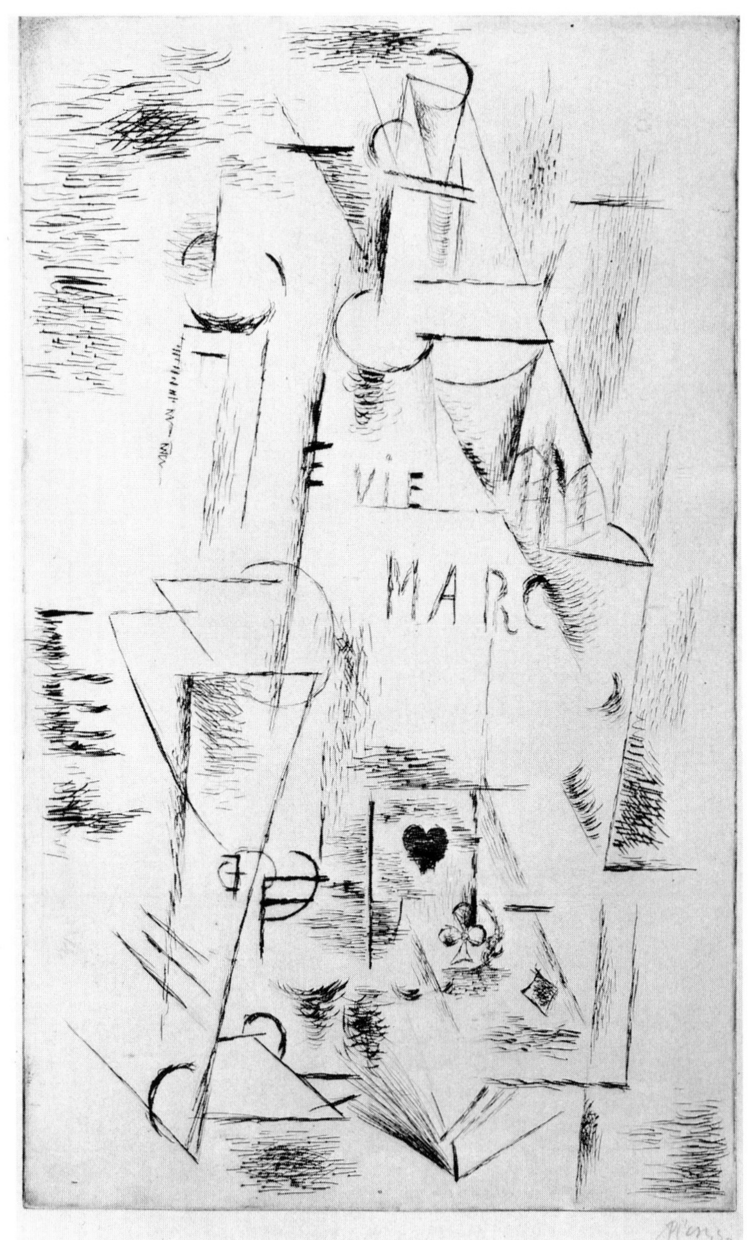

PICASSO

33 Still Life with Bottle, 1911–12

Drypoint, 50 × 30.5 cm ($19\frac{11}{16}$ × 12 in)

Collection, The Museum of Modern Art, New York

Acquired through the Lillie P. Bliss Bequest

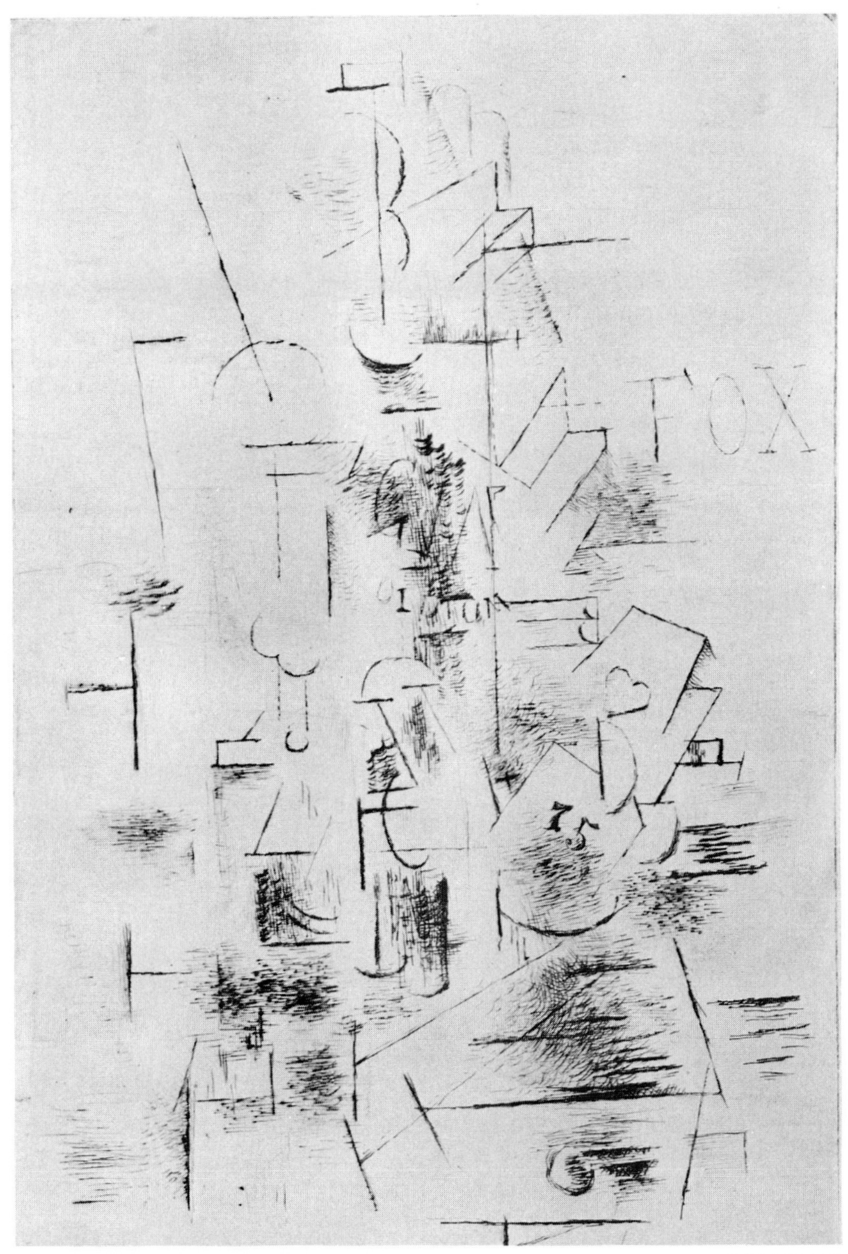

BRAQUE

34 Fox, 1911–12

Drypoint and etching, 54.8 × 38 cm (21½ × 15 in)

Collection, The Museum of Modern Art, New York

Purchase Fund

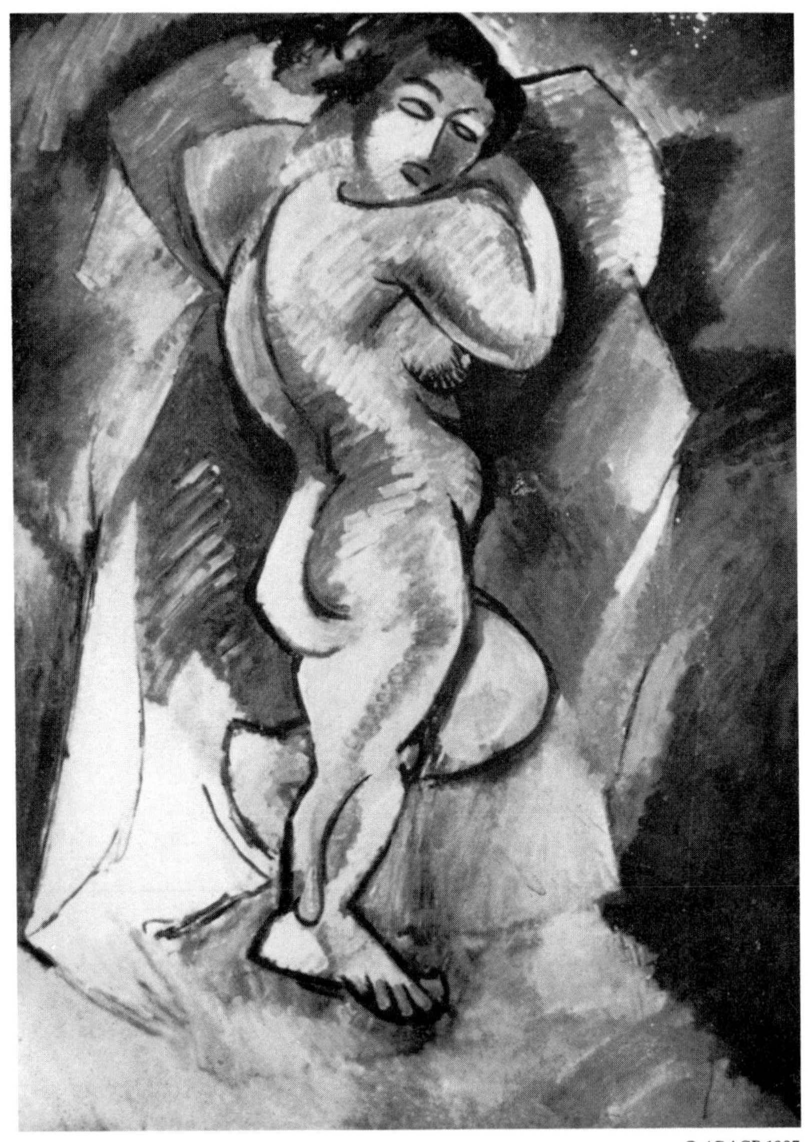

BRAQUE
35 Grand Nu, 1908
Oil, 141.6 × 101.6 cm (55¾ × 40 in)
Collection M. Alex Maguy, Paris

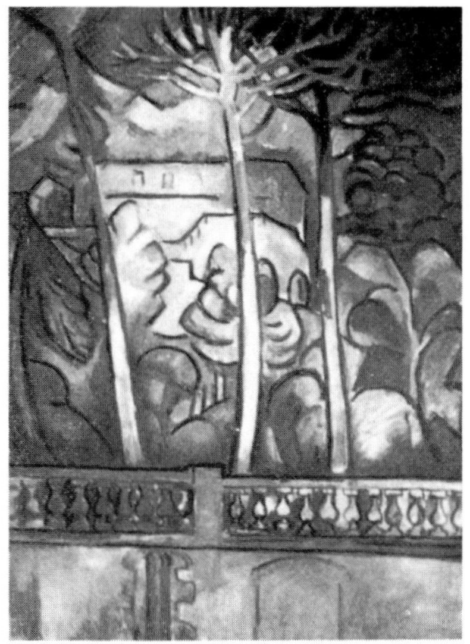

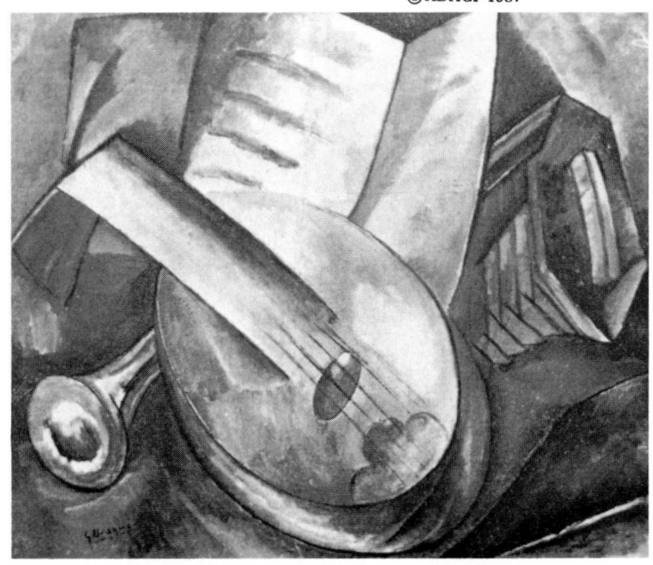

BRAQUE

36A View from the Hotel Mistral, 1907
Oil, 80 × 59.7 cm (31½ × 23½ in)
Private Collection, New York

36B Still Life with Musical Instruments, 1908
Oil, 50.1 × 60.9 cm (19¾ × 24 in)
Private Collection

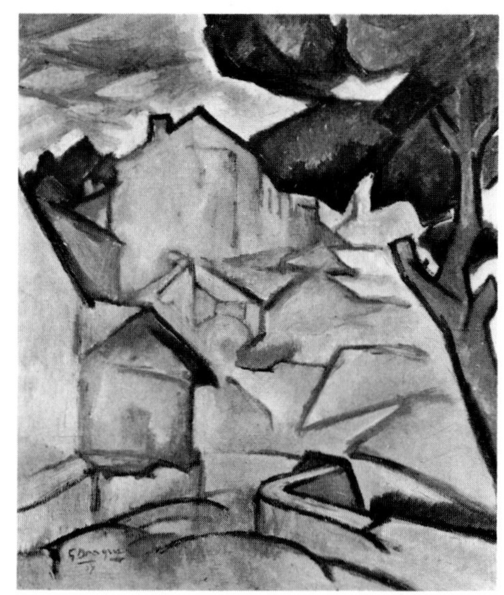

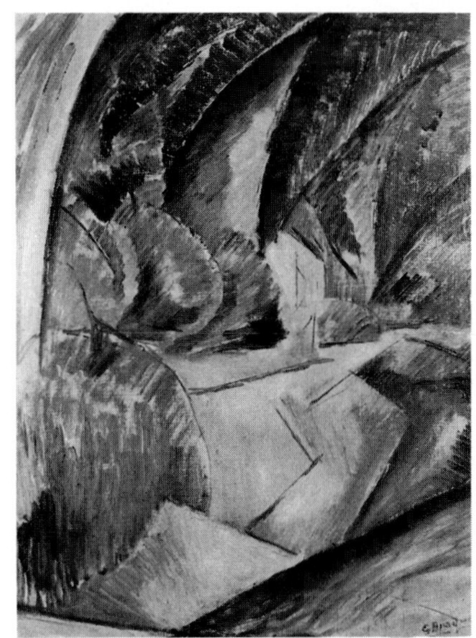

BRAQUE

37A Landscape with Houses, 1907
Oil, 54 × 46 cm (21¼ × 18⅛ in)
Private Collection

37B La Route de l'Estaque, 1908
Oil, 46 × 38.1 cm (18⅛ × 15 in)
Musée National d'Art Moderne, Paris

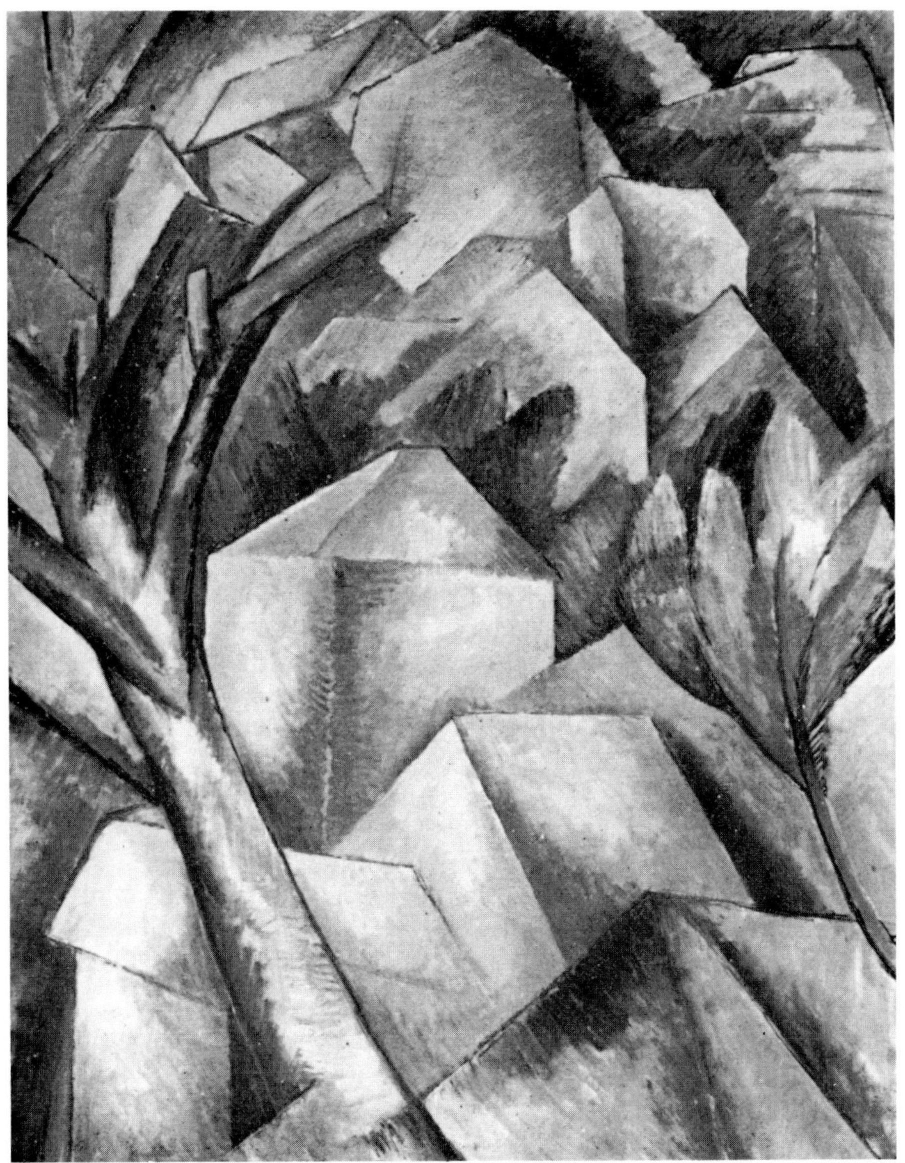

BRAQUE
38 Maisons à l'Estaque, 1908
Oil, 73 × 60.3 cm (28¾ × 23¾ in)
Kunstmuseum, Berne, Rupf Foundation

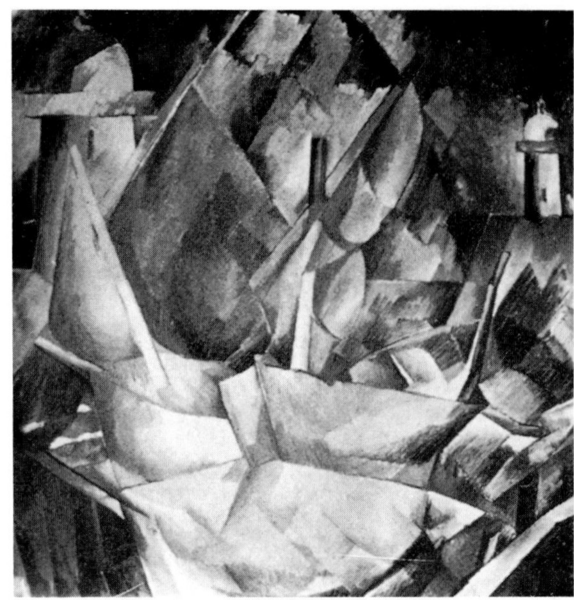

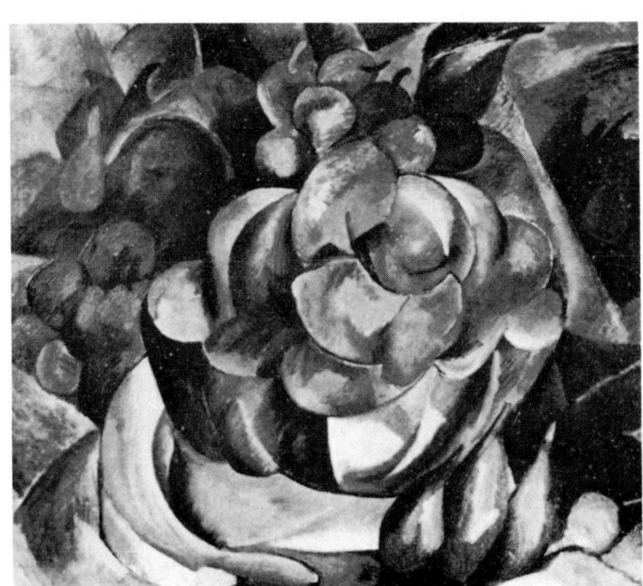

BRAQUE

39A Le Port (Harbour in Normandy), 1909
Oil, 81.3 × 81.3 cm (32 × 32 in)
The Art Institute of Chicago

39B Still Life with Fruit Dish, 1908–9
Oil, 52.7 × 64.1 cm (20¾ × 25¼ in)
Moderna Museet, Stockholm

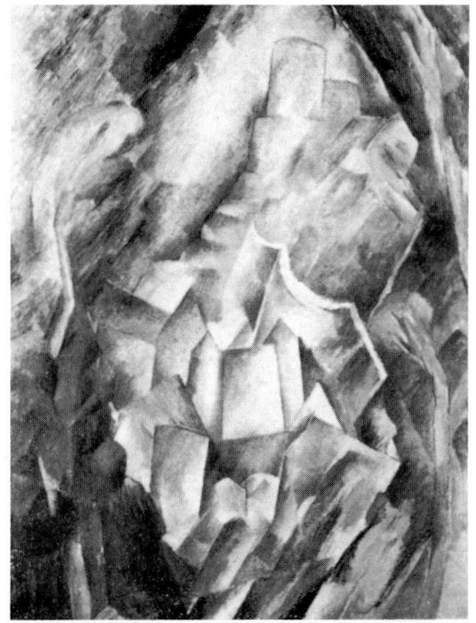

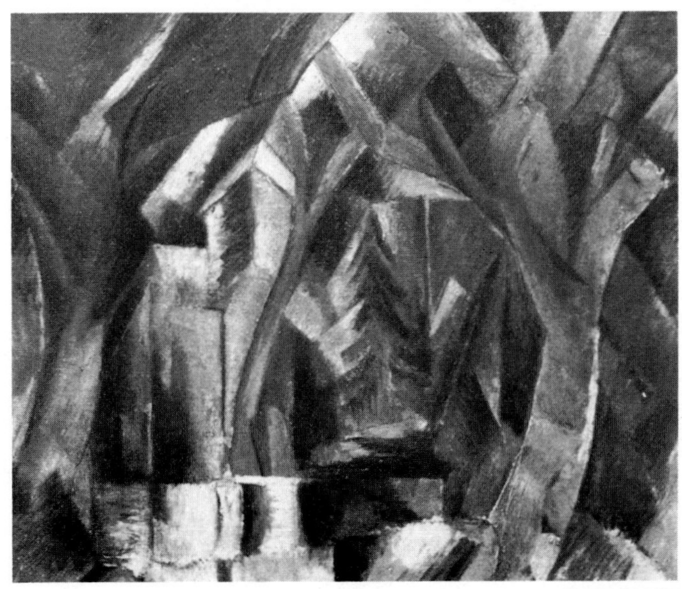

BRAQUE

40A Landscape, La Roche Guyon, 1909
Oil, 92 × 73 cm (36¼ × 28¾ in)
Stedelijk Van Abbe Museum, Eindhoven

40B Landscape, Carrières Saint-Denis, 1909.
Oil, 40.6 × 45.4 cm (16 × 17⅞ in)
Private Collection

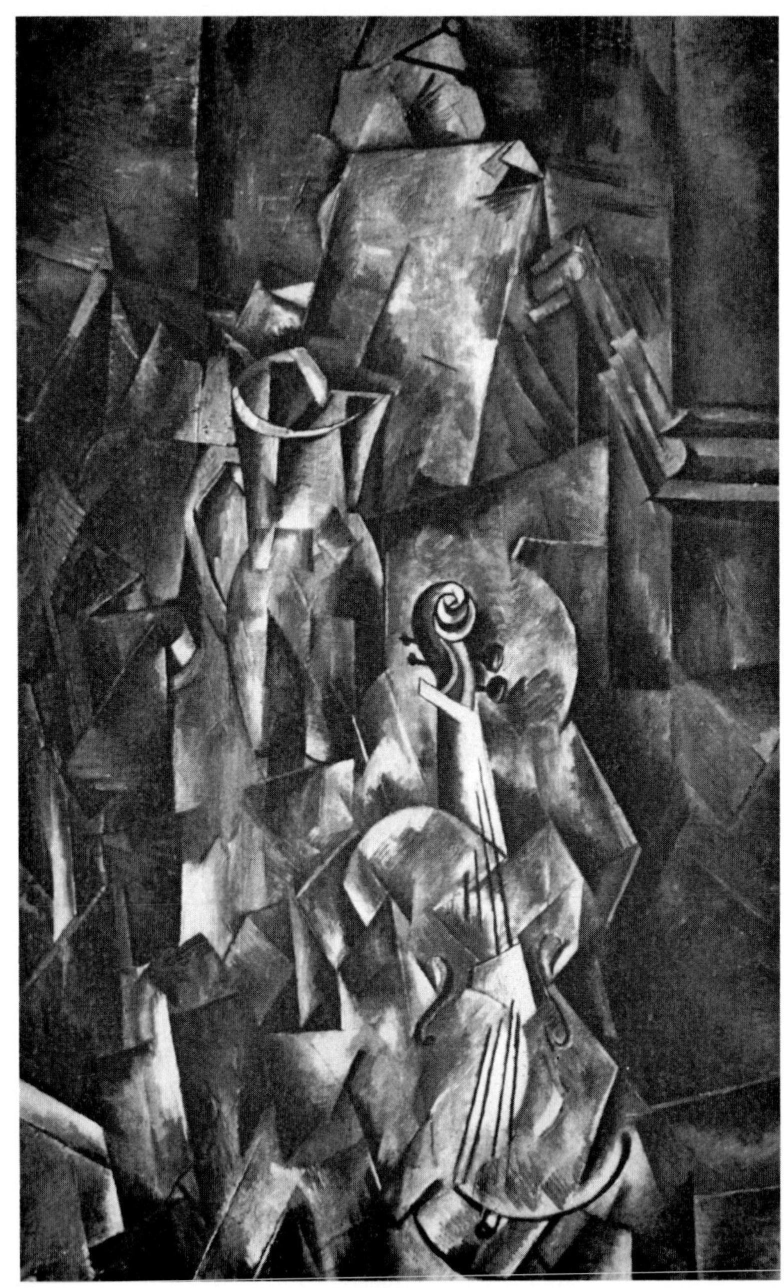

BRAQUE
41 Violon et Cruche, 1910
Oil, 118.1 × 73 cm (46½ × 28¾ in)
Kunstmuseum, Basel

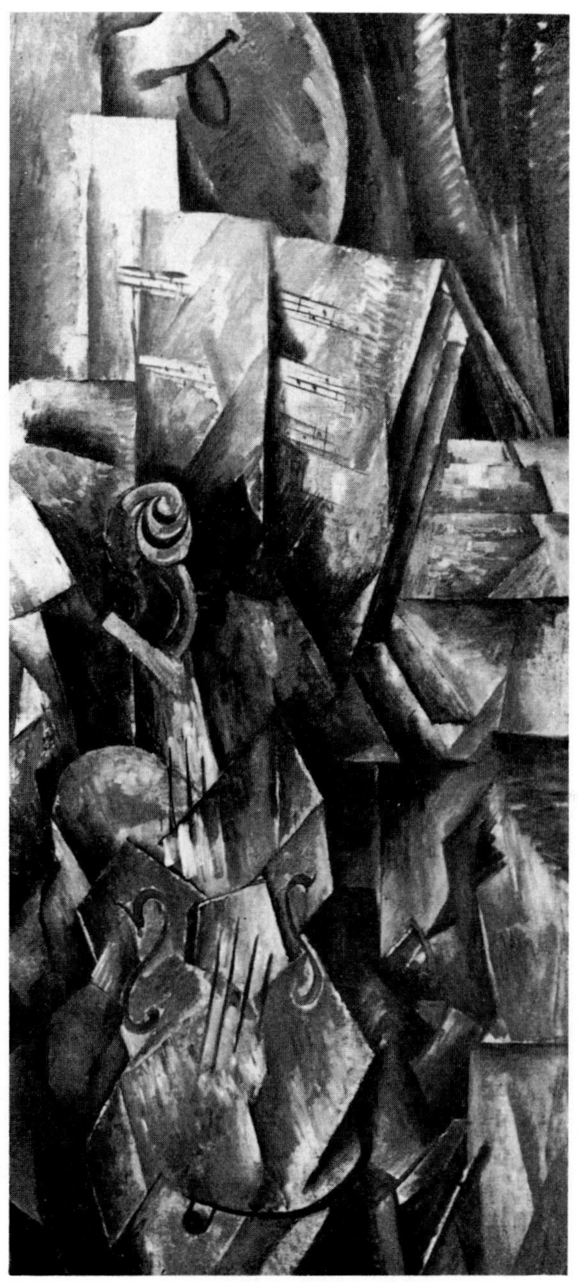

BRAQUE

42 Violin and Palette, 1910

Oil, 91.1 × 42.2 cm (35⅞ × 16⅝ in)

Solomon R. Guggenheim Museum, New York

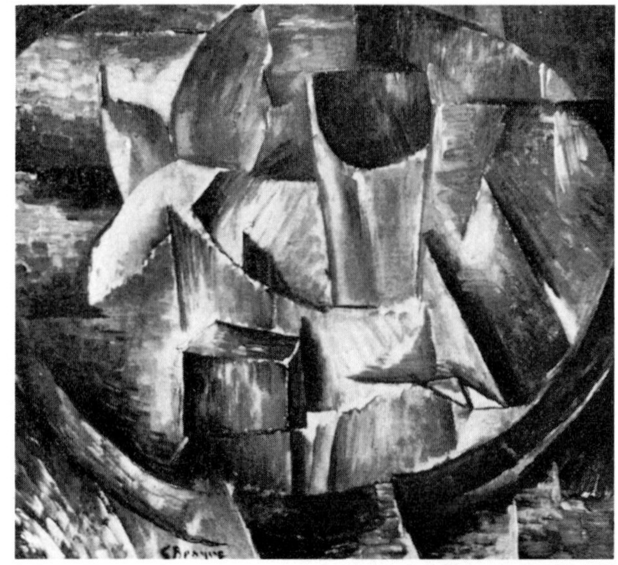

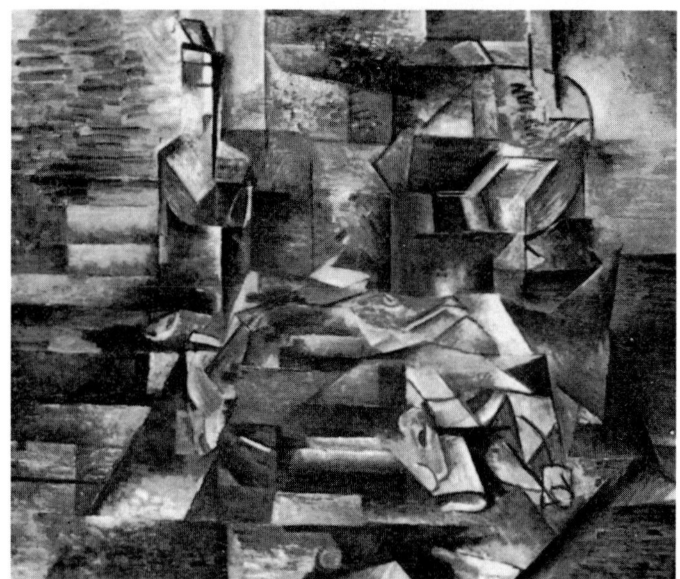

BRAQUE

43A Glass on a Table, 1910

Oil, 34.9 × 38.7 cm (13¾ × 15¼ in)

Collection Lady Hornby, London

43B Les Poissons, 1910

Oil, 72.4 × 59.7 cm (28½ × 23½ in)

Tate Gallery, London

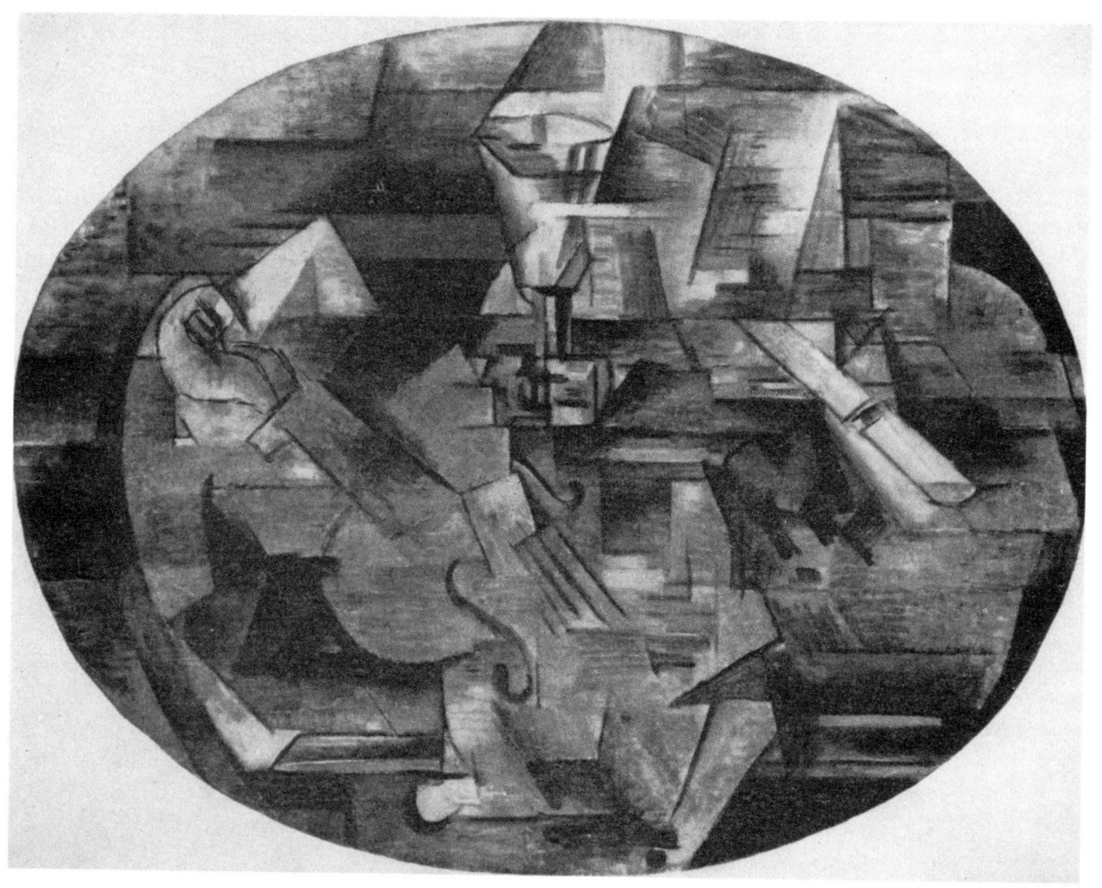

BRAQUE
44 Violin and Glass, 1910–11
Oil, 50.8 × 67.3 cm (20 × 26½ in), oval
National Gallery, Prague

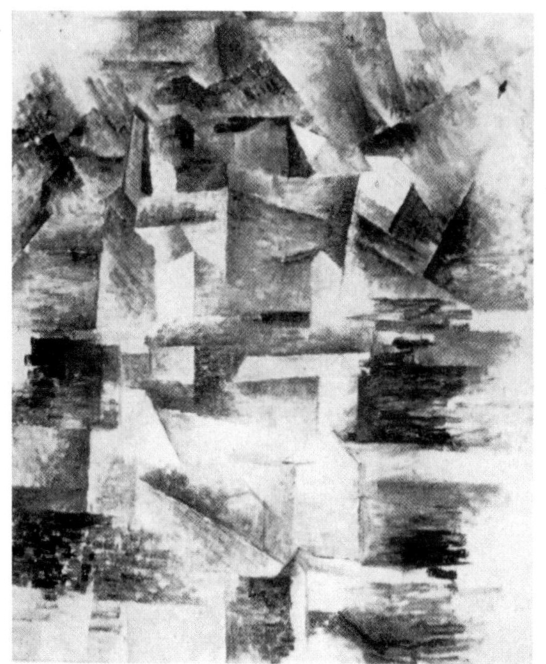

BRAQUE
45A Les Usines de Rio Tinto, 1910
Oil, 64.7 × 53.3 cm (25½ × 21 in)
Musée National d'Art Moderne, Paris

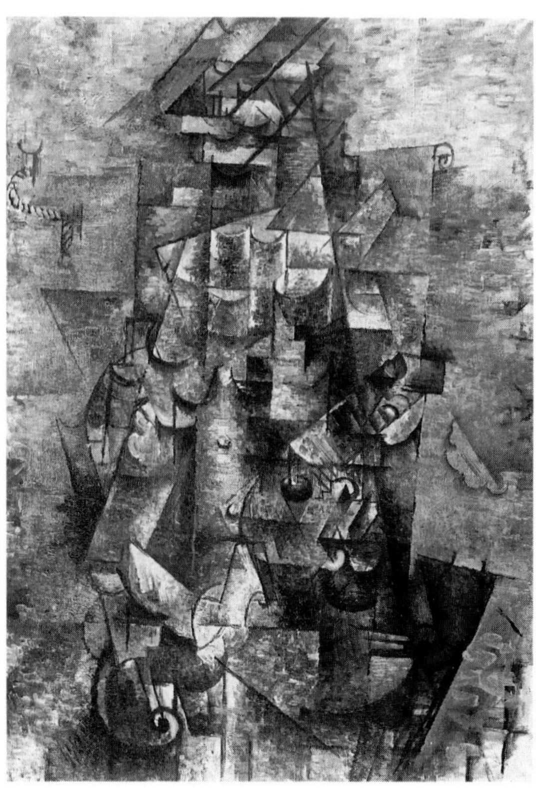

BRAQUE
45B Man with a Guitar, 1911
Oil, 116.2 × 80.9 cm (45¾ × 31⅞ in)
Collection, The Museum of Modern Art, New York
Acquired through the Lillie P. Bliss Bequest

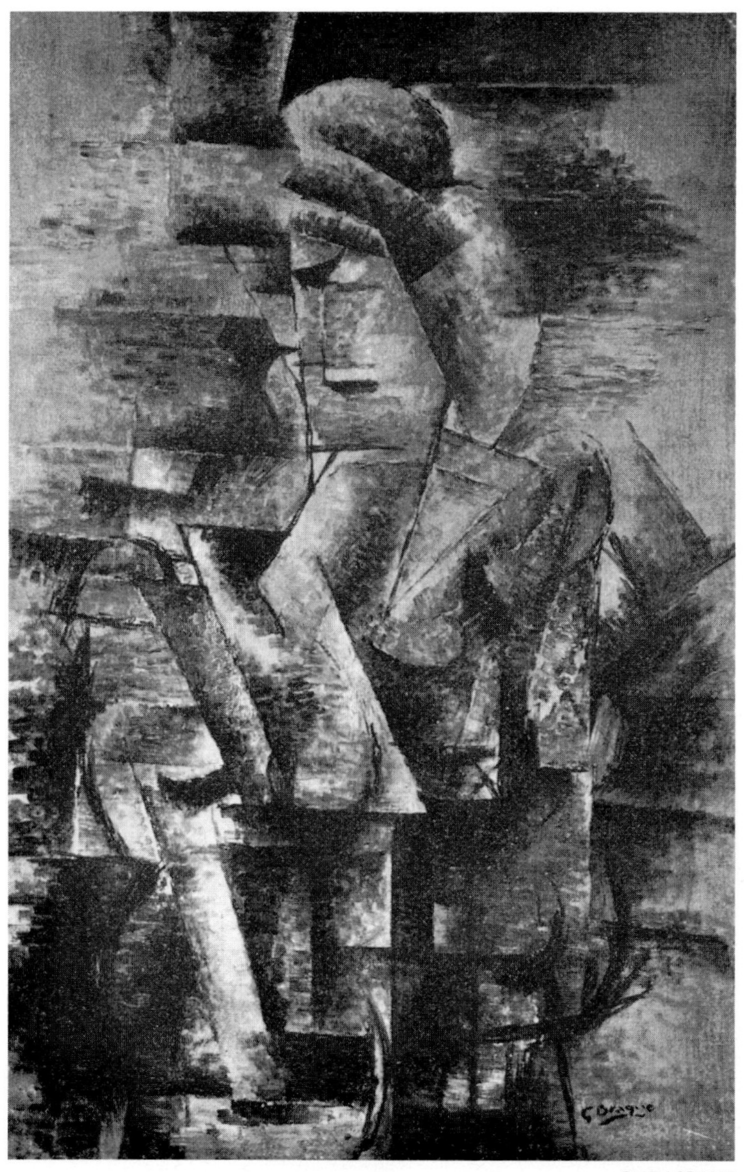

BRAQUE

46 Female Figure, 1910–11

Oil, 90.1 × 59.7 cm (35½ × 23½ in)

H. Carey Walker Foundation, New York

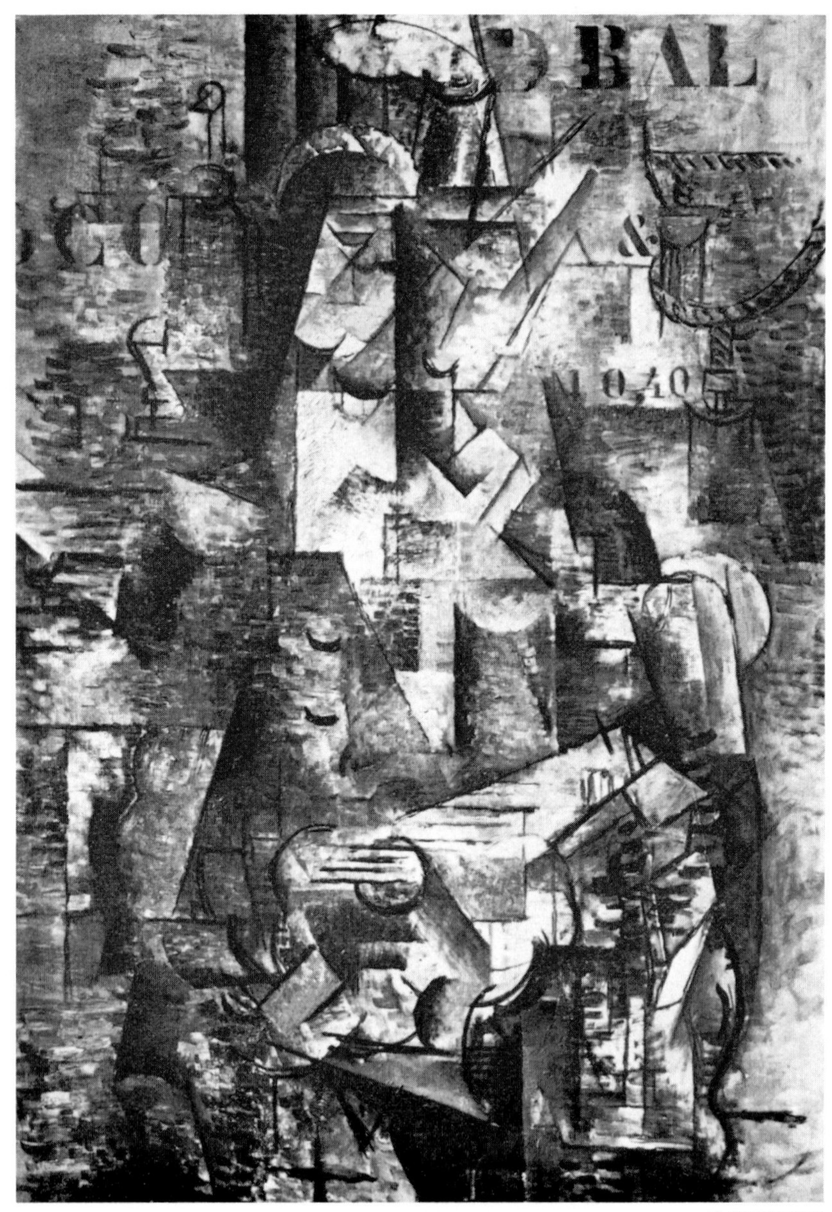

BRAQUE

47 Le Portugais, 1911

Oil, 116.2 × 81.3 cm (45¾ × 32 in)

Kunstmuseum, Basel

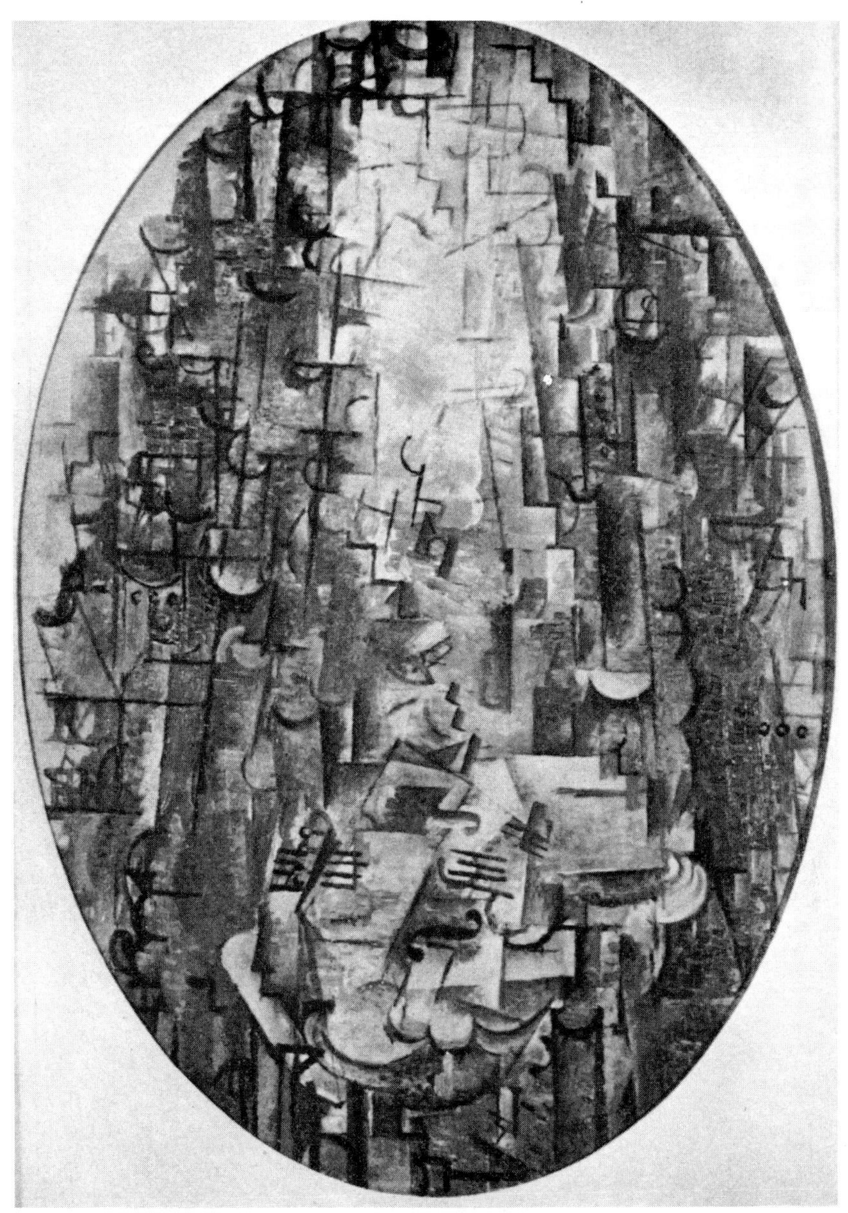

BRAQUE
48 Man with a Violin, 1911
Oil, 99.7 × 71.1 cm (39¼ × 28 in)
Bührle Collection, Kunsthaus, Zurich

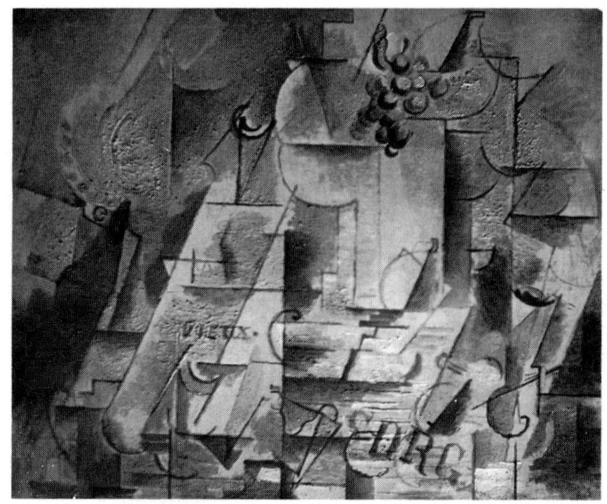

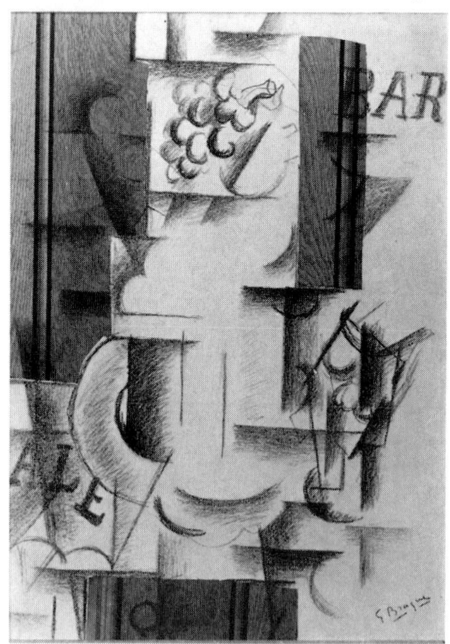

BRAQUE

49A Fruit Dish, Bottle and Glass, 1912
Oil and sand, 60.3 × 73.6 cm (23¾ × 29 in)
Private Collection, Paris

49B Compotier et Verre (Fruit Dish and Glass), 1912
Papier collé, 60.9 × 45.1 cm (24 × 17¾ in)
Private Collection

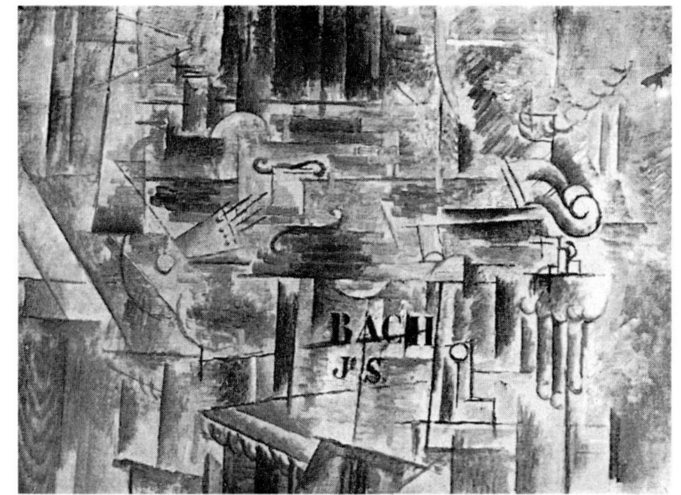

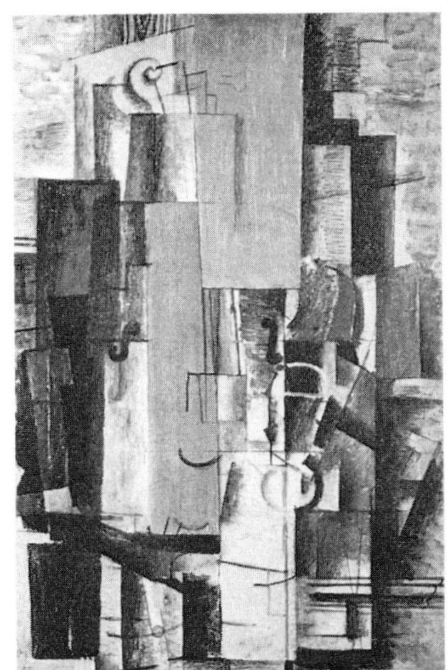

BRAQUE

50A Hommage à J. S. Bach, 1912
Oil, 54 × 73 cm (21¼ × 28¾ in)
Sidney Janis Collection, New York

50B Composition (The Violin), 1913
Oil, 80.6 × 54.6 cm (31¾ × 21½ in)
Private Collection

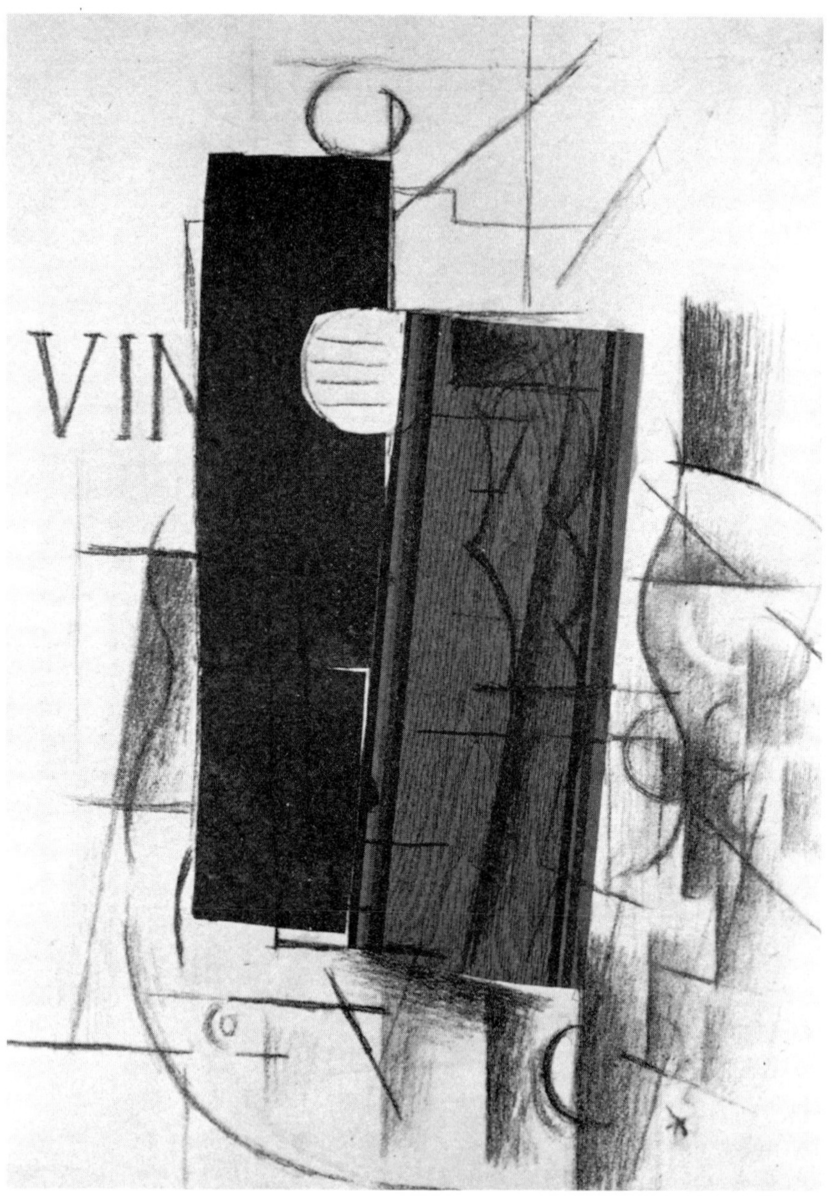

BRAQUE

51 Still Life with Guitar, 1912–13

Papier collé, 58.7 × 43.8 cm ($23\frac{1}{8} \times 17\frac{1}{4}$ in)

Louise and Walter Arensberg Collection, Philadelphia Museum of Art

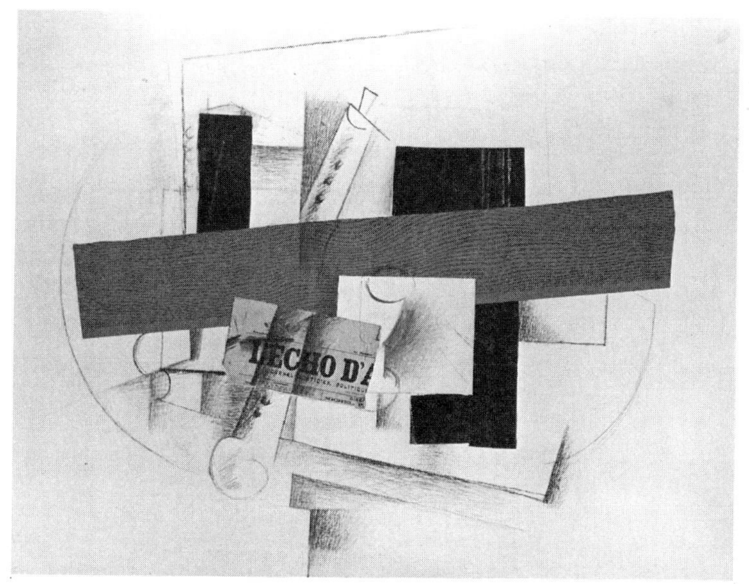

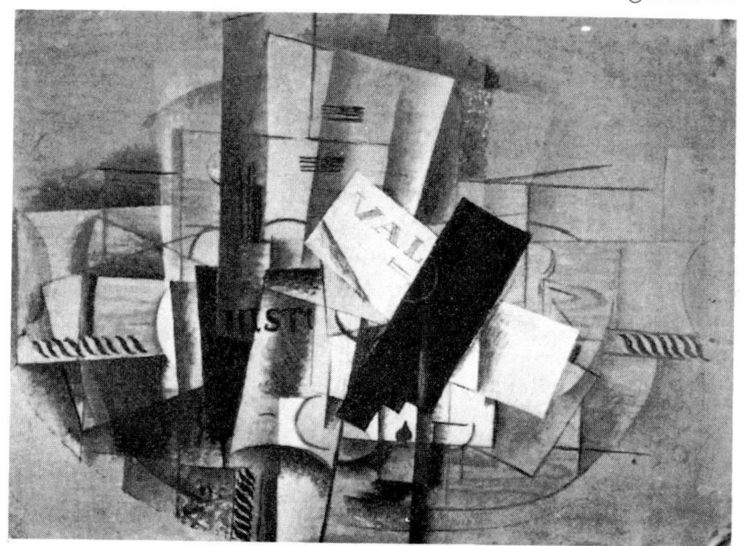

BRAQUE

52A Clarinet, 1913

Papier collé, charcoal, chalk and oil, 95.2 × 120.3 cm (37½ × 47⅜ in)

Museum of Modern Art New York
Nelson D. Rockefeller Bequest

52B La Table du Musicien, 1913

Oil and pencil, 65.1 × 92 cm (25⅝ × 36¼ in)

Kunstmuseum, Basel

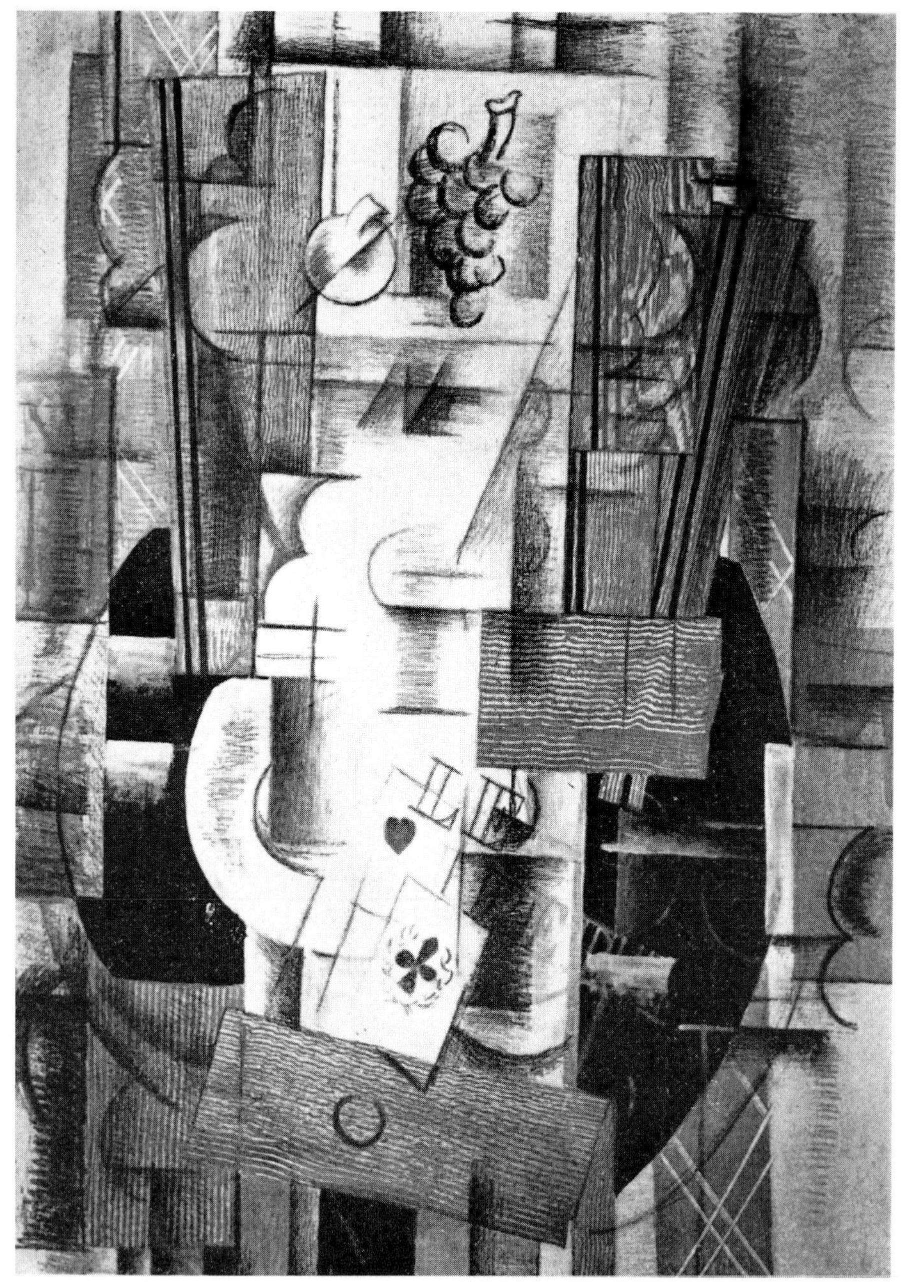

BRAQUE
53 Still Life with Playing Cards (Composition à l'As de Trèfle), 1913
Oil and charcoal, 81.3 × 59.7 cm (32 × 23½ in)
Musée National d'Art Moderne, Paris

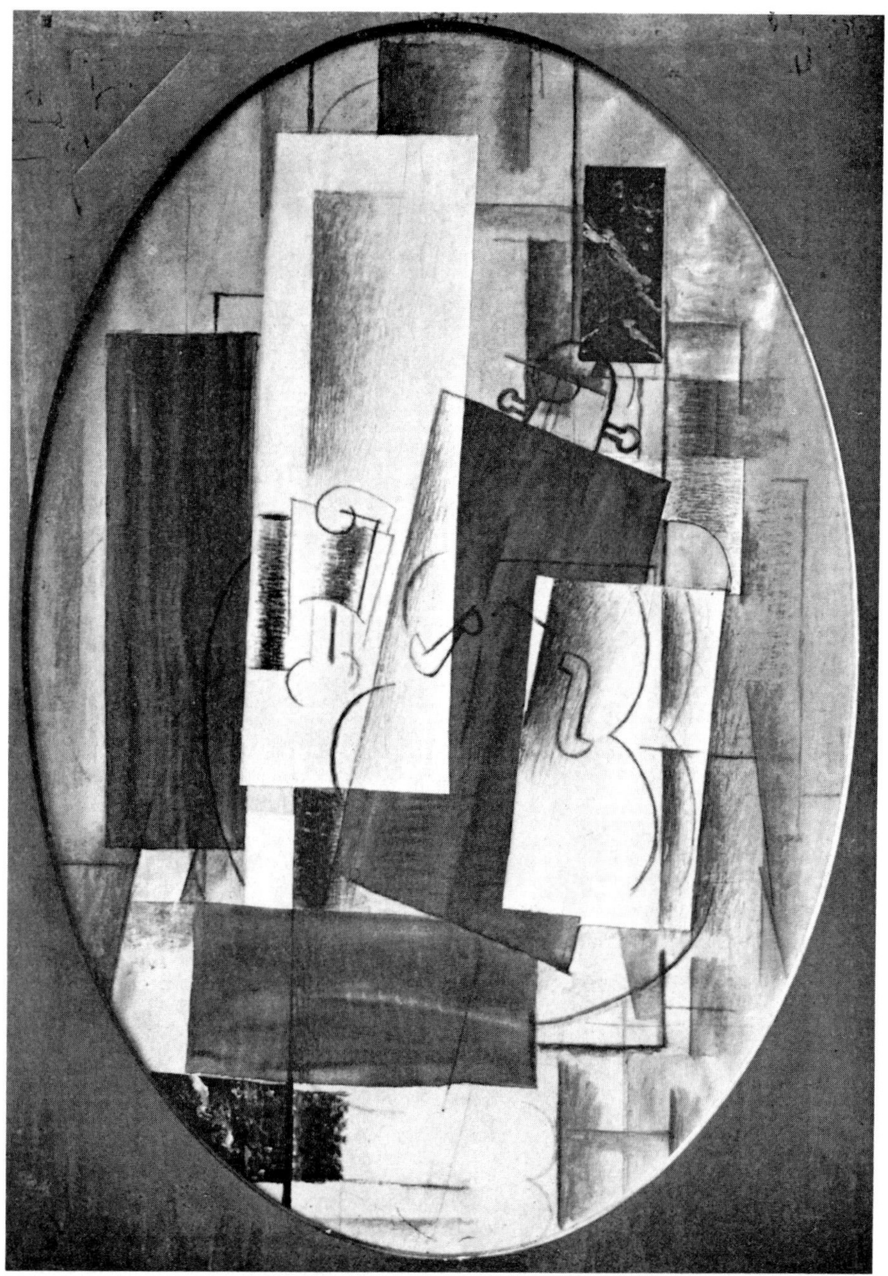

BRAQUE
54 Violon et Verre, 1913
Oil, 116.2 × 80.6 cm (45¾ × 31¾ in)
Kunstmuseum, Basel

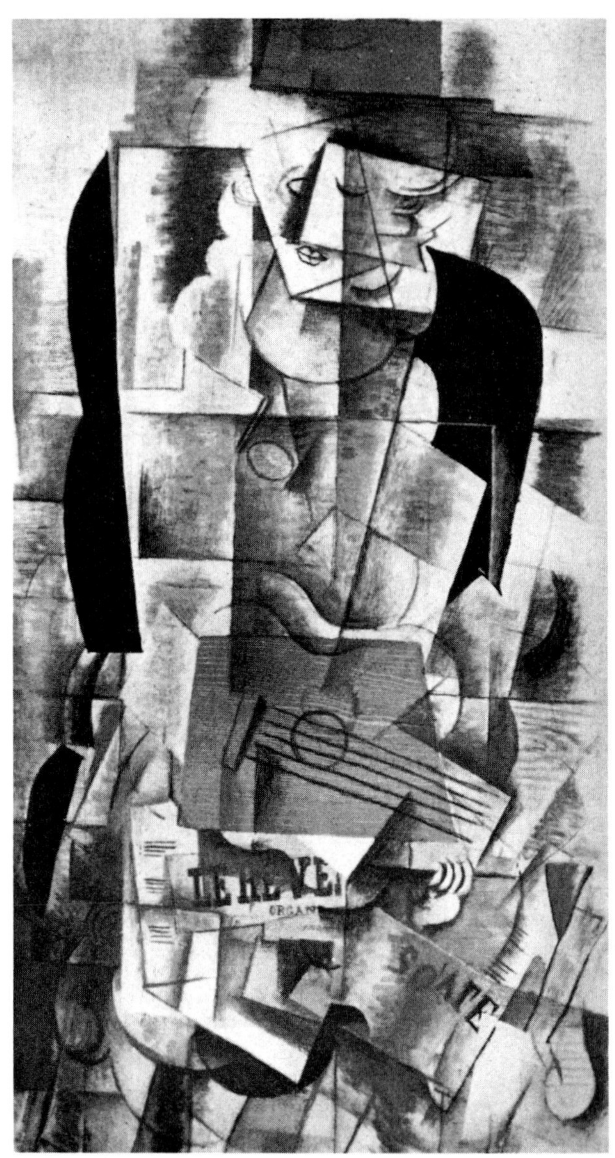

BRAQUE
55 Woman with a Guitar, 1913
Oil, 130.2 × 73.6 cm (51¼ × 29 in)
Musée National d'Art Moderne, Paris

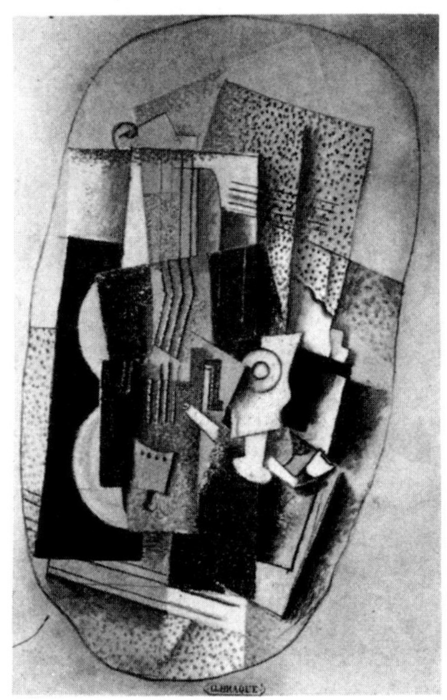

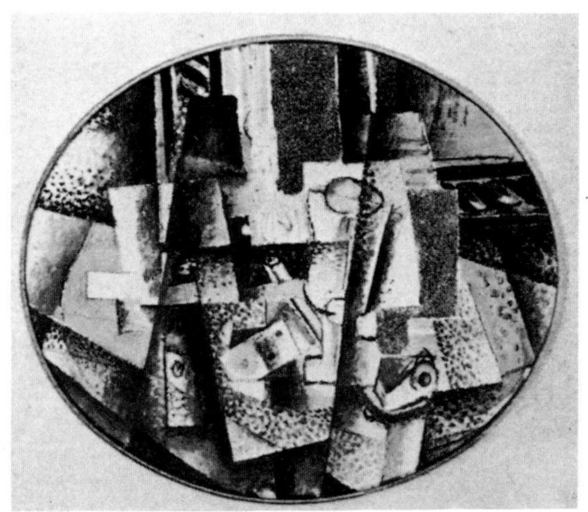

BRAQUE

56A Music, 1914

Oil with gesso and sawdust, 91.4 × 59.7 cm (36 × 23½ in)

Philips Collection, Washington, D.C. (Katherine Drier Gift)

56B Still Life (Nature Morte à la Pipe), 1914

Oil with sand and gesso, 38.1 × 45.7 cm (15 × 18 in)

Girardin Collection, Petit Palais, Paris

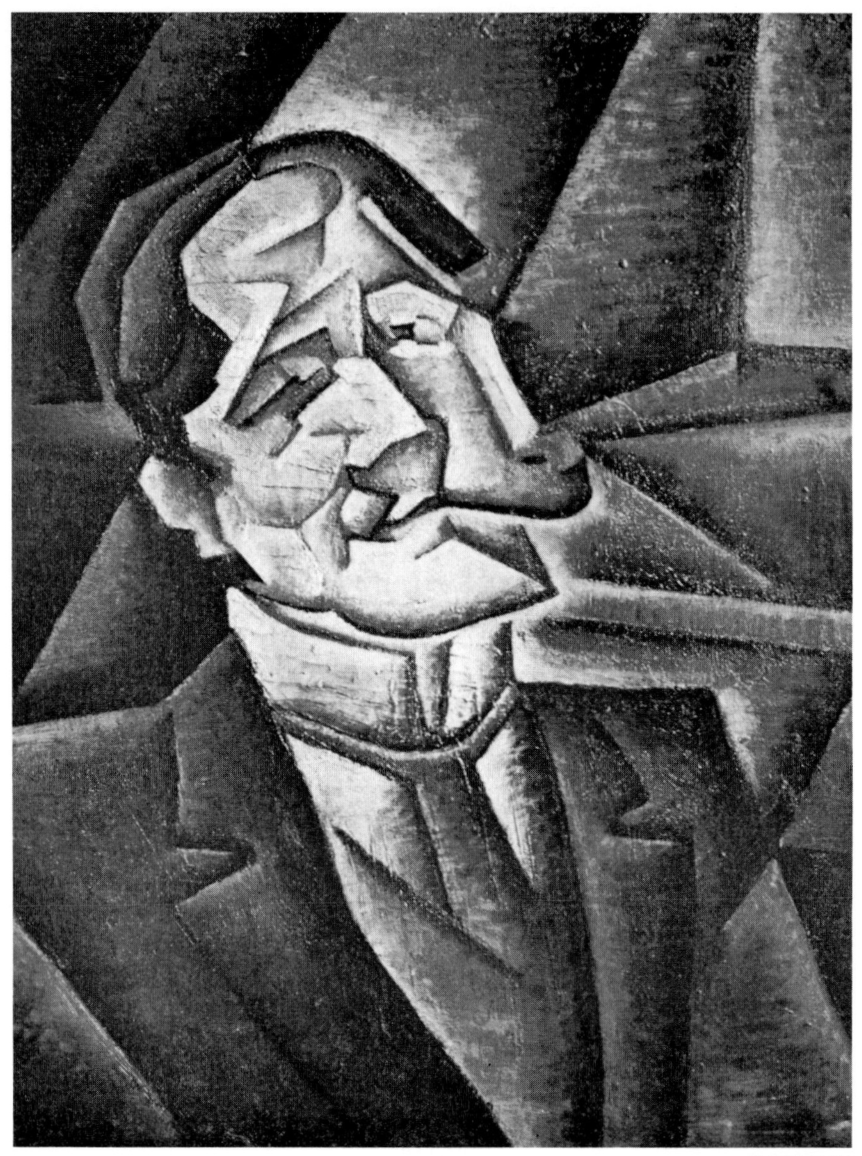

GRIS

57 L'Homme à la Pipe, 1911

Oil, 53.3 × 45.7 cm (21 × 18 in)

Collection Mr and Mrs Jacques Gelman, New York

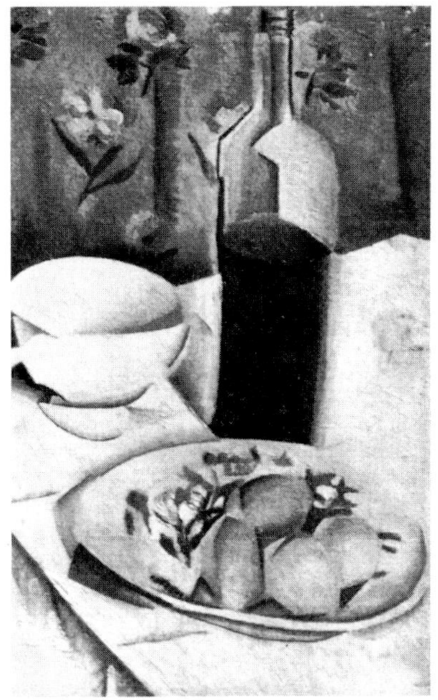

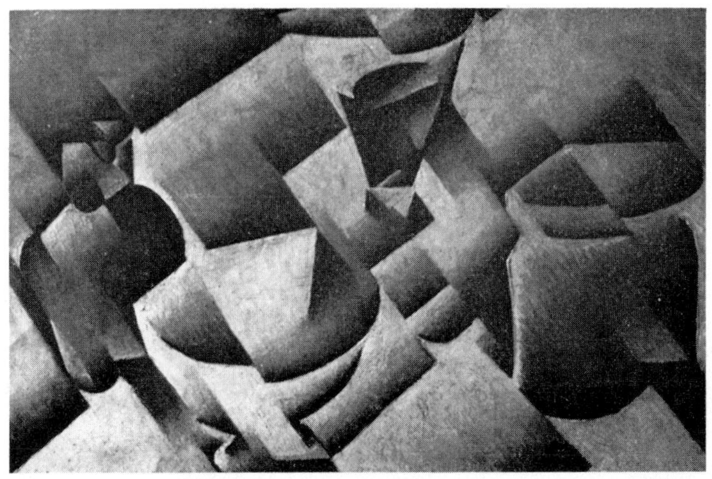

GRIS

58A The Eggs, 1911
Oil, 57.1 × 38.1 cm (22½ × 15 in)
Staatsgalerie, Stuttgart

58B Still Life with Cylindrical Pot, 1911
Oil, 33 × 51.4 cm (13 × 20¼ in)
Rijksmuseum Kröller-Müller, Otterlo

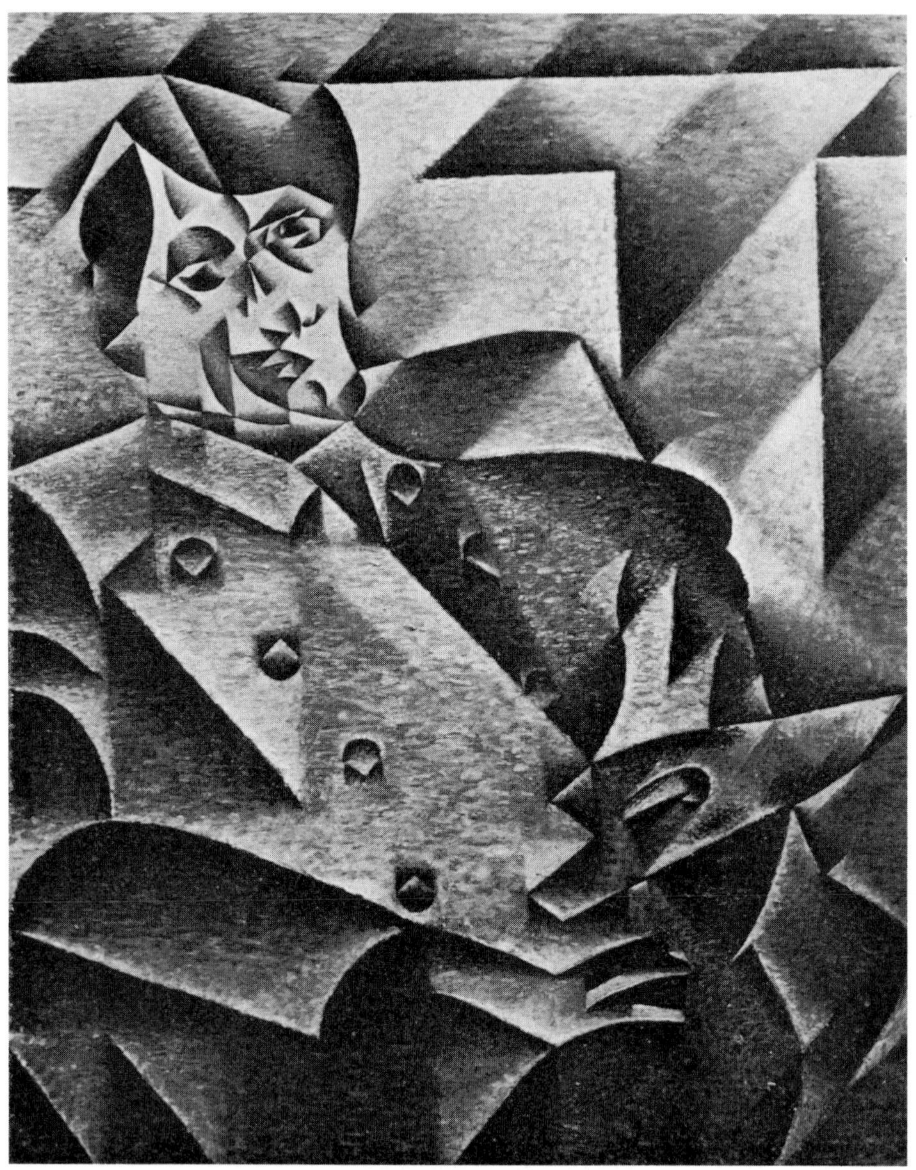

GRIS
59 Hommage à Picasso (Portrait of Picasso), 1911–12
Oil, 94 × 74.9 cm (37 × 29½ in)
The Art Institute of Chicago. All rights reserved

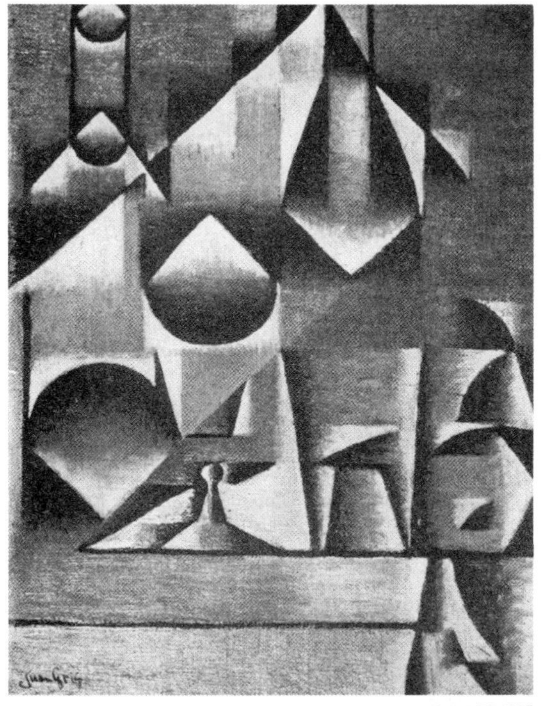

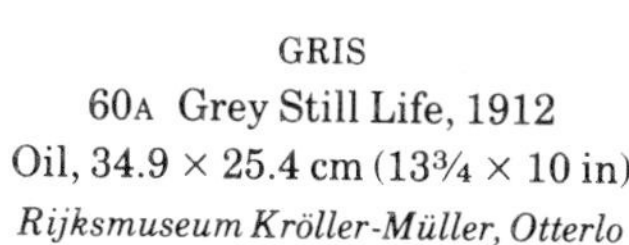

GRIS

60A Grey Still Life, 1912

Oil, 34.9 × 25.4 cm (13¾ × 10 in)

Rijksmuseum Kröller-Müller, Otterlo

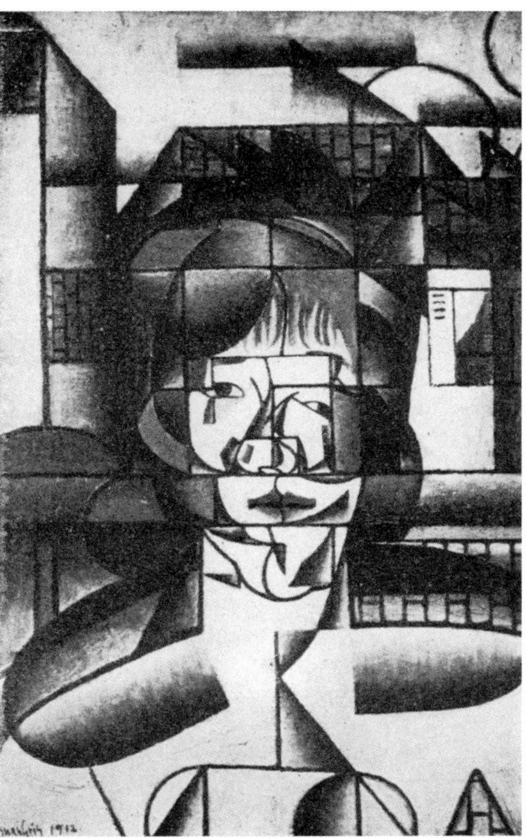

GRIS

60B Portrait of Germaine Raynal, 1912

Oil, 55.9 × 36.2 cm (22 × 14¼ in)

Private Collection, Paris

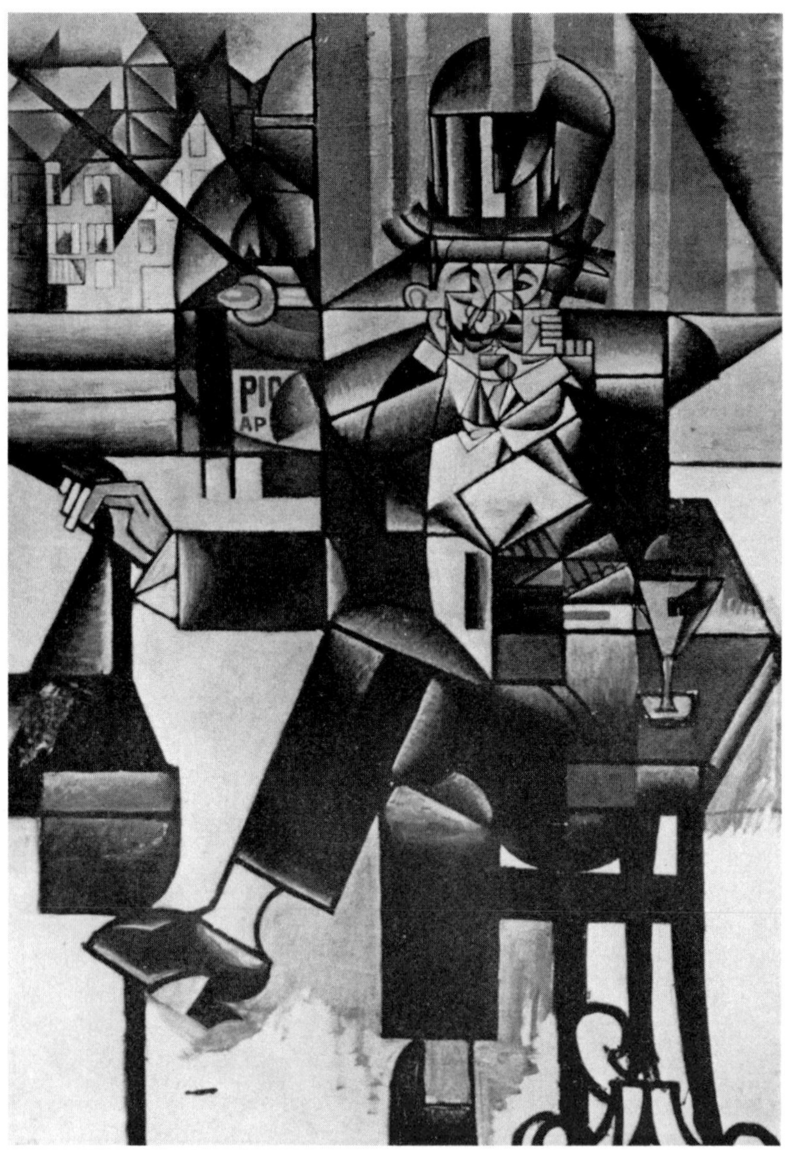

GRIS

61 The Man in the Café, 1912

Oil, 128.2 × 87.9 cm (50½ × 34⅝ in)

Louise and Walter Arensberg Collection, Philadelphia Museum of Art

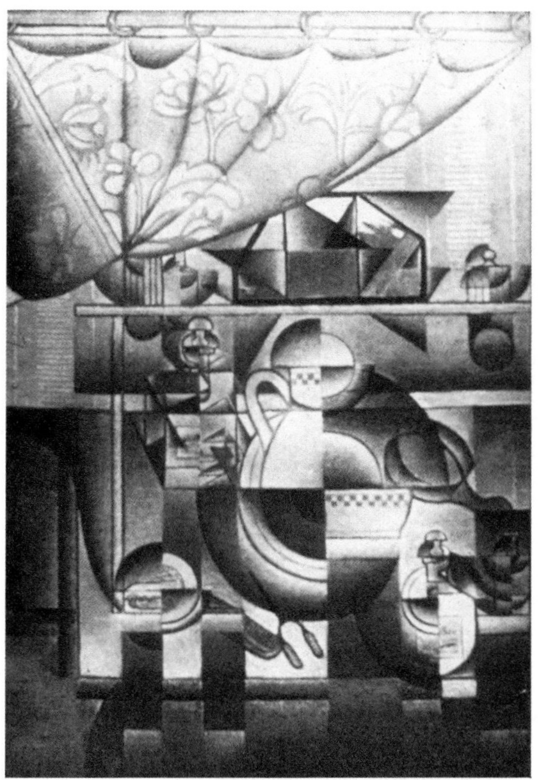

GRIS

62A Le Lavabo, 1912
Oil with mirror and *papier collé*,
132.1 × 90.1 cm (52 × 35½ in)
Private Collection

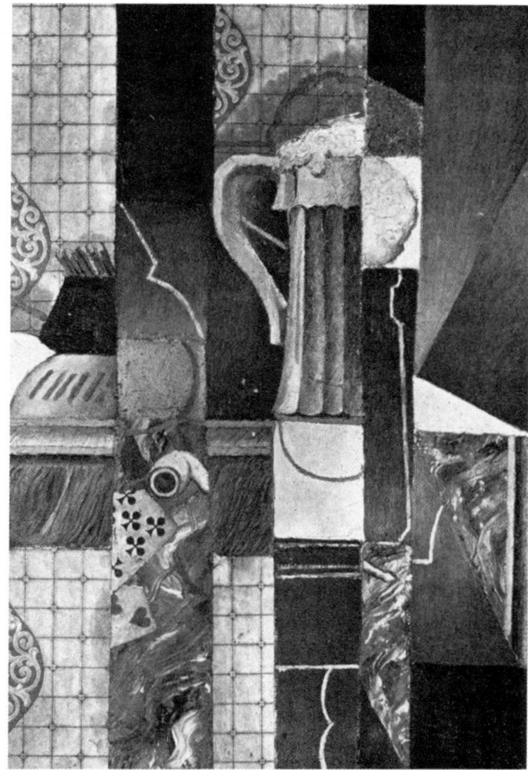

GRIS

62B Glass of Beer and Playing Cards, 1913
Oil and *papier collé*, 52 × 36.8 cm (20½ × 14½ in)
Columbus Gallery of Fine Arts (Howald Collection), Columbus, Ohio

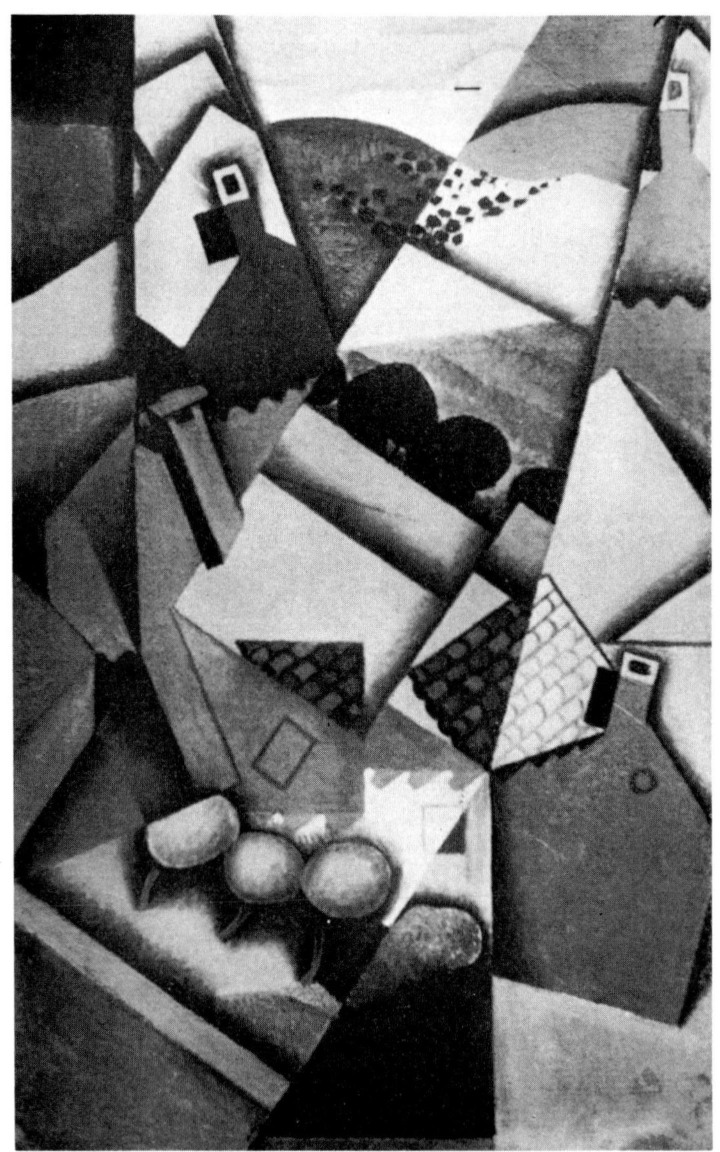

GRIS
63 Landscape at Céret, 1913
Oil, 100.3 × 64.7 cm (39½ × 25½ in)
Private Collection, Spain

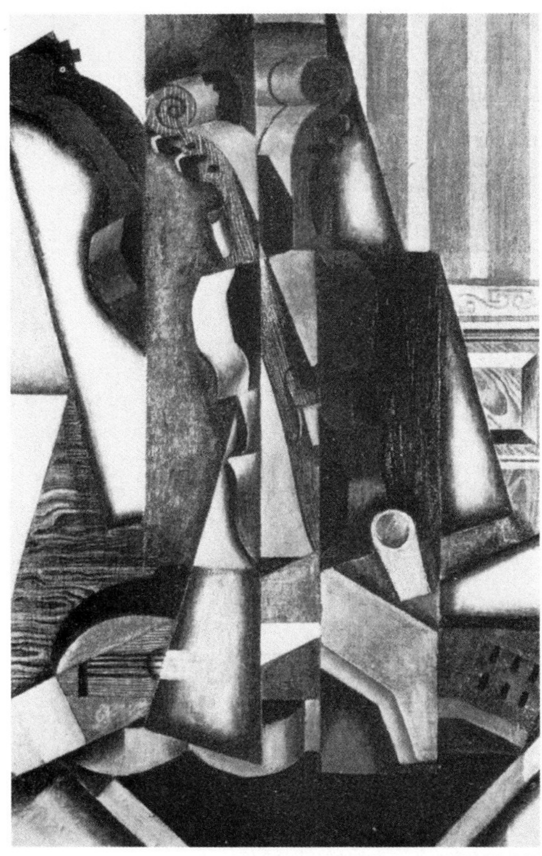

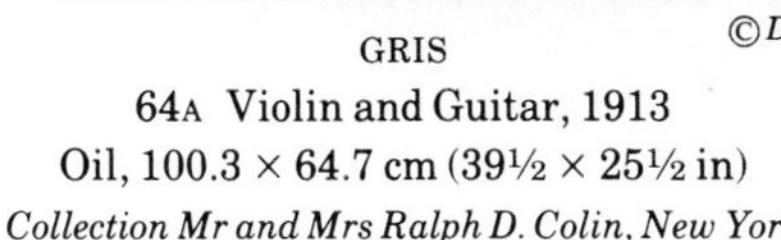

GRIS

64A Violin and Guitar, 1913

Oil, 100.3 × 64.7 cm (39½ × 25½ in)

Collection Mr and Mrs Ralph D. Colin, New York

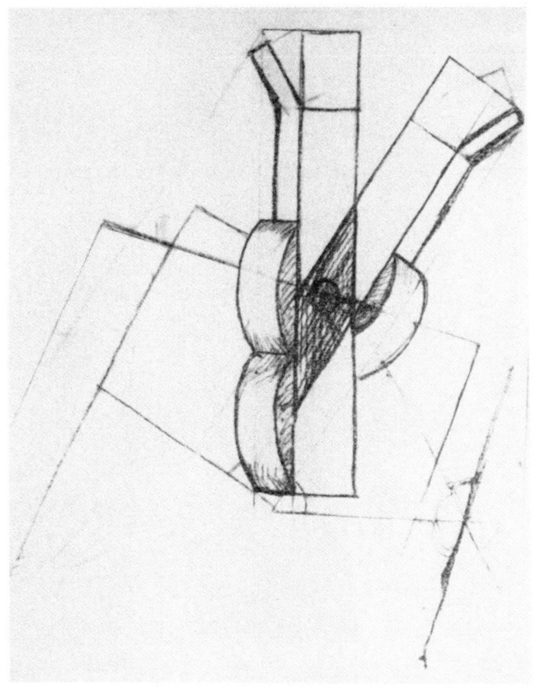

GRIS

64B The Guitar, 1913

Charcoal on paper, 30 × 22 cm (11¾ × 8¾ in)

Private Collection, France

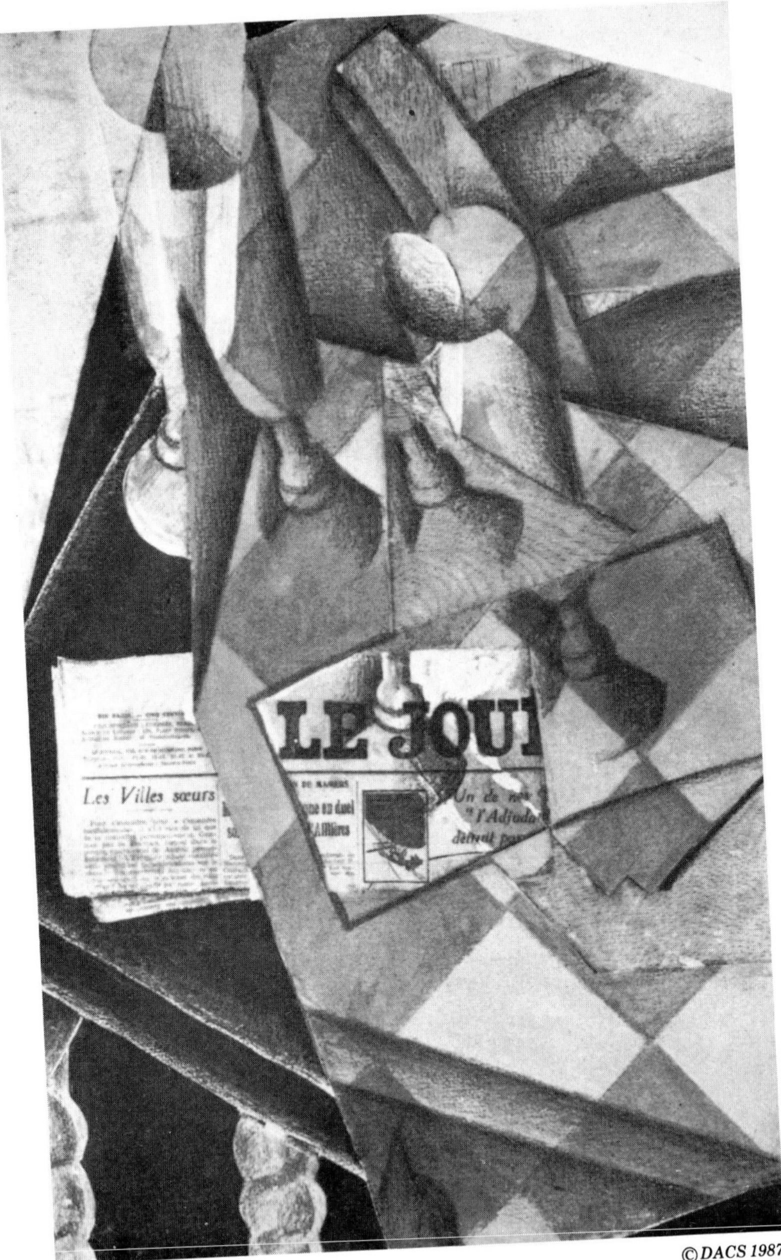

GRIS

65 Glasses and Newspaper, 1914

Papier collé, 60.9 × 38.1 cm (24 × 15 in)

Smith College Museum of Art, Northampton, Mass.

(Gift of Joseph Brummer)

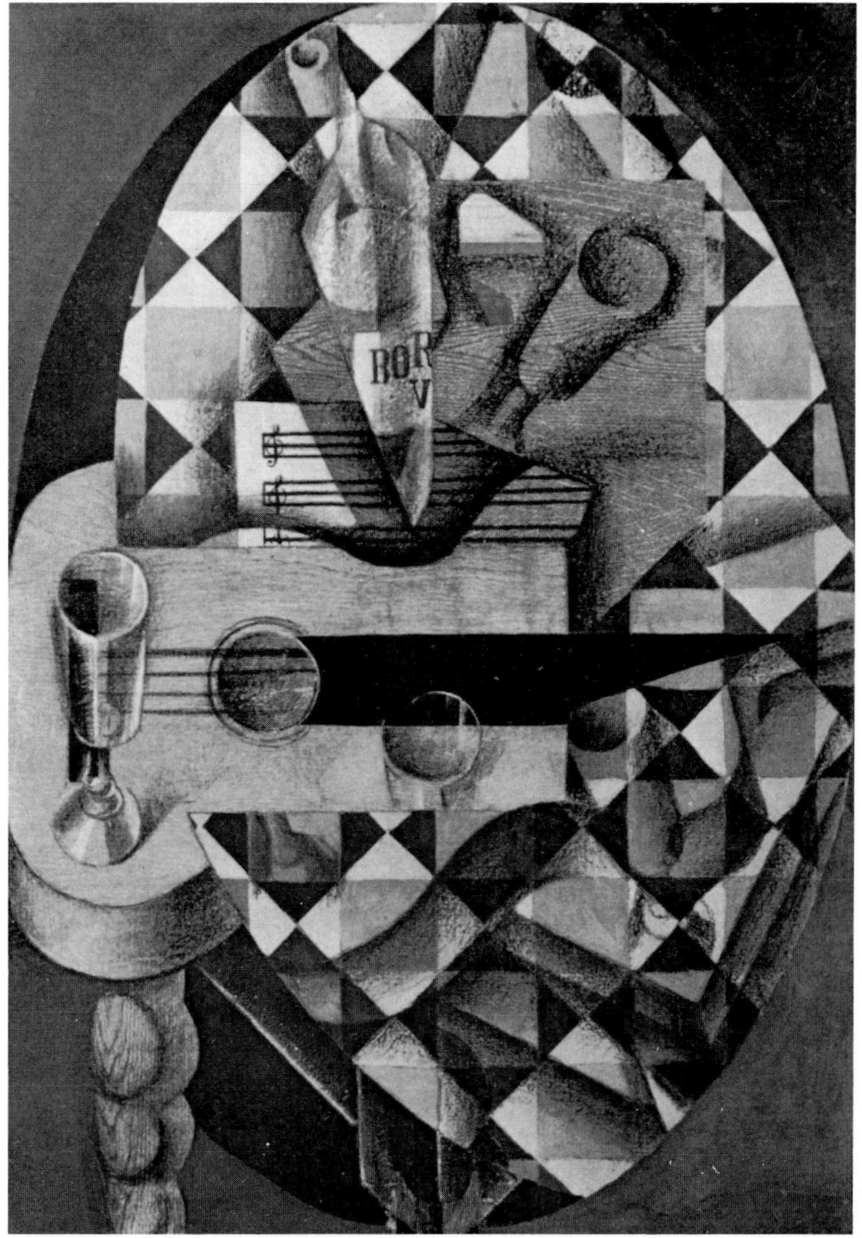

GRIS

66 Guitar, Glasses and Bottle, 1914

Papier collé, 91.4 × 64.7 cm (36 × 25½ in)

Private Collection, New York

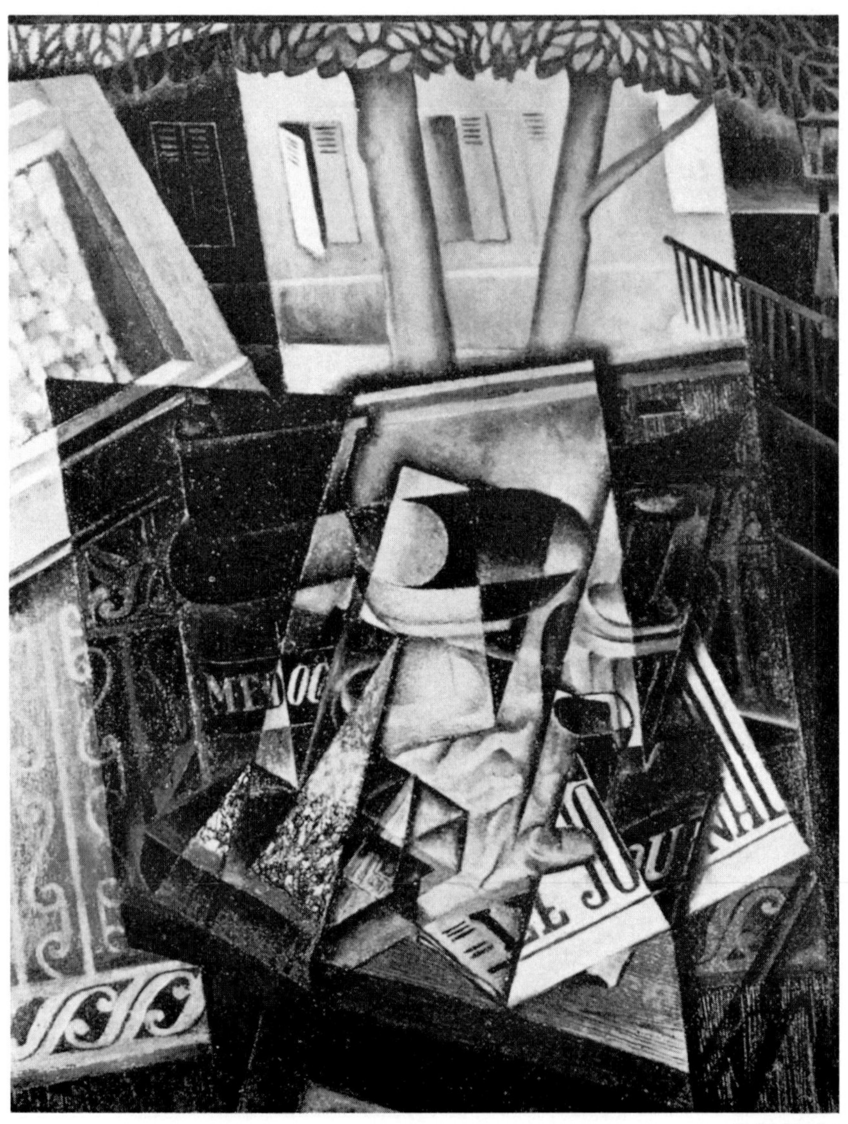

GRIS

67 Still Life in Front of an Open Window, 1915

Oil, 116.2 × 88.9 cm (45¾ × 35 in)

Louise and Walter Arensberg Collection, Philadelphia Museum of Art

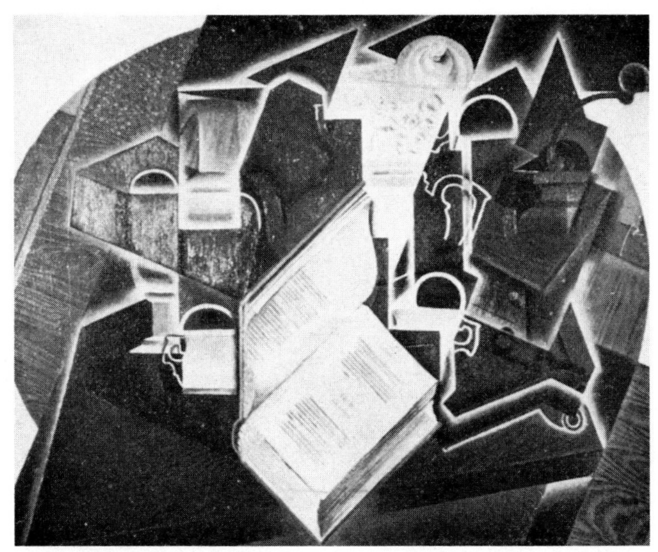

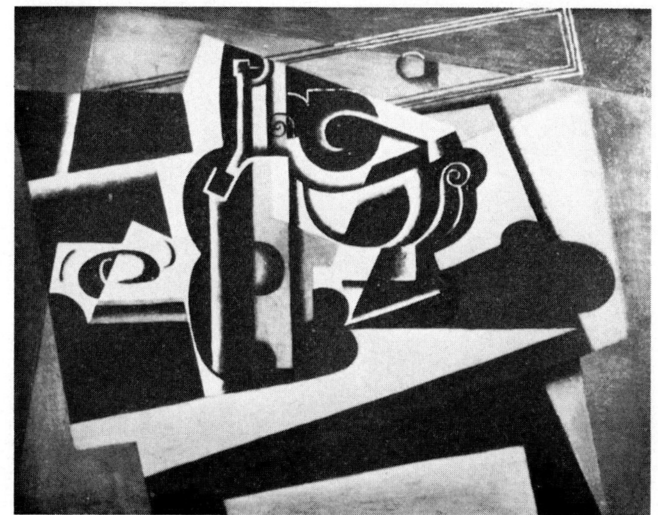

GRIS

68A Livre, Pipe et Verres, 1915
Oil, 93.3 × 73.6 cm (36¾ × 29 in)
Collection Mr and Mrs Ralph D. Colin, New York

68B Bouteille et Compotier, 1917
Oil, 93.3 × 73.6 cm (36¾ × 29 in)
Institute of Art, Minneapolis

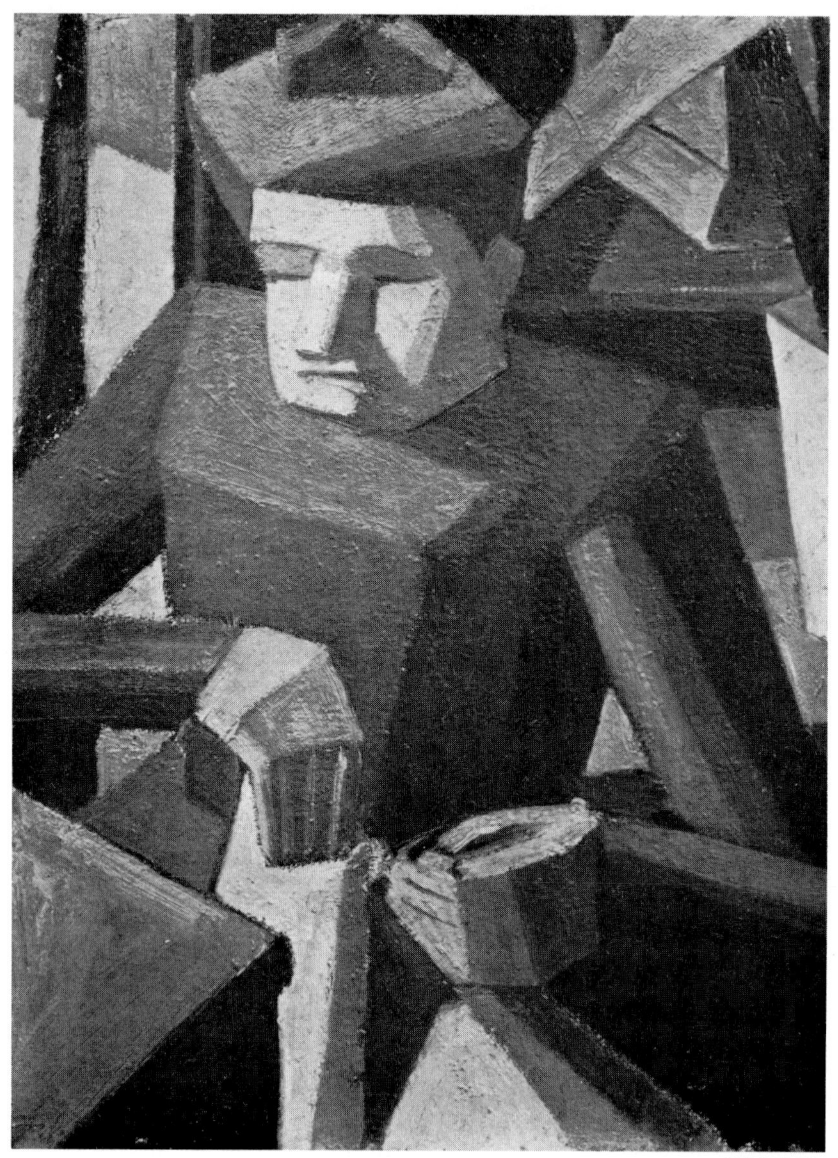

LÉGER
69 La Couseuse, 1909
Oil, 73 × 54.6 cm (28¾ × 21½ in)
Private Collection, Paris

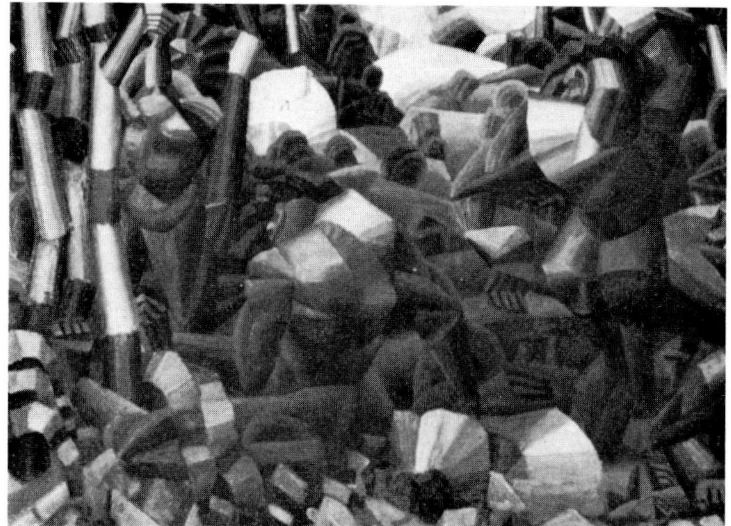

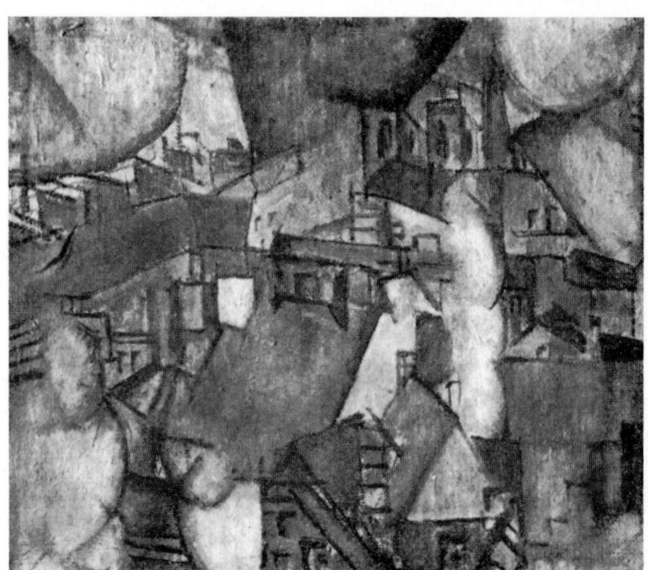

LÉGER

70A Nus dans un Paysage, 1909–11
Oil, 121.9 × 172.7 cm (48 × 68 in)
Rijksmuseum Kröller-Müller, Otterlo

70B Fumées sur les Toits, 1910
Oil, 66.7 × 55.9 cm (26¼ × 22 in)
Collection Mr Richard Weil, New York

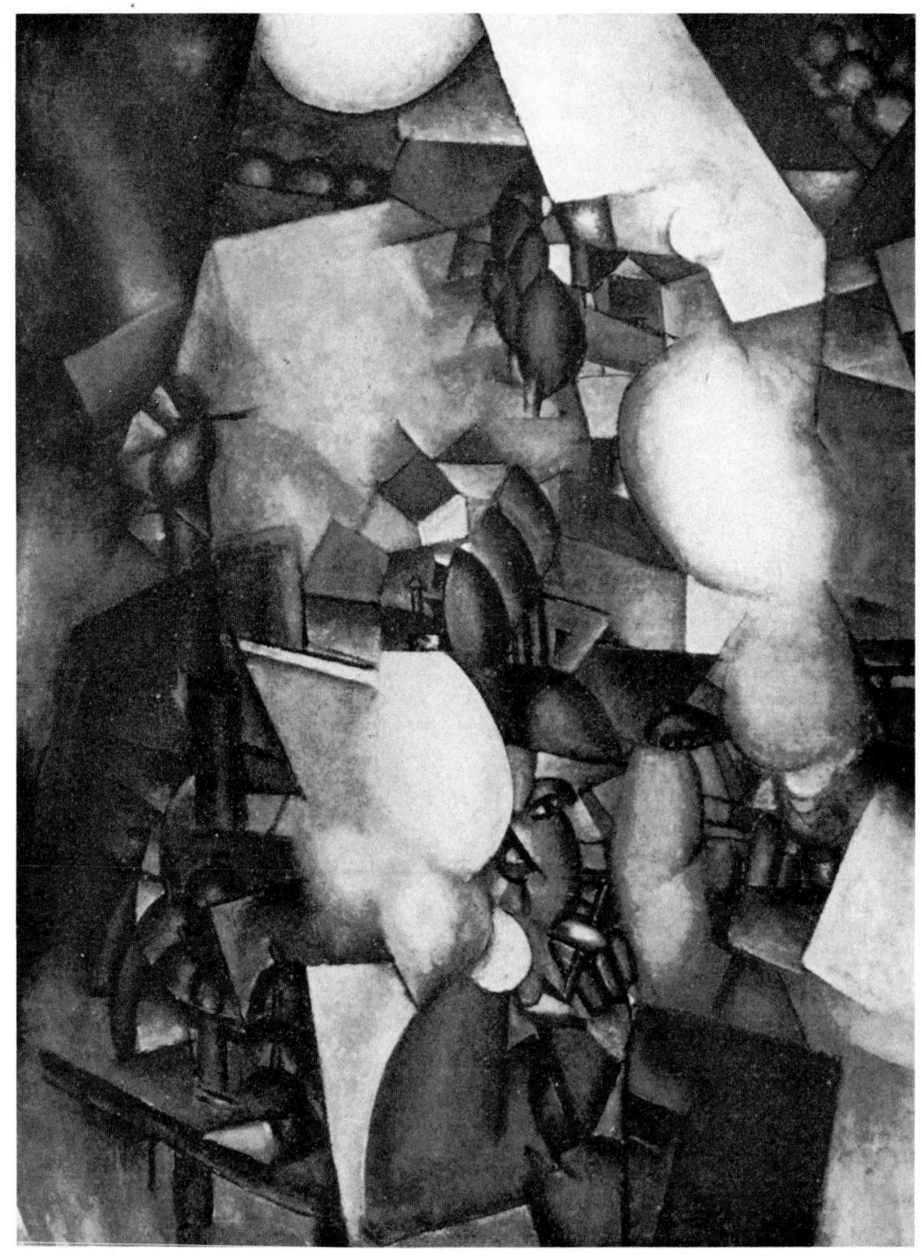

LÉGER

71 Les Fumeurs, 1911

Oil, 129.2 × 96.5 cm (50⅞ × 38 in)

Solomon R. Guggenheim Museum, New York

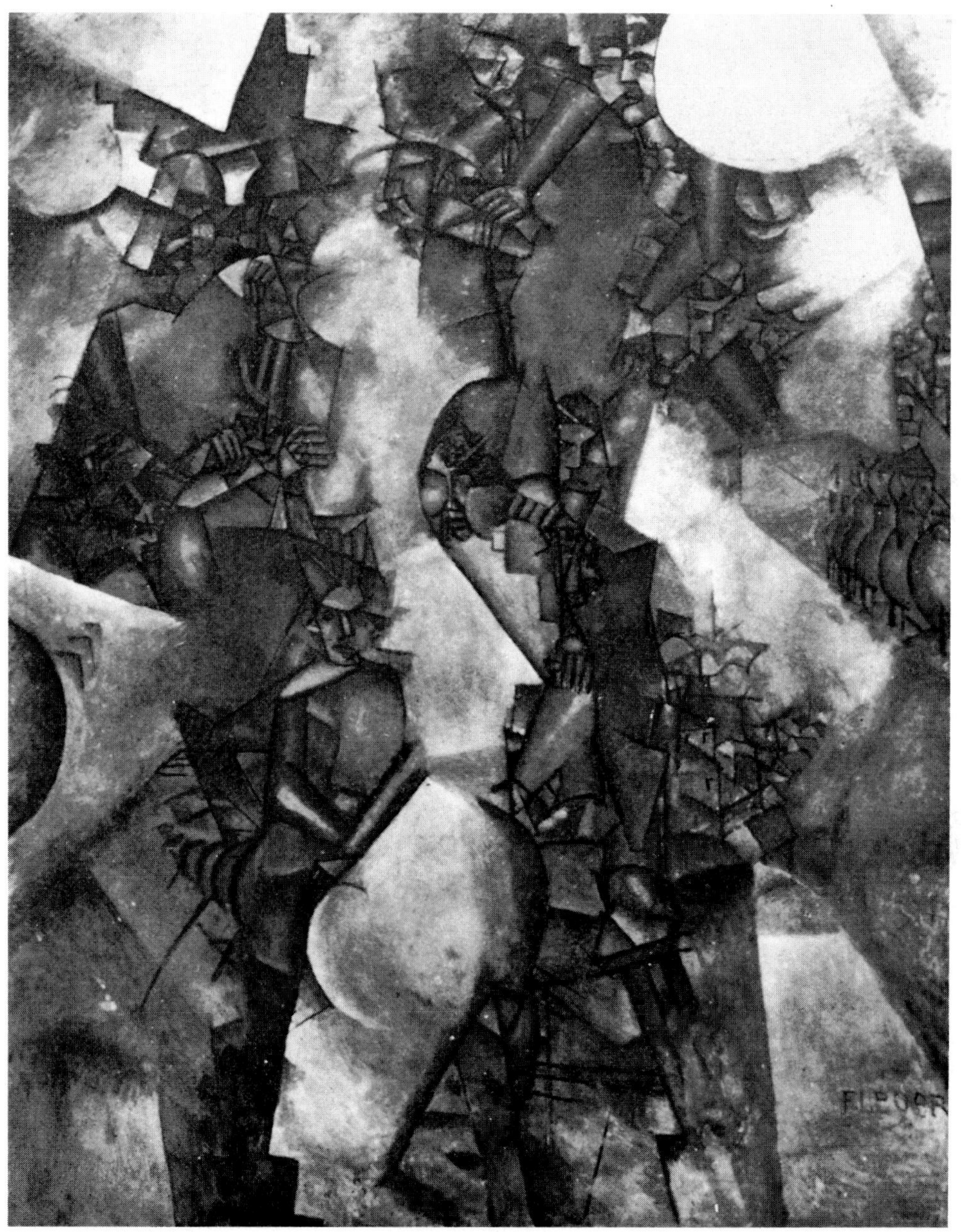

LÉGER

72 La Noce, 1911–12

Oil, 408 × 327 cm (160⅝ × 128¾ in)

Musée National d'Art Moderne, Paris

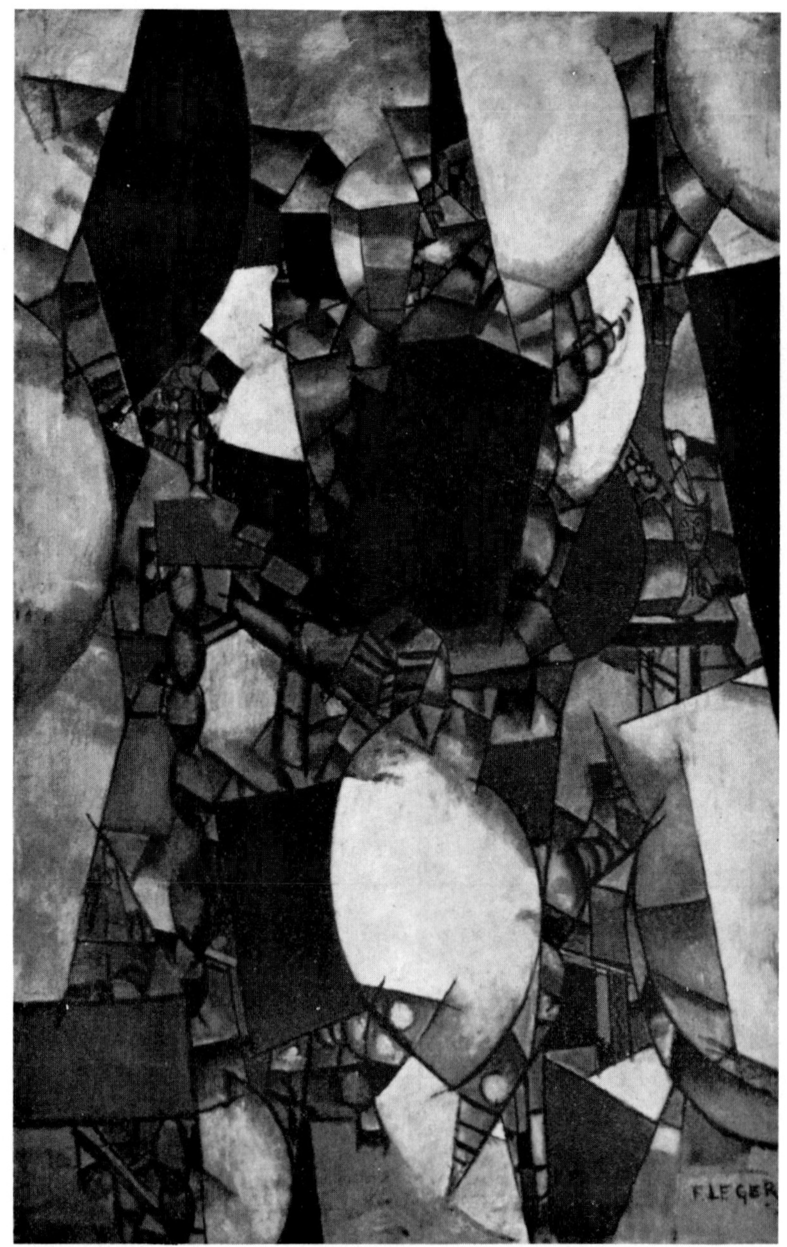

LÉGER
73 La Femme en Bleu, 1912
Oil, 193 × 132.1 cm (76 × 52 in)
Kunstmuseum, Basel

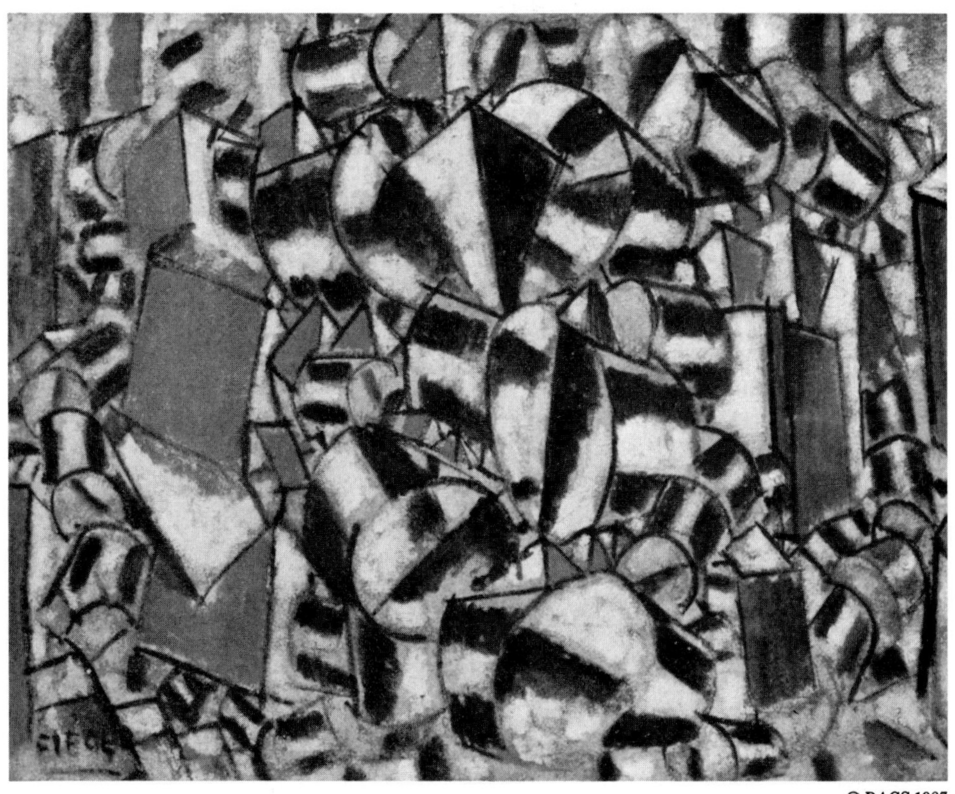

LÉGER
74 Contrastes de Formes, 1913
Oil, 99 × 125.1 cm (39 × 49¼ in)
Solomon R. Guggenheim Museum, New York

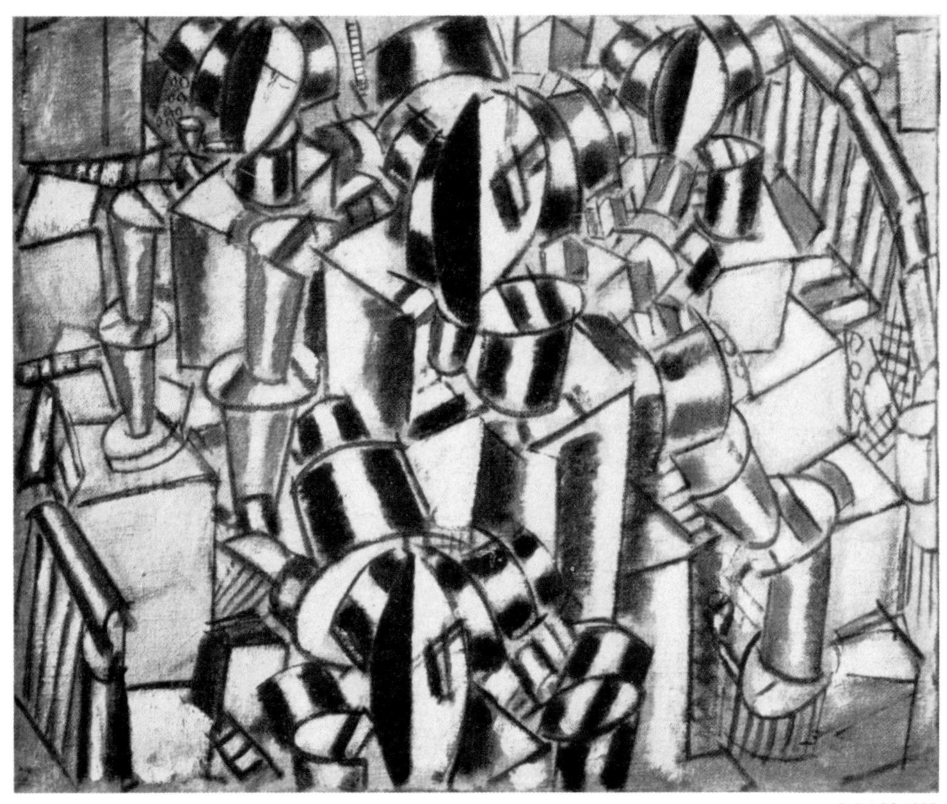

LÉGER
75 L'Escalier, 1914
Oil, 88.9 × 124.4 cm (35 × 49 in)
Kunstmuseum, Basel

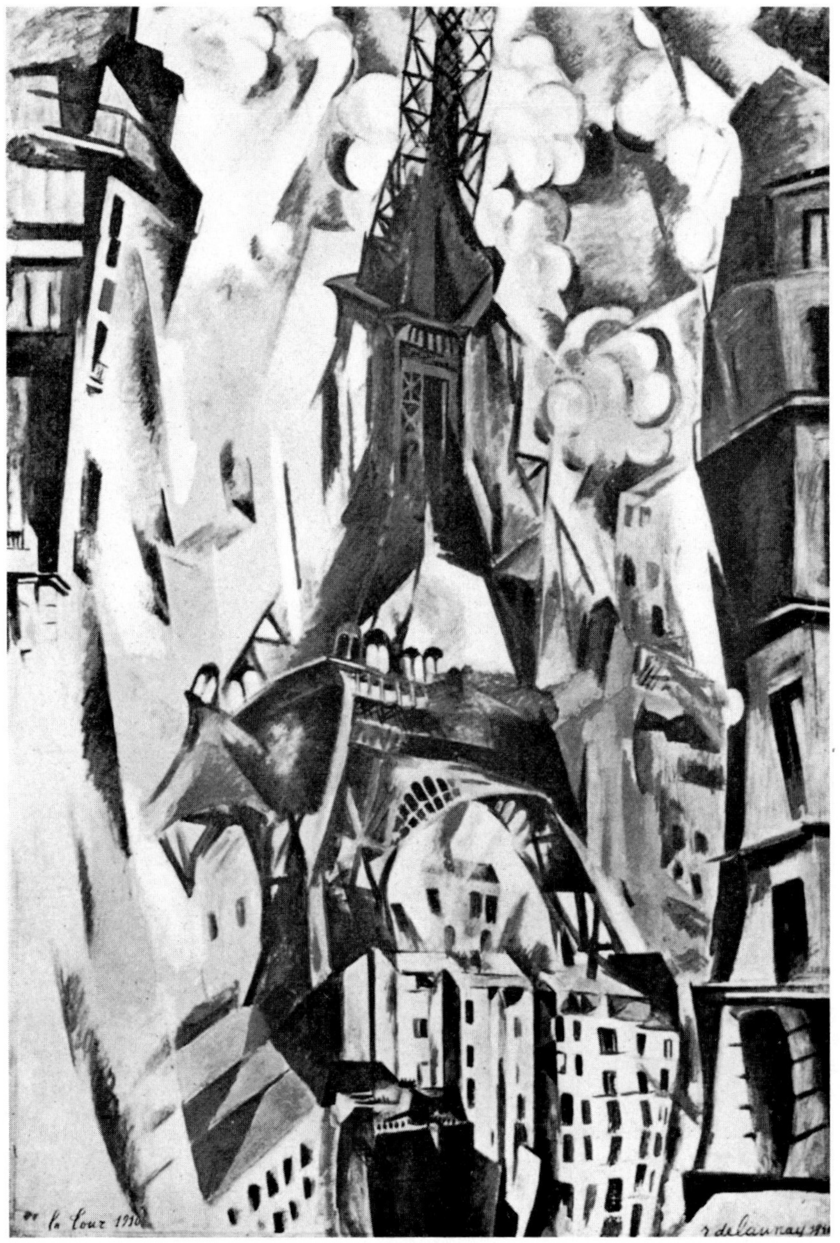

DELAUNAY

76 The Eiffel Tower, 1910

Oil, 201.9 × 138.4 cm (79½ × 54¼ in)

Solomon R. Guggenheim Museum, New York

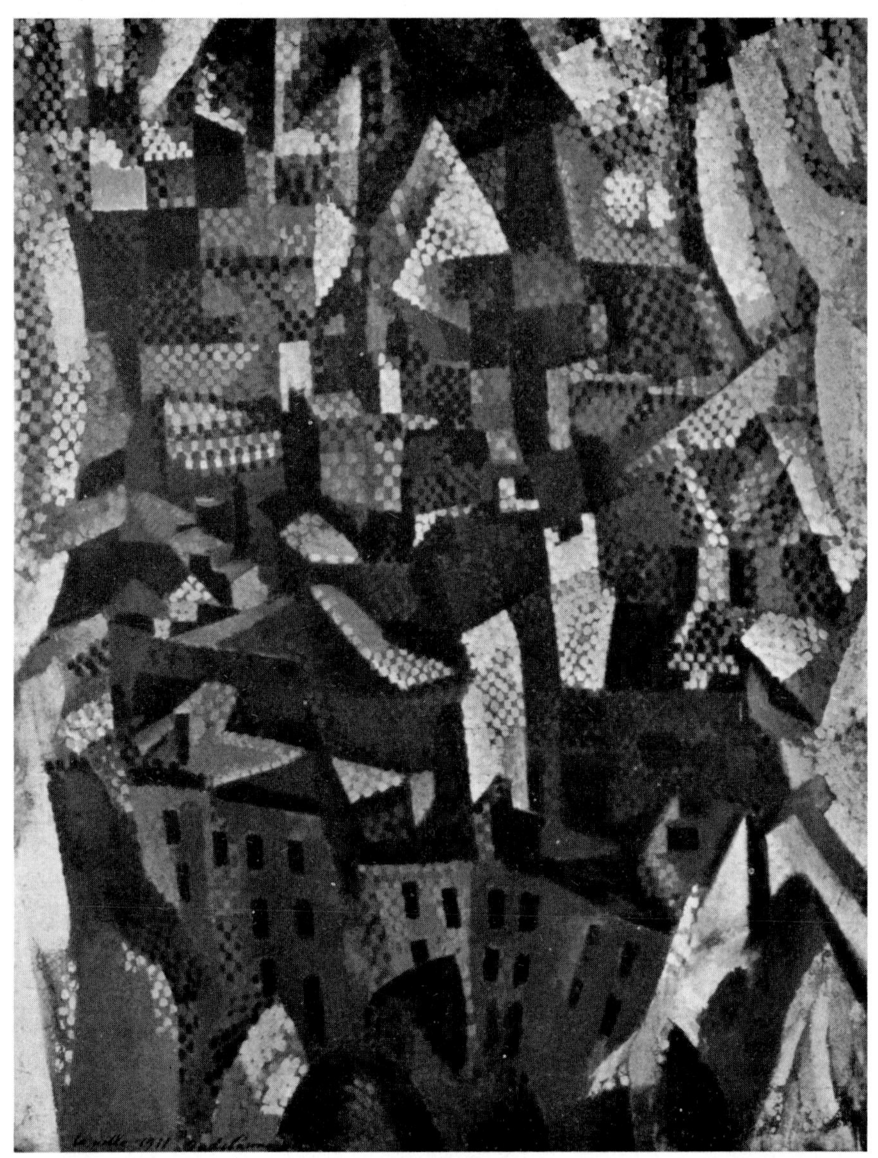

DELAUNAY
77 La Ville, 1911
Oil, 144.8 × 111.7 cm (57 × 44 in)
Solomon R. Guggenheim Museum, New York

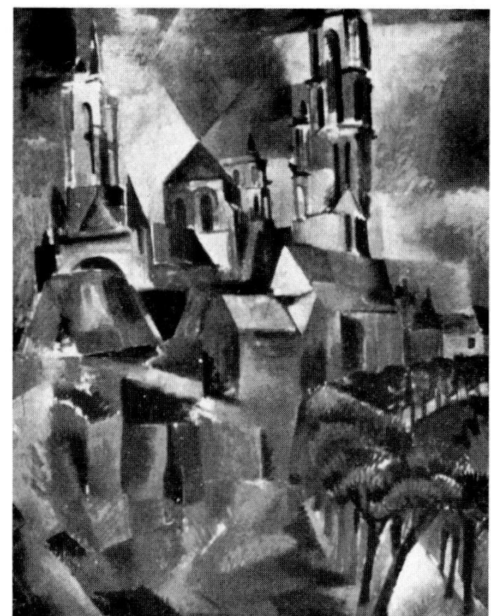

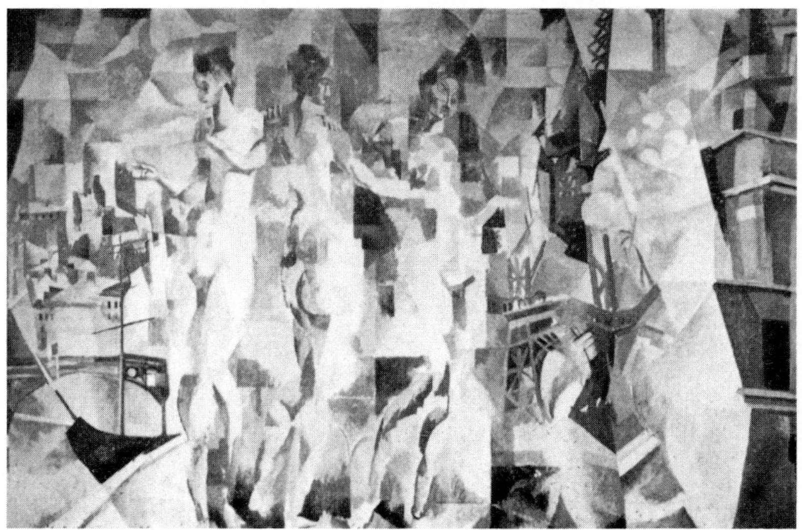

DELAUNAY

78A Les Tours de Laon, 1912
Oil, 161.9 × 129.8 cm (63¾ × 51⅛ in)
Musée National d'Art Moderne, Paris

78B La Ville de Paris, 1912
Oil, 265.4 × 402.6 cm (104½ × 158½ in)
Musée National d'Art Moderne, Paris

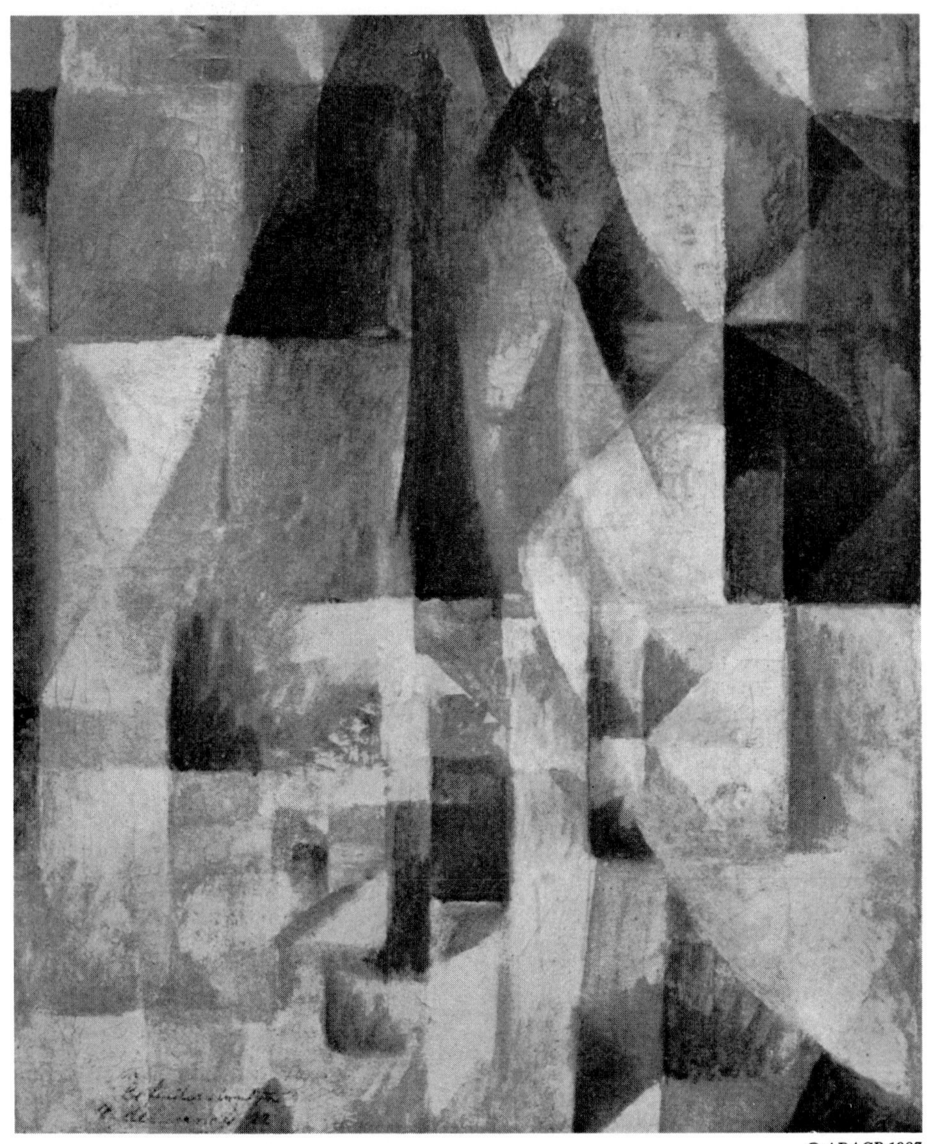

DELAUNAY

79 La Fenêtre, 1912

Oil, 55.2 × 46.6 cm (21¾ × 18⅜ in)

Solomon R. Guggenheim Museum, New York

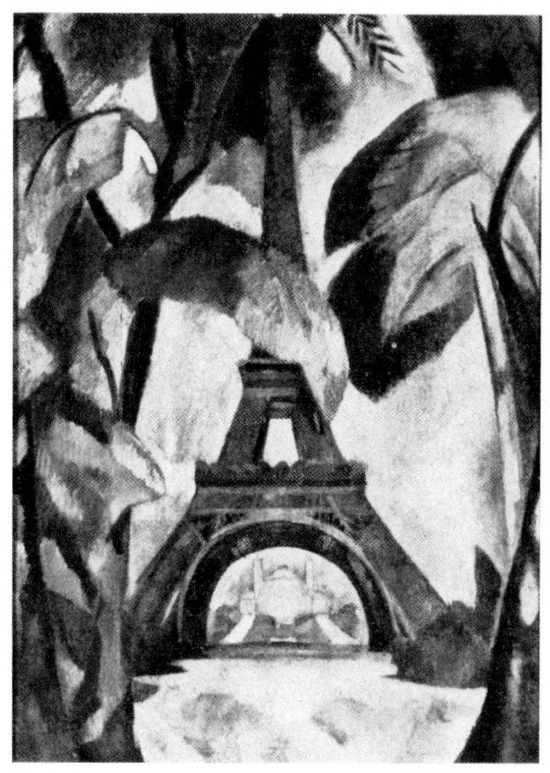

DELAUNAY

80A The Eiffel Tower, 1909

Oil, 96.5 × 70.5 cm (38 × 27¾ in)

Louise and Walter Arensberg Collection, Philadelphia Museum of Art

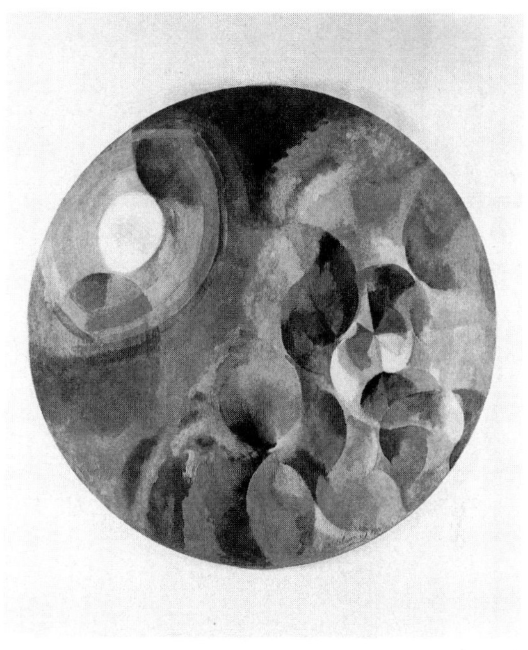

DELAUNAY

80B Simultaneous Contrasts: Sun and Moon, 1912–13

Oil, 135.5 cm (53 in) in diameter

Collection, The Museum of Modern Art, New York
Mrs Simon Guggenheim Fund

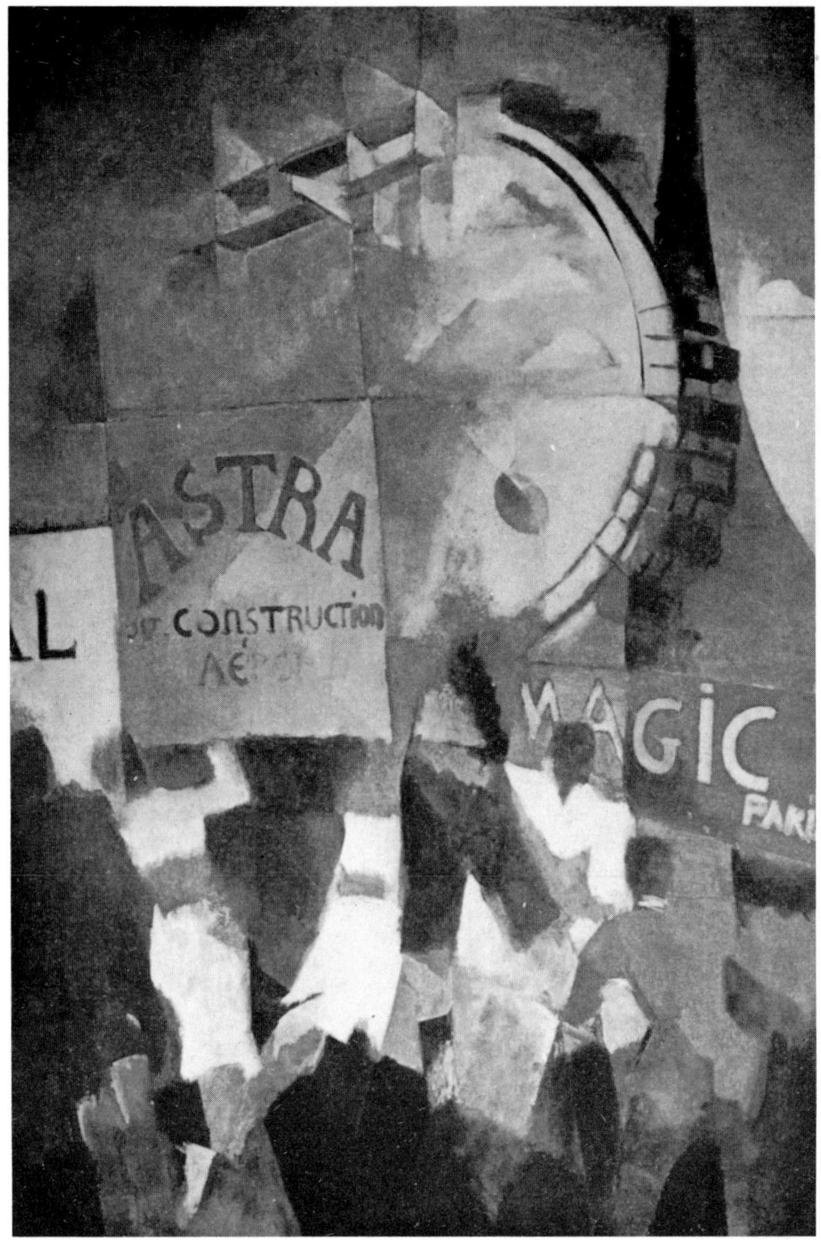

DELAUNAY

81 L'Equipe de Cardiff, 1912–13

Oil, 196.2 × 129.8 cm (77¼ × 51⅛ in)

Stedelijk Van Abbe Museum, Eindhoven

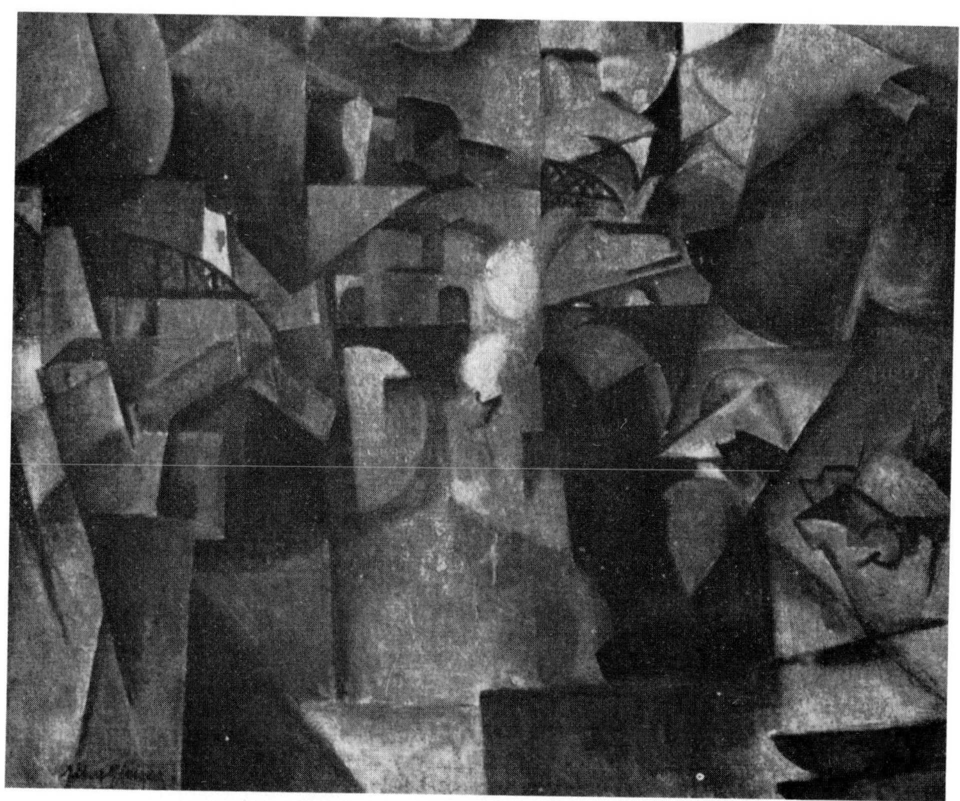

GLEIZES

82 The Bridges of Paris, 1912

Oil, 58.4 × 71.7 cm (23 × 28¼ in)

Museum des 20 Jahrhunderts, Vienna

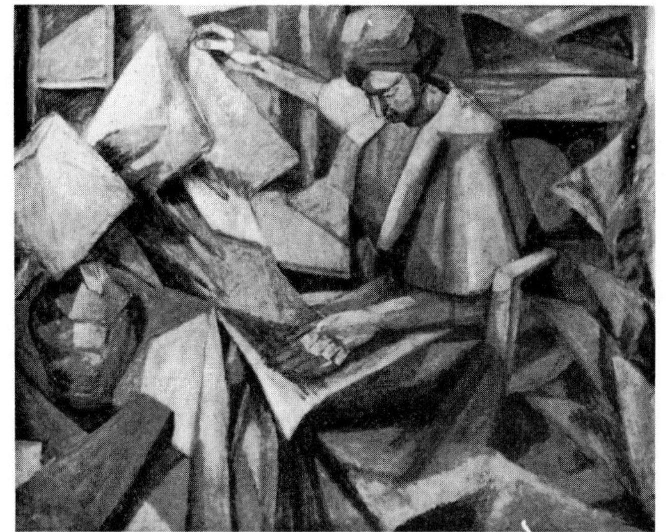

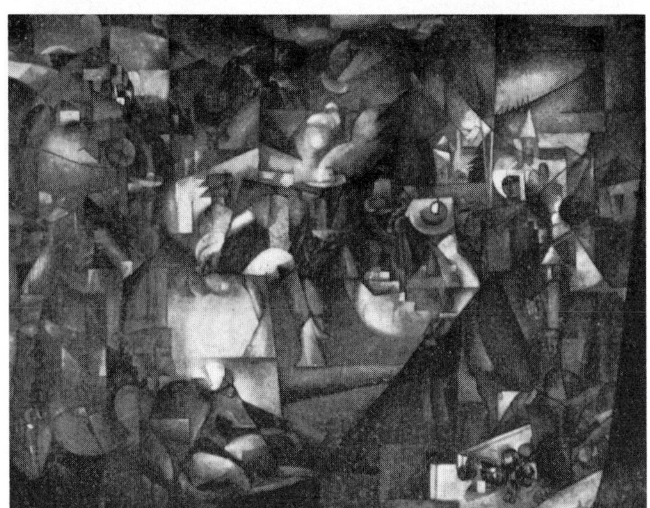

GLEIZES

83A La Femme aux Phlox, 1910–11
Oil, 81.3 × 100 cm (32 × 39⅜ in)
Museum of Fine Arts, Houston

83B Le Dépiquage des Moissons (Harvest Threshing), 1912
Oil, 269.2 × 352.7 cm (106 × 138⅞ in)
Solomon R. Guggenheim Museum, New York

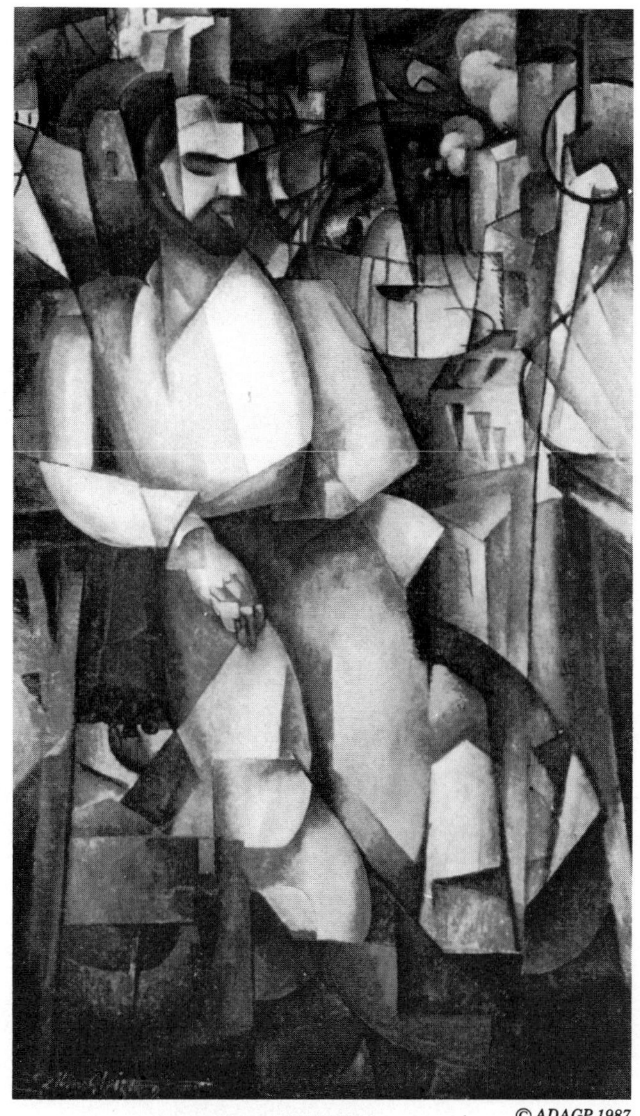

GLEIZES

84 L'Homme au Balcon, 1912

Oil, 195.6 × 114.9 cm (77 × 45¼ in)

Louise and Walter Arensberg Collection, Philadelphia Museum of Art

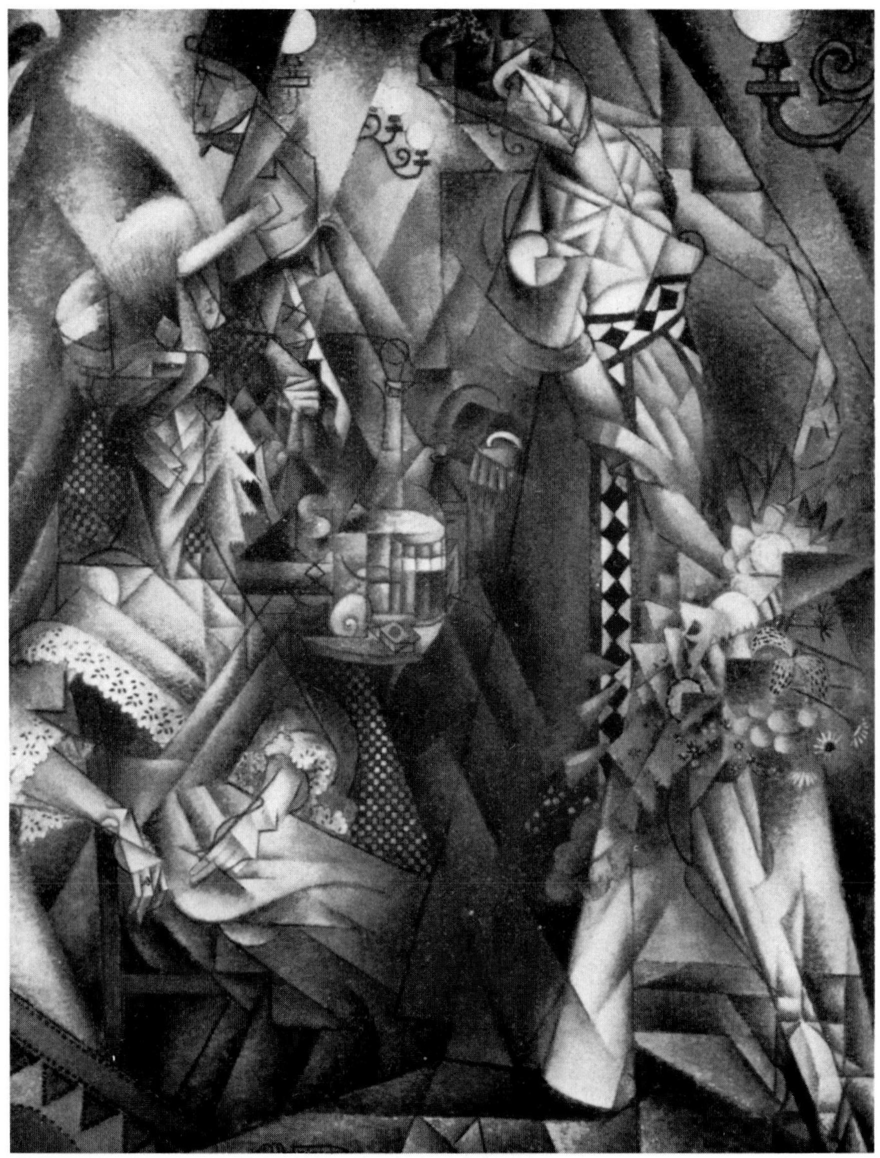

METZINGER
85 La Danseuse au Café, 1912
Oil, 144.8 × 113 cm (57 × 44½ in)
Albright Knox Gallery, Buffalo

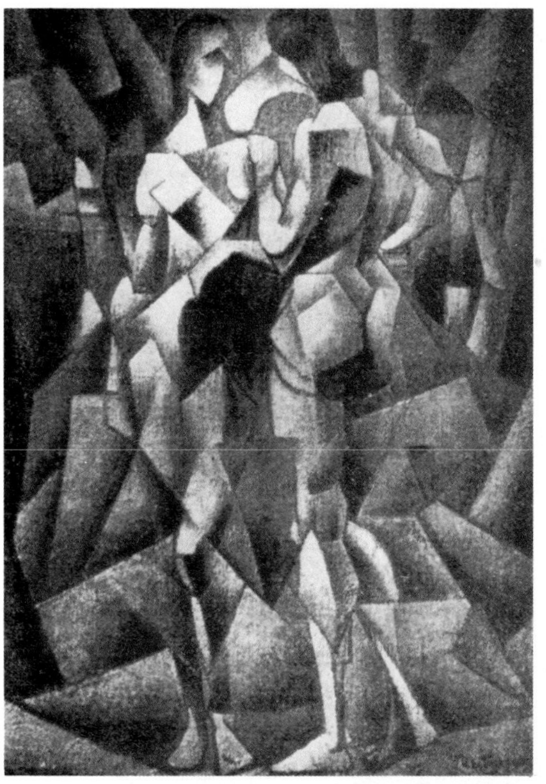

METZINGER
86A Two Nudes, 1910–11
Oil
Present whereabouts unknown

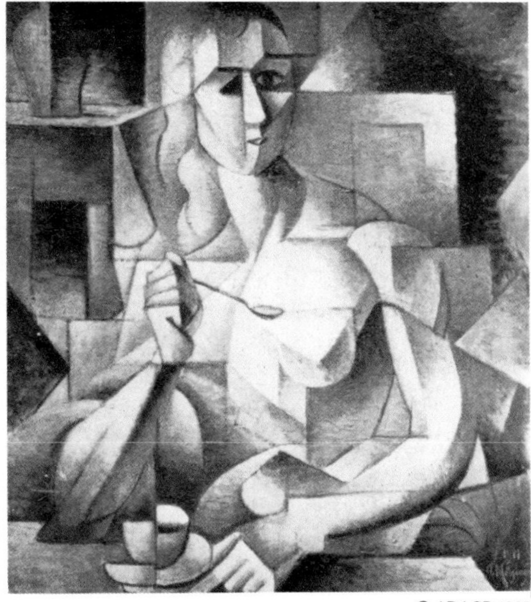

METZINGER
86B Le Goûter, 1911
Oil, 75.5 × 69.5 cm (29¾ × 27⅜ in)
Louise and Walter Arensberg Collection, Philadelphia Museum of Art

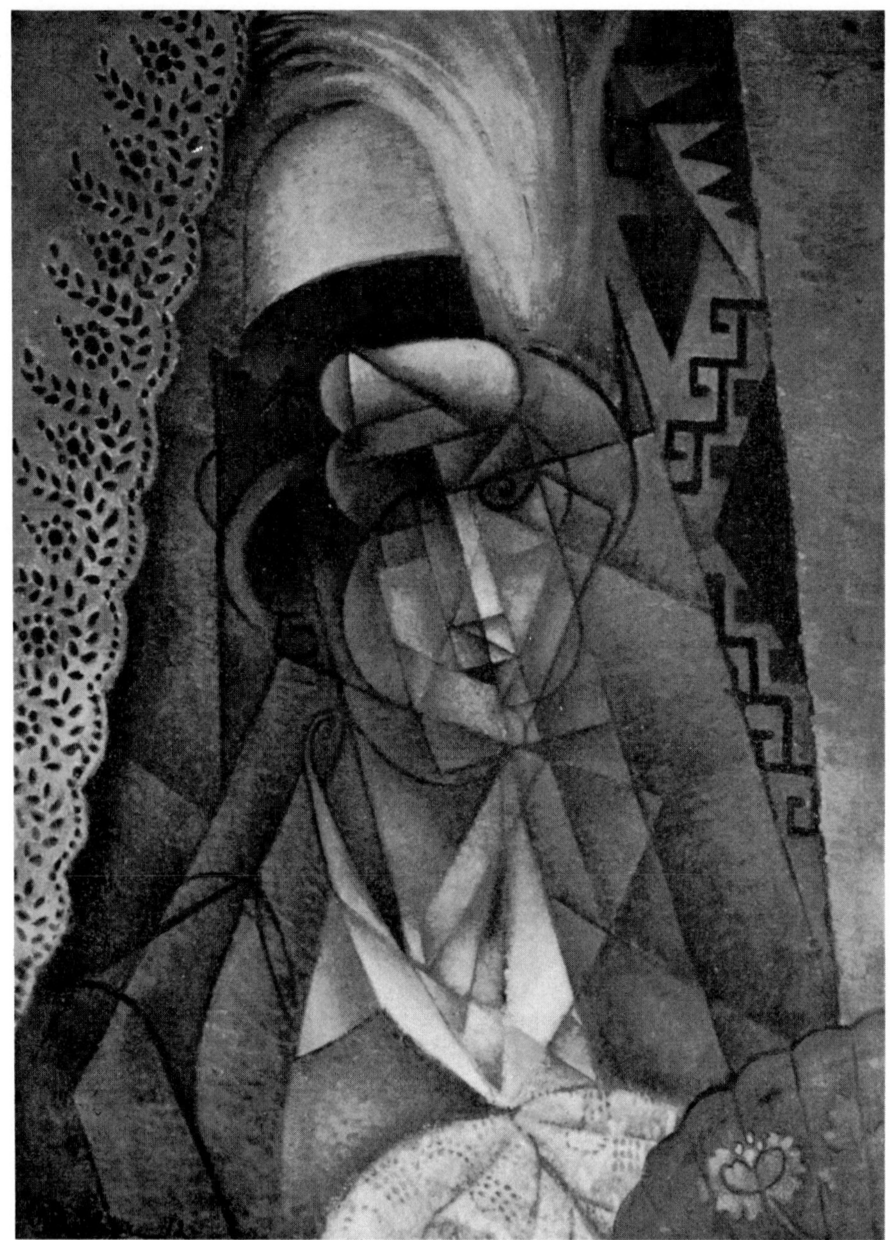

METZINGER
87 La Plume Jaune, 1912
Oil, 73 × 54 cm (28¾ × 21¼ in)
Collection Mr R. S. Johnson, Chicago

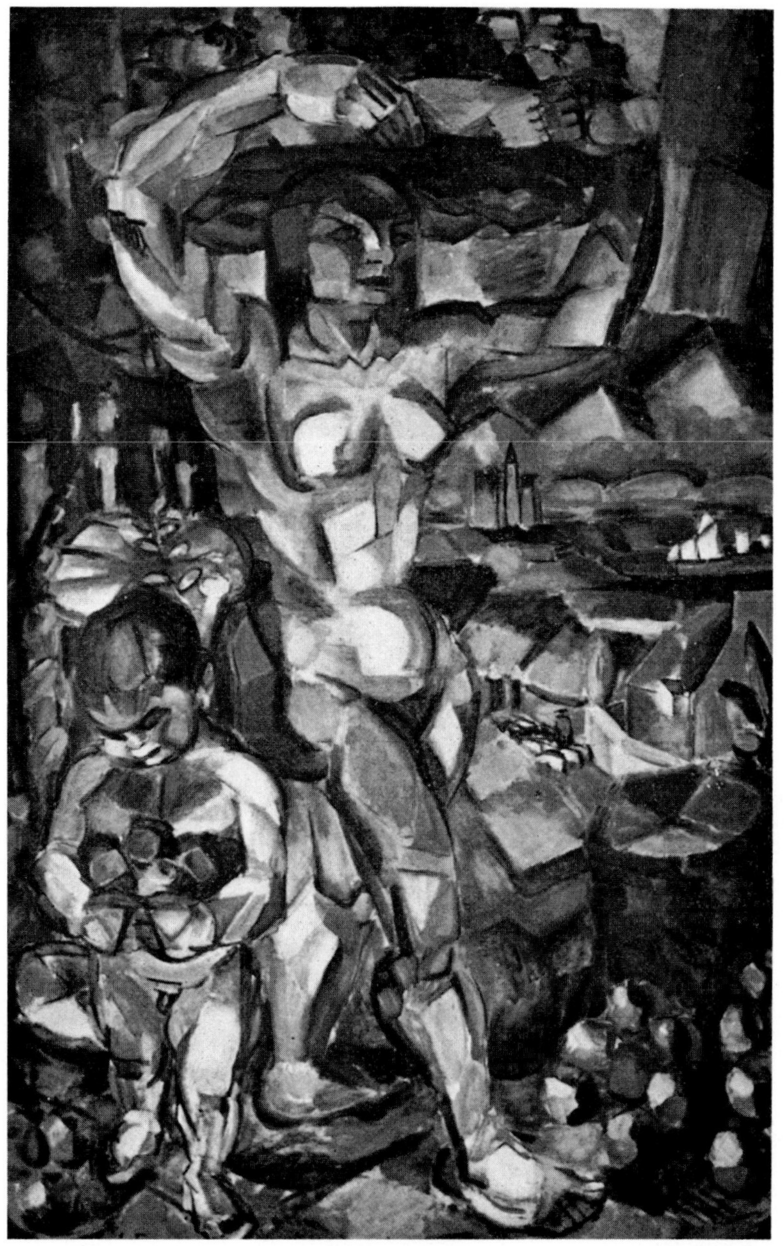

LE FAUCONNIER
88 L'Abondance, 1910–11
Oil, 318.7 × 195.6 cm (125½ × 77 in)
Gemeente Museum, The Hague

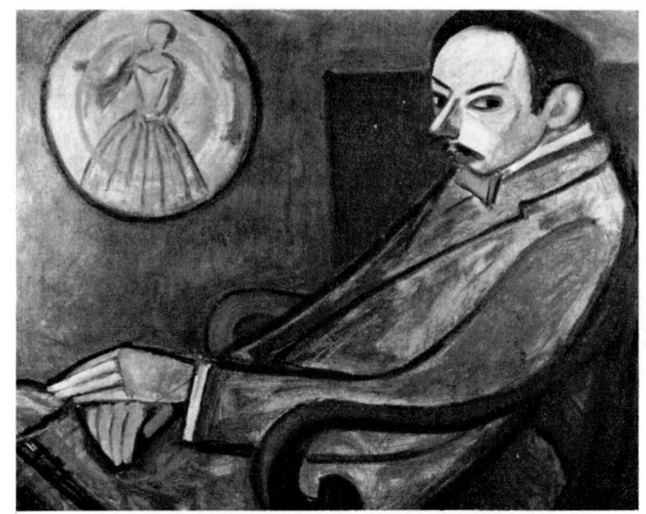

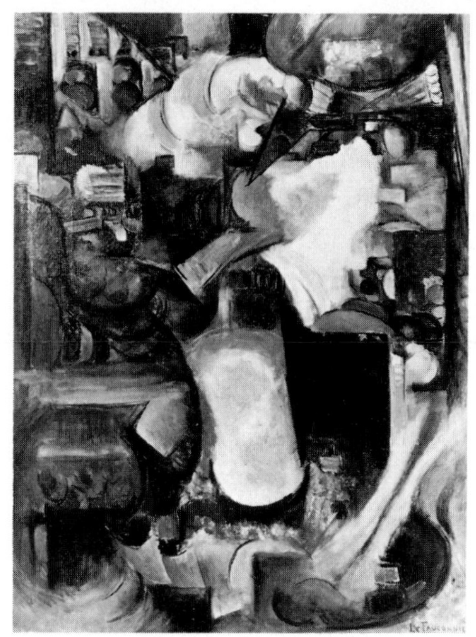

LE FAUCONNIER

89A Portrait of Jouve, 1909
Oil, 81×100cm (32½×40 in)
Musée National d'Art Moderne, Paris

89B The Huntsman (Chasseur), 1912
Oil, 158.1 × 117.8 cm (62¼ × 46⅜ in)
Collection, The Museum of Modern Art, New York
Gift of Mr and Mrs Leo Lionni

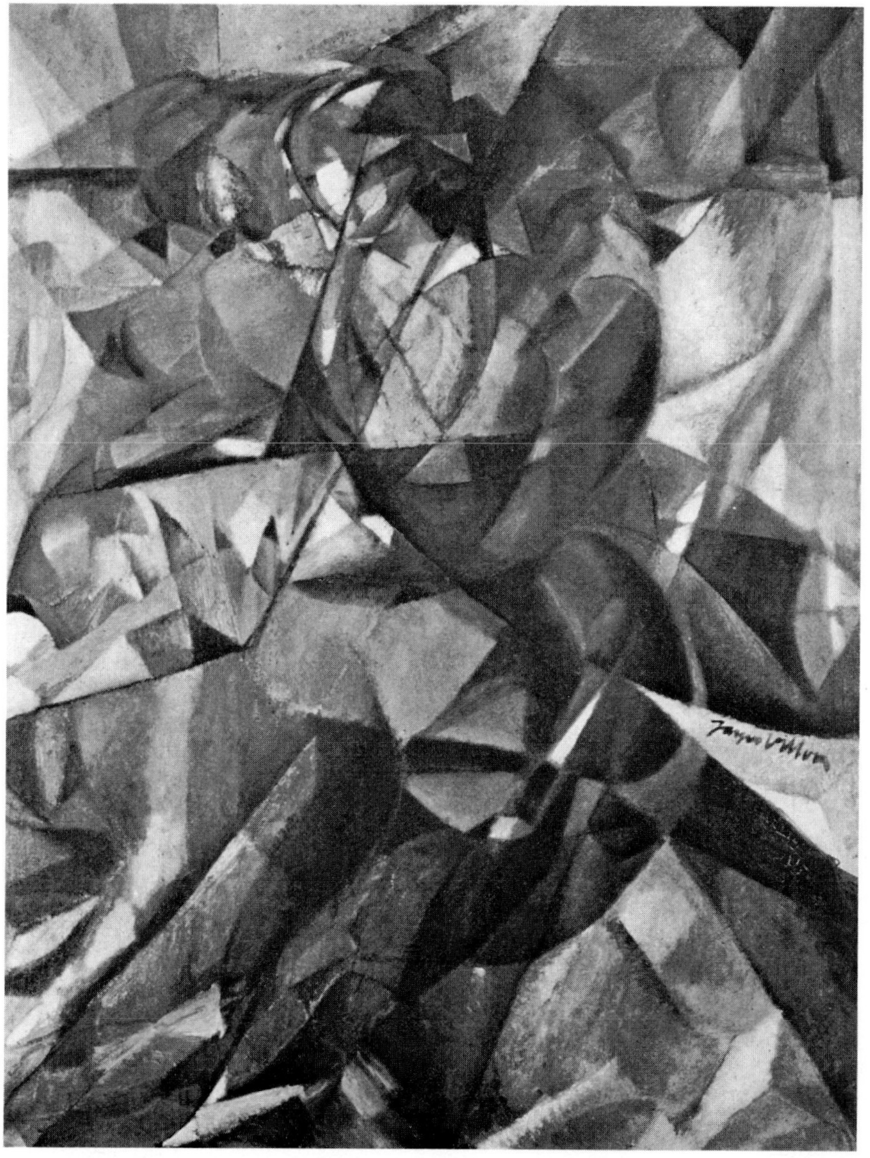

VILLON

90 Young Woman, 1912

Oil, 146.7 × 114.3 cm ($57\frac{3}{4}$ × 45 in)

Louise and Walter Arensberg Collection, Philadelphia Museum of Art

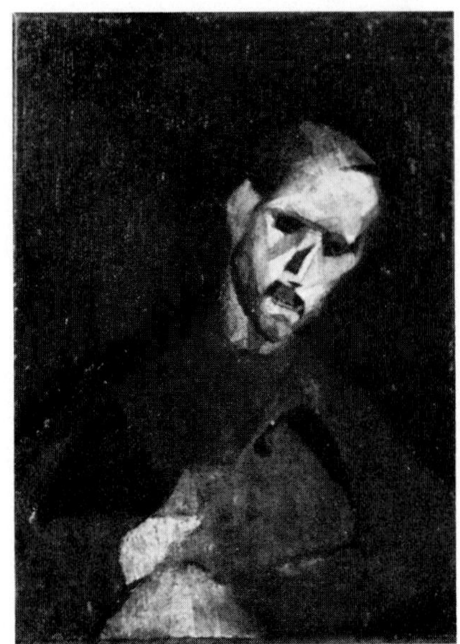

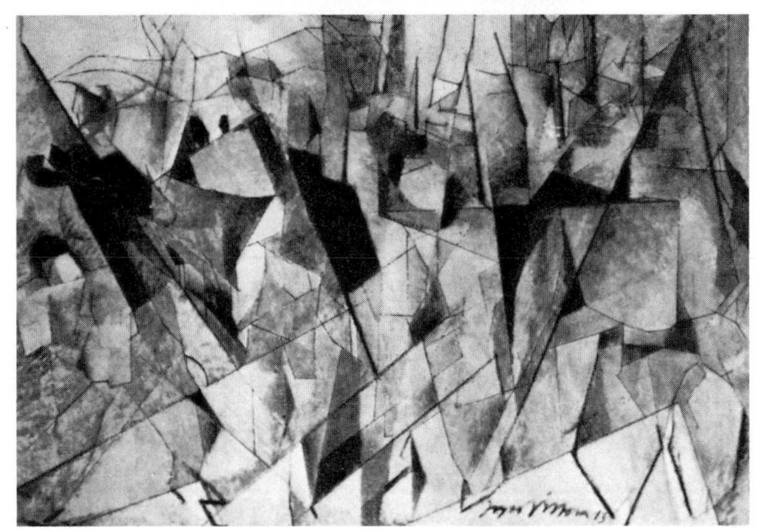

VILLON

91A Portrait of Duchamp-Villon
Oil, 34.9 × 26.6 cm (13¾ × 10½ in)
Musée National d'Art Moderne, Paris

91B Soldats en Marche, 1913
Oil, 64.7 × 91.4 cm (25½ × 36 in)
Musée National D'Art Moderne, Paris

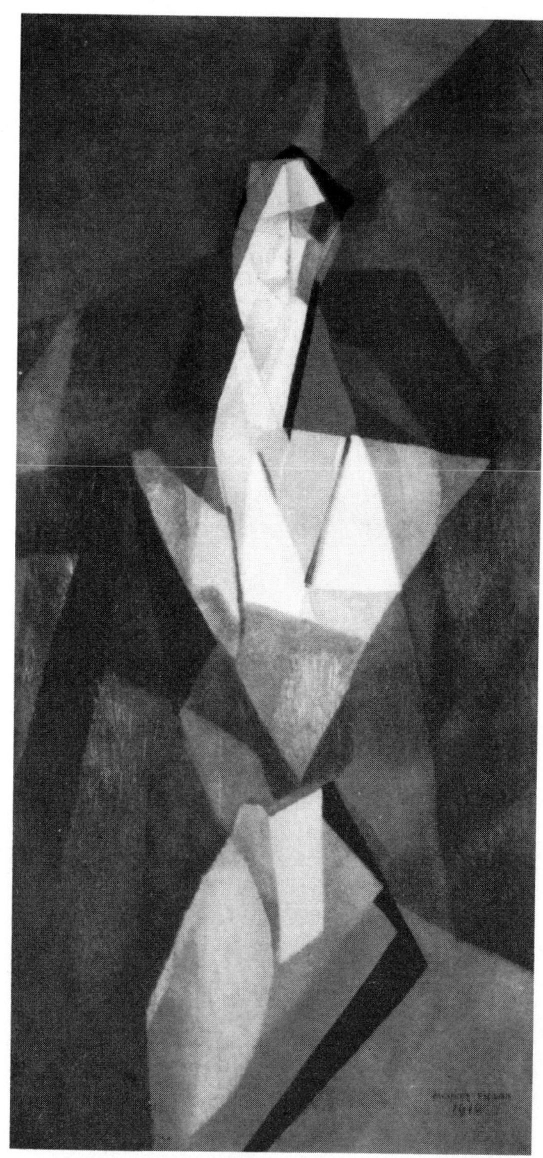

VILLON

92 La Femme Assise, 1914.

Oil, 198.7 × 95.2 cm (78¼ × 37½ in)

Collection Galerie Louis Carré, Paris

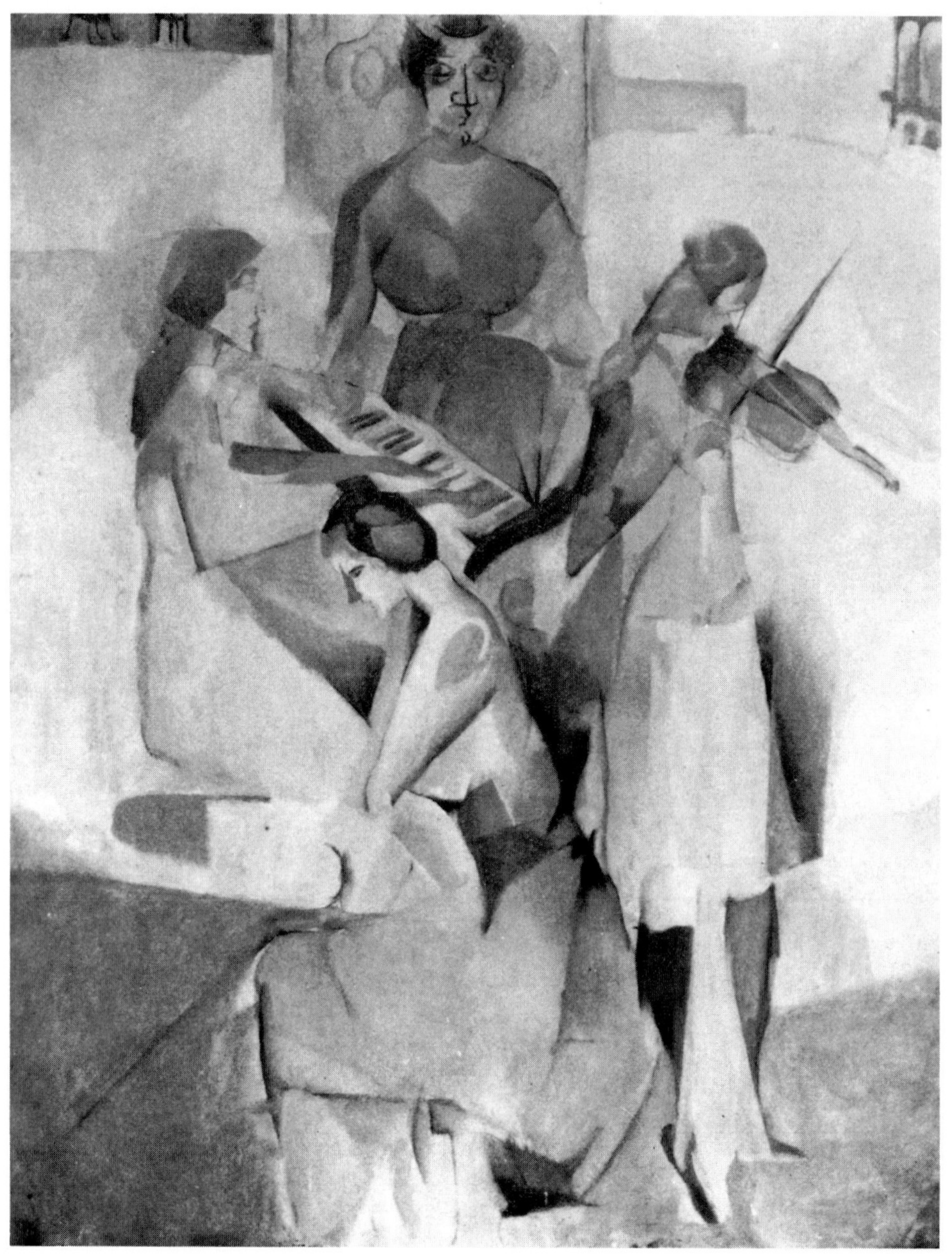

DUCHAMP
93 The Sonata, 1911
Oil, 144.8 × 113 cm (57 × 44½ in)
Louise and Walter Arensberg Collection, Philadelphia Museum of Art

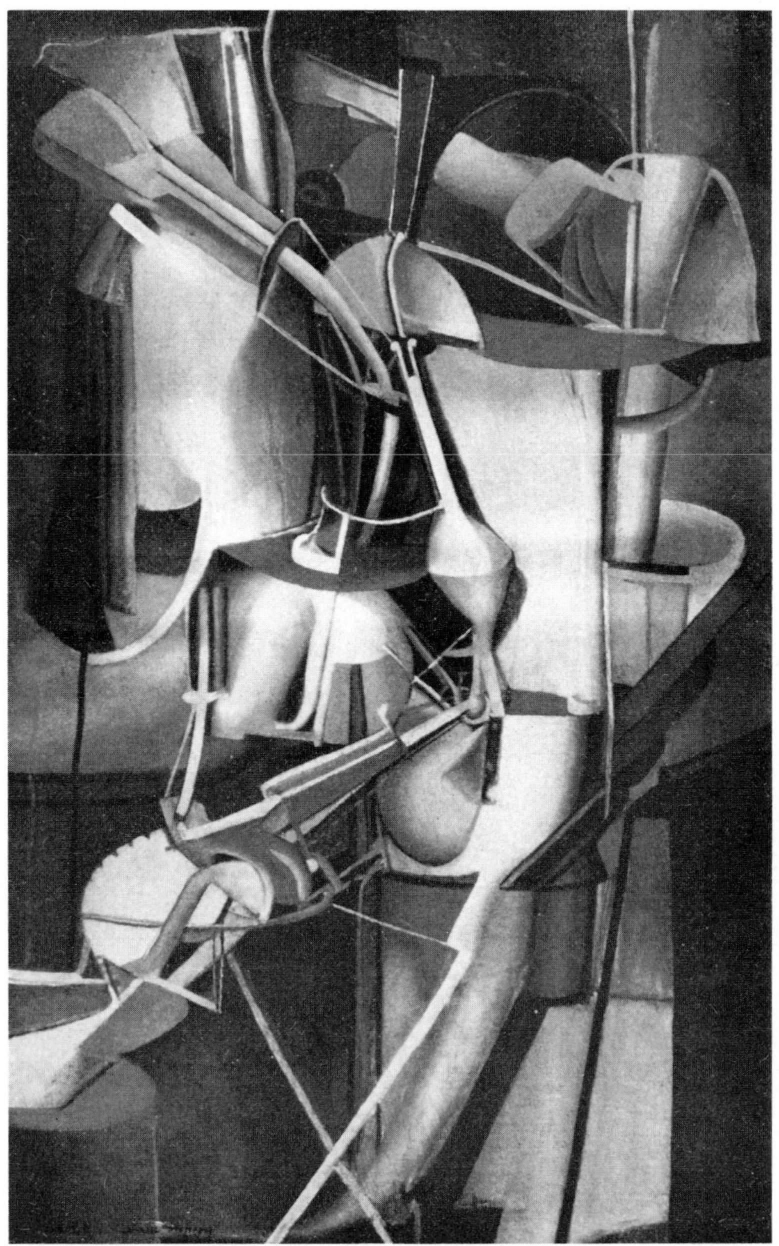

DUCHAMP
94 The Bride, 1912
Oil, 88.9 × 55.2 cm (35 × 21¾ in)
Louise and Walter Arensberg Collection, Philadelphia Museum of Art

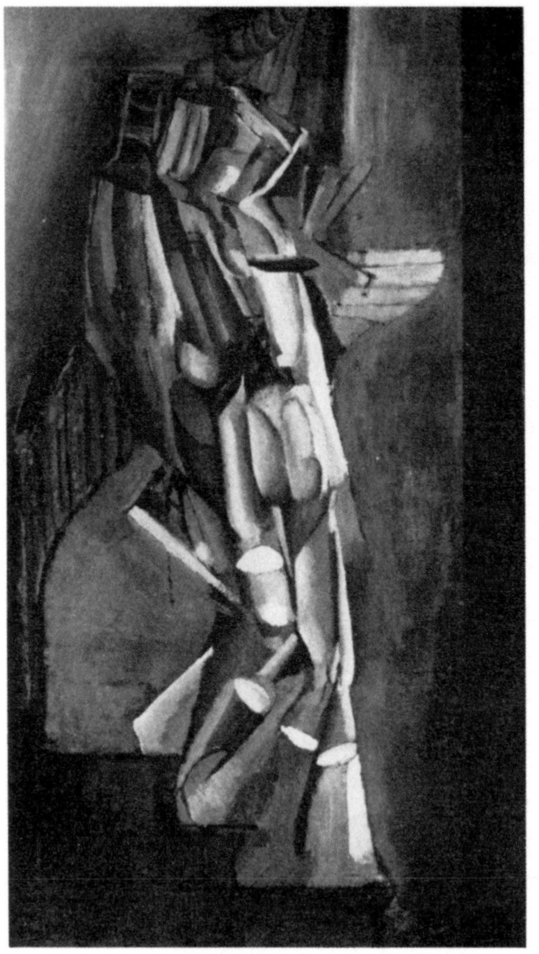

DUCHAMP

95A Nude Descending a Staircase, no. 1, 1911
Oil, 95.9 × 59.7 cm (37¾ × 23½ in)
Louise and Walter Arensberg Collection, Philadelphia Museum of Art

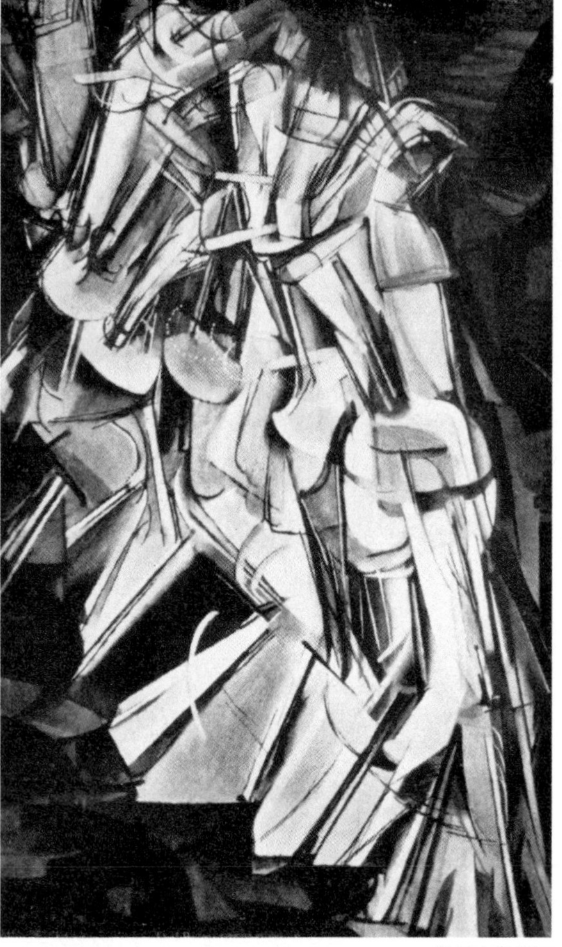

DUCHAMP

95B Nude Descending a Staircase, 1912
Oil, 147.3 × 88.9 cm (58 × 35 in)
Louise and Walter Arensberg Collection, Philadelphia Museum of Art

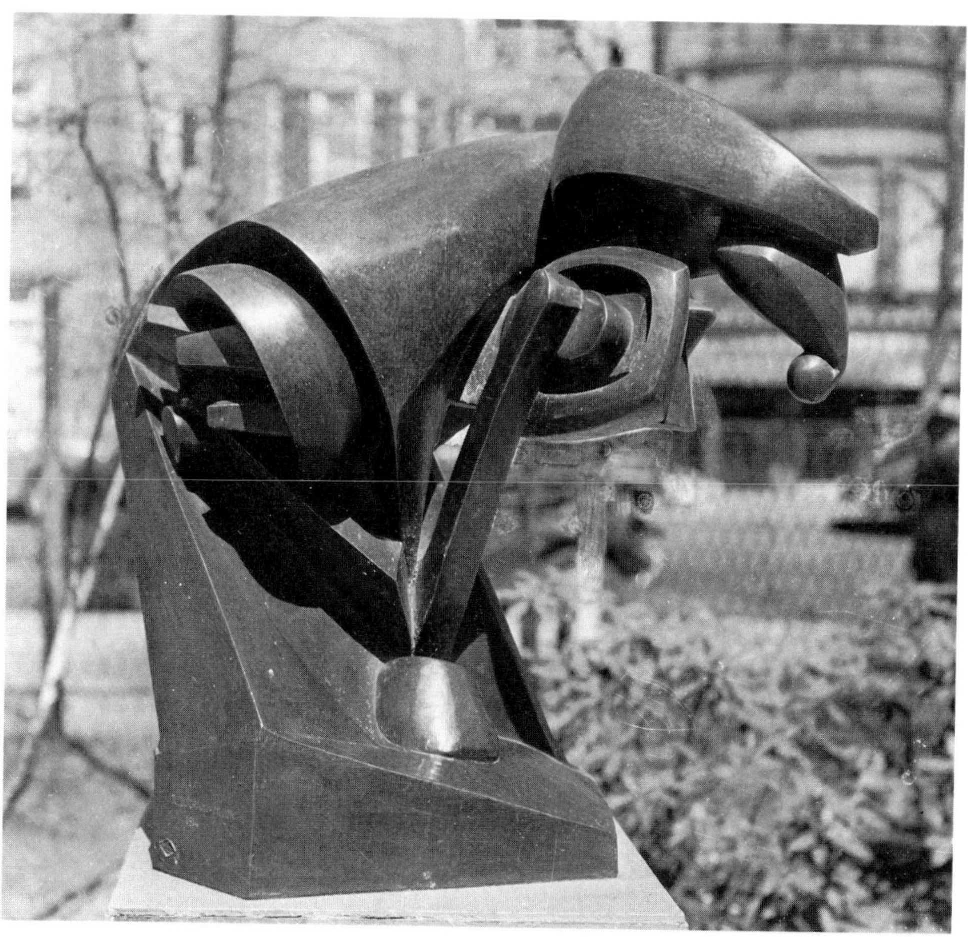

DUCHAMP-VILLON
96 The Horse (Le Cheval), 1914
Bronze (cast *c.*1930–1), height 101.6 cm (40 in)
Collection, The Museum of Modern Art, New York
Van Gogh Purchase Fund

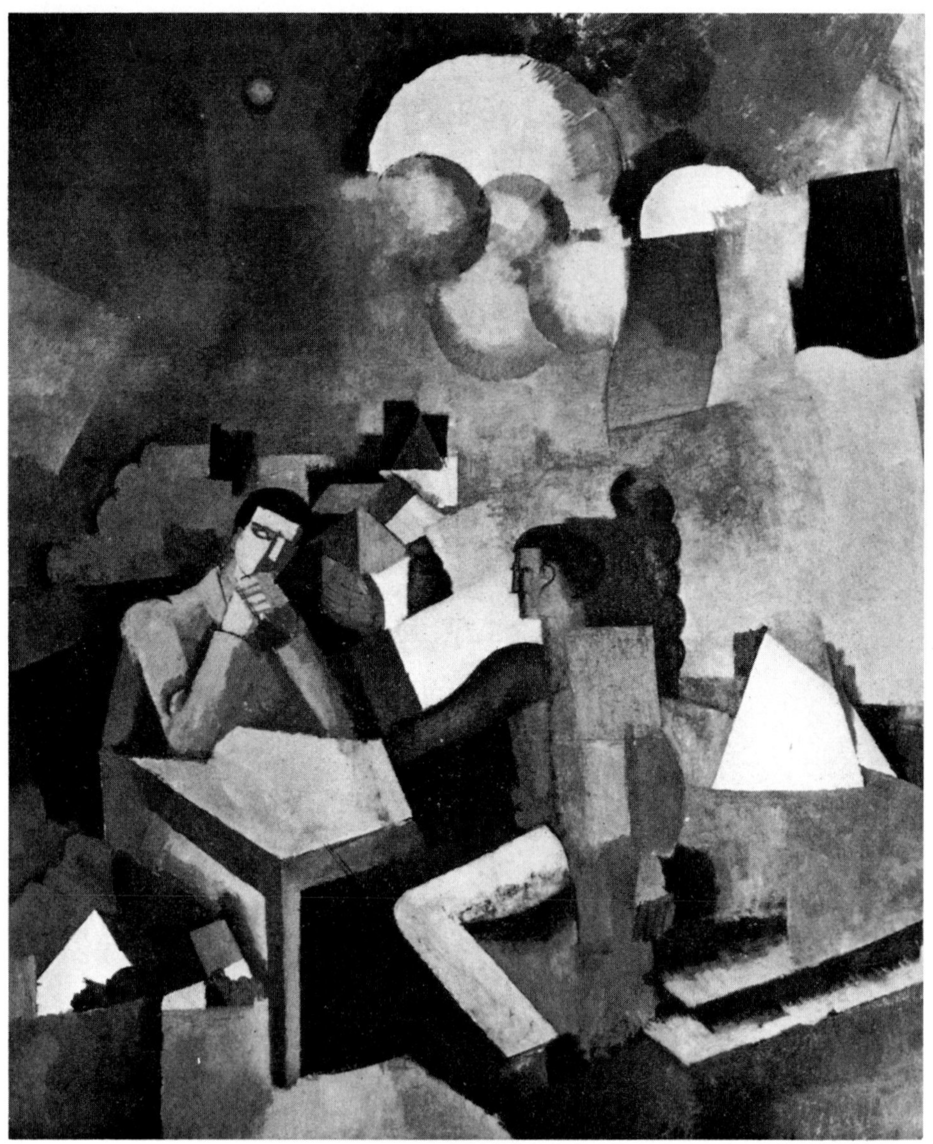

LA FRESNAYE
97 La Conquête de L'Air (The Conquest of the Air), 1913
Oil, 235.9 × 195.6 cm (92⅞ × 77 in)
Collection, The Museum of Modern Art, New York
Mrs Simon Guggenheim Fund

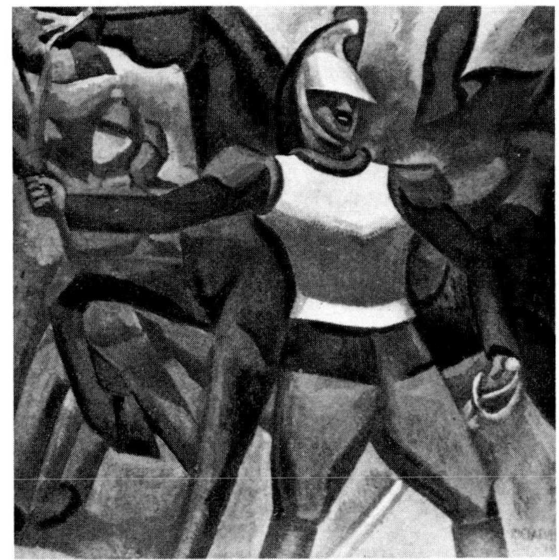

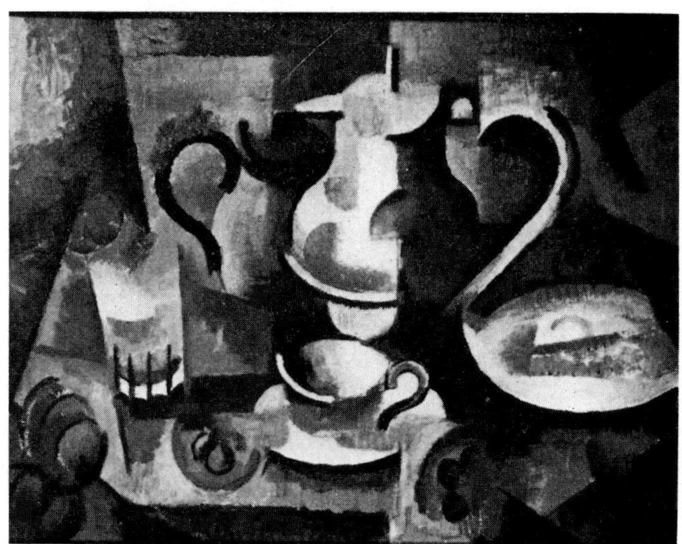

LA FRESNAYE

98A Le Cuirassier, 1910–11
Oil, 180.3 × 180.3 cm (71 × 71 in)
Musée National d'Art Moderne, Paris

98B Nature Morte aux Trois Anses, 1912
Oil, 40 × 64.7 cm (15¾ × 25½ in)
Girardin Collection, Petit Palais, Paris

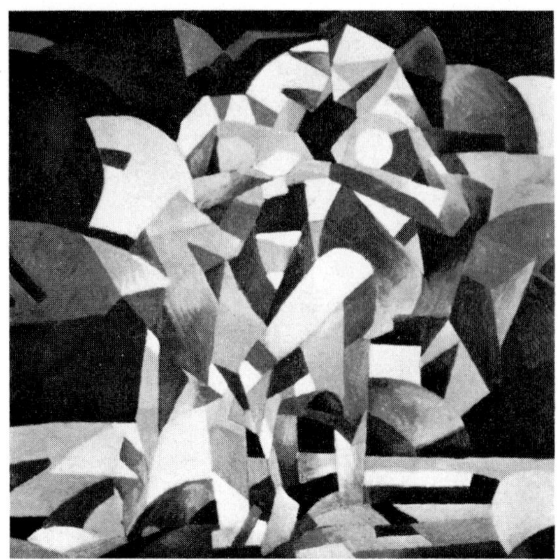

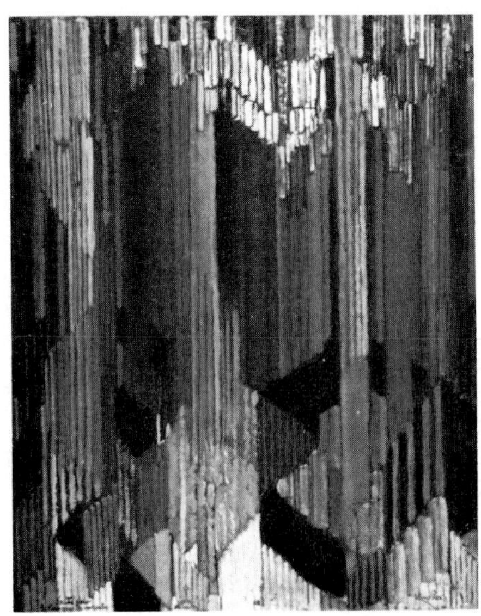

PICABIA

99A Danseuses à la Source, 1912

Oil, 120.6 × 120.6 cm (47½ × 47½ in)

Louise and Walter Arensberg Collection, Philadephia Museum of Art

KUPKA

99B Le Langage des Verticales (study), 1911–12

Oil, 77.4 × 62.8 cm (30½ × 24¾ in)

Collection Galerie Louis Carré, Paris

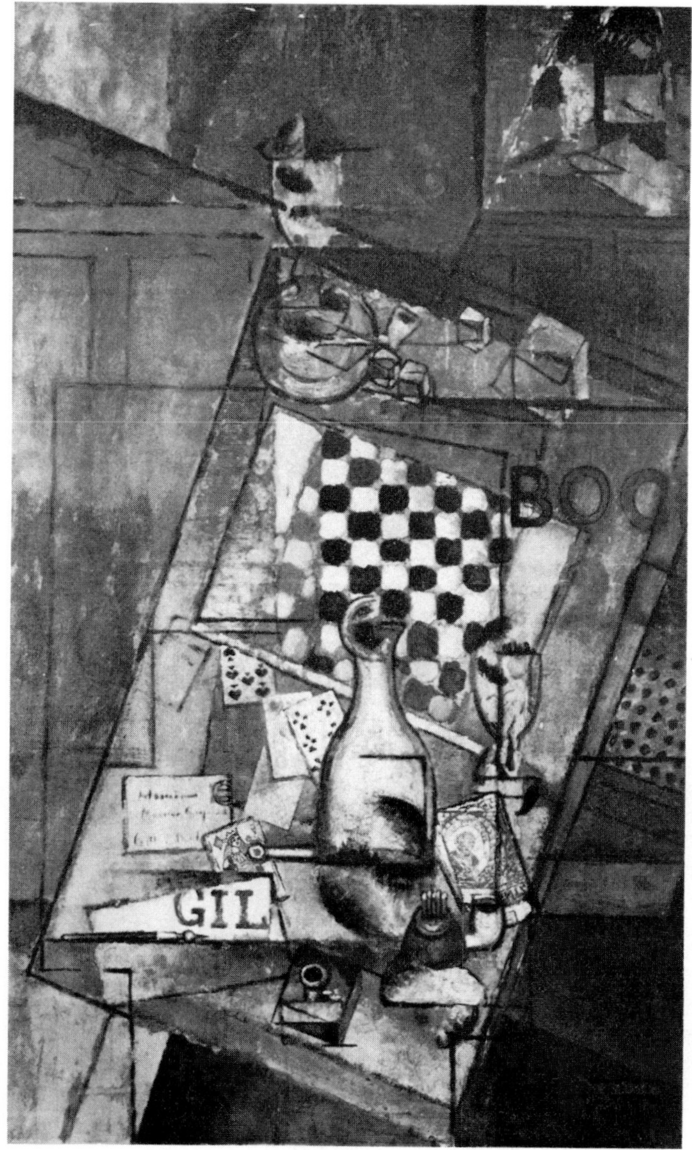

MARCOUSSIS

100 Nature Morte au Damier, 1912

Oil, 217.5 × 147.6 cm (85⅝ × 58⅛ in)

Musée National d'Art Moderne, Paris

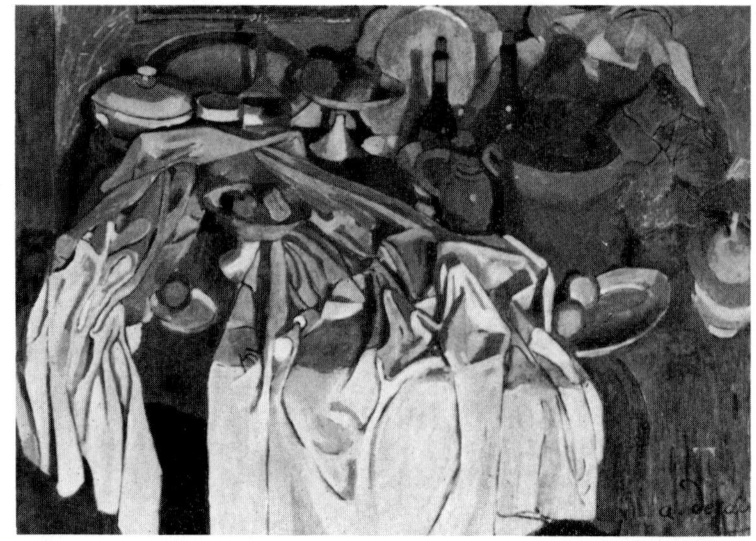

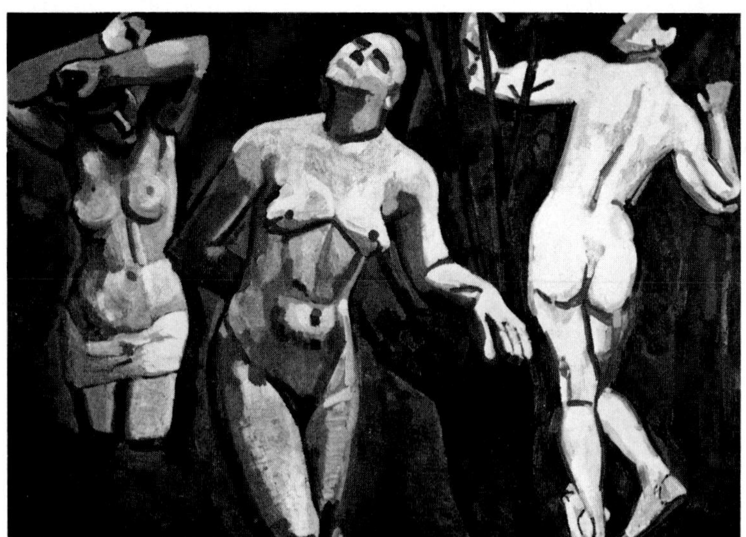

DERAIN

101A Still Life, 1904

Oil, 101.6 × 106.7 cm (40 × 42 in)

Private Collection, Paris

101B Baigneuses (Bathers), 1906–7

Oil, 132.1 × 195 cm (52 × 76¾ in)

Collection, The Museum of Modern Art, New York

William S. Paley and Abby Aldrich Rockefeller Funds

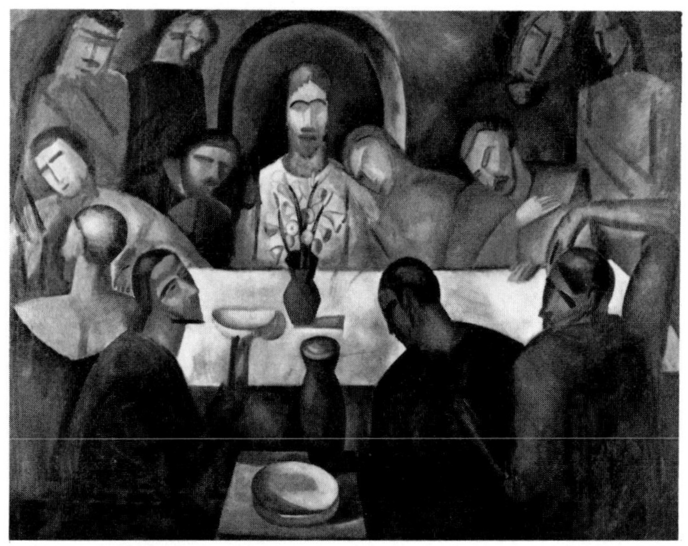

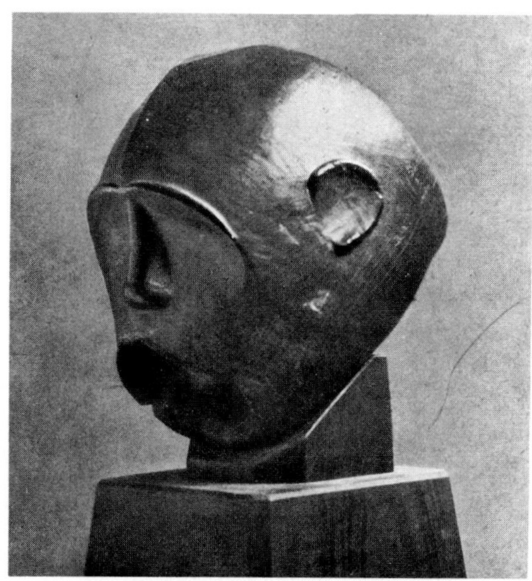

DERAIN

102A The Last Supper, 1911(?)–13

Oil, 220 × 280 cm (86⅝ × 110¼ in)

102B Head of a Monkey (?), Ubangi (?), Central African Republic. Wood

Private Collection

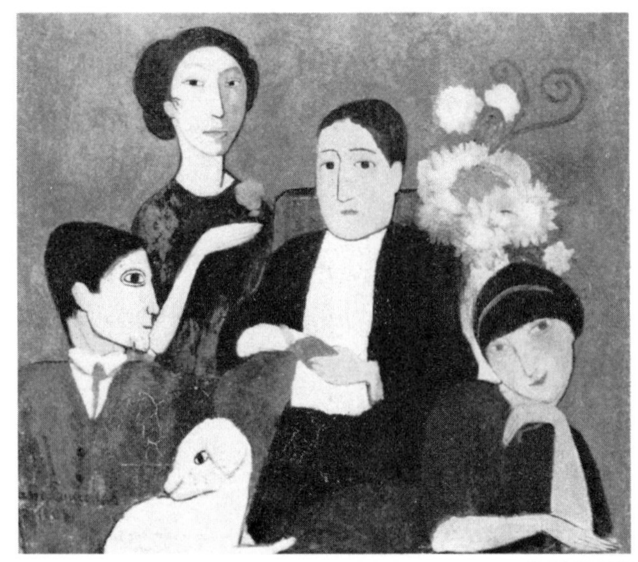

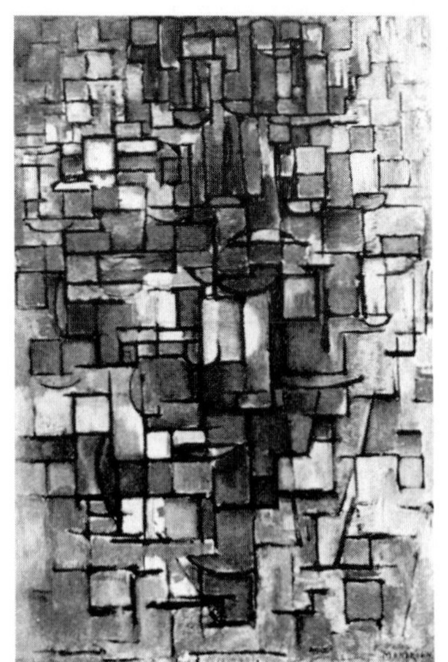

LAURENCIN

103A Group of Artists, 1908 (Self portrait with Apollinaire, Picasso and Fernande Olivier)
Oil, 51.1×103cm (25½×31⅞ in)
Cone Collection, Baltimore Museum of Art

MONDRIAN

103B Composition, 1913
Oil, 95.9 × 64.1 cm (37¾ × 25¼ in)
Rijksmuseum Kröller-Müller, Otterlo

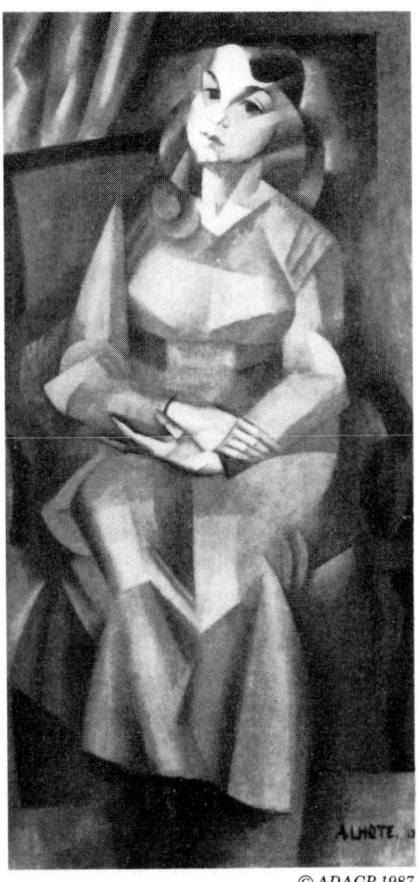

LHOTE

104A Portrait of Marguerite, 1913

Oil, 162.5 × 92.1 cm (64 × 36¼ in)

Marlborough Gallery, London

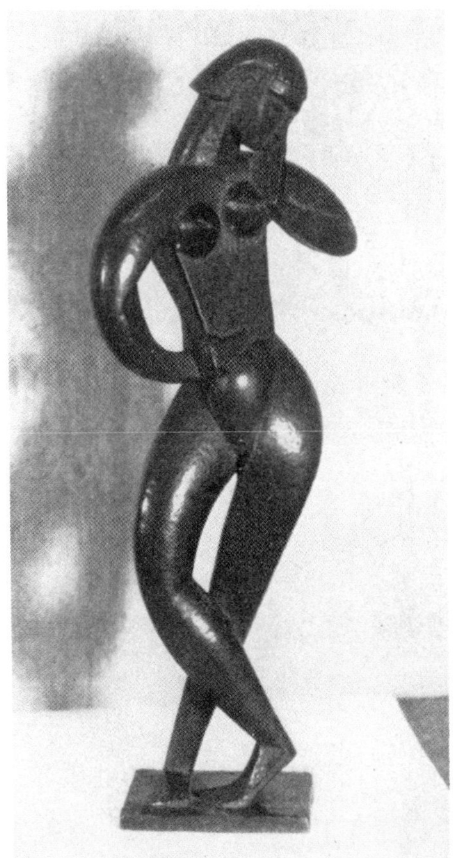

LIPCHITZ

104B Danseuse, 1913–14

Bronze, height 62.2 cm (24½ in)

Girardin Collection, Petit Palais, Paris

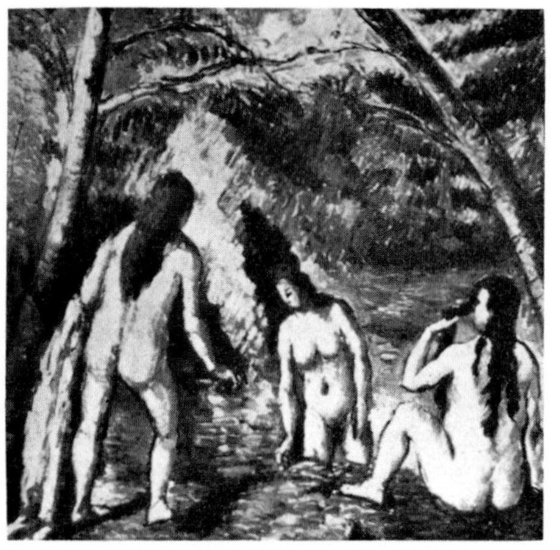

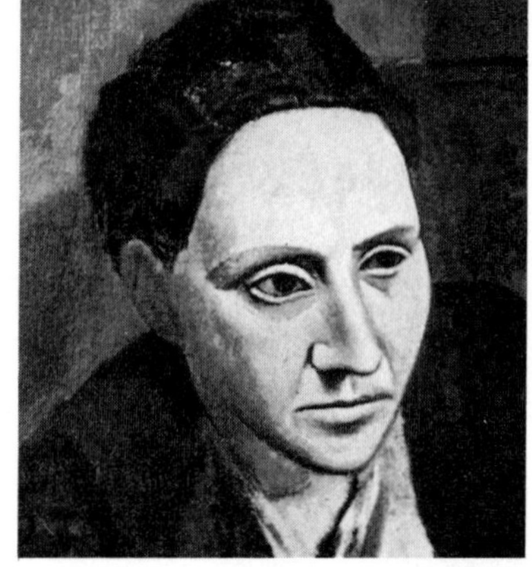

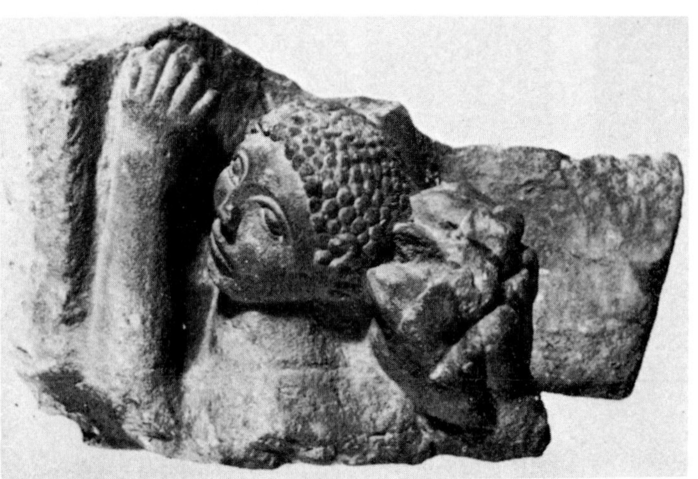

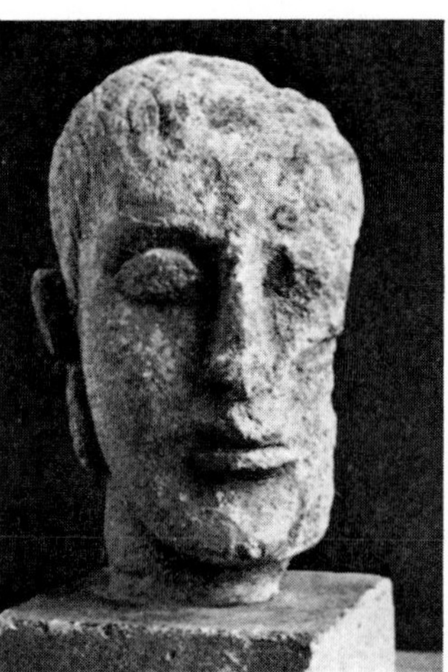

CÉZANNE
105A Trois Baigneuses
Oil, 50.1 × 50.1 cm (19¾ × 19¾ in)
Petit Palais, Paris

PICASSO
105B Portrait of Gertrude Stein, 1906 (detail of head)
Metropolitan Museum of Art, New York

105C Hunting Scene. Iberian Sculpture (Osuna)
Museo Arqueológico, Madrid

105D Head of a Man (full face view). Iberian Sculpture
Museé des Antiquités National, St-Germain-en-Laye

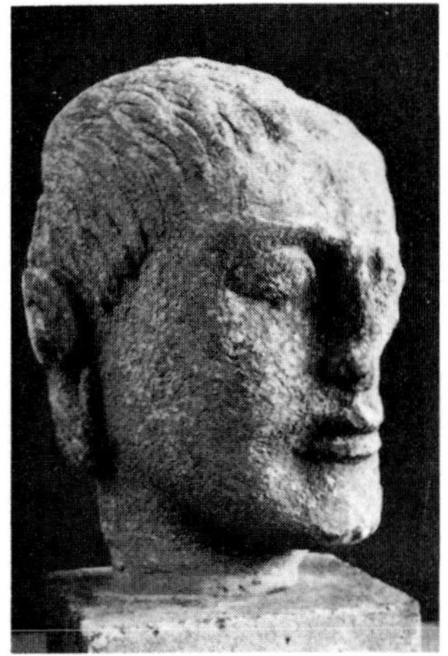

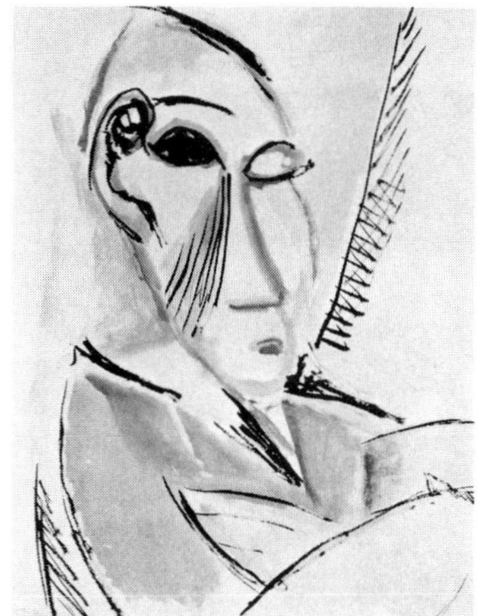

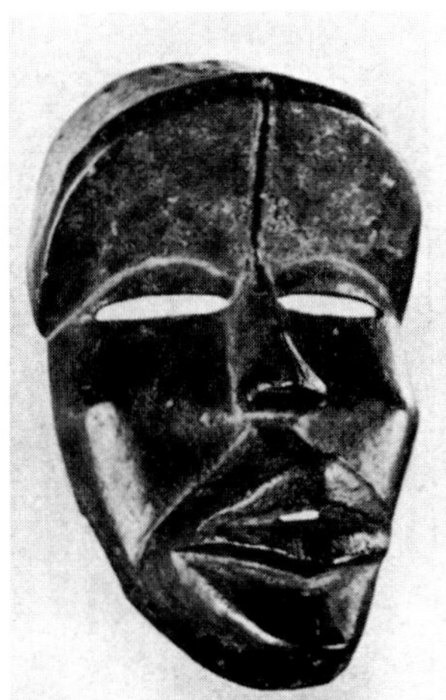

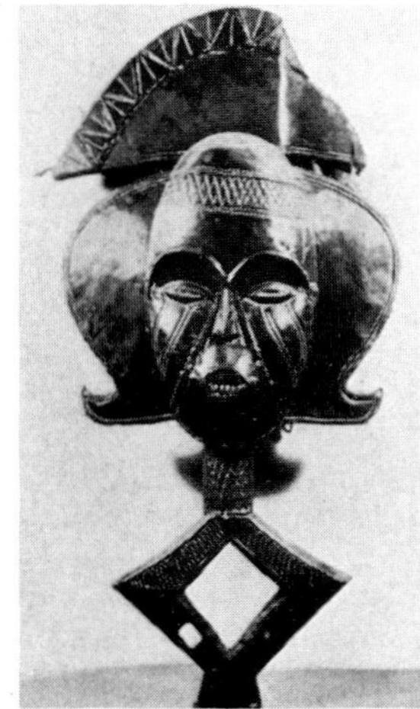

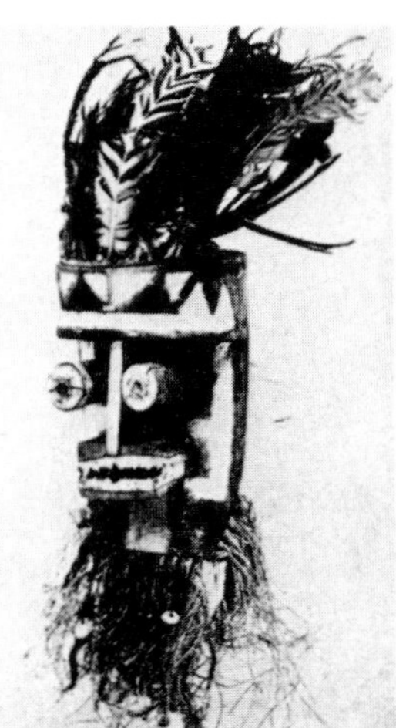

PICASSO

106A Head of a Man (three-quarter view). Iberian Sculpture
Museé des Antiquités Nationals, St-Germain-en-Laye

106B Head of a Man, 1907
Ink and watercolour, 60.3 × 47 cm (23¾ × 18½ in)
Collectiòn, The Museum of Modern Art, New York
A. Conger Goodyear Fund

106C Wooden Mask, Dan, Ivory Coast
Musée de l'Homme, Paris

106D Bronze ancestral figure from the French Congo
British Museum, London

106E Grebo Ceremonial Mask, Sassandra, Ivory Coast
Musée de l'Homme, Paris

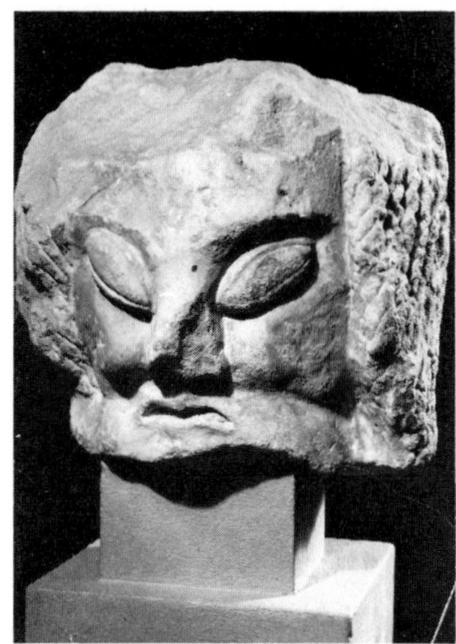

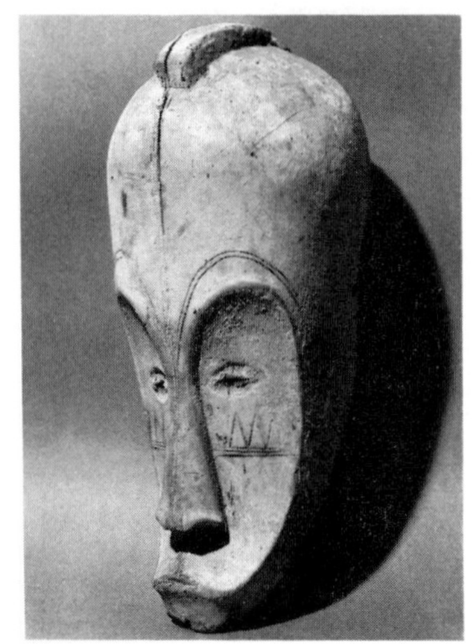

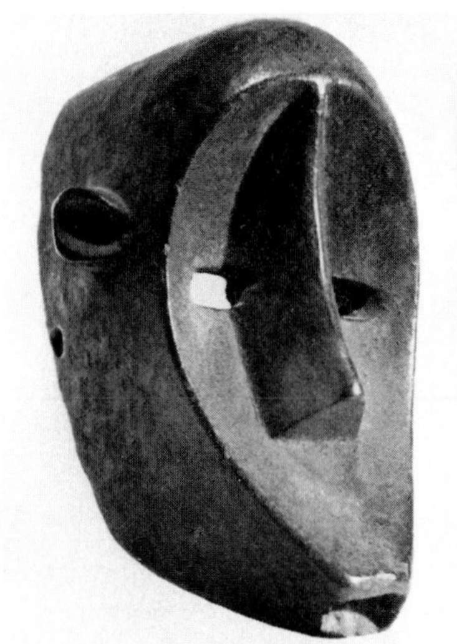

107A Head of a Woman. Iberian Sculpture
Museo Arqueológico, Madrid

107B Mask, Fang, Gabon. Wood
Vérité Collection, Paris

107C Mask, Bambara, Mali. Wood
Private Collection, Italy

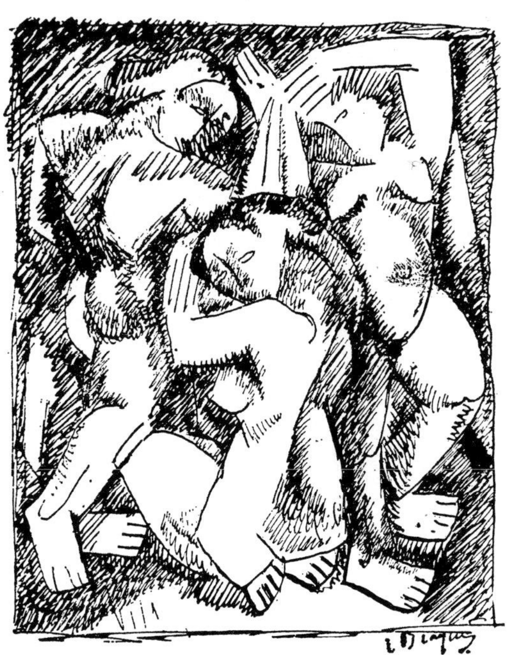

BRAQUE

108A Three Women, 1907. Ink on paper

Lost

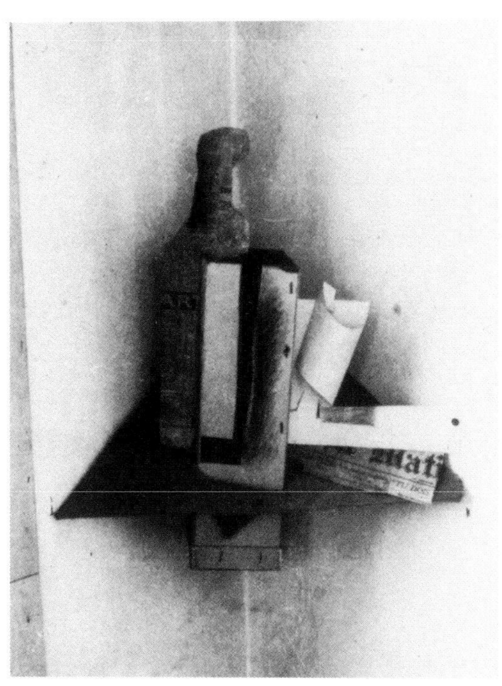

BRAQUE

108B Cardboard and Paper Construction, 1914

Destroyed

RACECHANGES

RACE AND AMERICAN CULTURE

Arnold Rampersad and Shelley Fisher Fishkin
General Editors

Love and Theft: Blackface Minstrelsy and the American Working Class
Eric Lott

The Dialect of Modernism: Race, Language, and Twentieth-Century Literature
Michael North

Bordering on the Body: The Racial Matrix of Modern Fiction and Culture
Laura Doyle

"Who Set You Flowin'?": The African-American Migration Narrative
Farah Jasmine Griffin

"Doers of the Word": African-American Women Speakers and Writers in the North (1830–1880)
Carla Peterson

Race, Rape, and Lynching: The Red Record of American Literature, 1890–1912
Sandra Gunning

Scenes of Subjection: Terror, Slavery, and Self-Making in Nineteenth-Century America
Saidiya V. Hartman

Racechanges: White Skin, Black Face in American Culture
Susan Gubar

Race: The History of an Idea in America, New Edition
Thomas F. Gossett

Psychoanalysis and Black Novels: Desire and the Protocols of Race
Claudia Tate

Black Hunger: Food and the Politics of U.S. Identity
Doris Witt

The New Red Negro: The Literary Left and African American Poetry, 1930–1946
James Edward Smethurst

New-slave Narratives: Studies in the Social Logic of a Literary Form
Ashraf H. A. Rushdy

RACECHANGES

White Skin, Black Face in American Culture

SUSAN GUBAR

OXFORD UNIVERSITY PRESS
New York Oxford

Oxford University Press

Oxford New York
Athens Auckland Bangkok Bogotá Buenos Aires Calcutta
Cape Town Chennai Dar es Salaam Delhi Florence Hong Kong Istanbul
Karachi Kuala Lumpur Madrid Melbourne Mexico City Mumbai
Nairobi Paris São Paulo Singapore Taipei Tokyo Toronto Warsaw

and associated companies in
Berlin Ibadan

First published in 1997 by Oxford University Press, Inc.
198 Madison Avenue, New York, New York 10016

First issued as an Oxford University Press paperback, 2000.

Oxford is a registered trademark of Oxford University Press

Library of Congress Cataloging-in-Publication Data
Gubar, Susan, 1944–
Racechanges: white skin, black face in American culture /
Susan Gubar.
p. cm. — (Race and American culture)
Includes bibliographical references and index.
ISBN 0–19–511002-1
ISBN 0–19–513418-4 (Pbk.)
1. Afro-Americans in popular culture. 2. Blackface entertainers—United States—History—20th century. 3. Arts, Modern—20th century—United States. I. Title. II. Series.
NX652.A37G83 1997 305.8'00973—DC20 96-28151

1 3 5 7 9 8 6 4 2

Printed in the United States of America
on acid-free paper

For Donald Gray

CONTENTS

LIST OF ILLUSTRATIONS ix

PREFACE xiii

1. ADVENTURES IN THE SKIN TRADE 3
2. SPIRIT-MURDER AT THE MOVIES 53
   Blackface Lynchings
3. MAKING WHITE, BECOMING BLACK 95
   Myths of Racial Origin in the Harlem Renaissance
4. DE MODERN DO MR. BONES 134
   (and All That Ventriloquist Jazz)
5. PSYCHOPATHOLOGIES OF BLACK ENVY 169
   Queer Colors
6. WHAT WILL THE MIXED CHILD DELIVER? 203
   Conceiving Color Without Race
7. THE EDIBLE COMPLEX 240
   A Postscript

NOTES 263

WORKS CITED 293

INDEX 313

ILLUSTRATIONS

CHAPTER 1

Figure 1.1	Janiform Vase	4
Figure 1.2	White Face of Janiform Vase	4
Figure 1.3	Black Face of Janiform Vase	4
Figure 1.4	Man Ray, *Noire et blanche* (Black and white)	7
Figure 1.5	Man Ray, *Noire et blanche*, negative version	8
Figure 1.6	Hannah Höch, *Entführung* (Abduction)	9
Figure 1.7	Hannah Höch, *Denkmall II: Eitelkeit* (Monument II: Vanity)	9
Figure 1.8	Engraving of Ellen Craft	14
Figure 1.9	Carrie Mae Weems, *Mirror, Mirror*	16
Figure 1.10	Pears' Soap Advertisement	22
Figure 1.11	Annie Leibovitz, *Whoopi Goldberg*	23
Figure 1.12	David Wayne and Keenan Wynn in *Finian's Rainbow*	26
Figure 1.13	Godfrey Cambridge in *Watermelon Man*	28
Figure 1.14	James Whitmore in *Black Like Me*	29
Figure 1.15	Portrait of Beethoven	32
Figure 1.16	*The Morphing of Queen Elizabeth*	33
Figure 1.17	*Rebirth of a Nation*	34
Figure 1.18	*The Emperor of Abyssinia and His Suite*	35
Figure 1.19	*White Like You,* from Dick Gregory, *What's Happening?*	36
Figure 1.20	Herbert M. Cole, *White Man*	39
Figure 1.21	Man Ray, *Noire et blanche*, vertical pose	49
Figure 1.22	Charles Cullen, *Tableau*	50
Figure 1.23	Robert Mapplethorpe, *Ken Moody and Robert Sherman*	50
Figure 1.24	Jean-Paul Darriau, *Red, Blond, Black, and Olive*	51

CHAPTER 2

Figure 2.1	Bing Crosby and Marjorie Reynolds in *Holiday Inn*	54
Figure 2.2	Walter Long in *The Birth of a Nation*	58
Figure 2.3	Ralph Lewis and Mary Alden in *The Birth of a Nation*	60
Figure 2.4	George Siegmann and Lillian Gish in *The Birth of a Nation*	62
Figure 2.5	"The Fiery Cross of Old Scotland's Hills!" from Thomas Dixon, *The Clansman*	64
Figure 2.6	Gus captured by the Klan in *The Birth of a Nation*	64
Figure 2.7	Al Jolson with May McAvoy in *The Jazz Singer*	67
Figure 2.8	Al Jolson with Eugenie Besserer in *The Jazz Singer*	69
Figure 2.9	Al Jolson, partially unmasked, in *The Jazz Singer*	70
Figure 2.10	Al Jolson in the final scene of *The Jazz Singer*	71
Figure 2.11	Publicity Poster of "Warner Bros. Supreme Triumph"	74
Figure 2.12	*Entartete Musik*, Adolf Hitler's poster for the Nazi exhibition of "degenerate" art	76
Figure 2.13	Eddie Cantor in *Kid Millions*	77
Figure 2.14	*Life* magazine photo of "Buck and Wing"	80
Figure 2.15	*Life* magazine photo of Bing Crosby playing Dan Emmett in *Dixie*	80
Figure 2.16	*Life* magazine photo of "a fear-crazed Negro boy" rescued by soldier from a Detroit mob	80
Figure 2.17	Martha Raye in *College Holiday*	83
Figure 2.18	Shirley Temple in *The Littlest Rebel*	87
Figure 2.19	Fred Astaire at start of "Bojangles of Harlem" number, *Swing Time*	89
Figure 2.20	Fred Astaire in "Bojangles of Harlem" number, *Swing Time*	89
Figure 2.21	Freeman Gosden and Charles Correll as Amos 'n' Andy in *Check Double Check*	90
Figure 2.22	Judy Garland and Mickey Rooney in *Babes in Arms*	91
Figure 2.23	Ronald Colman as Othello in *A Double Life*	92
Figure 2.24	Bing Crosby and Marjorie Reynolds in *Dixie*	93

CHAPTER 3

Figure 3.1	"Stop the world, I want to get on!," from Dick Gregory, *What's Happening?*	99
Figure 3.2	Richard Bruce Nugent, *Drawings for Mulattoes—Number 1*	108
Figure 3.3	Richard Bruce Nugent, *Drawings for Mulattoes—Number 2*	109

Figure 3.4 Richard Bruce Nugent, *Drawings for Mulattoes—Number 3* 110
Figure 3.5 Richard Bruce Nugent, *Drawings for Mulattoes—Number 4* 111
Figure 3.6 Billy Kersands in *Callender's (Georgia) Minstrels* 112
Figure 3.7 Bert Williams in blackface 113
Figure 3.8 Josephine Baker in *Chocolate Dandies* 115
Figure 3.9 Florence Mills in *Dixie to Broadway* 117
Figure 3.10 Paul Robeson with Phi Beta Kappa Key, Rutgers University 120
Figure 3.11 Paul Robeson in *Voodoo* 120
Figure 3.12 Paul Robeson in *Voodoo* 120
Figure 3.13 Josiah Priest, "The Family of Noah" 128

CHAPTER 4
Figure 4.1 Stella Bowen, *Hands of Edith Sitwell with Mask* 145
Figure 4.2 Barbara Ker-Seymer, Nancy Cunard with veil 151
Figure 4.3 Cecil Beaton, Nancy Cunard in feathers 151
Figure 4.4 Cecil Beaton, Nancy Cunard with bangles 151
Figure 4.5 Cover designed by Man Ray of *Henry Music* 153
Figure 4.6 Miguel Covarrubias, *A Prediction* 154

CHAPTER 5
Figure 5.1 Robert Mapplethorpe, *Man in Polyester Suit* 173
Figure 5.2 Cover of *The White Negro* 179
Figure 5.3 Carl Van Vechten, *Saint Sebastian* 184
Figure 5.4 Francis Picabia, *Oiseau et tortue* 185
Figure 5.5 Dick Gregory, "You can't marry my sister . . ." from Dick Gregory, *What's Happening?* 187
Figure 5.6 Barbara Ker-Seymer, Nancy Cunard solarization 201
Figure 5.7 Barbara Ker-Seymer, Nancy Cunard in neck gear 201

CHAPTER 6
Figure 6.1 Édouard Manet, *Olympia* 217
Figure 6.2 Pablo Picasso, *Parody of Manet's "Olympia"* 219
Figure 6.3 Larry Rivers, *I Like Olympia in Black Face* 219
Figure 6.4 Pablo Picasso, *Les demoiselles d'Avignon* 220
Figure 6.5 Marlene Dietrich as King Kong in *Blonde Venus* 222
Figure 6.6 Marlene Dietrich as Fay Wray in *Blonde Venus* 222
Figure 6.7 Horace Pippin, *Mr. Prejudice* 238

CHAPTER 7

Figure 7.1	Gene Wilder and Richard Pryor in *Silver Streak*	251
Figure 7.2	Steve Martin in *The Jerk*	251
Figure 7.3	Iké Udé, *Norma Jean*	253
Figure 7.4	Iké Udé, *Man in Polyester Suit*	255

COLOR INSERT (following page 168)
Eve, *Time* magazine cover girl
Robert Colescott, *Eat Dem Taters*
Robert Colescott, *George Washington Carver Crossing the Delaware*
Robert Colescott, *Shirley Temple Black and Bill Robinson White*
Robert Colescott, *Les demoiselles d'Alabama: Vestidas*
Robert Colescott, *Knowledge of the Past Is the Key to the Future (St. Sebastian)*

PREFACE

After a dignified WASP medievalist from an Ivy League university confided in an airport bar that her eminent husband spoke "black talk" to their dog, I began to expect white people to respond to a description of my project with some kind of confession about the prominence of clandestine racial parodies in their own lives. An Irish-Catholic college administrator exhibited his perfected Stepin Fetchit shuffle; an Italian physician whispered his secret black nickname, intoning it à la Kingfish; a Jewish friend from college expressed delight that her dark complexion and kinky hair led Parisians to fete her (since her looks had only incited wary glances in the segregated neighborhood of her native Bronx); still another Jewish friend explained how bewildered (even abandoned) she felt when her sister—who socialized only with the black friends of her African-American husband—began identifying herself as a person of color and echoing the street cadences of the Harlem neighbors among whom she resided. "Zi Zigga ZUMbah ZUMbah ZUMbah, / Zi Zigga ZUMbah ZUMbah ZAY!": After months spent writing about the centrality of cross-racial mimicry in twentieth-century culture, I found myself less shocked, more bemused at a wedding reception when an ersatz "Zulu Warrior Chant," presumably taught to the paterfamilias of a Southern family by General Patton during the Second World War, was performed, accompanied by rhythmic hand-clapping and foot-stomping, by all his sons, sons-in-law, and grandsons.

That white people often engage in silly, sexy, sleazy, and sometimes sinister cross-racial masquerades was made manifest by impersonations that were often rendered within my extended family as well. White kids who went to inner-city schools on the East Coast did not necessarily get a better education than those who went to lily-white, small-town midwestern schools in the heart of Hoosier heaven except in one area, or so it seemed to me, comparing the extensive multiracial experiences of my friends' children with the more limited ones of my own.

> Ugh! Ungowah!
> Your Momma needs a shower,
> Your Daddy needs a shave!

I said it,
I meant it,
I'm here to represent it.

Imitating the black kids in their New York City school, two honorary nieces performed their quasi-rap, quasi-cheer—"My back is breakin' / My belt's too tight / My booty's shakin' from left to right"—with an exuberant hilarity that came in part from the transgressive pleasure they savored in violating their own staunch convictions about its political incorrectness.

At a young age, after all, the girls had been brought up by their liberal parents—cherished friends of mine—to respect the right of African Americans to represent themselves. Yet they nevertheless reveled in a performance more savvy but just as ideologically suspect as my older daughter's frequent endearment to me at moments of parting: "I loves ya, honey," Molly would belt out, "but you'ze de WRONG color." She had taken in my stories about a childhood friend named Theresa who used to joke about my being the only white kid on the block and had made Theresa's language part of what in Molly's post-college days she now calls her own "idioverse." Having seen "blacks" mostly in movies like *Holiday Inn* (which features Bing Crosby dancing in blackface on Lincoln's birthday), Molly at the age of five or six felt pretty sure that Lincoln had been the first African-American President of these United States. Who said it, who meant it, who is here to represent it for people of color?

The answer, as everybody knows, is that whites have said what it meant to be black and have represented African Americans throughout the nineteenth and twentieth centuries. Although there has been a great deal of much needed scholarship documenting the history of black thinkers and artists lecturing, writing, and performing so as to demonstrate the intellectual and aesthetic acumen of the race not only to white audiences and readers but also to black ones, the humanity and the subjectivity of African Americans have often been staged by white people performing blackness. That whites have hardly produced flattering pictures of their black contemporaries has, of course, contributed to embarassment and anger over such portrayals. Simultaneously figured and disfigured, African Americans who were symbolically presented may have felt their race effectively erased in aesthetic productions—photographic, filmic, poetic, fictional—that always teetered on the edge of grotesque stereotyping and appropriation.

As the common determination to remain anonymous of the WASP scholar, the Irish administrator, the Jewish physician, the Southern paterfamilias, and the two adolescents indicates and as my opening anecdotes are meant to imply, my own interest in the ways and means by which—as well as the reasons why—white people imitate African Americans has been piqued by white people's determination to keep such exhibitions secret because of our shared belief that they are (or would be considered) wrong, unethical, degrading to real black people. What appears striking about those scenes of cross-racial impersonation, it seems to me, is the great divide between the highly censored, staid propriety with which people of conscience speak publicly about race and the private expression of far more disrespectful, indecorous attitudes felt to be vaguely shameful or shocking, a gap quite conscious and common in many white people's lives. Although the American imagination has repeatedly returned to figures attempting to cross the color line, although the recent appearance of newsletters and magazines entitled *New People* and *INTERRACE* attests to a growing population of biracial people, the pressures to separate black from white remain extensive.

The racial mutations and metamorphoses discussed in the pages to come have little to do with actual changes in melanin and sometimes have even less to do with real African Americans. Instead, they illuminate the psychology of whites who have evolved through a series of oppositional identities predicated on black Others. The "black" in the chapters that follow—not always or even usually an African-American human being—operates as a generic commodity constructed by the white imagination for white people. The pertinacity of our vocabulary of a racial duality of whiteness versus blackness—though it flies in the face of multiple ethnicities as well as clear visual evidence of a spectrum of shades and hues of complexion—reflects Manichean ideologies that have profoundly shaped aesthetic achievements in the twentieth century, ideologies that inform the manifold racial impersonations that I call "racechanges" and that I trace through the pages of this book.

As I worked on this project during this last decade of the twentieth century, many items in the news convinced me of its timeliness. Michael Jackson's infamous lightening of his skin was only the most obvious evidence of the ongoing evolution of passing traditions (rooted in Euro-American overvaluations of whiteness). Similarly, Ted Danson's shocking use of blackface at a Friars' Club roast was only the most conspicuous testimony of lasting taboos against minstrelsy (founded on Euro-American devaluations of blackness). When Susan Smith's description of the "black man" who stole her car and her two babies (strapped into the back seat) resulted in a composite drawing of the suspect, detectives began to surmise that she had performed a racechange so as to conceal her own crime by exploiting prevailing stereotypes about black criminality: "If you took off the stocking cap and narrowed his lips," police thought about the sketch, "he looked an awful lot like Smith's estranged husband, David" (*Newsweek*, Nov. 14, 1994, p. 28). According to many white TV addicts, O. J. Simpson entered his trial "as a fellow white man and grew darker as the proceedings went on" (*Time*, Oct. 16, 1995, p. 43).

In popular as well as elite art forms, too, racial masquerade and racechange appeared to play a crucial role for white men and women. Although the percentage of African-American undergraduates in college populations decreased throughout the last decade, many white kids displayed fashions from the ghetto, proof positive of the phenomenon Cornel West calls "the Afro-Americanization of white youth" (121): Some self-proclaimed "whiggers" sported cornrows, dreadlocks, or shaved scalps featuring razored designs; others flaunted baggy jeans, baseball hats worn backwards, or clunky, unlaced basketball shoes. During the same period that the movie *Soul Man* (1986) depicted a white student obtaining entrance into Harvard's Law School by impersonating a black and thus gaining affirmative action support, a group of musicians calling themselves Young Black Teenagers consisted of white rappers claiming affinities with black culture. On the USA cable channel weeknights, the syndication *Quantum Leap* featured a central character bounding into the bodies of oppressed people, with one episode showing the white hero becoming a black man at a segregated Southern lunch counter; in another he turns into an African American involved in an interracial romance during the Watts riot. The popular television series *Northern Exposure* included several episodes in which white Chris dreams his black brother Bernard's dreams, a signal of their interlaced subjectivities.

In 1993, two phenomena (that I contextualize in my introductory chapter) dramatically underscored the importance of cross-racial patterns of imagery. *Time* magazine featured a cover devoted to "The New Face of America," a computer-created portrait of a "new Eve" whose racial and ethnic features reflected the Anglo-Saxon, Middle Eastern, African, Asian, Southern European, and Hispanic countenances used to produce the composite image. At the same time, the Fox channel broadcast to some twenty-seven countries Michael Jackson's music video "Black or White," in which a white boy uses the heavy metal music his father dislikes to blast pater into an Africa peopled by tribesmen who metamorphose into Balinese and Native American dancers. Using the same Morph 2.0 computer program the editors of *Time* employed, Jackson next filmed a sequence of faces—black and white, female and male, Asian and Native American—blending into one another.

A couple of years later in a different riff on race, black actors on both sides of the Atlantic starred in *Hot Mikado*, a swing adaptation of Gilbert and Sullivan's 1885 use of ersatz Japanese characters to satirize the foibles of the British. Toward the end of 1995, Colin Powell's daughter, Linda Powell, performed in Douglas Turner Ward's play *Day of Absence* (1965), a satire about race relations with an all-black cast in "a reverse minstrel show done in white-face" (29), while the denouement of the movie *Devil in a Blue Dress* unmasked its light-skinned *femme fatale* as an African-American passer, and John Travolta starred with Harry Belafonte in *White Man's Burden*, Demond Nakano's film about an America populated by a wealthy black elite and an angry, dispossessed white underclass. At the time this manuscript was being read by its editor at Oxford University Press, ads started appearing for a movie called *A Family Affair*, in which Robert Duvall discovers that he has a black brother, James Earl Jones. On the day the copyeditor phoned to say she had finished her work on this manuscript, *The New Yorker* published Henry Louis Gates, Jr.'s article "White like Me" about "Anatole Broyard [who] wanted to be a writer, not a black writer. So he chose to live a lie rather than be trapped by the truth." As one acquaintance put it about the brilliant reviewer and memoirist, "He was black when he got into the subway in Brooklyn, but as soon as he got out at West Fourth Street he became white" (66–67).

To what extent, I wondered, were such racechanges motivated by multiple fantasies, propelled by various dynamics of desire. What were the motives, where did the pleasures reside in the psychology of racechange? Opinions about even one instance of cross-racial impersonation could vary quite sharply. About Anatole

Broyard, for instance, some felt he was simply "anti-black," while others saw him as a master of "self-creation" (74). Although the "whiggers" sought liberation from the numbing decorum of middle-class white suburbia, the central character in *Quantum Leap* aspired to some sort of identification with the injustly oppressed Other, as did the producers of *Day of Absence*, *Devil in a Blue Dress*, *White Man's Burden*, and *A Family Affair*. Derogation clearly impelled Susan Smith and the creator of *Soul Man*; however, Chris and Bernard on *Northern Exposure* seemed to represent the wish of whites for a utopian cross-racial union or mutuality. Michael Jackson's video ends with the rubric "Prejudice is ignorance," and *Time* magazine's racially mixed, computerized cover girl was put together to dramatize what the editors called "the impact of multiethnic marriage, which has increased dramatically in the U.S. during the last wave of immigration."

Yet despite such purportedly libertarian purposes, the networks censored footage of Jackson smashing store windows while *Time*'s cover girl sent the libertarian theorist Donna Haraway into "a dyspeptic attack of political correctness" at diversity paradoxically transfigured into a numbing, "utter homogenity" (364). Perhaps her chagrin is best explained by a Dutch couple surprised to discover that in vitro fertilization had given them one light- and one dark-skinned baby because a technician unwittingly reused a pipette that still contained some sperm from a Caribbean donor. Wilma and Willem Stuart—dismayed because "Brown people have a smaller chance to get a decent job in our society. They can't get a bank loan like white people"—questioned the possibility of the enlightened multi-ethnicity glamorized by morphed computer images: "Every time the right-wingers and racists in Parliament open their mouths," the non-biological father of the darker child admitted, "I am frightened" (*Newsweek*, July 3, 1995, p. 38).

When I began thinking about the historical and aesthetic precursors of such startlingly diverse racial permutations, the most stimulating critic addressing the issue of white psychology vis-à-vis blacks was Toni Morrison, whose pioneering *Playing in the Dark* concluded with an analysis of Ernest Hemingway's *Garden of Eden*, specifically a passage in which Hemingway's blond-haired heroine attempts to transform herself into an "African girl." Curiously, in the second volume of *No Man's Land: The Place of the Woman Writer in the Twentieth Century*, Sandra Gilbert and I had discussed Hemingway's novel in terms of sexual transmutations, entirely ignoring the experiments of its heroine on the color line. While it may seem like a simple step to move from a project that included a book entitled *Sexchanges* to one called *Racechanges*—both investigations into the transgressing of boundaries, the liminal spaces between categories—I had blinded myself in *Sexchanges* to even the most flagrant performance of racechange.

Why? Was the subject of transracial crossing more taboo than that of transvestism or transsexuality? Not only has the blatant racism of minstrelsy (quite reasonably) made white impersonations of blacks seem shameful, it has also (less sensibly) spilled over to discourage scholarship about its ongoing impact on American culture. Just as inhibiting, various intransigent categories at work in contemporary cultural criticism (as it is practiced in the academy) would deem such an investigation if not unthinkable then suspect. Women (and only women) are supposed to write feminist criticism, while blacks (and only blacks) are supposed to produce works in African-American studies and only lesbians or gay men are supposed to publish in queer theory. In captious article after article published in scholarly journals, hyper-conscientious academics attack approaches inattentive to the differences between multiply hyphenated subjectivities (or subject positions), arguing that such undertakings should not ignore nor privilege nor metaphorize race, class, gender, and sexual orientation. So who was entitled to write—or who would dare claim to be entitled to write—about autobiographers born Jewish who identified themselves as black or straight, middle-class authors in thrall to working-class, homosexual fantasies, or interracial lines of aesthetic influence between men and women of letters? Ironically, though, the boundaries of area studies and their methodologies have begun to be policed more rigidly at a time when many other scholars have become fascinated, on the one hand, with the elasticity or permeability of categories of race and gender and sexual preference and, on the other, with the transgressive or liminal aesthetic experiments produced throughout our cultural history.

Besides dealing with transracial performances usually considered unacceptable or indefensible, this study explores the creative endeavors of men as well as women, of blacks as well as whites—not in an effort to elide differences between them but rather to engage such differences. To some scholarly readers, therefore, my speculations may seem grounded in subjects too diverse, while to others they will seem undertheorized. I took both these risks quite consciously in an effort to enliven my topic for that phantom of desire haunting all writers, the figure Virginia Woolf called "the common reader." I therefore attempted to avoid the aridity of academic jargon, to substitute in its stead wherever possible the allure of visual treatments of the trope of racechange. Rather than seeking to romanticize racial masquerades that indubitably discount African-American subjectivity, I want my study to illuminate the powerful attraction of black people and their culture within the white imagination as well as the imaginative centrality of the color line for African-American artists. Film analyses, literary interpretation, and cultural studies in this context document white insecurity as well as status anxiety, a subject that will increase in importance when more whites realize that they (we) constitute each year a smaller percentage of the world population.

What does it mean, though, that white fascination with black culture comes at a time when the lives of many African-American men and women are so imperiled? At the present moment, sociologists cite harrowing statistics documenting this society's fatal effects on its black citizens: Blacks, who make up about 12 percent of the U.S. population, are overrepresented in prisons (some 45 percent of inmates) and as victims of crime (approximately 50 percent of murder victims), but underrepresented in colleges (receiving only about 5 percent of awarded bachelor's degrees); three times as likely to be unemployed as whites, African-Americans are nearly four times as likely to live in poverty. Although it will always be tricky to turn attention away from such injustice and onto those who may benefit from it, a focus on whites understandably engages the issue of white remorse about racial inequality, which turns out to be a more significant motive in twentieth-century aesthetic productions than many critics have realized.

As Shelby Steele explains about the historical advantage white Americans know they have derived from the subjugation of blacks, "racial guilt simply accompanies the condition of being white in America" (81). I suspect, too, that such shame will continue to play a major role in our contemporary society, where suicide and black-on-black homicide vie as the leading causes of death for young black men. Statistics confirming equally dire conditions in earnings, life expectancy, and imprisonment appear in a book entitled *Young, Black, and Male in America*, whose subtitle—*An Endangered Species*—cannot be dismissed as Draconian. The so-called "Million Man March" took place the week after a Washington-based Sentencing Project broke the news that one out of three black men aged 20 to 29 was in jail, paroled, or on probation. That the mid-nineties has witnessed the publication of *The Bell Curve*, with its biologizing of racially defined mental capacity, as well as legislative assaults against affirmative action, attests to a growing backlash among whites about the ethnic diversity the culture increasingly exhibits. (Significantly, one paperback response to *The Bell Curve* features a racechanged cover image composed of a biracial male face with African features prominent in the lower half and European features in the upper half, an iconography that extends a long tradition of identifying the European with the mind, the African with the mouth).

Thanks to a generation of brilliant African-American critics—thinkers like Henry Louis Gates, Jr., bell hooks, Toni Morrison, Michele Wallace, and Patricia J. Williams—these issues have entered the work of literary scholarship with a nuanced but deeply ethical sophistication upon which I hope to draw and to which I am profoundly indebted. I have also been influenced by Leslie Fiedler's insight in *Waiting for the End* about Americans. "Born theoretically white, we are permitted to pass our childhood as imaginary Indians, our adolescence as imaginary Negroes, and only then are expected to settle down to being what we really are: white once more" (*Waiting*, 134). While I was writing this book, the related work of Michael Awkward, Diana Fuss, Eric Lott, Michael North, and Michael Rogin appeared in print and shaped my thinking. Of course, though, as my subtitle and the pages following attest, my greatest intellectual debt is to Frantz Fanon, whose *Black Skin, White Masks* continues to serve as a source of inspiration for scholars studying the guilt-ridden psychologies of racism.

Although Fanon consistently universalizes the masculine perspective, his application of psychoanalytic concepts to the construction of racial subjectivity has encouraged critics to study race and gender as reciprocal, interactive categories. Elizabeth Abel's "Black Writing, White Reading: Race and the Politics of Feminist Interpretation," Anthony Gerard Barthelemy's *Black Face Maligned Race: The Representation of Blacks in English Drama from Shakespeare to Southerne*, Gail Ching-Liang Low's "White Skins/Black Masks: The Pleasures and Politics of Imperialism," David Roediger's "White Skins, Black Masks: Minstrelsy and White Working Class Formation before the Civil War," Michael Rogin's *Black-*

face, White Noise: Jewish Immigrants in the Hollywood Melting Pot, and Kaja Silverman's "White Skin, Brown Masks: The Double Mimesis; or With Lawrence in Arabia" all attest to Fanon's far-reaching influence and elaborate the chiasmus of his title. Evoking Fanon's rhetorical parallelism enables these studies to other whiteness, to race it, to denaturalize those dominant ideologies that make whiteness virtually invisible. Similarly, for me racechange became a trope that made whiteness as startlingly visible as blackness has historically been. In addition, Diana Fuss's comment that the comma in Fanon's title "allows simultaneously for an essentialist and a constructionist reading" foregrounds my own effort to question the association of race with biology while at the same time recognizing the ways in which racial categories have hinged on skin color (*Essentially Speaking*, 75).

What I set out to study about whites is a psychology of entitlement but also of guilt that men and women display quite differently in racial masquerades, with white men almost exclusively playing blacks on stage and screen, and white women of letters more focused on the relationship between race, sexuality, lineage, and reproduction. That I have not followed a reversal of Fanon's formula to subtitle this project "White Skin, Black Masks" means that I want to draw attention to a blurring of boundaries involved in racial masquerades: When white people portray African Americans, they embody (and displace) them. The phrase "Black Face" is meant to invoke the history of burnt cork in minstrelsy, vaudeville, and film, but also the transfiguring effect of the staging of blackness on white subjectivity. Put simply, it is not nearly as easy to take off a black face as it is to remove a black mask.

I also hope that this study might extend recent insight into the indebtedness of mainstream American culture to African-American people, a case made most assiduously by Ann Douglas, George Hutchinson, and Eric Sundquist, who argue that we can only represent American literature by integrating the canon so as to comprehend the dialectic between white and black works of art. From this perspective, black productions can hardly be ghettoized from white. Andrew Ross, citing some examples before the commerce between white rock 'n' roll and black rhythm and blues, calls hybrid cultural productions "miscegenated" and describes "Elvis's rockabilly hair, greased up with Royal Crown Pomade to emulate the black 'process' of straightening and curling, itself a black attempt to look 'white'" (68). What does it mean, then, that on the Oprah Winfrey show, a young black singer named L. D. Shore gained fame as "the Black Elvis," an African American imitating a white man imitating black singers? Or, for that matter, that one of the finest performers of Klezmer music—folktunes from the Polish-Jewish *shtetl*—is the African-American entertainer Don Byron?

Because of Michelle Shocked's recognition of the crossover dynamic at work in her own performances, the white singer, seeking to call attention to the "real 'roots'" of her tunes, initially wanted to present her record *Arkansas Traveler* (1991) with a coverphoto of herself "wearing blackface." Deciding against any image that might provide grist for hatemongers, she nevertheless explained in her album notes that "'blacking up' should be done correctly" in "a context of true respect for the cultures we ape." No wonder that Marlon T. Riggs asks, "What is, after all, the 'black' in black pop culture?" As Riggs goes on to speculate,

> how do Marky Mark and Vanilla Ice and Charley Pride and Living Colour fit within our frames of reference? That is, the first two kinda sound black but ain't, and the last two are black but don't sound like it, if you know what I mean. So—I mean this seriously—what is the marker of blackness in our pop culture? (104)

Unlike Ross and Riggs, I will be focusing primarily on the pre-seventies decades of the twentieth century and I will be dealing not with music but instead with films, poetry, fiction, painting, photography, and journalism; nevertheless, I raise comparable issues about the markers of whiteness and blackness in our high culture. For though, according to Stuart Hall, "there's nothing that global postmodernism loves better than a certain kind of difference" (23), I hope to show that turn-of-the-century movie makers, modernist poets, and midcentury novelists and journalists as well as contemporary photographers and painters also savored what Hall calls "a touch of ethnicity, a taste of the exotic, . . . 'a bit of the other'" (23).

At certain times and within certain genres, we shall see that the fascination of white artists with difference makes no difference at all, based (as it is) on consuming (cannibalizing) the Other. Tasting a bit of the Other becomes nothing but a sound bite. At other moments and within some milieus, however, it may provide a fleeting glimpse into what we (as individuals and as citizens of the United States) have to gain culturally from the risky Whitmanesque enterprise of trying to contain (without confining) multitudes. Although the Other often collapses into the self-same because of a kind of societal absorption or cultural assimilation, sometimes it provides the opportunity to unravel bounded definitions of the self, opening the self up to its own alarming alterity, moving us as spectators or readers toward (a possibly dystopic, possibly utopian) transracial consciousness. The performance artist Anna Deavere Smith, who plays the roles of Lubavitcher women as well as Haitian men, Korean store owners as well as El Salvadorian revolutionaries in *Fires in the Mirror* (1993) and *Twilight* (1994), has explained that she created her "documentary theater" so that "the reenactment, or the reiteration of a person's words" would "teach [her] about that person" (*Fires*, xxvi). Using the language and cadences of people she had interviewed about their reactions to racial conflicts in the Crown Heights neighborhood of Brooklyn and Los Angeles, Deavere Smith attempts to make the "frame of reference for the other . . . *be* the other," to learn "about the other by being the other" (xxvii).

In the process of writing, I have learned about the Other from many others, generous friends and colleagues who provided intellectual stimulation and intriguing suggestions: Richard Bauman, Linda Charnes, Eva Cherniavsky, Shehira Davezac, Linda David, Dyan Elliott, Jonathan Elmer, Alice Falk, Mary Favret, Tom Foster, Reginald Gibbons, Geoffrey Hartman, James Justice, Walter Kalaidjian, Tricia Lootens, Herb Marks, Portia K. Maultsby, Andrew Miller, Carolyn Mitchell, Andrea Most, Betty Rose Nagel, James Naremore, Cornelia Nixon, Gene Rice, Alvin Rosenfeld, Chris Sindt, Werner Sollors, Jan Sorby, Jayne Spencer, Paul

Strohm, and Susan Suleiman. I profited, too, from working with a group of smart graduate students: Louise Bernard, Kelly Burns, Kyeong-Hee Choi, Radiclani Clytus, Laura Dawkins, Christian Fahlen, Elena Glasberg, Melissa Valiska Gregory, Jonathan Hillman, Joan Hope, Renata Kobetts, Lori Landay, Mary Lane, Susan Moke, Betsy Oster, Liedeke Plate, Marguerite Rippy, Maia Saj Schmidt, Naoko Sugiyama, Abigail Sutton, Beth Sutton-Ramspeck, Robert Richardson, Ashley Tidey, Natasha Vaubel, and Ellen Weinauer.

The Lilly Library and the Black Film Center Archives, both at Indiana University; the Indianapolis Art Museum; and the Beinecke Rare Book Library provided indispensable research help, as did Peter Gordon, chief Curator of the San Jose Museum of Art; Mary Corliss and Terry Geesken at the Museum of Modern Art in New York; Paul Cox in the Picture Library, National Portrait Gallery, London; Dott. Giovanni Scichilone at the Museo di Villa Giulia in Rome; Richard Barrios at Photo-Fest; John Wessel at the Wessel O'Connor Gallery; and Ron Jagger of the Phyllis Kind Gallery. For a grant that made it possible for me to devote myself full-time to this project for an entire academic year, I am exceptionally grateful to the National Endowment of the Humanities. To helpful administrators at Indiana University—Kenneth Gros Louis, George Walker, Morton Lowengrub, and Kenneth Johnston—I give thanks for professional support. The encouragement of Diana Finch at the Ellen Levine Agency and the excellent editing of T. Susan Chang at Oxford University Press buoyed me up when I worried about the sensitivity of the subjects I was broaching.

With respect to those readers kind enough to comment so attentively and extensively on sections of this manuscript—Elizabeth Abel, Judith Kegan Gardiner, Sandra M. Gilbert, Ray Hedin, Carolyn Heilbrun, Eric Lott, Nancy K. Miller, Toni Morrison, Michael Rogin, Judith Roof, and Robyn Wiegman—I can only express my gratitude for the time and thought you so generously gave to me as well as my hope that the final product has profited from your insightful suggestions. Along with the late Elliot Gilbert, Sandra taught me what I knew about critical writing when I began this work, and I will always remain dazzled by her unfailing wit, her staunch intellectual integrity. Especially to Nancy, whose poise and humor were a constant source of inspiration, I owe my pleasure in the revising of this text.

On the home front, the outstanding research assistance I received from Katharine Ings went far beyond the usual checking of notes and shlepping of books to include scholarly sleuth work and critical discoveries. Aided by Rahul Mehta and Joellyn Ausanka at Oxford University Press, Anna Meek's help with the manuscript was exemplary. On a daily basis, I gained immeasurably from my dear friend Mary Jo Weaver, whose fortitude and kindness encouraged me "to boldly go" on this first solo flight. The amiable companionship of Julie Gray and Beau cheered me on, as did the downtown savvy of Susannah Gray and John Lyons. In addition, the unflagging energies of my mother, Luise David, turned her into an indefatigable source of information and inspiration. About Molly (now known as Marah) and Simone Gubar, I can only marvel: Their contribution took the form of enlivening ideas and stimulating texts as well as salutary reminders of the limits of my thinking. With their intelligence and good sense, they serve as a beacon for their sometimes misguided but always appreciative mother.

Finally, I dedicate this book to Donald Gray, whose brilliant editorial skills and cultural insights continually enliven and challenge my speculations. His curiosity and wisdom about the interplay among aesthetics, history, and ethics have taught me how to think, even as they have made him an inspiring model. Eccentric though it may seem, this book is my way of saying thank you for "The hourly kindness, the days' common speech, / The habitual content of each with each."

RACECHANGES

[T]he problem of the Twentieth Century is the problem of the color-line.

—W.E.B. Du Bois

One evening an actor asked me to write a play for an all-black cast. But what exactly is a black? First of all, what's his color?

—Jean Genet

What one's imagination makes of other people is dictated, of course, by the laws of one's own personality and it is one of the ironies of black-white relations that, by means of what the white man imagines the black man to be, the black man is enabled to know who the white man is.

—James Baldwin

Black slavery enriched the country's creative possibilities. For in that construction of blackness and enslavement could be found not only the not-free but also, with the dramatic polarity created by skin color, the projection of the not-me. The result was a playground for the imagination. What rose up out of collective needs to allay internal fears and to rationalize external exploitation was an American Africanism—a fabricated brew of darkness, otherness, alarm, and desire that is uniquely American. (There also exists, of course, a European Africanism with a counterpart in colonial literature.)

—Toni Morrison

To his white European patients, [Frantz] Fanon is ineluctably black—"the Negro doctor." To his black Algerian patients, Fanon is white: a French-educated, upper-middle-class professional who cannot speak the language.

—Diana Fuss

1

ADVENTURES IN THE SKIN TRADE

> [H]ow difficult it sometimes is to know where the black begins and the white ends.
>
> —Booker T. Washington

> [N]ot only must the black man be black; he must be black in relation to the white man. Some critics will take it on themselves to remind us that this proposition has a converse. I say that this is false. The black man has no ontological resistance in the eyes of the white man.
>
> —Frantz Fanon

Can human beings (and the cultures they create) be defined as either black or white? Or are most human beings (and the cultures they create) both black and white? These are the questions that seem to be posed by fascinating artifacts about race which survive from ancient times in the form of Janiform vases depicting the heads of Europeans and Africans. Dating back to 510 B.C., the two faces on one such Italian urn embody a study in racial contrast which is constructed by juxtaposing, feature by feature, a white and a black woman (Fig. 1.1). Seen in profile, hair, nose, lips, chin, jewelry (or its absence), and neck suggest that racial difference—not merely skin deep—dictates physiognomy, perhaps even psychology. Antithetical, the abutting heads seem to set the women at odds, for each looks out from her own perspective in a direction that dooms her never to see the other. Hardly a melting pot, the vessel portrays the races as distinct, separate, unamalgamated. Yet the burden of the ornamented pail shared by the two heads signifies a commonality eerily echoed by the two handles that come into view when the artifact is presented in either frontal position (Figs. 1.2 and 1.3). The white face now hides the black, the black the white. Somewhat like two sides of one coin, the dual faces constitute one head, one being, whose mysteriously doubled features speak to the complementarity of Western and African images of womanly beauty, of domestic supportiveness, or even of the biological capacity of the female to contain life as well as life-giving fluids. In this context, the salient, silent form of the urn communicates a teasing truth about racial comingling, fusing, intermixing.

As in Keats's famous "Ode on a Grecian Urn," the vase from ancient Tar-

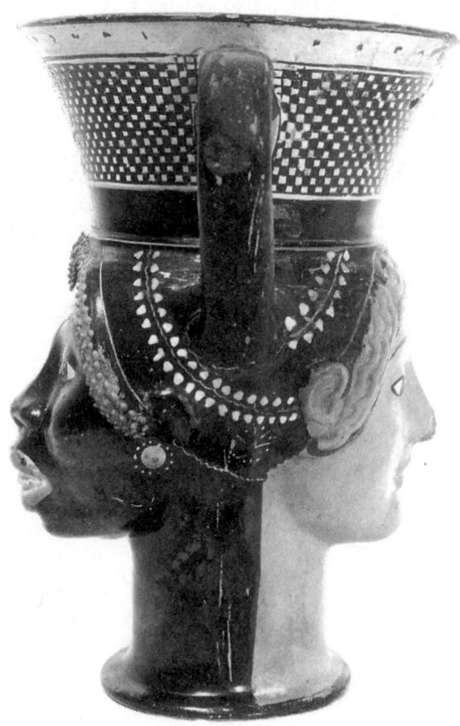

Figure 1.1 Janiform Vase (510 B.C.), Museo di Villa Giulia, Rome. Courtesy of Archeologica per L'Etruria Meridonale.

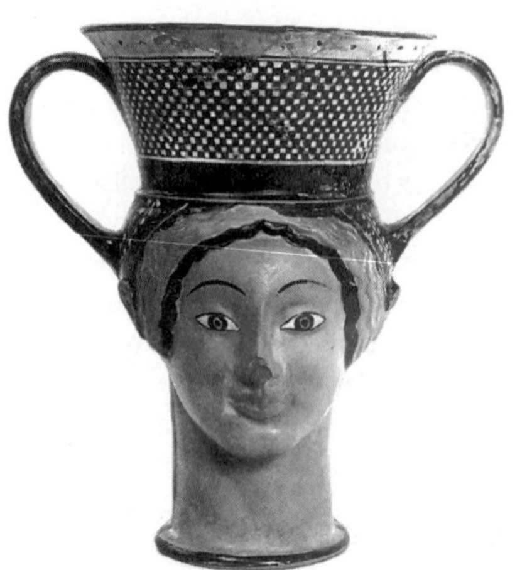

Figure 1.2 White Face of Janiform Vase

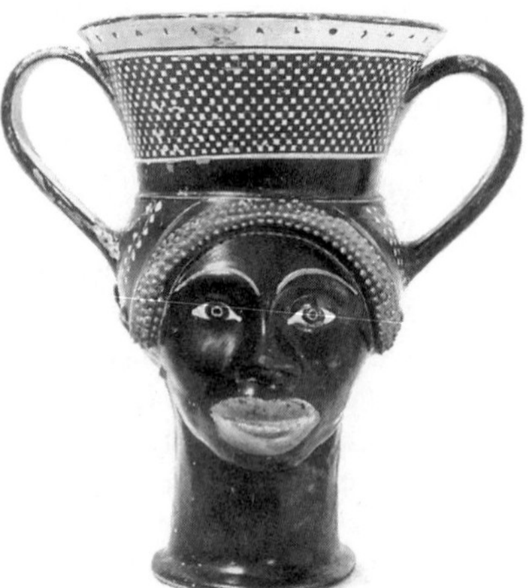

Figure 1.3 Black Face of Janiform Vase

quinia—or what we see as contemporary viewers looking at the vase—could be said to tell us all we know and all we need to know,[1] in this case about the contradictory disposition of racial representation in Western art. On the one hand, European and American artists have stressed the rigid boundaries separating race from race, while, on the other, they have documented racial interconnectedness and mutuality. Similarly, the two epigraphs for this chapter juxtapose the view (of Frantz Fanon) that race constitutes a rigid bifurcation with the belief (of Booker T. Washington) that race needs to be understood as a graduated spectrum. Imagining race—a category that has promulgated stories about civilization and nation, about family and identity—spawns an absorption with purity and pollution, integrity and hybridity, unity and plurality, sameness and difference. Throughout modern times, artists in virtually all media have meditated on racial relationships using multifaceted figures composed of ethnic comparisons, contrasts, and metamorphoses.

Though certainly conceptualizations of race have not remained static since the creation of the Janiform pail in ancient times, reading the vase now demonstrates how configurations of corporeal traits contributed to a black/white divide that paradoxically provoked in people on each side of it various transgressive maneuvers, much as has the arranging of the world into male and female.[2] Indeed, to Simone de Beauvoir, a thinker as obsessed with the inequality consigned to the Other as Fanon and Washington were, the urn might suggest "deep similarities between the situation of woman and that of the Negro," though it also implicitly challenges the all-too-common assumption that "woman" is white, "Negro" male (xxiii). Just as numerous sexual narratives were used to justify or explain the subjection of women, by the end of the nineteenth century stories about civilization and nation, about family and identity generated by racial imaginings exploited ideas about purity and pollution, integrity and hybridity, unity and plurality, sameness and difference that contributed to the subordination of whole populations.[3] By the twentieth century, when images of transvestism, androgyny, hermaphroditism, and transsexuality multiplied to negotiate the gender gap, what I am calling racechange had become a crucial trope of high and low, elite and popular culture, one that allowed artists from widely divergent ideological backgrounds to meditate on racial privilege and privation as well as on the disequilibrium of race as a category.

Racechange: The term is meant to suggest the traversing of race boundaries, racial imitation or impersonation, cross-racial mimicry or mutability, white posing as black or black passing as white, pan-racial mutuality. Over the past several decades, Americans have been repeatedly informed by psychologists and sociologists that the classification of peoples into Asians, blacks, Hispanics, and whites has no basis in science or biology, but such "folk taxonomies" persist, indicating how many individuals have not really been able to internalize such a proposition.[4] Racechange provides artists in diverse media a way of thinking about racial parameters. Just as the Tarquinian urn can be said to stress the rigid borders separating the races as well as the easy commerce between them, representations of racechange test the boundaries between racially defined identities, functioning paradoxically to reinforce and to challenge the Manichean meanings Western societies give to color. To begin with its most ambivalent and thus benign twentieth-century manifestation, racechange may be best viewed outside the American context that will elsewhere take precedence in this chapter and this book, specifically through a glance at the work of two Continental visual artists. For the experimental photographs and photomontages of Man Ray and Hannah Höch exemplify the instability and centrality of racechanging iconography in the modern period, and they do so by continuing to meditate on the relationship "between the situation of woman and that of the Negro."

During the first half of the twentieth century, Man Ray returned to the Janiform design to depict the juxtaposition of black and white faces because this aesthetic form could sustain doubleness, based, as it was, on the idea of the two-faced god Janus, a deity who stood at (and for) portals. A modernist riff on the Tarquinian urn, Man Ray's *Noire et blanche* (Black and white) series of images (1926)—with its juxtaposition of Anglo and African, light and dark forms of beauty—simultaneously postulates and traverses a gulf between African and European races and cultures. In the most distinctive of the photographs with this title, the illuminated, pale skin of Man Ray's model (Kiki de Montparnasse) can be read as an either/or statement about race since it contrasts with the dark, obdurate stone of the black head she holds with her hand (Fig. 1.4). Whereas the living face has all the marks of European urbanity—the flapper's tight cap of lacquered hair as well as her penciled brows and lashes, powdered lids, lipstick bow-mouth, and hint of an earring—the sculpted mask displays its African difference: With its symmetrically designed hair or helmet, its almost nonexistent mouth, and its half-opened, half-closed eyes, this artifact appears markedly less realistic, more stylized than the photograph Ray takes of it. An *objet*, the dark talis hints that, as Fanon speculates, black subjectivity has no ontological reality for whites. Thus, Kiki possesses the fetish—her hand exhibits it—because the picture counterpoints *Noire* with *blanche*, savage with civilized, black with white, the fad of *negritude* during the twenties with the art of photography which enabled modernist artists to appropriate or assimilate the crafts of alien and presumably primitive cultures.

But of course this photograph (as well as the others Man Ray produced on this theme) also emphasizes the *et* of his title, the both/and of race, suggesting the interchangeability or fungibility of model and mask. Light and dark heads alike cast shadows on the surface upon which they rest. Given Kiki's closed eyelids, both are blind, the objects rather than the subjects of the gaze. If anything, the stone head contains more agency than the person since its verticality appears to decapitate her. Though Kiki presumably has the superior consciousness of humanity, she is horizontal, as if asleep or dead, while the upright mask appears paradoxically more alert. In addition, Kiki's make-up, hairdo, and modeling mean she is just as constructed as the African icon, just as "framed" by Man Ray's "shot." Indeed, consenting to her erotic objectification, she endorses a colonization as complete as that of the exotic object. Nor, given his pseudonym, could this photographer be unself-conscious about man's (voyeuristic) rays. Or so Kiki's prone face—"made up" like a Japanese mask—suggests, since it looks like a rare shelved artifact.

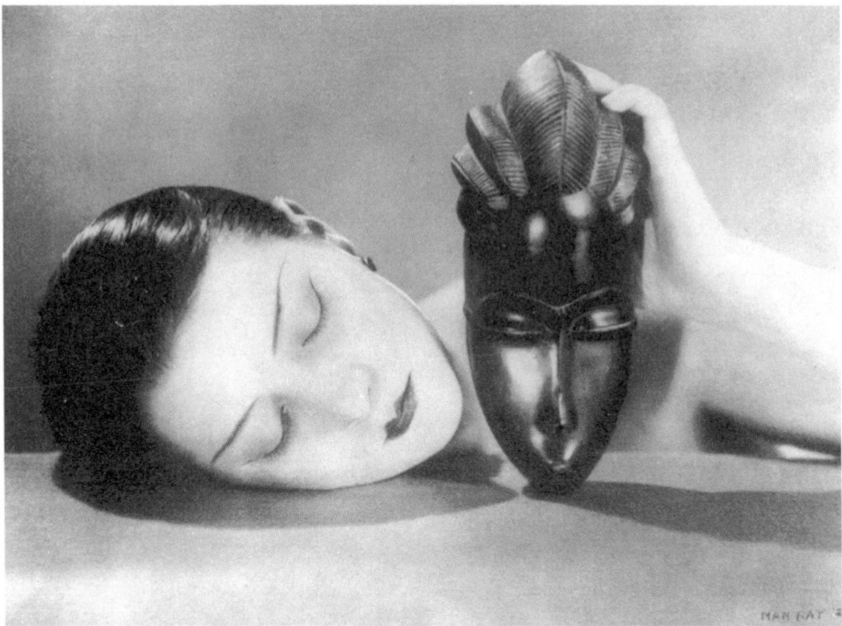

Figure 1.4 Man Ray, *Noire et blanche* (Black and white, 1926), gelatin-silver print, 6¾ × 8⅞ in. Copyright © Man Ray Trust-ADAGP/ARS, 1997.

From this perspective, the hand of Kiki represents less an act of ownership than an indication of bonding or camaraderie, a touching connection that links two fetishized objects of otherness, the beauty of blackness *and* of white femininity killed into art.

The negative version of *Noire et blanche*—switching lights and darks—graphically emphasizes the photographer's accord with Booker T. Washington's point that it is sometimes "difficult . . . to know where the black begins and the white ends" (267): Here the now illuminated mask is foregrounded, as if it might be slipped over Kiki's face (Fig. 1.5).[5] As in several other "solarizations" Man Ray produced, the effect is spectral, even apocalyptic. The inanimate object gains animation while the presence of the living model is reduced to a ghostly absence. Hannah Höch, a friend of Man Ray's and a theorist of cultural hybridity, extended his experimental variations on the Janus form which reinforce even as they challenge normative racial polarization. In *Entführung* (Abduction, 1925), Höch cut out a photograph of a roughly carved African animal statue on which several figures sit, placed it on a larger base, and substituted a New Womanly face for one of the primitive heads; eclipsing the original Other, an image of the self—the modern profile—stands out with startling whiteness, positioned backward on the sculpted body of an African female (Fig. 1.6). Paradoxically, then, the native travelers are facing forward, while the amazed modernist looks backward (as indeed Höch does) to a primitive past

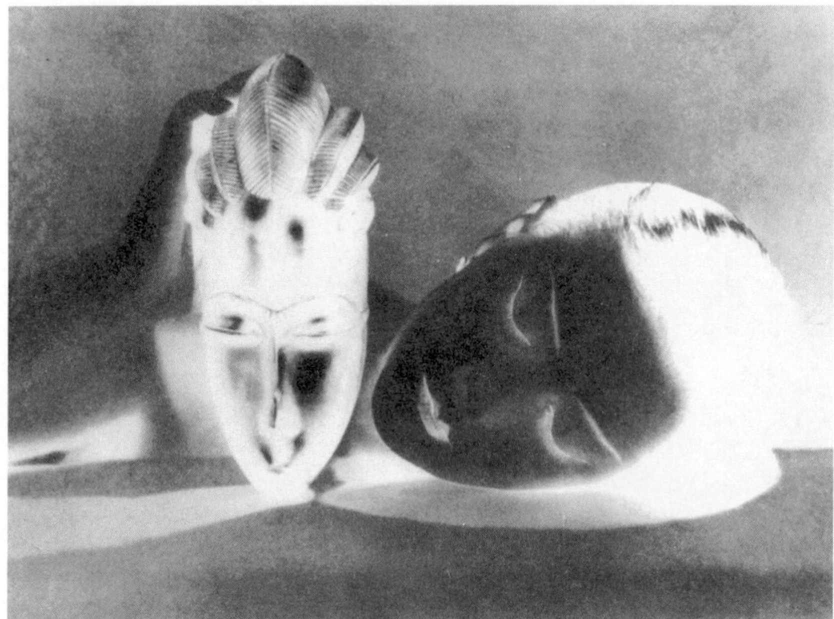

Figure 1.5 Man Ray, *Noire et blanche* (1926), negative version. Copyright © Man Ray Trust-ADAGP/ARS, 1997.

she seeks to excavate even as she criticizes how her contemporaries—artists and anthropologists—have reconstructed it. Despite modernist quests for an Ur-mythology grounded in the physicality of ancient, exotic cultures, Höch's New Woman remains a self divided, cut off from the body, a talking head.

Many of Höch's other collages in her Ethnographic Museum series mix so-called primitive sculptures of dark materials given traditionally African shapes with photographed white body parts. Framed within their frames by sculptural bases, pedestals, or platforms, Höch's discordant montages display "the arbitrariness of all canons of beauty, both familiar and exotic," as Maud Lavin puts it (166). According to Lavin, Höch's "humanistic linking of the subjecthood of Western and tribal peoples through montaging body parts" enabled her to consider the uncanny relationship between women commercialized as commodity fetishes, exhibited as mannequins, and primitives commercialized as ethnographic fetishes, exhibited as freaks (167–68). *Denkmall II: Eitelkeit* (Monument II: Vanity, 1926) features the legs of a naked, posturing white woman attached to what looks like an ancient black, androgynous fetish (Fig. 1.7); *Mutter* (1930) creates a number of facial plains in a cubist portrait that reveals the interplay of multicultural forms that seem to muffle or suppress subjectivity; *Fremde Schönheit I* (Strange Beauty, 1929) presents a seductively posed nude topped by a wrinkled (looming but possibly shrunken) head whose eyes look magnified through the oversized spectacles that underscore the viewer's own act of voyeurism. In all these works the juxta-

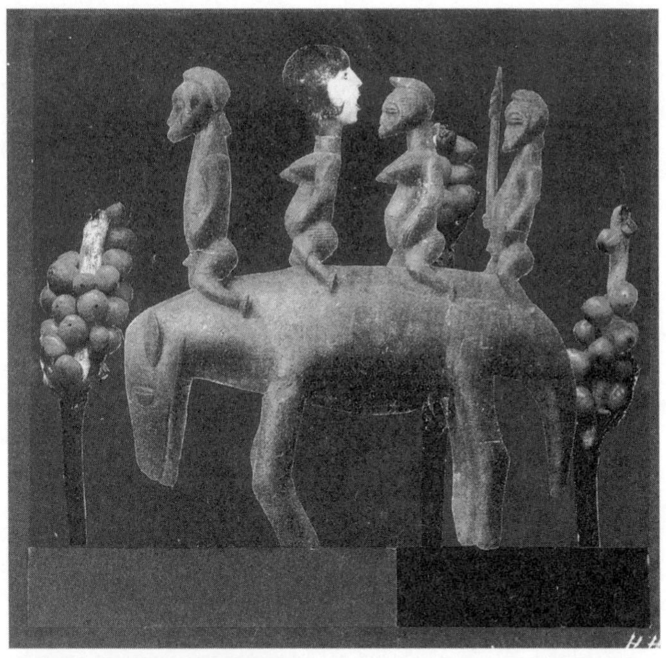

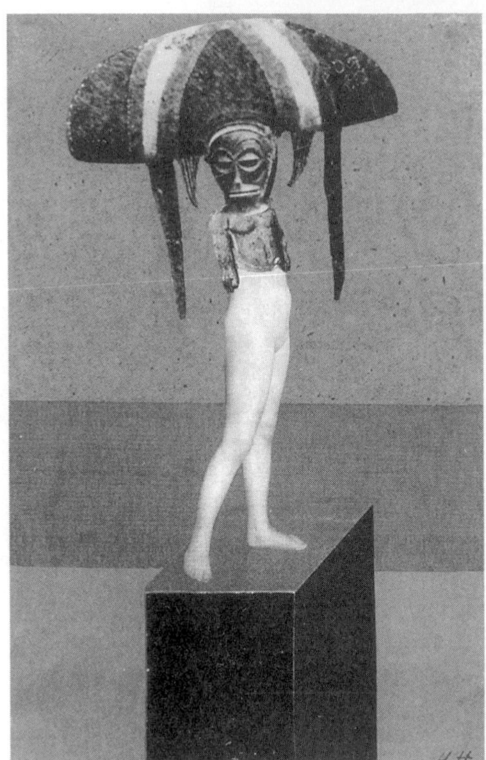

Figure 1.6 *(Above)* Hannah Höch, *Entführung* (Abduction, 1925), collage, 19.5 × 20 cm. Copyright © 1997 Artists Rights Society (ARS), New York / VG Bild-Kunst, Bonn; courtesy of Kupferstichkabinett Staatliche Museum Preussiche Kulturbesitz, Berlin.

Figure 1.7 Hannah Höch, *Denkmall II: Eitelkeit* (Monument II: Vanity, 1926), collage, 25.8 × 16.7 cm. Copyright © 1997 Artists Rights Society (ARS), New York / VG Bild-Kunst, Bonn; courtesy of Rossner-Hoch, Backnang, Germany.

positions between human and other-worldly body parts, symbolic and realistic corporeal configurations, combine to create sometimes funny, sometimes grotesque aliens. Using biracial imagery to meditate on the mind-body problem, Höch sought to confront the difficulty of knowing "where the black begins and the white ends," even as she studied the appropriation of the primitive that marks the ways in which race is codified when the African blatantly lacks "ontological resistance" or interiority.

If ambivalence distinguishes the Janiform design as well as its namesake, the Roman god of portals, Janus, whose doorways stand as entrances or exits, contradiction resides in the character of the racechanger, a shape-shifter who took center stage in the modern cultural arena. "I want to be your African girl," croons the blond-haired heroine of Ernest Hemingway's *Garden of Eden* (begun in the 1940s), explaining to her white lover the tanning process she has utilized to darken her skin. The experimental photographs of Man Ray and Hannah Höch may seem far removed from Hemingway's cross-racial impersonator or from Vachel Lindsay exploiting purportedly black rhythms to recite his popular poem "The Congo" (1914) or from the reincarnation of the dead, white Patrick Swayze in the living, black body of Whoopi Goldberg in the movie *Ghost* (1990); however, the shifty iconography of racechange has enabled artists working in diverse media and with quite different purposes to traverse racial boundaries and question racial presuppositions. The "trick" of racial metamorphosis participates in the illicit, the liminal, the transgressive, the outré, the comic, or the camp. Not simply mimetic, racechange is an extravagant aesthetic construction that functions self-reflexively to comment on representation in general, racial representation in particular. To the extent that racechange engages issues of representation, it illuminates the power issues at stake in the representation of race.

In the chapters to come, the permutations of racechange provide a means to measure altering societal attitudes toward race and representation. Of course racial crossover and ventriloquism have long been recognized in music, especially in the history of popular music. One thinks immediately of what Andrew Ross calls "miscegenated" musical productions generated by the interaction of white performers and African-American traditions—Benny Goodman's swing, Elvis Presley's rock 'n' roll, or Vanilla Ice's rap—as well as those created by black artists (say, Charley Pride and Living Color) whose productions "don't sound" black to an astute listener like Marlon T. Riggs, who is led to ask, "What is the marker of blackness in our pop culture?" (Ross, 68; Riggs, 104). Julie Dash's movie *Illusions* (1983) emphasizes the cross-racial dynamics at work in the music industry by presenting a behind-the-scenes view of a black singer's voice dubbed onto footage of a white, lip-synching actress. But what about the other, earlier aesthetic forms racechange often took? More specifically, how did the legacy of slavery and discrimination in the history of the United States shape the patterns racechange acquired among Man Ray's and Hannah Höch's American contemporaries?

The pages that follow spotlight white actors sporting burnt cork in pioneering twentieth-century films; black artists investigating the origins of color in literature and the visual arts; white poets exploiting black vernacular to speak as if from an

African-American subjectivity, as well as white patrons representing themselves through the language of the Harlem Renaissance writers they supported; white journalists blackening their faces in political pranks; and novelists, essayists, and painters envisioning sexually deviant whites as queerly colored or imagining parents of one race giving birth to babies who look like they belong to another. These are the phenomena I will use to identify the centrality of racechange in twentieth-century literature and art. As in the Tarquinian vase, the Man Ray photographs, and the Hannah Höch photomontages, racechanging imagery deploys sexual iconography to create a host of provocative connections and tensions between conceptions of race and those of gender. In any case, however, such figures are hardly the ones that first come to mind when the subject of racial impersonation is addressed.

On the one hand, the most notorious and arguably the most influential instance of racechange—one that still remains taboo because of its overt racism—appeared on the nineteenth-century minstrel stage, where white actors ridiculed African Americans. On the other hand, the most morally acceptable representation of racechange—indeed, the only one that has received extensive attention from literary scholars—surfaced in so-called "passing" novels, in which African-American characters masqueraded as white so as to assimilate into mainstream culture.[6] I begin with such black figures transforming themselves into whites because, as the writers to be discussed in this chapter demonstrate, this type of racechange functions as *the* crucial subscript of a supremacist society. Even before the passing novels of the Harlem Renaissance, black-to-white racechange played a decisive role in American culture. That we sympathize with light-skinned blacks passing as white to gain their rights and responsibilities and that we revile white people masquerading as black to mock African-American culture: This asymmetry clearly speaks to the devaluation of blackness, the overprivileging of whiteness in European and American culture.[7]

Yet regardless of which race engages in the charade and with what motive, twentieth-century performances of racechange depend on the two factors this introduction seeks to establish: first, the ways in which a culture that systematically devalues blackness and establishes whiteness as the norm effectively endorses, even enforces, black-to-white racechange; second, that historically such racial metamorphoses nevertheless (and paradoxically) constituted a crucial tactic used by civil libertarian activists and artists as a means of disentangling the category of race from skin color. In a society that teaches "If you're white, you're right" but "if you're black, get back," adventures in the skin trade often involve politically progressive blacks and whites trading places: blacks to gain the privileges of whites, whites to dramatize the privations of blacks, and both to unmask the arbitrariness of the system that accords those privileges. What, then, of the modernist ambiguities Man Ray and Hannah Höch achieved in photomontages which recapture the teasing equivocations of the Janiform urn? What, too, of the label of prejudice that has firmly (and rightly) attached itself in contemporary times to minstrelsy?

Although racism necessarily influences American thinking about racechange, just as it has contaminated the reputation of racechange, we will see the ways in which even—and perhaps especially—in the context of racism, racial impersonation can operate as a saving strategy, one that enabled African Americans' survival and fueled their satire. Indeed, this chapter attempts to demonstrate that artists from Claude McKay to Adrienne Kennedy depict African-American characters effectively instructed by American society that they will be inducted into it as full citizens with complete personhood only if (in the words of George Schuyler's title) they manage to be "black no more." In addition, writers from Charles Chesnutt to Virginia Woolf suggest that whites can understand the effect of this lesson on African Americans only if they temporarily become "black like me" (to adopt the phrase John Howard Griffin borrowed from Langston Hughes to entitle a best-seller about Griffin's venture across the color line). This liberal traffic across the color line makes us appreciate why and how throughout the twentieth century white impersonations of blackness functioned paradoxically both as a deeply conservative (even racist) as well as a shockingly radical (sometimes anarchic) mode of cultural production, one that has played a complicated role in film, fiction, poetry, painting, and photography.

If You're White, You're Right

A racechange imperative—from black to white—lurks in the very subordination of blackness to whiteness at the center of racist ideology, whether it appears in the British context of colonialism or the American of slavery. Consider, for example, the beginning of Blake's famous poem "The Little Black Boy" (1789):

My mother bore me in the southern wild,
And I am black, but O! my soul is white;
White as an angel is the English child,
But I am black as if bereav'd of light. (ll. 1–4)

The word "but," which clusters around the word "black," repeatedly implies that Blake's speaker experiences his race as a catastrophe, his complexion grievously at odds with his soul's color. Because Blake's boy is taught by his mother that his dark body and sun-burnt face are like a "cloud" or a "shady grove" in which he can learn to bear God's light and heat, His love and goodness, the black speaker concludes about the paradise he will ultimately share with a white boy, "I'll stand and stroke his silver hair, / And be like him, and he will then love me" (ll. 27, 28). Not only is skin colored "black" embodied (unlike the soul), it also signifies absence of light (unlike whiteness, which is imagined as the totality of light).[8]

More recently, Caryl Churchill's play *Cloud 9* (1984) dramatized the schizophrenia of Blake's speaker by casting a white actor to play the role of a colonized black servant. In the first act devoted to displaying the farcical ideologies of English imperialism in Africa, Churchill's Joshua sounds strikingly similar to "The Little Black Boy":

My skin is black but oh my soul is white.
I hate my tribe. My master is my light.
I only live for him. As you can see,
What white men want is what I want to be. (4)

Alienated from their native religions, their families, their own interests and bodies, Blake's "Little Black Boy" and Churchill's Joshua exhibit the psychological damage Fanon diagnosed in his classic book *Black Skin, White Masks* (1952), specifically his view that the colonized man of color thinks about himself, "There is no help for it: I am a white man. For unconsciously I distrust what is black in me, that is, the whole of my being" (191). A crisis of "corporeal reconfiguration" is inflicted on people of color, who are subjected to the "mirror" of an idealized whiteness that makes blackness horrific (Silverman, 27, 29).

"And be like him, and he will then love me"; "What white men want is what I want to be": Heaven for the black boy or man means obtaining the love of his white peer which is in turn predicated on the eradication of difference, the appearance of resemblance. Within the context of slavery, of course, such a resemblance could become a crucial means of survival. William and Ellen Craft's *Running a Thousand Miles for Freedom* (1860) describes the only possible solution to the horror of slavery as an escape route made possible by Ellen Craft's looking "almost white" (2). Disguised as an invalid gentleman, Ellen could be accompanied by her dark-skinned husband when she played the role of master to his slave. In case either her illiteracy or her smooth countenance might betray her, Ellen Craft bound up her right hand in a sling and wore a handkerchief over her cheeks. Although free Negroes existed in the South, William Craft explains, "every coloured person's complexion is *prima facie* evidence of his being a slave; and the lowest villain in the country, should he be a white man, has the legal power to arrest, and question, in the most inquisitorial and insulting manner, any coloured person, male or female" (36).

As if William Craft understood the allure of Ellen's race- and sexchange, he reproduced a picture of her as the frontispiece of his escape narrative, explaining that he managed to obtain his mother's freedom in part by selling the engraving of his disguised wife (Fig. 1.8). With her top hat, cravat, spectacles, and short hair, Ellen in the portrait does not wear the poultice that she used to hide the smoothness of her face, and, therefore, as Ellen Weinauer has pointed out, the engraving displays not really Craft's "wife in the disguise in which she escapes" (*Running*, 12) but, instead, an enigmatic, indeterminate figure—quasi-performer, quasi-performed—contesting the stability of gendered and racial categories of identity (50, 52). And certainly the allure of this creature is sustained as long as the (truly feminine) Ellen Craft plays the role of the (fictionally masculine) master, for she seems attractively emboldened, even spiritually strengthened, though she weeps and swoons when she dons feminine garb and declines back into the position of the childish, invalid wife (79). Even when only impersonated, whiteness (like maleness) confers power as well as privilege, whereas blackness (like femaleness) conveys subordination as well as dependency. Paradoxically, then, in the condition of slavery Ellen Craft gained the status of becoming her husband's "master," while his joyous arrival at a state of "freedom" inaugurated her feminized confinement.

In the clarity with which it presented whiteness as a symbol of personal autonomy, *Running a Thousand Miles for Freedom* establishes black-to-white racechange as a bid for freedom, one that would be made again by Homer Plessy at the

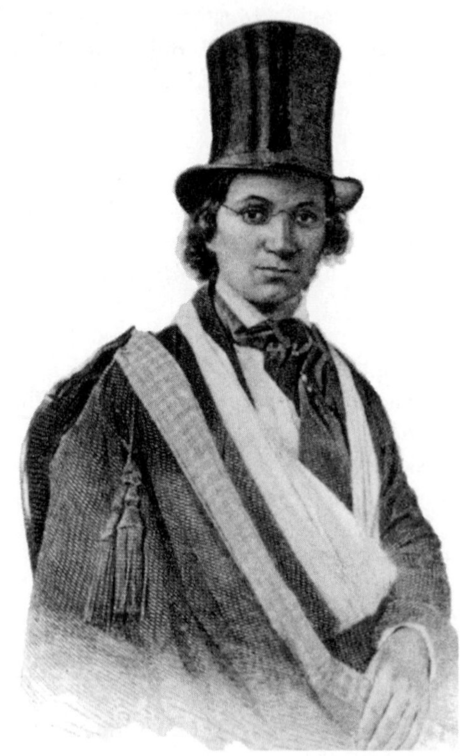

Figure 1.8 Engraving of Ellen Craft. First published in the *London Illustrated News* (19 April 1851), and used as frontispiece of William and Ellen Craft, *Running a Thousand Miles for Freedom* (1860).

end of the nineteenth century when he challenged Louisiana's segregated railroad car law by using his light complexion to gain access to the whites-only car and then announcing himself a Negro. Plessy's contention against Jim Crow seating—that his being only one-eighth Negro and able to pass entitled him to ride in seats reserved for whites—was rejected by the Supreme Court. Although the Court's landmark decision in favor of "a separate-but-equal doctrine" in *Plessy v. Ferguson* (1896) legalized segregation, Plessy had used impersonation to undercut the notion that skin color could simply be conflated with racial identity.[9] Because a figure like Plessy was able to pass for white, he could choose to be black; nevertheless, it is still the case that because he was not able to decide to be white, Plessy could only pretend to be white.[10] In other words, culture or social context shapes racial identity without completely replacing biological definitions of race.

Walter White, a prominent spokesperson for the National Association for the Advancement of Colored People (NAACP) during the 1930s and 1940s, anticipated this point in his autobiography, *A Man Called White* (1948), which begins with the following two, incongruent sentences: "I am a Negro. My skin is white, my eyes are blue, my hair is blond" (3). For White, "There is magic in a white skin; there is tragedy, loneliness, exile, in a black skin" (3). Yet, imbued with the conviction that he can only pretend to be white, the paradoxically named White chooses to be black, tracing his claimed cultural identity back to an incident in his thirteenth year when he and his father were saved from attack during the 1906 race riot in Atlanta because of their light complexions. At the very moment, they fully comprehended the depth of their alienation from white society; for the same reason that they were assured safety—that is, their skin color—father and son could only stand and watch "a lame Negro bootblack" clubbed to death on the street (9). When it later looked like the mob was making for his family's house and his father handed him a gun, White explains, he knew that

> I was a Negro, a human being with an invisible pigmentation which marked me a person to be hunted, hanged, abused, discriminated against, kept in poverty and ignorance, in order that those whose skin was white would have readily at hand a proof of their superiority, a proof patent and inclusive, accessible to the moron and the idiot as well as to the wise man and the genius. No matter how low a white man fell, he could always hold fast to the smug conviction that he was superior to two-thirds of the world's population, for those two-thirds were not white. (11)

The fact that Walter White felt the need to explain why he did not take advantage of his light complexion and renounce his allegiance to the Negro community marks the power of the condition the contemporary novelist Charles Johnson has called "epidermalized Being" (*Oxherding Tale*, 52).

Whereas Walter White chose to be black and refused to pretend to be white, both Ellen Craft and Homer Plessy utilized a mode of masquerading that resembles the tactics of central characters in turn-of-the-century and twentieth-century passing novels whose costumes of disguise demonstrate the fluidity of racial categories no longer connected to skin color. The slave mother of Mark Twain's *The Tragedy of Pudd'nhead Wilson* (1894), for instance, saves her light-skinned infant from being sold down the river by placing him in the elegant baby clothes and cradle of her master's son, while divesting the legitimate heir of his necklace and putting him in her own child's unpainted pine cradle. Similarly, Jessie Redmon Fauset's *Plum Bun* (1928) features a fair-skinned heroine who simply changes her name and her neighborhood so as to pass herself off as white because whites "had power and the badge of that power was whiteness" (73). After Fauset's central character determines to get "acquainted with life in her own way without restrictions or restraint," she understands herself to be "young, she was temporarily independent, she was intelligent, she was white" (88).

Although such passing novels did contain subversive readings of whiteness, at least in part their authors used racechange to analyze the dynamics of racial envy and more specifically black women's adoption of white-defined standards of beauty. From Zora Neale Hurston's Mrs. Turner (in *Their Eyes Were Watching God* (1937)), who believes "We oughta lighten up de race" (135), to Toni Morrison's Pecola Breedlove (in *The Bluest Eye* (1970)), who drinks milk out of a Shirley Temple cup so as magically to gain storybook blue eyes, a female longing for racechange reflects the self-hatred bred by a racist society. In a photograph entitled *Mirror, Mirror* (1986–87), the contemporary artist Carrie Mae Weems comments on such socially induced self-loathing by presenting a black woman asking

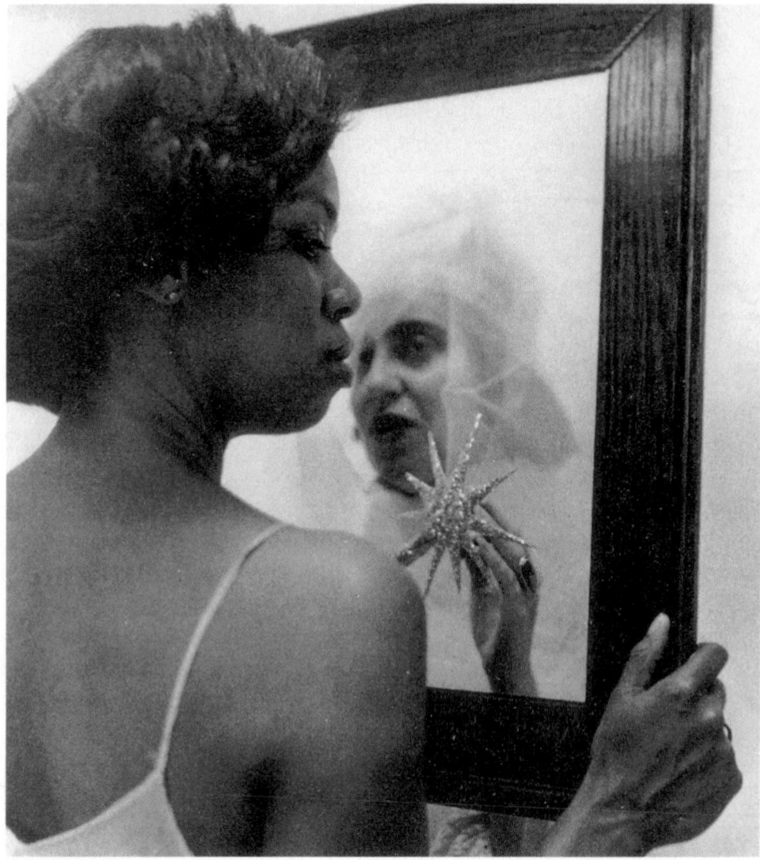

Figure 1.9 Carrie Mae Weems, *Mirror, Mirror* (1986–87), silver print, 20 × 16 in. Copyright Carrie Mae Weems; courtesy of PPOW, NY.

her mirror "who's the finest of them all?" and being told, "Snow White, you black bitch, and don't you forget it!!!" (Fig. 1.9). To be sure, because the wicked queen in the mirror looks more directly at the viewer than at the African-American girl, the evil stepmother may reflect the values of (the white) viewer more than those of the girl; and because the African-American girl looks aside, clutching the mirror as if in the next minute to shatter it, the Snow White tale may not be able to effect its damaging ends.[11] Yet the debilitating split image of "Snow White" and "the black bitch" illuminates and is in turned illuminated by a comment of Lorraine O'Grady's that uncannily serves to contrast Weems's photograph to the ancient urn from Tarquinia:

> The female body in the West is not a unitary sign. Rather, like a coin, it has an obverse and a reverse: on the one side, it is white; on the other, not-white or, prototypically,

> black. The two bodies cannot be separated, nor can one body be understood in isolation from the other in the West's metaphoric construction of "woman." White is what woman is; not-white (and the stereotypes not-white gathers in) is what she had better not be. (14)

Claude McKay's short story "Near-White" (1932) dramatizes the ways in which the breach between "Snow White" and the "black bitch" depends less on biology, more on ideology; less on visible signs of skin pigmentation, more on Manichean and transcendent ideas of whiteness versus blackness. Light-complexioned Angie Dove goes in search of romance and adventure in downtown Manhattan, much to the chagrin of her family in Harlem. Passing as white comes easily because "no tangible thing separated her from the respectable white audience down below, her features being whiter and more regular than many persons' who moved boldly and freely in the privileged circles of the Great Majority" (76). Since she displays no visible trace of "the stigmata of Africa" (86), she meets and eventually falls in love with a young man convinced that she is "the nicest, whitest little girl in the world" (99). Herself persuaded that "Prejudice is not stronger than love" (98), Angie determines to tell him the truth about her racial identity but is stopped after asking him to speculate about how he would feel if he found out he had been unwittingly involved with a quadroon or octoroon girl: "Me! I'd sooner love a toad!" (102).

This Jazz-age Cinderella—dancing nightly with a beau from whom she must escape at the close of the evening so as to keep her origins a secret—discovers that her kisses will never transform the Prince who (if he knew the truth) would consider her as repulsive as a toad. An anti-fairy tale, "Near-White" elaborates upon the passionate maxim of its heroine's mother: Speaking as one of the "light-colored ones," she asserts, "We hate [whites] more because we are *not* black" (95–97). What "near-whites" understand is the fictiveness of an oppressive system that generates the greatest hatred against "light-colored ones," a hatred based on fears about category confusion: Whites are "never sure about us, they can't place us" (96). "So close . . . and yet so far" from whites, "near-whites" prove that the color bar, though invisible, is nevertheless insurmountable. McKay strikes the point home by inundating the tale with references to Manhattan's melting pot society. The story begins with a song sensation launched by some "Yank or Yid" (72); continues with references to fashionable Spanish cabarets, German beer gardens, Arabian cafés run by Armenians, dance halls called the Pyramid; and concludes with Prince Charming assuring his doubtful date, "I'd love you if you were even Chinese!" (about which she muses, "Chinese! That was the lowest thing he could imagine" (101)). Yanks, Yids, Spaniards, Arabians, Armenians, Egyptians, and "even" Chinese have apparently managed to become "white," while whiter-than-white Angie remains as far away as "near-white."

The threat implicitly posed by Angie Dove on the marriage market is clearly related to her gender, since an unwitting husband could stand convicted of miscegenation, deemed a crime in many states until the 1957 decision in *Loving v. Virginia*. To be sure, the racial ambiguity of the "near-white" can be disturbing in male as well as female characters, or so William Faulkner's *Light in August* (1932) in-

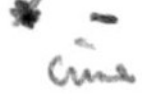

dicates. For the entire white community finds the "parchmentcolored" (304) Joe Christmas particularly dangerous since he cannot be categorized: "He never acted like either a nigger or a white man. That was it. That was what made the folks so mad" (386). However, women's role in reproduction caused female racial ambiguity to appear more sinister to those anxious about preserving the purity of a white patrilineage. Despite its liberal intentions, Jerome Kern and Oscar Hammerstein's *Show Boat* (originally produced on Broadway in 1927, made into a film in 1936, and revived in 1946 and 1994) inadvertently instructed audiences on the degradation a racechange from white to black entails for a sexually active (potentially reproductive) woman. The revelation that the light-skinned singer Julie is a "Negro" effectively makes her dispensable in the plot. First, after she and her white boyfriend Steve evade the charge of miscegenation by his cutting her hand and sucking her blood to prove he has more than "one drop" of "Negro blood" himself, the pair leave the showboat (on which they had been performing). Second, when she surfaces in the next act, Julie—abandoned by Steve and doomed to alcoholism—sacrifices a nightclub engagement so as to procure a job for the musical's white heroine and then disappears not only from respectable society but from any of the other characters' concern, an unnoticed casualty in the white community's happily-ever-after. As soon as her color is established, in other words, the beautiful and noble Julie suffers a series of catastrophes that ensure not only her demotion in the plot but the white heroine's promotion to center stage.

Given the entanglement of narratives like *Plum Bun*, "Near-White," and *Show Boat* with normative (white-defined) definitions of female attractiveness, it seems appropriate that the most extravagant racechange narrative to emerge from the Harlem Renaissance begins with a black man enthralled by a white woman. The hero of George Schuyler's freewheeling satire *Black No More* (1931) falls in love with a racist white woman whom he manages to marry only by turning himself white. And given the ways in which passing narratives conflate whiteness with life, blackness with life-in-death, it seems fitting that *Black No More* views the demise of blackness as the only viable solution for African Americans. As its title indicates, this tongue-in-cheek fantasy about a scientific method of triggering a "racial metamorphosis" (14) takes supremacist ideology to its logical conclusion by asking its readers to understand that freedom in America is predicated not only on whiteness but on the eradication of blacks. In a 1949 essay entitled "Has Science Conquered the Color Line?" Schuyler's distinguished contemporary Walter White outlined a similar point:

> Suppose the skin of every Negro in America was suddenly to turn white. What would happen to all the notions about Negroes, the idols on which are built race prejudice and race hatred? Would not Negroes then be judged individually on their ability, energy, honesty, cleanliness as are whites? (37)[12]

According to Schuyler, too, the only way for African Americans to achieve individuality, to avoid being viewed as racially representative, is through a color conversion. Schuyler further suggests that a hegemonic racechange script shapes American aesthetic values and political doctrines. Convincing blacks to believe in the superiority of the culture and characteristics of whites, this scenario effectively functions as a form of genocide, threatening to annihilate all African Americans.

To dramatize this idea, Schuyler centers attention on one black do-gooder, a Dr. Junius Crookman, whose studies of vitiligo—a disorder in skin pigmentation—lead him to perfect a method "of artificially inducing and stimulating this nervous disease at will" so as to "solve the American race problem" (27). Only three solutions remain available to African Americans facing that problem— " 'To either get out, get white or get along' " (27)—but most cannot or will not get out and many only barely get along. Determining therefore to get blacks white, Dr. Crookman places the thousands of interested customers he instantly attracts into "a cross between a dentist's chair and an electric chair" (34) so as to give them "the open sesame of a pork-colored skin" (35), even though it cannot yet be genetically transferred to their offspring. A "Race Man," the good doctor is convinced that "if there were no Negroes, there could be no Negro problem" (54).

Huge electric signs represent the commercialization of racechange in this economically astute novel:

> A black face was depicted at the lower end of the arrow while at the top shone a white face to which the arrow was pointed. First would appear the outlines of the arrow; then, BLACK-NO-MORE would flash on and off. Following that the black face would appear at the bottom and beginning at the lower end the long arrow with its lettering would appear progressively until its tip was reached, when the white face at the top would blazon forth. After that the sign would flash off and on and the process would be repeated. (43–44)

Because of the success of Dr. Crookman's business, hair-straightening parlors and whitening chemical concerns go bankrupt, but so do the various leaders of the black intellectual establishment—Santop Licorice of the once-flourishing Back-To-African Society (Marcus Garvey) and Dr. Shakespeare Agamemnon Beard, founder of the National Social Equality League (W.E.B. Du Bois)—since the citizens who once supported them are quickly disappearing. Ironically, then, the supposedly libertarian black intelligentsia, what Du Bois called the "talented tenth," oppose the Black-No-More entrepeneurs' plan for "chromatic emancipation" (87) as fervently as do the Klannish Knights of Nordica, whose members dread unwitting racial intermarriage and miscegenation.

When once-black Max Disher turned white Matthew Fisher joins the Knights of Nordica and marries its founder's daughter, he gains leadership through black-baiting for capitalists: Poor white workers are kept so busy worrying about "Negro blood" (130) and "white nigger" (128) labor competition that they forget to organize. Convinced that even a fiction about the "presence of the Negro as an under class" can continue to keep white workers underpaid and yet nonunionized, Matthew preaches racial supremacy, although "practically all the Negroes [left] are white" (158). But his success feels fragile because of his dread at his wife's producing a dark son, a fear that evaporates when a series of political maneuvers expose the racially mixed descent of the Democratic party and of the Knights of Nordica's leaders, who admit, "We're all niggers now" (193). Not only does

Matthew's racist wife believe her own ancestry may have caused the color of her baby, she also begins to use artifical methods to make herself look darker because in Schuyler's brave new world racism takes an odd twist. When it is discovered that "the new Caucasians were from two to three shades lighter than the old Caucasians" (218) (in other words, that "the blacks were whiter than the whites" (219)), prejudice against exceedingly pale people erupts and the marketing of face powders named "*L'Afrique*" as well as the wearing of "Egyptienne Stain," "Zulu Tan," or just plain charcoal (222) come into vogue.

As in the case of Matthew's wife, the Democratic antagonists of Dr. Crookman's Black-No-More enterprise discover how dangerous it is to be white no more when it is revealed that their own families derive from mixed racial inheritances. After two luckless Democrats try to escape Washington incognito by wearing blackface, they land amid "the most truly Fundamentalist of all the Christian sects in the United States" (203), whose preacher has asked for a sign from God consisting of "a nigger for his congregation to lynch" (208). The townfolk therefore greet the two blackfaced strangers with joy: "Niggers! Praise God! The Sign! Lynch 'em!" (213). Saved after they manage to reveal their pale skins, the doomed duo are next exposed as "damned Demmycratic candidates [who] is niggers" (215) and so their adventure ends with them stripped, their ears and genitals cut off, their bodies ignited on a pyre, their flesh roasted, and then their skeletons ransacked for souvenirs.

Schuyler's mordant indictment of Americans' virulent racism found disturbing confirmation in the fate of the daughter he and his white wife enthusiastically raised as an exemplar of "hybrid vigor" who would break down racial barriers. Some thirty years after the publication of *Black No More* and the birth of Philippa Schuyler, the talented, biracial pianist passed as the white Felipa Monterro not only to gain acceptance in the segregated world of classical music but also because, as she herself put it, "I will be accepted as a person not as a strange curiosity" and because being called "a Negro" would bring a "taint" and thus "30 more miserable years" (Talalay, 224). If the contemporary reviewer and memoirist Anatole Broyard passed in order "to be a writer, not a black writer," his racial imposture also hints that whiteness remains "the default position" for individuality, whereas blackness continues to be attached to the concept of race, of a race type, and thus to racial prejudice (Gates, "White," 66, 75).

"It don't matter if you're black or white," Michael Jackson has sung to popular acclaim at the end of the twentieth century; however, his own reaction to vitiligo adds proof to the continued timeliness of *Black No More*'s satire. Instead of darkening white blotches, as most patients do, Jackson whitened and westernized all of his features. Writing in the early fifties, Frantz Fanon described actual scientific schemes strikingly similar to those employed by Michael Jackson and by Schuyler's fictive Dr. Crookman:

> For several years certain laboratories have been trying to produce a serum for "denegrification"; with all the earnestness in the world, laboratories have sterilized their test tubes, checked their scales, and embarked on researches that might make it possible for the miserable Negro to whiten himself and thus to throw off the burden of that corporeal malediction. (111)

Set in the colonized locales Fanon studied, Julia Blackburn's novel *The Book of Colour* (1995) includes a reminiscence about a father who took on the work of "denegrification" every night when he washed his son's face "with a mixture of peroxide and the juice of a lemon" because the boy had "'been out in the sun, that is why your skin is too dark'" (8–9). Recently, when a black woman, married to an Italian, had a white woman's egg implanted in her womb so their offspring would be "spared the misery of racism," the science of "denegrification" horrified the legal theorist Patricia J. Williams, causing her to imagine black women serving as surrogate mothers and making more efficient the production of racially profitable white babies. As if bringing home the renewed relevance of Schuyler's narrative, Williams views this scenario as "nothing less than the transformation of the social difficulty of being black into an actual birth defect, an undesirable trait that technology can help eliminate" (*Rooster's Egg*, 241).

Back in the nineteenth century, illustrations of countless European and American soap commercials sold cleanliness as godliness by portraying blacks (often toddlers) attempting a racechange by trying to wipe away the dirt and grime of blackness, as did many pictures in children's books (Fig. 1.10). The critic Anne McClintock has argued about Victorian Pears' Soap ads that the purification of the physical body becomes a metaphor for the rejuvenation of the body politic. In the first frame of the bathing scene displayed on one such advertisement, the magic of soap promises to "regenerate the Family of Man by washing from the skin the very stigma of racial and class degeneration"; however, the second frame—in which the bathed child's body has undergone a lightening but his face has not—demonstrates that the white boy as an agent of historical progress cannot completely induct his "lesser brother" into the civilities of the European Enlightenment: "In the Victorian mirror," McClintock explains, "the black child witnesses his predetermined destiny of imperial metamorphosis but remains a passive racial hybrid, part black, part white, brought to the brink of civilization" (213) but never fully inducted or assimilated into it.

At the beginning of the twentieth century in middle America, Madame C. J. Walker (neé *Breedlove*) established her multi-million-dollar fortune by selling lightening creams that could be used on the body as well as the face and straightening solutions for the hair. Elsewhere, Fanon calls such "denegrification" methods a kind of "lactification" whereby whitening the race saves it from "falling back into the pit of niggerhood" (47), a process not unrelated to Pecola *Breedlove*'s great thirst for milk in *The Bluest Eye*. The brilliant photograph of Whoopi Goldberg taken by Annie Leibovitz shows the actress immersed in a tub of milk and thereby jokes about the grotesque imperatives/impossibilities of "lactification" (Fig. 1.11). Again, and in a manner as risible as Schuyler's narrative, the connection is made between racechange and death, for whiteness will only prevail when Whoopi's entire body—her legs, arms, face, and especially her nose and mouth—will be submerged beneath its surface. Is she grinning or grimacing, waving or drowning in her milk bath?

No wonder that Langston Hughes produced a brief but pointed satire of narratives in which characters seek to pass themselves off as white so as to gain social

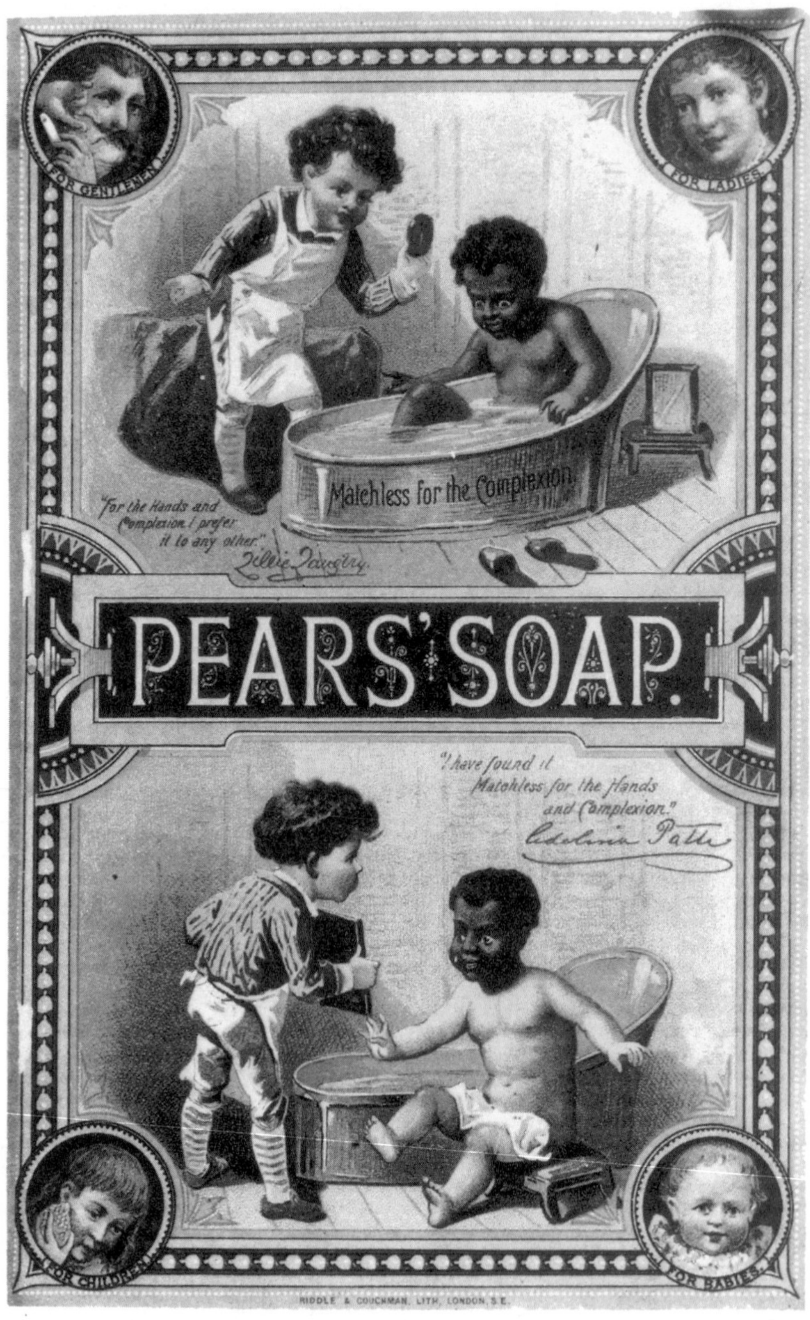

Figure 1.10 Pears' Soap Advertisement of the Victorian Period. Courtesy of Unilever.

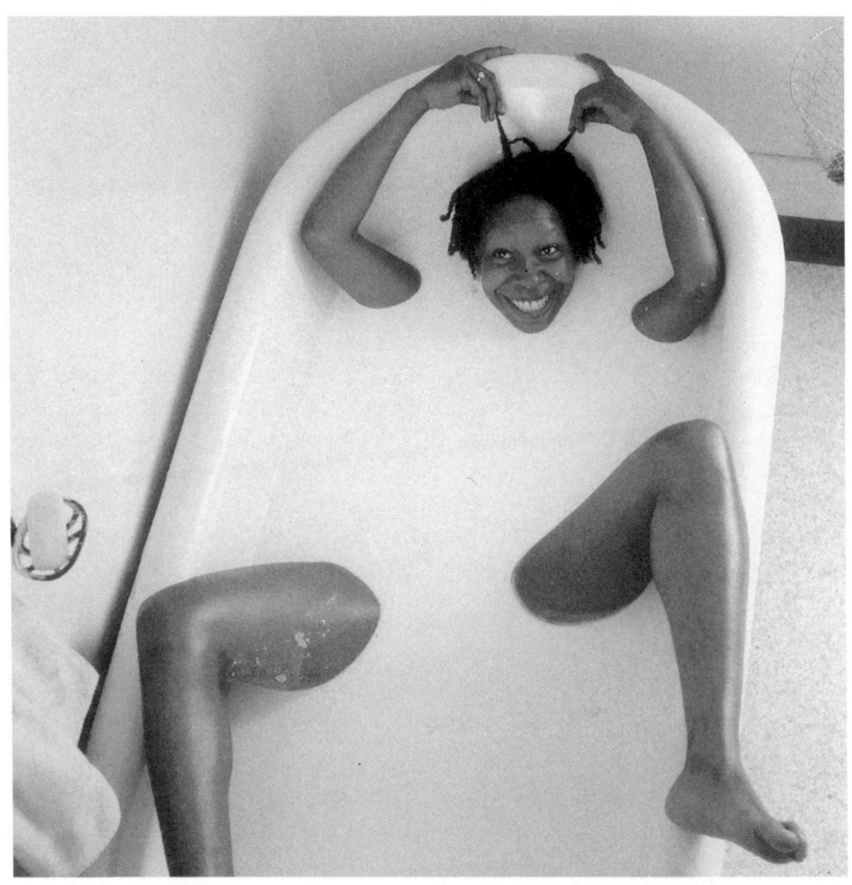

Figure 1.11 Annie Leibovitz, *Whoopi Goldberg*. Copyright © 1986 Annie Leibovitz/Contact Press Images.

acceptance and status. In "Limitations of Life" (1938), a parody of the very successful passing novel *Imitation of Life* (1933) by Fannie Hurst as well as its popular movie renditions, Hughes criticizes those conventions simply by transposing them. According to Hughes, the conventional passer of, say, Hurst's novel—a white wannabe—reinscribes the devaluation of blackness articulated by characters from Blake's "Little Black Boy" to Churchill's Joshua. What would happen if white people felt so ugly and worthless, so dependent on blacks for approval and financial success that they either dedicated themselves to serving blacks or attempted to transform themselves into blacks? What if the overvaluation of whiteness that causes blacks to pass as white were replaced by a privileging of blackness that motivated whites to try to turn black?[13]

In Hurst's popular tear-jerker, a large black woman named Delilah works as a domestic for a white woman and together they successfully market the pancakes Delilah makes; but in the process this twentieth-century mammy loses the affections of her very light-complexioned daughter who—somewhat like McKay's Angie Dove—seeks to pass as white and therefore will not recognize her mother until "too late": that is, Delilah's (ornate) funeral.[14] *The Bluest Eye* underlines the connection between Hurst's portrait of the passer and a racially marked ideal of (white) beauty when one of Morrison's characters confuses the name of the novel's heroine, Pecola, with the movie protagonist, Peola, the "mulatto girl [who] hates her mother 'cause she is black and ugly but then cries at the funeral" (67). Attempting to uncover the absurd racial assumptions of this maternal melodrama, Langston Hughes simply reverses racial markers. For Hughes, an imitation of whites leads to an imitation life for blacks that can only be understood as a limitation. He counters that limitation by switching the tables and producing a spoof that takes off on the image of a white Aunt Jemima on the box of pancake flour in Mammy Weaver's kitchen.

Wealthy Mammy Weaver (carrying a Metropolitan Opera program and speaking "perfect English with Oxford accent") is greeted in her elegant Harlem residence by blond Audette Aubert (Claudette Colbert played the passer in one of the movies), who falls all over herself in grateful servitude: "Mammy Weavers, ah been waintin' up for you-all. Ah thought you might like some nice hot pancakes before you-all went to bed" (656). Although Mammy, who has just come from the Mimo Club (where she dined on lobster à la Newburg), declines, she lets Audette rub her feet and sympathizes with the plight of her fair daughter who has been "lyin' out in de backyard in de sun all day long tannin' herself, ever day, tryin' so hard to be colored." When Audette is asked what she wants in exchange for all of her services—as nurse, cook, housekeeper, mother surrogate—this ideal domestic refuses a day off or a nice home of her own. Instead, all she wants "is a grand funeral when I die." What makes Delilah so very loveable in Hurst's *Imitation of Life*—a selflessness bordering on masochism in her service to whites—appears ludicrous when the races are switched around.[15] What makes Delilah's daughter a prototypical tragic mulatto—the contradiction between her "lowly" origins (the black mother) and her "high" aspirations (the white world)—seems equally absurd when played out through a character who seeks to pass as black.

Whereas Hughes's sketch uses humor, Adrienne Kennedy's experimental one-act play *Funnyhouse of a Negro* (1964) exploits surrealism to uncover the murderous logic of Western culture's racechange imperative. Its central character, Negro-Sarah, is haunted by ghostly white avatars of herself like the Duchess of Hapsburg and Queen Victoria Regina, surrogates who wish to be told "of a royal world where everything and everyone is white and there are no unfortunate black ones" because they "know" that "black is evil and has been from the beginning" (5). Wearing identical alabaster masks, both begin the play with "frizzy hair, unmistakably Negro kinky hair" (6), and both suffer the humiliation of alopecia. Negro-Sarah's original wish "not to be" and her ultimate fate as a suicide find their analogue in the baldness of her alter egos, for the falling out of wild kinky hair symbolizes the infantilization of black people (bald like babies), the castration of black people (shorn like Samson of power), the violation of black people (the rape of their locks), the disease of black people (suffering hair loss due to illness), and the premature decrepitude of black people (aging before their time).

If You're Black, Get Back

While some black characters seek to become white so as to gain privileges ("If you're white, you're right"), other white characters are turned black so they will understand and sympathize with the plight of those who are told "if you're black, get back." Just as Hughes's Audette Aubert exhibits the psychological masochism of the prototypically black mammy, just as Schuyler's fable concluded with white politicians suffering the fate (of lynching) more usually accorded blacks, a number of reform-minded writers attempted to educate whites about what Fanon called the "corporeal malediction" of color by presenting narratives of white-to-black racechanges that place racists in black people's shoes and thereby teach them that race matters most unfairly. Although the switch seems like a reversal—whites turning black instead of blacks turning white—it sometimes attests to the very same values, of whiteness and rightness, blackness and backness. An early and late example of this type of racechange—a story in Charles W. Chesnutt's *The Conjure Woman* (1899) and an episode in the musical comedy *Finian's Rainbow* (1947)—can stand here for liberal efforts to promote a kind of racial negative capability that would attenuate the virulence and violence of white supremacists. Yet, as in Schuyler's novel, blackness can remain anathema in this tradition, especially when it is inflicted as a punishment fitting the crimes of inhumane whites. Only when the boundaries separating black and white are perceived as demonstrably permeable does racial mutability lead to the undermining of race itself as a category.

Chesnutt's "Mars Jeems's Nightmare" is a tale told in dialect by the ex-slave Julius about a plantation owner whose cruelty leads one slave to consult "Aun' Penny, de free-nigger cunjuh 'oman" (76), who pounds up roots to be stirred into the master's okra soup. The next morning Master Jeems goes away on business, after describing to his overseer Master Johnson how his "niggers is gittin' monst'us triflin' en lazy en keerless" and advising his second-in-command "ter make a reco'd dat 'll show w'at kinder oberseah you is" (79). Naturally, Johnson takes this as a hint to overwork and underfeed the slaves. Predictably too, when a brash new slave is bought and brought to the house, Johnson responds to his backtalk and ineptitude by chaining, starving, beating, and finally selling him down river. Aunt Peggy is horrified to learn "'bout dis noo nigger bein' sol' 'erway" (87) and manages to get a conjured sweet potato to him just in time. The very next day, a transformed, repentant Master Jeems appears. Having suffered the "nightmare" of being the "noo nigger," he awakens a "noo man" (98), firing Johnson and making work bearable, play possible for his lucky slaves.

Though it may be difficult to determine how the spelling of "noo" marks a different pronunication of the word "new," clearly it is meant to stand for a visible mark of the difference vernacular makes. The frame tale—written in standard English—clarifies the elderly ex-slave-narrator's moral. At the beginning of Chesnutt's story, the white couple who find Julius's grandson careless, lazy, and untrustworthy fire the boy; after hearing about Master Jeems's nightmare, the wife decides to give the grandson another chance. Imagining the horror of Jeems's change from free master to abused slave makes it possible to think about the human subjectivity of blacks not only for the wife in the frame tale but also by extension for Chesnutt's white readers as well. Exactly this boon born of racechange occurs in *Finian's Rainbow*, where the racism of Senator Billboard Rawkins—played in the 1968 movie by Keenan Wynn—is punished when he is turned black and forced to experience the humiliations daily suffered by African Americans (Fig. 1.12).

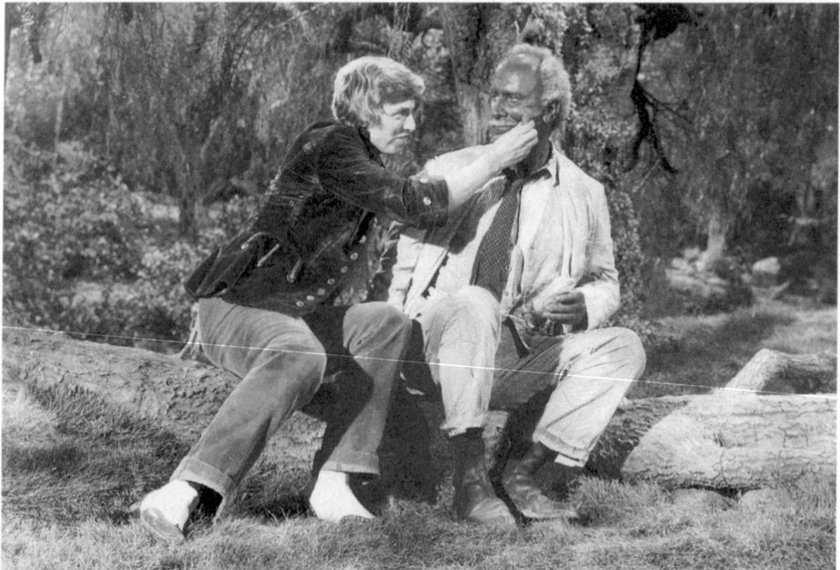

Figure 1.12 David Wayne and Keenan Wynn in *Finian's Rainbow* (1968). Courtesy of Museum of Modern Art Film Stills Archive.

Initially the bigoted master of an anachronistic Southern plantation, white Senator Rawkins had himself enforced a grotesque racechange upon his servants, one that turned proud African Americans into fawning darkies. When college-educated Howard took a job with the Senator, for example, the dark-skinned young man was taught how to act like a servile "boy." A white staff member set himself up as a role model—a kind of imitation Negro—for the new domestic by giving "a quick course in Southern-julep-serving, based on the minstrel tradition of Dixie shuffle and exaggerated accent": "Yousah julep, suh, Mr. Rawkins, suh, all frosted and minty—yawk, yawk!" Since a white man models black masculinity for an African American, racechange here, as elsewhere, questions authenticity, sincerity, and integrity, implying there is no single or stable racial identity. A black person is instructed to imitate a white counterfeiting blacks who are mimicking . . . . (A comparably vertiginous moment occurs in Douglas Sirk's version of *Imitation of Life* (1959) when a white actress pretending to be a light-skinned mulatto copies whites simulating blacks.)[16] In a fitting plot reversal, then, *Finian's Rainbow* manufactures a whimsical wish (magically implemented by a leprechaun) that triggers an epidermal metamorphosis, forcing the Senator to experience the vulnerability, injustice, and fear inflicted on blacks until he eventually manages to find happiness by joining a nomadic barbershop quartet. After the rapacious, mendacious Senator is subjected to the insults of discriminatory attitudes he had himself touted, he becomes a "better person," one who comprehends the injustice and arbitrariness of white supremacy.

As in Chesnutt's "Mars Jeems's Nightmare" and *Finian's Rainbow*, a racechanging script operates pedagogically to raise white consciousness about American racism in Melvin Van Peebles's movie *Watermelon Man* (1970). Here a white insurance salesman insensitive to racial injustice is played by (a heavily made-up) Godfrey Cambridge, who wakes up one night to the shocking realization that he has undergone a racial metamorphosis that proves to be longer and more disorienting than the "nightmare" he initially takes it to be. After various attempts at lightening his complexion fail—including milk baths that produce frames anticipating Annie Leibovitz's photo of Whoopi Goldberg (Fig. 1.13)—Cambridge suffers the indignities some African Americans commonly experience in everyday existence. Instead of his daily run for the bus being taken as a ritual sporting event, it immediately elicits the assumption of his criminality from neighbors and law enforcement officials alike. Because of his skin color, the Job-like Cambridge loses his children, his wife, his house, his job. At the end of the film, rage against injust persecution drives him to a mysterious room—a health club? a martial arts studio? a storeroom for janitors?—where he is last seen with a group of chanting black men brandishing mops and brooms in a quasi-African war ritual.

Precisely the advancing of racial consciousness that prompted Van Peebles's satire motivated the racechanges of two white journalists inspired by the civil rights movement. When in 1959 John Howard Griffin—and, later, following his example, Grace Halsell—traveled through the South as an African American, he was attempting to understand the nature of racial prejudice in this country: "How else except by becoming a Negro could a white man hope to learn the truth?" (7).

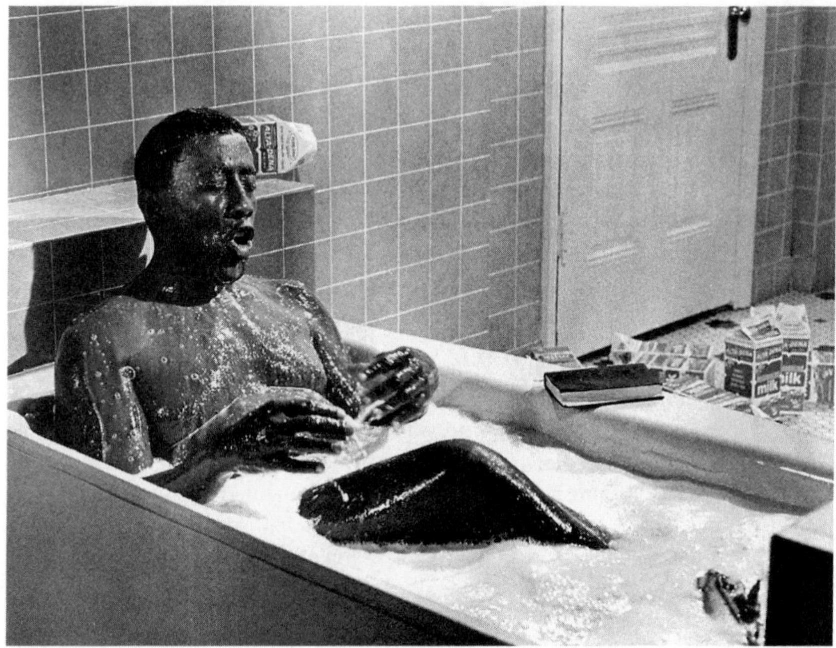

Figure 1.13 Godfrey Cambridge in *Watermelon Man* (1970). Courtesy of Photofest.

In *Black Like Me* (1961), one of the first and most commercially successful instances of so-called "new" journalism, Griffin recounted his use of a treatment developed for victims of vitiligo and of a skin stain to effect a transformation that seemed to "imprison" him in the dark "flesh of an utter stranger, an unsympathetic one with whom I felt no kinship" (15), a process presumably more effective than the burnt cork that hardly disguises white James Whitmore in the 1964 movie version of *Black Like Me* (Fig. 1.14). At times experiencing the invisibility of black citizens (too unimportant to be noticed), at times the hypervisibility of black citizens (too out of place to go unnoticed), Griffin became horrified, on the one hand, by the fact that "the Negro is part of the black mass, the white is always the individual" (48) and, on the other, by the racist "hate stare" (52), a look of passionate but eerily "unreasonable contempt" (87).

After Griffin returned to his white identity so as to publicize his findings, he was hung in effigy by anonymous members of his community: "a dummy, half black, half white, with [his] name on it and a yellow streak painted down its back, was hanging from the wire" (149). Later named a "lynching" (150), this ritual sacrifice implies that befriending African Americans subjects the white liberal to their fate. Of course the death and disappearance of a number of white civil rights activists in the sixties—most famously Michael Schwerner—drove home this point. Toni Morrison's *Beloved* (1987) makes a similar claim about white abolitionists during Civil War times: The egalitarian Edward Bodwin is termed a "bleached nigger" and his face is "shoe-blackened" by his proslavery enemies (260). About his own "experiment" in blackness, Griffin believed that according to most people "because I was a Negro for six weeks, I remained partly Negro or perhaps essentially Negro" (156). This perception helps explain both the strength and the weakness of *Black Like Me*'s journalistic experiment. For Griffin grounds his social critique on his evolving distrust of his own white privileges and of the depravity of vicious white stereotyping of African Americans; but the extraordinary popularity of a book that became a staple in junior high and high school classrooms depended upon Griffin's assumption that he could speak for black people and the persistence of white readers in assuming black people incapable of elaborating upon their own experiences (Wald, 154).

Grace Halsell—a White House staff writer during the Johnson administration—describes in *Soul Sister* (1969) a meeting she arranged with Griffin before her own journey, first to Harlem and later through Mississippi, as a black woman. At the time, in the spring of 1968, Griffin had undergone surgery because "certain bones were disappearing" which the doctors replaced with steel (21). Jokingly categorized as "a work of art" by his surgeon, Griffin did not attribute the disintegration of his bones to the doses of trimethyl psoralen or the exposure to ultraviolet rays he used for his racechange. Nor does Grace Halsell, who follows this same procedure to darken her skin. Yet after his death, a number of obituaries implied that Griffin had been slowly killed by the process he had undertaken to "pass over"

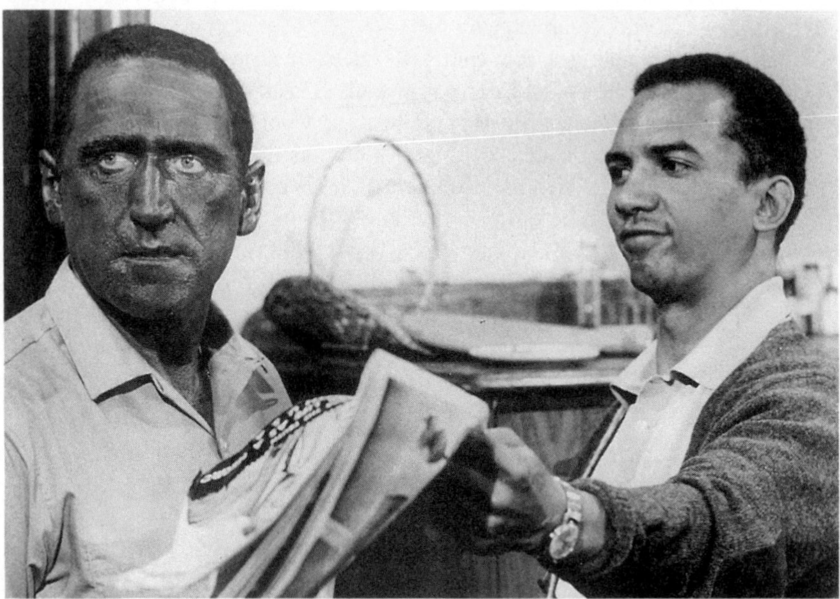

Figure 1.14 James Whitmore in *Black Like Me* (1964). Courtesy of Photofest.

(Griffin, 12), a phrase that associates passing with passing over from life to death or passing out. Perhaps rumors of Griffin's death-due-to-passing reflect a widespread belief that, as Isaac Julien has put it, "crossing racial lines usually results in punishment" (263), or, indeed, that it *should* result in punishment.

Certainly, before and after their passing episodes, both Griffin and Halsell suffered from a kind of racial schizophrenia. Like Halsell, who describes herself as "two persons" or a being "cast in a twin, paradoxical role of oppressor and oppressed," Griffin experienced himself as "two personalities, two sets of eyes, two bodies" containing "a single human heart in conflict with itself" (Halsell, 220–21). At least in part, their self-division derives from a conviction that "self-segrega[tion] . . . pains and cripples the white American . . . even more than the black American" (Halsell, 221). (Fanon also believed that "the Negro enslaved by his inferiority, the white man enslaved by his superiority alike behave in accordance with a neurotic orientation" (60)). Both Griffin and Halsell gain not only sympathy or understanding but a sense of community, profound societal insights, and a conviction of moral self-worth when "turned" black. Similarly, white Senator Rawkins in *Finian's Rainbow* was selfish, conniving, and cutthroat; however, black Rawkins gains in sympathy and love for his fellow creatures. Plus, he's got rhythm. (It was precisely the musicality of black communities that led Alan Lomax to put on blackface so he could accompany Zora Neale Hurston—the two thereby evading white authorities, not fooling African Americans—to collect material for the Music Division of the Library of Congress.[17]) When blackness is valued as intrinsically worthwhile or superior, racechange from white to black can be re-envisioned as a way to transform not only the individual conscience or consciousness but also our conceptualization of the major icons, myths, and institutions of European and American culture.

Rather than replicating a conventional system of representation that Others blacks, a number of artists and thinkers use cross-racial strategies to underline African cultural centrality in Western civilization. Countee Cullen's "The Black Christ" (1929) performs a racechange on Jesus, as do many paintings of the Harlem Renaissance in which the blackness of Jesus bespeaks his spiritual grace under inexplicable but murderous oppression.[18] From Jean-Paul Sartre's *Black Orpheus* (1963) to Angela Carter's *Black Venus* (1985), from Martin Bernal's *Black Athena* (1987, 1991) to China Galland's *Longing for Darkness: Tara and the Black Madonna* (1990), twentieth-century critical and creative speculations reinvent Western legends in such a way as to restructure our ideas about race and culture. The most ambitious of these—*Black Athena*—argues that Greek civilization resulted from Afroasiastic influences so that, for instance, the city name of Athens as well as the divinity Athena derive from Egyptian and Semitic sources. Rooted in black experience but reinvented by racist historians who wished to attribute the glory that was Greece to European or Aryan colonization, Western civilization itself, according to Bernal's widely acclaimed book, underwent an extraordinary whitewashing, a racechange from black to white.[19]

If the major myths of Europeans and Americans could be imagined as black stories, so might the founding narratives of popular culture. A number of modern musical productions have used racechange to ask, what differences does color make? Transforming *Carmen*'s cigarette factory and enthralling toreador in nineteenth-century Seville to a parachute factory and seductive fighter in twentieth-century America, *Carmen Jones* (1943, 1954 film) follows Bizet's script closely enough to suggest that the logic of erotic thralldom will work itself out inexorably on the lives of men and women, regardless of racial, geographic, or historical factors.[20] Just as Gilbert and Sullivan's *Mikado* (1885) had utilized racechange to spoof the English in the guise of the Japanese, two adaptions—entitled *The Swing Mikado* (1923) and *The Hot Mikado* (1939)—employed African-American performers to blast all notions of racial stereotyping, as did the the 1995 production mounted by David H. Bell, first for Washington, D.C.'s, Ford's Theatre and then for London's Queen's Theatre: blacks lampooning Brits playing Asians. When Frank Baum's *The Wonderful Wizard of Oz* (1900) and the Judy Garland film version surfaced on Broadway as *The Wiz* (1975), an all-black musical hit, some critics viewed Dorothy's trip from Kansas to the Emerald City as a metaphor for the great migration, the Wicked Witch of the West as a slave-mistress, the Emerald City as a superhip Harlem, and the Wiz himself as a hustling Sly Stone or Walt Frazier (Rollins). The use of black singers in the leading male roles of Peter Sellars' production of *Don Giovanni* (1991) engaged audiences in examining their preconceptions about race and promiscuity. Such exuberant transformations of white scripts redefine the color line that W.E.B. Du Bois saw as the central problem of the twentieth century as an inspiring opportunity for aesthetic innovation.

More focused on the unacknowledged creative contributions of African Americans to literary history, Shelley Fisher Fishkin's *Was Huck Black?* (1993) asks whether the model for Huck Finn's voice was a black child and thereby draws attention to the cross-racial lines of influence that Eric Sundquist sees at work in many of the most classic of nineteenth-century American texts, that Ann Douglas and George Hutchinson trace in the most modernist of twentieth-century American texts. For several decades, such speculations about hidden black roots have fueled discussions, for example, about artists like Beethoven, Alexander Pushkin, and Alexander Dumas. In a curious, three-volume meditation on *Sex and Race* (1944), the provocative cultural enquirer J. A. Rogers reproduced a painting of Beethoven as well as descriptions of his "swarthy" complexion and "flat broad nose" to argue that "there is not a single shred of evidence to support the belief that he was a white man neither from those who knew him nor from his biographers" (III: 306; Fig. 1.15). In more recent times, in a chapter of *White Man Listen!* (1957) devoted to "The Literature of the Negro in the United States," Richard Wright first claims that Pushkin and Dumas were "Negro" and then that, because they were fully integrated into their respective cultures, "no matter what the color of their skins, they were not really Negroes. One was a Russian, the other was a Frenchman" (75). Wright shows how arbitrary the color line is, how easily it can be abrogated.

Although an antithetical concern for recovering hidden racial roots may motivate the genealogist seeking to map her own family tree, this sort of a quest can also result in a conviction about the unreliability, permeability, or fictiveness of

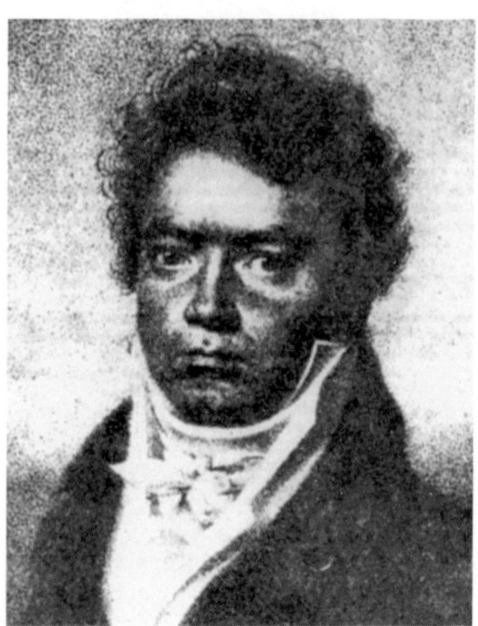

Figure 1.15 Portrait of Beethoven in J. A. Rogers, *Sex and Race* (1944).

racial labels. In "Passing for White, Passing for Black," the conceptual artist Adrian Piper describes any search into the ancestral past as "full of guesswork, false leads, blank spots and mysteries. For just as white Americans are largely ignorant of their African—usually maternal—ancestry, we blacks are often ignorant of our European—usually paternal—ancestry" (228). Such ignorance, at times (but certainly not always) an offshoot of the sexual exploitation of female slaves by white masters, may be more common than usually supposed. According to some geneticists, 95 percent of "white" Americans have varying degrees of black heritage and 75 percent of all "African" Americans have at least one white ancestor. In other words, concludes another genealogist named Shirlee Taylor Haizlip, "many Americans are not who they think they are; hundreds of thousands of white people in America are not 'white'" (15). For Piper, castigated as a "paleface" (216) by visibly black and white acquaintances alike, as for Haizlip, what happened in their families "calls into question the concept of color as a means of self-definition" (Haizlip, 15).

If "you look white, act white, live white, vacation white, go to school white, marry white and die white," perhaps race is "simply a matter of context," concludes Haizlip, while Piper wonders "whether the very idea of racial classification is a viable one," whether the concept of race might soon become "obsolete" (247).[21] A comparable argument for disentangling definitions of race from skin color is mounted by two contemporary scholars who also point to cases of mistaken racial identity. In 1982, a light-skinned plaintiff named Susie Guillory Phipps, who lived her life believing she was white, failed in her law suit against the Louisiana Bureau of Vita Record; the bureau refused to change the racial classification on her birth certificate from black to white. Michael Omi and Howard Winant conclude that the case "illustrates the inadequacy of claims that race is a mere matter of variations in human physiognomy, that it is simply a matter of skin color" (54). If this is so, then racial folk taxonomies based on complexion may soon become antiquated.[22] Unlike Homer Plessy and Walter White, who subscribed to the idea that they could only pretend to be white (because of the one-drop rule), the lawsuit of Phipps as well as the speculations of Haizlip and Piper intimate that the dangerous concept of race itself might be detonated when color no longer codes it. The indeterminacy of racial categories, breaking down either/or approaches to difference, would generate an appreciation of pan-ethnic, transracial persons of unclassifiable colors, fitting citizens of a syncretic society.

A technological analogue to such transgressive imaginings about racial mutability or pigment mutations beyond the confines of racial categories, the new computer program Morph (for metaMORPHosis) mixes features in such a way as to produce a picture of, say, Queen Elizabeth as a woman of color (Fig. 1.16).[23] The regal symbol of an empire upon which the sun would not set in the nineteenth century is melded through the magic of modern science with the physiognomy of those colonized. Similarly, like a number of United Colors of Benetton ads, the computer-generated, multicultural picture of Eve that appeared on the cover of *Time* magazine to illustrate America's "New Face" in the 1990s stressed the enticing glamor of ethnic diversity. The image produced by combining the features of Anglo-Saxons (15%), Middle Easterners (17.5%), Africans (17.5%), Asians (7.5%), Southern Europeans (35%), and Hispanics (7.5%) led one staff member to fall in love: "It really breaks my heart that she doesn't exist," exclaimed a journalist enthralled by this cybergenetic, multi-ethnic offspring (see color insert and Fig. 1.17).[24] Just as the chart of the 49 progeny produced from various combina-

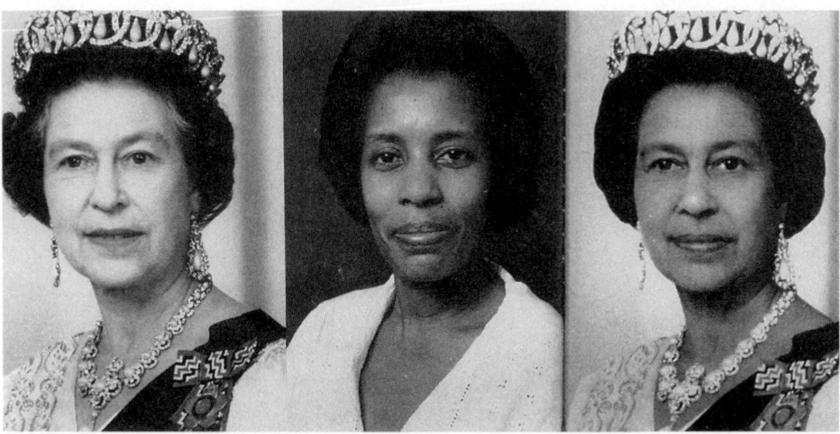

Figure 1.16 *The Morphing of Queen Elizabeth* (1994), courtesy of COLORS magazine (Issue #4 Race).

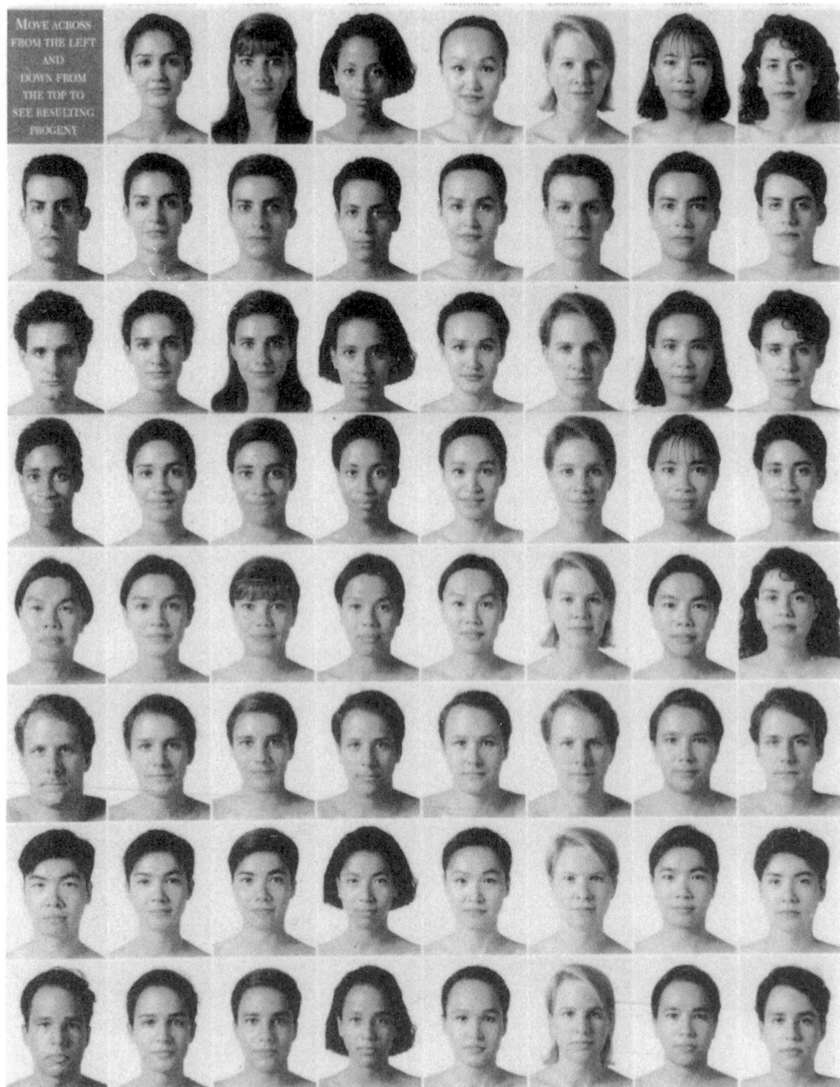

Figure 1.17 *Rebirth of a Nation* in *Time* magazine (Special Issue, Fall 1993). Courtesy of *Time* magazine.

tions of seven ethnicities is titled *Rebirth of a Nation* so as to establish itself as a retort to the racism of a founding film like *The Birth of a Nation*, the *Time* magazine cover seems to be subscribing to the moral conveyed not only by the morphed sequence of ethnic dancers in Michael Jackson's music video "Black or White" (1993) and the morphed Asian, Native-American, male, female, African-American, and Euro-American faces that conclude it but also by its take-home message: "Prejudice is ignorance."

Endeavoring to prove the speciousness of disabling racial pigeonholes, political pranksters had imagined such racial transformations long before they could be seen on a T.V. or computer screen. The earliest manifestation of Virginia Woolf's contempt for patriotism and militarism found expression in a racial masquerade that signaled her alienation from British imperialism. The so-called "*Dreadnought* hoax" occurred in 1910 when Woolf (then Virginia Stephen), her brother Adrian, and several of their friends dressed up as the emperor of Abyssinia and his entourage for an official inspection of one of the most famous ships in the British fleet (Fig. 1.18). The group was given a full tour of HMS *Dreadnought* and offered a twenty-one-gun salute as well as a Guard of Honour for their inspection. In native garb and blackface, Woolf the Abyssinian dignitary makes a mockery not only of a preeminent symbol of British military superiority but also of the rites and rituals of imperial etiquette, the pious inanities of ambassadorial amenities. Clearly the bold impudence of this send-up expresses the racial privilege of a group of intellectuals convinced of their right to take a holiday from whiteness so as to thumb their noses at even the highest authorities. Aware of the whiteness beneath the disguise, Woolf and her friends probably relished, on the one hand, the excitement of their hidden identities as British citizens and, on the other, the exhibition of the ex-

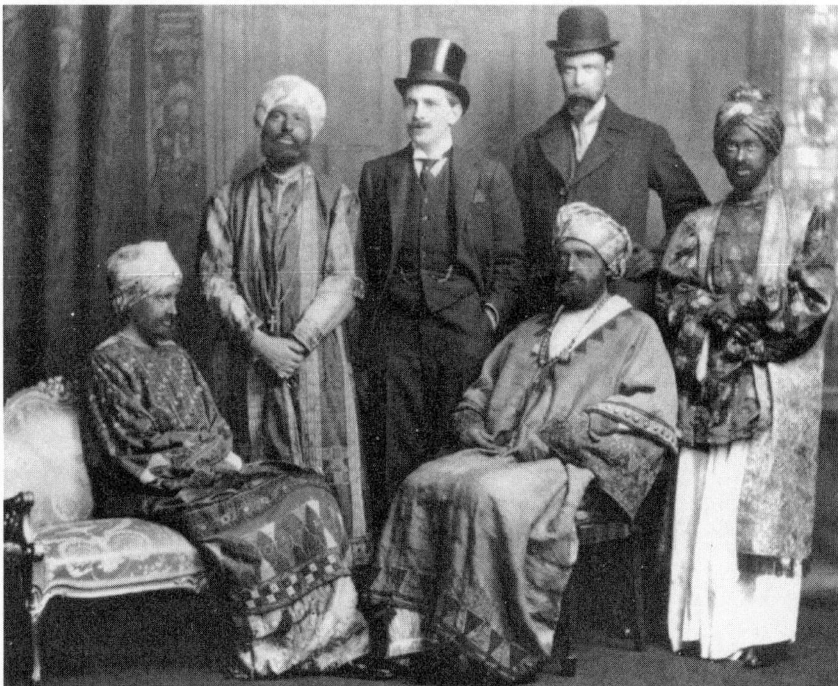

Figure 1.18 *The Emperor of Abyssinia and His Suite*, from the *Daily Mirror* (Wednesday, February 16, 1910). Standing, left to right: Guy Ridly, Horace de Vere Cole, Adrian Stephen, Duncan Grant. Seated, left to right: Virginia Stephen, Anthony Buxton.

oticized natives they enacted.[25] Still, presenting herself as the Other, the youthful writer established the anti-establishment sympathies that would fuel her subsequent pacifism and feminism.[26]

Anarchic or antic, the racechanger breaks taboos and pays the price with societal censure, as Woolf did, or with psychological self-division, as Griffin and Halsell did. However, what Griffin conceded in an afterword to his book—"The day was past when black people wanted any advice from white men" (177)—suggests that even the most high-minded, idealistic motivations will not save white impersonators of blackness from violating, appropriating, or compromising black subjectivity in a way that will inevitably rebound against the ethical integrity of whites, a point Dick Gregory makes in a racechanging parody of *Black Like Me* (Fig. 1.19). If *White Like You* is "the story of a Mississippi sharecropper who painted himself white and moved to Arizona" (wearing his patchwork overalls and toting watermelons), then perhaps *Black Like Me* presented just as blatant a counterfeit—even a stereotype—of African-American men.

Using the same title but skewed differently, Eddie Murphy's "White Like You" sketch for *Saturday Night Live* (1989) shows a made-up Murphy penetrating be-

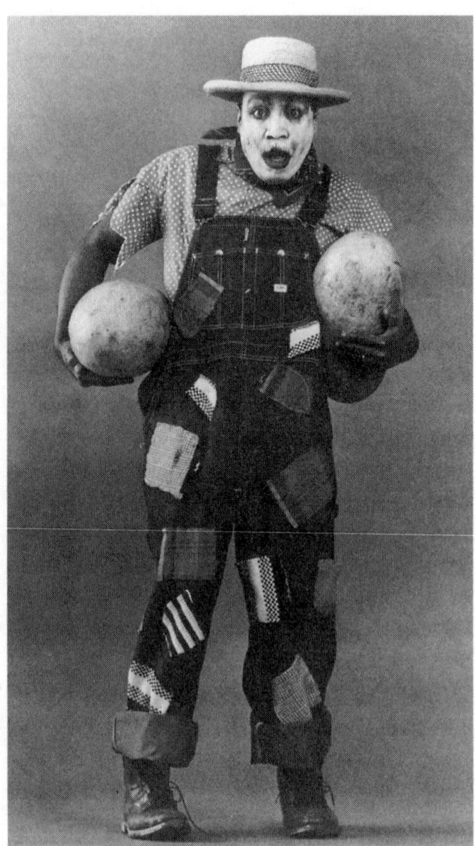

Figure 1.19 *White Like You*, from Dick Gregory, *What's Happening?* (Dutton 1965), photographs by Jerry Yulsman. Courtesy of Dick Gregory.

hind the facades erected before black people to understand that whites bond with each other, support each other, acclaim each other as if they were members of a club or a conspiracy. For example, the whitefaced Murphy boards a bus on which only one visibly black passenger sits surrounded by silent commuters ignoring each other; as soon as the black gets off, all the whites turn to each other and begin partying, leading Murphy to speculate that all his friends should resort to cosmetics as well. One of Langston Hughes's short sketches, "Who's Passing for Who?" (1952), is equally sardonic, though in his case about the uncertainty and indeterminacy racial masquerades spawn and also the asymmetrical racial values that make passing morally acceptable only for blacks, never for whites. Whether or not whites pretend to be black in order to learn more about the mores and morals of African-American communities, according to Hughes, the counterfeit is a cheat that robs black people of their dignity and their right to privacy.

In a Harlem club, Hughes describes how he and his friends encountered some white people visiting from Iowa. When a brown-skinned man knocks down a blond woman, the red-haired man from Iowa gets up to protect her; however, he stops when he is informed "she's colored" (31). Hughes's companions are horrified that the Iowa man wouldn't defend a woman from a brute, "no matter what race she may be" (32), and banish him from the cabaret. After some speculation that the abused woman might have been "just passing for colored" and a discussion of several passing novels by Harlem Renaissance writers, the remaining white couple explain that they have "just been *passing* for white for the last fifteen years" (33) so as to make more money. "All at once," Hughes explains, "we dropped our professionally selfconscious 'Negro' manners . . . and kidded freely like colored folks do when there are no white folks around" (33). At the end of the episode, as they are getting into a cab, the tourists explain that they are really white: "We just thought we'd kid you by passing for colored a little while—just as you said Negroes sometimes pass for white." Not knowing which way he and his friends have been fooled, Hughes ends on an uneasy note:

> Were they really white—passing for colored? Or colored—passing for white?
>
> Whatever race they were, they had had too much fun at our expense—even if they did pay for the drinks.

Who is conned by whom and for what purpose? Hughes implies that it is one thing for blacks to impersonate whites, quite another for whites to masquerade as blacks. He feels exploited, his culture invaded and spied upon, his authenticity at risk. And of course he is addressing a taboo still very much with us. Eddie Murphy elicits laughs when he uses the satiric tradition of racechange to impersonate Mr. Rogers in his parodic "Mr. Robinson's Neighborhood." Asking little boy and girl viewers if they know the meaning of two important words in the 'hood, he pulls on his cardigan, laces his shoes, faces the camera, and earnestly mouths the phrase "Eviction Notice." Even when Eddie Murphy puts on white make-up, it only signals a kind of antic clownishness, as in the photograph of Dick Gregory;[27] however, the minstrel in blackface remains a taboo emblem of reactionary white supremacy whose shock value was seriously underestimated recently by a companion of Whoopi Goldberg. Despite the imprimatur of Goldberg and the anything-goes atmosphere of a Friars Club roast, the actor Ted Danson could not get away with a Jolsonesque appearance in blackface that caused talk show host Montel Williams to view the event as a rally for the KKK and that led New York City Mayor David Dinkins to protest jokes "way over the line" (*Times*, Oct. 12, 1993).[28]

Perhaps the title of Fanon's classic attack on racism, *Black Skin, White Masks*, explains this asymmetry by suggesting that black-skinned people have to wear white masks. "[N]ot only must the black man be black," Fanon claimed; "he must be black in relation to the white man." And to those who would argue that this proposition has a converse, Fanon replied emphatically, "this is false. The black man has no ontological resistance in the eyes of the white man" (110). Despite Fanon's characteristic erasure of the black woman, he astutely maps in racial terms the difference that clusters around the issue of volition or agency. Ellen Craft needed to pass in order to obtain her freedom, whereas Virginia Woolf did so in a puckish prank; McKay's and Schuyler's characters can obtain life and latitude only by being black no more, while Hughes's Harlem tourists are motivated merely by a titillating voyeurism. In other words, racial impersonation and masquerading are a destiny imposed on colonized black people who *must* wear the white mask—of customs and values, of norms and languages, of aesthetic standards and religious ideologies—created and enforced by an alien civilization. "We wear the mask that grins and lies, / It hides our cheeks and shades our eyes,—": Paul Laurence Dunbar's poem speaks for the heroine of Jessie Fauset's *There Is Confusion* (1924), who can dance the part of America on a Broadway stage only if she wears a white mask, and for the black actors of Jean Genet's *The Blacks* (1960), whose imposed white masks hardly conceal but effectively intensify their racial rage.

A sardonic photograph that illuminates the title of James Clifford's *The Predicament of Culture: Twentieth-Century Ethnography, Literature, and Art* (1988) can serve here to summarize Fanon's, Dunbar's, Fauset's, and Genet's point. "*White Man*" (1982), which the author originally placed between the introduction and the first chapter, now graces the cover of the paperback edition (Fig. 1.20). Herbert M. Cole's picture displays a black man sardonically masquerading as a white man. The dark hands of the marginalized Nigerian hold a pencil and notebook to record African customs. The covered face of the subject—strikingly similar to the draped and thus blinded heads of René Magritte's portrait of a kiss joining two curtained, faceless lovers in *Les amants* (*The Lovers*) (1928)—has rendered Cole's subject invisible, silenced, even criminalized in his concealment. Astride a kerchief tied around the black man's brow rides the white man's head, a kind of amiably arrogant figurehead or hood ornament featuring the power of the white man's implacable gaze under a Doctor-Livingston-I-Presume hat. Like Fanon, this black-turned-white racechanger might think about himself, "There is no help for it: I am a white man. For unconsciously I distrust what is black in me, that is, the whole of my being" (191).

At the same time, however, the impersonator uses his face-change ironically as a weapon or retaliation against his colonization. Clearly the Doctor-Livingston observer-recorder is a satiric portrait of The Anthropologist whose geographical

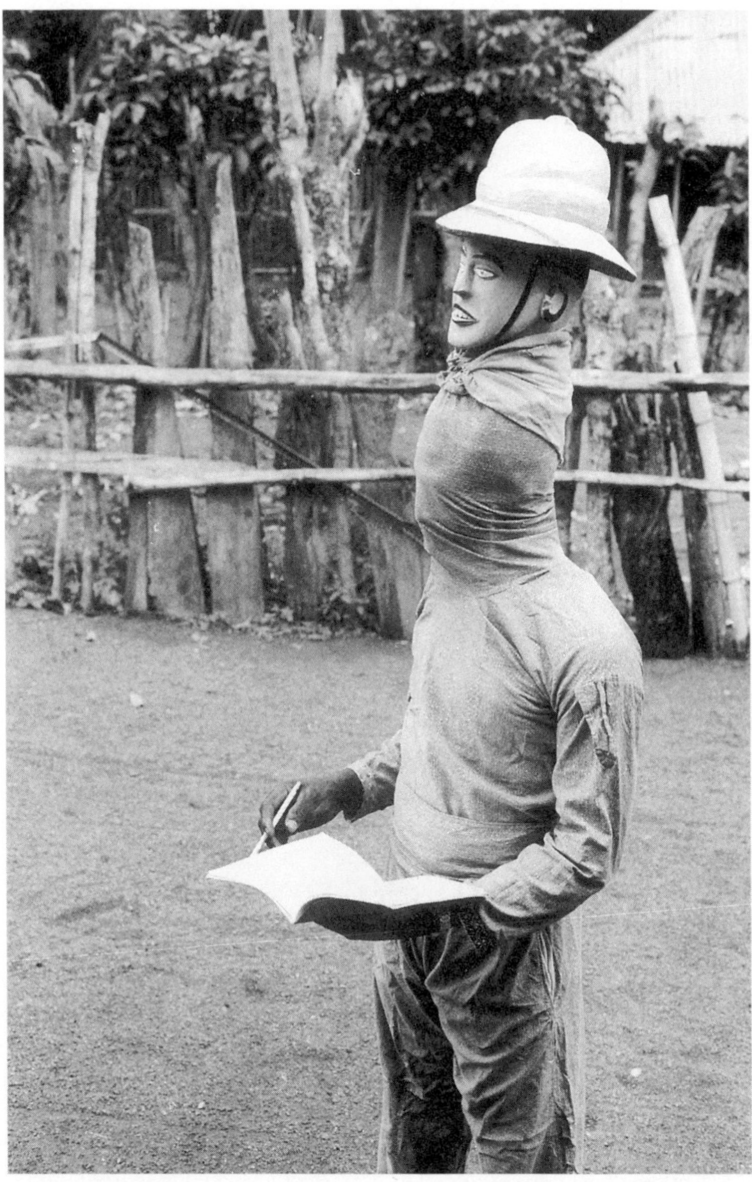

Figure 1.20 Herbert M. Cole, *White Man*, photograph of Onyeocha, a performer at Igbo masquerades, south-east Nigeria (1982). Courtesy of Herbert M. Cole and UCLA Museum of Cultural History.

and authorial incursions name and colonize the "exotic" or "native" or "primitive" Other. The hierarchical connection between the white explorer-author and the muffled black head reflects a relationship of dominance that entombs black reality even as it inscribes it. Bearing the white man as his burden, the black man is effaced by the colonizer, though it is possible to see a retaliation at work here, for whiteness appears impaled on the stake of the black body. The very concept "white man" depends on the subordinated black body, a point that helps illuminate the extraordinary importance of racial impersonation in the evolution of Western art produced by and for whites. Not an image of complementarity like the Janiform vase, Cole's picture captures a profoundly ambiguous and unstable imbalance buttressed throughout several centuries of global history: the black man elevating himself to the white man he mocks; the white man dependent on the black man he surmounts.

The Ethics of Racechange

What does it mean for the white scholar to enter into the intellectual marketplace of the skin trade? Is the critic of racechange—like The Anthropologist—guilty of silencing black subjects or is she an apologist for white co-optation of black culture? As the Igbo masquerade hints, the predicament of Western culture consists in its appropriation not only of black physical bodies but also of muffled black presences. The ambivalent twoness of the Janiform vase is hierarchized here, the black subordinated to the white. Certainly, too, the white-to-black racechanges to be analyzed in the subsequent chapters of this book contributed to the silencing and objectification of black people. Even though, as the preceding sections of this introduction attempted to show, a "white skin, black face" scenario could work toward libertarian ends, most people today would agree with John Howard Griffin and Langston Hughes that the time for racial impostures has passed. Yet because we have become a society more aware of how insulting such impersonations can be, the time for studying racial imitations has now begun.

For if the concept of whiteness depends—as Cole's image suggests it does—on the appropriation of black beings, then perhaps one of the predicaments of white culture has resided in its blindness about its dependency on represented (and thus effaced) black bodies. Although taboos against white impersonations of blackness need to be understood, they should not stop us from appreciating the extent to which twentieth-century Western culture is indebted to African and African-American tropes, images, mimicries, and masks. "The Negro is comparison" (211), Fanon argues elsewhere in *Black Skin, White Masks*, again insisting that this comparison is one inflicted only on black consciousness; however, we shall see that at certain moments the white person must be white in relation to the black, that the "Negro is comparison" for whites, even if (perhaps especially when) blacks have no ontological resistance in the eyes of whites.[29]

One of Fanon's most interesting interpreters, Homi Bhabha, puts it this way:

> The representative figure of [colonial] perversion . . . is the image of post-Enlightenment man tethered to, *not* confronted by, his dark reflection, the shadow of colonized

> man, that splits his presence, distorts his outline, breaches his boundaries, repeats his action at a distance, disturbs and divides the very time of his being. (44)

The staging of the ambivalence of the colonizer cannot be conflated with the performance of the ambivalence of the colonized; however, the recurrence of racechange allows us to see the extent to which Euro-Americans remained tethered to a dark reflection that splits and distorts their being. Although impersonation has functioned as a fate imposed upon or a strategy adopted by the disempowered, it has also operated as a means or method of disempowering others, of Othering others.[30] Indeed, the long history of racechange demonstrates that no single effect, no simple ideology can be said to emanate from a trope that embodies the slipperiness of metamorphosis in its adoptions or adaptions as well as in its historical evolution.

Hemingway's darkening heroine in *The Garden of Eden* (who tries to transform herself into an "African girl") is the character deployed by Toni Morrison to conclude her brilliant critical book, *Playing in the Dark* (1992), a summons for critics to study the uses to which dark and light images have been put by the white imagination. Responses to Morrison's call, the chapters that follow set out to understand the psychological, aesthetic, and ethical dimensions of cross-racial mimicry and imagery in the American canon. Yet, from antiquity to present times, Western culture's fascination with racial imitation, transformation, and mutability has gone unnoted because of embarrassment at what we have rightly been taught to view as racist activity and because of generalized discomfort over images that invoke while breaching conventional boundaries.[31] On the one hand, cross-racial masquerades rely upon strategies of commodification that have historically been used by whites to subordinate people of color; and, on the other hand, they disturb not only those who wish to police the parameters of racial categories (keeping black and white in strictly segregated separate spheres) but also those who wish to eradicate altogether the demarcations of racial categories (draining the very terms "black" and "white" of efficacy). In short, such racechanges have remained largely invisible because characters like Hemingway's blond African could trace their genealogical ancestry back to the minstrel and because of a recent theoretical emphasis on the fictionality of all racial categories.

To take this last matter first, a study of cross-racial impersonation may appear vexed from the perspective of current critical efforts to underscore the diversity of ethnicities and the social construction of race, for recent scholarship has tended to view stable racial categories as essentialist or biologistic, smacking (in other words) of the racism that put racial vocabularies into place during the Enlightenment.[32] At least in part to consolidate the so-called rainbow coalition of multi-hued people, "color" has recently made a comeback in popular as well as critical parlance, returning after "colored" gave way to "Negro," "Negro" to "black," "black" to "Afro-American," and "Afro-American" to "African American." Henry Louis Gates's "personal statement" for his Yale application nicely captures the rapidity of changing fashions of nomenclature: "My grandfather was colored, my father was Negro, and I am black," explained the now prominent spokesperson for

"Afro-American Studies" (in an account included in his recent memoir, significantly entitled *Colored People* (201)).

How can we write or speak about "black" and "white," proponents of the rainbow coalition might ask, in the context of Egyptian, Armenian, Sri Lankan, or Jamaican ethnicities? Some time ago, Joel Williamson expressed it this way: "There are, essentially, no such things as 'black' people or 'white' people" (522). As Robyn Wiegman—speculating about racial categories rendered "real" through "naturalizing" descriptions of the body—puts it, "making the African 'black' reduces the racial meanings attached to flesh to a binary structure of vision," thus imprisoning African Americans in a "prisonhouse of epidermal inferiority" (4, 11).[33] Given the empirical unreality of black and white, don't many of us feel the way the autobiographical writer Jane Lazarre does when she experiences herself as either "colorless" or "multicolored, some combination outside the known spectrum with no name to hold [us] down"? (*Worlds*, xiv). "Color" may be in vogue because it rejects the lure of ethnic absolutism, accepting in its stead (an also now fashionable) hybridity or plurality.

However, I do not restrict myself to the more stylish of these words because I seek to consider the imaginative prevalence black-and-white racial polarities have attained in modern culture. Curiously, an obsession with "racial purity" or "racial authenticity" has characterized not only right-wing fascist rhetoric in the twentieth century but also left-wing civil rights politics. Although such biologically and nationally based concepts of racial difference have been dubbed essentialist by contemporary theorists,[34] recent descriptions of the social construction of race sometimes seem too facile, or so a growing number of sophisticated interlocutors in the conversation about racial politics have begun to realize.[35] As Diana Fuss has argued, race—"a variable and flexible term"—may work "as a political concept" even when it is known to be "a biological fiction" (*Essentially Speaking*, 91). Neither an illusion nor a fact, race operates in a manner similar to gender—as a complex of meanings transformed by political frameworks.[36] Though race may be a fiction, in other words, it remains what Wallace Stevens called a Supreme Fiction that has exploited the corporeal body to put in place, sustain, and justify powerful systems of inequality. In both political and aesthetic realms, an iconography of ethnic absolutism has been abrogated and sustained by cross-racial intermixing, creolization, and impersonation. Drawing on a growing corpus of work on the racial significance of whiteness, I use the terms "black" and "white" throughout this book to accentuate the persistent power these categories have continued to exert, a power that speaks to the recalcitrance of the Western imagination, its recondite refusal to heed demythologists of racial definitions.[37] One major way the African was "made" black, in other words, was achieved through a series of racechanges undertaken by performers and artists who established whiteness as an escape from "the prisonhouse of epidermal inferiority" (Wiegman, 11).

But if the language of this study proves dated, what could be more anachronistic or retrograde than one of its primary subjects: whites masquerading as blacks? The second inhibition related to this study, then, pertains to the historical origins of whites' impersonations of blacks. The first channel white masquerades of blackness took, minstrelsy founded American entertainment by turning African Americans into figures of fun. No wonder that one of the most brilliant scholars of racial impersonation has claimed that almost any approach to this subject remains suspect: "To attack blackface (who would now defend it?)," Michael Rogin has speculated, "may simply be another way of putting it on" ("Blackface, White Noise," 438). What seems particularly ghastly about minstrelsy, of course, is that this white impersonation of blackness refuses black people intellectual agency or cognitive capacity.

In a 1992 radio interview about the importance of representation, Paule Marshall explained, "Once you see yourself truthfully depicted, you have a sense of your right to be in the world" (Funderburg, 9). Conversely, many racechange performances teach a cruel lesson to black audiences. When you repeatedly see yourself falsely depicted, you have no sense of your right to be in the world, or, indeed, you gain a conviction that you cannot, do not, should not exist. At its most sinister, in blackface performances, racechange taught precisely this lesson, for the white actor in burnt cork obsessively erased black subjectivity in a guilty reenactment of the murderous dynamics at work in a racist society. Yet simply to ignore cross-racial masquerades because they are psychologically damaging is, on the one hand, to miss an opportunity to examine one of the most pervasive and influential modes of racism in Western culture and, on the other, to lose the chance of understanding the different ideological work done by racial representation. As ethically disturbing as they are, such white masquerades of blackness nevertheless have had a checkered past that clarifies not only the dynamics of racial stereotyping and the psychology of racism but also the creative impact of race on the Anglo-American imagination.

Paradoxically, modernist racechange—so often subversive in its intent, so often avant-garde in its setting—finds its historical roots in exceptionally popular and virulently racist entertainments undertaken primarily by and for white men. In the commercially successful and technologically innovative movies featuring blackface actors that are analyzed in the second chapter of this book, minstrel and vaudeville traditions produce a gratingly abrasive compound of aesthetically fascinating but ethical repulsive scripts. The remaining pages of *Racechanges*—attending to the tendency of male artists to approach the subject through dramatic forms of impersonation while women of letters for the most part remain more absorbed by issues of lineage and inheritance—recount various artistic efforts of twentieth-century artists to grapple with the Othering blackface symbolically inflicted on African Americans. Like Man Ray and Hannah Höch, the African-American artists discussed in Chapter 3 attempted (in different ways and with varying degrees of success) to right the wrong of white privilege in the 1920s, in the case of the Harlem Renaissance thinkers by creating myths of racial origin that explained (without justifying) the historical fact of white supremacy. In Chapter 4, I discuss their white contemporaries, modernists who used black talk as back talk, exploiting cross-racial ventriloquism to establish—and then question—their identification with what had been rendered Other by their own culture.

The last two chapters concentrate more explicitly on the interactive influences of race and gender in racechange scripts. Especially in the period after World War II, I argue in Chapter 5, white men and women of letters pathologized and eroticized the black man—on whom was projected a criminalized yet alluring form of masculinism. Because white men and women of letters oscillated between wanting to become and wishing to have such a figure, their work tends to link the blurring of racial borderlines with the transgressive collapsing of homosexual and heterosexual categories. At the same time, as the last chapter demonstrates, birth stories about new breeds composed of mixed races enabled a host of writers to focus on mothers of one race giving birth to babies that look like they belong to another so as to see what the racechanged baby's reception might tell us about the possibilities of a post-racist society. That my meditations on the libertarian potentiality of racechange consistently encountered discouragingly recalcitrant scripts made it necessary to append the final chapter, a postscript in which I speculate that—despite its contributions to racist totalizing—racechange continues to hold out an aesthetic possibility of bridging the gap between blacks and whites.

What does it mean that racechange informs the most retrograde and the most revolutionary—the most conventional and the most experimental—works of art in the twentieth century? Whether as a manifestation of guilt, a form of pleasure, or a kind of guilty pleasure, white privilege plays itself out through almost obsessive racial masquerading. That the minstrel tradition established the parameters of racechange in America, a tradition shockingly incompatible with the benign impartiality of the Tarquinian urn and its equivocal faces, suggests the impossibility of collapsing the aesthetically pleasurable into the ethically acceptable or of associating racial impersonation with any monolithic ideological design—or, for that matter, of defining racism itself as a monochromatic phenomenon. Given what Homi Bhabha calls "the *ambivalence* of mimicry" (86), we need to understand white masquerades as a mockery of and menace to the Other, as an assertion of difference, but also a form of competition, as an admission of resemblance, a gesture of identification or solidarity, even a mode of self-mockery. Or so the centrality of Jews in the history of racechange—as performers and writers—will illustrate. For, just as Simone de Beauvoir began *The Second Sex* not only by comparing "the situation of woman and that of the Negro"—"the eternal feminine" with the "black soul"—but also by likening both with the situation of "the Jew" and "the Jewish character" (xxiii), racechanging conventions enabled artists from manifold traditions to relate nuanced comparative stories about various modes and gradations of Othering.

America's first national theater, first talking pictures, first radio shows, and first "new" journalism as well as Europe's first experimental literature, painting, and photography: All were marked by various forms of cross-racial performance, most frequently whites masquerading as Africans or African Americans. Historically, white *posing* counters black *passing*. Often, in other words, the white poser flagrantly exhibits the artifice of the performance, its theatrical falsity, while the black passer seeks to screen or camouflage signs of a discrepancy between hidden identity and outer appearance. Unlike the "passing" tradition, in which African Americans attempted to produce mimetically realistic replicas of Euro-Americans, whites posing as blacks often emphasized the spurious or ersatz caricature they created. Like the complicated motives of minstrelsy described by Eric Lott, nineteenth-century extravaganzas that both mock and celebrate the power of blacks, racial impersonations in the twentieth century stage white ambivalence about African Americans and their culture. The critic Susan Willis has speculated that "blackface is a metaphor for the commodity" (189) and we will see that blackface in the movies, blackface on the black faces of African-American Broadway entertainers, and various aesthetic transmutations of blackface flirt with even as they defend against the black Other, who becomes a kind of commodity fetish for white people.[38] To the fetishized, the process can only be perplexing, posing problems for real human beings harnessed to or assimilated into weirdly evocative images and stereotypes. However, for those whites shopping not only in low but also in high cultural markets, the shifting, shifty images of the fetish adorn the closet where the self slips on, tries out, purchases, or discards the outrageous costumes of its various incarnations. Unlike black people, who often had to adopt white masks to gain their rights and privileges, white people have chosen various modalities of racial impersonation, which in the course of the century have evolved from mockery to mimicry to an emphasis on inter-racial mutuality and mutability—not replacing mockery with mimicry or mimicry with mutuality but eventually playing out all three modes. More specifically, *Racechanges* traces an evolution from the mean mockery of blackface in the movies through the adulatory mimicry of the ersatz primitivism found in modernist verse and fiction, from the confused erotics of black envy during the post-World War II period to the loving emphasis on inter-racial mutuality at work in contemporary narratives of the mixed child.

That white artists continue to be fascinated with the permeable boundaries of racial markers means that their work documents their indebtedness to African-American culture. A consideration of white appropriation of black images therefore uncovers the extent to which mainstream American culture, no longer Anglo-American, has moved in the course of this century to becoming not only indebted to black aesthetic forms and traditions but itself profoundly African American.[39] Such a fusion holds out the promise of future reciprocity and respect, in the place of past thievery and scorn. A post-racist society cannot possibly come into being until Americans comprehend how the dualism of "black" versus "white" has operated to hide the cross-racial dynamics of our interwoven cultural pasts. To some extent, as we have seen, *COLORS*' computerized photo of a black Queen Elizabeth, Michael Jackson's morphed multi-ethnic sequence of faces in his instantaneously popular 1993 music video, and *Time*'s computerized portrait of a cybergenetic Eve dramatize racial merging as well as the reconfiguration of ideas about race. Indeed, a wish to celebrate a multi-ethnic diversity that would facilitate the "Rebirth of a Nation" informs all these "Morphies," whose eyes and lips, skin and hair represent 50–50 combinations of the physical characteristics of their African or Asian, Hispanic or Anglo-Saxon progenitors. Despite the recycling of such tried and tired terms as "Queen of the Empire" and "Eve," morphing postulates a visual elasticity beyond racial dualism, encouraging viewers to consider the ramifications of appreciating color divested of the category of race. The electronic melding of images produces perceivably new, transracial beings that resist old racial categories.

It would be wrong to conclude this first chapter on such an optimistic note, however. For even at its most utopian, racechange often fails to dislodge psychological and aesthetic structures generated by what Winthrop Jordan's title calls the prevailing arrangement of *White Over Black*. Although Michael Jackson overtly advertised his music video "Black or White" as an attack on prejudice, network officials objected to the violence of its conclusion and therefore cut footage of the superstar taking a crowbar and smashing car and store windows (bearing fascist and racist graffiti). And as sagacious a thinker as Donna Haraway found herself plummeted into "a dyspeptic attack of political correctness" upon gazing on the *Time* cover bearing the new Eve's face (364). Judging "the sense of utter homogeneity that emanates from *Time*'s matrix of diversity" nothing but "numbing," Haraway protests against its "evacuation of histories of domination and resistance," equates it with "the replicants for sale" in the futuristic movie *Blade Runner* (1989), and argues that this Eve "ensures the difference of no difference in the human family" (366). By emphasizing especially in its African and Hispanic faces blended or moderated skin tones as well as mostly Caucasian features, the genealogy of *Time*'s cybernetic cover girl hints that her creators eschew extremes as unattractive. Similarly, Patricia J. Williams looked at the depiction of Queen Elizabeth as a black woman (and other Benetton ads in which "the Pope becomes Chinese, Arnold Schwartzenegger becomes 'a negro'") to wonder at "this sifting through the jumbled jewelry box of cultural assets, selected body parts, and just the right accessories": Do such assemblages signify "the whole self" or the disembodiment of "No one"? (*Rooster's Egg*, 242–43).

Probably the most brilliant painter to exploit racechange, Robert Colescott, would endorse Haraway's and Williams's skepticism, for he proves just how far off the promised end of a post-racist society remains in his two most satiric works: *Eat Dem Taters* (1975) and *George Washington Carver Crossing the Delaware: Page from an American History Textbook* (1975). The first of these, a racechanged version of Van Gogh's *The Potato Eaters* (1885), hints at theft by reminding us of what one critic calls "the already Negroid features of the down-trodden peasants" in the original (Sims, 4, see color insert). Not simply a picture of the parallel oppressions of black sharecroppers and European peasants, Colescott's painting proves that the exploitation of the European peasant received its due in the dignified portrait produced by Van Gogh; however, American blacks suffer the added indignity of a representation that scornfully presents them happily embracing their impoverishment. The characters seated around the table in *Eat Dem Taters* look less like African Americans, more like white minstrels' depictions of African Americans. Similarly, in *George Washington Carver Crossing the Delaware: Page from an American History Textbook* (see color insert), the cook and the banjo player, the fisherman and the drunkard, and the wench displaying her bare bottom recall the characters of minstrelsy.

While Emanuel Leutze's original, *Washington Crossing the Delaware* (1851), testifies to the historic liberation of America by its first national leader, Colescott's parody takes one of the few black men to enter the history books—George Washington Carver—and places him in a ship of fools; that is, among the African Americans more often taught to whites: "the menial workers—Stepin Fetchits, Aunt Jemimas, boot blacks," in Colescott's words (Sims, 4). With its river so allusive of freedom and its cottony ice flows, the contemporary parody of *Washington Crossing the Delaware* contrasts the myth of freedom established by the founding fathers with the reality of slavery, even as it slyly hints that minstrelsy's version of African Americans provided the founding origins of American culture. Taken together, both of Colescott's racechanged paintings address African-American impoverishment as poverty and as the deprivation inflicted by degrading representations. At the same time, Colescott points a finger at the aesthetic past, reminding us that black figures have been marginalized and exploited as symbols or caricatures in the great masterpieces of Western civilization. Through the use of comic book images and parodic narration, post-modernist or in-your-face arrogation becomes a way of subverting earlier, clandestine appropriations of the African-American body, but it also provides a vehicle for placing African-American figures at the very center of the history of Western art and of American culture.

Yet what would happen if we approached Colescott's canvases without knowledge of his racial identity? Wouldn't they appear to be deeply unethical in their stereotyping of African Americans? This is precisely the question racechanging productions often pose as well as the query Henry Louis Gates, Jr., encourages us to ask in his provocative essay on "'Authenticity,' or the Lesson of *Little Tree*," which starts off with the irony that the best-selling *Education of Little Tree* was touted and taught in Native American literature courses as a true story composed by the grandson of Cherokees until it was discovered that the pseudonym Forrest Carter hid one Asa Earl Carter, a Ku Klux Klan terrorist and author of Governor George Wallace's famous speech "Segregation now . . . Segregation tomorrow . . . Segregation forever." From white abolitionists who composed ersatz slave narratives to the many male novelists who wrote not only about but through the consciousness of their heroines, authorly interlopers have refused to heed any border patrols in the realm of the imagination. "Ethnic transvestism" is the clever phrase coined by Werner Sollors to describe the "many fake ethnic writers, from the times of Henry Harland, who published 'Jewish' novels under the pen name Sidney Luska, to the recent case of Daniel James, who wrote 'Chicano' stories under the assumed name Danny Santiago and fooled critics for a while" (*Beyond Ethnicity*, 252).[40]

Is it true that the genuine, authentic, sincere experience of, say, an ethnic group can be expressed only by one of its own or are we too often entrapped by what Nancy K. Miller calls "as-a" criticism (20); and if we expect artists and scholars to confine themselves "as a black" to black writing or "as a lesbian" to lesbian writing, aren't we just putting into place another form of segregation now, tomorrow, and forever? Besides, what would such a protestation mean and to what extent could it deliver? The folklorist Roger Abrahams has shown, after all, that so-called "authenticating stories"—in which writers like Joel Chandler Harris, Lafcadio Hearn, Mark Twain, and George Washington Cable "make righteous claims to have learned major portions of their repertoires from specific black performers"—constituted just one more formulaic "way of establishing one's credentials as a vernacular artist, whether on the minstrel stage, the lecturer's platform, or the written page" (142–43). Like these, most authenticating maneuvers remain qualified strategies that can never completely certify legitimacy, for creative artists—even those telling stories from their own social repertoires—never fully possess or contain their creations;[41] even with the best intentions, they must invent characters and locales more or less than themselves and their places of origin. What the artists engaged in the conventions of racechange do is spotlight the discrepancy between creator and creation, performer and repertoire, usually by making obvious the white person behind the black persona, for example, or, more paradoxically, the black face behind the black mask. We do read Colescott's painting differently once we interpret it in terms of the racial identity he espouses, and that very difference is a mark of how vertiginously disabling racist iconography remains: The African-American artist who mocks grotesque caricatures of blacks finds himself replicating the most pernicious white representations.

If, as Richard Dyer has argued, "the invisibility of whiteness colonises other norms—class, gender, heterosexuality, nationality"—and if it "also masks whiteness as itself a category" (46), racechanges like those performed by Colescott make whiteness visible. (In Colescott's framework, it makes us see the canvases of Van Gogh and Leutze in a new way.) Finally, then, I have decided to close this introductory chapter with several images that help us envision the respect so flagrantly, pointedly violated in Colescott's paintings (as well as to instate a contrast to the Janiform faces looking in opposite directions at the start of this book and to illustrate an ongoing fascination with racechanging iconography). Consider, then, the images of racial interdependence developed by a striking series of portraits in which white and black faces are presented in parallel—rather than oppositional—poses.

One version of Man Ray's *Noire et blanche* makes the mirroring between model and mask quite explicit. The upright Kiki looks toward (leans into) the mask as if seeking her own alter self, the uncanny and unknown originatory psyche she always glimpses at the corner of her eye but can never fully comprehend (Fig. 1.21). Because Kiki's hand and cheek now embrace and encircle the mask, the two figures appear in the position of doubles, a twinning that eludes hierarchized racial and sexual categories. Two portraits that bring the homoerotic more explicitly into play through inter-racial doubling are Charles Cullen's "Tableau" (1927) and Robert Mapplethorpe's "Ken Moody and Robert Sherman" (1984), for the male profiles seem not really like two versions of one self so much as like two lovers in an intimate coupling (Figs. 1.22 and 23).

The visual emphasis on sameness—in positioning, in gender—infuses the racial contrasts here with a tantalizing tension so that blackness and whiteness perform the function of (hetero)sexualizing the couple. Its campy stars and rising sun, its swooning white man fondled and framed by his black partner, make Cullen's draw-

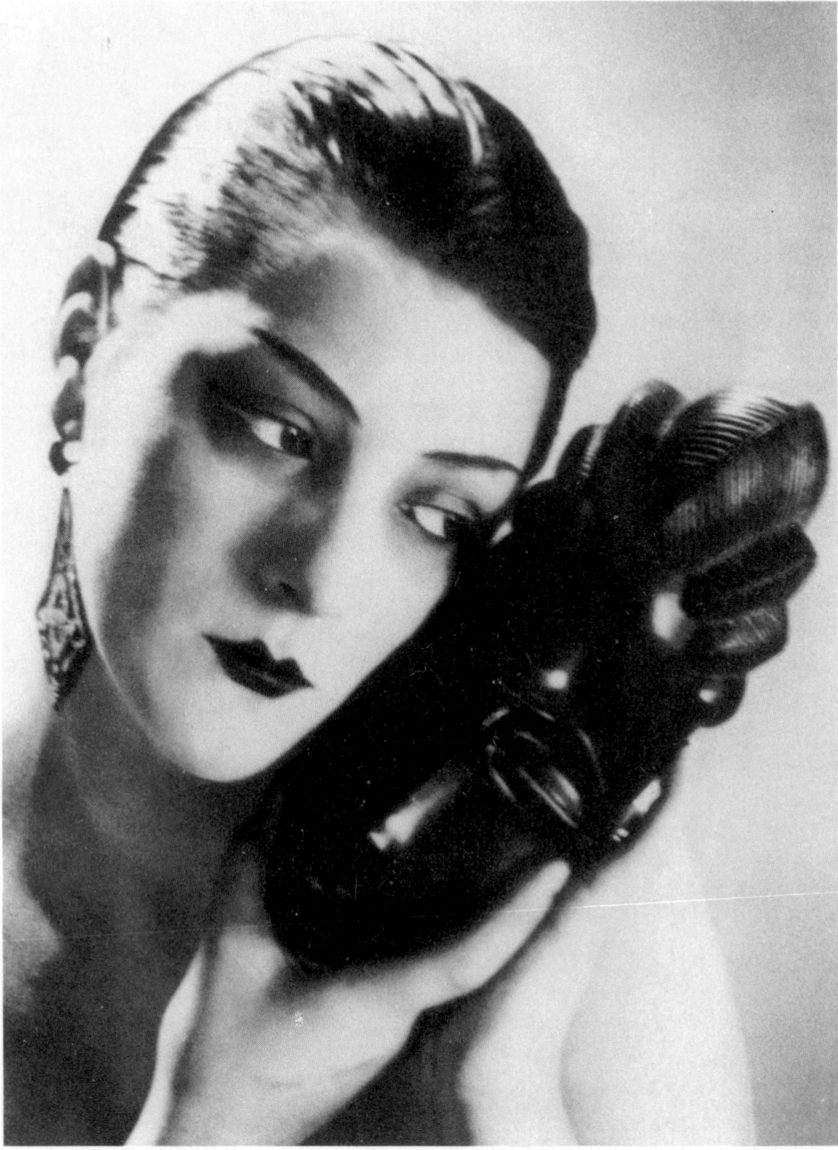

Figure 1.21 Man Ray, *Noire et blanche* (1926), vertical pose. Copyright © Man Ray Trust-ADAGP/ARS, 1997.

ing presage a glitzy new day, a show time of theatrically demonstrable, rapturous strutting. Mapplethorpe's more thrilling, more somber photograph meditates on the serious intent shared by its subjects' hauntingly interlaced subjectivities, an intensity of vision that highlights their vulnerability as the object of our gaze. As if the photographer were meditating on Fanon's belief that "European civilization is

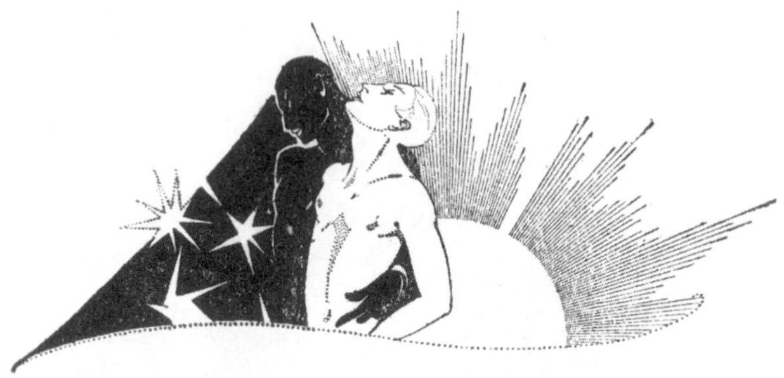

Figure 1.22 Charles Cullen, *Tableau* (1927). Copyright © Armistad Research Center, Tulane University, New Orleans, administered by Thompson and Thompson, New York.

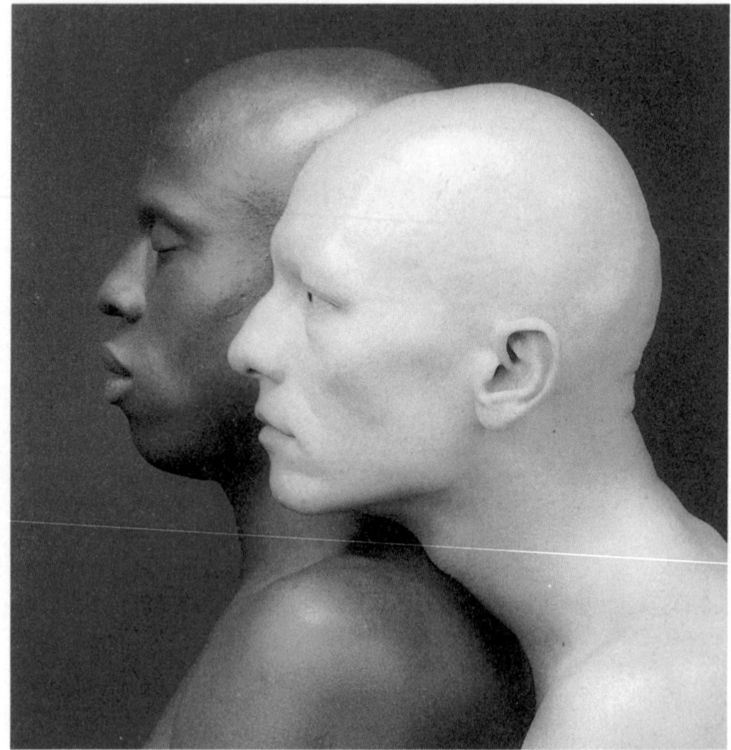

Figure 1.23 Robert Mapplethorpe, *Ken Moody and Robert Sherman* (1984), platinum print. Collection of Aaron and Barbara Levine. Copyright © 1984, The Estate of Robert Mapplethorpe/courtesy A+C Anthology.

characterized by the presence . . . [of] the Negro who slumbers in every white man" (187), the models' bald skulls make them seem universal, representative of a splitting in the psyche, for the open-eyed white man appears like a protector of his more vulnerable, sleeping black companion.

Less erotic but just as resistant to hierarchical valences are the curious postmodern totem poles next to the major highway that connects Bloomington, Indi-

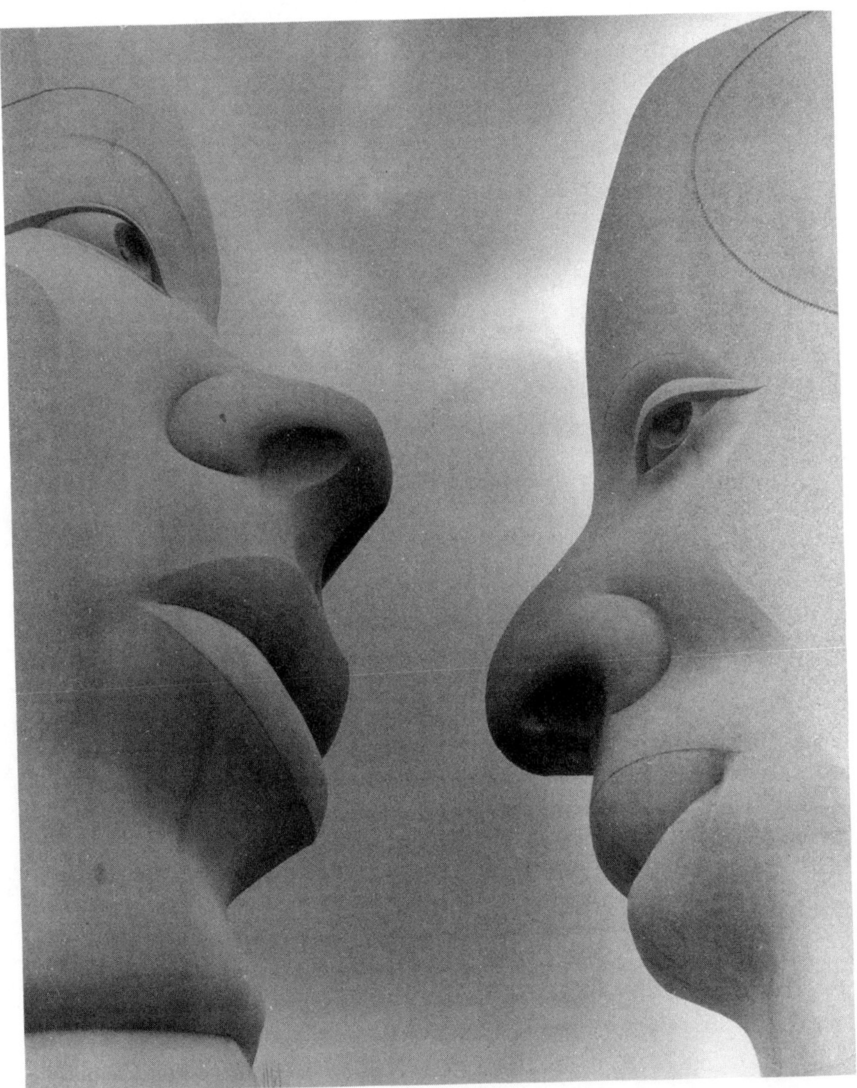

Figure 1.24 Jean-Paul Darriau, *Red, Blond, Black, and Olive* (1980), 14-foot limestone sculpture commissioned by Mayor Frank McClosky of Bloomington, Indiana. Photo by Kevin Hutchinson; courtesy of Jean-Paul Darriau.

ana, to the state capital: two limestone columns or pillars, riffs on Janiform emblems of racechange. Here racially marked faces—neither antithetical (positioned in opposite directions) nor parallel (looking in the same direction)—peer at each other. Jean-Paul Darriau's sculpture *Red, Blond, Black, and Olive* (1980) displays Native American, Caucasian, African, and Asian profiles, each head (of course) sharing the same beige-gray colors of the stone quarried in this region of the country, each here absorbed in an act of attention toward the other (Fig. 1.24). "The proximity of the Other is the face's meaning," the ethical philosopher Levinas has rather mysteriously mused. Attempting to capture the defenseless vulnerability and exposure of the face, Darriau's sculpture seems to illuminate Levinas's point: "The face before me summons me, calls for me, begs for me, as if the invisible death that must be faced by the Other, pure otherness, separated, in some way, from any whole, were my business" (82, 83).

The racechanges to be examined in this book do make commercially profitable business out of the Other, but they can also make the Other the ethical business of whites. At their most clarifying, racial masquerades illuminate manifold factors within the psyche and the society that converge to construct Otherness, powerful forces which, as Ursula Le Guin has observed, fatally conspire to impoverish our moral being:

> If you deny any affinity with another person or kind of person, if you declare it to be wholly different from yourself—as men have done to women, and class has done to class, and nation has done to nation—you may hate it, or deify it; but in either case you have denied its spiritual equality, and its human reality. You have made it into a thing, to which the only possible relationship is a power relationship. And thus you have fatally impoverished your own reality. You have, in fact, alienated yourself. (99)

Yet the odd paradox of this study consists of the puzzling (even disquieting) inconsistency that exactly what has depleted and challenged our ethical integrity has enriched our cultural inheritance. Just as paradoxically, we shall see that claims of sameness can be quite as destructive as those of difference. To revise Le Guin, "if you [affirm an] affinity with another person or kind of person, if you declare it to be wholly [the same as] yourself," you may also have "denied its spiritual equality, and its human reality." The pages that follow testify to the dialectical collisions and collusions between morality and Western megalomania played out in the arena of racial metamorphosis.[42]

2

SPIRIT-MURDER AT THE MOVIES

Blackface Lynchings

> The disaster of the man of color lies in the fact that he was enslaved.
>
> The disaster and the inhumanity of the white man lie in the fact that somewhere he has killed man.
>
> —Frantz Fanon

> The return of the dead is a sign of a disturbance in the symbolic rite, in the process of symbolization; the dead return as collectors of some unpaid symbolic debt.
>
> —Slavoj Žižek

A still from Irving Berlin's *Holiday Inn* (1942) encapsulates the point of this chapter, even as it provides a reminder of the longevity of blackface as America's favorite form of racechange (Fig. 2.1). Wearing burnt cork, Crosby here dances the part of (a now "African-American") President Lincoln with his companion appearing as a parodic pickaninny complete with cornrows, pinafore, and pantaloons. As is often the case late in its history, the use of blackface has presumably only been justified by the need for a disguise: In an earlier scene, a jealously possessive Crosby broke out the "bootblacking" so as to hide his attractive dancing partner from his rival, Fred Astaire. But as also often happens, an excess of meaning attends the assumption of burnt cork, in this instance after the blond-haired dancer bemoans the make-up as a "punishment" visited upon her for dreaming about "how pretty" she would look at the Inn on the occasion of Lincoln's birthday. Not at all a mimetically realistic disguise, her racechange contrasts black skin with white wig to make her look like a singular anomaly.

Shades of the prisonhouse of American history close upon the subsequent production number (which is supposed to parallel Fred Astaire's firecracker hoofing on the Fourth of July in the same movie). For Crosby's part-plantation minstrel, part-Lincoln struts a dance of emancipation to celebrate the liberation presumably effected by the Civil War. But the very assertion of black freedom supposedly in-

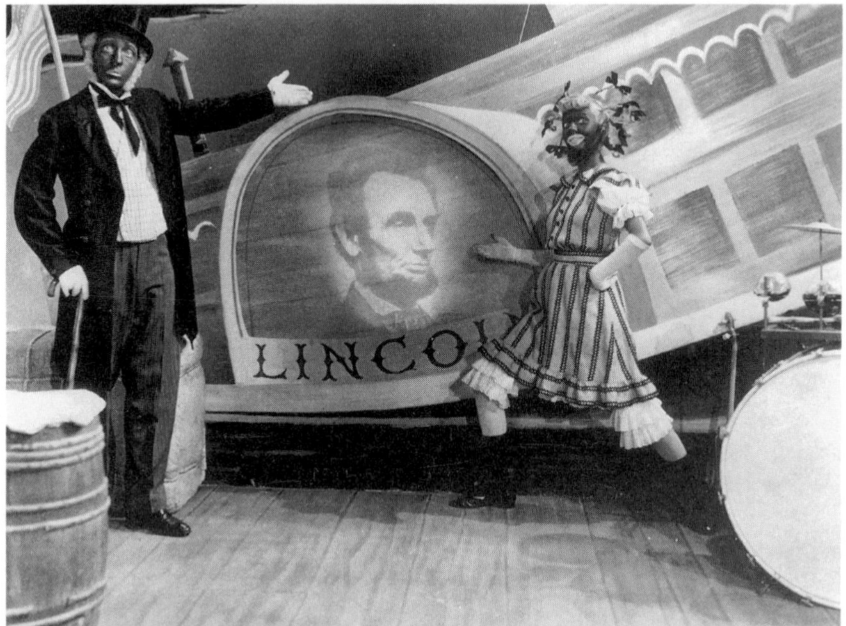

Figure 2.1 Bing Crosby and Marjorie Reynolds in *Holiday Inn* (1942). Courtesy of Museum of Modern Art Film Stills Archive.

augurated by President Lincoln is undercut by the grinning, singing, prancing Tom and Topsy and by the chorus crooned in the kitchen by the stereotypical Mammy—"Who was it set the darkie free?"—and answered by the chirping black children in her abundant lap: "Abraham! Abraham!" As the etiology of blackface and the genealogy of the blackface actor will demonstrate, racechanges shaped by the early movies constitute a cosmetic approach to white compunction about the abuses of slavery as well as the failures of Reconstruction. During the period when the nonwhite, Africanlike presence Toni Morrison calls "the Africanist persona" (*Playing in the Dark*, 6) became highly charged, on the one hand, with exotic and criminally deviant valences and, on the other, with clownish and childlike ones, blackface illuminates the longterm effects of slavery and in particular white people's efforts to repeat, rationalize, camouflage, confess, or repair the grievous injury inflicted on blacks by international and national forms of subjugation.

"Everyone seems to think that the Negro is easily imitated when nothing is further from the truth," Zora Neale Hurston once mused about would-be white racechangers. "Without exception," she continued, "I wonder why the black-face comedians *are* black-face; it is a puzzle—good comedians, but darn poor niggers" ("Characteristics," 186). As she herself intimates, the answer to this question had less to do with realism and more to do with white psychology. Hurston's good-humored protest addresses the "puzzle" of motivation and in particular the "puzzle" of white people's cross-racial performances to which Ralph Ellison returned in his analysis of "the Negro as national scapegoat." According to Ellison, even seemingly fun-loving portrayals of African Americans stage what he called "a ritual of exorcism." The "joke" a racechanging actor shares with his audience in minstrel and vaudeville halls constitutes a "yoke" for those caricatured, as Robert Colescott's paintings of grotesquely stereotyped black figures slyly illustrated in the last chapter ("Change the Joke," 49, 48).

When taken together, Hurston's and Ellison's reactions hint that racial impersonation serves a unique function for white people, not so much mimetic as punitive or purgative: a way of replaying the subordination of black people as well as exonerating it. If, as Frantz Fanon has commented in *Black Skin, White Masks*, the psychology of blacks differs from that of whites, then throughout the twentieth century blacks continue to suffer from their past enslavement while whites remain haunted by the killing fields of their history: "The disaster and inhumanity of the white man lie in the fact that somewhere he has killed man." Whereas cultural imperialism causes people with black skin to internalize white-defined standards or to don white masks, the minstrel tradition and its offshoots on stage and screen uncover a psychological mechanism that motivates people with white skin to assume the coloration of those they have colonized.

Although the picture of the Janiform vase which appears in the opening pages of this book represents the ambivalent doubleness of racial contrasts, holding out the promise that cross-racial iconography could function as an emancipatory force in history, a far more malevolent mode of racechange became extraordinarily popular in the nineteenth-century minstrel show, and it was this blackface performance of racechange that shaped the film industry when it emerged at the beginning of the twentieth century. Despite the common assumption that minstrelsy declined at the turn of the century, it profoundly influenced America's first movies and musicals, raising questions about the degree to which these apparently new and innovative genres contained and sustained conventional structures of oppression. Not only did minstrel shows play an important role in the social fabric of many small towns in America; not only did minstrelsy continue to appear in large city productions into the 1990s; it also influenced many art forms not generally associated with it.[1]

The surprising importance of blackface on stage and screen, I will argue in this chapter, arises from the dynamics of white guilt generated by the racially inflected psychological patterns so brilliantly captured by Fanon's contrast between the "disaster" troubling "the man of color," who inherits a history of enslaving systems that annihilated his personhood as well as his genealogy, and the quite different "disaster" haunting "the white man," who confronts the culpability of his own lethal past. Fanon's dramatic formulation of the white man's guilty consciousness that "somewhere he has killed" can be extended by linking it to Patricia J. Williams's analysis of what she calls "the spirit murder" of twentieth-century racism. Williams's *The Alchemy of Race and Rights* introduces this concept in a meditation on the case of a black civil rights worker stabbed thirty-nine times, an act she views as "not merely" body murder but as "spirit murder" (73). In her legal "diary," Williams wonders "what it was that would not die, what could not be killed by the fourth, fifth, or even tenth knife blow; what sort of thing would not die with the body but lived on in the mind of the murderer?" (72).

Within the conceptual framework provided by Fanon and Williams, the exceptional popularity of blackface suggests that it functioned as one method of repeatedly obliterating the black body, substituting in its stead not only the white body but also the white man's parodic imitation-black-body. Could it be, in other words, that the tenacity with which performers and audiences clung to blackface is not unrelated to what motivated the spirit-murder of the civil rights worker who was stabbed thirty-nine times: "What the murderer was trying to kill was a part of his own mind's image, a part of himself and not a real other" (72). Williams's phrase rings true with respect to the creation of the "darkie" played by so many white men on stage and screen. For besides displacing the body of an actual black person, white actors' performances replaced that body with a projection of the white mind, namely a knavish or foolish character clearly accountable for (culpable of) past wrongs. Thus, what blackface entertainers attempted to annihilate was white responsibility for a past injurious to African Americans, "the symbolic debt" they owed the dead (to use the language of Slavoj Žižek).

An act/art that came into being during slavery and reached its peak of popularity during its turbulent aftermath, blackface provides insight into the culpable mental condition of a genocidal society. "Why do the dead return?" asks Žižek in his study of contemporary horror films, and he answers, "*because they were not properly buried*" (23). If, as my second epigraph warns, the not-properly-buried dead come back "as collectors of some unpaid debt," perhaps blackface performances, which justify white oppression of blacks (by making African Americans look so evil or so foolish that they must be the guilty party), dramatize a horrific return of the displaced black body—now paradoxically borne on and reborn in the white body. Such a return or mimetic mirroring provides evidence of white consternation about the transparency of the lie blaming African Americans for their own suppression. In Žižek's terms, whites who have refused to pay their debt or admit their liability to the (African-American) dead continue to be haunted by them. Uncannily, as we shall see, this haunting took the form of a reenactment that encased the white actor inside the black's role as scapegoat. After the Emancipation, blackface performers effectively colluded in what Trudier Harris considers the work of lynching, namely "to keep Blacks contained politically and socially" (19). If lynching staged a spectacle that sought to discipline its black audience while it communalized whites by "territorializing the black body" (Wiegman, 13), we will see that blackface stages a comparable scenario. No wonder, then, that lynching played a prominent role in early Hollywood films which were promoted through gruesome advertising copy: "Hear His Moans and Groans, Price One Cent."[2]

Paradoxically, even in nonviolent movies the blackface performer who effectively attempted to avoid accountability for racial injustice bore the burden of the Undead in/on his own body. Thus, this historically important form of racial impersonation constitutes not only a crime of spirit-murder, not only a justification for that crime as well as a displacement of responsibility for it, but also an odd reprisal or punishment, at times, curiously, a reparation or mode of mourning. For we shall see that even as the blackface performer metaphorically sacrificed a black character, he himself enacted the role of scapegoat, much as had his precursors on the minstrel stage. This chapter will explore the crucial role blackface played in two foundational movies in America's film industry—the first blockbuster and the first talkie—before turning back to the historical roots of blackface on the minstrel stage and then forward to its later evolution in Hollywood. To the extent that blackface proliferated a series of white lies about the subjection of African Americans in American culture, it whitewashed past and present injustices. That it did so within movies depending upon repetitive symbolic lynchings of the black male body attests to the centrality in early film scripts of camouflaged scenes of racial subordination. The phrase "repetitive lynchings" sounds like a case of overkill and is meant to because, as Virginia Woolf once put it in a different context, "it is far harder to kill a phantom than a reality" (240) and the fictitious nature of this celluloid black specter kept it alive, creeping back to haunt the white imagination.[3] Only in later modes of racechange did the victims of racism begin to receive the equivalent of a decent burial in aesthetic productions that attempt to recapture an equanimity comparable to that of the Tarquinian urn and in so doing confront the trauma of the innocent suffering of African Americans in order to absorb that scandal into the nation's historical memory.

The Birth of a Nation's Movie Industry

Two seemingly antithetical uses of blackface in two of the most important movies produced in this country at the start of its rich cinematic history illuminate the centrality of racial impersonation in American cultural history. The first film masterpiece, *The Birth of a Nation* (1915), and the first talkie, *The Jazz Singer* (1927), used blackface in apparently opposed ways, the former featuring the blackface actor as criminal, the latter as clown. In addition, though audiences today may find Jolson's film suspiciously patronizing about African Americans, *The Jazz Singer* presented itself as a liberal contrast in matters of racial ideology to the overt racism of *The Birth of a Nation*. While Griffith portrayed blackface characters as sexual predators out to destroy the nation by polluting white womanhood, Warner Brothers produced a blackface entertainer seeking to please white America by crooning to his "Mammy." Whereas Griffith followed his source, the novels of Thomas Dixon, to depict most of his black characters as looming bucks menacing weakened whites, Jolson on bended knee signified a tried and true, tamed Uncle Tom. Yet ultimately, the criminality and the clownishness of the stage Negro in both films operated as a form of character assassination or spirit-murder that provided a bizarre justification or penance for the lynchings all too common in this same period of time.

Most of the portraits of African Americans in Griffith's still shockingly racist film corroborate the assertion of its second intertitle that (in a characteristically disingenuous euphemism) "the *bringing* of the African to America planted the first *seeds* of disunion" (emphasis mine). Quite a bit later in the film a would-be rapist (acted by Walter Long in blackface) attempts to sow such seeds. *The Birth of a*

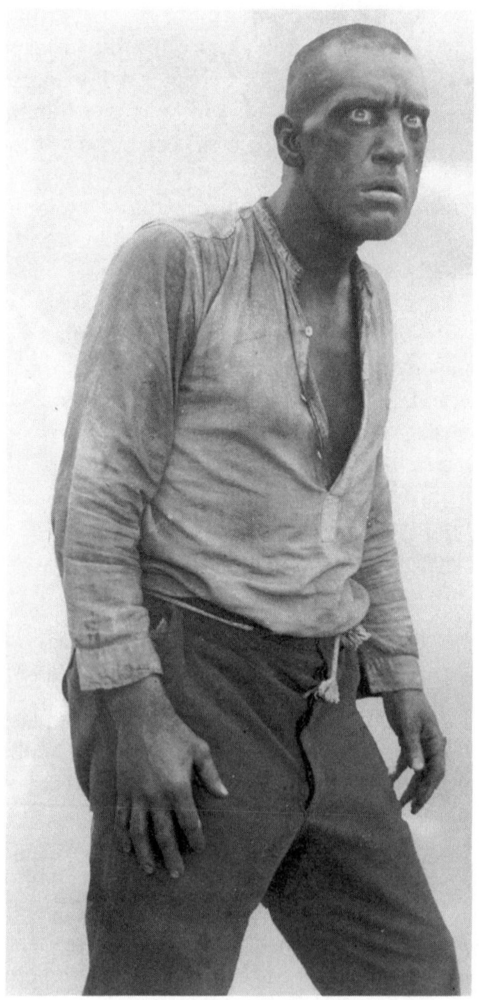

Figure 2.2 Walter Long as Gus in *The Birth of a Nation* (1915). Courtesy of Museum of Modern Art Film Stills Archive.

Nation's Gus pursues the innocent, youthful, white Flora Cameron (Mae Marsh) in a pine forest, stalking her as camera shots shift rapidly back and forth between her spontaneous, joyful wanderings in the woods and his prowling chase. Carrying a water bucket instead of a basket, the frolicking girl prancing off the beaten track plays Little Red Riding Hood to his Big Bad Wolf. According to Griffith's biographer, Walter Long was instructed to run doubled-over with a sort of "animalistic scuttle" and to gargle with a bottle of hydrogen peroxide so as to create the effect of foaming at the mouth (Schickel, 232, Fig. 2.2).[4]

After Flora hurls herself suicidally down a precipice in the forest rather than submit to Gus's bestial pursuit—"For her who had learned the stern lesson of honor we should not grieve that she found sweeter the *opal gates of death*" (Title 1093)—her brother recovers and cradles her broken body. Soon, too, this paradigmatic Southern hero, the Little Colonel of the Cameron family, finds "inspiration" watching white children under a sheet frightening (predictably terrified) pickaninnies at play and so decides to organize the mighty Ku Klux Klan whose white knights will redeem the honor of good girls like Flora by revenging themselves against the bestial black rapist and whose final ride-to-the-rescue would allow Griffith to film on a grand scale. "Instead of saving one poor little Nell of the Plains," he explained, "this ride would be to save a nation" (Schickel, 213).[5]

And, of course, in his sexual criminality Gus typifies the other blackface characters from whom the nation must be saved, two of whom are attached to the Northern senator Austin Stoneman, the deluded antagonist of the pastoral South, here typified by the Cameron family. With melodramatic symmetry, Pennsylvanian Stonemans and South Carolinian Camerons visit, befriend, and fall in love with each other before the Civil War; after its outbreak, however, the brothers of one family will murder the brothers or be rescued by the sisters of the other family, as Union and Confederate armies clash on the battlefields of the war. Based upon Thaddeus Stevens, the Pennsylvanian Republican deeply committed to racial equality in the Congress, Stoneman represents those misguided Northerners whose commitment to the liberation of the slaves inflates blacks with insolence and threatens to undermine the stability of the nation. Both Stoneman's mulatto mistress, Lydia Brown, and his mulatto henchman, the amazingly named Silas Lynch, act like lascivious predators whose hideously dominant sexuality affects and reflects their overweening political ambition.

Austin Stoneman's decision to commit himself to the radical Republican cause is first influenced by his housekeeper-mistress, who wishes to ferment rebelliousness in Southern blacks after the Civil War. We initially see Lydia Brown aspiring to social equality while presiding over the events in Stoneman's Northern residence, specifically a visit from Charles Sumner, who puts her in her place as a housekeeper by refusing to behave as if she were the mistress of the house. As soon as Sumner departs, Lydia falls into a paroxysm of rage, furious at the social slight and apparently determined to exploit this or any other incident to strengthen her hold over Stoneman. Ranting and raving, ripping her own clothing, repeatedly spitting and collapsing, she seems like a classic hysteric or madwoman, but it soon becomes clear that she will use her torn dress to pin blame on the unsuspecting Sumner, casting suspicion on him in Stoneman's eyes even as she fawns, caresses, and flatters her unsuspecting master (Fig. 2.3). The chapter of *The Clansman* (1905) devoted to Lydia is entitled "The First Lady of the Land" because Dixon wished to emphasize how this "sinister," "catlike," "sphinx" would "cast a shadow across the history of a great nation," becoming as Stoneman's consort "the arbiter of its social life," her self-serving, mendacious "ethics the limit of its moral laws" (94).

But in the movie Stoneman is blinded even more effectively by his other mulatto companion, the evocatively named Lynch who seeks (with Stoneman's approbation and the furtive glee of Lydia) to gain national leadership. Played by George Siegmann in blackface, Lynch looks like a cross between Orson Welles and Dan Ackroyd, puffing up as he gains political power and becomes Lieutenant

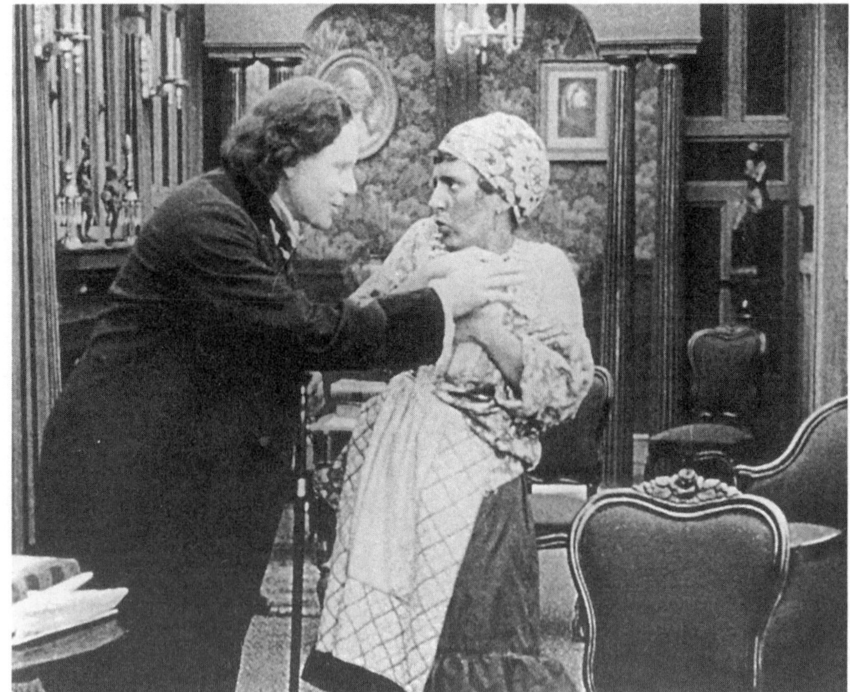

Figure 2.3 Ralph Lewis as Austin Stoneman with Mary Alden as Lydia Brown in *The Birth of a Nation.* Courtesy of Museum of Modern Art Film Stills Archive.

Governor of South Carolina. A leader of the black party, Lynch along with his cohorts manages to pervert democracy in America—we are shown black people stuffing the ballot box, disenfranchising whites, and murdering other black citizens who refuse to toe the black party's line—and it soon becomes clear why Lynch has his name. In the weird, topsy-turvy world of *Birth of a Nation*, African Americans themselves are presented as the guilty lynchers, turning their adversaries into "the helpless white minority." And so through the coalition of "negroes and carpetbaggers," Lynch rules a black-dominated state house of representatives whose rowdy black members pontificate while chomping on peanuts or joints of meat, downing both with intermittent swills of liquor. When a (predictable and presumably unnerving) bill for intermarriage is passed, it become apparent that the traitorous Lynch wants to marry not just any old white woman but Stoneman's own beautiful daughter, Elsie (presumably a fitting punishment for a Northerner made to understand that his egalitarian platform inevitably rests upon miscegenation, which in turn means the loss of racial "purity").

Richard Schickel argues about the portrayals of Gus, Lydia Brown, and Lynch that Griffith's decision to use make-up which "cannot and does not fully transform" his white actors into Negroes mitigates the film's racism. "He must have been aware that if a white man was playing a black man there was no way to disguise that fact" (233). And to the modern viewer, the blackface performances do seem parodically stereotypical, obviously designed to inspire the effect Thomas Dixon wanted, "to create a feeling of abhorrence in white people, especially white women against colored men" (Geduld, 98–99). At least in part, then, the black-faced actors look like what they are, namely (nasty) white people's (nasty) idea of blacks. However, part of the film's eerie effect derives from the use of "real" black extras: cavorting slaves on the antebellum plantation, carousing Northern soldiers disrespectfully bullying whites off the streets. At times, too, it is difficult to tell if blackface is being used: for example, in the case of those trusty and true family servants, the Camerons' loyal, loving Mammy and Uncle Tom. And the nefarious mulattos of the Stoneman residence can appear oddly light-skinned in some versions of the film, with Lydia Brown looking less like the nineteenth-century tragic mulatto and more like the nineteenth-century exotic Jewess. In the context of this potential confusion, the white masks of the Klan provide clarification, setting in order the chaos that threatens to contaminate Aryan culture.[6]

That misrule achieves a climax toward the close of the film when the screen is filled with multiple images of white men tarred and feathered, white husbands beaten with rifles by black soldiers, white citizens delivered from jail into the howling rage of the mob. A representative white father, the patriarch of the exemplary Southern Cameron family—miraculously still alive, despite the deaths of two of his sons in the Civil War and the suicide of his little Flora—is forced to take shelter in a wooden shack. The once and future master of a magnificent ancestral mansion cowers in a log cabin after having been arrested by Lynch and paraded in chains before his former slaves for the crime of possessing a Klan outfit; rescued by "loyal black souls," he owes his escape to the Mammy and Uncle Tom of his household and to the two Union veterans who share their refuge. As one intertitle puts it, "The former enemies of North and South are united again in common defence of their Aryan birthright." But united where, if not inside what looks suspiciously like an Uncle Tom's cabin? Within the brave new world ruled by Lynch's law, Griffith suggests, the slave quarters will confine white gentlemen regardless of their regional or political loyalties, reducing their families to hostages and chattel—unless, that is, they are rescued by the Klan.

Indeed, just as earlier in the film Elsie Stoneman went to President Lincoln to obtain a pardon for her true love (the young Cameron son) during the war, it becomes clear that Lynch has taken Lincoln's place when she petitions the Lieutenant Governor to free the Camerons from their cabin and is subjected to the lewd indignities of his lust (Fig. 2.4).[7] Unlike Griffith's gentle Lincoln, however, Lynch heeds not Elsie's plea for clemancy. With Elsie locked up and cowering in Lynch's office, a title informs us that he proposes to "build a Black Empire and you as a Queen shall sit by my side." While the camera cuts back and forth between a horrified Elsie pounding at or flinging herself against the door and the Clansmen galloping along tree-shaded roads, another title explains that "Lynch, drunk with wine and power, orders his henchmen to hurry preparations for a forced marriage." The camera lovingly returns over and over again to an image of the vulnerable Lillian Gish imprisoned, gagged, and bound, all swooning purity and terror in her white

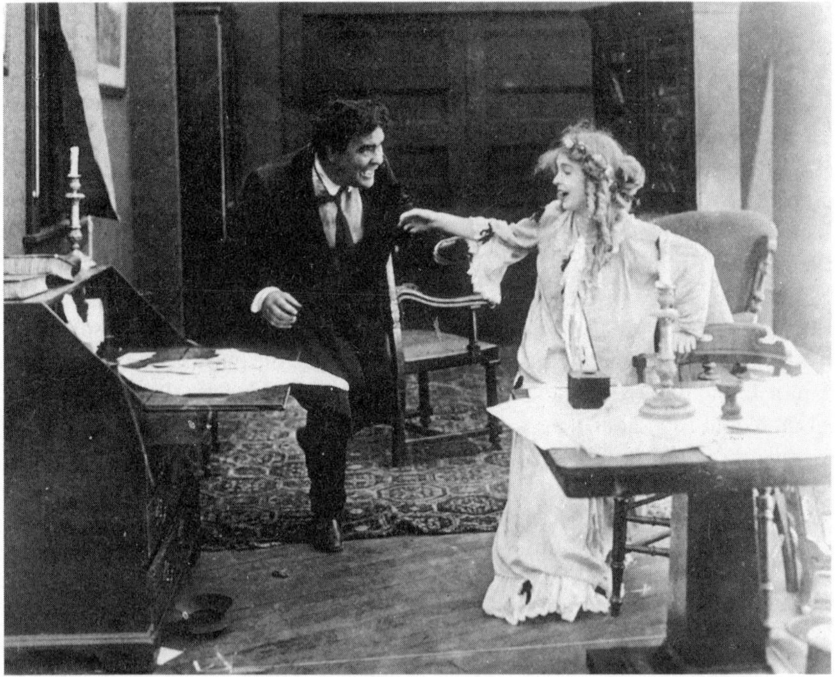

Figure 2.4 George Siegmann as Silas Lynch and Lillian Gish as Elsie Stoneman in *The Birth of a Nation*. Courtesy of Photofest.

flowing dress, threatened by a black fist, fainting in a dishevelled, fragile heap of grace under pressure.[8]

Exactly why Mr. Lynch insists on continuing to behave in this bullying manner remains beyond rational comprehension, except to justify Griffith's narrative conclusion.[9] If the first section of *The Birth of a Nation* closes with the senseless violence between North and South during the Civil War, the second part ends with the morally justified—even divinely sanctioned—violence of whites against blacks in a veritable race war. To vindicate the victimized Flora, to save the endangered Elsie, to rescue the captured patriarch of the Camerons—in other words, to reestablish traditional definitions of white femininity and masculinity—Gus, Lydia, Lynch, and indeed all black people must be destroyed. Given the use of scenes clearly marked as "Historical Facsimiles" (Sherman's march to the sea, the assassination of President Lincoln) as well as the periodic enactment of historic tableaux (all of which are touted as documentary in their accuracy), the film's claims to veracity easily spill over to camouflage pernicious racial ideology as pious race truth.[10] Rapid cutting after the Klan's "trial," "conviction," and murder of Gus—with shorter and shorter shots of the Camerons' cabin surrounded by black troups and Elsie Stoneman gagged in Lynch's study—emphasizes the compensatory solution to what one critic calls the "paranoid fantasies of white sexual inadequacy" that fuel this melodrama (Cripps, 51).

Thus, when white robes float over the moonlit roads of South Carolina at the end of the show to rescue Mr. Cameron from the slave cabin and Elsie Stoneman from the lustful Lynch, white crowds in cities all across America cheered what amounts to a Christian crusade for law and order. The rousing orchestration (teetering on the edge of Wagner's "Ride of the Valkyries") and the massive number of horses and riders involved, as well as the heroic, heraldic camera angles, transform this Nordic trek from a chase-to-the-rescue into an apocalyptic conflagration. A contrast to the tragic internecine destruction of the Civil War, the military mission of the Klan evokes cowboys come to slay the heathen Indians; the sheriff's posse about to reclaim a frontier town-gone-wrong; Arthurian knights out to win the tournament, protect the grail, man the round table, and assure the purity and honor of their ladies. As in the last illustration in Dixon's novel, though, the Clansman cum cowboy-sheriff-knight retains the moral stature of crusader (Figs. 2.5 and 2.6). It seems appropriate that one of Griffith's actor-riders was the soon-to-become famous director of westerns John Ford and that this was the first movie to be shown at the White House, dubbed (by President Wilson) "history written in lightning" (to which he added, "And my only regret is that it is all true" (Schickel, 268–70)).

History as whitening but also as a kind of electrocution. With night-riders in white sheets featured on posters—crosses emblazoned on each breast, hooded like their horses—with one publicity ploy involving hired horsemen, garbed in Klan robes, galloping through city streets, Griffith's film saved the endangered white femininity of Elsie Stoneman and the equally imperiled white masculinity of Cameron *père* through an Oedipal solution that issued a death sentence to black people, especially black men. Fearful white male insufficiency—the murder of Lincoln as well as the jeopardized paternity of all the other white men in the melodrama—threatens the continuity of the White House, of patriarchal genealogy itself. In opposition to the upstart pseudo-son Lynch and his Black Empire stand the true heirs apparent of the Invisible Empire, wearing their phallic hats, wielding their potent swords, and as spectral, invincible, and unified in their galumphing columns as any Lacanian would want. What accompanies the destruction of the criminalized bodies of Gus and Lynch, then, is an epithalamium: The wedding of the Cameron and Stoneman families reunifies South with North to deliver the birth of one nation under God, indivisible. With the dead Gus dumped on Lynch's doorstep, with Lynch himself in the hands of the Clan, Stoneman and Cameron descendants can unite in sexual unions to save the national Union from "Africanization."[11]

Like love and marriage, blackface and white hood seem to go together in Griffith's film. Two odd moments late in the movie explain why. First, at one point we are informed that blackfaced white actors on screen represent not African Americans but white spies using disguise to infiltrate the hegemonic black party so as to uncover its stratagems. Second, after the little Colonel as Clansman comes to res-

Figure 2.5 "The Fiery Cross of Old Scotland's Hills!" from Thomas Dixon, *The Clansman* (1905).

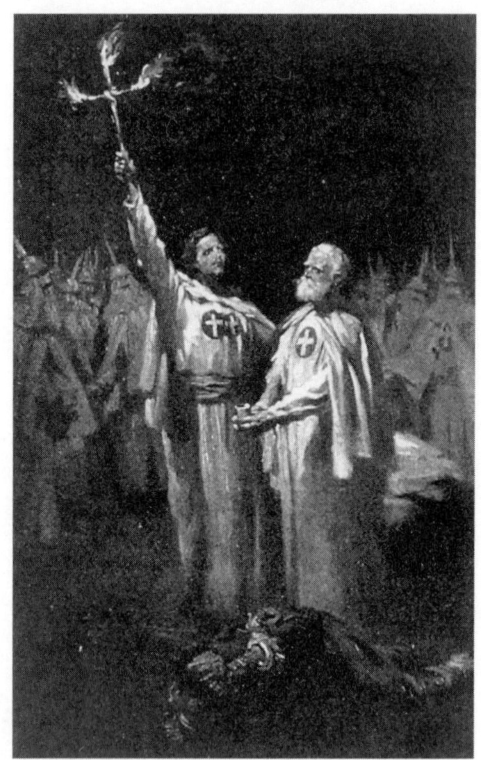

Figure 2.6 [*Below*] Gus captured by the Klan in *The Birth of a Nation*. Courtesy of Museum of Modern Art Film Stills Archive.

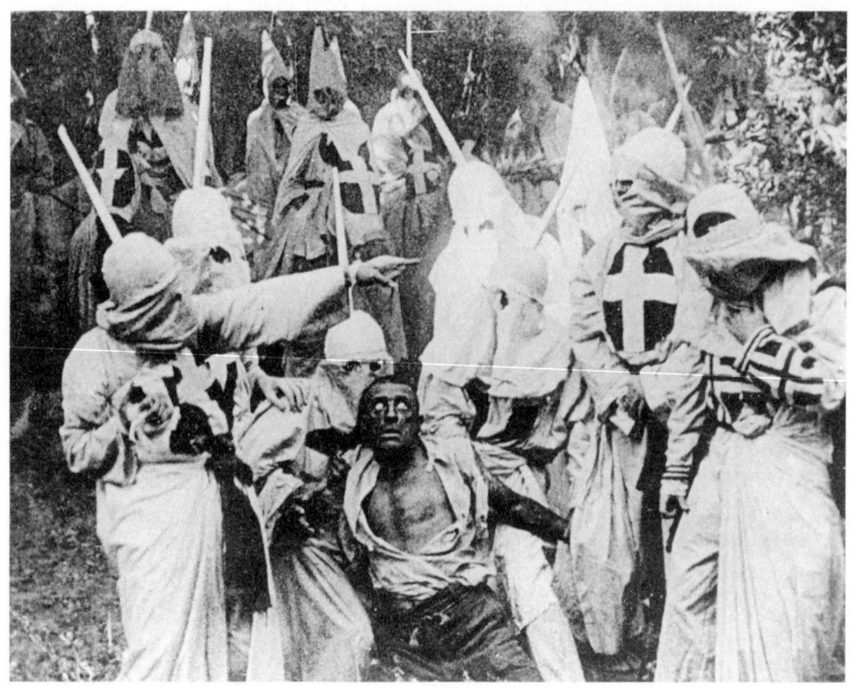

cue Elsie Stoneman, he finds it necessary to assure her of his identity by raising his hood so she can see his face. Taken together, the scenes remind viewers of the potential for racial confusion. Indeed, blackface itself might be considered a symbolic defense against such (inevitable) complications. Since it may be impossible to "tell" if a person is actually of black descent—especially in the context of the "one drop rule" (defining a person with just one "drop" of "black" blood as racially Other)—complexion is neither an infallible nor a stable index of race, while blackface assures audiences that difference is visible, always encoded in the same way, skin-deep. Also, given the evil roles played by the characters of African-American descent in Griffith's narrative, perhaps blacks are so polluting that they ought not to come into contact with white actors at all; maybe "that kind" of inhumanity should be represented only through surrogates, like the totemic symbols or fetishes used to stand for and ward off evil spirits in exorcist rituals.

From this perspective, blackface insures the 100 percent certifiable purity of an all-white cast/community of film actors and makers, unsullied by the threat of miscegenation against which they preach. And indeed, though a few African-American leads and some black extras were employed in the making of his movies, Griffith explicitly forbad any "black blood" in actors who touched white actresses, rejected players who had skin blemishes on their faces, and experimented with what he called "hazy photography," placing a white sheet beneath the actor's feet while a bright light would illuminate the body from above, thus, in his words, "eras[ing] imperfections" (May, 83, 76). That Lydia Brown just disappears from the film while Gus and Lynch must be destroyed so as to redeem the honor of Flora Cameron and Elsie Stoneman indicates that the real problem for Griffith, a man who late in his life claimed to have loved only one person, his father, is the black man and the threat he poses to the white patriarch as well as his lineage.[12] When the Klan victory ensuring the lynching of Gus and Lynch is followed by *Birth of a Nation*'s concluding images of a surrealistic Mars turning before our eyes into Christ-the-Clansman, we are meant to understand that the Prince of War will metamorphose into the Prince of Peace only when race war has brought victory to the white son, whose resurrection (erection) requires the sacrificed (castrated) black body.

The birth of the American nation and of its film industry is predicated upon the death of African Americans. Indeed, blackface marks that hope, the time when the only blacks will really be whites, whose blackness can be washed off like a cosmetic or paint. As warpaint, then, blackface constitutes a white declaration of war on blacks. Just as important, using blackface to portray the evil of blacks meant turning the victims into the perpetrators of racial violence, the lynched into the lynchers or the disenfranchized domestic servant into the "First Lady of the Land." Since the transparency of the lie underlines white culpability, blackface discloses the crime it was meant to conceal. Yet John Hope Franklin has pointed out—by explaining that William J. Simmons decided to realize his plans to revive the Klan when the film opened in Atlanta—that "*Birth of a Nation* was the midwife in the rebirth of the most vicious terrorist organization in the history of the United States" (431). Understandably, critics at the time of the film's release decried it as a "spiritual assassination" (Hackett, 163), for blackface in Griffith's film attempted to move African Americans from slavery to servitude by whitewashing American history.

The Atonement of the Jazz-Jew

While African Americans threaten the death of the American nation in Griffith's film, African Americans seem to epitomize America in *The Jazz Singer*, for Jolson as Jakie Rabinowitz manages to assimilate—to transform himself into Jack Robin, to extricate his fate from the control of his father, Cantor Rabinowitz, and to win the shiksa he loves—by defying his father's pious injunctions and appearing on stage wearing burnt cork.[13] Primarily blackface operates mimetically in *The Birth of a Nation*, marking a (supposedly) realistic difference between the races; however, in *The Jazz Singer* burnt cork is merely theatrical make-up. Whereas the former film preaches racial hatred, moreover, the latter counsels racial respect not only between gentiles and Jews but also between the cultures of whites and blacks.

The leering, lusty blackfaced Gus, Lydia, and Lynch must be tramped under the crusading hooves of Christ and his Clansmen; yet the meek and mild blackfaced Jolson on bended knee, with arms outstretched, looks somehow childlike, submissive, sorrowful, even Christlike. As Michael Rogin points out, though, the apparent opposition between *Birth*'s attack on miscegenation and *Jazz*'s promotion of inter-racial marriage hides the ways in which the latter "facilitates the union of Gentile and Jew, not white and black" ("Blackface," 420). Taking this point one step further, I want to claim that both films participate in a common task that illuminates the link between travesties of American justice and of African-American culture.[14] If *The Birth of a Nation* impersonates black men so as to justify their lynching, *The Jazz Singer* represents black masculinity also to unman, in this case by substituting infantilized "boy" for aggressive "buck" and thereby reenacting spirit-murder in its own, albeit different register. Yet if *The Birth of a Nation* uses blackface to effect a kind of spiritual assassination, *The Jazz Singer* remains haunted by the need to atone for that crime. Together, both films explain the popularity of the blackface performer who could dramatize for white audiences contradictory responses to the shame of a supremacist society.

"Orchard Street would have had some difficulty in recognizing Jakie Rabinowitz of Beth-El choir under the burnt cork of Jack Robin": so reads Title 49 of *The Jazz Singer* right after the first planned close-up of Jack Robin in blackface, applauding in the wings as he watches his girlfriend and patron Mary Dale complete her dance routine on stage (Carringer, 80). In the scene that follows (which was played in whiteface), Mary tells a doting but shy Jack about a new theatrical engagement that will launch her career, and although he congratulates her, he silently suffers because of their impending separation. From this point on, Jack's stage self becomes associated with his secondary position: his thralldom to Mary as well as his tormented contrition about his professional aspirations. The pattern of Mary's authority and Jack's admiring but dumb acquiescence recurs when they meet again, this time not in Chicago but in New York. An indebted Jack gets his

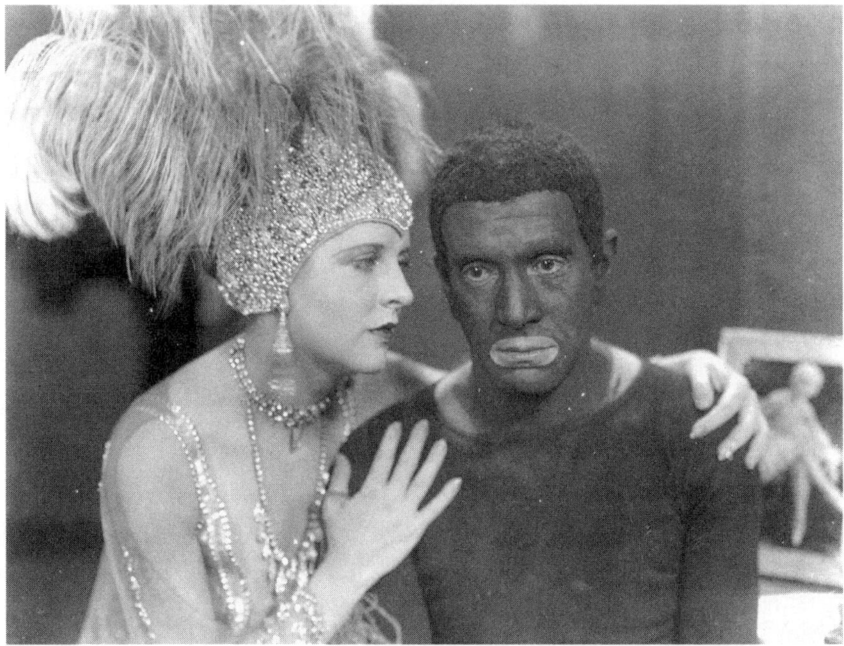

Figure 2.7 Al Jolson as Jack Robin with May McAvoy as Mary Dale in *The Jazz Singer* (1927). Courtesy of Museum of Modern Art Film Stills Archive.

break on Broadway because of Mary, and she is the one who invites him to the dinner that will eventuate in their engagement. Repeatedly, bashful Jack the impoverished ingenue gratefully admits to plucky Mary the established celebrity that he owes whatever success he will achieve to her patronage. Throughout their courtship, then, Mary's New Womanly determination and autonomy contrast with the hesitations and dependency of Jack. Unlike the blackface which hypermasculinizes in *The Birth of a Nation*, in *The Jazz Singer* burnt cork contributes to the already ongoing infantilization of its central character (Fig. 2.7).

Before and after he darkens his countenance, tears repeatedly course down Jack's cheeks, one sign of an effeminacy long attributed to the loyal, pious, long-suffering Uncle Tom.[15] As a young boy, Jakie cowers before and sobs after a beating inflicted by his orthodox father who has hauled him out of a bar and punished him for singing "raggy" songs.[16] He runs away, but not before taking tearful leave of his mother's portrait. Weeping is also part of his singing style: When he sings "jazz," there is said to be a "tear" in his voice; when his father advises a young boy to chant "with a sigh—like you are crying out to your God," he remembers how Jakie "had a voice like a angel." At the climax of Jack's bathetic self-displays, his most melodramatic self-division, the film introduces a scene in which Jack smears on blackface. Backstage for the last rehearsal of his first Broadway show and only hours before Yom Kippur, he completes the make-up by donning a wig of cropped wool; although he promises Mary to do his best for the show, the background music launches into a schmaltzy version of "I'd walk a million miles for one of your smiles, my Mammy."

Seated at his make-up mirror, a remorseful Jack envisions his father in the synagogue and hears the strains of "Kol Nidre." The putting on of blackface occurs when Jack seems most in need of parental approval, narcissistically watching himself being surveyed, passive with respect to Mary, and anxious about his professional aspirations. Although he agrees with Mary that his career must come first, the songs of his people are "tearing at [his] heart," rendering him vulnerable when his mother and Yudelson the Kibitzer (a synagogue *macher*) enter to make their plea. Embracing his mother (who sighs, "Jack, this isn't you"), the blackened Jack looks to Yudelson like Jack's "shadow" (originally in Alfred A. Cohn's film script his "nigger"). Papa is dying at home, we are told by a weeping Mama; sunset and Yom Kippur only two hours away! Who will sing the prayers? (Fig. 2.8).

Wiping his eyes, pulling away from his mother, Jack dons shirt and jacket, moves on stage and sings (to the disgust of the original story-writer) a number about mother-love which elicits Mama's emotional admission that her boy belongs in show business or (as she puts it) "to the world":

> Mother, I wandered away,
> breaking your heart.
> Now I'm grown up,
> Mother of mine.
> When friends all doubt me,
> I still have you,
> Somehow you're just the same.
> Mother divine,
> With your arms around me,
> I know I'm not to blame . . . .

After being congratulated at the rehearsal—"Wonderful, Jack! You were actually crying!"—Jolson wipes a hand across his weeping eyes, leaving a streak on his face. Though he glimpses in the enthusiastic reaction of the cast an impending professional triumph, the realization that his mother has left the theater and that his father is close to death casts him down. The camera zooms in and fades out as he sits alone in his dressing room, removes his wig, and lets his blackened, inconsolable face drop into his hands (Fig. 2.9). The next scene plays out Jack's self-division in whiteface an hour or so later within the patriarchal death chamber.

Again, Jack's eyes are "streaming" and his shoulders "shaking convulsively with suppressed sobs" (128). Kneeling by his father's bedside, Jack is joined by Mary and the show's backer, both of whom worry that he will "queer" himself on Broadway if, instead of opening, he gives into his mother's request to sing "Kol Nidre" at the synagogue adjoining the cantor's apartment. As Mama lights the Sabbath lights and Jack worries that he hasn't sung in the temple since a child, Yudelson promises him, "What a little boy learns, he never forgets." Jack's divided loyalties are represented by Mama and Yudelson the Kibitzer on one side of the screen,

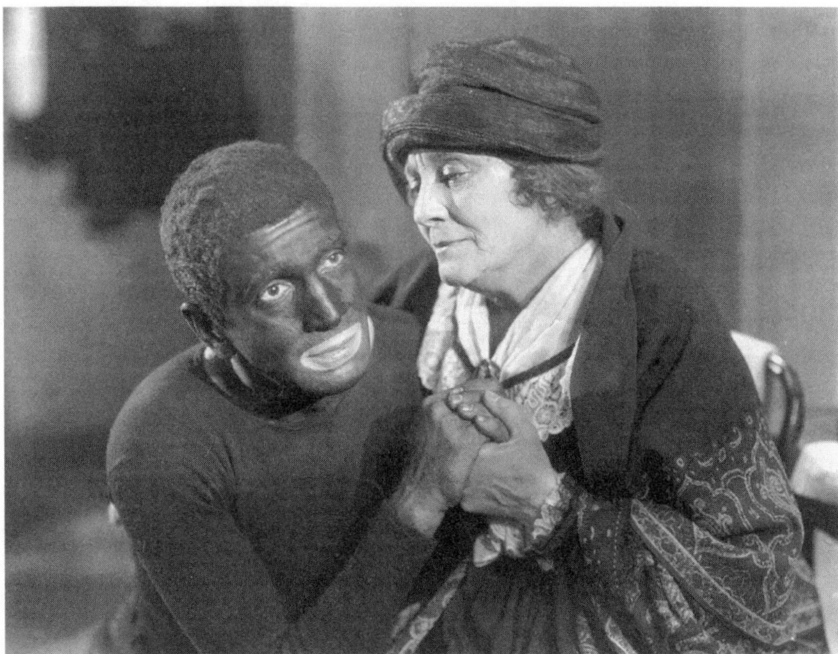

Figure 2.8 Al Jolson as Jack with Mama (Eugenie Besserer) in *The Jazz Singer*. Courtesy of Museum of Modern Art Film Stills Archive.

the backer and Mary on the other. Synagogue or stage? Skullcap and prayer shawl or blackface and wig? "Kol Nidre" or "Mammy"? Jewish orthodoxy and separatism or assimilation into mainstream American culture and intermarriage? The familial duties of childhood or the personal ambitions of maturity? The traditions of the past or the innovations of the future? Obviously, the black and white faces of Jack emphasize his self-division, his divided loyalties, his sense of doubleness or duplicity.

In the scene of Oedipal resolution that the screen treatment used as its conclusion, we see Cantor Rabinowitz dying, Mama weeping by the bed ("we have our son again"), and Mary listening too as the camera cuts next door to Jolson in rabbinical robes at the altar. Jack's chanting of the most plaintive passages of the "Kol Nidre" elicits Mary's judgment that "It's his last time in [the synogogue]. He *has* to come back to us." What was supposed to be the final shot shows Jack sorrowfully praying and visited by the spectral appearance of the (now dead) cantor whose misty form blesses the son and then disappears. The young man has managed to take on his father's roles and robes, an act of contrite, filial submission that will free him to defy paternal injunction in a brave new future world of Jewish assimilation. By dutifully relinquishing his Broadway opening night, Jack makes amends for his parricidal rebellion against Cantor Rabinowitz and thus the dead but propitiated father blesses his rebellious but penitent son.

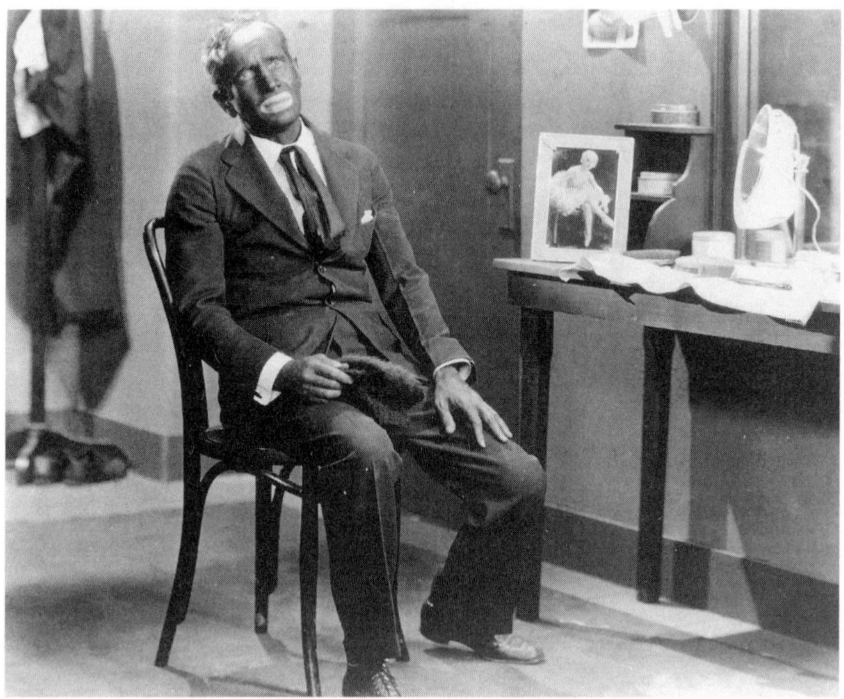

Figure 2.9 Al Jolson, partially unmasked, in *The Jazz Singer*. Courtesy of Museum of Modern Art Film Stills Archive.

The movie caps this planned ending with Jack appearing on stage at the Winter Garden in blackface, and again Oedipal victory is emphasized, as Mary radiates approval from the wings and Mama beams from the audience. If on Yom Kippur Jack atones for his betrayal of his Jewish origins, in the next and last scene he reaps its benefits, doing what Jolson's audiences expected him to do. In the process of filming Jolson's racial impersonation in "My Mammy," moreover, *The Jazz Singer* demonstrates how this type of racechange effectively colludes in the sort of spirit-murder performed in Griffith's *The Birth of a Nation* even as it proves the persistence of minstrelsy on the vaudeville stage and the movie screen. "My heart strings travel around Al-a-bammie": Jolson's Uncle Tom typifies the nostalgic slave returning to happy-go-lucky plantation times. Just as earlier Jolson's blackface was associated with his feminization, it is conflated now with the boy-child arrested in a pre-Oedipal moment of maternal bonding. Both of the songs Jolson sings in blackface are focused on the mother, indicating that staged blackface signifies a protected arena in which men can be boys.

Jolson in burnt cork is "a-comin'" to the smiles of his "Mother O'Mine" or his "Mammy" (Fig. 2.10). His outstretched arms, his pleading on bended knee, his passionate declaration of loyalty and love, his whitened and widened mouth, his effort to gain the approval of his mother and girlfriend: All these unman as effectively as hypermasculinization and castration do in Griffith's film.[17] As in Jack's first song in *Coffee Dans*, "Dirty Hands, Dirty Face" (about a part-devilish, part-angelic little boy), blackface provides white men a playful and temporary make-believe place to regress to an infantilized or effeminized bonding with (phantom) black boys or with a lost pre-Oedipal boyhood. At one and the same time Huck Finn and Jim, Jack corroborates Leslie Fiedler's point that Americans are "Born theoretically white" but permitted to pass their "adolescence as imaginary Negroes" (*Waiting for the End*, 134), even as Jack's two faces prove Yudelson correct: The blackened entertainer is the white performer's "nigger."

Therefore, the Jolson who had already made his reputation as a blackface belter and the Jack Robin based on that historic Jolson are masculinized by the feminized part of the slave their art masters. The final scene of *The Jazz Singer* confers upon Jack his mother's approbation, his girlfriend's adoration, and his own status as a successful white male adult. While the represented darkie is infantalized, the representing ventriloquist is empowered (only white boys have Mammies, after all) and allowed to win the girl who symbolizes the American success story by first posing, then defusing the visual threat of Mama or Mary coupling with a black man (only white men relinquish their Mammies for white Mommy-surrogates). As Rogin argues, the Warner Brothers production thus holds out the promise that acceptance of interfaith marriages between Jews and Christians can ward off inter-racial marriages between blacks and whites.

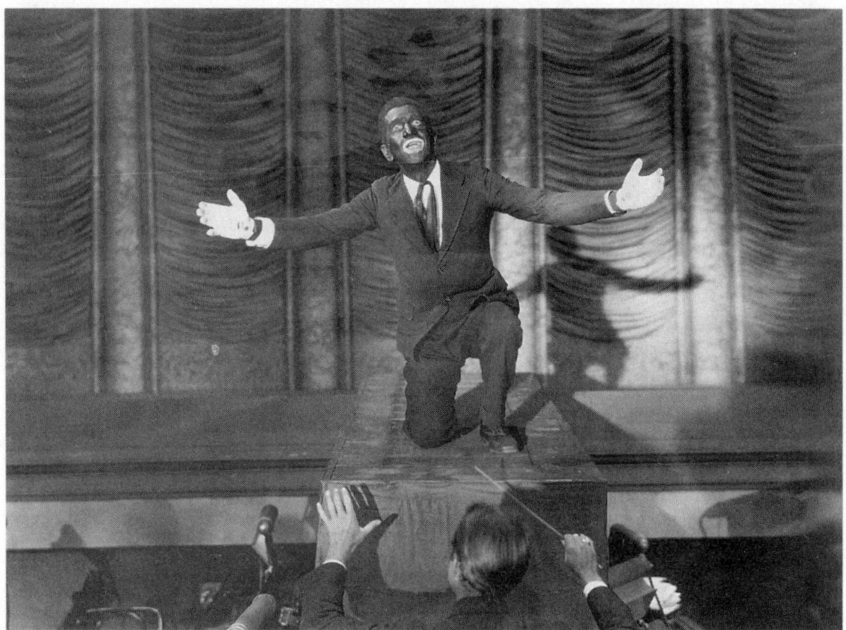

Figure 2.10 Al Jolson in the final scene of *The Jazz Singer*. Courtesy of Photofest.

But if burnt cork flirts with boyishness as well as miscegenation, *The Jazz Singer* also asks, what is the relationship between Jews, black mimicry, and African Americans? Oddly, blackface here seems to stage a mourning over precisely the injust spirit-murder it repeatedly enacts. An anti-semitic review written by Aldous Huxley picks up on the idea of mother love to examine the connection between the Jewish and jazzy faces of Jolson. According to Huxley, "dark and polished young Hebrews, whose souls were in those mournfully sagging, seasickishly undulating melodies of mother love," created characteristically "Jewish contributions to modern popular music" (Huxley, 58). Here the often-noted absence of "real" jazz from *The Jazz Singer* signifies the presence of the Jew-as-Jazz, the Jew-as-black. Not only such blackface Jewish stars as Sophie Tucker, Eddie Cantor, George Jessel, and Jolson himself but also Jewish "swing" composers and musicians like George Gershwin, Irving Berlin, Jerome Kern, and Benny Goodman forged links between the cultures of "dark Hebrews" and blacks. What Ann Douglas calls "Black art in whiteface" may or may not have been generated by the commonality she claims between Jewish and African-American music; however, the success of white blackface performers did coincide with the years of black exile from musical theater (354, 358, 362).

Despite the displacement of blacks by Jews, various intertitles and speeches in *The Jazz Singer* create analogues between Jewish and black cultures. The very first title before the long shot of New York's East Side ghetto explains that its daily life throbs to "the rhythm of music that is older than civilization." Raphaelson, the author of the original story, believed that jazz, with its "rhythm of frenzy staggering against a symphonic background," must be understood "principally [as] prayer" (23). But if jazz is a kind of secularization of prayer, the movie portrays prayer as a type of worldly performance: In Chicago, Jack sees a billboard that attracts him to a concert of Cantor Rosenblatt singing sacred songs on stage. When explaining to his father the importance of his career, then, Jack argues that his songs mean "as much to *my* audience" as his father's prayers mean to his synagogue's congregation. Though Jack's new "religion" consists of the belief that "the show must go on," he fervently affirms about his vaudeville sound, "There's something in my heart—maybe it's the call of the ages—the cry of my race." Finally, when Mary overhears his chanting of the "Kol Nidre," she dubs him "a jazz singer—singing to his God."

Curiously, *The Jazz Singer*'s narrative about Jewish assimilation addresses questions of passing more rigorously than does the racial impersonation at its end. After all, Jakie Rabinowitz has to change his name, his clothes, his hair, his accent so as to distinguish himself from his paternal origins. As a Jewish Mama's boy, Jakie lives out in his life the infantilization of the stereotypical black boy. Guilt over selling out his family and its history, over what kinds of betrayals and compromises the American success story entails, about defying the paternal law ("Stop" is the only word Cantor Rabinowitz actually can be heard to speak in the Vitaphone medium), about replacing the Jewish mother with the *shiksa*, Jewish guilt—the gift that keeps on giving—drips from this melodramatic plot, splashing over in its typical excess onto the plight of the black who is not as free as the Jew to make all these profitable compromises of assimilation. For clearly Jack's success depends on the privileges of his white skin, his ability to "pass" as a gentile.

Of course Jewish assimilation itself involves remorse over the betrayal of one's roots as well as the white lies entailed in masquerades of passing. Jews certainly knew that such an assimilation/impersonation gained immigrants (including but not exclusively Jewish ones) acceptance by virtue of their proving themselves to be not-black. What better way for a "dark" Hebrew to employ in demonstrating his not-blackness than by putting on blackface as a spectacularly theatrical act? "The price the white man paid for his ticket [for passage from the Old to the New World] was to become white": James Baldwin's point infuses the end of *The Jazz Singer* where racechange enables the Warner Brothers' American hero to wash himself white by siphoning off Otherness from the Hebrew to the African. To revise those historic first words spoken in this premier talkie ("Wait a minute. You ain't heard nothin' yet!"), you ain't seen nothing yet; you thought those guys with beards and prayer shawls in the synagogue looked *verkocktah*, but wait a minute; at least they're not *schvartzehs*! If the African American is dramatized as Otherness incarnate, then surely the Jew who plays him becomes less Other, more centrally human. In *The Jew's Body*, Sander Gilman makes the point with this question: "Does black-face make everyone who puts it on white?" (238). To be white in *The Jazz Singer* is to need to define oneself as neither orthodox Jew nor black. As in *The Birth of a Nation*, ultimately the American certifies his identity by proving himself not African-American.

Uncannily, though, in blackface Jolson looks like he is doing penance for the fact that ethnic acceptance and integration into American society are attained by stereotyping or scapegoating black people. Perhaps the poignancy of Jack's portrait in blackface depends on an inescapable consternation about one ethnic group rising at the expense of another as well as the more obvious icongraphy of the funnyman facade hiding a bleeding heart. Does *The Jazz Singer* focus from beginning to end on Yom Kippur because this holiday originated in the substitution of a scapegoat for a human sacrifice? That the film counterparts rabbinic ceremonies on Yom Kippur with blackface performances on Broadway raises this question, if only on a visceral level. "May all the people of Israel be forgiven including all the strangers who live in their midst, for all people are at fault": The words of the "Kol Nidre" prayer make explicit the moral urgency of mourning over past misdeeds so as to gain absolution. Penitential like the ashes of Ash Wednesday or the sackcloth and ashes of Nineveh, burnt cork evokes the dust of the grave, reparation for past losses and lapses, all of which find analogues in a soundtrack that returns not only to "Kol Nidre" but also to "Yahrzeit," the prayer for the dead. For if blackface signifies the death of Otherness (the cantor is dead, long live the entertainer!; Mama is displaced, long live the shiksa!), it reminds us that the Jew, standing in the place of the stigmatized African American, suffers the scapegoated Other's fate even as he inflicts a violence on the absent Other, a point to which a publicity poster for the movie testifies (Fig. 2.11).

As Rogin points out about this famous image, "Black holes in space fragment, stand in for, and render invisible the broken-up, absent black body" ("Blackface,"

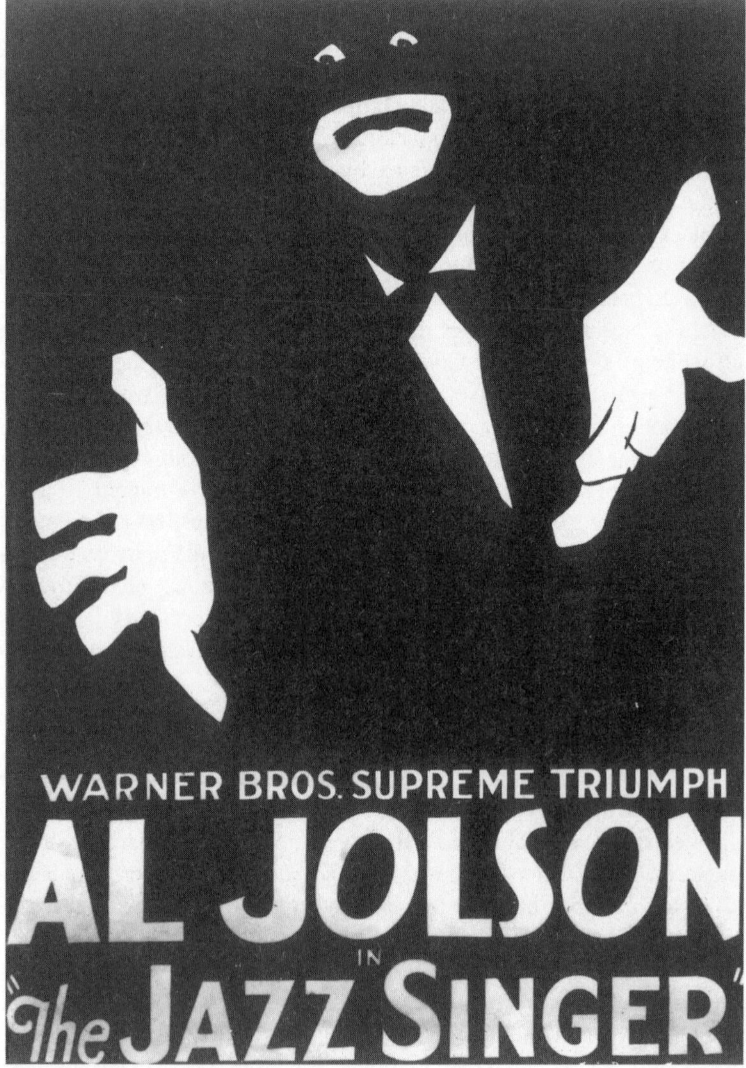

Figure 2.11 Publicity Poster of "Warner Bros. Supreme Triumph." Courtesy of Museum of Modern Art Film Stills Archive.

429). It is possible to view the character presented here as falling back into a pit of darkness, the hands outstretched and reaching for help. From this vantage, the eyes look terrified, the mouth less the all-too-familiar racist grin so much as gaping open in anguish or in a scream of terror. Grasping at air, the hands reach out, but the body vanishes into the background. Like the Undead or living dead who Žižek describes "as sufferers, pursuing their victims with an awkward persistence, colored by a kind of infinite sadness" (22–23), the melancholy Jack Robin seems "colored by a kind of infinite sadness."[18] Given the context of Yom Kippur, Jolson-in-blackface resembles a human (not a symbolic) sacrifice or the sacrifice effected by animalizing the scapegoated Other who evokes the figure Dorothy Sayers called "The Human Not Quite Human". One caption might be, "Don't shoot until you see the whites of their eyes."

Although Jewish anguish assuredly is not the point of the picture, it lies just beneath the surface of black exploitation, interfusing the image with ambiguity. If the enigmatically connected Jakie Rabinowitz, Jack Robin, and Al Jolson as blackfaced performers appear to suffer the torture they inflict on the black male body, such a mirroring finds shocking confirmation in another poster from a later age (Fig. 2.12), for its central image proves the elasticity of racist suppositions. With an earring that recalls the gypsies and homosexuals endangered in Nazi Germany as well as the more overt Jewish star, the part-bug, part-Jiminy Cricket figure sneakily peers out of the shadows. The prominent star and saxophone attribute the decadence of jazz to the contaminating collaborations of subhuman Jews and blacks; if *The Jazz Singer* had tried to assimilate its Jewish hero into mainstream society by stressing the distance between the (white) performer and the (black) performed, the Nazi poster collapsed the two back into one. In the "Degenerate Art Exhibit" that toured the Third Reich, the image of the "Jazz-Jew" demonstrates that the division of labor meant to be executed by blackface never could successfully divide the dark Hebrew from the African or, for that matter, the white from the black.

The Anatomy of Blackface

Together, *The Birth of a Nation* and *The Jazz Singer* use blackface to put into circulation dramatically contradictory attitudes toward color. In particular, burnt cork articulates two jostling propositions made by whites about blacks, a syntax which contributes to supremacist ideology: "We can be (like) them" versus "They need not exist." The actors who played the parts of, say, Gus, Lynch, and Jack use their white bodies to take on the aura of the not-there black body of the Other, simultaneously erasing and reproducing, slaying and resurrecting him. As Philippe Lacoue-Labarthe, following René Girard, has explained, "the origin of desire is mimesis—mimetism—and no desire is ever forged that does not at once desire the death or disappearance of the model or 'exemplary' personage that gave rise to it" (102). Similarly, "*every* identification involves a degree of symbolic violence," Diana Fuss argues, because identification—like representation—entails the "process of killing off the other in fantasy in order to usurp the other's place" (*Identification Papers*, 9). Racial mimesis of the Hollywood variety engages white impersonators in a love-hate relationship, for the wish to represent the absent black body intersects with the desire not only to replace it but also to obliterate it with a surrogate that is debased as well as debasing.

Blackface in both films presents the black as (eventually, inevitably) castrated, lacking, wounded, feminized, a mark of meaning and not a maker of meaning, an object on display for the visual gratification of whites, a construction of white ac-

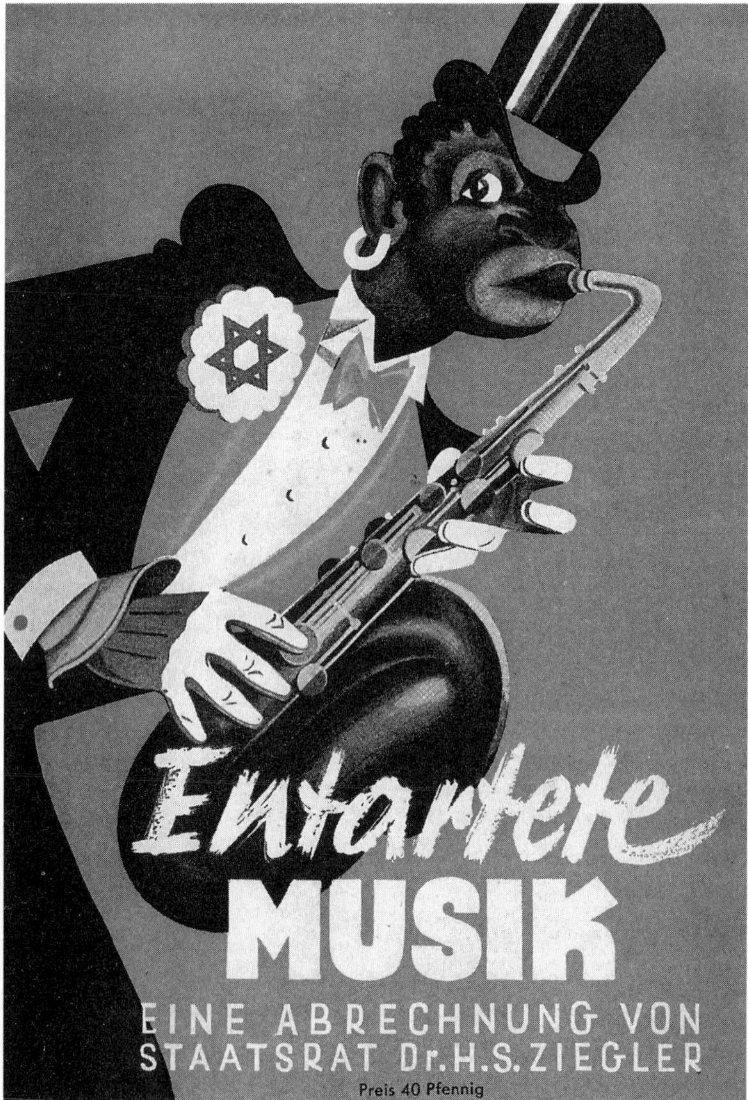

Figure 2.12 *Entartete Musik*, Adolf Hitler's 1938 poster for the Nazi exhibition of "degenerate" art. Los Angeles County Museum of Art, The Robert Gore Rivkind Center for German Expressionist Studies, purchased with funds provided by Anna Bing Arnold, Museum Associates Acquisition Fund, and deaccession funds.

tors for white audiences, a nonbeing. Within the darkened movie theater, with its screen filled with shadows and lights, blackface allowed white audiences to enjoy looking at a black person without having actually to see one; it allowed them to assure themselves about the inferiority of (especially) black men by re-enacting the devaluation or disavowing it. If, as one historian has argued, "Minstrelsy is negrophobia staged as negrophilia, or vice versa, depending on the respective weight of the fear or attraction" (Ostendorf, 81), the hypermasculinized buck of *Birth of a Nation* and the undermasculinized boy of *The Jazz Singer* sustain minstrel conventions, setting both negrophobia and negrophilia in the context of the Oedipal dilemma with its attendant anxieties about successful maturation into white manhood. Whether darkness signifies endings or beginnings, death or birth, lynching or infantilization, the rampant sexuality exorcised in Griffith's film counterpoints the childlike innocence exhibited on stage in the Warner Brothers production.

In addition, both *The Birth of a Nation* and *The Jazz Singer* frame the blackfaced man and the white woman as the paradigmatic couple which must be shot—that is, posed in order to be deposed or disposed of—as it is in many less famous movies (like, for example, *Kid Millions* with Eddie Cantor (1934, Fig. 2.13)). The breaking of racial taboos can be enjoyed even as the righting of racial order will (predictably, certainly) be established. But the blackfaced man/white woman couple—be it Gus and Flora Cameron, Lynch and Elsie Stoneman, or Jack Robin and Mary Dale—also theatricalizes precisely the sexual paranoia that helped establish Jim Crow laws and that was used to justify lynchings at the end of the nineteenth century and the beginning of the twentieth. Perhaps for this reason *The Birth of a Nation* and *The Jazz Singer* can be used to establish an uncanny connection between lynching, on the one hand, and, on the other, the popular traditions of minstrelsy as well as its Hollywood manifestations. Looking backward to Victo-

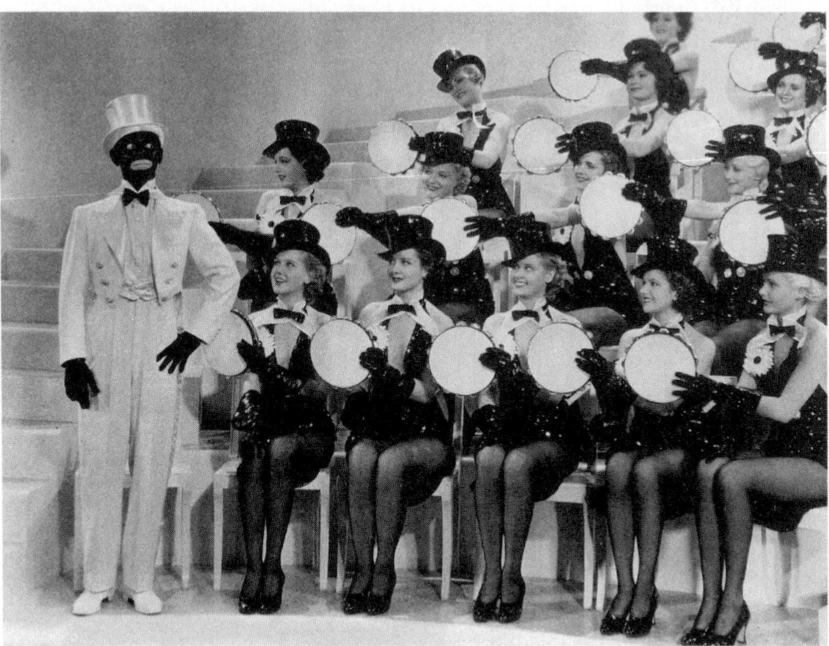

Figure 2.13 Eddie Cantor in *Kid Millions* (1934). Courtesy of Photofest.

rian minstrelsy and forward to the continued use of blackface in later twentieth-century movies, *The Birth of a Nation* and *The Jazz Singer* remain pivotal texts for understanding the curious mirroring between public performances of torture inflicted on the black body and the staging of punitive blackface representations.

Although most historians of minstrelsy date its demise with the turn of the century, the history of blackface in modern movies continues traditions that date back to Civil War times in America, to the Renaissance in Europe. Fittingly, then, the period in our history associated with "Jim Crow legislation"—that is, the end of the nineteenth century and the first half of the twentieth century when segregation was legal in this country—derives its name from the early Negro minstrel performance of "Daddy" Rice who, some time between 1828 and 1831, became a hit impersonating a rheumatic slave entertainer:

> First on de heel tap, den on de toe,
> Ebery time I wheel about I jump Jim Crow.
> Wheel about and turn about and do jis so,
> And ebery time I wheel about I jump Jim Crow. (Wittke, 26)

That the legal doctrine of separate but equal took its name from minstrelsy may or may not intimate public awareness about segregation as a farcical form of equality. However, from today's perspective, that tenet enacts a kind of unconscious repetition of the minstrel's insulting portrait of the less-than-equal darky.

One often cited pun from early minstrelsy indicates that white performers were not unaware of the economic incentive for their mimetic violence: The question "Why is we niggas like a slave ship on de Coast of Africa?" is answered with the rejoinder, "Because we both make money by taking off the negroes" (Roediger, 119). The modicum of truth in this joke consists of understanding the take-off of slavery and that of cross-racial parody as replicating forms of commodification for commercial exploitation. If we place Ralph Ellison's view of "the Negro as national scapegoat" in the context of such economic use, blackface performances justify and reenact racial exploitation. Add to this idea Philippe Lacoue-Labarthe's and René Girard's theories about a mimetic process that diverts violence onto symbolic objects so as to restore harmony to the society, and blackface becomes the secular rite by which a surrogate (black) victim is hung in effigy by the white community, thus deflecting violence's objectives away from that community.

In this next section, before returning to Hollywood's use of blackface, I want briefly to anatomize the various ways in which blackface performances can be considered a symbolic rite of scapegoating, the flip side of lynching: burnt cork instead of charred flesh, the grin and the grimace of pain, bulging eye balls, and twitching limbs or stiffness of body parts. For blacking up in even seemingly benevolent movies can be interpreted not only as a historical continuation of Victorian minstrelsy but also as an uncanny enactment of a punitive supremacist ideology.[19]

Historians disagree over the number of people lynched in America during the turn of the century. Whether one counts 3,724 people lynched in the United States from 1889 through 1930 (Raper, 1) or 4,951 between 1882 and 1927 (Harris, 7), the notion of representational violence remains grotesquely pertinent. The connection between the physical violence of lynching and the mimetic violence of blackface is probably best encapsulated in the July 5, 1943, issue of *Life* magazine that features stills from the nostalgic "bio-pic" movie *Dixie* (1943), in which Bing Crosby played minstrel man Dan Emmett, as well as photographs of African Americans beaten by white mobs in the worst race riot since 1919: 31 dead, more than 600 injured, and 1800 arrested (Figs. 2.14–2.16). Through mimetic mimicry, the gothic effects of scapegoating inflicted on the Other are played out on the body of the white impersonator, turning blackface not simply into a justification for ideologies perpetuating segregation or supremacy but paradoxically also into a symbolic form of punishment, a compulsive admission of guilt, the figurative payment of a debt to the dead.

Burnt Cork/Charred Flesh

Whether as warpaint or penitential ashes, burnt cork draws attention to its own artifice, just as it did in Victorian times when advertisements pictured dignified, aristocratic-looking white performers (dressed in formal evening attire) counterpointed by images of the strumming and strutting Zip Coons they impersonated in a kind of temporary slumming. Once again, a nineteenth-century joke emphasizes the nonmimetic effrontery of blackface as well as the ways in which such artifice constituted not only a brief installment of symbolic death or mourning but also a flirtation with feminization. "Why am I like a young widow?" a minstrel-comic would ask and then answer, "Because I do not stay long in black" (Toll, 40).

"With white face," a *London Illustrated News* explained about minstrelsy, "the whole affair would be intolerable. It is the ebony that gives the due and needful color to the monstrosities [and] the breaches of decorum" (Wittke, 54). Although blackface in film frequently attends narratives of disguise or camouflage, cosmetically darkened skin is as often conflated with mud or grease or coal as with make-up; it is smeared on like tar, soot, dirt, or feces, enabling the wearer to regress back to what one critic calls "the height of polymorphous perversity" through "infantile play with excrement or dirt" (Roediger, 118). Its color sometimes called "ebony," sometimes "mahogany," sometimes "chocolate," the complexion of the face links the performer to commodity objects. At times associated with bootblack, metaphorically burnt cork turns the top of the body (the head) into the toe, consciousness into physicality, human skin into animal hide or leather.[20]

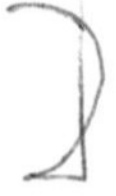

In Fannie Hurst's short story "The Smudge" (1922), about a woman who uses burnt cork to play the role of "buxom negro" maids on Broadway but who also manufacturers "Brown Cold Cream—Guaranteed Color-fast—Mulatto, Medium, Chocolate," the make-up transforms her into "a black crocodile" on stage, a stark contrast to the lead actress's "fair" narcissus and to her own "fair" daughter (146, 157). Yet "For everything fair" that her daughter possesses, the blackfaced mother "had brownly paid" (147). Hurst's tale revolves around the mother's "dark secret" (149), a secret about an illegitimate affair or an illegitimacy in racial origin conflated with the "brown mud" she wears, as well as the mother's dread that the mud will "smudge" and thereby pollute her daughter (151). As Rogin puts it, "Dirt

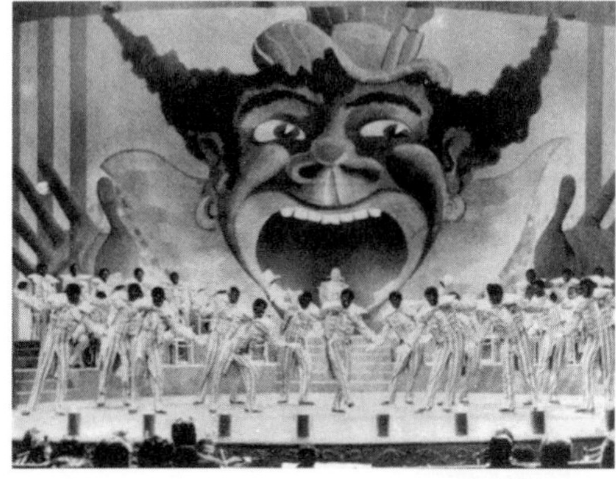

Figure 2.14 *Life* magazine photo of "Buck and Wing" (June 15, 1943). Courtesy of *Life* magazine.

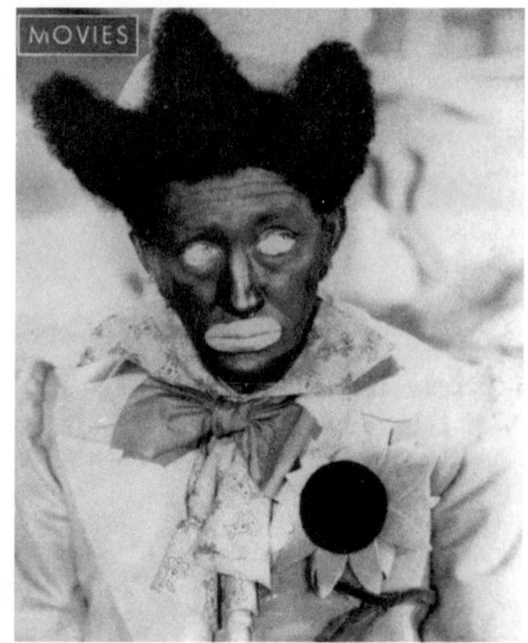

Figure 2.15 *Life* magazine photo of Bing Crosby playing Dan Emmett in *Dixie*. Courtesy of *Life* magazine.

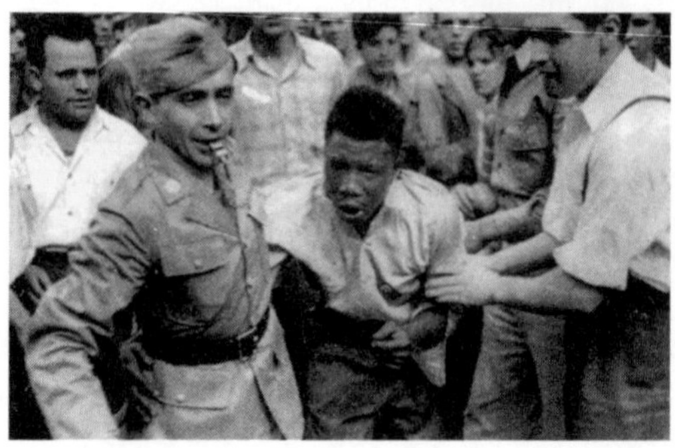

Figure 2.16 *Life* magazine photo of "a fear-crazed Negro boy" rescued by soldier from a Detroit mob. Courtesy of *Life* magazine.

was the magical, transforming substance in blackface carnivalesque (particularly transgressive for the blackface Jew, since the term *ham actor* originated from the use of ham fat to wipe off burnt cork)" ("'Democracy,'" 7). The opposite of purity and chastity, blackface signals not only the degradation of physicalization but (as it seems in the picture of Bing Crosby playing Dan Emmett in *Dixie*) also the penalty or penance of being covered over with mud, of being buried alive.

Just as linked to the base and the physical, the minstrel's Renaissance ancestor—the trickster-servant harlequin—often appeared in *commedia dell'arte* shows wearing a rough, bushy, or hirsute half-mask or carrying a phallus to link him to the satyr (Nicoll, 69; Gates, 61). Like the harlequin's dark mask, the black head of the minstrel sits atop an alien trunk (the contrast between head and body often marked by huge ties, bows, or collars), a signature of a kind of physical decapitation/castration. According to some critics, the harlequin's role became so stylized that he simply pointed to one of the black patches on his suit to become invisible (Gates, *Figures in Black*, 51). If the blackened body part looks like absence imposed (through burial or eradication or a process of petrifying or putrefying),[21] burnt cork on the face means a brain-dead minstrel who becomes all body. Blackface destroys the human subject on stage, replacing it with the black Other as corporeal object whose insignificance makes him invisible (like a pet, a servant, a child, a corpse) or hypervisible (like a pet, a servant, a child, a corpse). In popular skits performed in civic centers and town halls, hypervisible performers were sometimes called "unbleached American citizens" while invisible members of the cast were described as "so dark that they cannot be seen."[22]

The Grin/The Grimace of Pain

According to Carl Wittke, minstrel performers exercised great care in fixing their distended mouths, "for there was a rather widely accepted superstition among them that they would be unable to work properly in their acts unless this part of their make-up was perfect" (141). Red or white in outline, the large lips of the blackface performer connect him to the clown and, like the clown, he mocks language, reducing it to the physical either through dance, mime, gesture, instrumentation (horn, banjo, tambourine, bones) or by fracturing sense into highflown nonsense, pretentious malapropisms, and ungrammatical repetitions that emphasize its mere materiality. The "cork black, white-lipped, white gloved and 'derby'd'" minstrels in Leonard Bernstein and Alan Jay Lerner's musical *1600 Pennsylvania Avenue* (1976) engage in the prattling patter of bombastic incomprehensibility, their pretentiousness always destined to plummet them into nonsense:

UNCLE SAM: Well, Mr. Greenback, one must be pholocifical.
MR. GREENBACK: You mean lisophosical.
UNCLE SAM: I mean sifopholical. (369)

Accompanying the linguistic mistakes of the fool, the smile of the black man, according to Fanon, signals "Service with a smile, every time"; the grin "'as we see it—as we make it—always means a *gift*,'" he explains, quoting another thinker on the subject (Fanon, 49). The large lips of the minstrel—which Mark Twain described as "thickened and lengthened with bright red paint to such a degree that their mouths resemble slices cut in a ripe watermelon"—functioned historically to placate white guilt about slavery (*Autobiography*, 61): Look how happy those darkies are; they are not forcibly owned but give themselves freely as a gift to their masters! Sardonically or stereotypically, Gertrude Stein referred to "the wide, abandoned laughter that makes the warm broad glow of negro sunshine" throughout her most famous portrait of black life, "Melanctha" (1909, 340).

Later in his book, Fanon describes himself as "battered down by tom-toms, cannibalism, intellectual deficiency," but claims "above all else" to have been bludgeoned by "'Sho' good eatin'" (112). What the stage Negro craves are "lip-smacking," "mouth-watering" pork, chicken, and watermelon. Yet, as Fanon's comments about cannibalism and eating imply, smiling lips also represent white fear of black retaliation, white dread of being gobbled up by black people. An early minstrel song entitled "Gal from the South" typifies the conflation of oral and sexual appetites:

One morning massa goin' away,
He went to git his coat,
But neither hat nor coat was there,
For she had swallowed both;
He took her to a tailor shop,
To have her mouth made small,
The lady took in one long breath,
And swallowed tailor and all. (Lott, 26)

Large lips above the neck signify large lips below, placing minstrel performers—all (of course) male—under the sign of the engulfing, cannibalistic female, a form of temporary license the comedienne Martha Raye could tap in a film like *College Holiday* (1936; Fig. 2.17).[23]

Insatiable like that of an infant or an animal or a woman, the large mouth threatens to engorge what it cannot possibly digest. A blackface performer in Melville's *Confidence-Man* (1857) illustrates the ways in which the grin of the minstrel mimes the tortured grimace of the body in pain. A white man impersonates a "grotesque negro cripple" with his head thrown back and his mouth open—"at once target and purse"—to catch coins in "a strange sort of pitch-penny game"; "nearly always he grinned, and only once or twice did he wince" (16). Greedy like an animal, this human piggy bank symbolizes the black impersonator as repository of/for racial commodification. According to the French theorist Bataille, "human life is still bestially concentrated in the mouth" (59). Though the gaping mouth which signifies gross appetities can cannibalize just about anything (tailors, coins, watermelon), what it gives out is the false coin of malapropisms, pomposities, non sequiturs. Target and purse are, of course, exactly what the blackface performer makes of the African American.

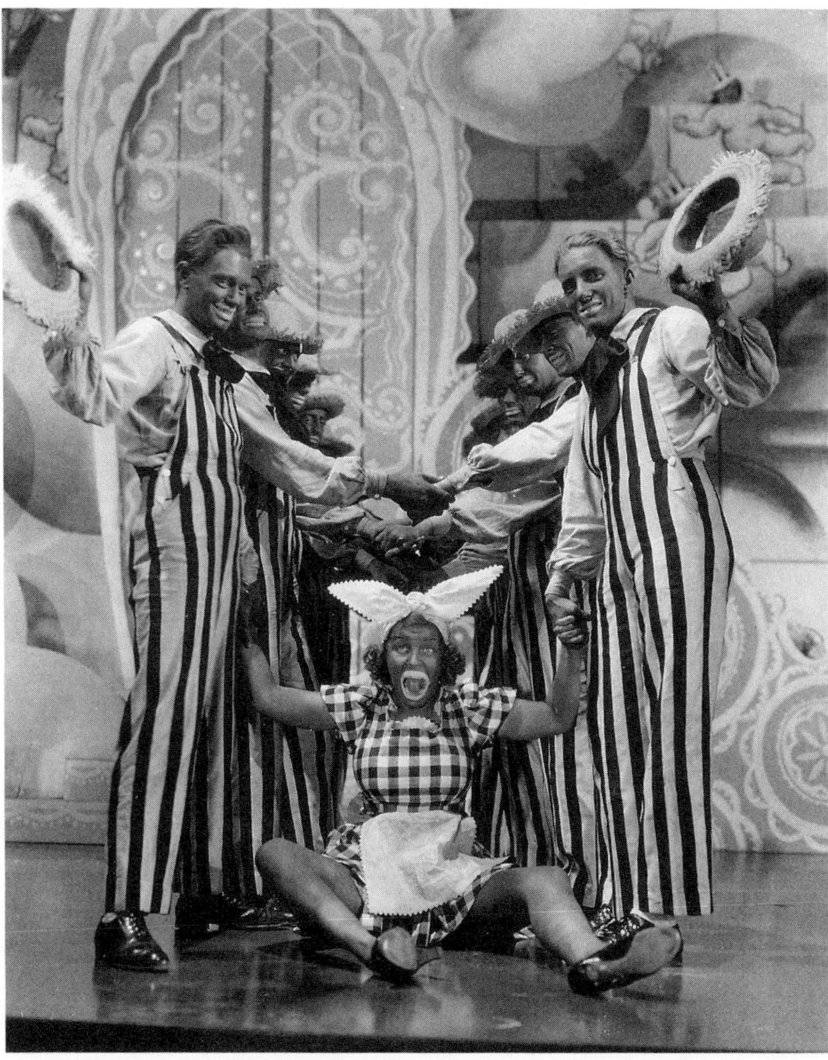

Figure 2.17 Martha Raye in *College Holiday* (1936). Courtesy of Photofest.

Bulging Eyes

When Hurst's mother in burnt cork blackens her eyelids, the trick turns her "good gray eyes" into "popping whites" (158). Characteristic expressions of astonishment, stupidity, fear, or delight on the actor wearing burnt cork mimic a look as easily understood to stand for strangulation and terror. Rolling or bulging white eyes may appear frenzied at least in part because enormous collars, oversized suits, and huge shoes made the minstrel look like he was drowning in his borrowed togs, doomed by the black dandy's misbegotten efforts to dress up in (an inevitably tawdry) effort to ape "his betters." The patchquilt costume or one composed of the Harlequin's geometrical suit of dark and light triangles created a checkered effect, setting off the contrast between black skin and white eyes and emphasizing the contradictory, disabling tension of the minstrel's being.

Indeed, such eyes belie the grin, or so Flannery O'Connor's description in the short story "The Artificial Nigger" (1955) implies. A plaster figure of "a Negro sitting bent over on a low yellow brick fence" was obviously "meant to look happy because his mouth was stretched up at the corners but the chipped eye and the angle he was cocked at gave him a wild look of misery instead" (268). Like O'Connor's statue of a Negro—which exists, according to her white characters, because "They ain't got enough real ones here. They got to have an artificial one"—blacked-up actors could be viewed as figures reified into "artificial niggers"[24] whose abundance might have prompted Gertrude Stein's apparently unmotivated aside in *Tender Buttons* (1914): "needless are niggers" (494).

Twitching Limbs/Stiffness of Body Parts

Two nineteenth-century observers of minstrelsy stressed the odd energy that seemed to surge through the minstrel's body parts. A New York editor who witnessed "Daddy" Rice's acting of "our American Negro" found himself most impressed by "such a twitching-up of the arm and shoulder! It was *the* Negro, par excellence" (Wittke, 31). And Charles Dickens, visiting New York, watched the famous Juba who danced "with two left legs, two right legs, two wooden legs, two wire legs, two spring legs—all sorts of legs and no legs—" (91). Eric Lott has discussed the "stiffness and extension of arms and legs" (as well as "coattails, hanging prominently between characters' legs, and personae . . . often pictured with sticks or poles strategicaly placed near the groin") as annoucements of "unsuccessful sublimations of sexual desire" (*Love and Theft*, 117, 120). Lott persuasively emphasizes the ways in which the black phallic figure of minstrelsy hints at homosexual attraction, male identification, and male rivalry. Just as noteworthy are the ways in which this phallicism transforms the entertainer's leg or arm into a prosthesis, enacting the rigidity that is rigor mortis, the stiffness of death. Frenzied but jerky in motion, the black figure who looks like a wind-up toy or mechanical doll on stage grotesquely shudders his way through death throes or convulsions that recall bodies hung, burnt alive, or dismembered in lynching performances.

When taken together, the anarchic impropriety and licentiousness of the minstrel verify Nathan Irvin Huggins's point that this performer offered a respite from the self-sacrifice and self-restraint of America's aggressive achievement ethic, "creating a distance between white men's normative selves (what they had to be) and their natural selves (what they feared but were fascinated by)" (357). Enjoying a holiday from the work ethic, the white actor nevertheless punished himself (at least symbolically) for the forbidden pleasure he took in physicality and freedom. Just as the minstrels' gags about slaves gagged African Americans, Hollywood blackface was only one but a quite effective means of maintaining racial subordination long after the passage of the Thirteenth and Nineteenth Amendments, a method that paradoxically played out the suffering of the victim on the body of the victimizer.[25] A ritual of exorcism, blackface episodes within Hollywood movies often display a curious combination of bodily pain and pleasure, physical confinement and release, bringing into modern times what Lott calls "the dialectical flickering of racial insult and racial envy" that shaped nineteenth-century minstrel impersonations (18). Always, such scenes return to the tropes we have already seen as central in *The Birth of a Nation* and *The Jazz Singer*, illuminating what Lott (in the title of his book on minstrelsy) calls "love and theft," a dynamic in blackface movies that teeters on a love/hate axis.

In "The Artificial Nigger," O'Connor dramatizes the community/communal solidarity effected by that dynamic when a feuding white grandfather and his grandson are reunited through their discovery of the "plaster figure of a Negro." After the old man mutters, "They ain't got enough real ones here. They got to have an artificial one," he feels its effect as a "dissolving [of] differences [between whites], like an action of mercy" (269). Suffering the fate O'Connor elsewhere described as "clownishness and captivity,"[26] the lineaments and physical attributes of "the artificial nigger" on stage and screen scapegoated blacks to bring together whites, testified to white guilt about the process, and eerily visited a suitable punishment for that guilt on the white body of the performer. Nor are such rituals of scapegoating over and done with: In *A Trap for Fools* (1989), Amanda Cross (aka Carolyn Heilbrun) presented a villainous university administrator casting suspicion onto African-American faculty by blackening his face before committing his murders. Nor are they simply fictional: In October of 1993, two teenagers dressed in Ku Klux Klan costumes attended a Halloween party at Yosemite High School (in Oakhurst, California) with a friend in blackface—whom they pretended to lynch. They won prizes for their costumes, though the school's principal soon regretted his decision to allow them to attend.

That blackface performances justified and replicated white violence against the black body is a point made brilliantly at the turn of the century by the plot of Charles W. Chesnutt's novel *The Marrow of Tradition* (1901). The degenerate aristocrat Tom Delamere puts on the long blue coat with brass buttons and plaid trousers of his grandfather's faithful black servant, Sandy Campbell, first to imitate "the quaintness of the darky dialect and the darky wit," then to dance "a buck dance" before admiring Northern visitors (118). Later in the novel, Tom again dresses as Sandy to rob his own aunt, an act that results in Sandy's imprisonment for murder and his near lynching. "He is black, and therefore guilty," one character explains (199). But the "example" of burning Sandy "would be all the more powerful if we got the wrong one," another white reveals; "It would serve notice on the niggers that we shall hold the whole race responsible for the misdeeds of each individual" (182). Blackface served that notice as well.

Hollywood's "Artificial Nigger"

From a host of take-offs and sequels of *The Jazz Singer* to more experimental, contemporary films, American movies have continued to exploit blackface. To begin with, *The Singing Fool* (1928), *Wonderbar* (1934), *A Song to Remember* (1945), *Rhapsody in Blue* (1945), and *The Jolson Story* (1946) sustained a tradition to which Danny Thomas (in 1952), Jerry Lewis (in 1959), and Neil Diamond (in 1980) returned in revisions of the original story.[27] From Moran and Mack in *Why Bring That Up?* (1929) and Laurel and Hardy in *Pardon Us* (1931) to *The Dolly Sisters* (1945) and *Somebody Loves Me* (1951), blackface played a prominent part in comedy and in musical production numbers. More recently and satirically, Brian De Palma directed *Hi, Mom!* (1970), in which Robert De Niro joins a theater of cruelty troupe that stages an audience-participation play, "Be Black, Baby": After whitefaced black actors dab dark paint on the faces of the white spectators so they can experience what it means to be black, members of the audience are then beaten, robbed, and raped. But of course such a grotesque scene reflects contemporary discomfort with the convention of blacking up which—in its heyday during the thirties—produced a number of movies that repeatedly returned to justify, reenact, or expiate the spiritual murder of American Americans and the eradication of their history.

Like Bing Crosby's burnt-cork number in *Holiday Inn*, Shirley Temple's use of blackface in *The Littlest Rebel* (1935) illustrates the uncanny way in which Hollywood movies that exploit racechange obsessively dwell on the inheritance of the Civil War, often to effect reversals that legitimized American slavery. After the sound track opens the credits with "Dixie" and "Old Folks at Home," *The Littlest Rebel* presents Shirley Temple as one cute little Virgie (Virginia? Virgin?), the pampered only child of an aristocratic Southern family threatened first when the father must ride off to join the Confederate Army and later when the territory surrounding their plantation is occupied by Union soldiers. Once the powerful Yankees arrive, striking fear in blacks and whites alike, all scramble to hide food and family treasures in a secret room that will also provide a hiding place for Shirley T. and a pickaninny-companion. The net result of the subsequent blackface scenes mark the true victims, villains, and heroes of the Civil War as white; African Americans just quake in terror as they watch on the sidelines, rooting for their genteel, gentle masters and mistresses.

To begin with, Shirley Temple appears safe only when she can become (as unintimidating or insignificant as any) black (slave). Looking to beat the white Confederates, Union soldiers won't hurt slaves, one black actor explains, even as his stereotypical cowardice shuffles him into a coat closet discovered by the Union troops (though they leave him unharmed, a testimony to the fact that blacks have nothing to fear but fear itself). Far more vulnerable but now wrapped in an Aunt Jemima bandana, Shirley can temporarily survive because of the dark varnish furnished by "Bixby" shoe polish, a preserver of the spirit of "Dixie" that would send those Northerners "away, away" (Fig. 2.18). But the true "white" character of that spirit cannot so easily be hidden: When the officer in charge takes her for a slave,

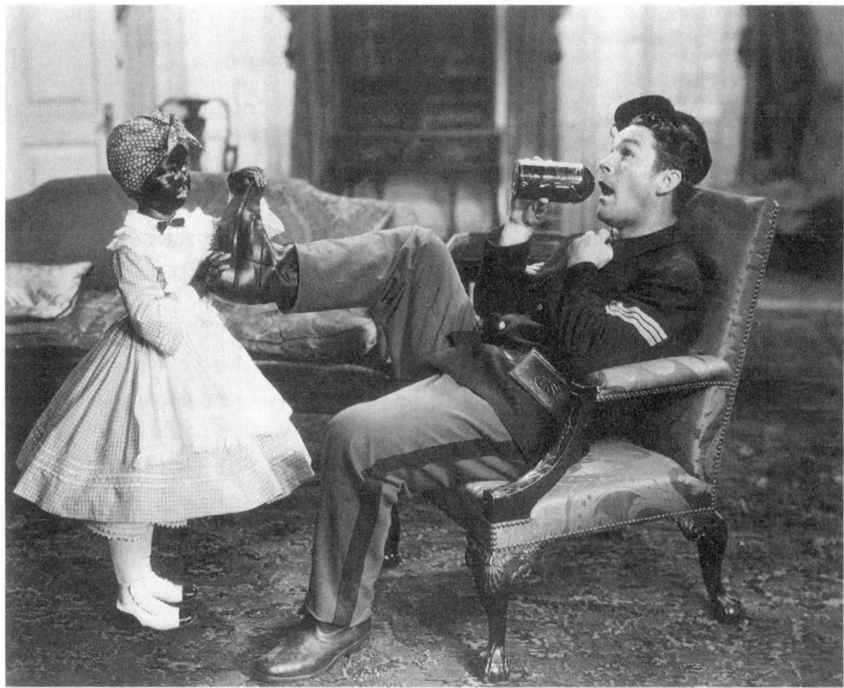

Figure 2.18 Shirley Temple as Virgie in *The Littlest Rebel* (1935). Courtesy of Museum of Modern Art Film Stills Archive.

sits down, and orders her to remove his boots, her plucky revolt against his injust possession of her father's house takes the form of pushing him off the chair. Rebellion is a white affair, bred of the privilege that makes it impossible for Shirley to adopt the role of subservient slave. A scuffle between her and the toppled officer results in the smudging of her polish, revealing a white-and-black blotched face.

The phrase "littlest rebel" gets applied to Shirley by the much more humane, kindly Yankee high commander who arrives on the scene just in time to administer justice. In this version of the Southern experience, good white men put bad white men on the whipping post. In a revision of the lashing usually imposed on slaves, the beneficent Union officer in charge orders his offensive subordinate to be whipped until he bleeds. Further erasing the dye around her eyes, Shirley earns her title, proving her intrepidity at precisely the moment she is revealed as only a make-believe pickaninny, an "artificial nigger" (to use O'Connor's sardonic phrase). As in *The Birth of a Nation* and *Holiday Inn*, Lincoln himself eventually makes an appearance in *The Littlest Rebel*. Drawing Shirley T. onto his lap and murmuring "Tell me about it," Honest Abe turns shrink here, issuing a pardon (not only for her imprisoned father but also for her imprisoned father-surrogate, the good Yankee officer) that proves the Civil War was waged to free white men. An even more direct character assassination is performed on African Americans through the portrait of its best representative, the wonderful dancing partner and trusty servant Uncle Billy (played by Bill Robinson) For though he hides Shirley in the secret room, Uncle Billy leaves tell-tale signs that lead to her detection (a skirt hanging out of the door) and becomes so fearful of the Northern troops that he drops a pitcher, inadvertently drawing attention to the hiding place. As in *The Jazz Singer*, blacks are childish, fearful, vulnerable; they can be saved only by the protection and authority furnished by whites.

That even the brilliant Bill Robinson is implicated in the character assassination of *The Littlest Rebel* and the other movies he made as Shirley Temple's playmate may be the source of the pathos in Fred Astaire's tribute to him in "Bojangles of Harlem," his only blackface performance and the climax of *Swing Time* (1936). A visually astonishing moment occurs at the start of this production number when a gigantic black face metamorphoses into the soles of two huge feet and then splits apart (in what Arlene Croce calls "a bad moment of 'amputation'" (107)) as enormous trousered legs (described by Croce as "long . . . guard rails") are separated and hauled off by a chorus of beauties, revealing just at the crotch area none other than Fred Astaire in burnt cork (Figs. 2.19 and 2.20). Clearly invoking the minstrel phallicism of big black feet and stiff prosthetic legs, the scene seems to imply that Astaire feels he cannot fill the shoes of his major black precursor, and so *Swing Time* works off Griffith's vision of the African American as threateningly potent. Indeed, the plot surrounding the scene furnishes the reasons for white men's fear that they cannot fill the black man's pants.

Swing Time begins with a marriage (of convenience, not love) postponed when Astaire's fellow dancers take his trousers away to be cuffed; only cuffed trousers are the vogue, they explain after drawing them on an advertised pair of pants. It ends with a similar trick played on Astaire's rival for his true love, the band leader about to marry Ginger Rogers. This Latin lover relinquishes his trousers when Astaire convinces him they must be cuffed, realizes his mistake, and dons the pants of his black servant, but they fall down because they are way too big for him. White men (even those with Latin blood) find black men daunting sexual competitors, the movie seems to hint. Significantly, then, Astaire puts burnt cork on after Ginger Rogers and he have kissed, and her lipstick has left a striking mark near his mouth. Though the kiss itself cannot be seen—it takes place behind a convenient door—clearly the smudge of sex (lipstick) leads directly to the trace of race (blackface) and to a dance that manages to express sexual envy as well as aesthetic indebtedness or even belatedness.

As a form of homage, then, "Bojangles of Harlem" addresses feelings of rivalry and emulation; Bill Robinson becomes Fred Astaire's role model, but Astaire's efforts to dance with (enormous) shadowed legs projected on a wall behind him prove that he cannot anticipate nor imitate nor control their motions. (That Thomas Rice's most famous Jim Crow act was his "shadow dance," in which a child actor in blackface emulated his every move, places Astaire's performance squarely in the minstrel tradition.[28]) A tribute to Robinson that admits he was scaled down to dance with Shirley Temple, *Swing Time* equates blackness with carnival, hinting

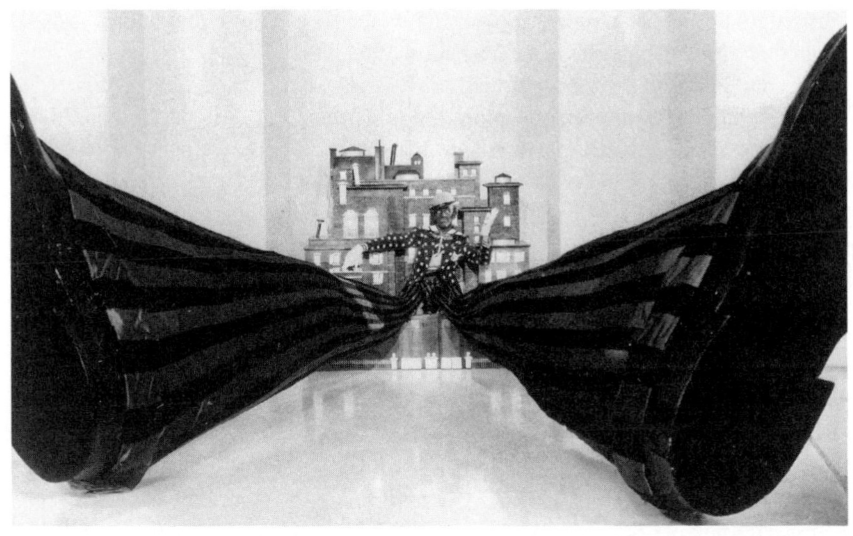

Figure 2.19 Fred Astaire at start of "Bojangles of Harlem" number, *Swing Time* (1936). Courtesy of Museum of Modern Art Film Stills Archive.

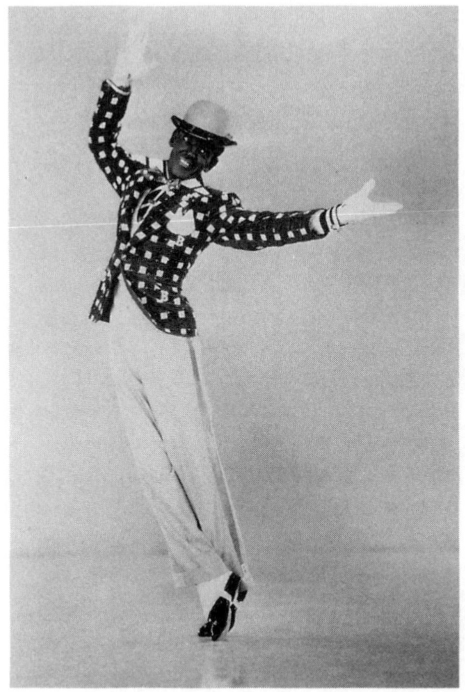

Figure 2.20 Fred Astaire in "Bojangles of Harlem" number, *Swing Time*. Courtesy of Museum of Modern Art Film Stills Archive.

that only on holidays or honeymoons can white people enjoy the bodily joy and grace that imbue Bojangles even in shadow.

By containing blackface within either stock vaudevillean comedy or historical episodes that self-consciously capture the minstrelsy "of old," Hollywood managed to recycle the form. An example of the first type of recycling—the recasting of humorous minstrel strutting and stuttering—Freeman F. Gosden and Charles V. Correll's *Check and Double Check* (1930) displays the ignorant buffoonery of Amos 'n' Andy, partners in Harlem's Air Taxi Company, within a plot that allows the two blackface comics to bumble into rescuing the paternal inheritance of the endangered son of their beloved white benefactor back in the memorialized, cherished South (Fig. 2.21). An example of the second—the historicizing of a minstrel episode—the characters in search of a finale in *Babes in Arms* (1939)—including Judy Garland and Mickey Rooney—perform a blacked-up number singing "My Daddy Was a Minstrel Man" (Fig. 2.22) because they remain loyal to the past, much as they do in its sequel, *Babes on Broadway* (1941) or in Crosby's depiction of Dan Emmett in *Dixie*. *Swing Time* is unusual in its deployment of blackface within a framework that at least implicitly questions the uses to which white America had put black culture. The white entertainer feels dwarfed by his belatedness (in relation to Robinson as a precursor) and his inadequacy (vis-à-vis black artistry), or so Astaire's doomed efforts to keep up with the brilliant background dancing legs imply.

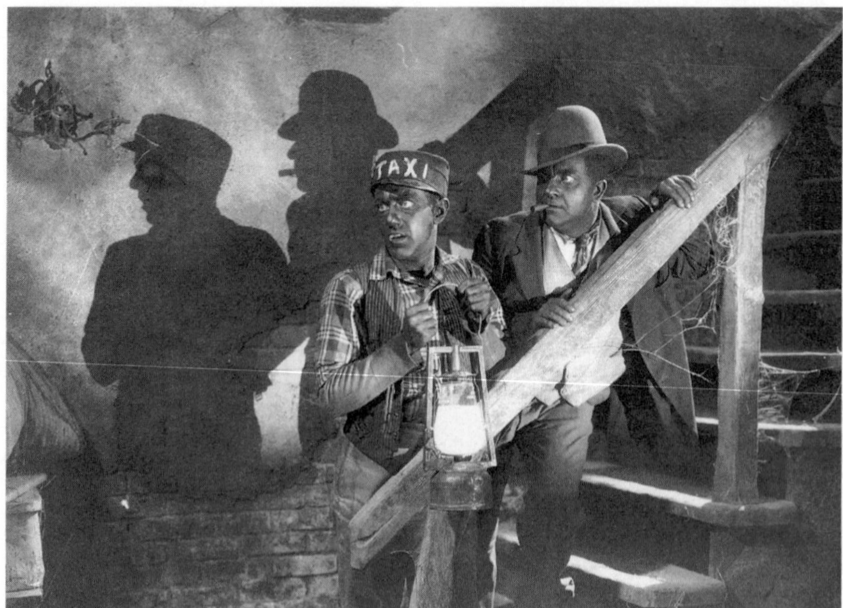

Figure 2.21 Freeman Gosden and Charles Correll as Amos 'n' Andy in *Check Double Check* (1930). Courtesy of Museum of Modern Art Film Stills Archive.

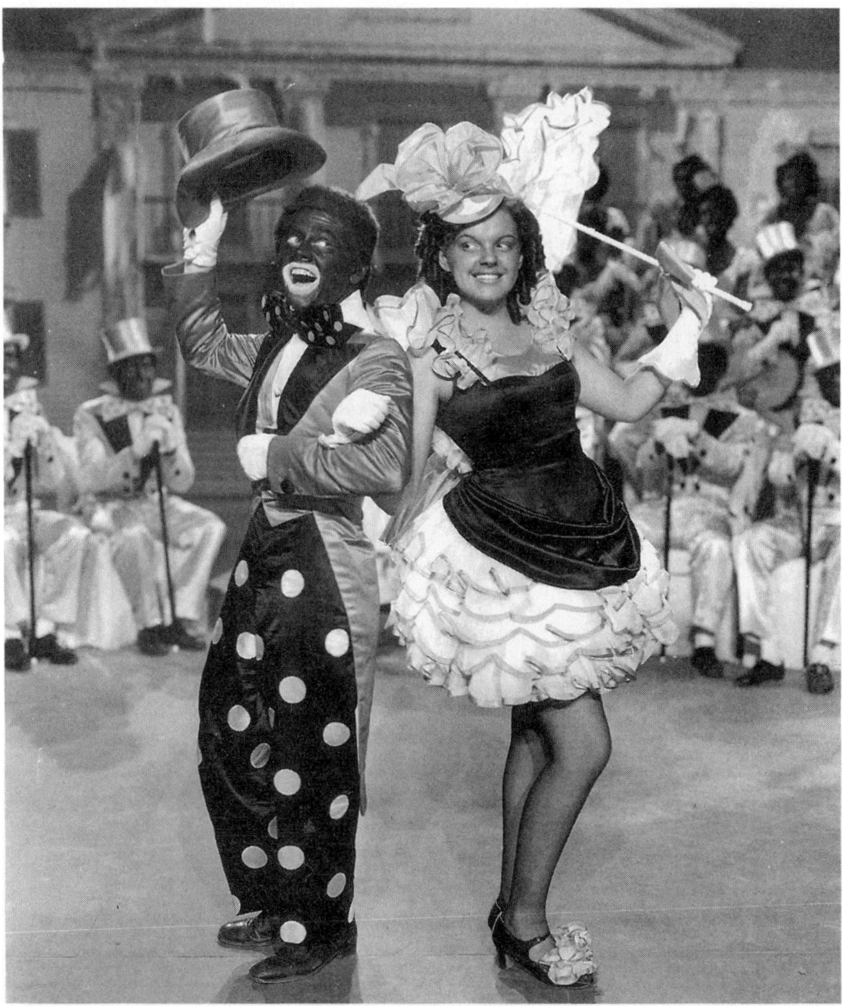

Figure 2.22 Judy Garland and Mickey Rooney in *Babes in Arms* (1939). Courtesy of Museum of Modern Art Film Stills Archive.

Although racist in other respects, the Marx brothers' movie *A Day at the Races* (1937) shares with *Swing Time* a use of blackface that attends to the racial remorse of a supremacist society. During a blatantly stereotypical musical interlude of prancing plantation darkies who are first held up as an object lesson of happy spontaneity, then led by a piping Harpo in a parade of "Gabriel," and finally depicted jitterbugging and blowing their horns to "All God's Children Got Rhythm," the black community exemplifies free-for-all antics (in accord with those of the anarchic Marx brothers themselves). When the bad guys show up (the law and the rich), Groucho and his two brothers hide beneath a wagon and use its axle grease to anoint their faces so as to escape detection. A number of curious ironies here and at the close of the movie draw attention to the guilt of an inequitable society. First, when the law arrives, the black folk scurry off, protesting their innocence but clearly assuming that they will be judged guilty of wrong-doing simply by virtue of the color of their skin. Second, when the Marx brothers in burnt cork finally manage to nail the bad guy in the barn, he is shown left in a stall with a bit in his mouth, a torture that recalls those practiced on slaves treated like horses or cattle. Third, at the end of the movie, the winning horse, High Hat, is identified as the Marx brothers' pick only after mud is wiped off the number he wears. "I haven't seen so much mud since the last election": Groucho's crack at dirty politics does not deflect from the visual point that High Hat will be denied his victory so long as he appears covered in black.

That people are what they pretend to be, that whites miming an Africanist presence will somehow undergo a moral racechange that blackens their character: This is the more typical point of burnt cork and the subject of *A Double Life* (1947), featuring Ronald Colman as the British actor (Tony) who gets caught up and confused by his theatrical role as the Moor in Shakespeare's *Othello* (Fig. 2.23). Although Shakespeare's drama attempted to reverse Renaissance stereotypes by presenting the white Iago as the villain who lures the innocent, dark-skinned hero into evil, *A Double Life* exploits blackface to reinforce the racist identification of blackness with madness and damnation. As in minstrel or vaudeville convention, it is

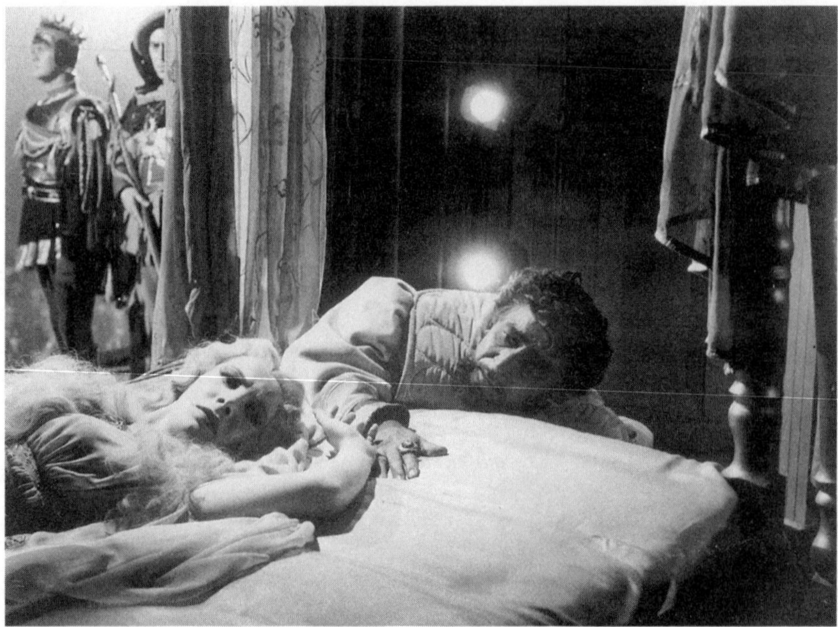

Figure 2.23 Ronald Colman as Othello in *A Double Life* (1947). Courtesy of Museum of Modern Art Film Stills Archive.

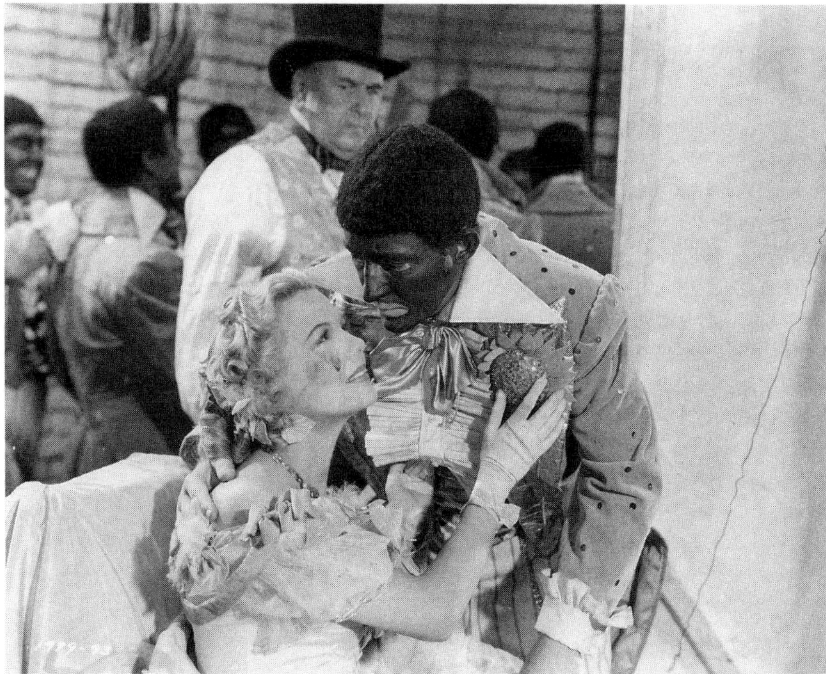

Figure 2.24 Bing Crosby and Marjorie Reynolds in *Dixie* (1943). Courtesy of Photofest.

the mouth that speaks of a voracious, destructive orality that would feed off and swallow the whole white world and in particular the world of white femininity. Seeing his own reflection in a window as the face of the black character he plays on stage, Tony becomes embroiled in a love-hate plot with two women: his classy ex-wife Brita (Signe Hasso) and the sexy waitress Pat Kroll (Shelley Winters). Jealous of Brita (who plays Desdemona to his Othello), he devises and practices a suffocating "kiss of death" in their final bedroom scene, but he actually perfects and uses it to murder her working-class surrogate, Pat.

Just as actors of nineteenth-century minstrel versions of *Othello* jumped Jim Crow between scenes, even those modern approaches to *Othello* that sought to celebrate diversity or Otherness tend to participate in the dynamics of spirit-murder implicit in the blackface tradition. When Laurence Olivier got ready for his part in *Othello* (1965), he explained the transformation blackening triggered within him as a kind of incorporation or even enslavement of the Other:

> Black all over my body, Max Factor 2880, then a lighter brown, then Negro No. 2, a stronger brown. Brown on black to give a rich mahogany. Then the great trick: that glorious half-yard of chiffon with which I polished myself all over until I shone . . . . I am, I . . . I am Othello . . . but Olivier is in charge. The actor is in control. The actor breathes into the nostrils of the character and the character comes to life. For this mo-

> ment in my time, Othello is my character—he's mine. He belongs to no one else; he belongs to me. When I sigh, he sighs. When I laugh, he laughs. When I cry, he cries. (158–59)

Thus Othello becomes Olivier's monster, a slave to the actor's magisterial artistry. How paradoxical, as Timothy Murray has pointed out, that Olivier's make-up can be seen on screen rubbed off onto the fair face of his Desdemona whose smudged cheek puts the lie to precisely the constructing and effacing of difference that blackface undertakes (112). That same type of smudge appears on the cheek of Marjorie Reynolds, presumably smeared off the blackfaced Bing Crosby in *Dixie* (Fig. 2.24). Alive and well, harlequin continues to perform the role immortalized for him by Joseph Conrad in his modernist classic about race, *Heart of Darkness*, ushering us into the darkness at the heart of the white imagination.

3

MAKING WHITE, BECOMING BLACK

Myths of Racial Origin in the Harlem Renaissance

Can the Ethiopian change his skin
  or the leopard his spots?
Then also you can do good
  who are accustomed to do evil.
—Jeremiah 13:23

Whereas men affirm this colour was a Curse, I cannot make out the property of that name, it neither seeming so to them, nor reasonably unto us; for they take so much content therein, that they esteem deformity by other colours, describing the Devil, and terrible objects, White.
—Thomas Browne, *Pseudodoxia Epidemica*

Just a few years ago, two scholars at Kenyon College excavated evidence that the Confederate anthem "Dixie Land," popularized by the white minstrel Dan Emmett (who claimed authorship), was actually composed by two black musicians, Ben and Lew Snowden.[1] The controversy typifies debates over scholarly evaluations of minstrelsy as a popular art form tapping authentic African-American traditions or as one reflecting the sexual repression and negrophobia of whites.[2] Could minstrelsy be effectively adopted and adapted by African-American artists or would it prove inexorably debilitating, even demeaning to them? Though, as Houston Baker has declared, "it is, first and foremost, the mastery of the minstrel mask by blacks that constitutes a primary move in Afro-American discursive modernism" (*Modernism and the Harlem Renaissance,* 17), the answer to both these questions remains a resounding "yes" in the cultural achievements produced during the oddly named Harlem Renaissance; that is, in a period of astonishing productivity for African-American artists, one that never remained bounded by Harlem and that should not be considered a rebirth (re-naissance) because there simply was no earlier opportunity for comparable creativity.

What both positive answers reveal is the double bind behind the questions. To adopt minstrelsy is to collude in one's own fetishization; but to relinquish efforts to adapt it is to lose completely a cultural past appropriated by whites. The problem facing African-American writers, entertainers, and visual artists was further complicated by the way in which the minstrel played out the age-old philosophic conundrum of mind-body dualism by presenting the white mime as the mind, the mimicked black as the body. A parable about the dynamics of cultural imperialism, composed by the Nobel award-winning dramatist Wole Soyinka, is worth quoting at some length here since it racializes that dualism, exposing the difficulty it poses for African Americans.

Soyinka's allegory begins by reinventing Conrad's Kurtz in *Heart of Darkness* as Descartes "in his pith-helmet, engaged in the mission of piercing the jungle of the black pre-logical mentality with his intellectual canoe":

> As our Cartesian ghost introduces himself by scribbling on our black brother's—naturally—*tabula rasa* the famous proposition, "I think, therefore I am," we should not respond, as the negritudinists did, with "I feel, therefore I am," for that is to accept the arrogance of a philosophical certitude that has no foundation in the provable. . . . I cannot imagine that our "authentic black innocent" would ever have permitted himself to be manipulated into the false position of countering one pernicious Manicheism with another. He would sooner, I suspect, reduce our white explorer to syntactical prospositions by responding: "You think, therefore you are a thinker. You are one-who-thinks, white-creature-in-pith-helmet-in-African-jungle-who-thinks and, finally white-man-who-has-problems-believing-in-his-own-existence." (*Myth, Literature,* 138–39)

Like Descartes, the minstrel writes a sentence on the black body that excludes African Americans from rationality, reducing them instead to physicality, desire, animality, entertainment. According to Soyinka, "I feel, therefore I am"—the acceptance of the minstrel persona—remains an inadequate response to the Cartesian "I think, therefore I am" because this proposition perpetuates "Manicheism" and also because it is "unprovable." Countering the "negritudinists," the African thinker advises the colonized to focus attention back on the motives, needs, and anxieties of the colonizer.

Many participants in the Harlem Renaissance anticipated the tactic advocated by Soyinka. They trained their attention on the neurotic motivations of whites and in particular on their dread of nonbeing, their need to turn toward African Americans as if toward being itself so as to negate white nothingness with a something destined always to elude. If a Cartesian thinker-ghost had monopolized the word "thinking" for himself, the black (taken to be a) *tabula rasa* could comment sardonically on the motivation of the white thinker's fearful alienation from the physical or natural. Curiously, however, an appreciable number of African-American writers also embraced the negritudinist "I feel, therefore I am" and did so at least sometimes in a manner that evades the naiveté against which Soyinka warns. Through a kind of "black black impersonation," some artists performed white people's conceptions of the stage Negro with a defensive irony that called attention to the artifice of the role.[3] If the only revolt against the Cartesian's "I think, therefore I am" consisted in scribbling the antithetical word "feeling" on the body of the black *tabula rasa*, then that body could perform such a script so as to comment sardonically upon the artifice of the physical or natural as an adopted pose.

Regardless of this swerve from Soyinka, most of the participants in the Harlem Renaissance would have agreed with him about the perplexity of their situation within a culture that denied them the very authority they sought to attain as authors. Whether African-American artists debunked white colonizers or glamorized colonized blacks, they anticipated Soyinka's attempt to counter the destructive effects of white supremacist logic. Perhaps for this reason, namely the problem of their color, often they returned to myths of origin about the nature of race, stories that fall under the rubric of "ethnogenesis."[4] Not "Who am I?" but "Why am I?" and especially "Why am I black?" are questions that repeatedly motivate and shape their achievements. Throughout history, of course, originatory myths have been used to account for creation, sexual subordination, even the geographical location of nations; however, in the twentieth century, Western culture has been polka-dotted by stories about the origins of color, many of which attempt to explain not only the experiences but also the existence of African Americans.

Two miniatures of such moments, one at the beginning of modern times and one within contemporary memory, can be used to bracket this period and capture the sense of frustration black people attributed to their entrapment in an alien and alienating white society. First, in Mark Twain's *Pudd'nhead Wilson* (1898), the light-skinned son who discovers he has a slave mother and wishes he were dead asks,

> "Why were niggers *and* whites made? What crime did the uncreated first nigger commit that the curse of birth was decreed for him? And why is this awful difference made between white and black?" (44)

Second, in an example of the "American Negro's New Comedy Act" of the 1960s, the following exchange between an unemployed black man and God returns to a similar question:

> "Tell me, Lord, how come I'm so black?"
> "You're black so that you could withstand the hot rays of the sun in Africa."
> "Tell me, Lord, how come my hair is so nappy?"
> "Your hair is nappy so that you would not sweat under the hot sun in Africa."
> "Tell me, Lord, how come my legs are so long?"
> "Your legs are long so that you could escape from the wild animals in Africa."
> "Tell me, Lord, what the hell am I doing in Chicago?" (Boskin, 222)

Tragic or comic in tone, such narratives about color record a sense of bewilderment ("Why" or "Tell me, Lord") at the injustice of racial subordination (the "crime" or "curse of birth"), the inadequacy of explanatory ideologies ("this awful difference"), and feelings of dislocation ("what the hell am I doing . . . ?"). Although they are strikingly dissimilar, both the lament of the character authored by the white writer and the joke of the stand-up black comic function something like the naive child's response in "The Emperor's New Clothes," for they question the obvious: Why more than one type of skin color? Why the enslavement or subordination of one race to another? Radical though they are in this regard, however, both remain conventional in their addressing blackness—not whiteness—as the problem in need of a solution or rationalization. "Can the Ethiopian change his skin?" asks Jeremiah, not "Can the Israelite change his?"[5] Even when a seventeenth-century skeptic like Thomas Browne rejected the notion that "a mighty and considerable part of mankinde, should first acquire and still retain the glosse and tincture of blacknesse" because of a "curse of God" (274), he admitted that this logic prevailed among his contemporaries. Nor did he ask why a considerable part of mankind should first acquire the gloss of whiteness.

Blackness may still be conceptualized as the problem because, as Andrew Hacker puts it in *Two Nations: Black and White, Separate, Hostile, Unequal*, "being white has a worth" (31). Hacker illustrates the point with a markedly fantastic racechange fable he tells college students so as to gauge by their reactions the estimate they place on their own skin tones. They will be visited by an official who admits a mistake has been made; each of them was supposed "to have been born black":

> So at midnight tonight, you will become black. And this will mean not simply a darker skin, but the bodily and facial features associated with African ancestry. However, inside you will be the person you always were. Your knowledge and ideas will remain intact. . . . [B]eing born to the wrong parents was in no way your fault. Consequently, [the official's] organization is prepared to offer you some resonable recompense. (32)

When asked to name a sum of money appropriate for this compensation, many of Hacker's undergraduates felt "it would not be out of place to ask for $50 million or $1 million for each coming black year," leading him to state that in contemporary culture "to be white is to possess a gift whose value can be appreciated only after it has been taken away" (32).[6] A similar point is made by a visually savvy use of racechange imagery: Dick Gregory's self-portrait in whiteface entitled "Stop the world, I want to get on!" hints at the privileges in class and in confidence that accompany whiteness (Fig. 3.1). But why does whiteness constitute an asset, blackness a debit? How and when did it come about that whiteness was experienced as desirable, a blessing, blackness a dreaded curse?

Perhaps inevitably, the overvaluation of white over black in Western culture has meant that most etiological accounts of color take whiteness as a starting point or standard, blackness as a deviance or devolution. In addition, given recent critical speculations about the fictionality of race and the inadequacy of representing the spectrum of diverse colors through the simple binary of white and black, such myths of racial origin may seem reductive, even biologically essentialist. Yet this type of story enabled twentieth-century artists to meditate on the relationship between "Descartes" and the "jungle"—Euro-American and African civilizations—while illuminating the imaginative centrality of race in our cultural history. In particular, originatory narratives about race often exploit images of racial meta-

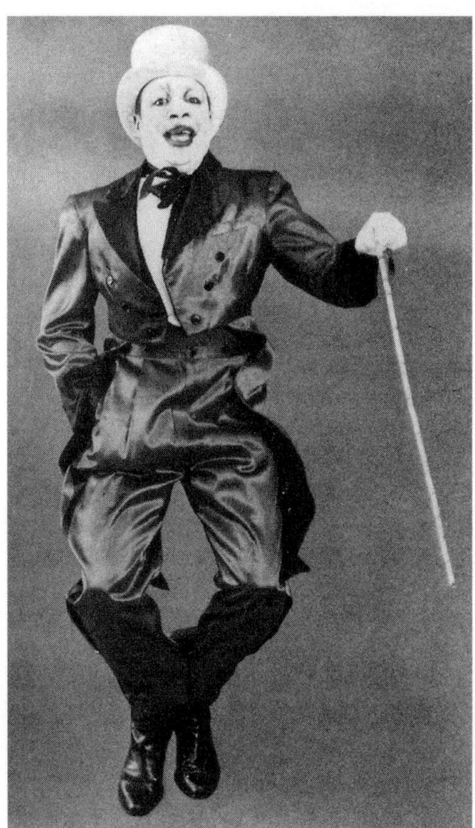

Figure 3.1 "Stop the world, I want to get on!," from Dick Gregory, *What's Happening?* (Dutton 1965), photographs by Jerry Yulsman. Courtesy of Dick Gregory.

morphosis: "Tonight, you will become black." While, as we have seen, blackface impersonations justified and even reenacted the subordination of African Americans, Ur-myths of racechange surfaced to interrogate, subvert, or topple racist stereotypes. During the Harlem Renaissance—from the teens through the early thirties—they even enabled some artists to wonder aloud, "Can the Israelite change his skin?" or to create an atmosphere in which some spectators might worry, "Lord, how come I'm so white?" Black modernists who deployed originatory fables of racechange to defamiliarize race relations sought to explain the inexplicable, to narrate the irrational, to confront and confound the "awful difference . . . between black and white."

Produced in the 1920s, the verse of Anne Spencer, the drawings of Richard Bruce Nugent, and the early dramatic work of Zora Neale Hurston can serve to establish a complex set of prevailing twentieth-century attitudes toward color, although these quite different achievements have gone largely ignored by cultural historians.[7] Taken together, the myths of ethnogenesis they fashion lay bare the structure of racial domination that infiltrates all manner of thinking and in so doing offers alternative ways of imagining the relationship of white to black. Anne Spencer's verse and Richard Bruce Nugent's prints stand for a newly militant effort among African-American artists to right the wrongs of history by reversing normative valuations of color: Some artists of the Harlem Renaissance accomplished this the way Spencer did, through a scathing vilification of whiteness, while others achieved it the way Nugent did, through the glorification (really the glamorization) of blackness. As if using the same logic as that of Soyinka, Spencer and Nugent analyze the Cartesian ghosts of Western culture that have framed the mind-body problem in racial terms. For Spencer and Nugent, black is the color of natural energy or primacy, while white is the color of unnatural entropy or belatedness. In other words, black being counters white nothingness, and both artists lay bare what the "white-man-who-has-problems-believing-in-his-own-existence" experiences during his encounters within "the jungle of the black," namely the insecurity that motivates cultural imperialism.

When placed alongside the achievements of their contemporaries, Spencer's critique of whiteness and Nugent's valoration of blackness link racial identity to performance. Whereas black characters imitating whites in passing narratives contributed to the deflation of whiteness, African-American entertainers imitating whites imitating blacks staged the valorization of blackness. Thus, two racechanging creatures emerge from Spencer's and Nugent's subversive approach to the etiological primacy of color: The former's angry account of the fall from a paradise of color hinges on the doomed "ex-coloured" character, while the latter's fanciful study of a colorful paradise regained deploys the resilient "re-colored" character. Noteworthy though the efforts of Spencer, Nugent, and some of their peers were, however, they pale when juxtaposed with Hurston's much more disturbing portrait of racechange. For, by drawing upon the most recalcitrant foundational narrative about color in Western civilization, Hurston dramatizes the impossibility of evading the negritudinist proposition, "I feel, therefore I am." In the process, she clarifies the ways in which hegemonic myths of originatory racechanges functioned historically to justify and even abet the subjugation of people of color by setting in place the political and spiritual systems that defined whiteness as an asset and a blessing, blackness as a debit and a curse.

Paradise Lost: Ex-Colored and Excoriated

What is the basic relationship of blackness to whiteness and why is it that black has been dominated by white? The first stanza of Anne Spencer's poem "White Things"—which appeared in a 1923 issue of *The Crisis*—strikingly disentangles preponderance from power, majority from might, in its meditation on these questions:

> Most things are colorful things—the sky, earth, and sea.
>   Black men are most men; but the white are free!
> White things are rare things; so rare, so rare
> They stole from out a silvered world—somewhere.
> Finding earth-plains fair plains, save greenly grassed,

They strewed white feathers of cowardice, as they passed;
The golden stars with lances fine,
The hills all red and darkened pine,
They blanched with their wand of power;
And turned the blood in a ruby rose
To a poor white poppy-flower. (ll. 1–11)

Beginning with black human beings, Spencer's poem subversively locates whiteness as an aberration. Most of the earth and its inhabitants are colored so where did the whites come from and why, asks the poet, is the white race "free"?

Unlike black men in Spencer's poem, whose color complements the green plains, golden stars, red hills, darkened pines, and ruby rose of nature, the white race appears unnatural: Whiteness is represented by "things," rather than beings, things which are "rare" and alien, as if from a "silvered" world elsewhere. Interlopers on the earth, the whites steal (creep out) into the world of sky, earth, and sea so as to steal (appropriate) it by steeling for warfare. Indeed, the first stanza ends with a cluster of images of destruction: "white feathers of cowardice," used throughout World War I to encourage men to volunteer for the front and almost certain death; the "wand of power" as a magical, magisterial phallus or weapon; the blood drained from the bleached, blanched "white poppy-flower." Rare, expensive, silver white things have devolved by the end of the stanza to "poor" white things, for the "wand" of white power blanches or bleaches, leaching color from the earth.

In the second and final stanza of "White Things," the stealing of the whites moves beyond pilfering and pillaging to the systematic murdering of a lynch mob:

They pyred a race of black, black men,
And burned them to ashes white; then,
Laughing, a young one claimed a skull,
For the skull of a black is white, not dull,
But a glistening awful thing
Made, it seems, for this ghoul to swing
In the face of God with all his might,
And swear by the hell that sired him:
"Man-maker, make white!" (ll. 12–20)

When the fire of the pyre changes black into white, life turns into death, burnt flesh and skin become ashes, heads revert to glistening skulls. In this nightmare conclusion, a ghoulish "young one" swings such a skull "In the face of God" and demands that this deity "make" the world and its inhabitants "white" or, in James Weldon Johnson's term, "ex-coloured." Spencer concludes her poem, then, with a scene of lugubrious drollery reminiscent of the fates of Gus and Silas Lynch in *The Birth of a Nation*. Her ghastly Descartes/Kurtz responds to the jungle as a suitable setting for a scapegoating ritual from a theater of cruelty not unlike the lynchers dancing "round the dreadful thing in fiendish glee" at the end of Claude McKay's sonnet "The Lynching" (1920).

As a statement about the psychology of racism, Spencer's poem suggests that the marginalization of whites, their insecurity at being a minority, their guilt at appropriating a world in which they feel alien, their envy of a natural beauty not their own, all these factors combine to cause the murderous mastery of imperialist violence. Here whiteness resembles cowardice or fear and its reaction-formation, domination.[8] According to one of the very few critics who interpret Spencer's verse, "the mad desire of a minority race to destroy everything unlike itself" triggers acts of terrorism against African-American men and women (Honey, 9–10). Reversing normative ethical and spiritual valuations of color, Spencer hints that the white race should be associated with evil. For the "ghoul" who swears "by the hell that sired him" utters not a pious prayer but a daemonic curse that God "make white," and "white" rhymes here with "might." The only hope the poem holds out persists in the quotation marks of the last line which contain the possibility that the God who made (black) men (not white ghouls) is a deity of color who will refuse to hear or heed the deadly malediction.

A powerful protest poem, "White Things" illustrates exactly how extraordinary a cultural moment occurred during the Harlem Renaissance because this poem traverses normative stories about race. By starting with a "colorful" world peopled by "Black men," Spencer topples the usual view of beginnings offered by traditional myths of racial origin. Throughout classical and early modern times but most explicitly in Ovid's *Metamorphoses* (ca. 8 A.D.), dark complexions and not light were explained by the climate. Ovid's myth of racial origin recounts how Phaethon overcame the objections of his father, the sun god Phoebus, drove his father's chariot, suffered a panic attack, lost control, and scorched the universe: "It was then, as men think, that the peoples of Aethiopia became black-skinned, since the blood was drawn to the surface of their bodies by the heat" (77). In the wasteland context—Libya dries up into a desert, nymphs bewail lost pools of water, river banks catch fire, intense heat melts the sands, and "Great cracks yawn every where" (79)—black skin embodies the misrule resulting from a mere boy-mortal attempting a god's manly job. Even when color was not explicitly associated with catastrophe, race itself became identified with dark and not light epidermis, a premise that explains why Thomas Browne, who rejected all the prevailing racial expositions of his culture including that of climate, wondered not over the existence of whites but instead "Why some men, yea and they a mighty and considerable part of mankinde, should first acquire and still retain the glosse and tincture of blacknesse" (274). It is hard to imagine Soyinka's Descartes in his pith-helmet peering into the black pre-logical jungle and asking, "How come I'm so white?"

Unlike most earlier speculations, Spencer's poem operates under the radical assumption that black people are the "first" race in the sense that they are the originatory, natural people inhabiting a landscape of their own; the whites—Promethean and Satanic—are second-comers, sly and destructive thieves. She therefore attributes racism to white belatedness, the anxieties of whites about entering a world of green, gold, red, dark, and ruby rose colors, all of which are born and born alive, while whiteness is produced by and through death. At its most gruesome Spencer's poem implies that, though colors simply exist, whiteness must be manufactured out of sacrificed black bodies. If blacks turn white only in death, perhaps white men are dead men, ghoulish ghosts in a silvered world of Unbeing.

As so often in satiric portrayals of lynching, whites are the savages who engage in cannibalism, the human sacrifice of pyring a race. The poet therefore sees the advancing, colonizing culture of whiteness as one grotesquely committed to transforming black into white and in the process murdering nature, killing colorful lives into ashen, blanched things.

According to Spencer, then, white culture dedicates itself to genocidal racechange, reducing black heads to white skulls, for no other reason than the need of whites to assert dominion. As Trudier Harris has explained about the lynchings that occurred between 1880s and 1920s, this ritual remained "fixed in a mental perception of [whites] as superior to other human beings," not (as during ancient times) in the belief that a scapegoat was necessary to insure the survival of a society endangered by drought, pestilence, or famine (12). The theories of W.E.B. Du Bois add up to a similar point in his extension of the thinking of *Souls of Black Folk* (1903) to "The Souls of White Folk" (1910), for in the later piece Du Bois simply defines "whiteness [as] the ownership of the earth, forever and ever, Amen," a perverted "religion" that he describes as a transmutation of the accident of skin color into a register of superiority (339).

"Make white!": Racechange surfaces as the crucial imperative of Western culture, the mandate upon which all other prerogatives depend, one which the black poet deplores. In this respect, "White Things" epitomizes a critique of Western society sustained not only by Spencer's contemporary, George Schuyler (whose analysis of racechange as genocide in *Black No More* was discussed earlier), but also by Jean Toomer. In one of the short, imagistic poems he included in *Cane* (1923), Toomer linked America's racechange imperative "Make white!" to lynching. Through its grotesque personification of those who perpetrate racial violence, "Portrait in Georgia" hints that the hurt inflicted on victims boomerangs to damage the victimizers:

Hair—braided chestnut,
   coiled like a lyncher's rope,
Eyes—fagots,
Lips—old scars, or the first red blisters,
Breath—the last sweet scent of cane,
And her slim body, white as the ash
   of black flesh after flame. (29)

Brilliantly collapsing several planes of meaning, Toomer presents a woman (with hair, eyes, lips, breath, and a slim body catalogued as in a love sonnet); an illness much like advanced stages of syphilis (scars, red blisters); and lynching (a coiled rope, fagots to fuel the flame).[9] The pathologized portrait of Georgia that emerges is a sexchanged personification of the character Anne Spencer called the "ghoul," here a murderous *femme fatale*. Like a syphilitic whore, this deathly dame demands the sacrifice of the black man who undergoes a racechange from black flesh into white ash because of a fiery consummation in "flame[s]" that invoke the hot passion of the miscegenation used to justify such scapegoating but also the whole burnt offering of the sacrificed body, which is the literal meaning of the word holocaust. To fall from the primacy of color into the hell of whiteness is to be excoriated, a word connoting condemnation that literally means being stripped of one's skin. In the shocking protests of Spencer and Toomer, whiteness emerges as simply the fantastic, destructive belief in superiority Du Bois had analyzed in "The Souls of White Folk." White ash is all that remains of black flesh after flame. For, as Walter Benn Michaels notes, "whiteness is produced by (rather than produces) the burning of black flesh" in a poem that turns out to be a "narrative of the origins of racial difference, a narrative in which white bodies are depicted as the consequence of violence against black bodies" (61–62).

Although novels about African-American characters trying to make themselves look white ultimately do contribute to the sort of critique of whiteness Anne Spencer, Jean Toomer, and W.E.B. Du Bois mounted, at first glance the passing genre appears to be quite conservative in its identification of whiteness with human dignity. After all, light-complexioned characters born in black families manage to escape the social stigma and professional restrictions placed on African Americans by pretending to be white. When the young boy of James Weldon Johnson's *The Autobiography of an Ex-Coloured Man* (1912) is shocked to discover from his darker mother that he is a "nigger," he knows that "she gave me a sword-thrust . . . which was years in healing" (19) because he experiences color as a "label of inferiority" (190). A similar wound of color pains the heroines of Jessie Fauset's *Plum Bun* and Nella Larsen's *Passing* (1929), both of whom reject this "label of inferiority" through white impersonation. From Charles W. Chesnutt's *The House Behind the Cedars* (1900) to the movies *Pinkie* (1949) and *Lost Boundaries* (1949), narratives about characters crossing the color line establish the material benefits accorded whites as a major plot motivation.

However, subsequently encased inside a hostile white culture, most passers are displayed feeling cut off from a nurturing black world. Making themselves white (though born black), they become "tragic mulattos," suffering a psychological and cultural splitting that reduces them to self-destructive liminality. Since whiteness ends up bringing them nothing but ontological insecurity, they ultimately experience their racechange as a kind of life-in-death, and thus endure exactly the doom analyzed by Spencer. Different as they seem from Spencer's poem, therefore, passing novels do contribute to the poet's satire on whitening as deadening when the passer loses a sense of social community, psychological coherence, and genealogical continuity. On this last count, the female imposter in particular suffers anxieties about those offspring she might produce whose skin tones could betray the secret she seeks to hide, and thus her counterfeit alienates her from the possibility of the life she contains within her. Her trajectory is one of homesickness: Beginning in a state of dis-ease at her confining black origins, she ends up after her traffic in an invalid white culture sick over her inability to return to those origins.

In this sense, the passer—neither black nor white—remains "ex-coloured." Since, as Michelle Cliff points out, "Passing demands a desire to become invisible. A ghost-life" (*Claiming an Identity*, 21), it brings into narrative the fragmentation and alienation so central to modernism. James Weldon Johnson's evocative term hints that cross-racial impersonation does not constitute a gain in whiteness so much as a haunting estrangement from colorful origins. The ex-colored heroine of Larsen's *Passing*, imbued with longing "to see Negroes, to be with them again, to talk with them, to hear them laugh" (200), typifies the ways in which the assumption of a spurious white identity catapults the black central character into a desire for a life-affirming reconnection to the African-American community. For to be ex-colored is to be Xed out or canceled: The X in ex-colored marks the burial spot of the excoriated, excommunicated living dead who can be reanimated only by a returning to color. Ultimately, the masquerade of whiteness undertaken by the passers of James Weldon Johnson, Jessie Fauset, and Nella Larsen deflates whiteness itself as a kind of masquerade because the passers comprehend exactly the gratuitous privileges, the almost religious assumption of election, Du Bois associated with "The Souls of White Folk."

Only the most threatening circumstances would lead a character into the excoriated excommunication of the "ex-coloured." When James Weldon Johnson's light-skinned boy grows up and decides to become "an ex-coloured man," it is at least in part because he witnesses the type of lynching scene described by Anne Spencer and Jean Toomer. Curiously, what he feels is horror not at the lynchers but at the lynched. Smelling the stink of burnt flesh, he experiences a "great wave of humiliation and shame . . . that I belonged to a race that could be so dealt with" (188):

> it was not discouragement or fear or search for a larger field of action and opportunity that was driving me out of the Negro race. I knew that it was shame, unbearable shame. Shame at being identified with a people that could with impunity be treated worse than animals. For certainly the law would restrain and punish the malicious burning alive of animals. (190–91)[10]

Another passing character in Fauset's *Plum Bun* experiences the same illogical revulsion: Having seen her innocent husband shot, his fingers and toes and ears cut off by "Souvenir hunters," this woman believes blacks are "cursed, otherwise why should we be so abused, so hounded?" (289–90). As if recycling a line about such anxiety that appears in Robert Browning's dramatic monologue "'Childe Roland to the Dark Tower Came,'" the characters of James Weldon Johnson and Fauset suspect that they or their race "must be wicked to deserve such pain" (l. 84).

Behind the twentieth-century slandering of color, these passages and Spencer's and Toomer's poems suggest, lurks the ignominious puzzle of victimization. Why were black people "treated worse than animals," why have they been enslaved or burnt alive by whites? Despite taboos of political solidarity that would censure such speculations, Spencer, Toomer, Johnson, and Fauset hint at the repugnance felt by some African Americans about the burden of their own history, a self-loathing spawned by the suspicion that somehow black people "deserved" or "acquiesced in" their fate, a dread that blackness has been inextricably contaminated by the unbearable shame of innocent suffering. By daring to write about such shame, of course, Spencer and Johnson reduce it to a sham, the scandal of a lying culture that would cover up the even more ignominious puzzle of why whites victimize blacks. What puts the lie to race shame, too, is the resourceful resiliency of the passer dedicated to survival. Through inventive self-fashioning, the passer reveals the deceitfulness of any script that would assign to blacks a sacrificial role.

Such tricky self-fashioning points to the last devaluation of whiteness to be discussed here, one derived from the color blindness induced by assumptions of white privilege. In African-American literature of the Harlem Renaissance, as in the Crafts' slave narrative *Running a Thousand Miles for Freedom*, passing characters, impersonators of whiteness, function like con artists who can move across the color line and return back again to tell their tale of trickery. Although their white companions are almost always duped, their knowing black relatives and friends watch the show with various degrees of relish, resentment, or remorse. At two points in *Passing*, Larsen's heroine meditates on the ease with which black people can fool whites. First, when she is herself passing, Irene thinks,

> White people were so stupid about such things for all that they usually asserted that they were able to tell; and by the most ridiculous means, finger-nails, palms of hands, shapes of ears, teeth, and other equally silly rot. They always took her for an Italian, a Spaniard, a Mexican, or a gipsy. Never, when she was alone, had they even remotely seemed to suspect that she was a Negro (150).

Skin, hair, fingernails, palms fail to register any visible evidence pertaining to race, making the category radically indeterminate. Destabilizing racial categories as well as the privileges founded upon them, the passing plot implies that "when 'race' is no longer visible, it is no longer intelligible" because (as Elaine Ginsberg puts it), "if 'white' can be 'black,' what is white?" (8).

Second, at a party where Irene's friend is passing, she explains to a white spectator that nobody can tell, "Not by looking," and then qualifies this assertion by explaining that especially white people cannot tell: "There are ways," she admits, "But they're not definite or tangible" and certainly not to the white gaze. In addition, "It's easy for a Negro to 'pass' for white. But I don't think it would be so simple for a white person to 'pass' for coloured" (206). In Fannie Hurst's novel *Imitation of Life*, as in the film versions of it (by John M. Stahl in 1934 and by Douglas Kirk in 1959), the light-complexioned Sarah Jane's imposture—a rebellion against her black mother's servile adherence to the role of mammy—goes undetected by whites unless she is exposed by her mother. (More recently, in Julie Dash's movie *Illusions,* a black singer whose voice is dubbed in for white women filmed lip-synching explains to the passer who is her producer, "They can't tell the way we can.") Why can blacks see racial truths that elude whites? Why do whites suffer a color blindness that makes the "ex-coloured" person unidentifiable?

Perhaps Soyinka's Descartes sees a blank slate in the jungle inhabitants because of a sightlessness linked to his propensity to project what he fears himself to be onto others. Larsen's plot corroborates her heroine's insights into the illogic of racial assumptions that allow "an Italian, a Spaniard, a Mexican, or a gipsy" to be labeled "white" by "fay" witnesses ignorant of the drama in which they are themselves involved. White people, who assume what they see is white because they can imagine personhood only in terms of their own whiteness, suffer a lapse in imagination also evident in their inability to pass as black. "How can you tell who is black?" asks Judy Scales-Trent, a professor of law who has recently published *Notes of a White Black Woman* (1995), and she goes on to add that the stigma keeping gay people in the closet resemble those that keep African-Americans with white skin inside what we might call a racial closet (88–89). Still, the color blindness of whites who "Make white" inadvertently licenses the black tricksters' illicit acts, their mimetic mockery. For, as James Weldon Johnson put it, "the coloured people of this country know and understand the white people better than the white people know and understand them" (22). Like Anne Spencer and Jean Toomer (as well as the protagonists of numerous slave narratives before them), he believed that such understanding was a necessary survival skill.

Paradise Regained: Black Black Impersonation

Whereas Spencer's poem uses racechange in a myth of origin to protest against Western civilization's genocidal determination to "Make white!," Richard Bruce Nugent's four "Drawings for Mulattoes" can be interpreted as an etiological narrative about the interdependence of black and white in the evolution of American culture, for his pictures of racechange hold out the possibility of mutuality instead of domination, indeed of interracial creativity. If Spencer's poetry epitomizes the protest literature that delegitimized whiteness in the Harlem Renaissance, Nugent's drawings represent the ways in which many artists of the period theatricalized race not only to valorize blackness but also to undercut stable racial definitions, thereby linking the crucial concept of the newly glamorized New Negro with the newness of modernism. To return to Soyinka's formulation, although Spencer and the black impersonators of whiteness in passing novels protest against white anxiety about nonbeing, Nugent and the black impersonators of blackness so prevalent in the early twentieth-century entertainment industry dramatize the ways in which African Americans stage fullness of being.

Printed in Charles S. Johnson's collection *Ebony and Topaz* (1927), Nugent's prints can be read as a series about ethnogenesis that moves from depictions of the primitive to images of civilization, all of which emphasize the primacy of blackness as well as the aesthetic centrality of Africa in the evolution of twentieth-century Western culture. In opposition to George Santyana, who censured American culture for leaping from barbarism to decadence without the intervening stage of civilization, Nugent portrays Western civilization as an enticing amalgam of barbarism and decadence. Drawing number 1 locates itself in Africa, but because mannered forms similar to those of Aubrey Beardsley, Erté, and art deco seem to stylize this landscape, the very notion of the "primitive" or the "barbaric" is put in question (Fig. 3.2). Three naked figures—the central one caught in dance? in ritual? in oration?—are separated by vertical lines that might be the bark of trees but that simultaneously look like totem poles or abstract, baroque panels of geometrical design. In the beginning, according to Nugent (as according to Spencer), was the black race; from its community or its representive figure (captured in the three different frames) a sense of mobility and physical exuberance emerges that contrasts with the fixity of the next drawing.

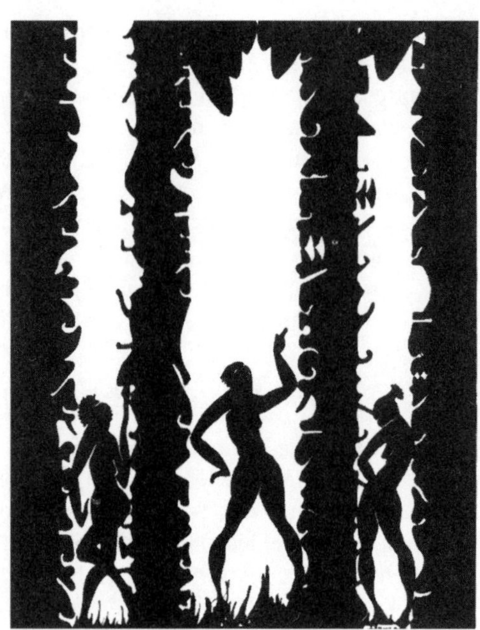

Figure 3.2 Richard Bruce Nugent, *Drawings for Mulattoes—Number 1*. Courtesy of Fisk University.

In drawing number 2, Nugent produces two images of racechange, one masculine and the other feminine (Fig. 3.3). The half-white, half-black woman in the bottom center of this picture—an ersatz, sexy Venus on the half-shell—may seem like a version of the jungle dancers in the first drawing. But here she appears encased inside the double-faced male head that, like the god Janus, looks both ways. And the features of this two-faced head reverse normative racial markers, for the dark face positioned next to palm trees has a Roman profile while the white face positioned next to industrialized beams has an African profile. Because the dancer has been removed from the African landscape and repositioned inside a mysteriously doubled patriarchal head, one could view this picture as a meditation on dislocation or exile. The African dancer almost looks as if she has been incorporated, internalized, or repressed inside the consciousness of the black-and-white male psyche.

One telltale aspect of this gestalt complicates and enriches such a reading, namely the odd extension of the white face's lips which look weirdly exaggerated. When we consider the exceptional importance of the lips in the portrayal of the minstrel—the grin of the blackfaced white performer who drew thick lines around a mouth often held or painted or photographed as gaping wide open—Nugent's drawing associates the idea of Africa with Western presence (the face on the left) and the transmission of the African to the Western world with a stereotyping of the black man (the face on the right). Can lips like these extended ones speak? Put another way, the drawing poses another question: Does the white man's burden consist of bearing the culpability for appropriating Africa (the profile on the left) and displacing Africans not only from their homeland but also from a sense of authentic interiority (the profile on the right)? And does such guilt create a kind of neurotic self-division? In a picture that rings changes on the two faces of ancient Janiform vases, Richard Bruce Nugent seems to meditate on Du Bois's influential notion of "double consciousness":

> One ever feels his twoness—an American, a Negro; two souls, two thoughts, two unreconciled strivings; two warring ideals in one dark body, whose dogged strength alone keeps it from being torn asunder. (Du Bois, *Souls of Black Folk*, 8–9)

Implicitly, too, Nugent asks, Who suffers double-consciousness, the black man, as Du Bois thought, or the white?[11]

The dancers of the first two pictures coalesce into the central focus of Number 3, another figure of racechange positioned against a background of stylized, black-and-white contrasts (Fig. 3.4). Nugent splices together the black naked dancer with the white flapper in her striped, two-piece outfit, complete with a high heel. The primitive energies of the jungle-dancer appear combined with the liberated sexuality of the New Woman. And again Nugent complicates any simple notion of twoness, for we are given the frontal portrait of the black-and-white performer except for her buttocks, skirt, and the back of her leg. Anatomically impossible, this creature thus emerges with various geometrical dimensions or planes on view in something like the manner of a cubist subject or a *Yellow Book* take on one of René Magritte's surrealistic creatures. Yet though we see "around" her, she remains mys-

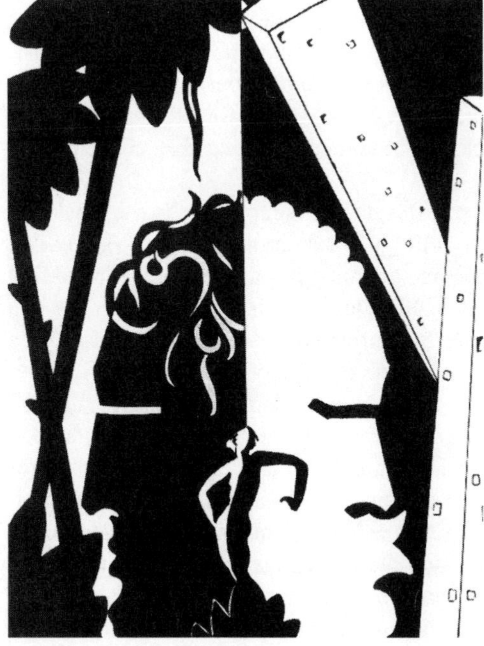

Figure 3.3 Richard Bruce Nugent, *Drawings for Mulattoes—Number 2*. Courtesy of Fisk University.

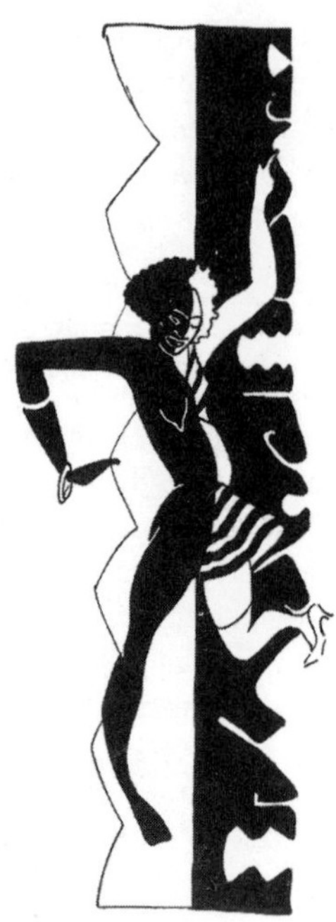

Figure 3.4 Richard Bruce Nugent, *Drawings for Mulattoes—Number 3*. Courtesy of Fisk University.

teriously Other, a composite of African and Western, old and new impulses, a fitting citizen of the place Ann Douglas calls *Mongrel Manhattan*. The clothing of the flapper and the breast of the African dancer appear to gender her female; however, the position of the muscled black leg (as well as the droop of the breast) seem almost satyr-like. As Walter Kalaidjian has pointed out, Nugent's "interracial images of the urban mulatto" recode "what was a conflicted figure of racial 'passing' and black 'double-consciousness' into a more subversive, cosmopolitan sign" (68).

Exactly the hermaphroditic quality of this dancer is replicated in the black and white chorus line at the bottom of the fourth and last drawing (Fig. 3.5). Wearing high heels but as naked and exuberant and androgynous as the women in the first drawing, these dancers again indicate that the Jazz Age offers the possibility of a recovery of African origins. In the central forms here, racechange appears as a playful reinterpretation of the traditional masks of tragedy and comedy. With a design reminiscent of the covers of sheet music, Nugent displays signs of the cabaret (the treble clef, musical notes, the (stage?) door) and a jungle scene (trees, masks, naked dancers), invoking song and dance numbers for jazz or blues nightclubs or the Broadway shows of the twenties. In this world of commodified African artifacts, which is the mask, which the face? Is the New Woman only a facade, the veneer removed here to reveal the flesh-and-blood black woman? Or do these two stylized images—neither tragic, nor comic, but highly reminiscent of Man Ray's *Noire et blanche* photographs—signify the ways in which the (black or white) feminine is put on display as an aesthetic spectacle? Linking gender with drama, the sequence also emphasizes the theatricality of race, the ways in which we are taught to impersonate ideas of color and its absence.

Taken as a whole, Nugent's series of prints questions whether the move from the African landscape to the Broadway stage or Harlem club is one of evolution or devolution, progress or decline and for whom. Perhaps the development is cyclical, a matter of the return in contemporary times of the far-away-and-long-ago repressed. Or is such a movement itself an illusion since Africa is "always already" represented through the lens of the downtown musical or uptown cabaret? What the diaspora means for artists like Richard Bruce Nugent is the impossibility of telling an etiological story about roots in an ancient Africa without at the same time inscribing the ways in which one's vision of the primitive must be filtered through a modernity marked by complete assimilation in American society. Any myth of

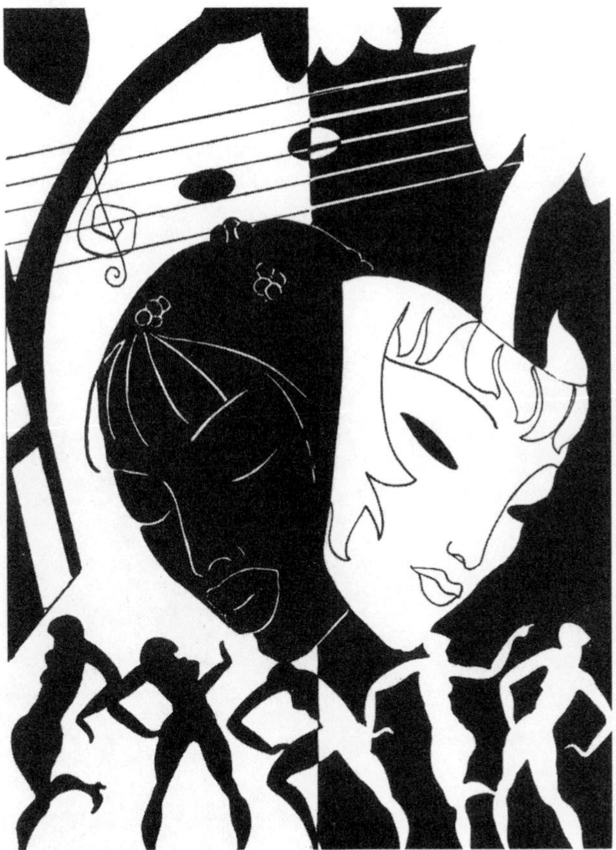

Figure 3.5 Richard Bruce Nugent, *Drawings for Mulattoes—Number 4*. Courtesy of Fisk University.

origins, Nugent suggests, must understand the African past as well as the more recent African-American slave past and the American present as several layers of meaning on a palimpsest, each calling the authority and integrity of the other into question.

Naked jungle dancers, sinuous flappers tapping the energies of ancient tribal rhythms, masked entertainers singing the praises of antebellum times on the plantation: By the twenties, American culture here and in Paris had been saturated by such images, often (as in Nugent's case) produced by black artists influenced by white precursors, patrons, or audiences. If the devaluation of whiteness undertaken by the artists of the Harlem Renaissance frequently assumed the form of black characters impersonating whites in passing novels, the glamorization of black origins associated with an urban and urbane cult of *negritude* led artists to adopt the configuration of blacks impersonating whites impersonating blacks—a kind of black black impersonation. Whereas the critique of whiteness helped form the "ex-coloured" character who had fallen from the paradise of color, we shall see that the romanticized staging of blackness helped shape what we might call the "re-colored" figure who regains the paradise of origins by fusing the past with the present.

As early as the 1870s, Billy Kersands exhibited what one observer called a "copiousness of mouth and bredth of tongue that no white man could ever expect to rival" (Toll, 254; Fig. 3.6). Filling his mouth with billiard balls or a coffee cup and saucer, he was rumored to have quipped to Queen Victoria, "If God ever wanted my mouth any bigger, he would have to move my ears" (M. Watkins, 114). His

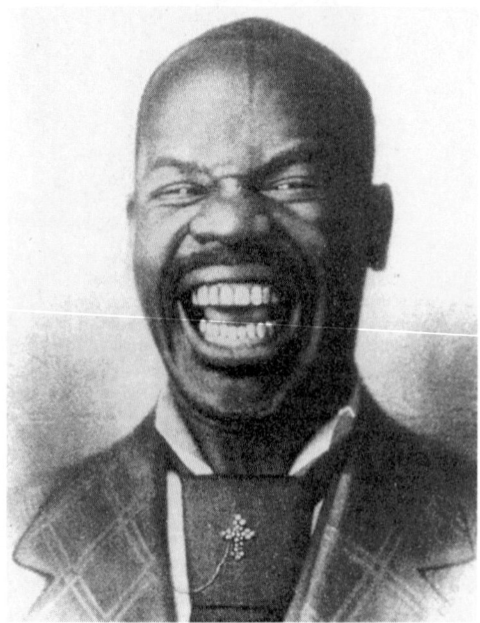

Figure 3.6 Billy Kersands in *Callender's (Georgia) Minstrels.* Courtesy of the Billy Rose Theatre Collection, The New York Public Library for the Performing Arts, Astor, Lenox and Tilden Foundations.

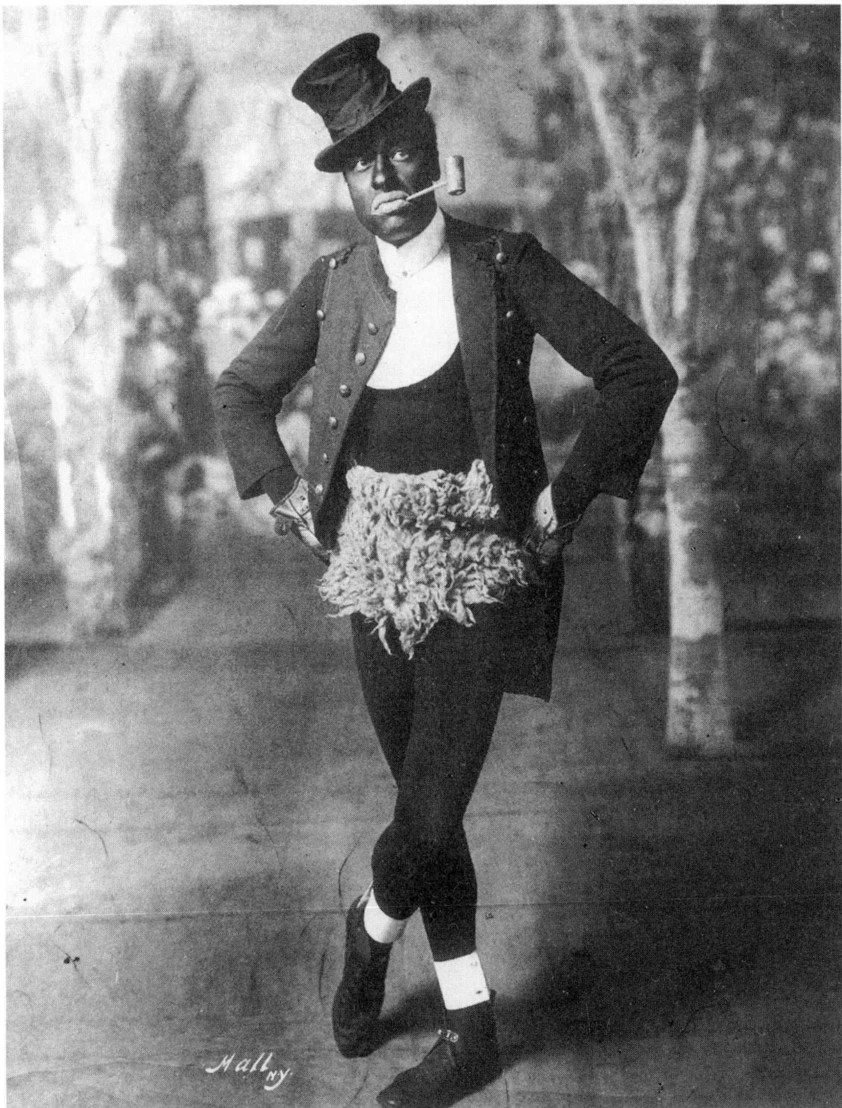

Figure 3.7 Bert Williams in blackface. Courtesy of Frank Driggs Collection.

self-presentation clearly mirrors the caricatures produced by white minstrels in blackface. At the turn of the century, black entertainers like Bert Williams and George Walker continued to imitate white minstrels who had "blacked up" to mimic and mock the dialect, music, and dance of African Americans throughout the second half of the nineteenth century (Fig. 3.7). Advertised as "Two Real Coons," Williams and Walker presented the "strutting dandy" and the "shuffling darky" of minstrelsy (Alkire, 36–37). A comment by Walker captures the vertiginous interactions of white and black theatrical representations of African Americans. "My idea was always to *impersonate my race just as they are*," Walker explained, in a glitch of thinking which he went on to illuminate: "The colored man has never successfully *taken off* his own humorous characteristics, and the white impersonator often overdoes the matter" (emphasis mine; D. Gilbert, 284). Understandably enmeshed in such mimicries, the black entertainer Ernest ("The Unbleached American") Hogan remained haunted until the end of his successful career by the smash success of the "humorous" ditty he composed, "All Coons Look Alike to Me" (1890; Woll, 4).

Racist as the influence of minstrel productions was, the staging of race resulted in what Eric Lott calls its "carnivalizing" (226); white appropriation of African or slave cultural forms could be re-manufactured by the black performer in ways paradoxically both demeaning and empowering. During the twenties, the new phenomenon of Broadway musicals featuring black actors—*Shuffle Along* (1921), *Dixie to Broadway* (1924), *The Chocolate Dandies* (1924), *Africana* (1927), and *Blackbirds of 1928*—presented contemporary numbers (the cakewalk, the black bottom, the tango, the Charleston, the lindy hop) as if they were modifications of plantation or African choreography and thus ironically drew upon what Mark Twain in his autobiography praised as the "glad and stunning surprise" of the white-produced, white-performed "nigger show" (64).[12] So popular were these productions that "It's Getting Dark on Old Broadway," a song included in the *Ziegfeld Follies of 1922*, claimed that New York's theater district was undergoing a racechange; "the very famous dazzling White-Way night lights" were "growing dimmer" because the arts of America's premier northern urban center were shaped by those of the pre-industrial, rural south:

> Ev'ry cafe now has the dancing coon.
> Pretty choc'late babies
> Shake and shimmie ev'rywhere
> Real dark-town entertainers hold the stage,
> You must black up to be the latest rage.
>
> Yes, the great white way is white no more,
> It's just like a street on the Swanee shore. (Woll, 76)

Despite commercial success and exhilarating visibility, the first generation of black Broadway stars must have known that they were tapping widespread assumptions "that Negroes have . . . a special theatrical genius" (Huggins, 245) as well as minstrel and vaudeville stereotypes that found their way even into presumably jubulent production numbers like "It's Getting Dark on Old Broadway." Stories and pictures of the blackened black face of Bert Williams convey the weird series of travesties set in motion, but perhaps a photograph of Josephine Baker in blackface best captures the black performer's wry awareness of her entanglement in this process (Fig. 3.8). Cross-eyed and thus willfully blind to the spectacle she has made of herself, she derisively displays herself as an antic figure of foolish fun.[13] If the shuffling, grinning blackfaced minstrel ridiculed African Americans

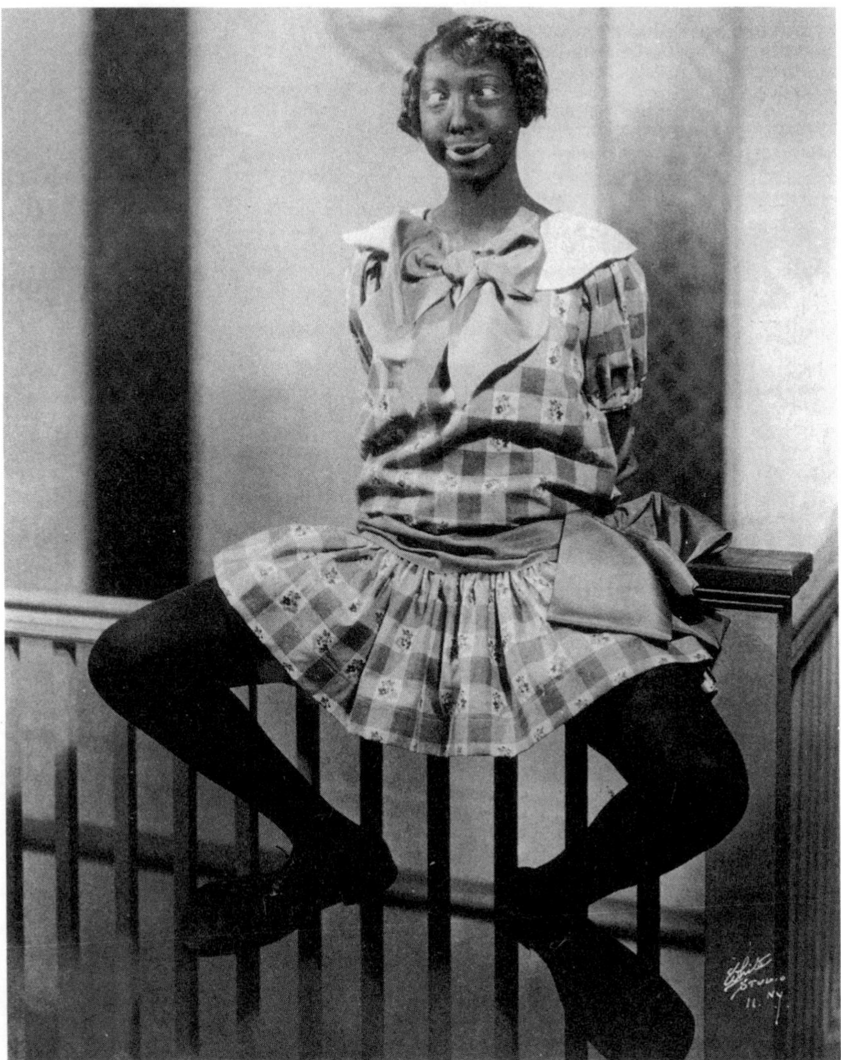

Figure 3.8 Josephine Baker sporting blackface in *Chocolate Dandies* (1925). Courtesy of the Billy Rose Theatre Collection, The New York Public Library for the Performing Arts, Astor, Lenox and Tilden Foundations.

as lazy, superstitious, childish, or sexually loose, Baker's pose burlesques the mockers through self-mockery. And throughout her career, Baker sauced her sexy numbers with comically exaggerated, antic gestures that distanced her from the sexual frenzy she was putting on display.

That display, of course, was promoted by the more widely circulated pictures of Baker which attest to her ability to transform the supposed atavism, carnality, and exuberance of the stage Negro into a self-glamorizing iconography of *negritude*. A genius at generating striking advertisements, the woman Picasso called the "Nefertiti of now" inspired the architect Adolf Loos to design a house for her that conjures up "the stripes of an African zebra" and stimulated the architect Le Corbusier to honor her by "appearing at a costume ball in blackface and with a circle of feathers around his waist" (G. Watkins, 135). Whether posed with a leopard or slithering on her belly like a snake, whether naked on all fours like a monkey or dressed only in a skirt of dangling bananas, Baker presented herself with boyishly short, cropped hair and daringly exposed, fashionably small breasts as an oxymoronic icon of the newly primitive. Just as capable as Baker of turning the famed rhythms of Africans and African Americans into a vertiginous mobility, Valerie Snow, Florence Mills, Ethel Waters, Nina Mae McKinney, and the chorus lines of girls they danced with on stage or screen "wiggle[d] and shim[mied] in a fashion to outdo a congress of eels, and they [flung] their limbs about without stopping to make sure that they [were] fastened on" (quoted in Huggins, 289). To the delight of many observers, such choruses consisted of "every colour and combination that our race goes through," including "blonds and girls with blue eyes, grey eyes, right through to what they used to call cafe-au-lait to dark-skins" (O'Connor, 9).

Proving "for the first time [that] . . . black was beautiful," as Janet Flanner explained (xx), Baker typified the ways in which all these performers manipulated the iconography of the flapper-as-savage, welding it to the image of the dangerously alluring, exotic-erotic-neurotic *femme fatale*: As one book about her puts it, Baker became a cross between "the 'Douanier' Rousseau of the music-hall, a living Gauguin, [and] the 'Black Venus' of Baudelaire" (O'Connor, 119). To be sure, Baker's white peers in the pioneering schools of modern dance—Loie Fuller, Isadora Duncan, Martha Graham, and Ruth St. Dennis—also found themselves transformed into avatars of the *femme fatale*. But Baker's merging of the modern or the new with the primitive or African complements Nugent's picture of the flapper-as-satyr. Almost as successful at melding the past with the contemporary and just as determinedly oxymoronic, Florence Mills dressed as the spirit of Dixie (Fig. 3.9) and sang hilariously inappropriate but flamboyantly spirited songs about those good old plantation days gone by:

On my pillow at night,
I see fields of white
And mammy's songs and stories, I recall.
Dixie scenes all pass before me
And I live my childhood it seems.
At the close of each day
Mister dream-man I pray
Bring back my Dixie dreams. ("Dixie Dreams")[14]

As Phyllis Rose explains about Josephine Baker's prominence in the twenties, when American culture "turned a face to Europe, that face was black" (80), but America's facial racechange repeatedly depended upon black black impersonation. During the twenties, dancers and singers were only the most visible of black

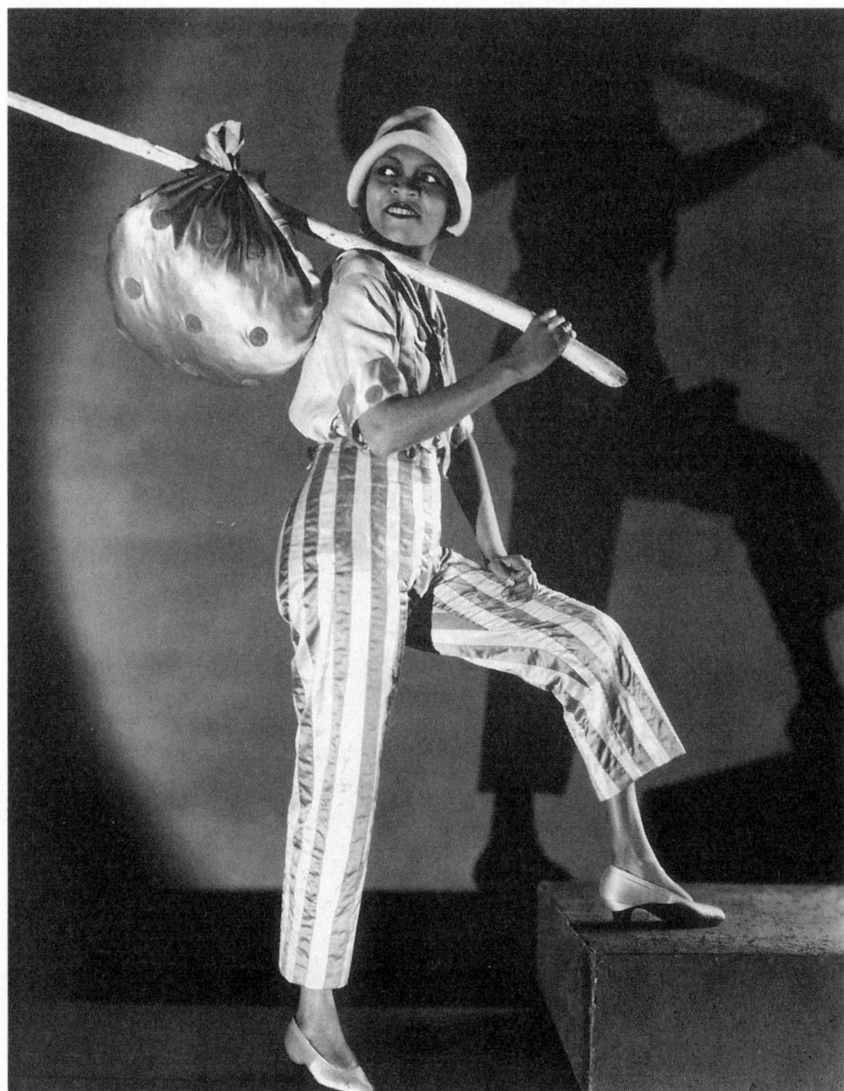

Figure 3.9 Florence Mills in *Dixie to Broadway* (1924). Courtesy of the Schomburg Center for Research in Black Culture, The New York Public Library, Astor, Tilden, and Lenox Foundations.

artists subjected to but also drawing upon the kind of fetishization Baker and Mills sometimes seemed to encourage from fans. In the process and with varying degrees of irony, musicians and poets proposed genealogical links between the African-American present and the African-American or simply African past. Yet like Langston Hughes, most proponents of racial uplift were aware that Duke

Ellington and his Jungle Band, playing at the Kentucky or Cotton Clubs, could not be heard by ordinary Negro patrons unless they were rich like A'Lelia Walker or famous like Bojangles. Although many of the writers of the Harlem Renaissance sought to affirm their African origins and slave histories less sardonically, such attempts left them open to charges of regression, cultural nostalgia, or simply bad faith. Hughes's poem "Afro-American Fragment" (1930) admits about American blacks' relation to African roots that "Not even memories" survive "alive / Save those that history books create, / Save those that songs / Beat back into the blood—" (129). Countee Cullen, seeking to link himself to a cultural heritage elsewhere, could ask hopefully, "What is Africa to me?" However, Waring Cuney would implicitly answer "not much": About a Harlem girl who might be made aware of her beauty "If she could dance naked under palm trees / And see her image in the river," Cuney concluded, "But there are no palm trees / On the street, / And dish water gives back no images" (99).

Because black artists suffered from a sense of "always looking at [themselves] through the eyes of" whites, modern attempts to recover African-American slave culture or African roots could plummet black actors into the paradox of recycling a highly commodified primitivism eroticized and appropriated by whites and thus catering to prurient stereotypes. As in Virgil Thompson's opera based on Gertrude Stein's *Four Saints in Three Acts* (1934–35), for example, American blacks appeared as one more exotic or experimental sales pitch in performances composed for and by whites. In a 1936 production for the WPA's Negro Theatre Project that Orson Welles called a "Negro Version" but that has been come to be known as his "Voodoo" *Macbeth*, feudal Scots were transported to nineteenth-century Haiti and the three witches turned into voodoo priestesses attended by forty-three celebrants (McCloskey, 410). However, the news commentator Edward R. Murrow, objecting to the drums and chants that pulsed throughout the production, disparaged its "blackface attitude" (France, 70).

Despite her own unconscious racism, Gertrude Stein examined the relationship between such fetishization and racechange in a passage of *The Autobiography of Alice B. Toklas* (1933) that focuses on the other American Negro who was in vogue with Europeans during the twenties, Josephine Baker's male counterpart, Paul Robeson. The famous black singer—sent by Carl Van Vechten to Stein's salon—understands "american values and american life as only one in it but not of it could know them." In other words, like Stein herself Robeson gained insight into American culture by remaining aloof and alienated from it. However,

> as soon as any other person came into the room *he became definitely a negro*. Gertrude Stein did not like hearing him sing spirituals. They do not belong to you any more than anything else, so why claim them, she said. He did not answer. (224; emphasis mine)

Though Stein's subsequent contention that "the african is not primitive, he [*sic*] has a very ancient but a very narrow culture and there it remains" (224) partakes of the same placidly stupid condescension about racial "types" that can be found elsewhere in her work, her record of Robeson's racial metamorphosis hints at the complexity of his situation. When refusing to answer Stein's question, is the Northern born and trained artist politely acquiescent, mutely resistent, or really in accord with his hostess about the fictitiousness of his relationship to nineteenth-century, Southern spirituals? Precisely such a question is raised if we contrast three photographs that document Robeson's black black impersonations: one taken in 1919 in which the decorous Rutgers University undergraduate sports his Phi Beta Kappa key, and the other two, shot during a summer vacation from Columbia Law School, showing Robeson looking carnivalesque in harlequin or minstrel pants and striking a bizarrely militant pose in ersatz African regalia for a production of the review *Voodoo* (Figs. 3.10–3.12). The juxtaposition of such images makes poignant Stein's subsequent diagnosis "that negroes were not suffering from persecution, they were suffering from nothingness," an analysis that begins to address the ontological confusion which might accompany performances of blackness by entertainers like Robeson.

Certainly Stein's testimonial that Robeson "became definitely a negro" links racechange to self-consciousness, spectatorship, and performance. From Williams, Walker, and Hogan to Baker and Robeson, black entertainers put on color with or without the help of burnt cork. In the literature of the Harlem Renaissance, the possibility of becoming not "ex-coloured" but re-colored as "definitely a negro" finds a fictive setting in bar scenes where what Claude McKay called "Jungle jazzing" leads to a surrealistic racechange that presages a return to origins, a reverting to "primitive joy" (*Banjo*, 58). After the heroine of Nella Larsen's *Quicksand* (1928) feels "drugged" by the "extraordinary music, blown out, ripped out, beaten out" in a Harlem cabaret, she returns to everyday consciousness with "a shameful certainty that not only had *she been in the jungle*, but that she had enjoyed it . . . [though] *She wasn't, she told herself, a jungle creature*" (59; emphasis mine). Less disgusted with herself but just as aware of "becoming definitely a negro," in "What It Means to Be Colored Me" (1926) Zora Neale Hurston imagines herself sitting in "The New World Cabaret with a white person, [and] *my color comes.*" Jazz causes her to "dance wildly inside myself; I yell within, I whoop; I shape my assegai above my head, I hurl it true to the mark *yeeeeooww*! I am in the jungle and living in the jungle way" (154; first emphasis mine).

Hurston's savage sentiment—"I want to slaughter some thing—give pain, give death to what, I do not know"—inevitably buttresses the idea that black people have obtained only a "veneer [of what] we call civilization." Yet, as Barbara Johnson has pointed out, the folklorist—who was herself often castigated for telling "lies" and "playing the darky"—maintains some degree of irony about this reversion to type by describing her color not as a biological complexion but as a cosmetic rainbow of hues: With her face "painted red and yellow" and her body "painted blue," Hurston presents her coming and going color as an aesthetic phenomenon that could be manipulated, a form of black black impersonation (154). Just as Baker established a seductive image out of the juxtaposition of herself as New Woman/savage or jungle beast/flapper, Robeson and Hurston negotiated between cosmopolitan, continental sophistication and "becoming definitely a negro" by letting "color come." One of Ann Douglas's contentions in *Terrible Honesty: Mongrel Manhattan in the 1920s* establishes a context to understand that negotia-

Figure 3.10 Paul Robeson with Phi Beta Kappa Key, Rutgers University, 1919. From *The Whole World in His Hands: A Pictorial Biography of Paul Robeson* (Citadel Press 1981); courtesy of Paul Robeson, Jr.

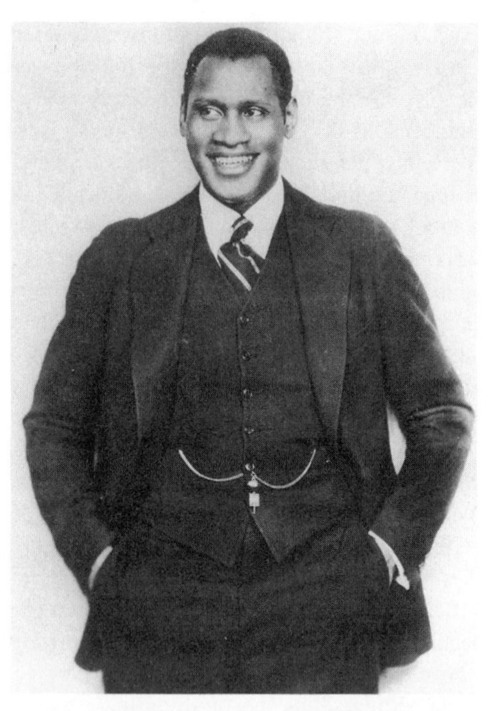

Figure 3.11 *(Below, left)* Paul Robeson in *Voodoo* (London 1922). From *The Whole World in His Hands: A Pictorial Biography of Paul Robeson* (Citadel Press 1981); courtesy of Paul Robeson, Jr.

Figure 3.12 *(Below, right)* Paul Robeson in *Voodoo* (London 1922). From *The Whole World in His Hands: A Pictorial Biography of Paul Robeson* (Citadel Press 1981); courtesy of Paul Robeson, Jr.

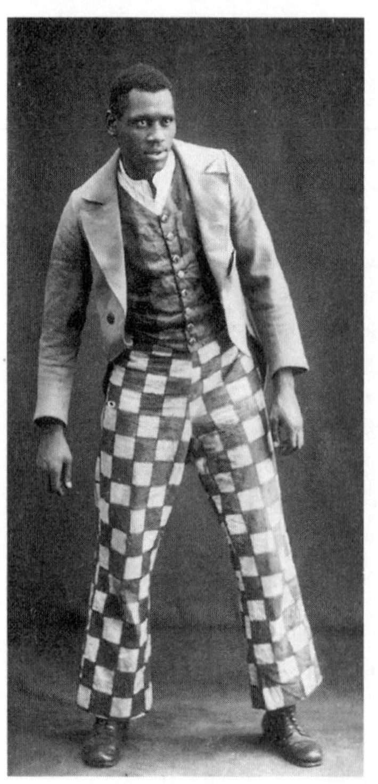

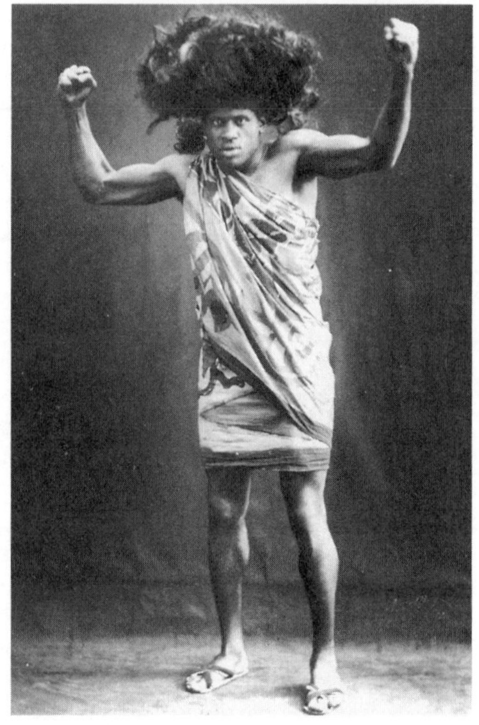

tion: "If actual blacking up, Eddie Cantor-style, decreased in the 1920s, blacking up, speaking metaphorically, increased dramatically" (78). With all the performances of Baker, Robeson, and Hurston, as with Nugent's "Drawings for Mulattoes," the faintly disturbing effect of blacks blacking up derives from their teetering on the edge of the stereotypical and thereby drawing attention to what in another context Eric J. Sundquist calls "the painful entanglement between cultural self-determination and racist domination," an entanglement that requires complex "cultural negotation[s]" on the part of African Americans (449–50). How did Hurston feel when she could get seated at a restaurant with her traveling companion, Fannie Hurst, only when the white novelist introduced the aspiring black writer as "Princess Zora"? Or when the folklorist signed letters written to her patron "Your Pickanniny, Zora"?

Yet it is pointless to censure such negotiations because they remain inevitable, a sign of the interwoven strands—indeed, the indistinguishable fabric—of African-American and American cultures. At their most optimistic, moreover, the flapper-cum-savage (Baker) and the concert-singer-cum-slave (Robeson) sought to instruct America about the allure of "twoness": Unlike the analysis of Du Bois which presented the "dark body" (assumed to be male) "torn asunder," the art of Josephine Baker and Paul Robeson enacted the exciting energy of "twoness—an American, a Negro; two souls, two thoughts, two unreconciled strivings." Richard Bruce Nugent, together with Aaron Douglas, examined this same sense of twoness by producing red and blue murals on the walls of basement cabarets which functioned something like Escher prints. Under one light, an African past could be seen, but under another a modern cityscape would emerge (Wirth, 16). Also mapping this "twoness," Nugent's drawings in *Ebony and Topaz* picture it less as the "strife" or "warring" inside the schizophrenic black male psyche and more as a cultural condition of blacks and whites, men and women, and a condition of modernity that could enrich as well as test the limits of conventional categories.

From this perspective, it seems significant that Nugent's contribution to the landmark issue of *Fire!!*, the 1926 journal "devoted to Younger Negro Artists," consisted of what has been called "the first literary work on an openly homosexual theme to be published by an Afro-American writer" (Wirth, 16). A stream-of-consciousness story about a drug-induced fantasy, "Smoke, Lilies and Jade" centers on a man equally attracted to male and female lovers, convinced that "one *can* love two at the same time . . . ." (39).[15] Like Baker, who often appeared in public dressed in men's clothing, and like Florence Mills, who took the part of the groom on the Broadway stage, Nugent played with twoness by opting for "both/and" instead of "either/or" and celebrating the sexchanges of bisexuality. Nor was he unusual in this regard since, as Ann Douglas has pointed out, "most of the best-known black male writers in the New York scene were homosexual" (97). Still, loving two in the "Drawings for Mulattoes" mostly means loving the biracial contrasts created by the twoness of racechange. Interlaced or counterpointed, black and white exist in dizzying relationships that make either/or, better/worse thinking simply inadequate. Du Boisian "double consciousness"—so often taken as a sign of schizophrenic confinement—becomes transmuted into inclusive, nondichotomized artistry.

American society, Nugent and his peers suggest, had been so profoundly shaped by blacks as to have generated a culture of double consciousness for all of its citizens; every American's culture, in other words, is intrinsically "African American." A far more optimistic narrative about origins than Anne Spencer's, Nugent's series implies that the black race—uprooted and stereotyped though it has been—infuses Western culture with the inventions and energies of song, of dance, of theatricality or what these days is dubbed performativity. Indeed, Nugent's series intimates that race itself consists of performances and therefore participates in the mobility, the mutability, and the aestheticism of dance and drama. The Jazz Age foregrounds as most mutable, most mobile, most aesthetic the previously maligned "mulatto." No longer tragic, the mulatto whose color can come and go taps origins to emerge as a trope of racechange and the epitome of the archaic hybridity of the modern, the primitive audacity of the new.

Perpetual Exile: The Curse of Color

Yet the context in which Richard Bruce Nugent's drawings appeared somewhat qualifies this optimistic interpretation. Sandwiched between two articles—one on "Phantom Color Lines" and the other on "The Changing Status of the Mulatto"—the prints are integrated into the volume *Ebony and Topaz* through their title. But to the dismay of the author of "The Changing Status of the Mulatto," racists have attributed the "conspicuously successful" lives of mulattos to "a marked superiority rooting in the fact of a white ancestry and relationship" (107). Just as depressing, although the writer of "Phantom Color Lines" believes that African Americans can better their economic lot by admitting that "a large share of the Negro's failure to secure employment is his own fault," he admits that some white Northerners continue to justify job discrimination by invoking the persistent claim that "cold weather cannot be endured by sons of Ham from the torrid regions of the South" (102). Just how "changed" is the "status of the mulatto"? How "phantom" are "color lines"? In fact, how "New" is the "Negro"?

The passing allusion to Ham takes on prominence elsewhere in *Ebony and Topaz*, specifically in Zora Neale Hurston's contribution *The First One* (1927), a short play based on folkloric elaborations upon the biblical character of Ham and far less optimistic about race than her essay "How It Feels to Be Colored Me." Unlike Spencer and Nugent, who produced libertarian myths about the origin of color, Hurston neither delegitimized whites nor legitimized blacks. By tackling one of the most pervasive, pernicious legends of racial origin in Western culture, Hurston directly challenged the idea that black people in the twenties were experiencing a "Renaissance" or giving birth to a "New Negro" race. For, as in so many revisionary modernist texts by, say, James Joyce, T. S. Eliot, and H. D., *The First One* insists that the archaic stories which continue to exert their power over the twentieth-century imagination resist the efforts of artists to "make it new." In Hurston's case, that resistance complicates the attempts of activists as well and clarifies the recalcitrant structures of racism that continue to warp the lives of blacks and whites alike. From the severe point of view of Hurston's play, Spencer's defamation of white and Nugent's glamorization of black remain compensatory, belated, and doomed efforts to disentangle the black race from its secondariness. Despite Hurston's valiant struggle with the most influential and racist originatory myth of Western culture, we shall see that her revisionary play eventually reassembles the ghastly contours of the age-old minstrel mask.

Though the Bible story of Ham's crime (of seeing Noah's nakedness), Noah's curse (against parental disrespect), and the subsequent punishment of Ham's son Canaan (when he is condemned to slavery) contains no mention of skin pigmentation at all, Hurston's drama about the first racechange draws on a long and complex history of biblical exegesis that exploited the narrative not only to explain the existence of people of color but also to justify their bondage. In the Ur-story, Shem, Ham, and Japheth—the sons of Noah who survived the flood in the ark—ultimately provide the generations who will people the entire world. According to the Bible, one day Noah became drunk and lay "uncovered in his tent," where Ham saw his nakedness and spoke about it to his brothers. After Shem and Japheth took a garment upon their shoulders, walked "backward and covered the nakedness of their father," Noah awakened and understood "what his youngest son had done" so he pronounced the famous sentences: "Curse be Canaan; a slave of slaves shall he be to his brothers" and "Blessed by the Lord my God be Shem; and let Canaan be his slave" (Genesis 10: 26–27). Even though color or complexion never appears in the Bible passage, even though Canaan (not Ham) is (inexplicably) cursed, the story very quickly found elaborators who used it to justify the slavery of Africans identified as Ham's descendants. Because "the view of Africa as a continent condemned to eternal servitude was eminently suited to a theological assessment of slavery," Jan Nederveen Pieterse has explained, the identification of Africa with Ham and with divinely ordained servitude "remained the most popular explanation of slavery" well into the nineteenth century (44).

While Anne Spencer's poem used racechange to protest the genocidal whitening of Western society, while Nugent's drawings employed it to imagine a new amalgam of ancient African and modern American cultures, Hurston's achievement was to make their projects seem utopian at best, specious at worst. For she hints that the twentieth-century imagination continues to identify people of color with Ham and with divinely sanctioned bondage. By beginning with a white race that makes black come into being as an affliction, Hurston grappled with an Ur-story about racechange that established the juridical justification of slavery as well as the ethical underpinnings behind twentieth-century ideologies of white supremacy. The Bible's sacralization of beginnings made ethnogenesis a particularly complicated problem for Hurston. Although she valiantly struggled to rescue the biblical myth from the bigoted uses to which it had been put by a long line of interpreters, ultimately the ubiquitous racism of that textual history resisted her efforts to make it new.

A one-act dramatic revision of Genesis 9:18–27, *The First One* elaborates on the biblical narrative, supplying new details and changing the meaning of others. On the third-year anniversary of their survival after the appearance of the rainbow covenant, Hurston's Noah and his wife and his sons (all married now) return to the

Valley of Ararat in order "to commemorate [their] delivery from the flood" (81). Immediately, Hurston's dialogue contrasts the temperaments of the two older brothers, Shem and Japheth, with that of the youngest, Ham. The former two clearly represent the work ethic—their days have been spent farming the fields and the vineyards, supplying meat for the offering, making the "dingy" robes they wear—while Ham, his wife (here called Eve), and their baby epitomize the ethos of play or artistry. Sporting white goat-skins, shiny green wreaths, and scarlet garlands, they bring flowers and music to the ritual, offering to "dance before Jehovah and sing joyfully upon the harp that [Ham] made of the thews of rams" (81).

Mrs. Shem and Mrs. Japheth—like Eve, they are entirely of Hurston's invention—put the plot in motion. Their jealousy of Noah's affection for the child of his old age stirs up dissension among the brothers. This, along with the naming of Ham's wife, makes *The First One* read like an echo of the garden of Eden story. As an interpreter of Genesis, then, Hurston emphasizes the ways in which the Noah-Ham story reiterates some of the same tropes as those in the account of the fall from paradise: the crime of (Eve's) disobedience or (Ham's) disrespect for authority and the subsequent punishment (exacted by God or Noah); the act of ingesting (Adam and Eve's eating the fruit or Noah's drinking the fruit of the vine), followed by (the first couple's or Ham's) seeing of nakedness and expulsion. After Hurston's Noah gets drunk, so as to drown out painful memories of the destruction wrecked by the flood, Mrs. Shem and Mrs. Japheth overhear the inebriated Ham laughing inside his father's tent and muttering as he emerges from it about "The old Ram" who "has had no spring for years" (84). As in the story of Eve's temptation of Adam, it is the women in Hurston's retelling who hatch the plot that brings disaster, goading their husbands to gain Noah's vineyards and flocks by reporting Ham's behavior to Noah, the self-proclaimed "Lord of the world" (82), who then acts like the God of the garden, cursing and casting out.

An enraged patriarch ("shall the lord of the Earth be mocked? Shall his nakedness be uncovered and he be shamed before his family?" (85)), Noah makes his proclamation without knowing the name of the perpetrator of the crime. First, Hustom's aged father pronounces a sentence about skin color that never appears in the Hebrew Bible: The scoffer "shall be accursed. His skin shall be black!" Next Noah adds the curse of slavery that does have a basis in Genesis: "He shall serve his brothers and they shall rule over him" (85). Departing from the biblical narrative completely, Hurston then portrays the immediate remorse of all concerned, their unsuccessful efforts to "unsay" or "Unspeak the Curse" (86). Finally, Ham—"horrified" and "stupefied" at the discovery that he is black—is brought his (now also) black child by Eve and the three of them are sent into exile by Noah: "Arise and go out from among us that we may see thy face no more, lest by lingering the curse of thy blackness come upon all my seed forever" (88). Disturbingly, in a number of respects Hurston's play appears more misogynist and racist than the original Genesis story, for *The First One* repeatedly conflates the color black with malediction and expulsion from the human (white) community, even as it blames this punishment on female ambition. The first racechange here constitutes a fall from the paradise of a whiteness so primordial that it remains invisible, unnamed, taken for granted, naturalized.

Just as significant, the biblical Noah curses not Ham but Ham's son, Canaan, who is to become "slave of slaves . . . to his brothers" (9: 25), while Hurston has Noah denounce the culprit directly and only by indirection his child (who also turns black). This last difference between the plot of Genesis and that of *The First One* points to the ways in which contradictions in the bibilical account are smoothed over or resolved by Hurston.[16] In addition, the ancient account does not even allude to complexion in general or to Africans in particular and thus in the Bible bondage remains unrelated to color. Indeed, because "the table of nations" (Genesis 10:1–32) implies that the entire human race—scattered all over the globe, different in its ethnicities and complexions—comes from the single family of Noah, the Bible can be said to embrace the idea of the essential unity of humankind. Yet by the time Hurston came to write *The First One*, the so-called "curse of Ham"—"the curse that never was," in Gene Rice's evocative phrase—functioned as a veritable lynchpin in the justification of American slavery at least in part because ancient commentaries set in place a racist account of the appearance of the first black human being and the first racechange. Only an understanding of these noxious elaborations upon the Ur-text can elucidate what would seem to be Hurston's apparent complicity in using the story to justify the expulsion of blacks from political power and spiritual primacy. What such a contextualization establishes, surprisingly, is how—within the confines of this noisome textual history—Hurston struggled to supply a potentially liberating counter-commentary, a midrash of her own.

How did Ham get his color? The name itself is "etymologically related to the word *hm*, 'warm,' 'hot' (from *hmm*, 'to become warm, hot'), or derived from the Egyptian Keme, 'the black land' (a name for ancient Egypt)" (*The Anchor Bible Dictionary*, III, 31). Because, as Ovid's tale in *Metamorphosis* illustrates, climatic causation had been used to explain a complexion thought to be burnt by the sun, Western commentators may have conflated heat and color. According to biblical ethnographic ideas, the descendants of Ham's sons—Cush (Ethiopians), Misraim (Egyptians), Put (Libyans), and Canaan (Canaanites)—occupied lands south and west of Israel. Early commentaries on the Bible often assume that Ham's "seeing" of Noah's nakedness must be read as a euphemism for some other, more heinous crime, thus linking the curse against Canaan to the outlawed sexual offenses attributed to the Canaanites in Leviticus (18: 24–30). In this way, sexual practices defined as the moral failure of the Canaanite people were used to justify the otherwise reprehensible notion that the (innocent) son Canaan is punished for the sins of his father, Ham.[17]

At least some of the conjectures about the actual crime committed by Ham led early thinkers in Talmudic, Midrashic, and other rabbinical sources (from the second to the fifth centuries A.D.) to transform the Noah-Ham-Canaan tale into a pernicious racechange narrative. Rabbinic commentaries on Genesis in Bereshith Rabbah link Ham's offense against Noah with castration and bestiality, conflating the evil of both acts with darkness:

> R. Huna said in R. Joseph's name: (Noah declared), "you have prevented me from begetting a fourth son, therefore I curse your fourth son." R. Huna also said in R. Joseph's name: "you have prevented me from doing something in the dark (cohabitation), therefore your seed will be ugly and dark-skinned." R. Hiyya said: "Ham and the dog copulated in the Ark, therefore Ham came forth black-skinned while the dog publicly exposes its copulation. . . . " (Midrash Rabbah-Genesis cited in Copher, 232)[18]

These interpretations, the source of many later ideological uses to which the Noah-Ham-Canaan story was put, contain several crucial motifs: a justification of the curse of Canaan in terms of an Oedipal struggle between a rivalrous Ham and the father he renders impotent or castrated; an identification of dark skin with ugliness; the stigmatizing of black skin, now linked not only with bestiality but also with bestial sexuality.

Other influential commentaries on Ham's seeing Noah unclothed conflate voyeurism with the act of castrating, attributing both to dark-skinned people and their supposed phallicism; the following passage, in which the speaker is Noah-the-judge ruling against his son, is produced by Robert Graves and Raphael Patai from various ancient sources:[19]

> "because you twisted your head around to see my nakedness, your grandchildren's hair shall be twisted into kinks, and their eyes red; again, because your lips jested at my misfortune, theirs shall swell; and because you neglected my nakedness, they shall go naked, and their male members shall be shamefully elongated." Men of this race are called Negroes; their forefather Canaan commanded them to love theft and fornication, to be banded together in hatred of their masters and never to tell the truth. (Graves and Patai, 121)

Hair "twisted," eyes "red," lips that "swell," the male member "shamefully elongated": The black (male) body appears to be a body in pain, a torture it is said to earn by virtue of the crime of looking and laughing at Noah's nakedness and unmanning him. Dedicated to theft, fornication, hatred, and lies: The black (male) mind is demonized as a mind of the damned. Early interpretations of the Genesis story so besmirched the reputation of Ham that in one midrashic passage "sodomy has been added to Ham's crimes" (Graves and Patai, 122). Said to have "defiled" and "mutilated" his father, to have "preven[ted] procreation," to have committed incest with either his father or his mother, Ham became the embodiment of the sexual evil attributed to black men throughout the Middle Ages and the Renaissance.[20]

Before and after 1773, when Phillis Wheatley, the first poet-slave of the New World, wrote in "On Being Brought from Africa to America" (1773)—

> Some view that sable race with scornful eye:
> "Their colour is a diabolic dye."
> Remember, Christians, Negroes black as Cain
> May be refined and join the angelic strain (ll. 5–8)

—the "'diabolic dye'" of the mark God set on Cain had merged with that on Ham and Canaan.[21] This, despite the fact that the mark in Genesis reflects God's efforts to protect Cain during his wanderings. One century later, Joseph Smith—the author of the *Pearl of Great Price* (1851) and founder of the Mormon church—put into practice doctrines that supported slavery, forbade racial intermarriage, and denied the priesthood to blacks because he believed that "all the Canaanites were blackened, . . . they were the seed of Cain, and from them spring the Egyptians via Egyptus (a black Canaanite married to Ham), preserving a black race descended from both Cain and Ham" (Mellinkoff, 79).[22] Following this imaginative line of speculation, defenders of slavery like one John Fletcher of Louisiana could present Ham's sin as miscegenation: Ham had married into the race of Cain, whose skin had turned black because of his murdering of Abel (H. Seldon Smith, 131).

Predictably, then, the biblical narrative of Noah's curse became especially attractive to Americans seeking to justify slavery as a divinely inspired and sanctioned institution. If the natives of Canaan, polluted because of their purported sins of disrespect or castration or what were castigated as various modes of sexual perversion ranging from incest to sodomy, could be thought of as no longer meriting their own lands or as in need of Israel's superior ethical leadership, the blacks of the South could be contaminated by their genealogical relation to Ham or Canaan and thereby converted into the moral burden of their white masters. Although New World theologians disagreed about the relationship between Ham, Canaan, and African Americans, they nevertheless repeatedly invoked the Bible either to defend or attack the institution of slavery.[23] As Theodore Weld observed in his antislavery tract *The Bible Against Slavery* (4th edition 1838), the "prophecy of Noah is the *vade mecum* of slaveholders and they never venture abroad without it" (H. Sheldon Smith, 130).

Even the most arcane and bizarre theories about racial origins tended to return to the story of Noah's curse. One example will suffice here. Josiah Priest's *Slavery as It Relates to the Negro, or African Race* (1843) begins in what we would today consider a politically correct manner, but then quickly degenerates. Adam and his progeny were all born red until God mysteriously decided to make Japheth white and Ham black (Fig. 3.13). Alas, for the latter, the name "not only signified *black* in its literal sense, but pointed out the very disposition of his mind": Demonstrating his etymological inventiveness, Priest argues that Ham means "*heat* or *violence* (murder, war, butcheries, and even *cannibalism*)" as well as "deceit, dishonesty, treachery, low mindedness, and malice" (33). This ingenious scholar then finds the words "*cursed Ham*" in the Bible and claims that they mean "he had been *always* a bad person, even from childhood; for let it not be forgotten, that Ham, at the very time he did that act [of laughing at his father], was more than 100 years old" (79). Why God would have bothered to create "such a race thus low in the scale of human existence . . . is more than can be known by human research" (83) and must simply be accepted in terms of "one of the great facts of God's jurisprudence among men [which] appears to be the *judicial* appointment of the black race to slavery" (83–84).[24]

Whether or not Hurston read any of these texts, her culture was saturated with allusions to them. Actually, though pseudo-scientific explanations of racial difference at the turn of the century displaced theological ones, as recently as 1959 the author of a book about *The Bible and Race* explained that some people exploit "the

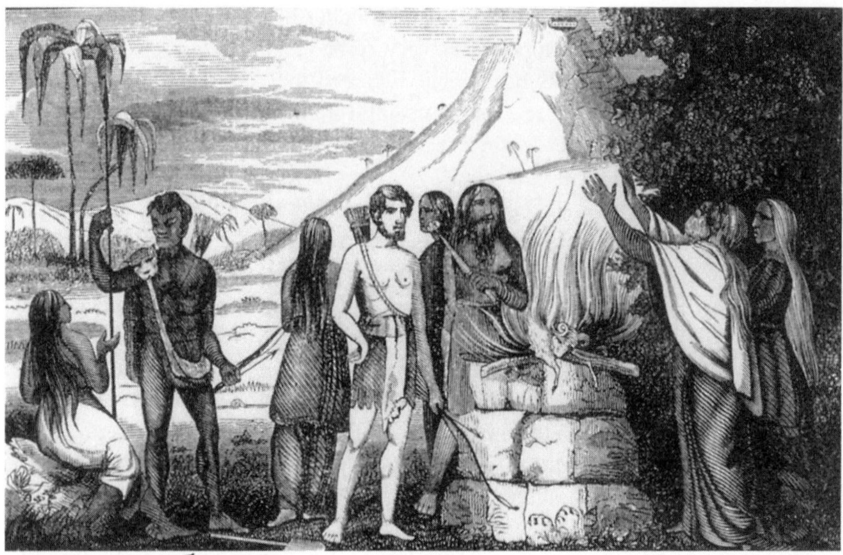

Figure 3.13 Josiah Priest, "The Family of Noah," in his *Slavery as It Relates to the Negro, or African Race* (1843).

curse of Canaan, frequently erroneously referred to as 'the curse of Ham,'" to argue that "the Negro, as a descendant of Ham, is destined by God to fill permanently a subservient place in society" (Maston, 105). As late as 1963, James Baldwin realized that, "according to many Christians, I was a descendant of Ham, who had been cursed, and that I was therefore predestined to be a slave. . . . my fate had been sealed forever, from the beginning of time" (*Fire Next Time*, 50).[25] Similarly, in his 1986 Nobel lecture, Wole Soyinka described "apartheid's mentality" as "The sons of Ham on the one hand, the descendants of Shem on the other. The once pronounced, utterly immutable curse" (12). Interpreting the myth of "the first one" as an injurious attack on African Americans (or a kind of forecast of "the last one"), the dramatist Suzan-Lori Parks brings in a character greeted as "HAM BONE HAM BONE" whose every other word is "SOLD" in her surrealistic play *The Death of the Last Black Man* (1992).

Although ultimately *The First One* does give off some such disturbing resonances, although it appears more misogynist and racist than the Bible, Hurston could be said to correct rabidly racist misreadings of Genesis. God does not pronounce the curse of color in *The First One*; as in the Bible, the sentence issues only from the mouth of a man. Thus, the oath loses divine sanction. More, the curse in Hurston's play comes from an intoxicated Noah who is suffering amnesia and a hangover. When woken up out of his drunken sleep after the cursing of Ham, a contrite Noah says, "I know of no curse" (86) and immediately joins the rest of the community in asking God to undo it. And as with the curse, so with the crime. Although biblical exegetes viewed Ham's crime of seeing the naked father not only as disrespect but also as a veiled allusion to a variety of sexual perversions, Hurston's Ham—as tipsy as his dad—simply talks to himself (more than to his brothers) when he emerges from Noah's tent and says, "Our Father has stripped himself, showing all his wrinkles. Ha! Ha! He's as no young goat in the spring" (84). Indeed, right after this speech, Ham passes out. Not especially respectful or modest in their motives, Shem and Japheth are propelled by wives who merely use the talk about "a father so mocked and shamed by his son" (84) to cover up the profit motive. In *The First One*, the acquisitive efforts of Mrs. Shem and Mrs. Japheth, the mainspring of the plot, turn attention to the relationship between paternity, private property, and slavery.[26]

For Hurston, then, the biblical narrative offers an opportunity to meditate on derision, the dishonoring of paternal authority, ownership, and bondage. Her play invites us to read the inauguration of an ethical justification for slavery as an Oedipal script set in a decidedly patriarchal framework. Just as Oedipus was guilty of murdering his father, Ham's crime consists of laughing at the phallus, a laughter in part motivated by the revelation that the young man is now ready to supersede his father. Though he is "as a young ram in the Spring" (83), Noah is "The old Ram" with "no spring for years" (84).[27] In his rebelliousness against the patriarch, Ham embodies a devotion to playfulness over and against work, a potentially anarchic and libidinal pleasure principle over and against a rigid, super-egoistic reality principle. The youngest of the three children, a favorite, and (in his singing as well as his dedication to honesty and pleasure) a bit of a fool, Ham functions as a truth-teller, somewhat like Shakespeare's Cordelia, with Mrs. Shem and Mrs. Japheth resembling Goneril and Regan. And, as in *King Lear*, in *The First One* the division of the father's goods among three offspring causes the rivalry between siblings that brings dissension and grief. If Ham plays the role of Oedipus, then, it is a Cordelia-like, fool-like Oedipus, a feminized "anti-Oedipus" who refuses to enter into a murderous rivalry with the father because he has no wish to become (like) the father.

As a statement about the psychology of bondage, Hurston's play suggests that paternal anxiety about potency as well as genealogical claims to legitimacy and property motivate racial subjugation. Laughing at the phallus is the outrage; disrespect for the father (even when the father has earned it) will be punished in the patrilineal, patri-centered ancient world. Slavery or white supremacy is the result of the law of the (insecure, out-of-control) father outraged and determined to assert authority and control over his family, his property, and his future. "Isn't laughter the first form of liberation from secular oppression?" Luce Irigaray has asked. "*Isn't the phallic tantamount to the seriousness of meaning?*" Like Irigaray, who speculates that women transcend "the sexual relation . . . 'first' in laughter" (163), Hurston imagines laughter as the irreverent crime of "the first one." As do Hélène Cixous and Julia Kristeva, Hurston presents laughter as the "volcanic" capacity to "break up the 'truth'" of a "phallogocentric order" (Cixous, 258) or as "what lifts inhibitions by breaking through prohibitions" (Kristeva, 224).

From this perspective, the black race derives from anti-patriarchal men—a fool or a youngest son or an anti-Oedipus—whose love of the sensual pleasures of life—which include the arts of music and dance as well as the beauties of nature—threatens the status quo and must therefore be repressed by a system that requires conformity to the rules of an anxiously defensive white patriarch. From this perspective, too, Eve and Ham at the end of the play—dedicated to music, laughter, and fun—function like precursors of Hurston's Janie and Tea Cake in *Their Eyes Were Watching God.* For the outcast couple's Dionysian joyousness and playfulness contrast sharply with the gloom of the whites on stage, all of whom have been traumatized by the horrors of the flood in the past and now by the mortifications of the injust curse: Noah looking "tragically stern," his other offspring appearing "ghastly," and his wife sobbing her dedication to a Jehovah who refuses to right the wrong of Noah's rash oath (88). Exhausted and demoralized, the white family, visibly suffering guilt over the wrongful fate inflicted on the "first one," endures the doleful spiritual consequences of its expulsion of Ham and his progeny from the human community. Ironically, too, though Noah and his family ask Jehovah to set a rainbow in the heavens as a sign of redemption, though they hopefully ask each other "do ye see colors appear?" (87), Ham's appearance as a man of color only repulses them.

Attractive as is such a reading of the subversiveness of *The First One*, it cannot fully account for the effect of Hurston's early effort at revisionary mythmaking. To be sure, Hurston's biographer, Robert Hemenway, interprets *The First One* as a play "pok[ing] fun at all those who take seriously the biblical sanction for racial segregation" (68) and he thereby suggests that the comedy contrasts Ham's innocent mirth with the materialism and cunning that do him wrong and do him in. A drunken old man mistakenly curses a tipsy son: how silly a basis for proclaiming a totalizing racial difference that would support slave systems. In the context of the play's authorial signature (Hurston's fame today as a subversive, black-affirming mythologist) or in the context of the play's African-American audience (Hurston's own awareness of her readers' suspicions about the misuses to which the Ham passage had been put), perhaps it can be understood as satiric. Unfortunately, however, such a reading too easily glosses over the ways in which *The First One* falls into the unprovable, Manichean "negritudinist" position encapsulated by Soyinka in the sentence "I feel, therefore I am." After all, Hurston emphasizes Ham's dreamy inability to comprehend his state of expulsion at the end. Noah prays, "If Jehovah keeps not the covenant this time, if he spares not my weakness, then I pray that Ham's heart remains asleep forever" (87). And when the rainbow fails to appear, it is clear that God will not undo the curse, so Eve says, "Let us go before you awake and learn to despise your father and your God" (88).

At the end of the play, Ham goes off stage and the audience is left wondering about a future awakening. Will the black race never confront the stigma of its fate, will it simply accept the rash injuries of the white father and the white father's God?[28] The happy-go-lucky Ham seems to submit with a grin to his injust exclusion from the human community. Indeed, after Hurston's Eve tells Ham, "Look at thy hands, thy feet. Thou art cursed black by thy Father," Ham embarks on his exile in true minstrel style, strumming his harp and blithely singing. What are we to make of the author's attitude toward her material? Has she subscribed to a view that the black race is so damned, so execrated as to be cursed by color and also by unconsciousness, a dumb submission to malediction, a mollified "shucks but let's go make hay while the sun shines"?

In the nineteenth century, Ham did play a role in comic songs of minstrelsy like this one about the origins of the banjo:

> Now Ham, de only nigger dat was runnin' on de packet,
> Got lonesome in de barber ship, an' couldn't stan' de racket
> So for to amuse himself he steamed some wood and bent it
> An soon he had a banjo made, de first dat was invented.

Curiously, however, this song could be viewed as less racist than Hurston's script since the minstrel Ham is not made black for any sin but instead is excluded from Noah's community *because* of his color. And, as William Stowe and David Grimsted point out in their discussion of stump sermons about color transformation on the stage, other minstrel speeches subversively presented Adam, Eve, and their children as originally black; after an angry God seeks out the guilty Cain, in one of their examples, the murderer "got frightened, and he turned white; and dis de way de first white man cum upon dis earth! And if it had not been for dat dar nigger Cane, we'd nebber been trubbled wid de white trash 'pon de face of dis here circumlar globe" (92).

Paradoxically, if myths of racial origin on the minstrel stage could poke fun at the overvaluation of whiteness, one of the most famous artists of the Harlem Renaissance could buttress the devaluation of blackness. Deeply implicated in the racist ideologies permeating nineteenth-century uses of the Bible, *The First One* can be said to perpetuate ideas about the ugliness, the secondariness, and the carnality of black people. For, as in Countee Cullen's poem "The Shroud of Color" (1925), Ham could say, "My color shrouds me in, I am as dirt / Beneath my brother's heel" (26). Not only is color a source of horror, not only is it created and then castigated by a white community, but at his first entrance on stage and at his last exit, Ham sings, "I am as a young ram in the Spring / Or a young male goat" (83). Like the harlequin carrying his club, Hurston's Ham counters his social liminality by touting his sexual prowess. Besides this clearly compensatory overvaluation of the physical, what does it mean that the black race is defined by Hurston solely in male terms? Until the end of the play, Eve remains white; the only other racechange besides Ham's is his son's.

A white Eve (not a temptress but a real helpmate here), a black man, and a black child constitute the first family of the black diaspora at the end of the play. Although it might be nice to think that Hurston slyly suggests that "black" has historically been conceptualized in terms of the black man, her first bi-racial family endorses the erasure of the black woman even as it seems to submit to the credo, "I feel, therefore I am." To gloss over the ways in which Hurston's text is embroiled in the history of its Ur-text would be to lose the significance of a play like this being produced by one of the foremost artists of the Harlem Renaissance, a writer whose early and late works exhibit a deep commitment to the liberation efforts of black women and men. The pervasive racism of the culture that grudgingly contained and misnamed the Harlem Renaissance inexorably molded even its most crafty advocates.[29]

Later in her career, during the prolific and creative years she spent in the 1930s, Hurston produced several versions of another etiological story about race that also presented the genesis of color as an error. *Mules and Men* (1935) includes a tall tale told by one "Gold" about the day God decided to "give everybody they color" and "He send de angels, Rayfield and Gab'ull," because he was tired of waiting for the "niggers" to show up:

> They hunted all over Heben till dey found de colored folks. All stretched out sleep on de grass under de tree of life. So Rayfield woke 'em up and tole 'em God wanted 'em.
>
> They all jumped up and run on up to de th'one and they was so skeered they might miss sumpin' they begin to push and shove one 'nother, bumpin' against all de angels and turnin' over foot-stools. They even had de th'one all pushed one-sided.
>
> Go God hollered "Git back! Get back!" And they misunderstood Him and thought He said, "Git black," and they been black ever since. (32–33)

Hardly a curse, blackness is just a blunder, the result here not of a crime but of simple exuberance and misunderstanding. Yet the oddity of Gold's "lie" consists of her inability to conceptualize people before color. In addition, her account of how "de colored folks" jumped up and then misunderstood God, thereby getting "black" instead of "back," hints that blacks are kept back by their color.

In a 1937 version of a chapter later revised for publication in Hurston's autobiography, *Dust Tracks on a Road* (1942), the same fable surfaces, but this time told directly by the author. Hurston explains how God looked at various portions of the multitude in front of him, proclaiming some "red people" and others "yellow" and "white" and finally wondering aloud to Gabriel about "miss[ing] some hosts":

> "You go hunt 'em up and tell 'em I say they better come quick if they want any color. Fool with me and I won't give out no more." So Gabriel went round everywhere hunting till way after while he found the lost multitudes down by the Sea of Life asleep under a tree. (305–6)

From here the "Get back!" "Get black!" story resumes, but in what a different modality. Instead of "and they been black ever since," Hurston writes in her own voice: "So they got black and just kept the thing agoing" (306). For color, though still nothing but a mistake, is clearly desirable here and Hurston uses her parable to conclude "we are no race. We are just a collection of people who overslept our time and got caught in the draft" (306).

All narratives about how people "got" black or white or red or yellow defamiliarize color by providing an explanation for it. In contrast to the more strenuously original images of racial origins crafted by Spencer and Nugent, however, Hurston returned to hegemonic stories of ethnogenesis that had functioned so effectively as subordinating decrees of bondage that even her revisionary efforts to make them work for (rather than against) African Americans remained in part baffled. Sadly, what Alain Locke called "the timid conventionalism which racial disparagement has forced upon the Negro mind in America"—what I would term the powerful conformity which America's racial disparagement forced upon all its citizens—did at times hamper the imaginations of even some of the most inventive, irreverent of twentieth-century artists. One of the greatest songs Fats Waller made famous, "Black and Blue," echoes "The First One" in its conflation of color with punishment: "I'm white inside, But that don't help my case," the lyrics of Andy Razaf state; "Cause I can't hide, What's in my face." As if composed for Hurston's Ham, the song asks, "What did I do, to be so black and blue?" and then it attests to Ham's belief that "My only sin is in my skin." Struggling to construct positive interpretations of inherited narratives that present color negatively, Waller—like Hurston—remained caught up in tensions that continue to typify the efforts of even the most progressive thinkers about race.

Yet the aesthetic energies with which such artists as Anne Spencer, Richard Bruce Nugent, and Zora Neale Hurston imbued the black race nevertheless contributed to the incursion of the African-American into Western literary traditions. Locke's belief that the "artistic discovery of African art came at a time when there was a marked decadence and sterility in certain forms of European plastic art expression, due to generations of the inbreeding of style and idiom" (258), explains why and how African forms transformed the paintings of Matisse, Picasso, Derain, and Utrillo, the sculpture of Epstein, Lipschitz, and Modigliani, the poetry of Guillaume Apollinaire and Blaise Cendrars (the artists cited in Locke's essay "The Legacy of the Ancestral Arts"). One contemporary critic points to the paradox in Locke's attempt to convince "the Negro to stop imitating reactionary Europeans and to start imitating progressive ones" (Michaels, *Our America*, 86), though of course Locke assumed black artists would derive from Africa an ancestral legacy that might bring them in touch with their own origins. Unbeknownst to Locke, however, many white poets writing at the same time he produced *The New Negro* (1925) adopted African cadences and African-American idioms to revitalize the "decadence and sterility" of European linguistic expression, indeed to cure or at least invigorate the "white-man-who-has-problems-believing-in-his-own-existence." With much less right to assert direct kinship with African culture than Locke, the lost generation associated with high modernism managed to find itself in what its members took to be ancient tribal rhythms and futuristic urban slang to which these writers (acknowledged they) could lay no legitimate claim.

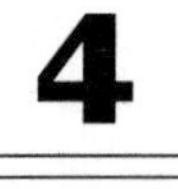

DE MODERN DO MR. BONES

(and All That Ventriloquist Jazz)

Oh! tis consummation
Devoutly to be wished,
To end your heartache by a sleep;
When likely to be dished,
Shuffle off your mortal coil,
Do just so,
Wheel about and turn about
And jump Jim Crow.
—Anonymous Minstrel

De fust great epitaph was written by Homer . . . He wrote de "Oddity." It is de story ob Ulysses. We know Ulysses' las' name—it was Grant. De "Oddity" is written in heroic cutlets wid miasmatic feet. Does you know what a miasmatic foot is? Well, dat is de meter. An' I don' mean de gas meter an I don' mean de water meter. It mean de heavenly meateor what comes shootin' from de stars.

—Anonymous Minstrel

—Mr Bones, you too advancer with your song,
muching of which are wrong.
—John Berryman

Why did Gertrude Stein take "the first definite step away from the nineteenth century and into the twentieth century in literature" by writing not only about but also as "Melanctha the negress" (Stein, 50)? What does it mean that the outrageous promoters of the Dada movement banged on drums while performing "Negergedichte" or "Negro poems" in the Cabaret Voltaire's 1916 avant-garde shows in Zurich? Is there a connection between Vachel Lindsay's frenzied recitation of "The Congo" at a banquet sponsored by Harriet Monroe's magazine *Poetry* and the patron Carl Van Vechten's decision to title his novel about Harlem after the speech of a Lennox Avenue character who declares, "I jes' nacherly think dis heah is Nigger Heaven" (15)? Or between T. S. Eliot's use of the nickname "Possum" (or Pound's of "Brer Rabbit") and Nancy Cunard's creation of footnotes for works she composed in African-American slang? How much and what kind of meaning should we assign to William Carlos Williams' placing toward the conclusion of *Paterson* (1946–1958) this quotation from *Really the Blues* (1946), the memoir of a jazz musician named Mezz Mezzrow who was born Jewish but considered himself Negro: "You could dig the colored man's real message and get in there with him. . . . inspiration's mammy was with me" (221)?

Certainly many of the white proponents of modernism immersed themselves in black culture and in particular in various attempts at a racial ventriloquism they associated with linguistic experimentation. Nor is this surprising if we take to its logical conclusion a point that Ralph Ellison made about black dialect. Considering the efforts of Americans to distinguish the New World from the Old, Ellison noted the importance of "the vernacular which gave expression to that very newness of spirit and outlook of which the leaders of the [American] nation liked to boast" ("Going to the Territory," 142). During the era in which Pound's injunction to "Make It New" resounded, black language practices—as they had been encoded by earlier (often white-authored) texts—offered an irresistible strategy for revitalizing the stale conventionalities of traditional forms, giving resonance to James Baldwin's assertion that "he who would enter the twenty-first century must come by way of me" (Baker, *Modernism*, 61).

In his contribution to Nancy Cunard's *Negro* anthology (1934), the composer George Antheil historicized this phenomenon of the blackening of the arts in painting (Gauguin, Picasso) and music (Stravinsky, Dvořák):

> The great war had come and gone, we had been robbed and ransacked of everything; and we were on the march again. Therefore we welcomed this sunburnt and primitive feeling, we laid out blankets in the sun and it killed all of our civilized microbes. The Negro came naturally into this blazing light, and has remained there. The black man (the exact opposite color of ourselves) has appeared to us suddenly like a true phenomenon. Like a photograph of ourselves he is the sole negative from which a positive may be drawn. (351)

Even before World War I, of course, the Negro (usually imagined as male) had become in the white mind a symbol of natural spontaneity, healthy exuberance, physical rhythms, the genuine or authentic. "Our fascination with the native," the cultural studies critic Rey Chow explains, has often been "a desire to hold on to an unchanging certainty somewhere outside our own 'fake' experience" (53). Indeed, it was precisely the prejudicial logic of such a stereotype of the vital authenticity of the primitive that led black writers to eschew dialect during the period white poets embraced it.

Most of the African-American contemporaries of Lindsay and Van Vechten rejected black vernacular as politically and aesthetically retrograde because it reinforced an image of the ignorant, stumbling, bumbling fool whose ungrammatical malapropisms were spouted by the blackfaced minstrel. Lest natural spontaneity or healthy exuberance slide into the stupidity usually attributed to animals and children, it had to be renounced or denounced. In other words, to offset a damaging view of black intellectual inferiority, some African-American writers in the first quarter of the twentieth century exhibited a kind of hypercorrect conventionality. According to Henry Louis Gates, Jr., many of the Harlem Renaissance poets extensively borrowed the forms of white poetry while eschewing what was singular about the speech of blacks (*Figures*, 181).[1] With the work of Langston Hughes and Sterling Brown providing the obvious exception to the rule, it is paradoxical that just as black dialect disappeared from the verse produced by African Americans, it surfaced with surprising vitality in the compositions of their white contemporaries.[2]

This may be why the only scholarly attention the phenomenon of racial ventriloquism has received comes by way of disapproval. Michael North's useful *The Dialect of Modernism*—with its documentation of the black talk white modernists used in their revolt against authoritarianism—views such appropriations as a "slumming in slang" that perpetuates racial slurs as well as the privileged position of whites (82). Similarly, Aldon Lynn Nielsen's important *White American Poets and the Racial Discourse in the Twentieth Century* reads twentieth-century white poets' "objectification of the racial other" as "romantic racism" (11).[3] Along with Marianna Torgovnick's *Gone Primitive*, these books demonstrate that the minstrel tradition, the fiction of Harriet Beecher Stowe (*Uncle Tom's Cabin* (1852)), the folklore of Joel Chandler Harris (*Uncle Remus* (1881), *The Tar-Baby* (1904), and *Uncle Remus and Br'er Rabbit* (1906)), and the movies based on Edgar Rice Burroughs's series (*Tarzan of the Apes* (1912)) were phenomenally popular and influential, shaping modernist writers' representations of black speech and contributing to racist stereotypes that placed Africans as well as African Americans outside the bounds of culture by associating blackness with ineptitude, passivity, or savagery. As Torgovnick has pointed out, the primitive is defined as "different from (usually opposite to) the present" so as to fulfill the needs of the present: "Voiceless, it lets us speak for it. It is our ventriloquist's dummy—or so we like to think" (9).

Yet in the "black literature" composed by twentieth-century white authors, the white poet or novelist speaks through the African dummy's mouth in a black talk that often presents itself as back talk. That is, most writers exploiting black rhythms and vernacular felt themselves to be tapping a dissident lexicon of subversive power, one at odds with the hegemonic cadences of mainstream culture as well as their own normative conformity to it. To the African-American reader, such an undertaking may seem like just another form of stereotypical appropriation. About John Berryman's famous decision to play the roles of Tambo and Bones "in that needful black idiom / offending me," Michael Harper flatly decides, "your ear lied. / *That slave in you was white blood forced to derision*" (10; emphasis his). Notwithstanding his ethical condemnation ("your ear lied"), Harper's analysis provides a clue for understanding the psychological and historical designs of racial ventriloquism in the modern minstrelsy of Berryman's poetic precursors; it also illuminates the major role linguistic racechanges played in the lives and works of several highly influential white patrons of the Harlem Renaissance. Ralph Ellison's reactions to Berryman's use of dialect supply a comparable lead when the novelist explained that despite his "preference" for "idiomatic rendering" and despite his "suspicion that Berryman was casting me as a long-distant Mister Interlocutor—

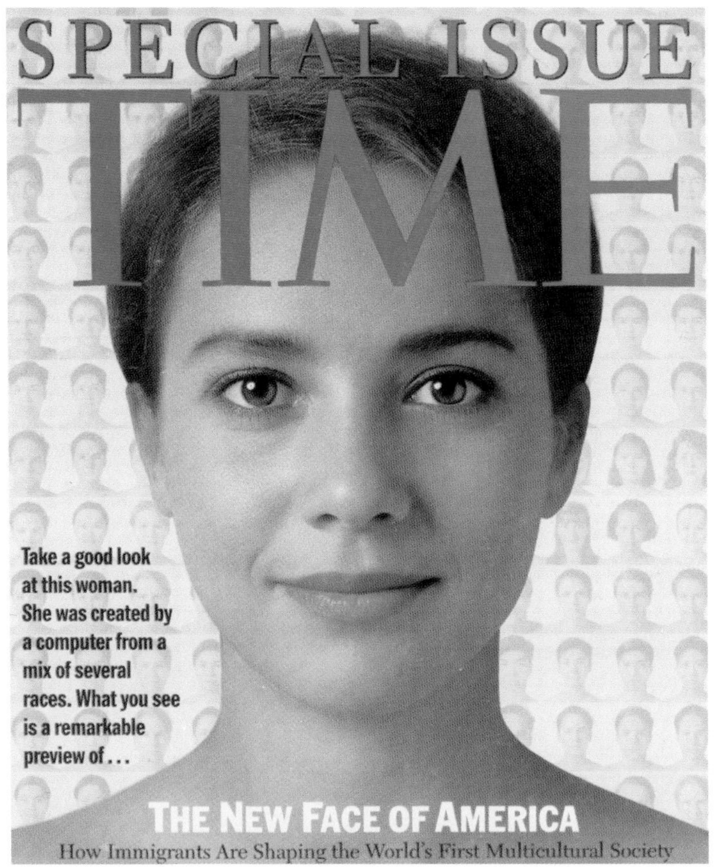

Eve, *Time* magazine cover girl. Special Issue, Fall 1993. Courtesy Time-Life.

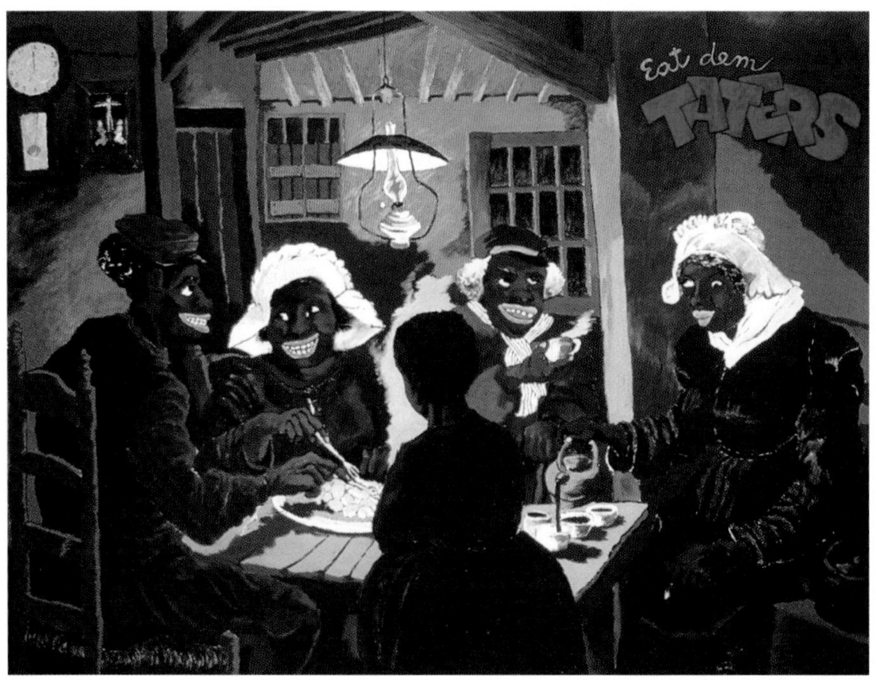

Robert Colescott, *Eat Dem Taters* (1975). Acrylic on canvas, 59 x 79 in. Courtesy Phyllis Kind Gallery, New York and Chicago.

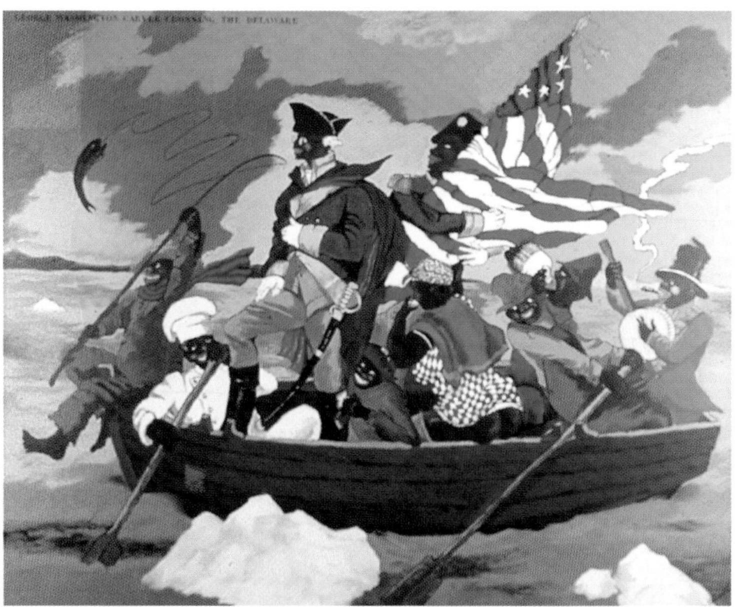

Robert Colescott, *George Washington Carver Crossing the Delaware: Page from an American History Textbook* (1975). Acrylic on canvas, 54 x 108 in. Courtesy Phyllis Kind Gallery, New York and Chicago.

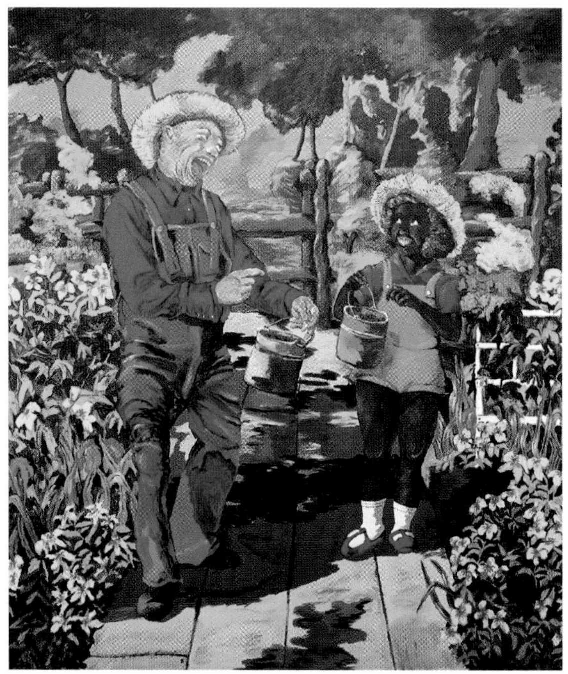

Robert Colescott, *Shirley Temple Black and Bill Robinson White* (1980). Acrylic on canvas, 84 x 72 in. Courtesy Phyllis Kind Gallery, New York and Chicago.

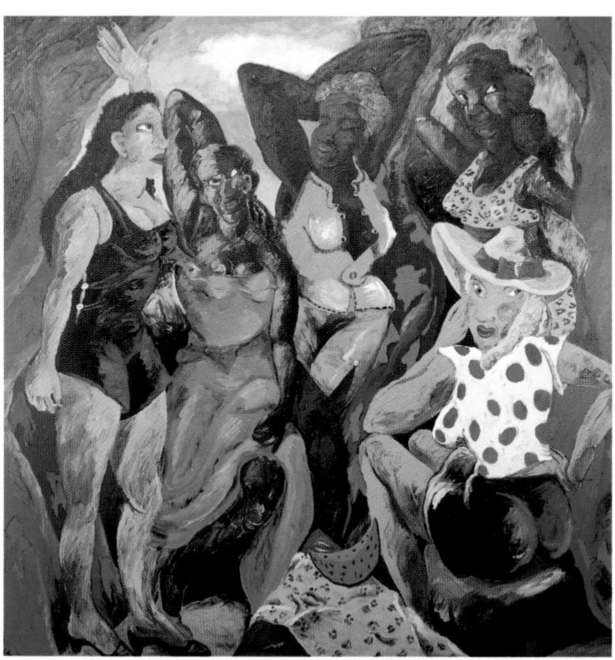

Robert Colescott, *Les demoiselles d'Alabama: Vestidas* (1985). Acrylic on canvas, 96 x 92 in. Courtesy Phyllis Kind Gallery, New York and Chicago.

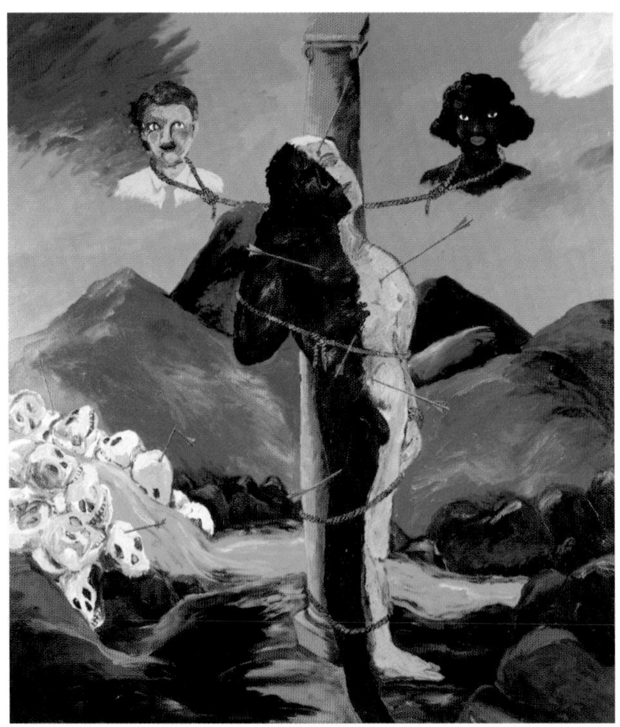

Robert Colescott, *Knowledge of the Past Is the Key to the Future (St. Sebastian)* (1986). Acrylic on canvas, 84 x 72 in. Courtesy Phyllis Kind Gallery, New York and Chicago.

or was it Mister Tambo?—" in the *Dream Songs*, Ellison himself "wasn't about to let the poetry of what [Berryman] was saying be interrupted by the dictates of my ear for Afro-American speech" (Mariani, *Dream Song*, 387). Though, like Harper, we might find fault with any appropriation by whites of black-inflected language and though, like Ellison, we might find such simulations inadequate as "idiomatic rendering[s]" of "Afro-American speech," we may have to admit that some of the most banal *and* some of the most brilliant experiments in twentieth-century poetry relied on cross-racial ventriloquism.

Perhaps because of its outrageous reliance on patently unrealistic or blatantly racist stereotypes, black English in twentieth-century literature contributes to the carnivalesque effect produced by pointedly self-parodic texts that seek to disrupt by mixing genres as well as lexical registers. As is the case in the fictional technique that the Russian theorist Bakhtin called "parodic stylization," the "intentions of the represent*ed* discourse are at odds with the intentions of the represent*ing* discourse" (364; emphasis mine). The printed white word contains and frames the represented speech of blacks, with the resulting collage contrasting belated written and originatory oral modalities often, as George Antheil had intuited, to dramatize the search of a society sickened by "civilized microbes" for a radiation-type therapy or cure derived from the blazing intensity of the African. In other words, black speech has a kind of fresh vitality that turns against the staid, stale, stupid decorums of the King's English. The very necessity of swerving toward subversive black talk, which holds out the possibility of reviving tediously traditional language forms, reveals the poverty and dessication of white culture. Whether conceived to be as ancient as African chants (what in this chapter I will call "Boomlay BOOM") or as new as African-American slang (what, following many, I term "Dis and Dat"), the vivacity or verve of African rhythms and African-American vernacular posed a threat to the established order for some as well as a promise for others. Indeed, in the pages to come we will note an ideological shift in emphasis over the course of the twentieth century: Black diction, which is repeatedly identified with a pre- or post-civilized energy, first tends to be exploited by practitioners who vilify it as anathema to Western civilization and only later in the century is it reimagined as redemptive.

But, regardless of their politics, all texts exploiting racial ventriloquism inevitably shuttle between defending against and welcoming energies of Otherness. The African-oral is written as if it hardly understands itself (and thus it must be desperately in need of the white writer who condescends to express it); however, the African-oral is supposed to capture primordial, essential meanings (and thus the mysterious potency of its energies captivate the white scribe).[4] What John Edgar Wideman identifies as the "high density of 'sound effects'" in folk narratives—performative strategies such as onomatopoetic words, syncopation, dialogue, phatic chants, word repetitions, rhetorical questions, parallel phrases, call and response patterns, notations indicating a percussive delivery, rhyme—finds its way into modern texts composed in imitation African rhythms (Boomlay BOOM) and African-American vernacular (Dis and Dat) that deride blacks but also backfire to mock white society as well as the white writer himself (74).

Though Wideman has argued that "*difference* in the dialect tradition clearly signaled *deficiency*" (60), improper grammar, eccentric orthography, slovenly pronunciation, comic malapropisms, and far-fetched words could also point to *difference* as *deviance* at a historical moment when alienated Euro-American writers sought to escape the horror, the horror of Western civilization and what it had wrought. Defying the efforts of scholars to distinguish the cadences and lexicons rooted in the speech of real slaves from the bogus stage-Negro vernacular created by whites, the literature of modernism problematizes such a clear-cut division.[5] Similarly, the Africanist presence in experimental twentieth-century literature often stands not only for the new and the old but also for the genuine as well as the ersatz. Although, as Chow puts it, "our fascination with the native" reflects "a desire to hold on to an unchanging certainty somewhere outside our own 'fake' experience," many twentieth-century white artists understood that such a figure for the authentic was of their own making and thus simply another form of fakery.

In the passage from the *Negro* anthology quoted above, after all, Antheil stated that blacks appeared "*like* a true phenomenon" (emphasis mine). Embedded, as it usually is, within the hegemonic diction of the poet's culture, black talk signals the wish to represent the authentic and the flagrant impossibility of doing so. Modernist experimentation in racial ventriloquism therefore needs to be distinguished from, say, the black slave narratives produced by white abolitionists or other crossover texts that attempted verisimilitude so as to pass their authors off as authentically colored.[6] Instead, what we confront in reading Lindsay's or Cunard's or Mezzrow's renditions of African or African-American language are so obviously pidgin versions of the Other or are so pointedly marked as foreign (thus in need of translation) that they force us to come to terms with the profound ideolectical differences which render all people incapable of communicating.[7] To the extent that exaggerated stereotyping increasingly calls attention to white authors' inability to represent the black Other, the works of later-twentieth-century writers self-consciously meditate on their failure to represent the white self. For if the writer cannot understand or render the Other, the work demonstrates that we cannot understand *any* other or, for that matter, each other. What Michael Harper diagnosed as "*white blood forced to derision*" constitutes the gothic self-mockery of this heteroglossia, a poetics based on a curious impasse: the wish to engage the authenticity of the Other—to call it into being—and the fated sense that such an effort is doomed from the start.[8]

That so many racial ventriloquists—like Lindsay and Cunard, Mezzrow and Berryman—would have viewed themselves as ardent advocates of racial equality complicates our understanding of their motives. Perhaps in this regard bell hooks furnishes the best framework for understanding how racial ventriloquism operates as an attempted racechange:

> The desire to make contact with those bodies deemed Other, with no apparent will to dominate, assuages the guilt of the past, even takes the form of a defiant gesture where one denies accountability and historical connection. Most importantly, it establishes a contemporary narrative where *the suffering imposed by structures of domination on those designated Other is deflected* by an emphasis on seduction and longing where

> the desire is not to make the Other over in one's image but *to become the Other*. (*Black Looks*, 25; emphasis mine)

Even as black rhythmic and lexical styles enabled many modernists to estrange language, they offered a (broken) promise that the white writer could become the Other and so often enmeshed practitioners in various fantasies of racechange. The race for modernity was African, according to a number of twentieth-century poets, patrons, and their more contemporary successors, many of whom sought to speak for and even as the blacks they (knew they only) pretended to be.

Modern Minstrelsy's Boomlay BOOM

For what reason is attention to the sufferings imposed by structures of domination deflected into a desire to become the Other or at least a desire to play at being the Other temporarily, as an inspiring experiment or exciting interlude? bell hooks supplies one answer: to assuage the guilt of the past or deny accountability for it. A related explanation is furnished by the anthropologist Renato Rosaldo:

> A person kills somebody, and then mourns the victim. In more attenuated form, someone deliberately alters a form of life, and then regrets that things have not remained as they were prior to the intervention. At one more remove, people destroy their environment, and then they worship nature. In any of its versions, imperialist nostalgia uses a pose of "innocent yearning" both to capture people's imaginations and to conceal its complicity with often brutal domination. (69–70)

After the slave system efficiently destroyed African culture and bodies, after the minstrel shows and blackface films effectively repeated an act of spirit-murder against African Americans, the basis for white guilt hardly needs to be explained. However, Rosaldo's concept of "imperialist nostalgia" illuminates the reasons why pseudo-African and African-American intonations functioned paradoxically as a form of complicity with brutal domination and as a compensatory lament deploring such domination. Since, as Adrienne Rich has remarked in a different context, "nostalgia is only amnesia turned around" ("Turning," 306), one face of imperialist nostalgia is what one might call imperialist amnesia.

Throughout the twentieth century, American, expatriate, and British poets used standard English inflected by rhythms marked as African in works overtly complicitous with brutal domination while others exploited African-American dialect to deplore such domination. Though they vary in their ideological designs and in their linguistic experimentation, early and later deployments of African rhythms, on the one hand, signal nostalgia for the oral, the originatory, the primordial, the real, the genuine; on the other hand, they denote white writers' consciousness that they are using not an undiluted but a minstrel-speak version of black talk that melds the genuine to the ersatz, generating a spurious speech to which the white imagination will perpetually be condemned. Among practitioners of what I am calling the Boomlay BOOM (ersatz African rhythms produced with standard English lexicons), Vachel Lindsay, Edith Sitwell, and T. S. Eliot illuminate the dynamics of imperialist nostalgia and amnesia even as they demonstrate the major role racial ventriloquism played in poetic experimentation. Despite their assaults on the culture and identity of black people, the reader's attention is deflected onto the taboo racechanges with which these racial ventriloquists flirt.

"Every kind of a war-drum ever heard. Then a Minstrel's Heaven, then a glorified Camp Meeting. Boomlay Boomlay Boomlay Boom!": This was how Vachel Lindsay described the "Congo piece" he began writing after visiting "vaudeville [and] . . . at last grasp[ing] what those painted folks are up to" (Ruggles, 210–11). Indeed, Lindsay believed that, given Americans' hatred of verse, the poet could aquire a sizable public only by cashing in on the popularity of, say, Bert Williams's ragtime hit "My Castle on the Nile"—"Inlaid diamonds on de flo', / A baboon butler at mah do'"—and thus producing the "Higher Vaudeville." "I am inventing a sort of ragtime manner that deceives [the audience] into thinking they are at a vaudeville show," Lindsay explained, although he admitted, "I have all my life abhorred" vaudeville (Yatron, 115; Ruggles, 211). Juba dancers at the Chicago World's Fair contributed to the rhythms of the poem, but so did his father's reading of *Uncle Remus*, Conrad's description of the "mighty big river . . . resembling an immense snake uncoiled" in *Heart of Darkness*, and Carlyle's query in *The French Revolution*:

> Does not the Black African take of Sticks and Old Clothes what will suffice and of these, cunningly combining them, fabricate for himself an Eidolon (Idol, or *Thing Seen*), and name it *Mumbo-Jumbo*? (6)

The patently grotesque logic of "The Congo"'s narrative depicts American blacks as genealogically linked to a sinister, heathen African race but able ultimately to be redeemed through Christianity. The first two sections—"Their Basic Savagery" and "Their Irrepressible High Spirits"—therefore move back and forth between twentieth-century American Negroes and primordial African savages. In Part I, "Fat Black bucks in a wine-barrel room" pay obeisance to the Congo God of destruction, Mumbo-Jumbo, as do "Tattooed cannibals [who] danced in files." A boisterous Negro subculture in America ("Barrel-house kings, with feet unstable, / Sagged and reeled and pounded on the table") remains tethered to an Africa figured as barbaric cannibalism ("the boom of the blood-lust song / And a thigh-bone beating on a tin-pan gong" (3)). Similarly, in Part II, "cake-walk royalty," juba dancers, a baboon butler, and a parrot band perform to the raucous delight of "witch men . . . with a sinister air" (5). The final solution appears in the last section, "The Hope of Their Religion," which moves to "the slums of the town" where a "good old negro" preaches to a congregation whose members repent "their stupor and savagery and sin and wrong" (6) so that "Mumbo-Jumbo will die in the jungle" and "Pioneer angels" can clear the way for a neat and clean "Congo paradise" (6). Ludicrous in the transparency of its racism, "The Congo" supplies its poet the role of missionary, shouldering the white man's burden to kill the African god who threatens to "hoo-doo" Western civilization.

The text of "The Congo"—with its stereotypically black rhythms glossed by directorial reading instructions in the prose marginalia—recalls Bakhtin's description of the clash between represent*ing* discourses that demolish represent*ed* languages in "parodic stylization" (364). From this perspective, the onomatopoetic and phatic words, syncopation, repetition, and percussive delivery of "The Congo" effectively ridicule and condemn the religious traditions and aesthetic styles identified as African and African-American. But the listeners who laughed at Lindsay's first performance were probably not tickled so much by its racism as by his flamboyantly weird delivery, just as those who made it his signature act were less enthralled by its message, more by the frenzied rolling of his eyes, the shooting of his hands, the rising of his voice to a whoop or a yelp and its falling to a whisper. Written accounts of Lindsay's impassioned performances as well as extant recordings make him sound like a versifying Al Jolson.[9] Curiously, too, the enormous popularity of the poem seemed to punish Lindsay for his cross-racial impersonation by forcing him repeatedly to stand in the place of the Other: Determined not to accede to the public's demands, he explained, "'I will *not* be a *slave* to my yesterdays'" (Ruggles, 412).

"People destroy their environment, and then they worship nature": If we apply the logic of Rosaldo's thinking about imperialist nostalgia to modernist heteroglossia, it becomes clear that Lindsay demonizes African Americans and then reveres their animated vitality (which he himself stages), for the effect of "The Congo" depends less on its genocidal plot and more on the verbal exuberance of its "high density of 'sound effects'" derived from African and African-American folk conventions. Pounding and singing, laughing and beating, preaching and prancing are the activities attributed within the poem to blacks but actually undertaken by the white performer. One passage, to be recited "with growing speed and sharply marked dance-rhythm," requires the white poet-performer to replicate the strutting of the black cake-walkers being described:

> And they pranced with their butterfly partners there,
> Coal-black maidens with pearls in their hair,
> Knee-skirts trimmed with the jassamine sweet,
> And bells on their ankles and little black feet. (5)

With their percussive four beats, these lines emphasize the pageantry, color, and vitality of a black culture that can never be fully captured through the pallor of print, but that the performer-poet seeks to replicate.

It does seem as if the topic of the poem gave Lindsay and his audience permission to engage with verbal intensity not just in "romantic racism" or "slumming in slang" but also in the mimetic rivalry of an incantatory chanting, singing, hymning, humming, slapping, drumming. All of "The Congo"'s lines aspire to the insistent, nonsensical condition of "Boomlay, boomlay, boomlay, BOOM." That is, the sense of the language is drained away by the repetition of sounds and words, by the alliteration, rhyme, and especially the preeminence of a rhythm so insistent it taps, claps, or drums through words. Phonetic similarity replaces semantic significance, as the ethnocentric effort to dethrone the African spiritual rituals of Mumbo Jumbo boomerangs to jettison the Western poet into his own mumbo jumbo of gibberish. Understandably, then, the strong beat and syncopation of Lindsay's "Higher Vaudeville" led Edgar Lee Masters to refer to "The Congo" as

"Beethoven jazz" (324).[10] Its prose gloss turns the text into a score, explaining to actor-chanters the speed, intonation, pitch, pausing, accents, emphasis, tone, emotion, and song tunes advisable for an effective performance. "With a touch of negro dialect and as rapidly as possible toward the end," one such stage direction reads (5).

Yet a "touch of negro dialect" that can be turned on, then turned off proves how consciously Lindsay wrote as a white for whites. That Lindsay understood himself to be involved in a less than authentic "Study of the Negro Race"—his subtitle to the poem and purported purpose in composing it—finds evidence throughout. First "Their" savagery, "Their" spirits, and "Their" religion: The pronoun of the section titles illustrates his acknowledged distance from the race he attempts to delineate. Second, the drunken barrel-house kings with their silk umbrellas and the cake-walking royalty would be instantly recognizable as types of the minstrel dandy. Third, Lindsay concedes that he and other whites have manipulated black representation: Ancient African voo-doo becomes "A roaring, epic, *rag-time tune*," a product of the contemporary Western imagination; the "negro fairyland" inhabited by the cake-walkers appears by "A *minstrel* river" (4). Finally, it is possible to read the end of the poem as an admission that white efforts to control black representation will be doomed to failure. Although the conclusion of "The Congo" emphatically states that the god of Africa is dead, a far-away vulture speaks the last lines of the poem: "Mumbo-Jumbo will hoo-doo you. / Mumbo . . . Jumbo . . . will . . . hoo-doo . . . you." To be recited in a "penetrating, terrified whisper," these broken phrases bespeak the author's admission that his curse poem will fail to extirpate the alien powers of Otherness that haunt his imagination and shape his artistry.

Lindsay is often ignored in histories of twentieth-century poetry because judged to be exceptionally reactionary in his racism. However, he was much more liberal than many of his poetic contemporaries and he first performed "The Congo" at a Lincoln Day banquet held in Springfield.[11] When Lindsay justified his pacifism during World War I, he said he would rather have died "of his own will mount[ing] a blazing pyre . . . by the side or in place of some black who had not trial by jury" than in the trenches (Ruggles, 250). "By the side or *in the place of some black*": Lindsay's self-sacrificial fantasy of racechange informed the poet's conviction that "the only way to end lynching would be to thrust yourself into the thick of such a mob and *make the men slay you instead of the Negro*. 'When they realized what they had done,'" Lindsay was supposed to have said, "'their hearts would be touched, their consciences shocked'" (Ruggles, 138; emphasis mine).[12] Even in the midst of describing the destructive ferocity of African savagry, Lindsay's "Congo" contains lines blaming black violence on white imperialism, including a grisly injunction that we "Listen to the yell of Leopold's ghost"; the Belgian King's exploitation of the Congo earns him "demons . . . / Cutting his hands off, down in Hell" (4). Although the booming drumbeats of "black bucks" and "barrel-house kings" lead Lindsay to explain, "THEN I had religion, THEN I had a vision. / I could not turn from their revel in derision" (3), he feels nothing but derision for the well-earned sufferings of King Leopold II punished in hell.

But if Lindsay cannot be discounted on account of virulent racism, neither can he be categorized as if outside the label "modernism," even though he is often presented as a formally conservative poet whose populist enthusiasm marked him as the very opposite of the experimental, elitist modernists. As prominent a poet as William Butler Yeats, commending "the half-sung, half-spoken delivery of such vaudeville acts as Tambo and Bones dialogues, which had an apparent spontaneity, and a quick-fire, incantatory rhythm," stated at the *Poetry* banquet recitation that "all that survived in America of the much-to-be-desired 'primitive singing of poetry' and the Greek lyric chant was American Vaudeville and Vachel Lindsay" (Massa, 231). Precisely "the half-sung, half-spoken delivery" of Tambo and Bones dialogues drew experimental writers rarely linked either to American vaudeville or Vachel Lindsay, at least in part because black talk enabled them to enact their estrangement from the pieties and proprieties of Western culture, to mark their awareness that such an alienation never guaranteed any bona fide alternative to Western culture, and to engage in unraveling meaning-making itself.[13]

What distinguishes the poetry of Boomlay BOOM in the twentieth century is its nonsensical hilarity, its anarchic incomprehensibility. When modernist writers heeded "The rattle of the bones, and chuckle spread from ear to ear," as T. S. Eliot did in *The Waste Land* (II.186), they used racial impersonation simultaneously to make the old new and the new old. And they did so by exploiting two of Lindsay's strategies: First, as Edith Sitwell's "Gold Coast Customs" (1928) illustrates, they produced incantatory mumbo jumbo by sustaining (what they thought to be) percussive African rhythms, emphasizing sound at the expense of sense; second, as T. S. Eliot's *Sweeney Agonistes* (1926–27) demonstrates, they set those rhythms within the framework of vaudeville and in so doing uncovered the links between the projects of modernism and minstrelsy, both of which exploited nonsense to ridicule the high seriousness of Western culture's monuments of unaging intellect.

Sitwell shared with Lindsay a fascination with Boomlay BOOM, though "Gold Coast Customs" seems even more saturated with revulsion at the knocking of savage bones on the portals of civilization than is "The Congo." When in the late forties Humphrey Searle, a practitioner of the twelve-tone scale and student of Webern, composed a musical setting to "Gold Coast Customs," he used a particularly full percussion section—two side drums, tenor drum, bass drum, tom-tom, triangle, cymbals, gong, and so on—to establish what one critic calls "the ground rhythm of the African tom-tom which gives the poem its rhythmical unity" (Singleton, 73). And Searle himself explained that "in the last movement at 'Bahunda, Banbangala, Barumbe, Bonge' (Section 24), whip, rattle, bass drum, two piccolos and a shouting chorus make an effect suggested by an African war-chant, whistled and shouted to the accompaniment of tom-toms and clapped hands" (Singleton, 74). He was drawing on a tradition of *musique nègre* that had shaped Stravinsky's *Le Sacre du printemps* (1913) and his *Ragtime* (1918), Milhaud's *La Creation du monde* (1924), and Poulenc's *Rapsodie nègre* (1917), in which a voice "singing only four pitches in a descending scalar pattern" recites such lines as "tota nou nou, nou nou ranga / lo lo lulu ma ta ma sou" (G. Watkins, 105).[14]

Echoes of the percussive, four-beat alliterative lines of "The Congo" toll in the opening of Sitwell's poem in which "Munza rattles his bones in the dusk, / Lurking in murk because he must" (7). Only the first explanatory note (on an Ashantee custom of killing slaves so as to use their blood in funeral services for the rich) and the closing footnote (documenting King Munza's reign in 1874 over the Monbuttoo) make any sense at all out of her mumbo jumbo. Instead of sense, sound links the three phantasmagoric settings of "Gold Coast Customs": the Ashantee tribal ceremonies, the decadent parties of one Lady Bamburgher, and a dock scene of sailors and prostitutes. Presented as if a poetic version of cinematic montage, all three share inexplicable but convulsive images of cannibalism, animality, corruption, and degeneration. As in the work of Lindsay, once again we have the narrative logic of a text that condemns black people for a fatal physicality at odds with morality or spirituality: According to Sitwell's notes, "The Negroes indulge [their] perfect contempt for humanity" in their "devouring of human flesh" (61).

A protest against the spiritual cannibalism of the postwar period, "Gold Coast Customs" condemns European civilization for its resemblance to Africa. Black mud, white bones and skulls, rotting flesh, devouring worms, monkey skins, rat-fat souls, and plague spots proliferate here, as there. But, as in "The Congo," the odd paradox emerges that the poet's voice finds its source of energy in (an albeit grotesquely stereotyped) Africa, "the threshold where history began" (16), an originatory place that keeps the poet enthralled by the "The cannibal drums [which] still roll in the mud / To the bones of the King's mother laved in blood." Sitwell herself seems to intuit the oddity of cross-racial identification early in the poem: The speaker refers mysteriously to "A bugbear bone that bellows white / As the ventriloquist sound of light" (8). Once again, an erstatz primitivism fuels modernist experimentation, for the poet repeatedly, passionately ventriloquizes "the bellowing bones" (28): "Rattle and beat what seemed a drum, / Rattle and beat it with a bone" (21). While most of the many photographed and painted portraits of Edith Sitwell emphasized her pallor and asceticism, a 1934 oil by Stella Bowen appears to invoke "Gold Coast Customs" by showing Sitwell's famously aristocratic hands grasping a black mask over her white face (Fig. 4.1).[15]

As if explaining the genealogy of "The Congo" and "Gold Coast Customs," T. S. Eliot once argued that "Poetry begins . . . with a savage beating a drum in a jungle" ("Beating of a Drum," 12).[16] But what Eliot's work lays bare is how self-consciously indebted the practitioners of the Boomlay BOOM tradition remained to flauntingly unreal representations of the primitive derived from minstrelsy, vaudeville, music halls, and Hollywood films.[17] Just as "The Congo" hinted at Lindsay's guilty awareness that he was engaged in an ersatz form of linguistic racechange, Eliot—who had prefaced "The Hollow Men" (1925) with Conrad's "*Mistah Kurtz—he dead*"—exploited "the hollow ring" of appropriated but admittedly spurious discourses.[18] This paradigmatic modernist, who accepted the nicknames Possum, Uncle Tom, and Tar Baby from Ezra Pound (himself nicknamed Br'er Rabbit)[19] and who for many years wrote pornographic verses about "King Bolo and His Great Black Queen," was drawn to black talk as a forbidden language that would enable him simultaneously to express and deride his most secret and fearful fantasies, or so a femicidal drama composed during the disintegration of his first marriage indicates.

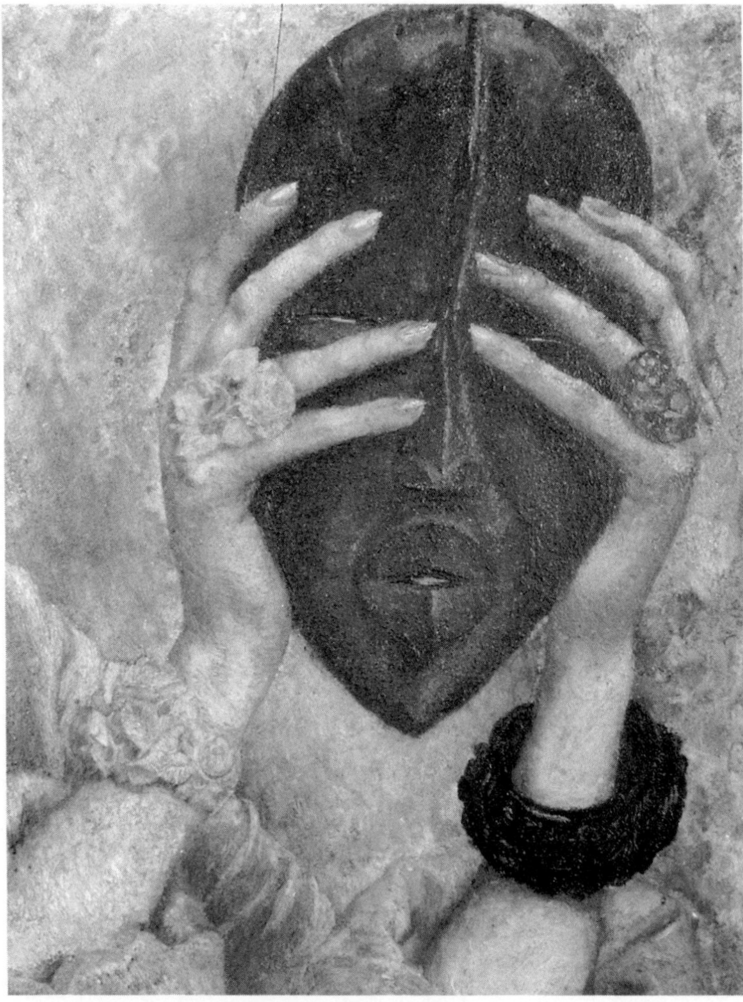

Figure 4.1 Stella Bowen, *Hands of Edith Sitwell with Mask* (1934), oil. Courtesy of David Higham Associates.

After completing *The Waste Land*, Eliot used the minstrel endmen Tambo and Bones, music-hall dialogue and song, insistent rhythms, incantatory repetition of nonsense words, and descriptions of a cannibal island to frame an unfinished pastische that he considered "the most original of his compositions" (Ackroyd, 146). Published only in fragmentary form, *Sweeney Agonistes* appears at first quite different from "The Congo" or "Gold Coast Customs" in subject at least; however, it was supposed to be accompanied by light drum taps to accentuate the beats; one of its first readers, Arnold Bennett, called it a "jazz play" (Everett, 248); and Eliot himself later titled it "Fragment of a Comic Minstrelsy" (North, 87). As Barbara Everett has pointed out, the two verse dialogues that Eliot completed contrast the super-literacy of epigraphs from Aeschylus and St. John of the Cross with the subliteracy of American speech to establish what she calls "the medium of the comic demotic" (251).

Originally titled *Wanna Go Home, Baby?* and often read as a statement about modernist homelessness, the hallucinatory action of *Sweeney Agonistes* occurs in a rented flat occupied by Doris and Dusty. In Part I, "Fragment of a Prologue," these two smart tarts read their fortunes in cards, à la Madame Sosostris; they are then visited by a number of gentlemen callers who explain that they will not settle down because they find London "*a little too gay*" (19; emphasis mine).[20] The stress on misrule—geographic and sexual—surfaces again at the start of Part II, "Fragment of an Agon," in which Sweeney appears, threatening to carry Doris off to a cannibal isle: He wants to "gobble" her up and "convert" her "Into a stew. / A nice little, white little, missionary stew" (23). The cannibal island itself he imagines as the antithesis of London—no gramophones, no motor cars; when Sweeney emphasizes the nothingness to which he wishes to convey Doris, she replies, "I'd be bored." Doris's ennui presumably spells Western alienation from nature and from the ontological grounds of being, a tedium that may also mask her dread that she would really "be bored"—sexually or violently penetrated. "A woman runs a terrible risk," Doris admits, as Sweeney recounts tales of lurid sex crimes against female victims kept in baths of Lysol.

Minstrel and music hall numbers enabled Eliot to articulate and ridicule misogynist impulses he labeled barbaric or primitive at a time when he resented the demands made by his increasingly hysterical and unhappy wife.[21] The flagrant factitiousness of vaudeville, its zany unreality, allowed Eliot to intimate that modern man will never be able to capture the exhilarating primacy of the primitive. Although, as Sweeney explains, "Any man might do a girl in / Any man has to, needs to, wants to / Once in a lifetime, do a girl in" (28), this latter-day seedy thug will never manage to take Doris to the cannibal isle upon which such a consummation could be more than wished, for his island is comprised entirely out of the never-never land of vaudevillean stagecraft, or so the songs of "Snow and Swarts" indicate. As if to emphasize the showy theatricality of music hall scripts not to be taken too seriously, one such song—a version of "Under the Bamboo Tree," whose lyrics were composed in 1902 in a collaboration that included James Weldon Johnson—is performed by "Swarts as Tambo, Snow as Bones."

Even as the contrast of black (German *schwartz*) and white (snow or cocaine) reveals that their prototype is the harlequin (sporting his checkered costume, his black mask, and his phallic scepter), the two endmen make a mockery of realistic faith in any genuine state of nature

Where the Gauguin maids
In the banyan shades
Wear palmleaf drapery
Under the bam
Under the boo
Under the bamboo tree. (25–26)

The music hall status of Eliot's Tambo and Bones signals the impossibility of Sweeney enacting his femicidal fantasies. Minstrelsy stands, on the one hand, for the endurance of murderous instincts in the psyche of Western man and, on the other, the degeneration of such masculinism to a farcically improbable show-stopper possible only "Under the bam / Under the boo" where "Two live as one/ One live as two" (20).[22] (That the first black minstrel, Juba, advertised his "Imitation Dances" by explaining he would "give correct Imitation Dances of all the principal Ethiopian Dancers in the United States. After which he [would] give an imitation of himself" (Toll, 43) indicates how fully immersed minstrel mimicry was in artifice from its very inception.)

Inhabiting a fallen linguistic realm, Eliot's characters—haunted by guilt at their murderous desires and using a language contaminated by racial guilt—end up with the dissolution of all relationships and with the entropic deterioration of language into the nihilistic clowning of Vachel Lindsay's higher vaudeville: "Hoo / Hoo / Hoo / Knock Knock Knock" (31).[23] Just as the minstrels ridiculed high culture in their jumble of mistaken words and their mock pomposity, constructing burlesques that made a travesty of Western traditions, *Sweeney Agonistes* turned to minstrelsy as a remedy for but also a sign of the dessication of Western culture. Nihilistic hilarity at a hodge-podge of jostling registers—Biblical quotations and music hall patter, vaudeville slapstick and "coon" songs, jazz numbers and slang syncopations—emanates from otherwise quite different minstrel and modernist texts, in Eliot's case clearly motivated by the perplexity of a sense of masculine insufficiency that finds no outlet for rage against women. In more general terms, though, it is surprising how minstrel and modernist productions share a fascination with incongruity, given the obvious contrast between the popular stage and the abstruse experiments of the avant-garde.

The jumbled parodies that I used as the first two epigraphs of this chapter show how American popular culture in the nineteenth century used blackface performances to reinvent the Old World's culture in the irreverent New World's image. Just as Hamlet's suicidal soliloquy about what dreams may come after "we have shuffled off this mortal coil" degenerates into the choreographic imperative to "Shuffle off your mortal coil, / Do just so, / Wheel about and turn about / And jump Jim Crow," Eliot's *Waste Land* performs a "Shakespeherian Rag" (II.128); just as Homer's *Odyssey* devolves in minstrel-speak into the "oddity," while heroic couplets become "heroic cutlets" and poetic meter becomes the "gas meter" or the "heavenly meateor," *The Waste Land* transforms Marvell's "But at my back I always hear / Time's winged chariot hurrying near" into "But at my back in a cold blast I hear / The rattle of the bones, and chuckle spread from ear to ear" (III.185–86) while Eliot's next work substituted the thuggish Sweeney for Milton's heroic *Samson Agonistes*.

A comparable incongruity characterizes the beginning of *Sweeney Agonistes* (Aeschylus and St. John of the Cross) and its ending (the "Hoo / Hoo / Hoo" in "FULL CHORUS"). Through repetition and an insistence on sound over sense, the minstrel and the modernist drained high cultural texts of their seriousness, thereby making a travesty of the classical and biblical touchstones of Western civilization. According to Raymond Williams, the avant-garde often attempted "to dispense with language altogether, as too hopelessly compromised," or to substitute what Artaud called "'a different language of nature,'" which Williams equates with "vaudeville" (70).[24] In its anarchic glee at constructing a pastiche of incoherent bits and bites from high and low culture, the modernist's signifying shared common cause with the minstrel's flirtation with nonsense, his tendency to shore fragments against or amid the ruins.[25]

Given many modernists' alienation from conventional, linear, logical, causal structures of aesthetic forms and modes of intellection, it is hardly surprising that a number of Eliot's contemporaries were drawn to what has been called the "altiloquent speech" of stage blacks, a language full of sound and fury but signifying next to nothing. Gertrude Stein's booming repetition of the word "always" in "Melanchta"—"you so stupid *always* to me and *always* just bother with your *always* asking to me" (408, emphasis mine)—represents one deployment of the Boomlay BOOM that is linked to minstrelsy through the image of another (disturbingly stereotypical) refrain: "the wide, abandoned laughter that makes the warm broad glow of negro sunshine." If to one of Stein's critics the moralizings of her Negro hero sound like "the voice of the white bourgeoisie coming through a black mannikin," another hears in the "libidinous blues" of Melanctha herself "the stirrings of white desire passed through a fictive veil of blackness" (Nielsen, 28). In any case, that William Carlos Williams wrote the line "Drum, drum, drum, drum, drum" in "Ol' Bunk's Band" (1948, II.149) and that Gregory Corso composed the line "BING BANG BONG BOOM bee bear baboon" in "Bomb" (1958; 179) proves that the Boomlay BOOM tradition of Lindsay, Sitwell, Eliot, and Stein ended not with a whimper but with a BOOM and a baboon.[26]

Attraction to a sang-froid shaped by the drumming chants, incomprehensible incantations, and ersatz murmurs of countless stage endmen and screen cannibals catapulted writers from Lindsay to Corso into displaying the centrality of modernist minstrelsy in the evolution of twentieth-century poetry, clarifying the uses served by a nonwhite, Africanlike presence in the white imagination. Their racial ventriloquism might be considered a type of body language, stream-of-consciousness, free association, automatic writing, hermetic definition, or any other number of outré linguistic formulations. For the white imagination, a resonant imagery of artistry resides in the black man Hart Crane imagined wandering "Between his tambourine, stuck on the wall, / And, in Africa, a carcass quick with flies" ("Black Tambourine," 1926). As if negotiating between the minstrel tradition of the tambourine and the fly-infested African carcass, as if seeking—in the words of Hart Crane—"to dye" words "with a peculiarity of meaning" (*Letters*, 77), the proponents of Dada broadcast the bankruptcy of European aesthetic traditions with "Negro poems" or *Negergedichte*: "TRABADYA LA MODJERE MAGAMORE MAGAGERE TRABADJA BONO" was recited in the Cabaret Voltaire to the poundings of a big bass drum and punctuated with what one critic calls the "bones-in-the-nose" of a periodic "umbah-umbah" (Marcus, *Lipstick Traces*, 19).

The Patrons' Dis and Dat

During the twenties and thirties, the pseudo-Africanism of the Boomlay BOOMers was most strikingly embodied on the person of Nancy Cunard, a poet turned editor whose money and influence helped white as well as black artists. In many of the celebrated pictures taken of her, Cunard—sporting her personal trademark of African bracelets—looks like she is about to embark on a trip to Lindsay's Congo, Sitwell's Gold Coast, or Eliot's cannibal isle for a photo op to illustrate Rosaldo's concept of imperialist nostalgia. And Cunard also employed black talk, although her use of it exemplifies the second type of linguistic experimentation generated in the twentieth century by racial ventriloquism, namely the exploitation not of African rhythms but of African-American slang by patrons and poets alike. In the same years that two white vaudevillians, Freeman Gosden and Charles Correll, produced *Amos 'n' Andy* on the radio (that is, from 1925 until 1932), writers like Cunard, Carl Van Vechten, and e. e. cummings eschewed the Boomlay BOOM for Dis and Dat, repudiating ersatz African rhythms so as to focus on equally factitious African-American idioms.

If attraction is filtered through revulsion against the African in Lindsay's, Sitwell's, and Eliot's racial ventriloquism, at first glance Cunard's passionate commitment to reversing the defamation of non-European cultures seems to transform her imitation of African ways into a sincere, unmitigated form of flattery. Indeed, Cunard's image is informed by the same dedication to civil rights that shaped her heated attacks against racial prejudice in her scathing broadside "Black Man and White Ladyship" (1931), a defense of her partnership with the black musician Henry Crowder, and in her monumental *Negro* anthology, a massive collection of anthropological, ethnographic, historical, critical, poetic, personal, and pictorial documents on the achievements of Africans, West Indians, South Americans, and African Americans composed by some 150 contributors, two-thirds of them black. Although critics of the publishing venture tended to use racechange to slander the anthologist—"Auntie Nancy's Cabin—Down Among the Black Gentlemen of Harlem" ran the headline of a particularly egregious article in the *Empire News* (Chisholm, 278–79)—Cunard had "lived to see black become less black and white turn less white through shame," or so her friend Solita Solano claimed (Solano, 77). Constantin Brancusi's portrait of Nancy Cunard (1925–27), reflecting his preoccupation with ovoid, abstract forms over and against personal features, alludes to her fascination with and commitment to African and African-American artistry by invoking his earlier sculpture, *The White Negress* (1923); as one critic explains, "something of Nancy's gaity is captured in the crowning whorl, which appears to represent a more vivacious version of the topknot in *The White Negress*" (G. Watkins, 169).

The racechanging possibilities apparent in both of Brancusi's works had always haunted Cunard's imagination. As the six-year-old child of a British shipping magnate, she once recalled, she had dreamed about "Africans dancing and drumming around me, and I one of them, though still white, knowing, mysteriously enough, how to dance in their own manner" (Cunard, *Grand Man*, 140). Barbara Ker-

Seymer's shot of the adult Cunard—linking the fur collar with the tiger-striped background and juxtaposing the black turban and its dark netting with the pale face—mixes primitive and modern, savage and civilized to present the exotically erotic Cunard as a wild and gamey hybrid (Fig. 4.2). As if participating in the higher vaudeville of "The Congo," "Gold Coast Customs," or *Sweeney Agonistes*, Cunard in a Cecil Beaton photograph sports a plumed headdress and, again photographed by Beaton, she is positioned before black and white polka dots, exhibiting bangled arms and a glossy skullcap (evoking the brilliantined hair of Josephine Baker), signs of the carnivalesque (Figs. 4.3 and 4.4), for here totemic items marked as Other flaunt the campy self-costuming at play. The outré bangles, wig, and feathers emphasize precisely the ontological fullness of being that Cunard attributed to black people:

> it is the zest that the Negroes put in, and the enjoyment they get out of, things that causes one more envy in the ofay. Notice how many of the whites are unreal in America; they are *dim*. But the Negro is very real; he is *there*. (*Negro*, 69)

Yet despite her admiration for the vitality of African Americans (typically engendered male in her mind), Cunard's envious self-fashioning hints at the same ambivalent dynamic at work in the poems of, say, Lindsay, Eliot, and Sitwell. The very model of the modern woman, Cunard (in Beaton's pictures especially) reeks of a sophistication and privilege based on displaying the highly commodified, commercialized merchandise of difference. In her bad-girl self-displays, she might be imagined as miming sexual slavery within the *tableaux vivant* of a classy brothel or, in more contemporary terms, modeling the goods on sale in a *Banana Republic* brochure or selling the perfume *Safari* in Bloomingdale's. Similarly, her use of black slang (ofay is pig latin for foe and a term for whites) bespeaks her appropriation of a culture very much not her own.

The phrase "*Fay, Ofay, Fagingy Fagade*: a white person" appears in the glossary entitled "Some Negro Slang" and attached to one of Cunard's contributions to her *Negro* anthology (75). So do several other terms that could have easily been used against her. Was she a "*Jig-chaser*: white person who runs after Negroes" (76)? A prototype of "*Miss Ann, Mr Eddie, Mr Charley*: wealthy social white people" (76)? Cunard's list of defined expressions calls attention to the white patron's schizophrenic self-loathing, her fascination with—but also hesitancy about—speaking the language of the Other. The word "*Boody*" Cunard glosses as a "lighthearted term for what Mommer does her loving with" (75). "Mommer" here resonates with the desire to represent black experience and the difficulty of doing so, as does the tonal glitch of the coy "*Tail, a piece of*: see *Boody*" (77). In addition, Cunard's earnest insistence that many Negroes in New York use "finger-language" (78) and speak "Sanguadny," a "distinct language" invented by them in the theatrical world and incomprehensible to "evil *ofays*"—including herself—testifies to the weird distortions bred by her fervid fantasies about black linguistic power.

Perhaps most notably in the poem "Equatorial Way," Cunard used black slang, in this case too (as so often evident in her work) associated with a male persona. The dedication for her edition of Henry Crowder's musical scores, *Henry Music* (1930), "Equatorial Way" displays her anxieties about such linguistic appropria-

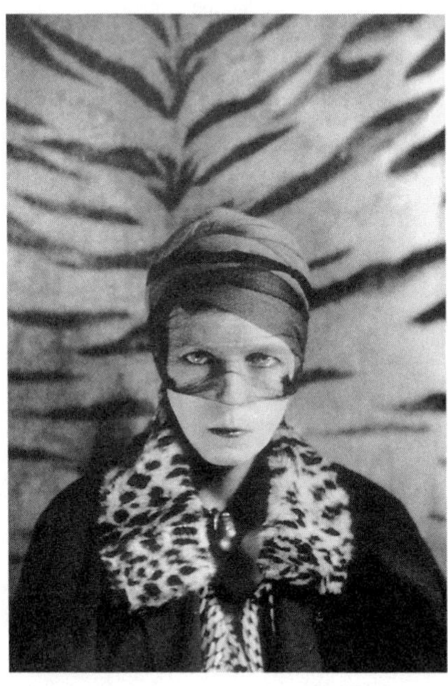

Figure 4.2 Barbara Ker-Seymer, Nancy Cunard with veil (1930). Photography Collection, Harry Ransom Humanities Research Center, The University of Texas at Austin; courtesy of Barbara A. Roett.

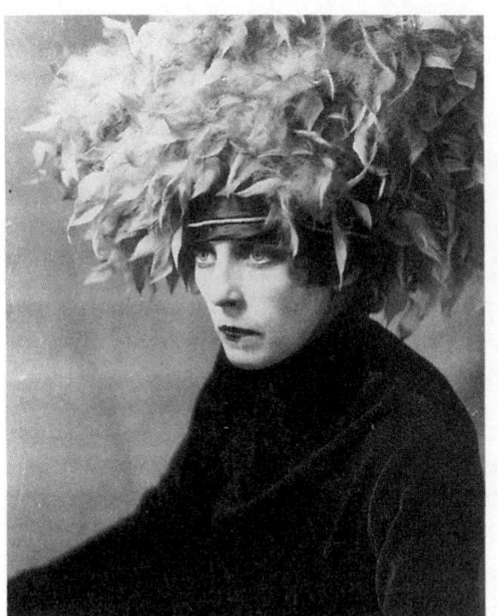

Figure 4.3 Cecil Beaton, Nancy Cunard in feathers. Kay Boyle Collection, Special Collections/Morris Library, Southern Illinois University at Carbondale.

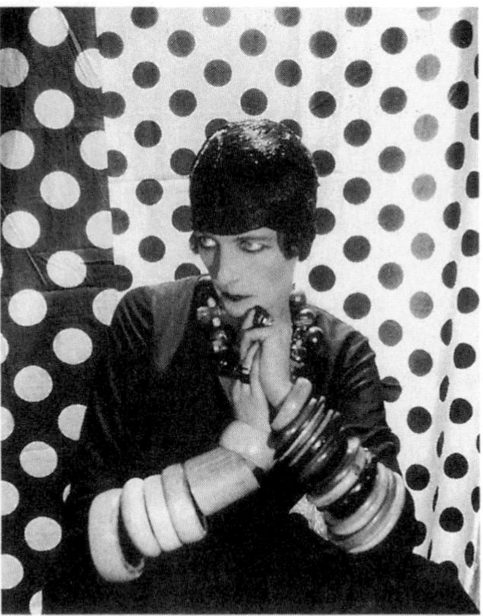

Figure 4.4 Cecil Beaton, Nancy Cunard with bangles. Courtesy of Sotheby's Belgravia.

tion, again through definitions (here provided in numbered footnotes set in parentheses and sprinkled throughout the poem). Cunard's speaker sets out to leave "cotton lands, / Ole-stuff coons in Dixie bands," as he travels "To where the Congo waters roll":

> This aint no (4) white man's nigger
> *Nor was*—but I've grown bigger
> The further away from you
> Further, longer away from you
> My (5) cracker moon.

The notes define "white man's nigger" as "A cringing or dispirited negro playing up to, i.e. bullied by whites" and "cracker" as "southerners with violent prejudice apt to explode."

The jacket of the volume in which this poem appears displays precisely the odd mixture of "love and theft" that Eric Lott sees at work in nineteenth-century minstrelsy and that reverberates through Cunard's black talk (Fig. 4.5). On the one hand, with a photomontage designed by Man Ray, Cunard produced a book honoring her lover's musical creativity that features a handsome portrait of the man himself. On the other, his shoulders seem oddly burdened by what look to be more of the African bracelets that are piled at the bottom of the picture. If these are the bangles on her own arms (if she is standing hidden behind him), they seem ominously to weigh him down like a kind of head- or neckbrace reminiscent of punitive devices in slavery. Has Henry Crowder been shackled by Nancy Cunard's patronage, turned into a "white [woman's] nigger"? Were the other black artists she supported so tethered? In ancient Rome, *Webster's New World Dictionary* explains, a patron was "a person who had freed his slave but still retained a certain paternal control over him."

Precisely this sort of tension makes even Cunard's most radical contributions to the Harlem Renaissance appear at times sinister. In her *Negro* anthology, for example, she included W.E.B. Du Bois's essay on "Black America" (explaining that "So-called black America is of every conceivable hue and shade, and white America is by no means 'lily-white'" (152)), but prefaced the contribution with a parochial attack on Du Bois's "Reactionary Negro Organization," in which she invoked the standards of the Communist Party to judge the NAACP and find its leader wanting. Although numerous satiric portraits of Cunard may have been in part motivated by racist and sexist resentment at her revolutionary values and lifestyle, what still emerges from them is a portrait of a vamp who used her social status, her money, and her promiscuity to work her willful ways.[27] Comparable ironies might speak, too, through Janet Flanner's recollection of seeing Henry Crowder's bruised face and being told what happened: "Just braceletwork, Miss Janet," Crowder was supposed to have said with the linguistic shuffle (feigned or not) of the paid escort into which he had declined. Or in Harold Acton's equally damning recollection that Cunard would instruct Crowder to "Be more *African*," only to receive the musician's plaintive reply, "But I *ain't* African. I'm *American*" (Chisholm, 186). As Ann Douglas astutely puts it, in Crowder's memoir, *As Won-*

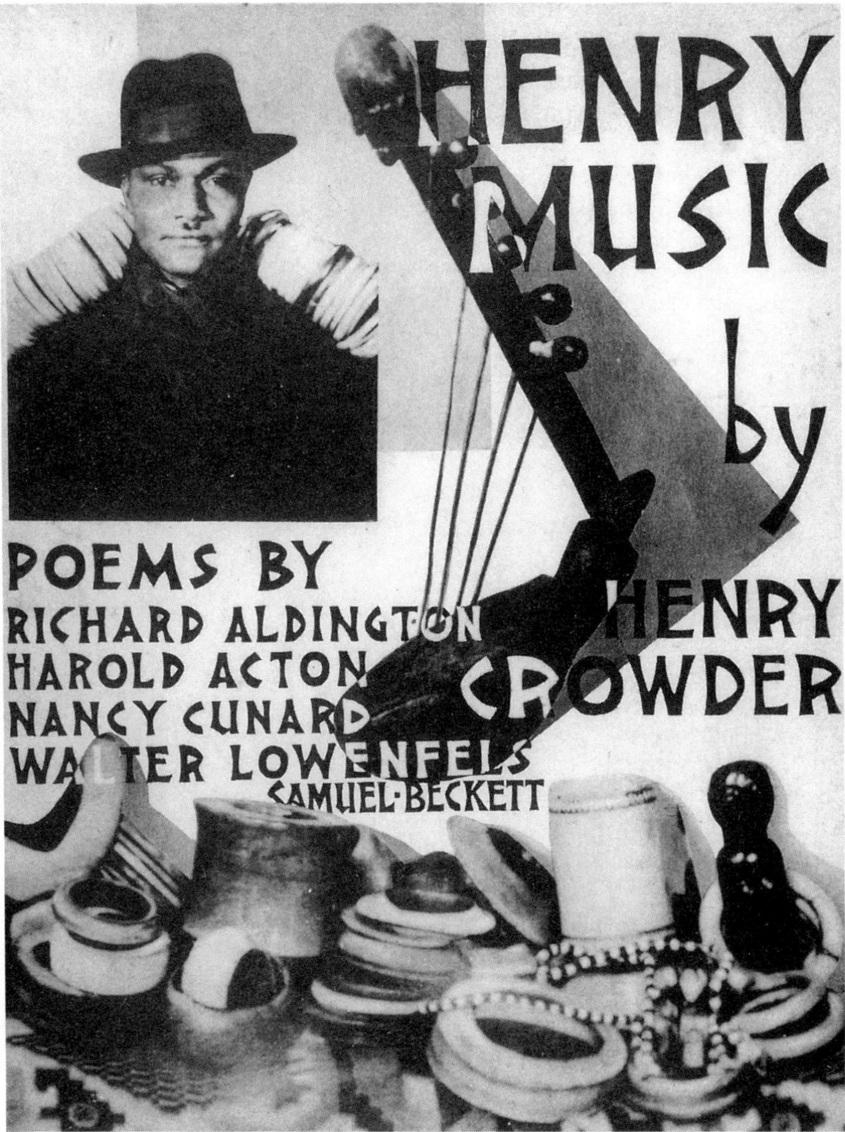

Figure 4.5 Cover designed by Man Ray of *Henry Music* (1930). Courtesy of Lilly Library, Indiana University.

derful as All That? (composed in 1935), "it is Nancy who plays the savage, Crowder the civilized role; she's the aggressor, he's the victim" (278).

Curiously, the other major patron of the Harlem Renaissance, Carl Van Vechten, also became notorious for a Dis and Dat ventriloquism that threatened to fetishize African-American difference. Although Cunard prided herself on a realism about race that she felt Van Vechten lacked, her attraction to "the zest" and "enjoyment" of being "very real" clearly propelled his "addiction" to African Americans (Kellner, *"Keep,"* 7).[28] Before and after the controversy set in motion by the publication of his portrait of Harlem, the bestselling novel *Nigger Heaven* (1926), Carl Van Vechten attained the same notorious identity in America that Cunard achieved in Europe, becoming a principal publicity icon of racechange during the Jazz Age (even as he publicized Harlem celebrities and visitors in his astonishingly numerous photographic portraits). A popular song of the time, "Go Harlem," advised listeners to "Go inspectin' like Van Vechten!" and he did attend Harlem's nightclubs, transvestite costume balls, and A'lelia Walker's 136th Street salon so frequently that (though he traveled by cab and at night) *Vanity Fair* claimed he was getting a heavy tan (Kellner, *Carl Van Vechten,* 198). Ignoring the fair complexion and blond hair of the Midwesterner, Miguel Covarrubias produced several caricatures which capture not so much Van Vechten in blackface as Van Vechten the African American.

Titled "A Prediction" (Fig. 4.6), one of Covarrubias's images prophesies that the color of the Harlemites with whom Van Vechten fraternized would somehow rub off on him. A different racechange narrative was told by Avery Hopwood, whose cautionary remarks to readers of *Nigger Heaven* sardonically hint that the

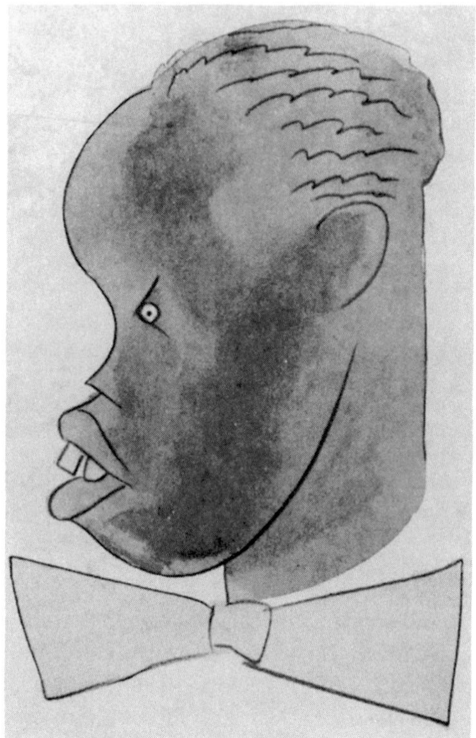

Figure 4.6 Miguel Covarrubias, *A Prediction.* Courtesy of Beinecke Library, Yale University.

whiteness of Van Vechten was a fiction: "I am explaining," Hopwood confided to Van Vechten, "that you really see little of Harlem, these days, but that you saw a great deal of it before you *passed.* They are all so surprised to hear about your Negro strain, but I tell them that your best friends *always knew*" (Kellner, *Carl Van Vechten,* 221). Similarly, in Rudolph Fisher's novel *The Walls of Jericho* (1928) a character patterned on Van Vechten declares, "'Downtown I'm only passing. These,' he waved grandiloquently [at blacks], 'are my people'" (117). Another cartoon by Covarrubias captures Van Vechten engaged in a strenuous version of the lindy hop, the black bottom, or the Charleston, again as a black man. Exactly this emphasis on Van Vechten's commonality with African Americans imbues Zora Neale Hurston's affectionate comment that "If Carl was a people instead of a person, I could then say, these are my people" (Kellner, *Carl Van Vechten,* 207).

The brouhaha over its title demonstrates, however, that the language of *Nigger Heaven* and in particular its white author's use of black vernacular shocked many readers. Van Vechten's father objected, as did W.E.B. Du Bois, to what the latter called "an astonishing and wearisome hodgepodge of laboriously stated facts, quotations and expressions" (Kellner, *Carl Van Vechten,* 209). Yet the novel influenced Claude McKay's landmark narrative, *Home to Harlem* (1928), regardless of his boast that "what I write is urged out of my blood. / There is no white man who could write my book" (*Selected Poems,* 50). And a number of powerful, independent black thinkers not only condoned but actually collaborated in Van Vechten's Dis and Dat. James Weldon Johnson, Walter White, and Rudolph Fisher read the galley proofs of *Nigger Heaven* for what they referred to as authenticity; Langston Hughes provided original lyrics to replace lines from the deleted song *Shake That Thing* (for which Van Vechten had forgotten to get copyright permission). Describing the process of revision before publication, Van Vechten's biographer calls "the working over of dialect . . . almost mathematical, as in the change from the conventional and inaccurate 'Dis am Nigger Heaven' to 'Dis heah is Nigger Heaven'" (220). Van Vechten, who used his connections in black cultural circles to engage in what Sollors calls "ethnic transvestism," produced a text that—like those purportedly real slave narratives authored by white abolitionists and unlike the more flagrantly ersatz productions of his contemporaries—raises crucial questions about who has what right to deploy racially inflected lexicons and experiences; however, even his collaborative work with African-American authorities displays subtle markings of its white author's unease at his linguistic appropriations.

"Ah calls et, specherly tonight, Ah calls et Nigger Heaven! I jes' nacherly think dis heah is Nigger Heaven" (15): A Lenox Avenue prostitute delivers this line early in the novel; yet—as if to underline the author's discomfort—a footnote later concedes that "While this informal epithet is freely used by Negroes among themselves, not only as a term of opprobrium, but also actually as a term of endearment, its employment by a white person is always fiercely resented" (26). Another sign of uneasiness may be the exploitation of what is called "eye dialect" in a contradictory manner: that is, "*Ah* calls et" but "*I* jes' nacherly think." A 1926 article in *The Crisis,* "The Negro in Art: How Shall He Be Portrayed?" by Van Vechten, further demonstrates his awareness of his precarious position as a linguistic trespasser whose borrowings might be viewed as poaching:

> Are Negro writers going to write about this exotic material while it is still fresh or will they continue to make a free gift of it to white authors who will exploit it until not a drop of vitality remains? (Kellner, "*Keep*," 65)

Clearly Van Vechten understood that his own aesthetic project would be judged a form of vampirism, draining the last drops of vitality out of fresh black material and eventually earning him the name "Von Vampton" in Ishmael Reed's satiric novel *Mumbo Jumbo* (1972).[29]

Whether or not their critics were justified in accusing them of vamping or vampirism, Cunard and Van Vechten combined outrage against racial injustice with a deep regard for African-American culture, a mixture of motives that distanced them from their (white) origins, providing them entrance into—but not citizenship in—another (black) country. Like Cunard, who denied personal accountability for a past injurious to black people while asking her white audience to shoulder such responsibility, Van Vechten used black talk to exhibit his commonality with the Other. Like Cunard's list, "Some Negro Slang," the vocabulary index at the end of *Nigger Heaven* signals identification (the white insider who understands the slang of blacks) and estrangement (the white newcomer or foreigner who admits his Ur-community of white readers will be mystified by such argot). In other words, the linguistic inventory as a genre registers the tension at work in twentieth-century racial ventriloquism. From *arnchy* (a person who puts on airs) and *August ham* (watermelon) to *struggle-buggy* (Ford) and *unsheik* (divorce), the slang of *Nigger Heaven* places on exhibit black linguistic strangeness, though Van Vechten's glossary flaunts more self-parodic playfulness than Cunard's, even sending the reader on a wild goose chase: "*boody*: see hootchie-pap" as well as "*hootchie-pap*: see boody" (285–86).

Taken together, Cunard and Van Vechten can stand for a generation of white artists crossing over into racially ghettoized material (often for libertarian as well as aesthetic reasons) and in the process deploying Dis and Dat: Waldo Frank in *Holiday* (1923), Eugene O'Neill in *All God's Chillun Got Wings* (1924), Sherwood Anderson in *Dark Laughter* (1925), DuBose Heyward in *Porgy* (1925), Marc Connelly in *The Green Pastures* (1930), and of course George Gershwin in *Porgy and Bess* (1935).[30] Notwithstanding their various levels of knowledge and sensitivity about black culture, all these white ventriloquists of dialect revert to the predicament of Cunard's line in "Equatorial Way": "This aint no white man's nigger." The very gestures they make toward ethnographic authenticity are set off by signs of their awareness that their counterfeits were plagiarized, sham, or simply simulated. With its grammatical and spelling mistakes—its double negatives, loss of final letters, appropriation of ghetto lingo, and give-and-take backchat—Cunard's Dis and Dat smacks of minstrelsy, as do any number of passages from *Nigger Heaven*.[31]

In the period when Freeman Gosden and Charles Correll made *Amos 'n' Andy* a smash hit with both white and black audiences, a number of white poets inadvertently displayed imperialist nostalgia and amnesia in their deployment of a racial ventriloquism that assumed with Cunard that whites are "unreal" or "*dim*" whereas blacks are "very real." Thus, William Carlos Williams's "Shoot It Jimmy!" (1923) sought to "Get the rhythm" of "Banjo jazz" (I.216). Wallace Stevens, who compared colonist to colonized in "Nudity at the Capital" and "Nudity in the Colonies" (1936), signed at least one personal letter with the name Sambo.[32] Two years after hearing Lindsay recite at the *Poetry* banquet, Carl Sandburg began a poem whose first lines are "I am the nigger. / Singer of songs . . . " ("Nigger," 23) and later he recorded the speech of a woman describing another "woman what / hustles / Never keeps nothin' / For all her hustlin'" ("Harrison Street Court," 64). Just as Amos 'n' Andy's "Recordin' to my figgers in de book" or "You gotta be repaired for that" perpetuated minstrel traditions, the Dis and Dat talk that surfaced in the work of white poets reveals (as strikingly as did the verse of Boomlay BOOM) minstrelsy's impact on modern literary diction. Possibly the most popular show ever broadcast on radio and still considered "the first great radio show," *Amos 'n' Andy*'s favorite sayings ("Ain't dat sumptin'" and "Holy mackerel") changed the nation's speech patterns, just as their malapropisms cracked up white as well as black audiences ("I denies the allegation," Kingfish pontificated to the judge, "and I resents the alligator").[33]

That a fine line divides comic hilarity from grotesque stereotyping becomes clear in the particularly gruesome evidence of minstrelsy's influence on e. e. cummings's surrealistic play *Him* (1927), specifically in the play-within-the-play composed by the blocked artist-hero (who is cummings's surrogate and named in the objective case, Him). One scene prefaces a black ensemble singing and dancing "Frankie and Johnie" with a dialogue between two "coalblack figures" engaged in the phatic patter of minstrelsy:

MALE(*Nervously*): Who you nigga?
FEMALE (*Looking up, answers lazily*): Ahs de ground.
MALE (*Apprehensively*): Who de ground?
FEMALE (*Proudly*): Ahs de ground.
MALE (*Fearfully*): Wot, you de ground?
FEMALE (*Insolently*): Yas ahs de ground, ahs de ripe rich deep sweet sleek an sleepy ground, de G-R-O-U-N-D GROUND. (49)

After a censor rises in the audience to stop their vulgarities, he is frightened out of the theater by Frankie showing him an amputated penis or, as this proleptic Lorena Bobbitt puts it, "The BEST PART OF THE MAN / WHO DONE ME WRONG" (56).[34]

Although the above dialogue matches the racist stereotypes produced by minstrelsy's ridicule of the grammatical mistakes, confused pomposities, and malapropisms of Tambo and Bones, the avowedly liberal cummings turned to the demotic energy he sought to tap in black talk as an antidote to the hypocrisy and sterility of standard English, for—like Cunard—cummings believed about blacks, "Theys sO alive," a conviction meant to boomerang against the ontological inferiority or dimness of whites (*Complete Poems*, 622). As with the Boomlay BOOM works, Dis and Dat slang illustrates the ways in which twentieth-century racial ventriloquism recycled nineteenth-century minstrel traditions by playing them out in the campy, nihilistic cadences of "the rattle of the bones, and chuckle spread from ear to ear." Like the practitioners of Boomlay BOOM, the twentieth-century speakers of Dis and Dat denied black people verbal intentionality or integrity and then paradoxically lauded that lacking as a kind of anarchic playfulness. Therefore, like the minstrels, modernist ventriloquists repeatedly returned to touchstone texts about race and in doing so re-inscribed the association of African Americans with pre-linguistic being. Just as the minstrels obsessively recycled *Uncle Tom's Cabin*, for example, e. e. cummings produced a ballet entitled *Tom* (1931) that amounts to modernist minstrelsy.[35]

Cummings's exuberant African-American characters in *Tom* continued to be mysteriously inclined to the atavistism so evident among the inhabitants of Lindsay's "Congo" and Sitwell's "Gold Coast," or, for that matter, Heyward's Catfish Row, whose jubulent Dis and Dat community remains as "Exotic as the Congo, and still able to abandon themselves utterly to the wild joy of fantastic play" (115). Yet in his later work, cummings seems to be striving for a more sensitive approach to racial ventriloquism, one that would take hold in the literature produced after the Second World War. Consider the jazzy rhythms of a poem cummings published in 1940, verse inflected by the enormous impact of black music embodied in

one slipslouch twi
tterstamp
coon wid a plon
kykerplung
guit
ar

The guitar player, a jazz man—who "sho am / wick / id"—stands for a wickedness associated with the powerful forces of the Freudian id, with inebriation and "joy (eye kinely thank yoo)" (*Complete Poems*, 519). Like so many practitioners of Boomlay BOOM as well as Dis and Dat, cummings falls under the influence of jazz, drugs, and urbanity and thereby follows the advice he proffered in another poem where he urges his readers to "touch the black skin / of an angel named imagination" (639). In their admittedly racist deployments of minstrelsy, the ventriloquists of modernism nevertheless touched their muse and found the source of their inspiration to be black.

Self-Derisive Black Talk

The effect of the blues and of jazz on white ventriloquists from the forties on can be demonstrated most effectively through the achievement of Milton "Mezz" Mezzrow, a musician whose 1946 autobiography dramatizes the evolving relationship between racial ventriloquism and racechange. At the end of his memoir *Really the Blues* (whose very title highlights the problem of authenticity), Mezzrow provided a glossary like those of Cunard and Van Vechten, defining his own name, "The

Mezz," as "*the best brand of marihuana; anything unusually good*" (376), a term immortalized in the song "If You're a Viper": "Dreamed about a reefer five foot long, / The mighty mezz but not too strong" (215). Mezzrow, whose book includes a fairly long account of various "Jive" sessions with a "translation" provided in an appendix (354–60), had been born Jewish in Chicago and called a "nigger-lover" in the South.[36] After a prison stint in 1918, he quickly came to believe about the other inmates that he "not only loved those colored boys, but I was one of them—I felt closer to them than I felt to the whites" so

> I was going to spend all my time from then on sticking close to Negroes. They were my kind of people. And I was going to learn their music and play it for the rest of my days. *I was going to be a musician, a Negro musician*, hipping the world about the blues the way only Negroes can. (18; emphasis mine)

And at the triumphant moment he enters the "serene exaltation" of playing "real authentic jazz" with his clarinet, he does become Jimmy Noone, Johnny Dodds, Sidney Bechet, Tubby Hall, Baby Dodds, Zutty Singleton, King Oliver, Tommy Ladnier, "and yes, Louis too, the one and only Pops, the greatest of them all" (322–23).

Yet in his capacity as an autobiographer Mezzrow himself admits the difficulty of his linguistic position: Street "lingo has to be *heard*, not seen"; even if written down, it "would sound like plain gibberish"; for "how can any outsider latch on to the real flavor of a secret code in which *tick twenty* means ten o'clock and *line forty* means the price is twenty dollars; friends are addressed as *gate* or *slot*, verbal shorthand for *gatemouth* and *slotmouth*, which are inner-circle racial jokes to begin with" (220)? A sea change occurs between the transcription of jive—

SECOND CAT: Never no crummy, chummy. I'm gonna lay a drape under the trey of knockers for Tenth Street and I'll be on the scene wearin' the green (216)

—and its translation:

SECOND CAT: I never lie, friend. I'm going to bring a suit to the pawnshop to raise ten dollars, and I'll show up with some money. (355)

Like his heightened awareness of the difficulties of shuttling between two languages, his sexual explicitness, his fascination with black music, and his absorption with drugs, Mezzrow's comprehension of the overwhelming racism of white society signals not a break so much as a shift in emphasis in the deployment of racial ventriloquism after the Second World War. Mezzrow, who was drawn to the "feeling of brotherhood" in Harlem, believed that "the oppression that rules" the lives of African Americans "has caused a kind of fraternity to spring up"; being black means being "at the bottom of the pile, with all the weight of white society crushing you" (228). William Carlos Williams, who in *Paterson* wryly explained that everything he had written was for "the birds / or Mezz Mezzrow" (221), was also drawn to racial ventriloquism as a means to establish a fraternity with an oppression that generated great music.[37]

After hearing Bunk Johnson's jazz band in 1945, Williams began work on "Boogie woogie writing" (84), a project related to his earlier view that African Americans were imbued with an authenticity bred of their existential nothingness; *In the American Grain* (1925) included, too, Williams's predictive declaration, "I wish I might write a book of [the black man's] improvisations in slang" (211) as well as his tribute to the African-American minstrel Bert Williams. Williams's attraction to black music and to the black Williams found an outlet in a collaborative work he set out to write in a jazzy, impromptu manner,[38] a novel entitled "Man Orchid" about a racechanging character who claims "I am black. Therefore I am white. Black, white. White black. Ampersand, quicksand: what's the difference?" (101). A study of the schizophrenia of American culture, the work suggests some sensitivity about racial identity, or so this meditation on its title indicates:

> Why the orchid?—to begin with. There's the old, tiresome and at bottom snobbish literary assumption that the Negro in America is an exotic bloom. Negro equals jungle. Despite the fact that he has been here longer than the second, third, even ninth generation Eurp [*sic*] European—Negro equals jungle. Then why doesn't the ofay bank president of German descent equal Black Forest? the Rutherford doctor of Welsh descent equal the cromlechs? or Welsh rarebit? (111)

Although many white writers of Williams's generation and of the next exploited black dialect after midcentury, they did so with an intensified apprehension about reductive stereotypes. As in the modernist period, during the second half of the twentieth century African rhythms and African-American vernacular assuage the burden of the past, denying accountability for guilt, but with more ideological footwork indicative of white sympathy for black oppression. "Look at me," postmodernist novelists and poets seem to say, "so deeply committed to alienation, so Other-identified as to be black." Curiously, though, their racial ventriloquism increasingly also exhibits an extraordinary self-consciousness about (their own collusion in) the racist roots of a discourse that maintains the subordination of people of color, a knowledge in part fashioned by the slang permeating the productions of the beat generation, whose artists made talking black/talking back *au courant* among dissidents. It was no accident that a so-called "holy barbarian" like Allen Ginsberg began his monumental beat poem *Howl* (1956) by describing his hysterical, naked, mad comrades "dragging themselves through the negro streets" or that he phrased his protest against "America" (1956) in terms of his identification with scapegoated African Americans: "America I am the Scottsboro boys" (l. 60).[39]

Yet the two mid-century writers who most brilliantly tackled the problematic ethics of racial ventriloquism—one in fiction, one in poetry—went far beyond the beats in the subtlety of their analyses. William Faulkner and John Berryman explore the comic demotic as a manifestation of the self-derision bred by white guilt about racial injustice. Ventriloquism's minstrel comedy becomes black humor in the works of both: Faulkner's tragic fiction satirizes humor at the expense of blacks as one more indication of a white stupidity and arrogance so profound as to call into question his own aesthetic project; Berryman's verse teeters always on the absurdly horrific, the grotesque, the painful exposure of the white speaker's linguistic bad faith. What fascinates both writers is their own entanglement in—attraction toward but also revulsion against—a racial ventriloquism they know to be damaging to African Americans and unscrupulous for Euro-Americans, though endlessly enticing. Both achieved the consummate feat of their artistry by representing their realization that their effort to find in an Africanist presence an escape from their own fake experiences would be a doomed undertaking.

The title story of Faulkner's *Go Down, Moses* (1940) shrewdly contrasts the languages of whites and blacks throughout, concentrating especially on the guilt-ridden, Harvard-educated lawyer Gavin Stevens's inability to comprehend the grief Mollie Worsham Beauchamp expresses over her dead grandson. Drawing upon the old spiritual that furnishes Faulkner's title, Mollie's incantatory lament with her brother—

> "Sold him in Egypt and now he dead."
> "Oh yes, Lord. Sold him in Egypt."
> "And now he dead."
> "Sold him to Pharaoh." (363)

—silences, flusters, and excludes the white lawyer, even as it expresses her understanding that this plea for a savior to "let my people go" comes too late for Butch, the lost grandchild, "now he dead." Baffled but sympathetic, Stevens sets out to enlist the charity of the white community to pay for Butch's funeral.

Beginning with an image of a black man incarcerated after killing a Chicago policeman and eventually executed, Faulkner's story ends with a telling moment that diagnoses racial ventriloquism as a reflex of white shame over the lasting, debilitating inheritance of slavery. That legacy means both the hardened grandson and the mourning grandmother are in danger of losing their voices. The brief sketch of Butch's few moments before execution portrays a fated gangster or gambler, complete with lacquered hair, fawn-colored flannel suit, and "a voice which was anything under the sun but a southern voice or even a negro voice" (351).[40] But the powerful "negro voice" of his grandmother is also threatened by the end of the narrative when the editor of the town newspaper explains to Stevens how Mollie had requested him to print the story of her grandson's death and funeral:

> "She said, 'Is you gonter put hit in de paper?"
> "What?"
> "That's what I said," the editor said. "And she said it again: 'Is you gonter put hit in de paper? I wants hit all in de paper. All of hit.'" (364–65)

Three aspects of this request strike the editor as ludicrous: that Mollie does not understand the details of her grandson's shameful end, that she cannot read, and that she speaks differently from him. By depicting a white man parodying the speech of a black woman—not in her own diction (as represented in the story) but in conventional black dialect—Faulkner examines racial impersonation as an act of violence comparable to that at work in the dynamics of blackface. "'Is you gonter put hit in de paper?'" becomes a kind of death sentence or spirit-murder. For the newspaper editor distances himself from the Other (she is so different from me) through incorporation (I can be her) that effectively destroys (she need not exist). If Mollie has been erased by the editor's impersonation of her, does she serve as an index of Faulkner's authorial arrogance as well? Are the African-American characters Faulkner created a reflex of his guilty awareness that he is not the Other and, indeed, that his linguistic transgressions have helped to Other black people?

Like the writing of the obituary which Mollie would not be able to read, the recording of the editor's mimicry of Mollie's speech effectually marks Faulkner's recognition of the iniquity of his own ventriloquism—because, of course, Mollie's speeches in the narrative (as "directly" presented earlier) have also been constructed by a white man, namely, Faulkner himself. As if producing evidence of his own continued entanglement in debilitating racial lies, Faulkner's tale sentimentalizes the charity of whites—the townspeople generously respect and fund Mollie's wish for a funeral in spite of their condescending incomprehension—and thereby deflects the reader's attention away from Mollie's tragedy. The reader ends up weeping over the pathos of the town's efforts at restitution rather than the black community's losses. In "Go Down, Moses," the author of numerous African-American characters presents the ethical complications behind minstrelsy's ongoing influence, casting suspicion on the art of racial ventriloquism that served as the basis of his own artistry and that soon brought so much flack to William Styron for *The Confessions of Nat Turner* (1967).

It seems paradoxical that the contributors to *William Styron's Nat Turner: Ten Black Writers Respond* (1968) agreed with Styron's own statement that "most Southern white people *cannot* know or touch black people," that the contemporary African American "may feel that it is too late to be known, and that the desire to know him reeks of outrageous condescension" (Styron, 135). Of course, the brouhaha at the publication of Styron's fictionalized account of a slave insurrectionist proved that the civil rights movement had intervened to usher in a period inhospitable to whites' use of black talk: During the early fifties, the NAACP managed to force CBS to suspend production of the hugely successful TV adaptation of *Amos 'n' Andy*.[41] Seeking to cancel both the TV and radio versions, NAACP critics believed the "show tends to strengthen the conclusion among uninformed and prejudiced people that Negroes are inferior, lazy, dumb, and dishonest" (M. Watkins, 521).

So we must understand the Tambo and Bones routines interspersed throughout the poems of Berryman's *The Dream Songs* (1964, 1968) as part of the stubborn depravity of its main character, Henry, and not just a manifestation of the liberal sympathy his author claimed when he described his identification with Jews and blacks who suffer the stigma of difference: "I feel extremely lucky to be white" (Linebarger, 85), Berryman explained, demonstrating his understanding of what today is called white privilege. A devotee of Bessie Smith, Victoria Spivey, and Teddy Grace, Berryman resembled cummings and Williams in his effort to utilize jazz and blues rhythms. Given his sensitivity to racism and his appreciation of black culture, Berryman surely understood the points Patricia J. Williams has recently made about "black speech" which is invariably marked "as low-status" when used by whites: that it is "very annoying to us black people," that it "makes most of you white people sound ridiculous," and that any attempt to "'sound like' should probably be avoided" (*Rooster's Egg*, 199–200).

Yet Berryman persisted in what he knew to be an especially degrading form of racial ventriloquism, a fact made evident by the major impact on him of Carl Wittke's book on minstrelsy, *Tambo and Bones*: "'GO IN, BRACK MAN, DE DAY'S YO' OWN,'" taken from *Tambo and Bones*, stands as the first epigraph of *77 Dream Songs*. The sentiment voiced here and throughout Berryman's *Dream Songs* often sounds liberal or even radical; however, the language adopted is that of a highly contaminated Dis and Dat.[42] Indeed, so adulterated is Berryman's black talk that it calls attention to the act of ventriloquism, foregrounding its status as a debased imitation and thereby its tendency to veer into a performance something like a drag show. Take, for example, the opening of this poem about the failure of integration after the historic 1954 Supreme Court decision:

> Afters eight years, be less dan eight percent,
> distinguish' friend, of coloured wif de whites
> in de School, in de Souf.
> —Is coloured gobs, is coloured officers,
> Mr Bones. Dat's nuffin? —Uncle Tom,
> sweep shut yo mouf,
>
> is million flocking from de proper job,
> de fairest houses & de churches eben.
> —You may be right, Friend Bones.
> Indeed you is. Dey flyin ober de world,
> de pilots, ober ofays. (60)

The first speaker, Henry, rarely talks in black talk, but here he uses it to protest against segregation in Southern schools. After being questioned by the second speaker about advances in the military, Henry calls his interlocutor an Uncle Tom and earns his agreement that job, housing, and even religious discrimination will result in some kind of race warfare. The poem ends with the two men sadly concurring, "mos peoples gonna *lose*."

Who are these two amicable antagonists doing this linguistic drag? In an introductory note Berryman describes Henry as "a white American in early middle age sometimes in blackface, who has suffered an irreversible loss and talks about himself sometimes in the first person, sometimes in the third, sometimes even in the second; he has a friend, never named, who addresses him as Mr Bones and variants thereof." Not to be confused with the poet, Henry House or Henry Cat or Huffy Henry finds a critic, a comforter, a companion in his counterpart, who frequently employs black talk, playing Tambo to Henry's Bones. Like earlier practitioners of Boomlay BOOM and Dis and Dat, Berryman remains fascinated by the ways in which racial ventriloquism unmakes meaning. The second poem, dedicated to Daddy Rice, who jumped Jim Crow in 1828, remains incomprehensible mumbo jumbo in its use of slang ("The jane is zoned!"), its opting for sound over sense ("Have ev'ybody head for Maine, / utility-man take a train?"), its ungrammatical syntax and nonreferential pronouns ("Arrive a time when all coons lose dere grip, / but is he come?"), and its puns ("Poll-cats" for people who vote or collectors of poll-tax or the cutters of poles/trees).[43] Toward the end of *The Dream Songs*, the poet admits, "These Songs are not meant to be understood, you understand. / They are only meant to terrify & comfort" (366).

Why would Berryman focus his verse on injustice—social, political, racial—in a language so polluted with the guilt of past oppressions? Or, as Aldon Lynn Nielsen phrases this question, "How seriously can readers take an argument for the recognition of the rights of Afro-Americans when that argument is couched in derisive terms and made in the course of an oneiric 'coon show'?" (143). But perhaps readers are meant to take seriously not simply the civil rights contentions but their incongruent relation to the contemptuous framework in which they appear, a framework that mordantly measures the failure of even the most sympathetic Euro-Americans. At least in part, the self-consciously white Berryman represents his predominantly white audience's stereotypical image of blacks so to examine one of his major obsessions and the one upon which his greatness as a confessional poet rests, namely, the difficulty of altering what is known to be destructive, the compulsive nature of evil, the recalcitrance of subjectivity despite the enlightenment furnished by reason, the inflexibility of habits known to be deleterious. Dis and Dat's retrograde pleasures give Berryman a chance to display his addiction to a host of damaging activities he knows to be harmful not only to himself (drinking, whoring around, smoking, suicidal abjection) but also to the culture at large (consumerism, militarism, racism).

To begin with, though, *The Dream Songs* presents the relationship of Tambo and Bones as a consolation, for Tambo provides solace, ballast, companionship, and a sense of perspective for the usually anguished Henry. Whenever Henry gets overly melodramatic, morbid, or maudlin, Tambo grounds him in the easy intimacy of the practical and everyday. In some poems, then, Tambo plays shrink or father confessor to Mr. Bones as patient or sinner, though neither exhibits much hope for a cure:

> The glories of the world struck me, made me aria, once.
> —What happen then, Mr. Bones?
> if be you cares to say. (26)

Later in the sequence when Henry, going out the door with his "cigs," his "flaskie," and his "crystal cock," asks a blessing, Tambo's realism brings him down to earth:

> —Mr. Bones,
> you makes too much
> démand. I might be 'fording you a hat:
> it gonna rain. (64)

Lusty Henry—as in "Love her he doesn't but the thought he puts / into that young woman / would launch a national product"—encounters Tambo's exasperated, avuncular deterrents: "—Mr. Bones, *please*" (69).[44] Vaudevillean give-and-take recaptures an easy, playful bonding between men, adding credence to Leslie

Fiedler's insight about Americans that they are "Born theoretically white," but "are permitted to pass . . . [their] adolescence as imaginary Negroes" (134). Its inane energies also serve as a kind of antidote to depressing seriousness as well as a reminder that the world is a stage and the show must go on. In the midst of what Henry calls the "lonely whines" he whips out in times of "fleeing double"—that is, seeing double and fleeing trouble and being so muddled as not to be able to say which—Tambo calls for a song and dance (114). At Henry's grief over a childhood loss, Tambo offers a handkerchief and advice: "now set / your left foot by my shoulder, all that jazz, / . . . hum a little, Mr. Bones" (76).

One of the rare poems in which Tambo predominates focuses on the central tragedy of Berryman's life, the suicide of his father during his youth, but does so by framing the memory with vaudevillean trappings that counteract bathos:

> —That's enough of that, Mr. Bones. *Some* lady you make.
> Honour the burnt cork, be a vaudeville man,
> I'll sing you now a song
> the like of which may bring your heart to break:
> he's gone! and we don't know where. (143)

The poem focuses on the child's sense of abandonment and guilt by shifting between Tambo's "you was just a little" and Henry's plaintive "He was going to swim out, with me forevers." Only through the distance created by this dual fictionalization of himself, only through the banter of these two blackfaced endmen going through the paces of their numbers, is the pain of recollection bearable for the poet. A corrective to melancholia, Tambo stands for endurance and survival not by ignoring pain or injustice but by joking about it. He is a self-defined "pro-man," strutting "out from the wings" even and especially when "it's curtain-call" time (220).

"Harms and the child I sing": Berryman's neologisms in what he calls his "minstrelsy" (231) allow him to bumble into insights, here the conflation between arms and harm, man and child (149). Similarly, Tambo's garbled, punning supposition that Henry's "got a lessen up your slave" (84) rings true for Berryman, too: minstrelsy's enslaved characters furnish him with lessons from a Blakean Bible of Hell to teach in a fallen language that lessens the humanity of blacks and whites alike. Throughout *The Dream Songs*, racial impersonation flaunts itself as an ersatz, campy form of drag. Though Tambo parenthetically remarks about their routines "Some time we'll do it again, / in whiteface" (220), blackface emphasizes the vulgarity, the speciousness, the pointlessness of Berryman's surrealistic actors and their routines. Mr. Bones is Berryman's fanciful penis, his prancing skeleton, engaged in an endlessly entertaining dance of love and death, providing cheap thrills not only for those readers Sylvia Plath called "the peanut-crunching crowd" but also to divert his own attention away from the end he always craved ("Lady Lazarus," 26).

"Negroes, ignite! you have nothing to use but your brains" (232). Each parodic substitution in this line echoes with the original to elaborate upon Berryman's comment on the legacy of racial ventriloquism he had inherited. Negroes, the workers of the white imagination, should give up on the Marxist hope of uniting and ignite instead, in fighting or rioting, in rage or in creative energy, or so Henry proclaims in a poem about his struggle to stay off the sauce, to wait upon the Lord, to free his life by controlling his fate. With nothing to lose and everything to gain, blacks should use what they have, for only their brains or what Blake called "mental strife" can break down the chains that bind them. Or perhaps blacks should lose their brains because their minds retard the liberating act of igniting. But of course such prosey translations fall into precisely the platitudes and pieties Berryman abhorred as a vacuous mode of liberal self-certification; "When the mind dies," he admonished sardonically, "it exudes rich critical prose" (170). And, in fact, Berryman remained unconvinced that brains (black or white) could break the chains of societal habits or personal additions.

Tambo's response to Henry's painful efforts to remain sober and receive religious certitude allows Berryman to racialize his thoughts about physical failing, spiritual falling. Calling for a drink—"one-two, the old thrones / topple, dead sober. The decanter, pal! / Pascal, we free & loose"—Henry haplessly fails, falling back into his old ways, reaching for a drink but also refusing Pascal's reasoning about the existence of God. Pascal probably drops into this poem about the dark night of the soul, placing "cagey bets" with the poet, because his belief in God was based on his view that there was nothing to lose and everything to gain from such a wager. Just as the poet stubbornly and irrationally refuses such a consolation of philosophy, "Negroes" (also with nothing to lose, everything to gain) will be no more successful in their quest for social freedom than he in his quest for the rectitude of sobriety and faith. Though the garbled language of Dis and Dat made it inevitable that Berryman would be misconstrued, his levity signifies his helpless acquiescence in a sordid discourse, a corrupt social order.

Embedding himself in a debased linguistic past so as to dramatize the hopelessness of the libertarian causes he championed, Berryman analyzed the self-derisive fatalism he felt about himself as a promoter of a grievous past. Tambo's retort to Mr. Bones—"you too advancer with your song, / muching of which are wrong" (99)—stands as a final epigraph for a self-reflexive tradition of racial ventriloquism that testifies to the acknowledged inability of white artists to represent the black Other and, by extension, the white self that longs to escape solipsism by knowing (or owning its own) Otherness. For Berryman, the failure to find a language to break out of his own and civilization's doomed patterns returns him repeatedly to the inauthenticity of whites talking black. What the modernists viewed as a dialect of energy and liberation had become a dead-end, a self-conscious register of corruption for the post-modernist. Berryman's achievement consists in laying bare the drollery and despair that infiltrate racial parodies in the lives of Euro-Americans who feel driven to speak what they suspect they cannot feel: the tantalizing interiority of the Other.

In contemporary times, admissions of white guilt about linguistic racechange often present white black talk either as an indefensible but enthralling trope of condescension or of exploitation. John Barth's *The Floating Opera* (1956, 1967) offers a good example of the former analysis in its conclusion which features the

"Ethiopian Tidewater Minstrels" show. Barth's suicide-obsessed hero, the aptly named Todd (*tod* is German for death), immediately understands the pathetic attraction of the "knights of the burnt cork" (238):

> Tambo and Bones vindicated our ordinariness; made us secure in the face of mere book learning; their every triumph over Mr. Interlocutor was a pat on our backs. Indeed, a double pat: for were not Tambo and Bones but irresponsible Negroes? (239)

Curiously, however, the climactic performance of *Adam's Original & Unparalleled Floating Opera* convinces the melancholy Todd not to commit suicide and does so in part by persuading him of the senselessness not only of living but of dying. Precisely the nihilistic hilarity, the threadbare facticity and absurdity of the actors' impersonations on the showboat provide an ironic but sustaining image of the games people play not only in art but in life.

Far more disturbing in its analysis of black talk as a sexual exploitation and perversion of whites is Bernard Malamud's *The Tenants* (1971), a meta-critical novel about two novelists, the Jewish one named Lesser but usually called "the writer," and the African American named sometimes Bill Spearmint, sometimes Willie Shakespear, but usually called "the black." The work of fiction Bill begins composing includes a chapter about his drunken mother and

> an ofay who liked to pretend to talk nigger talk. It made him feel good to do it though it was fake black talk. He did not come from the South, he came from Scranton, Pa. He came to my mama because she charged one dollar and it wasn't before long that he used to get it for free. (94–95)

As the narrative slips from third to first person and we enter Bill's autobiographical account of the humiliations of his mother and of himself as a child witness, the horror of the ofay's "nigger talk" feels like a kind of rape.

In Bill's text, the white man (known as Rubber Dick because of his "big prick") returns one night when the mother is gone. Offering money to the nine-year-old black boy—"Heah's a quotah mo. Now unzip mah pants and the money is yo's. Bof the dime and the quotah"—Rubber Dick makes a proposition terrifying to Willie, but somehow less horrifying than his fake black talk:

> "Don't take it out, please," I asked him.
>
> "Not till you show me kin you open yo mouf wide an covah yo teef wif yo lips like this."
>
> He showed me how to cover my teeth.
>
> "I will do it if you stop talking nigger talk to me."
>
> He said honey he would, and also I was a smart boy and he loved me very much.
>
> He was talking like a whitey again. (96)

For the black author of the scene, mourning the childhood degradations he had suffered, the bought boy manages to obtain—with his mouth made into a receptacle for the white man—some control over the white man's speech. A gruesome deal is struck; ersatz black talk relinquished, white semen accepted. But the white creator of the black writer of the scene stands accused by it of verbal propositions condemning blacks to an enforced prostitution comparable to the sexual abuse of children, for Malamud knows himself to be Lesser, realizes that in writing about Bill he is writing about the sort of man who "do not wish his words to be in your book" (195), and understands too that minstrel nightmares—"What he done did see, / He gnawin this white bone, / What that you eatin, Mr. Bones?" (133)—continue to haunt not only his characters' imagination but also his own. As the plot of *The Tenants* progresses and the black and white central characters trade places in an antagonistic *folie à deux* that can lead only to their common annihilation, each "feels"—but cannot speak—"the anguish of the other" (211).

5

PSYCHOPATHOLOGIES OF BLACK ENVY

Queer Colors

> That the PENIS of an African is larger than that of an European has, I believe, been shewn in every anatomical school in London. Preparations of them are preserved in most anatomical museums; and I have one in mine.
>
> —Dr. Charles White

> [T]he Negro is fixated at the genital; or at any rate he has been fixated there. Two realms: the intellectual and the sexual. An erection on Rodin's *Thinker* is a shocking thought. One cannot decently "have a hard on" everywhere. The Negro symbolizes the biological danger; the Jew, the intellectual danger.
>
> —Frantz Fanon

> "You know how I'd like to fuck her now? I just realized—if I could get into a *spade bag* . . . like if I could pretend to be a spade . . . yeah, that's it, *spade-rape bag*. You think she'd lie still for some *burnt cork*, B.?"
>
> —Terry Southern

On its July 27, 1994, cover, a notorious issue of *Time* magazine—featuring a "photo-illustration" of O. J. Simpson's mug shot that darkened his skin, blurred his features, and thickened the stubble on his chin—transformed one of America's most beloved athletes into the country's most familiar bogeyman. Its designer, Matt Mahurin, used a computer to produce the illustration because he wanted "a more somber photo, for a compelling story—an American tragedy" (*Herald-Times*, June 22, 1994, p. A3). Like Dreiser's novel of that name, the American tragedy to which the cover legend referred is domestic violence, in the Simpson case the wife-battering that allegedly ended in the death of Nicole Brown Simpson. But perhaps another tragedy, one of racial violence against men, is enacted by the reproduction itself, specifically through its use of blackface to execute a character assassination. Blacken the man, *Time* magazine implies, and you simultaneously drain him of moral discernment while accentuating his physicality, thus intensifying his brawn even as you criminalize it.

Unlike the colonized subject analyzed in Fanon's psychological study of racism, a black man who adopts the culture of the civilizing nation and thus "becomes whiter as he renounces his blackness, his jungle" (18), O. J. Simpson seemed "to many whites" like "a fellow white man [who] grew darker as the proceedings went on" (*Time*, Oct. 16, 1995, p. 43). Mahurin's illustration, then, functioned something like the portrait of Dorian Gray, predicting the hero's fall from grace. As hypermasculinized as the blackface rapists Gus and Lynch in *The Birth of a Nation*, Simpson is nevertheless arrested like the ineffective, boyish Jolson in *The Jazz Singer*, for the mug shot frames the man, transforming him into a mugger whose macho days are numbered. As Fanon slyly hints in one of my epigraphs, the biological danger posed by the black man's "hard on" paradoxically exempts him from modeling the perfection epitomized by Rodin's *Thinker*. As the passage of dialogue from Terry Southern's novel *Blue Movie* (1970) intimates, then, white people could project masculinist proclivities and misogynist antipathies onto personified "*spade-rape bag[s]*."[1]

That the stereotype of the black rapist coexists with the equally resilient image of the black eunuch; that behind the "buck" of, for example, *The Birth of a Nation* lurks the "boy" of, for instance, *The Jazz Singer* means the image of the black man has displayed both an intensification and a diminishment of masculinity. Two powerfully disturbing portraits of black men created by white artists—one fictional, one photographic—furnish primal scenes of instruction in which the displaying of male genitalia reveals the anxieties that shape contradictory constructions of black masculinity and that explain the nature of explicitly sexual fantasies of racechange during the second half of the twentieth century. In particular, Saul Bellow's novel *Mr. Sammler's Planet* (1970) and Robert Mapplethorpe's photograph "Man in Polyester Suit" (1980) deploy shockingly explicit images that, on the one hand, correlate black male subjectivity with the body and specifically with the penis, an association that has obviously contributed to the idea of the hypermasculinized black stud; on the other hand, by virtue of exposing the black penis for/to the white gaze, both artists deflate it, thereby self-consciously participating in the manifold ways in which a racist culture wrests authority and symbolic power from African Americans.

Bellow and Mapplethorpe muster the gruesome logic that stimulates eroticized fantasies of racechange in the post-World War II period. Put in Lacanian terms, this reasoning supposes that the black man who *is* his penis neither has nor ever will have the phallus.[2] To be sure, as any orthodox Lacanian would immediately interject, all men have penises, but none possesses the phallus. Not a real organ but instead an attribute of power or meaning, the phallus remains a signifier beyond the reach of all human beings. Yet, as Jane Gallop has pointed out in her cleverly entitled "Phallus/Penis: Same Difference," ever since Freud termed the woman's version of the castration complex "penis envy," the phallus belonging to the ideal other has been confused with the penis of an embodied male subject (124).[3] That male subject whose penis often seemed to embody the phallus was of course implicitly white. What Bellow and Mapplethorpe lay bare in their quite different ways is how the black man provides what—taking a clue from Edward Carpenter—we might call an Intermediate Type, a fantastic image of a nonphallic penis or an anti-establishment masculinism, one that repels the novelist but attracts the photographer.[4]

Mr. Sammler's Planet, Bellow's study of an Eastern European Holocaust survivor in New York City, dramatizes its central character's alienation as he attempts to inhabit a world he can only partially affirm after having been literally buried alive by the Nazis during the Second World War. Early in the novel, Sammler intently observes a black pickpocket who eventually sees the aging immigrant watching him. Acknowledging his fascination in the crime but fleeing the scene, Sammler finds himself confronted by the criminal in the lobby of his apartment building. Although the African American "no more spoke than a puma would," he delivers a silent message or warning:

> The black man had opened his fly and taken out his penis. It was displayed to Sammler with great oval testicles, a large tan-and-purple uncircumcised thing—a tube, a snake; metallic hairs bristled at the thick base and the tip curled beyond the supporting, demonstrating hand, suggesting the fleshly mobility of an elephant's trunk, though the skin was somewhat iridescent rather than thick or rough. (49)

"It was displayed": The passive voice here hints that the black man himself does not or cannot control his bestial penis. Because "The thing was shown with mystifying certitude," even "lordliness," Sammler responds to the "shock" of this experience by wondering "what was the object of displaying the genitalia?" and by recalling a scene of phallic exhibitionism attributed to a President of the United States who demanded to know from representatives of the press "whether a man so well hung could not be trusted to lead his country" (66). What power of intimidation and violence links the black pickpocket and the white Commander-in-Chief, mesmerizing Sammler?

To some extent, Sammler's voyeurism accords romance to the "princeliness" of the black con man ostensibly motivated by "an idea of *noblesse*" (294), one indication that the survivor prefers the somewhat iridescent genitals of the pickpocket to the messiness of female sexuality: "Females were naturally more prone to grossness, had more smells, needed more washing, clipping, binding, pruning, grooming, perfuming, and training" (36). Still, metallic and tubelike, the uncircumcized black penis in its rank physicality faintly repels the fastidious immigrant so understandably terrified of weaponry but also of nature, of the earthly tomb into which the Nazis had once long ago thrown him as if dead. Given "the sex ideology" of the day, the black man's "huge piece of sex flesh, half-tumescent in its pride," may symbolize "superlegitimacy or sovereignty" to the bankrupt society at large. But to sardonic Sammler, who has mastered the lessons of the body in pain, it quickly descends to the level of ridiculous physical protuberances: snakes, elephants' trunks, and anteaters' snouts (55).

The scene of exposure in *Mr. Sammler's Planet* is not unrelated to an infamously sardonic query put by Bellow that implicitly sets the terms civilization and Africa in opposition: "Who is the Tolstoi of the Zulus?"[5] According to squeamish Sammler, "the sexual ways of the seraglio and of the Congo bush" would contaminate

Enlightenment ideals (of "Liberty, Fraternity, Equality"), substituting in their stead such presumably immoral, inane principles as "Adultery," "the rights of women," "the unity of the different races affirmed," and "the right to be uninhibited, spontaneous, urinating, defecating, belching, coupling in all positions . . . " (32–33). For the displaced European, as for his creator, "the peculiar aim of sexual niggerhood for everyone" (162) must be defeated because the "superlegitimacy" of the black man's organ merely reflects corrupt social values—the lying, cheating, bullying criminality that saturates American culture from the bottom to the top, from the petty thief on the street to the President in the White House. Yet the fact that the pickpocket is last seen in Bellow's book struggling for possession of a camera (which contains shots of his pickpocketing activity) and bloodied from a beating inflicted at Sammler's instigation hints at the black prince's vulnerability. He has to be rescued eventually by the conscience-stricken philosopher king, Sammler, or he would be pummeled to death.[6] Despite the "intense animal pressing-power, the terrific swelling of the neck and the tightness of the buttocks" of this walking muscular member of society, he is last seen prostrate on the pavement, his face crushed, his skin gashed, his cheeks bloodied, fully liable to painful intimations of his own mortality.

With its focus on a bared black penis jutting out of the trunk of an otherwise fully clothed man, Robert Mapplethorpe's "Man in Polyester Suit" (Fig. 5.1) almost seems to place the viewer in the position of Sammler surprised in his lobby even as it meditates on Bellow's concluding vision of the black man vanquished by his inability to wrest control over the shots a camera has taken of his crimes. For Mapplethorpe draws attention to the ways in which African-American men have been refused jurisdiction over the representation of their own sexuality. Decapitated, the model of Mapplethorpe's audacious photograph stands disclosed, though fully clothed, symbolized by his sex. Indeed, the shocking contrast between the costume of culture (at least mythologically created to cover the sexual parts) and the exhibited sexual organ highlights the exposed flesh. The thrill of an erotic photo of an exposed man posing for the male photographer in part derives from the camera's height and angle, which brings the Sammler-like voyeur to his knees, situating him quite definitively and respectfully at eye level with what's central here, the sex that is the point of the picture, the male/male desire that connects Mapplethorpe and his subject.

Yet, as if he were a suspect or a specimen, the model's face must be hidden from view. As in cartoons of dressed-up animals, moreover, his relaxed penis emerges out of the suit like the tail of a puma or the trunk of an elephant or the snout of an anteater, biological nature putting the lie to the costume of culture. And the title emphasizes the generic disposition of this "Man" not in *a* specific outfit but instead "in Polyester Suit," wording that puts on display an ethnographic oddity (like "Animal in Human Clothing"). The sex at the center of the picture simply is the man who merely wears the polyester suit. Paradoxically, the visual evidence of masculinity here—because it exists for the viewer's inspection—emasculates the passive object of the photographer's gaze. A portrait of the signified, not the signifier, a picture of a visible and physical object rather than a veiled symbol of law

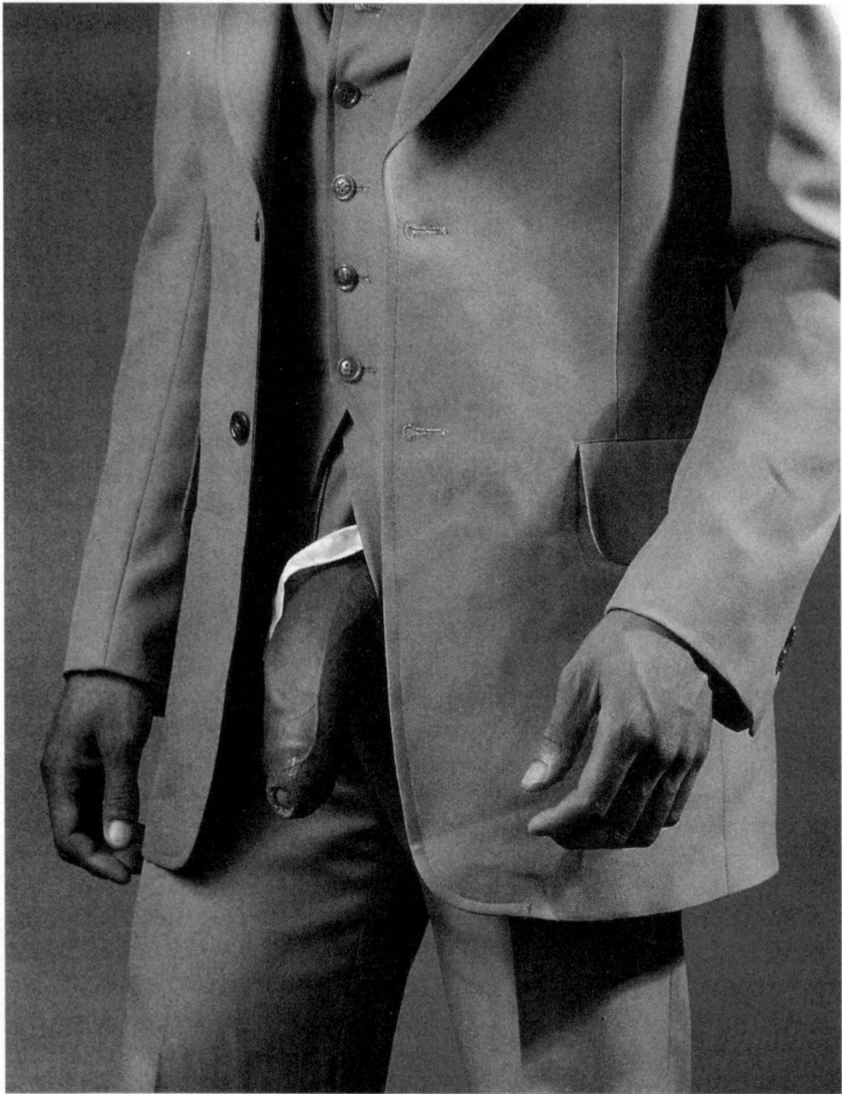

Figure 5.1 Robert Mapplethorpe, *Man in Polyester Suit* (1980), unique gelatin silver print, 40 × 30 in. Collection of Baldwin Fong. Copyright © 1980, The Estate of Robert Mapplethorpe/courtesy of A+C Anthology.

or lack, the photograph disempowers. For the "dark-veined, heavy thing" that is the literal penis, as Nancy K. Miller points out, remains "prosaic," unmediated by highminded concepts of the symbolic order that cluster about the magisterial phallus (145). Even the most standardized clothes of Western culture cannot fashion Mapplethorpe's headless model into a properly authoritative man.

What is it about this particular picture—as well as the many other images in the

Black Book (1986) collection—that makes it seem even more dangerous than far more violent, contorted shots like, for instance, the photographer's self-portrait with a whip handle inserted into his anus? Does "Man in Polyester Suit," endorsing the view of the eighteenth-century Dr. Charles White that "the PENIS of an African is larger than that of an European," prove that Mapplethorpe took the picture because he simply wanted to "have one" in his own possession? Emasculating by hypermasculinizing its subject, the photograph could—by fixing him at the physical level of the penis—contribute to those dangerous mythologies of black male predation on white women that were often used to warn against miscegenation or to justify lynching at the turn of the century.[7]

By means of cropping and lighting, Kobena Mercer and Isaac Julien have argued, the camera's fetishistic attention to one body part "affirms and denies that most fixed of racial myths in the white man's mind: that all black men have got bigger willies than he has" (150).[8] Excessive sexuality or an inability to control sexual passion—often imagined in terms of the large penis—has always characterized the male Other, be he a Jew, a homosexual, or a black.[9] So the decapitated trunk of the subject seems to deprive the man in the suit of subjectivity. Mindless matter devoid of morals or manners, "the Negro is eclipsed"—to use Fanon's phrasing—for "He is turned into a penis. He *is* a penis" (120). No wonder that one critic has linked this photograph to Mapplethorpe's penchant for "domineering erotic routines," especially "coprophagy" (since its "compulsory diet of excrement" symbolically punished black lovers for "their crime in having caused him to desire them" (Conrad 90)).

Still, the model clearly has consented to this pose which just as obviously occurs within the careful lighting of a studio. As Richard Avedon understood about the photographic studio which isolates people from their environment, subjects there "become in a sense . . . symbolic of themselves" (Sontag, 187). In addition, symmetry in Mapplethorpe's design stresses the representative content and artifice of the shot. A studied piece of white shirt peeks out of the fly to frame the penis, much as the skin on the shaft sets off the hidden head, much as the delicately veined hands balance the delicately veined "third hand," displaying the sensitivity of flesh as opposed to the real insult here: the clueless polyester. With its subject's quarter-angled pose, arms slightly bent, the image does seem "a parody of men's fashion photography of the Sears catalog school" (Sante, 46). An enemy of the synthetic respectability postulated by the cheap fabric of the suit, the model—like the photographer—thumbs his metaphorical nose at the viewer, flaunting his flagrant defiance of the rules. Therefore the picture puns on the word "exposure" in sexuality and in photography. Who is the pervert here: the black man exposing himself or the white photographer making his exposures; the people who enjoy the picture or the critic who reproduces it in her book? In other words, is the prurience of the viewer addressed by Mapplethorpe and his model, as if they were saying to the likes of Saul Bellow and his Mr. Sammler, "This is how you whites really see all blacks"?[10] Does black skin mean whites see no face at all?

What nauseates Bellow and fascinates Mapplethorpe is an uncanny, different kind of masculinism, an excessively physical masculinity stripped of traditionally patriarchal privilege. Certainly the sexual fantasies of racechange composed by white men and women from midcentury on return over and over again to the black penis-not-a-phallus, ringing changes on a phenomenon I am calling "black envy" to invoke Freud's idea of "penis envy."[11] Since American culture denied most black men "the Name of the Father"—the genealogical, linguistic, economic authority traditionally signified by the phallus—the black man excommunicated from the symbolic suffered an iconographic devolution into the penis incarnate and then was pathologized by whites fearful or ashamed about their own representational violence. Because of such double binds, however, the black man who had historically been denied the patronymic and defined as three-fifths of a citizen could also offer an alternative, alluring model of the masculine, one lacking oppressive claims to a restrictive superiority.[12] When what Mira Schor considers the prevalent "pattern of diminishing or hiding the penis" was finally broken by twentieth-century painters, sculptors, and photographers, the represented biological appendage could unveil the phallus, undermining its power (6, 15). If, as Schor speculates, "black men may be allowed big penises because, in the myopia of a Eurocentric culture, they are *denied* the *phallus* of language and history" (12), they might become especially resonant images of an unmediated, illegal, anarchic eroticism.

Whereas Freud wrote about a penis envy that supposedly only affected women, I will focus here on the black envy expressed by white men and women of letters who have imagined blackness as a renegade, masculine Third Sex divested of patriarchal entitlement (a mode of thinking that fetishizes black men even as it effectively obliterates the existence of black women).[13] During the period following the Second World War, when conventional models of masculinity had proved themselves demonstrably destructive and outdated, the trope of the penis-not-a-phallus became especially glamorous as a way of flirting with titillating alternatives to normative heterosexuality. As in Bellow's *Mr. Sammler's Planet* and Mapplethorpe's "Man in Polyester Suit," the genital distinctiveness ascribed to the black man by the white homosexualizes their bond: Sammler's spying on the pickpocket bespeaks a voyeuristic pleasure the black character intuits; even though he conceals his subject's face, Mapplethorpe wants the "Man in Polyester Suit" out, at least as out as the photographer himself is. Precisely the intensification and diminishment of masculinity characteristic of the African American's image also frequently mark the male homosexual (typecast, say, as macho biker or effete fairy) and blackness does at times take on the color of deviance for white writers. As we shall see, the strange combination of hypersexuality and emasculation may even oddly lesbianize the black man. The penis-not-a-phallus makes the black male character neither traditionally male nor female, neither paternal nor maternal, and so he provides the white imagination with an escape route from the boredom of the family romance, the pieties and proprieties of customary roles.

The essays and novels discussed in these pages affiliate the mutability of racechange with the flexibility of transgressive and difficult to categorize erotic desires.[14] Pathologized, the imagined black stud—on whom are projected criminalized or perverted forms of masculinity—can become a model for whites (what they want to become) or an erotic object (what they wish to have) and so the texts in which he appears tend to collapse heterosexual and homosexual categories as they blur racial borders. Racial ambiguity, in other words, attends sexual ambivalence and vice-versa. To the greater or lesser degree that sexual and racial suppleness prompts anxiety, essayists and novelists exhibit more or less pronounced cases of what Eve Kosofsky Sedgwick calls "definitional panic" (167). "Color me queer," the racechangers in this chapter seem to say, or "queerness colors me," though their white creators vary in the extent to which apprehension leads them to annihilate the representative of deviance.

The second half of this chapter will describe how the magnetism of such a scenario shaped portraits of racechange as sexchange in fiction by Ernest Hemingway and Lois Gould, specificially the former's *Garden of Eden* (c. 1946–61) and the latter's *A Sea-Change* (1976) in which white female characters live out their wish to become black men. However, first we will see that the black penis-not-a-phallus also fascinated such writers as Norman Mailer, Jack Kerouac, and John Howard Griffin, who uncover a psychopathology of fear, admiration, and envy of—as well as identification with and attraction toward—the black stud during the fifties and sixties. Queer colors are the object of fascination, but the subjects enthralled are mostly straight writers who wish to take a holiday from the banality of heterosexual roles. Just a holiday though: The metaphorically perverse only looks like it will threaten the status quo, for it ends up strengthening the satisfying closure of a heterosexually defined happily-ever-after. Initially in these narratives, disgust with traditional gender roles turns white men and women toward a perversity that in turn attaches itself to the racechanged character; however, eventually the blackness of the Third Sex works to retain difference and thus ultimately to enable a heterosexuality otherwise imperiled.

Throughout both sections of this chapter, the mutability implicit in racechange scenarios inflects sexuality with an elusive pliancy; conversely, the blurring of normative categories of eroticism contributes to the permeable boundaries of racial borderlines. Flirting with the idea of breaking taboos against interracial love and same-sex desire, the authors and characters in thrall to black envy temporarily eschew the boring categories "black," "white," "straight," "gay" for scenarios propelled by more slippery, seductive terms. "What alternative to the phallus is there?" Jessica Benjamin has inquired in her study of domination and desire. The fantasy of the penis-not-a-phallus has clearly been debilitating to actual African-American people; yet it illuminates the titillating uses to which the Other has been put in narratives tapping black envy to imagine eros outside the standard Oedipal plot. Enthralled by a traditionally retrograde racial script, writers like Mailer, Hemingway, and Gould seem to ask, "What's love got to do with it?" when sadism, masochism, fetishism, sodomy, adultery, regression, and polygamy are just so much more fun.

The White Negro's Desire for the Black Man

In a meditation entitled "The Black Boy Looks at the White Boy," about his intermittent friendship with Norman Mailer, James Baldwin approached the odd double bind of black men imbued with hypothetical sexual powers even as they are drained of political or social potency:

> I think that I know something about the American masculinity which most men of my generation do not know because they have not been menaced by it in the way that I have been. It is still true, alas, that to be an American Negro male is also to be a kind of walking phallic symbol: which means that one pays, in one's own personality, for the sexual insecurity of others. The relationship, therefore, of a black boy to a white boy is a very complex thing. (217)

Menaced by "the" American masculinity, Baldwin feels himself sufficiently removed from it to analyze it; because of white men's "sexual insecurity," the African American remains always a "*walking* phallic *symbol*," a symbol for whites that never possesses the phallus in its own right.[15] Understandably, then, Baldwin condemns Mailer's impassioned essay "The White Negro" (1957) as an instance of an "antique vision" of blacks. Indeed, Baldwin bases his "resistance to the title" on his suspicion that "the sorely menaced sexuality of Negroes" is maligned by Mailer "in order to justify the white man's own sexual panic" (230).

The "sexual panic" so evident in Mailer's essay includes white men's fears about impotence, emasculation, sexual ineptitude, physical inferiority, and whiteness as well as "homosexual panic," the term Sedgwick uses to describe heterosexual men's fear of homosexuality.[16] For Mailer's attraction to the pathologized image of the black stud teeters between admiration of a role model and desire for an erotic partner. Just as important, Mailer's racechanging fantasy of a "White Negro," which enabled him to play out his rebellion against traditional definitions of masculinity as well as his attraction to illicit forms of eroticism, typifies a racial crossover that accelerated in the late forties and fifties to flower in the sixties. Describing this phenomenon, Malcolm X explained that "A few of the white men around Harlem, younger ones we called 'hippies,' acted more Negro than Negroes" (94). The Otherness of the "White Negro" enabled Mailer to lay the groundwork for the beats and beatniks, the hippies and yippies who so often took the black man as a model for their rebellion against the bourgeois respectability of the authoritarian white patriarch. Racechange for Mailer and his followers empowered them to experience, on the one hand, their revulsion against conventional sex roles and, on the other, their attraction to outlawed alternatives to them. Although Baldwin's indictment of "The White Negro"'s "offensive nonsense" captures the pathos of Mailer's effort to become "hip," Baldwin failed to see the ways in which the white writer's black envy accords with the black novelist's own sense of what it means to be "a Negro man" (232), let alone a white boy looking at a "walking phallic symbol."

Panic, specifically panic about outworn masculine roles, informs the very beginning of Mailer's essay with its horror at concentration camps, atom bombs, and a Western "civilization founded upon the Faustian urge to dominate nature" (583). For Mailer, what emerged out of the Second World War was an acknowledgment that "no matter how crippled and perverted an image of man was the society he had created, it was nonetheless his creation" (583). Composed at the end of the fifties, the essay—attributing the "conformity and depression" of the period to fear and a collective failure of nerve—begins with white self-loathing and a crisis in male identity. The existentialist hipster who emerges as a new hero out of this landscape offers the only hope of masculine survival:

> *if one is to be a man*, almost any kind of unconventional action often takes disproportionate courage. So it is no accident that *the source of Hip is the Negro* for he has been living on the margin between totalitarianism and democracy for two centuries. (585; emphasis mine)

As Baldwin intuited, Mailer identifies black culture with sex and primitivism: "Jazz is orgasm" (586), he insists; "Hip is the sophistication of the wise primitive in a giant jungle" (589), he intones. And the hipster-Negro is also criminalized into a "psychopath [who] murders—if he has the courage—out of the necessity to purge his violence" (593). Childlike in his nihilism, beyond good and evil, the hipster-Negro could as easily be a left-wing revolutionary as a fascist: "Hip . . . is the affirmation of the barbarian for it requires a primitive passion about human nature to believe that individual acts of violence are always to be preferred to the collective violence of the State" (601). How new is the hipster-Negro if in him is only reinscribed the stereotype of the oversexed, psychopathic, aggressive barbarian typified by a character like Gus in *Birth of a Nation*—even though these attributes are now valued positively rather than negatively?[17] To the extent that its author was "in the grip of a bad case of the I've-got-the-pseudo-anglo-saxon-technological-male menopausal-twentieth-century-civilized man's blues" (as Michele Wallace puts it (42)), the concept of the White Negro offensively stereotypes black culture.

It seems appropriate that a photographic negative appears on the cover of the book version of Mailer's essay (Fig. 5.2) since its central figure is, in the words of one critic, "an inverted image" of the Other whose devalorized attributes (primitivism, violence, insanity) were simply revalorized as emblems of alienation from dominant cultural norms (Mercer, "Skin Head," 21). Two precursors of Mailer—Hart Crane and e. e. cummings—flirted with exactly such a "strategic self-othering" through fantasies of the physically daunting black outsider (Mercer, "Skin Head," 21). Hart Crane's terrified dream of finding himself floating in a canoe or rowboat toward a waterfall concludes with his seeing a naked Negro on a nearby shore, a black man whose huge penis convinces Crane of his own insignificant genitals, "tiny as a baby's" (Unterecker, 501). Similarly, when e. e. cummings is imprisoned in *The Enormous Room* (1922), he encounters another inmate more confident than the poet could ever be, "a beautiful pillar of black strutting muscle" whose grin and musical laugh create an "effect on the spectators [which] was instantaneous; they roared and danced with joy" (197).

One narrative line interwoven in Crane's and cummings's accounts is unraveled by Sherwood Anderson's story "The Man Who Became a Woman" (1923) when a scared and lonesome young man is found by "two big buck niggers" who take him for the girl he fears himself to be (219).[18] Part castration anxiety, part projection, part desire, the image of the formidable Other reinforces Crane's and cummings's insecurity about their own deficiency, but it also speaks of a wish cummings silent-

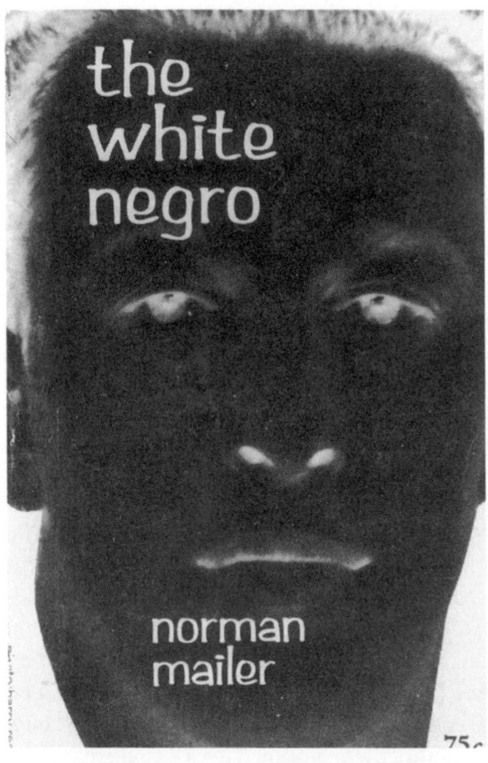

Figure 5.2 Cover of *The White Negro*. Copyright © 1960 by City Lights Books, reprinted by permission.

ly puts to the grinning, strutting black muscle (so reminiscent of minstrelsy's version of the African American): If only in the privacy of his mind, cummings prays to Jean, "Take me up (carefully;as if I were a toy)and play carefully with me,once or twice,before I and you go suddenly all limp and foolish" (*sic*; 214). The homosexual subtext—hardly acknowledged yet so thinly veiled—means that the potent black Other offers the promise of a tender companion who is not female as well as respite from self-loathing for the white man who seeks to be like the Other, to be with the Other, to be loved by the Other, as indeed Norman Mailer does throughout "The White Negro." Several factors may get lost in too quick a condemnation of Mailer's polemic: first, his appreciation of subversive survival skills conditioned by the oppression of African Americans; second, the open secret of his desire for some kind of sexualized union with black men.

At the close of "The White Negro," Mailer describes "the most intense conditions of exploitation, cruelty, violence, frustration, and lust" that bred the Negro's "passionate instinct about the meaning of life" (604). The hipster needs to absorb "the existentialist synapses of the Negro" (587) because the African American always has understood the dangerous edge upon which he attempted to live his precarious life. Anti-social and rebellious in the theater of the present, the hipster can learn survival strategies by modeling himself upon "the Negro [who] knows more about the ugliness and danger of life than the White" (602). Like Lenny Bruce, the comedian Jonathan Miller called the "sick white negro," Mailer ridiculed liberal platitudes about American justice to dramatize the ongoing history of racial persecution. Like Bruce, too, Mailer admired the tenacity of black people faced with constant discrimination as well as what he lauded as their nihilistic disillusionment about American culture.

Despite his loathing of Mailer's essay, Baldwin comes very close to Mailer's view of the existentialist wisdom and grit conferred on African Americans by their marginalization in a culture out to destroy them. Baldwin believes that

> to become a Negro man, let alone a Negro artist, one had to make oneself up as one went along. This had to be done in the not-at-all-metaphorical teeth of the world's determination to destroy you. The world had prepared no place for you, and if the world had its way, no place would ever exist. (*Nobody*, 232)

Although he realizes that society has prepared no place for *anyone*, Baldwin knows about white delusions of grandeur and in particular about white men who (assuming "the world is theirs") "expect the world to help them in the achievement of their identity" (232). In other words, he shares with Mailer a belief that the exile and consequent self-fashioning of black men glamorize them with Byronic alienation, Joycean cunning, and the grace under pressure Hemingway named the model of courage.

What Mailer adds to this mix is a Lawrentian blood consciousness infused by his own cross-racial desire. According to Mailer, the "Negro, not being privileged to gratify his self-esteem," chose instead to derive from "perversion, promiscuity, pimping, drug addiction, rape . . . a morality of the bottom" (594). Connecting the "emergence of the Negro" with the eruption of a psychic rebellion "against the anti-sexual foundation of every organized power in America" (603), he fantasizes about congress between whites and Negroes:

> In such places as Greenwich Village, *a ménage-à-trois* was completed—the bohemian and the juvenile delinquent came face-to-face with the Negro, and the hipster was a fact in American life. If marijuana was *the wedding ring, the child* was the language of Hip. . . . And *in this wedding of the white and the black* it was the Negro who brought the cultural *dowry*. (586; emphasis mine)

Leslie Fiedler has described the longing that imbues *Huckleberry Finn*, the Leatherstocking novels, and *Moby Dick* as the wish that "Our dark-skinned beloved will take us in . . . when we have been cut off, or have cut ourselves off, from all others" (150). Isolated and alienated, Mailer's bohemian and juvenile delinquent also dream of their "acceptance at the breast [they have] most utterly offended" (Fiedler, "Come Back," 151). Fiedler's "notion of the Negro as the unblemished bride" (148) informs Mailer's longing for the "wedding" of white and black men, where the Negro furnishes the "dowry" and a new mulatto language emerges to express the rebellious thoughts of the outlawed hybrid.[19]

A figure of the Not-Yet-Born out of male bonding, the White Negro would speak this miscegenated tongue. A racechanging simulacrum emerging out of a drug dream of mutability, the hipster becomes the fantasy son of three coupling white and black men. With its Man Ray look of a negative, the photograph on the copy

berg's pioneering essay on Van Vechten's "Queer Collection" demonstrates, have scholars realized that this celebrated promoter of the Harlem Renaissance put together some twenty scrapbooks of pictures and newspaper clippings that constitute "homemade sex books, early and private forerunners of Madonna's best-seller" (28). Two portraits of Saint Sebastian—one with a white model, one with a black—justify Weinberg's view that "changing the race of [the] model raises disturbing associations. For us today, the tied arms and outdoor setting might evoke less the early-Christian martyr than a modern lynching" (36; Fig. 5.3).

That the patron of the Harlem Renaissance was drawn to Sebastian seems hardly surprising, since this third-century martyr served as the patron saint of a masochistically inflected homosexuality for many artists. The staging of his sanctification usually features a beautiful, naked youth whose flesh is riddled with arrows in a scene that extends suspense by protracting suffering; the mixture of pain due to phallic penetration and pleasure in transcendence made Sebastian a particularly resonant prototype of the ecstatic torment of a supreme erotic experience. With his eyes shut and his arms clutching the stake or tree against which he is impaled, the black model in Van Vechten's picture looks ravished in both senses of the word: raped and sent into ecstasies. Like Mapplethorpe's photographs in the *Black Book*, however, Van Vechten's racechanged "shot" of Sebastian hints that when a white boy looks at a black boy he may manage to dislodge the more traditional figure of the fetishized female nude only by glamorizing the (already potentially subordinated) black subject as a model of feminized masochism. As curvaceous as a woman, black St. Sebastian sports two arrows strategically placed on either side of his genitals, making a V, something like the iconic V for Venus or vagina. Though he is supposed to appear thrilled at being pierced by the skewed arrows, Van Vechten's target of opportunity—displayed like sexual meat—may seem uncomfortably scapegoated or skewered (something like shish kebab).

If Van Vechten performs a racechange on St. Sebastian to intensify the thrill at arresting time before saintly reward or sexual consumation, Francis Picabia's gouache *Oiseau et tortue* (Bird and turtle, 1949; Fig. 5.4) presents its strangely colored central figure to hint at an androgynous sexuality. The hermaphroditic and biracial center of attention here—neither black nor white, neither male nor female—engages in a kind of life or death struggle as if to establish new categories of being that would violently rescind the ordinary either/or binaries of gender, sexual orientation, and race. Using the trope of the spotted Negro, Picabia draws attention to achromatism, usually held to be hideous or a sign of illness but here a signature of the fluid boundaries between what are often taken to be distinct species or kinds of being.[25] The mottled skin denotes a hybridity comparable to the bisexuality of the body, intimating that racechange and sexchange together undo conventional modes of being and seeing. Once again, in other words, the strangely colored White Negro—like Edward Carpenter's Intermediate Type—annuls the polarity of standard gender categories.

In supposedly straight contexts, too, black becomes a color favored to figure deviant forms of eroticism that defy ordinary heterosexual plots. In fact, racial Otherness guards against sexual Otherness; for white men of letters, an enticing black

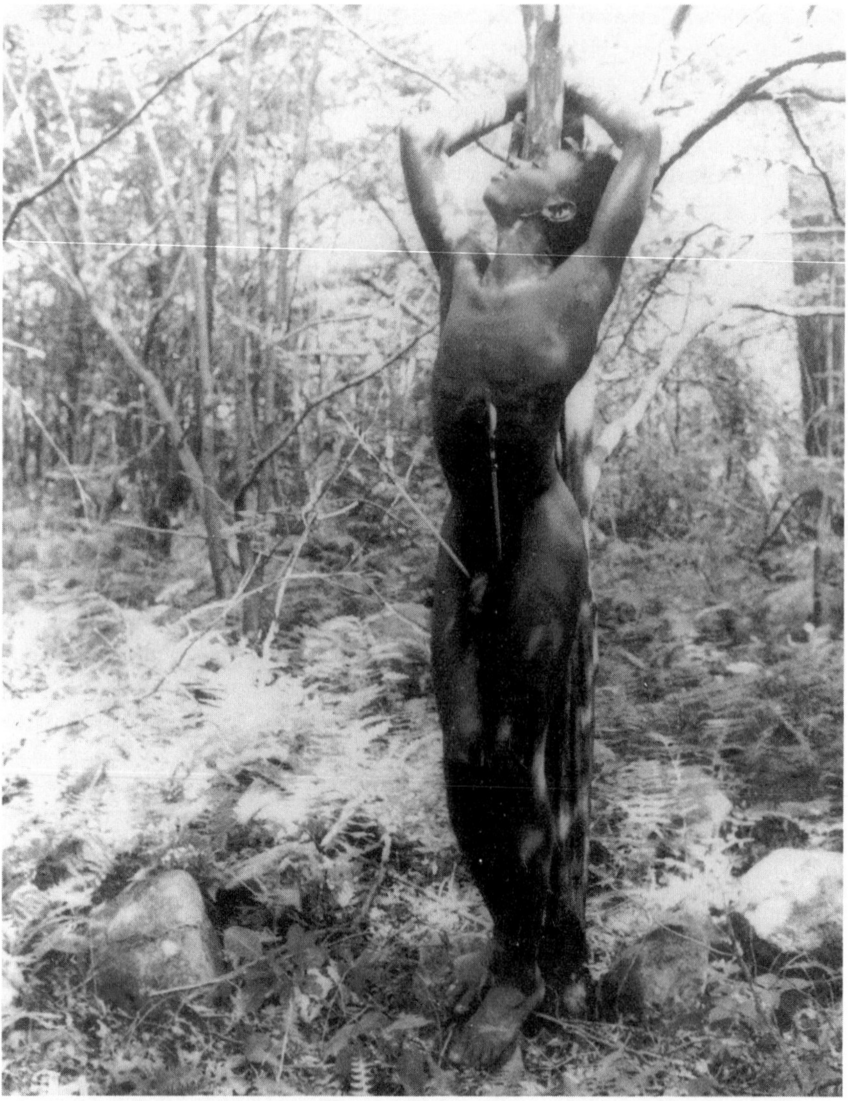

Figure 5.3 Carl Van Vechten, *Saint Sebastian.* Courtesy of Beinecke Library, Yale University. Courtesy of Joseph Solomon, Executor of the Estate of Carl Van Vechten.

masculinity can defend against women. The most aggressively heterosexual book to exhibit black envy is Jack Kerouac's *On the Road* (1957), especially in a passage later hailed by Eldridge Cleaver as symptomatic of white youth's "rejection of the conformity which America expected" (72). The third section begins with the narrator, Sal Paradise, strolling in the "violet dark," wishing he "could exchange worlds with the happy, true-hearted, ecstatic Negroes of America" (149):

> At lilac evening I walked with every muscle aching amongst the lights of 27th and Welton in the Denver coloured section, *wishing I were a Negro*, feeling that the best the white world had offered was not enough ecstasy for me, not enough life, joy, kicks, darkness, music, not enough night. (148; emphasis mine)

As in *The Subterraneans* (1958), where he describes his "old dream of wanting to be vital, alive like a Negro or an Indian or a Denver Jap or a New York Puerto Rican" (70), Kerouac was disgusted by what he took to be white rationality and self-consciousness.

Drugs, jazz, and male bonding with the innocent but scapegoated victims of racism, all to be found on "the negro streets" Ginsberg walked when declaring "I am the Scottsboro boys" typify the wish for some sort of racechange in consciousness that animated the beat generation. *On the Road* describes what happens when Sal meets up with his white buddy Dean Moriarty, who immediately deserts

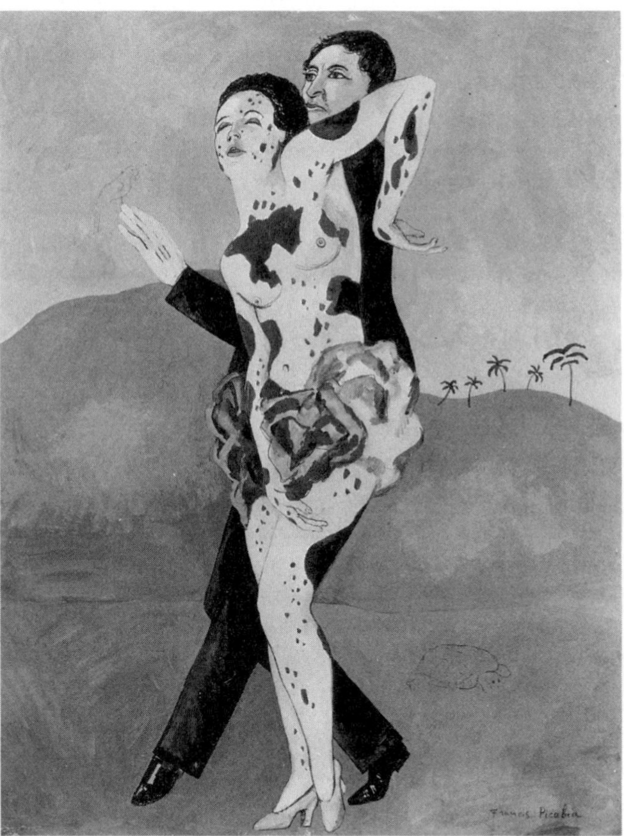

Figure 5.4 Francis Picabia, *Oiseau et tortue* (Bird and turtle, 1925–27), gouache on paper, 25¾ × 19¾ in. Courtesy of the Metropolitan Museum of Art, Alfred Stieglitz Collection, 1949.

his pregnant wife and baby, putting "bitterness, recriminations, advice, morality, sadness—everything . . . behind him" so as to embrace "the ragged and ecstatic joy of pure being" (161). In a sawdust saloon filled with "colored men in Saturday-night suits" (162), Dean almost seems to copulate with an orgasmic tenorman:

> Dean was directly in front of him with his face lowered to the bell of the horn, clapping his hands, pouring sweat on the man's keys, and the man noticed and laughed in his horn a long quivering crazy laugh, and . . . finally the tenorman decided to blow his top and crouched down and held a note in high C for a long time as everything else crashed along and the cries increased and I thought the cops would come swarming from the nearest precinct. Dean was in a trance. (163)

Notwithstanding Kerouac's intermittent put-downs of "queers," the same love that joins white hero and black musician also flourished between white buddies on the roads they took to flee from family responsibilities in general, wives and children in particular. Just as Sal, staring at Dean who gazes back at Sal, often feels something "click" between them, many photographs of their prototypes—Kerouac himself and Neal Cassady—present the duo with arms entangled, looking boyishly fraternal. As Paul Goodman knew, "Beat culture, unlike the American standard of living, is essentially for men" (185), a point presumably made too by the camaraderie fostered by jazz and drugs.

Curiously, even the enemies of "The Know-Nothing Bohemians" adopted the rhetoric of cross-racial longing. The phrase just quoted is the title of Norman Podhoretz's 1958 attack on Ginsberg and Kerouac (and specifically the latter's "idyllic picture of Negro life" so similar to Southern attempts "to convince the world that things were just as fine as fine could be for the slaves" (311)). Yet Podhoretz's essay "My Negro Problem—And Ours" (1963) contains the same stock of black envy spiced with a dash of homoeroticism evident in "The White Negro" and *On the Road*:

> just as in childhood *I envied Negroes* for what seemed to me *their superior masculinity*, so *I envy them* today for what seems to be their superior physical grace and beauty. I have come to value physical grace very highly and I am now capable of *aching with all my being when I watch a Negro couple* on the dance floor, or *a Negro playing* baseball or basketball. They are on the kind of terms with their own bodies that I should like to be on with mine, and for that precious quality they seem blessed to me. (99; emphasis mine)[26]

Podhoretz represents himself as a liberal in race matters, one who would even learn—if necessary—to let his sister or daughter marry "one" (101). But the ache he feels while watching Negro athletes may mean the hypothetical sister or daughter has been put in place as a kind of surrogate. In one of the stills Dick Gregory includes in his satiric book on American racism in the sixties, *What's Happening?* (1965), the black comic hints as much about the sexually hidden motives of even the most prejudiced of law enforcement officers (Fig. 5.5). "You can't marry my sister," the white sheriff explains to the black aristocrat, "but if you're as rich as you look, you can marry me."

From the fifties and sixties on, libertarians and bigots alike shared an obsessive

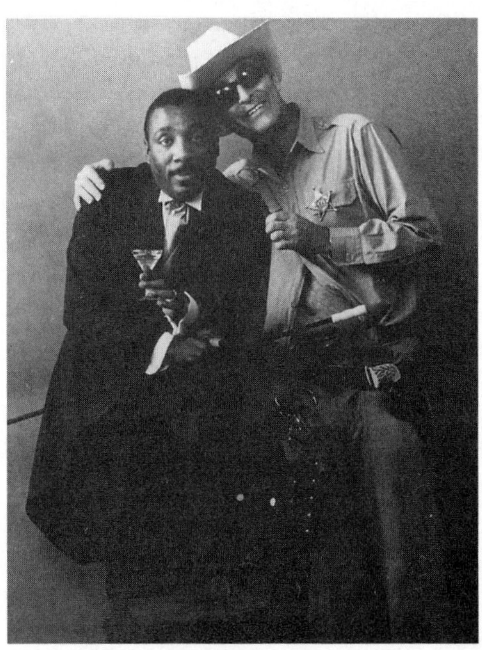

Figure 5.5 Dick Gregory, "You can't marry my sister, but if you're as rich as you look, you can marry me," from Dick Gregory, *What's Happening?* (Dutton 1965), photographs by Jerry Yulsman. Courtesy of Dick Gregory.

black envy. Indeed, the allegedly enlightened Podhoretz's aching admiration recalls the reactions of the racist Southerners who pass the blackened, hitch-hiking John Howard Griffin on the road during the daylight, but stop to pick him up after dark. This disturbing section of *Black Like Me* castigates the pornographic imagination of white men, their "morbid curiosity about the sexual life of the Negro" whom they see "as an inexhaustible sex-machine with oversized genitals and a vast store of experiences, immensely varied" (85). A kind of confessional, the dark car at night becomes a "ghoulish" place of white men's "pantings" as they take to "hounding" Griffin for his "sexual reminiscences" (85). Significantly, then, white men are shown propositioning a presumably black man to hear his accounts of sex. As if situating himself in the voyeuristic place of Bellow's Sammler or Mapplethorpe's camera, one especially prurient driver who "had never seen a Negro naked" asks Griffin to expose himself; after he is refused, the young man feels the need to explain, "I wasn't going to do anything to you. . . . I'm not a queer, or anything" (89).[27] If we return to the Terry Southern quotation at the start of this chapter, keeping in mind the absence of women from the scenes of Griffin's dialogues, it may seem that the speaker who wants to "pretend to be a spade" is less excited by the fantasy female figure to be raped than by the act of actually "get[ting] into a *spade bag*."

Cases of white men's black envy make strange bedfellows in popular American culture during the second half of the twentieth century. According to Greil Marcus, early rock 'n' roll "must have been a bit like a white foray into darktown, a combination of a blackface minstrel show and night riding—romantic as hell, a little dangerous, a little ridiculous" (*Mystery Train*, 176). Though Elvis Presley didn't need to exile himself from his own community as Mezz Mezzrow and Johnny Otis "and so many *real white Negroes*" did (182; emphasis mine), the King nevertheless remained indebted to the black music upon which he drew, as did Jimmie Rogers, Dock Boggs, and Bob Dylan. Assessing the ethics of that debt, Marcus asks, "What *does* Huck owe Jim, especially when Jim is really Huck in blackface and everyone smells loot?" (180). "Elvis was sexy," according to one popular music historian, "not clean-cut, wholesome, white-bread, Hollywood sexy but sexy in the aggressive earthy manner associated by whites with black males" (George, 62–63). The prominence of black cultural forms, which "served as a model for middle-class youths in the 1950s," may explain why "bad" teens ("hoods" as well as "beats") wore "black turtleneck shirts, black stockings, black sunglasses" (Breines, 19, 148).

Mick Jagger and Keith Richards—as if confirming Marcus's view of rock 'n' roll as white forays into darktown—initially bonded over their mutual obsession with Chuck Berry and Muddy Waters; however, during their first tour of the States a mistaken Murray the K warned them "there was not much hope for them in America because if Americans wanted the music of Chuck Berry and Muddy Waters they would listen to the original, and anyway white people most certainly did not want what was considered 'nigger music.' . . . And it would not be realistic to hope that black people would want to listen to young Englishmen playing the blues" (Schofield, 68). Another type of England's youth culture, "the mods" in mid-sixties London displayed "an emotional affinity with black people" that "was transposed into style," according to Dick Hebdige: The (blatantly stereotyped) model of "the Black Man" made possible the view that "work was insignificant, irrelevant; vanity and arrogance were permissible, even desirable qualities, and a more furtive and ambiguous sense of masculinity" could be achieved through "a sleight of hand, through 'soul'" (Hebdige 53–54).

Black envy—so prevalent in rock music's metaphorical blackface—shaped the civil rights movement as well. In a 1964 interview with Bradford Daniel for *The Progressive*, John Howard Griffin described the "intellectual fad" of white liberals as a kind of love affair with African Americans: "liberals . . . embrace all Negroes because they are Negroes"; they "tend to adopt the attitude: 'You bring the whiskey and I'll bring the Negro,' to a party or a meeting" (15).[28] Not only were various quests for countercultural authenticity imagined in terms of an archaic Africa, the pathologized hypervirility of the black man continued to propel the imaginations of political activists from widely divergent perspectives.[29] According to Michele Wallace, who believes that "the manhood America finally conceded to blacks was the manhood of a psychopath" (48), the "curiously psychopathic energy at work in the black man's pursuit of his manhood (Black Power)" derived from the influence of Norman Mailer's fantasies on militants like LeRoi Jones and Eldridge Cleaver (47, 39): "Yes, white men were perversely obsessed with the black man's genitals but the obsession turned out to be a communicable disease and in the sixties black men came down with high fevers" (73).

For Jones (later Amiri Baraka) and Cleaver, in turn, the supermasculinization of the black power movement could lead to the virulent homophobia of the former's comment that "Most American white men are trained to be fags" (*Home*, 216) or of the latter's judgment that "Homosexuality is a sickness, just as are baby-rape or wanting to become the head of General Motors" (110).[30] Cleaver's subsequent effort to market "real men's pants," featuring large and dangling cotton-stuffed codpieces, serves as a symbol of what the social critic Stanley Crouch calls "the priapic version of black 'manhood' that slithered from behind the black power movement's fly" (106–7). As if to confirm the idea that racism may be rooted not only in white men's jealous imagining of black macho but also in their racechanging impersonations of that macho, the writings of the ex-KKK leader and recurrent Republican candidate David Duke include *African Atto*, a street-fighting manual for urban blacks that he wrote under the pseudonym Mohammed X in order to collect the names of black militants.[31]

What Does the Lesbian White Negro Want?

Despite their manifold differences, the common project of Norman Mailer, Jack Kerouac, Norman Podhoretz, John Howard Griffin, and Eldridge Cleaver—their effort to locate through black men a dissident masculinity before or beyond the phallic—demonstrates its limits in their unconscious but not therefore less emphatic contempt for women. To become racially Other somehow licenses violence against women. Obviously, Mailer's flirtation with a "morality of the bottom" ratified "perversion, promiscuity, pimping, drug addition, rape" (603) in ways that could easily constitute a danger for the sex he considered secondary. In other words, the supposedly revolutionary renegade often shares with the authoritarian men against whom he rebels a scorn for women whose femininity is equated with castration. Although, as Jane Gallop has pointed out, "To distinguish penis from phallus would [appear to] be to locate some masculinity that does not necessarily obliterate the feminine" (125), women *are* eclipsed in such texts as "The White Negro" and *On the Road*. What happens when the psychopathology of black envy surfaces not in a white male but in a white female context? Here, too, we will see that queer colors—though attractive as one aspect of a seductive revolt against traditional and debilitating gender roles—nevertheless ultimately play themselves out in scenarios that continue to identify women with castration and that oddly end up buttressing heterosexual as well as racist structures.

Given the long history of the black stud/white female victim in propaganda and pornography, it is no wonder that white women have written quite openly about their fear of the "*spade-rape bag*." Indeed, a touchstone psychoanalytic essay about femininity begins with a meditation on the meaning of such dread. Joan Rivière's "Womanliness as a Masquerade" (1929)—which argues that "women who wish for masculinity may put on a mask of womanliness to avert anxiety and the retribution feared from men" (35)—includes a case study of an intellectually proficient woman who believes her ambitions supplant her father, who propitiates father-figures by flirting, and who associates such flirtation with a youthful fantasy:

> This phantasy . . . had been very common in her childhood and youth, which had been spent in the Southern States of America; if a negro came to attack her, she planned to defend herself by making him kiss her and make love to her (ultimately so that she could then deliver him over to justice). But there was a further determinant of the obsessive behaviour. In a dream . . . she was in terror alone in the house; then a negro came in and found her washing clothes, with her sleeves rolled up and arms exposed. She resisted him, with the secret intention of attracting him sexually, and he began to admire her arms and caress them and her breasts. (37)

Rivière goes on to explain what she takes to be the dream's meaning: The girl was alone in the house because she had killed her parents so she dreaded their retribution and she defended herself from charges of ambitiousness by playing a menial role, thereby disguising herself as "merely a castrated woman" (38). Convinced that her intellectual gifts have turned her into a man, she feigns femininity by means of flirtatious ogling.

Rivière remains perfectly satisfied with her conflating of the white parents so feared by the daughter with the phantom Negro breaking in: Both are frighteningly powerful and therefore must be assuaged with seductive coquetting.[32] But what if the girl's "*making* [the negro] kiss her and make love to her" or resisting "with the secret *intention of attracting* him sexually" (emphasis mine) can be read as a way of rebelling against the authority of the white parents, finishing them off? If the young woman's intellectual displays are experienced as an apprehensive "possession of the father's penis," perhaps she longs to entice the black man to take up her cause. Put another way, just as she wishes for an intellectual proficiency equal to—but not identical with—the father's, she dreams of aligning herself with a black masculinity equal to—but not identical with—the father's. Conceivably, then, she wishes to join with the black man, become part of the black man, become the black man, to exploit him as an instrument to complete the castration of the white father. Two novels by Ernest Hemingway and Lois Gould propose exactly such a dynamic. More surprising than representations of white women's anxieties about the black rapist are portraits hinting that—like white men—white women are also capable of flirting with the stereotype of the black renegade, identifying with it, and thus relishing the fantasy of getting into a "*spade-rape bag*."

In other words, white men were not alone in their desire to model themselves on the dark stud. Male- and female-authored heroines also enact their own misogyny through the figure of the black penis-not-a-phallus. This is a misogyny women experience because of their alienation from a demeaning, secondary, trivializing, weakening construction of femininity, a femininity that makes women feel vulnerable and frightened, dependent upon feigned flirations and in need of paternal protection.[33] Both Hemingway's *Garden of Eden* and Gould's *A Sea-Change* present portraits of female characters nauseated by such an enfeebling femininity and driven by anxieties about their subordination to revenge themselves against men. In revolt against the same gender polarity that disgusted the White Negro, Hemingway's and Gould's heroines appear to reject the rational reality principle of the father (or conventionally masculine) as well as the intimacy, emotionalism, and affectivity of the mother (or traditionally feminine). By means of a black envy that causes them to darken themselves, they stage racechange as a sexchange that turns them into White Negroes, queer hipsters or outlaws who compete with white men for white women. This is why in both these texts the lesbian looks so dark and so male. Paradoxically, then, we will see that even the most seemingly seditious racechange narratives ultimately work to support a compromised, endangered heterosexuality.

Turning dark in *The Garden of Eden* and *A Sea-Change* means turning queer; both Hemingway's and Gould's heroines uncover bizarre slippages between lesbianism, transsexuality, blackness, and heterosexual sadism. For Hemingway's Catherine Bourne and Gould's Jessie Waterman, to become black means gaining seditious, prohibited, masculine potency; however, it also means a fugitive status that continues to subject them to political as well as social marginality. Disrupting the patriarchal order, the rebellious lesbians in these two novels at least temporarily refute traditional sexual arrangements, but only by employing the profoundly retrograde racial configuration of the pathologized black stud.

Hemingway, who worked on the posthumously published *Garden of Eden* from 1946 until his death in 1961, used his title to point to the mythic design upon which he hung his narrative of "an intelligent woman uncontrollably envious of her husband's success as a writer" (to use the prefatory words of the editor who helped shape—by cutting—the only version that is now available in print).[34] Pen and penis envy motivate Catherine, David Bourne's bride of three weeks, who interrupts their idyllic swimming and fishing, their Edenic eating and sleeping and lovemaking during a honeymoon in Avignon to embark on "a wonderful dangerous surprise": "I'm going to be changed," she explains before going off to get her hair "cropped as short as a boy's" (12, 14–15). The boy's haircut leads directly to transgression—"Dave, you don't mind if we've gone to the devil, do you?"—and the fall is a sexual one. When Catherine takes on the character of "Peter," asking David to become "my girl Catherine," she effects her temptation through the act of sodomy:

> He lay there and felt something and then her hand holding him and searching lower and he helped with his hands and then lay back in the dark and did not think at all and only felt the weight and the strangeness inside and she said, "Now you can't tell who is who can you?" (17)

The "dark magic of the change" at first only occurs at night, but Catherine wants "to be darker" and that wish forecasts the impossibility of her containing the process that will inexorably lead, as in the original myth, to shame, recrimination, and expulsion. "I'll be your African girl," she vows, dedicating herself to getting "darker than an Indian" and "further away from other people" (30).[35] Yet the tanning process that blackens Catherine's skin demonstrates that the "African girl" she wants to be is "Peter" penetrating David. Nor is Hemingway's association of "dark" or "African" ways with sodomy eccentric. Throughout *Women in Love*

(1921) as well as his later essays, Hemingway's English counterpart describes sodomy as "the African process." According to D. H. Lawrence, "African degradation" occurs at "the darkest, deepest, strangest life-source . . . at the back and base of the loins."[36] As Diana Fuss has shown, Freud also established his theories about the origin of culture by equating "primitivity and homosexuality" as the "inversions" that had to be repressed or made taboo (*Identification Papers,* 36).

For Catherine, being black means attaining the pleasure of becoming physically active in the penetration of her lover without claiming the legitimacy or respectability of any socially sanctioned authority. Indeed, she seeks precisely the psychopathic violence and nihilistic courage of Mailer's alienated hipster. After another haircut followed by bouts of anxiety about sex- and racechanges that hook her like a compulsion or addiction, it becomes clear that Catherine's need to "be a boy" requires David's "change" into "my dearest only girl" (56), illustrating Hemingway's tendency to imagine homosexuality in heterosexual terms. Given her nickname, "Devil," Catherine would use her transgressive seductions to bear David Bourne away to a sexual wilderness where he will be reborn as a girl. When he submits to having his hair cut just like hers and then lightened to a color of no color, something like her pearls, he finds it futile to fly from the hell which is himself. For, unlike Samson, he has voluntarily and knowingly submitted to the rape of his locks.

After being turned into a twin image of Catherine and playing her role in bed, David looks in the mirror and admits responsibility for the change: "Don't ever say anyone tempted you or that anyone bitched you," he advises himself, because "You like it" (84–85). With their brown skin and their lightened hair, the pair looks not only like each other but also like Man Ray's photographic "solarizations" or the cover of Mailer's "The White Negro," as if their outré reversals mean to highlight their refusal to conform to conventional gender and race roles, their playing with a dangerous androgyny and hybridity. The punk contrast Catherine designs between the couple's tanned skin and the whitening of their hair emphasizes their self-made, artificial, singular being, her cosmetological effort to break not only sexual and racial taboos but also normative physiological types. As Toni Morrison explains in her reading of the novel, "Catherine is both black and white, both male and female" and thus destined for madness (*Playing*, 87–88). All too predictably, then, the next "dark change" the "African girl" instigates involves her taking a female lover.

When Catherine brings Marita into the relationship, David's passive, pensive query—"Whose girl is she?"—indicates that Catherine enjoys having Marita as an erotic partner, but Catherine also relishes playing the man by bringing a gift to her girl David ("I brought you a dark girl for a present," she tells him (103)); in addition, she savors being one of two lovers for her husband David ("be nice to your girls," she instructs him (103)). Just as her turning David into a kind of twin gives the marriage a tang of incest, the *ménage à trois* breaks several taboos, allowing Catherine to flirt with adultery, lesbianism, polygamy. In her compulsion to experience whatever sexual permutations and combinations she can imagine, this licentious "African girl" recalls Lawrence's meditation on a West African fetish, a female statue that represents

> mindless, progressive knowledge through the senses, knowledge arrested and ending in the senses, mystic knowledge in disintegration and dissolution, knowledge such as the beetles have, which live purely within the world of corruption and cold dissolution. (*Women in Love*, 330)

For a while, David allows the two girls "to take turns" with him as he is drained of agency by Catherine's demonic invention of competing life stories that redirect his aesthetic energies onto herself. What can save our hero from what Lawrence calls "knowledge in dissolution, the African knowledge," not to mention "knowledge such as the beetles have"? Although living with two wives would be allowed "in Africa if I was registered Mohammedan" (144), David increasingly sees Catherine as neurotically flaunting her economic support of him and complaining either that she is not allowed to read the stories she has financed or labeling them "bestial" and "horrible" (157). But as he resumes work on his writing David luckily finds a way back to a reborn masculininity, conveniently allowing "Hemingway to play out the familiar male fantasy of converting a lesbian to another way of sexuality" (Comley and Scholes, 97). To add piquancy to David's victory, he does so by winning Marita away from Catherine, reestablishing as normative his heterosexuality as well as his imaginative autonomy, and banishing Catherine to the hinterlands where any Eve turned Lilith belongs.

No wonder that Marita happily recovers from (sick) homosexuality to attain (sound) heterosexuality. To begin with, she herself views lesbianism as "only something girls do because they have nothing better" (120). So as to confirm a Victorian diagnosis of homosexuality as masturbatory self-abuse, Catherine's sexual experimentation, affecting her like a drug, leaves her feeling empty, dead, hollow, exhausted. Headed for a breakdown, Hemingway's heroine inhabits a wired, weird world in which colors are too bright, time seems speeded up, and bouts of hectic alcoholism follow enervating periods of lassitude. Her nemesis is soon nicknamed "Heiress" and "Haya" ("the one who blushes, the modest one" (142)) by a David who sees where his future lies, for Marita serves as an antidotal, sacerdotal Mary to Catherine's transgressive Eve-turned-Lilith, making his fall a fortunate one indeed. Significantly, David rescues himself from mindless African dissolution by writing African tales reminiscent of Hemingway's own hunting tales and those of his major precursor, Rudyard Kipling. Indeed, the last quarter of the published version of *The Garden of Eden* progresses by splicing the main plot of the novel—Catherine's breakdowns, her increasing hostility toward David's writing and his affair with Marita, her climactic burning of the only copy of his writing, and her abject note on leaving the newly constituted couple—with David's interpolated narrative about his father on an elephant hunt. Why does Hemingway shuttle the reader between a feminized Europe in an erotic present and a masculine Africa in an adventurous past?

The autobiographical story upon which David works so assiduously concerns a young boy's trip with his father and his father's native guide, Juma, to track an ancient elephant that the soon repentant David and his dog, Kibo, had glimpsed one mystic night in the moonlight: "The bull wasn't doing anyone any harm and now we've tracked him to where he came to see his dead friend and now we're going to kill him. It's my fault. I betrayed him" (181). The adult David completes "a very young boy's story" by noting about his central character, "The elephant was his hero now as his father had been for a long time" (201). Why does the murder of the elephant in the interpolated tale lead directly to Catherine's burning of David's manuscripts in the main narrative and her expulsion from his future?[37] Does David's participation in the crime of (writing about) murdering the elephant somehow lead to punishment exacted by Catherine, an act which in turn requires her own annihilation?

Catherine hints at a wildness she shares with the ancient, huge mammal in an excised portion of the manuscript: "you are lucky to have a wife that is a wild animal instead of a domestic animal," she informs David (Ms. 1/1/23–24). Like the elephant, hunted for his ivory tusks, "the darkest white girl in the world," who sports hair so blond it looks "just like ivory" (169) and who ascribes her ability to get dark to her "lion color" (30), seems doomed. After David the writer records the murder of the elephant, Catherine returns to act "for" the repressed, destroying David's tale. She merits her own destruction because she represents the male author's dependency upon dangerously unmanning sources of inspiration. Just as the young boy David loved but learned to accept his complicity in the betrayal of the elephant, the grown-up David loves but learns he must vanquish his "African girl." Presenting a portrait of the artist as colonizer, Hemingway admits with some guilt his reliance on an Otherness with which he cannot abide: African wilderness/sexual wildness furnish the aphrodisiac to fuel the writing that sentences them to extermination.

Yet, unlike David, who cannot be persuaded by Catherine to write about her escapades, Hemingway *does* focus much of his novel on Catherine. In so doing and also by making David's African tale so nostalgic, Hemingway gains several degrees of distance from his hero. Closer to the self-consciously ersatz "African girl," Hemingway marks his awareness of a primitivism constructed by the Western imagination and therefore already compromised by producing David's tale as a parodically formulaic initiation story. Like Catherine, Hemingway mourned a father dead by suicide, experienced cross-dressing that turned him into an androgynous twin (of his sister), and believed that good writers should destroy much of their writing. Indeed, just as Catherine recalls Catherine Earnshaw of *Wuthering Heights* in her passionate belief that she is David, David is Catherine and so is Hemingway himself, who uses Catherine's female gender to camouflage the ways she encodes his own fascination with sexual transgression. The African queen of *The Garden of Eden* is queer, Hemingway's drag persona. (Paradoxically, such a lesbian self-image can be understood as oddly bracing Hemingway's view of his heterosexuality as if he were exclaiming "even if I were a woman, I'd still desire women—not men, never men.")

Dramatizing Hemingway's contradictory version of himself as imperialist and as lesbian, *The Garden of Eden* remains surprisingly fair-minded in its analysis of the sexual antagonism of its protagonists. Catherine at her most seductively sinister lavishes attention on David—"Let me feel your hair girl . . . . you have lovely lips. Shut your eyes girl"—so as to teach him "it isn't so easy to be a girl if you're really one. If you really feel things" (86). To some extent, then, both the race- and the sexchange are contextualized by her wish to write or paint and her knowledge that she cannot execute her aesthetic ambitions, except on herself. Being typed as a girl means being "a god damned bore" as well as "Scenes, hysteria, false accusations, temperament" (70), so her crafty plots reflect her nervous, nihilistic efforts to circumvent the creative nullity she experiences as a woman.[38]

Black envy in *The Garden of Eden* is pen and penis (not phallus) envy; Catherine's wish to become the darkest white girl merges with her desire to become her husband's twin, depraved seducer, or Devil (not her husband's husband, father, or God). Yet because body parts other than the penis—hands, hair, skin—as well as symbolic accoutrements—a car, a female lover, money—allow her to appropriate masculine powers, it may be possible to appraise Catherine's response to the narcissistic wound of femininity as a quest not for a penis and not for a phallus (which Lacan associates with law, authority, legitimacy) but for an illicit substitute that disguises that wound while still leaving a trace of its threat.[39] This formulation would identify blackness as a fetish—a sexually overvalued part of the body or inanimate object—just as it is in the photographs of Man Ray and the photomontages of Hannah Höch. Not a phallic symbol, a fetish is a substitute for the missing penis, which is exciting precisely because it is "seen as authentically different from the missing penis" (Bersani and Dutoit, 68). Blackness as a fetish gives Catherine something comparable to, evocative of, but different from male genitalia.

In any case, however, Hemingway ultimately punishes Catherine's Satanic ambition, for he retains the conventional notion that the white man with a penis should have the phallus or the fetish, the signifying power and authority. Even at her darkest Catherine remains merely a male manqué, an imitation boy (Peter) who will never grow into a man. Women's anxiety about powerlessness takes a quite different turn in Lois Gould's more surrealistic *A Sea-Change* whose heroine also dreams of aligning herself with a black masculinity equal to—but not identical with—the father's. Like Rivière's patient and Hemingway's Catherine, Gould's central character wishes to become the black man to complete the castration of the white father. But the female novelist grants this wish, depicting her white heroine undergoing a fully actualized sex- and racechange. Whether or not Gould read Hemingway's short story "The Sea Change" (1938)—an encapsulated version of *The Garden of Eden* about a tanned, short-haired young woman's decision to leave her male partner for another woman as well as his helpless chagrin at this turn of events—Gould's *Sea-Change* deflates Hemingway's fantasy of converting the sick lesbian into a healthy heterosexual, meditating instead on the threat to masculine perogative racially transgressive sexchanges inaugurate.[40]

Gould's Jessie Waterman is imbued with fury generated by envy of men and feminine self-loathing. In a dreamlike flashback of a scene that may or may not have actually occurred but that recurs throughout the narrative, Jessie remembers being subjected to the terrifying breaking and entering of a *b*lack *g*unman she calls B.G. What horrifies her about the episode is her terror when B.G. caressed her breasts with his gun as well as her physical responsiveness when she followed his orders and embraced it with her mouth, felt it entering her smoothly, "sliding it, so easily, as if into a lubricated holster" (83), calling it by her husband's name, Roy (from *roi*, French for king). The twofold effect of the nightmarish experience involves a confusion of cocked gun and gunning cock, of rapist and husband, of sex and death: "Roy had come Ah, Jessie, Ahh, red-and-black, her blood and B.G.'s cock/gun Roy had come exploding finally Ah Jessie Ahh" (122). The conflation of masculinity with femicidal sadism, femininity with masochistic victimization inevitably results in a revulsion against heterosexuality. Because the phallus/penis/gun—"Loaded aiming at you"—slips into the place of the camera which previously ruled Jessie's modeling career, she becomes increasingly alienated by the condescending, philandering husband—"a relic from the golden age of misogyny" (30)—who had kept her in this job and who (in some of the surrealistic retellings of the primal scene) colludes with B.G. in the rape.

But if the initial reaction to the haunting assault is revulsion, the more lasting is a mounting desire for retaliation which triggers a grotesque rebirth, a schizophrenic twinning along the lines of the brutal Mr. Hyde's emergence out of the benevolent Dr. Jekyll. (That one film version of Stevenson's Gothic tale performs a racechange on Mr. Hyde helps to explain the novella's influence on *A Sea-Change*, as do more contemporary interpretations of its doubling as an encoded approach to homosexual liasons.[41]) Described as "nursing her secret, which grew inside her like a tumor or a monstrous child" (24), Jessie (bearing her embryonic alter-ego) moves to remote Andrea Island with her daughter, Robin, and her stepdaughter Diane. Although the old vulnerable Jessie-identity seems "rooted, attached like a vestigial organ" (25), the new hardened B.G.-identity responds to the freedom of her commuting husband's removal by annihilating the "Soft, pliant core that would yield, would give way" (104). Besides the body-building exercising in which she devotedly engages, the hurricane Minerva fosters the evolution of Jessie into B.G. Named after the goddess of war, the storm turns Jessie into the veteran B.G. on an island named for andro or male.[42] Indeed, its fury obviously functions as the objective correlative of Jessie *Waterman*'s wish for a "real female weapon," like "quakes, volcanoes, whirlpools, cyclones. Even ocean currents. Powerful sucking devices in a female form" (47).

What actually transforms Jessie racially and sexually is a repetition of the act of rape—a reenactment with Jessie in control, first positioning herself again in the position of the raped victim and then in the place of the raping victimizer. At the beginning of this process, she engages the attentions of her friend Kate by trying out various sadistic erotic advances. As her attraction to Roy indicates, Kate stands for an earlier, more submissive version of Jessie. But by kissing Jessie's breasts, the enthralled Kate can still call the "skeleton" feminine Jessie out of the "closet" that the black gunman B.G. fears he has become (111). To prove B.G. more than just a closet, Jessie first notes that Kate seems attracted by the temporarily waylaid coastguardsman Leo Bailey (and even more fascinated when she discovers he had participated once in a gang bang). Then Jessie sets up a *ménage à trois*. Getting Kate so drunk that she passes out, Jessie impersonates her friend, urging Bailey to engage in "hate-fucking" her "Hard, and cold, and very fast" until Jessie "tore open beneath him, until he broke her like a cheap toy" (120–1). Because this murderous act kills off the feminine Jessie, the person who emerges "would never again perceive the touch of her body, of her breasts, as an assault. . . . Here I am, B.G." (121).

Breaking into Kate's room, like entering Kate's body, gives B.G. his identity: "Slip in through the narrow opening of the sliding glass door. He would like the feel of that, the tightness squeezing him" (129). Out of the closet, Gould's violent White Negro is beyond the pale, something like Hyde in his demonic dedication to aggression. Using his gun on Kate as it had been used on Jessie, B.G. then holds it up to Leo Bailey's face: "Clean it for me, Surfman. Leo Bailey did that too" (134). Thus Jessie as the black gunman gets Leo Bailey to become complicitious in precisely the mysterious way Roy had been earlier and in the process blackmails the coastguardsman to secrecy. Displaying a satanic aggression that silences white men and women, B.G. talks black: "Aint no *but*, man" (134), he tells Leo; "I don't study about love, baby. I just know what I got to have to make it" (144), he whispers to Kate. An incarnation of precisely the sexual symbolism Baldwin decried, B.G. embodies the ferocity of Jessie Waterman's hatred of her earlier femininity, her leaping into "a *spade-bag*" not substantially different from the one that so attracted Terry Southern's hero.

With daughter and stepdaughter in tow, relocating to the even more remote Reef Island under cover of the supposed demise of Mrs. Jessie Waterman, the black gunman who names himself *Kil*roy reconstitutes his family, which goes unrecognized by the searching Roy. Whereas Hemingway's Catherine remains at best an imitation boy, Gould's B.G. becomes a stud powerful enough to compete successfully with the white patriarch. An anti-king in his liminal realm, the black, male Jessie inhabits a borderline place in culture, an outlaw who survives by virtue of his commitment to a control he can exert over a succession of women who fill in for the absent Kate. At the close of the novel, B.G. is joined by Kate, who embraces thralldom as her fate. In this triumphant sado-masochistic consummation, Gould bleakly suggests that the sea-change of sex- and racechange constitutes no change in gender arrangements at all. Thus *A Sea-Change* concurs with Jane Gallop's quip, "Penis, phallus—same difference." Black man, white man—same difference too. What does it mean that Jessie's anxieties about masculinity and revulsion against normative heterosexuality have issued in racechanging scenarios that ultimately restore the most sadomasochistic form of heterosexual coupling as well as the founding couple of racist propaganda: the black male rapist, white female victim?

The title of Gould's novel refers the reader to its epigraph about the physiological sexchanges of coral-reef fish in warm coastal areas; however, like Hemingway's "The Sea Change" it also invokes Shakespeare's *Tempest* (1623), a play about a number of transformations on a magical island and in particular a song of

Ariel's that T. S. Eliot had placed at the center of *The Waste Land* (1922) and Sylvia Plath had located at the center of her book of verse *Ariel* (1965):

> Full fathom five thy father lies,
> Of his bones are coral made;
> Those are pearls that were his eyes;
> Nothing of him that doth fade,
> But doth suffer a sea-change
> Into something rich and strange.
> Sea-nymphs hourly ring his knell . . . (I.ii.397–404)

Gould, who clearly shared Eliot's and Plath's fascination with transformation, remained particularly absorbed by the issue of domination. The novelist uses the patriarchal Roy and the renegade B.G. to call attention to Prospero's rule in Shakespeare's play, to Caliban's servitude to Prospero, and to the relationship between that subordination and rape fantasies. After the magus robbed Caliban of his inheritance (the island which belonged to Caliban's mother, Sycorax), the native attempted to use sexual assault to take revenge against his colonizer, or so Prospero claims. His accusation—"thou didst seek to violate / The honour of my child"—meets with Caliban's implicit admission of guilt: "O ho, O ho! would't had been done! / Thou didst prevent me—I had peopled else / This isle with Calibans" (I.ii.346–51).[43]

Like Shakespeare, Gould may be found guilty of further cementing the chains that link ethnic difference with animality and a fearsome sexual aggression. Like Caliban, an inferior being "on whose nature / Nurture can never stick" (IV.i.188–9), B.G. remains stubbornly unregenerate, cursing the tyranny that brutalizes him, seeking a cruel revenge against the white patriarch by seizing the women men like Roy control. Unlike Shakespeare, though, Gould presents the native/rapist as a *white* fantasy. To this extent, her meditation on racechange in *A Sea-Change* uncovers the secret longing that imbues even the most racist imaginings of the black Other. Robert Browning used the figure of "Caliban upon Setebos" (1864) to make a similar point. His Caliban, musing upon the God who made him, illuminates the dynamics of creation that impelled Shakespeare to create Caliban but that also motivates whites to construct blackness in the shape of, say, B.G.:

> He would not make what he mislikes or slights,
> An eyesore to Him, or not worth His pains:
> But did, in envy, listlessness, or sport,
> Make what Himself would fain, in a manner, be—
> Weaker in most points, stronger in a few,
> Worthy, and yet mere playthings all the while,
> Things He admires and mocks too—that is it. (ll. 59–65)

If B.G. embodies what Lois Gould and her heroine would fain be, he establishes not only the strength of their revulsion against feminization but also the allure of the black rogue who can compete through sheer willfulness and badness with the patriarchal power of the white father. Yet since B.G. takes the place of Roy in the ownership of Kate, he proves that, even when the white father is buried five fathoms deep down in death, he subsists through psychic metamorphoses that continue to haunt the minds not only of men but also of women. Since nothing of the patriarch fades—he suffers a sea-change only when played in blackface by a white woman—B.G./Jessie and Kate as a couple hardly adumbrate a brave new world. On the one hand, the central female characters of Hemingway and Gould may simply be understood as a sign of these authors' homophobic, racist identification of white lesbians and black men with sick sadism. On the other, to the extent that both Catherine and Jessie are motivated to forge their plots about lesbianism and blackness because of their revulsion against the passivity and vulnerability they associate with white femininity, they may illuminate one racialized psychological strain that turns erotic love toward domination.[44]

Racechange fantasies, which put both Catherine and Jessie in touch with taboo, masculine impulses, allow Hemingway and Gould to elaborate upon the logic of Fanon, who views "the Negro" as "the predestined depository" of the white girl's aggression, arguing that "the fantasy of rape by a Negro is a variation of this emotion: 'I wish the Negro would rip me open as I would have ripped a woman open'" (179). Unfortunately, however, Fanon simply counters the debilitating myth of the black rapist with the equally disturbing myth of the white woman's desire to be raped (Fuss, *Identification Papers*, 156). Both Hemingway and Gould ground the desire to be a rapist and the desire to be raped in their female characters' hatred of white femininity. In *The Garden of Eden* and *A Sea-Change*, the logic goes something like this: White women's abhorrence of feminization leads to a projection of that hatred onto the penis-not-a-phallus and a fantasy of becoming the dark Third or Intermediate Sex. What this analysis adds to Fanon's is the idea that the Negro is the depository of the white girl's conflicted aggression against her own femininity.

Like Freud, Hemingway and Gould connect lesbianism with the wish for a penis or a penis substitute. But Freud's propensity to see "the lesbian as masculine solves the problem of lesbian sexuality by rendering it as essentially heterosexual" (Roof, *A Lure of Knowledge*, 211), whereas black envy—the wish for a black penis—creates a mixed figure in *The Garden of Eden* and *A Sea-Change*, for the lesbian is a woman who thinks she has an erotic power capable of successfully competing with—but not the same as—white men's. Still, to the extent that race triggers sexchanges and so functions to maintain difference (to allay anxieties about representing lesbian sameness), both Hemingway and Gould reiterate Freud's tendency to collapse lesbian sexuality into the heterosexual paradigm. Indeed, racechange as sexchange transforms lesbianism into heterosexuality: Instead of two women coupling, the portrait of lesbianism provided by Hemingway consists of dark "Peter" (Catherine) with "his girl" (David), just as Gould presents "B.G." (Jessie) with "his" girl (Kate). As Judith Roof has demonstrated using many other narratives, "the metaphorically perverse both threatens to short-circuit and leads toward a satisfying, very heterosexual closure" (*Come as You Are*, xxxiv).

Next to both novels' association of primitivism and deviancy, moreover, lurks the iconography of slavery—locks and chains, whips, head constraints and hoods, leather straps. In addition, the fact that slaves were forced to submit to sexual acts has imaginatively fused the sadomasochistic to racial impersonation, regardless of which role is adopted (since, as Gould points out, the parts of dominator and dominated can be switched). White female characters like Jessie and Kate, enthralled by the idea of a dominator, exhibit the masochism dramatized in a series of disturbing photographs of Nancy Cunard taken by Barbara Ker-Seymer, a German photographer, and recently brought to the attention of scholars by Jane Marcus.[45] Both the "solarizations" and the traditional shots display a starved creature Marcus terms "a white slave" whose neck is encircled by beaded necklaces that appear to strangle, bind, or leash her (Figs. 5.6 and 5.7). According to Marcus's analysis, this "reenactment of black slave bondage in the self-staging of [a] white body" should be read "as a site for political protest against racism" and not "as a perverse pornography": Cunard "really meant the performance of bondage to signify her political bonding with black culture" (42). Maybe.

However, if we interpret this racechanging figure more skeptically as Jessie Waterman at the start of her dreadful intimacy with B.G. or as Kate at the end of her equally appalling mating with Jessie-turned-B.G., then the mimicry of slavery Cunard performs stages the female White Negro's desirous encounter with the "*spade-rape bag*." Cunard's eroticizing of a master/slave psychology could be said to perpetuate racial and sexual scripts of thralldom that bequeath only the most degrading form of power to men, that of sexual domination; only the most demeaning form of submission to women, that of anorexic self-abasement. Although Gould's characters see the black man as a sadist while Cunard views the female slave as a masochist, both glamorize the sadomasochistic deviance of color.

Like the photos of Cunard, then, the conclusion of Gould's *A Sea-Change* implies that, as Sylvia Plath put it, "Every woman adores a Fascist, / The boot in the face, the brute / Brute heart of a brute like you" ("Daddy," l.48–50). Inveighing against "the black man who / Bit [her] pretty red heart in two," Plath is motivated by grief and rage to perform a racechange on the father to whom she remains enthralled even as she determines to plant "a stake in [his] fat black heart" (l.53–55, 76). Once again in the history of racechanging iconography, as it did in *The Jazz Singer*, Jewishness emerges to play an unforeseeable (if erratic) part, for Plath pits the black, male Nazi against the white, female Jew. Whereas Norman Mailer's and Saul Bellow's quite different engagements with the Negro construct the American Jew's masculinity, Jewishness is marked feminine in Plath's work. But all three writers continue to equate blackness with what Fanon called "the biological danger" of the penis, Jewishness with "the intellectual danger" of subjectivity itself.

Because "Peter" or "B.G." or the "black man who / Bit my pretty red heart in two" does not exist, white people will supply, invent, or become him. Addressing white fearful projections about the penis-not-a-phallus, Adrian Piper's cross-dressing performance in the early seventies, *Mythic Being*, included notes explaining how her Afro, bell bottoms, and dark glasses made her

> swagger, stride, lope, lower my eyebrows, raise my shoulders, sit with my legs wide apart on the subway, so as to accommodate my protruding genitalia. (Golden, 26)

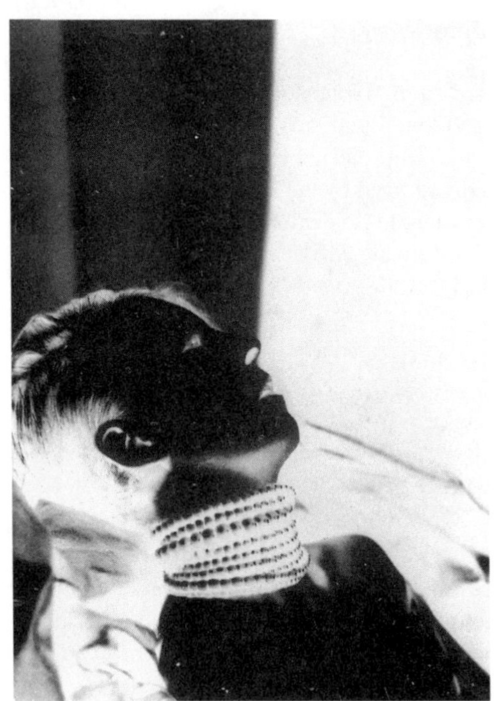

Figure 5.6 Barbara Ker-Seymer, Nancy Cunard solarization. Photography Collection, Harry Ransom Humanities Research Center, The University of Texas at Austin; courtesy of Barbara A. Roett.

Figure 5.7 (*Below*) Barbara Ker-Seymer, Nancy Cunard in neck gear. Photography Collection, Harry Ransom Humanities Research Center, The University of Texas at Austin; courtesy of Barbara A. Roett.

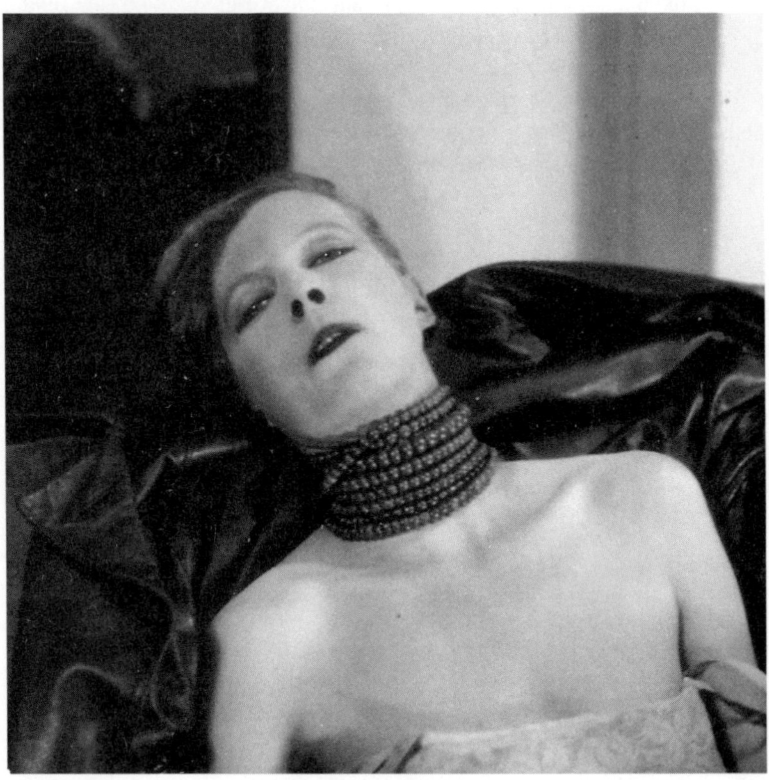

And the portrait of herself she created from *Mythic Being* contains the words "I embody everything you most hate and fear." Similarly, Piper's later installation *Four Intruders Plus Alarm Systems* (1980) projected slide and sound images of black men as interlopers, images predetermined by the same white fears and fantasies Toni Morrison addresses in her fiction (Golden, 26). Most pointedly, Morrison's *Sula* (1973) includes a speech by a male character who seems to be meditating on the consequences of the black "*spade-rape bag*" for black men:

> White men love you. They spend so much time worrying about your penis they forget their own. The only thing they want to do is cut off a nigger's privates. And if that ain't love and respect I don't know what is. And white women? They chase you all to every corner of the earth, feel for you under every bed. I knew a white woman wouldn't leave the house after 6 o'clock for fear one of you would snatch her. Now ain't that love? They think rape soon's they see you, and if they don't get the rape they looking for, they scream it anyway just so the search won't be in vain. (103)

Besides illuminating the reasons why O. J. Simpson's picture underwent a darkening and why, even more recently, Susan Smith depicted the "murderer" of the children she herself actually killed as a black man, the logic of such bitter testimony explains the sophisticated imagery of Bellow's *Mr. Sammler's Planet* and Mapplethorpe's "Man in Polyester Suit." As these and most of the other texts explored in this chapter prove, white fixation on the black penis has contributed not only to the blackmailing of the black man (the criminalizing of his sexuality) but also to the eclipse of the black woman, supplanting her from creative and critical view. Yet we will see in the next chapter that when she does come into focus, the African-American woman's image is less framed by an obsession with the magnetism of any one of her body parts, more focused on the question of who lays claim to the productions of her womb.

WHAT WILL THE MIXED CHILD DELIVER?

Conceiving Color Without Race

[T]he basic error of white comments about their own oppression is the assumption that they *know* the nature of their enslavement. This cannot be so, because if they really knew, they would liberate themselves by joining the revolution of the black community. They would destroy themselves and be born again as beautiful black people.

—James Cone

I almost felt the baby grow inside me, and I suddenly felt completely Black. . . . in that moment, walking down the street full of people who were miraculously unaware of the change in me, resting my hand lightly on my belly, I was as Black as anyone.

—Jane Lazarre

In my body were many bloods, some dark blood, all blended in the fire of six or more generations. I was, then, either a new type of man or the very oldest. . . . If I achieved greatness of human stature, then just to the degree that I did I would justify *all* the blood in me. If I proved worthless, then I would betray all.

—Jean Toomer

Shirley Temple Black and Bill Robinson White, a 1980 acrylic, is one of Robert Colescott's more sardonic experiments in racechange (see color insert). Picking berries on a garden path, a darkened Shirley and a lightened Bill pause to glance at each other, perhaps the moment before they will break out in a tap dance routine. As in so many of his other paintings, this picture converts characters traditionally portrayed as white into blacks, switching the races so as to ridicule, first, our assumptions about white hegemony in cultural scripts and, second, the caricaturing that infects almost all depictions of African Americans in mass-produced as well as elite art. Here the coincidence of Shirley Temple's married surname serves as Colescott's sly pretext for her racial metamorphosis. In a discussion of this painting recorded on the video *Robert Colescott: The One Two Punch* (1993), the artist explains that he was wondering what kind of society ours might have been if Shirley Temple had been black: What if America's sweetheart during the thirties were a little dark child?

Had we grown up with stories treasuring the sweetness of black children, Colescott's painting intimates, many of the other scripts that govern public and private life might have been less dangerous to the welfare of African Americans. Instead, of course, we expect to see the pampered white child at the center of a narrative in which she is waited on by the devoted black domestic. Shirley Temple frolicking with Bojangles typifies the coupling of white child/black adult-servant which is rendered so frequently that it has moved to the very center of American cultural history. From youthful Huck accompanied by Nigger Jim to adolescent Scarlett O'Hara costumed by her Mammy, the white youth attended by the black adult spells out a number of disturbing ideological lessons. Not only are blacks somehow childlike in their fawning dependency, but authority accrues to whiteness, which even at its most vulnerable and ignorant masters blackness. Were the tables turned, it would be whites who might have to struggle with anxieties about their insufficiency and debasement into a grateful servitude.

In part, Shirley Temple's whiteness can be attributed to the exclusion of blacks from the Blakean or Wordsworthian figure of the child as embodied wisdom, spontaneity, and joy, as if a people condemned to perpetual childishness must be robbed of childhood itself. Thus in *The Bluest Eye*, when Toni Morrison's outcast Pecola seeks the milk of human kindness reserved for a cherished offspring, she tries to lighten herself by drinking from a Shirley Temple cup. Loathing Shirley Temple, Pecola's healthier, less socialized friend, Claudia, believes instead that Bojangles is her friend, uncle, daddy, and that he "ought to have been soft-shoeing it and chuckling with" her (19). From the baby in the barn depicted in Renaissance paintings to *Alice in Wonderland* and the Bobbsey twins, from Valentine cupids and cherubs to the Snow Whites, Pinocchios, and Little Bo Peeps of fairy tales and nursery rhymes, the normative child of Western culture appears white (at least until quite recently).[1] If only inadvertently, the white child who figures as the protagonist in stories with a multiracial cast of characters attests to the centrality of the white race. Black mother surrogates could serve as wet nurses and mammies, black domestics could become "uncles" or "aunts"; however, they were supposed to lavish their attention on the well-being of the white heir apparent. Equally to the point, the beneficent surrogate parenting performed by the desexualized black caretaker drained away the threat of interracial sexuality (which might contaminate the "purity" of white lineage).

It is striking in this regard that, even though the racechanged Shirley Temple seems to grant Morrison's Claudia her wish of soft-shoeing it and chuckling with her very own Bojangles, Colescott's metamorphosed characters continue to suffer the consequences of racist imagery: Shirley Temple does not appear simply darkened, Bojangles simply lightened in skin tone.[2] Instead, racial transformation eroticizes the couple, draining away their innocence and infusing them with a vaguely perverse ribaldry. Why does the prancing Robinson White seem to be leering at the equally coquettish and rather hefty Temple Black? Does their berry picking hint at the saying "the darker the berry the sweeter the juice"? As one of the curators of Colescott's shows has remarked, "the older black man" had been so "effectively emasculated" by the Uncle Tom role as "to pose no sexual threat to American white females," but his racechange into a white fieldhand grants the Robinson figure potential virility (Sims, 5). At the same time, though, *is* Robinson simply whitened in Colescott's painting or does his lightening immediately jettison him into a minstrel role? In overalls—with the familiar gaping mouth, bowed legs, and glowing eyes—Colescott's Bill occupies a liminal position on the color line; whether a white man impersonating a black or a light-skinned black man, he ogles the dark child who grins back at him and together they illustrate an imagistic amplitude or physicalization that robs African-American girl children of their childhood. When the adorable Shirley Temple turns black, she devolves into soon-to-be gobbled up sexual food for a lecherous uncle-daddy. The one-two punch Colescott's work administers by switching the expected color of the child pertains to the shocking stories it uncovers about race and sex, a maneuver that male and female, black and white writers exploit in a curious narrative translation of Colescott's trope, namely the appearance of a child whose skin color appears unexpected or unprecedented, at odds with that of its parents.

Like Colescott, fiction writers from Kate Chopin and Jean Toomer to Gloria Naylor brood over the significance of the racechanged child in terms of sexuality, lineage, and cultural empowerment. What does it mean if the newborn baby looks visibly different from its parents, looks like it comes from another race? Would a white Mr. and Mrs. Temple feel about a mysteriously swarthy daughter that she decreased their value or even comprised an embarrassment that should be destroyed or disowned? What if the child attests to the amalgamation of races that had been declared not simply unwelcome but downright illegal? Until 1967 many states decreed interracial marriage a criminal act and its mixed-race offspring illegitimate.[3] In addition, the "one drop rule" meant that after the 1920 census all mulatto children were defined as black and thus disappeared as an identifiable group. Buttressing the "one drop rule" as well as many states' laws against miscegenation, turn-of-the-century eugenicists argued that "the result of the mixture of two races, in the long run, gives us a race reverting to the more ancient, generalized, and lower type. . . . The cross between a white man and a negro is a negro" (Doyle, 16). Thus, the mixed child produced by interracial relationships became conceptually inconceivable. As Colescott also hints, Shirley Temple has to be either white or black. In an autobiographical book published in 1994, Maureen Reddy, the white wife of a black man who writes about their children, points out that even today school applications, federal government documents, medical records, census reports, and job applications do not recognize "biracial" as a category (75).

Yet precisely a fascination with such a transgressive term shapes the way in which racechange played itself out in plots about the mixed child that surfaced repeatedly in twentieth-century fiction. This outlawed creature, according to Jane Lazarre, "has stalked the white nightmare for all of American history, born at times of transcending love, at others of twisted desire, a creature who threatens the boundaries we have drawn around ourselves—the hybrid" (*The Mother Knot*, 45).

Although Jean Toomer's denial of his African-American identity, his claim that "many bloods" ran in his veins, has been viewed as aberrant or retrograde,[4] the birth story of new breeds composed of mixed races appears with startling frequency possibly because it enabled both mainstream and African-American artists to meditate on the idea of color without race. Was that idea a nightmare or a dream come true?

In the interest of righting past wrongful thinking about miscegenation, one might hope that the dark infant demonized by white parents early in this period would reappear trailing clouds of glory later in the twentieth century, that the light-skinned child born to black parents would be dislodged from the center of their desires at the end of the century. And something like this paradigm shift does occur. Whereas early artists worry over the traditional problem of who will deliver the dark child, later ones consider the more fantastic, even apocalyptic forms of deliverance the dark child might hold out to or for society. Indeed, we shall see that the image of a white woman mothering, nursing, or tending the African-American baby eventually surfaced in imaginative literature as a sign of white efforts to offset a history of conflictual racial Othering. Nor is it surprising that the image of the unexpectedly colored infant has recently been so positively revalued because few people today are racially "pure," in any sense of that word. Not simply admonitions against choosing one identification over and against another, not merely vindications of the "mulatto" or "half-breed" previously shamed as a racial traitor, fictional meditations on the mixed child exploit racechange to elaborate upon Jean Toomer's awareness of how "many bloods" run through the veins of most people. At their most optimistic, some of these narratives—attempting to envision a post-racist time—celebrate the permeable boundaries between mother and hybrid child as a panracial antidote to racism, an intersubjective solution to the violence of a racist past.

Less predictable, though, are those black and white authors of the racechanged offspring who remain bleak about the redemptive possibilities of its subversive plot. For the multiracial child may inherit as its birthright only the lies, secrets, and silences that threaten not merely its well-being but its life and society's future. "To the Child, she held herself, her life, accountable" ("One Child," 362): The language in which Alice Walker praises the poet Muriel Rukeyser can be applied to the ethic adopted by most of the authors in this tradition, a maternal ethic which explains why so many of them are women. In contrast to most of the other race mutations studied in this book, the peculiar force of the child of a startling color depends upon a phenomenon neither chosen nor willed. The offspring's out-of-place, uncanny complexion means that racechange—not merely an impersonation, not volitional—ceases to be playful, speculative, or temporary and instead simply poses a challenge to a society organized in such a way as to deny the ambiguously raced child the familial space that accords personal and public identity. Since, as Fanon puts it, "the family is a miniature of the nation" (142), writers from Kate Chopin to Gloria Naylor resemble Rukeyser and Walker in finding in their elegiac writing about the racechanged child an alternative to the less constructive forms of rage that they feel at national injustices. Their accountability to the hybrid offspring (innocent but judged guilty) shapes their scathing portraits of family values based on racial taxonomies proved irrational, even vicious.

"Writing saved me," Walker explains, "from the sin and *inconvenience* of violence" ("One Child," 369). In the most embittered scripts, the racechanged baby taps the anger of African-American writers and the guilt of their white contemporaries, all of whom understand that, as Walker again puts it, "black children are to have less in their world so that . . . white children will have more" (374). Such anger and guilt are only enhanced by the secret the biracial infant holds, namely the lie commingled bloodlines put to historical accounts of a segregated culture. At their most optimistic, however, narratives about the racechanged baby hold out the promise of a redemptive transracial consciousness that does not merely mimic existing racial categories but transgressively traverses them. Taken together, then, stories about the mixed child hauntingly posit a variation on Jean Genet's assertion that "In white America the Blacks are the characters in which history is written. They are the ink that gives the white page its meaning" (*Prisoner of Love*, 213).[5] African Americans, according to the authors in this tradition, are the characters in which the genealogies of America were written in ink that most public or national histories attempted to blot out but that can be traced to discern different tellings of our common heritage.

The Color of Desire

Kate Chopin's 1892 story "Désirée's Baby" will serve as a touchstone for narrative use of the mixed-race child in this chapter because Chopin uses fairy-tale motifs and a set of ironic reversals to compose what amounts to multiple parables about interracial genealogy. This often anthologized tale turns on a shock administered to mother, father, and relatives when the most desirable of desired babies, born of a woman herself allegorically linked to desire, undergoes a racechange that transforms the infant from a valued beloved into an unwanted outcast. Each of the reversals that conclude Chopin's brilliant story (so similar to those devised by Maupassant and O'Henry) epitomizes alternative approaches to the narrative of the racechanged child. Yet in both ironic twists, the baby of desire and, indeed, desire itself remain doomed to extinction because they contradict warped definitions of the permissible in a segregated society. The clash between desire and the permissible plays itself out in the ironic contradictions between reproduction and the family. Family values which are firmly grounded in dualistic racial categories endanger life, liberty, and the pursuit of happiness, according to Chopin's tale, since a familial investment in racial dualism effectively murders desire (which knows no racial restrictions) as well as life itself.

The story begins with one Madame Valmonde who, going to visit Désirée and her baby, reflects back many years to Désirée herself as a toddler mysteriously found sleeping under a stone pillar. Madame Valmonde and her husband, accepting the foundling as a providential response to their childlessness, watched the girl grow "to be beautiful and gentle, affectionate and sincere."[6] With perfect fairy-tale logic, we are immediately told that eighteen years later, when Désirée stood before that very same stone pillar, she was immediately sighted by the aristocratic Armand Aubigny. Just returned from his early life and education in France, the young man deems Désirée the object of his desire. Despite her obscure origins and his own proud heritage, Armand determines on the marriage. Once this flashback account of past events ends, the visit of Madame Valmonde occurs and we are shown her consternation at looking at the infant: "This is not the baby! . . . . the child has grown, has changed," she exclaims.

Although at this point Désirée herself sees no transformation and remains delighted by her husband's pleasure at the appearance of a male offspring, soon she notices "an awful change in her husband's manner" as well as "an air of mystery among the blacks" toward whom his severity has increased. The inevitable scene of instruction occurs when the young mother watches her three-month-old baby being fanned by one of the children of a slave named La Blanche, a "little quadroon" boy. After Désirée "looked from her child to the boy who stood beside him, and back again; over and over," her "blood turned like ice in her veins, and a clammy moisture gathered upon her face." Asking her husband, "What does it mean?" Désirée is told "the child is not white; it means that you are not white." When she interjects that her hand is whiter than Armand's, he sneers, "As white as La Blanche's." The shocked wife's letter to her stepmother explaining, "I am not white. . . . I shall die" results in Madame Valmonde's loving offer of shelter; however, Désirée—feeling her husband's words stabbing her soul, wearing only a thin white garment—departs with her child, disappearing "among the reeds and willows that grew thick along the banks of the deep, sluggish bayou; and she did not come back again."

As Du Bois explained in "The Souls of White Folks" (the racechanged version of his more famous *Souls of Black Folk*), a "religion of whiteness" preaches that "whiteness is the ownership of the earth, forever and ever, Amen!" (339) so the now black Désirée must be expunged. The first, Ophelia-type ending of the story establishes the tale as a statement about the fatality of black maternity for mother and child. Désirée, engaged in an act of infanticide, commits suicide because her child's color reflects back, as in a glass darkly, to teach her that her light epidermis conceals her "real" racial identity and because she understands that (in a slave economy) her infant follows the condition of the mother into the dispossession spelled by namelessness. Thus, Chopin foregrounds patrilineage to examine the exclusion of blacks from kinship, property, and identity. That Désirée was "nameless" when she arrived at the stone pillar, that Armand possesses "one of the oldest and proudest" of names in Louisiana, and that at first Armand delights in "a boy, to bear his name": All these demonstrate the legitimacy of the white man, as does Désirée's demotion to La Blanche, whose light skin (because on a "black"-defined person) exemplifies not purity so much as legal blankness.[7]

Since there is no space appointed for the mixed offspring or for the baby's double, Désirée herself, they leave the world of culture to merge into the anonymity of nature. Although a son, her nameless child is as cut off as she from any kinship system and thus he is disinherited and fatally ungendered.[8] Always a baby, he will never grow to become a boy or a man. A statement about slavery as the death not only of Désirée and her baby but of desire itself, Chopin's narrative attributes the destruction of desire to the racially marked limits of the idea of the family. The black baby proves that Armand defines the family not in terms of the reproduction of children or even inheritors but in terms of the production of whiteness; biological offspring designated as not white must be excluded from membership.[9] The racially mixed infant who is labeled black signifies the white father's sexual rights over black women and his economic control over mother and child as well as his repudiation of paternity; the racechanged baby embodies the African-American mother's physiological tie to the child as well as her inability to protect it.

But of course the tale Chopin picks up after the blank space on the page and the passage of several weeks revises the first ending of Désirée's expulsion as an outcast black by performing yet another racechange. Burning a cradle, a priceless layette, silk and velvet gowns, bonnets and gloves in a kind of funeral pyre, Armand fanatically sets out to purify the presumably polluted space of the plantation. As if his wife were a witch or sorceress, he annihilates the costume of culture that disguised Désirée's alien identity, itself a threat to the purity of his lineage. In an all-consuming rage, Armand also sets fire to the letters Désirée had sent him. Then he sees the remnant of an old letter from the same drawer, a letter from his mother to his father: "'I thank the good God for having so arranged our lives that our dear Armand will never know that his mother, who adores him, belongs to the race that is cursed with the brand of slavery.'" Reading becomes his undoing because Chopin seeks to link the act of reading writing with larger issues about the interpretation of physical features.

When earlier Armand had read the baby's dark complexion as a sign of Désirée's race, he assumed the baby's materiality was maternal while its symbolic place in society was paternal. Then, banishing Désirée and her baby, he acted on what Patricia Yaeger calls "the temporal distance between insemination and parturition," which is an equally immense conceptual distance, as suggested by the adage "Mama's baby, Papa's maybe" (285). In other words, Armand saw visible links between Désirée and the baby, not between the infant and himself. If, as James Joyce put it, "paternity is a legal fiction," it could be abrogated; the child was effectively divorced by Armand when he cast Désirée out. Ironically, though, Armand discovers that he has fashioned a destiny for Désirée more justly suited to himself. Even more ironic, he suffers the fate of becoming Désirée's baby (just as his wife had in the earlier ending) at the moment he understands himself to be guilty of the "brand" he attaches to his offspring. Not the child, but he is born of a white man and a black woman. As readers, now, we reinterpret his earlier life in France as a sign of (what else?) the illicit sexuality of his parents. Visual as well as familial markers function so ambiguously that a pale wife has been defined as black while a dark husband has been taken to be white. The end of the tale effectively divides physiology from race, complexion from origin, making the visual unreliable. Indeed, though many readers assume that Armand's black matrilineage somehow turns Désirée white, the race of Chopin's heroine remains stubbornly indeterminate. Notwithstanding the predilection of most interpreters of the narrative, there is no logical reason to assume that since Armand is black, Désirée must be white.[10]

Because of that indeterminacy, "Désirée's Baby" manages to encapsulate a cluster of twentieth-century scripts about the dark child whose skin color does not match that of his parents: (1) narratives about white fathers and black mothers; (2) narratives about racially indeterminate women (who ought not become mothers); (3) narratives about black fathers and white mothers. As in the various conclusions of "Désirée's Baby," until very recently most artists depict the mixed offspring expelled from the human community or sentenced to undeserved suffering and almost certain death. As in its first ending, moreover, the majority of stories about biological hybridity have tended to center on the baby born of a white father and a black mother (to which this chapter will next turn). For Armand's original supposition has remained the normative one; the belief that the dark baby must be conceived within the black maternal body was a logic determined by the economy of slavery in which white masters established sexual rights over black female slaves. As if taking revenge for the innocent but helpless infant, Chopin's plot punishes Armand for his murderous arrogance and the punishment fits the crime. But vengeance may be carried out by hybrid characters themselves when the baby grows up to wage war against the white father who gives even as he denies love to the mother, life to the child.

Oedipal Rage Against the White Father

Although Ann Douglas has argued that "Freud's theories of what he called 'the family romance,' the tortured triangle of mother, father, and child that produces the Oedipus complex, had little to do with the African-American experience" (95), stories about the biracial child born of a white father and a black mother repeatedly return to Oedipal struggles.[11] Both white and black writers understand that the annihilation of desire dictated by the family's romance with white lineage necessarily breeds retaliatory fantasies in the dispossessed offspring; however, the plots they fashion respond differently to the dissonant appearance of the child born into a family in which it does not fit. Whereas such white writers as Mark Twain and William Faulkner reject or put off the promise of the biracial offspring who poses a threat to the white family, the African-American authors Marita Bonner and Langston Hughes indict a racist system which damages or imperils the future such children promise to bring into being.

Twain's *Pudd'nhead Wilson* provides a paradigm of the Oedipal rage for revenge instilled in the biracial son of a black single mother. The pale complexion of Twain's central character here, the light-skinned Tom who was born to the slave Roxy and switched with her master's heir in infancy, gives his mother the opportunity to save him from slavery. Pampered as his wealthy uncle's inheritor, Tom exhibits all the character flaws instilled by faulty upbringing, although Twain's ambiguous story also hints that the immorality of this cowardly liar and sneak should be attributed to a "native viciousness" (20) related to his genetic background. Whether because of nurture or nature, at a climactic point in the novel Tom blackens his face with burnt cork, arms himself with an Indian knife, creeps downstairs into his surrogate father's study to steal his money, and reacts quickly to hearing the old man's cries of help: "Without hesitation he drove the knife home—and was free" (94), a phrase that expresses his Oedipal revenge against the man who stands in the place of his father, the authority whom he seeks to supplant. That even the best of white fathers jeopardizes mother and child by means of his power of excommunicating them from (the security of) the family is what fosters interracial hatred and intergenerational rivalry.[12]

Far more equivocal about what the ex-slave Harriet Jacobs called the "tangled skeins" of "the genealogies of slavery" (121), William Faulkner examines the psychology of Twain's position when he considers the reasons why the white family represses the mixed child who threatens if not the father directly then the old patrilineal ways. The story "Delta Autumn" in *Go Down Moses* (1942) evocatively presents a woman who appears to be white, who turns black before the eyes of the aging Isaac (Ike) McCaslin, and who holds in her arms a biracial baby (whose father is McCaslin's white relative Roth Edmonds). Though she sounds like "a Northerner" (343), the mysterious mother mentions an aunt taking in washing, thereby providing a clue that leads Ike to look at "the pale lips, the skin pallid and dead-looking yet not ill, the dark and tragic and foreknowing eyes" and proclaim her "a nigger"; in the same passage, he also thinks about inter-racial unions, "*Maybe in a thousand or two thousand years in America, . . . but not now!*" (344).

The blanket-swaddled bundle must be trundled off, along with the woman who is paid to leave and told to marry a black man. That Ike has divested himself of his inheritance in order to expiate the sins of his grandfather—who begot a child upon his own slave daughter—makes this act exceptionally ironic. Horrified by a social order in which white privilege shapes ownership of property, family, and law, the compensation Ike McCaslin offers mother and child nevertheless remains only money, exactly the reparation his grandfather profferred to his biracial offspring as a way of paying them off for disowning them: Cash *"was cheaper than saying My son to a nigger . . . "* ("The Bear," 258). Although Faulkner's central character has renounced his white inheritance as contaminated, Ike McCaslin's withdrawal from the nameless young woman—herself a living embodiment of his grandfather's miscegenation—dramatizes his continued entrapment in a shameful past that has not paid adequate restitution. Thus, the mother of "Delta Autumn" carries not only the baby but the moral weight of the tale.[13] Not accepting the infant that would bring the bifurcated lines of the family together means that Faulkner's representative patriarch is doomed to remain entrapped in an exhausted, guilty past.

If in different ways Twain and Faulkner make the family the victim of the out-of-place child, African-American authors sympathize with the rage of the child against a familial system that dispossesses, or so the rivalrous feelings expressed in a poem entitled "Mulatto" (1925) by Claude McKay suggest:

> Because I am the white man's son—his own,
> Bearing his bastard birth-mark on my face,
> I will dispute his title to his throne,
> Forever fight him for my rightful place.

As in Twain's novel, at the end of McKay's poem the speaker is spurred on by hate to determine on the murder of his father:

> When falls the hour I shall not hesitate
> Into my father's heart to plunge the knife
> To gain the utmost freedom that is life. (*Passion*, 126)

Two contemporaries of McKay's, Marita Bonner and Langston Hughes, published racialized revisions of the Oedipal story that examine the patricidal anger of a mulatto child. In particular, Bonner's "One Boy's Story" (1927) almost reads like an allegory about the self-destructiveness this author presents as paradigmatic in all biracial boys' psychosexual development.

The eleven-year-old child who is the central character of Bonner's resonant narrative, Donald Gage, lives with his seamstress mother, dimly aware of their liminal status as people of color in the white town. Although he knows one of her customers, a childless Mrs. Swyburne, observes him sadly, wishing she could have a son just like him, the well-behaved Donald refrains from explaining she cannot, "Cause I'm colored and you aren't" (80). Visits from Mr. Swyburne perplex him, but the books he brings intrigue the boy who becomes especially absorbed by tales about "Orestes who went home from the Trojan War and found his mother had married his father's brother so he killed them" and "about Oedipus—a Greek too—who put out his eyes to hurt himself because he killed his father and married his mother by mistake" (81–82). In response to the child's fascination with epic heroes, Mr. Swyburne proudly exclaims "he has the blood" and the reader understands—even though Donald does not yet—that the white man is his biological father and that his mother is trying to extricate herself from the ongoing relationship she has maintained with him.

When Mrs. Gage's vain attempts to break away from the white father of her son issue in a fight with Swyburne that is witnessed by Donald, he takes out his slingshot and aims a stone that kills the man. Less like David stalking Goliath, more like Oedipus who unwittingly murdered his father at the crossroads and equally unknowingly embraced his mother, Donald finds the touch of his mother fatal. Her hold impales him on her breast pin, which first scratches his mouth and then sticks into his tongue. The resulting infection means that to save his life he will have to lose his tongue and the ability to speak. About the "black stump" in his mouth, "shaped like a forked whip," Donald sometimes pretends, "I am Orestes with the Furies' whips in my mouth for killing a man. . . . I am Oedipus and . . . I cut it out for killing my own father" (91). But what Bonner best captures in this grotesque tale is the unmanning of Donald. A sign of castration, the cut-off tongue links Donald not only to the maimed yet heroic Oedipus and Orestes but also to the silenced, raped Philomel (whose tongue is cut so she cannot accuse her powerful rapist, a king).

Just as Désirée's baby never grows up, "One Boy's Story" tells the narrator's story of remaining a lost boy.[14] From its very first sentence—"I'm glad they got me shut up in here"—to its conclusion, Donald is trapped and silenced by a father who lays claim to his mother but relinquishes any familial tie. The Oedipal crisis cannot be resolved because the biological father refuses to perform the societal function of the father—refuses, that is, to provide the name, property, status, home, protection, or education that would enable the son to secede him. The story of the son who cannot become a man ends not only with patricidal fury but with a fatal identification with the African-American mother who—despite her loving kindness—inflicts a wounding dispossession. At the end, the hybridity of Bonner's central character breeds self-consuming rage as well as painfully enforced silence: "I am bearing my Furies and my clipped tongue like a Swyburne and a Gage—'cause I am both of them" (91).

Langston Hughes's historical play *Mulatto: A Tragedy of the Deep South* (1931)—like the story "Father and Son" (1933) based on it—turns on exactly the psychosexual dynamic described by Twain, McKay, and Bonner, a variation on the theme of the mulatto tragically doomed to illegitimacy and schizophrenia. As such critics as Judith Berzon, Werner Sollors, and Heather Hathaway have pointed out, Greek themes of incest and obscure familial origins accrue in American literature to melodramas of the "tragic mulatto" in a racially divided society. Hughes' Bert, the mixed son of Colonel Norwood with "proud thin features like his father's," finds himself treated as his father's slave (2). His mother, the black housekeeper on the plantation and mistress of Colonel Norwood, becomes convinced their son is mad when he grandly struts about asking, "Isn't this my old man's house? Ain't I his son and heir?" (15). Although he repeatedly exclaims, "I'm not a nigger, Colonel Tom. I'm your son," the master of the plantation insists, "Nigger women don't know the fathers. You're a bastard" (23). Earlier in their lives, too, the conflict of father and son occurred over naming. Bert received his first physical punishment when the Colonel "beat him for callin' him 'papa'" (14). Their struggle escalates until the son murders his father and then commits suicide to escape a lynching mob.

According to his mother, Cora, Bert represents countless others: "White mens, and colored womens, and little bastard chilluns—that's de old way of de South— . . . mixtries, mixtries" (30–31); mixes of blood, mixed-up ancestries, mysterious (family) trees. The son in Hughes's play dies on his mother's bed, arrested in the maternal realm, no less fatally divided from the symbolic order of (white) masculine legitimacy than Bonner's Donald. Named after the mythic Greek maiden abducted and raped by the god of the underworld, Cora is right that Bert stands for other doomed characters, even in Hughes's own *oeuvre*. The tormented figure of Hughes's poem "Mulatto" (1927), for example, speaks lines that echo those of Bert—*"I am your son, white man!"*—while the father sounds like Colonel Norwood: *"You are my son! / Like hell!"* (100). Similarly, the speaker of the poem "Cross" (1925), who is "neither white nor black," looks upon his old man's death "in a fine big house" and his mother's "in a shack," wondering not only where he will die but how he can live in the doublecross of his biracial inheritance (58–59).

To "mixtries," the white father must seem a little more than kin, but less than kind. Whether murdered, maddened, ungendered, or simply expelled from the human community, the biracial offspring in narratives about the white father/black mother remains disinherited, hidden from public history, a shameful burden or secret.[15] In a novel entitled *Kindred* (1979) that looks back on American slavery, Octavia E. Butler weighs the origins of the biracial child in illegitimacy and rape against what Jacobs called the "tangled skeins" of slavery's ongoing genealogies. A curious blend of historical slave narrative and science-fiction time travel, the work features a contemporary black woman named Dana who shuttles between southern California in the 1970s and an antebellum plantation in Maryland. In particular, she is snatched back to the past so as to rescue her white progenitor, slave owner Rufus Weylin, who must live and mate with his slave Alice Greenwood until their child Hagar is born. That it is Hagar who will give birth to a lineage (eventuating ultimately in the birth of Dana) evokes the biblical slave-girl Hagar as a prototypical black single mother: Used by Abraham as a surrogate when his wife Sarah is sterile, Hagar is expelled with her illegitimate son Ishmael.[16] As a genealogical statement, *Kindred* portrays the one bit of hope it proffers when—after the death by hanging of Alice—her children begin to call Rufus "Daddy" (253), a sign of his new willingness to acknowledge familial ties that in turn allows Dana to win for them certificates of freedom. Despite the family's romance with whiteness, American history is written in the ink of mated (not married) black and white characters.[17]

Racial Ambiguity and (Childless) Prostitution

If we turn away from Armand's conventional idea of the narrative and toward the second conclusion of "Désirée's Baby," Chopin's far less traditional ending remains more openly ambiguous than her first, for though we presumably know that Armand is the black father of the mixed child, we remain unsure about Désirée's racial background. In this regard, the story resists racial categories altogether. The "dark" baby and father have undergone a racechange from white to black; however, the orphan Désirée remains a figure as nebulous and elusive as desire itself. We had thought her black when she departed for the sluggish bayou; we may have labeled her white when the dark color of her baby was assumed to be the result of Armand's black mother; ultimately, however, we cannot ascertain her own lineage and the baby's dark color may be derived from both parents' mysteriously distant or unknown African lineage.

Perhaps, like the author of a recent autobiography entitled *Notes of a White Black Woman*, Désirée would describe herself as "living on the margins of race" because she believes herself to be "a black American with white skin"; or perhaps Désirée would describe herself as "living on the margins of race" because she assumes herself to be outcast as a white woman who has entered into a sexual relationship with "a black American with white skin" (Scales-Trent, 7). In either case, her indeterminate status means that a definitively color-coded culture must deny her maternal status since her offspring threatens to contaminate the racial purity of white lineage. The racially mutable figure of Désirée, destined at the end to a kind of perpetual oscillation or an unending series of racechanges, establishes a curious link between the white woman defined as illegitimate in her sexuality and the African-American woman, the fallen and the black female, because to bear an unexpectedly colored baby is to register oneself as fallen or sexual—an available black woman, a degenerate white woman—and thus (paradoxically) unfit for motherhood. When doubled with black women—as two potential aspects of one self or as mistress and maid—white women's eroticism, lawlessness, and primitivism are multiplied. For the cultural assumption remained, as one widely read nineteenth-century natural historian put it, that "Negresses carry voluptuousness to a degree of lascivity unknown in [the European] climate."[18]

In its protest against the damning of biracial affiliations and its radical refusal to spell out the secret of Désirée's genealogy, Chopin's tale resembles Charles Chesnutt's "White Weeds" (1974), a story unpublished in his lifetime which also insists on the unstable racial identity of its heroine. Indeed, a female character of obscure origins who is about to be married to an established Professor Carson of Danforth University functions in Chesnutt's narrative as if she were the nemesis Chopin's Désirée might have desired for Armand. The story evolves as a series of mysterious vignettes revolving around Professor Carson's alarm concerning an anonymous letter slandering his wife-to-be followed by his depression after the wedding and subsequent death. Why is Professor Carson's funeral surrealistically staged by his widow as a lavish wedding ceremony, complete with love songs and a casket made to resemble a couch, the "Wedding March" from *Lohengrin*, and Mrs. Carson clad in bridal array?

Only later does the reader discover that the tormented groom had told his bride about the letter's "monstrous calumny," although no one "looking at [her] fair face . . . [could] believe that one drop of Negro blood coursed through [her] veins" (401). Like Armand, in other words, the Professor feared that his fair wife was African American. Again like Armand, Professor Carson insisted that "men and women are either white or black. Those who are not all white are all black," but his bride refuses to give him any assurance that she does not derive from black lineage. Instead, with Jamesian ambiguity she insisted, "I shall certainly not deny it" (402). As if acting out a rebelliousness one might wish for Chopin's heroine, Mrs. Carson persists in precisely the unknowability of racial identity that the orphaned Désirée actually embodies. At least one reason why Professor Carson's bride refuses to reveal the secret of her racial ancestry has to do with the sexual impact of racechange on a woman: It would eroticize or even prostitute her.

Professor Carson's abhorrence—"Nothing could ever make me feel that the touch of a Negress was not pollution"—comes from his mother's suffering when her husband, a planter with numerous slaves, took "some poor unfortunate of color" as his mistress (402). A promise at the maternal deathbed that he would never commit "this sin" causes the fastidious Professor to seek the assurance of his wife about her whiteness. Her refusal to do so apparently leads not only to their alienation in marriage but also to his morbidity and death. In both the funeral-qua-wedding and the title, whiteness—emblematizing an obsessive, self-destructive anxiety about blood stains and strains—takes on the color of grief. Like Miss Havisham in Dickens's *Great Expectations* (1861), Mrs. Carson marks the wedding day as the inauguration of a life-in-death, the commencement of a broken heart. Wearing white weeds, the widow also connects the death of her marriage with the consummation of her desire. Since Mrs. Carson's marriage had been a living death, her husband's death means life to her. The source of the narrative's power derives from its heroine's refusal to accept race as a definition of identity—even if, *especially if*, that identity is maternal and thus capable of producing what Professor Carson calls "children . . . show[ing] traces of their descent from an inferior and degraded race" (402).[19]

The fact that ontological insecurity destroys Professor Carson, who finds himself maddened by his inability to tell if the woman in his bed is a respectable wife or an illicit whore, suggests the fragility of men's control over their future racial lineage. Given the uncertainty of his bride's background, he only knows that she must never become the mother of his children. To admit to being an African American would put the mother and her children beyond the pale. Thus, Mrs. Carson's stubborn silence constitutes a refusal to move along the trajectory of Désirée from sanctification to demonization, from the representative of home to the emblem of homelessness. Yet black or white, Chopin's heroine—as the mother of a dark child—is doomed, exactly as her predecessor La Blanche had been. If black, she devolves into sexual chattle; if white, she must be stigmatized for having been possessed by a black man. Since Désirée remarks that her husband can hear their baby crying "as far away as La Blanche's cabin," perhaps Armand has retained La Blanche as his whore after his wedding, a fate he may have set aside for Désirée, too, once he suspected her of African ancestry.[20]

Exactly this path paved by racechange—from propriety to prostitution—constitutes the progress of the biracial child Amantha Starr of Robert Penn Warren's historical novel *Band of Angels* (1955). The only daughter of a nameless, dead woman and a devoted white planter who neglected to manumit her, Amantha plummets from Edenic freedom to hellish bondage at her father's death when she is enslaved to be sold to pay his debts. At several points in the narrative, Warren's light-skinned heroine experiences a jolting, jarring form of racechange. Like the "ex-coloured man" who narrates James Weldon Johnson's passing narrative and who feels himself "growing black and thick-featured and crimp-haired" when he reveals his African-American roots (204), at certain moments Amantha looks at herself, seeing

> the stain of the black blood swelling through my veins—yes, I actually saw some such picture in my head, a flood darkening through all the arteries and veins of my body—no, a stain spreading in a glass of clear water. (228)

At a later point in the book, however, when the young woman attempts to identify herself with black characters, she feels as if

> a strong galvanic current had been passed through my being to jerk me out of my torpor, to jerk me scrambling up, not in fear, in some deeper necessity, uttering the unplanned words, the words that burst out of me.
>
> The words were: "I'm not nigger, I'm not nigger—I'm white." (332)

Perpetually oscillating in her racial identity, Amanda knows as completely as did Désirée and Mrs. Carson that to be "nigger" for a woman means being sold as

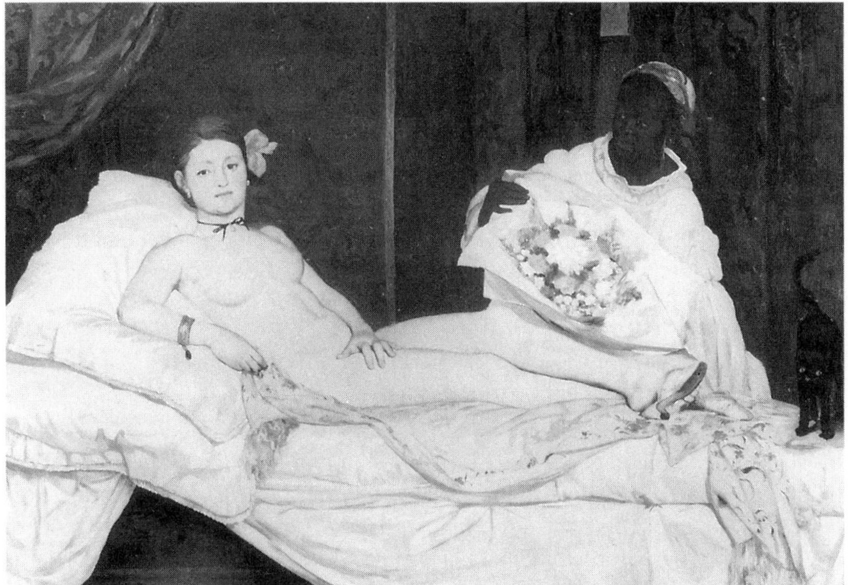

Figure 6.1 Édouard Manet, *Olympia* (1863). Courtesy Musée d'Orsay, Paris.

sexual merchandise,[21] a form of exploitation which was buttressed by nineteenth-century icongraphy in art and in medicine. As Sander Gilman has demonstrated, aesthetic and anatomical imagery linked "two seemingly unrelated female images—the icon of the Hottentot female and the icon of the prostitute" (206). Perhaps for this reason, racechange when it occurs in the white female of the species tends to physicalize, much as it did in Colescott's portrait of "Shirley Temple Black." The same dynamic is at work in the racechanges performed on two touchstone paintings, both of which established links between the black female body and white prostitution: Édouard Manet's *Olympia* (1863) and Pablo Picasso's *Les demoiselles d'Avignon* (1907). Although Gilman quite reasonably uses Manet's famous portrait of *Olympia* (Fig. 6.1) to establish the connection between women, sex for sale, and nonwhites, the racechanging parodies of this picture produced by Picasso and Larry Rivers make the point even more explicit.

The black cat coupled with the black maid on the extreme right of Manet's original painting stand for the "pussy" which the thin model coyly hides beneath her hand but which the hefty servant offers the viewer in the shape of a bouquet symbolizing the female genitals and echoed by the exotic flower worn in her mistress's hair. A revision of and homage to Titian's *Venus of Urbino* (1538), Manet's canvas plays various tones of white (the naked skin of the courtesan, rumpled sheets and pillows, silk robe and slippers) against many dark tones (the brown skin of the Negress, dark green curtains, black alley cat). Carrying the gift from a past or future gentleman caller, the maid eyes the mistress as if replicating the gaze to which the mistress brazenly attends, the voyeuristic stare of the spectator who is placed in the position of next client or departing caller. (No wonder that in *Fremde Schönheit* (discussed in the opening chapter) Hannah Höch bestows such huge though sunken eyes upon her reinvention of Manet's model.) Theodore Reff has demonstrated that *Olympia*, which "seems in fact to mark the real beginning of modern art" (59), brings together a heady Baudelairean brew of "la Venus noire," "fleurs du mal," and a witchy feline fetish, a blend of animal magnetism and moral indifference, ostentatious luxury and commodified primitivism dependent on the doubling of the white courtesan and her black attendant (91–94).

As Marianna Torgovnick points out, both Picasso's *Parody of Manet's "Olympia"* (Fig. 6.2) and Rivers's *I Like Olympia in Black Face* (Fig. 6.3) equate blackness with prostitution and a more explicit physicality (102). In Picasso's canvas, the dark female figure's pronounced thighs and belly as well as her exposed pubic hair emphasize her fleshliness (in contrast to the thinner white model at the center of Manet's painting and the emaciated customers in Picasso's). By producing a picture of himself pointing at the reclining Negress, Picasso stresses his self-consciousness about his own absorption with the African as the subject of modern art. In Rivers's parody, reciprocity in black and white means that when black turns white, white turns black. Not merely a portrait of a single prostitute, the scene has become a whorehouse or harem, complete with titillating interracial lesbian overtones.[22] Playing with the same sort of oscillating racechanges that doom Chopin's and Chesnutt's heroines, Picasso and Rivers produce canvases that oddly medicalize their subjects, hinting at hospital beds, patients anatomically displayed as curiosities, and attendant visitor-voyeurs. Female sexuality, whether black or white, appears vaguely aberrant or even potentially contaminating. If, as Lorraine O'Grady has remarked, the female body, like a coin, has an obverse and a reverse side—"White is what woman is; not-white . . . is what she had better not be"—then the impossibility of separating the two dooms both to pollution (14); it dooms both to childlessness as well, since the pariah's "sterility" stands iconographically in opposition to the sacred mother's "fertility."

Many critics have observed that Picasso's *Les demoiselles d'Avignon* (originally called "The Brothel of Avignon" and partially inspired by *Olympia*) fits Iberian, African, or Oceanic masks onto the inhabitants of a Parisian bordello to conflate the Otherness of primitivism with the Otherness of female sexuality (Fig. 6.4). Like *Parody of Manet's "Olympia"* and *I Like Olympia in Black Face*, Picasso's modernist breakthrough—undertaken soon after his trip to the ethnographic collections at the Trocadero—can be linked to syphilophobia since original drafts of the picture include a dessicated male figure as well as a doctor.[23] As the Africanization of the faces deepens toward the right side of the canvas in the head of the standing *demoiselle* (whose features most resemble the masks of tribal peoples), what William Rubin calls "the unprecedented *brut* or raw coloring and the slashing painterly attack" become more evident, emphasizing the physicality of the oil medium itself (*Les demoiselles*, 105). By destylizing or fleshing out black female figures, Robert Colescott's *Les demoiselles d'Alabama: Vestidas, 1985* (see color insert) ridicules not only Picasso's sexual anxieties but also modernist commodi-

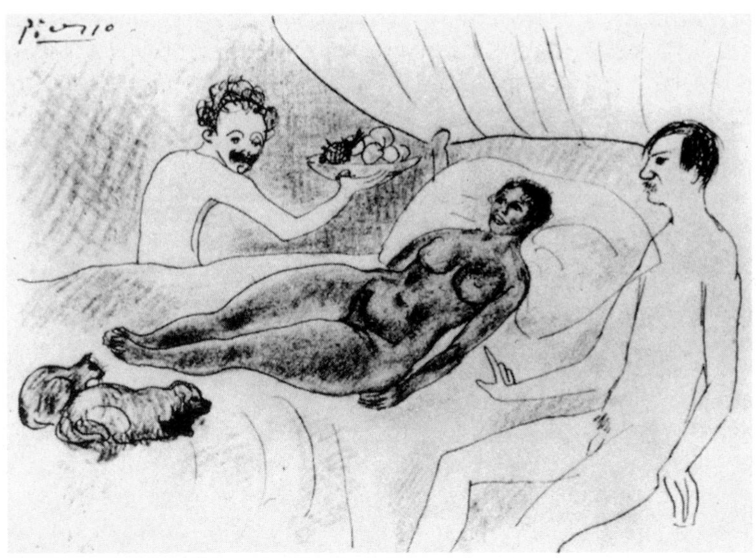

Figure 6.2 Pablo Picasso, *Parody of Manet's "Olympia"* (1907). Copyright © 1989, ARS N.Y./SPADEM.

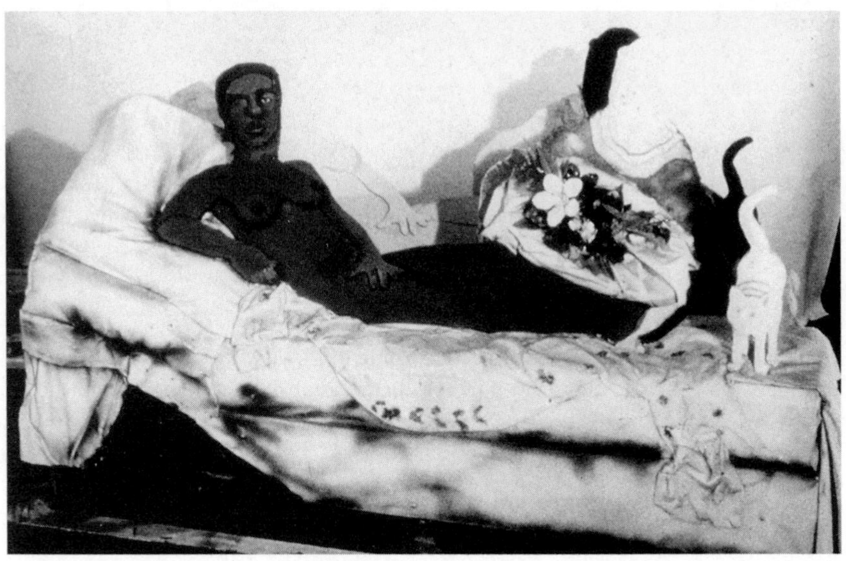

Figure 6.3 Larry Rivers, *I Like Olympia in Black Face* (1970), mixed media construction, $71\frac{5}{8} \times 76\frac{3}{8} \times 39\frac{3}{8}''$. Copyright © 1996 by Larry Rivers/Licensed by VAGA, New York. Collection, Musée National d'art Moderne, Centre Georges Pompidou, Paris; courtesy ARS N.Y.

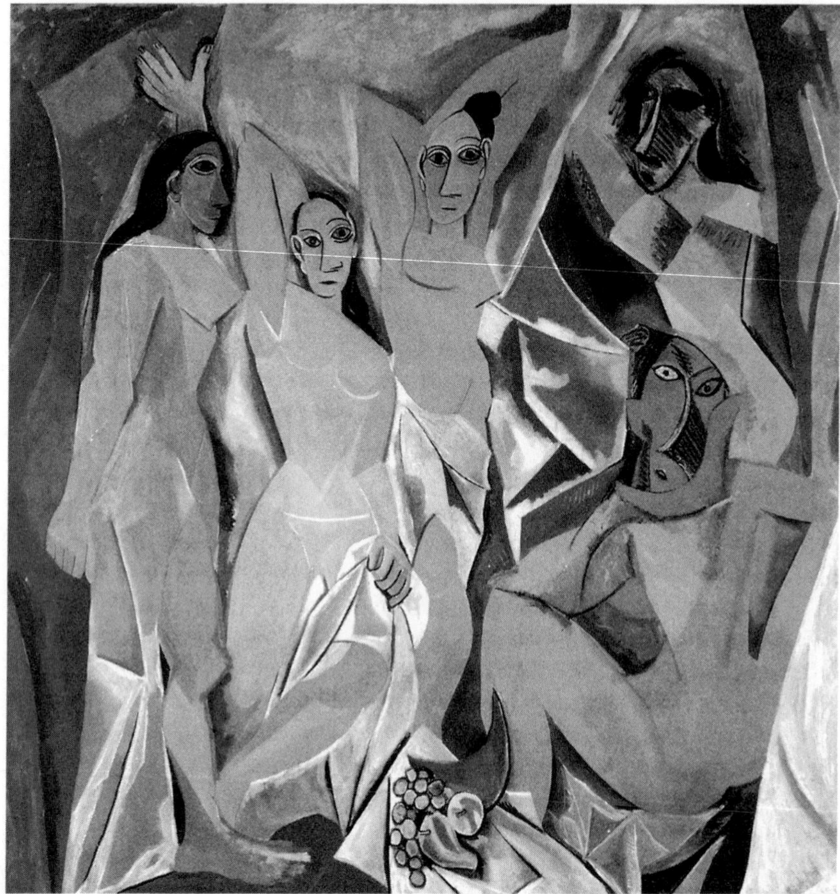

Figure 6.4 Pablo Picasso, *Les demoiselles d'Avignon*, Paris (June–July 1907), oil on canvas, 8′ × 7′8″. Copyright © 1996 The Museum of Modern Art, New York, acquired through the Lillie P. Bliss Bequest.

fications of women and of Africans. According to Lowery S. Sims, "Colescott deabstracts the Picasso composition . . . , which was abstracted under the influence of African art, and he restores these female apparitions to their original European painterly manifestations" (8). Since Picasso used African art to make European conventions abstract, Colescott moves Picasso's Africanism back toward European images. From Colescott's point of view, "the irony is partly that what most people (including me) know about African conventions comes from Cubist art"; he goes on to ask, "Could a knowledge of European art be so derived as well?" (Sims, 8).

Colescott's question can be answered in the affirmative after we note that removing the masks from the prostitutes in the whorehouse involves depicting their various colors, costumes, and body shapes in such a manner as to make the whore strutting her stuff for the male customer evoke the slave on an auction block. In the fleshly passivity of their line-up, there is something slavish about the prostitute, something prostituted about the slave. Whereas Picasso used geometric planes and abstraction to emphasize the stylized constructedness of even the naked body and thus degendered his subjects, Colescott employs a combination of realistic and comic book techniques to stress the materiality of his decidedly female models. His picture thereby insists that the object of the Western gaze has always been female and that the reified, fetishized female model remains a crucial convention in European art. Colescott centrally locates a wedge of red—a berry? a watermelon?—that mimics the shape of minstrelsy's smiling lips as well as the lipstick-red lips of the whores, thus linking both with the lower (vaginal) lips proferred to anyone in the market for forbidden fruit.

That the trollop on the left looks a bit like Picasso only underlines Colescott's critique of the uses to which the Spanish modernist put African and female images.[24] Taken together with *Olympia* and her racechanged avatars, *Les demoiselles d'Alabama*'s subjects continue to make the mixed child inconceivable since the prostitute in art and in literature may bring pleasure or pain, orgasm or syphilis, but she rarely bears children into the world. Only childlessness insures that a racially indeterminate lineage will not pollute pure origins, as Chesnutt's Professor Carson understood. In the case of *Olympia* and her progenitors, pets, not babies, appear on her bedsheets, embodiments of her willingness to submit herself not only to a devolution into physicality but also to ownership. Zora Neale Hurston's phrase "The 'Pet' Negro System" (1943) adds resonance to Dorothy Sayers's definition of the feminine as "the human-not-quite-human," and together they hint at the reciprocity between the white prostitute and the dark Other singled out for affection by its owner. J.-J. Grandville's parodic version of *Olympia*, entitled *I Was Lazy* (1842), graphically identifies the model reclining on her couch with her pet; the face of the human figure is quite definitively that of a cat (Reff, 72).

The white woman who has trafficked in darkness is not simply prostituted and animalized but also twinned with black women so as to suggest a range of perversities from bestiality to lesbianism. As with the black stud stereotype, the hypersexuality of the Africanist female could take bizarre shapes, as it does perhaps most notoriously in the "Hot Voodoo" nightclub number of Josef von Sternberg's movie *Blonde Venus* (1929) after Marlene Dietrich strips off a gorilla suit and sports a blond Afro while gyrating to jungle drum beats in front of a chorus line of African-American women decked in black Afros. When Dietrich removes her gorilla suit to show the cabaret audience her white hands and face, she herself becomes an amalgam of Fay Wray and King Kong (Figs. 6.5 and 6.6). Both beauty and beast, Dietrich half in, half out of her ape costume recalls the transformation of She-Who-Must-Be-Obeyed at the end of Rider Haggard's late Victorian best-seller *She* (1887). His exquisite heroine, Ayesha, devolves into a wrinkled, brown female animal, "no larger than a big ape" (308). Like Haggard's She, Dietrich—encircled by gyrating black women toting spears (threatening castration) and

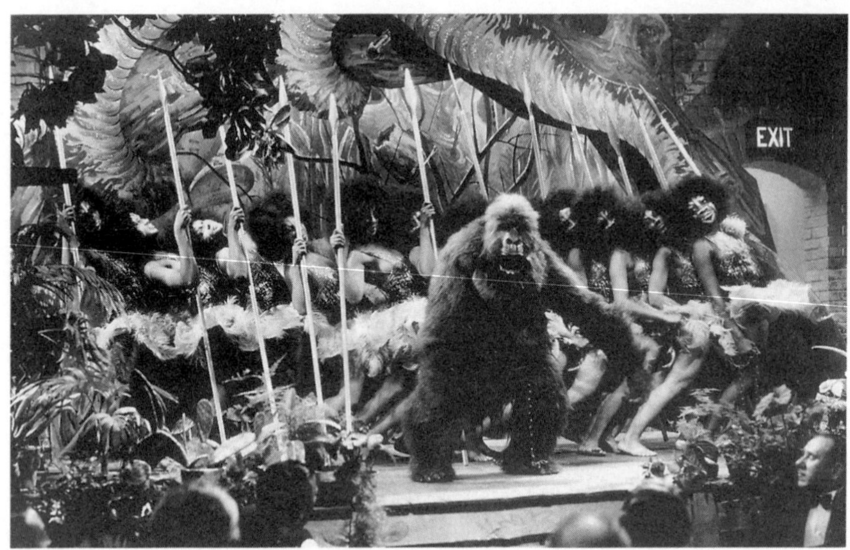

Figure 6.5 Marlene Dietrich as King Kong in *Blonde Venus* (1929). Courtesy of Museum of Modern Art Film Stills Archive.

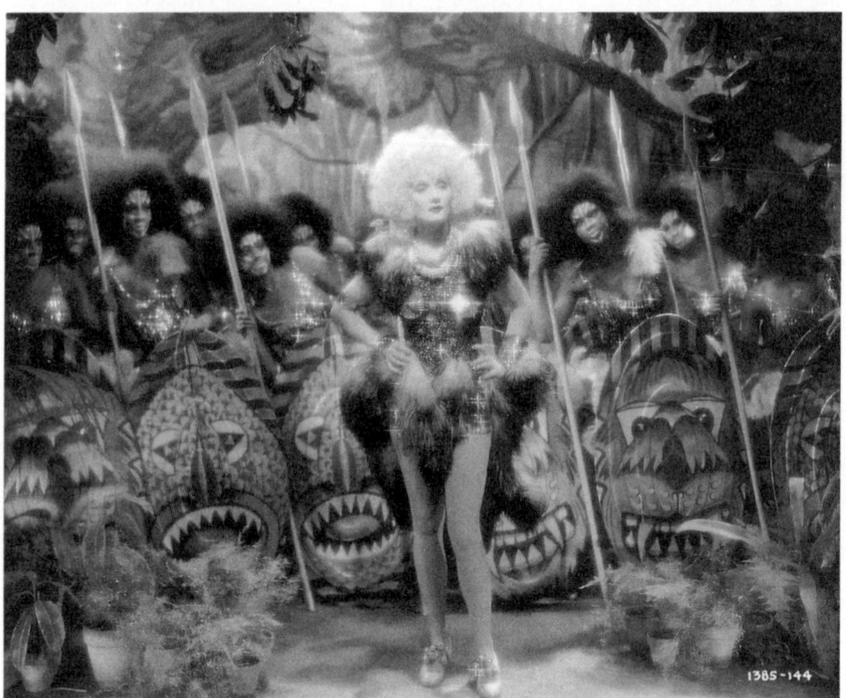

Figure 6.6 Marlene Dietrich as Fay Wray in *Blonde Venus* (1929). Courtesy of Museum of Modern Art Film Stills Archive.

shields painted with vagina dentata (more castration)—no longer knows right from wrong because those insidious "voodoo" drums have caused her conscience to "take a vacation." To the extent that the weary irony and the German-inflected English of her performance-within-the performance emphasize the star's jaded distance from Africa, it is hardly surprising that Dietrich reminds one of her most perceptive critics of the role model for Haggard's She-Who-Must-Be-Obeyed, namely "what the Mona Lisa had been for Walter Pater—a tantalizing, enigmatic woman framed by a decadent gloom, whose face hinted at delicious perversities" (Naremore, 143).

Not only does the "Hot Voodoo" number insinuate that the races are two species—the white one human, the black not—but what Freud called "the dark continent" of female sexuality surfaces in these frames to mark the heroine's role as *femme fatale* as well as her abdication of her maternal respectability.[25] Like Manet's *Olympia*, the nightclub scene brings together a Baudelairean brew of animal magnetism, "la Venus noire," and commodified primitivism through the doubling of the white courtesan and her Africanist attendants. As Dietrich is surrounded by a chorus line of partially naked showgirl-natives, the woman famous for emanating an eroticism that floated free of gender appears to pose the threat and the promise of color released from race in a degenerate (but titillating) deviancy. Reduced to a widow or a whore, robbed of maternity, or simply animalized, the white woman coupled with blackness typifies what Calvin C. Hernton calls the "slut concept," the idea that "any white woman with a Negro [is considered] fair game" (53).[26] Even in the thinking of a critic as savvy as Hernton, the view prevails that "it is the racial meaning of Negro sexuality, in all of its pornography, that the white woman *expects* and *demands* when she becomes intimate with a Negro" (50), whether or not "a Negro" is the male of the species, as Hernton assumes. When the character he calls "the White-Negro woman" undergoes a racechange, she "has that 'gyrating gait,' that bouncing of the shoulders as she talks, that slur in the voice, that earthy twirl in her pelvis when she dances . . ." (51).[27]

The Pre-Oedipal Union of White Mother, Dark Baby

To turn to a final interpretation of the conclusion of Chopin's tale, what if Désirée's baby is born of a black father and a white mother? Such a denouement is, of course, the most shocking of all, from a historical perspective, because the idea of a black father/white mother was made unspeakable during slavery and Reconstruction. In *Incidents in the Life of a Slave Girl*, Harriet Jacobs explains that, although the infant of a black mother immediately became the property of the white father, the baby born of a white mistress who selected a slave on the plantation to be the father of her child would be smothered at birth or banished from sight (81). No wonder that even the most racist eugenicist admonitions—"The cross between a white man and a negro is a negro"—take for granted the white father, black mother. Not only the privations suffered by the central character of the first published novel by an African American but also the obscurity of the book itself—it disappeared into oblivion for more than a century—may be related to Harriet Wilson's depiction in *Our Nig* (1859) of an interracial marriage between a white wife and a black husband. Both the presences and the absences in twentieth-century literature imply that the mandates of a history of slavery and lynching still operate. Significantly, however, transgressive narratives about the white mother/black offspring eventually issue in a libertarian script, one that imbues the multiracial child with an almost magical transracial aura.

An especially evocative, lyrical story about dark children born to a white mother, which appears near the beginning of Jean Toomer's classic *Cane* (1923), captures the calamitous as well as the potentially redemptive aspects of the white mother/black child dyad. An opening and closing paragraph—

> Becky was the white woman who had two Negro sons. She's dead; they've gone away. The pines whisper to Jesus. The Bible flaps its leaves with an aimless rustle on her mound. (7)

—brackets the tale, functioning like a refrain or an epigraph, so as to establish the sketch as an elegy of a pariah. White and black communities alike ostracize Becky after the first "Negro son" was engendered by what the whites in the town call a "Damn buck nigger" and what the blacks call a "Low-down nigger with no self-respect." Gossip from both sides conspires to destroy Becky's sanity, though she does not reveal the father's identity (and thereby saves him from the lynching other sections of *Cane* describe). Against the crime of miscegenation and racial disloyalty, blacks and whites "joined hands to cast her out" onto a "narrow strip of land between the railroad and the road," a location fitting her liminal status in the town.

But like other scapegoats, Becky takes on magical significance to those who have exiled her. Although "No one ever saw her," train passengers throw papers on the "Ground islandized between the road and railroad track," something like the prayers strewn on religious shrines, while townsfolk secretly bring her sweet potatoes and corn, something like offerings or propitiations. When her five-year-old boy appears carrying a dark baby, everyone knows but no one says anything about the second child, for people had told themselves "that Becky now was dead" (8). The pronoun "we" surfaces in this section of the narrative to make it clear that the community remains monolithic in its scorn of the "Sullen and cunning" boys who, in turn, curse white and black people alike. Since the young men don't know or care if they are "White or colored" and since neither racial group will take them in, Becky's sons "answered black and white folks by shooting up two men and leaving town." The departure of the renegades leads to the repeated refrain "O pines, whisper to Jesus" as the narrator explains the community's dread that Becky's ghost haunts the cabin.

One Sunday, on a trip home from a neighboring church, an unnamed but now individualized narrator sees his horses frightened as they come onto Becky's cabin. Terrified himself, he witnesses the ground trembling as a ghost train rumbles by and the chimney falls down with a hollow thud. A glance at the door tells him and his companion, Barlo, that Becky would have been buried by the bricks, if she were in there: "I thought I heard a groan. Barlo, mumbling something, threw his Bible on the pile" (9). As a number of readers have explained, Becky becomes invisible because her racial transgression has broken the ban against cross-racial mothering; however, she also becomes a haunting, even shamanistic presence, indeed the spirit of the place that both black and white people placate, feed, worship (Baker, *Singers of Daybreak*, 59; Doyle, 84). Like Désirée, Becky remains an outcast whose dark children blackened her character. But Toomer's prose poem insists it is the very unthinkability of Becky's life story that obsesses the racially segregated community.[28]

Refusing to accept the idea of black babies born of white maternal bodies, both blacks and whites isolate, punish, and then bow down to the woman who incarnates their secret desires. Like the return of the repressed, Becky's spectral life-in-death on the edge of town transmutes her into an uncanny haunting presence. Just as Becky moves from scapegoat to saint, the figure of the white mother of the dark child evolves from pariah to madonna over the course of the twentieth century. The identity of her child, too, undergoes a transformation, as the move from the term "mulatto" (meaning a sterile mule) to the terms "mixed," "hybrid," "biracial," and "multi-ethnic" demonstrates. Through the story of a woman made into a taboo—consecrated but forbidden, polluted but sacred—Toomer provides a framework for understanding the relative silence of imaginative writers on the narrative of the white mother of the mixed child, a silence maintained until very recently. Even when that silence was broken, the narrative seems at first to have generated grotesquely incommensurate, Gothic consequences.

Countee Cullen's lament in his poem "Near White" (1925)—that those "Ambiguous of race . . . stand/ By one disowned, scorned of another"—underscores the fates of fictional and nonfictional products of the white mother, black father (*Color*, 11). At the turn of the century, according to Ida B. Wells, apocryphal stories about the members of integrated clubs giving birth to black babies were used to warn white women against including African Americans in their ranks. That monitory tales cautioning against the dangers of miscegenation endured long into the century Bessie Head's *A Question of Power* (1973) proves.[29] For the African writer's autobiographical novel presents a protagonist told about her biracial origins by a school principal who seems to see them as legal proof of the girl's culpability:

> "We have a full docket on you. You must be very careful. Your mother was insane. If you're not careful you'll get insane just like your mother. Your mother was a white woman. They had to lock her up, as she was having a child by the stable boy, who was a native." (16)

The quintessential victim of racism, Head's heroine is viewed as a half-breed or untouchable. A character in Zora Neale Hurston's novel *Jonah's Gourd Vine* (1934) illuminates the same dynamic at work in American society when he explains, "dese half-white niggers [are thought to have] got de worst part uh bofe de white and de black folks" (9), a claim sustained in contemporary times by one Gregory Howard Williams—the "whitest colored boy" most people had seen—who attributed the prejudice he experienced while growing up in the Midwest during the 1950s to whites' revulsion against the "'bestial mongrel mulatto'" (93).[30]

Notwithstanding the persistence of pessimistic accounts of the biracial offspring, in recent times several contemporary literary women brood on the story of the biracial child born of the white mother so as to induce a kind of redemptive racechange in the psychology of nonblack readers. If "among politically committed and enlightened whites," as Adrian Piper has contended, "the inability to acknowledge their probable African ancestry is the last outpost of racism" (234), then white parenting of black children may constitute one vanguard in a movement of changing racial consciousness. According to Piper, "for whites to acknowledge their blackness is . . . much the same as for men to acknowledge their femininity and for Christians to acknowledge their Judaic heritage. It is to reinternalize the external scapegoat through attention to which they have sought to escape their own sense of inferiority" (235). How better reinternalize the external scapegoat than by bearing the black baby within the white body? How better acknowledge blackness than by giving birth to, nursing, or nurturing the black child?

Such contemporary women of letters as Marilyn Hacker, Jane Lazarre, Sherley Anne Williams, and Grace Paley engage nonblack readers in imagining their African ancestry by celebrating consciousness of color without race, transcendent epiphanies achieved through the image of the dark child fostered by the white parent. In the place of the warring father and Oedipal son, they excavate the pacific pre-Oedipal bonding of mother and baby to delineate the possibilities not only of fluid ego boundaries between self and Other but also blurred racial boundaries between white mother and biracial infant. Implicitly agreeing with James Baldwin's belief that one cannot "cease playing a role simply because one has begun to understand it" (*Price of the Ticket*, 291), these contemporary poets and fiction writers envision the interdependence as well as the merging of races through the complicated two-in-oneness of the mother/child dyad, a couple which leads them to meditations similar to Baldwin's reflection that "each of us, helplessly and forever, contains the other—male in female, female in male, white in black, and black in white" (*Price of the Ticket*, 690).

Marilyn Hacker and Jane Lazarre, writing respectively in autobiographical verse and prose forms, depict the pregnancy of the white mother, the birth of the dark child as an awakening into a consciousness different from the normative one of racial conflict or competition. Bearing the multiracial child delivers the mother into a new conception of not simply admitting or acknowledging but embracing and loving difference. Representative of much of her work on this subject, Hacker's sonnet about the birth of her biracial daughter deserves to be quoted in full:

"I'm pregnant," I wrote to her in delight
from London, thirty, married, in print. A foolscap sheet scrawled slantwise with one minuscule
sentence came back. "I hope your child is white."
I couldn't tear the pieces small enough.
I hoped she'd be black as the ace of spades,

though hybrid beige heredity had made
that as unlikely as the spun-gold stuff
sprouted after her neonatal fur.
I grudgingly acknowledged her "good hair,"
which wasn't, very, from my point of view.
"No tar brush left," her father's mother said.
"She's Jewish and she's white," from her cranked bed
mine smugly snapped.
She's Black. She is a Jew.

Rebellious toward her aged, ill mother, Hacker identifies her delight in the mysterious child she is carrying with her pleasure in her own authority and authorship. "Thirty, married, in print," she writes a letter about her pregnancy and imagines a baby "black as the ace of spades." Her mother's conventionally prejudiced response arrives in a "minuscule sentence" "scrawled" on "A foolscap sheet" only to be torn into small pieces. Although the mother-to-be worries about "hybrid beige heredity" on the father's side, her mother-in-law appears to be pleased that there is "no tar brush left." Firmly rejecting the terms of her mother and her mother-in-law, Hacker's poem turns into a love sonnet in its last line of welcome where the child's transracial identity cannot be summed up in one sentence but needs two separate but equal declarations on the page, both combined in the unprecedented mix of the child.[31] The "unlikely . . . neonatal fur" sprouting on Hacker's baby signals its unpredictable difference from what had come before and presages the older child's color of "gold on lion-gold" in a later poem where the mother-poet directly claims that "mixed races swell the lexicon," generating new words and new perceptions like that of the "Bedouin for *sand*, or Eskimo / for *snow*" (45).

Just as giving birth to the biracial child alienates Hacker from the conventional racial consciousness of her cranky mother and mother-in-law, the white writer Jane Lazarre in *The Mother Knot* feels herself undergoing a racechange when she realizes she is pregnant with her black husband's child: "Resting my hand lightly on my belly, I was as Black as anyone" (18). But it is not until the birth of her baby that her identification with the infant effectively alienates her from white people, specifically when she witnesses incomprehensible white fear of blackness. At the hospital where her first son is born, she watches the nurses holding her boy and notes "the same fear lurking around the edges of their faces as I had seen in other white faces, in town, in stories, in our housing complex, when they spoke of Bobby Seale," a civil rights activist just as unintimidating as her infant son because incarcerated at the time (45). In her confessional novel *Worlds Beyond My Control* (1991), Lazarre's shameful awareness of white people's unfounded fear of African Americans jettisons her fictional surrogate into a series of racechanges in consciousness.

Because the heroine's son Daniel understands that white people do not perceive him or his father as persons but instead witness only color, Julia begins to feel "her skin is scorched by their blackness, like a branding iron would scorch her skin. Her skin seems to go up in smoke from a body that is hot, wounded" (95). Although her other son, Anthony, composes a poem about "*Warring races divided / yet in-*

side of me / the two races beautifully united," Julia wonders if her husband ever regrets that he married someone white, only to be charmed by his mock shock: "—Oh my God . . . You're white?" (100–101). Terrified throughout her writing about letting her children go out into a world especially inhospitable to black young men, Julia nevertheless learns from them to imagine clay roads inside her body turning into rich layers of mud and being transformed until she is "as black and blue" as her husband and children: "I am black inside where loss, language, and courage will root for as long as I live" (176). As if writing from the position of one of Lazarre's sons and imbued with precisely the sense of biracial subjectivity that fascinates her, James McBride—one of twelve siblings brought up by a black father and a Jewish mother who defined herself as not "white" but simply "light-skinned"—explains in his memoir, *The Color of Water* (1996), that as a child he "would have preferred that Mommy were black"; however, as as adult "I feel privileged to have come from two worlds. My view of the world is not merely that of a black man but that of a black man with something of a Jewish soul" (15, 79).

In an analysis of precisely the taboo Hacker, Lazarre, and Ruth McBride Jordan have broken, Patricia J. Williams asks a series of resonant questions about white mothering of black children:

> Is there not something unseemly, in our society, about the spectacle of a white woman mothering a black child? A white woman giving totally to a black child; a black child totally and demandingly dependent for everything, sustenance itself, from a white woman. The image of a white woman suckling a black child; the image of a black child sucking for its life from the bosom of a white woman. The utter interdependence of such an image; the merging it implies; the giving up of boundary; the encompassing of other within self; the unbounded generosity and interconnectedness of such an image. (*Alchemy*, 226–27)

Elsewhere, envisioning a way to "integrate this world from the inside out," Williams argues that "We must shake up biological normativity" and goes so far as to "suggest guerrilla insemination to challenge the notion of choice" (the privileging of white characteristics); "it will be disembodied black seed that will swell white bellies; the symbolically sacred vessel of the white womb will bring the complication home to the guarded intimacy of white families, and into the madonna worship of the larger culture" (*Alchemy*, 188). (Such seemingly outré ideas take on plangency in the context of cases like that of Wilma and Willem Stuart, the Dutch couple whose experience with in-vitro fertilization produced one light- and one dark-skinned baby because a technician unwittingly reused a pipette that still contained sperm from a previous insemination.[32])

Probably the most ironic approach to the taboo described by Williams surfaces in a brilliant short story by Muriel Spark about the racial limits of Western culture's madonna worship as well as its mythology about the maternal instinct. "The Black Madonna" (1960) focuses on a couple of progressive Catholics—Raymond and Lou Parker—whose liberalism is unmasked by the horror they experience at their bringing a black baby into the world. Even at the beginning, Spark's tale juxtaposes the patronizing Parkers' befriending of two Jamaicans with certain strains in the relationship. After a visit to Lou's impoverished sister, for example, black Henry Pierce has the temerity to compare her psychology to "the slum mentality . . . back home," but Lou resents the comparison; "what a cheek *him* talking like a snob. At least Elizabeth's white" (13). Or, again, when the other Jamaican, Oxford St. John, looks at the glass in her kitchen and refers to himself as black, "Lou thought . . . it was not the thing to say" (13). Yet the Raymonds continue to pray for the welfare of the two immigrants, and after those prayers are met by the aesthetically distinctive icon in their parish church, Lou and Raymond "decided to put in for a baby to the Black Madonna" (16). Of course their prayers are answered in a manner they could hardly expect.

Appearing "terribly red" at first (20), the newborn is perfect, yet the couple is shocked to discover "the baby will certainly be brown, if not indeed black" (21). Lou refuses to feed the infant, an enraged Raymond wonders if it was Oxford who is to blame, Lou's sister informs them of color on her father's side, but nothing placates the horrified pair. "If it was anyone else's child I would think it was all right," Raymond explains; "It's just the thought of it being mine, and people thinking it isn't" (26). Lou agrees, declaring to a neighbor, "Imagine it for yourself, waking up to find you've had a black baby that everyone thinks has a nigger for its father" (26). When they put the baby up for adoption, the priest says it is the "*right*" thing to do, though it would have been a "*good*" thing to have kept it. The difference between "right" and "good" is the contrast between the facade of liberalism Lou and Raymond practice and the love they cannot find within themselves. The black Madonna seems to work the will of "a coloured God [who] is not asleep," playing exactly the trick on the priggish couple that they deserve. When "the symbolically sacred vessel of the white womb" swells with "black seed," it brings home the complications of unacknowledged racism, as Williams predicted it would. Spark's madonna is black because in this satirist's view racism has incapacitated whites, proven them incapable of loving—or mothering—the Other.

Like Patricia J. Williams, though more cynically, Muriel Spark broods on the possibility of the interdependence of mother and child, the permeable boundaries between mother and infant, posing an antidote to racism in a fostering of the Other within the self. Similarly, in *Dessa Rose* (1986), Sherley Anne Williams's imaginative account of a nineteenth-century slave rebellion, the "unseemly" scene of a white woman suckling a black child first horrifies the baby's slave mother but eventually foreshadows reciprocity between blacks and whites. Here, a runaway who has just given birth, the eponymous Dessa, awakes in shock to witness a white woman nursing the black newborn. Miss Rufel, a mother and a plantation mistress presiding over a refuge for runaways, had responded to the tiny, bloodied baby with painful intensity and "only when his cries were stilled and she looked down upon the sleek black head, the nut-brown face flattened against the pearly paleness of her breast, had she become conscious of what she was doing" (105). Embarrassed, she feels "somehow vindicated" by the confusion of the African Americans in her household, though mortified, too, "at becoming wet nurse for a darky" (106). What wins out is the pleasure the white mistress takes at "the contrast between [the infant's] mulberry-colored mouth and the pink areola surrounding her nipple, between his caramel-colored fist and the rosy cream of her breast" (106).

At first Dessa's vision of Rufel nursing her baby goes "against everything she had been taught to think about white women but to inspect that fact too closely was almost to deny her own existence" (123). However, Rufel clearly acts this way in gratitude and reciprocity for the acts of kindness of her Mammy. Indeed, because of the goodness of this shadowy figure as well as the white woman's growing awareness that she knew nothing at all about Mammy as a person in her own right, rueful Rufel expects "all darkies to be like Mammy. *Like family*" (135; emphasis mine). Eventually, just as the mistress begins to admit her ignorance about Mammy, to concede that kinship had been forced on Mammy, even the resentful and understandably wary Dessa learns that Rufel "wasn't that foolish. But where white peoples look at black and see something ugly, something hateful, she saw color" (184). Finally, together with other runaways, Rufel and Dessa enter into a con game on slaveholders, with Rufel playing the role of "Mistress" and Dessa playing the role of "Mammy." The fictiveness of their impersonations has been underscored not only by a series of complex disagreements and dialogues they have sustained about Mammies and mothers but also by the fact that Rufel has actually functioned as Mammy for Dessa's baby.[33]

Besides shaking up what Patricia J. Williams calls "biological normativity," the racechanged baby nursed by its loving mother or mother surrogate holds out the promise of difference not simply recognized but relished. Writing about what the mother-infant couple teaches, the psychologist Jessica Benjamin points out that "In getting pleasure *with* the other and taking pleasure *in* the other, we engage in mutual recognition" (126). The "intersubjective mode where two subjects meet"—mother and child, man and woman, black and white—negotiates between separateness and relatedness, bounded and unbounded possibilities, holding out some future solution to past conflictual sexual or racial Othering. For this reason, the nurtured biracial child can become a utopian icon of transracial consciousness. One of the happiest subjects interviewed in Lise Funderburg's *Black, White, Other: Biracial Americans Talk about Race and Identity* (1994) explained that she feels "ahead of everybody else . . . because I'm already mixed. I have this hidden theory that eventually everybody in the world is going to be mixed with something or another, so I got a jump on it" (298).[34]

Grace Paley would agree with the biracial son in Lazarre's *Worlds Beyond My Control* about the mixed child representing "*Warring races divided / yet inside of me / the two races beautifully united*" and with Lise Funderburg's optimistic subject. Indeed, in two quite different stories, Paley uses the hybridity of the mixed race child to capture the possibility of a redemptive future truce in race warfare. As narrated by its central character, an aged Jewish pharmacist, "Zagrowsky Tells" (1985) examines a miraculous transformation from racial hate to racial love. Accompanied by his black five-year-old grandson Emanuel, Zagrowsky tells his story to Faith, a woman who once many years earlier had picketed his store because he refused to serve African Americans or kept them waiting or served them rudely. Although he admits that he had wanted "to discourage" black people from moving into the neighborhood, although he used to respond to interracial couples with "Ugh—disgusting! It shouldn't be allowed!" (158, 165), he clearly has learned to love "raising a little boy brown like a coffee bean" (159). Convinced that his wife's nervousness has given his daughter Cissy her mental illness—he believes that "genes . . . [are] where the whole story is written down" (154)—Zagrowsky is shocked when she finds herself pregnant in the mental institution to which she has been confined and impregnated by "a black man with a green thumb"—the gardener (169). At first, the old man thinks to himself, "I can't stand it. I refuse. Out of my Cissy, who looked like a piece of gold, would come a black child" (168), but soon the child becomes his "little best friend" (169), convincing Zagrowsky that "long ago we were mostly dark" and "there are plenty black Jews" (171).

Just as Jean Toomer looked upon *Cane* as "a spiritual fusion analogous to the fact of racial intermingling" (Hutchinson, "Jean Toomer," 231), the biracial offspring in Paley's work holds out the promise of a mystical merging. The hybrid child becomes a messianic wonder worker in the gospel according to Zagrowsky but also in the good news of "At That Time, or The History of a Joke" (1981). In the earlier story, Faith finds newborn faith in a child named Emanuel (Hebrew for messiah) born to a mother who used to sing Handel's *Messiah*, especially two songs: "One is about the Gentiles will see the light and the other is, Look! a virgin will conceive a son" (162). Zagrowsky, who himself believes that the boy is "a golden present" from "Egypt," is told by Faith that Emanuel is born from Ishmael who is born from Abraham's union with Hagar (the slave of his barren wife, Sarah). As in Octavia Butler's *Kindred*, the biblical story of Hagar identifies African-American women with an enforced surrogacy that could be defined as rape, single parenthood, exile, and radical encounters with divinity. In any case, the dark child earlier despised and rejected becomes an uncanny savior.

Composed in a more tongue-in-cheek style, the postmodernist fable "At That Time, or The History of a Joke" takes up the idea of the dark child as a messiah in a technologically advanced time when "most people were willing to donate organs" and one woman received a uterine transplant only immediately to discover that her womb held "a darling rolled-up foetus": "It was unfurled in due time and lo! it was black as the night which rests our day-worn eyes." Again the child is a herald of redemption, as the aptly named scientist Dr. Heiliger calls out "see how the myth of man advances on the back of technological achievement and behold without conceiving a virgin has borne a son." All the people celebrate except for certain Jews weeping "It is not He!" As always, the Jews are right. After the authorities take away their TVs and shortwaves, the doctor admits, "Yes, it is a girl. A virgin born of a virgin." Paley's parodic parable concludes with the joy of the world, for "By that time, sexism and racism had no public life, though they were still sometimes practiced by adults at home."

On the one hand, as if elaborating upon Charlotte Perkins Gilman's view that male-authored religions were death-centered while female-created spiritualities would be birth-centered, Paley envisions the holy black girl's umbilicus becoming a spiritual symbol to put next to that of the cross; on the other, she imagines the stiff-necked Jews still discontented, exclaiming "we need another Virgin Birth like our blessed dead want cupping by ancient holistic practitioners." That with varying degrees of joy, anxiety, and hilarity Hacker, Lazarre, and Paley mythologize dark babies in explicitly Jewish contexts reflects the many artistic links between blacks and Jews, associations embodied at the start of the century in the cross-racial artistry of performers like Irving Berlin, Sophie Tucker, Eddie Cantor, and Al Jolson; at midcentury, connections manifest in Norman Mailer's "White Negro," and at its close in Anna Deavere Smith's *Fires in the Mirror* (1993), a dramatic performance in which the talented actress impersonates Lubavitchers and blacks at war in the Crown Heights section of Brooklyn. As Deavere Smith's play proves, it would, of course, be foolish to ignore divisions between and within African-American and Jewish communities during the past several decades, including charges of paternalism leveled against Jewish supporters of civil rights, accusations of anti-Semitism aimed at black leaders, and outrage about racialized class boundaries that have kept a greater percentage of African Americans than Jews in poverty. Indeed, Jewish–black racechanges often address precisely these tensions. In addition, however, the mythologizing of the Jewish, black child suggests that the discourse of Judaism—by traversing ethnic, religious, regional, and racial categories—might set the stage for less agonistic approaches to difference.[35] (It seems significant, in this regard, that Fanon modeled his ideas about racism on Sartre's study *Anti-Semite and Jew*.[36])

For such women of letters as Muriel Spark and Sherley Anne Williams, as for Hacker, Lazarre, and Paley, the hybridity of the child signals an apocalyptic racial consciousness, a distinct rupture from the past into an unprecedented, strange, post-racist future. According to Lise Funderburg, biracial people "necessarily have to break new ground in their own relationships" since they can never replicate their family of origin, "that intersection of two separate groups" (197). Empowering whites to experience the individuality of the Other on a visceral level, the mixed children of contemporary fiction usher into being a rejuvenated world order not further away than the middle of the next century when white Americans will constitute a minority of the national population.

Black Parents and the Racechanged Offspring

In 1972, when the National Association of Black Social Workers passed a resolution against the adoption of black children by white parents, it issued what F. James Davis has called "a ringing endorsement of the one-drop rule" (129). Arguing that black children need role models to gain confidence in their identities, the social workers considered the racial match between parent and child "essential to maintaining pride in the black ethnic identity" (168). By 1995, interracial adoptions were officially or unofficially barred in 43 states (*Newsweek*, Feb. 13, 1995).[37] From the perspective of the National Association of Black Social Workers, do fantasies of the unpredictably colored baby simply illuminate one more nefarious attempt at white appropriation of black bodies or one more representation of white authority over black? Have the most scrupulously imaginative efforts at restitution for the long history of suffering inflicted by whites on blacks only transmuted the childishness and primitivism which were attributed to African Americans so as to justify whites playing a role *in loco parentis*?

By trying to fashion scripts in which African Americans affect the lives of whites personally, in which family responsibilities are restructured along interracial lines, in which racial competition is replaced by interracial nurturance that benefits both parent and child, authors of the narrative of the white-mothered black offspring seek to escape the dynamics of Othering that permeate racism. Supplanting Shirley Temple, the mixed child appears as a Blakean "Infant Joy" or a Wordsworthian "best Philosopher" or "Nature's Priest." Yet of course such black and white thinkers as Patricia J. Williams and Grace Paley understand that the terms with which they describe the organic revolution they seek remain inevitably contaminated by the culture they inhabit. *Charitas* could devolve into charity; parenting into patronizing.[38] Too often, Patricia J. Williams explains, "gray babies" under a "waved banner of aggressive miscegenation" become "the optimist's antidote to everything" (*Rooster's Egg*, 189–90). Despite loving intentions, then, creators of a story about whites bearing, birthing, or nursing black offspring could be accused of slipping back into the habit of whites defining themselves vis-à-vis subordinated black bodies.

Recently, as if defending against imperializing encounters, a number of writers have revised the narrative of the racechanged child by imagining its appearance within the black family. Whereas historically literature records white families depreciating the gift of black life, at times (albeit infrequently) it has included imaginative accounts of blacks devaluing the gift of white life.[39] When the white child is imagined inexplicably materializing in the black family, it can create exactly the response of shock, alarm, even horror generated by the dark offspring in characters like Chopin's Armand and Hughes's Colonel Norwood, for the light-skinned child may be rejected as a denial or abandonment of (black) origins. Though it is hardly surprising that celebrating blackness can entail demonizing whiteness, even the lightest baby in the black family remains inescapably, categorically African American (because of the ongoing influence of the "one-drop rule"). This asymmetry means that white racism never translates simply into black racism; even black parents bent on killing their light offspring cannot simply be accused of hostility against whites, for they collude in a culture hostile primarily to African Americans.

The striking contrast between Zora Neale Hurston's play *Color Struck* (1926) and Alyce Miller's short story "Color Struck" (1994) exemplifies a shift in narrative treatment of the light-skinned child born to the black mother. At the beginning of the drama produced during the Harlem Renaissance, Hurston's insecure heroine, Emma, remains firmly convinced that her dark skin color makes her unlovable. For this reason, she has rejected a black lover (jealously believing John desirous of lighter women) and has given birth out of wedlock to a child whose complexion suggests that the father is white. Years later, after John has returned to express his devotion again, Emma remains so blinded by overvaluations of whiteness (so "color-struck") that she lets her sick daughter die, rather than leave her alone with him in order to go for a doctor; the ailing child is condemned to death because the mother believes her suitor would molest the bedridden girl. Apparently, a light epidermis—even on a feverish little girl—casts an inexorably alluring spell. Exemplifying the sort of psychotic racial self-hatred Hurston would go on to examine in the character of Mrs. Turner in *Their Eyes Were Watching God*, the color-struck mother effectively murders the light child she has brought into the world.

Just as disturbed by the eruption of whiteness in the family as Emma is enthralled by it, the parents in Alyce Miller's story "Color Struck" are shocked by the appearance of their third child. For the mother Caldonia, a caesarian birth has contributed to her sense that the white "child had not really come out of her own body" (108) but was instead some kind of ghastly "mix-up" (128) or "blunder, a genetic contretemps" (110). Although Caldonia had read an article entitled "White Couple Gives Birth to Black Baby," she cannot simply reverse its message to comprehend her own situation because "a black woman's baby, no matter how light, would always be black" (110). According to the estranged mother, the child, who seems "cold and foreign" (110), a "tiny wriggling shrimplike creature," must be tended in the dark like "a household plant" (120) or a shameful secret. Haunted by her fear that she will never be able to love the child, Caldonia cannot find a name for the infant even weeks after the birth. If Hurston's mother adores whiteness (though she kills it), Miller's finds it vaguely repulsive (though she nurtures it).

When her brother's date arrives at Thanksgiving and turns out to have the coloring of the baby, Caldonia's extended family coos over the "same pretty complexion" they share (125), but Caldonia remains upset and calls the baby "albino" not simply to signify its sensitivity to light but to indicate her refusal to conform to their "color-struck" values (122–23). Arranging "the baby's pink mouth at her brown breast" (147), she sees that the white girlfriend will never respond to the advances of her dark brother, and she does not "know which was worse, going through life toward blindness or going through life white. In a way, it was kind of the same thing" (128). Caldonia's wish to name the baby Ebony is greeted by her husband with incredulity; however, the final sentence of the story—"she wasn't blaming anyone but herself for the pinch in her heart that prevented her from running right upstairs and calling the child by her rightful name" (129)—suggests, on the one hand, that the baby must be named Ebony so as to be loved within the black family and, on the other, that nobody knows the child's name.

Throughout the narrative of the racechanged child, of course, a fascination with the new child signals an interest in imagining the parent-self reborn with an altered demeanor. In other words, the child can be read as an avatar embodying one of the parent's potential futures. For Alyce Miller's central character, the slippage between whiteness and a disabling albinism means such a rebirth constitutes a genetic mistake.[40] The white-self emerges again as a fallen one in two dystopic reveries on what racial rebirth might mean for the African-American poet. June Jordan's "What Would I Do White" (1967) and Lucille Clifton's "my dream about being white" (1987) use racechange fantasies to identify whiteness with a kind of ghostly invisibility or insubstantial nonbeing. Jordan answers the question of her title with a poem that can be summed up in the word "nothing." If she were "full / of not exactly beans," she would forget her furs, ignore the doorman, and "inspire big returns to equity / the equity of capital I am / accustomed to accept." The final couplet—"I would do nothing. / That would be enough."—hints that the white woman on view as a decorous object, unproductive except as a kind of investment or commodity, is herself nobody. Similarly, in Clifton's dream of being white, negativity abounds. With "no lips" and "no behind," the poet reborn white finds herself "wearing / white history / but there's no future / in those clothes" so she strips and wakes up dancing. Like Soyinka, Jordan and Clifton hint at a black fullness of being, white nothingness that could propel precisely the anxieties among Euro-Americans that in turn lead to obsessive racial mimicries and masquerades.

Inevitable as retaliatory devaluations of whiteness (like those of Jordan and Clifton) may be, their insufficiency as a response against racism is examined by Gloria Naylor, whose ambitious novel *Linden Hills* (1985) provides a sort of coda to this chapter through its meditation on the vertiginous destructiveness of racial impersonation for the African-American community. Here the legitimate but shockingly light-skinned baby born into a black family is as despised as the dark child in slave times. Though endowed with the "same squat bowlegs, the same protruding eyes and puffed lips" as his father, the son's white complexion makes him appear to his father like "a ghostly presence that mocked everything his fathers had built" (18). As in Alyce Miller's tale, then, the child goes unnamed, but in this case for the first five years of life. Clearly Naylor, like Miller, is interested in the idea of black replications of white racism. Ultimately, however, both writers insist that even the lightest or the most assimilated African Americans remain categorized as implacably, essentially black. Ironically, only when black people try (unsuccessfully) to model themselves on whites in *Linden Hills* do they learn to loath difference; only when black people imitate whites do they commit the crime of murdering Otherness. Naylor's highly paradoxical novel thus turns on mimicry and mirroring, racial impersonation as a dead end.

A revision of Dante's *Inferno*, *Linden Hills* describes a wealthy black suburb whose citizens pay for their success with various forms of torment, from suicide and infidelity to loveless marriages and a sense of lifelessness. When blacks model their communities on the competitive, entrepreneurial system of whites, the resulting racechange kills or perverts. The select families chosen to receive mortgages are given "a thousand years and a day to sit right there and forget what it means to be black" (16), somewhat like Nathan Hare's *Black Anglo-Saxons* (1965), those "social schizophrenics" who—because they are black on the outside, white on the inside—are dubbed "Oreos." Although advertised as a "beautiful, black wad of spit right in the white eye of America," Linden Hills "wasn't black; it was successful" (9, 17). Following up on this grotesque logic, one of its fanatically conformist citizens, hungry for professional advancement in the white business world, makes "his blackness . . . disappear" by avoiding sex and controlling his diet so as to regulate his bowel movements (102–4). Similarly, a top executive at IBM kills herself after selling her soul to the corporation, while a lawyer suffers a life-in-death marriage when he relinquishes his male lover to defuse homophobic rumors that threaten his career.

At the bottom of this sordid, sad world, in the very pitch of power, is Satanic Luther Nedeed's house, surrounded by a frozen lake and given the number 999 because in this neighborhood up is down (the wealthier houses are lower down the hill) and 666 is the sign of the beast.[41] Unlike his ancestors who wed light-skinned brides, each of whom produced one very dark and froglike son, a duplicate of the father, Luther Nedeed married a dark "shadow" of a woman, Willa Prescott Nedeed, who has given birth to a white child resembling her grandmother. Because Luther considers the boy a bastard or because his wife has failed in her appointed task to recreate him, Nedeed incarcerates his wife and son in the basement, a kind of underworld beneath the hell of his house. Willa survives in part by interpreting the documents left behind by wives of earlier Nedeeds—diaries, photographs, cookbooks—whose stories reveal the effacement through which they submitted to their husbands' denial of their value as anything except what Margaret Homans calls "disposable machines for replicating men" (369).

The death of the six-year-old boy, a dead end for the Nedeed line, awakens the complicitous Willa, who finally realizes that she has herself walked down the steps into the basement and so she can walk back up. Carrying her ghostly white son, Willa revolts against the slavery inflicted on herself and on all the other wives of Nedeed men. In a brilliant revision of Charlotte Brontë's *Jane Eyre*, where maddened Bertha Mason Rochester escapes her confinement in the attic of the ancestral mansion of Thornfield Hall and climbs to the roof to set it afire, Willa ascends from the basement to struggle with her husband and in the process sets the house afire. Her dead white child serves as an emblem of the deathliness of the psychological racechanges that created Linden Hills in the first place. In other words, the son dies because he was always destined to be merely a simulacrum or copy of whiteness, a symbol of the fatality and futility of the black middle class's effort to prove itself "just like" whites. Significantly, Willa's boy is murdered by the black man who wants to "forget what it means to be black": A white impersonator, Luther Nedeed becomes the apotheosis of evil when he acts like Chopin's Armand and Hughes's Colonel Norwood, refusing to father the son he masters. That he destroys himself and his lineage in the process proves that black racism remains a contradiction-in-terms for Naylor; it injures only black people and thus perpetuates the hurts inflicted by white racism.[42]

Eventually, the ghost story Naylor tells eulogizes all the rejected children haunting the conscience of the nation. As Lillian Smith once put it, "Little ghosts playing and laughing and weeping on the edge of the southern memory can be a haunting thing" (120). Whether unexpectedly dark or light, then, racechanged children in fiction act as ghostly instructors on the subject of the family's romance with whiteness. In his meditation on "Family Romances" (1909), Freud claimed that most children remain persuaded for a good portion of their early lives that their mundane biological parents could not possibly be their real parents, for a magisterial sense of privilege and power endows young children with the fantasy that they must derive from royal lineage. Children convinced that they have an Emperor and Empress for father and mother demote their actual parents into mere caretakers, substituting in their stead exaulted parents of "better birth," altogether "grander people" (76–77). If we read this psychological trope not only in the Oedipal context provided by Freud but also in the framework of most psychologists' belief that babies and young children do not register any awareness of a racial identity, narratives of the racechanged child suggest that all colored but unraced babies are mismatched with parents pledging allegiance to a single racial identity. The shock administered by stories of racechanged children has everything to do with startling representations of the monochromatic adult self at odds with its own uncannily colorful embodiments.

Perhaps no African-American visual artist has presented a better portrait of the comforting familiarity of stultifying, monochromatic racial identities than Horace Pippin in his painting *Mr. Prejudice* (1943), a picture portraying a world split in two (Fig. 6.7). This ironic treatment of what one critic calls "the threat to wartime unity posed by the persistence of racial segregation in the United States" places the central image of the Allied effort in the Second World War, the V-for-Victory, so as to divide blacks from whites (Wilson, 61). Black soldiers and sailors, black artisans and workers occupy the left side of the canvas with the towering figure of the Statue of Liberty as their avatar. White soldiers and craftsman, workers and farmers occupy the right side of the picture with the towering figure of a Ku Klux Klansman as their avatar. Although mirroring goes on (between Islamic fundamentalist and Klansman, for instance), interchanges and racechanges remain impossible between black and white citizens or cultures. To insure widened divisions, white Mr. Prejudice drives a wedge into the very crux of the V, threatening to transform wartime unity into postwar divisiveness. Neither the prewar idea of the melting pot of assimilation nor the postwar ideal of the salad bar of cultural pluralism seems feasible in a framework that so severs America. That bigotry is personified as a "Mr." and that all the figures except the stone statue are male highlight the iconography of the V which traditionally stands not only for wartime victory but also for the vagina, the virgin, Venus herself, the female generative principle. Read this way, Pippin's canvas imagines a wounding penetration, an injurious rape presaging the destruction of the womb, the place of reproduction. As writers from Chopin to Toomer, from Spark to Naylor understood, perhaps only the annihilation of life and love itself will insure a lasting divorce between black and white.

Although the history of racechange in the twentieth century attests to repeated attempts to imagine racial mutations that confirm, attack, confound, or move beyond the conventional meanings of black and white in America, racial polarity has a kind of obdurate recalcitrance, a stubborn and stupid obstinacy that withstands such imaginings. Perhaps such permutations remain thin and partial because they so often assume the priority or superiority of white over and against black or because of the flimsiness of aesthetic phenomena vis-à-vis the material recalcitrance of race relations in the United States. With none of the redeeming value it displays in, say, Picabia's portrait of the androgynous White Negro, racechange crucifies in Robert Colescott's most tragic approach to the subject. His biracial figure returns to the "mixtries" of Langston Hughes through the saint sanctified by Carl Van Vechten to merge the homosexual as a blameless victim of heterosexual society with the hybrid as a casualty of racist society. Executed in what one critic calls

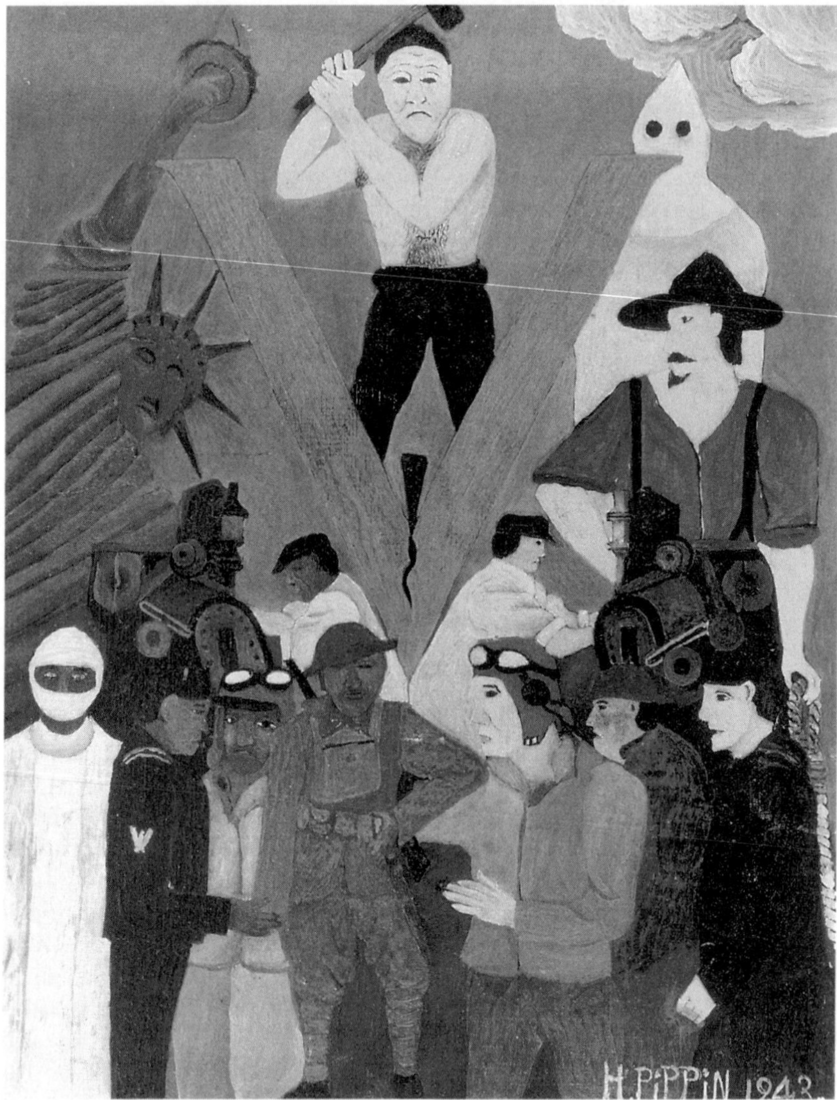

Figure 6.7 Horace Pippin, *Mr. Prejudice* (1943), oil on canvas, 18 × 14 in. Gift of Dr. and Mrs. Matthew T. Moore; courtesy of the Philadelphia Museum of Art.

a "luridly Neo-Expressionist style," Colescott's painting "Knowledge of the Past Is the Key to the Future (St. Sebastian)" (1986; see color insert) explicitly applies the St. Sebastian figure and the White Negro to the trope of the tragic mulatto or self-divided hermaphrodite (Johnson, 149). The central figure, whose left half is a black man and whose right half is a white woman, appears bound and pierced, in part because of a schizophrenic splitting of the biracial, bisexed body.

Above the central figure, two heads—tethered together—signify the attachments between black women and white men in America, bonds that bind. Whether a portrait of the historical reality of interracial coupling (a coercive white master exercising his right to rape the black female slave) or a picture of the main subject's familial genealogy (a voluntarily entered-upon union), the "not" of miscegenation turns the marriage "knot" into a lynching rope or a murderous noose. Such a genealogy, social or personal, casts the Saint as an outlaw, strung up as a sacrifice, subjected to the torment of becoming an enigmatic contradiction-in-terms, a Du Boisian icon of warring "double consciousness." Fixed in a living hell of gender and racial tensions, Colescott's racechanged offspring will join his only companions, the skulls on the bottom left of the canvas that foretell the inexorable fate of all those who abrogate conventional categories defining difference. Within the barren valley of the shadow of death that is Western civilization, the solid, sullied flesh of whites and blacks alike brings only pain, the sole release its melting away to reveal macabre skeletons with their rictus of a grin. Saint Sebastian is only the latest in a long line of martyrs. Outlawed, criminalized, and then worshipped, the saint punished for sexual, racial transgressions suffers the martyrdom of an ambiguous racial and sexual identity that defies normative classifications. Strapped to his stake, Colescott's protagonist experiences the color line Du Bois considered the central problem of the twentieth century as only a lash.

7

THE EDIBLE COMPLEX

A Postscript

> I conceive there is more barbarism in eating a man alive than in eating him dead. . . .
>
> —Montaigne

> The Negro is America's metaphor.
>
> —Richard Wright

> Of every hue and caste am I. . . . I resist any thing better than my own diversity.
>
> —Walt Whitman

> In the relation of the self (the same) to the Other, the Other is distant, he is the stranger; but if I reverse this relation, the Other relates to me as if I were the Other and thus causes me to take leave of my identity. . . . When thus I am wrested from myself, there remains a passivity bereft of self (sheer alterity, the other without unity).
>
> —Maurice Blanchot

Born white and Jewish, the chameleon-hero of Woody Allen's *Zelig* (1983) subsequently becomes not only black and Native American but also Irish, Italian, Mexican, and Chinese; judged a "triple threat" by the Ku Klux Klan, he embodies the "hybridity, impurity, intermingling, the transformation that comes of new and unexpected combinations of human beings" to which an intrepid Salman Rushdie dedicated his *Satanic Verses* (1988).[1] When Steve Martin starts a comic film by recalling "I was born a poor black child," when Karl Lagerfeld photographs the model Naomi Campbell as a black Scarlett for a fashion collection presented with a *Gone with the Wind* twist, even flippant contemporary approaches to racechange appear to tap its subversive potential, disrupting the racist complacency many earlier deployments bolstered. The performance artist Adrian Piper, who meditates in her essays on whether the idea of race might soon become obsolete, put together the exhibit and the volume *Colored People* (in 1987 and 1991 respectively) by coloring and categorizing sixteen people's photographs according to such moods as "scarlet with embarrassment" or "tickled pink." Also fascinated with the anarchic promise of double-crossing the color line, Iké Udé used computer graphics to produce in his *Celluloid Frames* exhibit (of 1995) racechanged versions of one of Marilyn Monroe's most famous images and one of Mapplethorpe's most infamous in order to criticize the tendency of consumer culture to portray "difference as 'damned otherness.'" Like a surprising number of writers and film-makers working at the close of this century, Piper and Udé concretize the denaturalizing of race implicit in the idea of racechanges as well as the diverse roles they have played over time in manifold settings and media.

Denaturalizing: To translate Simone de Beauvoir's famous remark about femininity from a context of gender to a framework of race, racechange demonstrates that one is not born but becomes a white; one is not born but becomes a black. Diversity: Cross-racial imitations have appeared in startlingly different contexts throughout the pages of this book. Although racial masquerades seem murderous in their intent as they enact replacement (of the self for the Other), they appear loving as they emphasize resemblance (of the self with the Other). Conscious or unconscious, voluntary or involuntary, racial impersonations can be set within homosexual, heterosexual, bisexual, and ambiguously sexual scenarios. Not always the sites of erotic investment, they may constitute a political venture. We have seen, too, that cross-racial fantasies appear in nonironic, mimetic frameworks or they parade a parodic excess that turns them into self-mocking performances. Some racial masquerades act to police boundaries; however, others abrogate definitional limits. In various contexts and media, racial representations teeter between identification (the wish to be the Other), desire (the wish to have the Other), and disavowal (the wish to disengage from the Other).

Yet, oddly and disturbingly, cross-racial impersonations have often sustained racist conceptualizations. Why did the denaturalizing potential and diversity of racechange so rarely find egalitarian expression?[2] In earlier chapters, I have primarily emphasized the motives for racechange; however, what exactly are its effects? If I ask and answer a question usually put to doctoral students defending their completed dissertations in the humanities—how did the material surprise you in the course of your writing?—I have to admit to finding myself somewhat alarmed that racechange (as employed by artists from D. W. Griffith to Zora Neale Hurston, from Mark Twain to Fannie Hurst and William Faulkner, from Vachel Lindsay and T. S. Eliot to Lois Gould) remained circumscribed so often within narratives that either endorse or acquiesce in racist totalizing as well as the social injustices such totalizing validates. I want to speculate in this postscript on why racechange has served racist ends in this country's cultural past before I conclude by claiming that its structure nevertheless continues to hold out the promise of bridging the gap between black and white. What I will end up suggesting, then, is that racechange has historically buttressed the very totalizing that its dynamic calls into question. Thus the liberating potential of racechanging iconography is only now being tapped in various performances, meditations, films, and art works that use cross-racial imagery to enact or envision post-racist ways of being and perceiving.

Racist Totalizing

One of the more bizarre moments in Edgar Allan Poe's *The Narrative of Arthur Gordon Pym* (1837) occurs in an episode that forecloses any possibility of cross-racial interaction when a captive cannibal opens his lips to disclose black teeth. To the white hero who finds himself floating in a canoe in the Antarctic Ocean at the end of Poe's unfinished narrative, the dark-skinned savage appears so violently terrified by whiteness that he goes into convulsions, first, at the sign of a linen handkerchief and, then, as a fine white powder resembling ashes begins to fall from an apocalyptic sky. After being questioned about the motives of his countrymen in destroying Pym's companions, Nu-Nu's dread incapacitates him from affording a rational reply:

> He still obstinately lay in the bottom of the boat; and, upon our reiterating the questions as to the motive made use only of idiotic gesticulations, such as raising with his forefinger the upper lip, and displaying the teeth which lay beneath it. These were black. We had never before seen the teeth of an inhabitant of Tsalal. (194)

Not just skin deep, racial difference permeates and saturates all aspects of being, dividing Europeans from Africans anatomically, genetically, skeletally, absolutely.[3] The mark of racist totalizing inflicted by a fictional trope like black teeth on a character such as Nu-Nu depends on a simple mental trajectory. By the word "totalizing," I mean that trajectory to encompass two assumptions: that all blacks are alike and also that all blacks are completely and immutably different, utterly distinct from whites. (I use blacks in the place of those racially totalized since whites in America remain in the default position of a humanity presumed to be raceless.) The idea of race as absolute or monolithic—the notion that racial dissimilarity permeates every cell, each gene, all internal and external organs of the body, even its skeletal frame—surfaced repeatedly in Western history. For example, Poe's account summarizes a commonplace mindset described by Frantz Fanon with characteristic surrealism:

> And there one lies body to body with one's blackness or one's whiteness, in full narcissistic cry, each sealed into his own peculiarity. . . . (45)

As in the paintings of Horace Pippin and Robert Colescott that were reproduced in the last chapter, race operates decisively and divisively the way species does, to sunder the human race.

On Nu-Nu's home island of Tsalal, we are told, nothing white or light-colored was to be found. Similarly, Nu-Nu's black teeth accentuate difference, in this telling case the deviancy of his mouth which in turn draws attention back to his idiotic (yet somehow obstinate) silence as well as the obscene tastes of his bloodthirsty, barbaric people.[4] Yet of course Nu-Nu's cannibalism camouflages the engorging dynamics of a white creativity that incorporates Africanist presences to reproduce them for its own purposes. Like Lynch, the black politician in *The Birth of a Nation* who wants to lynch white people exactly as much as his creator sought to expunge blacks, the supposed orality of Poe's savage captive screens the exorbitant appetites of a white author whose racial representations are themselves a form of cannibalism; with a nod toward Sigmund Freud and bell hooks, we might term this dynamic "the edible complex."[5] The first epigraph of this postscript—Montaigne's critique of imperialists horrified by cannibalism yet themselves guilty of torturing natives "under the pretense of piety and religion"—remains pertinent vis-à-vis the dynamics of representation.

A quick glance confirms the fact that such different and differently situated thinkers as Herman Melville, Robert Lowell, and Thomas Jefferson meditated on a totalizing that permeated American thought and that in turn explains why racechange has historically served racist ends. At the very center of Herman Melville's fascinating "Benito Cereno" (1856), the tale of a slave mutiny, the brilliant rebel leader Babo strikes terror into the heart of his white captain not only by murdering the Spaniard's cocaptain and displaying the dead man's bones on the bow (substituted for the ship's figurehead), but also by exulting in the whiteness of the skeleton (which Babo uses to prove his triumph over this particular white man and white privilege in general): "The Negro Babo" asks Benito Cereno repeatedly about his cocaptain's remains "whether, from its whiteness, he should not think it a white's" (111). Just as Babo almost gets away with his conspiracy by playing on racist propositions (through his black black impersonation of a fawningly solicitous slave), his exultant display of the white bones uncovers the racist totalizing of his would-be enslavers. In contrast to the black skull and crossbones raised by the insurrectionary Africans in Robert Lowell's 1965 dramatic adaptation of Melville's tale stands the chalk-white skeleton dressed up in Benito Cereno's clothes and hailed by the slaves on board the ship:

> He is a white because his bones are white!
> He is a white because his bones are white! (208)

Although Lowell's Babu harbors some hope that Thomas Jefferson, the "King" of the American "Republic, would like to free his slaves," the rebel leader is immediately disabused of that illusion: "Jefferson [is] a gentleman and an American," which means "He's not lifting a finger to free his slaves" (195). And even a glimpse at the relatively liberal meditations of Thomas Jefferson in *Notes on the State of Virginia* (1787) provides evidence that he had internalized not simply the most transparently utilitarian platitudes about slaves—that they "require less sleep" or feel "griefs [that] are transient"—but also a racist totalizing based upon immutable physical distinctions purportedly permeating all aspects of being:

> Whether the black of the negro resides in the reticular membrane between the skin and scarf-skin, or in the scarf-skin itself; whether it proceeds from the colour of the blood, the colour of the bile, or from that of some other secretion, the difference is fixed in nature, and is as real as if its seat and cause were better known to us. And is this difference of no importance? Is it not the foundation of a greater or less share of beauty in the two races? (138)

According to Jefferson, beauty cannot reside in "that eternal monotony . . . , that immoveable veil of black which covers all the emotions of the other race" (138).[6] To be sure, Jefferson sounds relatively moderate when he admits that "The opinion, that [blacks] are inferior in the faculties of reason and imagination, must be hazarded with great diffidence" (143). Still, he strikes a far more ominous tone when he melds race with species, judging the preference of slaves for whites to be as uniform "as is the preference of the Oran-ootan for the black women over those of his own species" (138).

As with fictional characters so with real people—at least with respect to the wound of such totalizing. Although Fanon tries on a "tight smile" when a little girl points at him—exclaiming to her mother "Look, a Negro!"—the psychiatrist admits that he "made myself an object" and that this process felt like "an amputation, an excision, a hemorrhage that spattered my whole body with black blood" (112). Like Nu-Nu's black teeth, Fanon's black blood signifies his complete Otherness; however, he stages that estrangement in the context of his internalization of a totalizing "racial epidermal schema" projected on him by whites, one requiring very thick skin indeed from the point of view of the person seeking (without much hope) to extricate himself from a position of alterity. How should we position cross-racial passing and posing in terms of racist totalizing?

Especially before civil rights legislation, affirmative action programs, and the emergence of a substantial black middle class, the white imagination tended to conform to the pattern of an edible complex that depends upon totalizing, picturing blacks as so saturated by Otherness that their disruptive, demonized energies had to be contained since they threaten the status quo. Several decades ago, Zora Neale Hurston compared her own situation to that of whites; regardless of her entanglement in prejudicial modes of conceptualizing race, her conclusion that whites remained victims of the fears they projected onto blacks still rings true today:

> The position of my white neighbor is much more difficult [than mine]. No brown specter pulls up a chair beside me when I sit down to eat. No dark ghost thrusts its leg against mine in bed. (153)

Brown specters and dark ghosts haunting the house of the white imagination attest to many artists' sometimes conscious, sometimes unconscious efforts to buttress privileges made fragile by the inevitable awareness produced in a democratic society that such entitlements are indefensible. Often in the American past, racechanges—undertaken by white artists for a variety of motives—testify to the construction of an Otherness compulsively annihilated.

Despite the anarchic potential of racechange, then, the aggregate of epidermal fungibility, or what I am tempted to call "epidermatics," almost always seems historically to have resulted in the subordination, muting, or obliteration of the Other. Whether driven by identification or disidentification, racechanges spotlight the crucial question posed by Diana Fuss in her recent book *Identification Papers*: "How can the other be brought into the domain of the knowable without annihilating the other *as other*—as precisely that which cannot be known?" (4). Like the politics that Fuss sees at work in Fanon's analysis of the violence of identification, cross-racial impersonations have illuminated "the material practices of exclusion, alienation, appropriation, and domination that transform other subjects into subjected others" (14). The paradox of this study is that they did so despite the wildly divergent, conscious aims of performers.

Here, then, are the equations that constitute the edible complex shaping seemingly antithetical attempts at cross-racial impersonation. They must be read with some attention to numbering, for the first Proposition 1 begins with resemblance while the second Proposition 1 antithetically starts with disavowal. Indeed, the first Proposition 1 looks like the most libertarian form of racechanging mutability whereas the second Proposition 1 looks like the most racist form of totalizing. Yet, if scanned as two sequences, they shockingly end up in the same irrationally monistic place:

1. I am like the Other.
2. I display my similarity to the Other.
3. I am the same as the Other.
4. I admit the Other within me.
5. I contain the Otherness of the Other within me.

—6. I represent the Other.

5. I contain the Otherness of the Other outside me.
4. I expel the Other outside me.
3. I am the opposite of the Other.
2. I display the Otherness of the Other.
1. I am nothing like the Other.

Starting from startlingly opposed attitudes toward Otherness, the subject nevertheless subjects the Other to ownership or control. If "I" represent the "Other," the "Other" is "my" construction. (The prohibition against graven images of divinity in the Hebrew Bible or the fear among some peoples that a photograph constitutes a form of soul-snatching might help contextualize the idea that representation poses the threat of violation.)

Whether one begins with internalization or externalization of the Other, identification or disavowal of identification, professed amity or enmity, the logic of the self that occupies the position of the universally representative, representing subject ends us possessing or dispossessing, engulfing or expelling Otherness. A catch-22 or double bind, the syntax of self and Other inevitably leads to the disappearance of the Other's Otherness.[7] Regardless of the route by which it is attained, the central Proposition 6 inexorably transmutes the Other into a surd or a voiceless sound. Thus, the history of representations of racechange provides a cautionary tale about the expropriating mechanics of mimesis in general. More specifically, the cross-racial masquerades presented in this book often tally the same irrational numbers, though they are motivated by widely divergent desires and dreams. Like those vegematics advertised on late-night television, epidermatics grind out with mindless rapidity identical, predictable patterns and shapes (bringing to mind the old adage, "no matter how you slice it . . . ").

Although white representations of blackness have moved in the course of the twentieth century from the mean mockery of blackface through the adulatory mimicry of imperialist nostalgia, from the confused erotics of black envy to the loving emphasis on interracial mutuality and mutability at work in narratives of the mixed child and in visual graphics of morphed hybrid beings, even the best-intentioned and most aesthetically exuberant imitations veer into incorporations that threaten to obliterate the Otherness of the Other: not just *The Birth of a Nation* but also *Swing Time*, not just Vachel Lindsay's "The Congo" but also John Berryman's *The Dream Songs*, not just Saul Bellow's *Mr. Sammler's Planet* but also Norman Mailer's "The White Negro," not just Al Jolson's but also Virginia Woolf's and John Howard Griffin's use of blackface, not just Mark Twain's *Pudd'nhead Wilson* but also Kate Chopin's "Désirée's Baby." (In an elegaic manner comparable to that adopted by Chopin, the racechanging works of such black artists as Anne Spencer, Charles Chesnutt, George Schuyler, Marita Bonner, Jean Toomer, and Gloria Naylor make this same point.) In other words, the purported politics of racechangers can vary dramatically, but the ethical problem that structures their performance tends to remain constant.

Keeping this in mind, what does it mean to return to the idea articulated in my introduction that America's first national theater, first motion pictures, first radio shows, and first new journalism as well as Europe's first experimental literature, painting, and photography were all marked by forms of cross-racial impersonation? Has a significant aspect of the evolution of modern Euro-American culture been achieved through the edible complex and the muting or what bell hooks calls "the eating" of the Other? Just as *The Birth of the Nation* and the birth of the nation's film industry depended upon staging the death of African Americans, could one contend that the genesis of twentieth-century radio, new journalism, experimental poetry, modernist painting, and avant-garde photography hinged at least in part on representations that possessed or dispossessed, engulfed or expelled the black Other? Edward Said's argument about European modernism—that its most prominent characteristics derive from collisions between Western society and native cultures constituted by the colonized—can be extended to twentieth-century American aesthetic productions which repeatedly framed themselves in terms of multiple collusions in the persistent disparity in power between the white and the black (188–91).

Though I have not told the whole story of black passing and white posing, though I have refrained from a teleological plot with a comic or tragic resolution, I have found myself returning again and again to a question this study cannot answer, the ethical inquiry at the center of cross-racial interaction: How can white people understand or sympathize with African-Americans without distorting or usurping their perspective? In the conclusion to her book about theorizing race and gender, Robyn Wiegman raises the same problem about "the transformatory hope of identifying with the pain and suffering of others [which] seems ever more bound to an imperialistic cast," and she goes on to ask, "is this the only fate for identification?" (200) Perhaps most of the racechanges recounted in these pages answer this question positively because they operate so intransigently within the categories of a sovereign, autonomous selfhood defined through whiteness and an Other colored black. As Fuss puts it,

> To invoke "the Other" as an ontological or existentialist category paradoxically risks eliding the very range and play of cultural differences that the designation is intended to represent. Reliance upon the Other as a categorical imperative often works to flatten rather than to accentuate difference. (*Identification Papers*, 144)

The query "How can white people understand or sympathize with African-Americans without distorting or usurping their perspective?" too glibly assumes that there is such a perspective. Indeed, how can one posit a genuine, uncontaminated white cultural identity or a unique black racial autonomy, given the cross-racial entanglements and influences mapped throughout these pages? What the history of racechange teaches is that race and color are not immutable categories but classifications with permeable boundaries. Or, to put it another way, that neither black nor white fill-in-the-blank—artistic productions, experiences, groups of people—can be understood as unitary, entire, monolithic, coherent. Although the epidermatics of cross-racial performances would flatten all cross-racial experiments to the level of the same evil white conspiracy, a recognition of their complex inflections and rhetorics makes for a more intricate comprehension of how those experiments arbitrate or violate racial perimeters.

Transraciality

Only by understanding the complex heterogeneity hidden beneath the terms "I" and "Other" can we avoid facile assumptions about a single, homogenized subjectivity or Otherness. When the manifold sorts of differences—beyond those of complexion—multiply, perhaps the monolithic dualism that set the stage for twentieth-century racechanges can break down. Yet—and this is a big "yet"—"color has long been a powerful tool for assimilative erasure of class, religion, history, most ethnicity, gender and sexual orientation," or so Patricia J. Williams has observed (*Rooster's Egg*, 188–89). Besides leveling many other differences, pigmentation has monotonously played into Western culture's favorite mind-body dualism. For too long the human face has been white, the object-face black—as, for example, in Man Ray's photographs. (A glance back at some of Hannah Höch's photomontages confirms her effort to undermine this equation.) As a number of racechanging productions analyzed in this book intimate, the African American has been more deeply inflected by an homogenized Otherness than other admittedly othered groups; the category "black" takes on what Patricia J. Williams calls "irreducibility" in the racist imagination (192).

In *The Jazz Singer* or Claude McKay's "Near White," we have seen, blacks function as precisely the limits by which other others (Jews and Chinese) could be accepted into American society as white. Antithetically, blackness—when plastered on other others—serves to extend their marginalization: On the Renaissance stage, according to James Shapiro, Jews were demonized as blackamoors; in contemporary times, according to Bharati Mukherjee, Indians in Toronto are asked, "Why don't you go back to Africa?" (38). Yet if we break down the terms "black" and "white," will the proliferation of more differences evade the fate of simply refining the taxonomy by which we other others? Will dividing "white" into, say, working-class, second-generation, lapsed Catholic, Irish-American afford more than just more claustrophobic pigeonholes? Or can an ineffable attentiveness to precisely those differences resistant to our analogizings save us from the erasures of Othering, as Wiegman has speculated (179–202)?

Whether "the Other" becomes an individuated "you" or multiply defined "others," a shift in syntax combined with attentiveness to differences resistant to our analogizings might help make the relationship between "black" and "white" bidirectional. As the world population becomes darker and the Euro-American becomes simply another other, such two-way traffic encourages self and other to change places, so "the Other relates to me as if I were the Other" (Blanchot, 18). What can be said on behalf of the performances studied in this book is that they provide an explanation for, even a prognostication of, that future evolution. For regardless of its historic contamination in racist totalizing, the structure of cross-racial impersonation poses a dialectic between self and Other that posits a third term, pointing toward "transraciality," a word Michael Awkward uses "to describe the adoption of physical traits of difference for the purpose of impersonating a racial other" (19). To distinguish the concept from the various modes of cross-racial passing and posing we have reviewed thus far, I would stress the ways in which transracial performers seek neither to become the Other (blending into or integrating within the Other's community like a passer) nor to flaunt their alienation from the Other (ridiculing the Other's mores like a poser). The word "cross-racial" means crossing over racial demarcations; however, the word "transracial" should imply dwelling within racial borderlands.

Securely positioned in the place of neither the self nor the Other, the racechanger demonstrates through the motility of performance how impossible it is to ascribe fixed meanings to racial or, for that matter, gendered differences (19–20). To the "either/or, both/and" with which I began this book, the transraciality of the racechanger posits a "neither/nor"—not in the conflicted, sad cadences of the "tragic mulatto" whose neither white nor black spells disastrous exile but in the flagrantly foreign heterogeneity implied by Rimbaud's "*Je est un autre*" ("I is an other") with its call for the acknowledgment not simply of accepting the Other but, as Julia Kristeva puts it, "of *being in his [or her] place*, and this means to imagine and make oneself other for oneself" (*Strangers* 13). In the thirties, the surrealist artist Claude Cahun explained her racechanging, sexchanging self-portraits by describing her principal pleasure as dreaming about alterity: "To imagine that I am another" (Phillips, 39). A whimsical approach to the vertiginous instability of "transraciality" might be furnished by the panethnic chameleon of Woody Allen's *Zelig* who, in the words of Ella Shohat and Robert Stam, "renders syncretism visible by offering us a figure who is at once Woody Allen, and therefore White and Jewish, *and* Black, Indian, Chinese, and Irish" (238). Or, for that matter, Mel Brooks's *Blazing Saddles* (1972) where whites sing "Ole Man River" and blacks sing "I Get No Kick from Champagne." Another and the one Awkward uses is provided by Michael Jackson.

Because the transraciality of a figure like Michael Jackson—"the radical revision of one's natural markings and the adoption of aspects of the human surface (especially skin, hair, and facial features) generally associated with the racial other"—insists on the mysteriousness of the racial other's cultural life, it distinguishes itself from passing: In Awkward's view, then, it may constitute "a distinct cultural and scopic possibility in our time" (181).[8] To the extent that cross-racial performers neither abandon origins nor pass into the other group's world, they create a new (volatile and not necessarily unified) racial category. In terms of its most liberating potential and despite its history, then, trans-racial transgressions can crack open any monolithic notion one might have about the coherent racial self. Two recent avant-garde films explore the scopic possibilities transraciality holds out by making white viewers self-conscious about the uses to which they put racial categories.

So blatantly post-modern is the performance artist Sandra Bernhard in her approach to the recalcitrant mysteriousness of the Other's cultural life that she sardonically turns her gaze onto herself as a prototypical white subject enraptured by black envy; she thereby seeks to dramatize the extent to which whiteness depends upon appropriative and patently synthetic presentations of blackness. From its beginning, Bernhard's movie *Without You I'm Nothing* (1990) melds racechange with sexchange when the camera pans away from a white man in eighteenth-century costume playing Bach on a spinet to a contemporary black woman picking up the same piece. Repeatedly filmed in a cabaret and introduced to bored black patrons by an MC who keeps misnaming her "Sarah Bernhardt," Bernhard—through heavily ironized performances, some in blackface—never captures anyone's attention, despite what Stanley Kauffmann calls her "guilt-cum-envy toward blacks" (26).

What the self-satirizing routines enact is Bernhard's understanding that her wish to gain the adulation of blacks is as morally reprehensible as her adulterated versions of their artistry. Invariably a bit off, the shuck and sham of Bernhard's ersatz racial concoctions remind us that it is only us whites playing black people for our own narcissistic purposes (though Bernhard teerers on the edge of an imitative fallacy that rebounds against her own egomania).[9] The film's title captures some of the paradoxes at work in white psychology, a line of thinking (within the mind of the white entertainer brooding on her black precursors and audience) which might be captured this way:

> Because "*Without you* I'm nothing," I desire you more than anything; however, because "*I am nothing* without you," I resent the way you make me feel dependent on you for my very existence. In fact, my loathing of myself for my dependency on you is only matched by my hatred of you. And so let me remind you, for once and all, that "*Without me* you're nothing." I am at the center here so count yourself lucky that I make and re-make you up, rescuing you from the nothingness to which you must remain ontologically wedded. Only when we both agree that "*You're nothing* without me" will it become apparent that "*I'm something* with or without you (aren't I?)."

Another recent movie, entitled *Suture* (1993), dramatizes the instability of transraciality—and by extension of such transgressively malleable figures as Jean

Toomer and Mezz Mezzrow—through the odd juxtaposition between the color blindness of its characters and an inevitable awareness of racial markers on the part of the viewing audience. A decent but impoverished African-American man named Clay suffers amnesia after his nefarious but wealthy white brother Vincent unsuccessfully attempts to stage his own death by murdering Clay. Placed inside Vincent's locale by deluded doctors and friends, the confused Clay inhabits his brother's identity, living his white brother's life without any of Vincent's acquaintances ever in any way noticing the racechange the scoundrel has undergone. In other words, we-the-viewers repeatedly see the African-American Clay being mistaken for his white brother Vincent.

After an enamored white woman praises the Greco-Roman beauty of Clay's nose and the slimness of his lips, the black man who has stepped into the white man's shoes decides to become Vincent, even though an avuncular psychiatrist warns that such an abrogation of Clay's originatory identity will lead to catastrophic consequences. When Vincent returns to reclaim his privileged life, Clay murders him and becomes him (even though Clay's memory has returned and he knows now who he "really" is). By the film's conclusion, Clay's happily-ever-after proves the shrink wrong, just as all of the characters' obliviousness about color hints that we viewers are stuck in old-fashioned notions about the significance of the visibility or the stability of racial identity, categories which in fact have no substantive reality within the world of the film. The black Clay therefore need not "pass" as the white Vincent since the African-American assumes and plays his brother's roles without in any way altering his dark complexion or African-American features.

Different though they are in terms of aesthetic ambitiousness and mass marketing, Hollywood films have recently exploited various types of transracial narratives to complicate normative notions about the color line. In *Silver Streak* (1976), *The Jerk* (1979), and *Heart Condition* (1990), for example, transraciality triggers the reversals in perspective that racechanges often deploy. *Silver Streak*'s Richard Pryor mentions Al Jolson when he instructs Gene Wilder on how to disguise himself as a black man to evade police looking for a white suspect, so it is hardly surprising that, shoe polish and shades and radio notwithstanding, Wilder remains unable to display the rhythmic acumen necessary to pass (Fig. 7.1). This same lacking is what tells Navin R. Johnson (aka Steve Martin) that he is not the natural-born child of his black parents (Fig. 7.2). *The Jerk*, which opens with Martin explaining "I was born a poor black child," includes a flashback to the "jump down, turn around, pick a bail of cotton" jamboree of Navin's childhood when his mother's confession about his adoption makes him burst out crying in horrified disbelief: "You mean, I'm going *to stay* this color?" *Heart Condition* remains just as sardonic about white deficiency when chubby, sweaty Bob Hoskins receives the heart of healthy, handsome, but murdered Denzel Washington. After Hoskins's racist buddies joke about the sort of organ transplant he really wants by displaying a huge black dildo on his hospital bedside tray, Hoskins-with-a-black-heart regains his lost soul by saving the child Denzel Washington fathered with the vulnerable white woman Hoskins had himself failed to foster at an earlier time of his life.

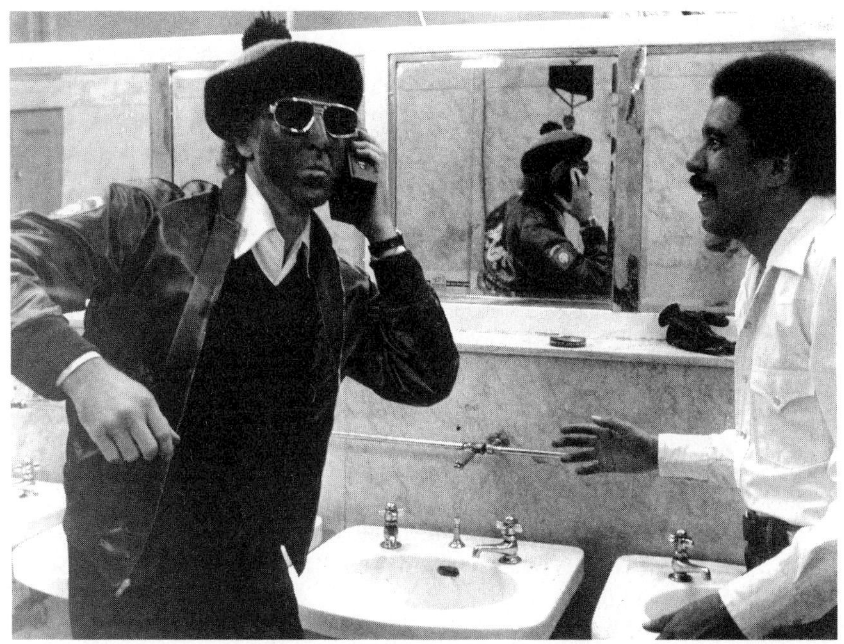

Figure 7.1 Gene Wilder and Richard Pryor in *Silver Streak* (1976). Courtesy of Photofest.

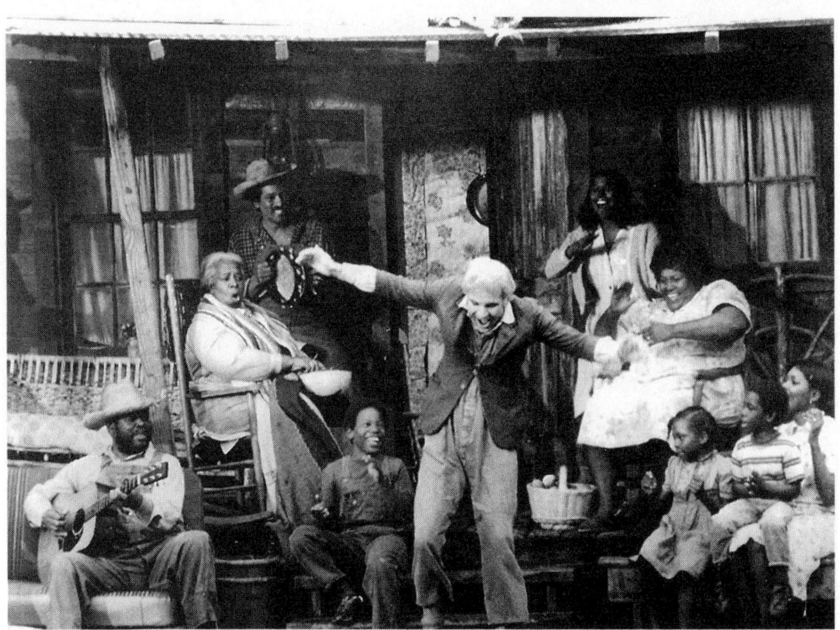

Figure 7.2 Steve Martin in *The Jerk* (1979). Courtesy of Museum of Modern Art Film Stills Archive.

The importance of transraciality in popular media may be bound up with what the novelist Trey Ellis views as a new phenomena extending the Black Arts movement into the eighties and nineties, namely the emergence of what he calls the "cultural mulatto," a figure "educated by a multi-racial mix of cultures [who] can also navigate easily in the white world" and who "no longer need[s] to deny or suppress any part of our complicated and sometimes contradictory cultural baggage to please either white people or black" (235). Ellis, pointing to the class basis of this new "post-bourgeois" movement, locates its origins in the production of a critical mass of black college graduates who are the children of college graduates (237). From the films of Spike Lee and the rap of Fishbone to the novels of Terry McMillan, samples of what Ellis jokingly calls the NBA (the New Black Aesthetic) empower a skeptical take on earlier black nationalist movements, flouting any "positivist black party line": Playwright George C. Wolfe's parodies of *A Raisin in the Sun* (1961) and *For Colored Girls* (1975) in his brilliantly satiric *The Colored Museum* (1987), for instance, refuse to whitewash the intricate experiences of African Americans whether or not white and/or black audiences (for whatever reason) wish to be given sanitized positive role models (236). When the extraordinary tap-dancer Savion Glover choreographed "The Uncle Huck-a-Buck Song" for his Broadway hit *Bring in 'Da Noise, Bring in 'Da Funk* (1996), he depicted what he judged to be Bill Robinson's limited repertoire as a reflex of his white audiences' demands on a black performer. Sardonically living out the dream of the little black girls in *The Bluest Eye*, Glover himself—mincing behind a life-size, floppy Shirley Temple doll strapped to his hands and feet—dances with a Bojangles who can be only as versatile as his racist viewers will allow.

As if exemplifying Ellis's vision of the cultural mulatto's multicultural mixing of traditions, Adrian Piper and Iké Udé focus on the portrait as a genre that can unravel racialized presuppositions about identity. Piper's *Colored People* consists of photographic self-portraits that sixteen subjects ("equal numbers of people of color and euroethnics, women and men") took in eight different shots of themselves, "each expressing facially the corresponding colloquial metaphor of color as mood." Presumably Piper herself colored them in as "Tickled Pink" or "Scarlet with Embarrassment," "Purple with Anger" or simply "Blue," "Green with Envy" or "Jaundiced Yellow," "White with Fear" or "Black Depression." The childlike strokes of crayon lines criss-crossing faces—often not staying within the heads' boundaries, at times looking weblike, at times like a cloud or a vise—connect people together on the basis of fleeting feelings fixed and framed.

The colored people in Iké Udé's *Celluoid Frames* are featured in movie posters created for nonexistent films through computer graphics. One such ad, "Norma Jean," features a familiarly posed but racechanged Marilyn Monroe fighting to keep her billowing dress from exposing her panties; though African American, "Norma Jean" remains quite definitively the movie star Marilyn Monroe (Fig. 7.3), an off-hand homage to Andy Warhol's marketing of multicolored Marilyns. The title of this ersatz poster for a "virtual" movie emphasizes the woman with bronze skin and dark hair who pre-existed the marketed Monroe. As Udé himself puts it, "the dark-haired beauty Norma Jean passed when she became the Snow-White

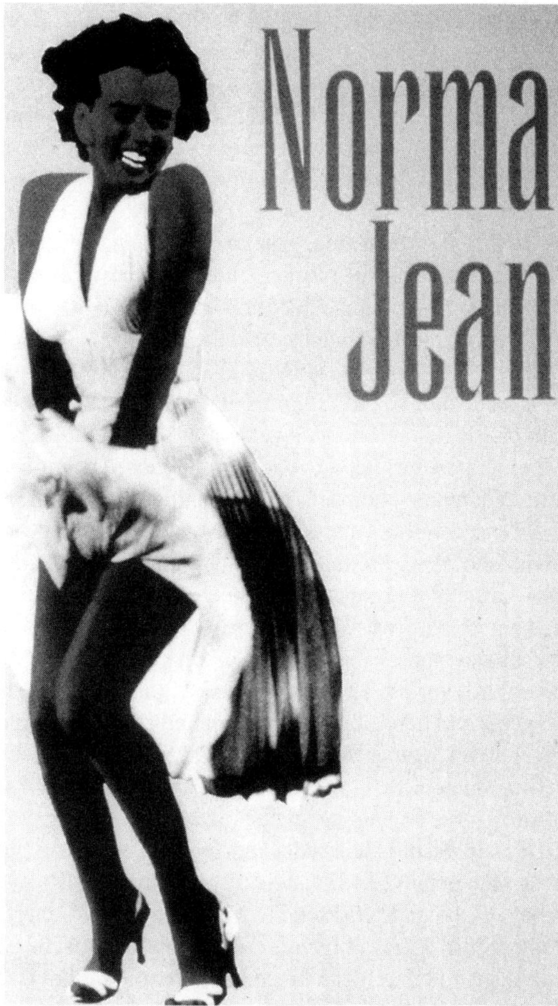

Figure 7.3 Iké Udé, *Norma Jean* (1995), from the *Celluloid Frames* series, cibachrome print, 34″ × 48″, computer manipulated photography. Courtesy of Wessel O'Connor Gallery.

Monroe, much as Madonna did too and via the same bottle of peroxide."[10] That the executive producer is listed in the print below as "Material Girl" or that the production design is said to be by "Peroxide Magic" makes clear and abundant sense.

But what does Udé mean by listing the director of photography as "Leni Riefenstahl" or the editor as "Himmler" or the director as "The Fuhrer"? Seeking to eliminate their "darker roots," both Monroe and Madonna opted for a form of blond ambition that bought into a Nordic notion of beauty, for "the bestselling blond embraces notions of the Aryan whiter-than-white." An article in Udé's aply named magazine *aRUDE* explains about the marketing of Monroe as blond Venus, "Hollywood played Bosnia and she was ethnically cleansed" (33). Just as dedicated as Iké Udé to exhibiting what Kobena Mercer terms "the unfinished business of the post-Civil Rights era" and specifically to confronting the issue of ethnic cleansing, Daniel Tisdale's 1988 series of images *Post-Plantation Pop* contrasts "before" and "after" shots of several icons of ethnicity (like Harriet Tubman and Paul Robeson) so that the retouched, glamorized, often Westernized photocopy "documents the inexorable power of mass culture to drain off the aura of ethnic iconicity—and hence to 'deracialize' identity—all the better to colonize and cannibalize difference, and thus homogenize and hegemonize it under the supremacy of sameness" (Mercer, *Welcome to the Jungle*, 161).

Udé's most parodic approach to "ethnic iconicity," his "Man in Polyester Suit," exhibits a circumcised and racechanged version of Mapplethorpe's "Man in Polyester Suit" as a movie poster that attributes production design to "Newth Gengrich," editing to "Clarence Thomas," and directing of photography to "Jessey Elms," presumably to connect repressive right-wing censorship or self-righteous respectability with shockingly sexualized productions (Fig. 7.4). Mapplethorpe's black-and-white "artistic" photograph has been reproduced and colorized on a computer screen and therefore could presumably be mass marketed and plastered on the walls of subway and bus stations or urban construction sites all over the first, second, and third worlds. The contrast Udé highlights between the dark suit and the pinkish penis and hands brings out Mapplethorpe's allusion to Sloan Wilson's sociological novel *Man in the Gray Flannel Suit* (1955); popularized in the Gregory Peck film version, this critique of the corporate organization man's affluence, conformity, and cowardice in the fifties has been extended by Mapplethorpe's and his successor Udé's audacious retort to bourgeois puritanism. That the timidity of the Man in the Gray Flannel Suit is not unrelated to the vulgar bravado and abusiveness of the male character in Mary McCarthy's short story "Man in the Brooks Brother Shirt" (1941) suggests that repression must be gauged in terms of economic privilege and that it can breed sexual exploitation. Because Udé has circumcised the photographer's subject, he hints at a class (as well as a complexion) change. Is it more upsetting for white viewers to see a white, possibly Jewish, probably middle-class (or even (pardon the expression) pointedly professional) penis than one that always already embodied nothing but the brutishness of the black man?[11]

Just as Udé features various racechanged and sexchanged portraits of himself on the covers of parodic versions of *GQ* ("Conservative Skirts for the Working Man") and *Town & Country* ("The Noble Savage Is Dead") to stress not only the self's "constant want of re-invention" but also the need to affirm a "reverence for difference that will redeem and liberate us" (35), the art critic Thomas McEvilley has argued, "One is bound to betray one's own specific ethnic inheritance in the attempt to open oneself to the reality of others." He therefore goes on to advocate developing "the ability to switch value frameworks and cognitive frameworks at will"; "the search for the Other then is a search for the newness of one's changing

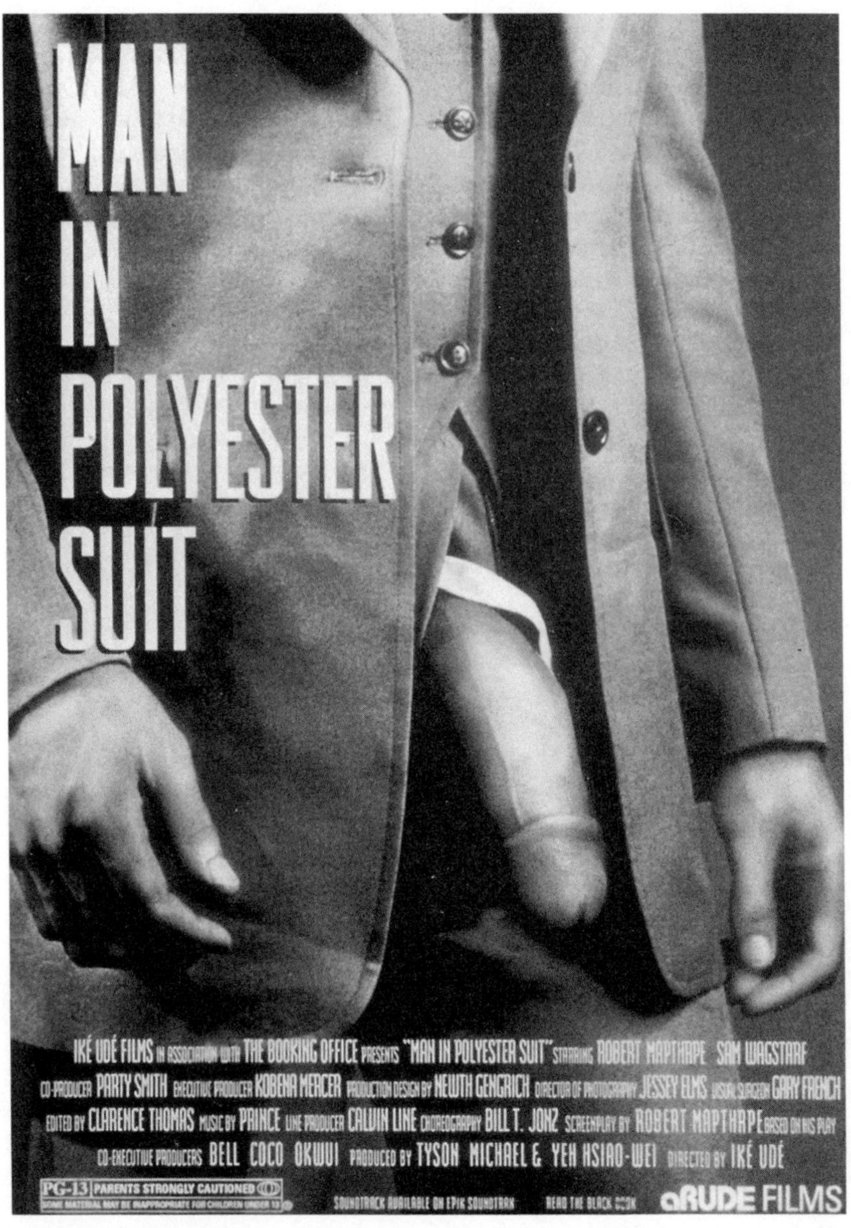

Figure 7.4 Iké Udé, *Man in Polyester Suit* (1995), from the *Celluloid Frames* series, cibachrome print, 34″ × 48″, computer manipulated photography. Courtesy of Wessel O'Connor Gallery.

self" (99–100, 104) or one's own transraciality. If we return to the issues raised by the propositions governing epidermatics, or epidermal fungibility, from the perspective of the transraciality at work in Udé's computer graphics and McEvilley's speculations, the central statement of the edible complex would itself undergo a transformation, for the self that represents the Other does not merely supplant others but also presents Otherness again. In other words, although the "re" in representation signifies *dis*placement of the Other, it also signifies a *re*placement staged by the self put in the position of reenacting Otherness again and with a difference. Who knows, racechange may go on to become a crucial aesthetic means of comprehending racial distinction without entrenching or denying it, as it does in the transracial skits of the white performance artist Eleanor Antin (whose personae include the Black King, the Black Ballerina, and the Black Nurse) and of the comics Eddie Murphy, Lily Tomlin, Billy Crystal, and Whoopi Goldberg. Just as their stand-up routines contrast inner being and outer appearance to disrupt racial totalizing, the avant-garde plays of Caryl Churchill, Adrienne Kennedy, and Suzan-Lori Parks reverse the mechanics of Othering in the way Blanchot describes in my final epigraph.

"Few people speak a language about race that is not their own," the performance artist Anna Deavere Smith cautions in her introduction to *Twilight: Los Angeles, 1992*, adding, "If more of us could actually speak from another point of view, like speaking another language, we could accelerate the flow of ideas." Documentary theater involves Deavere Smith in listening to and then repeating the stories of a host of very different people responding to a crisis like the L.A. riots. According to her, working aesthetically and psychologically both within and beyond the "boundaries of ethnicity" might "develop multifaceted identities" as well as "a more complex language": "Our race dialogue desperately needs this more complex language" (xxv). The consciousness she seeks involves neither the flattening-out of differences into samenesses nor their exaggeration into ghettoized partitions but awareness of the sometimes harmonious, sometimes cacophonous connections between related (not equated) narratives.[12]

"One aspect of symbolic inversion may be to break people out of their culturally defined, even biologically ascribed, roles," Victor Turner has commented. Just as psychologists employ sociodrama as a therapeutic technique that assigns to patients the roles of those with whom they are in conflict, ritual or dramatic symbolic inversion may topple age or sex or status barriers "to teach the meaning of the generic humanity; so that each person becomes the joker in the pack, the card who can be all cards, the method actor" (287–88). In addition, racechange uncovers the illusion of racial autonomy or purity, the inexorable reality of racial interdependency. Flying in the face of all insistences on racial totalizing or ethnic purity, transracial mutations put the lie to ideas of cultural homogeneity or authenticity, suggesting instead that mixing, merging, borrowing, and adapting remain inevitable and creative in the realm of the aesthetic. Pastiche and collage and parody, so characteristic of racechange representations, criss-cross the ethnic divides constructed by historians, abrogating all efforts at compartmentalizing discrete ethnic or racial productions. Cross-cultural, dialogic artistic productions address the analogies, competitions, frictions, juxtapositions, and distinctions between traditions that are thereby rendered strangely unfamiliar and new.

The influence of black culture on white (and vice versa) has such dizzying interactional effects that an artist like Colescott can play with the idea of an African-American painter translating hegemonic images of whites into portraits of blacks who in turn were created by whites. Questions of ethics—such as, should an ethnically specific tradition or genre be appropriated by outsiders?—operate on the illusion that cross-racial interactions can be regulated. Whether or not they *should* be, American history suggests that they *cannot* be.[13] What Barbara E. Johnson has called "*cultural* apartheid" remains impossible "once cultures enter dialogue, or conflict": "Cultures are not containable within boundaries" ("Response," 42). If, as the folklorist Roger Abrahams posits about the Civil War period, "the motives of the Southern white dancers who engaged in the black jig at the end of their formal dances are not that removed from those of the white bluesman, rapper, or break dancer," then the dynamic driving contemporary American culture may consist of an endless oscillation between white "aficionados of stylistically alternative performances" who adopt a distinctly Afro-American style and the invention of new, singular styles within black communities (157). From this perspective, many American aesthetic enterprises participate in what Sollors calls "ethnic transvestism," especially those produced by artists who endorce Walt Whitman's vision of himself (and by extension his view of humanity) as colored by "every hue and cast" and resisting "any thing better than my own diversity."[14]

It seems significant, finally, that several racechanging episodes help the theorist Patricia J. Williams whittle away at the "irreducibility of the category of 'black'" (*Rooster's Egg*, 192) that elsewhere in her critical writing understandably distresses her. In one such scenario, she finds herself in a hip-hop dance class populated entirely by Japanese so adept that she knows immediately that she is "in deep hip-hop trouble" (193). Williams undergoes three racechanges. When she enters the studio, she becomes "conspicuously black" and is taken for "The Real Thing"; however, after her ineptitude demonstrates that she is as far removed from hip-hop "as any American white person," she finds herself undergoing a whitening until she returns to the street where "I was completely black again" (194). Since the Japanese dancers (whose martial arts influenced hip-hop) were more enmeshed in this black cultural form, it was theirs, but she "couldn't help feeling that it was more 'mine' than 'theirs,' even though I had no claim" (194). Surprised—somewhat like Hurston in "How It Feels to Be Colored Me"—"to feel both so black *and* so *white*," Williams sees the event as an ambiguous "example of cultural hybridity that reasserts a co-optive status quo, or one that exceeds the limits of the body to imagine the harmonious potential of borrowed community" (192–93).

Williams's second reverie about racechange returns to the issue of black and Jewish relations that have so frequently shaped the history of cross-racial imaginative influence. She recalls seeing the vividly colorful paintings of an Auschwitz survivor, exquisitely lush in their brightness, but "in every last one of them there was a space of completely bare canvas, an empty patch in the shape of a human being." To the painter's wife, the bare patch presents the tragedy of unfinished work; to Williams, it means "the erasure of humanity that the Holocaust exacted" (*Rooster's Egg*, 209). The law scholar later has a dream that depends on the arrival of an intervening letter: A sister sends Williams "a microfiche copy of a property listing from the National Archives, documenting the existence of our enslaved great-great-grandmother." In her subsequent dream of the survivor's paintings,

> all those vivid landscapes with the bare body-shapes, and suddenly my great-great-grandmother appeared in the middle of each and every one of them. Suddenly she filled in all the empty spaces, and I looked into her face with the supernatural stillness of deep recollection. From that moment, I knew exactly who she was—every pore, every hair, every angle of her face. I would know her everywhere. (209)

Cultural property and cultural identity remain paradoxically both fixed and fused through Williams's powerful meditations on the vertiginous surprises of an appreciation of cultures not one's own that strains against simple appropriative gestures to aim instead at a kind of palimpsestic homage. The surd at the center of the survivor's paintings, the empty patch in the shape of a human being, remains a bare spot on his canvas but also becomes the only space poignant enough to hold Williams's own hurtful past. Beyond a politics of coexistence and what she calls "the handwringing about subject position" (118), Williams's negotiations hint at a visionary diversity that intensifies the reality of each unique inheritance.

Neither an erasure of the survivor's anti-figure by Williams's enslaved ancestress nor a conflation of the two, the dream refuses to reduce the Jewish experience of the Holocaust to the African-American experience of slavery or vice versa. Incommensurate, each heritage retains its own image, its own integrity. Yet the dream keeps the two figures and experiences in some sort of conversation—something like the momentary illumination that Fanon sees as the only solution to the separatism he imagines as two bodies, black and white, lying side by side:

> And there one lies body to body with one's blackness or one's whiteness, in full narcissistic cry, each sealed into his own peculiarity—with, it is true, now and then a flash or so, but these are threatened at their source. (45)

Uncannily, in a flash of insight threatened at its source Williams recognizes her relative—"I knew exactly who she was. . . . I would know her everywhere"—when the great-great-grandmother appears set in the foreign space of another's most poignant context of loss. Should the Auschwitz survivor be able to see his anti-figure filled in by Williams's apparition, would he, too, "know her" or own her as a redemptive reincarnation of what he had feared destroyed? Even if he viewed Williams's use of his space as appropriative, might he understand how appropriate it would seem from her point of view as a marker of "borrowed community"? Given this logic, would he have asked the question voiced by Bernard Malamud's Job-like Manischevitz: "So if God sends to me an angel, why a black?" (47).

Not in any way definitive, Bernard Malamud's vision of racechange in his story "Angel Levine" (1958) will nevertheless furnish the penultimate image of racial mutation in this extended study of the troubling friction between the aesthetics and ethics of the skin trade that helped to shape American culture in the twentieth century. Although in *The Tenants* Malamud finds no solution to inter-racial animosity, in this tale he gains sufficient distance from it to gauge the possibilities of achieving dialogues of understanding in a syncretistic society. After suffering as many reverses as he can possibly stand—a fire in his shop, a son dead in war, a runaway daughter, a wife wasting before his eyes—Manischevitz is visited by one Alexander Levine, a "bona fide angel of God, within prescribed limitations" (46). A disbeliever initially, Malamud's Jewish sufferer goes to Harlem in search of the black angel only when further misery breaks down his skepticism. First he sees "four Negroes wearing skullcaps" and reading "the Holy Word"—"On de face of de water moved de speerit"—and then he finds an inebriated, carousing Levine—spruced up in "shiny new checkered suit, pearl-gray derby, cigar, and big, two-tone button shoes"—to whom Manischevitz must summon all his conviction to attest "I think you are an angel from God" (52–53, 54–55). The parodic black talk of the worshippers at the Harlem Ark, like the Harlequin pimp suit in the all too familiar honky-tonk, reflects only the most obvious forms of stereotyping in this story. Yet the proliferating ironies of the tale's final line—Manischevitz's marveling to his now cured wife, "Believe me, there are Jews everywhere" (56)—disrupt all racial complacencies. For probably one of the least remarkable aspects of the remarkable character of Angel Levine is his Jewishness.

Why is Malamud's Job not astonished that he joins the ranks of the biblical immortals—Abraham and Lot—when his grief produces a sign from God? Why is he not amazed that such a phenomenon as Jewish angels still exist, no less that they visit the earth? Shouldn't he be surprised that simply and only his own act of believing in the divine presence can empower Levine's agency? Why does this contemporary Jew never express any shock about the uncanniness of natural supernaturalism when Angel Levine manages not only to heal his wife but also to ascend to heaven on what look like "a pair of magnificent black wings" (56)? Instead, the miracle that blacks are not goyim takes precedence in Manischevitz's mind, much to the amusement of his creator.[15] Parochial though he may be, Manischevitz has derived a lesson from his racechanged angel that demonstrates what extraordinary magic it would take to transform individual cultural consciousness into a multicultural conscience adequate to American society: Whether or not Malamud and his readers agree, Manischevitz operates under the assumption that crucial meanings reside not simply in the cultural or ethnic or religious heritage he claims as his past but also in their continual entanglement in issues of self-definition.[16]

Yet of course Malamud would no more ascribe to the idea that cultural identity can ever fully stand for subjectivity or personhood than would Patricia J. Williams. Like Henry Louis Gates, Malamud and Williams would probably "rebel at the notion that I can't be part of other groups, that I can't construct identities through elective affinity, that race must be the most important thing about me" (Gates, *Colored People*, xv). Shedding the excessive physicality and sexuality usually attributed to blackness, Malamud's Angel Levine refutes Western notions of whiteness as purity, absence, the universality accorded discorporated being. An intoxicated

Manischevitz has been guarded and guided by an immortal spirit in the shape of a human body, an uncanny better and othered self. If not he then his creator understands that racial dialogues and interactions begin to evolve when the bloated term "white" no longer is allowed to stand for spirituality or identity.[17] To repeat a point I made earlier, only by understanding the complex heterogeneity hidden beneath the term "self" or "one" or "I" can we avoid facile assumptions about a single, homogenized Otherness.

Is Manischevitz himself white, when his spiritual doppleganger is black? Since there are African-American Jews, can't there be—aren't there also—Canadian Islamics, Italian Buddhists, Ethiopian and Korean Catholics? And how are they related to Islamic Canadians, Buddhist Italians, and Catholic Ethiopians or Koreans? Of course blacks and Jews remain different (since Malamud does not deny blackness by putting it into an Old Testament costume), but neither absolutely nor diametrically so. And if blacks are Jews then Jews can be blacks, and after such knowledge, who can keep the categories sequestered? Manischevitz's black angel underscores the mystic manner in which we understand our relatedness to each other or the ways in which interiority never collapses simply into socially ascribed, racial or ethnic or gender or class positions.

This, it seems to me, is the point of John Edgar Wideman's albino character Brother Tate in *Sent for You Yesterday* (1983), a novel about a man described as "lighter than anybody else" who nevertheless "wasn't white," but whose "color changed." Whereas albinism for Ralph Ellison's *Invisible Man* (1952) eventually means being turned "transparent" by a "cruel, invisible ray" (434), for Wideman's narrator it signifies the fear that seeks out color as a category so as to camouflage the real terror about the common vulnerability all fleshly things remain heir to:

> I was a little afraid of him, afraid I'd see through him, under his skin, because there was no color to stop my eyes, no color which said there's a black man or a white man in front of you. I was afraid I'd see through that transparent envelope of skin to the bones and blood and guts of whatever he was. (15)[18]

The pervasive color-coding of human beings does assuage—but cannot defend against—generalized discomfort about the susceptible, live organism pulsing behind the fragile "envelope of skin." Albinism makes Brother Tate into something like an empty patch in the shape of a human body, one so alarming to a community organized along separatist lines that his light-colored, six-year-old son is burned to death as a human sacrifice.

"Depending on the time of day, on how much light was in a room, on how you were feeling when you ran into Brother Tate, his color changed" (15). In this regard, Wideman's seemingly eccentric character typifies the syncretic or hybrid self—the physical and aesthetic mutability of the racechanger whose performances undermine the notion that any racial type can posit a unified or fixed or epistemologically privileged term. The passage I have used as a second epigraph to this coda—Richard Wright's famous claim that "the Negro is America's metaphor"—sounds strikingly similar to Fanon's assertion that "The Negro is comparison" (211). Metaphor: the substitution of the one for the other, from the

Greek *metaphora*, meaning transport. Ideas about who constitutes "the one," what functions as "the other," and how such a substitution signifies transmute mysteriously under the pressure of those changing faces of every hue and caste that use their "elective affinities" to put the lie to "cultural apartheid." What will happen to our society when we understand Americans as not necessarily white or black people in thrall to the transporting figures of the edible complex?

NOTES

Epigraph Page: Du Bois, *Souls of Black Folk*, vii; Genet, *Blacks*, 3; Baldwin, *Notes of a Native Son*, 150; Morrison, *Playing in the Dark*, 38; Fuss, *Identification Papers*, 164.

Chapter 1. Adventures in the Skin Trade

Epigraphs: Washington, 100; Fanon, 110.

1. I am not making an argument about racial equality in ancient Tarquinia, although Frank M. Snowden, Jr., views the image of blacks in the ancient world as "highly favorable," claiming that "white-black relationships differ[ed] markedly from those that have developed in more color-conscious societies" (vii).

2. On the history of race defined as a binary, see Jordan, *White over Black*, and JanMohamed, "The Economy of Manichean Allegory."

3. See Donna Haraway's meditation on "category confusion" and the way in which it has affected racial taxonomies in American history.

4. A recent article on "Mixed Blood" in the popular magazine *Psychology Today*, for example, explains that "our categories for the racial classification of people arbitrarily include certain dimensions (light versus dark skin) and exclude others (rounded versus elongated bodies). There is no biological basis for classifying race according to skin color instead of body form—or according to any other variable, for that matter. . . . race is a myth" (Jefferson M. Fish, Nov./Dec. 1995: 57).

5. Two portraits of André Breton that Man Ray shot in the thirties testify to his continued interest in racechange and sexchange: Breton as his own negative image and Breton as a cross between a nun and an aviator. Man Ray also produced a number of pictures of white faces peering through black netting or abstract white forms striated with black shadows. See Man Ray, *Man Ray: Photographs*, 65, 114, 161.

6. To be sure, minstrelsy and its offshoot, blackface in the movies, have received quite a bit of attention, mostly from American historians; however, literary critics have tended to confine their investigations into cross-racial masquerade to African-American passing characters.

7. According to James Weldon Johnson in *The Autobiography of an Ex-Coloured Man*, "it cannot be so embarrassing for a coloured man to be taken for white as for a white man to be taken for coloured; and I have heard of several cases of the latter kind" (172–73).

8. Victor Burgin explains that when the color white as "the sum totality of light" is contrasted with black as "the total absence of light," "elementary optical physics is recruited to the psychotic metaphysics of racism in which white is 'all' to black's 'nothing'" (70).

9. F. James Davis argues that, though the Plessy case is no longer law, "the nation's legal definition of who is black remains unchanged" since that time: *Who Is Black?*, 9.

10. I have profited from Walter Benn Michaels's analysis of the transformation of race into an identity and a culture at the beginning of the twentieth century in *Our America*, 122.

11. I am indebted to Christine Froula's speculations on this image.

12. In "Has Science Conquered the Color Line," White quotes this passage (written three years earlier) but now explains that "science is near making such a dream a reality" through monobenzyl ether of hydroquinone, which dermatologists have used to clear up discolorations of the skin.

13. Joyce Carol Oates exploits this same sort of technique throughout her play "Negative" (1991) in which "racial stereotypes are reversed, as in a photograph negative" (60).

14. See Lauren Berlant, "National Brands/National Body," in *Comparative American Identities*, 110–40.

15. Curiously, Hughes's satire turns into a series of sexual jokes when Mammy's male companion asks Audette for "some of that fine white bread" and then settles for pancakes with "jelly" on his.

16. Mary Ann Doane discusses this paradoxical scene in which Sarah Jane "assumes the expectations about blackness which are imposed upon her. She becomes the representation of blackness which is implicitly contrasted with her passing" (237). More specifically, a white actress playing a mulatto passer speaks the black talk she identifies with precisely the African-American culture this character seeks to disavow.

17. Hemenway points out that "The idea was not to fool black folks—who must have been amused by the strange sight—but to present a uniform color to white passersby" (211).

18. Recent evidence of ongoing concern about the iconography of Christainity appears in James McBride's *The Color of Water* (1996) where a Jewish mother tells her black son that God's spirit "doesn't have a color . . . God is the color of water" and where later another son protests against pictures of a white Jesus: "If they put Jesus in this picture here, and He ain't white, and He ain't black, they should make him gray. Jesus should be gray" (39, 41).

19. According to the late Senegalese writer Cheikh Anta Diop, European culture derives from Egypt and Egypt is African. Euclid and Cleopatra were black; the pyramid, hieroglyphics, the cult of the sun king were all the achievements of black Africa. Such theorists clearly were reacting against the view of, say, Arnold Toynbee in *A Study of History* who claimed that the only one of the races which did not make a creative contribution to civilization was the black race.

20. Perhaps because the black singers are so passionately reminiscent of their operatic prototypes in the film version of *Carmen Jones*, their diction—when it falls into stereotypical "dis and dat"—seems not simply ludicrous but demeaning.

21. See Walter Benn Michaels's discussion of Piper's essay in which he asks about her definition of being black as being identified by a white racist society as black: "On what grounds, then, can someone who is *not* identified by that society as black be said to be black?" (*Our America*, 133).

22. Omi and Winant argue that the concept of race cannot be reduced to an essence but that it also cannot be imagined as a mere illusion. In other words, even if there is nothing

fixed or objective or biological about race, it still plays a crucial role in structuring the social world.

23. According to Russell E. Coon, Chicago's Field Museum reopened its permanent Egyptian collections in 1988, including an interactive display labeled "See Yourself as an Ancient Egyptian." "Peering into a semi-reflective glass case, viewers confronted their own countenances, Egyptianized by the superimposition of a curly black wig and 'Egyptian' make-up" (11).

24. While *Rebirth of a Nation, Computer-Style* appears to revel in the "morphies" created out of a "straight 50–50 combination of the physical characteristics of their progenitors," it is interesting that the editors explain, "One of our tentative unions produced a distinctly feminine face—sitting atop a muscular neck and hairy chest." Clearly disturbed by the hermaphroditism of this image, they conclude, "Back to the mouse on that one."

25. Gail Ching-Liang Low describes the phenomenon of cultural cross-dressing from Sir Richard Burton to the Lawrence of Arabia legend in these terms which are borrowed from Robert Stoller's treatment of transvestism (where the cross-dresser relishes his awareness of his hidden maleness and thus plays at being a woman with the phallus) (96–97).

26. It is interesting that *Orlando* (1928), Woolf's novel about sexchange, depicts its hero becoming a heroine when she has joined with the gipsies, thus undergoing a racechange as well.

27. The artist Adrian Piper presented herself in whiteface and with a penciled mustache as "white man" in *Some Reflective Surfaces*, first performed in 1975. See Adrian Piper on "Passing for White, Passing for Black" (241) as well as Amelia Jones.

28. According to *Rolling Stone* magazine (March 10, 1994), John Mellencamp's video "When Jesus Left Birmingham" is the first from which MTV has censored faces. Mellencamp was asked to put computer-scrambled squares over parts of the video where guitarist David Grissom appears in blackface and backing vocalist Roberta Freeman appears in whiteface (18).

29. Ashley Tidey, in her dissertation-in-progress, puts it this way: "The white, in Fanon's view, does not have to 'be' anything for the black. The white man, is, in fact, unable to see the black man. This observation, however, does not discredit the fact that the white's identity is affected by that which he cannot identify/see. . . . [T]he white *does* define himself in relation to the black—*even though* he does not or cannot or refuses to 'see' the black. We must recognize, in other words, what the white does not: that is, that he (the white) not only projects his own anxieties, fears, and doubts onto the black but also that he introjects, figuratively speaking, the racial other" (Chapter 2, 51).

30. As Anne McClintock explains, "different forms of mimicry such as passing and cross-dressing deploy ambiguity in different ways," and she goes on to caution that "critical distinctions are lost if these historically variant cultural practices are collapsed under the ahistorical sign of the same" (65).

31. Until the historical and critical work of such thinkers as Robert Toll, Eric Lott, Michael Rogin, and Toni Morrison, white impersonations of blackness have gone largely ignored by American cultural historians because of morally important taboos that censure such spectacles and that also (though less reasonably) discourage analysis of them.

32. See Guillaumin, 37–67. She demonstrates "how belief in the physical existence of race is really an archetypal attitude of pseudo-materialism" (37). In addition, Anthony Appiah in "The Uncompleted Argument: Du Bois and the Illusion of Race" explains that race is a fiction with no empirical or scientific basis.

33. Eve Sedgwick's analysis of the arbitrariness of gender binaries in *Legacies* makes a similar point.

34. See Paul Gilroy's somewhat sardonic discussion of theorists who tout "the effluent from a constituted subjectivity that emerges contingently from the endless play of racial signification" (36).

35. For a discussion of the social construction of race that explains how obdurate that construction remains in contemporary America, see Guillaumin, "The Idea of Race," and Wiegman, Chapter 1. In *Essentially Speaking*, Diana Fuss includes a chapter that describes what is at stake in the argument over de-essentializing race for such critics as Henry Louis Gates, Jr., Houston Baker, and Barbara Christian (73–96). Fuss's last chapter of *Identification Papers* furnishes an excellent meditation on the implications of Fanon's racial analyses for the critic also interested in gender.

36. According to Omi and Winant, too, one should "avoid both the utopian framework which sees race as an illusion we can somehow 'get beyond,' and also the essentialist formation which sees race as something objective and fixed, a biological datum" (55). They argue that race must be understood as a "complex of social meanings constantly being transformed by political struggle" (55).

37. Although I do not want to fall into the fallacy of "chromatism," the term Gayatri Spivak uses to describe the problem of reducing race to the question of visible difference in skin color (235), twentieth-century narratives about skin color uncover the evolution of the meaning of the term "race."

38. See Susan Willis, who defines blackface "as a metaphor for the commodity" (189), and Homi Bhabha, who views "the racial stereotype of colonial discourse in terms of fetishism" (74).

39. In other words, this study accords with Eric Sundquist's belief that, although the black and white traditions in literature have been and can continue to be seen as separate, ultimately "they form a single tradition" (22). So-called "American culture" has become so embedded within and saturated by conventions generated by its black citizens that one may foresee a future in which it will be indistinguishable from "African-American culture." To be sure, black culture may always derive ways of differentiating itself from the white mainstream. And, of course, there are ways that mainstream culture continues to define itself in exclusionary terms and along racial lines.

40. What was recently described "as the worst hoax in the history of Australian publishing" illuminates the ongoing centrality of this issue. Susan Demidenko admitted that "her book *The Hand That Signed the Paper*, an account of the role of Ukrainians in atrocities against Jews during the Holocaust, was not based on her own family's history, as she had long insisted in defending the book's veracity." Not Ukrainian at all, Helen Darville (the pseudonomous Dimidenko) was the child of well-educated British immigrants to Australia. (*New York Times*, Sept. 26, 1995).

41. Consider the lesbian critic who is not Jewish writing about Gertrude Stein or the black critic who is not Islamic writing about Malcolm X. To match the "subject position" of the critic with that of the artist would inevitably involve the infinite regress that a Derridean would identify with an "abyssal question." Obviously, too, authors of narrative cannot posssibly limit themselves to the creation of characters only reflective of their ethnic, class, or social background, even if they tried to. In other words, as I argue in the last chapter, crossover work remains inevitable.

42. I am revising Andrew Sarris's famous observation that "the dramatic conflict in a Welles film often arises from the dialectical collision between morality and megalomania," mindful that Wells demonstrated a fascination with racial imaginings in his efforts to produce a version of Joseph Conrad's *Heart of Darkness*, in his production of a "Voodoo" *Mac-*

beth (discussed in Chapter 3), and in his blackface portrayal of *Othello*. For background on these matters, see Guerric DeBona.

Chapter 2. Spirit-Murder at the Movies

Epigraphs: Fanon, 231; Žižek, 23.

1. An exception to the notion that minstrelsy remained a nineteenth-century form is Mark A. Reid's argument that the most pervasive subtypes of African-American comedy in film retain various hybrid forms of minstrelsy: *Redefining Black Film*, 19–43. As recently as April 13–15, 1995, *The Minstrel Show*, a production of the Dance Center of Columbia College, Donald Byrd, and the Group, ran at the Shubert Theatre in Chicago.

2. See the discussion in Cripps, 25 and 14, and in M. Watkins, 185–86. The ways in which *Uncle Tom's Cabin* evolved through various silent and then sound movies has begun to be studied by Michele Wallace, who points out that the first movie in which Uncle Tom was played by a black actor also revises Stowe's plot in a scene where a black man responds directly against slavery by shooting and killing a white.

3. Woolf's comments about the phantom of the Angel in the House appear in "Professions for Women." I am suggesting that the blackface actor in films functions like a ghost in the movie house.

4. In Dixon's novel, Gus actually rapes the girl, and the act is described in bestial imagery evocative of *Dracula*: "A single tiger-spring, and the black claws of the beast sank into the soft white throat and she was still" (304).

5. According to Michael Rogin, the original version of the movie probably followed *The Clansman* and portrayed Gus raping Flora before she leaps to her death. Also, he explains that audiences in Los Angeles and the South saw footage of Gus's castration, now lost or unavailable but recorded by Seymour Stern: "'The Sword Became a Flashing Vision,'" 277–78.

6. Robert Lang argues that the villainy of Lynch "originates in the fact that he is neither white nor black—that is, he is worse than black." In other words, Lang sees the mulatto as the "living embodiment of a disturbance in the melodramatic field, in which one is *either* white *or* black" (20).

7. See Walter Benn Michaels, who argues in "The Souls of White Folk" that "The invisible Empire of the Knights of the Ku Klux Klan arises in rebellion against the 'visible' empire of the North and its black soldiers like the rapist 'Gus' who, as his full name—Augustus Caesar—makes clear, is to be regarded as an imperial storm trooper. In *The Clansman*, then, white Americans are understood not as imperialists but as the victims of imperialism" (187).

8. Lillian Gish explained that she was chosen over another actress because she was "very blonde and fragile-looking. The contrast with the dark man evidently pleased Mr. Griffith, for he said in front of everyone, 'Maybe she would be more effective than the mature figure I had in mind.'" Quoted by Rogin, "The Sword Became a Flashing Vision," 267.

9. Richard Schickel "does not believe" that Lynch wishes "to carry [Elsie] off and work his will upon her at leisure." Indeed, he attributes Lynch's motivation to shame and fear of being ridiculed for his proposal, imagining that his "true intention may be to kill her rather than allow her to expose his terrible secret, which is not that he lusts after her but that he truly loves her" (234).

10. Mimi White points out that one supposed "historical facsimile" of the state house of representatives in 1871 is based on a photograph of that House in 1870: "A gap between the source and the filmic representation is . . . immediately evident in the title-card itself, which situates events in 1871 and the source in 1870, prior to the depicted scene." See her "*The Birth of a Nation*: History as Pretext" in Lang, 218.

11, According to Dixon's preface to *The Clansman*, Thaddeus Stevens attempted "to Africanize ten great States of the American Union" after Lincoln's assassination.

12. It seems significant in this regard that although white minstrel performers like the celebrated Francis Leon produced seductive images of black women, no comparably attractive representation of black men appeared in nineteenth-century and turn-of-the-century minstrelsy. A Wood's Theatre playbill illustrates how black women—though often libeled and stereotyped—could appear attractive while black men always look grotesque; see Toll, 77.

13. The contrast between the earliest masquerades in black on British and American stages speaks to the divergence between blackface in *The Birth of a Nation* and in *The Jazz Singer*. The first black impersonators on the English-speaking stage played a satanic, black Aaron, the Moor in Shakespeare's *Titus Andronicus,* who would soon be outstripped in popularity by the less evil but equally destructive Othello; however, one of the first native American roles written for blackface on the American stage was the part of a fool named Sambo who would soon be eclipsed in popularity by dramatic renditions of Harriet Beecher Stowe's less silly but equally naive Uncle Tom. See the discussion of all these characters in Leonard, passim. On the use of blackface in early English literature (Renaissance emblem books and on the Jacobean stage), see Boose, 49–50, and Beemer, passim.

14. The commonality of the two movies is forecast by curious historical connections between Griffith and Jolson. After the appearance of *The Birth of a Nation* and before the filming of *The Jazz Singer*, Griffith planned to make a movie tentatively entitled either *Black and White* or *Mammy's Boy*, a crime story starring Al Jolson as an innocent detective using the appearance of a "guilty black face" to exonerate a falsely accused man (Geduld, 167). Another of Griffith's projects—*The Romance of a Jewess* (1908)—focused on the intermarriage of Jew and gentile at the center of *The Jazz Singer*. This odd coupling of Griffith and Jolson recurred when Jolson first approached Griffith with the idea of dramatizing Samson Raphaelson's story "The Day of Atonement" (Carringer, 12).

15. Theodore Tilton's famous remark that the black race is equal in moral faculties to the white woman and thus superior to white men—"The negro race is the feminine race of the world"—appears in *The Negro* (1863) and is often cited (for example in bell hooks, "Feminism Inside," 131).

16. Eric Lott has pointed out to me that this scene resembles a rape, "with Pop pulling off his belt and charging after Jakie into the bedroom, out of which the crying boy will shortly emerge" (private correspondence).

17. A telltale mistake in the written treatment of Jack's blackface suggests his feminization: Jack "goes up and takes [his mother's] hands in his. He starts to kiss her, then, remembers her [*sic*] make-up" (Carrianger, 120). Also, the word "queer"—used by Mary and the backer to stop Jack from giving into his family—seems to warn against an unmanly passivity.

18. I am indebted to Melissa Valiska Gregory for pointing out the resonance of this passage with respect to the Jolson poster and for discovering the next very striking image.

19. A good description of the standard late-nineteenth-century minstrel show appears in Huggins, 249–50. After a rousing opening number, blackfaced performers sat in a row in

the careless costume of Jim Crow (the rough barbarian) and the ruffled super-stylishness of Jim Dandy (the urban effete). The center man, called the interlocutor and sometimes remaining in whiteface, engaged the end men, Mr. Bones and Mr. Tambo, in comic routines: jokes, political speeches, sermons. The "olio" followed with songs and dances. A grand finale usually closed the show.

20. No wonder, then, that the name Sambo has been traced back to the sixteenth-century word "zambo," a type of monkey whose antics were considered natural, and that one of the first musical works in America, *The Disappointment* (1767), featured a comic black character called "Raccoon" (Boskin, 38 and 70).

21. Darkened skin itself might signify disappearance by evoking body parts charred by fire or gone dead from gangrene, as they do to the boy child of William Faulkner's *As I Lay Dying* (1930): Observing one brother's burnt back and another's gangrened leg, Vardaman thinks they "looked like a nigger's" (224).

22. Alexander Saxton quotes Harry McCarthy, *Deeds of Darkness* (1876), *Dick's Ethiopian Scenes* (1879), and Bert Richards's *Colored Senators, an Ethiopian Burlesque* (23).

23. A similar song performed by Moore & Burgess Minstrels in England describes a mouth, "a caution to see, / A better provision store never could be," which the singer has not found a way to kiss because "I'm afraid to go near her, I'm sure to be drowned" (Pickering, 197).

24. Claire Kahane argues that the young boy Nelson and his grandfather Mr. Head in O'Connor's story identify with the plaster figure of the Negro and thereby achieve "an acceptance of helplessness and mutual dependency": "O'Connor implies that they themselves are 'artificial niggers,' powerless and afraid before the contingencies of a threatening world" (183).

25. Alexander Saxton explains that the banjo song published in New York in 1863 is sung by a character who would like to respond to "Abram Linkum" by buying "up all de niggers—de niggers—de colored African-American citizens" in order to sell them; he then finds it "Geographically and emotionally" quite close to the maiming and lynching of blacks on the sidewalks of New York during the draft riots of the same year.

26. See O'Connor, "Judgement Day," 539.

27. In "'Democracy and Burnt Cork,'" Michael Rogin points out that by the mid-1930s, the genre had turned to backstage musicals about putting on a show or retrospective biographies of the central figures in the history of American popular music (4).

28. As Eric Lott has commented to me, however, the background legs are unable to keep up with Astaire and they end up giving in and going away. If the legs represent Robinson's, perhaps he is shown throwing in the towel, unable to compete with the brilliant Astaire (private correspondence).

Still, the background and foreground oscillate so as to produce doubling between the two dancers. To the extent that Fred Astaire's dance number pays homage to Bojangles, it differs from other productions that simply appropriated black arts. See Carol J. Clover on the film *Singin' in the Rain* (1952) with its "moralizing surface story . . . a guilty disavowal of the practices that went into its own making" (725). Clover argues that the film apparently looks at the immorality of appropriating another person's voice but really it rips off (without crediting) the dancing bodies of black men. Whereas "there was a perverse honesty to traditional blackface" which "does point to where credit might be due" (740), *Singin' in the Rain* "doesn't-but-does know" that the musical art upon which it depends is African-American in origin (742).

On Rice's "shadow dance," see M. Watkins, 84.

Chapter 3. Making White, Becoming Black

Epigraphs: Bible; Browne, 281.

1. See Sacks and Sacks.

2. See, for example, Houston Baker's rejection of Constance Rourke's assessment of the authenticity of minstrel traditions in *Modernism and the Harlem Renaissance*, 17.

3. I am indebted to Sandra M. Gilbert's ideas about "female female impersonation" here; see our *Letters from the Front*, chapter 2.

4. Werner Sollors, quoting Andrew Greeley's use of the term "ethnogenesis," explains that the word "nicely combines an organic sense (people, birth) with a faint biblical echo (Genesis) and helps to sacralize beginnings" (*Beyond Ethnicity*, 57). For a discussion of early American as well as Greek, Native American, and Islamic black-white founding myths, see the chapter on "Origins" in Sollors's forthcoming book *Neither Black nor White and Yet Both: Thematic Explorations of Interracial Literature.*

5. See Bailey. Insistent about grounding a positive black self-image on recalcitrant biblical texts, the scholar Cain Hope Felder argues about the famous Jeremiah passage that "To Jeremiah and to his listeners, it is unthinkable that the Cushites would want to change the way they look"; indeed, "the use of [Ham's descendants] in this passage suggests that Israel should use the Cushites as 'yardsticks' for assessing themselves." For Cain, the Ethiopians or Cushites and the leopard "have learned the advantages of being who they are, rulers of territories who are respected by and awesome to their neighbors," and because they have "no incentive for change," they are used to explain the situation of the people of Judah who "liv[ing] the life of sinning have learned the advantages of being sinners" (177).

Cain's exegetical acrobatics cannot hide the fact that Jeremiah's famous rhetorical questions are structured so as to equate the Ethiopian's color and the leopard's spots with sin: just as the Cushite cannot change his skin or the leopard his spots, the evil-doer cannot become virtuous.

6. Patricia J. Williams quotes a twenty-year-old study about "The Economics of the Baby Shortage" that created a controversy when its authors, Judge Richard Posner and his associate Elizabeth Landes, argued, "Were baby prices quoted as prices of soybean future are quoted, a racial ranking of these prices would be evident, with white baby prices higher than nonwhite baby prices" (*Rooster's Egg*, 217).

7. Even though Hurston's accomplishments won prizes during her lifetime and her novel *Their Eyes Were Watching God* has attained centrality in the college curriculum, her early work—like the poems of Spencer and the graphics of Nugent—has gone virtually unnoticed. Neither Spencer nor Bruce published a collection of their works in their lifetimes, compositions which remain obscure (especially in the latter's case) because still scattered in journals, and neither one has yet received the scholarship which might illuminate the shape of their careers. Spencer, who lived reclusively with her mother and husband in Lynchburg, Virginia, was mentored by James Weldon Johnson; Richard Bruce, the pseudonym for Bruce Nugent, moved from Washington, D.C., to New York City, pursuing a more flamboyantly public life during which he was befriended by Georgia Douglas Johnson, Langston Hughes, Wallace Thurman, and Aaron Douglas.

8. Maureen Honey explains that Spencer composed the poem after reading about a pregnant woman who was tortured by a lynch mob while trying to protect her husband who had killed a racist employer (9–10).

9. The word "fagot" most obviously stands for the wood that fuels the mob's violent burning of the black body; however, it also resonates with the British meaning of fag—a

boy who acts as a servant for another boy in a higher class—and the slang term for homosexual. Sugar cane takes on the ominous resonance of caning in this context.

10. As many critics have suggested, of course, it is possible to read the "ex-coloured" man's revulsion against the black victim as an index of his identification with whites and of the irony his author directs against him.

11. Ashley Tidey refashions Du Bois's term to comprehend a comparable (though different) form of what she calls "white double consciousness."

12. Anne Douglas includes a description of the ways in which *Shuffle Along* represented a return to minstrelsy in *Mongrel Manhattan*, 378.

13. According to Watkins, Pigmeat Markham was one of the last comics to work in blackface in the 1950s, and audiences were astonished to find (when he relinquished the burnt cork) that "he was actually darker than the makeup he had used" (p. 133).

14. But Mills also played the groom for the bridal production number "Mandy, Make Up Your Mind" and insisted on her rights to artistic independence, explaining, "I'm the despair of stage managers who want a player to act in a groove. No grooves for me. The stage isn't large enough for me at times" (Woll, 102, 106).

15. James De Jongh mentions two novels, *Strange Brother* (1931) by Blair Niles and *The Young and the Evil* (1933) by Charles Henri Ford and Parker Tyler that include descriptions of Harlem's gay scene (34).

16. Most biblical commentators examine a series of enigmas in this text. If Ham was guilty of disrespect toward his father, why is Canaan cursed? Why is Ham mentioned as the youngest son in one verse and listed as the second of three in another? Did Noah have three or four sons? Why does Noah counter his curse of Canaan with a blessing that Japheth "dwell in the tents of Shem"? By glossing over such confusions or dissolving them, Hurston's tale represses the ideological pressures that probably shaped the evolution of the text. As Cain Hope Felder has speculated, "Many of the difficulties within this passage find a solution once we allow the possibility that the original version of Genesis 9:18–27 referred only to Ham and his error and that a later version of the story, motivated by political developments in ancient Palestine, attempted to justify the subjugation of Canaanites by Shem's descendants (Israel) and those of Japheth (Philistines)" (131).

17. Therefore, as Umberto Cassuto has argued, "The Canaanites were to suffer the curse and the bondage not because of the sins of Ham, but because they themselves acted like Ham, because of their own transgressions, which resembled those attributed to Ham in this allegory" (155).

18. For an illuminating commentary on these passages and the uses to which they have been put, see Rice, 5–27. In "The Curse of Ham: A Case of Rabbinic Racism?," David M. Goldenberg argues that "the source of anti-Black prejudice in western civilization" has been "found in rabbinic literature" and he goes on to exonerate the Rabbinic writing from this charge. Not race but skin color was the subject of folktales that simply express a "somatic norm preference" for lighter complexions. In addition, faulty translations as well as enigmatic texts have contributed to the unfair charge of Jewish racism. See the collection on blacks and Jews edited by Jack Salzman and Cornel West (Oxford University Press, forthcoming).

19. Copher cites the sources of Graves and Patai as Sanhedrin 108B and *Tanhumaa Noah* 13, 15.

20. By the end of the thirteenth century in England, an otherwise quite liberal attack on the slavery of men of free ancestry in the *Mirror of Justices* contained a defense of the subjugation of serfs because "this serfage . . . comes from the curse which Noah pronounced

against Canaan, the son of his son Ham. . . . And thus are men serfs by divine law and this is accepted by human law and confirmed by canon law" (D. B. Davis, 97).

Winthrop D. Jordan's point, though in need of qualification, remains an important one: "It is suggestive that the first [widespread] Christian utilizations" of Talmudic and Midrashic sources came during a period of "overseas exploration" (18). On sixteenth- and seventeenth-century writers' approach to the origins of blackness vis-à-vis climatological and biblical explanations, see Boose, 42–44.

21. On the conflation of Cain and Ham, see J. Friedman, 99–105. He sees the basis of the metaphoric identification of Ham and Cain in the Middle Ages as a result of certain parallels in their stories: Each was a bad brother and son, lived before the earth was populated, and produced a cursed line. "The descendants of Cain and Ham seem, indeed, to have become ubiquitous by the thirteenth century, and almost any person or people viewed with distaste or hostility by a Christian writer was likely to receive honorary membership in their family, as genealogy was used to justify an unfriendly or suspicious attitude toward the peoples who dwelt on the fringes of the medieval Latin world" (103).

For another biblical identification of darkening with the sorrow of a curse, see Job 28–31:

> I go about blackened, but not by the sun;
> I stand up in the assembly, and cry for help.
> I am a brother of jackals,
> and a companion of ostriches.
> My skin turns black and falls from me,
> And my bones burn with heat.
> My lyre is turned to mourning,
> and my pipe to the voice of those who weep.

22. See "Selections from the Book of Moses," in which the following passage appears:

> 23 The land of Egypt being first discovered by a woman, who was the daughter of Ham, and the daughter of Egyptus, which in the Chaldean signifies Egypt, which signifies that which is forbidden;
> 24 When this woman discovered the land it was under water, who afterward settled her sons in it; and thus, from Ham, sprang that race which preserved the curse in the land. (Abraham 1:23–24) in J. Smith, 31.

23. On the one hand, in his 1791 sermon on "The Injustice and Impolicy of the Slave Trade" Jonathan Edwards, Jr., argued that the curse of Canaan "had no reference to the inhabitants of Guinea, or of Africa in general"; on the other, in his 1724 book on the *Present State of Virginia* the Reverend Hugh Jones viewed Africans as "descendants from some of the sons of *Canaan*," a race "in an especially Manner hateful to God" (J. Washington, 316, 395).

24. Disturbing as Josiah Priest's account of Genesis may seem, it looks benign in contrast to that of Dr. Samuel A. Cartwright, whose "Unity of the Human Race Disproved by the Hebrew Bible" appeared in the August 1860 issue of *De Bow's Review*. In Cartwright's surreal analysis, Ham was not the natural father but instead the "head man, manager, or overseer" of Canaan, who (like the serpent in the Garden) was not a member of the white (superior) race derived from Adam but instead a representative of a pre-Adamic breed ("the *naphesh chaiyal*" of Genesis 1:24 in which the Lord brings forth "living creatures" along with "cattle and creeping things and the beast of the earth" (129)). In the Garden, "Adam selected his slaves from that portion of the *naphesh chaiyah*, or inferior races, who had the hardest masters in the world—the serpents" (133). After Cain killed Abel, he corrupted the

Adamic race through miscegenation with this inferior race: "That they were black is inferred from the mark they put upon Cain" (134). In any case, God cursed Canaan (and not Ham) because Canaan was part of the "snake-worshipping race," a race that exhibits "no resentments for being flogged"; one "that liberty makes . . . miserable instead of happy"; one that resembles the snake crawling in the dust because it is a tribe of "*knee-benders*, literally and metaphorically, knee-benders in mind and body" (135).

25. In *The Fire Next Time*, Baldwin criticized not only Christianity for its racism but also Islam, and in particular its myth of origin that describes prehistory as all-black and depicts whites as the product of an experiment Allah allowed the Devil to perform (81).

26. At least one early commentator on slavery had used the Bible in a comparable way. The jurist Sir Edward Coke believed "That Bondage or Servitude was first inflicted for dishonouring of Parents: For Cham the Father of Canaan . . . seeing the Nakedness of his Father Noah, and shewing it in Derision to his Brethren, was therefore punished in his Son Canaan with Bondage." At the time of the flood, "all Things were common to all," but afterward battles arose and "then it was ordained by Constitutions of Nations . . . that he that was taken in Battle should remain Bond to his taker forever, and he to do with him, all that should come of him, his Will and Pleasure, as with his Beast, or any other Cattle, to give, or to sell, or to kill" (W. Jordan, 55–56).

27. Similarly, just as Oedipus unwittingly slept with his mother, Ham was accused of all kinds of sexual perversions, including incest with his parents. According to one seventeenth-century exegete, Ham's sin of looking on his father's nakedness should be interpreted as having "incestuous relations with one's mother; so Canaan was the child of Noah's wife and Ham" (Allen, 78). According to Robert Graves and Raphael Patai, moreover, the myth of Noah's three brothers "is related to the Greek myth of how five brothers . . . conspired against their father Uranus," who is castrated by one of them (122).

28. Also important, the absence of a covenant brings up the apocalyptic possibility of another flood. Since the first flood is described in horrific terms that recall the Second Passage—Noah drinks so as to forget the deathly waters "And bodies floating face up!" (83)—perhaps the crimes of slavery will bring about another catastrophe.

29. It is hardly surprising that Hurston got caught up in the contradictions of the biblical myth of origin. More recently, in *The African Origin of Civilization* (trans. 1974), Cheikh Anta Diop argues,

> If we assembled end to end all the Biblical quotations in Western works referring to the curse on Ham's progeny, they would without exaggeration be numerous enough to fill a library. In contrast, rare are the quotations pointing out the fact that the Egyptians belong among Ham's descendants. (246)

For Diop, "the ethnic designation of Ham and his progeny is implied in the etymology of the word used in Genesis" and proves that "a Negro Egypt" gave birth to Western civilization (45). According to Diop, Ham is "blackened" by subsequent commentators as "the ancestor of the Negroes," but then he is "whitened whenever one seeks the origin of civilization" (9).

Chapter 4. De Modern Do Mr. Bones (and All That Ventriloquist Jazz)

Epigraphs: quoted in Brown, 382; quoted in Haywood, 80; and Berryman, 99. Here and at the end of this chapter, I use the poem number (not the page number) that appears at the top of each of the verses in *The Dream Songs*, the one-volume edition of *77 Dream Songs* and *His Toy, His Dream, His Rest*.

1. Gates goes on to say, "Far too often, their models were not of the first order; these black mockingbirds did not supersede the creations of their borrowed forms." Similarly, to the editor of one anthology of black women's poetry from this era, the work seems "sentimental and stilted" in form (Honey, 32). So that they would represent the race in a politically correct manner, black writers were often encouraged by their mentors to conform to established aesthetic standards or congratulated for doing so. Countee Cullen's 1927 *Caroling Dusk* anthology touted Jessie Fauset's debts to the Sorbonne and Lewis Alexander's reliance on haiku forms as well as Anne Spencer's use of imagism. Benjamin Brawley's review of "The Negro Literary Renaissance" rejected vers libre, jazz, blues, or vernacular influences.

More recently, in the Program Notes of Shange's *Sassafrass, Cypress and Indigo* (1976), the author explains "i cant count the number of times i have vicerally wanted to attack deform n maim the language that i waz taught to hate myself in/the language that perpetuates the notions that cause pain to every black child as he/she learns to speak of the world & the 'self'": quoted in Baker, *Workings of the Spirit*, 170–71.

2. Of course, the same argument cannot be made about prose fiction, given Zora Neale Hurston's extensive use of dialect in her stories and novels.

3. Although anyone interested in the subject of racial ventriloquism remains indebted to North, Nielsen, and Torgovnick, I am suggesting that they do not fully appreciate the extent to which white practitioners of black talk are themselves highly critical of their own language performances. An exception to those who disapprove of cross-racial linguistic experimentation is Sylvia Wallace Holton, *Down Home and Uptown*, which furnishes many and interesting readings of black speech in the writings of American whites.

4. My language here draws upon a related meditation on dual linguistic registers in the essay "Quotations of Voices" in Certeau, esp. 159–63.

5. The point Shelley Fisher Fishkin makes about American literature can thus be extended to modernist literature in general: "The laws against miscegenation have been struck from the books. But unwritten laws prevent critics from acknowledging how fully black and white voices and traditions have mingled to create what we know as 'American' culture." See Fishkin, 142. Her comment also points to the unwritten history of how white writers read and were affected by black authors as well as unwritten theories about the dynamics of cross-racial influence.

6. In "'Authenticity,' or the Lesson of *Little Tree*," Gates describes the 1836 slave narrative of Archy Moore which was written by the white historian Richard Hildreth; *Autobiography of a Female Slave* (1857), a novel composed by the white woman Mattie Griffith; and the purportedly true narrative composed by the ersatz slave James Williams.

7. This discussion is based on an analysis of miscommunication within marriages (Mairs, 114). Mairs goes on to say about miscommunication in relationships that, although we tend to say, "I know exactly what you mean," most of us should admit, "I, for one, don't know exactly what I mean, much less what you mean."

8. As Michel de Certeau put it in a different context, "The written discourse which cites the speech of the other is not, cannot be, the discourse of the other" (78).

9. Lindsay recorded his poems in January 1931 under the auspices of Columbia University (Ruggles, 408).

10. Ann Massa quotes the poet explaining that he "always hated Jazz" and so he disavowed this approach to his poetry (235). As with the Higher Vaudeville analogy, Lindsay suffered attraction and repulsion to the experimental techniques he shared with popular American artists, black and white.

11. In 1909 Lindsay composed a story entitled "The Golden Face People" (printed in

The Crisis) about a future America conquered by the Chinese in which he examined the dynamics of racial subordination and clearly did so because he sympathized with the plights of minorities in America.

12. Lindsay's conflicted attitude toward his performances illuminates the complexities of his cross-racial identification. Although he was "used up in shouting" what people always wanted to hear, although after each performance he suffered bouts of vertigo and depression, the dramatizations acted on him "like alcohol" (Ruggles, 305, 307). That Lindsay is quoted as describing the appeal of his tours "as a splendid and unending drunkenness" (Cusic, 22) and that he eventually committed suicide by drinking Lysol dramatize the toll of what Michael Harper diagnosed as "*white blood forced to derision*."

13. To some extent, of course, such a linguistic crossover reflects many early twentieth-century attempts at verbal strangeness—multiple classical allusions, say, or the effort to make language aspire to the conditions of music or painting—and to some extent, too, racial ventriloquism manifests a fascination with border crossings that led exiled and expatriated writers to "unhouse" language, to use George Steiner's term. Closest in kind might be the influence of Asian traditions on, say, Ezra Pound and Amy Lowell. Yet unlike linguistic Otherness in the fashion of the far East, which tends toward understated elegance, simplicity of diction, sparsity of verbal brushstrokes, linguistic Otherness in the fashion of the black emphasizes ridiculously ornate and baroque structures of address or hilariously nonsensical ones.

14. Glenn Watkins describes Louis Bruenberg's musical rendition of Lindsay's *The Daniel Jazz* as a "fusion of Viennese chromaticism with ragtime and the blues" (180).

15. Significantly, too, the frontispiece design for Sitwell's *Façade*, a 1919 gouache by Gino Severini, featured the figures of two harlequins. See Salter, 54.

16. See Yeomans, 267–75, for an account of Eliot's use of black-defined rhythms: 267–75. James Clifford links literary modernism to the beginning of modern anthropology in *Predicament of Culture*.

17. Eliot recurrently turned to dialect (white working-class or black), as in "He Do the Police in Different Voices" (the epigraph of Part I of the drafted *Waste Land*) and in the quotation that opens "The Hollow Men": "Mistuh Kurtz—he dead." More to the point, the original version of *The Waste Land* began with vaudevillean tunes—"Meet me in the shadow of the watermelon Vine / Eva Iva Uva Emmaline" (*Facsimile*, 5)—and the completed text included references not only to the "rattle of the bones" but also to the popular tune about Mrs. Porter's daughter (who washed her "feet in soda water" (III.200)).

18. The phrase comes from Michelle Shocked, whose notes to *Arkansas Traveler* (1992) claim that "a blackface tradition is alive and well hidden behind a modern mask. I believe that 'blackening up' should be done correctly; as an exploration for the source of that hollow ring we mistakenly believe was immaculately conceived in Las Vegas, and in a context of true respect for the cultures we ape."

19. Both Nielsen and North devote pages to Pound's use of black vernacular in the *Pisan Cantos*: *Reading Race*, 66–72 and *The Dialect of Modernism*, 91–99.

20. As early as 1700, the word "gay" means addicted to social dissipations, though it does not take on the notion of homosexuality until the mid-twentieth century.

21. His notes about the play describe the murder and reappearance of one Mrs. Porter, while the first London stage production presented Sweeney pursuing the screaming Doris with a razor, to the horror of Vivienne Eliot (Gordon, 57–58). I am indebted to Sandra Gilbert for her work done on this play in *No Man's Land* but also for the scholarship she produced with Elliot Gilbert on Eliot's relationship to his first wife. Robert Crawford explains that Doctor F. L. Sweany was featured in an ad that fascinated the young Eliot in which men

"lacking in energy, strength and vigor" are offered a remedy for their sense that they are "wasting away" (28).

22. Repeatedly encouraging Doris to "Let Mr. Sweeney continue his story" about doing a girl in, Swarts and Snow bring intimations of death to Doris when she sees them as "spades"—the suit of the coffin.

23. Crawford cites a letter to Michael Roberts, July 19, 1935 (in the Berg), in which Eliot explains that Lindsay's work might pave the way for better things (161).

24. As Donald J. Gray has shown, it was probably the antic dispensing with normative sense in minstrel songs that attracted the consummate nonsense poet Lewis Carroll to minstrelsy; his early version of "The Mock Turtle's Song"—"Salmon come up! Salmon go down! / Salmon come twist your tail around!"—echoes the popular (ribald) "Sally, Come Up":

Sally come up! Sally go down!
Sally come twist your heel around!
De old man he's gone down to town—
Oh Sally come down de middle.

25. I have used the word "signifying" here to indicate an odd resemblance between the parodic gleefulness of overtly racist minstrel numbers and the impact of the signifying structures Henry Louis Gates, Jr., finds in the African-American tradition (*Figures*, 242). Within the Dis-and-Dat songs popular in the nineteenth century, many focused on high cultural figures:

To Boston Part I den sail roun,
Dey said de Dickens was in town;
I ax dem who de Dickens was
Dey sed 'twas massa Pickwick Box.
Ring de Hoop! an blow de horn!
Massa Dickens eat de corn.

This particular song is quoted in Wasserstrom, 343.

26. The efforts of the Boomlay BOOMers cannot be conflated but nevertheless dovetail with what D. H. Lawrence sought in the Etruscan tongue, namely words resonant with "some of Africa's imperturbable sang-froid" ("Cypresses," 296), for they display precisely Lawrence's alienation against the hollowness of traditional European vocabularies.

27. Cunard's very real contributions to Africans and African Americans may have been obscured by the notoriety she achieved when her highly publicized bad girl escapades broke all the gender rules of the day. She was supposed to have inspired a number of fictional *femmes fatales*, from Lady Brett Ashley in Hemingway's *The Sun Also Rises* (1926) and Lucy Tantamount in Aldous Huxley's *Point Counter Point* (1928) to the "lecherous octopus" qua "erotic boa constrictor" Constance in Richard Aldington's short story "Now Lies She There" in *Soft Answers* (1932).

28. Cunard's essay "Harlem Reviewed" (1934) fulminates against "Van Vechten and Co. [who] have made a revolting and cheap lithograph, so that Harlem, to a large idle-minded public, has come to mean nothing more whatsoever than a round of hooch-filled nightclubs after a round of 'snow' (cocaine) filled boudoirs" (*Negro*, 67–75).

29. As if to ward off such criticism, Van Vechten included an analysis of his novel's title by its gloomily Byronic hero—one Byron Kasson—who exclaims about "Nigger Heaven" that "We sit in our places in the gallery of this New York theatre and watch the white world sitting down below in the good seats in the orchestra. Occasionally they turn their

faces up towards us, their hard, cruel faces, to laugh or sneer, but they never beckon" (149). Surely Langston Hughes was right; Van Vechten understood "that old segregated heaven . . . Ain't no heaven at all" (Kellner, "*Keep A-Inchin'*," 9–10). In addition, as college-educated Byron's speeches prove, Van Vechten allows class and social contexts to define which black characters do and do not speak Dis and Dat.

Van Vechten's crucial role in the Harlem Renaissance may have been downplayed "by design," as Bruce Kellner indicates, because of the wish of scholars to promote an image of independent black consciousness. During his lifetime, many black intellectuals and artists praised Van Vechten's contributions to the civil rights cause and to the black arts in America. See Kellner, "*Keep A-Inchin'*," 11–12.

30. How many of the racial ventriloquists in this generation shared the embarrassment experienced by Connelly, one wonders, when words written as a lamentation—a forlorn God says, "I ain't comin' down to help you. I'm jest in de dozens and wanta feel a little better, dat's all"—received "audible reactions" from his cast of black actors: Although Connelly believed "in the dozens" meant "greatly depressed, one actor discreetly informed him that in Harlem 'you say it when someone is sleeping with his aunt'" (Connelly, 175). More ominous is the story told about the black actor playing the central character of O'Neill's *The Emperor Jones* (1920), specifically his effort to substitute the words "black baby" for the term "nigger"; the playwright (noted for his liberalism) threatened him: "If I ever catch you rewriting my lines again, you black bastard, I'm going to beat you up" (Bogard, 134).

31. Consider, for example, a conversation at the beginning of *Nigger Heaven* between two friends who play the numbers:

> What nummer?
> Seven-Nine-Eight.
> Whah you find et?
> Off'n a gal's fron' do'.
> Commin' ut?
> Goin' in. Ah went out duh back winder. Her daddy done come home widout writin'.
> Hush mah mouf!
> Ah doan mean mebbe. (4)

Dialect markers standardized in the nineteenth-century are quite apparent here: changes in *th* ("the" becomes "duh" and "mouth" becomes "mouf"), loss of final letters ("front" becomes "fron'"), nasalization ("going" becomes "goin'"), eye dialect ("maybe" become "mebbe"), loss of words ("Whah you find et?"), reduction of consonant clusters ("don't" becomes "doan"), an alternative verb system (where "came" would be expected "done come home" appears), and phonological substitutions ("et" for "it"). Given the context of cuckoldry and gambling, the vaudevillean give-and-take backchat links black street talk with laziness, ignorance, boastful strutting, much as it had been in the nineteenth-century minstrel show and the turn-of-the-century music hall.

32. See the letter dated December 3, 1908 in H. Stevens, 199. See also "Exposition of the Contents of a Cab," in which "Victoria Clementina, negress," brings to Stevens's mind "savage blooms; // Thridding the squawkiest jungle" (*Opus Posthumous*, 41).

33. See M. Watkins, 276 and 278, as well as Gates, *Colored People*, 23.

34. A second scene, drawing upon homophobic as well as racist burlesque conventions, features a "Roman" drama about two centurions shooting craps and joined first by an Ethiopian and then by "two Fairies in scarlet togas": "If daze anything worse than Christians," exclaims the slave, "it certainly am peddyrasts" (66). The exceptional homophobia

at work here comes into focus in the context of cummings's later explanation that the scene was about Bert Savoy, a comedian who appeared in Broadway musicals, and cummings's own conviction about the link between homosexuality and fascism; "in my experience, enthusiastic advocates of any form of totalitarianism are inclined to be nothing-if-not-queer, mentally if not otherwise" (Norman, 221).

35. See *Uncle Tom's Cabin* (1852), by George L. Aiken and George C. Howard, one of the first musical adaptations of the novel. It is interesting to compare minstrels' punning on the novel's cast and its settings so as to drain Stowe's jeremiad of polemical substance—

We wur cakes.
What kind ob cakes wur we?
Jist black cakes.
What kind ob cakes is Little Eva?
Angel Cake!
An Massa St. Clair
An eclair (Toll, 94)—

—with e. e. cummings's script which seeks to revive the libertarian plea of Stowe's best-seller; however, in the process he sustained minstrel stereotypes of the physicality and atavism of black people. On *Uncle Tom's Cabin* as staged by minstrels, see also M. Watkins, 95.

36. Mezzrow explains about Ted Lewis, Sophie Tucker, Eddie Cantor, and Al Jolson that they "were heebs, and the boys had the feeling that we should all stick together and not knock the big names of 'our' race. I didn't go for that jive at all; being a Jew didn't mean a thing to me." His "real brothers" were "the colored musicians," and "not a lot of beat-up old hamfats who sang and played a commercial excuse for the real thing. I never could dig the phony idea of a race—if we were a 'race'—sticking together all the way, even when it meant turning your back on what was good or bad" (49).

37. Nielsen and North discuss Williams's contribution to the *Negro* anthology, "The Colored Girls of Passenack—Old and New," in the context of Williams's various recollections in prose and verse of voyeuristic scenes in which he spies at black servants as well as Williams's fascination with the black minstrel Bert Williams (Nielsen, 72–84, and North, 150–161).

38. See the account of this project by Mariani in "Williams' Black Novel," which explains that the prototype of Man Orchid was one Bucklin Moon whom Williams believed to be a light-skinned black but who was, in fact, Dutch.

39. *Holy Barbarians* was the title of a book about the beats composed by Lawrence Lipton. The beats' attitudes toward the black man as a kind of prototypical renegade are discussed in Chapter 5.

40. The loss of his "negro voice" may have begun with the loss of his home on the Edmonds's place, as Mollie explains: Butch was exiled from home for petty thievery. But it was surely accelerated afterward when a policeman in Jefferson felled him in the act of breaking and entering a store, causing him to curse "through his broken mouth, his teeth fixed into something like furious laughter through the blood" (354). From the beginning to the end of his brief life, Mollie's grandson has been constructed into a Butch: a butcher of other men, a man who will be butchered, but also a hyper-masculinized stud.

41. See Brasch for a discussion of the "more Standard than Black English" used on the TV show (224). Although *Amos 'n' Andy* was not renewed after its 1952–53 run, CBS syndicated the films to local television stations so the episodes continued to be aired. See Ely, 238–39.

42. On the issue of Berryman's ignorance of actual black experience, see Canarroe, who argues nevertheless that "Berryman's feelings of kinship actually are sincere, touchingly so, expressing the self-mockery of a victim, and that if his diction is at times exploitative his motives were nevertheless sound" (104).

43. A heroic effort to understand this poem is made by Kathe Davis, 30–45.

44. According to one reader, Berryman—"by giving his Conscience a black voice"—embodied through "a white face in blackvoice" the "sustained reproof that white America faces from its dialectic companion, blackness" (Vendler, 57).

Chapter 5. Psychopathologies of Black Envy

Epigraphs: quoted in Hoch, 52; Fanon, 165; Southern, 198.

1. When in *The Tenants* Bernard Malamud named his reclusive white writer Lesser and his bellicose black novelist took the pseudonym Will Spear, the narrative turned the depiction of their relationship into an analysis of dualism in which the (white) mind finds itself divided from and diminished by the fearful potency of the (black) body. In Fanon's terms, the Jewish intellectual menace confronts the Negro biological threat. Yet that Will Spear's most horrific memory involves being forced to perform fellatio and that Lesser robs Will of his girlfriend clearly undercuts the identification of the black man with the phallic spear.

2. See Gwen Bergner's excellent discussion of Fanon which examines the ways in which colonialism allocates social power according to skin color instead of penis possession: "To say that the phallus corresponds to whiteness is not to unhinge the phallus from the penis but to complicate the association. Racial and gender privilege are so intertwined that Fanon evokes castration to describe racial disempowerment" (79).

3. As Diana Fuss explains in *Essentially Speaking*, the Lacanian phallus remains "metonymically close to the penis and derives much of its signifying importance from this by no means arbitrary relation. It is precisely because a woman does not have a penis that her relation to the phallus, the signifying order, the order of language and the law, is so complicated and fraught with difficulties" (8).

4. Carpenter's phrase is meant to describe those beings "occupying an intermediate position between the two sexes" (185), people whose homosexuality makes them deviate from normative definitions of either the feminine or the masculine. It is interesting in this regard that Jean-Joseph Goux has recently argued that Greek philosophy did not equate the phallus with the penis but instead aligned it with the *logos*. In my formulation, then, the hyperbolic penis of the black man, his inflated virility, paradoxically ties him to the body, separating him from the phallus or *logos* (discussed in Silverman, 30–31).

5. See Atlas, 111. Significant in this regard is the response of Brent Staples to the novel: "Bellow wanted the dick remembered. He returned to it again and again as a symbol of spiritual decay. . . . I expected more of a man who could see to the soul. I expected a portrait of myself, not as the beast I'd been made out to be, but as who I was at heart" (220).

6. I am disagreeing with an interesting reading proposed by Stanley Crouch, who argues that Mr. Sammler is turned into a man by the red blood of the pickpocket wounded in the street, for he understands that "The thief is no longer a dandified puma or an animal, but a human being vulnerable to the hysteria at the nub of injustice" (108).

7. As Allen Ellenzweig has pointed out, "to view with irony Mapplethorpe's attitudes toward his black males may be a luxury only the gay white viewer can afford" (138).

8. See also Mercer, "Skin Head Sex Thing," 1–23. At the Playwrights Horizons on Theater Row in New York in December 1995, four new one-act plays entitled *Black Ink*

included Ed DuRante's "Man in Polyester Suit," a play about two friends, one black and one white, who attempt to come out and to out each other.

9. See the chapter on "Race and Sexuality: The Role of the Outsider," in Mosse, 133–52.

10. That the photo exposes whites (rather than blacks) is partially related to the fact that Milton Moore, Mapplethorpe's model and lover, is as uncircumcised as the pickpocket in Bellow's novel, which means that the shaft of the penis covers the head; still undisclosed, his penis could be said to be only peeking out of the foreskin.

Recently, in "Looking for Trouble," Kobena Mercer reversed his original belief that the photograph stereotyped black men (352, 354).

11. From Vachel Lindsay's "fat black bucks" to Cunard's "nigger . . . grown bigger," the black of modernism was masculine but hopelessly emasculated vis-à-vis white power, as was evident in Chapter 4.

12. In her consideration of the history of African-American culture in the context of Lacanian issues, "Mama's Baby, Papa's Maybe," Hortense Spillers explains that "'Family' as we practice and understand in 'in the West'—the vertical transfer of a bloodline, of a patronymic, . . . from *fathers* to *sons* and in the supposedly free exchange of affectional ties between a male and a female of *his* choice—becomes the mythically revered privilege of a free and freed community." Thus, "legal enslavement removed the African-American male not so much from sight as from *mimetic* view as a partner in the prevailing social fiction of the Father's name, the Father's law" (74 and 80).

13. In the chapter on the "male male impersonator" in *Letters from the Front*, Sandra Gilbert and I discuss "male penis envy," a phrase we derive from Joseph Heller and Woody Allen.

14. Although, as Eve Kosofsky Sedgwick has argued, "the gender of object choice . . . has remained as *the* dimension denoted by the now ubiquitous category of 'sexual orientation'" (8), racechange scripts clustering around black male sexuality call into question traditional binary definitions of hetero- versus homosexualities (much as Sedgwick herself does when in *Epistemology of the Closet* she poses some pungent, funny alternative ways of categorizing human sexuality).

15. Thus, Morris Dickstein encapulates Baldwin's thematic project in the sentence, "How unbearably poignant . . . that he, the black man, so cruelly undermined, should ironically remain the mythical phallus, the object of the deepest sexual fantasies and expectations of white people" (169). Dickstein also makes the point that Baldwin served as a precursor for Mailer: *Advertisements for Myself* appeared four years after *Notes of a Native Son*, and Mailer's *Armies of the Night* "was quite deliberately Mailer's *Fire Next Time*" (162).

16. See Sedgwick's discussion of this term as "a name for 'a structural residue of terrorist potential, of *blackmailability*, of Western maleness through the leverage of homophobia'" in *Epistemology*, pp. 19–22.

17. An isolated rebel without a cause, the hipster-Negro-dummy through whom speaks the ventriloquist Norman Mailer makes the white writer sound kind of foolish when he boasts, "I am just one cat in a world of cool cats" (589). The "primitive vocabularies" (599) he self-consciously exhibits—with "words like go, and make it, and with it, and swing" (596)—appear dated, forced, adding verisimilitude to Baldwin's anecdote about some "Negro musicians" complaining that "the only trouble with that cat [Mailer] is that he's white" (231). In addition, Mailer's vignette about an illiterate "Negro friend" sustaining a discussion with an intellectual white girl "by swinging with the nuances of her voice" (586–87) is patronizing at best. Finally, the novelist resembles a puerile Raskolnikov when he justi-

fies the "courage" of murdering a "weak fifty-year-old man" as an attempt to violate private property and introduce "a dangerous element into one's life" (593).

18. Earlier in Anderson's tale, the narrator sees his face in a looking-glass over a bar and sees "a girl's face, and a lonesome and scared girl too" (207); although he explains he is "not any fairy" (209), the boy cannot find a voice to protest against the black men who think his body "pretty white and slender . . . like a young girl's body" and later speculates about his silence, "It may be that I was too ashamed of having turned into a girl and being afraid of a man to make any sound" (223).

19. A useful discussion of Fielder's anxious turn from "the homosexual" to "the homoerotic" in his formulation of interracial fraternity in American fiction appears in Wiegman, 149–78.

See, too, Joseph A. Boone's critique of orientalist homoerotics and in particular his analysis of the sexual contacts between white gay men and brown boys in the Near East. As with the white male/African-American male dynamic, here too the gay man's "object of desire remains simultaneously same and other, a source of troubling and unresolved identification and difference" (91). On Mailer's later reaction against what he himself called "his love affair with the Black soul, a sentimental orgy at its worst," see Wallace, 49.

20. In this respect, Mailer anticipates a comparable phenomenon Wiegman has mapped in popular movies and TV shows, namely the ways in which "the image of interracial fraternity [came] to signify the post-civil rights era" (149–50).

21. Analyzing slippages between homosexuality and homosocial relationships between women, Rich's "lesbian continuum" refers only to the ways in which women slide from sisterly and maternal forms of loving into same-sex sexual relationships. Since a girl's first love object is usually the mother, Rich argues, the basis for her loving is a same-sex relationship. Most theorists agree that homosexuality remains more firmly bracketed away from heterosexuality in the psychology of men. I refrain from using Eve Kosofsky Sedgwick's word "homosocial" to describe nongenital bonding between men because the slide from social to sexual language makes it impossible to distinguish homosocial from homosexual attachments in many of the texts imbued by black envy. Perhaps in the post-World War II period, blackness calls into being a taboo against miscegenation that makes possible the blurring of the hetero-/homosexual dichotomy Sedgwick sees as so crucial in Western culture.

22. The best discussion of this story and its connection not only to Mailer's boxing fantasies but also to *An American Dream* is Messenger, "Norman Mailer." Although here Mailer sounds curiously sophisticated in his recognition that no safe space of straight confidence exists, in "The Homosexual Villain" he testifies with a kind of stilted silliness to his amazing realization that "*My God, homosexuals are people too*" (225). Bad faith reeks from the prefatory remarks about Mailer's reaction on being asked to write the piece—"*I didn't know the first thing about homosexuality*"—and from the liberal breast-beating within it: "I did not *know* any homosexuals because obviously I did not want to" (223). Indeed, evaluating this essay, Mailer himself later viewed it as "the worst article I have ever written, conventional, empty, pious, the quintessence of the Square" (221).

23. In this regard, it would be interesting to study the difference between brown and black. Tapping the homosexual tradition established from Sir Richard Burton to Laurence of Arabia to Virginia Woolf (whose Orlando undergoes a racechange before the sexchange that turns him into her), the gay beats often played out their homosexuality in Morocco, Tangiers, Algiers, Mexico.

24. The blackening of the homosexual functioned historically as a kind of character assasination. During his tour in America, for example, racialized caricatures of Oscar Wilde

appeared in a number of newspapers and popular books, as if to indicate that the average American citizen conflated decadent homosexual and tawdry black tastes which were thought to mirror each other in their flamboyant, bizarre vulgarity. According to Wilde's biographers, students at the University of Rochester and Yale University hired black men, dressed them in formal attire with kid gloves, and paid them to parade in the lecture halls visited by the English speaker (Ellman, 184).

25. See the discussion of blots, spots, and skin in Stafford, 294–320. Michelle Cliff describes "The Girl from Martinique": "A piece of cloth wrapped her breasts and wound itself behind her . . . . she was *parti-colored* . . . . Patches of black bumped against ivory." A "checkerboard of a woman," she appears in a freak show (76). One of the earliest discussions of achromatism appears in Jefferson's *Notes on a State of Virginia*, 70–71.

26. Whether or not Podhoretz "had a clear crush" on Mailer, as Jules Feiffer once claimed (Manso, 269), his legitimizing of "The White Negro" with the *Partisan Review* crowd may have been related to his sharing with Mailer an appreciation of the beauty of black masculinity.

27. Lott notes that Norman Mailer's codification of "the renegade ethic of male sexuality conceived out of and projected onto black men" resurfaces in "the homosocial nature of the dialogues" of *Black Like Me*: "In these conversations," Lott explains, "white men's interest in black male sexuality is mediated by but also identifies them with the white women black men are supposed to crave" ("White Like Me," 487). Yet the racial voyeurism at work here slips easily out of the slick category of homosociality into homosexuality, since women may not even be mentioned.

28. Similarly, as Andrew Ross has observed, such countercultural spokesmen as the Yuppie leader Jerry Rubin and the electronic technology promoter Marshall McLuhan paid "Rousseauistic tributes" to a primitivism figured as African (123).

29. In Melvin Van Peebles's movie *Watermelon Man,* the white racist who wakes up to discover that he has turned black shadowboxes in the mirror with the fighter he fancies he has become and then quickly looks down into his pants (though he knows "that's an old wives' tale"). The same sort of scene occurs in the movie *Soul Man*, where a girl peeks down the pants of her blacked-up lover to see the difference race makes.

30. See Henry Louis Gates, Jr., on the homophobia of black nationalism in "Black Man's Burden," 78–79.

31. On Duke, see *Newsweek*, Nov. 18, 1991, pp. 24–28. Despite the pacifist leanings of its founder, Robert Bly, the Wild Man movement of the nineties encouraged men to come into contact with the savage self within by playing bongo drums and visiting sweat houses in the wilderness.

32. Jean Walton remarks on the fact that, for Rivière, "Only the imagined attacker's gender is significant, not his race" ("Re-Placing Race," 782) and further argues that "Rivière's indifference to the racialized components of her patient's fantasies is reproduced with a striking monotony by her feminist successors" (800). The white woman's fantasy of a Negro intruder propels the sex games of Joanna Burden in *Light in August* where Joe Christmas is supposed to act as if he is breaking into her house through a window until he finds her hiding in a closet or an empty room or beneath certain shrubs; "She would be wild then, in the close, breathing halfdark without walls, with her wild hair, each strand of which would seem to come alive like octopus tentacles, and her wild hands and her breathing: 'Negro! Negro! Negro!'" (285).

33. I have discussed this concept more fully in "Feminist Misogyny." In relation to women's attraction to the beats during the fifties, see Breines, esp. 127–66.

34. The 1500-page manuscript can be read in the Hemingway Collection at the Kennedy Library in Boston, Massachusetts. For a discussion of it, see Spilka as well as Comley and Scholes. Despite the ways in which the paperback version "went too far in concealing the darkness of this text" (Comley and Scholes, 103), I have confined my comments mostly to the edited version because it has necessarily become the classroom text of this work.

35. As Comley and Scholes explain, the manuscript includes more references to Catherine's Africanism. She tells Marita that first she was "a Kanaka. Now I'm working to be Somali" (98). Similarly, although David advises Marita, "Don't try and make yourself like a Wakamba or M'Bulu girl," he quickly agrees that "We'll go to Africa tonight" (99).

36. See Cornelia Nixon's discussion of sodomy, 44–49, 153–54, 223–28. Also Ford, 189–205.

37. Morrison explores the counterpoint between the two narratives at the end of *The Garden of Eden* by explaining, "Africa, imagined as innocent and under white control, is the inner story; Africanism, imagined as evil, chaotic, impenetrable, is the outer story" (*Playing in the Dark*, 89).

38. A likeness of Zelda Fitzgerald, who explained the tanning craze in *Save Me the Waltz* (1932) by declaring that "beautiful brown people . . . seem so free of secrets" (85), Catherine in this respect dramatizes the tragic incompatibility between white femininity and creative freedom.

39. Countering notions of the lesbian phallus, de Lauretis proposes a model of perverse desire based on fetishism. The lesbian subject, neither refusing nor accepting castration, disavows it, adopting masculinity as a fetish because "masculinity alone carries a strong connotation of sexual desire for the female body" (204, 243). See also Grosz, 39–54, and Adams, 261. Of course, all these speculations diverge from Freud's view that the fetishist is male. Naomi Schor explains that fetishism may function as a strategy for women: "By appropriating the fetishist's oscillation between denial and recognition of castration, women can effectively counter any move to reduce their bisexuality to a single one of its poles" (98).

40. In *The Garden of Eden* manuscript, Catherine thinks about her sexual changes as sea changes: "we must have the sun to make this sea change. The sea change was made in the night and it grows in the night and the darkness that she wants and needs now grows in the sun" (quoted in Comley and Scholes, 93).

41. *Dr. Jekyll and Mr. Hyde*, directed by Rouben Mamoulian with Fredric March, Miriam Hopkins, and Rose Hobart (1932) presents a character whose otherness teeters between black and Asian characteristics. For a homosexual interpretation of *Dr. Jekyll and Mr. Hyde*, see Showalter, *Sexual Anarchy*, 105–26.

42. See Rubenstein, "Intersexions," and Showalter, "Rethinking the Seventies," 249: "B.G. is both [Jessie's] demon lover and her own repressed violent potentiality."

43. On the uses to which Octave Mannoni and other theorists of colonization have put *The Tempest*, see Loomba, 149.

44. In her analysis of the tendency of erotic love to become domination, Jessica Benjamin links that drift to masculine psychosexual development:

> The need to sever the identification with the mother in order to be confirmed both as a separate person and as a male person—and for the boy these are hard to distinguish—often prevents the boy from recognizing his mother. She is not seen as an independent person (another subject), but as something other. . . . (76)

Using the novels of Hemingway and Gould, we could rewrite this script to explain lesbian sadism:

> The need to sever the identification with [the feminine] in order to be confirmed . . . as a separate person [which means being] a male person . . . often prevents [the young woman] from recognizing [her] mother [or any woman]. She is not seen as an independent person (another subject), but as something other.

45. Although I am disagreeing with Jane Marcus's reading of these photographs, I am indebted to her scholarship in "Bonding and Bondage."

Chapter 6. What Will the Mixed Child Deliver?

Epigraphs: Cone, 186; Lazarre, *Mother Knot*, 17–18; Toomer quoted in D. Turner, xiii.

1. An exception to this rule is Topsy in *Uncle Tom's Cabin*, but it is worth observing that she was not born but "jes grew"; in other words, unsure of her own origins, she appears to be a fact or force of nature rather than an individuated child.

In *Vicious Modernism*, James De Jongh discusses a poem by Barbara Bellow Watson entitled "Echoes in a Burnt Building" that reimagines Alice reborn as black in a burned-out Wonderland (181).

2. Susan Willis makes a somewhat different point about Morrison's Claudia and racechange when she argues that Christie, the Barbie doll's black equivalent, "is not wholly unlike the inception of a black Shirley Temple doll." According to Willis, however, such black "replicants" are "devoid of cultural integrity" (183–84).

3. In *Loving v. Virginia*, the United States Supreme Court struck down laws against interracial marriage which existed in sixteen states at that time. As Naomi Zack explains in *Race and Mixed Race*, "At one time or another before 1957, thirty-eight states had laws against marriage between blacks and whites" (77). For historical background on attitudes toward miscegenation and mulattoes, see Williamson, *New People*. That miscegenation has been taboo throughout this country's past links American racism to South African apartheid, a system which reclassified the white partner of a black person as "colored."

4. George Hutchinson points out that Henry Louis Gates, Jr., associates Toomer's insistance on his status as a mulatto with sexual lack when he claims, "Toomer's was a gesture of racial castration, which, if not silencing his voice literally, then at least transformed his deep black bass into a false soprano" (228).

5. This statement about Genet's feeling that the disappearance of blacks would make the United States "nothing" to him, appears late in the book which opens with the comment "When I said the Blacks were the characters on the white page of America, that was too easy an image: the truth really lies where I can never quite know it, in a love between two Americans of different colour" (*Prisoner of Love*, 3).

6. Because this story is so very short and so very often anthologized, I've refrained from including page numbers parenthetically in the text.

7. For a fuller account of this dynamics, see Peel, 223–37.

8. Hortense Spillers's important essay, "Mama's Baby, Papa's Maybe" informs this discussion, in particular her idea that slavery inflicted a process of ungendering.

9. See Zack, 34, for a discussion of the American white family as a "private institution for breeding white people." According to the "one drop rule," to be white is to have no black relatives at all; to be black is to have only one distant black ancestor. As Langston Hughes's character Simple deadpans, "That drop is really powerful" (*Simple Takes A Wife*, 85).

10. To be sure, the model for Chopin's tale was Loca Sampite, the white wife of one Al-

bert Sampite (with whom Chopin had an affair) and a woman who—whem deserted by her husband—simply went back to her mother with her children (Toth, 215).

11. See especially Sollors, "'Never Was Born,'" and Hathaway. Hathaway argues, "The desire to kill the father for sleeping with the mother is intensified by the rejection of the 'black' son by the 'white' father because of racial 'impurities.' The violation of identity caused by miscegenation exacerbates oedipal motivations" (154).

12. In Harriet Jacobs's slave narrative, the autobiographical heroine Linda uses blackface to disguise herself to reach a safe hiding place in her grandmother's garret. Her determination to win freedom for herself and her children does not really require that she don a sailor's outfit and blacken her face with charcoal, as she walks through the streets of the town where "The father of my children came so near that I brushed against his arm; but he had no idea who I was" (172). Whereas Jacobs's protagonist uses blackface to reach a safe hiding place in a scene where burnt cork signals the deflation of black interiority to a racial brand or the devolution of personhood to property in a slave economy, Tom's blackened face seems to signify a murderous depravity innate in the mixed child.

13. That the mother's tale is framed by the shooting of a doe—by hunters instructed by McCaslin to understand that one should not hunt does "because if we did kill does in a few years there wouldn't even be any bucks left to kill" (331)—means that Faulkner views the expulsion of mother and child as a tragic loss for white as well as black generations, which in any case cannot really be distinguished in the mixed generations to come. Ike McCaslin's discovery of Roth Edmonds' miscegenation with a "doe . . . that walks on two legs" (321) teaches the old man that his own ancestry will endure only into a diminished future in the blood lines of kindred repudiated as family.

14. When a black man shows up in town and then at his mother's house, Donald—who has seen "no colored men"—responds to his predictable questions by explaining he wants to grow up to become "A colored man" (83–84). But the African-American man reacts to the linking of Mrs. Gage's name with Swyburne's by cursing "Nigger women" and the outraged boy hits him. Finally, the story suggests that the biracial son understands the black man's hostility when he says "Nigger women" (85), for the black man has been displaced and replaced by the shadowy white father and Donald will therefore never grow up to become a "colored man."

15. An evocative refrain from Toomer's *Cane* makes a similar point:

> rock a-by baby . . .
> Black mother sways, holding a white child on her bosom.
> when the bough bends . . .
> Her breath hums through the pine cones. (84)

The black mother disempowered, helpless against the catastrophe awaiting her offspring, or the black mother surrogate retaliating, surviving the catastrophe awaiting the infant she has wet-nursed or adopted: In either case the child comes down, cradle and all.

In Nadine Gordimer's short story "The Moment before the Gun Went Off" (1991), the narrative of the biracial offspring of white father and black mother remains a not-growing-up tale, a plot of childhood's end, of infant mortality. Gordimer's black mother stands silently with her eyes downcast at the grave of her son because, as her secret sexual union with a white man is meant to indicate, she cannot do anything but comply with her own hidden exploitation under South Africa's system of apartheid. See also the discussion of Hurston's play *Color Struck* (1926) at the end of this chapter.

16. Though expelled by Abraham, Hagar is promised by God that her son Ishmael will

also found a great nation. See Delores S. Williams's extended discussion of the Hagar story in *Sisters in the Wilderness*, 15–33.

17. Finally, after witnessing Hagar's freedom and thus the survival of her matrilineage, Dana exacts revenge by acting as a female Oedipus, murdering her white progenitor and struggling back through the thick wall of the past into his future, at the cost of her left arm (cut off at precisely the spot the master's fingers had grasped). Joining the slave narrative with H. G. Wells's plot of time travel, Butler manages to foreshorten "the distance between now and then," as Robert Crossley put it in his Introduction to *Kindred*, (Butler, xxiii).

18. The rest of the quote attributes the voluptuousness of black women to "their sexual organs [which] are much more developed than those of whites." J. J. Virety, *Histoire naturelle du genre human*, 3 vols. (Paris, 1824), II: 150, is quoted by Reff, 92. Reff explores the role of "the Negress" in paintings where she clearly signifies exoticism and eroticism.

19. As in Chesnutt's "Her Virginia Mammy" (1899), where a black mother withholds her identity from her daughter and even impersonates the girl's mammy, female silence underscores the tension between interracial desire and the family as a producer of whiteness. Similarly, in George Washington Cable's novella "Madame Delphine" (1881), a quadroon mistress swears that her daughter is not her child (again, so the girl can make a respectable match).

20. See Anna Shannon Elfenbein's discussion of "Désirée's Baby" (127–31).

21. After one trader insinuates, "A prettty girl like you are, maybe some young buck down in Louisianna'll buy you—one of those French fellers down there—and you know what he'll do?—do you know now? . . . He'll ——— you" (65), Amantha—though she had never heard the "vile word" spoken before—hears it ring "like a bell with all the clarity of knowledge, or rather, with the clarity of nightmare knowledge" (*Band of Angels*, 65). It seems worth mentioning that, even if only through the title, this text again alludes to *Hamlet*.

22. One of the paintings thought to lead to *Les demoiselles d'Avignon* is entitled *The Harem*, a 1906 oil in which Picasso shows "four nude Fernandes" who are bathing in a room (Rubin and Seckel, 35).

23. See the discussions of North, 67–70, and Torgovnick, 102. Also see Foster for a discussion of William Rubin's show "Primitivism" at the Museum of Modern Art, an attempt to qualify the "debased art-historical notion of causal influence" that replaced it with the vague notion of "affinity" (182–83). Foster points out that Picasso understood the African fetishes were used as weapons and perhaps himself appropriated them so as to use Otherness to ward away others (women, death, the primitive itself). Rubins discusses Picasso's anxieties about syphilis and the evolution of the figures of the sailor and the student (see esp. 55–60).

24. See Langston Hughes's meditation on Picasso's cubism and sexual diseases in "Cubes" (*Collected Poems*, 175–76).

25. When the stuttering black waiter explains to a customer that he wouldn't "be here" if the gorilla were real, *Blonde Venus* seems to hint that the fetishization of the stage Africanist presence keeps actual African Americans in their subservient place.

In her excellent discussion of this film, Mary Ann Doane reads the movie in the context of Freud's phrase—"dark continent"—which appears in "The Question of Lay Analysis" and is used to describe the psychology of girls who "'feel deeply their lack of a sexual organ that is equal in value to the male one'" (210). Also useful is Tania Modleski's analysis, 127–29.

26. Foregrounding the logic that informs all these works, Alice Walker's *Meridian* (1976) meditates on the ways in which the white woman in a black context becomes prostituted. A chapter entitled "Of Bitches and Wives" presents a black man living with a white

woman he would never marry and explaining, "It's just a matter of pussy. That's all. Just a matter of my *personal* taste in pussy," though he views his personal taste as an aspect of racial politics because "This is war, man, *war!* And all's fair that fucks with the suckers' minds!" (136). Here the sexualized white woman has undergone a kind of species change in the battle between black and white men.

Elsewhere in *Meridian*, another white female character attached to a black man, Lynne Rabinowitz, realizes that she can be raped because black men assume she is "fucking every nigger in sight" (163). That the six-year-old child of Lynne Rabinowitz and her black husband Truman Held suffers a horrible death clearly dramatizes the fatality of their inter-racial partnership. Although Lynne had been drawn to the black community because "to her black people had a unique beauty, a kind of last-gasp loveliness, which, in other races, had already become extinct" (157), she is abandoned by her white parents (who count her dead because of her inter-racial marriage) and by her black husband (whose best friend rapes her).

27. The instability of female racial identity functions as a kind of Rorschach test in Toni Morrison's short story "Recitatif" (1982), an experimental tale that provides highly ambiguous social details upon which readers must build racial categories. For though we are told that one of Morrison's central characters comes "from a whole other race" and that together the two girls look like "salt and pepper" (445–46), Morrison removes or confuses racial codes. In a fascinating introspection on her critical response to the story, Elizabeth Abel has explained that she took "the amplitude of the sexualized body" of one character as evidence of black skin; her racial iconography, it turned out, hinged "on the construction of embodiedness" (473–74). But, as we have seen and as Abel herself knows, fleshliness or physicalization—the amplitude or embodiedness of the prominently sexualized female body—has historically been raced black.

28. Therman B. O'Daniel points out that Becky breaks the taboo of miscegenation but also defies the pressure of the town which would have lynched the man she refuses to name. In addition, he identifies her name with Rebecca, whose sons, Jacob and Esau, quarreled over the stolen birthright because of course Becky's sons have their birthrights stolen by the town (230 and 408).

29. I am indebted to Laura Dawkins for pointing out this passage in Wells, 270–71.

30. Gregory Howard Williams describes the racechange he and his brother were supposed to undergo when his father (who had passed as Italian) explained that his marriage to their white mother was over: "In Virginia you were white boys. In Indiana you're going to be colored boys" (33). Warned that "crackers . . . [will] beat the hell out of you," Williams and his brother are also told that "Colored don't like half-breeds either." And the author admits that "Nobody liked the half-breeds" (38) because of TV Westerns but also because the "'white nigger' baby" was "a daily reminder . . . of the forbidden and unforgivable star-crossed union between black and white" (62).

31. See also Hacker's use of Harriet Tubman as a poetic mask in "Part of a True Story" and "Inheritances," where she compares the slavery of race (experienced by her husband's family) to the slavery of class (experienced by her own), both in *Assumptions*, 25–28 and 33–34.

32. According to *Newsweek* (July 3, 1995), the story ends on an upbeat note when the white couple is "heartened" by the way in which the biological father of the dark child reacted to the news: "The first question he asked was, 'Do they love the child?'" (38).

33. See Rushdy and McDowell for more extended analyses of the novel.

34. Adrian Piper quotes Perry, *Another Present Era*: "She really thought everyone would be like her some day, neither black nor white, but something in between. It might take

decades or even centuries, but it would happen. And sooner than that, racism and the concept of race itself would become completely obsolete" (247).

35. On the very complicated relationship between Jews and blacks, see Rogin, *Blackface*, 251–68 as well as see Cornel West's foreword to Anna Deavere Smith, *Fires in the Mirror*, xvii-xxii and Takaki, 406–9.

36. See esp. pp. 115–22 of *Black Skin, White Masks*.

37. Elizabeth Bartholet explains in her chapter on "Adoption and Race" that "Racial matching policies represent a coming together of powerful and related ideologies—old-fashioned white racism, modern-day black nationalism, and what I will call 'biologism,' the idea that what is 'natural' in the context of the biological family is what is normal and desirable in the context of adoption" (93). She concludes about the large number of black children in need of homes (because the black adoptive families demanded by policies remain unavailable) that "the current racial matching regime, by barring and discouraging white parents from transracial adoption rather than welcoming them in the agency doors, denies adoptive homes to large numbers of minority children" (101). Finally, she argues that "Current racial matching policies are in conflict with the basic law of the land on race discrimination" (106).

38. Consider the popularity of a group of TV shows that presented the cute little black child adopted by white parent surrogates: *Webster, Diff'rent Strokes*, etc.

39. Such a devaluation is related to resistance to oppression. One thinks, for example, of Elizabeth Barrett Browning's dramatic monologue "The Runaway Slave at Pilgrim's Point" (1850) in which an infanticidal slave mother maddened by rape exclaims, "I am black, you see,—/ And the babe who lay on my bosom so, / Was far too white, too white for me" (I.113–15) so she retaliates by murdering the too-white infant.

40. Grounding her political disaffection from whiteness in a colonized past, Michelle Cliff in *Claiming an Identity They Taught Me to Despise* also views whiteness as a mistake, for she uses the same language Jean Rhys's heroine exploits in *Wide Sargasso Sea* (1966) to identify racial lightening with the degradation of sexual colonization:

> White cockroaches
> white niggers
> quadroons
> octoroons
> mulattos
> creoles
> white niggers. (44)

41. For an extensive reading of Dante's influence, see Catherine C. Ward.

42. As Henry Louis Gates, Jr., has explained in his response to Homan's "The Woman in the Cave," "the confusing phenomenon of the black bourgeois" in Naylor's novel may be modeled on white affluence without its citizens ever becoming integrated into white society; mimicry does not collapse into identity "(Linden Hills, the same as its white echelons of corporate success; Scarsdale in blackface)" (618–19).

All the characters in *Linden Hills* remain entrapped in structures that preexist their individual existences, enforcing identities upon them. To the extent that their thwarted lives demonstrate how different structures of domination operate to suppress difference differently, they exhibit the fear that keeps Naylor's closeted homosexual from risking a new life. Indeed, the speech composed of Whitman's lyrics about "the love of comrades" that marks the demise of the homosexual couple's union can be extended to encompass the leap of faith none of her characters dare to make:

> The way is suspicious—the result uncertain, perhaps destructive;
> You would have to give up all else—I alone would expect to be your God, sole and exclusive,
> Your novitiate would even then be long and exhausting,
> *The whole past theory of your life, and all conformity to the lives around you, would have to be abandon'd*;
> Therefore release me now, before troubling yourself any further—(88; emphasis mine)

Although Naylor insists on the complex incongruence of the various binds imposed by color, class, gender, and sexual orientation, all her characters fear the uncertainty of leaving behind the comforting familiarity of the known, even though the known consists of systems of oppression damaging to body and soul. What "conformity to the lives around you" means in the racial terms that closet African Americans in *Linden Hills* is the double bind of trying to appear similar to or different from whites.

Chapter 7. The Edible Complex

Epigraphs: Montaigne, 185; Wright, 74; Whitman, *Song of Myself*, 16 ("I am of old and young, of the foolish as much as the wise"), lines 346, 349; Blanchot, 18.

1. *Newsweek*, Feb. 12, 1990, p. 52.

2. Indeed, what does it mean that racist dualisms seem more effectively challenged by racechanges in physiological rather than in cultural venues? Despite the efforts of many theorists to debiologize race so as to emphasize the possibility of socially reconstructing nonracist values, the most optimistic racechange scenarios seem to involve actual or electronically imagined physical (not social) transformations that are visible to the eye: the hybrid child, the morphed image. At the present moment, when magazines devote many words and pictures to illustrating the propositions that inter-racial marriages have escalated from 310,000 to more than 1.1 million in the past two decades and that the incidence of births of mixed-race babies has multiplied 26 times as fast as that of any other group (*Time*, 142, no. 21 (Fall 93): 64), we may find ideas about race forced to shift because of transformations situated more in the genetic than in the political realm. (Needless to say, however, "the simplistic antidote of More Miscegenation" cannot counter the past "pervasive anti-miscegenist horror of tainted bloodlines," as Patricia J. Williams has warned, at least in part because that horror was preceded by judicial justifications of miscegenation between white men and their "chattle" during slave times (190–91).)

3. Lest such a view appear happily fantastic or anachronistic—ensconced in a mythic past—consider the story told by the Mississippi bluesman Big Bill Broonzy about a man in his home town called Mister White whose property was surrounded by a white fence:

> Trees, he painted them white, up as fur as he could git . . . And all the cattle . . . uh, and the sheeps, the goats, and the hogs, and the cows, mules, horses, and everything on his place was white. And any time that his cow, or his goat or whatsonever it was have a black colt, anything like that . . . he'd give it to the niggers. He didn't want nothing on his plantation black, see. . . .

When a state highway is run through his plantation, Mr. White builds a bypass and puts up a sign entitled *Negro Turn* so as to ensure the purity of his place. Though told as a hilarious tall tale to the folklorist Alan Lomax, Broonzy's account describes the psychology of separatism.

The CD *Blues in the Mississippi Night* (as told to and recorded by Alan Lomax) features Memphis Slim, Bill Broonzy, and Sonny Boy Williamson, who tell stories about African Americans led to refer to white mules as "Mister Mule" and asking for a can of Prince Albert tobacco (which had a picture of that white man on the can) with the sentence "Gimme can of Mister Prince Albert."

4. John Carlos Rowe argues that Nu-Nu's dead corpse functions as one aspect of "Poe's poetic mastery, his poetics of postmodern colonialism" in his reading of *Pym* (132).

5. Besides Freud's Oedipus complex, I am alluding to bell hooks's stimulating essay "Eating the Other" in *Black Looks*, 21–39.

6. It is interesting to juxtapose these passages with the novel written about Jefferson's slave mistress, Sally Hemings. In William Wells Brown's *Clotel; or, The President's Daughter* (1853), an abolitionist text centers on the child Jefferson fathered as a symbol of the injustice of slavery. See Sollors, *Ethnicity*, 225.

7. Diane Elam examines Derrida's claim that "This obligation to project the other's otherness is not merely a theoretical imperative" in the final chapter of *Feminism and Deconstruction*, 111.

8. See also Fuchs, 23–24.

9. See the useful comments of bell hooks on the film's conclusion and specifically her argument that the bored black woman has no need of Bernhard's performance and thus inscribes her ironic condemnation of her own efforts to perform blackness (esp. 38) and of Jean Walton, who points out that the black woman, filmed reading Harold Bloom's *Kabbalah and Criticism*, remains linked through Jewishness to the white star (in "Sandra Bernhard," esp. 254).

10. Phone conversation with the artist, March 18, 1996.

11. Another project undertaken by Udé, who clearly focuses on the importance of commercialized Hollywood images in his native Nigeria and elsewhere, involves an experiment in living art for which he constructed a magazine kiosk to display *Glamour*, *Mirabella*, and *Town & Country* magazines whose covers feature his own face transmuted through a series of costumes and cosmetics into multiple racial and sexual guises.

12. When during the 1980s and '90s an all-white New York theatrical troup called the Wooster Group used burnt cork—in reenactments of Pigmeat Markham's blacked-up vaudeville routines juxtaposed with a videotaped performance of Wilder's *Our Town* and in Eugene O'Neill's *The Emperor Jones* staged with a blackfaced actress playing the title role—they did so precisely to draw attention to the ironies of racial representation. I am indebted to Andrea Most for information on the Wooster Group. Shohat and Stam discuss what they call "the possibilities of epidermically incorrect casting in *Seeing Double* (1989), a San Francisco Mime Troupe play" about Israeli-Palestinian conflict (191).

13. In this regard, see Sollors's essay "A Critique of Pure Pluralism," in which he argues that "the ethnic perspective"—when taken exclusively as an emphasis on a writer's descent—"all but annihilates polyethnic art movements, moments of individual and cultural interaction, and the pervasiveness of cultural syncretism in America" (256).

14. Perhaps this is the reason why Charles Johnson's novels about slavery remain fascinated with what he calls "the theater of tattoes" in which his characters read "the profound mystery of the One and the Many" (*Oxherding Tale*, 195–6). Both *Oxherding Tale* (1982) and *Middle Passage* (1990) hinge on an "epiphany of skin," a vision of phantasmagoric images on epidermis that dramatize the boundaries and borders Americans perpetually race and erase (Gysin 289).

15. See the somewhat different reading of this tale in Ozick, 43.

16. For Malamud, as for Williams, the fact that cultural identities have been shaped by

lethal forms of racism—that anti-Semitism inflects Judaism with a self-subverting definition of Jewish-American identity and racism stamps blackness with a self-subverting definition of African-American identity—does not abrogate their persisting power over definitions of selfhood, though it does complicate their impact. Walter Benn Michaels asks in the last footnote of his book, "What exactly would be lost if everybody in Quebec stopped speaking French or if no one ever again thought of himself or herself as a Jew?" and answers that something of value might be lost "but that identity is never lost" (182); Malamud, like so many of the artists involved in racechanges, would have disagreed.

17. David Lloyd examines "the persistence of racism" as "an effect of ideological interpellation: approximation to the position of the Subject, theoretically available to all regardless of 'race or creed,' in fact requires the impossible negation of racial or cultural differences" (86).

18. I am indebted to the discussion of Wright and Wideman in Gysin, 293.

WORKS CITED

Abel, Elizabeth. "Black Writing, White Reading: Race and the Politics of Feminist Interpretation." *Critical Inquiry* 19, no. 3 (Spring 1993): 470–98.

Abrahams, Roger D. *Singing the Master: The Emergence of African-American Culture in the Plantation South*. New York: Penguin, 1992.

Ackroyd, Peter. *T. S. Eliot: A Life*. New York: Simon and Schuster, 1984.

Adams, Parveen. "Of Female Bondage." In *Between Feminism and Psychoanalysis*, ed. Teresa Brennan, 247–65. London and New York: Routledge, 1989.

Aiken, George L., and George C. Howard, *Uncle Tom's Cabin*. Ed. Thomas Riis. New York: Garland Publishing, 1994.

Alkire, Stephen Robert. "The Development and Treatment of the Negro Character as Presented in American Musical Theatre 1927–1968." Ph.D. diss., Michigan State University, 1972.

Allen, Don Cameron. *The Legend of Noah*. Urbana: Univ. of Illinois Press, 1949.

The Anchor Bible Dictionary. Vol. 3. Ed. David Noel Freedman. New York: Doubleday, 1992.

Anderson, Sherwood. "The Man Who Became a Woman." In *Horses and Men*, 185–228. New York: B. W. Huebsch, 1923.

Appiah, Anthony. "The Uncompleted Argument: Du Bois and the Illusion of Race." *Critical Inquiry* 12, no. 1 (Autumn 1985): 21–37.

Atlas, James. "Allan Bloom: Chicago's Grumpy Guru." *New York Times Magazine* (Jan. 3, 1988): 111.

Awkward, Michael. *Negotiating Difference: Race, Gender, and the Politics of Positionality*. Chicago: Univ. of Chicago Press, 1995.

Bailey, Randall C. "Africans in Old Testament Poetry and Narratives." In Felder, 165–86.

Baker, Houston A., Jr. *Long Black Song: Essays in Black American Literature and Culture*. Charlottesville: Univ. Press of Virginia, 1972.

———. *Modernism and the Harlem Renaissance*. Chicago: Univ. of Chicago Press, 1987.

———. *Singers of Daybreak: Studies in Black American Literature*. Washington, D.C.: Howard Univ. Press, 1974.

———. *Workings of the Spirit: The Poetics of Afro-American Women's Writing*. Chicago: Univ. of Chicago Press, 1991.

Bakhtin, M. M. *The Dialogic Imagination: Four Essays*. Ed. Michael Holquist, trans. Caryl Emerson and Michael Holquist. Austin: Univ. of Texas Press, 1992.

Baldwin, James. "The Black Boy Looks at the White Boy." In *Nobody Knows My Name: More Notes of a Native Son*, 169–90. New York: Dial Press, 1961.

———. *The Fire Next Time*. New York: Dial Press, 1963.

———. *Notes of A Native Son*. New York: Dial Press, 1972.

———. *The Price of the Ticket*. New York: St. Martin's, 1985.

Barth, John. *The Floating Opera and the End of the Road*. New York: Anchor, 1967.

Bartholet, Elizabeth. *Family Bonds: Adoption and the Politics of Parenting*. New York: Houghton Mifflin, 1993.

Beauvoir, Simone de. *The Second Sex*. Trans. H. M. Parshley. New York: Knopf, 1953.

Beemer, Suzy. "'Assay the Power You Have': Compromised Subjectivities and English Renaissance Literary Women." Ph.D. diss., University of Nebraska, 1996.

Bellow, Saul. *Mr. Sammler's Planet*. New York: Penguin, 1977.

Benjamin, Jessica. *The Bonds of Love: Psychoanalysis, Feminism, and the Problem of Domination*. New York: Pantheon, 1988.

Bergner, Gwen. "Who Is That Masked Woman? or, The Role of Gender in Fanon's *Black Skin, White Masks*." *PMLA* 110, no. 1 (Fall 1994): 75–88.

Berlant, Lauren. "National Brands/National Body: *Imitation of Life*." In *Comparative American Identities: Race, Sex, and Nationality in the Modern Text*, ed. Hortense J. Spillers, 110–40. New York: Routledge, 1991.

Bernstein, Leonard, and Alan Jay Lerner. "1600 Pennsylvania Avenue: A Musical Play about the Problems of Housekeeping." Typescript libretto from the Indiana University School of Music, 1976.

Berryman, John. *The Dream Songs*. New York: Farrar, Straus & Giroux, 1990.

Bersani, Leo, and Ulysse Dutoit. *The Forms of Violence*. New York: Schocken, 1985.

Berzon, Judith. *Neither White nor Black: The Mulatto Character in American Fiction*. New York: New York Univ. Press, 1978.

Bhabha, Homi. *The Location of Culture*. New York: Routledge, 1994.

Blackburn, Julia. *The Book of Colour*. London: Jonathan Cape, 1995.

Blake, William. *Poems of William Blake*. Ed. W. H. Stevenson. London: Longman, 1971.

Blanchot, Maurice. *The Writing of the Disaster*. Trans. Ann Smock. Lincoln and London: University of Nebraska Press, 1995.

Bogle, Donald. *Toms, Coons, Mulattoes, Mammies, and Bucks: An Interpretive History of Blacks in American Films*. New York: Continuum, 1989.

Boime, Albert. *The Art of Exclusion: Representing Blacks in the Nineteenth Century*. Washington and London: Smithsonian Institution Press, 1990.

Bonner, Marita. "One Boy's Story." In *Frye Street & Environs*, ed. Joyce Flynn and Joyce Occomy Stricklin, 78–91. Boston: Beacon Press, 1987.

Boone, Joseph A. "Vacation Cruises; or, The Homoerotics of Orientalism." *PMLA* 110, no. 1 (Fall 1995): 89–107.

Boose, Lynda E. "'The Getting of a Lawful Race': Racial Discourse in Early Modern England and the Unrepresentable Black Woman." In *Women, "Race," and Writing in the Early Modern Period*, ed. Margo Hendricks and Patricia Parker, 35–54. New York: Routledge, 1994.

Boskin, Joseph. *Sambo: The Rise and Demise of an American Jester*. New York: Oxford Univ. Press, 1986.

Brasch, Walter M. *Black English and the Mass Media*. Lanham, New York, London: Univ. Press of America, 1981.

Breines, Wini. *Young, White, and Miserable: Growing Up Female in the Fifties*. Boston: Beacon, 1992.

Brown, Ray B. "Shakespeare in American Vaudeville and Negro Minstrelsy." *American Quarterly* 12, no. 3 (Fall 1960): 374–91.

Browne, Thomas. *Pseudodoxia Epidemica; or, Enquiries into Very Many Received Tenents, and Commonly Presumed Truths*. 2nd ed. London: A. Miller, for Edw. Dod and Nath. Ekins, 1650.

Browning, Elizabeth. *The Poetical Works of Elizabeth Barrett Browning*. Ed. Ruth M. Adams. Boston: Houghton Mifflin, 1974.

Browning, Robert. *The Poetical Works of Robert Browning*. With an intro. by G. Robert Stange. Boston: Houghton Mifflin, 1974.

Burgin, Victor. "Paranoiac Space." *New Formations* 12 (Dec. 1990): 62–73.

Butler, Octavia E. *Kindred*. Intro. by Robert Crossley. Boston: Beacon Press, 1988.

Canarroe, Joel. *John Berryman*. New York: Columbia Univ. Press, 1977.

Carlyle, Thomas. *The French Revolution*. Centenary Edition. London: Chapman and Hall, 1937.

Carpenter, Edward. *Selected Writings*. Vol. 1: *Sex*. London: Gay Modern Classics, 1984.

Carringer, Robert L. *The Jazz Singer*. Madison: Univ. of Wisconsin Press, 1979.

Cartwright, Dr. Samuel A. "Unity of the Human Race Disproved by the Hebrew Bible," *De Bow's Review* 29 (vol. 4, no. 2): 129–36.

Cassuto, Umberto. *A Commentary on the Book of Genesis, Part II*. Trans. Israel Abrahams. Jerusalem: Magnes Press, Hebrew University, 1964.

Certeau, Michel de. *The Practice of Everyday Life*. Trans. Steven Rendeall. Berkeley: Univ. of California Press, 1984.

Chesnutt, Charles W. "Her Virginia Mammy." In *"The Wife of His Youth" and Other Stories of the Color Line*, 25–59. Ann Arbor: Univ. of Michigan Press, 1968.

———. *The House Behind the Cedars*. New York: Penguin, 1993.

———. *The Marrow of Tradition*. New York: Penguin, 1993.

———. "Mars Jeems's Nightmare." In *The Conjure Woman*, 54–102. Ridgewood, N.J.: Gregg Press, 1968.

———. "White Weeds." In *The Short Fiction of Charles W. Chesnutt*, ed. Sylvia Lyons Render, 391–404. Washington: Howard Univ. Press, 1981.

Chisholm, Anne. *Nancy Cunard*. New York: Alfred A. Knopf, 1979.

Chopin, Kate. "Désirée's Baby." In *The Awakening and Selected Stories*, 189–94. New York: Penguin, 1983.

Chow, Rey. *Writing Diaspora: Tactics of Intervention in Contemporary Cultural Studies*. Bloomington: Indiana Univ. Press, 1993.

Churchill, Caryl. *Cloud Nine*. New York: Routledge, 1987.

Cixous, Hélène. "The Laugh of the Medusa." In *New French Feminisms*, ed. Elaine Marks and Isabelle de Courtivron, 245–63. Amherst: Univ. of Massachusetts Press, 1980.

Cleaver. Eldridge. *Soul on Ice*. New York: McGraw-Hill, 1968.

Cliff, Michelle. *Bodies of Water*. New York: Dutton, 1990.

———. *Claiming an Identity They Taught Me to Despise*. Watertown, Mass.: Persephone Press, 1980.

Clifford, James. *The Predicament of Culture*. Cambridge, Mass.: Harvard Univ. Press, 1988.

Clifton, Lucille. "my dream about being white." In *Next New Poems*. Brocksport, N.Y.: BOA, 1987.

Clover, Carol J. "Dancin' in the Rain." *Critical Inquiry* 21, no. 4 (Summer 1995): 722–47.

Comley, Nancy R., and Robert Scholes. *Hemingway's Genders: Rereading the Hemingway Text*. New Haven: Yale Univ. Press, 1994.

Cone, James. *A Black Theology of Liberation*. Philadelphia and New York: J. B. Lippincott, 1970.

Connelly, Marc. *Voices Offstage: A Book of Memoirs*. New York: Holt, Rinehart and Winston, 1968.

Conrad, Peter. "The Devil's Disciple: The Art and Artifice of Robert Mapplethorpe." *The New Yorker* (June 5, 1995): 85–91.

Cooley, John. "White Writers and the Harlem Renaissance." In *The Harlem Renaissance: Revaluations*, ed. Amritjit Singh, William S. Shiver, and Stanley Brodwin, 13–22. New York: Garland, 1989.

Coon, Russell E. "Writing on Ancient Egypt: The Practices and Politics of Egyptomania." Ph.D. diss. proposal, Indiana University 1995.

Copher, Charles B. "Three Thousand Years of Biblical Interpretation with Reference to Black Peoples." *Journal of the Interdenominational Theological Center* 13 (Spring 1986): 225–46.

Corso, Gregory. "Bomb." In *The Penguin Book of the Beats*, ed. Ann Charters, 174–78. New York: Penguin, 1992.

Craft, William and Ellen. *Running a Thousand Miles for Freedom*. London: W. Tweedie, 1860.

Crane, Hart. *Letters of Hart Crane and His Family*. Ed. Thomas S. W. Lewis. New York: Columbia Univ. Press, 1974.

Crawford, Robert. *The Savage and the City in the Work of T. S. Eliot*. Oxford: Clarendon Press, 1987.

Cripps, Thomas. *Slow Fade to Black: The Negro in American Film, 1900–1942*. London: Oxford Univ. Press, 1977.

Croce, Arlene. *The Fred Astaire and Ginger Rogers Book*. New York: Galahad Books, 1972.

Cross, Amanda [Carolyn Heilbrun]. *A Trap for Fools*. New York: Ballantine, 1989.

Crouch, Stanley. *The All-American Skin Game; or, The Decoy of Race*. New York: Pantheon, 1995.

Crowder, Henry. *Henry-Music*. N.p.: Hours Press, 1930.

Cullen, Countee. *Color*. New York: Harper & Brothers, 1925.

cummings, e.e. *Complete Poems*. 2 vols. Great Britain: Macgibbon and Kee, 1968.

———. *The Enormous Room*. New York: Liveright, 1978.

———. *Him*. New York: Liveright, 1927.

———. *Tom*. In *Three Plays and a Ballet*, ed. George J. Firmage. New York: October House, 1967.

Cunard, Nancy. *Grand Man: Memoirs of Norman Douglas*. London: Secker and Warburg, 1954.

———. *Negro: An Anthology*. London: Wishart, 1934.

Cuney, Waring, "No Images." In *American Negro Poetry*, rev. ed., ed. Arna Bontemps, 98–99. New York: Hill and Wang, 1974.

Daniel, Bradford. "Why They Can't Wait: An Interview with a White Negro." *The Progressive* (July 1964): 15–19.

Davis, David Brion. *The Problem of Slavery in Western Culture*. Ithaca: Cornell Univ. Press, 1966.

Davis, F. James. *Who Is Black?: One Nation's Definition*. University Park: Pennsylvania State Univ. Press, 1991.

Davis, Kathe, "'Honey Dusk Do Sprawl': Does Black Minstrel Dialect Obscure *The Dream Songs*?" *Language and Style: An International Journal* 18, no. 1 (Winter 1985): 30–45.

DeBona, Guerric, O.S.B. "Into Africa: Orson Welles and *Heart of Darkness*." *Cinema Journal* 33, no. 3 (Spring 1994): 16–34.

De Jongh, James. *Vicious Modernism: Black Harlem and the Literary Imagination*. Cambridge: Cambridge Univ. Press, 1990.

De Lauretis, Teresa. *The Practice of Love: Lesbian Sexuality and Perverse Desire*. Bloomington: Indiana Univ. Press, 1994.

Diamond, Stanley. *In Search of the Primitive: A Critique of Civilization*. New Brunswick: Transaction Books, 1974.

Dickens, Charles. *American Notes and Pictures from Italy*. Intro. Sacheverell Sitwell. London: Oxford Univ. Press, 1966.

Dickstein, Morris. *Gates of Eden: American Culture in the Sixties*. New York: Basic Books, 1977.

Dijkestra, Bram. *Idols of Perversity: Fantasies of Feminine Evil in Fin-de-Siècle Culture*. New York: Oxford Univ. Press, 1986.

Diop, Cheikh Anta. *The African Origin of Civilization*. Trans. Mercer Cook. New York: Lawrence Hill, 1974.

Dixon, Thomas. *The Clansman*. New York: Doubleday, Page, 1905.

Doane, Mary Ann. *Femmes Fatales: Feminism, Film Theory, Psychoanalysis*. New York: Routledge, 1991.

Douglas, Ann. *Terrible Honesty: Mongrel Manhattan in the 1920s*. New York: Farrar, Straus and Giroux, 1995.

Doyle, Laura. *Bordering on the Body: The Racial Matrix of Modern Fiction and Culture*. New York: Oxford Univ. Press, 1994.

Du Bois, W.E.B. *The Souls of Black Folk*. Millwood, N.Y.: Kraus-Thomson, 1973.

———. "The Souls of White Folk." *The Independent* 69, no. 3220 (Aug. 18, 1910): 339–42.

Dunbar, Paul Laurence. "We Wear the Mask." In *American Negro Poetry*, rev. ed., ed. Arna Bontemps, 14. New York: Hill and Wang, 1974.

Dyer, Richard. "White." *Screen* 29, no. 4 (1988): 44–64.

Elam, Diane. *Feminism and Deconstruction: Ms. en Abyme*. New York: Routledge, 1994.

Elfenbein, Anna Shannon. *Women on the Color Line: Evolving Stereotypes and the Writings of George Washington Cable, Grace King, Kate Chopin*. Charlottesville: Univ. of Virginia, 1989.

Eliot, T. S. "The Beating of a Drum." *Nation and the Athenaeum* 34 (Oct. 6, 1926): 12–13.

———. *Sweeney Agonistes*. London: Faber & Faber, 1932.

———. *The Waste Land, a Facsimile and Transcript*. Ed. Valerie Eliot. New York: Harcourt Brace Jovanovich, 1971.

Ellenzweig, Allen. *The Homoerotic Photograph: Male Images from Durieu/Delacroix to Mapplethorpe*. New York: Columbia Univ. Press, 1992.

Ellis, Trey. "The New Black Aesthetic." *Callaloo* 12 (Winter 1989): 233–43.

Ellison, Ralph. "Change the Joke and Slip the Yoke." In *Shadow and Act*, 45–59. New York: Random House, 1964.

———. *Going to the Territory*. New York: Random House, 1987.

———. *Invisible Man*. New York: Random House, 1952.

Ellmann, Richard. *Oscar Wilde*. New York: Alfred A. Knopf, 1988.

Ely, Melvin Patrick. *The Adventures of Amos 'n' Andy: A Social History of an American Phenomenon*. New York: Free Press, 1991.

Everett, Barbara. "The New Style of *Sweeney Agonistes*." *Yearbook of English Studies* 14 (1984): 243–63.

Fanon, Frantz. *Black Skin, White Masks*. Trans. Charles Lam Markmann. New York: Grove Weidenfeld, 1967.

Faulkner, William. *As I Lay Dying*. New York: Viking, 1990.

———. "The Bear," "Delta Autumn," and "Go Down, Moses." In *Go Down, Moses*, 183–315, 319–48, 351–65. New York: Vintage, 1970.

———. *Light in August*. New York: Vintage, 1987.

Fauset, Jessie Redmon. *Plum Bun: A Novel Without a Moral*. Boston: Pandora, 1985.

Felder, Cain Hope, ed. *Stony the Road We Trod: African American Biblical Interpretation*. Minneapolis: Fortress Press, 1991.

Fiedler, Leslie. "Come Back to the Raft Ag'in, Huck Honey!" In *An End to Innocence: Essays on Culture and Politics*, 142–51. Boston: Beacon Press, 1952.

———. *Waiting for the End*. New York: Stein and Day, 1964.

Fish, Jefferson M. "Mixed Blood." *Psychology Today* (Nov./Dec. 1995): 55–61, 76, 80.

Fisher, Rudolph. *The Walls of Jericho*. New York and London: A. A. Knopf, 1928.

Fishkin, Shelley Fisher. *Was Huck Black?: Mark Twain and African-American Voices*. New York: Oxford Univ. Press, 1993.

Fitzgerald, Zelda. *Save Me the Waltz*. Carbondale: South Illinois Univ. Press, 1967.

Flanner, Janet. *Paris Was Yesterday, 1925–1939*. Ed. Irving Drutman. New York: Viking, 1972.

Ford, George H. *Double Measure: A Study of the Novels and Stories of D. H. Lawrence*. New York: Holt, Rinehart and Winston, 1965.

Foster, Hal. *Recordings: Art, Spectacle, Cultural Politics*. Seattle: Bay Press, 1985.

France, Richard. *The Theatre of Orson Welles*. Lewisburg: Bucknell Univ. Press, 1977.

Franklin, John Hope. "'Birth of Nation'"—Propaganda as History." *Massachusetts Review* 20, no. 3 (Autumn 1979): 417–33.

Fredrickson, George. *The Black Image in the White Mind: The Debate on Afro-American Character and Destiny, 1817–1914*. New York: Harper, 1971.

Freud, Sigmund. "Family Romances" (1909). In *Collected Papers*, vol. 5, ed. James Strachey, 74–76. London: Hogarth Press and the Institute of Psycho-Analysis, 1950.

Friedman, John Block. *The Monstrous Races in Medieval Art and Thought*. Cambridge: Harvard Univ. Press, 1981.

Friedman, Lester D. *Unspeakable Images: Ethnicity and the American Cinema*. Urbana and Chicago: Univ. of Illinois Press, 1991.

Fuchs, Cynthia J. "Michael Jackson's Penis." In *Cruising the Performative: Interventions into the Representation of Ethnicity, Nationality, and Sexuality*, ed. Sue-Ellen Case, Philip Brett, and Susan Leigh Foster, 13–33. Bloomington: Indiana Univ. Press, 1995.

Funderburg, Lise. *Black, White, Other: Biracial Americans Talk about Race and Identity*. New York: William Morrow, 1994.

Fuss, Diana. *Essentially Speaking*. New York: Routledge, 1989.

———. *Identification Papers*. New York: Routledge, 1995.

Gallop, Jane. "Phallus/Penis: Same Difference." In *Thinking Through the Body*, 124–33. New York: Columbia Univ. Press, 1988.

Gates, Henry Louis, Jr. "'Authenticity' and the Lesson of *Little Tree*." *New York Times Book Review* (Nov. 24, 1991).

———. "The Black Man's Burden." In *Black Popular Culture, a Project by Michele Wallace*, ed. Gina Dent, 75–83. Seattle: Bay Press, 1992.

———. *Colored People, a Memoir*. New York: Random House, 1994.

———. *Figures in Black: Words, Signs, and the "Racial" Self*. New York: Oxford Univ. Press, 1987.

———. "Significant Others, a Response to Margaret Homans." *Contemporary Literature* 29, no. 4 (1988): 606–23.

———. "White Like Me," *The New Yorker* (June 17, 1996): 66–81.

Geduld, Harry M. *The Birth of the Talkies*. Bloomington: Indiana Univ. Press, 1975.

Genet, Jean. *The Blacks*. Trans. Bernard Frechtman. New York: Grove Press, 1960.

———. *Prisoner of Love*. Trans. Barbara Bray. London: Picador, 1989.

George, Nelson. *The Death of Rhythm and Blues*. New York: Pantheon, 1988.

Gilbert, D. *American Vaudeville, Its Life and Times*. New York: McGraw-Hill, 1940.

Gilbert, Sandra M., and Susan Gubar. *Letters from the Front*. New Haven: Yale Univ. Press, 1994.

———. *Sexchanges*. New Haven: Yale Univ. Press, 1989.

Gilman, Sander L. "Black Bodies, White Bodies: Toward an Iconography of Female Sexuality in Late Nineteenth-Century Art, Medicine, and Literature." *Critical Inquiry* 12, no. 1 (Autumn 1985): 204–42.

———. *Difference and Pathology: Stereotypes of Sexuality, Race, and Madness*. Ithaca: Cornell Univ. Press, 1986.

———. *The Jew's Body*. New York: Routledge, 1991.

Gilroy, Paul. *The Black Atlantis: Modernity and Double Consciousness*. Cambridge: Harvard Univ. Press, 1993.

Ginsberg, Allen. *Collected Poems, 1947–1980*. New York: Harper & Row, 1984.

Ginsberg, Elaine K. "Introduction: The Politics of Passing." In *Passing and the Fictions of Identity*, ed. Elaine K. Ginsberg, 1–18. Durham: Duke Univ. Press, 1996.

Golden, Thelma. "My Brother." In *Black: Representations of Masculinity in Contemporary American Art*, ed. Thelma Golden, 19–43. New York: Whitney Museum of American Art, distributed by Harry N. Abrams, 1994.

Goldenberg, David M. "The Curse of Ham: A Case of Rabbinic Racism?" In *Struggles in the Promised Land: Towards a History of Black-Jewish Relations in the United States*, ed. Jack Salzman and Cornel West. New York: Oxford Univ. Press, forthcoming.

Goldwater, Robert. *Primitivism in Modern Art*. New York: Vintage, 1967.

Gordimer, Nadine. "The Moment before the Gun Went Off." In *Jump and Other Stories*. New York: Penguin, 1992.

Gordon, Lyndall. *Eliot's New Life*. New York: Farrar, Straus and Giroux, 1988.

Gould, Lois. *A Sea-Change*. New York: Farrar, Straus and Giroux, 1976.

Graves, Robert, and Raphael Patai. *Hebrew Myths: The Book of Genesis*. New York: Greenwich House, 1983.

Gray, Donald J. "The Uses of Victorian Laughter." *Victorian Studies* 10, no. 2 (Dec. 1966): 145–76.

Gregory, Dick. *What's Happening?* Photographs by Jerry Yulsman. New York: E. P. Dutton: 1965.

Griffin, John Howard. *Black Like Me*. New York: Signet, 1976.

Grosz, Elizabeth A. "Lesbian Fetishism?" *differences* 3, no. 2 Special Issue on Queer Theory, ed. Teresa de Lauretis (1991): 39–54.

Gubar, Susan. "Feminist Misogyny: Mary Wollstonecraft and the Paradox of 'It Takes One to Know One.'" *Feminist Studies* 20, no. 3 (Fall 1994): 453–74.

Guillaumin, Colette. "The Idea of Race and Its Elevation to Autonomous, Scientific and Legal Status." In *Sociological Theories: Race and Colonialism*, 37–67. Paris: UNESCO, 1980.

Gysin, Fritz. "Predicaments of Skin: Boundaries in Recent African American Fiction." In *The Black Columbiad: Defining Moments in African American Literature and Culture*, ed. Werner Sollors and Maria Diedrich, 286–97. Cambridge: Harvard Univ. Press, 1994.

Hacker, Andrew. *Two Nations: Black and White, Separate, Hostile, Unequal.* New York: Charles Scribner's Sons, 1992.

Hacker, Marilyn. *Assumptions*. New York: Alfred A. Knopf, 1985.

Hackett, Francis. "Brotherly Love." In *The Birth of a Nation*, ed. Robert Lang, 161–63. New Brunswick: Rutgers Univ. Press, 1994.

Haggard, H. Rider. *She*. New York: Hart, 1976.

Haizlip, Shirlee Taylor. *The Sweeter the Juice*. New York: Simon & Schuster, 1994.

Hall, Stuart. "What Is This 'Black' in Black Popular Culture." In *Black Popular Culture, a Project by Michele Wallace*, ed. Gina Dent, 21–33. Seattle: Bay Press, 1992.

Halsell, Grace. *Soul Sister*. Greenwich, Conn.: Fawcett Crest, 1969.

Haraway, Donna J. "Universal Donors in a Vampire Culture: It's All in the Family: Biological Kinship Categories in the Twentieth-Century United States." In *Uncommon Ground*, ed. William Cronon, 321–66. New York: Norton 1995.

Hare, Nathan. *The Black Anglo-Saxons*. London. Collier-Macmillan, 1965.

Harper, Michael S. *Images of Kin: New and Selected Poems*. Urbana: Univ. of Illinois Press, 1977.

Harris, Trudier. *Exorcising Blackness: Historical and Literary Lynching and Burning Rituals*. Bloomington: Indiana Univ. Press, 1984.

Hathaway, Heather. "'Maybe Freedom Lies in Hating': Miscegenation and the Oedipal Conflict." In *Refiguring the Father: New Feminist Readings of Patriarchy*, ed. Patricia Yaeger and Beth Kowaleski-Wallace, 153–67. Carbondale: Southern Illinois Univ. Press, 1989.

Haywood, Charles. "Negro Minstrelsy and Shakespearean Burlesque." In *Folklore and Society: Essays in Honor of Benjamin A. Botkin*, ed. Bruce Jackson, 77–92. Hatboro, Pa.: Folklore Association, 1966.

Head, Bessie. *A Question of Power*. Portsmouth, N.H.: Heinemann, 1974.

Hebdige, Dick. *Subculture: The Meaning of Style*. London: Methuen, 1987.

Hemenway, Robert E. *Zora Neale Hurston*. Urbana: Univ. of Illinois Press, 1980.

Hemingway, Ernest. *The Garden of Eden*. New York: Collier Books, 1986.

———. "The Sea Change." In *The Complete Stories of Ernest Hemingway*, 302–5. New York: Charles Scribner's Sons, 1987.

Hernton, Calvin C. *Sex and Racism in America*. New York: Grove Weidenfeld, 1988.

Heyward, DuBois. *Porgy*. N.p. New York: Grosset & Dunlap with George H. Doran, 1925.

Hoch, Paul. *White Hero, Black Beast: Racism, Sexism and the Mask of Masculinity*. London: Pluto Press, 1979.

Holton, Sylvia Wallace. *Down Home and Uptown: The Representation of Black Speech in American Fiction*. Rutherford, N.J.: Fairleigh Dickinson Univ. Press, 1984.

Homans, Margaret. "The Woman in the Cave: Recent Feminist Fictions and the Classical Underworld." *Contemporary Literature* 29, no. 3 (1988): 369–402.

Honey, Maureen, ed. *Shadowed Dreams: Women's Poetry of the Harlem Renaissance*. New Brunswick: Rutgers Univ. Press, 1989.

hooks, bell. *Black Looks: Race and Representation*. Boston: South End Press, 1992.

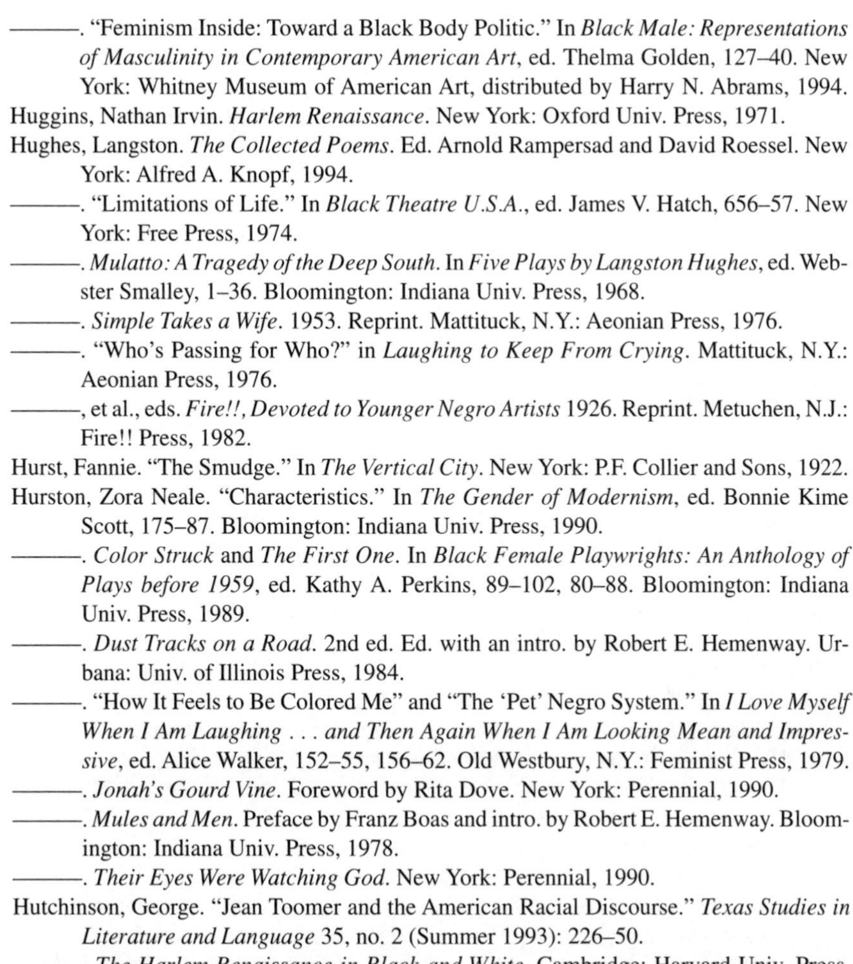

———. "Feminism Inside: Toward a Black Body Politic." In *Black Male: Representations of Masculinity in Contemporary American Art*, ed. Thelma Golden, 127–40. New York: Whitney Museum of American Art, distributed by Harry N. Abrams, 1994.

Huggins, Nathan Irvin. *Harlem Renaissance*. New York: Oxford Univ. Press, 1971.

Hughes, Langston. *The Collected Poems*. Ed. Arnold Rampersad and David Roessel. New York: Alfred A. Knopf, 1994.

———. "Limitations of Life." In *Black Theatre U.S.A.*, ed. James V. Hatch, 656–57. New York: Free Press, 1974.

———. *Mulatto: A Tragedy of the Deep South*. In *Five Plays by Langston Hughes*, ed. Webster Smalley, 1–36. Bloomington: Indiana Univ. Press, 1968.

———. *Simple Takes a Wife*. 1953. Reprint. Mattituck, N.Y.: Aeonian Press, 1976.

———. "Who's Passing for Who?" in *Laughing to Keep From Crying*. Mattituck, N.Y.: Aeonian Press, 1976.

———, et al., eds. *Fire!!, Devoted to Younger Negro Artists* 1926. Reprint. Metuchen, N.J.: Fire!! Press, 1982.

Hurst, Fannie. "The Smudge." In *The Vertical City*. New York: P.F. Collier and Sons, 1922.

Hurston, Zora Neale. "Characteristics." In *The Gender of Modernism*, ed. Bonnie Kime Scott, 175–87. Bloomington: Indiana Univ. Press, 1990.

———. *Color Struck* and *The First One*. In *Black Female Playwrights: An Anthology of Plays before 1959*, ed. Kathy A. Perkins, 89–102, 80–88. Bloomington: Indiana Univ. Press, 1989.

———. *Dust Tracks on a Road*. 2nd ed. Ed. with an intro. by Robert E. Hemenway. Urbana: Univ. of Illinois Press, 1984.

———. "How It Feels to Be Colored Me" and "The 'Pet' Negro System." In *I Love Myself When I Am Laughing . . . and Then Again When I Am Looking Mean and Impressive*, ed. Alice Walker, 152–55, 156–62. Old Westbury, N.Y.: Feminist Press, 1979.

———. *Jonah's Gourd Vine*. Foreword by Rita Dove. New York: Perennial, 1990.

———. *Mules and Men*. Preface by Franz Boas and intro. by Robert E. Hemenway. Bloomington: Indiana Univ. Press, 1978.

———. *Their Eyes Were Watching God*. New York: Perennial, 1990.

Hutchinson, George. "Jean Toomer and the American Racial Discourse." *Texas Studies in Literature and Language* 35, no. 2 (Summer 1993): 226–50.

———. *The Harlem Renaissance in Black and White*. Cambridge: Harvard Univ. Press, 1995.

Huxley, Aldous. "Silence Is Golden." In *Do What You Will*. New York: Doubleday, Doran, 1929.

Irigaray, Luce. *This Sex Which Is Not One*. Trans. Catherine Porter with Carolyn Burke. Ithaca: Cornell Univ. Press, 1985.

Jacobs, Harriet. *Incidents in the Life of a Slave Girl*. New York: Oxford Univ. Press, 1988.

JanMohamed, Abdul R. "The Economy of Manichean Allegory: The Function of Racial Difference in Colonialist Literature." *Critical Inquiry* 12, no. 1 (1985): 59–87.

Jefferson, Thomas. *Notes on the State of Virginia*. Ed. William Peden. New York: W. W. Norton, 1954.

Johnson, Barbara. "Thresholds of Difference: Structures of Address in Zora Neale Hurston." *Critical Inquiry* 12, no. 1 (1985): 278–89.

———. "Response to Henry Louis Gates, Jr." In *Afro-American Literary Study in the 1990s*, ed. Houston A. Baker, Jr., and Patricia Redmond 39–44. Chicago: Univ. of Chicago Press, 1989.

Johnson, Charles. *Oxherding Tale*. Bloomington: Indiana Univ. Press, 1982.

Johnson, Charles R. *Black Humor*. Chicago: Johnson Publishing, 1970.

Johnson, James Weldon. *Autobiography of an Ex-Coloured Man*. New York: Vintage, 1989.

Johnson, Ken. "Colescott on Black & White." *Art in America* (June 1989): 148–53, 187.

Jones, Amelia, "Postfeminism, Feminist Pleasures, and Embodied Theories of Art." In *New Feminist Criticism*, ed. Joanna Frueh, Cassandra L. Langer, and Arlene Raven, 16–41. New York: Harper-Collins, 1991.

Jones, LeRoi (Amiri Baraka). *Home: Social Essays*. New York: William Morrow, 1966.

Jordan, June. "What Would I Do White." In *No More Masks*, ed. Florence Howe, 264–66. New York: HarperPerennial, 1993.

Jordan, Winthrop D. *White over Black: American Attitudes toward the Negro, 1550–1812*. Kingsport: Univ. of North Carolina Press, 1968.

Julien, Isaac. "Black Is, Black Ain't: Notes on De-Essentializing Black Identities." In *Black Popular Culture, a Project by Michele Wallace*, ed. Gina Dent, 255–63. Seattle: Bay Press, 1992.

Kahane, Claire. "The Artificial Niggers." *Massachusetts Review* (Spring 1978): 183–98.

Kalaidjian, Walter. *American Culture Between the Wars: Revisionary Modernism and Postmodern Critique*. New York: Columbia Univ. Press, 1993.

Kerouac, Jack. *On the Road*. New York: New American Library, 1957.

———. *The Subterraneans*. New York: Grove, 1958.

Kauffmann, Stanley. "Books & the Arts: Her Life and Times." *New Republic* 203, no. 1 (July 2, 1990): 26–27.

Kellner, Bruce. *Carl Van Vechten and the Irreverent Decades*. Norman: Univ. of Oklahoma Press, 1968.

———. *"Keep A-Inchin' Along": Selected Writings of Carl Van Vechten about Black Art and Letters*. Westport, Conn.: Greenwood Press, 1979.

Kennedy, Adrienne. *Funnyhouse of a Negro*. In *Adrienne Kennedy in One Act*. Minneapolis: Univ. of Minnesota Press, 1988.

Kristeva, Julia. *Revolution in Poetic Language*. Trans. Margaret Waller, intro. Leon S. Roudiez. New York: Columbia Univ. Press, 1984.

———. *Strangers to Ourselves*. Trans. Leon S. Roudiez. New York: Columbia Univ. Press, 1991.

Kuper, Adam. *The Invention of Primitive Society: Transformations of an Illusion*. London: Routledge, 1988.

Lacoue-Labarthe, Philippe. *Typography: Mimesis, Philosophy, Politics*. Ed. Christopher Fynsk, intro. Jacques Derrida. Cambridge, Mass.: Harvard Univ. Press, 1989.

Lang, Robert. "*The Birth of a Nation*: History, Ideology, Narrative Form." In *The Birth of a Nation*, 3–24. New Brunswick: Rutgers Univ. Press, 1994.

Larsen, Nella. *Quicksand and Passing*. Ed. Deborah E. McDowell. New Brunswick: Rutgers Univ. Press, 1986.

Lavin, Maud. *Cut with the Kitchen Knife: The Weimar Photomontages of Hannah Höch*. New Haven: Yale Univ. Press, 1993.

Lawrence, D. H. "Cypresses." In *The Complete Poems*, ed. Vivian de Sola Pinto and F. Warren Roberts, 296–98. New York: Penguin, 1984.

———. *Women in Love*. New York: Penguin, 1982.

Lazarre, Jane. *The Mother Knot*. New York: McGraw-Hill, 1976.

———. *Worlds Beyond My Control*. New York: Dutton, 1991.

Le Guin, Ursula K. *The Language of the Night: Essays on Fantasy and Science Fiction*. New York: G. P. Putnam's Sons, 1979.

Leonard, William Torbert. *Masquerade in Black*. Metuchen, N.J.: Scarecrow Press, 1986.

Lindsay, Vachel. *The Congo and Other Poems*. New York: Dover Thrift Editions, 1992.

Linebarger, J. M. *John Berryman*. New York: Twayne, 1974.

Lipton, Lawrence. *The Holy Barbarians*. New York: Julian Messner, 1959.

Lloyd, David. "Race under Representation." *Oxford Literary Review* 13, nos. 1–2 (1991): 62–94.

Locke, Alain. "The Legacy of the Ancestral Arts." In *The New Negro*, ed. Alain Locke, 254–67. New York: Atheneum, 1968.

Loomba, Ania. *Gender, Race, Renaissance Drama*. Manchester: Manchester Univ. Press, 1989.

Lott, Eric. *Love and Theft: Blackface Minstrelsy and the American Working Class*. New York: Oxford Univ. Press, 1993.

———. "White Like Me: Racial Cross-Dressing and the Construction of American Whiteness." In *Cultures of United States Imperialism*, ed. Amy Kaplan and Donald E. Pease, 474–95. Durham: Duke Univ. Press, 1993.

Low, Gail Ching-Liang. "White Skins/Black Masks: The Pleasures and Politics of Imperialism." *New Formations* 9 (Winter 1989): 83–104.

Lowell, Robert. "Benito Cereno." In *The Old Glory*, 135–214. New York: Farrar, Straus & Giroux, 1968.

McBride, James. *The Color of Water: A Black Man's Tribute to His White Mother*. New York. Riverhead, 1996.

McClintock, Anne. *Imperial Leather: Race, Gender and Sexuality in the Colonial Context*. New York: Routledge, 1995.

McCloskey, Susan. "Shakespeare, Orson Welles, and the 'Voodoo' *Macbeth*." *Shakespeare Quarterly* 36, no. 4 (Winter 1985): 406–16.

McDowell, Deborah E. "Negotiating Between Tenses: Witnessing Slavery after Freedom—*Dessa Rose*." In *Slavery and the Literary Imagination*, ed. Deborah E. McDowell and Arnold Rampersad, 144–63. Baltimore: Johns Hopkins Univ. Press, 1989.

McEvilley, Thomas. *Art and Otherness: Crisis in Cultural Identity*. New York: McPherson, 1992.

McKay, Claude. *Banjo*. New York: Harper and Brothers, 1929.

———. "Near-White." In *Gingertown*, 72–104. New York: Harper and Brothers, 1932.

———. *The Passion of Claude McKay: Selected Poetry and Prose, 1912–1948*. Ed. Wayne F. Cooper. New York: Schocken, 1973.

Mailer, Norman. *Advertisements for Myself*. New York: G. P. Putnam's Sons, 1959.

———. "Ten Thousand Words a Minute." *Esquire* 59 (Feb. 1963): 109–20.

———. "The White Negro." In *The Penguin Book of the Beats*, ed. Ann Charters, 581–605. New York: Penguin, 1993.

Mairs, Nancy. *Ordinary Time: Cycles in Marriage, Faith, and Renewal*. Boston: Beacon, 1994.

Malamud, Bernard. "Angel Levine." In *The Magic Barrel*. New York: Farrar, Straus & Cudahy, 1958.

———. *The Tenants*. New York: Pocket Books, 1972.

Manso, Peter. *Mailer: His Life and Times*. New York: Simon and Schuster, 1985.

Mapplethorpe, Robert. *Robert Mapplethorpe's Black Book*. New York: St. Martin's Press, 1986.

Marcus, Greil. *Lipstick Traces*. Cambridge: Harvard Univ. Press, 1989.

———. *Mystery Train: Images of America in Rock 'n' Roll Music*. New York: E. P. Dutton, 1975.

Marcus, Jane. "Bonding and Bondage: Nancy Cunard and the Making of the *Negro* Anthology." In *Borders, Boundaries, and Frames: Cultural Criticism and Cultural Studies*, ed. Mae Henderson, 33–63. New York: Routledge, 1995.

Mariani, Paul. *Dream Song: The Life of John Berryman*. New York: William Morrow, 1990.

———. "Williams' Black Novel." *Massachusetts Review* (Winter 1973): 67–75.

Massa, Ann. *Vachel Lindsay: Fieldworker for the American Dream*. Bloomington: Indiana Univ. Press, 1970.

Masters, Edgar Lee. *Vachel Lindsay: A Poet in America*. New York: Biblo and Tannen, 1969.

Maston, T. B. *The Bible and Race*. Nashville, Tenn.: Broadman Press, 1959.

May, Larry. *Screening Out the Past: The Birth of Mass Culture and the Motion Picture Industry*. New York: Oxford Univ. Press, 1980.

Mellinkoff, Ruth. *The Mark of Cain*. Berkeley: Univ. of California Press, 1981.

Melville, Herman. "Benito Cereno." In *Billy Budd and Other Stories*. New York: Houghton Mifflin, 1970.

———. *The Confidence-Man*. London: Penguin, 1990.

Mercer, Kobena. "Looking for Trouble." In *The Lesbian and Gay Studies Reader*, ed. Henry Abelove, Michele Aina Barale, and David M. Halperin, 344–59. New York: Routledge, 1993.

———. "Skin Head Sex Thing: Racial Difference and the Homoerotic Imaginary." *New Formations* 16 (Spring 1992): 1–23.

———. *Welcome to the Jungle: New Positions in Black Cultural Studies*. New York: Routledge: 1994.

Mercer, Kobena, and Isaac Julien. "Race, Sexual Politics and Black Masculinity." In *Male Order: Unwrapping Masculinity*, ed. Rowena Chapman and Jonathan Rutherford, 97–164. London: Lawrence and Wishart, 1988.

Messenger, Christian K. "Norman Mailer: Boxing and the Art of His Narrative." *Modern Fiction Studies* 33, no. 1 (Spring 1987): 85–104.

Mezzrow, Milton "Mezz," and Bernard Wolfe. *Really the Blues*. New York: Random House, 1946.

Michaels, Walter Benn. "Race into Culture: A Critical Genealogy of Cultural Identity." *Critical Inquiry* 18 (Summer 1992): 655–85.

———. *Our America: Nativism, Modernism, and Pluralism*. Durham: Duke Univ. Press, 1995.

———. "The Souls of White Folk." In *Literature and the Body: Essays on Populations and Persons*, ed. Elaine Scarry, 185–209. Baltimore: Johns Hopkins Univ. Press, 1988.

Miller, Alyce. "Color Struck." In *The Nature of Longing*, 106–29. Athens: Univ. of Georgia Press, 1994.

Miller, Nancy K. *Getting Personal: Feminist Occasions and Other Autobiographical Acts*. New York: Routledge, 1991.

Miller, Jonathan. "The Sick White Negro." *Partisan Review* 7.6 (Spring 1963): 149–55.

Modleski, Tania. *Feminism Without Women: Culture and Criticism in a "Postfeminist" Age*. New York: Routledge, 1991.

Montaigne, Michel de. "Of Cannibals." In *The Essays*, vol. 1, trans. Jacob Zeitlin. New York: Alfred A. Knopf, 1934.

Morrison, Toni. *Beloved*. New York: Plume, 1988.

———. *The Bluest Eye*. New York: Plume, 1994.

———. *Playing in the Dark: Whiteness and the Literary Imagination*. Cambridge, Mass.: Harvard Univ. Press, 1992.

———. "Recitatif." In *The Before Columbus Foundation Fiction Anthology: Selections from the American Book Award*, ed. Ishmael Reed, Kathryn Trueblood, and Shawn Wong, 445–64. New York: W. W. Norton, 1992.

———. *Sula*. New York: Plume, 1982.

Mosse, George L. *Nationalism and Sexuality: Middle-Class Morality and Sexual Norms in Modern Europe*. Madison: Univ. of Wisconsin Press, 1985.

Mukherjee, Bharati. "An Invisible Woman." *Saturday Night* (March 1981): 36–40.

Murray, Timothy. *Like a Film: Ideological Fantasy on Screen, Camera and Canvas*. London and New York: Routledge, 1993.

Naremore, James. *Acting in the Cinema*. Berkeley: Univ. of California Press, 1988.

Naylor, Gloria. *Linden Hills*. New York: Penguin, 1985.

Nicoll, Allardyce. *The World of Harlequin, a Critical Study of the Commedia dell'arte*. Cambridge: Cambridge Univ. Press, 1963.

Nielsen, Aldon Lynn. *Reading Race: White American Poets and the Racial Discourse in the Twentieth Century*. Athens: Univ. of Georgia Press, 1988.

Nixon, Cornelia. *Lawrence's Leadership Politics and the Turn Against Women*. Berkeley: Univ. of California Press, 1986.

Norman, Charles. *e.e. cummings: The Magic-Maker*. Indianapolis: Bobbs-Merrill, 1972.

North, Michael. *The Dialect of Modernism: Race, Language and Twentieth-Century Literature*. New York: Oxford Univ. Press, 1994.

Nugent, Richard Bruce. "Drawings for Mulattoes." In *Ebony and Topaz: A Collection*, ed. Charles S. Johnson, 103–6. Freeport, N.Y.: Books for Libraries Press, 1971.

———. "Smoke, Lilies and Jade." In Hughes, ed., *Fire!!*, and reprinted under the pseudonym Richard Bruce in Nathan Irvin Huggins, *Voices from the Harlem Renaissance*, 99–110. New York: Oxford Univ. Press, 1995.

Oates, Joyce Carol. "Negative." In *Skin Deep: Black Women and White Women Write about Race*, ed. Marita Golden and Susan Richards Shreve, 60–86. New York: Doubleday, 1995.

O'Connor, Flannery. "The Artificial Nigger" and "Judgement Day." In *Collected Short Stories of Flannery O'Connor*, 531–50. New York: Farrar, Straus and Giroux, 1972.

O'Connor, Patrick. *Josephine Baker*. Boston: Little, Brown, 1988.

O'Daniel, Therman B. *Jean Toomer: A Critical Evaluation*. Washington, D.C.: Howard Univ. Press, 1988.

O'Grady, Lorraine. "Olympia's Maid: Reclaiming Black Female Subjectivity." *Afterimage* (1992): 14–23.

Olivier, Laurence. *On Acting*. New York: Simon and Schuster, 1986.

Omi, Michael, and Howard Winant. *Racial Formation in the United States*. New York: Routledge & Kegan Paul, 1986.

Ostendorf, Berndt. *Black Literature in White America*. Sussex, Engl.: Harvester Press, 1982.

Ovid. *Metamorphoses*. Vol. 1. Trans. Frank Justus Miller. Cambridge, Mass.: Loeb Classical Library, 1984.

Ozick, Cynthia. "Literary Blacks and Jews." In *Blacks and Jews: Alliances and Arguments*, ed. Paul Berman, 42–75. New York: Dell, 1994.

Paley, Grace. "At That Time, or The History of a Joke" and "Zagrowsky Tells." In *Later the Same Day*. New York: Farrar, Straus and Giroux, 1985.

Parks, Suzan-Lori. *The Death of the Last Black Man in the Whole Entire World*. In *The American Play, and Other Works*, 99–131. New York: Theatre Communications Group, 1995.

Peel, Ellen. "Semiotic Subversion in "Désirée's Baby." *American Literature* 62, no. 2 (June 1990): 223–37.

Phillips, Christopher. "'To Imagine That I Am Another.'" *Art in America* 80 (July 1992): 92–93.

Pickering, Michael. "Mock Blacks and Racial Mockery: The 'Nigger' Minstrel and British Imperialism." In *Acts of Supremacy: The British Empire and the Stage, 1790–1930*, ed. J. S. Bratton, Richard Allen Cave, Breandan Gregory, Heidi J. Holder and Michael Pickering, 179–236. Manchester: Manchester Univ. Press, 1991.

Pieterse, Jan Nederveen. *White on Black: Images of Africa and Blacks in Western Popular Culture*. New Haven: Yale Univ. Press, 1992.

Pifer, Ellen. "'Two Different Speeches': Mystery and Knowledge in *Mr. Sammler's Planet.*" *Mosaic: A Journal for the Interdisciplinary Study of Literature* 18, no. 2 (Spring 1985): 17–32.

Piper, Adrian. "Passing for White, Passing for Black." In *New Feminist Criticism: Art Identity Action*, ed. Joanna Frueh, Cassandra L. Langer, and Arlene Raven, 216–47. New York: Harper Collins, 1991.

Plath, Sylvia. *The Collected Poems*. New York: Harper Colophon, 1981.

Podhoretz, Norman. "The Know-Nothing Bohemians." *Partisan Review* 25, no. 2 (Spring 1958): 305–18.

———. "My Negro Problem—And Ours." *Commentary* 35 (1963): 93–101.

Poe, Edgar Allan. *The Narrative of Arthur Gordon Pym*. New York: Hill and Wang, 1977.

Price, Sally. *Primitive Art in Civilized Places*. Chicago: Univ. of Chicago Press, 1989.

Priest, Josiah. *Slavery as It Relates to the Negro, or African Race*. New York: Arnow, 1977.

Ray, Man. *Man Ray Photographs*. Intro. Jean-Hubert Martin. New York: Thames and Hudson, 1991.

Reddy, Maureen T. *Crossing the Colorline: Race, Parenting, and Culture*. New Brunswick, N.J.: Rutgers Univ. Press, 1994.

Reff, Theodore. *Manet: Olympia*. New York: Viking Press, 1977.

Reid, Mark A. *Redefining Black Film*. Berkeley: Univ. of California Press, 1993.

Rice, Gene. "The Curse that Never Was (Genesis 9:18–27)." *Journal of Religious Thought* 24 (1972): 6–27.

Rich, Adrienne. "Compulsory Heterosexuality and Lesbian Existence." In *Women: Sex and Sexuality*, ed. Catharine R. Stimpson and Ethel Spector Person, 62–91. Chicago: Univ. of Chicago Press, 1980.

———. "Turning the Wheel." In *The Fact of a Doorframe: Poems Selected and New, 1950–1984*, 305–10. New York: W. W. Norton, 1984.

Riggs, Marlon T. "Unleash the Queen." In *Black Popular Culture, a Project by Michele Wallace*, ed. Gina Dent, 99–105. Seattle: Bay Press, 1992.

Rivière, Joan. "Womanliness as a Masquerade." In *Formations of Fantasy*, ed. Victor Burgin, James Donald, and Cora Kaplan, 45–61. London: Methuen, 1986.

Robert Colescott: The One Two Punch. Written and directed by David Irving, created and produced by Linda Freeman. Chappaqua, N.Y.: L&S Video, 1993.

Roediger, David R. *The Wages of Whiteness: Race and the Making of the American Working Class*. London: Verson, 1991.

Rogers, J. A. *Sex and Race: Negro-Caucasian Mixing in All Ages and All Lands*. 3 vols. St. Petersburg, Fla.: Helga M. Rogers, 1952, 1967.

Rogin, Michael. "Blackface, White Noise: The Jewish Jazz Singer Finds His Voice." *Critical Inquiry* 18, no. 4 (Spring 1992): 417–53.

———. *Blackface, White Noise: Jewish Immigrants in the Hollywood Melting Pot.* Berkeley: Univ. of California Press, 1996.

———. "'Democracy and Burnt Cork': The End of Blackface, the Beginning of Civil Rights." *Representations* 46 (Spring 1994): 1–34.

———. "'The Sword Became a Flashing Vision': D.W. Griffith's *The Birth of a Nation.*" In Lang, ed., *Birth of a Nation*, 250–93.

Rollins, Bryant. "Does '*The Wiz*' Say Something Extra to Blacks?" *New York Times* (Dec. 28, 1975).

Roof, Judith. *Come as You Are: Sexuality and Narrative.* New York: Columbia Univ. Press, 1996.

———. *A Lure of Knowledge: Lesbian Sexuality and Theory.* New York: Columbia Univ. Press, 1991.

Rosaldo, Renato. *Culture and Truth: The Remaking of Social Analysis.* Boston: Beacon Press, 1989.

Rose, Phyllis. *Jazz Cleopatra: Josephine Baker in Her Time.* New York: Vintage, 1991.

Ross, Andrew. *No Respect: Intellectuals and Popular Culture.* New York: Routledge, 1989.

Rowe, John Carlos. "Poe, Antebellum Slavery, and Modern Criticism." In *Poe's Pym: Critical Explorations*, ed. Richard Kopley, 117–38. Durham: Duke Univ. Press, 1992.

Rubenstein, Roberta. "Intersexions: Gender Metamorphosis in Angela Carter's *The Passion of New Eve* and Lois Gould's *A Sea-Change.*" *Tulsa Studies in Women's Literature* 12, no. 1 (Spring 1993): 103–18.

Rubin, William, Helene Seckel, and Judith Cousins. *Les Demoiselles d'Avignon.* New York: Museum of Modern Art, distributed by Harry N. Abrams, 1994.

Rubin, William, ed. *"Primitivism" in 20th-Century Art.* 2 vols. New York: Museum of Modern Art, 1984.

Ruggles, Eleanor. *The West-Going Heart: A Life of Vachel Lindsay.* New York: W. W. Norton, 1959.

Rushdy, Ashraf H. A. "Reading Mammy: The Subject of Relation in Sherley Anne Williams' *Dessa Rose.*" *African American Review* 27, no. 3 (1993): 365–89.

Sacks, Howard and Judith. *Way Up North in Dixie, a Black Family's Claim to the Confederate Anthem.* Washington, D.C.: Smithsonian Press, 1993.

Said, Edward. *Culture and Imperialism.* New York: Vintage, 1994.

Salter, Elizabeth. *Edith Sitwell.* London: Oresko Books, 1979.

Sampson, Henry T. *Blacks in Blackface: A Source Book on Early Black Musical Shows.* Metuchen, N.J.: Scarecrow Press, 1980.

Sandburg, Carl. *Complete Poems.* New York: Harcourt, Brace & World, 1950.

Sante, Luc. "The Unexamined Life." *New York Review of Books* 42, no. 18 (Nov. 15, 1995): 42–47.

Saxton, Alexander, "Blackface Minstrelsy and Jacksonian Ideology." *American Quarterly* 27 (1975): 3–21.

Scales-Trent, Judy. *Notes of a White Black Woman: Race, Color, Community.* University Park: Pennsylvania State Univ. Press, 1995.

Scarry, Elaine. *The Body in Pain.* New York: Oxford Univ. Press, 1985.

Schor, Mira. "Representations of the Penis." *M/E/A/N/I/N/G* 4 (Nov. 1988): 3–17.

Schor, Naomi. "Female Fetishism." In *Bad Objects: Essays Popular and Unpopular*, 93–100. Durham: Duke Univ. Press, 1995.

Schickel, Richard. *D. W. Griffith.* London: Pavilion Books, 1984.

Schofield, Carey. *Jagger.* New York: Beaufort Books, 1985.

Schuyler, George. *Black No More*. With a new foreword by James A. Miller. Boston: Northeastern Univ. Press, 1989.

Sedgwick, Eve Kosofsky. *Epistemology of the Closet*. Berkeley: Univ. of California Press, 1990.

Shakespeare, William. *The Tempest*. In *William Shakespeare, the Complete Works*, ed. Alfred Harbage, 1373–95. Baltimore, Md.: Penguin, 1972.

Shohat, Ellan, and Robert Stam. *Unthinking Eurocentrism: Multiculturalism and the Media*. London and New York: Routledge, 1994.

Showalter, Elaine. "Rethinking the Seventies: Women Writers and Violence." In *Women and Violence in Literature*, ed. Katherine Anne Ackley, 237–54. New York: Garland, 1990.

———. *Sexual Anarchy: Gender and Culture at the Fin de Siècle*. New York: Viking, 1990.

Silverman, Kaja. *The Threshold of the Visible World*. New York: Routledge, 1996.

Sims, Lowery S., and Mitchell D. Kahan. *Robert Colescott: A Retrospective, 1975–1986*. San Jose: San Jose Museum of Art, 1987.

Singleton, Geoffrey. *Edith Sitwell: The Hymn to Life*. London: Fortune Press, 1961.

Sitwell, Edith. "Gold Coast Customs." In *Gold Coast Customs*. London: Duckworth, 1929.

Smith, Anna Deavere. *Fires in the Mirror: Crown Heights, Brooklyn, and Other Identities*. New York: Anchor, 1993.

———. *Twilight: Los Angeles, 1992*. New York: Anchor, 1994.

Smith, H. Seldon. *In His Image, But . . . : Racism in Southern Religion, 1780–1910*. Durham, N.C.: Duke Univ. Press, 1972.

Smith, Joseph. *The Pearl of Great Price (as Revealed to J. Smith, June 1830–February 1831)*. Salt Lake City: Church of Jesus Christ of Latter-Day Saints, 1985.

Smith, Lillian. *Killers of the Dream*. New York: W. W. Norton, 1949.

Snowden, Frank M., Jr. *Before Color Prejudice: The Ancient View of Blacks*. Cambridge: Harvard Univ. Press, 1983.

Solano, Solita. *Nancy Cunard: Brave Past, Indomitable Rebel, 1896–1965*. Ed. Hugh Ford. Philadelphia: Chilton, 1968.

Sollors, Werner. *Beyond Ethnicity: Consent and Descent in American Culture*. New York: Oxford Univ. Press, 1986.

———. "A Critique of Pure Pluralism." In *Reconstructing American Literary History*, ed. Sacvan Bercovitch, 250–69. Cambridge: Harvard Univ. Press, 1986.

———. *Neither Black Nor White Yet Both*. New York: Oxford Univ. Press, 1997.

———. "'Never Was Born': The Mulatto, an American Tragedy." *Ethnicity and Literature* 27, no. 2 (Summer 1986): 293–316.

Sontag, Susan. *On Photography*. New York: Farrar, Straus and Giroux, 1977.

Southern, Terry. *Blue Movie*. London: Calder & Boyars, 1973.

Soyinka, Wole. *Myth, Literature and the African World*. Cambridge: Cambridge Univ. Press, 1976.

———. "This Past Must Address Its Present" (the 1986 Nobel Lecture). *Statement: Occasional Papers of the Phelps-Stokes Fund*, no. 3 (March 1988).

Spark, Muriel. "The Black Madonna." In *The Go-Away Bird and Other Stories*, 1–27. Philadelphia and New York: J. B. Lippincott, 1960.

Spencer, Anne. "White Things." In the *Norton Anthology of Literature by Women*, ed. Sandra M. Gilbert and Susan Gubar, 1367. New York: W. W. Norton, 1996.

Spilka, Mark. "Hemingway's Barbershop Quintet: The *Garden of Eden* Manuscript." *Novel* 21, no. 1 (Fall 1987): 29–55.

Spillers, Hortense. "Mama's Baby, Papa's Maybe." *diacritics* 17, no. 2 (Summer 1987): 65–81.

Spivak, Gayatri. "Imperialism and Sexual Difference." *Oxford Literary Review* 8, nos. 1–2 (1986): 225–40.

Stafford, Barbara Maria. *Body Criticism: Imaging the Unseen in Enlightenment Art and Medicine*. Cambridge, Mass.: MIT Press, 1991.

Staples, Brent. *Parallel Time: Growing Up in Black and White*. New York: Pantheon, 1994.

Steele, Shelby. *The Content of Our Character*. New York: HarperPerennial, 1990.

Stein, Gertrude. *The Autobiography of Alice B. Toklas*, "Melanctha," and *Tender Buttons*. In *Selected Writings of Gertrude Stein*, ed. Carl Van Vechten. New York: Vintage Books, 1974.

Stevens, Holly. *Souvenirs and Prophecies: The Young Wallace Stevens*. New York: Alfred A. Knopf, 1977.

Stevens, Wallace. *The Collected Poems*. New York: Vintage, 1982.

———. *Opus Posthumous*. Ed. Samuel French Morse. New York: Alfred A. Knopf, 1957.

Stowe, William F., and David Grimsted. "White-Black Humor." *The Journal of Ethnic Studies* 3, no. 2 (Summer 1975): 78–96.

Street, Brain V. *The Savage in Literature: Representations of "Primitive" Society in English Fiction 1858–1920*. London: Routledge & Kegan Paul, 1975.

Styron, William. "This Quiet Dusk." *Harper's* 230, no. 1379 (April 1965): 135–46.

Sundquist, Eric J. *To Wake the Nations: Race in the Making of American Literature*. Cambridge, Mass.: Harvard Univ. Press, 1993.

Takaki, Ronald. *A Different Mirror: A History of Multicultural America*. Boston: Little, Brown, 1993.

Talalay, Kathryn. *Composition in Black and White: The Tragic Saga of Harlem's Biracial Prodigy*. New York: Oxford Univ. Press, 1995.

Tidey, Ashley. "Reflections Across the Color Line: White Double Consciousness and the Heritage of Slavery." Ph.D. diss., Indiana Univ., 1996.

Tischler, Barbara L. "Europa Jazz in the 1920s and the Musical Discovery of Harlem." In *The Harlem Renaissance: Revaluations*, ed. Amritjit Singh, William S. Shiver, and Stanley Brodwin, 185–94. New York: Garland, 1989.

Toll, Robert C. *Blacking Up: The Minstrel Show in Nineteenth-Century America*. New York: Oxford Univ. Press, 1974.

Toomer, Jean. *Cane*. Ed. Darwin T. Turner. New York: W. W. Norton, 1988.

Torgovnick, Marianna. *Gone Primitive: Savage Intellects, Modern Lives*. Chicago: Univ. of Chicago Press, 1990.

Toth, Emily. *Kate Chopin*. New York: William Morrow, 1990.

Turner, Darwin. "Introduction" to Toomer, *Cane*, ix–xxv. New York: Liveright, 1975.

Turner, Victor. "Comments and Conclusions." In *The Reversible World: Symbolic Inversion in Art and Society*, ed. Barbara A. Babcock, 276–95. Ithaca: Cornell University Press, 1978.

Twain, Mark. *Autobiography*. Ed. Charles Neider. New York: Harper, 1959.

———. *Pudd'nhead Wilson and Those Extraordinary Twins*. Ed. Sidney E. Berger. New York: W. W. Norton Critical Edition, 1980.

Udé, Iké. "The Unknown Norma Jean: Monroe's Darker Roots." *aRUDE* 2, no. 1 (1996): 32–35.

Unterecker, John. *Voyager: A Life of Hart Crane*. London: Anthony Blond, 1970.

Van Vechten, Carl. *Nigger Heaven*. New York: Alfred A. Knopf, 1926.

Vendler, Helen. *The Given and the Made: Strategies of Poetic Redefinition*. Cambridge: Harvard Univ. Press, 1995.

Wald, Gayle. "'A Most Disagreeable Mirror': Reflections on White Identity in *Black Like Me*." In Ginsberg, ed., *Passing and the Fictions of Identity*, 151–77.

Walker, Alice. "One Child of One's Own: A Meaningful Digression Within the Work(s)." In *In Search of Our Mothers' Gardens*, 361–83. New York: Harcourt Brace, Jovanovich, 1983.

———. *Meridian*. New York: Pocket Books, 1976.

Wallace, Michele. *Black Macho and the Myth of the Superwoman*. New York: Verso, 1990.

Walton, Jean. "Re-Placing Race in (White) Psychoanalytic Discourse: Founding Narratives of Feminism." *Critical Inquiry* 21, no. 4 (Summer 1995): 775–804.

———. "Sandra Bernhard: Lesbian Postmodern or Modern Postlesbian?" In *The Lesbian Postmodern*, ed. Laura Doan, 244–61. New York: Columbia Univ. Press, 1994.

Ward, Catherine C. Ward. "Gloria Naylor's *Linden Hills*: A Modern *Inferno*." *Contemporary Literature* 28, no. 1 (1987): 67–81.

Ward, Douglas Turner. *Happy Ending and Day of Absence*. New York: Dramatists Play Service, 1966.

Warren, Robert Penn. *Band of Angels*. New York: Random House, 1955.

Washington, Booker T. *Up from Slavery*. New York: Penguin, 1986.

Washington, Joseph R., Jr. *Anti-Blackness in English Religion 1500–1800*. New York: Edwin Mellen, 1984.

Wasserstrom, William. "Cagey John: Berryman as Medicine Man." *Centennial Review* 12(1968): 334–54.

Watkins, Glenn. *Pyramids at the Louvre: Music, Culture, and Collage from Stravinsky to the Postmodernists*. Cambridge: Harvard Univ. Press, 1994.

Watkins, Mel. *On the Real Side: Laughing, Lying, and Signifying—The Underground Tradition of African-American Humor That Transformed American Culture, from Slavery to Richard Pryor*. New York: Touchstone, 1995.

Weinauer, Ellen M. "'A Most Respectable Looking Gentleman': Passing, Possession, and Transgression in *Running a Thousand Miles for Freedom*." In Ginsberg, ed., *Passing and the Fictions of Identity*, 37–56.

Wells, Ida B. *Crusade for Justice: The Autobiography of Ida B. Wells*. Ed. Alfreda Duster. Chicago: Univ. of Chicago Press, 1970.

Weinberg, Jonathan. "'Boy Crazy': Carl Van Vechten's Queer Collection." *Yale Journal of Criticism* 7, no. 2 (1994): 25–51.

West, Cornel. *Race Matters*. New York: Vintage, 1994.

Wheatley, Phillis. *The Collected Works*. Ed. John Shields. New York: Oxford Univ. Press, 1988.

Wheeler, David L. "Helping Mixed-Race People Declare Their Heritage: Portrait of Terry P. Wilson." *Chronicle of Higher Education* (Sept. 7, 1994): A8.

Whitman, Walt. *Leaves of Grass*. Ed. Jerome Loving. New York: Oxford Univ. Press, 1990.

White, Mimi. "*The Birth of a Nation*: History as Pretext." In Lang, ed., *The Birth of a Nation*, 214–24.

White, Walter. "Has Science Conquered the Color Line?" Reprinted from *Look* in *Negro Digest* (Dec. 1949): 37–40.

———. *A Man Called White: The Autobiography of Walter White*. New York: Arno Press and the New York Times, 1969.

Wideman, John Edgar. "Charles Chesnutt and the WPA Narratives: The Oral and Literate Roots of Afro-American Literature." In *The Slave's Narrative*, ed. Charles T. Davis and Henry Louis Gates, Jr., 59–77. New York: Oxford Univ. Press, 1985.

———. *Sent for You Yesterday*. London: Allison & Busby, 1984.

Wiegman, Robyn. *American Anatomies: Theorizing Race and Gender*. Durham: Duke Univ. Press, 1995.

Williams, Delores S. *Sisters in the Wilderness: The Challenge of Womanist God-Talk*. Maryknoll, N.Y.: Orbis Books, 1993.

Williams, Gregory Howard. *Life on the Color Line: The True Story of a White Boy Who Discovered He Was Black*. New York: Dutton, 1995.

Williams, Patricia J. *The Alchemy of Race and Rights: Diary of a Law Professor*. Cambridge, Mass.: Harvard Univ. Press, 1991.

———. *The Rooster's Egg: On the Resistance of Prejudice*. Cambridge: Harvard Univ. Press, 1995.

Williams, Raymond. *The Politics of Modernism: Against the New Conformists*. London: Verso, 1989.

Williams, Sherley Anne. *Dessa Rose*. New York: Berkeley, 1987.

Williams, William Carlos. *The Collected Poems*. Vols. 1 and 2. Ed. A. Walton Litz and Christopher MacGowan. New York: New Directions, 1986, 1988.

———. *In the American Grain*. New York: New Directions, 1956.

———. "Man Orchid." *Massachusetts Review* (Winter 1973): 77–117.

———. *Paterson*. New York: New Directions, 1963.

Williamson, Joel. *The Crucible of Race*. New York: Oxford Univ. Press, 1984.

———. *New People: Miscegenation and Mulattoes in the United States*. New York: Free Press, 1980.

Willis, Susan. "I Shop Therefore I Am: Is There a Place for Afro-American Culture in Commodity Culture?" In *Changing Our Own Words: Essays on Criticism, Theory, and Writing by Black Women*, ed. Cheryl A. Wall, 173–95. New Brunswick: Rutgers Univ. Press, 1991.

Wilson, Judith. "Scenes of War." In *I Tell My Heart: The Art of Horace Pippin*, 56–69. Philadelphia: Pennsylvania Academy of the Fine Arts, 1993.

Wirth, Thomas H. "Richard Bruce Nugent." *Black American Literature Forum* 19 (Spring 1985): 16.

Wittke, Carl. *Tambo and Bones: A History of the American Minstrel Stage*. New York: Greenwood Press, 1968.

Woll, Allen. *Black Musical Theatre: From Coontown to Dreamgirls*. Baton Rouge: Louisiana State Univ. Press, 1989.

Woolf, Virginia. "Professions for Women." In *The Death of the Moth and Other Essays*, 235–42. Orlando, Fla.: Harcourt Brace, 1942.

Wright, Richard. *White Man, Listen!* Garden City, N.Y.: Anchor Books, 1964.

X, Malcolm. *The Autobiography of Malcolm X*. With the assistance of Alex Haley. New York: Ballantine Books, 1992.

Yaeger, Patricia. "The Poetics of Birth." In *Discourses of Sexuality: From Aristotle to AIDS*, ed. Domna C. Stanton, 262–96. Ann Arbor: Univ. of Michigan Press, 1992.

Yatron, Michael. *America's Literary Revolt*. New York: Philosophical Library, 1959.

Yeomans, W. E. "T. S. Eliot, Ragtime, and the Blues." *University Review—Kansas City* 34 (1968): 267–75.

Zack, Naomi. *Race and Mixed Race*. Philadelphia: Temple Univ. Press, 1993.

Žižek, Slavoj. *Looking Awry: An Introduction to Jacques Lacan Through Popular Culture*. Cambridge, Mass.: MIT Press, 1992.

INDEX

PAGE NUMBERS IN ITALICS REFER TO ILLUSTRATIONS.

Abolitionism, 28–29, 138
Abraham (biblical character), 214, 231, 259
Abrahams, Roger, 47–48, 257
Acton, Harold, 152
Adam (biblical character), 124, 127
Adoption: of black children, 232
Advertisements for Myself (Mailer), 181
Aesthetics: and transraciality, 258–60
Africa: and black envy, 193–95; as dark continent, 223; and Ham (biblical character), 123; influence on American/Western culture of, 30–31, 107–22; as masculine, 193; and prostitution, 217, 218, *219*, 220, *220*; and sexuality, 223. *See also* Animalism; Jungle
African Americans. *See* Blacks
Africana (musical), 114
"Afro-American Fragment" (Hughes), 118
Albinos, 260
The Alchemy of Race and Rights (Patricia Williams), 55–56
Alienation: and black black impersonation, 118; and black envy, 178, 180, 190, 192, 196; and black talk, 138, 143; and mixed children, 227; and passing, 104–5; and racist totalizing, 244–45
"All Coons Look Alike to Me" (song), 114
All God's Chillun Got Wings (O'Neill), 156
Allen, Woody, 240, 248
Les Amants (The Lovers) (Magritte), 38
"America" (Ginsberg), 160
"American Negro's New Comedy Act," 97–98
American/Western culture: African/black influence on, 30-31, 45, 107–22; black alienation from, 143; and black talk, 143; as death, 239; and ethics of racechange, 47; interdependence of blacks and whites in evolution of, 107; and minstrelsy, 147; origins of, 47; schizophrenia of, 160
Amos 'n' Andy (radio show), 149, 156, 157, 162. *See also* Correll, Charles V.; Gosden, Freeman F.
Anderson, Sherwood, 156, 178–79, 181
Androgyny, 5, 183, 192, 194
"Angel Levine" (Malamud), 258–60
Animalism, 194, 221, *222*, 223
Antheil, George, 135, 137
Anti-Semite and Jew (Sartre), 232
Anti-Semitism, 232
Antin, Eleanor, 256
Apartheid: cultural, 257, 261; and Noah's curse, 128
Ariel (Plath), 198
"The Artificial Nigger" (O'Connor), 84, 85
"Artificial niggers": in film, 84, 86–94
Astaire, Fred, 53–54, 88, *89*, 90
"At That Time, or The History of a Joke" (Paley), 231
Authenticity, 47–48, 138, 256. *See also* Racial purity
"'Authenticity,' or the Lesson of *Little Tree*" (Gates), 47
The Autobiography of Alice B. Toklas (Stein), 118–19
The Autobiography of an Ex-Coloured Man (Johnson), 104, 105, 216
Avedon, Richard, 174
Awkward, Michael, 248, 249

Babes in Arms (film), 90
Babes on Broadway (film), 90, *91*
Baker, Houston, 95
Baker, Josephine, 114–16, *115*, 117, 119, 121, 150
Bakhtin, M. M., 137, 140–41
Baldwin, James, 73, 128, 135, 176–78, 180, 197, 226
Band of Angels (Warren), 216–17
Barth, John, 166–67

Baum, Frank, 31
Beardsley, Aubrey, 107
Beat generation, 160, 177, 184–86, 188. *See also* Ginsberg, Allen; Kerouac, Jack
Beaton, Cecil, 149–50, *151*
Beauvoir, Simone de, 5, 44, 241
Beethoven, Ludwig von, 31, *32*
Bell, David, 31
Bellow, Saul, 170–72, 174–75, 187, 200, 202, 246
Beloved (Morrison), 28–29
Benetton advertisements, 33, 46
"Benito Cereno" (Melville), 243
Benjamin, Jessica, 176, 230
Bennett, Arnold, 145
Berlin, Irving, 72, 232. See also *Holiday Inn*
Bernal, Martin, 30
Bernhard, Sandra, 249
Bernstein, Leonard, 81
Berry, Chuck, 188
Berryman, John, 136–37, 138, 160–61, 162–66, 246
Berzon, Judith, 213
Besserer, Eugenie. See *The Jazz Singer*
Bhabha, Homi, 40–41, 44
Bible: and racist totalizing, 245. *See also specific character*
The Birth of a Nation (film), 34, 70, 73, 75, 77, 85, 87, 101; and black envy, 170, 178; discussion about, 57–66; and minstrelsy, 77–78; pictures of, *58*, *60*, *62*, *64*; and racist totalizing, 242, 246
Black Anglo-Saxons (Hare), 235
Black Arts movement, 252
Black Athena (Bernal), 30
Black black impersonation: and blackface, 112–14, *113*, 114–16; and gender, 108, 109–11; and Harlem Renaissance, 96–97, 100, 107–22; and minstrelsy, 108–9, 112–14; and modernism, 107; and origination myths, 107–12
"Black and Blue" (song), 133
Black Book (Mapplethorpe), 183
"The Black Boy Look at the White Boy" (Baldwin), 176–78
"The Black Christ" (Cullen), 30
Black envy: and black women, 175; and crime, 170, 172, 174, 178, 202; and femininity, 189–202; and hipster, 177, 178, 179, 180, 181, 182, 191; and homosexuality, 175, 176, 177, 179, 181, 182–83, 186, 192, 193; and lesbianism, 175, 189–202; and masculinity, 170–71, 173, 174–75, 177, 182, 183–84, 186, 193, 195–200; and penis, 172–75, *173*, 176, 182, 189, 190, 195, 196, 197, 199, 200, 202; and phallus, 175, 176, 177, 182, 183, 189, 190, 195, 196, 197, 199, 200, 202; and racial superiority, 181, 198, 199, 200; and racism, 185, 189, 197, 200; and sadism, 191, 196, 197, 199, 200; and stereotypes, 170, 178, 190; and Third Sex, 175, 176, 199; and transraciality, 249; and white guilt, 194; and White Negro, 191; and white women, 189–202; and women, 175, 187, 189, 202
Black intelligentsia, 19
Black Like Me (film), 28, *29*
Black Like Me (Griffin), 28–30, 36, 187
The Black Madonna (Spark), 228–29
"Black Man and White Ladyship" (Cunard), 149
Black men: and black black impersonation, 121; and blackface, 76; glamourization of, 180; and Noah's curse, 126; schizophrenia of, 121; as sexual threats to white men, 88, 177; White Negro desire for, 176–89. *See also* Black envy
Black nationalism, 252
Black No More (Schuyler), 18–20, 25, 38, 103
Black power movement, 188–89
Black Skin, White Masks (Fanon), 13, 38, 40, 55
Black talk: and beat generation, 160; and blackface, 165; and Boomlay BOOM, 137, 139–48, 149, 157–58, 163; and civil rights movement, 162, 164; and Dis and Dat, 137, 149–58, 163, 164, 166; and ethics, 162; as forbidden, 144; and Harlem Renaissance, 136; and minstrelsy, 135, 136, 139, 143, 146, 147–48, 152, 156, 157, 158, 160, 162, 165, 168; as mocking of white society, 137; and modernism, 134–48, 158, 160, 166; in music, 10; and patrons, 149–58; and racial subordination, 135–36, 139, 160, 168; and racism, 136, 140, 141, 142, 159; self-derisive, 138, 158–68; and sexuality, 146, 167–68; and stereotypes, 135, 136, 137, 138, 140–41, 144, 157, 160, 162, 164; as threat to established order, 137; and vaudeville, 140, 141–42, 143, 146, 148, 165; and white guilt, 139, 147, 160, 161–62, 164, 166
"Black or White" (Jackson music video), 34, 45, 46
Black, White, Other (Funderburg), 230
Black women. *See* Prostitution; Women: black
Blackbirds of 1928 (musical), 114
Blackburn, Julia, 21
Blackface, 154; ambivalence of, 44; anatomy of, 75–86; and "artificial nigger," 84, 86–94; and black black impersonation, 112–14, *113*, 114–16; and black envy, 85, 199; and black inferiority, 76; and black talk, 135, 139, 147, 165; and bulging eyes, 83–84; and burnt cork/charred flesh, 79, 81; and clownishness, 57, 66–75, 81; and colonialism, 55; and crime, 57–66, 169, 170; and cultural imperialism, 55; and death of Other, 73, 75, 79, 84; and devaluation of blackness, 76; economic use of, 78; and erasure of subjectivity of blacks, 43; and ethics of racechange, 43, 44, 45; and evil of blacks, 65, 92–93; and feminization, 70–71, 75, 79; in

film, 53–94; functions/purposes of, 54, 56; and grin/grimace of pain, 81–82; and homosexuality, 84; and infantilization, 67, 71, 72; and Jews, 66–75; and love-hate relationship, 85; and lynchings, 56, 78–79, 84, 85; as make-up, 66; and masculinity, 67, 71, 75, 77; and minstrelsy, 55, 76–77, 78, 79; and miscegenation, 65; and negrophobia, 76–77, 82; and punishment, 56–57, 79, 81; and racial subordination, 55, 57, 85, 99; and racist totalizing, 246; and scapegoats, 54–55, 57, 73, 75, 78–86; and sex, 57–66, 77; and slavery, 54; and spirit murder, 93–94; and stereotypes, 61, 73; and "symbolic debt," 56; and transraciality, 249; and twitching limbs/stiffness of body parts, 84–85; and violence, 85, 161; and visibility of race, 65, 81; as war on blacks, 65; and white guilt, 55, 79, 82, 85, 92; and white supremacy, 78. See also *The Birth of a Nation*; *The Jazz Singer*
"Blackface, White Noise" (Rogin), 43
Blackness: as blunder, 132; as carnival, 88, 90, 114; celebration of, 233; changes in representations of, 245–46; and color as means of defining race, 32–33; for comparisons, 40–41; as curse, 98, 122–33; devaluation of, 11, 12–25, 76, 98, 100, 131; as deviant, 98, 175; distrust of, 38; as fetish, 195; glorification/glamourization of, 100, 112, 116, 123; and hidden racial roots of whites, 31–32; of Jesus, 30; and madness, 92–93; and neurotic orientation, 30; as norm, 100, 101–2; parodies of, 36–37, *36*; privileging of, 24; as problem in need of solution/rationalization, 98; prostitution equated with, 218; as punishment, 25, 30, 53; and racist totalizing, 242; and role of African culture in western civilization, 30–31; superiority of, 30; as ugly, 126; and white man as burden, 38, 40. *See also* Passing
Blacks: as America's metaphor, 260; and black black impersonation, 108; blame on, 56; as comparison, 260; as deserving of abuse/pain, 105; desexualization of, 204, 205; eradication/erasure of, 18–19, 38, 43, 131, 175, 202; as evil, 65, 92–93; as first race, 102; inferiority of, 243–44; as lynchers, 60; marginalization of, 47; and mixed children, 207–14; as mothers, 207–14; objectification of, 40; as parents of white children, 232–39; as perverters of democracy, 60; as servants, 204, 205, 229–30; silencing of, 40; as surrogate mothers, 204, 229–30; and *tabula rasa*, 96, 106; white sympathy and understanding of, 246. *See also* Black men; *specific person or topic*
The Blacks (Genet), 38
Blade Runner (film), 46
Blake, William, 12, 13, 24, 166
Blazing Saddles (film), 248
Blonde Venus (film), 221, *222*, 223
Blue Movie (Southern), 170
Blues music, 158, 159, 162, 188
The Bluest Eye (Morrison), 15, 21, 24, 204, 252
Boggs, Dock, 188
Bojangles, 118, 204, 252
"Bojangles of Harlem" (Astaire routine), 88, *89*, 90
"Bomb" (Corso), 148
Bonner, Marita, 210, 212–13, 246
The Book of Colour (Blackburn), 21
Boomlay BOOM, 137, 139–48, 149, 157–58, 163
Bowen, Stella, 144, *145*
Brancusi, Constantin, 149
Bring in 'Da Noise, Bring in 'Da Funk (musical), 252
Brontë, Charlotte, 236
Brooks, Mel, 248
Brown, Sterling, 136
Browne, Thomas, 97–98, 102
Browning, Robert, 105, 198
Broyard, Anatole, 20
Bruce, Lenny, 179–80
Burroughs, Edgar Rice, 136
Butler, Octavia E., 214, 231
Buxton, Anthony, 35, *35*

Cabaret Voltaire, 134, 148
Cable, George Washington, 48
Cahun, Claude, 248
Cain (biblical character), 126–27
"Caliban upon Setebos" (Browning), 198
Cambridge, Godfrey, 27, *28*
Campbell, Naomi, 240
Canaan (biblical character), 123–31
Cane (Toomer), 224–25, 231
Cannibalism, 82, 144, 146, 242–43, 254
Cantor, Eddie, 72, 77, *77*, 232
Carlyle, Thomas, 140
Carmen (Bizet opera), 31
Carmen Jones (film), 31
Carpenter, Edward, 170–71, 183
Carter, Angela, 30
Carter, Asa Earl. *See* Carter, Forrest
Carter, Forrest (aka Asa Earl Carter), 47
Cartesianism, 96–97. *See also* Descartes, René; Mind-body problem
Castration, 189, 190, 212, 221, 223
Celluloid Frames (Udé), 241, 252–54, *253*, *255*
Censorship, 254
"Change the Joke" (Ellison), 55
Check and Double Check (film), 90, *90*
Chesnutt, Charles W., 12, 25–26, 27, 104, 246; and blackface, 85; and prostitution, 215–16, 218, 221
"'Childe Roland in the Dark Tower Came'" (Browning), 105

Children: adoption of black, 232; and black servants, 204, 229–30; pre-Oedipal bonding of mother and, 223–32; stereotypes of, 204; white as norm for, 204. *See also* Mixed children; Temple Black, Shirley
The Chocolate Dandies (musical), 114, *115*
Chopin, Kate: and mixed children, 205, 206, 207–10, 214–15, 216, 218, 223, 233, 236, 237; and racist totalizing, 246
Chow, Rey, 135, 138
Churchill, Caryl, 12–13, 24, 256
Civil rights: and black envy, 181, 182, 188; and black talk, 162, 164; and Jews, 232; and racial purity, 42; and "spirit-murder," 55–56; and whites passing as blacks, 27–29
Civil War, 257. See also *The Birth of a Nation*
Cixous, Hélène, 129
The Clansman (Dixon), 57, 59, *64*. See also *The Birth of a Nation*
Class issues, 188, 232, 244, 252, 254
Classical Greece and Rome. *See* Greek mythology; Tarquinian vase
Cleaver, Eldridge, 184, 188, 189
Cliff, Michelle, 104
Clifford, James, 38
Clifton, Lucille, 234–35
Cloud 9 (Churchill), 12–13, 24
Clowns, 57, 66–75, 81
Cohn, Alfred A., 68
Cole, Herbert M., 38, *39*, 40
Cole, Horace de Vere, 35, *35*
Colescott, Robert: *Les demoiselles d'Alabama: Vestidas* by, 218, 220, 221; *Eat Dem Taters* by, 46; *George Washington Carver Crossing the Delaware* by, 46–47, 48; and mixed children, 203–5, 217; and racial subordination, 55; and racist totalizing, 242; *Saint Sebastian* by, 237–38, 239; *Shirley Temple Black and Bill Robinson White* by, 203–5, 217; and transraciality, 257; and White Negro, 237–39. *See also* color insert
College Holiday (film), 82, *83*
Colman, Ronald, 92–93, *92*
Colonialism: and artist as colonizer, 194; and black talk, 157; and blackface, 55; blackness as retaliation against, 38, 40; and ethics of racechange, 40–41; and mind-body problem, 96–97; and racist totalizing, 246; and transraciality, 254; and whiteness as norm, 12–13. *See also* Imperialism
Color. *See* Skin color
"Color Struck" (Alyce Miller), 233, 234, 235
Color Struck (Hurston), 233–34
The Color of Water (McBride), 228
The Colored Museum (Wolfe), 252
Colored People (Piper), 240–41, 252
Comedy. *See* Blackface; Minstrelsy
Computer graphics, 241, 252–54, *253*, 256
The Confessions of Nat Turner (Styron), 162
Confidence Man (Melville), 82
"The Congo" (Lindsay), 10, 134, 140–43, 144, 147, 150, 158, 246
The Conjure Woman (Chesnutt), 25
Connelly, Marc, 156
Conrad, Joseph, 94, 96, 140, 144
Consciousness: double, 109, 110, 121, 122, 239; and transraciality, 256; of whites, 25–27
Correll, Charles V., 90, *90*, 149, 156
Corso, Gregory, 148
Covarrubias, Miguel, 154, 155, *155*
Craft, William and Ellen, 13, *14*, 15, 38, 106
Crane, Hart, 148, 178, 181
Crime: and black envy, 170, 172, 174, 178, 202; and blackface, 57–66, 169, 170
Cripps, Thomas, 63
Croce, Arlene, 88
Crosby, Bing: in *Dixie*, 79, *80*, 81, 90, *93*, 94; in *Holiday Inn*, 53–54, *54*, 86
Cross, Amanda, 85
Cross dressing, 13, *14*, 200, 202. *See also* Transvestism
"Cross" (Hughes), 213
Crouch, Stanley, 189
Crowder, Henry, 150, 152–53
Crystal, Billy, 256
Cubist art, 220
Cullen, Charles, 48–49, *50*
Cullen, Countee, 30, 118, 131, 225
Culture: and cultural apartheid, 257, 261; and cultural hybridization, 257; and cultural mulatto, 252; and cultural pluralism, 237; and ethics of racechange, 43; influence of black culture on popular, 30–31; influence of black and white on each other's, 257; popular, 30–31, 43; and racial stereotyping, 31; and transraciality, 257–58, 259
cummings, e. e., 149, 157–58, 162, 178–79, 181
Cunard, Nancy: and black talk, 134–35, 138, 149–50, *151*, 152–54, 156, 157; KerSeymer's photographs of, *151*, 200, *201*
Cuney, Waring, 118

Dada movement, 134, 148
Dance. *See* Minstrelsy; *specific person, film, or musical*
Daniel, Bradford, 188
Danson, Ted, 38
Dante, 235
Dark Laughter (Anderson), 156
Darriau, Jean-Paul, 51–52, *51*
Dash, Julie, 10
Davis, F. James, 232
A Day at the Races (film), 91–92
De Niro, Robert, 86
Death: of African Americans in film, 246; and black talk, 144, 167; and blackface, 65, 73, 75, 79, 84; and denegrification, 21; and ex-colored, 103–4; life-in-, 74–75, 104, 215–16, 224–25; and mixed children, 208–9, 215–16,

224–25, 235, 236; and origination myths, 102–4; and passing, 29–30, 104; Western civilization as, 239; whiteness associated with, 102–3
The Death of the Last Black Man (Parks), 128
Deavere Smith, Anna, 232, 256
"Degenerate Art Exhibit" (Nazi poster), 75, *76*
"Delta Autumn" (Faulkner), 211
Democracy: blacks as perverters of, 60
Les demoiselles d'Alabama: Vestidas (Colescott), 218, 220, 221. *See also* color insert
Les demoiselles d'Avignon (Picasso), 217, 218, 220, *220*
Denaturalizing, 241
Denkmall II: Eitelkeit (Monument II: Vanity) (Höch), 8, *9*, 10
Descartes, René, 96, 101, 102, 106
"Désirée's Baby" (Chopin), 205, 206, 207–10, 214–15, 216, 223, 233, 236, 246
Dessa Rose (Sherley Anne Williams), 229
Dialect. *See* Black talk
Diamond, Neil, 86
Dickens, Charles, 84, 215
Dietrich, Marlene, 221, *222*, 223
Dinkins, David, 38
Dis and Dat, 137, 149–58, 163, 164, 166
"Dixie" (Confederate anthem), 95
Dixie (film), 79, *80*, 81, 90, *93*, 94
Dixie to Broadway (musical), 114, 117, *117*
Dixon, Thomas, 57, 59, 61, 63, *64*
The Dolly Sisters (film), 86
Don Giovanni (film), 31
"Double consciousness," 109, 110, 121, 122, 239
A Double Life (film), 92–93, *92*
Douglas, Aaron, 121
Douglas, Ann, 31, 72, 110, 119, 121, 152–53, 210
"Drawings for Mulattoes" (Nugent), 107–12, *108*, *109*, *110*, *111*, 116, 121, 123
"*Dreadnought* hoax," 35–36, *35*, 38
The Dream Songs (Berryman), 162–66, 246
Du Bois, W.E.B., 19, 103, 155; and double consciousness, 109; and mixed children, 208; and NAACP, 152; and passing, 104, 105; and race as gradation, 31, 152, 239
Duke, David, 189
Dumas, Alexander, 31
Dunbar, Paul Laurence, 38
Dyer, Richard, 48
Dylan, Bob, 188

Eat Dem Taters (Colescott), 46. *See also* color insert
Ebony and Topaz (Charles S. Johnson), 107, 121, 122
Eliot, T. S., 122, 197–98, 241; and black talk, 134, 139–40, 143, 144, 145–48, 149, 150
Elizabeth (queen of Great Britain), 33, *33*, 45, 46
Ellington, Duke, 117–18
Ellis, Trey, 252
Ellison, Ralph, 54–55, 78, 135, 136–37, 260
Emmett, Dan, 95. *See also Dixie*
England, 188
The Enormous Room (cummings), 178
Entführung (Abduction) (Höch), 7–8, *9*
"Equatorial Way" (Cunard), 150, 152, 156
Erté, 107
Ethics: and black talk, 162; of racechange, 40–52, 246; and transraciality, 257
Ethnic cleansing, 254
"Ethnic transvestism," 47, 155, 257
Ethnicity: and transraciality, 254, 256, 257
Ethnogenesis. *See* Origination myths
Ethnographic Museum series (Höch), 8, 10
Eugenics, 205, 223
Europe: as feminine, 193
Eve (biblical character), 124, 131, 193
Everett, Barbara, 145–46
Ex-colored, 100–107, 112, 216
Existentialism, 179, 180, 247

"Family Romances" (Freud), 236–37
Family. *See* Mixed children; slavery; *specific biblical character*
Fanon, Frantz, 6, 56, 170; and black envy, 174, 199, 200; and black is comparison, 40; and "corporeal malediction," 25; and "corporeal reconfiguration," 13; and denegrification, 20, 21; and ethics of racechange, 45, 49, 51; and family as miniature nation, 206; and mixed children, 232; and neurotic orientation, 30; and psychology of blacks and whites, 55; and race as rigid bifurcation, 5; and racist totalizing, 242, 244–45; and smile of blacks, 81–82; and transraciality, 258, 260; and volition or agency issues, 38; and white guilt, 55
Fantasies: about being white, 234–35; and black envy, 190, 198; and masquerades, 241; and mixed children, 236–37
"Father and Son" (Hughes), 213
Fathers: and black envy, 195–200; and mixed children, 207–14; and Oedipal Rage, 210–14; whites as, 207–14
Faulkner, William, 17–18, 160, 161–62, 181–82, 210, 211, 241
Fauset, Jessie Redmon, 15, 18, 38, 104, 105
Femininity/feminization: and black envy, 189–202; and blackface, 70–71, 75, 79; as castration, 189, 190; and Europe as feminine, 193; and Jews, 200
Femme fatale, 116
Fetish, 175, 193, 195, 221
Fiedler, Leslie, 71, 164–65, 180, 182
Film: African Americans in, 246; "artificial nigger" in, 86–94; blackface in, 53–94; and ethics of racechange, 43; influence of minstrelsy on, 55; minstrelsy in, 70, 76–78,

Film (*continued*)
90; spirit-murder in, 53–94; stereotypes in, 61, 73, 88, 91–92; and transraciality, 249–50. *See also specific film*
Finian's Rainbow (musical), 25, 26–27, *26*, 30
Fire!! (journal), 121
Fires in the Mirror (Anna Deavere Smith), 232
Fishbone, 252
Fisher, Rudolph, 155
Fishkin, Shelley Fisher, 31
Flanner, Janet, 116, 152
Flapper-cum-savage. *See* Baker, Josephine
The Floating Opera (Barth), 166–67
Ford, John, 63
Four Intruders Plus Alarm Systems (Piper), 202
Four Saints in Three Acts (Stein), 118
Frank, Waldo, 156
Franklin, John Hope, 65
Fremde Schönheit I (Strange Beauty) (Höch), 8, 10, 218
Freud, Sigmund, 192, 199, 210, 223, 236–37, 243
Funderburg, Lise, 230, 232
Funnyhouse of a Negro (Kennedy), 25
Fuss, Diana, 42, 75, 192, 244–45, 246–47

"Gal from the South" (song), 82
Galland, China, 30
Gallop, Jane, 170, 189, 197
Garden of Eden (biblical), 124
The Garden of Eden (Hemingway), 10, 41, 176, 190–95, 197, 199, 200
Garland, Judy, 90, *91*
Garvey, Marcus, 19
Gates, Henry Louis, Jr., 41–42, 47, 81, 136, 259
Gender: and black black impersonation, 108, 109–11; and curse of color, 131; and ethics of racechange, 43–44; and miscegenation, 17, 18; and racial subordination, 5, 6, 11; and transraciality, 248. *See also* Black men; Women
Genealogy, 31–32, 207–10
Genet, Jean, 38, 207
Genitals, 187, 188, 217. *See also* Penis; Phallus
Genocidal racechange, 103, 123. *See also* Schuyler, George
George Washington Carver Crossing the Delaware (Colescott), 46–47, 48. *See also* color insert
Gershwin, George, 72, 156
Ghost (film), 10
Gilbert and Sullivan, 31
Gilman, Charlotte Perkins, 231
Gilman, Sander, 73, 217
Ginsberg, Allen, 160, 182, 185, 186
Ginsberg, Elaine, 106
Girard, René, 75, 78
Gish, Lillian. See *The Birth of a Nation*
Glover, Savion, 252
Go Down, Moses (Faulkner), 161–62, 211
"Gold Coast Customs" (Sitwell), 143–44, 150, 158
Goldberg, Whoopi, 10, 21, *22*, 27, 37–38, 256
Goodman, Benny, 10, 72
Goodman, Paul, 186
Gosden, Freeman F., 90, *90*, 149, 156
Gould, Lois, 176, 190, 191, 195–200, 241
Grandville, J.-J., 221
Grant, Duncan, 35, *35*
Graves, Robert, 126
Great Expectations (Dickens), 215
Greek mythology, 212, 213. *See also* Tarquinian vase
The Green Pastures (Connelly), 156
Gregory, Dick, 36, *36*, 37, 98, *99*, 186, *187*
Griffin, John Howard, 12, 27–30, 36, 40, 176, 187, 188, 189, 246
Griffith, D. W., 241. See also *The Birth of a Nation*
Grimsted, David, 131
Grin/grimace, 81–82, 108–9
Guilt: of Jews, 72–73. *See also* White guilt

Hacker, Andrew, 98
Hacker, Marilyn, 226–27, 228, 232
Hagar (biblical character), 214, 231
Haggard, Rider, 221, 223
Hair, 25, 126, 195, 217, 218
Haizlip, Shirlee Taylor, 32, 33
Halsell, Grace, 27, 29, 30, 36
Ham (biblical character), 122, 123–31, 133
Ham actors, 81
Hamlet (fictional character), 147
Hammerstein, Oscar, 18
Hands, 144, *145*, 195
The Hands of Edith Sitwell (Bowen), 144, *145*
Haraway, Donna, 46
Hare, Nathan, 235
Harland, Henry. *See* Luska, Sidney
Harlem Renaissance: and black black impersonation, 96–97, 100, 107–22; and black talk, 136; Cunard's contributions to, 152; and curse of color, 131–32; and devaluation of whiteness, 112; and ethics of racechange, 43; and ex- colored, 100–107; and Jesus as black, 30; and mind-body problem, 96–97, 100; and minstrelsy, 95; misnaming of, 95, 131–32; and origination myths, 99, 102, 106, 131; and passing, 11, 37, 106; and white dread of nonbeing, 96, 100; and whiteness as norm, 11, 18. *See also specific artist or writer*
Harlequin, 81, 84, 94, 131, 146, 259
Harper, Michael, 136, 137, 138
Harris, Joel Chandler, 48, 136
Harris, Trudier, 56, 103
"Has Science Conquered the Color Line?" (Schuyler), 18
Hasso, Signe, 93

Hathaway, Heather, 213
Head, Bessie, 225
Hearn, Lafcadio, 48
Heart Condition (film), 250
Heart of Darkness (Conrad), 94, 96, 140, 144
Hebdige, Dick, 188
Hemenway, Robert, 130
Hemingway, Ernest, 10, 41, 176, 180, 190–95, 197, 199, 200
Henry-Music (Cunard and Crowder), 150, 152
Hermaphrodites, 5, 183, 237–38
Hernton, Calvin C., 223
Heyward, DuBose, 156, 158
Hi, Mom! (film), 86
Him (cummings), 157
Hipster, 177, 178, 179, 180, 181, 182, 191, 192. *See also* "The White Negro" (Mailer)
Höch, Hannah, 6, 7–8, *9*, 10, 11, 43, 195, 218, 247
Hogan, Ernest, 114, 119
Holiday (Frank), 156
Holiday Inn (film), 53–54, *54*, 86
"The Hollow Men" (Eliot), 144
Homans, Margaret, 236
Home to Harlem (McKay), 155
Homer, 147
Homosexuality: and beat generation, 186; and black black impersonation, 121; and black envy, 175, 176, 177, 179, 181, 182–83, 186, 189, 192, 193, 199; and blackface, 84; and ethics of racechange, 44; and ex-colored, 107; Freudian views of, 192; men's fear of, 177; and mixed children, 237; and racism, 237
Honey, Maureen, 102
hooks, bell, 138–39, 243, 246
Hopwood, Avery, 154–55
The Hot Mikado (musical comedy), 31
"Hot Voodoo" nightclub number (*Blonde Venus* film), 221, 223
Hottentots, 217
The House Behind the Cedars (Chesnutt), 104
"How It Feels to Be Colored Me" (Hurston), 119, 257
Howl (Ginsberg), 160
Huckleberry Finn (Twain), 71, 180, 204
Huggins, Nathan Irvin, 84
Hughes, Langston, 117, 237; and black black impersonation, 118; and black talk, 136, 155; and ethics of racechange, 40; and mixed children, 210, 212, 213, 233, 236; and passing, 37, 38; and whiteness as norm, 12, 21, 24–25
Hurst, Fannie, 24, 79, 81, 106, 121, 241
Hurston, Zora Neale, 155, 241; and black black impersonation, 119, 121; and blackface, 30, 54; and curse of color, 122–31, 132, 133; and mixed children, 225, 233–34; and origination myths, 99, 100; and prostitution, 221; and racial envy, 15; and racist totalizing, 244; and transraciality, 257
Hutchinson, George, 31
Huxley, Aldous, 72

I Like Olympia in Black Face (Rivers), 218, *219*
I Was Lazy (Grandville), 221
Identification Papers (Fuss), 244–45
Identity: race as definition of, 216–17, 232; and racist totalizing, 245–47;
and social context, 14–15; and transraciality, 250, 254, 256, 257–58, 259, 260
Illusions (film), 10, 106
Imitation of Life (film), 27
Imitation of Life (Hurst), 24, 106
Imperialism: and black envy, 194–95; and black talk, 139- 40, 141, 156–57; and black violence, 142; and blackface, 55; and mind-body problem, 96; and racist totalizing, 243, 246. *See also* Colonialism
In the American Grain (William Carlos Williams), 160
Incidents in the Life of a Slave Girl (Jacobs), 223
Infantilization: and blackface, 67, 71, 72
Inferno (Dante), 235
Intermarriage, 60, 127; and *The Jazz Singer*, 66–75. *See also* Miscegenation; Mixed children
Invisible Man (Ellison), 260
Irigaray, Luce, 129
Ishmael (biblical character), 214, 231
"It's Getting Dark on Old Broadway" (song), 114

Jackson, Michael, 20, 34, 45, 46, 248–49
Jacobs, Harriet, 211, 223
Jagger, Mick, 188
James, Daniel, 47
Jane Eyre (Brontë), 236
Janiform design, 6–10, 40, 48. *See also* Tarquinian vase; *specific artwork*
Janus (god), 6, 10, 108
Japan, 257
Japheth (biblical character), 123–31
Jazz, 72, 119, 158, 159, 162, 185, 186
Jazz Age, 110, 122
The Jazz Singer (film), 57, 77, 85, 88, 170, 200, 247; discussion about, 66–75; and minstrelsy, 77–78; pictures from, *67*, *69*, *70*, *71*, *74*
Jefferson, Thomas, 243–44
The Jerk (film), 250, *251*
Jessel, George, 72
Jesus: as black, 30
Jewelry, 200, *201*
Jews: and black envy, 200; and blackface, 66–75; and civil rights, 232; demonization of, 247; and femininity, 200; guilt of, 72–73; and Holocaust, 257–58; masculinity of, 200; and mixed children, 228, 230–32; and Noah's curse, 125–26; and passing, 72–73; and

Jews (*continued*)
racechange, 44; and transraciality, 247, 254, 257–60
The Jew's Body (Gilman), 73
Jim Crow laws, 77, 78, 163
Johnson, Barbara E., 119, 257
Johnson, Charles, 15
Johnson, Charles R., 98
Johnson, Charles S., 107
Johnson, James Weldon, 101, 104–5, 107, 146, 155, 216
Jolson, Al, 141, 232, 246, 250. See also *The Jazz Singer*
The Jolson Story (film), 86
Jonah's Gourd Vine (Hurston), 225
Jones, LeRoi, 188, 189
Jordan, June, 234, 235
Jordan, Ruth McBride, 228
Jordan, Winthrop, 46
Joyce, James, 122, 209
Juba (black minstrel), 84, 147
Juba dancers, 140
Julien, Isaac, 30, 174
Jungle: and black black impersonation, 119; and black talk, 144, 160; and origination myths, 101, 102, 106; and prostitution, 221, *222*, 223

Kalaidjian, Walter, 110
Kauffmann, Stanley, 249
Ken Moody and Robert Sherman (Mapplethorpe), 48, 49, *50*, 51
Kennedy, Adrienne, 12, 25, 256
Ker-Seymer, Barbara, *151*, 200, *201*
Kern, Jerome, 18, 72
Kerouac, Jack, 176, 184–86, 189
Kersands, Billy, 112–13, *112*
Kid Millions (film), 77, *77*
Kindred (Butler), 214, 231
King Lear (Shakespeare), 128
Kipling, Rudyard, 193
"The Know-Nothing Bohemians" (Podhoretz), 186
Krenek, Ernst, *76*
Kristeva, Julia, 129, 248
Ku Klux Klan, 57, 59, *64*, 237, 240. See also *The Birth of a Nation*

Lacoue-Labarthe, Philippe, 75, 78
Lagerfeld, Karl, 240
Language. *See* Black talk
Larsen, Nella, 104, 105, 106, 119
Laughter, 129
Laurel and Hardy, 86
Lavin, Maud, 8
Lawrence, D. H., 192, 193
Lazarre, Jane, 42, 205, 226, 227–28, 230, 232
Le Corbusier, 116
Le Guin, Ursula, 52
Leatherstocking novels, 180
Leibovitz, Annie, 21, *23*, 27
Lee, Spike, 252
Lerner, Alan Jay, 81
Lesbians, 175, 189–202, 218, 221
Leutze, Emanuel, 46–47, 48
Lewis, Jerry, 86
Lewis, Ralph. See *The Birth of a Nation*
Liberals, 187, 188
Libertarians, 245
Life magazine, 79, *80*
Light in August (Faulkner), 17–18
Lightening creams, 21
Lilith (biblical character), 193
"Limitations of Life" (Hughes), 21, 24, 25
Linden Hills (Naylor), 235–36
Lindsay, Vachel, 10, 241, 246; and black talk, 134, 138, 139–43, 144, 147, 148, 149, 150, 157, 158
Lips, 108–9, 126, 211, 221, 235, 242, 250
"The Literature of the Negro in the United States" (Wright), 31
"The Little Black Boy" (Blake), 12, 13, 24
The Littlest Rebel (film), 86–88, *87*
Living Color, 10
Living death, 74–75, 104, 215–16, 224–25
Locke, Alain, 132, 133
Lomax, Alan, 30
Long, Walter. See *The Birth of a Nation*
Loos, Adolf, 116
Los Angeles, California: riots in, 256
Lost Boundaries (film), 104
Lot (biblical character), 259
Lott, Eric, 45, 84, 85, 114, 152
Love-hate relationship, 75, 85
Loving v. Virginia (1957), 17
Lowell, Robert, 243
Luska, Sidney, 47
Lynching: and black talk, 142; and blackface, 56, 78–79, 84, 85; and blacks as lynchers, 60; and ex-coloured, 101, 103–4, 105; in film, 56, 57, 60; and origination myths, 103–4; and racist totalizing, 242; and sexual paranoia, 77; and whiteness as aberration, 101; and whiteness as death, 103
"The Lynching" (McKay), 101

McAvoy, May. See *The Jazz Singer*
McBride, James, 228
McCarthy, Mary, 254
McClintock, Anne, 21
McClosky, Frank, 51–52, *51*
McEvilley, Thomas, 254, 256
McKay, Claude: and black black impersonation, 119; and "The Lynching," 101; and mixed children, 211–12, 213; and passing, 17, 18, 38, 247; and racial subordination, 12; Van Vechten as influence on, 155
McKinney, Nina Mae, 116
McMillan, Terry, 252
Madness, 92–93, 192

Madonna, 225, 228–29
Madonna (singer), 253–654
Magritte, René, 38, 109
Mahurin, Matt, 169, 170
Mailer, Norman, 176–78, 179–82, 188, 189, 192, 200, 232, 246. *See also* "The White Negro"
Malamud, Bernard, 167–68, 258–60
Malcolm X, 177
"Man in the Brooks Brother Shirt" (McCarthy), 254
A Man Called White (White), 14–15
Man in the Gray Flannel Suit (Sloan Wilson), 254
"Man Orchid" (William Carlos Williams), 160
Man in Polyester Suit (Mapplethorpe), 170–71, 172–75, *173*, 187, 192, 202, 254
Man in Polyester Suit (Udé), 254, *255*
"The Man Who Became a Woman" (Anderson), 178–79, 181
Manet, Édouard, 217–18, *217*, 218, 223
Mapplethorpe, Robert: and black envy, 170–71, 172–75, *173*, 183, 187, 202; *Ken Moody and Robert Sherman* by, 48, 49, *50*, 51; *Man in Polyester Suit* by, 170–71, 172–75, *173*, 187, 192, 202, 254; and Otherness, 241; and transraciality, 254
Marcus, Greil, 187–88
Marcus, Jane, 200
Marriage. *See* Intermarriage
The Marrow of Tradition (Chesnutt), 85
"Mars Jeems's Nightmare" (Chesnutt), 25–26, 27
Marsh, Mae. See *The Birth of a Nation*
Marshall, Paule, 43
Martin, Steve, 240, 250, *251*
Marx brothers, 91–92
Mary (biblical person), 193
Masculinity: and Africa as masculine, 193; and black envy, 170–71, 173, 174–75, 177, 182, 183–84, 186, 188, 189, 193, 195–200; and black talk, 147; and blackface, 67, 71, 75, 77; degeneration of, 147; and ethics of racechange, 44; of Jews, 200
Masks/masquerades: and black envy, 189–90; and ex-colored, 100–107, 112, 216; and fantasies, 241; and mixed children, 235; and prostitution, 218, 220–21; and racist totalizing, 245; and re-coloured, 112–22; and replacement of self for Other, 241; and sexuality, 241. *See also* Blackface; *specific art work*
Masochism, 183, 196, 197, 200
Masters, Edgar Lee, 141–42
"Melanctha" (Stein), 82, 134, 148
Melville, Herman, 82, 180, 243
Mercer, Kobena, 174, 254
Messiah: dark child as, 231–32
Metamorphosis (Ovid), 102, 125
Metaphor: and transraciality, 260–61
Mezzrow, Milton "Mezz," 135, 138, 158–59, 188, 249–50
Michaels, Walter Benn, 104
Mikado (Gilbert and Sullivan), 31
Miller, Alyce, 233, 234, 235
Miller, Jonathan, 180
Miller, Nancy K., 47, 173
Mills, Florence, 116, 117, *117*, 121
Mimesis, 44–45, 75, 78, 85, 235. *See also* Blackface
Mind-body problem, 10, 96–97, 100, 247
Minstrelsy: and "artificial niggers" in film, 90; and black black impersonation, 108–9, 112–14; and black talk, 135, 136, 139, 143, 146, 147–48, 152, 156, 157, 158, 160, 162, 165, 168; and blackface, 55, 76–77, 78, 79; and curse of color, 123, 131; demise of, 78; and ethics of racechange, 41, 42–43, 44, 45, 47; in film, 70, 76–78, 90; grins in, 108–9; and Harlem Renaissance, 95; influence of, 11, 55; and mind-body problem, 96–97; and modernism, 143, 147–48, 158; as negrophobia, 76–77; and origination myths, 131; phallic figures in, 84; and prejudice, 11; as racist, 11; and stereotypes, 157; as taboo, 37–38; in vaudeville, 70; and Western culture, 147. *See also specific person or film*
Mirror, Mirror (Weems), 15–16, *16*
Mirroring, 223, 235, 237. *See also specific art work*
Miscegenation: in *The Birth of a Nation*, 60, 65, 66; and black envy, 180, 182; and blackface, 65; in film, 60, 65; and gender, 17, 18; laws against, 17, 18, 205; and mixed children, 205, 206, 211, 224, 225, 233; and Noah's curse, 127; and racial purity, 60. *See also* Intermarriage
Missionaries, 140
Mixed children: and adoption, 232; and black mothers/parents, 207–14, 232–39; and class, 232; and color of desire, 207–10; and death, 208–9, 215–16, 224–25, 235, 236; and ethics of racechange, 44, 45; and fantasies, 236–37; and Jews, 228, 230–32; and masquerades, 235; and maternal ethic, 206; as messiah, 231–32; and mimicry, 235; and mirroring, 235, 237; and Oedipus myth, 210–14, 223–32, 237; and one-drop rule, 205, 232, 233; and Other, 232; and paternalism, 232; and prostitution, 214–23; and racial purity, 214; and racism, 226, 229, 231, 232, 233, 235–36, 237; and redemption, 207, 226, 230–32; and scapegoats, 224–25, 226; and schizophrenia, 237–39; and skin color, 207–10; and slavery, 208–9, 214, 229–30; and white father, 210–14; and white guilt, 207, 211; and white mothers, 223–32, 233; and White Negro, 237–38; and white parents, 205, 206. *See also* Birth stories
Moby Dick (Melville), 180

Modernism: and black black impersonation, 107; and black talk, 134–48, 158, 160, 166; and curse of color, 133; and minstrelsy, 143, 147–48, 158; and racist totalizing, 246
Monroe, Harriet, 134
Monroe, Marilyn, 241, 252–54, *253*
Montaigne, Michel, 243
Monterro, Philippa. *See* Schuyler, Philippa
Montparnasse, Kiki de, 6–7, *7*, 48
Moran and Mack, 86
Mormonism, 126–27
Morph (computer program), 33–34, 45–46
Morrison, Toni: and "the Africanist persona," 54; and black envy, 192, 202; and ethics of racechange, 41; and mixed children, 204; and racial envy, 15, 21, 24; and whiteness as norm, 15, 21, 24; and whites passing as blacks, 28–29
The Mother Knot (Lazarre), 227
Mothers: blacks as, 204, 207–14, 229–30; pre-Oedipal bonding of children and, 223–32; and prostitution, 215; surrogate, 204, 229–30; whites as, 223–32, 233. See also *The Jazz Singer*
Movies. *See* Film
Mr. Prejudice (Pippin), 237, *238*
"Mr. Robinson's Neighborhood" (Murphy sketch), 37
Mr. Sammler's Planet (Bellow), 170–72, 174–75, 187, 202, 246
Mukherjee, Bharati, 247
Mulatto: A Tragedy of the Deep South (Hughes), 213
"Mulatto" (Hughes), 213
"Mulatto" (McKay), 211–12
Mulattoes: cultural, 252. *See also* Mixed children; Nugent, Richard Bruce; Passing
Mules and Men (Hurston), 132
Murphy, Eddie, 36–37, 256
Murray the K, 188
Murray, Timothy, 94
Murrow, Edward R., 118
Music, 10, 143, 187–88. *See also* Blues music; Jazz; *specific song or film*
Musicals: influence of minstrelsy on, 55. *See also specific musical*
Mutter (Höch), 8, 10
"My Mammy" (song), 57, 68, 69, 70
"My Negro Problem—And Ours" (Podhoretz), 186
Mythic Being (Piper), 200, 202

The Narrative of Arthur Gordon Pym (Poe), 242–43
National Association for the Advancement of Colored People (NAACP), 152, 162
National Association of Black Social Workers, 232
Native Americans, 47
Naylor, Gloria, 205, 206, 235–36, 237, 246
"Near White" (Countee Cullen), 225
"Near-White" (McKay), 17, 18, 38, 247
Negrification, 20–21
Negritude, 6, 112, 116, 130
Negro. *See* Blackness; Blacks
Negro (Cunard anthology), 135, 138, 149, 150, 152
"The Negro in Art: How Shall He Be Portrayed?" (Van Vechten), 155–56
Negrophilia, 76–77
Negrophobia, 76–77, 82, 95
New Black Aesthetic, 252
"New Face" of America (*Time* magazine cover), 33, 45, 46. *See also* color insert
"New Negro," 107, 122
The New Negro (Locke), 133
New Woman, 109, 110, 119
Nicoll, Allardyce, 81
Nielsen, Aldon Lynn, 136, 164
Nigger Heaven (Van Vechten), 154–56
Nihilism, 178, 180, 181, 192, 195
Noah (biblical character), 123–31
Noire et blanche (Black and white) (Ray), 6–7, *7*, *8*, 48, *49*, 109
Norma Jean (Udé), 252–54, *253*
North, Michael, 136
Notes of a White Black Woman (Scales-Trent), 214
"Nudity at the Capital" (Stevens), 157
"Nudity in the Colonies" (Stevens), 157
Nugent, Richard Bruce, 99, 100; and black black impersonation, 107–12, *108*, *109*, *110*, *111*, 116, 121, 122; and curse of color, 122, 123, 132, 133

O'Connor, Flannery, 84, 85, 87
Odyssey (Homer), 147
Oedipal patterns: and black envy, 182; and *The Jazz Singer*, 69–71, 77; and mixed children, 210–14, 237; and Noah's curse, 126, 128, 129–30; and rage at white father, 210–14; reconfigured as "Edible Complex," 242–61; and white mothers and dark babies, 223–32
Oedipus (mythical character), 212
O'Grady, Lorraine, 16–17, 218
Oiseau et tortue (Picabia), 183, *185*
Olivier, Laurence, 93–94
Olympia (Manet), 217–18, *217*, 221, 223
Omi, Michael, 33
"On Being Brought from Africa to America" (Wheatley), 126
On the Road (Kerouac), 185–86, 189
"One Boy's Story" (Bonner), 212–13
One-drop rule, 18, 33, 65, 205, 232, 233
O'Neill, Eugene, 156
Onyeocha, *39*
Orestes (mythical character), 212
Organ transplants, 250
Origination myths: and black black

impersonation, 107–22; and black talk, 144; and curse of color, 122–31; and death, 102–4; and ethics of racechange, 43; and ex-colored, 100–107; functions/purpose of, 98–99, 100; and Harlem Renaissance, 99, 102, 106, 131; and lynchings, 103–4; and mind-body problem, 96–97, 100; and minstrelsy, 131; and Noah's curse, 123–31; and racial subordination, 97–98, 99–100, 129; and racial superiority, 103; and racism, 102–3, 114, 128, 131–32; and stereotyping, 99; and "Why am I black?" question, 97–98
Ostendorf, Berndt, 76–77
Othello (fictional character), 92–93, *92*, 93–94
Other: annihilation of, 244–47; and blackface, 73, 75, 79, 84; death of, 73, 75, 79, 84; homogenization of, 247, 260; and masquerades, 241; and metaphor, 260–61; and mixed children, 232; Otherness of, 244–46; and racist totalizing, 244–47; and self, 229, 248, 256; and transraciality, 247–61
Otis, Johnny, 188
Our Nig (Harriet Wilson), 224
Ovid, 102, 125

Paley, Grace, 226, 230–32, 233
Pardon Us (film), 86
Parks, Suzan-Lori, 128, 256
Parody of Manet's "Olympia" (Picasso), 218, *219*
Passing: and alienation, 104–5; and black black impersonation, 110, 112; and black parodies of whiteness, 36–37, *36*; and blacks passing as whites, 11, 14–15, 17, 18–20, 44–45, 106–7; and death, 29–30, 104; effects on blacks of, 104–5; and ex-colored, 105–7; and fluidity of racial categories, 14–15; and Harlem Renaissance, 106; and Jews, 72–73; as morally acceptable for blacks, 11, 37; and *Plessy v. Ferguson*, 14; and psychological splintering, 104–5; and racial subordination, 104; and racist totalizing, 244; and transraciality, 248, 250; and victimization, 105–7; and voyeurism, 37, 38; white posing versus black, 44–45; and whiteness as norm, 14–15, 17, 18–20; and whites passing as blacks, 25–30, 35–36, *35*
Passing (Larsen), 104, 105, 106
"Passing for White, Passing for Black" (Piper), 32
Patai, Raphael, 126
Paternalism, 232. *See also* Fathers; Noah (biblical character)
Paternity, 208, 209
Paterson (William Carlos Williams), 135, 159
Patrons: and black talk, 134, 149–58
Pears' Soap advertisments, 21, *22*
Pen (writing): and black envy, 190–95
Penis: and black envy, 170–75, *173*, 176, 178, 182, 189, 190, 195, 196, 197, 199, 200, 202; and black talk, 165; and class, 254; and Noah's curse, 126; and transraciality, 254
Phallus: and "artificial niggers" in film, 88; and black envy, 170–71, 175, 176, 177, 182, 183, 189, 190, 195, 196, 197, 199, 200, 202; in minstrelsy, 84
Phipps, Susie Guillory, 32–33
Photography. *See specific photographer*
Picabia, Francis, 183, *185*, 237
Picasso, Pablo, 217, 218, *219*, *220*, 221
Pieterse, Jan Nederveen, 123–31
Pinkie (film), 104
Piper, Adrian, 32, 33, 200, 202, 226, 240–41, 252
Pippin, Horace, 237, *238*, 242
Plath, Sylvia, 165, 198, 200
Playing in the Dark (Morrison), 41, 54
Plessy, Homer, 13–14, 15, 33
Plessy v. Ferguson (1896), 13–14
Plum Bun (Fauset), 15, 18, 104, 105
Podhoretz, Norman, 186, 187, 189
Poe, Edgar Allan, 242–43
Poetry magazine, 134
Popular culture, 30–31, 43
Porgy and Bess (Gershwin), 156
Porgy (Heyward), 156, 158
"Portrait in Georgia" (Toomer), 103–4
Post-Plantation Pop (Tisdale), 254
The Potato Eaters (Van Gogh), 46
Pound, Ezra, 135, 144
The Predicament of Culture (Clifford), 38
"A Prediction" (Corvarrubias), 154, *155*
Prejudice, 11, 17, 20, 227, 237, *238*
Presley, Elvis, 10, 188
Pride, Charley, 10
Priest, Josiah, 127, *128*
Primitivism, 136, 178, 192, 194, 199, 218, 223. *See also* Jungle
Prostitution: and animalism, 221, *222*, 223; blackness equated with, 218; and castration, 221, 223; and doubling, 223; Hottentot as icon of, 217; and lesbianism, 218; and masks, 218, 220–21; and mixed children, 214–23; and mothers, 215; and primitivism, 218, 223; and racial ambiguity, 214–23; and slavery, 221
Pryor, Richard, 250, *251*
Psychoanalysis: and blackface, 54–55; and colonialism, 13; and corporeal reconfiguration, 13; differences in black and white, 55; and ethics of racechange, 43; and mixed children, 210–14; and neurotic orientation, 30; and whiteness as norm, 13. *See also* Freud, Sigmund; Oedipal patterns; Schizophrenia
Pudd'nhead Wilson (Twain), 15, 97–98, 210–11, 212, 246
Punishment: and blackface, 56–57, 79, 81; blackness as, 53; and mixed children, 210
Pushkin, Alexander, 31

"Queer Collection" (Van Vechten), 182–83
A Question of Power (Head), 225
Quicksand (Larsen), 119

Race: as classifications with permeable boundaries, 247; color without, 206; and gender, 5, 6, 11; as graduated spectrum, 5, 7; and identity, 216–17, 232; interdependency of, 48–49, *49*, *50*, 51–52, *51*, 226, 248, 256; as monolithic, 242, 247; as rigid bifurcation, 5; and sex, 203–5; skin color as definition of, 5, 7, 32- 33; as social context, 32; as Supreme Fiction, 42. *See also* Racechange
Race riots, 79, *80*, 256
Racechange: and black envy, 177; characteristics of, 5–6; and conservatism, 12; effects of, 241; ethics of, 40–52, *49*, *50*, 51–52, *51*, 246; evolution of, 245–46; functions/purposes of, 5–6, 10; genocidal, 103, 123; liberating potential of, 241; in music, 10; and radicalism, 12; and sexchange, 189–202, 248, 249, 254
Racial envy, 15–18, 45, 85, 88, 101–2. *See also* Black envy
Racial purity, 42, 60, 204, 206, 209, 214, 256
Racial subordination: and black talk, 135–36, 139, 160, 168; and blackface, 55, 57, 85, 99; and curse of color, 129; and gender, 5, 6, 11; and origination myths, 97–98, 99–100, 129; and passing, 104. *See also* Racial superiority
Racial superiority: and black envy, 181, 198, 199, 200; and blackface, 78; and curse of color, 122, 129; and ethics of racechange, 40–41; and Noah's curse, 123; and origination myths, 103; and white supremacy, 78, 123, 129, 181. *See also* Colonialism; Imperialism; Racial subordination; Whiteness: as norm
Racism: and African American survival, 11–12; and black black impersonation, 114; and black envy, 185, 189, 197, 200; and black talk, 136, 140, 141, 142, 159; and cross-racial impersonations, 241; and curse of color, 128, 131- 32; and homosexuality, 237; and minstrelsy, 11; and mixed children, 206, 226, 229, 231, 232, 233, 235–36, 237; and origination myths, 102–3, 114, 128, 131–32; and racist totalizing, 242–47, 256; romantic, 136, 141; and satire, 11–12; and transraciality, 247, 252; and violence, 206; and whiteness as norm, 12–25; and whites passing as blacks, 25–30. See also *The Birth of a Nation*; Prejudice
Racist totalizing, 242–47, 256
Rape: and black envy, 170, 187, 189, 190, 196–97, 199, 200, 202; and mixed children, 214
Ray, Man, 180; and black black impersonation, 109; and black envy, 192, 195; and ethics of racechange, 43, 48, *49*; and *Henry Music* cover, 150, 152, *153*; and *Noire et blanche*, 6–7, *7*, *8*, 10, 11, 48, *49*, 109; and transraciality, 247
Raye, Martha, 82, *83*
Razaf, Andy, 133
Re-coloured, 112–22
Really the Blues (Mezzrow), 135, 158–59
Rebirth of a Nation (*Time* magazine), 33–34, *34*, 45
Reconstruction. See *The Birth of a Nation*
Red, Blond, Black, and Olive (Darriau), 51–52, *51*
Reddy, Maureen, 205
Reed, Ishmael, 156
Reff, Theodore, 218
Religion, 140, 141, 260. *See also specific biblical character*
Reynolds, Marjorie, *93*, 94
Rhapsody in Blue (film), 86
Rice, Gene, 125
Rice, Thomas "Daddy," 78, 84, 88, 163
Rich, Adrienne, 139
Richards, Keith, 188
Ridly, Guy, 35, *35*
Riggs, Marlon T., 10
Rimbaud, Arthur, 248
Rivers, Larry, 217, 218, *219*
Rivière, Joan, 189–90
Robeson, Paul, 118–19, *120*, 121, 254
Robinson, Bill, 88, 203–5, 252
Rock 'n' roll, 187–88
Roediger, David R., 78, 79
Rogers, Ginger, 88
Rogers, J. A., 31, *32*
Rogers, Jimmie, 188
Rogin, Michael, 43, 66, 71, 73–74, 79, 81
Romantic racism, 136, 141
Roof, Judith, 199
Rooney, Mickey, 90, *91*
Rosaldo, Renato, 139, 141
Rose, Phyllis, 116
Ross, Andrew, 10
Rubin, William, 218
Rukeyser, Muriel, 206
Running a Thousand Miles for Freedom (Crafts), 13, *14*, 38, 106
Rushdie, Salman, 240

Sadism, 191, 196, 197, 199, 200
Said, Edward, 246
Saint Sebastian (Colescott), 237–38, 239. *See also* color insert
Saint Sebastian (Van Vechten), 183, *184*, 237–38, 239
Samson Agonistes (Eliot), 147
Sandburg, Carl, 157
Santiago, Danny. *See* James, Daniel
Santyana, George, 107
Sarah (biblical character), 214
Sartre, Jean-Paul, 30, 232

Satanic Verses (Rushdie), 240
Satire, 11–12
Sayers, Dorothy, 75, 221
Scales-Trent, Judy, 106–7, 214
Scapegoats: and black envy, 183, 185; and blackface, 54–55, 57, 73, 75, 78–86; and ex-colored, 101; and mixed children, 224–25, 226
Schickel, Richard, 58, 59, 60–61, 63
Schizophrenia: of American culture, 160; of black men, 121; and mixed children, 237–39; and passing, 30, 36, 104–5; and sexuality, 237–39
Schor, Mira, 175
Schuyler, George, 12, 18–20, 25, 38, 103, 246
Schuyler, Philippa, 20
Schwerner, Michael, 28
A Sea-Change (Gould), 176, 190, 191, 195–200
Searle, Humphrey, 143
Second Sex (Beauvoir), 44
Sedgwick, Eve Kosofsky, 176, 177
Self: definition of, 32, 259; hatred of, 15–16, 234; and Other, 229, 248, 256; and transraciality, 248, 249, 256, 259
Sellars, Peter, 31
Sent for You Yesterday (Wideman), 260
Separate-but-equal doctrine, 14, 78
Servants: blacks as, 204, 205, 229–30
Sex: and Africa, 223; in *The Birth of a Nation*, 57–66; and bisexuality, 121; and black black impersonation, 109, 121; and black men as threats to white men, 88; and black servants, 204, 205; and black talk, 146, 167–68; and blackface, 57–66, 77; and cannibalism, 146; and curse of color, 123–31; and lynchings, 77; and masks, 241; and negrophobia, 95; and Noah's curse, 123–31; and race, 203–5; and racial envy, 88; and schizophrenia, 237-39; and transraciality, 254. *See also* Black envy; Lesbians; Penis; Phallus; Rape; Sexchange
Sex and Race (Rogers), 31, *32*
Sexchange: and racechange, 189–202, 248, 249, 254; and transraciality, 248, 249, 254
"Shadow dance," 88
Shakespeare, William, 92–93, 128, 197–98
Shapiro, James, 247
She (Haggard), 221, 223
Shem (biblical character), 123–31
Shirley Temple Black and Bill Robinson White (Colescott), 203–5, 217. *See also* color insert
Shohat, Ella, 248
"Shoot It Jimmy!" (William Carlos Williams), 157
Show Boat (musical), 18
"The Shroud of Color" (Countee Cullen), 131
Shuffle Along (musical), 114
Siegmann, George. See *The Birth of a Nation*
Silver Streak (film), 250, *251*
Simmons, William J., 65
Simpson, O. J., 169–70, 202
Sims, Lowery S., 220
The Singing Fool (film), 86
Sirk, Douglas, 27
Sitwell, Edith, 139–40, 143–44, *145*, 148, 149, 150, 158
1600 Pennsylvania Avenue (musical), 81
Skin color: and black envy, 195; as classifications with permeable boundaries, 247; and climate, 125; curse of, 122–33; as definition of race, 5, 7, 32–33; of desire, 207–10; and Harlem Renaissance, 131–32; as means of self- definition, 32; and Noah's curse, 123–31; and sex, 123-31; and stain, 28; without race, 206. *See also* Blackness; Blacks; Mixed children; Passing; Whiteness; Whites
Slavery: biblical justification for, 123–31; and black envy, 199–200, *201*; and black talk, 139, 161; and blackface, 54; and ethics of racechange, 47; and mixed children, 208–9, 214, 229–30; and Mormonism, 127; narratives about, 138; and Noah's curse, 123–31; and prostitution, 221; and racist totalizing, 243; and transraciality, 258; white guilt about, 54, 82, 161; and whiteness as norm, 12, 13, *14*. *See also specific film*
Smith, Joseph, 126–27
Smith, Lillian, 236
Smith, Susan, 202
"Smoke, Lilies and Jade" (Nugent), 121
"The Smudge" (Hurst), 79, 81
Snow, Valerie, 116
Snowden, Ben and Lew, 95
Sodomy, 181
Solano, Solita, 149
Sollors, Werner, 47, 155, 213, 257
"Some Negro Slang" (Cunard), 156
Somebody Loves Me (film), 86
A Song to Remember (film), 86
Soul Sister (Halsell), 29
The Souls of Black Folk (Du Bois), 109, 208
"The Souls of White Folks" (Du Bois), 103, 104, 105, 208
Southern, Terry, 170, 187, 197
Soyinka, Wole, 96, 97, 100, 102, 106, 107, 128, 130, 235
Spark, Muriel, 228–29, 232, 237
Spencer, Anne, 99, 100–104, 105, 107, 122–23, 132, 133, 246
"Spirit-murder": and "artificial nigger" in film, 86; and *The Birth of a Nation*, 66; and black talk, 139, 161; and blackface, 93–94; in film, 53–94; and *The Jazz Singer*, 66, 70, 72; as penance for lynching, 57; and white guilt, 55–56
Stam, Robert, 248
Stein, Gertrude, 82, 84, 118–19, 134, 148
Stephen, Adrian, 35, *35*
Stereotypes: in *The Birth of a Nation*, 61; and

Stereotypes (*continued*)
black black impersonation, 108, 114, 122; and black envy, 170, 178, 190; and black talk, 135, 136, 137, 138, 140–41, 144, 157, 160, 162, 164; and blackface, 61, 73; of children, 204; in film, 61, 73, 88, 91–92; and minstrelsy, 157; and origination myths, 99; in popular culture, 31; and transraciality, 259
Stevens, Wallace, 42, 157
Stevenson, Robert Louis, 196
"Stop the world, I want to get on!" (Gregory act), 98, *99*
Stowe, Harriet Beecher, 136
Stowe, William, 131
Stuart, Wilma and Willem, 228
Styron, William, 162
The Subterraneans (Kerouac), 185
Sula (Morrison), 202
Sundquist, Eric J., 31, 121
Suture (film), 249–50
Swayze, Patrick, 10
Sweeney Agonistes (Eliot), 143, 145–48, 150
The Swing Mikado (musical comedy), 31
Swing Time (film), 88, *89*, 90, 246
"Symbolic debt," 56

Tableau (Charles Cullen), 48–49, *50*
Tambo and Bones (Wittke), 163
Tarquinian vase, 3, *4*, 5, 6, 11, 16–17; and black black impersonation, 109; and blackface, 55, 57; and ethics of racechange, 44
The Tempest (Shakespeare), 197–98
Temple Black, Shirley, 86–88, *87*, 203–5, 217, 233, 252
The Tenants (Malamud), 167–68, 259
Tender Buttons (Stein), 84
Terrible Honesty: Mongrel Manhattan in the 1920s (Douglas), 110, 119, 121
Their Eyes Were Watching God (Hurston), 15, 130, 234
There Is Confusion (Fauset), 38
Third Sex, 175, 176, 199
Thomas, Danny, 86
Thompson, Virgil, 118
"The Time of Her Time" (Mailer), 181
Time magazine: "New Face" of America on cover of, 33, 45, 46; *Rebirth of a Nation* in, 33–34, *34*, 45; Simpson picture in, 169–70, 202. *See also* color insert
Tisdale, Daniel, 254
Titian, 217
Toll, Robert C., 79
Tom (cummings), 158
Tomlin, Lily, 256
Toomer, Jean, 103–4, 105, 107, 205, 206, 224–25, 231, 237, 246, 249–50
Torgovnick, Marianna, 136, 218
Totalizing, racist, 242–47, 256
Transraciality, 247–61
Transvestism, 5; ethnic, 47, 155, 257. *See also* Sexchange
A Trap for Fools (Cross), 85
Trickster. *See* Harlequin
Tubman, Harriet, 254
Tucker, Sophie, 72, 232
Turner, Victor, 256
Twain, Mark, 15, 48, 82, 97–98, 114, 180, 241, 246; and mixed children, 210–11, 212, 213
Twilight: Los Angeles, 1992 (Deavere Smith), 256

Udé, Iké, 241, 252–54, *253*, *255*, 256
Uncle Remus (Harris), 136, 140
Uncle Tom's Cabin (Stowe), 136, 158

Van Gogh, Vincent, 46, 48
Van Peebles, Melvin, 27
Van Vechten, Carl, 118, 134, 149, 153–56, 182–83, *184*, 237–38
Vanilla Ice, 10
Vaudeville: and black black impersonation, 114; and black talk, 140, 141–42, 143, 146, 148, 165; and ethics of racechange, 43; minstrelsy in, 70
Venus of Urbino (Titian), 217
Violence, 78–79, 85, 142, 161, 189, 192, 206. *See also* Lynchings; Rape
Vitiligo, 19, 20, 28
"Voodoo" *Macbeth*, 118
Voodoo (musical), 119, *120*
Voyeurism, 37, 38

Walker, A'Leilia, 118, 119, 154
Walker, Alice, 206, 207
Walker, George, 113–14
Walker, Madame C. J., 21
Wallace, George, 47
Wallace, Michele, 178, 187, 188
Waller, Fats, 133
The Walls of Jericho (Fisher), 155
Warhol, Andy, 252
Warren, Robert Penn, 216–17
Was Huck Black? (Fishkin), 31
Washington, Booker T., 5, 7
Washington, Denzel, 250
Washington Crossing the Delaware (Leutze), 46–47, 48
The Waste Land (Eliot), 143, 147, 197–98
Watermelon Man (film), 27, *28*
Waters, Ethel, 116
Waters, Muddy, 188
Weems, Carrie Mae, 15–16, *16*
Weinauer, Ellen, 13
Weinberg, Jonathan, 182–83
Weld, Theodore, 127
Welles, Orson, 118
Wells, Ida B., 225
Western civilization. *See* American/Western culture

"What Would I Do White?" (June Jordan), 234
What's Happening? (Gregory), 186, *187*
Wheatley, Phillis, 126
White, Charles, 174
White, Walter, 14–15, 18, 33, 155
White guilt: and "artificial niggers" in film, 92; and black black impersonation, 109; and black envy, 194; and black talk, 139, 147, 160, 161–62, 164, 166; and blackface, 55, 79, 82, 85, 92; and blackness as norm, 101–2; and mixed children, 207, 211; and slavery, 161; and "spirit murder," 55–56; and transraciality, 249
White Like You (Gregory parody), 36, *36*
"White Like You" (Murphy sketch), 36–37
White Man (Cole), 38, *39*, 40
White man's burden, 140
The White Negress (Brancusi), 149
White Negro: and black envy, 191; and Colescott, 237–39; desire for Black Man by, 176–89; lesbian, 189–202; and mixed children, 237–38; Picabia portrait of, 237; women as, 223
"The White Negro" (Mailer), 177, 179–81, *179*, 186, 189, 192, 232, 246
White Over Black (Jordan), 46
White supremacy, 78, 123, 129, 181
"White Things" (Spencer), 100–103, 107
"White Weeds" (Chesnutt), 215–16
Whiteface, 98, *99*, 165
Whiteness: as aberration, 101; as burden to blacks, 38, 40; and death, 102–4; definition of, 103; demonization/vilification of, 100, 233; devaluation of, 106, 112, 233, 235; as escape from "epidermal inferiority," 42; as evil, 102; and neurotic orientation, 30; as norm, 11, 12–25, 30, 98; overprivileging of, 11; visibility of, 48. *See also* Passing; Whites
Whites: as fathers, 207–14; hidden racial roots of, 31–32; as mothers, 223–32, 233; nonbeing of, 96, 100; passing as blacks, 25–30, 35–36, *35*; racial envy of, 101–2; self-loathing of, 178, 179; sexual insecurity of, 88, 177; and sympathy and understanding of African Americans, 246; as victims of own fears, 244
Whitman, Walt, 257
Whitmore, James, 28, *29*
Whoopi Goldberg (Leibovitz), 21, *23*, 27
"Who's Passing for Who?" (Hughes), 37, 38
Why Bring That Up? (film), 86
Wideman, John Edgar, 137–38, 260
Wiegman, Robyn, 42, 56, 246, 248
Wilder, Gene, 250, *251*
Williams, Bert, 113–14, *113*, 114, 119, 140, 160
Williams, Gregory Howard, 225–26
Williams, Montel, 38
Williams, Patricia J.: and black talk, 162; and denigrification, 21; and ethics of racechange, 46; and mixed children, 228, 229, 230, 233; and spirit murder, 55–56; and transraciality, 247, 257–58, 259
Williams, Raymond, 148
Williams, Sherley Anne, 226, 229, 232
Williams, William Carlos, 135, 148, 157, 159–60, 162
Williamson, Joel, 42
Willis, Susan, 45
Wilson, Harriet, 224
Wilson, Sloan, 254
Winant, Howard, 33
Winters, Shelley, 93
Without You I'm Nothing (film), 249
Wittke, Carl, 81, 84, 163
The Wiz (musical comedy), 31
Wolfe, George C., 252
"Womanliness as a Masquerade" (Rivière), 189–90
Women: black, 38, 108, 131, 175, 202; and black black impersonation, 108; and black envy, 175, 187, 189–202; erasure of black, 38, 131, 175, 202; and ethics of racechange, 43–44; fantasies of, 190; racially indeterminate, 207–10; violence against, 189; white, 189- 202; as White Negro, 223. *See also* Gender; Mothers; Prostitution; *specific woman*
Wonderbar (film), 86
The Wonderful Wizard of Oz (film), 31
Woolf, Virginia, 12, 35–36, *35*, 38, 57, 246
World War II, 237
Worlds Beyond My Control (Lazarre), 227–28, 230
WPA Negro Theatre Project, 118
Wright, Richard, 31, 260

Yaeger, Patricia, 209
Yeats, William Butler, 143

"Zagrowsky Tells" (Paley), 230–31
Zelig (film), 240, 248
Žižek, Slavoj, 56, 74